# Financial Accounting for Managers

## FIRST EDITION

**WAYNE THOMAS**

*University of Oklahoma*

**MICHAEL DRAKE**

*Brigham Young University*

**JAKE THORNOCK**

*Brigham Young University*

**J. DAVID SPICELAND**

*University of Memphis*

Dedicated to

FINANCIAL ACCOUNTING FOR MANAGERS

Published by McGraw Hill LLC, 1325 Avenue of the Americas, New York, NY 10121. Copyright ©2023 by McGraw Hill LLC. All rights reserved. Printed in the United States of America. No part of this publication may be reproduced or distributed in any form or by any means, or stored in a database or retrieval system, without the prior written consent of McGraw Hill LLC, including, but not limited to, in any network or other electronic storage or transmission, or broadcast for distance learning.

Some ancillaries, including electronic and print components, may not be available to customers outside the United States.

This book is printed on acid-free paper.

1 2 3 4 5 6 7 8 9 LWI 27 26 25 24 23 22

ISBN 978-1-265-09449-2
MHID 1-265-09449-7

Cover Image: © *metamorworks/Getty Images*

mheducation.com/highered

# About the Authors

## WAYNE THOMAS

Wayne Thomas is the Senior Associate Dean for Faculty and Research Innovation and the David C. Steed Chair of Accounting at the University of Oklahoma, where he teaches introductory financial accounting, intermediate accounting, and MBAs. He received his bachelor's degree in accounting from Southwestern Oklahoma State University, and his master's and PhD in accounting from Oklahoma State University.

©Shevaun Williams & Associates

Wayne has won teaching awards at the university, college, and departmental levels, and has received the Outstanding Educator Award from the Oklahoma Society of CPAs. In addition to *Financial Accounting for Managers,* he also co-authors McGraw Hill's best-selling *Intermediate Accounting,* with David Spiceland, Mark Nelson, and Jennifer Winchel, and *Financial Accounting* with David Spiceland and Don Herrmann.

His primary research interests include accounting information in capital markets, techniques used by managers to manipulate earnings, the importance of financial disclosures, and financial statement analysis. He previously served as an editor of *The Accounting Review* and has published articles in a variety of journals, including *The Accounting Review, Journal of Accounting and Economics, Journal of Accounting Research, Review of Accounting Studies,* and *Contemporary Accounting Research.* He has won several research awards, including the American Accounting Association's Competitive Manuscript Award and the University of Oklahoma's highest research award, being named a George Lynn Cross Research Professor.

Wayne is married to Julee, and they have four kids, Olivia, Jake, Eli, and Luke. He enjoys sports (basketball, tennis, golf, biking, and ping pong), crossword puzzles, the outdoors, and spending time with his family.

## MICHAEL DRAKE

Michael Drake is the K. Fred Skousen Professor of Accounting in the BYU Marriott School of Business at Brigham Young University. Before joining BYU, he was on faculty in the Fisher College of Business at The Ohio State University and a doctoral student in the Mays Business School at Texas A&M University, where he was a Deloitte Foundation Doctoral Fellow. Prior to his graduate work, he worked in public accounting at Arthur Andersen and Ernst & Young.

Michael teaches financial accounting and financial statement analysis at the undergraduate, graduate, and executive levels and has won several teaching awards, including the MBA Core Professor of the Year award in several consecutive years and the BYU Marriott School Teaching Excellence Award.

Michael's primary research interest is in capital markets with a specific focus on the intermediaries and technologies that facilitate price formation. His research has been published in ©Savannah Sorenson/Brigham top academic journals, including the *Journal of Accounting and Economics, Journal of Accounting* Young University *Research, The Accounting Review, Contemporary Accounting Research, Review of Accounting Studies,* and *Management Science.* He has won several awards at the academy, university, and college level for his research, including multiple best paper awards and the BYU Young Scholar award. Michael currently serves on the editorial boards of *The Accounting Review* and *Contemporary Accounting Research.*

Michael is married to McKenzie, and they have five children, Gavin, Abbie, Quentin, Maxwell, and Hannah. He enjoys playing, coaching, and watching all sports.

## JAKE THORNOCK

Jake Thornock is a professor of accounting in the BYU Marriott School of Business at Brigham Young University and holds the John and Nancy Hardy Chaired Professorship. He joined BYU from the University of Washington, where he was a tenured associate professor of accounting and the PwC Faculty Fellow. Jake completed his doctoral studies at Kenan-Flagler Business School at the University of North Carolina, where he was awarded the William Delozier Fellowship for Outstanding Doctoral Student. He earned his undergraduate and master's degrees in accounting at BYU.

Jake has diverse research interests, including interest in taxation, tax havens, earnings information content, and information technologies. His research has been accepted for publication at the *Journal of Accounting and Economics, Journal of Accounting Research, The Accounting Review, Contemporary Accounting Research, Review of Accounting Studies, Journal of Finance, Journal of Financial Economics,* and *Management Science.* Jake's research has been cited or featured in the *Wall Street Journal, New York Times, Bloomberg Businessweek, Fox News,* and NPR, and has been presented at the IRS, the SEC, and a congressional subcommittee. Jake currently serves as an editor at *Contemporary Accounting Research.*

Jake has taught accounting at undergraduate and graduate levels. He was won several awards for teaching, mentoring, research, and innovation in the classroom. He also co-founded Accounting Coding Camp with Mike Drake and Josh Lee, which provides coding education to graduate students in accounting and finance.

Jake is married to Kerrie, and they have four children, Allie, Luke, Mia, and Josie. He enjoys audiobooks, enjoys college sports, and is an ardent fly fisherman.

## DAVID SPICELAND

David Spiceland is Accounting Professor Emeritus at the University of Memphis. He received his BS degree in finance from the University of Tennessee, his MBA from Southern Illinois University, and his PhD in accounting from the University of Arkansas.

Professor Spiceland's primary research interests are in earnings management and educational research. He has published articles in a variety of journals, including *The Accounting Review, Accounting and Business Research, Journal of Financial Research, Advances in Quantitative Analysis of Finance and Accounting,* and most accounting education journals: *Issues in Accounting Education, Journal of Accounting Education, Advances in Accounting Education, The Accounting Educators' Journal, Accounting Education, The Journal of Asynchronous Learning Networks,* and *Journal of Business Education.* David has received university and college awards and recognition for his teaching, research, and technological innovations in the classroom. David is a co-author on McGraw Hill's best-selling *Intermediate Accounting* text, with Mark Nelson, and Wayne Thomas.

David enjoys playing basketball, is a former all-state linebacker, and is an avid fisherman. Cooking is a passion for David, who served as sous chef for Paula Deen at a Mid-South Fair cooking demonstration.

# CELEBRATING STUDENT SUCCESS

Don't you love those moments when your students see the bigger picture of financial accounting? Or when they see the important role that financial reporting plays in business decisions and our society? The authors have developed *Financial Accounting for Managers* with this purpose in mind. Students will gain knowledge of not only how to account for particular transactions, but perhaps more importantly, how those transactions affect the financial statements and how those financial statements are critical to understanding the financial performance, health, and prospects of a company. After reading this book, students will see financial accounting as an information tool that will help them make better decisions in their careers.

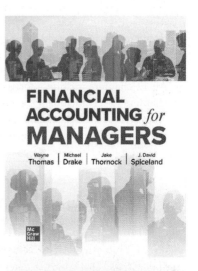

## SPICELAND/THOMAS ACCOUNTING SERIES

The Spiceland/Thomas Accounting series includes:

- *Financial Accounting 6e*
- *Intermediate Accounting 11e*
- *Financial Accounting for Managers 1e*

*Financial Accounting* and *Intermediate Accounting* have proven records of market-leading success by engaging a broad range of students, offering a wide array of resources necessary for building accounting concepts, and giving instructors the variety of tools they need to structure their unique courses.

*Financial Accounting for Managers* provides an exciting new book to the series with the addition of award-winning authors Michael Drake and Jake Thornock. Using the same proven Spiceland/Thomas approach, the text motivates student engagement by using modern companies, robust financial analysis sections, auto-graded real-world cases, and a focus on helping students see how financial statements are used to make business decisions. They also provide a flexible approach to accommodate various teaching styles, programs, and methods, including the extent to which debits and credits are considered.

The Spiceland/Thomas Accounting Series is fully integrated with McGraw Hill's Connect, an educational platform that seamlessly joins Spiceland/Thomas superior content with enhanced digital tools to deliver precisely what a student needs, when and how they need it.

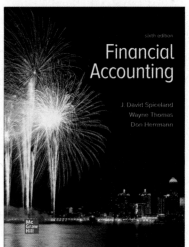

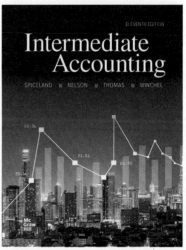

# A Flexible Approach

We recognize instructors have a wide variety of choices for topical coverage depending on their own preferences, course objectives, student mix, and length of the course. Because of this, instructors need flexibility in how much material to include in the course. *Financial Accounting for Managers* by Thomas, Drake, Thornock, and Spiceland has been designed to provide this flexibility. For example:

- Each chapter is designed to include fundamental topics in Parts A and B.
- For those instructors desiring expanded coverage of certain topics, some chapters contain Parts C and D, or Appendices.
- All end-of-chapter assignments are organized by Parts to simplify course development.
- All 12 chapters include a focus on the usefulness of financial statements to managers' decisions, and all of the topical chapters (5–11) include a specific analysis section using real-world companies. A comprehensive discussion of financial analysis is provided in Chapter 12.
- All chapters include a variety of cases and assignments to meet different course needs.

| | Chapter | Fundamental Parts | Expanded Parts | Analysis Section |
|---|---|---|---|---|
| Introduction | 1. Overview of Financial Reporting | A, B | C, App | |
| | 2. The Financial Statements | A, B | C, D | |
| Accounting Cycle | 3. The Accounting Cycle: During the Period | A, B | C | |
| | 4. The Accounting Cycle: End of the Period | A, B | C | |
| Topical Issues | 5. Revenue and Receivables | A, B | App | ✓ |
| | 6. Inventory and Cost of Goods Sold | A, B | App | ✓ |
| | 7. Long-Term Assets | A, B | App | ✓ |
| | 8. Investments | A, B | C | ✓ |
| | 9. Liabilities | A, B | App | ✓ |
| | 10. Stockholders' Equity | A, B | C | ✓ |
| | 11. Statement of Cash Flows | A, B | App | ✓ |
| Analysis | 12. Financial Statement Analysis | A, B | C | ✓ |

## DEBITS AND CREDITS?

Instructors also differ in whether to use debits and credits in teaching the course. The entire book and its assignment material have been written to accommodate both approaches.

All transactions are presented in the book showing their financial statement effects. Then, a separate call-out box, titled "DEBITS & CREDITS," shows related journal entries and T-accounts.

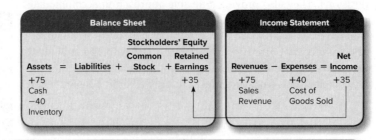

- Instructors **not covering** debits and credits can skip these call-out boxes.

- Instructors **covering** debits and credits can utilize these call-out boxes.

Additionally, all end-of-chapter assignment materials are available for both approaches by separating versions that use journal entries from those that do not. Assignments within the Brief Exercises, Exercises, and Problems ask students to identify the financial statement effects, while corresponding Journal Entries sections ask students to record the transactions using debits and credits. These corresponding assignments are cross referenced to make them easy to find.

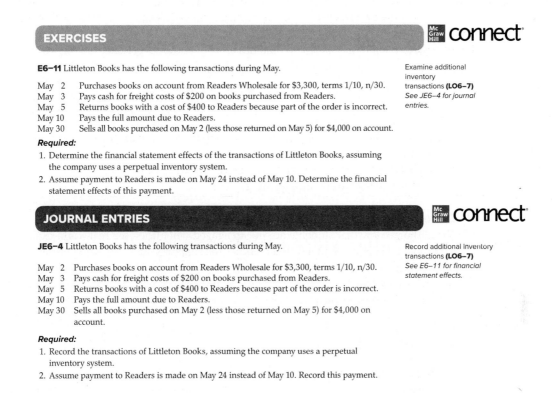

**EXERCISES**

**E6–11** Littleton Books has the following transactions during May.

| May 2 | Purchases books on account from Readers Wholesale for $3,300, terms 1/10, n/30. |
| May 3 | Pays cash for freight costs of $200 on books purchased from Readers. |
| May 5 | Returns books with a cost of $400 to Readers because part of the order is incorrect. |
| May 10 | Pays the full amount due to Readers. |
| May 30 | Sells all books purchased on May 2 (less those returned on May 5) for $4,000 on account. |

**Required:**

1. Determine the financial statement effects of the transactions of Littleton Books, assuming the company uses a perpetual inventory system.
2. Assume payment to Readers is made on May 24 instead of May 10. Determine the financial statement effects of this payment.

Examine additional inventory transactions **(LO6–7)**
*See JE6–4 for journal entries.*

**JOURNAL ENTRIES**

**JE6–4** Littleton Books has the following transactions during May.

| May 2 | Purchases books on account from Readers Wholesale for $3,300, terms 1/10, n/30. |
| May 3 | Pays cash for freight costs of $200 on books purchased from Readers. |
| May 5 | Returns books with a cost of $400 to Readers because part of the order is incorrect. |
| May 10 | Pays the full amount due to Readers. |
| May 30 | Sells all books purchased on May 2 (less those returned on May 5) for $4,000 on account. |

**Required:**

1. Record the transactions of Littleton Books, assuming the company uses a perpetual inventory system.
2. Assume payment to Readers is made on May 24 instead of May 10. Record this payment.

Record additional inventory transactions **(LO6–7)**
*See E6–11 for financial statement effects.*

## CASE-BASED INSTRUCTION

*Financial Accounting for Managers* offers a robust array of Brief Exercises, Exercises, and Problems to cover each chapter's topics. In addition, many instructors want to add cases, offering important real-world applications, to their in-class curriculum or take-home activities. *Financial Accounting for Managers* offers over 100 cases in its "Real World Perspectives" sections and dozens of Excel and Data Analytics assignments online, with each one auto-gradable in Connect, allowing additional decision-making practice for students and ease of grading for instructors. Our goal is to provide instructors with flexibility in the coursework they choose for their classes, ranging from knowledge-building assignments to real-world perspectives cases.

**REAL WORLD PERSPECTIVES**

| CASE TYPE | CASE DESCRIPTION |
|---|---|
| EDGAR | Analyze each chapter's topics through the lens of dozens of real-world financial statements and disclosure notes acquired from the SEC's EDGAR database. |
| Financial Analysis | Analyze the financial statements of Buckle and American Eagle for each chapter. |
| Comparative Analysis | Compare the financial statements of Buckle versus American Eagle for each chapter. |
| Ethics | Address ethical dilemmas facing managers in their financial reporting decisions. |
| Sustainability | Analyze real-world sustainability disclosures related to environmental, social, and governance issues. |
| Earnings Management | Demonstrate the incentives facing managers to aggressively use accounting estimates and judgments. |
| Great Adventures | Follow a single company through all chapters, adding topics as the story unfolds. |
| Excel | Learn the topical content while also learning Excel. |
| Data Analytics | Connect the chapter's content with technical analytics tools, including data visualization with Tableau. |

# CREATING FUTURE BUSINESS LEADERS

*Financial Accounting for Managers* combines years of author experience talking with business leaders, financial analysts, standard setters, auditors, and fellow accounting instructors across the country to ensure the book and its supplemental materials are consistent with what's being practiced in the business world and presented in such a way to help students be ready for business success. In keeping with this feedback, the authors have focused their approach on four key areas:

- Developing real-world perspectives and career-ready students
- Fostering decision-making and analysis skills
- Helping students focus on critical concepts
- Using technology to enhance learning

### Developing Real-World Perspectives & Career-Ready Students

The authors know that students are most engaged when they see real-world examples that are applicable to their lives and future careers. As the chapter's topics are being presented, references to real companies in the chapter's opening Feature Story and other related companies help keep topics relevant. Instructors can assign Real-World Perspective cases related to EDGAR Research, Financial Analysis, Comparative Analysis, Ethics, Sustainability, Earnings Management, and Great Adventures Continuing Problem. *Financial Accounting for Managers* offers more than 100 cases, with each one auto-gradable in Connect, allowing additional decision-making practice for students and ease of grading for instructors.

### Fostering Decision-Making and Analysis Skills

Companies today cite decision-making and analysis skills as top desired skills among recent graduates. Students are given opportunities to see real business decision-making practices in each chapter's Decision Maker's Perspectives and Manager Analysis boxes. Instructors can help students build their Excel, Tableau, and data visualization skills using a wide variety of Data Analytics and Excel assignments that are auto-gradable in Connect. Finally, the Great Adventures Continuing Problem progresses from chapter to chapter, encompassing the accounting issues of each new chapter as the story unfolds. These problems are also available in McGraw Hill Connect's General Ledger format.

### Helping Students Focus on Critical Concepts

Students check their understanding along the way by using Key Points within each Learning Objective and in-chapter Let's Review problems of the chapter's primary topics. These items prepare students to successfully complete the assigned end-of-chapter materials. Many Let's Review problems are complemented by videos. The Common Mistakes feature is a student favorite, helping them avoid mistakes that regularly trip up both learners and professionals.

### Using Technology to Enhance Learning

Today's students are comfortable online and seek out videos to aid their learning. *Financial Accounting for Managers* reinforces students' conceptual understanding with videos such as Let's Review, Interactive Illustrations, Concept Overview, and Applying Excel. Select end-of-chapter exercises are supplemented with Hints/Guided Example videos, and additional online resources like adaptive-learning SmartBook.

# DEVELOPING REAL-WORLD PERSPECTIVES & CAREER-READY STUDENTS

Students retain more information when they see how concepts are applied in the real world. Each chapter begins with a **Feature Story** that highlights real companies and offers business insights related to the material in the chapter. As the chapter's topics are being presented, references to the companies in the Feature Story and other related companies help keep topics relevant. The authors understand that students are best engaged when the discussion involves companies that students find interesting and whose products or services are familiar, such as **Apple**, **American Eagle Outfitters**, **Best Buy**, **Lululemon**, **Walmart**, **Disney**, and **Zoom**. In Chapter 12, full financial statement analysis is provided for **Nike** versus **VF Corporation**. The authors carry these real-world companies into the end-of-chapter material, asking students to analyze real-world situations. Over 100 real-world companies are featured in examples and assignments materials throughout the text.

The **Real World Perspectives** section of each chapter offers cases and activities that ask students to apply the knowledge and skills they've learned to actual, real-world situations. Students are placed in the role of decision maker, presented with a set of information, and asked to draw conclusions that test their understanding of the issues discussed in the chapters. All cases and activities are auto-gradable, meaning that McGraw Hill's Connect will automatically grade each case. Chapters contain: four Edgar Research, two Continuing Financial Analysis, Comparative Financial Analysis, Ethics, Sustainability, Earnings Management, and Great Adventures Continuing General Ledger cases, as well as Excel and Data Analytics cases that are available online.

---

## REAL WORLD PERSPECTIVES

**EDGAR Case**

### Norfolk Southern (ticker: NSC)

**RWP7–1** In EDGAR, find the annual report (10-K) for Norfolk Southern for the year ended December 31, 2019, and locate the note titled "7. Properties." Use the information in this note to answer the questions below.

**Required:**
1. Does the company have any assets that are *not* depreciated? If so, what are they?
2. What type of property has the highest depreciation rate?
3. Focus on Locomotives, which are one of Norfolk's major assets used in operations. Based on the stated depreciation rate, back into the implied service life of the company's locomotives.

Sustainability issues continue to have increasing importance for managers' decisions, not only related to environmental risks, but also the social and governance impact of their decisions. Chapter 1 introduces Sustainability Disclosures to set the stage, and Sustainability boxes are provided in the remaining chapters to highlight how the chapter's topics relate to environmental, social, and governance issues. A Sustainability Case using a real-world company can also be found in each chapter's Real World Perspectives assignment material.

 **SUSTAINABILITY**

The SASB aims to enable standardized, comparable reporting of sustainability metrics for many topics, including inventory sourcing. This goal of standardization and comparability implies that similar companies report similar sustainability measures in similar ways. Comparability will allow investors and other stakeholders to credibly assess and compare the quality of a company's sustainability numbers to other similar companies.

This issue can be seen in the SASB standards for the Apparel, Accessories & Footwear industry, which ask companies to disclose accounting metrics related to product inventory. The following table presents some of the important quantitative metrics requested by the SASB for apparel companies:

| Topic | Accounting Metric | Unit of Measure | SASB Code |
|---|---|---|---|
| Raw Material Sourcing & Innovation | Top five raw materials used in products | Metric tons | CN0501-03 |
| | Percentage of raw materials third-party certified to meet sustainability standards | Percentage (%) by weight | CN0501-04 |
| Labor Conditions in the Supply Chain | Percentage of suppliers beyond that have been audited to a labor code of conduct. | Percentage (%) | CN0501-05 |
| | Non-conformance rate for suppliers' labor code of conduct audits | Rate | CN0501-06 |
| Environmental Impacts in the Supply Chain | Percentage of supplier facilities with wastewater discharge meeting or exceeding legal requirements | Percentage (%) | CN0501-08 |
| | Percentage of suppliers who have completed an independent assessment on environmental data collection | Percentage (%) | CN0501-09 |

By encouraging the consistent measurement and disclosure of these important metrics, the SASB is aiming to improve practices on responsible inventory sourcing.

**Source:** https://www.sasb.org/wp-content/uploads/2015/09/CN0501_Apparel-Accessories-Footwear_Standard.pdf

# HELPING STUDENTS FOCUS ON CRITICAL CONCEPTS

**Critical Concepts**—It is crucial that students begin with a solid understanding of the role of financial accounting and the importance of financial statements to decision makers. For this reason, the first two chapters focus on building a framework for financial accounting (Chapter 1) and walking students through each primary financial statement (Chapter 2). Then, in Chapters 3 and 4, students work through the accounting cycle during the period and at the end of the period to understand how those financial statements are built. This sequence of coverage provides students with a solid foundation with which to tackle specific topics (Chapters 5 through 10) that are presented in general balance sheet order. The book finishes with coverage of cash flows (Chapter 11) and financial statement analysis (Chapter 12) to provide students a summary view of how the accounting information they've studied helps to understand a company's financial position and valuation.

**Let's Review** sections within each chapter test students' comprehension of key concepts. These short review exercises, with solutions, are intended to reinforce understanding of specific chapter material and allow students to apply concepts and procedures learned in the chapter prior to attempting their homework assignment. **Let's Review Videos** show students how to solve select exercises and model that approach for related homework.

The following is a list of accounts in alphabetical order and their balances for the Gav Paint Corporation at December 31, 2024:

**Let's Review**

| Account Title | Amount |
|---|---|
| Accounts payable | $170,000 |
| Accounts receivable, net | 180,000 |
| Bonds payable (due in 10 years) | 500,000 |
| Cash | 80,000 |
| Common stock | 400,000 |
| Intangible assets, net | 50,000 |
| Interest payable | 10,000 |
| Inventory | 300,000 |
| Investment in equity securities[a] | 50,000 |
| Notes payable[b] | 200,000 |
| Short-term investments | 60,000 |

**Common Mistakes** made by students and professionals are highlighted throughout each of the chapters. With greater awareness of the potential pitfalls, students can avoid making the same mistakes and gain a deeper understanding of the chapter material.

 **COMMON MISTAKE**

Some students confuse par value with market value. Par value is the legal capital per share that is set when the corporation is first established and actually is unrelated to "value." The market value per share is equal to the current share price. In most cases, the market value per share will far exceed the par value.

**Key Points** provide quick synopses of the critical pieces of information presented throughout each chapter.

 **KEY POINT**

External transactions are activities conducted between the company and other entities. The effects of these transactions on the financial position of a company are recorded in accounts. Accounts provide a record of all business activities related to a particular item. The balance of the account equals all activities that increase the account minus all activities that decrease the account.

# FOSTERING DECISION-MAKING & ANALYSIS SKILLS

**Manager Analysis** boxes are provided throughout each chapter and summarize why information presented in the chapter is important to managers. These boxes offer a framework of questions managers ask, the accounting information needed for reference, and possible analysis of that information.

## Manager Analysis

| Question | Accounting information | Analysis |
|---|---|---|
| How much profit is being generated from sales? | Profit margin | A higher profit margin indicates a company generates a higher net income per dollar of sales. |
| Is the company effectively generating sales from its assets? | Asset turnover ratio | A higher asset turnover indicates a company generates a higher sales volume per dollar of assets invested. |

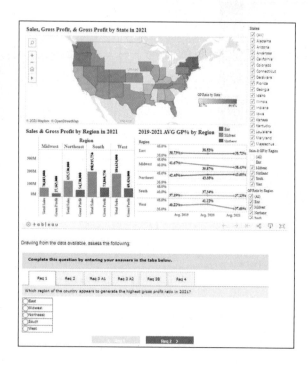

**Data Analytics** assignments are provided with each chapter. Instructors can visit Connect to find a variety of auto-graded Data Analytics questions that introduce students to seeing data presented in the types of visual formats they'll see in today's business environments. These exercises have been thoughtfully developed and scaffolded to build data analytics exposure and skills. Assignable, auto-gradable materials include:

- **Data Visualizations**—Familiarize students with data visualizations. Students interpret data in a static visual to answer accounting questions.
- **Tableau Dashboard Activities**—Easily introduce students to Tableau. Students learn to gather the information they need from a live embedded Tableau dashboard—no prior knowledge of Tableau needed.
- **Applying Tableau Cases**—Build student's data analytics skills. Students download an Excel file and build a Tableau dashboard with video tutorial guidance. Once they've completed their dashboard, they'll use it to answer auto-graded questions in Connect.

In today's environment, business graduates need to be well-equipped in analyzing data and making decisions. To address this need, each chapter includes **Decision Maker's Perspective** sections, which offer insights into how the information discussed in the chapters affects decisions made by investors, creditors, managers, and others.

**The Great Adventures Continuing Problem** progresses from chapter to chapter, encompassing the accounting issues of each new chapter as the story unfolds. These problems allow students to see how each chapter's topics can be integrated into the operations of a single company. Great Adventures problems are also available in McGraw Hill Connect's General Ledger format.

**Excel activities** and exercises foster career readiness by offering students hands-on training in multiple ways:

- **Integrated Excel** assignments pair the power of Microsoft Excel with the power of Connect. A seamless integration of Excel within Connect, Integrated Excel questions allow students to work in live, auto-graded Excel spreadsheets—no additional logins, no need to upload or download files. Instructors can choose to grade by formula or solution value, and students receive instant cell-level feedback via integrated Check My Work functionality.
- **Applying Excel** features in each chapter help build students' Excel skills, showing them how Excel can be used to make efficient calculations and analysis. Applying Excel video solutions housed in Connect complement the feature, allowing students to view the power of Excel to analyze business scenarios.

## Decision Maker's Perspective

### Limited Liability *and* Beneficial Tax Treatment

Wouldn't it be nice to get the best of both worlds—enjoy the limited liability of a corporation and the tax benefits of a sole proprietorship or partnership? An S corporation allows a company to enjoy limited liability as a corporation but tax treatment as a partnership. Because of these benefits, many companies that qualify choose to incorporate as S corporations. One of the major restrictions is that the corporation cannot have more than 100 stockholders, so S corporations appeal more to smaller, less widely held businesses.

Two additional business forms have evolved in response to liability issues and tax treatment—*limited liability companies* (LLCs) and *limited liability partnerships* (LLPs). Most accounting firms in the United States adopt one of these two business forms because they offer limited liability and avoid double taxation, but with no limits on the number of owners as in an S corporation.

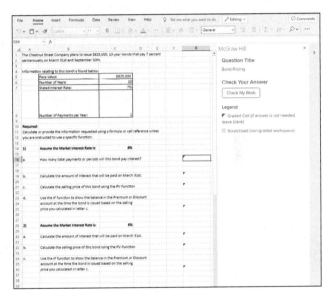

# USING TECHNOLOGY TO ENHANCE LEARNING

**Connect** and *Financial Accounting for Managers* are tightly integrated to continue honing students' conceptual understanding, problem-solving, decision-making, and analysis skills.

All end-of-chapter items in the textbook are built in the Connect platform. These items include feedback and explanations and many with **Hints/Guided Example Videos** to help students work through their homework in an effective manner.

## ASSESSMENT & PRACTICE: END-OF-CHAPTER AND TEST BANK

### Algorithmic Content & End-of-Chapter Assignments

A large set of algorithmic problems have been included, allowing students more opportunities for students to demonstrate their understanding.

Extensive end-of-chapter assignments are available in the text and Connect:

- Self-Study Questions
- Real World Perspectives
  - EDGAR cases
  - Financial analysis cases
  - Ethics cases
  - Sustainability cases
  - Earnings Management cases
  - Great Adventures continuing cases
- Brief Exercises
- Exercises
- Problems
- Journal Entries—Brief Exercises
- Journal Entries—Exercises
- Journal Entries—Problems
- Data Analytics & Excel cases (available online)

---

Using EDGAR (Electronic Data Gathering, Analysis, and Retrieval system), find the annual report (10-K) for Apple for the year ended September 28, 2019. Locate the "Consolidated Statements of Operations" (income statement) and "Consolidated Balance Sheets." You also may find the annual report at the company's website.

**Required:**
Determine the following from the company's financial statements:

1. What amount does the company report for accounts receivable? What does this amount represent?
2. What amount does the company report for accounts payable? What does this amount represent?
3. The company reports a single amount for "Other current liabilities" in the liability section of the balance sheet. What are some possible liabilities included in this amount?
4. What amount does the company report for common stock (including additional paid-in capital)? What does this amount represent?
5. Determine whether the company's total assets equal total liabilities plus total stockholders' (or shareholders') equity.
6. What amount does the company report for net sales? When a sale is made, does the company debit or credit the Sales Revenue account?
7. Do the company's total revenues exceed total expenses? By how much?

**Complete this question by entering your answers in the tabs below.**

| Required 1 | Required 2 | Required 3 | Required 4 | Required 5 | Required 6 | Required 7 |
|---|---|---|---|---|---|---|

| Accounts receivable | |
|---|---|
| The accounts receivable account represents the | |

< Required 1     Required 2 >

## Concept Overview Videos

Concept Overview Videos provide engaging narratives of chapter learning objectives in an assignable, interactive online format. These videos follow the structure of the text and match specific learning objectives within each chapter of *Financial Accounting for Managers*. Concept Overview Videos provide additional explanation and enhancement of material from the text chapter, allowing students to learn, study, and practice at their own pace. Assignable assessment questions paired with the videos help students test their knowledge, ensuring that they are retaining concepts.

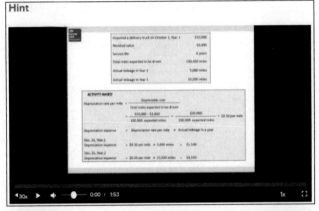

## Hints/Guided Example Videos

Hint/Guided Example videos are narrated, animated, and step-by-step walkthroughs of algorithmic versions of select exercises in Connect. Presented to the student as hints, Guided Examples provide just-in-time feedback, focused on the areas where students need the most guidance.

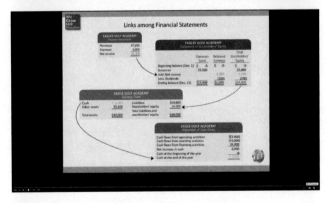

## Interactive Illustration Videos

Interactive Illustrations provide video-based explanations of key illustrations in the chapter. These videos transform a static illustration in the text into a dynamic, step-by-step walk through of the illustration, deepening students' understanding of the concepts or the calculations shown.

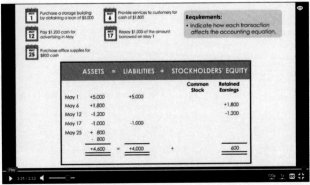

## Let's Review Videos

Let's Review videos relate to the Let's Review sections in the text, showing students how to solve certain exercises. In walking students through a particular scenario or question, these videos model how students can approach problem solving.

### Test Builder in Connect

Available within Connect, Test Builder is a cloud-based tool that enables instructors to format tests that can be printed or administered within a LMS. Test Builder offers a modern, streamlined interface for easy content configuration that matches course needs, without requiring a download.

Test Builder allows you to:

- Access all test bank content from a particular title.
- Easily pinpoint the most relevant content through robust filtering options.
- Manipulate the order of questions or scramble questions and/or answers.
- Pin questions to a specific location within a test.
- Determine your preferred treatment of algorithmic questions.
- Choose the layout and spacing.
- Add instructions and configure default settings.

Test Builder provides a secure interface for better protection of content and allows for just-in-time updates to flow directly into assessments.

### Remote Proctoring & Browser-Locking Capabilities

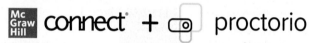 New remote proctoring and browser-locking capabilities, hosted by Proctorio within Connect, provide control of the assessment environment by enabling security options and verifying the identity of the student.

Seamlessly integrated within Connect, these services allow instructors to control students' assessment experience by restricting browser activity, recording students' activity, and verifying students are doing their own work.

Instant and detailed reporting gives instructors an at-a-glance view of potential academic integrity concerns, thereby avoiding personal bias and supporting evidence-based claims.

# A HEARTFELT THANKS

*Financial Accounting for Managers* would not be the same book without the valuable suggestions, keen insights, and constructive criticisms of the list of reviewers below. Each professor listed here contributed in substantive ways to the organization of chapters, coverage of topics, and selective use of pedagogy. We are grateful to them for taking the time to read each chapter and offer their insights.

We also acknowledge those reviewers who helped in the genesis of this text we appreciate your efforts!

Jon A. Baumunk, San Diego State University
Andrew Bird, Carnegie Mellon University
Edward Conrad, The University of Akron
Gregory L Davis, University of Illinois at Urbana–Champaign
Lucile Faurel, Arizona State University
Elisabeth Felten, DeSales University
Micah Frankel, California State University, East Bay
Diana Franz, University of Toledo
Henry Friedman, University of California, Los Angeles
Carla Hayn, University of California, Los Angeles
Joe Hatch, Lewis University

Dell Ann Janney, Culver-Stockton College
Jim Kimball, Endicott College
Cedric L. Knott, Colorado State University–Global
Sia Nassiripour, William Paterson University
Thomas P. O'Shea, Lewis University
Bo Ouyang, Penn State University at Great Valley
Usha Rackliffe, Emory University
Patricia Doran Walters, Texas Christian University
Harold E. Wright, Jr., The University of Alabama
Jia Wu, University of Massachusetts Dartmouth
Christian E. Wurst, Jr., Temple University

We also would like to acknowledge the many talented people who contributed to the creation of this text and thank them for their valuable contributions. Teressa Farough did a wonderful job accuracy checking our manuscript. Mark McCarthy of East Carolina University contributed a helpful accuracy check of the page proofs; we thank him for his speedy and insightful comments. We also appreciate the willingness of The Buckle, Inc., and American Eagle Outfitters, Inc., to allow us to use their companies' annual reports.

Ashley Newton of the University of Oklahoma did a wonderful job with the Test Bank, Concept Overview Videos, and Applying Excel video resources. Thanks to Shari Lynn Fowler of Indiana University–East for creating the PowerPoints. Jean Bissell did an outstanding job as Lead Subject Matter Expert for Connect; Beth Koblylarz and Teressa Farough and all of the staff at AnsrSource contributed their invaluable expertise as Connect reviewers.

We also appreciate the expert attention given to this project by the staff at McGraw Hill Education, especially Tim Vertovec, Vice President BEC Portfolio; Rebecca Olson, Excecutive Director; Noelle Bathurst, Senior Portfolio Manager; Lauren Schur, Marketing Manager; Christina Sanders, Lead Product Developer; Rachel Hinton, Assessment Product Developer; Kevin Moran, Director of Digital Content; Pat Frederickson, and Angela Norris, Lead Content Project Managers; Matt Diamond, Senior Designer; Traci Vaske, Senior Content Licensing Specialist; and Laura Fuller, Buyer.

# Instructors: Student Success Starts with You

## Tools to enhance your unique voice

Want to build your own course? No problem. Prefer to use an OLC-aligned, prebuilt course? Easy. Want to make changes throughout the semester? Sure. And you'll save time with Connect's auto-grading too.

**65%**
**Less Time Grading**

Laptop: McGraw Hill; Woman/dog: George Doyle/Getty Images

## Study made personal

Incorporate adaptive study resources like SmartBook® 2.0 into your course and help your students be better prepared in less time. Learn more about the powerful personalized learning experience available in SmartBook 2.0 at **www.mheducation.com/highered/connect/smartbook**

## Affordable solutions, added value

Make technology work for you with LMS integration for single sign-on access, mobile access to the digital textbook, and reports to quickly show you how each of your students is doing. And with our Inclusive Access program you can provide all these tools at a discount to your students. Ask your McGraw Hill representative for more information.

Padlock: Jobalou/Getty Images

## Solutions for your challenges

A product isn't a solution. Real solutions are affordable, reliable, and come with training and ongoing support when you need it and how you want it. Visit **www. supportateverystep.com** for videos and resources both you and your students can use throughout the semester.

Checkmark: Jobalou/Getty Images

# Students: Get Learning that Fits You

## Effective tools for efficient studying

Connect is designed to help you be more productive with simple, flexible, intuitive tools that maximize your study time and meet your individual learning needs. Get learning that works for you with Connect.

## Study anytime, anywhere

Download the free ReadAnywhere app and access your online eBook, SmartBook 2.0, or Adaptive Learning Assignments when it's convenient, even if you're offline. And since the app automatically syncs with your Connect account, all of your work is available every time you open it. Find out more at **www.mheducation.com/readanywhere**

> *"I really liked this app—it made it easy to study when you don't have your textbook in front of you."*
>
> - Jordan Cunningham, Eastern Washington University

Calendar: owattaphotos/Getty Images

## Everything you need in one place

Your Connect course has everything you need—whether reading on your digital eBook or completing assignments for class, Connect makes it easy to get your work done.

## Learning for everyone

McGraw Hill works directly with Accessibility Services Departments and faculty to meet the learning needs of all students. Please contact your Accessibility Services Office and ask them to email accessibility@mheducation.com, or visit **www.mheducation.com/about/accessibility** for more information.

Top: Jenner Images/Getty Images, Left: Hero Images/Getty Images, Right: Hero Images/Getty Images

# Contents in Brief

*Available online only

# Contents

# CHAPTER 6

## Inventory and Cost of Goods Sold 268

# CHAPTER 7

## Long-Term Assets 334

# CHAPTER 8

## Cash and Investments 392

# CHAPTER 9

## Liabilities 436

# CHAPTER 10

## Stockholders' Equity 502

# CHAPTER 11

## Statement of Cash Flows  552

# CHAPTER 12

## Financial Statement Analysis  610

*Available online only

# Financial Accounting for Managers

## CHAPTER ONE

# A Framework for Financial Accounting

**Learning Objectives**

### PART A: ACCOUNTING AS A MEASUREMENT/COMMUNICATION PROCESS

- ■ **LO1–1** Describe the two primary functions of financial accounting.
- ■ **LO1–2** Understand the business activities that financial accounting measures.
- ■ **LO1–3** Determine how financial accounting information is communicated through financial statements.

### PART B: THE DEMAND FOR FINANCIAL ACCOUNTING INFORMATION

- ■ **LO1–4** Describe the role that financial accounting plays in the decision-making process.
- ■ **LO1–5** Explain the need for accounting standards and the demand by investors and creditors for audited financial statements.

### PART C: THE SUPPLY OF FINANCIAL ACCOUNTING INFORMATION

- ■ **LO1–6** Understand the types of financial statement disclosures that companies provide in annual and quarterly reports.
- ■ **LO1–7** Understand the types of financial statement disclosures that companies provide in current reports.
- ■ **LO1–8** Understand the types of sustainability disclosures that companies provide.

### APPENDIX

- ■ **LO1–9** Explain the nature of the conceptual framework used to develop generally accepted accounting principles.

**Self-Study Materials**

- ■ Let's Review—Measuring business activities (p. 8).
- ■ Let's Review—Communicating through financial statements (p. 17).
- ■ The Bottom-Line (Key Points by Learning Objective) (p. 36).
- ■ Glossary of Key Terms (p. 37).
- ■ Self-Study Questions with answers available (p. 38).

## Feature Story

# Accounting: The Language of Business

Some of you reading this book may question if the material will be important for you in your future business careers. Perhaps you are planning a career in consulting, product management, marketing, supply chain, human resources, or finance and wondering why you have to learn accounting. You may even be thinking—*I don't want to be an accountant. I don't even plan to work closely with accountants. So why am I reading an accounting textbook?* We invite you to consider the following.

Managers, investors, lenders, suppliers, customers, and many others make important business decisions every day. These decisions relate to how a company grows, remains competitive in the marketplace, finances its operations, manages its operating costs, minimizes its risks, utilizes its resources, and generates profits for its owners, to name just a few. To make good decisions, these individuals need timely and reliable information. This is where accounting plays a critical role for business professionals. The primary functions of accounting are to measure the activities of a company and communicate those measurements to help individuals make good decisions. The better the information, the better the decisions.

Further, understanding accounting means understanding the language of business. When you speak that language, you'll be able to better communicate with others, which will allow you to make better decisions, help others make better decisions, and play a more influential role in creating a prosperous business.

Finally, you'll soon see how accounting reports help tell a company's story. Understanding the story plays a critical role in helping to shape the company's future. Accounting reports help reveal business success, failures, opportunities, challenges, risks, and uncertainties not otherwise known to the managers. The better you understand the stories told by the accounting reports, the better decisions you'll make to improve the company's future.

# ACCOUNTING AS A MEASUREMENT/ COMMUNICATION PROCESS
## Defining Accounting

■ **LO1–1**
Describe the two primary functions of financial accounting.

**Accounting is "the language of business."** It's the language companies use to tell their financial story. More precisely, accounting is a system of maintaining records of a company's operations and communicating that information to decision makers. The earliest use of such systematic recordkeeping dates back thousands of years to when records were kept of delivered agricultural products. Using accounting to maintain a record of multiple transactions allowed for better exchange among individuals and aided in the development of more complex societies.[1] In this book, you'll learn how to read, interpret, and communicate a company's financial story using the language of business.

Millions of people every day must make informed decisions about companies. Illustration 1–1 identifies some of those people and examples of decisions they make about the companies.

**ILLUSTRATION 1–1**

**Decisions People Make About Companies**

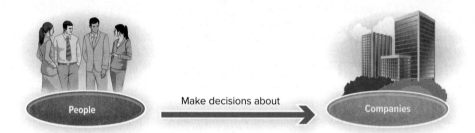

People — Make decisions about → Companies

1. **Investors** decide whether to invest in stock.
2. **Creditors** decide whether to lend money.
3. **Customers** decide whether to purchase products.
4. **Suppliers** decide the customer's ability to pay for supplies.
5. **Managers** decide production and expansion.
6. **Employees** decide employment opportunities.
7. **Competitors** decide market share and profitability.
8. **Regulators** decide on social welfare.
9. **Tax authorities** decide on taxation policies.
10. **Local communities** decide on environmental issues.

To make the decisions outlined in Illustration 1–1, these people need information. This is where accounting plays a key role. As Illustration 1–2 shows, accountants **measure the activities of the company and communicate those measurements to others.**

Accounting information provided for *internal* users (managers) is referred to as **managerial accounting;** that provided to *external* users is referred to as **financial accounting.** In this book, we focus on financial accounting. Formally defined, the two functions of financial accounting are to measure business activities of a company and then to communicate those measurements to *external* parties for decision-making purposes.

As you study the business activities discussed in this book, it is important to keep in mind the following "framework" for financial accounting. For each activity, ask yourself

1. How is the business activity being measured?
2. How is the business activity being communicated?

These are the two functions of financial accounting. You'll better understand *why* this process exists by thinking about *how* the measurements being communicated help people make better decisions.

---

[1]S. Basu and G. Waymire. 2006. Recordkeeping and Human Evolution. *Accounting Horizons* 20 (3): 201–229.

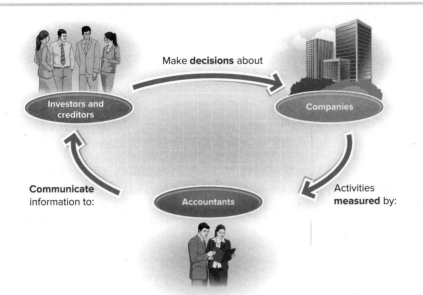

**ILLUSTRATION 1–2**

Framework for Financial Accounting

For example, **investors** want to make good decisions related to buying and selling their shares of the company's stock: Will the company's stock increase or decrease in value? The value of a stock is tied directly to the company's ability to make a profit, so what activities reflect the company's profitability? How should those activities be measured, and how should they be communicated in formal accounting reports?

As another example, **creditors** make decisions related to lending money to the company: Will the company be able to repay its debt and interest when they come due? How can debt activity be measured and how can it be communicated so that creditors better understand the ability of the company to have sufficient cash to repay debt and interest in the short term and the long term?

 **KEY POINT**

The two primary functions of financial accounting are to measure business activities of a company and to communicate information about those activities to investors and creditors and other outside users for decision-making purposes.

*User's Guide*
For learning objectives throughout this book, you will see boxed sections, like this one, titled *Key Point*. These boxed items will highlight the central focus of the learning objectives.

## Measuring Business Activities

Let's first look at the typical activities of a start-up business. We'll do this with a simple example. Suppose you and two associates (one a mechanical engineer and another a software engineer) want to start a business that sells and customizes robots for commercial use. The company will purchase generic robots from a manufacturer and then customize the robot (including hardware and software customization) to suit the specific needs of its customers. You name the company Eagle Robotics.

■ **LO1–2**
Understand the business activities that financial accounting measures.

Let's assume, after running some numbers, you estimate you'll need $1,500,000 to get the business up and running. You don't have that amount of money to start the business, so you start looking for investors. With their money, investors buy ownership in the company and have the right to share in the company's profits. Each share of ownership is typically referred to as a share of common stock. You develop a business proposal, explaining your target customers, funds needed, expected profits, and benefits your company will bring to the community. You pitch your idea to a private equity firm that agrees to invest $1,000,000 in your company in exchange for a 70 percent equity stake. The remaining 30 percent equity stake is divided equally among you and your two associates. Your company now has $1,000,000 from issuing common stock, which sometimes is referred to as contributed capital.

To raise the remaining cash needed, you turn to **creditors.** Creditors lend money to a company, expecting to be paid back the loan amount plus interest. Impressed by your business proposal and ability to raise funding from investors, a local bank lends you $500,000 with 12 percent annual interest, which you agree to repay within three years.

Now, with the $1,500,000 of cash obtained from investors and creditors, your company buys equipment. This equipment costs $240,000, leaving $1,260,000 cash for future use. At this point, your company has the following resources that can be used for operations.

| Cash | $1,260,000 | |
|------|-----------:|---|
| Equipment | 240,000 | **Resources** |
| | $1,500,000 | |

Who has the claims to the company's resources? Answer: The investors and creditors. Creditors have claims equal to the amount loaned to the company, $500,000. In other words, $500,000 of the company's resources are promised to the local bank. Investors have claims to all remaining resources, $1,000,000.

| Creditors (bank) | $ 500,000 | |
|------------------|----------:|---|
| Investors (common stock) | 1,000,000 | **Claims to Resources** |
| | $1,500,000 | |

We can see that the company has engaged in financing and investing activities, and it will soon begin operating activities.

- **Financing activities** include transactions with investors and creditors, such as issuing stock ($1,000,000) and borrowing money from a bank ($500,000).
- **Investing activities** include transactions involving the purchase and sale of resources that are expected to benefit the company for several years, such as the purchase of equipment for $240,000. With the necessary resources in place, the company is ready to begin operations.
- **Operating activities** will include transactions that relate to the primary operations of the company, such as providing products and services to customers and the associated costs of doing so, like rent, salaries, utilities, taxes, and advertising.

**Types of Business Organizations.**   Notice that you are both the manager and a stockholder of Eagle Robotics. You manage the resources of the company on behalf of all owners (stockholders, in this case), and you are also a stockholder, which helps align your interests with that of the other stockholders in the company. This is common in many start-up businesses. Mark Cuban, the owner of the Dallas Mavericks and a tech savvy entrepreneur, refers to a manager who also owns shares in the company as having "skin in the game." Companies that issue shares of stock often form as corporations.

A corporation is a company that is legally separate from its owners. The advantage of being legally separate is that the stockholders have limited liability. Limited liability prevents stockholders from being held personally responsible for the financial obligations of the corporation. Stockholders of Eagle Robotics can lose their investment of $1,000,000 if the company fails, but they cannot lose any of their personal assets (such as homes, cars, computers, and furniture).

A sole proprietorship is a business owned by one person; a partnership is a business owned by two or more persons. If you had decided to start Eagle Robotics alone, you could have formed a sole proprietorship, or you and your friends could have formed a partnership. However, because you did not have the necessary resources to start the business, being a sole proprietorship (or even one member of a partnership) was not a viable option. Thus, a disadvantage of selecting the sole proprietorship or partnership form of business is that owners must have sufficient personal funds to finance the business in addition to the ability to borrow money. Another disadvantage of being a sole proprietorship or partnership is that neither offers limited liability. Owners (and partners) are held personally responsible for the activities of the business.

A potential disadvantage of a corporation is *double taxation:* (1) the company first pays corporate income taxes on income it earns, and (2) stockholders then pay personal income taxes on income distributed to them from the company. There are many complexities in tax laws, and these laws are subject to change. For certain types of corporations and in certain instances, corporations may pay a higher or lower overall tax rate compared to partnerships and sole proprietors.

Because most of the largest companies in the United States are corporations, in this book we will focus primarily on accounting from a corporation's perspective. Focusing on corporations also highlights the importance of financial accounting—to measure and communicate activities of a company for investors (stockholders) and creditors (lenders, such as a local bank).

## ASSETS, LIABILITIES, AND STOCKHOLDERS' EQUITY

What information would Eagle's investors and creditors be interested in knowing to determine whether their investment in the company was a good decision? **Ultimately, investors and creditors want to know about the company's resources and their claims to those resources.** Accounting uses three measurement categories to describe such resources and claims.

Assets are the total resources of a company. At this point, Eagle Robotics has two assets—cash of $1,260,000 and equipment of $240,000—equaling total resources of $1,500,000. Of course, there are many other possible resources that a company can have, such as supplies, inventory for sale to customers, buildings, land, and investments. You'll learn about these and many other assets throughout this book.

Liabilities are amounts owed to creditors. Eagle Robotics has a liability of $500,000 to a bank. Other examples of liabilities would be amounts owed to suppliers, employees, utility companies, and the government (in the form of taxes). Liabilities typically include claims that must be paid by a specified date.

Stockholders' equity represents the owners' claims to resources. These claims arise from two primary sources: (1) contributions by the owners themselves and (2) net resources generated by company operations. To this point, Eagle Robotics has contributions from owners of $1,000,000.

The accounting equation in Illustration 1–3 shows the relationship among the three measurement categories. The equation shows that a company's assets equal its liabilities plus stockholders' equity. Alternatively, a company's resources equal creditors' and owners' claims to those resources.

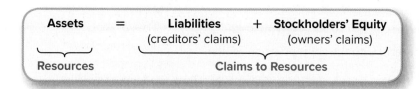

| Assets | = | Liabilities | + | Stockholders' Equity |
|---|---|---|---|---|
|  |  | (creditors' claims) |  | (owners' claims) |
| Resources |  | Claims to Resources |  |  |

ILLUSTRATION 1–3

The Accounting Equation

The accounting equation for Eagle Robotics would be

| Assets | = | Liabilities | + | Stockholders' Equity |
|---|---|---|---|---|
| (resources) |  | (creditors' claims) |  | (owners' claims) |
| $1,500,000 | = | $500,000 | + | $1,000,000 |

The accounting equation illustrates a fundamental model of business valuation. The value of a company to its owners equals total resources of the company minus amounts owed to creditors. Creditors expect to receive only resources equal to the amount owed them. Stockholders, on the other hand, can claim all of the company's resources in excess of the amount owed to creditors.

## REVENUES, EXPENSES, AND DIVIDENDS

Of course, all owners hope their claims to the company's resources increase over time. This increase occurs when the company makes a profit. Stockholders claim all resources in excess of amounts owed to creditors; thus, profits of the company are claimed solely by stockholders. We calculate a company's profits as the difference between revenues and expenses.

Revenues are the amounts recognized when the company sells products or provides services to customers. For example, when you or one of your employees provides services to a customer, the company recognizes revenue. However, as you've probably heard, "It takes money to make money." To operate the business, you'll encounter many costs.

Expenses are the costs of providing products and services and other business activities during the current period. For example, to operate the business, you'll have costs related to salaries, rent, supplies, and utilities. These are typical expenses of most companies.

*Common Terms*
Other common names for net income include *earnings* or *profit*.

Net income is the difference between revenues and expenses. All businesses want revenues to be greater than expenses, producing a positive net income and adding to stockholders' equity in the business. However, if expenses exceed revenues, as happens from time to time, the difference between them is a negative amount—a **net loss.**

You'll notice the use of the term *net* to describe a company's profitability. In business, the term *net* is used often to describe the difference between two amounts. Here, we measure revenues *net* of (or minus) expenses, to calculate the net income or net loss. If we assume that by the end of the first month of operations Eagle Robotics has total revenues of $375,000 and total expenses of $330,000, then we would say that the company has *net income* of $45,000 for the month.

Dividends are cash payments to stockholders. Suppose Eagle Robotics generated net income of $45,000 for the month. From these profits, let's suppose the company decides to make a cash payment of $14,000 to stockholders. The remaining $31,000 of resources are retained in the company to help grow future operations. Thus, when Eagle has net income of $45,000, stockholders receive a total benefit of $45,000, equal to $14,000 of dividends received and $31,000 retained in the company they own.

**Dividends Are Not an Expense.**   Recall earlier we defined expenses as the costs necessary to run the business to produce revenues. Dividends, on the other hand, are not costs related to providing products and services to *customers;* dividends are distributions (most often cash) to the *owners* of the company—the stockholders. Thus, dividends are not considered an expense of the business.

## Let's Review

*User's Guide*
*Let's Review* exercises test your comprehension of key concepts covered in the chapter text.

Match the term with the appropriate definition.

1. __F__ Assets
2. __C__ Liabilities
3. __E__ Stockholders' equity
4. __D__ Dividends
5. __B__ Revenues
6. __A__ Expenses

A. Costs of selling products or services.
B. Sales of products or services to customers.
C. Amounts owed.
D. Distributions to stockholders.
E. Owners' claims to resources.
F. Resources of a company.

*Solution:*

1. F; 2. C; 3. E;  4. D; 5. B; 6. A

In summary, the measurement role of accounting is to create a record of the activities of a company. To make this possible, a company must maintain an accurate record of its assets, liabilities, stockholders' equity, revenues, expenses, and dividends. Be sure you understand the meaning of these items. We will refer to them throughout this book. Illustration 1–4 summarizes the business activities and the categories that measure them.

**ILLUSTRATION 1–4**

Business Activities and Their Measurement

| Activities Related to: | Measurement Category | Relationship |
|---|---|---|
| • Resources of the company<br>• Amounts owed<br>• Stockholders' investment | • Assets<br>• Liabilities<br>• Stockholders' equity | Accounting Equation (A = L + SE) |
| • Distributions to stockholders | • Dividends | |
| • Sales of products or services<br>• Costs of providing sales | • Revenues<br>• Expenses | Net Income (R − E = NI) |

**KEY POINT**

The measurement role of accounting is to create a record of the activities of a company. To make this possible, a company must maintain an accurate record of its assets, liabilities, stockholders' equity, revenues, expenses, and dividends.

# Communicating through Financial Statements

We've discussed that different business activities produce assets, liabilities, stockholders' equity, dividends, revenues, and expenses, and that the first important role of financial accounting is to *measure* the relevant transactions of a company. Its second vital role is to *communicate* these business activities to those outside the company. The primary means of communicating business activities is through financial statements.

**■ LO1–3**

Determine how financial accounting information is communicated through financial statements.

Financial statements are periodic reports published by the company for the purpose of providing information to external users. There are five primary financial statements.

1.  Income statement
2.  Statement of stockholders' equity
3.  Balance sheet
4.  Statement of cash flows
5.  Statement of comprehensive income (when necessary)

These financial statements give investors and creditors the key information they need when making decisions about a company: Should I buy the company's stock? Should I lend money to the company? Is management efficiently operating the company? **Without these financial statements, it would be difficult for those outside the company to see what's going on inside the company.**

Let's go through a simple set of financial statements to see what they look like. We'll continue with our example of Eagle Robotics. Actual companies' financial statements report items you haven't yet encountered. However, because actual companies' financial information will be useful in helping you understand certain accounting topics, we'll sample them often throughout this book.

## INCOME STATEMENT

The income statement is a financial statement that reports the company's revenues and expenses over an *interval of time* (e.g., a month, quarter, or year). It shows whether the

**Common Terms**
Other common names for the income statement include *statement of operations*, *statement of income*, and *profit and loss statement*.

company was able to generate enough revenue during the period to cover the expenses of running the business. If revenues exceed expenses, then the company reports *net income:*

$$\text{Revenues} - \text{Expenses} = \text{Net Income}$$

If expenses exceed revenues, then the company reports a *net loss.*

On December 1, 2024, Eagle Robotics began operations. At the end of the first month of operations, Eagle Robotics reports its income statement as shown in Illustration 1–5.

**ILLUSTRATION 1–5**

Income Statement for Eagle Robotics

| EAGLE ROBOTICS Income Statement For the month ended December 31, 2024 | |
|---|---:|
| Revenue | $ 375,000 |
| Cost of goods sold | 250,000 |
| **Gross profit** | **125,000** |
| Operating expenses | 60,000 |
| **Operating income** | **65,000** |
| Interest expense | 5,000 |
| **Pretax income** | **60,000** |
| Income tax expense | 15,000 |
| **Net income** | **$ 45,000** |

Here are some specifics about Eagle's income statement:

- **Heading**—The heading includes the company's name, the title of the financial statement, and the time period covered by the financial statement. Because Eagle began operations on December 1, this income statement shows activity occurring *from* December 1 *to* December 31, 2024.
- **Revenues**—Eagle billed customers $375,000 for robot sales and customization services.
- **Gross profit**—Eagle has costs associated with the purchase of the generic robots from a supplier. The cost associated with the inventory sold to customers (or the "cost of goods sold") totaled $250,000 in December. After taking out the direct cost of the robots sold, Eagle has $125,000 left over. We call this amount the gross profit, which equals revenues minus cost of goods sold.
- **Operating income**—Eagle has other costs associated with operating its business including salaries, rent, supplies, etc. These operating expenses total $60,000 for the month of December. The operating expenses are subtracted from the gross profit to determine the company's operating income for the month. Eagle reports operating income of $65,000.
- **Pretax income**—Eagle also has expenses related to how it financed its business. Recall that Eagle borrowed $500,000 from a bank at 12% annual interest. The $5,000 in interest expense relates to the interest charge for the month of December and is subtracted from operating income to arrive at pretax income. Pretax income is also sometimes referred to as "income before income taxes."
- **Net income**—Finally, Eagle has to account for taxes. As discussed previously, corporations pay taxes to the government. For December, income tax expense is $15,000 or 25% of its pretax income amount. Income tax expense is subtracted from pretax income to arrive at net income. Eagle earned net income of $45,000 in the month of December.
- **Underlines**—In a financial statement, a single underline generally represents a subtotal, while a double underline indicates a final total.

The fact that Eagle reports a positive net income is, in some sense, a signal of the company's success. The company is able to generate more revenue from customers than the costs of running the business. Do you assume most companies sell their products and services for a profit? It's not as easy as you might think. In recent years, companies such as **Tesla, eBay, Uber, Boeing, General Electric, Wayfair, Fitbit,** and thousands of others have reported net losses.

**KEY POINT**

The income statement compares revenues and expenses for the current period to assess the company's ability to generate a profit from running its operations.

| Question | | Accounting information | | Analysis | |
|---|---|---|---|---|---|
| How can I tell if a company is profitable? | | Income statement | | If revenues exceed expenses, then a company has net income and is profitable. | |

**Manager Analysis**

*User's Guide*
*Manager Analysis* in chapter highlights specific decisions related to chapter topics that can be made using financial accounting information.

## STATEMENT OF STOCKHOLDERS' EQUITY

The statement of stockholders' equity is a financial statement that summarizes the changes in stockholders' equity over an interval of time. Stockholders' equity arises from two primary sources—common stock and retained earnings.

$$\text{Stockholders' Equity} = \text{Common Stock} + \text{Retained Earnings}$$

1. Common Stock (*external* source of equity) represents amounts invested by stockholders (owners) when they purchase shares of stock. The change in common stock over the period is shown as:

$$\text{Beginning Common Stock} + \text{New Issuances} = \text{Ending Common Stock}$$

2. Retained Earnings (*internal* source of equity) represent *all net income minus all dividends over the life of the company*. The change in retained earnings over the period is shown as:

$$\text{Beginning Retained Earnings} + \text{Net Income} - \text{Dividends} = \text{Ending Retained Earnings}$$

Think of retained earnings this way. A company that has net income has generated resources for owners through its operations. Those resources can either be returned to owners for their personal use (dividend payments) or retained in the business for future company use. From the company's perspective, we need to account for the total net income retained in the business. That's the balance of retained earnings. In each period, the beginning balance of retained earnings is updated for the current period's net income minus dividends to calculate ending retained earnings. This same calculation repeats each period.

Illustration 1–6 shows the statement of stockholders' equity for Eagle Robotics.

| EAGLE ROBOTICS Statement of Stockholders' Equity For the month ended December 31, 2024 | | | |
|---|---|---|---|
| | Common Stock | Retained Earnings | Total Stockholders' Equity |
| Beginning balance (Dec. 1)* | $          -0- | $     -0- | $          -0- |
| Issuance of common stock | 1,000,000 | | 1,000,000 |
| Add: **Net income for the period** | | 45,000 | 45,000 ← |
| Less: Dividends | | (14,000) | (14,000) |
| **Ending balance (Dec. 31)** | **$1,000,000** | **$31,000** | **$1,031,000** |

**ILLUSTRATION 1–6**

Statement of Stockholders' Equity for Eagle Robotics

From the income statement

*Beginning balances are zero only because this is the first month of operations for Eagle. Normally, beginning balances for Common Stock and Retained Earnings equal ending balances from the previous period.

Here are some specifics about Eagle's statement of stockholders' equity:

- **Heading**—The statement of stockholders' equity reports the activity for common stock and retained earnings over an *interval of time.* Similar to the income statement, the period of time in this example is December 1 to December 31, 2024.
- **Common Stock**—When Eagle begins operations on December 1, the balance of common stock is $0. This would be true of any company beginning operations. During December, Eagle issues $1,000,000 in common stock, so the balance of common stock increases by **$1,000,000**.

Accounting convention uses parentheses to signify an amount to be subtracted (such as dividends here).

- **Retained Earnings**—Retained Earnings also begins the first month of operations with a balance of $0. For the month of December, retained earnings increase by net income of **$45,000** and decrease by $14,000 for dividends paid to stockholders. We show the amount of net income in blue here to emphasize that it came from the income statement (Illustration 1–5). The ending balance of **$31,000** represents all net income minus all dividends over the life of the company, which is only one month to this point in our example.
- **Total Stockholders' Equity**—The third column shows that the two components—common stock and retained earnings—add to equal total stockholders' equity of **$1,031,000**.

*User's Guide*
Throughout each chapter, you will see sections titled Common Mistake. Information in these boxes will help you avoid common mistakes on exams, quizzes, and homework.

**COMMON MISTAKE**

Dividends represent the payment of cash but are not considered an expense in running the business. Students sometimes mistakenly include the amount of dividends as an expense in the income statement, rather than as a distribution of net income in the statement of stockholders' equity.

**KEY POINT**

The statement of stockholders' equity reports information related to changes in common stock and retained earnings each period. The change in retained earnings equals net income less dividends for the period.

**Statement of Retained Earnings.**    Notice the middle column of the statement of stockholders' equity in Illustration 1–6. This column sometimes is referred to as the *statement of retained earnings.* In practice, companies don't report retained earnings in a separate statement from common stock, so that's why we demonstrate the statement of stockholders' equity. Nevertheless, it's useful to see that this column highlights how net income (revenues minus expenses) from the income statement links to total stockholders' equity by adding to the balance of retained earnings.

**Manager Analysis**

| Question | Accounting information | Analysis |
|---|---|---|
| Was the change in stockholders' equity the result of external or internal sources? | Statement of stockholders' equity | When a company sells common stock, equity increases due to external sources. When a company has profits during the year in excess of dividends paid, equity increases due to internal sources. |

## BALANCE SHEET

The balance sheet is a financial statement that presents the financial position of the company on a particular date. The financial position of a company is summarized by the accounting equation (see Illustration 1–3):

$$\text{Assets} = \text{Liabilities} + \text{Stockholders' Equity}$$

As discussed earlier, this equation provides a fundamental model of business valuation. Assets are the resources of the company, and liabilities are amounts owed to creditors. Stockholders have equity in the company to the extent that assets exceed liabilities. Creditors also need to understand the balance sheet; it's the company's assets that will be used to pay liabilities as they become due. Illustration 1–7 shows the balance sheet of Eagle Robotics.

**ILLUSTRATION 1–7**

**Balance Sheet for Eagle Robotics**

**EAGLE ROBOTICS**
**Balance Sheet**
**December 31, 2024**

| Assets | | Liabilities | |
|---|---|---|---|
| Cash | $ 458,000 | Accounts payable | $ 14,000 |
| Accounts receivable | 287,000 | Salaries payable | 3,000 |
| Supplies | 4,000 | Income tax payable | 15,000 |
| Inventory | 500,000 | Interest payable | 5,000 |
| Other assets | 165,000 | Other liabilities | 82,000 |
| Equipment, net | 236,000 | Notes payable | 500,000 |
| | | Total liabilities | $ 619,000 |
| | | **Stockholders' Equity** | |
| | | Common stock | 1,000,000 |
| | | Retained earnings | 31,000 |
| | | Total stockholders' equity | 1,031,000 |
| Total assets | $1,650,000 | Total liabilities and stockholders' equity | $1,650,000 |

*Common Terms* Another name for the balance sheet is the *statement of financial position.*

From the statement of stockholders' equity

Here are some specifics about Eagle's balance sheet:

- **Heading**—The balance sheet reports assets, liabilities, and stockholders' equity at a *point in time,* in contrast to the income statement, which shows revenue and expense activities over an *interval of time.* For example, Eagle's income statement shows revenue and expense activity occurring *from* December 1 *to* December 31, 2024; its balance sheet shows assets, liabilities, and stockholders' equity of the company *on* December 31, 2024.
- **Assets**—These are the resources of a company. Eagle has total assets of $1,650,000. *Cash* is a resource because it can be used to make purchases. *Accounts receivable* is a resource because they represent the right to receive cash from customers that have already been provided products or services. *Supplies* include resources used to run the business, such as paper, cleaning supplies, and basic office materials. *Inventory* and *Equipment* are resources that can be used to provide sales and services to customers.
- **Liabilities**—These are the amounts owed by a company. Eagle has total liabilities of $619,000. These include amounts owed to regular vendors (accounts payable), as well as amounts owed for other items such as employee salaries, taxes to government agencies, interest, and bank borrowing (notes payable). Many liabilities are referred to as "payables" to signify amounts the company will "pay" in the future.
- **Stockholders' equity**—The difference between total assets and total liabilities of **$1,031,000** represents stockholders' equity. Total stockholders' equity includes the amount of common stock plus the amount of retained earnings from the statement of stockholders' equity. We show the stockholders' equity items in purple here to indicate they came from the statement of stockholders' equity (Illustration 1–6).
- **Accounting Equation**—Notice that the amounts listed in the "balance sheet" show that the accounting equation "balances."

The income statement is like a video (shows events over time), whereas a balance sheet is like a photograph (shows events at a point in time).

Total assets must equal
total liabilities and
stockholders' equity.

| Assets | = | Liabilities | + | Stockholders' Equity |
|---|---|---|---|---|
| (resources) | | (creditors' claims) | | (owners' claims) |
| **$1,650,000** | **=** | **$619,000** | **+** | **$1,031,000** |

**KEY POINT**

The balance sheet demonstrates that the company's resources (assets) equal creditors' claims (liabilities) plus owners' claims (stockholders' equity) to those resources on a particular date.

**Manager Analysis**

| Question | | Accounting information | | Analysis | |
|---|---|---|---|---|---|
| What are creditors' claims and owners' claims to the company's resources? | | Balance sheet | | The amount of total liabilities equals creditors' claims to the company's resources. The extent to which total assets exceed total liabilities represents owners' claims. | |

## STATEMENT OF CASH FLOWS

The statement of cash flows is a financial statement that measures activities involving cash receipts and cash payments over an interval of time. We classify all cash transactions into three categories that correspond to the three fundamental business activities—operating, investing, and financing.

- Operating cash flows include cash receipts and cash payments for transactions involving revenue and expense activities that arise during normal business operations during the period. In other words, operating activities include the cash effects of the same activities that are reported in the income statement to calculate net income. For this reason, the statement of cash flows presents a reconciliation of net income to operating cash flows.
- Investing cash flows generally include cash transactions for the purchase and sale of investments and long-term assets. Long-term assets are resources owned by a company that are thought to provide benefits for more than one year.
- Financing cash flows include cash transactions with lenders, such as borrowing money and repaying debt, and with stockholders, such as issuing stock and paying dividends.

Illustration 1–8 provides the statement of cash flows for Eagle Robotics. The statement shows the cash flows for each type of activity, with net cash inflows shown as positive amounts and net cash outflows shown in parentheses to denote negative amounts. Cash flows from operating activities are most often computed as net income adjusted for certain reconciling items that we'll cover later. Cash flows from investing and financing activities are computed as all cash inflows minus all cash outflows associated with those activities.

The total of the net cash flows from operating, investing, and financing activities equals the *net change in cash* during the period.

$$\text{Change in cash} = \text{Operating cash flows} + \text{Investing cash flows}$$
$$+ \text{Financing cash flows}$$

For Eagle, the net change in cash for December was an increase of $458,000. That amount equals the sum of its operating cash flows of −$788,000, investing cash flows of −$240,000,

*[handwritten: more than 1 year]*

**ILLUSTRATION 1–8**

**Statement of Cash Flows for Eagle Robotics**

Remember, amounts in parentheses indicate outflows of cash.

**EAGLE ROBOTICS**
**Statement of Cash Flows**
**For the month ended December 31, 2024**

| | | |
|---|---:|---:|
| Net Income | $ 45,000 | |
| Reconciling items | (833,000) | |
| Cash flows from operating activities | | $ (788,000) |
| Cash flows from investing activities | | $ (240,000) |
| Cash flows from financing activities | | $1,486,000 |
| **Net increase in cash** | | **$ 458,000** |
| Cash at the beginning of the period | | 0 |
| **Cash at the end of the period** | | **$ 458,000** |

← Included in the balance sheet

and financing cash flows of $1,486,000. The pattern of negative operating cash flows, negative investing cash flows, and positive financing cash flows is very common for start-ups. New companies generally have to make significant cash outlays to build-up inventory and to purchase equipment. We next add the beginning balance of cash. Because this is the first month of operations for Eagle, cash at the beginning of the period is zero. The ending balance of cash is the same as that reported in the balance sheet in Illustration 1–7. This reconciliation of the beginning and ending cash balances emphasizes that the statement of cash flows explains *why* the cash reported in the balance sheet changed from one period to the next.

 **KEY POINT**

The statement of cash flows reports cash transactions from operating, investing, and financing activities for the period.

# Decision Maker's Perspective

The statement of cash flows can be an important source of information to investors and creditors. For example, investors use the relationship between net income (revenues minus expenses) and operating cash flows (cash flows from revenue and expense activities) to forecast a company's future profitability. Creditors compare operating cash flows and investing cash flows to assess a company's ability to repay debt. Financing activities provide information to investors and creditors about the mix of external financing of the company.

*User's Guide*
*Decision Maker's Perspective* sections discuss the usefulness of accounting information to decision makers such as investors, creditors, and company managers.

## STATEMENT OF COMPREHENSIVE INCOME

The statement of comprehensive income measures changes in equity that arise from non-owner sources. Items that can potentially impact comprehensive income include gains and losses associated with investments in certain types of debt securities, certain types derivatives, pensions, and foreign currency translations. If a company, like Eagle Robotics, does not have any changes in equity from nonowner sources, then they are not required to prepare a statement of comprehensive income. We will discuss this statement in more detail in Chapter 2.

## THE LINKS AMONG FINANCIAL STATEMENTS

The financial statements are linked, because events that are reported in one financial statement often affect amounts reported in another. Many times, a single business transaction, such as receiving cash from a customer when providing services, will affect more than one of the financial statements. Providing services to a customer, for example, results in revenues recorded in the income statement, which are used to calculate net income. Net income, in turn, is reported in the calculation of retained earnings in the statement of stockholders'

equity. Then, the ending balance of retained earnings is reported in the balance sheet. **Thus, any transaction that affects the income statement ultimately affects the balance sheet through the balance of retained earnings.** The cash received from customers will be reported as part of the ending cash balance in the balance sheet and as part of operating cash flows in the statement of cash flows.

Illustration 1–9 shows the links among the financial statements of Eagle Robotics in Illustrations 1–5, 1–6, 1–7, and 1–8.

- Link [1] shows that net income from the income statement is reported in the statement of stockholders' equity as part of the calculation of retained earnings.
- Link [2] shows that after calculating the balance of retained earnings, the amount of total stockholders' equity can be reported in the balance sheet. Finally,
- Link [3] demonstrates that the balance of cash in the balance sheet equals the amount of cash reported in the statement of cash flows.

**ILLUSTRATION 1–9**

**Links among Financial Statements**

**EAGLE ROBOTICS**
**Income Statement**

| | |
|---|---|
| Revenues | $375,000 |
| Expenses | 330,000 |
| Net income | $ 45,000 |

**EAGLE ROBOTICS**
**Statement of Stockholders' Equity**

**[1]** Notice that the amount of net income in the income statement reappears in the statement of stockholders' equity.

[1]

| | Common Stock | Retained Earnings | Total Stockholders' Equity |
|---|---|---|---|
| Beginning balance (Dec. 1) | $ -0- | $ -0- | $ -0- |
| Issuance of common stock | 1,000,000 | | 1,000,000 |
| Add: **Net income for the period** | | 45,000 | 45,000 |
| Less: Dividends | | (14,000) | (14,000) |
| Ending balance (Dec. 31) | $1,000,000 | $31,000 | $1,031,000 |

**EAGLE ROBOTICS**
**Balance Sheet**

**[2]** Notice that the ending balance in the statement of stockholders' equity reappears in the balance sheet.

| | | | |
|---|---|---|---|
| Cash | $ 458,000 | Liabilities | $ 619,000 |
| Other assets | 1,192,000 | Stockholders' equity | 1,031,000 |
| | | Total liabilities and | |
| Total assets | $1,650,000 | stockholders' equity | $1,650,000 |

[2]

**EAGLE ROBOTICS**
**Statement of Cash Flows**

**[3]** Notice that the amount of cash in the balance sheet reappears as the ending cash balance in the statement of cash flows.

[3]

| | |
|---|---|
| Net Income | $ 45,000 |
| Reconciling items | (833,000) |
| Cash flows from operating activities | $ (788,000) |
| Cash flows from investing activities | (240,000) |
| Cash flows from financing activities | 1,486,000 |
| **Net increase in cash** | **458,000** |
| Cash at the beginning of the period | -0- |
| **Cash at the end of the period** | $ 458,000 |

Test your understanding of what you've read so far. The Computer Shop repairs laptops, desktops, and mainframe computers. On December 31, 2024, the company reports the following year-end amounts:

**Let's Review**

| Assets: | Cash | $10,000 | Revenues: | Service | $65,000 |
|---|---|---|---|---|---|
| | Supplies | 8,000 | | | |
| | Equipment, net | 26,000 | | | |
| | | | Expenses: | Rent | 6,000 |
| Liabilities: | Accounts payable | 4,000 | | Supplies | 14,000 |
| | Notes payable | 10,000 | | Salaries | 40,000 |

Additional information:

a. The balance of retained earnings at the beginning of the year is $7,000.

b. The company pays dividends of $1,000 on December 31, 2024.

c. Common stock is $15,000 at the beginning of the year, and additional shares are issued for $4,000 during 2024.

**Required:**

Prepare the (1) income statement, (2) statement of stockholders' equity, and (3) balance sheet.

**Solution:**

1. Income statement:

2. Statement of stockholders' equity:

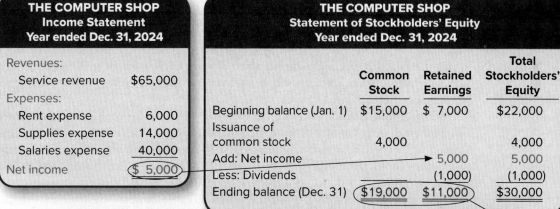

3. Balance sheet:

**KEY POINT**

All transactions that affect revenues or expenses reported in the income statement ultimately affect the balance sheet through the balance in retained earnings.

## PART B

# THE DEMAND FOR FINANCIAL ACCOUNTING INFORMATION

As discussed in Part A, accounting plays a critical role in communicating the financial story of a company. To this point, we've presented a simple look at how the financial story of a start-up company is measured and communicated to external users. Subsequent chapters will provide a more detailed view of this measurement and communication process. Before proceeding, it's important to understand a little more about the *demand* for accounting information by external users and the role of accounting in helping users to make decisions.

## Making Decisions with Accounting Information

■ **LO1–4**
Describe the role that financial accounting plays in the decision-making process.

In a free-enterprise economy, the majority of productive resources are privately owned rather than government owned. For the economy to operate efficiently, these resources should be allocated to enterprises that will use them best to provide the goods and services desired by society and not to enterprises that will waste them. The mechanisms that foster this efficient allocation of resources are the capital markets. We can think of the capital markets simply as a composite of all investors and creditors who provide funds to businesses who need them. Businesses go to the capital markets to obtain the cash necessary for the business to function and grow.

But how do investors and creditors identify the successful companies from the unsuccessful companies? How do they get the information necessary to make good investment decisions that help develop a prosperous society? Here's where financial accounting enters the picture. **Investors and creditors rely heavily on financial accounting information in making investment and lending decisions.**

Think of financial accounting as a special "language" that companies use to communicate financial information to capital market participants. The Pathways Commission of the American Accounting Association developed an illustration to help visualize this important role of accounting. As shown in Illustration 1–10, accounting provides useful information about economic activity to help produce good decisions and foster a prosperous society. Economic activity is complex, and decisions have real consequences, so critical thinking and many judgments are needed to produce the most useful accounting information possible.

### USEFULNESS OF FINANCIAL STATEMENTS

A recent survey of professional financial statement users (investors, creditors, analysts) examined the usefulness of the financial statements for six different decisions, including

1. Assessing the prospect of future cash flows.
2. Estimating firm value.
3. Identifying red flags.
4. Evaluating risks and uncertainties.
5. Assessing credit risk.
6. Evaluating management.

You can imagine that these decisions require reliable information, which you can get from the financial statements. The survey asked participants to assess the usefulness for these decisions of the five financial statements—balance sheet, income statement, statement

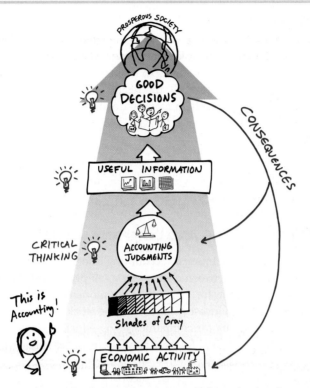

**ILLUSTRATION 1–10**

**Pathways Commission Visualization: "THIS is Accounting!"**

Reprinted with permission from the American Accounting Association.

of cash flows, statement of stockholders' equity, and statement of comprehensive income.[2] The survey participants assessed each statement on a scale of 1 (not important) to 5 (very important).

We present the survey results in Illustration 1–11.

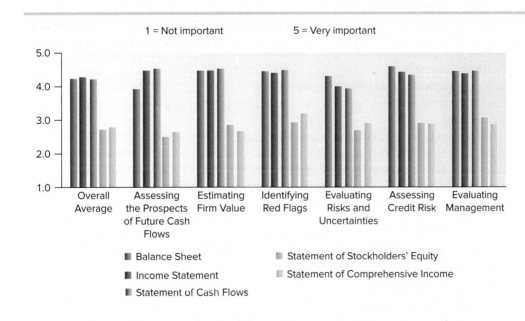

**ILLUSTRATION 1–11**

**Professional User Perceptions of Financial Statement Usefulness**

[2]Drake, M. S., Hales, J., & Rees, L. (2017). Disclosure Overload? A Professional-User Perspective on the Usefulness of General Purpose Financial Statements. *Contemporary Accounting Research* Vol. 36 (4).

The survey results reveal that the balance sheet, income statement, and statement of cash flows are all deemed to be important or very important to financial statement users for all tasks. The statement of stockholders' equity and the statement of comprehensive income are deemed to be less important than the other three statements. In Chapter 2, we discuss each of these statements in much more detail to learn more about the information investors and creditors can learn from each. Overall, the results of this survey indicate that financial accounting information is highly useful in making important information-based decisions.

 **KEY POINT**

Financial accounting serves an important role by providing information useful in investment and lending decisions.

## LINK BETWEEN ACCOUNTING AND COMPANY VALUE

To demonstrate the importance of financial accounting information to investment decisions, we can look at the relationship between changes in stock prices and changes in net income over the past 10 years. As an investor, you will make money from an increase in the stock price of a company in which you invest (you can sell the stock for more than you bought it). So as an investor, you are looking for companies whose stock price is likely to increase. Is there a way to find such companies? Interestingly, there is: **No other single piece of company information better explains companies' stock price performance than does financial accounting net income,** the bottom line in the income statement.

What if you could accurately predict which companies would have the largest increases in net income over the next year—that is, suppose you could predict the companies that will be above the 75th percentile in terms of their net income changes—and then you invested $1,000 in these companies? In contrast, what if instead you invested $1,000 in companies with the largest decreases in net income—that is, companies in the bottom 25th percentile in terms of their net income changes. Illustration 1–12 shows what would happen to your $1,000 investment over 10 years for each scenario.

You can see that if you had invested $1,000 in companies with the largest increases in net income, your investment would have increased to about $3,500 over the 10-year period. That's a 250% increase! If instead you had invested $1,000 in companies with the largest decreases in net income, your $1,000 investment would have shrunk to about $400 over this same period. This dramatic difference in the value of the investment demonstrates the importance of financial accounting information to investors. This book will provide you with a thorough understanding of how net income is calculated and presented in financial statements. As you can see from the illustration, if you are able to predict the change in financial accounting's measure of profitability—net income—then you can predict the change in stock prices as well.

Investors and creditors also use information reported in the balance sheet. For example, the liabilities section of the balance sheet reports *total debt.* Expanding debt levels limit management's ability to respond quickly and effectively to business situations. The "overhanging" debt, which involves legal obligation of repayment, restricts management's ability to engage in new profit-generating activities. Increased debt levels also increase interest payment burdens on the company. Failure to pay interest or to repay debt can result in creditors forcing the company to declare bankruptcy and go out of business. Understandably, then, investors and creditors keep a close eye on the company's debt level and its ability to repay.

 **KEY POINT**

No single piece of company information better explains companies' stock price performance than does financial accounting net income. A company's debt level is an important indicator of management's ability to respond to business situations and the possibility of bankruptcy.

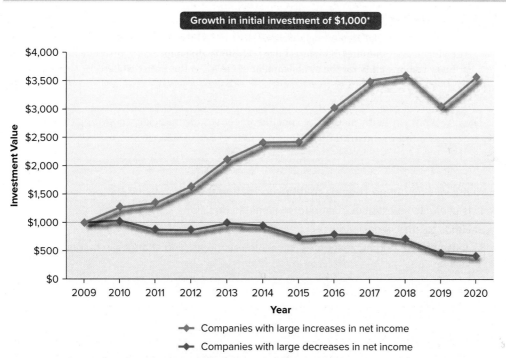

**Growth in initial investment of $1,000***

*Companies with large increases in net income*

*Companies with large decreases in net income*

*Amounts in this chart represent the investment growth based on the median stock return of each group each year. Companies in the top (bottom) group include the 25 percent of all U.S. listed companies with the largest increase (decrease) in net income. Each group has an average of about 1,700 companies per year.

**ILLUSTRATION 1–12**

Relationship between Changes in Stock Prices and Changes in Net Income over a 10-Year Period

## The Demand for Comparable Accounting Information

Because financial accounting information is so vital to investors and creditors, formal standards have been established. The rules of financial accounting are called generally accepted accounting principles, often abbreviated as GAAP (pronounced *gap*). The fact that all companies use these same rules is critical to financial statement users. It helps investors to accurately *compare* financial information among companies when they are making decisions about where to invest or lend their resources.

### STANDARD SETTING AND THE OBJECTIVES OF FINANCIAL REPORTING

The 1933 Securities Act and the Securities Exchange Act of 1934 were enacted after the stock market crash and ensuing Great Depression of the 1930s to restore investor confidence in financial accounting. The 1933 act sets forth accounting and disclosure requirements for initial offerings of securities (stocks and bonds). The 1934 act created a government agency, the **Securities and Exchange Commission (SEC).** The 1934 act gives the SEC the power to require companies that publicly trade their stock to prepare periodic financial statements for distribution to investors and creditors.

While Congress has given the SEC both the power and the responsibility for setting accounting and reporting standards for publicly traded companies, the SEC has delegated the primary responsibility for setting accounting standards to the private sector, currently the Financial Accounting Standards Board (FASB) (pronounced either by the letters themselves or as *faz-be*). The FASB is an independent, private-sector body with full-time voting members and a very large support staff. Members include representatives from the accounting profession, large corporations, financial analysts, accounting educators, and government agencies. Note that the SEC delegated only the responsibility, not the authority, to set these standards. The power still lies with the SEC. If the SEC does not agree with a particular standard issued by the FASB, it can force a change in the standard. In fact, it has done so in the past.

■ **LO1–5**
Explain the need for accounting standards and the demand by investors and creditors for audited financial statements.

For information about the activities of the Financial Accounting Standards Board, see its website, *www.fasb.org.*

**KEY POINT**

The rules of financial accounting are called generally accepted accounting principles (GAAP). The Financial Accounting Standards Board (FASB) is an independent, private body that has primary responsibility for the establishment of GAAP in the United States.

The FASB has explicitly stated the specific objectives of financial accounting. These objectives are presented in Illustration 1–13.

**ILLUSTRATION 1–13**

Objectives of Financial Accounting

*[handwritten: FASB = GAAP  IASB = IFRS]*

**Financial accounting should provide information that:**

1. Is useful to investors and creditors in making decisions.
2. Helps to predict cash flows.
3. Tells about economic resources, claims to resources, and changes in resources and claims.

Not all countries follow the same accounting and reporting standards. Many countries around the world follow broad standards set by the International Accounting Standards Board (IASB) and then often customized those standards to their particular country. The standards being developed and promoted by the IASB are called International Financial Reporting Standards (IFRS). The FASB and IASB have made several efforts to converge U.S. GAAP and IFRS, although some differences remain.

## THE DEMAND FOR CREDIBLE ACCOUNTING INFORMATION

For many businesses, there is a natural separation between those who run the business (managers) and those who own the business or finance operations (investors and creditors). This separation creates the need to ensure honest financial reporting. Managers may purposely provide misleading financial accounting information, called "cooking the books" for several reasons, such as to hide the poor operating performance of the company or to increase their personal wealth at stockholders' expense.

*Common Terms*
The auditor's report is also commonly referred to as the *auditor's opinion*.

To help ensure that management has in fact appropriately applied GAAP, the SEC requires independent outside verification of the financial statements of publicly traded companies. Such independent examination is done by auditors, who are *not* employees of the company, but who are hired by the company as an independent party to express a professional opinion of the extent to which financial statements are prepared in compliance with GAAP and are free of material misstatement. If auditors find material mistakes or fraudulent reporting behavior, then they require the company to correct all significant information before issuing financial statements. **Auditors play a major role in investors' and creditors' decisions by adding credibility to a company's financial statements.**

Auditors formally state their professional opinion about the financial statements in a report called the "Report of Independent Auditors." There are four basic types of auditor reports:

*[handwritten: 1. unqualified - best  2. unqualified w/ an explanatory or emphasis paragraph.  3. Qualified departure from GAAP  4) Adverse the worst]*

1. *Unqualified.* An auditor issues an unqualified or "clean" opinion when it is their opinion that the financial statements are presented in conformity with GAAP and free of material misstatement.

2. *Unqualified with an explanatory or emphasis paragraph.* An auditor believes the financial statements are in conformity with GAAP (unqualified), but the auditor feels that other important information needs to be emphasized to financial statement users.

3. *Qualified.* An auditor issues a qualified opinion when either the audit process has been limited (scope limitation), or there has been a departure from GAAP, but neither is of sufficient seriousness to invalidate the financial statements as a whole.

4. *Adverse.* An auditor issues an adverse opinion when the auditor has specific knowledge that financial statements or disclosures are seriously misstated or misleading. Adverse opinions are rare because auditors usually are able to persuade management to rectify problems to avoid this undesirable report.

Illustration 1–14 presents an excerpt from the auditor's report for **Tesla**. The auditor's report indicates that the financial statements for the period mentioned have been prepared in conformity with GAAP.

**ILLUSTRATION 1–14**

Excerpt from the Independent Auditor's Report of Tesla

**Tesla**
**Report of Independent Auditors (excerpt)**

To the Board of Directors and Stockholders of Tesla, Inc.

*Opinions on the Financial Statements and Internal Control over Financial Reporting*

We have audited the accompanying consolidated balance sheets of Tesla, Inc. and its subsidiaries (the "Company") as of December 31, 2020 and 2019 and the related consolidated statements of operations, of comprehensive loss, of redeemable noncontrolling interests and equity, and of cash flows for each of the three years in the period ended December 31, 2020, including the related notes (collectively referred to as the "consolidated financial statements").

In our opinion, the consolidated financial statements referred to above present fairly, in all material respects, the financial position of the Company as of December 31, 2020 and 2019, and the results of its operations and its cash flows for each of the three years in the period ended December 31, 2020 in conformity with accounting principles generally accepted in the United States of America.

/s/PricewaterhouseCoopers LLP

San Jose, California
February 8, 2021

We have served as the Company's auditor since 2005.

To further enhance the credibility of financial reporting, Congress established in 2002 the **Public Company Accounting Oversight Board (PCAOB).** The role of the PCAOB is to ensure that auditors follow a strict set of guidelines when conducting their audits of public companies' financial statements. The PCAOB is a government entity that, simply stated, "audits the auditors."

 **KEY POINT**

Auditors play a major role in investors' and creditors' decisions by adding credibility to a company's financial statements.

## AN ETHICAL FOUNDATION

Investors, creditors, government, and the general public rely on general ethical behavior among those who record and report the financial activities of businesses. A lack of public trust in financial reporting can undermine business and the economy.

The Sarbanes-Oxley Act (SOX), named for the two congressmen who sponsored the bill, provides for the regulation of auditors and the types of services they furnish to clients, increases accountability of corporate executives, addresses conflicts of interest for securities analysts, and provides for stiff criminal penalties for violators. These increased requirements have dramatically increased the need for good accounting and, at the same time, highlighted the value of accounting information to investors and creditors.

Important as such legislation is in supporting the ethical foundation of accounting, it is equally important that accountants themselves have their own personal standards for ethical conduct. Managers need to *develop* their ability to identify ethical situations and know the difference between right and wrong in the context of the accounting topics you will learn in this course. One of the keys to ethical decision making is having an appreciation for how your actions affect others.

When you face ethical dilemmas in your professional life (and indeed in your personal life), you can apply the following simple four-step framework as you think through what to do:

1. Understand the ethical decision you face.
2. Specify the options for alternative courses of action.
3. Identify the impact of each option on the stakeholders.
4. Make a decision.

For accountants, ethical decisions most often involve understanding how their actions affect amounts reported in the financial statements. An "Ethics Case" is included at the end of each chapter to give you an opportunity to practice this four-step process in the context of financial reporting.

 **KEY POINT**

The primary objective of financial accounting is to provide useful information to investors and creditors in making decisions.

**PART C**

# THE SUPPLY OF FINANCIAL ACCOUNTING INFORMATION

In Part B, we discussed why investors and creditors demand financial accounting information. We now discuss in more detail the many different types of financial accounting information that companies provide to capital markets—in other words, the *supply* of financial accounting information. While some investors and creditors may only be interested in the primary financial statements that we discussed in Part A, others demand more detail about the financial performance of the company, its financial position, and its prospects for the future. Companies supply additional financial accounting disclosures in annual and quarterly reports.

## Annual Reports

■ **LO1–6**
Understand the types of financial statement disclosures that companies provide in annual and quarterly reports.

At the end of each fiscal year, companies with public securities are required to provide stockholders with an annual report in a Form 10-K. Private companies are also often required to provide annual reports to lenders. The annual report includes the five primary financial statements: balance sheet, income statement, statement of cash flow, statement of stockholders' equity, and the statement of comprehensive income. Financial statements, though, are only part of the information provided in the annual report. Critical to understanding the financial statements and to evaluating a company's performance and financial health are additional disclosures included as part of the financial statements and also as part of the annual reporting requirements to the SEC.

The amount of information provided by annual report disclosures can be significant. For example, Tesla's most recent annual report filed with the SEC included five pages of financial statements followed by 61 pages of related disclosure notes. There were another 107 pages of disclosures related to business conditions, risk factors, legal proceedings, the company's stock performance, management's discussion and analysis, and internal control procedures. We discuss some of the annual report disclosures in the next section.

### DISCLOSURE NOTES

Some financial statement items include supporting discussion, calculations, and schedules in the notes following the financial statements. These disclosure notes are the most common means of providing disaggregated information or other additional information. For example, Tesla's balance sheet reports inventory of approximately $4.1 billion. Illustration 1–15 provides an excerpt of Telsa's inventory note that provides the disaggregation of inventory into its various categories: raw materials, work in process, finished goods, and service parts.

ILLUSTRATION 1–15

Excerpt from Tesla's Annual Report

**Tesla**
**Notes to the Financial Statements (excerpt)**

| ($ in millions) | December 31, 2020 |
| --- | --- |
| Raw materials | $1,508 |
| Work in process | 493 |
| Finished goods | 1,666 |
| Service parts | 434 |
| Total | $4,101 |

Most annual reports include a dozen or so additional notes on topics including investments, inventory, property and equipment, intangible assets, debt, leases, taxes, and employee compensation. We discuss and illustrate these in later chapters in the context of the related financial statement items.

The disclosure notes must include certain specific notes such as a summary of significant accounting policies, descriptions of subsequent events, and related third-party transactions, but many notes are fashioned to suit the disclosure needs of the particular reporting enterprise. Actually, any explanation that contributes to investors' and creditors' understanding of the results of operations, financial position, and cash flows of the company should be included. Let's take a look at just a few of these disclosure notes.

## SUMMARY OF SIGNIFICANT ACCOUNTING POLICIES

Typically, the first disclosure note consists of a summary of significant accounting policies that discloses some of the financial accounting choices the company makes. There are many areas where management chooses from among equally acceptable alternative accounting methods. For example, management chooses between different methods of accounting for inventory and for depreciation. The company also discusses its policies regarding the timing of recognizing revenues. Illustration 1–16 shows a portion of a typical summary note from a recent annual report of the Tesla.

Studying the summary of accounting policies note is an essential step in analyzing financial statements. Obviously, knowing which methods were used to derive certain accounting numbers is critical to assessing the adequacy of those amounts.

## MANAGEMENT'S DISCUSSION AND ANALYSIS

In addition to the financial statements and accompanying disclosure notes, each annual report requires a fairly lengthy discussion and analysis provided by the company's management. In this section, which precedes the financial statements and the auditor's report, management provides its views on significant events, trends, and uncertainties pertaining to the company's (a) operations, (b) liquidity, (c) capital resources, (d) off-balance sheet arrangements, and (e) critical accounting estimates. Although the management's discussion and analysis (MD&A) section may embody management's biased perspective, it can offer an informed insight that might not be available elsewhere. Illustration 1–17 contains a small portion of Tesla's MD&A in its annual report.

**ILLUSTRATION 1–16**

Excerpt from Tesla's
Summary of Accounting
Policies

**Tesla**
**Summary of Accounting Policies (excerpt)**

**Revenue Recognition**
We recognize revenue on automotive sales upon delivery to the customer, which is when the control of a vehicle transfers.

**Cash and Cash Equivalents**
All highly liquid investments with an original maturity of three months or less at the date of purchase are considered cash equivalents. Our cash equivalents are primarily comprised of money market funds.

**Property, Plant and Equipment**
Property, plant and equipment, including leasehold improvements, are recognized at cost less accumulated depreciation. Depreciation is generally computed using the straight-line method over the estimated useful lives of the respective assets.

**Research and Development Costs**
Research and development costs are expensed as incurred.

**Warranties**
We provide a manufacturer's warranty on all new and used vehicles, production powertrain components and systems and energy storage products we sell. In addition, we also provide a warranty on the installation and components of the solar energy systems we sell for periods typically between 10 to 25 years. We accrue a warranty reserve for the products sold by us, which includes our best estimate of the projected costs to repair or replace items under warranties and recalls when identified.

**ILLUSTRATION 1–17**

Excerpt from Tesla's
Management
Discussion and
Analysis

**Tesla**
**Management Discussion and Analysis (excerpt)**

**Overview and 2020 Highlights**
Our mission is to accelerate the world's transition to sustainable energy. We design, develop, manufacture, lease and sell high-performance fully electric vehicles, solar energy generation systems and energy storage products. We also offer maintenance, installation, operation and other services related to our products.

**Automotive**
We recently announced updated versions of Model S and Model X featuring a redesigned powertrain and other improvements. In 2021, we are focused on ramping these models on new manufacturing equipment, as well as production rates of Model 3 and Model Y, to at least the capacity that we have installed. The next phase of production growth will depend on the construction of Gigafactory Berlin and Gigafactory Texas, each of which is progressing as planned for deliveries beginning in 2021.

**Liquidity and Capital Resources**
As of December 31, 2020, we had $19.38 billion of cash and cash equivalents. Balances held in foreign currencies had a U.S. dollar equivalent of $6.76 billion and consisted primarily of euros, Chinese yuan and Canadian dollars. Our sources of cash are predominantly from our deliveries of vehicles, sales and installations of our energy storage products and solar energy systems, proceeds from debt facilities, proceeds from financing funds and proceeds from equity offerings.

**2020 Compared to 2019**
Automotive sales revenue increased $6.23 billion, or 31%, in the year ended December 31, 2020 as compared to the year ended December 31, 2019, primarily due to an increase of 129,268 Model 3 and Model Y cash deliveries despite production limitations as a result of temporary suspension of production at the Fremont Factory and Gigafactory Nevada during the first half of 2020. We were able to increase deliveries year over year from production ramping at both Gigafactory Shanghai and the Fremont Factory.

## COMPENSATION OF DIRECTORS AND TOP EXECUTIVES

The compensation large U.S. corporations pay its top executives is an issue of considerable public debate and controversy. Stockholders, employees, politicians, and the public in general sometimes question the huge pay packages received by company officials at the same time that more and more rank-and-file employees are being laid off as a result of company cutbacks. Contributing to the debate is the realization that the compensation gap between executives and lower-level employees is much wider in the United States than in most other industrialized countries.

A substantial portion of executive pay often is in the form of stock options or restricted stock awards. Executive stock options give an individual the right to buy the company's stock at a set price, regardless of how high the stock price rises. Restricted stock is a unit of stock given to an employee, but that unit of stock is not fully transferable until certain conditions are met (such as length of employment or attainment of performance goals). In recent years, restricted stock as a form of compensation has become more popular than stock options.

To help stockholders and others sort out the content of executive pay packages and better understand the commitments of the company in this regard, the SEC requires disclosures on compensation to directors and executives. A proxy statement is provided each year and includes compensation information for directors and top executives. The statement also invites stockholders to the annual meeting to elect board members and to vote on issues before the stockholders or to vote by proxy. Illustration 1–18 provides the compensation table for Tesla.

| Tesla Compensation Table | | | |
| --- | --- | --- | --- |
| **Name and Principal Position** | **Salary** | **Option Awards** | **Total** |
| Elon Musk, Chief Executive Officer | $ 56,380 | $2,283,988,504 | $2,284,044,884 |
| Jeffrey B. Straubel, Chief Technology Officer | 250,560 | 11,416,860 | 11,667,420 |
| Jerome Guillen, President Automotive | 301,154 | 17,450,897 | 17,752,051 |
| Deepak Ahuja, Former Chief Financial Officer | 501,923 | 5,708,430 | 6,210,353 |

**ILLUSTRATION 1–18**

**Excerpt from Tesla's Proxy Statement**

This note reveals that Elon Musk, the CEO of Tesla, earned a salary of $56 thousand and was awarded stock options with a value of $2.3 billion! However, it is important to recognize that these option awards are performance-based and that Elon Musk is not able to convert these options into cash because they have not yet "vested." The disclosure further reveals that a portion of these option awards become vested as the market value of Telsa hits certain milestones, such as doubling from its current market value of $50 billion to $100 billion. More options become vested as the market value grows in $50 billion increments thereafter (e.g., at $150 billion, $200 billion, etc.). All stock option awards become vested only when the market value of Tesla reaches $650 billion.

## AUDITOR'S REPORT

As discussed in Part B, independent auditors examine the financial statements and notes and then express an opinion as to whether the information is presented in accordance with GAAP and free of material misstatements. Illustration 1–14 provides an example of this report from Tesla. The auditor's report is included as part of the annual report.

## Quarterly Reports

Public companies are required to file quarterly financial statements with the SEC on Form 10-Q. These quarterly reports are similar to the annual reports in that they include a full set of financial statements and the management discussion and analysis (MD&A) section. However, the quarterly reports provide limited additional financial notes. The most recent quarterly report for Tesla includes 26 pages of additional notes compared to 61 pages of notes in the annual report. Quarterly reports are not audited by the independent auditors. Telsa makes this clear to financial statement users by stating that the statement is "unaudited" at the top of each of the financial statements.

**KEY POINT**

In addition to providing the primary financial statements, companies must also provide additional financial disclosures that provide disaggregated information and other additional information that supports the amounts reported in the financial statements. These additional disclosures also include a summary of significant accounting policies, descriptions of subsequent events, discussion of any related third-party transactions, management discussion and analysis, and information about executive compensation. For public companies, this information is provided annually to the SEC in a Form 10-K, and a subset of this information is provided each quarter to the SEC in a Form 10-Q.

## Current Reports

■ **LO1–7**
Understand the types of financial statement disclosures that companies provide in current reports.

In addition to filing annual reports on Form 10-K and quarterly reports on Form 10-Q, public companies must report certain major events on a more timely basis. These reports are called "current reports" and are filed with the SEC on Form 8-K. Companies generally have no more than four business days to file a current report once an event has taken place. Here are some examples of the types of events that should be reported in a current report.

The company has

- Publicly announced the results of quarterly and annual operations.
- Filed its quarterly or annual financial statements with the SEC.
- Entered into an agreement to acquire another company.
- Completed the acquisition or divestiture of another company.
- Delisted a security from a public exchange.
- Restated previously filed financial statements.
- A director or key officer that is departing.
- Declared bankruptcy.

Illustrations 1–19 and 1–20 provide examples of two current reports for Telsa. In the first example, Tesla is announcing that its financial results of the quarter ended September 30, 2020, have been released on its website. In the second example, Tesla discloses that it completed the sale of a new stock offering.

**ILLUSTRATION 1–19**

Excerpt from a Current Report of Tesla

> ### Tesla
> ### Current Report (excerpt)
>
> **Results of Operations and Financial Condition**
> On October 21, 2020, Tesla, Inc. released its financial results for the quarter ended September 30, 2020, by posting its Third Quarter 2020, Update on its website. The full text of the update is attached hereto as Exhibit 99.1 and is incorporated herein by reference.

> **Tesla**
> **Current Report (excerpt)**
>
> On December 9, 2020, Tesla, Inc. completed the sale of $5.0 billion (before commissions) of its common stock through its "at-the-market" offering program previously disclosed on December 8, 2020. The final settlement of the shares sold is expected to be completed by December 11, 2020.

**ILLUSTRATION 1–20**

Excerpt from a Current Report of Tesla

 **KEY POINT**

Public companies are required to disclose significant corporate events to the SEC within four days of occurrence in a current report called a Form 8-K. Common examples of significant corporate events include the announcement of financial results, the acquisition of a company, the divestiture of a company, or the departure of a director or key executive.

## Sustainability Disclosures

■ **LO1–8**
Understand the types of sustainability disclosures that companies provide.

Sustainability is defined as "corporate activities that maintain or enhance the ability of a company to create value over the long term" (SASB 2017).[3] In addition to providing the financial disclosures discussed previously in this chapter, many public companies now voluntarily provide sustainability disclosures that detail their policies, practices, and performance related to the sustainability of business operations. These disclosures provide information on the measurement, management, and reporting of these corporate activities. Stockholders demand sustainability information because they recognize that sustainability issues impact the current and future prospects of the company. Sustainability disclosures also provide information more broadly to other *stakeholders*, including creditors, employees, suppliers, governments, and the community, to help these parties better understand the impact of the company on society in general.

Sustainability disclosures are in their infancy. Presently, there is little uniformity across companies and little professional guidance, unlike for most mandatory GAAP disclosures. The Sustainability Accounting Standard Board (SASB) is an independent organization that sets reporting standards around sustainability reporting. Its stated mission is "to establish and improve industry specific disclosure standards across financially material environmental, social, and governance topics that facilitate communication between companies and investors about decision-useful information."[4] The SASB has developed unique standards for 77 different industries. These standards establish a minimal set of disclosures related to the industry's sustainability topics and metrics. These topics can be grouped into three broad categories: environmental disclosures, social disclosures, and governance disclosures.

**Environmental disclosures** focus on a company's environmental impact and generally relate to the issues noted in Illustration 1–21.

> **Environment**
>
> - Greenhouse gas (GHG) emissions
> - Air quality
> - Energy and fuel management
> - Water and waste management
> - Hazardous materials management

**ILLUSTRATION 1–21**

Examples of Environmental Issues

[3]https://www.sasb.org/wp-content/uploads/2020/02/SASB_Conceptual-Framework_WATERMARK.pdf
[4]https://www.sasb.org/about/

The most common environmental disclosure by most major companies is their greenhouse gas (GHG) emissions. In their sustainability disclosures, many companies disclose their actual emissions and then often compare these actual emissions to planned reductions. For example, **Coca-Cola** reports each year its greenhouse gas emission in total and per liter of product, as well as its progress toward its goal of a 25% reduction in emissions by 2030 from a 2015 base year. **Disney** provides a similar report, disclosing its progress in moving toward more renewable energy and away from fuel consumption, water usage, and waste production.

**Social disclosures** focus on issues of interest to broader stakeholders and society at large and generally relate to the matters noted in Illustration 1–22.

**ILLUSTRATION 1–22**

Examples of Social and Human Capital Issues

**Social & Human Capital:**

- Labor relations
- Fair labor practices
- Diversity and inclusion
- Employee health and safety
- Compensation and benefit
- Recruitment and retention
- Human rights
- Access and affordability
- Customer welfare
- Data security and customer privacy
- Fair advertising

Social disclosures cover dimensions of both social and human capital. For example, the SEC requires companies to disclose the ratio of the compensation of its chief executive officer (CEO) to the median compensation of all full-time employees. Many stakeholders are concerned that a significant pay gap between CEOs and their employees could reduce employee morale, lower productivity, and increase employee turnover. Each of these outcomes has potential negative consequences on the company and society in general. While a variety of metrics are used to calculate this ratio, and the ratio can fluctuate greatly each year depending on the form of CEO pay, the average ratio for S&P 500 companies in 2019 was 264-to-1. Some of the most astounding CEO ratios included **Dick's Sporting Goods** (1,487-to-1), **Starbucks** (1,675-to-1), **McDonald's** (1,939-to-1), and **Abercrombie & Fitch** (4,293-to-1).[5]

Diversity and inclusion are another major part of sustainability disclosures. Companies often report diversity metrics, such as the gender pay ratio. The gender pay ratio measures average male pay relative to average female pay. To the extent the ratio is out of balance, the company might not be able to retain qualified employees and may potentially suffer from reputational and legal costs. Similarly, companies disclose strategies and metrics related to diversity and equity. For instance, **Walgreens** states that "A diverse, equitable and inclusive organization is an essential part of [Walgreen's] business strategy" and reports metrics related to gender, racial and ethnic diversity across its leadership team and general workforce.[6] Many other types of disclosures are frequently reported to provide clarity concerning the treatment of employees—employee turnover rate, employee injury rate, temporary worker ratio, employee safety policy, and employee non-discrimination policy.

**Governance disclosures** include the company's actions and policies related to the division of power within the company such as the items noted in Illustration 1–23.

For example, most companies disclose the independence of their Board of Directors. Independent directors (sometimes referred to as outside members) are those individuals with no material interest in the company other than being on the board. Inside board

---

[5]https://aflcio.org/paywatch/company-pay-ratios
[6]https://www.walgreensbootsalliance.com/file-download/download/public/10251

ILLUSTRATION 1–23

Examples of
Governance Issues

**Governance:**

- Board independence
- Business ethics
- Conflicts of interest
- Competitive behavior
- Political influence
- Illegal practices

members often include company executives and major stockholders. While inside board members often have detailed information on the company's operations, independent board members are believed to act in better interest of stockholders and broader stakeholders. In 2020, **HP**'s 12-member board included 11 independent directors, 7 minorities, and 5 women.

Companies also may provide governance disclosures related to their ethical policies and procedures. Companies have incentives to signal their ethical conduct and willingness to take actions to reduce the risks of government fines and sanctions that would potentially hinder the company's operations. Another important governance disclosure in recent years is data privacy. With easy access to a large amount of customer data, many ethical issues have surfaced on how and whether companies should use their customers' data. For example, **Target** discloses its policy on how customer data are collected, used, protected, and shared. Nevertheless, Target also discloses that simply having a data privacy policy does not guarantee these data remain private. We provide an example of Target's data security and privacy disclosure note in Illustration 1–24.

Throughout the book, we discuss sustainability issues related to the various accounting topics that will make it clear how sustainability issues impact the financial system. At the end of each chapter, a sustainability case will give you an opportunity to examine recent sustainability disclosures from public companies in many different industries. These discussions and cases are designed to help you see that *sustainability issues are business issues*.

ILLUSTRATION 1–24

Excerpt from Target's
Disclosure of Data
Security and Privacy

**Information Security, Cybersecurity
and Data Privacy Risks (in part)**

We regularly receive and store information about our guests, team members, vendors, and other third parties. We have programs in place to detect, contain, and respond to data security incidents. However, because the techniques used to obtain unauthorized access, disable or degrade service, or sabotage systems change frequently and may be difficult to detect for long periods of time, we may be unable to anticipate these techniques or implement adequate preventive measures. In addition, hardware, software, or applications we develop or procure from third parties may contain defects in design or manufacture or other problems that could unexpectedly compromise information security, cybersecurity, and data privacy. Unauthorized parties may also attempt to gain access to our systems or facilities, or those of third parties with whom we do business, through fraud, trickery, or other forms of deceiving our team members, contractors, and vendors.

 **KEY POINT**

Many public companies voluntarily disclose information about their policies, practices, and performance related to the sustainability of business operations. This information generally relates to environmental issues, social issues, and governance issues.

## APPENDIX

■ **LO1–9**
Explain the nature of the conceptual framework used to develop generally accepted accounting principles.

# CONCEPTUAL FRAMEWORK

The FASB establishes financial accounting standards based on a **conceptual framework**, which you can think of as the "theory" of accounting. In much the same way that our nation's Constitution provides the underlying principles that guide the "correctness" of all laws, the FASB's conceptual framework prescribes the correctness of financial accounting rules. Having a conceptual framework provides standard setters with a benchmark for creating a consistent set of financial reporting rules now and in the future. It also provides others with a *written* framework so that everyone understands the underlying concepts that accountants are to consider in preparing and interpreting financial accounting information.

 **KEY POINT**

The conceptual framework provides an underlying foundation for the development of accounting standards and interpretation of accounting information.

In the chapter, we discussed the three objectives of financial accounting as outlined in the FASB's conceptual framework. Financial accounting should provide information that

1. Is useful to investors and creditors in making decisions.
2. Helps to predict cash flows.
3. Tells about economic resources, claims to resources, and changes in resources and claims.

To satisfy these objectives, financial reporting of accounting information should possess certain characteristics to be useful. What are the desired characteristics? Illustration 1–25 provides a graphical depiction of the qualitative characteristics of useful financial information.

**ILLUSTRATION 1–25**    Qualitative Characteristics of Useful Financial Information

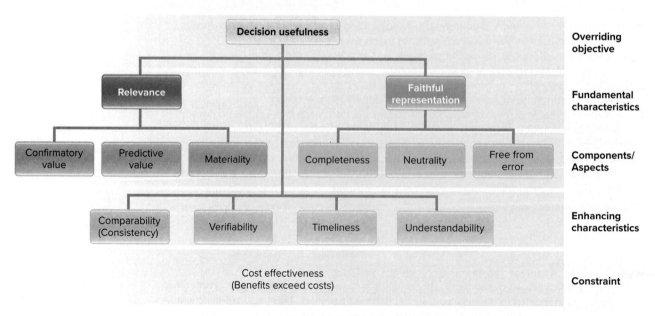

Notice that at the top of the figure is decision usefulness—the ability of the information to be useful in decision making. Accounting information should help investors, lenders, and other creditors make important decisions about providing funds to a company.

## FUNDAMENTAL QUALITATIVE CHARACTERISTICS

The two fundamental decision-specific qualitative characteristics that make accounting information useful are *relevance* and *faithful representation.* Both are critical. No matter how representative, if information is not relevant to the decision at hand, it is useless. Conversely, relevant information is of little value if it does not faithfully represent the underlying activity.

**Relevance.** To have relevance, accounting information should possess *confirmatory value* and/or *predictive value.* Generally, useful information will possess both of these components. For example, the ability of **Nike** to report a positive net income confirms that its management is effectively and efficiently using the company's resources to sell quality products. In this case, net income has *confirmatory value.* At the same time, reporting a positive and growing net income for several consecutive years should provide information that has *predictive value* for the company's future cash-generating ability.

*Materiality* reflects the impact of financial accounting information on investors' and creditors' decisions. Unless an item is material in amount or nature—that is, sufficient in amount or nature to affect a decision—it need not be reported in accordance with GAAP. Based on the concept of materiality, Nike probably does not record all its assets as assets. Most companies record assets such as wastebaskets and staplers as *expenses,* even though these items will benefit the company for a long period. Recording a $6 wastebasket as a current expense instead of a long-term asset for a multibillion-dollar company like Nike has no impact on investors' decisions. Thus, materiality is an aspect of the relevance characteristic with regard to values users deem significant in their decision-making process.

**Faithful representation.** To be a faithful representation of business activities, accounting information should be complete, neutral, and free from error. *Completeness* means including all information necessary for faithful representation of the business activity the firm is reporting. For example, when Nike reports inventory in its balance sheet, investors understand it to represent *all* items (and only those items) intended for sale to customers in the ordinary course of business. If the amount reported for inventory includes only some of the items to be sold, then it lacks completeness. Adequate note disclosure is another important component of completeness. Nike must disclose in the notes to the financial statements the method it used to calculate inventory reported on its balance sheet. (We discuss alternative inventory methods in Chapter 6.)

*Neutrality* means to be unbiased, and this characteristic is highly related to the establishment of accounting standards. Because of the topic and the nature of the business, sometimes a new accounting standard may affect one group of companies over others. In such cases, the FASB must convince the financial community that this was a *consequence* of the standard and not an *objective* used to set the standard. For example, the FASB requires that all research and development (R&D) costs be reported as an expense in the income statement, reducing the current year's net income. The FASB's objective in adopting this approach was not to weaken the financial appearance of those companies in R&D-intensive industries, such as telecommunications, pharmaceuticals, and software, even though that may have been an effect.

*Free from error* indicates that reported amounts reflect the best available information. As you'll come to find out in this course, some amounts reported in the financial statements are based on estimates, and the accuracy of those estimates is subject to uncertainty. Because of this, financial statements are not expected to be completely free of error, but they are expected to reflect management's unbiased judgments and due diligence in reflecting appropriate accounting principles.

**KEY POINT**

To be useful for decision making, accounting information should have relevance and faithful representation.

## ENHANCING QUALITATIVE CHARACTERISTICS

Four enhancing qualitative characteristics are comparability, verifiability, timeliness, and understandability. Comparability refers to the ability of users to see similarities and differences between two different business activities. For example, how does **Nike**'s net income compare with net income for other sports apparel companies such as **Under Armour**? Comparability also refers to the ability of users to see similarities and differences in the same company over time. How does Nike's net income this year compare to last year's? Closely related to the notion of comparability is consistency. Consistency refers to the use of similar accounting procedures either over time for the same company or across companies at the same point in time. Comparability of financial information is the overriding goal, while consistency of accounting procedures is a means of achieving that goal.

Verifiability implies a consensus among different measurers. For instance, different graders will arrive at the same exam score for multiple-choice tests, but they are more likely to differ when scoring essay exams. Multiple-choice tests are highly verifiable. The same idea holds in the business world. For example, the price Nike pays to purchase a trademark of another company is usually verifiable because there is an exchange of cash at a certain point in time. In contrast, the value of a patent for a new product or design that Nike develops internally over an extended period is more subjective and less verifiable.

Firms must also disclose information related to net income that is *timely*. Timeliness refers to information being available to users early enough to allow them to use it in the decision process. Large companies like Nike are required to report information related to net income within 40 days after the end of the quarter and within 60 days after the end of the year.

Understandability means that users must be able to understand the information within the context of the decision they are making. This is a user-specific quality because users will differ in their ability to comprehend any set of information.

**KEY POINT**

Four characteristics of financial reporting enhance its usefulness. These characteristics include comparability, verifiability, timeliness, and understandability.

## COST CONSTRAINT

Sometimes, certain information involves more time and effort than the information is worth. For example, if a friend asks what you did today, she probably wants to know the general outline of your day but does not want to hear a recital of every move you made. Similarly, there may be a cost constraint (limit) to reporting financial information.

The cost constraint suggests that financial accounting information is provided only when the benefits of doing so exceed the costs. For example, knowing the profit margin earned by Nike in each country provides decision-useful information to investors and creditors.

However, this information is also helpful to the company's current and potential competitors, such as Under Armour, as it makes its own expansion plans. The competitive costs of providing this information may outweigh the benefits.

## UNDERLYING ASSUMPTIONS

For the qualitative characteristics described above to be applied to accounting information, four basic assumptions must be made to support the existence of GAAP. As pictured in Illustration 1–26, they are (1) the economic entity assumption, (2) the monetary unit assumption, (3) the periodicity assumption, and (4) the going concern assumption.

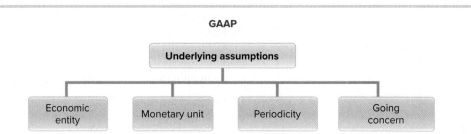

**ILLUSTRATION 1–26**

**Assumptions That Underlie GAAP**

**Economic Entity Assumption.**   The economic entity assumption states that we can identify all economic events with a particular economic entity. In other words, only business transactions involving Nike should be reported as part of Nike's financial accounting information. Another key aspect of this assumption is the distinction between the economic activities of owners and those of the company. For example, Nike co-founder and chair Phil Knight's personal residence is not an asset of Nike.

**Monetary Unit Assumption.**   Information would be difficult to use if, for example, we listed assets as "three machines, two trucks, and a building." According to the monetary unit assumption, in order to *measure* financial statement elements, we need a unit or scale of measurement. The dollar in the United States is the most appropriate common denominator to express information about financial statement elements and changes in those elements. In Europe, the common denominator is the euro. Nike has operations throughout the world, so it must translate all its financial information to U.S. dollars under the monetary unit assumption.

**Periodicity Assumption.**   The periodicity assumption relates to the qualitative characteristic of *timeliness*. External users need *periodic* information to make decisions. The periodicity assumption divides the economic life of an enterprise (presumed to be indefinite) into artificial time periods for periodic financial reporting. Corporations like Nike, whose securities are publicly traded, are required to provide financial information to the SEC on a quarterly *and* an annual basis. Quarterly reports are more timely, while annual reports allow the full application of GAAP.

**Going Concern Assumption.**   The going concern assumption states that in the absence of information to the contrary, a business entity will continue to operate indefinitely. This assumption is critical to many broad and specific accounting principles. It provides justification for measuring many assets based on their original costs (a practice known as the *historical cost principle*). If we knew an enterprise was going to cease operations in the near future, we would measure assets and liabilities not at their original costs but at their current liquidation values.

**THE BOTTOM LINE**

**LO1–1 Describe the two primary functions of financial accounting.**

The two primary functions of financial accounting are to measure business activities of a company and to communicate information about those activities to investors and creditors and other outside users for decision-making purposes.

**LO1–2 Understand the business activities that financial accounting measures.**

The measurement role of accounting is to create a record of the activities of a company. To make this possible, a company must maintain an accurate record of its assets, liabilities, stockholders' equity, revenues, expenses, and dividends.

**LO1–3 Determine how financial accounting information is communicated through financial statements.**

The income statement compares revenues and expenses for the current period to assess the company's ability to generate a profit from running its operations.

The statement of stockholders' equity reports information related to changes in common stock and retained earnings each period. The change in retained earnings equals net income less dividends for the period.

The balance sheet demonstrates that the company's resources (assets) equal creditors' claims (liabilities) plus owners' claims (stockholders' equity) to those resources on a particular date.

The statement of cash flows reports cash transactions from operating, investing, and financing activities for the period.

All transactions that affect revenues or expenses reported in the income statement ultimately affect the balance sheet through the balance in retained earnings.

**LO1–4 Describe the role that financial accounting plays in the decision-making process.**

Financial accounting serves an important role by providing information useful in investment and lending decisions.

No single piece of company information better explains companies' stock price performance than does financial accounting net income. A company's debt level is an important indicator of management's ability to respond to business situations and the possibility of bankruptcy.

**LO1–5 Explain the need for accounting standards and the demand by investors and creditors for audited financial statements.**

The rules of financial accounting are called generally accepted accounting principles (GAAP). The Financial Accounting Standards Board (FASB) is an independent, private body that has primary responsibility for the establishment of GAAP in the United States.

The primary objective of financial accounting is to provide useful information to investors and creditors in making decisions.

Auditors play a major role in investors' and creditors' decisions by adding credibility to a company's financial statements.

**LO1–6 Understand the types of financial statement disclosures that companies provide in annual and quarterly reports.**

In addition to providing the primary financial statements, companies must also provide additional financial disclosures that provide disaggregated information and other additional information that supports the amounts reported in the financial statements. These additional disclosures also include a summary of significant accounting policies, descriptions of subsequent events, discussion of any related third-party transactions, management discussion and analysis, and information about executive compensation. For public companies, this information provided annually to the SEC in a Form 10-K and a subset of this information is provided each quarter to the SEC in a Form 10-Q.

**LO1–7 Understand the types of financial statement disclosures that companies provide in current reports.**

Public companies are required to disclose significant corporate events to the SEC within four days of occurrence in a current report called a Form 8-K. Common examples of significant corporate events include the announcement of financial results, the acquisition of a company, the divestiture of a company, or the departure of a director or key executive.

**LO1–8 Understand the types of sustainability disclosures that companies provide.**

Many public companies voluntarily disclose information about their policies, practices, and performance related to the sustainability of business operations. This information generally relates to environmental issues, social issues, and governance issues.

**Appendix**

**LO1–9** Explain the nature of the conceptual framework used to develop generally accepted accounting principles.

The conceptual framework provides an underlying foundation for the development of accounting standards and interpretation of accounting information.

To be useful for decision making, accounting information should have relevance (confirmatory value, predictive value, and materiality) and faithful representation (completeness, neutrality and free from error).

Four characteristics of financial reporting enhance its usefulness. These characteristics include comparability, consistency, verifiability, and timeliness.

## GLOSSARY

**Accounting:** A system of maintaining records of a company's operations and communicating that information to decision makers. **p. 4**

**Accounting equation:** Equation that shows a company's resources (assets) equal creditors' and owners' claims to those resources (liabilities and stockholders' equity). **p. 7**

**Assets:** Resources of a company. **p. 7**

**Auditors:** Trained individuals hired by a company as an independent party to express a professional opinion of the conformity of that company's financial statements with GAAP. **p. 22**

**Balance sheet:** A financial statement that presents the financial position of the company on a particular date. **p. 12**

**Capital markets:** A composite of all investors and creditors who provide funds to businesses who need them. **p. 18**

**Common stock:** Amounts invested by stockholders when they purchase shares of stock; external source of equity. **p. 11**

**Comparability:** The ability of users to see similarities and differences between two different business activities. **p. 34**

**Consistency:** The use of similar accounting procedures either over time for the same company or across companies at the same point in time. **p. 34**

**Corporation:** An entity that is legally separate from its owners. **p. 6**

**Cost constraint:** Financial accounting information is provided only when the benefits of doing so exceed the costs. **p. 34**

**Decision usefulness:** The ability of the information to be useful in decision making. **p. 33**

**Dividends:** Distributions to stockholders, typically in the form of cash. **p. 8**

**Economic entity assumption:** All economic events with a particular economic entity can be identified. **p. 35**

**Expenses:** Costs of providing products and services and other business activities during the current period. **p. 8**

**Faithful representation:** Accounting information that is complete, neutral, and free from error. **p. 33**

**Financial accounting:** Measurement of business activities of a company and communication of those measurements to external parties for decision-making purposes. **p. 4**

**Financial Accounting Standards Board (FASB):** An independent, private body that has primary responsibility for the establishment of GAAP in the United States. **p. 21**

**Financial statements:** Periodic reports published by the company for the purpose of providing information to external users. **p. 9**

**Financing cash flows:** Cash transactions with lenders (borrowing and repaying debt) and stockholders (issue stock and paying dividends). **p. 14**

**Generally accepted accounting principles (GAAP):** The rules of financial accounting. **p. 21**

**Going concern assumption:** In the absence of information to the contrary, a business entity will continue to operate indefinitely. **p. 35**

**Income statement:** A financial statement that reports the company's revenues and expenses over an interval of time. **p. 9**

**International Accounting Standards Board (IASB):** An international accounting standard-setting body responsible for the convergence of accounting standards worldwide. **p. 22**

**International Financial Reporting Standards (IFRS):** The standards being developed and promoted by the International Accounting Standards Board. **p. 22**

**Investing cash flows:** Cash transactions for the purchase and sale of investments and long-term assets. **p. 14**

**Liabilities:** Amounts owed to creditors. **p. 7**

**Monetary unit assumption:** A unit or scale of measurement can be used to measure financial statement **elements. p. 35**

**Net income:** Difference between revenues and expenses. **p. 8**

**Operating cash flows:** Cash payments and receipts that arise during normal business operations. **p. 14**

**Partnership:** Business owned by two or more persons. **p. 6**

**Periodicity assumption:** The economic life of an enterprise (presumed to be indefinite) can be divided into artificial time periods for financial reporting. **p. 35**

**Relevance:** Accounting information that possesses confirmatory value and/or predictive value, and that is material. **p. 33**

**Retained earnings:** All net income minus all dividends over the life of the company; internal source of equity. **p. 11**

**Revenues:** Amounts recognized when the company sells products or services to customers. **p. 8**

**Sarbanes-Oxley Act (SOX):** Formally titled the Public Company Accounting Reform and Investor Protection Act of 2002, this act provides regulation of auditors and the types of services they furnish to clients, increases accountability of corporate executives, addresses conflicts of interest for securities analysts, and provides for stiff criminal penalties for violators. **p. 23**

**Sole proprietorship:** A business owned by one person. **p. 6**

**Statement of cash flows:** A financial statement that measures activities involving cash receipts and cash payments over an interval of time. **p. 14**

**Statement of comprehensive income:** Reports changes in equity that arise from nonowner sources. **p. 15**

**Statement of stockholders' equity:** A financial statement that summarizes the changes in stockholders' equity over an interval of time. **p. 11**

**Stockholders' equity:** Owners' claims to resources, which arise primarily from contributions by the owners and company operations. **p. 7**

**Sustainability disclosures:** Information about a company's policies, practices, and performance related to the sustainability of business operations. **p. 29**

**Timeliness:** Information being available to users early enough to allow them to use it in the decision process. **p. 34**

**Understandability:** Users must understand the information within the context of the decision they are making. **p. 34**

**Verifiability:** A consensus among different measurers. **p. 34**

## SELF-STUDY QUESTIONS

1. Based on the introductory section of this chapter, financial accounting also can be described as a way to **(LO1–1)**
   a. Tell the financial story of a company.
   b. Calculate the amount of taxes owed to the government.
   c. Determine employee satisfaction with their work environment.
   d. Measure the personal net worth of stockholders.

2. Financial accounting serves which primary function(s)? **(LO1–1)**
   a. Measures business activities.
   b. Communicates business activities to interested parties.
   c. Makes business decisions on behalf of interested parties.
   d. Both *a.* and *b.* are functions of financial accounting.

3. Resources of a company are referred to as **(LO1–2)**
   a. Liabilities.
   b. Stockholders' equity.
   c. Dividends.
   d. Assets.

4. Sales of products or services are referred to as **(LO1–2)**
   a. Assets.
   b. Revenues.
   c. Liabilities.
   d. Expenses.

5. Amounts owed by the company are referred to as **(LO1–2)**
   a. Expenses.
   b. Dividends.
   c. Liabilities.
   d. Assets.

6. Which financial statement conveys a company's ability to generate profits in the current period? **(LO1–3)**
   a. Income statement.
   b. Statement of cash flows.
   c. Balance sheet.
   d. Statement of stockholders' equity.

7. Which financial statement shows that a company's resources equal claims to those resources? **(LO1–3)**
   a. Income statement.
   b. Statement of stockholders' equity.
   c. Balance sheet.
   d. Statement of cash flows.

8. A company reports the following in its income statement: Total revenues of $500,000 and total expenses of $300,000. Which of the following is true? **(LO1–3)**
   a. Net income equals $200,000.
   b. Total dividends equal $200,000.
   c. Total assets equal $200,000.
   d. Total stockholders' equity equals $200,000.

9. A company reports the following in its balance sheet: Total assets of $800,000 and total liabilities of $700,000. Which of the following is true? **(LO1–3)**
   a. Net income equals $100,000.
   b. Total expenses equal $1,500,000.
   c. Total revenues equal $1,500,000.
   d. Total stockholders' equity equals $100,000.

10. Why does financial accounting have a positive impact on our society? **(LO1–4)**
    a. It entails a detailed transaction record necessary for filing taxes with the Internal Revenue Service (IRS).
    b. It allows investors and creditors to redirect their resources to successful companies and away from unsuccessful companies.

c. It prevents competitors from being able to steal the company's customers.

d. It provides a system of useful internal reports for management decision making.

11. The body of rules and procedures that guide the measurement and communication of financial accounting information is known as **(LO1–5)**

a. Standards of Professional Compliance

b. Code of Ethical Decisions (COED)

c. Rules of Financial Reporting

d. Generally Accepted Accounting Principles (GAAP).

12. Financial accounting and reporting standards in the United States are established primarily by the **(LO1–5)**

a. Securities and Exchange Commission (SEC)

b. Financial Accounting Standards Board (FASB)

c. International Accounting Standards Board (IASB).

d. The U.S. Congress.

13. Companies' annual reports are filed with the Securities and Exchange Commission (SEC) on an annual basis on form: **(LO1–6)**

a. 8-K

b. 10-K.

c. 10-Q.

d. S-1.

*Note: For answers, see the last page of the chapter.*

14. Which of the following statements is false with respect to companies' quarterly reports? **(LO1–6)**

a. Quarterly reports are audited by independent auditors.

rts include financial statements and

re required for public companies.

lude an MD&A section.

nies generally have to file
C after a major corporate

to all of the

es.

sues.

the two fundamental qualitative characteristics ...ied by the Financial Accounting Standards Board's (FASB) conceptual framework? **(LO1–9)**

a. Relevance and faithful representation.

b. Materiality and efficiency.

c. Comparability and consistency.

d. Costs and benefits.

*Krizzi@sunrise-detox.com*

---

## REAL WORLD PERSPECTIVES

### Nike (ticker NKE)

**EDGAR Case**

**RWP1–1** Visit **www.sec.gov/edgar** and search for the **Nike** annual report (10-K) for the year ended May 31, 2019, using EDGAR (Electronic Data Gathering, Analysis, and Retrieval system).

**Required:**

1. Locate the "Consolidated Balance Sheets" and answer the following questions:
   a. What is the amount of total assets for the most recent year?
   b. What is the amount of total shareholders' equity for the most recent year?
   c. Calculate total liabilities for the most recent year.
2. Locate the "Consolidated Statements of Income" and answer the following questions:
   a. What is the amount of revenue for the most recent year? Did it increase or decrease from the previous year?
   b. What is the amount of net income for the most recent year? Did it increase or decrease from the previous year?
3. Locate the "Consolidated Statements of Cash Flows" and answer the following questions:
   a. What is the amount of operating cash flows for the most recent year? How did the operating cash flow change from the previous year?
   b. What is the amount of investing cash flows for the most recent year? How did the investing cash flow change from the previous year?
   c. What is the amount of financing cash flows for the most recent year? How did the financing cash flow change from the previous year?

## Netflix Inc. (ticker: NFLX)

**RWP1–2** Visit **www.sec.gov/edgar** and search for the **Netflix** annual report (10-K) for the year ended December 31, 2019, using EDGAR (Electronic Data Gathering, Analysis, and Retrieval system).

***Required:***

1. Locate "Item 7. Management's Discussion and Analysis of Financial Condition and Results of Operations" and answer the following questions:
   a. Consolidated revenues for Netflix increased by 28% from the previous year. What is the breakdown of this increase between growth in average paying memberships and growth in the average monthly revenue per paying membership?
   b. What percent of Netflix revenues in the most recent year come from Latin America?
   c. How much did Netflix spend on marketing in the most recent year? What percentage of revenue is the marketing expense?
2. Locate "3. Balance Sheet Components" disclosure note and answer the following questions:
   a. What percentage of Netflix's "Total streaming content" is produced by Netflix (as opposed to licensed from other producers)?
   b. How much is in Netflix's "Buildings" account at the end of the most recent year?
3. Locate "4. Long-term Debt" disclosure note and answer the following questions:
   a. What is Netflix's total debt obligations at the end of the most recent year? Did it go up or down from the previous year?
   b. How much debt is due in less than one year?
4. Locate "8. Income Taxes" disclosure note. What is the "effective tax rate" of Netflix in the most recent year?
5. Locate the auditor's report titled "Report of Independent Registered Public Accounting Firm" and answer the following questions:
   a. Which accounting firm audits Netflix?
   b. Is the auditor of the opinion that the financial statements of Netflix are fairly presented?

## General Mills Inc. (ticker: GIS)

**RWP1–3** Visit **www.sec.gov/edgar** and search for the **General Mills** quarterly report (10-Q) for the quarter ended August 25, 2019, using EDGAR (Electronic Data Gathering, Analysis, and Retrieval system).

***Required:***

1. Is the quarterly report at August 25, 2019, for the first, second, third, or fourth quarter of the fiscal year?
2. Go to the "Consolidated Statements of Earnings." This statement reports the income statement for the three-month period ending August 25, 2019, and also presents a comparative income statement. Which quarter is used as the comparison quarter?
3. A typical annual report for General Mills includes approximately 20 disclosure notes. How many different disclosure notes are included in the quarterly report?

## Nordstrom Inc. (ticker: JWN)

**RWP1–4** Visit **www.sec.gov/edgar** and search for the **Nordstrom** current report (8-K) filed on April 8, 2020 (accession number ending 10090), using EDGAR (Electronic Data Gathering, Analysis, and Retrieval system).

***Required:***

1. What event triggered the filing of this current report?
2. What specific actions is the company taking to "proactively strengthen its financial flexibility and navigate through" the effects of this event?

## American Eagle Outfitters, Inc.

Continuing Financial Analysis Case

**RWP1–5** Financial information for **American Eagle** is presented in **Appendix A** at the end of the book.

*Required:*
1. Determine the amounts American Eagle reports for total assets, total liabilities, and total stockholders' equity in the balance sheet for the most recent year. Verify that the basic accounting equation balances.
2. American Eagle refers to its income statement using another name. What is it?
3. Determine the amounts American Eagle reports for net sales and net income in its income statement for the most recent year.
4. For investing activities, what is the item having the largest inflow and the item having the largest outflow for the most recent year reported in the statement of cash flows? For financing activities, what is the item having the largest inflow and the item having the largest outflow?
5. Who is the company's auditor? (See the Report of Independent Registered Public Accounting Firm.) What does the report indicate about the amounts reported in the company's financial statements?

## The Buckle, Inc.

Continuing Financial Analysis Case

**RWP1–6** Financial information for **Buckle** is presented in **Appendix B** at the end of the book.

*Required:*
1. Determine the amounts Buckle reports for total assets, total liabilities, and total stockholders' equity in the balance sheet for the most recent year. Verify that the basic accounting equation balances.
2. Buckle refers to its income statement using another name. What is it?
3. Determine the amounts Buckle reports for net sales and net income in its income statement for the most recent year.
4. For investing activities, what is the item having the largest inflow and the item having the largest outflow for the most recent year reported in the statement of cash flows? For financing activities, what is the item having the largest inflow and the item having the largest outflow?
5. Who is the company's auditor? (See the Report of Independent Registered Public Accounting Firm.) What does the report indicate about the amounts reported in the company's financial statements?

## American Eagle Outfitters, Inc. vs. The Buckle, Inc.

Continuing Comparative Analysis Case

**RWP1–7** Financial information for **American Eagle** is presented in **Appendix A** at the end of the book, and financial information for **Buckle** is presented in **Appendix B** at the end of the book.

*Required:*
1. Which company reports higher total assets?
2. Which company reports higher total liabilities? Does this always mean this company has a higher chance of not being able to repay its debt and declare bankruptcy? Explain.
3. What relevant information do total assets and total liabilities provide to creditors deciding whether to lend money to American Eagle versus Buckle?
4. Which company reports higher net income? Does this always mean this company's operations are more profitable? Explain.
5. What relevant information does net income provide to investors who are deciding whether to invest in American Eagle versus Buckle?

## Ethics

Ethics Case

**RWP1–8** Suppose an auditor has been paid $1,000,000 each year for the past several years to perform the audit of a company's annual financial statements. This company is the auditor's largest client. In the current year, the auditor notices that the preliminary income statement excludes certain expenses that typically are shown. When asked, management tells the auditor that these expenses do not reflect the company's true performance, so they will not be shown in this year's income statement. Plus, management informs the auditor it will be paying $1,200,000 for this year's audit, and management commits to using the auditor for at least five more years.

***Required:***

1. Understand the reporting effect: Does the audit arrangement described above have the potential to jeopardize the auditor's opinion of management's decision not to report certain expenses?
2. Specify the options: Are auditors employees of the company who must accept requests of management?
3. Identify the impact: Do investors, creditors, and others rely on the fair presentation of financial statements?
4. Make a decision: Should the auditor accept management's decision not to report the expenses this year?

**Continuing General Ledger Case**

## Great Adventures

(The Great Adventures problem continues in each chapter.)

**RWP1–9** Tony Matheson plans to graduate from college in May 2024 after spending four years earning a degree in sports and recreation management. Since beginning T-ball at age five, he's been actively involved in sports and enjoys the outdoors. Each summer growing up, he and his father would spend two weeks at a father/son outdoor camp. These fond memories are part of the reason he chose his major. He wants to remain involved in these outdoor activities and provide others with the same adventures he was able to share with his dad. He decides to start an outdoor adventure company. However, he's not sure he has the business background necessary to do this.

This is where Suzie Ramos can help. Suzie also plans to graduate in May 2024 with a major in business. Suzie and Tony first met their sophomore year and have been friends ever since as they share a strong interest in sports and outdoor activities.

They decide to name their company, Great Adventures. They will provide clinics for a variety of outdoor activities such as kayaking, mountain biking, rock climbing, wilderness survival techniques, orienteering, backpacking, and other adventure sports.

***Required:***

1. Tony and Suzie are concerned about personal liability from customers who are injured during outdoor adventure activities. Which of the three basic forms of business organization do you recommend for Great Adventures (sole proprietorship, partnership, or corporation)?
2. Great Adventures plans to maintain records of transactions in accounts such as Cash, Common Stock, Service Revenue, Salaries Expense, Accounts Payable, Equipment, Advertising Expense, Supplies, Salaries Payable, and Insurance Expense. (a) For each of these accounts, indicate whether the account would be reported in the balance sheet or income statement. (b) For accounts in the balance sheet, indicate whether it would be classified as an asset, liability, or stockholders' equity. (c) For accounts in the income statement, indicate whether it would be classified as a revenue or an expense.

## BRIEF EXERCISES

**Define accounting (LO1–1)**

**BE1–1** Indicate whether the definition provided is true or false.

**(True/False)** Accounting can be defined as:

1. _____ The language of business.
2. _____ A measurement/communication process.
3. _____ A mathematics course.

**BE1–2** Which of the following are the three primary business activities in which companies are involved? (Mark all that apply).

_____ Financing activities

_____ Outreach activities

_____ Compensation activities

_____ Operating activities

_____ Investing activities

_____ Funding activities

Identify the different types of business activities (LO1–2)

**BE1–3** Match each form of business organization with its description.

Identify the different forms of business organizations (LO1–2)

| Business Organizations | Descriptions |
|---|---|
| 1. _____ Sole proprietorship | a. Business owned by two or more persons. |
| 2. _____ Partnership | b. Entity legally separate from its owners. |
| 3. _____ Corporation | c. Business owned by a single person. |

**BE1–4** Match each account type with its description.

Recognize the different account classifications (LO1–2)

| Account Classifications | Descriptions |
|---|---|
| 1. _____ Assets | a. Sales of products or services. |
| 2. _____ Liabilities | b. Owners' claims to resources. |
| 3. _____ Stockholders' equity | c. Distributions to stockholders. |
| 4. _____ Dividends | d. Costs of selling products or services. |
| 5. _____ Revenues | e. Resources of a company. |
| 6. _____ Expenses | f. Amounts owed. |

**BE1–5** For each transaction, indicate whether each account would be classified in the balance sheet as (a) an asset, (b) a liability, or (c) stockholders' equity; in the income statement as (d) a revenue or (e) an expense; or in the statement of stockholders' equity as (f) a dividend.

Assign account classifications (LO 1–2)

| Account Classifications | Accounts | Related Transactions |
|---|---|---|
| 1. _____ | Rent expense | Cost of rent. |
| 2. _____ | Interest revenue | Interest earned on savings account. |
| 3. _____ | Dividends | Cash payments to stockholders. |
| 4. _____ | Land | Land used for operations. |
| 5. _____ | Accounts payable | Amounts owed to suppliers. |

**BE1–6** For each transaction, indicate whether each account would be classified in the balance sheet as (a) an asset, (b) a liability, or (c) stockholders' equity; in the income statement as (d) a revenue or (e) an expense; or in the statement of stockholders' equity as (f) a dividend.

Assign account classifications (LO1–2)

| Account Classifications | Accounts | Related Transactions |
|---|---|---|
| 1. _____ | Utilities payable | Amounts owed for utilities. |
| 2. _____ | Cash | Cash available for use. |
| 3. _____ | Salaries expense | Cost of salaries. |
| 4. _____ | Common stock | Shares of ownership sold to investors. |
| 5. _____ | Service revenue | Sale of services to customers. |

**BE1–7** Match each financial statement with its description.

Describe each financial statement (LO1–3)

| Financial Statements | Related Transactions |
|---|---|
| 1. _____ Income statement | a. Change in owners' claims to resources. |
| 2. _____ Statement of stockholders' equity | b. Profitability of the company. |
| | c. Change in equity from nonowner sources. |
| 3. _____ Balance sheet | |
| 4. _____ Statement of cash flows | d. Change in cash as a result of operating, investing, and financing activities. |
| 5. _____ Statement of comprehensive income | e. Resources equal creditors' and owners' claims to those resources. |

Determine the location
of items in financial
statements (LO1–3)

**BE1–8**   Determine on which financial statement you find the following items.

| Financial Statements | Items |
|---|---|
| 1. _____ Income statement | a. The change in retained earnings due to net income and dividends. |
| 2. _____ Statement of stock-holders' equity | b. Amount of cash received from borrowing money from a local bank. |
| 3. _____ Balance sheet | c. Revenue from sales to customers during the year. |
| 4. _____ Statement of cash flows | d. Gains from foreign currency translations. |
| 5. _____ Statement of compre-hensive income | e. Total amounts owed to workers at the end of the year. |

Identify different groups
engaged in providing
high-quality financial
reporting (LO1–5)

**BE1–9** Each of these parties plays a role in the quality of financial reporting. Match each group with its function.

| Groups | Functions |
|---|---|
| 1. _____ Financial Accounting Standards Board | a. Group that has been given power by Congress to enforce the proper application of financial reporting rules for companies whose securities are publicly traded. |
| 2. _____ International Accounting Standards Board | b. Independent, private-sector group that is primarily responsible for setting financial reporting standards in the United States. |
| 3. _____ Securities and Exchange Commission | c. Independent intermediaries that help to ensure that management appropriately applies financial reporting rules in preparing the company's financial statements. |
| 4. _____ Auditors | d. Body that is attempting to develop a single set of high-quality, understandable global accounting standards. |

Identify the
objectives of financial
accounting (LO1–5)

**BE1–10** Indicate which of the following are objectives of financial accounting.

| (Yes/No) | Objectives |
|---|---|
| 1. _____ | Provide useful information to investors and creditors. |
| 2. _____ | Guarantee businesses will not go bankrupt. |
| 3. _____ | Provide information about resources and claims to resources. |
| 4. _____ | Prevent competitors from offering lower-priced products. |
| 5. _____ | Provide information to help users in predicting future cash flows. |
| 6. _____ | Maximize tax revenue to the federal government. |

Understand what is
included in annual
reports (LO1–6)

**BE1–11** Which of the following financial statements is required to be included in a company's annual report filed with the Securities and Exchange Commission (SEC)? (Mark all that apply).

_____ Balance sheet.
_____ Income statement.
_____ Statement of executive compensation.
_____ Statement of cash flows.
_____ Statement of stockholder's equity.
_____ Statement of capital expenditures.
_____ Statement of sales revenue.
_____ Statement of comprehensive income.

**BE1–12** The management discussion and analysis (MD&A) section of a company's annual report generally includes (mark all that apply):

_____ Management's views on company operations.

_____ Management's views on the audit.

_____ Management's views on the uncertainties and risks the company faces.

_____ Management's views on company's use of resources.

_____ Management's views on pending litigation.

Understand what is included in MD&A **(LO1–6)**

**BE1–13** Which of the following statements best describes the purpose of a current report (Form 8-K) filed with the Securities and Exchange Commission (SEC):

_____ Current reports are filed with the SEC to ensure that capital providers understand management's current operating plans for the company.

_____ Current reports are filed with the SEC to ensure that capital providers are made aware of major corporate events on a timely basis.

_____ Current reports are filed with the SEC to ensure that capital providers understand management's current financing structure for the company.

_____ Current reports are filed with the SEC to ensure that capital providers know the most recent set of company policies.

Understand the purpose of current reports **(LO1–7)**

**BE1–14** Sustainability disclosures generally relate to all of the following issues except (mark all that apply):

_____ Social and human capital issues.

_____ Environmental issues.

_____ External audit issues.

_____ Governance issues.

Understand the purpose of sustainability disclosures **(LO1–8)**

**BE1–15** Match each of the components of relevance with its definition.

Identify the components/aspects of relevance **(LO1–9)**

| Components of Relevance | Definitions |
|---|---|
| 1. _____ Confirmatory value | a. Information is useful in helping to forecast future outcomes. |
| 2. _____ Predictive value | b. Information provides feedback on past activities. |
| 3. _____ Materiality | c. The nature or amount of an item has the ability to affect decisions. |

**BE1–16** Match each of the components of faithful representation with its definition.

Identify the components/aspects of faithful representation **(LO1–9)**

| Components of Faithful Representation | Definition |
|---|---|
| 1. _____ Free from error | a. All information necessary to describe an item is reported. |
| 2. _____ Neutrality | b. Information that does not bias the decision maker. |
| 3. _____ Completeness | c. Reported amounts reflect the best available information. |

## EXERCISES

Mc Graw Hill **connect**

**E1–1** The following provides a list of accounts and a list of business activities. Match the account with the business activity by indicating the letter that corresponds to the most appropriate business activity.

Identify the different types of business activities **(LO1–2)**

| Account | Business Activities |
|---|---|
| 1. Common stock | a. Operating |
| 2. Accounts receivable | b. Investing |
| 3. Equipment | c. Financing |
| 4. Inventory | |
| 5. Loans | |
| 6. Buildings | |

Identify account
classifications
and business
activities (LO1–2)

**E1–2** Falcon Incorporated has the following transactions with Wildcat Corporation.

| Transactions | Falcon's Related Account |
| --- | --- |
| 1. Falcon purchases common stock of Wildcat. | Investment |
| 2. Falcon borrows from Wildcat by signing a note. | Notes payable |
| 3. Falcon provides services to Wildcat. | Service revenue |
| 4. Falcon pays interest to Wildcat on borrowing. | Interest expense |

*Required:*

1. For each transaction, indicate whether Falcon would report the related account in the balance sheet or income statement.
2. For accounts in the balance sheet, indicate whether it would be classified as an asset, liability, or stockholders' equity. For accounts in the income statement, indicate whether it would be classified as a revenue or an expense.
3. Indicate whether each transaction is classified as operating, investing, or financing activity.

Identify account
classifications
and business
activities (LO1–2)

**E1–3** The transactions in this problem are identical to those in E1–2, but now focus on Wildcat.

| Transactions | Wildcat's Related Account |
| --- | --- |
| 1. Wildcat issues common stock to Falcon. | Common stock |
| 2. Wildcat lends to Falcon by accepting a note. | Notes receivable |
| 3. Wildcat receives services from Falcon. | Service fee expense |
| 4. Wildcat receives interest from Falcon on lending. | Interest revenue |

*Required:*

1. For each transaction, indicate whether Wildcat would report the related account in the balance sheet or income statement.
2. For accounts in the balance sheet, indicate whether it would be classified as an asset, liability, or stockholders' equity. For accounts in the income statement, indicate whether it would be classified as a revenue or an expense.
3. Indicate whether each transaction is classified as operating, investing, or financing activity.

Calculate net income
and stockholders'
equity (LO1–2)

**E1–4** Eagle Corp. operates magnetic resonance imaging (MRI) clinics throughout the Northeast. At the end of the current period, the company reports the following amounts: Assets = $50,000; Liabilities = $27,000; Dividends = $3,000; Revenues = $14,000; Expenses = $9,000.

*Required:*

1. Calculate net income.
2. Calculate stockholders' equity at the end of the period.

Calculate net loss
and stockholders'
equity (LO1–2)

**E1–5** Cougar's Accounting Services provides low-cost tax advice and preparation to those with financial need. At the end of the current period, the company reports the following amounts: Assets = $19,000; Liabilities = $15,000; Revenues = $28,000; Expenses = $33,000.

*Required:*

1. Calculate net loss.
2. Calculate stockholders' equity at the end of the period.

Prepare a basic balance
sheet (LO1–3)

**E1–6** Prepare an income statement for DEFT Corporation using the following balances at the end of December.

| Accounts | Balance |
| --- | --- |
| Liabilities | $20,000 |
| Expenses | 35,000 |
| Assets | 32,000 |
| Cash | 6,800 |
| Revenues | 42,000 |
| Dividends | 4,000 |

**E1–7** Prepare a balance sheet for DEFT Corporation using the same account information provided in E1–6.

Prepare a basic balance sheet (LO1–3)

**E1–8** LuLu Islands Inc. has $60 million in common stock and $25 million in retained earnings at the start of the year. During the year, LuLu reports net income of $15 million and paid dividends of $5 million. At the end of the year, LuLu still has $60 million in common stock. Prepare a statement of stockholder's equity at the end of the year.

Prepare a basic statement of stockholder's equity (LO1–3)

**E1–9** LuLu Islands Inc. reports a beginning cash balance of $16 million. LuLu also reports cash inflows of $32 million from operating activities, $5 million from financing activities, and a cash outflow of $12 million from investing activities. Calculate the ending cash balance of LuLu Islands.

Compute ending cash balance (LO1–3)

**E1–10** On December 31, 2024, Fighting Okra Cooking Services reports the following revenues and expenses.

Link the income statement to the statement of stockholders' equity (LO1–3)

| | | | |
|---|---|---|---|
| Service revenue | $75,000 | Rent expense | $10,600 |
| Postage expense | 1,500 | Salaries expense | 24,000 |
| Legal fees expense | 2,400 | Supplies expense | 14,500 |

In addition, the balance of common stock at the beginning of the year was $200,000, and the balance of retained earnings was $32,000. During the year, the company issued additional shares of common stock for $25,000 and paid dividends of $10,000.

*Required:*
1. Prepare an income statement.
2. Prepare a statement of stockholders' equity.

**E1–11** At the beginning of 2024, Artichoke Academy reported a balance in common stock of $150,000 and a balance in retained earnings of $50,000. During the year, the company issued additional shares of stock for $40,000, earned net income of $30,000, and paid dividends of $10,000. In addition, the company reported balances for the following assets and liabilities on December 31.

Link the statement of stockholders' equity to the balance sheet (LO1–3)

| Assets | | Liabilities | |
|---|---|---|---|
| Cash | $ 52,600 | Accounts payable | $ 9,100 |
| Supplies | 13,400 | Utilities payable | 2,400 |
| Prepaid rent | 24,000 | Salaries payable | 3,500 |
| Land | 200,000 | Notes payable | 15,000 |

*Required:*
1. Prepare a statement of stockholders' equity.
2. Prepare a balance sheet.

**E1–12** Squirrel Tree Services reports the following amounts on December 31, 2024.

Link the balance sheet to the statement of cash flows (LO1–3)

| Assets | | Liabilities and Stockholders' Equity | |
|---|---|---|---|
| Cash | $ 7,700 | Accounts payable | $ 9,700 |
| Supplies | 1,800 | Salaries payable | 3,500 |
| Prepaid insurance | 3,500 | Notes payable | 20,000 |
| Building | 72,000 | Common stock | 40,000 |
| | | Retained earnings | 11,800 |

In addition, the company reported the following cash flows.

| Cash Inflows | | Cash Outflows | |
| --- | --- | --- | --- |
| Customers | $60,000 | Employee salaries | $22,000 |
| Borrow from the bank (note) | 20,000 | Supplies | 4,000 |
| Sale of investments | 10,000 | Dividends | 6,500 |
| | | Purchase building | 62,000 |

*Required:*
1. Prepare a balance sheet.
2. Prepare a statement of cash flows.

**Compute missing amounts from financial statements (LO1–3)**

**E1–13** Each of the following independent situations represents amounts shown on the four basic financial statements.
1. Revenues = $27,000; Expenses = $18,000; Net income = _____.
2. Increase in stockholders' equity = $17,000; Issuance of common stock = $11,000; Net income = $12,000; Dividends = _____.
3. Assets = $24,000; Stockholders' equity = $15,000; Liabilities = _____.
4. Total change in cash = $26,000; Net operating cash flows = $34,000; Net investing cash flows = ($17,000); Net financing cash flows = _____.

*Required:*
Fill in the missing blanks using your knowledge of amounts that appear on the financial statements.

**Calculate the balance of retained earnings (LO1–3)**

**E1–14** During its first five years of operations, Red Raider Consulting reports net income and pays dividends as follows.

| Year | Net Income | Dividends | Retained Earnings |
| --- | --- | --- | --- |
| 1 | $1,700 | $ 600 | _____ |
| 2 | 2,200 | 600 | _____ |
| 3 | 3,100 | 1,500 | _____ |
| 4 | 4,200 | 1,500 | _____ |
| 5 | 5,400 | 1,500 | _____ |

*Required:*
Calculate the balance of retained earnings at the end of each year. Note that retained earnings will always equal $0 at the beginning of year 1.

**Calculate amounts related to the balance of retained earnings (LO1–3)**

**E1–15** Below are approximate amounts related to retained earnings reported by five companies in previous years.
1. **Coca-Cola** reports an increase in retained earnings of $3.2 billion and net income of $6.9 billion. What is the amount of dividends?
2. **PepsiCo** reports an increase in retained earnings of $3.4 billion and dividends of $2.6 billion. What is the amount of net income?
3. **Alphabet** reports an increase in retained earnings of $1.6 billion and net income of $1.6 billion. What is the amount of dividends?
4. **Sirius XM Satellite Radio** reports beginning retained earnings of −$1.6 billion, net loss of $1.0 billion, and $0 dividends. What is the amount of ending retained earnings?
5. **Abercrombie & Fitch** reports ending retained earnings of $1.56 billion, net income of $0.43 billion, and dividends of $0.06 billion. What is the amount of beginning retained earnings?

*Required:*
Calculate the answer to each.

**E1–16** Below are approximate amounts related to balance sheet information reported by five companies in previous years.

Use the accounting equation to calculate amounts related to the balance sheet (LO1–3)

1. **ExxonMobil** reports total assets of $228 billion and total liabilities of $107 billion. What is the amount of stockholders' equity?
2. **Citigroup** reports total liabilities of $1,500 billion and stockholders' equity of $110 billion. What is the amount of total assets?
3. **Amazon.com** reports total assets of $4.7 billion and total stockholders' equity of $0.3 billion. What is the amount of total liabilities?
4. **Nike** reports an increase in assets of $1.2 billion and an increase in liabilities of $0.3 billion. What is the amount of the change in stockholders' equity?
5. **Kellogg's** reports a decrease in liabilities of $0.34 billion and an increase in stockholders' equity of $0.02 billion. What is the amount of the change in total assets?

*Required:*
Calculate the answer to each.

**E1–17** Below are approximate amounts related to cash flow information reported by five companies in previous years.

Calculate missing amounts related to the statement of cash flows (LO1–3)

1. **KraftHeinz** reports operating cash flows of $3.6 billion, investing cash flows of $0.6 billion, and financing cash flows of −$4.2 billion. What is the amount of the change in total cash?
2. **Hillshire Brands** reports operating cash flows of $1.4 billion, investing cash flows of −$0.3 billion, and financing cash flows of −$1.4 billion. If the beginning cash amount is $0.7 billion, what is the ending cash amount?
3. **Performance Food Group** reports operating cash flows of $0.07 billion, investing cash flows of $0.63 billion, and a change in total cash of $0.04 billion. What is the amount of cash flows from financing activities?
4. **Smithfield Foods** reports operating cash flows of $0.60 billion, financing cash flows of $0.42 billion, and a change in total cash of $0.02 billion. What is the amount of cash flows from investing activities?
5. **Tyson Foods** reports investing cash flows of −$1.42 billion, financing cash flows of $1.03 billion, and a change in total cash of $0.02 billion. What is the amount of cash flows from operating activities?

*Required:*
Calculate the answer to each.

**E1–18** Below are concepts associated with the role of the auditor in financial reporting.

Understand the role of the auditor (LO1–5)

| Concept | Description |
| --- | --- |
| 1. _____ Securities and Exchange Commission | a. Phrase meaning to present misleading accounting information. |
| 2. _____ Need for auditing | b. Auditors are not employees of the company they audit. |
| 3. _____ Cooking the books | c. Responsible for applying generally accepted accounting principles (GAAP). |
| 4. _____ Management | d. Regulatory body that requires audits of all publicly traded companies. |
| 5. _____ Auditor | e. Separation of management from those who own the business or finance operations. |
| 6. _____ Independent | f. Party that reports on whether a company's financial statements are in accordance with GAAP. |
| 7. _____ Opinion | g. View expressed by an auditor as to the accuracy of a company's financial statements. |

*Required:*
Match each concept with its description.

**E1–19** Annual reports include which of the following *required* parts? (Mark all that apply).
_____ Income statements for each business segment.
_____ Auditor's report.

Understand what is included in annual reports (LO1–6)

_____ Disclosure notes.

_____ Financial statements for the entire company.

_____ Forecasts of future sales and net income.

_____ Biographies on each chief officer.

_____ An overview of the company's history.

_____ Management discussion and analysis.

_____ Executive compensation information.

**Understand what is included in quarterly reports (LO1–6)**

**E1–20** Quarterly reports include which of the following _required_ parts (mark all that apply):

_____ Income statements for each business segment.

_____ Auditor's report.

_____ Disclosure notes.

_____ Financial statements for the entire company.

_____ Forecasts of future sales and net income.

_____ Biographies on each chief officer.

_____ An overview of the company's history.

_____ Management discussion and analysis.

_____ Executive compensation information.

**Understand what is included in current reports (LO1–7)**

**E1–21** Which of the following events would likely require the company to file a current report (Form 8-K) with the Securities and Exchange Commission (mark all that apply):

_____ A flood severely damaged one of the company's three factories.

_____ One of the company's minor suppliers filed for bankruptcy.

_____ The company completed development of a new product.

_____ The CEO was fired and the search for a new CEO has begun.

_____ The company entered into an agreement with a private equity group to become a private company.

_____ The company increased salaries to all employees by an average of two percent.

_____ The financial statements from two years ago were not stated correctly and need to be restated.

_____ The company launched a major advertising campaign.

**Understand the purpose of sustainability disclosures (LO1–8)**

**E1–22** Which of the following topics would most likely be reported in a sustainability disclosure? (Mark all that apply).

_____ Information about the diversity among the board of directors.

_____ Information about the amount of wastewater avoided.

_____ Information about new research and development.

_____ Information about how foreign currency fluctuations affects the company.

_____ Information about greenhouse gas emissions of a factory.

_____ Information about capital expenditures.

_____ Information about contributions made to a political trade association.

_____ Information about the number of employee injuries.

**Identify the purpose of qualitative characteristics (LO1–9)**

**E1–23** The qualitative characteristics outlined in the FASB's conceptual framework include:

| Fundamental Characteristics | | Enhancing Characteristics |
|---|---|---|
| **Relevance** | **Faithful Representation** | g. Comparability |
| a. Confirmatory value | d. Completeness | h. Verifiability |
| b. Predictive value | e. Neutrality | i. Timeliness |
| c. Materiality | f. Free from error | j. Understandability |

Consider the following independent situations.

1. In deciding whether to invest in **Southwest Airlines** or **American Airlines**, investors evaluate the companies' income statements. _____

2. To provide the most reliable information about future sales, **Walmart**'s management uses an appropriate process to estimate the decline in inventory value each year. _____

3. In deciding whether to loan money, **Wells Fargo** uses balance sheet information to forecast the probability of bankruptcy. _____

4. **IBM** is required to issue public financial statements within 60 days of its year-end. _____

5. Employees of **Starbucks** can use the company's financial statements to analyze the efficiency with which management has conducted operations over the past year. _____

6. When first requiring firms to prepare a statement of cash flows, the FASB's intent was not to discourage or promote investment in the automobile industry. _____

7. When **Harley-Davidson** reports revenue for the year, the amount includes sales not only in the United States but also those outside the United States. _____

8. The amount of total assets reported by **General Mills** can be substantiated by its auditors. _____

9. The **Cheesecake Factory** prepares its balance sheet in a clear format using basic accounting terminology to allow users to easily comprehend the company's assets, liabilities, and stockholders' equity. _____

10. **Target** prepays $600 to rent a post office box for the next six months and decides to record the entire payment to Rent expense (instead of Prepaid rent) in the current month. _____

**Required:**
Determine which qualitative characteristic best applies to each situation. Note: Each of the 10 characteristics is used only once.

**E1–24** Below are the four underlying assumptions of generally accepted accounting principles.

*Identify business assumptions underlying GAAP (LO1–9)*

| Assumptions | Descriptions |
| --- | --- |
| 1. _____ Economic entity | a. A common denominator is needed to measure all business activities. |
| 2. _____ Going concern | b. Economic events can be identified with a particular economic body. |
| 3. _____ Periodicity | c. In the absence of information to the contrary, it is anticipated that a business entity will continue to operate indefinitely. |
| 4. _____ Monetary unit | d. The economic life of a company can be divided into artificial time intervals for financial reporting. |

**Required:**
Match each business assumption with its description.

## PROBLEMS

**P1–1** Below are typical transactions for **Hewlett-Packard**.

*Classify business activities (LO1–2)*

| Type of Business Activity | Transactions |
| --- | --- |
| 1. _____ | Pay amount owed to the bank for previous borrowing. |
| 2. _____ | Pay utility costs. |
| 3. _____ | Purchase equipment to be used in operations. |
| 4. _____ | Provide services to customers. |
| 5. _____ | Purchase office supplies. |
| 6. _____ | Purchase a building. |
| 7. _____ | Pay workers' salaries. |
| 8. _____ | Pay for research and development costs. |
| 9. _____ | Pay taxes to the IRS. |
| 10. _____ | Sell common stock to investors. |

**Required:**
Indicate whether each transaction is classified as a financing, investing, or operating activity.

**Assign account classifications (LO1–2)**

**P1–2** Account classifications include assets, liabilities, stockholders' equity, dividends, revenues, and expenses.

| Account Classifications | Accounts | Related Transactions |
|---|---|---|
| 1. _____ | Common stock | Sale of common stock to investors. |
| 2. _____ | Equipment | Equipment used for operations. |
| 3. _____ | Salaries payable | Amounts owed to employees. |
| 4. _____ | Service revenue | Sales of services to customers. |
| 5. _____ | Utilities expense | Cost of utilities. |
| 6. _____ | Supplies | Purchase of office supplies. |
| 7. _____ | Research and development expense | Cost of research and development. |
| 8. _____ | Land | Property used for operations. |
| 9. _____ | Income tax payable | Amounts owed to the IRS for taxes. |
| 10. _____ | Interest payable | Amount of interest owed on borrowing. |

*Required:*

For each transaction, indicate whether the related account would be classified in the balance sheet as (a) an asset, (b) a liability, or (c) stockholders' equity; in the income statement as (d) a revenue or (e) an expense; or in the statement of stockholders' equity as (f) a dividend.

**Prepare financial statements (LO1–3)**

**P1–3** Longhorn Corporation provides low-cost food delivery services to senior citizens. At the end of the year on December 31, 2024, the company reports the following amounts:

| | | | |
|---|---|---|---|
| Cash | $ 1,200 | Service revenue | $67,700 |
| Equipment | 29,000 | Salaries expense | 53,400 |
| Accounts payable | 4,400 | Buildings | 40,000 |
| Delivery expense | 2,600 | Supplies | 3,400 |
| Rent expense | 5,500 | Salaries payable | 800 |

In addition, the company had common stock of $40,000 at the beginning of the year and issued an additional $4,000 during the year. The company also had retained earnings of $18,200 at the beginning of the year.

*Required:*

Prepare the income statement, statement of stockholders' equity, and balance sheet for Longhorn Corporation.

**Understand the format of financial statements and the links among them (LO1–3)**

**P1–4** Below are incomplete financial statements for Bulldog, Inc.

**BULLDOG, INC.**
**Income Statement**
**Year ended Dec. 31, 2024**

| | |
|---|---|
| Revenues | $39,000 |
| Expenses: | |
| Salaries | (a) |
| Advertising | 6,000 |
| Utilities | 4,000 |
| Net income | (b) |

**BULLDOG, INC.**
**Statement of Stockholders' Equity**
**Year ended Dec. 31, 2024**

| | Common Stock | Retained Earnings | Total Stk. Equity |
|---|---|---|---|
| Beginning balance | $10,000 | $ 7,000 | $17,000 |
| Issuances | 1,100 | | 1,100 |
| Add: Net income | | (c) | (c) |
| Less: Dividends | | (3,000) | (3,000) |
| Ending balance | $11,100 | $10,000 | $21,100 |

**BULLDOG, INC.**
**Balance Sheet**
**Dec. 31, 2024**

| Assets | | Liabilities | |
|---|---|---|---|
| Cash | $ 4,000 | Accounts payable | (d) |
| Accounts receivable | 3,000 | **Stockholders' Equity** | |
| Supplies | 9,000 | Common stock | (e) |
| Equipment | 10,000 | Retained earnings | (f) |
| | | Total liabilities and | |
| Total assets | $26,000 | stockholders' equity | (g) |

*Required:*

Calculate the missing amounts.

**P1–5** Cornhusker Company provides the following information at the end of 2024.

Prepare financial statements (LO1–3)

| | |
|---|---|
| Cash remaining | $ 4,800 |
| Rent expense for the year | 7,000 |
| Land that has been purchased | 21,000 |
| Retained earnings | 12,400 |
| Utility expense for the year | 4,900 |
| Accounts receivable from customers | 7,200 |
| Service revenue recognized during the year | 37,000 |
| Salary expense for the year | 13,300 |
| Accounts payable to suppliers | 2,200 |
| Dividends paid to stockholders during the year | 3,200 |
| Common stock that has been issued prior to 2024 | 16,000 |
| Salaries owed at the end of the year | 2,400 |
| Insurance expense for the year | 3,500 |
| Retained earnings at the beginning of the year | 7,300 |

*Required:*

Prepare the income statement, statement of stockholders' equity, and balance sheet for Cornhusker Company on December 31, 2024. No common stock is issued during 2024.

**P1–6** The four underlying assumptions of generally accepted accounting principles are economic entity, monetary unit, periodicity, and going concern. Consider the four independent situations below.

Identify underlying assumptions of GAAP (LO1–9)

1. Jumbo's is a local restaurant. Due to a bad shipment of potatoes, several of the company's customers become ill, and the company receives considerable bad publicity. Revenues are way down, several of its bills are past due, and the company is making plans to close the restaurant at the end of the month. The company continues to report its assets in the balance sheet at historical (original) cost.

2. Gorloks Tax Services is owned and operated by Sam Martin. The company has the usual business assets: land, building, cash, equipment, and supplies. In addition, Sam decides to buy a boat for him and his family to enjoy on the weekends. Sam includes the boat as an asset in the balance sheet of Gorloks Tax Services.

3. Claim Jumpers International, a U.S.-based company, has operations in the United States and Europe. For the current year, the company purchased two trucks in the United States for $10,000 and three trucks in Europe for €20,000 (euros). Because of the differences in currencies, the company reported "Five Trucks" with no corresponding amount in the balance sheet.

4. Cobbers Etc. sells specialty music equipment ranging from African bongo drums to grand pianos. Because of the fluctuating nature of the business, management decides to publish

financial statements only when a substantial amount of activity has taken place. Its last set of financial statements covered a period of 14 months, and the set of financial statements before that covered a period of 18 months.

***Required:***

For each situation, indicate which of the underlying assumptions of GAAP is violated.

**Understand the components of the FASB's conceptual framework (LO1–9)**

**P1–7** Listed below are nine terms and definitions associated with the FASB's conceptual framework.

| Terms | Definitions |
|---|---|
| 1. _____ Completeness | a. Requires the consideration of the costs and value of information. |
| 2. _____ Comparability | |
| 3. _____ Neutrality | b. Ability to make comparisons between firms. |
| 4. _____ Understandability | c. Comprehending the meaning of accounting information. |
| 5. _____ Cost effectiveness | |
| 6. _____ Verifiability | d. Including all information necessary to report the business activity. |
| 7. _____ Decision usefulness | |
| 8. _____ Economic entity assumption | e. The business will last indefinitely unless there is evidence otherwise. |
| 9. _____ Going concern assumption | f. Recording transactions only for the company. |
| | g. Implies consensus among different measures. |
| | h. Accounting should be useful in making decisions. |
| | i. Accounting information should not favor a particular group. |

***Required:***

Pair each term with its related definition.

## DATA ANALYTICS

Visit Connect to view **Data Analytics** questions related to:

1. Applying Excel
2. Data Visualizations
3. Tableau Dashboard Activities
4. Applying Tableau

## ANSWERS TO THE SELF-STUDY QUESTIONS

1. a   2. d   3. d   4. b   5. c   6. a   7. c   8. a   9. d   10. b   11. d   12. b   13. b   14. a   15. c   16. c   17. a

# CHAPTER TWO

# 2 The Financial Statements

## Learning Objectives

### PART A: THE BALANCE SHEET

- **LO2–1** Describe the various asset classifications and measurement methods.
- **LO2–2** Describe the various liability and stockholders' equity classifications.
- **LO2–3** Understand the limitations of the balance sheet.

### PART B: THE INCOME STATEMENT

- **LO2–4** Describe revenues, expenses, gains, and losses.
- **LO2–5** Calculate the different measures of income.
- **LO2–6** Understand the limitations of the income statement.

### PART C: THE STATEMENT OF CASH FLOWS

- **LO2–7** Identify operating, investing, and financing cash flows.

### PART D: STATEMENTS OF STOCKHOLDERS' EQUITY AND COMPREHENSIVE INCOME

- **LO2–8** Understand the purpose of the statement of stockholders' equity.
- **LO2–9** Understand the distinguishing features of comprehensive income.

## Self-Study Materials

## Feature Story

# Lululemon: Growth through Comfortable Clothes . . . and Equity Financing

**Lululemon** sold its first pair of yoga pants in 1998 and has had steady growth ever since. Its latest annual report discloses global sales of over $3 billion. Part of the secret to its success is in signature fabric, trademarked as "Luon." Luon is a unique blend of polyester, nylon, and spandex that comes together to feel like cotton. Having a unique and comfortable product, however, is not enough to grow a business into a global icon. So how did the founder of Lululemon, Chip Wilson, grow his business into a well-known company with more than 400 locations and more than 15,000 employees? With the help of equity investors.

In 2007, Lululemon and its existing owners raised approximately $327 million in an initial public offering (IPO) of stock. The stock was expected to be priced at $10 to $12 per share at the initial offering, but actually went public at $18 per share, which shows the excitement of early investors. The company stated it would use a portion of the proceeds received from the IPO to open new stores, fund day-to-day operations, and achieve other corporate objectives.

Another surprising element of Lululemon's strategy is that the company has avoided taking out loans from banks or using other forms of debt. How did Lululemon finance its growth without taking on debt? The answer: by generating profits. Profits are a source of *internally* generated funds, a concept accountants call "retained earnings." Lululemon's most recent balance sheet discloses retained earnings of $1.8 billion! That means Lululemon has made cumulative profits of $1.8 billion over the years and reinvested those earnings back into the business.

As you can see, the narrative story of Lululemon is fascinating. In this chapter, we tell the *financial story* of Lululemon through the lens of the financial statements. By the end of the chapter, you will see the many insights and lessons financial statements can teach us about the financial position and performance of a company.

## PART A

# THE BALANCE SHEET

The balance sheet, sometimes referred to as the **statement of financial position**, presents an organized list of assets, liabilities, and equity. It's a freeze frame or snapshot of a company's financial position at the end of a particular day that marks the end of an accounting period. This is why it's called the balance sheet—it reports the balance of a company's assets, liabilities, and stockholders' equity *at a point in time*. Illustration 2–1 provides an example of a balance sheet for **Lululemon** (formally known as Lululemon Athletica Inc).

**ILLUSTRATION 2–1**

The Balance Sheet for Lululemon

| LULULEMON<br>Balance Sheet<br>As of February 2, 2020<br>($ in millions) | |
| --- | ---: |
| **Current assets:** | |
| Cash and cash equivalents | $ 1,093 |
| Accounts receivable, net | 40 |
| Inventories | 519 |
| Prepaid expenses | 156 |
| Total current assets | 1,808 |
| Property and equipment, net | 672 |
| Operating leases | 690 |
| Intangible assets, net | 24 |
| Other long-term assets | 87 |
| Total long-term assets | 1,473 |
| **Total assets** | **$3,281** |
| | |
| **Current liabilities:** | |
| Accounts payable | $    80 |
| Accrued expenses | 140 |
| Current lease liabilities | 129 |
| Taxes payable | 26 |
| Deferred revenue (gift cards) | 120 |
| Other current liabilities | 125 |
| Total current liabilities | 620 |
| Long-term liabilities: | |
| Non-current lease liabilities | 611 |
| Deferred taxes | 92 |
| Other long-term liabilities | 6 |
| **Total liabilities** | **$ 1,329** |
| | |
| Common stock | 1 |
| Additional paid-in capital | 355 |
| Retained earnings | 1,821 |
| Accumulated other comprehensive loss | (225) |
| **Total stockholders' equity** | **$ 1,952** |
| | |
| **Total liabilities and stockholders' equity** | **$3,281** |

The primary balance sheet elements are as follows:

- **Assets** are the *economic resources* of a company.
- **Liabilities** are the *economic obligations* of a company.
- **Equity** (or net assets), which is also called **stockholders' equity** or **shareholders' equity**, equals total assets minus total liabilities.

Illustration 2–2 provides the accounting equation, which is presented in the balance sheet and shows the relationship among assets, liabilities, and stockholders' equity. Included in the illustration are the subclassifications of each element. We will discuss each of these subclassifications next.

ILLUSTRATION 2–2
The Accounting Equation

| Assets | = | Liabilities | + | Stockholders' Equity |
|---|---|---|---|---|
| 1. Current assets | | 1. Current liabilities | | 1. Contributed capital |
| 2. Long-term assets | | 2. Long-term liabilities | | 2. Retained earnings |

## Assets

Assets are the economic resources of a company. The balance sheet classifies assets into two major categories:

- Current assets—those that are expected to provide a benefit within the next year.
- Long-term assets—those that are expected to provide a benefit for more than one year.

■ LO2–1
Describe the various asset classifications and measurement methods.

### CURRENT ASSETS

Current assets include cash and other assets that are expected to be converted to cash or consumed within one year from the balance sheet date, or within the normal operating cycle of the business if that's longer than one year. The operating cycle refers to the period of time from the purchase of inventory until the time the company collects cash from a customer from the sale of inventory.

Illustration 2–3 presents the current assets section of Lululemon's recent balance sheet. Current assets are typically listed in order of liquidity. The liquidity of an asset refers to how quickly it can be converted to cash.

ILLUSTRATION 2–3
Current Assets of Lululemon (Balance Sheet excerpt)

| LULULEMON Current Assets ($ in millions) | |
|---|---|
| Current assets: | |
| Cash and cash equivalents | $1,093 |
| Accounts receivable, net | 40 |
| Inventories | 519 |
| Prepaid expenses | 156 |
| **Total current assets** | **$1,808** |

**Cash and Cash Equivalents.** The most liquid asset, cash, is listed first in the balance sheet. Cash includes cash on hand and in banks available for use in the operations of the business. It also includes cash equivalents, which are defined as short-term investments with original maturities of less than 90 days. These investments are highly liquid—they are "equivalents" because they can be converted into cash quite easily.

**Accounts Receivables, Net.**   Accounts receivable result from the sale of goods or services on account. By "on account," we mean that goods and services are sold on credit rather than for cash. Accounts receivable often are referred to as *trade receivables* because they arise in the course of a company's normal trade. Accounts receivable usually are due in 30 to 60 days, depending on the terms offered to customers, and therefore are classified as current assets. The balance sheet reports "accounts receivable, *net*" because the amount presented is net of an allowance for uncollectible accounts. Historical patterns imply that some customers will not pay their accounts. The allowance for uncollectible accounts represents the amount of accounts receivable that the company expects not to collect.

**Inventory.**   Inventory for a wholesale or retail company consists of goods for sale to customers. For example, you buy goods such as athletic wear from Lululemon, organic food at **Costco**, and cars at **CarMax**. However, the inventory of a manufacturer, such as **Stryker**, will include not only finished goods but also goods in the course of production (work in process) and goods to be consumed directly or indirectly in production (raw materials). Inventory is reported as a current asset because it's typically sold within the operating cycle.

**Prepaid Expenses.**   A prepaid expense arises when a company pays cash in advance for an asset that won't be expensed until a future time. Examples are prepaid rent and prepaid insurance. For instance, if a company pays in advance for insurance coverage over a period of time, it has an asset called prepaid insurance. This asset will be expensed as the insurance expires over the period of coverage. Whether a prepaid expense is current or noncurrent depends on the period in which the item is consumed. Lululemon includes prepaid expenses in current assets because they will be consumed within a year.

## LONG-TERM ASSETS

When assets are expected to provide economic benefits for greater than a year, they are reported as *long-term* (or *noncurrent*) *assets*. Illustration 2–4 shows the long-term asset section of Lululemon's balance sheet.

**ILLUSTRATION 2–4**

Long-Term Assets for Lululemon (Balance Sheet excerpt)

| LULULEMON<br>Long-Term Assets<br>($ in millions) | |
| --- | --- |
| Property and equipment, net | 672 |
| Operating leases | 690 |
| Intangible assets, net | 24 |
| Other long-term assets | 87 |
| **Total long-term assets** | **$1,473** |

Long-term assets generally consist of the following types of assets:

1. Long-term investments
2. Property, plant, and equipment
3. Operating leases
4. Intangible assets
5. Other

**Long-Term Investments.**   Companies occasionally purchase investments in debt and equity securities of other corporations. These assets are classified as long-term when management does not intend to sell the securities in the next year. However, if management intends to sell these investments within the year, then they would be classified as current assets.

**Property, Plant, and Equipment.**   Virtually all companies own assets classified as property, plant, and equipment or ("PPE"). The common characteristics these assets share are that they are *tangible, long-lived,* and *used in the operations of the business.* Property, plant, and equipment often are the primary revenue-generating assets of the business.

Although "property, plant, and equipment" is the catch-all name for these assets, they also include land, buildings, computers, software, machinery, furniture, fixtures, and vehicles. Because these assets are used for more than one year, the amount reported in the balance sheet is determined using a concept called depreciation. Depreciation refers to the process of writing off a portion of the asset's original cost in each year the asset is used. The amount reported in the balance sheet becomes the difference between the original cost of the asset and the depreciation that has accumulated to that point in time. This difference is referred to as the *net* amount of property, plant, and equipment. The one exception to this approach is land, which does not depreciate over time and is reported simply at its original cost.

**Operating Leases.**   An operating lease represents the right to use an asset for a specified period of time. This is why operating leases are often referred to as "right-of-use" assets. In return for this right to use the asset, the company promises to make periodic cash payments with the intention of returning the asset at the end of the lease.

Operating leases with terms greater than one year are considered long-term assets that are reported separately from property, plant, and equipment on the balance sheet. For a company like Lululemon, these assets include contractual rights to use store and other retail locations, distribution centers, offices, and equipment. Operating leases are common in the retail apparel industry. Leasing also is popular in many other industries, such as the land used by **McDonald's** restaurants, planes flown by **Delta Airlines**, hotel rooms offered by **Marriott**, cell towers used by **AT&T**, and stores operated by **Walgreens**. Operating leases with terms less than one year are not reported as assets. Instead, operating lease costs are expense and included on the income statement.

**Intangible Assets.**   Some assets used in the operations of a business have no physical substance. These assets are appropriately called intangible assets. Many intangible assets grant an exclusive right to a company to provide a product or service, such as patents, copyrights, franchises, and trademarks.

Another common type of intangible asset, also reported by Lululemon, is *goodwill.* Goodwill isn't associated with any specific identifiable right, but instead arises when one company acquires another company. The amount reported for goodwill equals the acquisition price above the fair value of the identifiable net assets (total assets minus total liabilities) acquired.

**Other Long-Term Assets.**   This category of long-term assets (reported by most companies) represents a catch-all classification of long-term assets that were not reported separately in one of the other long-term classifications. This amount most often includes long-term prepaid expenses, called *deferred charges.* For instance, in its disclosure notes Lululemon reports that it deferred charges related to income taxes, as well as other long-term assets related to security deposits and cloud computing arrangements.

 **KEY POINT**

Current assets include cash and other assets that are reasonably expected to be converted to cash or consumed within one year from the balance sheet date, or within the normal operating cycle of the business if that's longer than one year. Long-term asset classifications include investments; property, plant, and equipment; operating leases; intangible assets; and other assets.

## ASSET MEASUREMENT

When you look at the assets presented in Lululemon's balance sheet in Illustration 2–1, you may be tempted to think that all the assets are measured in the same way. As it turns out, there is more than one way to measure an asset—in fact, there are several. Here are four common measurement methods:

1. Historical cost
2. Amortized cost
3. Net realizable value
4. Fair value
   - Market value
   - Present value

**Historical Cost.**   We often measure assets based on their *original transaction value,* that is, their historical cost. Historical cost equals the value of what is given in exchange (usually cash) for the asset at its initial acquisition. Land is probably the most common example of an asset measured at its historical cost—the value of land in the balance sheet is simply the original price paid for that land. Inventory also is measured at historical cost under normal circumstances.

**Amortized Cost.**   This method is closely related to the historical cost method. Amortized cost is the historical cost of an asset adjusted for the depreciation or amortization accumulated over its lifetime. Buildings, equipment, and many intangible assets are measured at their amortized cost, which is their original cost less the accumulated depreciation (or amortization) to date.

**Net Realizable Value.**   Some assets are measured at their net realizable value. Intuitively, net realizable value is the net amount of cash into which an asset could be converted in the ordinary course of business. Accounts receivable are measured by their net realizable value—that is, the amount a company can expect to receive when the asset is converted into cash.

**Fair Value.**   Many financial assets, such as short-term investments in stock of another company, are measured at fair value, a measurement concept that is both useful and controversial. Fair value is defined as the price that would be received to sell assets in an orderly transaction between market participants on a given date. A key aspect of this definition is its focus on the perspective of *market participants.* The nuance of fair value arises because different market participants might value the asset differently. As a result, there are several approaches for determining fair value. We will discuss two of these approaches: market value and present value.

When an asset is frequently bought and sold in an active market, such as a stock market, then the quoted market value of the asset can be used as the fair value of the asset. When an asset is not traded in an active market, then there is no reliable market value, and the fair value of the assets must be estimated. One way to estimate the fair value is by calculating the present value of the asset. Present value represents the value today of all future cash flows. Operating lease assets are reported initially using the present value of future lease payments. We explore the topic of present value in depth in Appendix C at the end of the text.

**KEY POINT**

The balance sheet uses at least four methods for measuring assets, including historical cost, amortized cost, net realizable value, and fair value. The method chosen depends on the nature of the asset.

# Liabilities

Liabilities are the economic obligations of the company. We classify them into two major categories:

■ **LO2–2**
Describe the various liability and stockholders' equity classifications.

- Current liabilities—those that are due within one year of the balance sheet date.
- Long-term liabilities—those that are due in more than one year.

Illustration 2–5 shows the liability section of Lululemon's balance sheet. Like assets, current liabilities are listed before long-term liabilities to better help investors and creditors understand the company's liquidity.

| LULULEMON<br>Total Liabilities<br>($ in millions) | |
| --- | --- |
| Current liabilities: | |
| Accounts payable | $   80 |
| Accrued expenses | 140 |
| Current lease liabilities | 129 |
| Taxes payable | 26 |
| Deferred revenue (gift cards) | 120 |
| Other current liabilities | 125 |
| Total current liabilities | 620 |
| Long-term liabilities: | |
| Noncurrent lease liabilities | 611 |
| Deferred taxes | 92 |
| Other long-term liabilities | 6 |
| **Total liabilities** | **$1,329** |

**ILLUSTRATION 2–5**

Total Liabilities for Lululemon (Balance Sheet excerpt)

## CURRENT LIABILITIES

Current liabilities are those obligations that are expected to be satisfied within one year. Current liabilities are typically ordered in the balance sheet by maturity date. The most common current liabilities are:

1. Accounts payable
2. Deferred revenues
3. Accrued liabilities
4. Current portion of long-term debt

**Accounts Payable.**   The obligation related to purchases of inventory or supplies on account is called accounts payable. The company can make purchases on account if it has a credit arrangement with the supplier allowing it to receive the inventory or supplies now, but pay for those items later. Accounts payable are usually paid within 30 to 60 days and typically do not incur interest charges.

**Deferred Revenues.**   When cash is received in advance from a customer for goods or services to be provided in a future period, it creates an obligation called deferred revenue (sometimes called *unearned revenue*). For example, Lululemon reports almost $100 million of deferred revenue when it receives cash in advance from customers for gift cards. The company does not report revenue until the obligation is satisfied when a customer uses the card and Lululemon provides the product.

**Accrued liabilities.**   Accrued liabilities, sometimes called *accrued expenses,* represent obligations created when expenses have been incurred but not yet paid. For example, a company might owe salaries at the end of the current year that won't be paid until the following year. In this case, the company would report *salaries payable* as an accrued liability in the current year's balance sheet (as well as the related salaries expense in the income statement). Lululemon reports $26 million of taxes payable, which represents an accrued liability because the company incurred the tax expense in the current year, but won't pay those taxes until the following year. Other common examples of accrued liabilities include interest payable, utilities payable, and legal fees payable.

**Current portion of long-term debt.**   The current portion of long-term debt refers to the portion of long-term notes, leases, mortgages, and bonds that is payable within the next year (or operating cycle, if longer). For example, a $1,000,000 note payable requiring $100,000 in principal payments to be made in each of the next 10 years is classified as a $100,000 current liability and a $900,000 long-term liability. Lululemon does not report having any debt due in the next year.

## LONG-TERM LIABILITIES

Long-term liabilities are those obligations that are expected to be satisfied in more than one year. There are many examples of long-term liabilities, including the following:

- Note—a long-term loan in which the company is the borrower.
- Bond—a formal debt security issued by the company to a debt market or group of investors.
- Lease—a financial obligation arising from an arrangement between two parties for the right to use an asset for a specified period of time.
- Pension obligation—the estimated financial commitment related to retirement benefits the company has promised to its current and former employees.

The disclosure notes related to long-term liabilities provide additional information about the liability. For instance, long-term could mean anything from 2 to 20, 30, or 40 years. Payment terms, interest rates, and other details needed to assess the impact of these obligations on future cash flows and long-term solvency are reported in a disclosure note. Lululemon reports three items in the long-term liabilities section. One of these items relates to its long-term leasing obligations. These are the payment obligations associated with operating lease assets reported earlier in the balance sheet. The other two long-term liabilities relate to taxes and miscellaneous long-term obligations that cannot be identified from that statement but are discussed in further detail in the disclosure notes.

 **KEY POINT**

Liabilities are the obligations of a company. They are classified as either current (due within one year) or long-term (due in more than one year).

## Stockholders' Equity

The final section of the balance sheet is the stockholders' equity section. Stockholders' equity is simply total assets minus total liabilities. Stockholders' equity has many different names, including shareholders' equity, owners' equity, book equity, or simply equity. Entities that are not established with traditional equity ownership, such as non-profits, will use the term *net assets.* For example, the non-profit organization, **Gates Foundation**, reports *net assets* of about $40 billion. What does that mean? It means its assets of $48 billion exceed its liabilities of $8 billion.

Illustration 2–6 presents the equity section for Lululemon.

| LULULEMON Stockholders' Equity ($ in millions) | | |
|---|---|---|
| Common stock | $ | 1 |
| Additional paid-in capital | | 355 |
| Retained earnings | | 1,821 |
| Accumulated other comprehensive loss | | (225) |
| **Total stockholders' equity** | | **$1,952** |

**ILLUSTRATION 2–6**

Stockholders' Equity for Lululemon (Balance Sheet excerpt)

Stockholders' equity for a corporation arises primarily from three sources:

1. Contributed capital
   - Common stock
   - Additional paid-in capital
2. Retained earnings
3. Accumulated other comprehensive income

**Contributed Capital.**   The amount that stockholders have invested in the company is called contributed capital. It's often partitioned into two parts: *common stock* and *additional paid-in capital*. It arises when the company issues stock to a public equity market, such as the NYSE or Nasdaq, or sells a portion of its equity to an outside party, such as a private equity investor.

The stockholders' equity section of Lululemon's balance sheet reports the full amount of contributed capital in two accounts—common stock and additional paid-in capital. In combination, these two amounts indicate that Lululemon has a total contributed capital balance of $356 million at the end of the year.

**Retained Earnings.**   The balance of retained earnings is the total net income over the life of the company minus all dividends paid out to stockholders. In other words, it's the accumulated lifetime profits a company has earned for its stockholders but has not distributed to those stockholders. Most companies don't distribute all of their earnings as dividends, and some companies do not pay any dividends at all. This means that any profits they generate in a given year are accumulated in the retained earnings account.

**Accumulated Other Comprehensive Income (AOCI).**   Accumulated other comprehensive income (loss) captures all other changes in stockholders' equity related to nonowner sources (those that are not captured by retained earnings). We will discuss this account in more detail later in the chapter.

**KEY POINT**

Stockholders' equity for a corporation arises primarily from three sources: (1) contributed capital—amounts invested by stockholders in the corporation, and (2) retained earnings—accumulated net income reported by a company since its inception minus all dividends distributed to stockholders, and (3) accumulated other comprehensive income—changes in stockholders' equity from nonowner sources.

# Limitations of the Balance Sheet

■ LO2–3
Understand the limitations
of the balance sheet.

Despite its usefulness in presenting a snapshot of the company's resources and obligations, the balance sheet has limitations. We will discuss two primary limitations:

1. The difference between a company's book value and its market value.
2. The potential misuse of estimates and judgments.

## BOOK VALUE VS. MARKET VALUE

One important limitation of the balance sheet is that a company's book value, its reported total assets minus total liabilities, usually *will not reflect the company's market value.* As discussed previously, market value represents the price at which something could be sold in an active market. In the case of a public corporation, market value is represented by the trading price of a share of the corporation's stock. We can get an idea of the corporation's overall market value (or *market capitalization*) by multiplying the share price times the number of shares outstanding.

Illustration 2–7 presents the average ratio of the market value to the book value for all U.S. public companies by industry. A ratio of 1.0 means that the two values are equal. We see here that the ratio for the average firm is above 1.0 in all industries, and in some cases, the ratio is greater than 3.0.

**ILLUSTRATION 2–7**

**The Ratio of Market Value to Book Value by Industry**

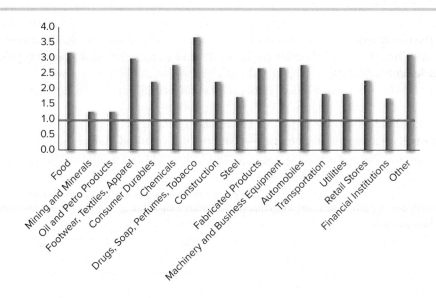

The three primary reasons a company's book value in the balance sheet will differ from its market value are:

1. Many assets, like land and buildings, are measured at their historical costs or amortized costs rather than amounts for which the assets could be sold. For example, suppose a company owns land and the amount for which the land could be sold increases. The increase in the land's fair value is not reported in the balance sheet, so it has no effect on the company's book value. However, to the extent the increase in the land's fair value is known by investors, that increase will be reflected in the company's market value.

2. Many economic resources of a company may not be reported as an asset in a company's balance sheet, such as trained employees, experienced management team, loyal customer relationships, and product knowledge. Investors understand the ability of these resources to generate future profits, and therefore these resources will

be reflected in a company's market value. These items, however, are not reported as assets in the current balance sheet and therefore are not reflected in book value.

3. Market values reflect investor's *expectations of future growth* of the company. Suppose, for example that investors receive new information that demand for the company's products have increased and will lead to higher future sales. The market value will increase to reflect the expectation of new growth, but this information will not impact the book value today.

In summary, even though the balance sheet *does not directly measure* the market value of the company, it provides valuable information that can be used to *help judge* market value.

## THE USE OF ESTIMATES IN THE BALANCE SHEET

Another limitation of the balance sheet is that many of the reported amounts are heavily reliant on *estimates and judgments rather than determinable amounts.* Here are some examples of the types of judgments and estimates that go into balance sheet amounts:

- Accounts receivable—the amount of receivables expected not to be collected.
- Inventory—the amount of inventory that is obsolete and cannot be sold.
- Property, plant, and equipment—the useful life of the asset.
- Investments—the fair value of the investment.
- Warranty reserves—the amount of warranty costs expected to occur in the future.
- Bonds payable—the fair value of the company's bond obligations.

Each of these estimates affects amounts reported in the balance sheet. If the estimates are biased or based on erroneous assumptions, the balance sheet will portray a distorted financial picture of the company. For example, **WorldCom** famously inflated the assets on the balance sheet by billions of dollars by inappropriately treating certain expenses (fees paid to use other telecommunication company networks) as capitalized assets.

**KEY POINT**

A limitation of the balance sheet includes stockholders' equity (book value) not equaling the company's market value. This occurs because many assets are measured at historical costs, some economic resources of the company are not reported as assets, and market values reflect expectations of future growth. Amounts in the balance sheet are also subject to management estimation error.

The following is a list of accounts in alphabetical order and their balances for the Gav Paint Corporation at December 31, 2024:

**Let's Review**

| Accounts | Amount |
|---|---|
| Accounts payable | $170,000 |
| Accounts receivable, net | 180,000 |
| Bonds payable (due in 10 years) | 500,000 |
| Cash | 80,000 |
| Common stock | 400,000 |
| Intangible assets, net | 50,000 |
| Interest payable | 10,000 |
| Inventory | 300,000 |
| Investment in equity securities[a] | 50,000 |
| Notes payable[b] | 200,000 |
| Short-term investments | 60,000 |

| Accounts | Amount |
|---|---|
| Prepaid expenses | 30,000 |
| Property, plant and equipment, net | 820,000 |
| Retained earnings | 250,000 |
| Salaries payable | 40,000 |

[a]The company intends to hold the $50,000 investment in equity securities for at least three years.
[b]The $200,000 note payable is a long-term loan, with $20,000 of the principal due on each July 1 for the next 10 years. Interest is payable each July 1.

**Required:**

Prepare a balance sheet for the Gav Paint Corporation at December 31, 2024. In particular, solve for current assets, total assets, current liabilities, total liabilities, and total stockholders' equity.

**Solution:**

**GAV PAINT CORPORATION**
**Balance Sheet**
**At December 31, 2024**

| | |
|---|---|
| Cash | $ 80,000 |
| Short-term investment | 60,000 |
| Accounts receivable, net | 180,000 |
| Inventory | 300,000 |
| Prepaid expenses | 30,000 |
| **Total current assets** | **650,000** |
| Property, plant and equipment, net | 820,000 |
| Intangible assets, net | 50,000 |
| Investments in equity securities | 50,000 |
| **Total assets** | **$1,570,000** |
| | |
| Accounts payable | $ 170,000 |
| Salaries payable | 40,000 |
| Interest payable | 10,000 |
| Current portion of long-term debt | 20,000 |
| **Current liabilities** | **240,000** |
| Notes payable | 180,000 |
| Bonds payable | 500,000 |
| **Total liabilities** | **920,000** |
| Common stock | 400,000 |
| Retained earnings | 250,000 |
| **Total stockholders' equity** | **650,000** |
| **Total liabilities and stockholders' equity** | **$1,570,000** |

## PART B

# THE INCOME STATEMENT

The income statement reports a company's profit (or loss) during a particular period (generally one year or one quarter). Profit equals revenues and gains minus expenses and losses. Unlike the balance sheet, which is a position statement *at a point in time*, the income statement measures activity *over a period of time*. For annual reporting, the income statement measures a company's income for a given year.

Illustration 2–8 provides the income statement for Lululemon. The amounts reported are for the 12-month period ending February 2, 2020, reflecting the revenues and expenses over this period of time.

ILLUSTRATION 2–8

Income Statement for Lululemon

**LULULEMON**
**Income Statement**
**For the fiscal year ended February 2, 2020**
**($ in millions)**

| | |
|---|---|
| Sales revenues, net | $3,979 |
| Cost of goods sold | 1,756 |
| **Gross profit** | 2,223 |
| Selling, general and administrative expenses | 1,334 |
| **Operating income** | 889 |
| Other income (expenses) | 8 |
| **Pretax income** | 897 |
| Income tax expense | 251 |
| **Net income** | **$ 646** |

## Components of Net Income

The income statement reports the revenues, expenses, gains, and losses that have occurred during the reporting period. The total amount of all revenues and gains minus the total of all expenses and losses equals **net income**. Next, we'll discuss each of the components of net income.

**■ LO2–4**
Describe revenues, expenses, gains, and losses.

### REVENUES AND EXPENSES

**Revenues.**   Revenues are the amount of resources generated by providing goods or services to customers during a given time period. For merchandising companies like Lululemon, the main source of revenue is sales revenue generated by selling merchandise inventory. Service companies such as **SalesForce** or **FedEx** generate revenue by providing services.

Companies typically report revenues for all product lines and geographic regions together in a single number. They will also report revenue *net* of any actual or predicted merchandise returns. The general rule is that revenue should be reported in the period that the goods and services are provided to customers for the amount a company is entitled to receive. Hence, the major challenges related to revenue are *when* it should be reported in the income statement and *how much* should be reported. We discuss these two issues in Chapter 5.

**Expenses.**   The costs incurred to generate revenue and run the business are called expenses. They represent the costs of providing goods and services. The general rule is that expenses should be reported in the period resources are used in operations. As a result, the timing of expenses should align with the timing of the revenues they help create.

Expenses can take just about any form—almost any costs incurred in the course of operations are considered expenses. These include:

- Cost of goods sold (COGS)—the purchase or manufacturing cost of merchandise inventory sold to customers.
- Cost of services—similar to COGS, costs incurred by a service or digital company directly related to delivering services and providing support to customers.
- Selling, general, and administrative expenses—a catch-all account that includes the costs of operations, including salaries, marketing, distribution, facilities maintenance, and depreciation.
- Interest expense—the cost of debt financing and other credit arrangements.
- Tax expense—the cost of all income taxes, including foreign, federal, and local income taxes.

### GAINS AND LOSSES

There are also two concepts that are highly related to revenues and expenses, respectively: gains and losses. Gains and losses are increases or decreases in income from transactions not classified as revenues or expenses. In general, these gains and losses do not reflect normal operating activities of the company, but they nevertheless represent transactions that affect a company's financial position. For example, consider the case when a restaurant chain sells several properties for an amount greater than their book value. This difference is reported as a gain, but it would be incorrect to consider this gain as a revenue because the gain occurred based on a transaction that was outside of the company's normal operations. Hence, revenues and expenses are linked to the normal operations of a company, while gains and losses are not. We will discuss many types of gains and losses throughout this book.

 **KEY POINT**

> The income statement reports the revenues, expenses, gains, and losses that have occurred during the reporting period. Revenues are the amount of resources generated by providing goods or services to customers during a given time period. Expenses are costs incurred to generate revenue and run the business. Gains and losses are increases or decreases in income from transactions not classified as revenues or expenses. The primary output of the income statement is net income.

## Measures of Income

■ LO2–5
Calculate the different measures of income.

While the concept of income is fairly straightforward, there are multiple ways to measure that concept. In this section, we'll discuss several measures of income followed by a discussion of two ways to present the income statement.

**Gross Profit.**   For a merchandising company like Lululemon, gross profit equals sales revenue minus cost of goods sold. For a services company like Salesforce, gross profit equals service revenue minus cost of services. The key to understanding gross profit lies in understanding the costs included in its computation. Cost of goods sold (or cost of services) includes the direct costs related to inventory (or services).

As a result, gross profit is a measure of profitability that links revenues directly to the costs needed to generate those revenues. It's the first measure of profitability presented in an income statement and provides a key, top-level measure of profitability for the company's primary business activities.

**Operating Income.**   Operating income includes gross profit less additional expenses related to the *operating activities* of the company. These additional operating expenses include items that are not direct costs related to inventory (or services), such as advertising, salaries, rent, utilities, supplies, and depreciation.

**Nonoperating Income.**   Nonoperating income includes revenues, expenses, gains, and losses related to investing and financing activities, not operating activities. For example, a manufacturer would include interest revenue, gains and losses from selling investments, and interest expense in nonoperating income. On the other hand, a financial institution like a bank would consider those items to be a part of operating income because they relate to the primary revenue-generating activities for that type of business. As shown in Illustration 2–8, nonoperating items often are included in the income statement under the heading *Other income (expense)*.

**Pretax Income.**   Pretax income is the sum of operating income and nonoperating income. This is the amount of profits before accounting for income taxes. Like individuals, corporations are income-tax-paying entities. Because of the importance and size of income tax expense (sometimes called the "provision for income taxes"), it's always reported on a separate line in corporate income statements.

**Net Income.**   The total amount of all revenues and gains minus the total of all expenses and losses equals net income. It's considered the company's "bottom line." Net income boils down the company's total performance over a given period to a single number, which makes it a useful summary statistic.

**Earnings per Share.**   Net income is reported in total dollars and represents the total profits that the company has generated for *all stockholders* during the period. However, for individual decision-making, investors want to know how much profit has been generated for *each stockholder.* To this end, we calculate earnings per share (EPS) as the amount of net income a company generates relative to the number of common shares outstanding.

EPS provides a convenient way for investors to link the company's profitability to the value of an individual share of ownership. EPS generally makes it easier to compare the performance of the company over time. However, EPS may not be comparable across companies if each company has issued a different number of shares. Larger companies may naturally have larger dollar amounts of net income, but they do not always generate more profit for each stockholder.

U.S. GAAP requires that public companies report two specific calculations of EPS: (1) basic EPS and (2) diluted EPS. Basic EPS equals total net income divided by the number of common shares outstanding. It is slightly more complicated than that, but we'll dive into those details later in Chapter 10. Basic EPS provides a measure of net income generated for each share of common stock during the period.

Diluted EPS incorporates the dilutive effect of all *potential* common shares in the calculation of EPS. Dilution refers to the reduction in EPS that occurs as the number of common shares outstanding increases as a result of certain securities outstanding, such as employee stock options or restricted stock units, that could dilute shares outstanding. Diluted EPS is a topic for more advanced accounting classes.

## INCOME STATEMENT FORMATS

There are two general approaches to formatting the income statement:

- The single-step format
- The multiple-step format

A single-step income statement groups all revenues and gains into a single subtotal. Then, expenses and losses are grouped and subtotaled. The difference between these two subtotals equals pretax income (also sometimes referred to as income from continuing operations before income taxes). Companies then subtract income tax expense to calculate net income.

The multiple-step income statement format reports a series of intermediate subtotals, such as gross profit, operating income, nonoperating income, and pretax income. Most companies provide income statements in this format, including Lululemon (Illustration 2–8).

A primary advantage of the multiple-step format is that it clearly separates operating and nonoperating items, which allows users to better assess a company's *core profitability. Operating income* provides a measure of profitability for core (or normal) operations, a key performance measure for predicting the future profit-generating ability of the company. Similarly, the classification of expenses into separate functions also provides useful information because it allows users to assess costs of differing types (e.g., depreciation vs. interest expense). *Pretax income* could be useful for comparing the performance of companies in different tax jurisdictions.

It's important to note that the difference between the single-step and multiple-step income statement is one of presentation. The bottom line, *net income,* is the same amount regardless of the format used. We use the multiple-step format for illustration purposes throughout the remainder of this book.

**KEY POINT** ――――――――――――――――――――――――――――――――――――

A single-step income statement groups all revenues and gains into a single subtotal, and all expenses and losses into a single subtotal (other than income tax expense), to calculate net income. A multiple-step income statement presents multiple measures of income, including gross profit, operating income, nonoperating income, pretax income, and net income.

## INCOME FROM DISCONTINUED OPERATIONS

Companies sometimes decide to sell or dispose of a component of their business. The operations of that business component are known as discontinued operations. What are some examples of discontinued operations? In recent years, **General Electric** sold its financial services businesses. **Campbell Soup Company** sold its European simple meals business to **Soppa Investments**. **Google** sold its Motorola Mobility smartphone subsidiary to **Lenovo**. **Procter & Gamble** sold its batteries division. These are all examples of discontinued operations.

By definition, profits from any discontinued operations will not continue in the future. If the discontinued operations represent a material component of the company, then the results from discontinued operations are reported separately in the income statement to allow financial statement users to more clearly understand results from *continuing* operations.

Illustration 2–9 presents the income statement of **Abbott Laboratories** that reported a discontinued operation.

**ILLUSTRATION 2–9**

Income Statement for
Abbott Laboratories

| ABBOTT LABORATORIES<br>Income Statement<br>For the fiscal year ended December 31, 2020<br>($ in millions) | |
|---|---:|
| Sales revenues, net | $34,608 |
| Cost of goods sold | 15,003 |
| Selling, general and administrative expenses | 11,828 |
| Research and development | 2,420 |
| Operating income | 5,357 |
| Other income (expenses) | (389) |
| Income from continuing operations before income taxes | 4,968 |
| Income tax expense | 497 |
| **Income from continuing operations** | **4,471** |
| **Income from discontinued operations, net of taxes** | **24** |
| **Net income** | **$ 4,495** |

The objective of reporting income from continuing operations is to inform financial statements users of which components of net income are continuing and which are not. Companies do this by separately reporting income from *continuing* operations (which for Abbott Laboratories is $4,471 million) and income from *discontinued* operations (which for Abbott Laboratories is $24 million).

# Limitations of the Income Statement

■ LO2–6
Understand the limitations
of the income statement.

Despite its usefulness in presenting a summary measure of performance, the income statement has limitations. We will discuss three primary limitations:

1. The inclusion of recurring and nonrecurring items.
2. The inclusion of operating and nonoperating items.
3. The potential misuse of estimates and judgments.

## THE INCLUSION OF RECURRING AND NONRECURRING ITEMS

The income statement contains items that are likely to recur in the future, but also some items that are unlikely to recur. Examples of recurring items include salaries expenses, advertising expense, and depreciation. Examples of nonrecurring items include one-time gains and losses on the sale of long-term assets, one-time changes to restructure the business, and unusual charges associated with unpredictable events such as floods. The presence of both recurring and nonrecurring items in the income statement can make it difficult for investors to predict what income will look like in the future. In other words, the income statement can include items that actually diminish its predictive value.

## THE INCLUSION OF OPERATING AND NONOPERATING ITEMS

The income statement also contains items related to core operations and items that are not, which we call nonoperating items. Examples of operating items includes sales revenue, cost of goods sold, depreciation, and salaries. These items are part of the core business of the company. Examples of nonoperating items relate to the investing and financing activities of the business. For example, a company may choose to invest some of its cash in a short-term security to make a modest return. Any income that results from this investment is considered nonoperating if the company is not in the business of making investments (as would be the case for a bank). Most companies also have financed some of their business through debt. Payments for interest are considered a nonoperating expense because they relate to a financing decision.

The good news is that the income statement does separate the operating income from the nonoperating income. Illustration 2–8 shows this separation for Lululemon, which shows that operating income effectively partitions the income statements into two segments: operating (revenues and expenses above operating income) and nonoperating (those below operating income). That said, it is important to recognize that the operating income and nonoperating income items are all presented in the income statement on a pretax basis and it is not clear from the statement how much tax expense relates to the operating and nonoperating items. This comingling makes it difficult to determine the portion of net income stemming from operating activities and the portion stemming from nonoperating activities.

## THE POTENTIAL MISUSE OF ESTIMATES AND JUDGMENTS

Like the balance sheet, many income statement items are based on the judgments and estimates of management, and therefore can potentially be manipulated or biased. Companies face strong incentives to show growth and profits. Furthermore, many company managers are compensated for achieving certain performance targets. These incentives can encourage managers to exercise their influence over accounting estimates to inflate reported profits in a way to achieve these targets.

Occasionally, companies are required to restate previously filed financial statements when it's determined that previously filed financial statements are misstated in some way. For example, in 2019, **Pareteum Corporation** announced that investors should no longer rely upon the company's financial statements released in 2018 and the first part of 2019 due to an overstatement in revenues. The company restated the financial statements, which resulted in a reduction of revenue of approximately $9 million in 2018 and $24 million in 2019. The restatement also impacted several other accounts, including cost of services and accounts receivable. Restatements can have significant consequences for the company. The stock price of Pareteum dropped by 59% on the news of the restatement, and a class action lawsuit was filed against the company. The most common restatements relate to managers over-estimating their revenues, and the second most common restatement relates to managers under-estimating their core expenses.[1] These restatements provide evidence of managers' efforts to inflate reported profits. We'll discuss managers' influence over earnings—including earnings management and non-GAAP earnings—in more detail in Chapter 12.

 **KEY POINT**

Limitations of the income statement include (1) inclusion of recurring and nonrecurring items, (2) inclusion of operating and nonoperating items, and (3) potential misuse of estimates and judgments. Each of these makes it difficult for investors to predict what income will look like in the future.

---

[1]Scholz, S. (2008). *The changing nature and consequences of public company financial restatements.* The Department of the Treasury (April).

**Let's Review**

The following is a list of accounts in alphabetical order for **Target** at February 2, 2019 ($ in millions):

| Accounts | Amount |
|---|---|
| Cost of sales | $53,299 |
| Depreciation and amortization expense | 2,224 |
| Income tax expense (from continuing operations) | 746 |
| Interest expense | 461 |
| Other nonoperating income | 27 |
| Profit from discontinued operations, net of tax | 7 |
| Sales revenue | 75,356 |
| Selling, general and administrative expenses | 15,723 |

**Required:**

Prepare a multiple-step income statement for Target at February 2, 2019.

**Solution:**

**TARGET CORP**
**Income Statement**
**For the year ended February 2, 2019**
**($ in millions)**

| | |
|---|---|
| Sales revenue | $75,356 |
| Cost of sales | 53,299 |
| **Gross profit** | **22,057** |
| Selling, general and administrative expenses | 15,723 |
| Depreciation and amortization expense | 2,224 |
| **Operating income** | **4,110** |
| Interest expense | (461) |
| Other nonoperating income | 27 |
| **Income from continuing operations before income taxes** | **3,676** |
| Income tax expense | 746 |
| **Income from continuing operations** | **2,930** |
| Profit from discontinued operations, net of tax | 7 |
| **Net income** | **$ 2,937** |

---

**PART C**

# THE STATEMENT OF CASH FLOWS

The statement of cash flows provides information about the cash receipts and cash payments of a company during a particular reporting period. The difference between cash receipts and cash payments represents the change in cash for the period. To help investors and creditors determine the type of transaction that gave rise to each cash flow, the statement of cash flows classifies all transactions affecting cash into one of three categories: (1) operating activities, (2) investing activities, and (3) financing activities.

In this chapter, we focus on the *intuition* underlying the statement of cash flows. The construction of the statement of cash flows and discussions of the different ways to present the operating section (direct and indirect methods) are presented in Chapter 11.

## Classifying Cash Flows

### CASH FLOWS FROM OPERATING ACTIVITIES

**■ LO2–7**
Identify operating, investing, and financing cash flows.

The inflows and outflows of cash that result from activities reported in the income statement are classified as cash flows from operating activities. These activities typically represent the normal day-to-day business operations of a company. Illustration 2–10 provides a list of some of the these activities.

ILLUSTRATION 2–10

Transactions Included in Cash Flow from Operating Activities

Cash *inflows* from operating activities:

- Sale of goods or services to customers.
- Interest and dividends from investments.

Cash *outflows* from operating activities:

- Purchase of inventory.
- Salaries, wages, and other operating expenses.
- Interest on debt.
- Income taxes.

The difference between the inflows and outflows is called *net cash flows from operating activities.*

Let's take a look at the operating section of the statement of cash flows for Lululemon in Illustration 2–11 to get a better idea of the information provided by the statement.

ILLUSTRATION 2–11

Statement of Cash Flows for Lululemon

### LULULEMON
### Statement of Cash Flows
### For the fiscal year ended February 2, 2020
### ($ in millions)

| | | |
|---|---:|---:|
| Cash flows from operating activities | | |
| Net income | $ 646 | |
| *Adjustments for noncash items included in net income* | 218 | |
| *Changes in operating assets and liabilities* | (195) | |
| **Net cash flows from operating activities** | | **669** |
| Cash flows from investing activities | | |
| Purchase of equipment | (283) | |
| Other investing activities | 3 | |
| **Net cash flows from investing activities** | | **(280)** |
| Cash flows from financing activities | | |
| Issuance of employee stock | 18 | |
| Taxes paid on employee stock issuance | (22) | |
| Stock repurchase | (173) | |
| **Net cash flows from financing activities** | | **(177)** |
| Net change in cash | | 212 |
| Cash balance, February 3, 2019 | | 881 |
| Cash balance, February 2, 2020 | | $1,093 |

Lululemon is generating positive cash flows from operations of $669 million. This implies that the cash inflows from selling its products exceeds the cash outflows needed to run operations. Positive operating cash flows generally indicate good financial health of the company because it suggests the company can pay its bills with funds generated by operations. Consistently negative operating cash flows cannot be sustained over time.

You'll notice the operating section of the statement of cash flows is constructed by starting with net income and then making adjustments to arrive at operating cash flows. These adjustments represent the difference between performance measured on a cash basis (operating cash flows) and performance on an accrual basis (net income). We briefly discuss these concepts next and then in more detail in Chapter 11.

**Cash Basis vs. Accrual Basis.**  As implied by the name, operating cash flows provide information about a company's operating performance. In Part B, we learned that the income statement also provides information about the operating performance of the company. What accounts for the difference between the measure of operating cash flows presented in the statement of cash flows and the measure of net income presented in the income statement?

It's first important to understand that the statement of cash flows and the income statement present information using a different *basis of accounting*. That is, the two statements are created using different accounting methodologies. The statement of cash flows uses a *cash basis* of accounting. This means that the statement of cash flows recognizes cash inflows and outflows based on the actual exchange of cash. The income statement uses an *accrual basis* of accounting. This means that the income statement recognizes revenues at the time goods and services are provided and recognizes expenses as resources are used in operations. The recognition of revenues and expenses does not necessarily depend on when the associated cash flows are received or paid.

For example, suppose a company sells goods to customers on account. The income statement reports sales revenue, but the statement of cash flows reports no cash inflows. This difference is captured by the change in the balance of accounts receivable. Similarly, a company may pay for supplies but not yet use those supplies. The statement of cash flows reports cash outflows, but the income statement reports no supplies expense until those supplies are used. The difference between cash paid for supplies and supplies expense is captured by the change in the balance of the supplies account. Also, some expenses, like depreciation expense, don't affect cash at all and aren't included as cash outflows from operating activities, but they are reported in the income statement and affect net income. Don't worry too much at this point if the concept of accrual-basis accounting is challenging to grasp. This entire book is designed to teach you about accrual-basis accounting, so you'll have plenty of time for this concept to sink in.

It's important to recognize that neither basis of accounting, cash basis or accrual basis, *is better*. They are both useful to investors and creditors. The income statement tells us about the economic profitability of the company over a period of time. The statement of cash flow tells us about the sources and uses of cash over that same period of time.

 **KEY POINT**

> The income statement and the statement of cash flows both measure operating performance, but with different methodologies. The statement of cash flows uses a cash basis of accounting to measure operating cash flows. The income statement uses an accrual basis of accounting to measure net income. Both statements are useful to investors and creditors.

## CASH FLOWS FROM INVESTING ACTIVITIES

Cash flows from investing activities include inflows and outflows of cash related to the acquisition and disposition of long-term assets used in the operations of the business (such as property, plant, and equipment) and some investment assets. The purchase and sale of inventory are not considered investing activities. Inventory is purchased for the purpose of being sold as part of the company's operations, so the purchase and sale of inventory are included with operating activities rather than investing activities. Illustration 2–12 provides a list of some of the common investing activities.

The difference between the inflows and outflows equals *net cash flows from investing activities*. A negative number here indicates the outflows exceeded the inflows and vice versa.

Returning to the investing activities section of the statement of cash flows for Lululemon (see Illustration 2–11), we can see that the company made capital expenditures for new equipment totaling $283 million and had other investing cash inflows of $3 million.

## CASH FLOWS FROM FINANCING ACTIVITIES

Cash flows from financing activities relate to the external financing of the company. Cash inflows occur when cash is borrowed from creditors or invested by owners. Cash outflows occur when cash is paid back to creditors or distributed to owners. The payment of interest to a creditor, however, is classified as an operating activity. Illustration 2–13 provides a list of some of the common financing activities.

ILLUSTRATION 2–12

Transactions Included
in Cash Flow from
Investing Activities

Cash *inflows* from investing activities:

- Sale of equipment, buildings, and other long-term assets used in the business.
- Sale of some investment securities.
- Collection of loans made by the company.

Cash *outflows* from investing activities:

- Purchase of long-lived assets used in the business. This amount is commonly referred to as capital expenditures or "capex."
- Purchase of investment securities, such as stocks and bonds of other entities.

**ILLUSTRATION 2–12**

Transactions Included
in Cash Flow from
Investing Activities

Cash *inflows* from financing activities:

- Sale of shares to owners (stockholders).
- Borrowing from creditors through notes, loans, mortgages, and bonds.

Cash *outflows* from financing activities:

- Dividends or other distributions to owners (stockholders).
- Repurchase of shares from owners (stockholders).
- Repayment of the principal amounts of debt to creditors (excluding trade payables that relate to operating activities).

**ILLUSTRATION 2–13**

Transactions Included
in Cash Flow from
Financing Activities

*Net cash flows from financing activities* equal the difference between the inflows and out-flows. Again, if the outflows exceed the inflows, this number will be negative. This is the case for Lululemon, which shows negative cash flows from financing (Illustration 2–11). The company spent $173 million to buy back its own stock (commonly called "stock repur-chases" or "stock buybacks"), received $18 million on the issuance of employee stock while paying $22 million in taxes for the employee stock issuance. We discuss stock repurchases in greater detail in Chapter 10.

**KEY POINT**

Investing cash flows include inflows and outflows of cash related to the acquisition and dispo-sition of long-term assets used in the operations of the business and some investment assets. Financing cash flows include inflows and outflows of cash related to creditors (primarily long-term debt) and investors (such as issuance of stock and distribution of dividends).

## CHANGE IN CASH

The final component of the statement of cash flows shows the change in cash for the fiscal period. The change in cash is simply the difference between the balance of cash at the end of the current period and the balance at the beginning of the current period (end of the last fiscal period). The change in cash should always equal the sum of cash flows from operating activities, investing activities, and financing activities.

Putting it all together, we learn that Lululemon generated enough cash flows from operations to fund all of their investing and financing activities. We learn this from the "Net change in cash" subtotal in Illustration 2–11, which shows a positive change in cash of $212 million. We learn from the final section of their statement of cash flows that the company started the year with $881 million in cash. After accounting for the $212 million increase in cash, the company ended the year with $1,093 million in cash.

## Let's Review

*Required:*

The following is a list of cash flows for LuLu Consulting. Indicate whether each cash flow would be categorized as an operating, investing or financing cash flow and calculate net cash flows for each type of activity.

Cash paid to employees for salaries, $200,000
Cash paid for new equipment, $168,000
Cash paid for dividends, $600,000
Cash received from the sale of a debt investment, $60,000
Cash paid to fly consultants to engagements, $100,000
Cash received from a new loan, 250,000
Cash paid for taxes, $4,500,000
Cash received from customers in advance of services, $6,500,000
Cash paid for supplies, $420,000
Cash received from an issuance of equity securities, $1,000,000

*Solution:*

| | Operating Cash Flow | Investing Cash Flow | Financing Cash Flow |
|---|---|---|---|
| Cash paid to employees for salaries | $ (200,000) | | |
| Cash paid for new equipment | | $(168,000) | |
| Cash paid for dividends | | | $(600,000) |
| Cash received from the sale of a debt investment | | 60,000 | |
| Cash paid to fly consultants to engagements | (100,000) | | |
| Cash received from a new loan | | | 250,000 |
| Cash paid for taxes | (4,500,000) | | |
| Cash received from customers in advance of services | 6,500,000 | | |
| Cash paid for supplies | (420,000) | | |
| Cash received from an issuance of equity securities | | | 1,000,000 |
| Net cash flows | $1,280,000 | $(108,000) | $ 650,000 |

## PART D

# STATEMENTS OF STOCKHOLDERS' EQUITY AND COMPREHENSIVE INCOME

The final two statements we discuss are the statement of stockholders' equity and the statement of comprehensive income. In Chapter 1, we discussed survey evidence that indicates financial statement users do not see the statement of stockholders' equity and the statement of comprehensive income as being as useful as the balance sheet, income statement, and statement of cash flows. This does not mean, however, that these two additional statements do not provide certain valuable information and should be ignored. We discuss each in turn.

## Statement of Stockholders' Equity

■ **LO2–8**
Understand the purpose of the statement of stockholders' equity.

The statement of stockholders' equity summarizes the changes in each stockholders' equity account during a particular reporting period. Recall from the discussion in Part A that there are three primary sources of equity reported in the balance sheet—contributed capital (common stock and additional paid-in capital), retained earnings, and accumulated other comprehensive income (AOCI). The balance sheet shows the amounts for these accounts as of a point in time (the last day of the fiscal period). The objective of the statement of stockholders' equity is to detail *the change in the balance* of these equity accounts from the beginning of the period to the end of the period.

Let's take a look at the statement of stockholders' equity for Lululemon to get a feel for some of the things we can learn from this statement. It is presented in Illustration 2–14.

| | Common Stock | Additional Paid-in Capital | Retained Earnings | AOCI | Total Stockholders' Equity |
|---|---|---|---|---|---|
| **LULULEMON** | | | | | |
| **Statement of Stockholders' Equity** | | | | | |
| **As of February 2, 2020** | | | | | |
| **($ in millions)** | | | | | |
| Beginning Balance | $1 | $315 | $1,347 | $(217) | $1,446 |
| Net income | | | 646 | | 646 |
| Foreign currency translation | | | | (8) | (8) |
| Stock-based compensation | | 42 | | | 42 |
| Stock repurchase | | (2) | (172) | | (174) |
| **Ending balance** | **$1** | **$355** | **$1,821** | **$(225)** | **$1,952** |

**ILLUSTRATION 2–14**

Statement of Stockholders' Equity for Lululemon

There are several insights we can learn from this statement:

1. The change in contributed capital is shown in the first two columns—*Common Stock* and *Additional Paid-in Capital*. There was no change in common stock in the current year, but Lululemon added $42 million in additional paid-in capital resulting from stock-based compensation. This column, along with the amount in the Retained Earnings column, shows that the company purchased its own stock for $174 million (we commonly call these "stock repurchases"). These stock repurchases reduce the number of shares that are traded in the market and can sometimes impact retained earnings. We'll dive into stock repurchases in Chapter 10.

2. The column labeled *Retained Earnings* reveals the company generated $646 million in net income during the year, which increases retained earnings. This amount ties directly to net income reported in the income statement (Illustration 2–8). This column also reveals that the company did not pay any dividends during the period. If they had, then this column would report a decrease in retained earnings associated with the dividends.

3. Finally, the statement includes a column for *AOCI*. The statement shows the company suffered a decline in AOCI of $8 million due to translation of foreign currency from its foreign operations.

As shown in the final column, total stockholders' equity of the company has increased over the year.

 **KEY POINT**

Ths primary components of stockholders' equity are contributed capital (common stock and additional paid-in capital), retained earnings, and accumulated other comprehensive income. The statement of stockholders' equity summarizes the changes in each of these stockholders' equity accounts.

# Comprehensive Income

You may have heard people refer to net income as the "bottom line." It turns out that there is another measure of income that comes after net income. This measure is called comprehensive income, which is a broader definition of income that includes *all* changes in equity that arise from both owner and nonowner sources.

■ **LO2–9**

Understand the distinguishing features of comprehensive income.

To understand the concept of comprehensive income, it's first important to understand that changes in stockholders' equity arise from two sources—transactions with owners (stockholders) and transactions with nonowners. Transactions with owners include events such as increasing equity by issuing stock to stockholders, decreasing equity by purchasing stock from stockholders, and paying dividends. All other changes in equity come from nonowner sources. So what do we mean by *nonowner* sources? The transactions that lead to changes in equity from nonowner sources include all transactions with customers, suppliers, employees, landlords, utility providers, and tax authorities, to name a few. Most of these transactions are reported as revenues, expenses, gains, and losses in the income statement and are used to calculate net income. However, there are a few gains and losses that arise from nonowners sources that are not reported in the income statement, but nevertheless affect equity. These other gains and losses are reported as other comprehensive income (OCI). Therefore, the broader concept of comprehensive income includes all of the items reflected in net income plus these *other* changes in stockholders' equity from nonowner sources:

**Comprehensive income = Net income + Other comprehensive income**

What types of items are included in *other comprehensive income?* These items tend to reflect gains and losses that are not part of core operations and are largely outside the control of management. These items include:

- Foreign currency adjustments.
- Unrealized ("paper") gains or losses on certain types of securities.
- Unrealized gains and losses on sophisticated derivative investments.
- Certain gains and losses associated with pension plans.

As you can see, these items are largely outside management's control because they tend to move with broader movements in the market. Changes in the value of these items, however, do impact the equity of the company, but standard setters have elected to keep them off of the income statement and instead include them in other comprehensive income.

Illustration 2–15 provides the statement of comprehensive income for Lululemon.

**ILLUSTRATION 2–15**

Statement of Comprehensive Income for Lululemon

**LULULEMON**
**Statement of Comprehensive Income**
**For the fiscal year ending February 2, 2020**
**($ in millions)**

| | |
|---|---|
| Sales revenues, net | $3,979 |
| Cost of goods sold | 1,756 |
| Gross profit | 2,223 |
| Selling, general and administrative expenses | 1,334 |
| Operating income | 889 |
| Other income (expenses) | 8 |
| Pretax income | 897 |
| Income tax expense | 251 |
| **Net income** | **646** |
| Foreign currency translation adjustment | (8) |
| **Comprehensive income** | **$ 476** |

As you can see, Lululemon presents its statement of comprehensive income as an extension of the income statement (see Lululemon's income statement in Illustration 2–8). We learn from the statement of comprehensive income that the company has one component of *other comprehensive income*—foreign currency translation adjustment. Lululemon operates in many different countries that use different currencies. When the value of those currencies changes in relation to the U.S. dollar, then it can either increase or decrease the value of the company. Because the loss related to fluctuation in foreign currencies represents a nontraditional change in equity, it's considered part of other comprehensive income.

The $8 million decrease related to foreign currency translation adjustment ties directly to the $8 million decrease we observed in the AOCI column of the statement of stockholders' equity presented in Illustration 2–14. Thus, net income is incorporated into total equity through the retained earnings account, and other comprehensive income items are incorporated into total equity through AOCI.

### KEY POINT

Comprehensive income is a broader definition of income that includes all revenues, expenses, gains, and losses arising from "nonowner transactions." Most revenues, expenses, gains, and losses are reported as part of net income in the income statement, while a few gains and losses are not reported as part of net income. These other gains and losses represent other comprehensive income items and are captured in accumulated other comprehensive income.

### SUSTAINABILITY

The five financial statements discussed in this chapter communicate important financial amounts and performance indicators to stakeholders. Similarly, the SASB encourages companies to identify and communicate financially material *sustainability* information to these stakeholders. This information includes sustainability performance metrics different from those you'd typically find in the financial statements.

For example, in its Environmental, Social, and Governance (ESG) report, **American Airlines** states the following:

> At American Airlines, we know that rigorous management of environmental, social and governance (ESG) issues is critical to the long-term success of our company and our planet. This includes effectively governing our business and holding ourselves accountable on a set of key issues that are important to our company and our stakeholders. It also means being responsive to our stakeholders and transparent about our performance.

American Airlines then reports the following performance metrics related to fuel-efficiency and emissions reported in the ESG report.

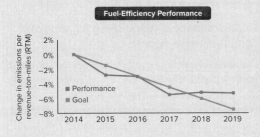
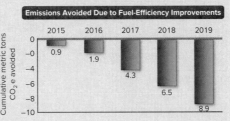

These types of sustainability performance disclosures help stakeholders to track and monitor the company's efforts to reduce its carbon footprint.

### THE BOTTOM LINE

**LO2–1** Describe the various asset classifications and measurement methods.

Current assets include cash and other assets that are reasonably expected to be converted to cash or consumed within one year from the balance sheet date, or within the normal operating cycle of the business if that's longer than one year. Long-term asset classifications include investments; property,

plant, and equipment; intangible assets; and other assets.

The balance sheet uses at least four methods for measuring assets, including historical cost, amortized cost, net realizable value and fair value. The method chosen depends on the nature of the asset.

**LO2–2  Describe the various liability and stockholders' equity classifications.**

Liabilities are the obligations of a company. They are classified as either current (due within one year) or long-term (due in more than one year).

Stockholders' equity for a corporation arises primarily from three sources: (1) contributed capital—amounts invested by stockholders in the corporation, (2) retained earnings—accumulated net income reported by a company since its inception minus all dividends distributed to stockholders, and (3) accumulated other comprehensive income (AOCI)—changes in stockholders' equity from nonowner sources.

**LO2–3  Understand the limitations of the balance sheet.**

A limitation of the balance sheet includes stockholders' equity (book value) not equaling the company's market value. This occurs because many assets are measured at historical costs, some economic resources of the company are not reported as assets, and market values reflect expectations of future growth. Amounts in the balance sheet are also subject to management estimation errors.

**LO2–4  Describe revenues, expenses, gains, and losses.**

The income statement reports the revenues, expenses, gains, and losses that have occurred during the reporting period. Revenues are the amount of resources generated by providing goods or services to customers during a given time period. Expenses are costs incurred to generate revenue and run the business. Gains and losses are increases or decreases in income transactions not classified as revenues or expenses. The primary output of the income statement is net income.

**LO2–5  Calculate the different measures of income.**

A single-step income statement groups all revenues and gains into a single subtotal, and all expenses and losses into a single subtotal (other than income tax expense), to calculate net income. A multiple-step income statement presents multiple measures of income, including gross profit, operating income, nonoperating income, pretax income, and net income.

**LO2–6  Understand the limitations of the income statement.**

Limitations of the income statement include (1) inclusion of recurring and nonrecurring items, (2) inclusion of operating and nonoperating items, and (3) potential misuse of estimates and judgments. Each of these makes it difficult for investors to predict what income will look like in the future.

**LO2–7  Identify operating, investing, and financing cash flows.**

The income statement and the statement of cash flows both measure operating performance but with different methodologies. The statement of cash flows uses a cash basis of accounting to measure operating cash flows. The income statement uses an accrual basis of accounting to measure net income. Both statements are useful to investors and creditors.

Investing cash flows include inflows and outflows of cash related to the acquisition and disposition of long-term assets used in the operations of the business and some investment assets.

Financing cash flows include inflows and outflows of cash related to creditors (primarily long-term debt) and investors (such as issuance of stock and distribution of dividends).

**LO2–8  Understand the purpose of the statement of stockholders' equity.**

The primary components of stockholders' equity are contributed capital (common stock and additional paid-in capital), retained earnings and accumulated other comprehensive income. The statement of stockholders' equity summarizes the changes in each of these stockholders' equity accounts.

**LO2–9  Understand the distinguishing features of comprehensive income.**

Comprehensive income is a broader definition of income that includes all revenues, expenses, gains, and losses arising from "nonowner transactions." Most revenues, expenses, gains, and losses are reported as part of net income in the income statement, while a few gains and losses are not reported as part of net income. These other gains and losses represent other comprehensive income items and are captured in accumulated other comprehensive income.

## GLOSSARY

**Accounts payable:** Obligations to suppliers for purchases of inventory or supplies on account. **p. 63**

**Accounts receivable:** The amount of cash owed to the company by its customers from the sale of goods or services on account. **p. 60**

**Accrued liabilities:** Expenses already incurred, but not yet paid (also sometimes called accrued expenses). **p. 64**

**Accumulated other comprehensive income (loss):** A component of stockholders' equity that reports the accumulated amount of other comprehensive income items in the current and prior periods. **p. 65**

**Amortized cost:** Historical cost of an asset less an adjustment for the depreciation or amortization that has accumulated over its useful life. **p. 62**

**Balance sheet:** A financial statement that presents the financial position of the company on a particular date. **p. 58**

**Basic EPS (Earnings per Share):** Net income divided by the actual number of common shares outstanding. **p. 71**

**Book value:** Total assets minus total liabilities. **p. 66**

**Cash equivalents:** Short-term investments with original maturities of less than 90 days. **p. 59**

**Cash flows from financing activities:** Inflows and outflows of cash resulting from transactions with capital providers (creditors and owners). **p. 76**

**Cash flows from investing activities:** Inflows and outflows of cash that result from the acquisition and disposition of long-term assets used in the operations of the business (such as property, plant, and equipment) and some investment assets. **p. 76**

**Cash flow from operating activities:** Inflows and outflows of cash that result from activities stemming from normal business operations that are reported in the income statement. **p. 74**

**Comprehensive income:** A broader definition of income that includes net income and all other changes in equity that arise from nonowner sources during the period. **p. 79**

**Contributed capital:** The amount that stockholders have invested in the company; consists of common stock and additional paid-in capital amounts. **p. 65**

**Current portion of long-term debt:** The portion of long-term debt (notes, bonds, mortgages, etc.) that is payable within the next year (or operating cycle if longer than one year). **p. 64**

**Deferred revenue:** Cash received in advance from customers for goods and services to be provided in the future. **p. 63**

**Depreciation:** Allocating the cost of a long-term asset to an expense over its service life. **p. 61**

**Diluted EPS (Earnings per Share):** Net income divided by the actual and potential number of common shares outstanding; potential common shares result from securities such as stock options or restricted stock units. **p. 71**

**Discontinued operations:** Operations that the company has decided to sell or discontinue in the future. **p. 72**

**Earnings per share (EPS):** Net income divided by the actual number of common shares outstanding. **p. 71**

**Expenses:**  Costs of providing products and services and other business activities during the current period. **p. 69**

**Fair value:** The price that would be received to sell an asset in an orderly transaction between market participants on a given date. **p. 62**

**Gains:** Increases in income from transactions not classified as revenues. **p. 69**

**Gross profit:** Sales revenue minus cost of goods sold (or service revenue minus cost of services for a service company) **p. 70**

**Historical cost:** The value of what is given in exchange for an asset at its initial acquisition. **p. 62**

**Income statement:** A financial statement that reports the company's profits during a particular reporting period, measured as revenues and gains minus expenses and losses. **p. 68**

**Income tax expense:** The amount of tax owed to governments for profits reported during the period. **p. 70**

**Intangible asset:** Assets used in business operations that have no physical substance and often involve an exclusive right of the company to provide a product or service. **p. 61**

**Inventory:** Items a company intends for sale to customers in the ordinary course of business. **p. 60**

**Liquidity:** Refers to how quickly an asset can be converted to cash. **p. 59**

**Losses:** Decreases in income from transactions not classified as expenses. **p. 69**

**Market value:** The value of an asset as quoted on an active market. **p. 62**

**Multiple-step income statement:** Presents the income statement as a series of intermediate subtotals including gross profit, operating income, nonoperating income, and pretax income. **p. 71**

**Net income:** The total amount of all revenues and gains minus the total of all expenses and losses. P. 70

**Net realizable value:** The net amount of cash into which an asset could be converted in the ordinary course of business. **p. 62**

**Nonoperating income:** Revenues, expenses, gains, and losses related to investing and financing activities.  **p. 70**

**Operating cycle:** The period of time from the purchase of inventory until the time the company collects cash from customers from the sale of inventory.  **p. 59**

**Operating income:** Gross profit minus all additional expenses related to the operations of the business. **p. 70**

**Operating lease:** The right to use an asset for a specified period of time. **p. 60**

**Other comprehensive income (OCI):** Gains and losses that arise from nonowners sources that are not reported in the income statement. **p. 80**

**Prepaid expense:** Cost of assets acquired in one period that are expensed in a future period. **p. 60**

**Present value:** The value today of all future cash flows. **p. 62**

**Pretax income:** Operating income plus nonoperating income. **p. 70**

**Property, plant, and equipment:** Tangible, long-term assets used in the operations of the business, such as land, buildings, equipment, machinery, furniture, and vehicles, as well as natural resources, such as mineral mines, timber tracts, and oil wells. **p. 61**

**Retained earnings:** All net income minus all dividends over the life of the company; internal source of equity. **p. 65**

**Revenues:** Amounts recognized when the company sells products or services to customers. **p. 69**

**Single-step income statement:** Presents the income statement by grouping all revenues and gains into a single subtotal,

all expenses and losses into another subtotal, and then differencing the two subtotals to equal pretax income. **p. 71**

**Statement of cash flows:** A financial statement that measures activities involving cash receipts and cash payments during a particular reporting period. **p. 74**

**Statement of stockholders' equity:** A financial statement that summarizes the changes in stockholders' equity during a particular reporting period. **p. 78**

## SELF-STUDY QUESTIONS

1. Which of the following assets is generally not classified as a current asset? **(LO2–1)**
   a. Inventory.
   b. Land.
   c. Accounts receivable.
   d. Prepaid expenses.

2. Which of the following is not an appropriate method for measuring various assets? **(LO2–1)**
   a. Historical cost.
   b. Fair value.
   c. Management's estimate of future value.
   d. Net realizable value.

3. In a classified balance sheet, liabilities are separated into two categories based on **(LO2–2)**
   a. The amount of the obligation to be satisfied—large versus small.
   b. To whom the obligation is owed—those inside versus those outside of the company.
   c. The nature of the obligation—determinable amount versus estimated amount.
   d. The length of time until the obligation is expected to be satisfied—less than one year versus more than one year.

4. Which of the following liabilities is generally classified as a long-term liability? **(LO2–2)**
   a. Notes payable.
   b. Accounts payable.
   c. Accrued liabilities.
   d. Deferred revenues.

5. The component of stockholders' equity that measures total net income over the life of the company minus all dividends paid out to stockholders is **(LO2–2)**
   a. Additional paid-in capital.
   b. Retained earnings.
   c. Accumulated other comprehensive income.
   d. Common stock.

6. Which of the following is a potential limitation of the balance sheet? **(LO2–3)**
   a. Some assets are reported at historical cost instead of their fair value.

   b. Many "economic resources" of a company may not be reported as an asset.
   c. Assets often do not reflect investors' expectations of future growth.
   d. All of the above are potential limitations of the balance sheet.

7. Estraik Corporation reports the following for its income statement: sales revenues, $12,000; cost of goods sold, $7,000; salaries expense, $2,500; interest expense, $500; income tax expense, $1,500. Compute net income. **(LO2–4)**
   a. $500.
   b. $1,000.
   c. $1,500.
   d. $2,500.

8. Gregory Driving Camp reports the following for its income statement: service revenues, $63,000; cost of sales, $31,000; marketing expenses, $8,000; selling and administrative expenses, $7,000; other expenses, $1,000; gain on investments, $3,000. Compute operating income. **(LO2–5)**
   a. $19,000.
   b. $16,000.
   c. $32,000.
   d. $17,000.

9. Which of the following is not one of the limitations of the income statement? **(LO2–6)**
   a. The inclusion of recurring and nonrecurring items.
   b. The inclusion of operating and nonoperating items.
   c. The potential for cash manipulation.
   d. The potential misuse of estimates and judgments.

10. The following information is available for Kaden Enterprises: net cash flows from financing activities, $4,000; net cash flows from investing activities; $(2,000); net cash flows from operating activities, $6,500. Compute the net change in cash for the period. **(LO2–7)**
    a. $500.
    b. $10,500.
    c. $12,500.
    d. $8,500.

11. Which of the following activities is classified as an operating cash flow? **(LO2–7)**
   a. Cash paid out in dividends.
   b. Cash received from selling equipment.
   c. Cash paid for stock repurchases.
   d. Cash received from customers from providing services.

12. Which of the following activities is classified as an investing cash flow? **(LO2–7)**
   a. Cash received from the sale of goods or services.
   b. Interest paid on debt.
   c. Cash paid to purchase inventory.
   d. Cash paid for property and equipment.

13. Which of the following activities is classified as a financing cash flow? **(LO2–7)**
   a. Cash received from the sale of merchandise inventory.
   b. Cash received from taking on long-term debt.
   c. Cash paid to purchase inventory.
   d. Cash paid for property and equipment.

*Note: For answers, see the last page of the chapter.*

14. Which of the following accounts is not reported in the statement of stockholders' equity? **(LO2–8)**
   a. Common stock.
   b. Short-term investments.
   c. Additional paid-in capital.
   d. Retained earnings.

15. DEFT Designs reports net income of $24,000 and the following additional information: foreign currency adjustments, $(1,000); unrealized loss on derivatives, $(2,000). Compute comprehensive income. **(LO2–9)**
   a. $21,000.
   b. $22,000.
   c. $26,000.
   d. $27,000.

16. Which of the following is never included in other comprehensive income? **(LO2–9)**
   a. Unrealized gains and losses on certain types of securities.
   b. Certain gains and losses related to pension plans.
   c. Gains and losses related to the sale of property and equipment.
   d. Foreign currency adjustments.

## REAL WORLD PERSPECTIVES

### Costco Wholesale Corporation (ticker: COST)

**EDGAR Case**

**RWP2–1** Visit www.sec.gov/edgar and search for the **Costco** annual report (10-K) for the year ended September 1, 2019, using EDGAR (Electronic Data Gathering, Analysis, and Retrieval system). Locate the "Consolidated Balance Sheets" and answer the following questions:

*Required:*
1. What is the amount of total assets for the most recent year?
2. What is the amount of total liabilities for the most recent year?
3. What is the amount of total stockholders' equity for the most recent year?
4. Do total assets minus total liabilities equal total stockholders' equity for the most recent year?
5. Calculate total non-current assets for the most recent year.
6. Did Costco's long-term debt increase or decrease from the prior year and by how much?
7. Did Costco's retained earnings balance increase or decrease from the prior year and by how much?

### Amazon (ticker: AMZN)

**EDGAR Case**

**RWP2–2** Visit www.sec.gov/edgar and search for the **Amazon** annual report (10-K) for the year ended December 31, 2019, using EDGAR (Electronic Data Gathering, Analysis, and Retrieval system). Locate the "Consolidated Statements of Operations" to answer questions 1–3 and the "Consolidated Statements of Cash Flows" to answer questions 4–6.

*Required:*
1. What is revenue for the most recent year? Did it increase or decrease over the prior year?
2. What is operating income for the most recent year? Did it increase or decrease over the prior year?
3. What is net income for the most recent year? Did it increase or decrease over the prior year?
4. Did operating activities produce positive or negative cash flows in the most recent year and what was the amount of the cash flow?

5. Did investing activities produce positive or negative cash flows in the most recent year and what was the amount of the cash flow?
6. Did financing activities produce positive or negative cash flows in the most recent year and what was the amount of the cash flow?

EDGAR Case

## AMC Entertainment Holdings (ticker: AMC)

**RWP2–3** Visit www.sec.gov/edgar and search for the AMC annual report (10-K) for the year ended December 31, 2019, using EDGAR (Electronic Data Gathering, Analysis, and Retrieval system). Locate the "Consolidated Statements of Stockholders' Equity" and answer the following questions.

*Required:*
1. What is total stockholders' equity at the end of the previous year?
2. What is total stockholders' equity at the end of the most recent year?
3. How did net income(loss) in the current year affect the balance in total stockholders' equity?
4. How did stock-based compensation awarded in the most recent year affect the balance in total stockholders' equity?

EDGAR Case

## Domino's Pizza Inc (ticker: DPZ)

**RWP2–4** Visit www.sec.gov/edgar and search for the Domino's annual report (10-K) for the year ended December 29, 2019, using EDGAR (Electronic Data Gathering, Analysis, and Retrieval system). Locate the "Consolidated Statements of Comprehensive Income."

*Required:*
1. Domino's reports positive net income and comprehensive income in the most recent year. Which of these two measures of income is greater?
2. Which item accounts for the difference between these two measures of income?

Continuing Financial
Analysis Case

## American Eagle Outfitters, Inc.

**RWP2–5** Financial information for American Eagle is presented in **Appendix A** at the end of the book.

*Required:*
1. What is the largest asset reported by American Eagle in the most recent year?
2. What is the largest liability reported by American Eagle in the most recent year?
3. What is American Eagle's sale growth percentage in the most recent year?
4. What is American Eagle's largest expense item in the most recent year?
5. What are American Eagle's operating cash flows in the most recent year?
6. How much cash did American Eagle pay for capital expenditures in property and equipment?

Continuing Financial
Analysis Case

## The Buckle, Inc.

**RWP2–6** Financial information for Buckle is presented in **Appendix B** at the end of the book.

*Required:*
1. What is the largest assets reported by Buckle in the most recent year?
2. What is the largest liabilities reported by Buckle in the most recent year?
3. What is Buckle's sale growth percentage in the most recent year?
4. What is Buckle's largest expense item in the most recent year?
5. What are Buckle's operating cash flows in the most recent year?
6. How much cash did Buckle pay for capital expenditures in property and equipment?

Continuing Comparative
Analysis Case

## American Eagle Outfitters, Inc. vs. The Buckle, Inc.

**RWP2–7** Financial information for American Eagle is presented in **Appendix A** at the end of the book, and financial information for Buckle is presented in **Appendix B** at the end of the book.

*Required:*

1. Which company reports higher current assets in the most recent year?
2. Which company reports higher current liabilities in the most recent year?
3. Calculate the ratio of current assets to current liabilities for these two companies in the most recent year (this ratio is called the "current ratio" and will be discussed in more detail in Chapter 9). Which company is better able to satisfy its current liabilities using current assets?
4. Which company has higher diluted earnings per share (EPS) in the most recent year? Is it always appropriate to compare earnings per share between two companies?
5. Which company had a greater dividend in the most recent year?

## Ethics

**RWP2–8** Suppose a company incurred $1 million in expenses related to the restructuring of its business. These expenses related to store closings and severance pay for terminated employees. Because the restructuring is going to cause the company to have a "bad year," the CFO would like to make it a "really bad year." The CFO encourages the chief accountant to over-estimate certain expenses and charges. The CFO explains "if we take the extra charges this year, then we don't have to report those charges in future years."

*Required:*

1. Understand the reporting effect: If the chief accountant follows the CFO's request, how will net income be affected in the current year? How will it be affected in future years?
2. Specify the options: If the chief accountant does not follow the CFO's request, how is the balance of retained earnings affected in the current year?
3. Identify the impact: Are investors and creditors potentially harmed by the CFO's suggestion?
4. Make a decision: Should the chief accountant follow the advice of the CFO?

## Sustainability

**RWP2–9** Go to the SASB website (**https://www.sasb.org/company-use/sasb-reporters/**) and search for **American Airlines**. Select American Airlines' sustainability report for the 2019–2020 period (publication year = 2020). Go to the subsection titled "Safety Performance" on page 34 and answer the questions that follow.

*Required:*

1. How many flights did American Airlines operate in 2019?
2. How many enforcement actions were levied against the company by government agencies in 2019?
3. What percentage of safety risks and hazardous situations identified by the company were mitigated on its "Mainline" flights?
4. Did the "Lost day rate" (days employees are away from work due to injury or illness) on "Mainline" flights increase or decrease from 2018 to 2019?

## Great Adventures

(This is a continuation of the Great Adventures problem from Chapter 1.)

**RWP2–10** Great Adventures plans to maintain records of transactions in accounts such as Cash, Common Stock, Service Revenue, Salaries Expense, Accounts Payable, Equipment, Advertising Expense, Supplies, Salaries Payable, and Insurance Expense.

*Required:*

1. For each of these accounts, indicate whether the account would be reported in the balance sheet or income statement.
2. For accounts in the balance sheet, indicate whether it would be classified as an asset, liability, or stockholders' equity.
3. For accounts in the income statement, indicate whether it would be classified as a revenue or an expense.

**BRIEF EXERCISES**

**Understand the timing of financial statements (LO2–1, 2–4, 2–7)**

**BE2–1** Indicate whether each financial statement reports amounts over a period of time or at a point in time.

| <u>Financial Statement</u> | <u>Timing</u> |
|---|---|
| 1. _____ Balance sheet | a. Over a period of time |
| 2. _____ Income statement | b. At a point in time |
| 3. _____ Statement of cash flows | |

**Identify asset measurement (LO2–1)**

**BE2–2** Indicate how each of the following assets would be measured under normal circumstances.

| <u>Asset</u> | <u>Measurement</u> |
|---|---|
| 1. _____ Equipment | a. Historical cost |
| 2. _____ Accounts receivable | b. Amortized cost |
| 3. _____ Land | c. Net realizable value |
| 4. _____ Inventory | d. Market value |
| 5. _____ Short-term investment in public company stock | e. Present value |
| 6. _____ Short-term investment in private company stock | |
| 7. _____ Buildings | |

**Identify balance sheet accounts (LO2–1, 2–2)**

**BE2–3** Indicate whether each account is reported in the balance sheet.

**(Yes/No) Balance Sheet Account?**

1. _____ Cash
2. _____ Service revenue
3. _____ Accounts payable
4. _____ Salaries expense
5. _____ Retained earnings
6. _____ Equipment
7. _____ Income tax expense
8. _____ Cost of goods sold
9. _____ Operating lease
10. _____ Sales revenue

**Prepare a balance sheet (LO2–1, 2–2)**

**BE2–4** KAT Productions reports the following amounts on December 31, 2024: retained earnings, $15,000; equipment, $38,000; accounts payable, $9,000; inventory, $15,000; notes payable, $20,000; common stock, $19,000; cash, $10,000. Prepare the balance sheet for KAT Productions.

**Prepare a balance sheet (LO2–1, 2–2)**

**BE2–5** AMT Tax Consulting reports the following amounts on December 31, 2024: accounts payable, $61,000; equipment, $90,000; operating lease, $10,000; accrued liabilities, $42,000, common stock, $55,000; retained earnings, $48,000; deferred revenues, $18,000; cash, $44,000; accounts receivable, $80,000. Prepare the balance sheet for AMT.

**Identify balance sheet classifications (LO2–1, 2–2)**

**BE2–6** Indicate whether each of the following assets and liabilities would be classified as current or long-term under normal circumstances.

| <u>Assets and Liabilities</u> | <u>Classification</u> |
|---|---|
| 1. _____ Prepaid rent | a. Current |
| 2. _____ Intangible assets | b. Long-term |
| 3. _____ Accounts payable | |
| 4. _____ Inventory | |
| 5. _____ Bond payable | |
| 6. _____ Equipment | |
| 7. _____ Accounts receivable | |
| 8. _____ Accrued liabilities | |
| 9. _____ Deferred revenues | |
| 10. _____ Cash | |

**BE2–7** Match the following limitations to the financial statement to which it applies.

Understand limitations of financial statements (LO2–3, 2–6)

**Limitation**

1. _____ Includes recurring and nonrecurring items.
2. _____ Book value does not necessarily capture market value.
3. _____ Subject to the potential misuse of estimates and judgments.

**Financial Statement**

a. Balance sheet
b. Income statement
c. Both

**BE2–8** KAT Productions reports the following amounts for the fiscal year: depreciation expense, $11,000; sales revenues, $100,000; other expenses, $5,000; loss on sale of equipment, $1,000; marketing expense, $8,000; cost of goods sold, $78,000. Compute net income for KAT Productions by preparing a single-step income statement for the year ended December 31, 2024.

Compute net income (LO2–4)

**BE2–9** AMT Tax Consulting reports the following amounts for the fiscal year: cost of services, $200,000; service revenues, $500,000; income tax expense, $38,000; gain on sale of investments, $10,000; maintenance expense, $25,000; advertising expense, $35,000; selling and administrative expenses, $66,000. Compute net income for AMT by preparing a single-step income statement for the year ended December 31, 2024.

Compute net income (LO2–4)

**BE2–10** The following information is available for Seamons Capital. Solve for the missing amounts.

Complete income statement (LO2–5)

**SEAMONS CAPITAL**
**Income Statement**
**For the year ended December 31, 2024**

| | |
|---|---:|
| Service revenues | $ ? |
| Cost of services | 150,000 |
| **Gross profit** | **166,000** |
| Selling and administrative expenses | 12,000 |
| Depreciation expense | 25,000 |
| **Operating income** | ? |
| Interest expense | 35,000 |
| Loss on sale of investments | 4,000 |
| **Pretax income** | ? |
| Income tax expense | 30,000 |
| **Net income** | **$ 60,000** |

**BE2–11** Match each measure of income with its description.

Understand different measures of income (LO2–5)

**Measure of Income**

1. _____ Gross profit
2. _____ Net income
3. _____ Operating income
4. _____ Pretax income

**Description**

a. All revenues minus all expenses.
b. Profits before accounting for income taxes.
c. Profits related to the operating activities of the company.
d. Profits directly related to the key costs needed to generate those revenues.

**BE2–12** Refer to information in BE2–8, compute gross profit and operating income. Show your answer in the form of a multiple-step income statement.

Compute different measures of income (LO2–5)

**BE2–13** Refer to information in BE2–9, compute gross profit and operating income. Show your answer in the form of a multiple-step income statement.

Compute different measures of income (LO2–5)

**BE2–14** The following information is available for Kaden Enterprises: the net change in cash for the period, $5,000; net cash flows from investing activities; $(2,000); net cash flows from operating activities, $6,500. Compute net cash flows from financing activities.

Understand components of net cash flows (LO2–7)

**Identify cash flow classifications (LO2–7)**

**BE2–15** Match each business activity with its description.

| Business Activities | Descriptions |
|---|---|
| 1. _____ Financing | a. Transactions related to revenues and expenses. |
| 2. _____ Investing | b. Transactions with lenders and owners. |
| 3. _____ Operating | c. Transactions involving the purchase and sale of productive assets. |

**Identify and compute operating cash flows (LO2–7)**

**BE2–16** D&D Company reports select items from its statement of cash flows. Identify those items related to operating activities and compute net cash flows from operating activities.

| Activity | Amount |
|---|---|
| Cash paid to purchase property | $400,000 |
| Cash from selling merchandise | 688,000 |
| Cash paid for income taxes | 135,000 |
| Cash received from a long-term note | 850,000 |
| Cash paid to repurchase stock | 100,000 |
| Cash received from sale of investments | 40,000 |
| Cash received from issuing equity shares | 500,000 |
| Cash paid to purchase merchandise | 710,000 |
| Cash paid to purchase investment securities | 50,000 |
| Cash paid in salaries and wages | 410,000 |

**Identify and compute investing cash flows (LO2–7)**

**BE2–17** Refer to the information in BE2–16. Identify those items related to investing activities and compute net cash flows from investing activities.

**Identify and compute investing cash flows (LO2–7)**

**BE2–18** Refer to the information in BE2–16. Identify those items related to financing activities and compute net cash flows from financing activities.

**Identify changes in stockholders' equity (LO2–8)**

**BE2–19** Identify whether each of the items below increases or decreases total stockholders' equity.

| | |
|---|---|
| 1. _____ Dividends | a. Increases stockholders' equity |
| 2. _____ Stock repurchases | b. Decreases stockholders' equity |
| 3. _____ Stock issuance | |
| 4. _____ Net income | |

**Understand statement of stockholders' equity (LO2–8)**

**BE2–20** M-E Drafting Inc. reports the following statement of stockholders' equity. Solve for the missing amounts.

| | Common Stock | Additional Paid-in Capital | Retained Earnings | Total Stockholders' Equity |
|---|---|---|---|---|
| Beginning balance | $5 | $995 | $  ? | $1,600 |
| Net income | | | 100 | 100 |
| Dividends | | | ? | ? |
| Stock repurchase | | ? | | ? |
| Ending balance | $5 | $980 | $660 | $1,645 |

**Understand net income and comprehensive income (LO2–4, 2–9)**

**BE2–21** Identify which of the income items below is reported in the income statement or statement of comprehensive income.

| Income Items | Statement |
|---|---|
| 1. _____ Cost of goods sold | a. Income statement |
| 2. _____ Gains on sale of equipment | b. Statement of comprehensive income |
| 3. _____ Marketing expense | |
| 4. _____ Foreign currency adjustments | |
| 5. _____ Depreciation expense | |
| 6. _____ Interest expense | |
| 7. _____ Pension plan gains and losses | |
| 8. _____ Income from discontinued operations | |
| 9. _____ Other income/expenses | |
| 10. _____ Unrealized gains and losses on derivatives | |

## EXERCISES

**E2–1** Wolfpack Construction has the following account balances on December 31, 2024.

Prepare a balance sheet (LO2–1, 2–2)

| Accounts | Balances |
|---|---|
| Equipment | $ 26,000 |
| Accounts payable | 3,000 |
| Salaries expense | 33,000 |
| Common stock | 11,000 |
| Land | 18,000 |
| Notes payable | 20,000 |
| Service revenue | 39,000 |
| Cash | 6,000 |
| Retained earnings | ? |

**Required:**

Use only the appropriate accounts to prepare a balance sheet.

**E2–2** Use the following information from the balance sheet of ELC Plumbing to determine the missing amounts.

Find missing balance sheet amounts (LO2–1, 2–2)

| | | | |
|---|---|---|---|
| Cash and cash equivalents | $40,000 | Accounts payable | $32,000 |
| Retained earnings | ? | Accounts receivable | 120,000 |
| Inventory | ? | Notes payable (due in 2 years) | 50,000 |
| Common stock | 100,000 | Property, plant and equipment (net) | ? |
| Total current assets | 235,000 | Total assets | 400,000 |

**E2–3** Indicate whether each of the following assets and liabilities typically should be classified as current or long-term: (a) accounts receivable; (b) prepaid rent for the next six months; (c) notes receivable due in two years; (d) notes payable due in 90 days; (e) notes payable due in five years; (f) patent.

Identify balance sheet classifications (LO2–1, 2–2)

**E2–4** The following are the typical classifications used in a balance sheet:

Identify balance sheet classifications (LO2–1, 2–2)

a. Current assets
b. Investments
c. Property, plant and equipment
d. Intangible assets

e. Current liabilities
f. Long-term liabilities
g. Contributed capital
h. Retained earnings

**Required:**

For each of the following balance sheet items, indicate the appropriate classification.

1. _____ Prepaid insurance
2. _____ Goodwill
3. _____ Equipment
4. _____ Deferred revenues
5. _____ Common stock
6. _____ Additional paid-in capital
7. _____ Accounts payable

8. _____ Accounts receivable
9. _____ Inventory
10. _____ Accrued liabilities
11. _____ Patent
12. _____ Building
13. _____ Dividends
14. _____ Notes payable (current portion)

**Identify asset and liability classifications.**
**(LO2–1, 2–2)**

**E2–5** McK Nursery, Inc., reports the following account balances on December 31, 2024: cash, $16,000; accounts receivable, $11,000; inventory, $25,000; equipment (net), $75,000; operating leases, $5,000; accounts payable, $14,000; salaries payable, $9,000; interest payable, $1,000; notes payable (due in 18 months), $30,000; common stock, $50,000.

**Required:**
Calculate total current assets and total current liabilities that would appear in the company's year-end balance sheet.

**Calculate retained earnings. (LO2–2)**

**E2–6** Refer to the situation described in E2–5. Determine the year-end balance in retained earnings for McK Nursery, Inc.

**Prepare a balance sheet and identify balance sheet classifications (LO2–1, 2–2)**

**E2–7** Refer to the situation described in E2–5. Prepare a classified balance sheet for McK Nursery, Inc.

**Prepare an income statement (LO2–4)**

**E2–8** Below are the account balances for Cowboy Law Firm on December 31, 2024.

| Accounts | Balances |
|---|---|
| Cash | $5,400 |
| Salaries expense | 2,200 |
| Accounts payable | 3,400 |
| Retained earnings | 3,900 |
| Utilities expense | 1,200 |
| Supplies | 13,800 |
| Service revenue | 9,300 |
| Common stock | 6,000 |

**Required:**
Use only the appropriate accounts to prepare an income statement.

**Prepare an income statement (LO2–4)**

**E2–9** MMT Corporation reports the following income statement items ($ in millions) for the year ended December 31, 2024: sales revenue, $2,106; cost of goods sold, $1,240; selling expense, $126; general and administrative expense, $105; interest expense, $40; and gain on sale of investments, $45. Income tax expense has not yet been recorded. The income tax rate is 25%.

**Required:**
Using the account balances, prepare a single-step income statement.

**Prepare an income statement (LO2–5)**

**E2–10** Refer to the situation described in E2–9. If the company's accountant prepared a multiple-step income statement, what amount would appear in that statement for (a) operating income and (b) nonoperating income?

**Prepare a multiple-step income statement (LO2–5)**

**E2–11** Refer to the situation described in E2–9. Using the account balances, prepare a multiple-step income statement .

**Determine different measures of income (LO2–5)**

**E2–12** The following information for Jedgy Corp. is provided:

| | |
|---|---|
| Service revenue | $400,000 |
| Gain on sale of equipment | 3,000 |
| Cost of services | 180,000 |
| Selling and administrative expenses | 45,000 |
| Interest expense | 24,000 |
| Income tax expense | 28,000 |

**Required:**
Determine the following: (a) gross profit, (b) operating income, (c) pretax income, and (d) net income by preparing a multiple-step income statement.

**E2–13** The following information relates to **Uber**'s income statement in a recent year.

Determine different measures of income (LO2–5)

| UBER Income Statement | |
|---|---:|
| Revenues | $14,147 |
| Cost of revenues | 7,208 |
| **Gross Profit** | ? |
| Operating expense | 2,302 |
| Marketing expense | 4,626 |
| Research and development expense | 4,836 |
| General and administrative expense | 3,299 |
| Depreciation expense | 472 |
| **Operating loss** | ? |
| Interest expense | (559) |
| Other income | 694 |
| **Pretax income** | ? |
| Income tax expense | 45 |
| **Net loss** | ? |

*Required:*
Solve for the missing amounts.

**E2–14** The following provides a list of transactions and a list of business activities.

Classify cash flows (LO2–7)

**Transactions**

1. _____ Borrow from the bank.
2. _____ Provide services to customers.
3. _____ Issue common stock to investors.
4. _____ Purchase land.
5. _____ Pay rent for the current period.
6. _____ Pay dividends to stockholders.
7. _____ Purchase building.

**Business Activities**

a. Financing
b. Investing
c. Operating

*Required:*
Match the transaction with the business activity by indicating the letter that corresponds to the appropriate business activity.

**E2–15** The statement of cash flows classifies all cash inflows and outflows into one of the three categories shown below and lettered from a through c.

Classify cash flows (LO2–7)

a. Operating activities
b. Investing activities
c. Financing activities

*Required:*
For each of the following transactions, use the letters above to indicate the appropriate classification category.

1. _____ Purchase of equipment for cash.
2. _____ Payment of employee salaries.
3. _____ Collection of cash from customers.
4. _____ Cash proceeds from notes payable.
5. _____ Purchase of common stock of another corporation for cash.
6. _____ Issuance of common stock for cash.
7. _____ Sale of equipment for cash.
8. _____ Payment of interest on notes payable.
9. _____ Payment of cash dividends to stockholders.
10. _____ Payment of principal on notes payable

**Identify and compute cash flows (LO2–7)**

**E2–16** France Consulting has the following cash transactions for the period.

| Activity | Amount | Inflow or Outflow? |
|---|---|---|
| Cash received from providing consulting services | $275,000 | |
| Cash paid for interest on debt | 15,000 | |
| Cash paid for income taxes | 45,000 | |
| Cash paid for salaries | 150,000 | |
| *Cash flows from operating activities* | ? | |
| Cash received from the sale of investments | 7,000 | |
| Cash paid for computing equipment | 40,000 | |
| *Cash flows from investing activities* | ? | |
| Cash received from a loan | 300,000 | |
| Cash paid to repurchase stock | 60,000 | |
| *Cash flows from financing activities* | ? | |
| *Net change in cash flows* | ? | |

**Required:**
1. Identify whether the cash transaction represents an inflow or an outflow of cash.
2. Solve for the missing amounts.

**Prepare the statement of cash flows (LO2–7)**

**E2–17** Tiger Trade has the following cash transactions for the year ended December 31, 2024.

| Accounts | Amounts |
|---|---|
| Cash received from sale of products to customers | $ 40,000 |
| Cash received from the bank for long-term loan | 45,000 |
| Cash paid to purchase factory equipment | (50,000) |
| Cash paid to merchandise suppliers | (12,000) |
| Cash received from the sale of an unused warehouse | 13,000 |
| Cash paid to workers | (24,000) |
| Cash paid for advertisement | (4,000) |
| Cash received for sale of services to customers | 30,000 |
| Cash paid for dividends to stockholders | (6,000) |

**Required:**
1. Calculate the ending balance of cash, assuming the balance of cash at the beginning of the period is $5,000.
2. Prepare a statement of cash flows. (Hint: For operating, investing, and financing activities, list the inflows and subtract the outflows to calculate net cash flows for each type of activity.)

**Prepare the statement of stockholders' equity (LO2–8)**

**E2–18** At the beginning of the year (January 1, 2024), Buffalo Drilling has $11,000 of common stock outstanding and retained earnings of $8,200. During 2024, Buffalo reports net income of $8,500 and pays dividends of $3,200. In addition, Buffalo issues additional common stock for $8,000.

**Required:**
Prepare the statement of stockholders' equity at the end of the year (December 31, 2024).

**Understand comprehensive income (LO2–9)**

**E2–19** JLT Industries reports the following information related to its other comprehensive income for the year.

| | |
|---|---|
| Net income | $    ? |
| Foreign currency adjustments | (490) |
| Unrealized loss on derivatives | (60) |
| Gain related to pension plan | 160 |
| Comprehensive Income | $5,750 |

**Required:**
Solve for net income.

**E2–20 Anthem, Inc.,** reports the following information related to its other comprehensive income ($ in millions):

Compute comprehensive income (LO2–9)

| | |
|---|---|
| Net unrealized gains/losses on investments | $680 |
| Net unrealized gains/losses on derivatives | (16) |
| Net gains/losses related to pension costs | 26 |

**Required:**
1. Compute other comprehensive income for Anthem for the year.
2. Based on net income of $4,807, calculate total comprehensive income for the year.

## PROGRAM PROBLEMS

Mc Graw Hill **connect**

**P2–1** Timpview, Inc., reports the following on December 31, 2024:

Prepare a balance sheet (LO2–1, 2–2)

| Account | Amount |
|---|---|
| Cash | $ 40,000 |
| Accounts receivable | 34,000 |
| Inventory | 75,000 |
| Prepaid rent (for the next 8 months) | 16,000 |
| Investment in equity securities (short term) | 10,000 |
| Machinery (net) | 134,000 |
| Patent (net) | 83,000 |
| Accounts payable | 8,000 |
| Salaries payable | 4,000 |
| Income taxes payable | 32,000 |
| Bonds payable (due in 10 years) | 200,000 |
| Common stock | 100,000 |
| Retained earnings | 48,000 |

**Required:**
Prepare a balance sheet for Timpview, Inc. Be sure to properly classify assets, liabilities and equity accounts.

**P2–2** Account classifications include assets, liabilities, stockholders' equity, dividends, revenues, and expenses.

Identify account classifications (LO2–1, 2–2, 2–4)

| Account Classifications | Accounts | Related Transactions |
|---|---|---|
| 1. _____ | Cash | Receive cash from customers. |
| 2. _____ | Service revenue | Provide services to customers. |
| 3. _____ | Supplies | Purchase supplies. |
| 4. _____ | Buildings | Purchase factory for operations. |
| 5. _____ | Advertising expense | Pay for cost of advertising. |
| 6. _____ | Equipment | Purchase equipment for operations. |
| 7. _____ | Interest expense | Pay for cost of interest. |
| 8. _____ | Accounts payable | Purchase supplies on credit. |
| 9. _____ | Dividends | Distribute cash to stockholders. |
| 10. _____ | Notes payable | Borrow from the bank. |

**Required:**
For each transaction, indicate whether the related account would be classified in the balance sheet as (a) an asset, (b) a liability, or (c) stockholders' equity; in the income statement as (d) a revenue or (e) an expense; or in the statement of stockholders' equity as (f) a dividend.

Identify account
classifications
(LO2–1, 2–2)

**P2–3** The following are the typical classifications used in a balance sheet.

a. Current assets
b. Investments
c. Property, plant and equipment
d. Intangible assets
e. Other assets

f. Current liabilities
g. Long-term liabilities
h. Contributed capital
i. Retained earnings

***Required:***

For each of the following 2021 balance sheet items, use the letters above to indicate the appropriate classification category. If the item is a contra account, place a minus sign before the chosen letter.

1. _____ Interest payable (due in 3 months)
2. _____ Franchise
3. _____ Accumulated depreciation
4. _____ Prepaid insurance (for 2022)
5. _____ Bonds payable (due in 10 years)
6. _____ Current maturities of long-term debt
7. _____ Notes payable (due in 3 months)
8. _____ Long-term receivables
9. _____ Restricted cash (will be used to retire bonds in 10 years)

10. _____ Supplies
11. _____ Machinery
12. _____ Land (used in operations)
13. _____ Deferred revenue (for 2022)
14. _____ Copyrights
15. _____ Common stock
16. _____ Land (held for speculation)
17. _____ Cash equivalents
18. _____ Salaries payable

Prepare an income
statement (LO2–4, 2–5)

**P2–4** Sundance Investments reports the following information for the year ended December 31, 2024:

| Account | Amount |
| --- | --- |
| Sales revenue | $1,300,000 |
| Interest revenue | 30,000 |
| Gain on sale of investments | 50,000 |
| Cost of goods sold | 720,000 |
| Selling expense | 160,000 |
| General and administrative expense | 75,000 |
| Interest expense | 40,000 |
| Income tax expense | 130,000 |

***Required:***

1. Prepare a single-step income statement for Sundance Investments for the year.
2. Prepare a multiple-step income statement for Sundance Investments for the year.
3. Assuming 100,000 shares of common stock outstanding for the year, compute earnings per share (EPS).

Prepare an income
statement (LO2–4, 2–5)

**P2–5** ACC Partners reports the following information for the year ended December 31, 2024:

| Account | Amount |
| --- | --- |
| Subscription revenue | $2,350,000 |
| Interest revenue | 80,000 |
| Loss on sale of investments | 22,500 |
| Cost of sales | 1,200,300 |
| Loss on sale of property | 200,000 |
| Marketing expenses | 300,000 |
| General and administrative expense | 150,000 |
| Interest expense | 90,000 |

In addition, there were 160,000 shares of common stock outstanding throughout 2024. Income tax expense has not yet been recorded. The income tax rate is 25%.

**Required:**
1. Prepare a single-step income statement for ACC Partners for the year.
2. Prepare a multiple-step income statement for ACC Partners for the year.
3. Compute earnings per share (EPS).

**P2–6** Gator Investments provides financial services related to investment selections, retirement planning, and general insurance needs. At the end of the year on December 31, 2024, the company reports the following amounts:

*Prepare financial statements (LO2–1, 2–2, 2–4, 2–8)*

| | | | |
|---|---|---|---|
| Advertising expense | $33,500 | Service revenue | $127,600 |
| Buildings | 150,000 | Interest expense | 3,500 |
| Salaries expense | 65,100 | Utilities expense | 15,500 |
| Accounts payable | 6,400 | Equipment | 27,000 |
| Cash | 5,500 | Notes payable | 30,000 |

In addition, the company had common stock of $100,000 at the beginning of the year and issued an additional $11,000 during the year. The company also had retained earnings of $30,300 at the beginning of the year and paid dividends of $5,200 during the year.

**Required:**
Prepare the income statement, statement of stockholders' equity, and balance sheet for Gator Investments.

**P2–7** Below are incomplete financial statements for Bulldog, Inc.

*Understand financial statements (LO2–1, 2–2, 2–4, 2–8)*

**CYCLONE, INC.**
**Income Statement**
**Year ended Dec. 31, 2021**

| | |
|---|---|
| Revenues | (a) |
| Expenses: | |
| Salaries | $13,000 |
| Rent | 7,000 |
| Advertising | 5,000 |
| Net income | (b) |

**CYCLONE, INC.**
**Statement of Stockholders' Equity**
**Year ended Dec. 31, 2021**

| | Common Stock | Retained Earnings | Total Stk. Equity |
|---|---|---|---|
| Beginning balance | $14,000 | $7,000 | $21,000 |
| Issuances of stock | (c) | | (c) |
| Add: Net income | | 5,000 | 5,000 |
| Less: Dividends | | (d) | (d) |
| Ending balance | $17,000 | $8,000 | $25,000 |

**CYCLONE, INC.**
**Balance Shett**
**Dec. 31, 2021**

| Assets | | Liabilities | |
|---|---|---|---|
| Cash | $ 1,100 | Accounts payable | $4,000 |
| Supplies | (e) | **Stockholders' Equity** | |
| Land | 6,000 | Common stock | (g) |
| Building | 16,000 | Retained earnings | (h) |
| | | Total liabilities and | |
| Total assets | (f) | stockholders' equity | (i) |

**Required:**
Calculate the missing amounts.

Classify cash
flows (LO2–7)

**P2–8** Below are typical transactions for **Caterpillar Inc.**

| Type of Business Activity | Transactions |
|---|---|
| 1. _____ | Pay for advertising. |
| 2. _____ | Pay dividends to stockholders. |
| 3. _____ | Collect cash from customer for previous sale. |
| 4. _____ | Purchase a building to be used for operations. |
| 5. _____ | Purchase equipment. |
| 6. _____ | Sell land. |
| 7. _____ | Receive a loan from the bank by signing a note. |
| 8. _____ | Pay suppliers for purchase of supplies. |
| 9. _____ | Provide services to customers. |
| 10. _____ | Invest in securities of another company. |

Prepare statement of cash
flows (LO2–7)

**P2–9** The following summary transactions occurred for Shepa, Inc., for the year ended December 31, 2024:

| | |
|---|---:|
| **Cash Received from:** | |
| Sales to customers | $475,000 |
| Interest on investment | 6,000 |
| Collection of note receivable | 50,000 |
| Sale of investments | 30,000 |
| Issuance of notes payable | 202,000 |
| Sale of long-term asset | 40,000 |
| Issuance of equity | 228,000 |
| **Cash Paid for:** | |
| Purchase of inventory | $ 33,000 |
| Interest on notes payable | 5,000 |
| Purchase of equipment | 18,000 |
| Salaries to employees | 140,000 |
| Operating expenses | 25,000 |
| Dividends to stockholders | 20,000 |
| Purchase of supplies | 3,000 |
| Income and property taxes | 11,000 |
| Purchase of property | 400,000 |
| Repurchase of stock | 8,000 |

The balance of cash at the beginning of 2024 was $220,000.

***Required:***

Prepare a statement of cash flows for the year for Shepa Inc. (*Hint:* For operating, investing, and financing activities, list the inflows and subtract the outflows to calculate net cash flows for each type of activity.)

Prepare statement
of comprehensive
income (LO2–9)

**P2–10** Sundance Investments reports the following information related to stockholders' equity for the year ended December 31, 2024.

| Account | Amount |
|---|---:|
| Common stock, beginning of period | $ 10,000 |
| Additional paid-in capital, beginning of period | 990,000 |
| Stockholders' equity, beginning of period | 1,400,000 |
| Retained earnings, beginning of period | 400,000 |
| Dividends | 50,000 |
| Net income | 255,000 |
| Stock-based compensation | 10,000 |

*Required:*

Prepare a statement of stockholders' equity for Sundance Investments.

**P2–11** The Massoud Consulting Group reported net income of $1,354,000 for its fiscal year ended December 31, 2024. In addition, during the year the company experienced a positive foreign currency translation adjustment of $240,000 and an unrealized loss on debt securities of $80,000. The company's effective tax rate on all items affecting comprehensive income is 25%. Each component of other comprehensive income is displayed net of tax.

Prepare statement
of comprehensive
income (LO2–9)

*Required:*

Prepare a separate statement of comprehensive income for 2024.

## DATA ANALYTICS

Visit Connect to view **Data Analytics** questions related to:

1. Applying Excel
2. Data Visualizations
3. Tableau Dashboard Activities
4. Applying Tableau

## ANSWERS TO SELF-STUDY QUESTION

1. b    2. c    3. d    4. a    5. b    6. d    7. a    8. d    9. c    10. d    11. d    12. d    13. b    14. b    15. a    16. c

# CHAPTER THREE

# The Accounting Cycle: During the Period

**Learning Objectives**

| PART A: MEASURING BUSINESS ACTIVITIES |
|---|

- **LO3–1** Analyze the effects of transactions on assets, liabilities, and stockholders' equity.
- **LO3–2** Analyze the effects of transactions on revenues, expenses, and dividends.

| PART B: PREPARING PRELIMINARY FINANCIAL STATEMENTS |
|---|

- **LO3–3** Prepare a preliminary balance sheet and income statement.

| PART C: DEBITS AND CREDITS |
|---|

- **LO3–4** Record transactions in a journal using debits and credits.
- **LO3–5** Post transactions to the general ledger.
- **LO3–6** Prepare a trial balance.

**Self-Study Materials**

## Feature Story

### Walmart: Shelves of Business Transactions

**Walmart** opened its first store in Rogers, Arkansas, in 1962. By 1967, the company had increased to 24 stores totaling $12,600,000 in sales, and the following year it expanded operations to Missouri and Oklahoma. Today, Walmart is the world's largest retailer with over $500,000,000,000 in sales. (That's half a trillion dollars each year!) With more than 2.3 million employees worldwide, it's the largest private employer in the United States and Mexico and one of the largest in Canada. Each year Walmart purchases from over 100,000 vendors merchandise totaling nearly $400 billion. More than 265 million customers visit Walmart stores each week.

With billions of transactions with customers, suppliers, employees, and government agencies, how does Walmart's management keep track of the company's financial position? How do investors know whether the company is profitable and whether management is efficiently running the company? How do creditors know whether they should lend money to the company and whether the company will be able to pay its financial obligations as they become due?

To answer these questions, a system must be in place that can measure billions of transactions of Walmart, summarize those measurements in an efficient way, and then communicate them to management and other decision makers. These are the roles of financial accounting.

In this chapter, we review the measurement process financial accountants use to identify, analyze, record, and summarize transactions. We'll see that financial accounting involves assessing the impact that business transactions have on the company's financial position. These effects are then recorded in accounts. For example, all of Walmart's cash transactions (increases and decreases) are recorded in the Cash account. We then summarize all of the increases and decreases in an account over the accounting period to calculate the account's balance. A list of all account balances provides a summary picture of the company's current financial position and performance during the year.

Without the measurement process of financial accounting, it would be nearly impossible to analyze a company's operations. Having a firm grasp of this measurement process is key to your understanding of financial accounting.

# MEASURING BUSINESS ACTIVITIES

Recall from Chapter 1 that the two functions of financial accounting are to (1) measure business activities of the company and (2) communicate those measurements to external parties for decision-making purposes. The full set of procedures used to accomplish this two-step measurement/communication process is referred to as the accounting cycle. In this chapter, we'll focus on the procedures related to *measuring* business activities *during the accounting period*. In Chapter 4, we'll complete the accounting cycle by examining the remaining procedures that occur at the *end of the accounting period*.

## Effects of Transactions on Assets, Liabilities, and Stockholders' Equity

■ **LO3–1**
**Analyze the effects of transactions on assets, liabilities, and stockholders' equity.**

A company has business transactions with many different individuals and other companies. Examples are selling products to a customer, purchasing supplies from a vendor, paying salaries to an employee, and borrowing money from a bank. These transactions are often referred to as external transactions because they are conducted between the company and a separate economic entity. We need to measure these business transactions, so they can be communicated to investors, creditors, and other financial statement users.

The activities we want to measure are those that affect the financial position of the company. That means they affect the accounting equation you learned about in Chapter 1. Remember, the basic accounting equation shows that assets equal liabilities plus stockholders' equity. In other words, resources of the company equal claims to those resources by creditors and owners.

The basic accounting equation

| Assets | = | Liabilities | + | Stockholders' Equity |
|---|---|---|---|---|
| | | (creditors' claims) | | (owners' claims) |
| Resources | | Claims to Resources | | |

When **Walmart** borrows cash from a bank, its financial position is affected because assets (cash) increase and liabilities (the loan payable to the bank) increase. So, Walmart records that event in its accounting records. On the other hand, when Walmart hires Ralph as a front-door greeter, that action doesn't change the company's assets, liabilities, or stockholders' equity; Walmart's financial position is unaffected the day Ralph is hired, and until he begins work. Yes, Walmart hopes that hiring Ralph will favorably affect its financial position in the future, but the hiring itself does not.

The basic accounting equation must always remain in balance: The left side (assets) equals the right side (liabilities plus stockholders' equity). **Each transaction will have a dual effect.** If one side of the equation increases, then the other side of the equation increases by the same amount. That's what happens, for example, when Walmart borrows cash.

We'll measure the effects of a transaction on the financial position of a company using specific accounts. An account provides a record of the business activities related to a particular item. For instance, *asset accounts* include Cash, Supplies, and Equipment. All transactions affecting cash are recorded in the Cash account. When a company receives cash, an increase is recorded in the Cash account. When the company pays cash, a decrease is recorded in the Cash account. The balance of the account equals all increases minus all decreases. This is the way that all accounts work.

Examples of *liability accounts* include Accounts Payable, Salaries Payable, Utilities Payable, and Taxes Payable. Each of these accounts keeps a record of amounts owed as a result of the related transactions. Examples of *stockholders' equity accounts* include Common Stock and Retained Earnings.

**KEY POINT**

External transactions are activities conducted between the company and other entities. The effects of these transactions on the financial position of a company are recorded in accounts. Accounts provide a record of all business activities related to a particular item. The balance of the account equals all activities that increase the account minus all activities that decrease the account.

To see the effect of each transaction on the accounting equation, ask yourself these questions:

1. "What is one account in the accounting equation affected by the transaction? Does that account increase or decrease?"
2. "What is a second account in the accounting equation affected by the transaction? Does that account increase or decrease?"

After noting the effects of the transaction on the accounting equation, ask yourself this:

3. "Do assets equal liabilities plus stockholders' equity?"

The answer to the third question must be "yes."

Most business transactions affect only two accounts. However, there are some transactions that affect more than two accounts. They are known as *compound transactions.* We'll see an example of a compound transaction in this chapter, and we'll cover several more in later chapters.

**Example.**   The best way to understand the impact of a transaction on the accounting equation is to see it demonstrated by a few examples. In the first month of operations, Eagle Robotics had 10 external transactions. These transactions are summarized in Illustration 3–1.

| Transaction | Date | Description |
|---|---|---|
| (1) | Dec.  1 | Sell shares of common stock for $1,000,000 to obtain the funds necessary to start the business. |
| (2) | Dec.  1 | Borrow $500,000 from the local bank and sign a note promising to repay the full amount of the debt in three years. |
| (3) | Dec.  1 | Purchase equipment necessary for customizing robots, $240,000. |
| (4) | Dec.  1 | Pay one year of rent in advance for retail and warehouse space, $180,000 ($15,000 per month). |
| (5) | Dec.  6 | Purchase supplies on account, $14,000. |
| (6) | Dec. 12 | Purchase 15 robotics units as inventory, $750,000 ($50,000 per unit). |
| (7) | Dec. 17 | Sell 5 robots for cash, $70,000, and on account, $280,000. |
| (8) | Dec. 23 | Receive cash in advance from customers for customization services to be performed in the future, $100,000. |
| (9) | Dec. 28 | Pay employee salaries of $28,000 for the month of December. |
| (10) | Dec. 30 | Pay cash dividends of $14,000 to shareholders. |

**ILLUSTRATION 3–1**

External Transactions of Eagle Robotics

## TRANSACTION (1): ISSUE COMMON STOCK

To begin operations, Eagle Robotics needs cash. To generate cash from external sources, Eagle sells shares of common stock to investors for $1,000,000. In other words, the company receives cash of $1,000,000 from investors, who in turn become owners of the company by receiving shares of common stock.

Eagle Robotics                                      Stockholders

Stock Certificate

It's time to ask the three questions we asked earlier:

1. **"What is one account in the accounting equation affected by the transaction? Does that account increase or decrease?"**

   Answer: **Cash.** Cash is a resource owned by the company, which makes it an asset. The company receives cash from investors, so cash and total assets **increase** by $1,000,000.

2. **"What is a second account in the accounting equation affected by the transaction? Does that account increase or decrease?"**

   Answer: **Common Stock.**[1] Common Stock is a stockholders' equity account. Issuing common stock to investors in exchange for $1,000,000 cash increases the amount of common stock owned by the company's stockholders, so common stock and total stockholders' equity **increase**.

   Issuing common stock for cash increases both sides of the accounting equation:

**TRANSACTION (1)**

Initial investment of $1,000,000 by stockholders

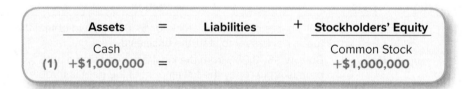

| **Assets** | = | **Liabilities** | + | **Stockholders' Equity** |
|---|---|---|---|---|
| Cash | | | | Common Stock |
| (1)  +$1,000,000 | = | | | +$1,000,000 |

3. **"Do assets equal liabilities plus stockholders' equity?"**

   Answer: **Yes.**

   Note that the accounting equation balances. If one side of the equation increases, so does the other side. We can use this same series of questions to understand the effect of *any* business transaction.

 **COMMON MISTAKE**

It's sometimes tempting to *decrease* cash as a way of recording an investor's initial investment. However, we account for transactions *from the company's perspective,* and the company *received* cash from the stockholder—an increase in cash.

---

[1]Common Stock is often referred to as Contributed Capital, representing contributions of capital from external investors. In Chapter 10, we will learn about different components of stockholders' equity, including contributed capital, common stock, preferred stock and additional paid-in capital.

## TRANSACTION (2): BORROW CASH FROM THE BANK

Seeking cash from another external source, Eagle borrows $500,000 from the bank and signs a note promising to repay the loan amount in three years.[2]

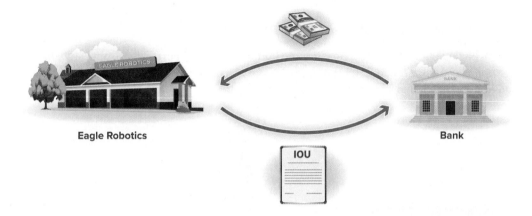

Eagle Robotics                                    Bank

IOU

1. **"What is one account in the accounting equation affected by the transaction? Does that account increase or decrease?"**

   Answer: **Cash.** Cash is a resource owned by the company, which makes it an asset. The company receives cash, so cash and total assets **increase.**

2. **"What is a second account in the accounting equation affected by the transaction? Does that account increase or decrease?"**

   Answer: **Notes Payable.** Notes payable represent amounts owed to creditors (the bank in this case), which makes them a liability. The company incurs debt when signing the note, so notes payable and total liabilities **increase.**

   Borrowing by signing a note causes both assets and liabilities to increase:

|        | Assets      | = | Liabilities   | + | Stockholders' Equity |
|--------|-------------|---|---------------|---|----------------------|
|        | Cash        |   | Notes Payable |   | Common Stock         |
| Bal.   | $1,000,000  |   |               |   | $1,000,000           |
| (2)    | +$ 500,000  |   | + $500,000    |   |                      |
| Bal.   | $1,500,000  |   | $ 500,000     |   | $1,000,000           |
|        | $1,500,000  | = |               |   | $1,500,000           |

**TRANSACTION (2)**

Borrow $500,000 from the bank and sign a three-year note

3. **"Do assets equal liabilities plus stockholders' equity?"**

   Answer: **Yes.**

After these two transactions, the accounting equation remains in balance. Notice that the $500,000 cash collected on the note adds to the $1,000,000 cash received from stockholders. The total resources of the company equal $1,500,000. Creditors' claims to those resources total $500,000, and the remaining $1,000,000 in resources were provided by stockholders.

Regardless of the number of transactions occurring during the period, the accounting equation always must remain in balance. For brevity, we do not address the three-question process for Eagle's remaining eight transactions, but you should ask yourself those questions until you feel comfortable with the process.

---

[2]Some banks and other lending institutions might require companies to have a history of profitable operations, rising cash balances, or other evidence of ability to repay prior to lending. Here, we'll assume Eagle's $1,000,000 cash generated from investments by stockholders gives the bank confidence in Eagle's ability to repay the debt.

**KEY POINT**

After each transaction, the accounting equation must always remain in balance. In other words, assets must always equal liabilities plus stockholders' equity.

## TRANSACTION (3): PURCHASE EQUIPMENT

Once Eagle obtains financing by issuing common stock and borrowing from the bank, the company can invest in long-term assets necessary to operate the business. Eagle purchases equipment needed to customize its robots for $240,000.

Eagle Robotics                    Supplier

Buying equipment causes one asset (equipment) to increase and another asset (cash) to decrease:

**TRANSACTION (3)**

Purchase equipment with cash, $240,000

| | Assets | | = | Liabilities | + | Stockholders' Equity |
|---|---|---|---|---|---|---|
| | Cash | Equipment | | Notes Payable | | Common Stock |
| Bal. | $1,500,000 | | | | | $1,000,000 |
| (3) | −$ 240,000 | +$240,000 | | | | |
| Bal. | $1,260,000 | $ 240,000 | | $500,000 | | $1,000,000 |
| | $1,500,000 | | = | | $1,500,000 | |

**COMMON MISTAKE**

Students sometimes want to *expense equipment* when it is purchased. Remember that equipment is an asset because it provides economic value in the future. Hence, when equipment is purchased, we record it as an *asset*. Later, as the asset is used over time, we record *depreciation expense*—but this is a topic for the next chapter.

Because purchasing one asset (equipment) with another asset (cash) has no effect on total assets, the accounting equation remains in balance.

## TRANSACTION (4): PAY FOR RENT IN ADVANCE

On December 1, Eagle signs an agreement to rent office space, as well as a large warehouse. At the time the agreement is signed, Eagle pays one year of rent in advance, $180,000, which amounts to $15,000 per month. Because the rent paid is for occupying space in the future, we record it as an asset representing a resource of the company. We call the asset *prepaid rent*. Other common examples of prepaid assets include prepaid insurance, prepaid advertising, and other prepaid services. These items often are purchased prior to their use.

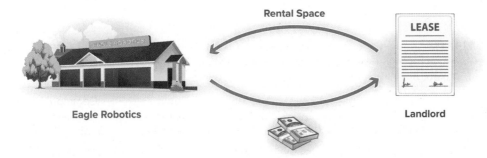

Paying rent in advance causes one asset (prepaid rent) to increase and one asset (cash) to decrease:

**TRANSACTION (4)**

Pay for one year of rent in advance, $180,000

| | Assets | | | = | Liabilities | + | Stockholders' Equity |
|---|---|---|---|---|---|---|---|
| | Cash | Prepaid Rent | Equipment | | Notes Payable | | Common Stock |
| Bal. | $1,260,000 | | $240,000 | | | | $1,000,000 |
| (4) | −$ 180,000 | +$180,000 | | | | | |
| Bal. | $1,080,000 | $ 180,000 | $240,000 | | $500,000 | | $1,000,000 |
| | | $1,500,000 | | = | | $1,500,000 | |

## TRANSACTION (5): PURCHASE SUPPLIES ON ACCOUNT

On December 6, Eagle purchases supplies on account for $14,000. The phrase *on account* indicates that the company does not pay cash immediately but promises to pay cash in the future. While supplies represent a resource of the company (an asset), the promise to pay the supplier (vendor) later is an obligation. We refer to a liability of this type, in which we purchase something on account, as an *account payable.* The term *payable* means "to be paid in the future." Thus, the Accounts Payable account is a record of amounts owed to specific people and companies to which we expect to pay cash in the future.[3]

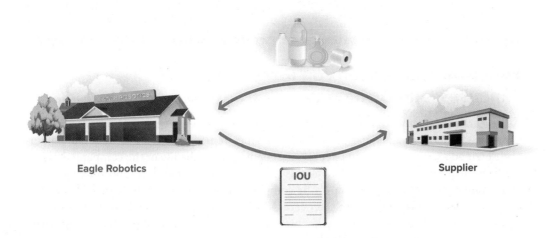

Purchasing supplies with the promise to pay cash in the future causes an asset (supplies) to increase and also causes a liability (accounts payable) to increase:

---

[3]Companies often purchase their supplies on account, usually being required to pay the invoice within 30 to 60 days. In some cases, new companies may be required to establish a relationship with the supplier or provide evidence of ability to repay before the supplier will provide supplies on account.

**TRANSACTION (5)**

Purchase supplies on account, $14,000

| | Assets | | | | = | Liabilities | | + Stockholders' Equity |
|---|---|---|---|---|---|---|---|---|
| | Cash | Supplies | Prepaid Rent | Equipment | | Accounts Payable | Notes Payable | Common Stock |
| Bal. | $1,080,000 | | $180,000 | $240,000 | | | $500,000 | $1,000,000 |
| (5) | | +$14,000 | | | | +$14,000 | | |
| Bal. | $1,080,000 | $14,000 | $180,000 | $240,000 | | $ 14,000 | $500,000 | $1,000,000 |
| | | $1,514,000 | | | = | | $1,514,000 | |

Later, when the company pays cash to those suppliers, an asset decreases (cash) and a liability decreases (accounts payable). Accounts payable decrease because those amounts are no longer owed to suppliers once the cash has been paid.

### TRANSACTION (6): PURCHASE INVENTORY WITH CASH

The business model of Eagle Robotics is to buy and sell robotics inventory and to provide customization of the robots it sells. At this point, Eagle is ready to purchase its first batch of robotics inventory. On December 12, Eagle purchases 15 robots at a cost of $50,000 each for a total of $750,000 in cash. Purchasing inventory with cash causes one asset (inventory) to increase and another asset (cash) to decrease:

**TRANSACTION (6)**

Purchase robotics inventory with cash, $750,000

| | Assets | | | | | = | Liabilities | | + Stockholders' Equity |
|---|---|---|---|---|---|---|---|---|---|
| | Cash | Supplies | Prepaid Rent | Inventory | Equipment | | Accounts Payable | Notes Payable | Common Stock |
| Bal. | $1,080,000 | $14,000 | $180,000 | | $240,000 | | $14,000 | $500,000 | $1,000,000 |
| (6) | −$ 750,000 | | | +$750,000 | | | | | |
| Bal. | $ 330,000 | $14,000 | $180,000 | $ 750,000 | $240,000 | | $14,000 | $500,000 | $1,000,000 |
| | | $1,514,000 | | | | = | | $1,514,000 | |

## Effects of Transactions on Revenues, Expenses, and Dividends

■ LO3–2

Analyze the effects of transactions on revenues, expenses, and dividends.

As we learned in Chapters 1 and 2, we can divide stockholders' equity into its two components—common stock and retained earnings. Common stock represents investments by stockholders. Retained earnings represents net income reported over the life of the company that has *not* been distributed to stockholders as dividends. Both common stock and retained earnings represent stockholders' claims to the company's resources. Next, we can split retained earnings into its three components—revenues, expenses, and dividends—where revenues and expenses will ultimately be represented as net income. Illustration 3–2 presents the expanded accounting equation, which shows these components.

Be sure to notice the effects of revenues, expenses, and dividends on retained earnings (and therefore on total stockholders' equity) in the expanded accounting equation:

1. We *add* revenues to calculate retained earnings. That's because revenues increase net income, and net income increases stockholders' claims to resources. **Therefore, an** *increase* **in revenues has the effect of increasing stockholders' equity in the basic accounting equation.**

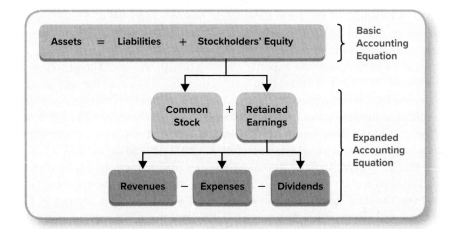

**ILLUSTRATION 3–2**

Expanded Accounting
Equation

2. We *subtract* expenses and dividends to calculate retained earnings. Expenses reduce net income, and dividends represent a distribution of net income to stockholders. Both expenses and dividends reduce stockholders' claims to the company's resources. **Therefore, an increase in expenses or dividends has the effect of** *decreasing* **stockholders' equity in the basic accounting equation.**

**KEY POINT**

The expanded accounting equation demonstrates that revenues increase retained earnings while expenses and dividends decrease retained earnings. Retained earnings is a component of stockholders' equity.

## TRANSACTION (7): SELL INVENTORY FOR CASH AND ON ACCOUNT

To see an example of how revenues and expenses affect the expanded accounting equation, let's look at transaction (7). Recall from transaction (6) that Eagle purchased robotics inventory for $50,000 per unit. Now, on December 17, Eagle sells five of those units at a price of $70,000 per unit for a total of $350,000. The customer pays $70,000 to Eagle in cash and promises to pay the remaining $280,000 within the next 30 days. Should Eagle record revenue for $70,000 (the amount of cash it received from the sale) or for the full $350,000? What expense should be recognized with the sale of inventory?

The revenue recognition principle states that companies recognize revenue (1) at the time they provide goods and services to customers (2) for the amount they are *entitled* to receive from those customers. Because Eagle has delivered the inventory to the customer, it

**TRANSACTION (7)**   Sell robotics inventory for cash and on account

| | Assets | | | | | | = | Liabilities | | + | Stockholders' Equity | | |
|---|---|---|---|---|---|---|---|---|---|---|---|---|---|
| | Cash | Accounts Receivable | Supplies | Prepaid Rent | Inventory | Equipment | | Accounts Payable | Notes Payable | | Common Stock | Retained Earnings | |
| Bal. | $330,000 | | $14,000 | $180,000 | $750,000 | $240,000 | | $14,000 | $500,000 | | $1,000,000 | | |
| (7) | +$70,000 | +$280,000 | | | | | | | | | | +$350,000 | Sales Revenue |
| | | | | | −$250,000 | | | | | | | −$250,000 | Cost of Goods Sold |
| Bal. | $400,000 | $280,000 | $14,000 | $180,000 | $500,000 | $240,000 | | $14,000 | $500,000 | | $1,000,000 | $100,000 | |
| | | | $1,614,000 | | | | = | | | | $1,614,000 | | |

is entitled to revenues for the entire sale amount of $350,000. This means that all $350,000 is recorded as revenue. At the same time, Eagle has received cash of $70,000 and has the right to receive cash of $280,000 in the future—kind of like an "IOU" from the customer. That right represents an asset called *accounts receivable*.

We also need to recognize the expense associated with the sale. The purchase of inventory was initially recorded as an asset in transaction (6). Because of the sale in transaction (7), the decline in inventory needs to be recorded. We reduce the Inventory account for the cost at which the inventory was initial recorded ($50,000 per unit, or $250,000 total for five units). The cost of the inventory sold represents a cost that was *used* in operations, so we need to record that cost in an expense account—*Cost of Goods Sold*.

Notice that an increase in Sales Revenue increases stockholders' equity by increasing the Retained Earnings account (+$350,000). At the same time, an increase to Cost of Goods Sold decreases stockholders' equity by decreasing the Retained Earnings account (−$250,000). The net increase to Retained Earnings is $100,000, and this is the same amount as the net increase in assets. Therefore, the basic accounting equation remains in balance (Assets = Liabilities + Stockholders' Equity).

As shown previously in Illustration 3–2, revenues are a component of retained earnings. When a company recognizes revenue, the amount of retained earnings (or net income) in the business increases. We can increase the balance of Retained Earnings by increasing its revenue component. Stated another way, an increase in revenues increases net income, which increases retained earnings, which increases total stockholders' equity:

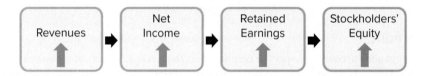

Expenses (such as Cost of Goods Sold) reduce net income and therefore reduce the balance of Retained Earnings, a stockholders' equity account. Stated another way, an increase in expenses decreases net income, which decreases retained earnings, which decreases total stockholders' equity:

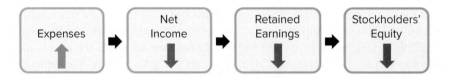

### TRANSACTION (8): RECEIVE CASH IN ADVANCE FROM CUSTOMERS

Eagle Robotics also makes money by customizing robots to the specific needs of its customers. In transaction (8), Eagle receives $100,000 in advance from a customer to provide customization services at some later date. The major accounting question is this: Can this $100,000 be considered revenue to Eagle at the time the cash is received? Not yet—Eagle can't report revenue from customization at the time it receives this cash because it has yet to provide those services to its customer. Recall that the revenue recognition principle states that revenue is recognized when goods and services are provided to customers. In transaction (8), receiving cash in advance from customers creates an obligation for the company to perform services in the future. This future obligation is a liability (or debt), most commonly referred to as *deferred revenue*.[4]

---

[4]Deferred revenue is sometimes referred to as unearned revenue. The use of the term "deferred revenue" is increasingly popular in practice and is more consistent with the FASB's 2014 update of the revenue recognition principle (ASU No. 2014-09), which eliminates the "earnings" process in defining revenue. The term "deferred revenue" is also helpful in emphasizing that revenue is initially deferred but will be recognized eventually when the service is provided.

**TRANSACTION (8)   Receive cash in advance from customers, $100,000**

| | | | Assets | | | = | | Liabilities | | + | Stockholders' Equity | |
|---|---|---|---|---|---|---|---|---|---|---|---|---|
| | Cash | Accounts Receivable | Supplies | Prepaid Rent | Inventory | Equipment | Accounts Payable | Notes Payable | Deferred Revenue | Common Stock | Retained Earnings |
| Bal. | $400,000 | $280,000 | $14,000 | $180,000 | $500,000 | $240,000 | $14,000 | $500,000 | | $1,000,000 | $100,000 |
| (8) | +$100,000 | | | | | | | | +$100,000 | | |
| Bal. | $500,000 | $280,000 | $14,000 | $180,000 | $500,000 | $240,000 | $14,000 | $500,000 | $100,000 | $1,000,000 | $100,000 |
| | | | $1,714,000 | | | | = | | | $1,714,000 | | |

**COMMON MISTAKE**

Don't let the account name fool you. Even though the term *revenue* appears in the account title for *deferred revenue,* this is not a revenue account. *Deferred* indicates that the company has yet to provide services even though it has collected the customer's cash. The company owes the customer a service, which creates a liability.

## TRANSACTION (9): PAY SALARIES TO EMPLOYEES

Companies incur a variety of costs in running the business. In transaction (9), Eagle pays salaries to employees for work in the current month. Because these salaries represent a cost of operations during the current period, Eagle records them in the current month as salaries expense of $28,000.

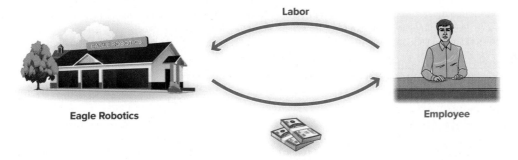

Labor

Eagle Robotics                                          Employee

Paying salaries for the current period causes an asset (cash) to decrease and stockholders' equity to decrease (and salaries expense to increase):

**TRANSACTION (9)   Pay salaries to employees, $28,000**

| | | | Assets | | | = | | Liabilities | | + | Stockholders' Equity | |
|---|---|---|---|---|---|---|---|---|---|---|---|---|
| | Cash | Accounts Receivable | Supplies | Prepaid Rent | Inventory | Equipment | Accounts Payable | Notes Payable | Deferred Revenue | Common Stock | Retained Earnings | |
| Bal. | $500,000 | $280,000 | $14,000 | $180,000 | $500,000 | $240,000 | $14,000 | $500,000 | $100,000 | $1,000,000 | $100,000 | |
| (9) | −$28,000 | | | | | | | | | | −$28,000 | Salaries Expense |
| Bal. | $472,000 | $280,000 | $14,000 | $180,000 | $500,000 | $240,000 | $14,000 | $500,000 | $100,000 | $1,000,000 | $72,000 | |
| | | | $1,686,000 | | | | = | | | $1,686,000 | | |

Notice that an *increase* in Salaries Expense results in a *decrease* in Retained Earnings (−$28,000). As a result, the accounting equation remains in balance, with both sides decreasing by $28,000.

Beyond salaries expense, companies have a number of other expenses. Most expense accounts are labeled with the word *expense* in the title. For instance, common expense accounts include Supplies Expense, Utilities Expense, Rent Expense, Advertising Expense, Interest Expense, and Insurance Expense. We saw in transaction (7) an example of an expense that did not have *expense* in the account title—Cost of Goods Sold.

## TRANSACTION (10): PAY CASH DIVIDENDS

The final transaction of Eagle Robotics for the month is the payment of a $14,000 cash dividend to stockholders. Recall from the previous chapter that a dividend represents a distribution to the owners (stockholders) of the company.[5]

**TRANSACTION (10)**    Pay dividends to stockholders, $14,000

| | Assets | | | | | | = | Liabilities | | | + | Stockholders' Equity | |
|---|---|---|---|---|---|---|---|---|---|---|---|---|---|
| | Cash | Accounts Receivable | Supplies | Prepaid Rent | Inventory | Equipment | | Accounts Payable | Notes Payable | Deferred Revenue | | Common Stock | Retained Earnings |
| Bal. | $472,000 | $280,000 | $14,000 | $180,000 | $500,000 | $240,000 | | $14,000 | $500,000 | $100,000 | | $1,000,000 | $72,000 |
| (10) | −$14,000 | | | | | | | | | | | | −$14,000 Dividends |
| Bal. | $458,000 | $280,000 | $14,000 | $180,000 | $500,000 | $240,000 | | $14,000 | $500,000 | $100,000 | | $1,000,000 | $58,000 |
| | $1,672,000 | | | | | | = | | $1,672,000 | | | | |

Paying dividends causes an asset (cash) to decrease and stockholders' equity to decrease (and dividends to increase):

**Like expenses, dividends reduce retained earnings, but dividends are *not* expenses.** Instead, dividends are distributions of part of the company's net income to the owners, reducing the amount of earnings that have been retained in the business. Therefore, an *increase* in Dividends results in a *decrease* in Retained Earnings (−$14,000). The accounting equation remains in balance, with both sides decreasing by $14,000. Because Retained Earnings is a stockholders' equity account, when retained earnings decreases, so does stockholders' equity:

 **COMMON MISTAKE**

Students often believe a payment of dividends to owners increases stockholders' equity. Remember, you are accounting for the resources *of the company*. While stockholders have more personal cash after dividends have been paid, the company in which they own stock has *fewer* resources (less cash).

---

[5]Normally a company wouldn't pay dividends after only a month in business, but we make this assumption here for purposes of illustration.

Illustration 3–3 summarizes all 10 of the month's transactions we just analyzed for Eagle Robotics. Notice that the accounting equation remains in balance.

**ILLUSTRATION 3–3    Summary of All 10 External Transactions of Eagle Robotics**

| | Assets | | | | | | = | Liabilities | | | + | Stockholders' Equity | | |
|---|---|---|---|---|---|---|---|---|---|---|---|---|---|---|
| | Cash | Accounts Receivable | Supplies | Prepaid Rent | Inventory | Equipment | | Accounts Payable | Deferred Revenue | Notes Payable | | Common Stock | Retained Earnings | |
| Dec. 1 | $0 | $0 | $0 | $0 | $0 | $0 | | $0 | $0 | $0 | | $0 | $0 | |
| (1) | +1,000,000 | | | | | | | | | | | +1,000,000 | | |
| (2) | +500,000 | | | | | | | | | +500,000 | | | | |
| (3) | −240,000 | | | | | +240,000 | | | | | | | | |
| (4) | −180,000 | | | +180,000 | | | | | | | | | | |
| (5) | | | +14,000 | | | | | +14,000 | | | | | | |
| (6) | −750,000 | | | | +750,000 | | | | | | | | | |
| (7) | +70,000 | +280,000 | | | | | | | | | | | +350,000 | Sales Revenue |
| | | | | | −250,000 | | | | | | | | −250,000 | Cost of Goods Sold |
| (8) | +100,000 | | | | | | | | +100,000 | | | | | |
| (9) | −28,000 | | | | | | | | | | | | −28,000 | Salaries Expense |
| (10) | −14,000 | | | | | | | | | | | | −14,000 | Dividends |
| | $458,000 | $280,000 | $14,000 | $180,000 | $500,000 | $240,000 | | $14,000 | $100,000 | $500,000 | | $1,000,000 | $58,000 | |
| | | | $1,672,000 | | | | = | | | | | | $1,672,000 | |

Bogey Incorporated has the following transactions during May:

**Let's Review**

May  1    Purchase a storage building by obtaining a loan of $5,000.
May  6    Provide services to customers for cash, $1,800.
May 12    Pay $1,200 cash for advertising in May.
May 17    Repay $1,000 of the amount borrowed on May 1.
May 25    Purchase office supplies for $800 cash.

*Required:*

Indicate how each transaction affects the accounting equation.

*Solution:*

| | Assets | = | Liabilities | + | Stockholders' Equity | |
|---|---|---|---|---|---|---|
| | | | | | Common Stock | Retained Earnings |
| May  1 | +$5,000 | | +$5,000 | | | |
| May  6 | +$1,800 | | | | | +$1,800 |
| May 12 | −$1,200 | | | | | −$1,200 |
| May 17 | −$1,000 | | −$1,000 | | | |
| May 25 | +$  800 | | | | | |
| | −$  800 | | | | | |
| | +$4,600 | = | +$4,000 | + | | +$  600 |

# PREPARING PRELIMINARY FINANCIAL STATEMENTS

**PART B**

Now that we've analyzed each of the 10 transactions for Eagle Robotics, we can summarize these transactions into a preliminary set of financial statements—namely, the balance sheet and income statement. We call these financial statements preliminary because some of the account balances may need further adjustments (a major subject of Chapter 4) before the financial statements are finalized.

■ **LO3–3**
Prepare a preliminary balance sheet and income statement.

Recall that a balance sheet captures the balances of all asset, liability, and stockholders' equity accounts at a given point in time. Thus, to create the preliminary balance sheet, we need to gather the balances of these accounts for Eagle Robotics. Fortunately, we have these balances available in the summary information provided in Illustration 3–3.

The format of the balance sheet follows the accounting equation: assets = liabilities + stockholders' equity. Hence, to begin, we'll gather the preliminary balances of each of the asset accounts: Cash, Accounts Receivable, Supplies, Prepaid Rent, Inventory, and Equipment. Together, these asset accounts make up total assets on the balance sheet.

| Assets | Balances |
|---|---|
| Cash | $ 458,000 |
| Accounts Receivable | 280,000 |
| Supplies | 14,000 |
| Prepaid Rent | 180,000 |
| Inventory | 500,000 |
| Equipment | 240,000 |
| **Total assets** | **$1,672,000** |

Next, we'll assemble the liabilities and stockholders' equity. The liability accounts include Accounts Payable, Deferred Revenue, and Notes Payable. The stockholders' equity accounts include Common Stock and Retained Earnings.

| Liabilities | Balances |
|---|---|
| Accounts Payable | $ 14,000 |
| Deferred Revenue | 100,000 |
| Notes Payable | 500,000 |
| **Total liabilities** | **$614,000** |

| Stockholders' Equity | Balances |
|---|---|
| Common Stock | $ 1,000,000 |
| Retained Earnings | 58,000 |
| **Total equity** | **$1,058,000** |

With these amounts, we've almost completed the preliminary balance sheet. Let's simply arrange the asset accounts on the left side and the liability and stockholders' equity accounts on the right side. The preliminary balance sheet is shown in Illustration 3–4.

**ILLUSTRATION 3–4**

Preliminary Balance Sheet

**EAGLE ROBOTICS**
**Balance Sheet (preliminary)**
**December 31, 2024**

| Assets | | Liabilities | |
|---|---|---|---|
| Cash | $ 458,000 | Accounts Payable | $ 14,000 |
| Accounts Receivable | 280,000 | Deferred Revenue | 100,000 |
| Supplies | 14,000 | Notes Payable | 500,000 |
| Prepaid Rent | 180,000 | **Total liabilities** | **614,000** |
| Inventory | 500,000 | | |
| Equipment | 240,000 | **Stockholders' Equity** | |
| | | Common Stock | 1,000,000 |
| | | Retained Earnings | 58,000 |
| | | **Total equity** | **1,058,000** |
| | | | |
| | | **Total liabilities and** | |
| **Total assets** | **$1,672,000** | **stockholders' equity** | **$1,672,000** |

This process of creating a preliminary balance sheet can be helpful for several reasons. First, it helps us to see that the account balances have been calculated appropriately; we know this because the balance sheet actually balances! That is, total assets amount to $1,672,000, while the sum of liabilities and stockholders' equity amount to $1,672,000. This also provides us some assurance that the transactions have been entered into the accounting system correctly. Second, it provides a basic understanding of the source of Eagle Robotics' assets—they were financed more from equity transactions than from transactions related to liabilities.

Notice that the balances of assets, liabilities, and equities do not match those from the balance sheet presented for Eagle Robotics in Chapter 1. The reason for the difference in these balances is that the balance sheet presented in Chapter 1 is finalized after completing the accounting cycle, while the balance sheet above represents a preliminary tally of the account balances prior to adjusting asset and liability accounts at the end of the year. We'll cover those topics in Chapter 4.

Now, let's turn to creating a preliminary income statement for Eagle Robotics for the year. Again, we'll lean on the summary information provided in Illustration 3–3. We'll focus on the accounts that affect the income statement—revenue accounts and expense accounts. Transaction (7) affected sales revenue for the year, and transactions (7) and (9) affected expenses. Note that the dividends paid for the year [transaction (10)] did not affect the income statement. Instead, dividends directly impacted the company's retained earnings, which is included in the preliminary balance sheet we created above. The preliminary income statement is shown in Illustration 3–5.

**ILLUSTRATION 3–5**

Preliminary Income Statement

| EAGLE ROBOTICS | |
|---|---|
| Income Statement (preliminary) | |
| For the month ended December 31, 2024 | |
| Sales Revenues | $350,000 |
| Cost of Goods Sold | (250,000) |
| Salaries Expense | (28,000) |
| **Net Income** | **$ 72,000** |

This process of creating a preliminary income statements provides us with an initial sense of the company's profitability. In its first month of business, Eagle Robotics has generated more revenues than expenses, leading to its net income of $72,000. Being profitable in its first month of operations is quite a feat for a start-up company! In Chapter 4, we'll discuss additional adjustments to revenues and expenses that are needed before finalizing the income statement.

 **KEY POINT**

A preliminary income statement can be created after all transactions during the period are recorded. It provides initial information on a company's profitability. A preliminary balance sheet can also be created after all transactions during the period are recorded. It provides information on the current balances of a company's resources (assets) and claims to those resources (liabilities and stockholders' equity).

# DEBITS AND CREDITS

**PART C**

As we saw in the previous section, transactions have the effect of increasing or decreasing account balances. While the terms *increase* and *decrease* are well understood, accountants more often use the terms *debit* and *credit* to indicate whether an account balance has increased or decreased. Here, we introduce those terms, discuss their effect on account balances, and show how we record transactions using debits and credits.

# Effects of Debits and Credits on Account Balances

■ **LO3–4**

Record transactions in a journal using debits and credits.

You can learn how to increase and decrease account balances using the terms debit and credit to better understand the language of accounting. Although debit and credit are derived from Latin terms, today **debit** simply means "left" and **credit** means "right." Their use dates back to 1494 and a Franciscan monk by the name of Luca Pacioli.

Look at the accounting equation in Illustration 3–6. Like every equation, there is a left-hand side and a right-hand side. Assets are on the left-hand side of the equal sign, while liabilities and stockholders' equity are on the right-hand side. In accounting terminology, **we refer to increases in assets as debits, and we refer to decreases in assets as credits.** For example, if a company receives cash (an asset), the balance of the Cash account increases, so we refer to the increase as a "debit to cash." We would refer to a decrease in cash as a "credit to cash."

**ILLUSTRATION 3–6**

Debit and Credit Effects on Accounts in the Basic Accounting Equation

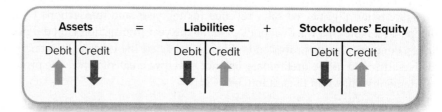

Just the opposite is true for liabilities and stockholders' equity. These accounts are on the right-hand side of the accounting equation. **We refer to increases in liabilities and stockholders' equity as credits, and decreases in those accounts as debits.**

 **COMMON MISTAKE**

Some students think the term "debit" *always* means increase and "credit" *always* means decrease. While this is true for assets, it is *not* true for liabilities and stockholders' equity. Liabilities and stockholders' equity increase with a credit and decrease with a debit. Further, students sometimes think that debit means "good" and credit means "bad"—this is also not true. Just remember that debit means left and credit means right—that's it!

 **KEY POINT**

For the basic accounting equation (Assets = Liabilities + Stockholders' Equity), assets (left side) increase with *debits*. Liabilities and stockholders' equity (right side) increase with *credits*. The opposite is true to decrease any of these accounts.

As we demonstrated in Illustration 3–2, we can expand the basic accounting equation to include the components of stockholders' equity (common stock and retained earnings) and the components of retained earnings (revenues, expenses, and dividends). Because common stock and retained earnings are part of stockholders' equity (right-hand side), it follows directly that we increase both with a credit, and decrease both with a debit.

For the components of retained earnings:

- **Revenues** increase retained earnings. Retained Earnings is a credit account, so we increase revenues with a credit.
- **Expenses,** on the other hand, decrease retained earnings. Thus, we do the opposite of what we do with revenues; we increase expenses with a debit.
- **Dividends,** similar to expenses, decrease retained earnings, so we increase dividends with a debit.
- For each of these components, **we do the opposite to decrease the balance.**

Illustration 3–7 summarizes the effects of debits and credits on the expanded accounting eqution.

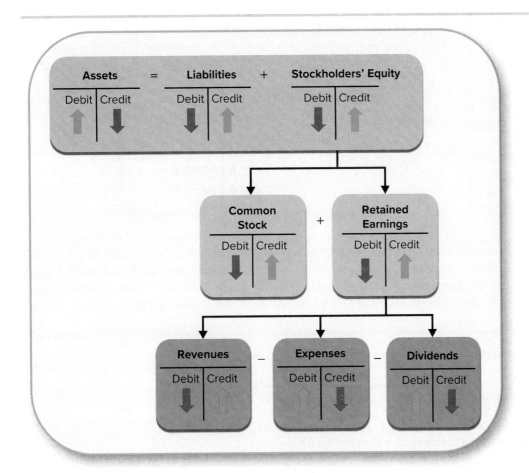

**ILLUSTRATION 3–7**

Debit and Credit Effects on Accounts in the Expanded Accounting Equation

**KEY POINT**

The Retained Earnings account is a stockholders' equity account that normally has a credit balance. The Retained Earnings account has three components—revenues, expenses, and dividends. The difference between revenues (increased by credits) and expenses (increased by debits) equals net income. Net income increases the balance of Retained Earnings. Dividends (increased by debits) decrease the balance of Retained Earnings.

## Manager Analysis

| Question | Accounting information | Analysis |
|---|---|---|
| How much profit has a company generated over its lifetime for its owners and retained for use in the business? | Retained earnings | The balance of retained earnings provides a representation of annual net income (revenue minus expenses) accumulated over the life of the company, less the total dividends distributed over the life of the company. |

Illustration 3–8 provides a simple memory aid that can help you remember debits and credits. Remember the acronym DEALOR and you'll be able to recall the effect that debits and credits have on account balances.

**ILLUSTRATION 3–8**

**Effects of Debit and Credit on Each Account Type**

| DEALOR | |
|---|---|
| **D**ividends | **L**iabilities |
| **E**xpenses | **O**wners' Equity |
| **A**ssets | **R**evenue |

Debit and Credit Rules:   Debit ↑   Credit ↑
                          Credit ↓   Debit ↓

**Common Terms**
Another name for stockholders' equity is *owners' equity*, since stockholders are the owners of a company.

In accounting terminology, debit means left, and credit means right. Let's split DEALOR into its left and right side. The three accounts on the left, or debit, side of DEALOR—Dividends, Expenses, and Assets—increase with a debit and decrease with a credit. In contrast, the three accounts on the right, or credit, side—Liabilities, Owners' (stockholders') equity, and Revenues—increase with a credit and decrease with a debit.

## Let's Review

Bogey Incorporated has the following transactions during May:

May  1   Purchase a storage building by obtaining a loan of $5,000.
May  6   Provide services to customers for cash, $1,800.
May 12   Pay $1,200 cash for advertising in May.
May 17   Repay $1,000 of the amount borrowed on May 1.
May 25   Purchase office supplies for $800 cash.

**Required:**

For each transaction, (1) identify the two accounts involved, (2) the type of account, (3) whether the transaction increases or decreases the account balance, and (4) whether the increase or decrease would be recorded with a debit or credit.

**Solution:**

| Date | (1) Accounts Involved | (2) Account Type | (3) Increase or Decrease | (4) Debit or Credit |
|---|---|---|---|---|
| May 1 | Buildings | Asset | Increase | Debit |
|  | Notes Payable | Liability | Increase | Credit |
| May 6 | Cash | Asset | Increase | Debit |
|  | Service Revenue | Revenue | Increase | Credit |

*(continued)*

*(concluded)*

| Date | (1)<br>Accounts Involved | (2)<br>Account Type | (3)<br>Increase or<br>Decrease | (4)<br>Debit or Credit |
|---|---|---|---|---|
| May 12 | Advertising Expense | Expense | Increase | Debit |
| | Cash | Asset | Decrease | Credit |
| May 17 | Notes Payable | Liability | Decrease | Debit |
| | Cash | Asset | Decrease | Credit |
| May 25 | Supplies | Asset | Increase | Debit |
| | Cash | Asset | Decrease | Credit |

## Recording Transactions in a Journal

We have just discussed whether the impact of an external transaction results in a debit or credit to an account balance. Next, we'll learn how to formally record transactions using those same debits and credits in a journal. A journal provides a chronological record of all transactions affecting a company. Prior to the widespread use of computers, companies recorded their transactions in paper-based journals. Thus, the term journal entry was used to describe the format for recording a transaction. Today, nearly all companies have easy access to computers, and paper-based journals have become obsolete, but journal entries continue to be made in a computerized accounting information system. Illustration 3–9 shows the format we'll use throughout the book to record a company's transactions.

| Date | | Debit | Credit |
|---|---|---|---|
| **Account Name** ................................................................ | | Amount | |
|     **Account Name** ........................................................ | | | Amount |
|     *(Description of transaction)* | | | |

**ILLUSTRATION 3–9**

**Format for Recording a Business Transaction or Journal Entry**

**COMMON MISTAKE**

Many students forget to indent the credit account names. For the account credited, be sure to indent both the account name and the amount.

The entry that records a transaction has a place for the date of the transaction, the relevant account names, debit amounts, credit amounts, and a description of the transaction. We first list the account to be debited; below that, and indented to the right, we list the account to be credited. The entry has two amount columns—one for debits, one for credits. Because the amounts always represent dollar amounts (not number of units, for example), the dollar sign ($) is not used. As you might expect, the left-hand column is for debits, and the right-hand column is for credits. A brief description of the transaction is customarily included at the bottom to leave an information trail for later reference if necessary.

Illustration 3–9 displays only one debit and one credit. However, it's certainly possible to have more than one debit or more than one credit in a journal entry as the result of a business transaction. These are known as *compound entries*. The important point is this: **For each journal entry, total debits must equal total credits.** This means that the sum of all numbers that are debited must equal the sum of all numbers that are credited. This is a nice way to check your work—if total debits do not equal total credits, something isn't right.

Think of recording a transaction as if you're writing a sentence form of the "accounting language." For example, recall in transaction (1) that "On December 1, Eagle Robotics sells shares of common stock to investors for cash of $1,000,000." Here is this same sentence presented in the form of a journal entry:

**TRANSACTION (1)**

Initial investment of $1,000,000 by stockholders

| December 1 | Debit | Credit |
|---|---|---|
| **Cash** *(+A)* ................................................................ | 1,000,000 | |
|     **Common Stock** *(+SE)* .................................................... | | 1,000,000 |
|     *(Issue common stock for cash)* | | |

Just as every English sentence uses at least one noun and one verb, every accounting sentence includes at least one debit and one credit. While not a formal part of recording transactions, we'll use a notation in parentheses beside the account name in Chapters 3 and 4 to help you get more familiar with the effect of debits and credits on the account balance. Thus, the entry shows that transaction (1) causes total assets to increase (+*A*) and total stockholders' equity to increase (+*SE*). Increases to assets are recorded with a debit, and increases to stockholders' equity are recorded with a credit. Learning how to read and write in the language of accounting can help you better communicate with accountants, managers, and many other professionals throughout the business world.

**KEY POINT**

For each transaction, total debits must equal total credits.

**COMMON MISTAKE**

Students sometimes hear the phrase "assets are the debit accounts" and believe it indicates that assets can only be debited. This is incorrect! Assets, or any account, can be *either* debited or credited. Rather, this phrase indicates that debiting the asset account will increase the balance and that an asset account normally will have a debit balance. Similarly, the phrase "liabilities and stockholders' equity are the credit accounts" does *not* mean that these accounts cannot be debited. They will be debited when their balances decrease. Rather, the phrase means that crediting the liabilities and stockholders' equity accounts increases their balances, and they normally will have a credit balance.

The formal account names used to record transactions in the journal are listed in the chart of accounts. Illustration 3–10 provides the chart of accounts for Eagle Robotics based on the 10 transactions covered to this point. Later, we'll introduce other transactions and accounts for Eagle. At the back of the book, you'll see a chart of accounts that includes all accounts used throughout the book.

**ILLUSTRATION 3–10**

Preliminary Chart of Accounts for Eagle Robotics

**EAGLE ROBOTICS**
**Chart of Accounts (preliminary)**

| Assets | Liabilities | Stockholders' Equity |
|---|---|---|
| Cash | Accounts Payable | Common Stock |
| Accounts Receivable | Deferred Revenue | Retained Earnings |
| Supplies | Notes Payable | **Dividends:** |
| Prepaid Rent | | Dividends |
| Inventory | | **Revenues:** |
| Equipment | | Sales Revenue |
| | | **Expenses:** |
| | | Cost of Goods Sold |
| | | Salaries Expense |

# Posting to the General Ledger

As discussed in the previous section, a journal provides in a single location a chronological listing of every transaction affecting a company. As such, it serves as a handy way to review specific transactions and to locate any accounting errors at their original source. But it's not a convenient format for calculating account balances to use in preparing financial statements. You don't need to stretch your imagination too far to see that even for a very small company with few transactions, calculating account balances from a list of journal entries would very soon become unmanageable. Just imagine how lengthy the journal would be for **Walmart.** If each sales transaction with a customer took about one inch of space, the journal would be over 150,000 miles long by the end of the year.

■ **LO3–5**
Post transactions to the general ledger.

To make the calculation of account balances more efficient, we need to collect all transactions, per account, in one location. We do this through a process called *posting*. Formally, posting is the process of transferring the debit and credit information from the journal to individual accounts in the general ledger. The general ledger provides, in a single collection, each account with its individual transactions and resulting account balance.

Illustration 3–11 presents a simplified version of the general ledger account, commonly referred to as a T-account. A T-account includes the account title at the top, one side for recording debits, and one side for recording credits. Consistent with our previous discussion of debits and credits, the left side of the T-account is the debit column, and the right side is the credit column. You can see that the name T-account comes from the natural T shape formed in the general ledger by the debit and credit columns.

| Account Title | |
|---|---|
| **Debits** | **Credits** |
| **Debit Balance** | **Credit Balance** |

**ILLUSTRATION 3–11**

Example of a T-account

After all individual transactions for the period are posted to the T-account, we present the ending net balance at the bottom on either the debit or credit side, depending on which total column amount is bigger.

After all individual transactions for the period are posted to a general ledger account, we **aggregate** these individual amounts to compute a single ending account balance. It is this process of measuring each transaction and then aggregating those measurements that allows efficient communication of accounting information to financial statements users.

Of course, computerized systems automatically and instantly post information from the journal to the general ledger accounts and calculate account balances. Here, we will see the formal process of recording transactions in a journal and then posting them to the general ledger by working through the 10 transactions of Eagle Robotics listed in Illustration 3–1.

## TRANSACTION (1): ISSUE COMMON STOCK

In transaction (1), Eagle issues common stock for $1,000,000 cash. As demonstrated in the previous section, Eagle records a debit to Cash and a credit to Common Stock in the journal. We debit Cash because it's an asset account, and asset balances increase with a debit. We credit Common Stock because it's a stockholders' equity account, and these balances increase with a credit.

Now, let's record the transaction in the journal and then post the debit and credit to the general ledger accounts.

**TRANSACTION (1)**

Initial investment of $1,000,000 by stockholders

| December 1 | Debit | Credit |
|---|---|---|
| Cash (+A) ......................................................................... | 1,000,000 | |
|    Common Stock (+SE) ................................................. | | 1,000,000 |
|    *(Issue common stock for cash)* | | |

| Cash | | | Common Stock | | |
|---|---|---|---|---|---|
| (1) | 1,000,000 | | | (1) | 1,000,000 |
| Bal. | 1,000,000 | | | Bal. | 1,000,000 |

Notice that posting involves simply moving the debit to Cash from the journal entry to a debit (or left side) in the Cash general ledger account, increasing its balance by $1,000,000. The credit to Common Stock from the journal entry becomes a credit (or right side) in the Common Stock general ledger account, increasing its balance by $1,000,000.

The first row of the general ledger account is the balance at the beginning of the period. In this case, the balance is $0 for both accounts because Eagle is just beginning operations.

### TRANSACTION (2): BORROW CASH FROM THE BANK

In transaction (2), Eagle borrows $500,000 cash from a bank. The company has an increase in cash (an asset) and an increase in the amount owed (a liability). Assets increase with a debit, so we debit Cash for $500,000. Liabilities increase with a credit, so we credit Notes Payable for $500,000. Let's record the transaction in the journal and then post the debit and credit to the general ledger accounts.

**TRANSACTION (2)**

Borrow $500,000 from the bank and sign a three-year note

| December 1 | Debit | Credit |
|---|---|---|
| Cash (+A)............................................................................. | 500,000 | |
|    Notes Payable (+L) ................................................. | | 500,000 |
|    *(Borrow cash by signing three-year note)* | | |

In the T-accounts below, we see that the balance in both accounts increases by $500,000. The balance of the Cash account is now $1,500,000, which includes $1,000,000 cash received from stockholders in transaction (1) plus $500,000 cash received from the bank in transaction (2). The balance of the Notes Payable account increases from $0 to $500,000.

| Cash | | | Notes Payable | | |
|---|---|---|---|---|---|
| (1) | 1,000,000 | | | (2) | 500,000 |
| (2) | 500,000 | | | | |
| Bal. | 1,500,000 | | | Bal. | 500,000 |

As we go through transactions (3)–(10) next, **notice how each individual transaction is recorded in the journal but then adds to or subtracts from the account's total balance in the T-account.**

## TRANSACTION (3): PURCHASE EQUIPMENT

In transaction (3), Eagle purchases equipment with $240,000 cash. The company has an increase in equipment (an asset) and a decrease in cash (an asset). Assets increase with a debit, so we debit Equipment for $240,000. Assets decrease with a credit, so we credit Cash for $240,000.

| December 1 | Debit | Credit |
|---|---|---|
| **Equipment** *(+A)*......................................................................... | **240,000** | |
| **Cash** *(−A)*................................................................. | | **240,000** |
| *(Purchase equipment with cash)* | | |

**TRANSACTION (3)**
Purchase equipment with cash, $240,000

| Equipment | | Cash | |
|---|---|---|---|
| **(3)  240,000** | | (1)  1,000,000 | **(3)  240,000** |
| | | (2)     500,000 | |
| Bal.  240,000 | | Bal.  1,260,000 | |

For Cash (a *debit* account), notice that the $240,000 *credit* decreases the balance from $1,500,000 to $1,260,000.

## TRANSACTION (4): PAY FOR RENT IN ADVANCE

In transaction (4), Eagle pays $180,000 cash for one year of rent. The company has an increase in prepaid rent (an asset) and a decrease in cash (an asset). Assets increase with a debit, so we debit Prepaid Rent for $180,000. Assets decrease with a credit, so we credit Cash for $180,000.

| December 1 | Debit | Credit |
|---|---|---|
| **Prepaid Rent** *(+A)*........................................................... | **180,000** | |
| **Cash** *(−A)*....................................................................... | | **180,000** |
| *(Prepay one year of rent with cash)* | | |

**TRANSACTION (4)**
Pay one year of rent in advance, $180,000

| Prepaid Rent | | Cash | |
|---|---|---|---|
| **(4)  180,000** | | (1)  1,000,000 | (3) 240,000 |
| | | (2)     500,000 | **(4) 180,000** |
| Bal.  180,000 | | Bal.  1,080,000 | |

## TRANSACTION (5): PURCHASE SUPPLIES ON ACCOUNT

In transaction (5), Eagle purchases supplies on account for $14,000. The company has an increase in supplies (an asset) and an increase in amounts owed to suppliers (a liability). Assets increase with a debit, so we debit Supplies for $14,000. Liabilities increase with a credit, so we credit Accounts Payable for $14,000.

| December 6 | Debit | Credit |
|---|---|---|
| **Supplies** *(+A)*.......................................................... | **14,000** | |
| **Accounts Payable** *(+L)*.................................................. | | **14,000** |
| *(Purchase supplies on account)* | | |

**TRANSACTION (5)**
Purchase supplies on account, $14,000

| Supplies | | Accounts Payable | |
|---|---|---|---|
| **(5)   14,000** | | | **(5)   14,000** |
| Bal.   14,000 | | | Bal.   14,000 |

Later, when the company pays cash to those suppliers, accounts payable (a liability) decrease so we would debit Accounts Payable, and cash (an asset) decreases so we credit Cash.

### TRANSACTION (6): PURCHASE INVENTORY WITH CASH

In transaction (6), Eagle purchases a batch of 15 robots at a cost of $50,000 each for a total of $750,000 in cash. Purchasing inventory with cash causes one asset (inventory) to increase and another asset (cash) to decrease, so we debit Inventory for $750,000 and credit Cash for $750,000.

**TRANSACTION (6)**

Purchase robotics inventory with cash, $750,000

| December 12 | Debit | Credit |
|---|---|---|
| **Inventory** *(+A)* ............................................................... | **750,000** | |
| **Cash** *(−A)* ..................................................................... | | **750,000** |
| *(Purchase robotics inventory with cash)* | | |

| Inventory | | Cash | | | |
|---|---|---|---|---|---|
| **(6)   750,000** | | (1)   1,000,000 | (3)   240,000 | | |
| | | (2)      500,000 | (4)   180,000 | | |
| | | | (6)   750,000 | | |
| Bal.   750,000 | | Bal.      330,000 | | | |

### TRANSACTION (7): SELL INVENTORY FOR CASH AND ON ACCOUNT

In the first part of transaction (7), Eagle sells inventory for $350,000, with $70,000 for cash and $280,000 on account. The company has an increase in cash (an asset) and an increase in accounts receivable (an asset). Because these are both asset accounts, we increase them with a debit—we debit Cash for $70,000 and debit Accounts Receivable for $280,000. Revenues increase with a credit, so we credit Sales Revenue for $350,000.

**TRANSACTION (7)**

Sell robotics inventory for cash and on account, $350,000

| December 17 | Debit | Credit |
|---|---|---|
| **Cash** *(+A)* ..................................................................... | **70,000** | |
| **Accounts Receivable** *(+A)* .......................................... | **280,000** | |
| **Sales Revenue** *(+R, +SE)* ............................................ | | **350,000** |
| *(Sell robotics inventory for cash and on account)* | | |

| Cash | | | | Accounts Receivable | | Sales Revenue | |
|---|---|---|---|---|---|---|---|
| (1)   1,000,000 | | (3)   240,000 | | **(7)   280,000** | | | **(7)   350,000** |
| (2)      500,000 | | (4)   180,000 | | | | | |
| **(7)        70,000** | | (6)   750,000 | | | | | |
| Bal.      400,000 | | | | Bal.   280,000 | | | Bal.   350,000 |

Notice that the increase to revenue also increases stockholders' equity. Recall from Illustration 3–7 that revenue is a component of retained earnings (an equity account).

In the second part of transaction (7), Eagle records the cost of inventory sold (an expense), as well as the reduction in inventory (an asset). The cost of inventory sold is an expense called Cost of Goods Sold, which increases with a debit of $250,000. The reduction in inventory is recorded with a credit to Inventory of $250,000.

| December 17 | Debit | Credit |
|---|---|---|
| **Cost of Goods Sold** *(+E, −SE)*............................................................ | **250,000** | |
| **Inventory** *(−A)*................................................................ | | **250,000** |
| *(Record cost of inventory sold)* | | |

**TRANSACTION (7)**

Record the cost of inventory sold, $250,000

| Cost of Goods Sold | | Inventory | |
|---|---|---|---|
| (7)   250,000 | | (6)   750,000 | (7)   250,000 |
| Bal.   250,000 | | Bal.   500,000 | |

Note that the two journal entries related to transaction (7) could be collapsed into a single journal entry—we've presented it here as two entries for purposes of illustration.

## TRANSACTION (8): RECEIVE CASH IN ADVANCE FROM CUSTOMERS

In transaction (8), Eagle receives $100,000 cash in advance from customers for robot customization to be provided in the future. Eagle has an increase in cash (an asset) and an increase in obligations to provide future services to its customers (a liability). Assets increase with a debit, so we debit Cash for $100,000. Liabilities increase with a credit, so we credit Deferred Revenue for $100,000.

| December 23 | Debit | Credit |
|---|---|---|
| **Cash** *(+A)*................................................................ | **100,000** | |
| **Deferred Revenue** *(+L)*................................................... | | **100,000** |
| *(Receive cash in advance from customers)* | | |

**TRANSACTION (8)**

Receive cash in advance from customers, $100,000

| Cash | | Deferred Revenue | |
|---|---|---|---|
| (1)   1,000,000 | (3)   240,000 | | (8)   100,000 |
| (2)      500,000 | (4)   180,000 | | |
| (7)        70,000 | (6)   750,000 | | |
| **(8)      100,000** | | | |
| Bal.      500,000 | | | Bal.   100,000 |

## TRANSACTION (9): PAY SALARIES TO EMPLOYEES

In transaction (9), Eagle pays $28,000 cash for employee salaries during the month. The company has an increase in employee costs for work in the current period (an expense) and a decrease in cash (an asset). Expenses increase with a debit, so we debit Salaries Expense for $28,000. Assets decrease with a credit, so we credit Cash for $28,000.

**TRANSACTION (9)**

Pay salaries to employees, $28,000

| December 28 | Debit | Credit |
|---|---|---|
| **Salaries Expense** *(+E, −SE)* ............................................................ | **28,000** | |
| **Cash** *(−A)* ................................................................. | | **28,000** |
| *(Pay salaries to employees)* | | |

| Salaries Expense | | Cash | | | |
|---|---|---|---|---|---|
| **(9)  28,000** | | (1)  1,000,000 | (3)  240,000 | | |
| | | (2)     500,000 | (4)  180,000 | | |
| | | (7)       70,000 | (6)  750,000 | | |
| | | (8)     100,000 | **(9)    28,000** | | |
| Bal.  28,000 | | Bal.     472,000 | | | |

## TRANSACTION (10): PAY CASH DIVIDENDS

In transaction (10), Eagle pays $14,000 in cash dividends to stockholders. The company has an increase in the Dividends account and a decrease in cash (an asset). Dividends increase with a debit, so we debit Dividends for $14,000. Assets decrease with a credit, so we credit Cash for $14,000.

**TRANSACTION (10)**

Pay cash dividends to stockholders, $14,000

| December 30 | Debit | Credit |
|---|---|---|
| **Dividends** *(+D, −SE)*.................................................................. | **14,000** | |
| **Cash** *(−A)* ................................................................. | | **14,000** |
| *(Pay cash dividends)* | | |

| Dividends | | Cash | | | |
|---|---|---|---|---|---|
| **(10)  14,000** | | (1)  1,000,000 | (3)  240,000 | | |
| | | (2)     500,000 | (4)  180,000 | | |
| | | (7)       70,000 | (6)  750,000 | | |
| | | (8)     100,000 | (9)       28,000 | | |
| | | | **(10)    14,000** | | |
| Bal.  14,000 | | Bal.     458,000 | | | |

**KEY POINT**

Posting is the process of transferring the debit and credit information from transactions recorded in the journal to individual accounts in the general ledger. A T-account is a simplified form of a general ledger account.

A summary of the external transactions that have been recorded in a journal for Eagle Robotics is provided in Illustration 3–12.

| | Debit | Credit |
|---|---|---|
| **(1) December 1** | | |
| **Cash** *(+A)* ............................................................................ | 1,000,000 | |
|    **Common Stock** *(+SE)* ................................................ | | 1,000,000 |
|    *(Issue common stock for cash)* | | |
| **(2) December 1** | | |
| **Cash** *(+A)* ............................................................................ | 500,000 | |
|    **Notes Payable** *(+L)* .................................................. | | 500,000 |
|    *(Borrow cash by signing three-year note)* | | |
| **(3) December 1** | | |
| **Equipment** *(+A)* ................................................................. | 240,000 | |
|    **Cash** *(−A)* ................................................................. | | 240,000 |
|    *(Purchase equipment for cash)* | | |
| **(4) December 1** | | |
| **Prepaid Rent** *(+A)* ............................................................ | 180,000 | |
|    **Cash** *(−A)* ................................................................. | | 180,000 |
|    *(Prepay one year of rent with cash)* | | |
| **(5) December 6** | | |
| **Supplies** *(+A)* .................................................................... | 14,000 | |
|    **Accounts Payable** *(+L)* ........................................... | | 14,000 |
|    *(Purchase supplies on account)* | | |
| **(6) December 12** | | |
| **Inventory** *(+A)* ................................................................... | 750,000 | |
|    **Cash** *(−A)* ................................................................. | | 750,000 |
|    *(Purchase robotics inventory with cash)* | | |
| **(7) December 17** | | |
| **Cash** *(+A)* ............................................................................ | 70,000 | |
| **Accounts Receivable** *(+A)* ............................................. | 280,000 | |
|    **Sales Revenue** *(+R, +SE)* ....................................... | | 350,000 |
|    *(Sell robotics inventory for cash and on account)* | | |
| **Cost of Goods Sold** *(+E, −SE)* ..................................... | 250,000 | |
|    **Inventory** *(−A)* ........................................................ | | 250,000 |
|    *(Record cost of inventory sold)* | | |
| **(8) December 23** | | |
| **Cash** *(+A)* ............................................................................ | 100,000 | |
|    **Deferred Revenue** *(+L)* ........................................... | | 100,000 |
|    *(Receive cash in advance from customers)* | | |
| **(9) December 28** | | |
| **Salaries Expense** *(+E, −SE)* ......................................... | 28,000 | |
|    **Cash** *(−A)* ................................................................. | | 28,000 |
|    *(Pay salaries to employees)* | | |
| **(10) December 30** | | |
| **Dividends** *(+D, −SE)* ....................................................... | 14,000 | |
|    **Cash** *(−A)* ................................................................. | | 14,000 |
|    *(Pay cash dividends)* | | |

**ILLUSTRATION 3–12**

Summary of Journal Entries Recorded for Transactions of Eagle Robotics

Illustration 3–13 provides the general ledger accounts after posting the journal entries summarized in Illustration 3–12. Account balances are in bold, and transaction numbers are shown in parentheses.

**ILLUSTRATION 3–13**    Posting of External Transactions of Eagle Robotics from Journal Entries to General Ledger Accounts

| Assets | | | = | Liabilities | + | Stockholders' Equity | |

**Assets** = **Liabilities** + **Stockholders' Equity**

**Cash**

| | | | |
|---|---|---|---|
| (1) 1,000,000 | (3) 240,000 | | |
| (2) 500,000 | (4) 180,000 | | |
| (7) 70,000 | (6) 750,000 | | |
| (8) 100,000 | (9) 28,000 | | |
| | (10) 14,000 | | |
| **Bal. 458,000** | | | |

**Accounts Receivable**

| | |
|---|---|
| (7) 280,000 | |
| **Bal. 280,000** | |

**Accounts Payable**

| | |
|---|---|
| | (5) 14,000 |
| | **Bal 14,000** |

**Common Stock**

| | |
|---|---|
| | (1) 1,000,000 |
| | **Bal. 1,000,000** |

**Retained Earnings**

| | |
|---|---|
| | 0 |
| | **Bal. 0** |

**Supplies**

| | |
|---|---|
| (5) 14,000 | |
| **Bal. 14,000** | |

**Prepaid Rent**

| | |
|---|---|
| (4) 180,000 | |
| **Bal. 180,000** | |

**Deferred Revenue**

| | |
|---|---|
| | (8) 100,000 |
| | **Bal. 100,000** |

**Dividends**

| | |
|---|---|
| (10) 14,000 | |
| **Bal. 14,000** | |

**Sales Revenue**

| | |
|---|---|
| | (7) 350,000 |
| | **Bal. 350,000** |

**Inventory**

| | |
|---|---|
| (6) 750,000 | (7) 250,000 |
| **Bal. 500,000** | |

**Equipment**

| | |
|---|---|
| (3) 240,000 | |
| **Bal. 240,000** | |

**Notes Payable**

| | |
|---|---|
| | (2) 500,000 |
| | **Bal. 500,000** |

**Cost of Goods Sold**

| | |
|---|---|
| (7) 250,000 | |
| **Bal. 250,000** | |

**Salaries Expense**

| | |
|---|---|
| (9) 28,000 | |
| **Bal. 28,000** | |

Transaction numbers are shown in parentheses.
Account balances are in bold.

## Let's Review

Bogey Incorporated has the following transactions during May:

May 1   Purchase a storage building by obtaining a loan of $5,000.
May 6   Provide services to customers for cash, $1,800.
May 12  Pay $1,200 cash for advertising in May.
May 17  Repay $1,000 of the amount borrowed on May 1.
May 25  Purchase office supplies for $800 cash.

*Required:*

1. Record each transaction.
2. Post the transactions to the Cash T-account, assuming a beginning cash balance of $2,500 on May 1.

*Solution:*

1. Record each transaction.

| May 1 | Debit | Credit |
|---|---|---|
| **Buildings** *(+A)* ..................................................... | **5,000** | |
| **Notes Payable** *(+L)* .............................................. | | **5,000** |
| *(Purchase building with note payable)* | | |

| May 6 | Debit | Credit |
|---|---|---|
| **Cash** *(+A)* .............................................................. | **1,800** | |
| **Service Revenue** *(+R, +SE)* ................................... | | **1,800** |
| *(Provide services for cash)* | | |

| May 12 | Debit | Credit |
|---|---|---|
| **Advertising Expense** *(+E, −SE)* ....................................................... | 1,200 | |
|     **Cash** *(−A)*.......................................................................................... | | 1,200 |
|     *(Pay for advertising)* | | |

| May 17 | Debit | Credit |
|---|---|---|
| **Notes Payable** *(−L)* ........................................................................ | 1,000 | |
|     **Cash** *(−A)*.......................................................................................... | | 1,000 |
|     *(Repay portion of note)* | | |

| May 25 | Debit | Credit |
|---|---|---|
| **Supplies** *(+A)* .................................................................................. | 800 | |
|     **Cash** *(−A)*.......................................................................................... | | 800 |
|     *(Purchase supplies for cash)* | | |

2. Post the transactions to the Cash T-account, assuming a beginning cash balance of $2,500 on May 1.

|  | Cash | | |
|---|---|---|---|
| Beginning balance | 2,500 | | |
| May 6 | 1,800 | | |
| | | 1,200 | May 12 |
| | | 1,000 | May 17 |
| | | 800 | May 25 |
| Ending balance | 1,300 | | |

## Trial Balance

After we've posted journal entries to the general ledger accounts, **the sum of the accounts with debit balances should equal the sum of the accounts with credit balances.** This is expected because debits were equal to credits for every journal entry posted to those ledger accounts. To prove this and to check for any errors in posting, we prepare a trial balance. A trial balance is a list of all accounts and their balances at a particular date, showing that total debits equal total credits. Another purpose of the trial balance is to assist us in preparing adjusting entries. We discuss adjusting entries in Chapter 4.

■ **LO3–6**
Prepare a trial balance.

Using the account balances calculated in Illustration 3–13, we can now prepare the trial balance of Eagle Robotics. The trial balance appears in Illustration 3–14. Notice that accounts are listed with the debit balances in one column and the credit balances in another column. Asset, expense, and dividend accounts normally have debit balances. Liability, stockholders' equity, and revenue accounts normally have credit balances. As expected, total debits ($1,964,000) equal total credits ($1,964,000).

**COMMON MISTAKE**

Just because the debits and credits are equal in a trial balance does not necessarily mean that all balances are correct. A trial balance could contain offsetting errors. For example, if we overstate Cash and Revenue each by $1,000, both accounts will be in error, but the trial balance will still balance, since the overstatement to Cash increases debits by $1,000 and the overstatement to Revenue increases credits by $1,000.

**ILLUSTRATION 3–14**

**Trial Balance of Eagle Robotics**

**EAGLE ROBOTICS**
**Trial Balance**
**December 31, 2024**

| Accounts | Debit | Credit |
|---|---|---|
| Cash | $ 458,000 | |
| Accounts Receivable | 280,000 | |
| Supplies | 14,000 | |
| Prepaid Rent | 180,000 | |
| Inventory | 500,000 | |
| Equipment | 240,000 | |
| Accounts Payable | | $ 14,000 |
| Deferred Revenue | | 100,000 |
| Notes Payable | | 500,000 |
| Common Stock | | 1,000,000 |
| Retained Earnings | | 0 |
| Dividends | 14,000 | |
| Sales Revenue | | 350,000 |
| Cost of Goods Sold | 250,000 | |
| Salaries Expense | 28,000 | |
| Totals | $1,964,000 | $1,964,000 |

Total debits equal total credits.

**Retained Earnings.**   Notice the balance of Retained Earnings in the trial balance is $0. As we explained earlier, retained earnings is a composite of three other types of accounts— revenues, expenses, and dividends. Those three accounts have balances at this point, but those balances haven't yet been transferred to the Retained Earnings account. This transfer is known as the *closing process,* and we will discuss it in Chapter 4. Since this is the first period of the company's operations, retained earnings will start at $0. As time goes by, the Retained Earnings account will accumulate a balance that is carried forward each period.

**Manager Analysis**

| Question | Accounting Information | Analysis |
|---|---|---|
| How does the accounting system capture the effects of a company's external transactions? | Journal entries General ledger Trial balance | The effects of external transactions are summarized by recording increases and decreases to general ledger accounts and summarizing them in a trial balance. |

## ORDER OF ACCOUNTS

The trial balance is used *for internal purposes only* and provides a check on the equality of the debits and credits. Because the trial balance is not a published financial statement to be used by external parties, there is no required order for listing accounts in the trial balance. However, most companies list accounts in the following order: assets, liabilities, stockholders' equity, dividends, revenues, and expenses. As we'll see in Chapter 4, the trial balance simplifies preparation of the published financial statements. Asset, liability, and stockholders' equity accounts are reported in the balance sheet. Dividends are reported in the statement of stockholders' equity. Revenue and expense accounts are reported in the income statement. Having the accounts listed in order of those classifications in the trial balance makes it easier to prepare the financial statements.

**KEY POINT**

A trial balance is a list of all accounts and their balances at a particular date. Debits must equal credits, but that doesn't necessarily mean that all account balances are correct.

 **THE BOTTOM LINE**

**LO3–1** Analyze the effects of transactions on assets, liabilities, and stockholders' equity.

External transactions are activities conducted between the company and other entities. The effects of these transactions on the financial position of a company are recorded in accounts. Accounts provide a record of all business activities related to a particular item. The balance of the account equals all activities that increase the account minus all activities that decrease the account.

After each transaction, the accounting equation must always remain in balance. In other words, assets must always equal liabilities plus stockholders' equity.

**LO3–2** Analyze the effects of transactions on revenues, expenses, and dividends.

The expanded accounting equation demonstrates that revenues increase retained earnings while expenses and dividends decrease retained earnings. Retained earnings is a component of stockholders' equity.

**LO3–3** Prepare a preliminary balance sheet and income statement.

A preliminary income statement can be created after all transactions during the period are recorded. It provides initial information on a company's profitability. A preliminary balance sheet can also be created after all transactions during the period are recorded. It provides information on the current balances of a

company's resources (assets) and claims to those resources (liabilities and stockholders' equity).

**LO3–4** Record transactions in a journal using debits and credits.

For the basic accounting equation (Assets = Liabilities + Stockholders' Equity), assets (left side) increase with debits. Liabilities and stockholders' equity (right side) increase with credits. The opposite is true to decrease any of these accounts.

The Retained Earnings account is a stockholders' equity account that normally has a credit balance. The Retained Earnings account has three components—revenues, expenses, and dividends. The difference between revenues (increased by credits) and expenses (increased by debits) equals net income. Net income increases the balance of Retained Earnings. Dividends (increased by debits) decrease the balance of Retained Earnings.

For each transaction, total debits must equal total credits.

**LO3–5** Post transactions to the general ledger.

Posting is the process of transferring the debit and credit information from transactions recorded in the journal to individual accounts in the general ledger. A T-account is a simplified form of a general ledger account.

**LO3–6** Prepare a trial balance.

A trial balance is a list of all accounts and their balances at a particular date. Debits must equal credits, but that doesn't necessarily mean that all account balances are correct.

## GLOSSARY

**Account:** A record of the business activities related to a particular item. **p. 102**

**Accounting cycle:** Full set of procedures used to accomplish the measurement/communication process of financial accounting. **p. 102**

**Chart of accounts:** A list of all account names used to record transactions of a company. **p. 120**

**Credit:** Right side of an account. Indicates a decrease to asset, expense, or dividend accounts, and an increase to liability, stockholders' equity, or revenue accounts. **p. 116**

**Debit:** Left side of an account. Indicates an increase to asset, expense, or dividend accounts, and a decrease to liability, stockholders' equity, or revenue accounts. **p. 116**

**External transactions:** Transactions the firm conducts with a separate economic entity. **p. 102**

**General ledger:** A collection of each account with its individual transactions and resulting account balance. **p. 121**

**Journal:** A chronological record of all transactions affecting a firm. **p. 119**

**Journal entry:** The format used for recording business transactions. **p. 119**

**Posting:** The process of transferring the debit and credit information from the journal to individual accounts in the general ledger. **p. 121**

**Revenue recognition principle:** Record revenue in the period in which we provide goods and services to customers for the amount the company is entitled to receive. **p. 109**

**T-account:** A simplified form of a general ledger account with space at the top for the account title, one side for recording debits, and one side for recording credits. **p. 121**

**Trial balance:** A list of all accounts and their balances at a particular date, showing that total debits equal total credits. **p. 129**

## SELF-STUDY QUESTIONS

1. Which of the following represents an external transaction? **(LO3–1)**
   a. Lapse of insurance due to passage of time.
   b. Use of office supplies by employees over time.
   c. Payment of utility bill.
   d. Salaries earned by employees but not yet paid.

2. Which of the following transactions has no effect on total assets? **(LO3–1)**
   a. Pay dividends to stockholders.
   b. Purchase inventory on account.
   c. Secure a loan to pay for new equipment.
   d. Purchase inventory with cash.

3. Which of the following transactions causes an increase in total assets? **(LO3–1)**
   a. Pay employee salaries for the current month.
   b. Pay dividends to stockholders.
   c. Issue common stock in exchange for cash.
   d. Purchase office equipment for cash.

4. Which of the following transactions causes an increase in stockholders' equity? **(LO3–2)**
   a. Pay dividends to stockholders.
   b. Obtain cash by borrowing from a local bank.
   c. Provide services to customers on account.
   d. Purchase advertising on a local radio station.

5. If a company has an increase in total expenses of $10,000, which of the following is possible? **(LO3–2)**
   a. Total liabilities decrease by $10,000.
   b. Total assets increase by $10,000.
   c. Total stockholders' equity increases by $10,000.
   d. Total assets decrease by $10,000.

6. If a company has an increase in total revenues of $10,000, which of the following is possible? **(LO3–2)**
   a. Total assets increase by $10,000.
   b. Total liabilities increase by $10,000.
   c. Total stockholders' equity decreases by $10,000.
   d. Either b. or c. is correct.

7. Which of the following would cause the preliminary balance sheet not to balance? **(LO3–3)**
   a. Increase assets; increase liabilities.
   b. Decrease assets; increase expenses.
   c. Increase assets; increase dividends.
   d. Decrease liabilities; increase revenues.

8. In the language of accounting, the term "debit" always means **(LO3–4)**
   a. Increase.
   b. Decrease.
   c. Left-hand side.
   d. Right-hand side.

9. A debit is used to increase which of the following accounts? **(LO3–4)**
   a. Utilities Expense.
   b. Accounts Payable.
   c. Service Revenue.
   d. Common Stock.

10. A credit is used to increase which of the following accounts? **(LO3–4)**
    a. Dividends.
    b. Insurance Expense.
    c. Cash.
    d. Service Revenue.

11. The purchase of supplies with cash would be recorded as **(LO3–4)**
    a. Debit Cash; Credit Supplies Expense.
    b. Debit Supplies; Credit Cash.
    c. Debit Cash; Credit Supplies.
    d. Debit Supplies Expense; Credit Cash.

12. The payment for utilities of the current month would be recorded as **(LO3–4)**
    a. Debit Cash; Credit Utilities Payable.
    b. Debit Utilities Expense; Credit Utilities Payable.
    c. Debit Utilities Expense; Credit Cash.
    d. Debit Utilities Payable; Credit Cash.

13. Providing services to customers on account for $100 is recorded as **(LO3–4)**

| | | |
|---|---|---|
| a. Accounts Receivable | 100 | |
|     Service Revenue | | 100 |
| b. Cash | 100 | |
|     Accounts Receivable | | 100 |
| c. Service Revenue | 100 | |
|     Accounts Receivable | | 100 |
| d. Service Expense | 100 | |
|     Accounts Payable | | 100 |

14. Posting is the process of **(LO3–5)**
   a. Analyzing the impact of the transaction on the accounting equation.
   b. Obtaining information about external transactions from source documents.
   c. Transferring the debit and credit information from the journal to individual accounts in the general ledger.
   d. Listing all accounts and their balances at a particular date and showing the equality of total debits and total credits.

15. A trial balance can best be explained as a list of
   a. The income statement accounts used to calculate net income. **(LO3–6)**
   b. Revenue, expense, and dividend accounts used to show the balances of the components of retained earnings.
   c. The balance sheet accounts used to show the equality of the accounting equation.
   d. All accounts and their balances at a particular date.

*Note: For answers, see the last page of the chapter.*

## REAL WORLD PERSPECTIVES

Mc Graw Hill **connect**

### Stryker, Inc. (ticker: SYK)

EDGAR Case

**RWP3–1** Visit www.sec.gov/edgar and search for the **Stryker** annual report (10-K) for the year ended December 31, 2019, using EDGAR (Electronic Data Gathering, Analysis, and Retrieval system). Locate its balance sheet, labeled "Consolidated Balance Sheets." Use this information to answer the questions below.

*Required:*

1. What amount did Stryker report for total assets, total liabilities, and total shareholders' equity as of the end of 2019?
2. Show that the basic accounting equation remains in balance using information from Stryker's balance sheet.
3. Based on the basic accounting equation, what proportion of Strkyer's "resources" is related to "creditors' claims" (liabilities) versus "owners' claims" (stockholders' equity)? What does this tell you about how Stryker finances its assets?

### Netflix, Inc (ticker: NFLX)

EDGAR Case

**RWP3–2** Visit www.sec.gov/edgar and search for the **Netflix** annual report (10-K) for the year ended December 31, 2019, using EDGAR (Electronic Data Gathering, Analysis, and Retrieval system). Locate its balance sheet, labeled "Consolidated Balance Sheets." Use this information to answer the questions below.

*Required:*

1. Think about the business model of Netflix. With that in mind, what are the "content assets"?
2. Assume that Netflix develops a costly new series costing $80 million. In addition, suppose they pay for 10% of these costs with cash, while the rest is financed with a liability labeled "long-term content liability." How would this transaction affect the accounting equation for Netflix?

### The Boeing Company (ticker: BA)

EDGAR Case

**RWP3–3** Visit www.sec.gov/edgar and search for the **Boeing** annual report (10-K) for the year ended December 31, 2019, using EDGAR (Electronic Data Gathering, Analysis, and Retrieval system). Locate its balance sheet, labeled "Consolidated Statements of Financial Position," and its income statement, labeled "Consolidated Statements of Operations." Use this information to answer the questions below.

*Required:*

1. Suppose that on January 1, 2020, Boeing sells one of its 777 series planes to Singapore Airlines on account—its first and only transaction on the first day of the fiscal year. The sales price is $400 million and the inventory cost $330 million to manufacture. Record the journal entry for this transaction.

2. Which account(s) in the income statement would increase or decrease as a result of this transaction?
3. Which account(s) in the balance sheet would increase or decrease as a result of this transaction? What is the new balance in these accounts?
4. Update the December 31, 2019, total amount of assets, liabilities and stockholders' equity to show that Boeing's balance sheet remains in balance after this transaction is properly recorded.

EDGAR Case

## Carmax, Inc (ticker: KMX)

**RWP3–4** Visit www.sec.gov/edgar and search for the Carmax annual report (10-K) for the year ended February 29, 2020, using EDGAR (Electronic Data Gathering, Analysis, and Retrieval system). Locate its balance sheet and income statement. Use this information to answer the questions below.

*Required:*
1. In the income statement, find total cost of goods sold (labeled "Total cost of sales") and use it to record the journal entry for cost of goods sold.
2. In the balance sheet, find the amounts reported for ending inventory in the current year and the previous year. Create a T-account for inventory and input the beginning and ending balances for the current year. Use the previous year's ending balance as the current year's beginning balance Using these balances and your answer in Requirement 1, solve for the missing value in the Inventory T-Account—this amount represents inventory purchases in the current year.
3. Record the journal entry for inventory purchases, using the amount calculated from Requirement 2 and assuming all inventory purchases are on account.

Continuing Financial Analysis Case

## American Eagle Outfitters, Inc.

**RWP3–5** Financial information for American Eagle is presented in **Appendix A** at the end of the book.

*Required:*
1. Calculate American Eagle's percentage change in total assets and percentage change in net sales for the most recent year.
2. Calculate American Eagle's percentage change in net income for the most recent year.
3. Did American Eagle issue any common stock in the most recent year?
4. Do you see the term debit or credit listed in the balance sheet? Which account types in the balance sheet increase with a debit and which ones increase with a credit?
5. Do you see the term debit or credit listed in the income statement? Which account types in the income statement increase with a debit? Which increase with a credit?

Continuing Financial Analysis Case

## The Buckle, Inc.

**RWP3–6** Financial information for Buckle is presented in **Appendix B** at the end of the book.

*Required:*
1. Calculate Buckle's percentage change in total assets and percentage change in net sales for the most recent year.
2. Calculate Buckle's percentage change in net income for the most recent year.
3. Did Buckle issue any common stock in the most recent year?
4. Do you see the term debit or credit listed in the balance sheet? Which account types in the balance sheet increase with a debit and which ones increase with a credit?
5. Do you see the term debit or credit listed in the income statement? Which account types in the income statement increase with a debit? Which increase with a credit?

Continuing Comparative Analysis Case

## American Eagle Outfitters, Inc. vs. The Buckle, Inc.

**RWP3–7** Financial information for American Eagle is presented in **Appendix A** at the end of the book, and financial information for Buckle is presented in **Appendix B** at the end of the book.

*Required:*

Determine which company's growth rate in total assets, net sales, and net income is greater. Why do you think this might be the case?

## Ethics

Ethics Case

**RWP3–8** Larry has been the chief financial officer (CFO) of Maxima Auto Service for the past 10 years. The company has reported profits each year it's been in business. However, this year has been a tough one. Increased competition and the rising costs of labor have reduced the company's profits. On December 30, Larry informs Robert, the company's president and Larry's closest friend for the past 10 years, that it looks like the company will report a net loss (total expenses will be greater than total revenues) of about $50,000 this year.

The next day, December 31, while Larry is preparing the year-end reports, Robert stops by Larry's office to tell him that an additional $75,000 of revenues needs to be reported and that the company can now report a profit. When Larry asks about the source of the $75,000, Robert tells him, "Earlier in the month some customers paid for auto services with cash, and with this cash I bought additional assets for the company. That's why the $75,000 never showed up in the bank statement. I just forgot to tell you about this earlier." When Larry asks for more specifics about these transactions, Robert mumbles, "I can't recall where I placed the customer sales invoices or the purchase receipts for the assets, but don't worry; I know they're here somewhere. We've been friends for a lot of years and you can trust me. Now, let's hurry and finish those reports and I'll treat you to dinner tonight at the restaurant of your choice."

*Required:*

1. Understand the reporting effect: What effect does reporting additional revenue have on reported profit?
2. Specify the options: If the additional revenue is not reported, do both Robert and Larry potentially lose benefits?
3. Identify the impact: Does reporting the additional revenue strengthen the company's financial appearance to those outside the company?
4. Make a decision: Should Larry report the additional revenue without source documents?

## Great Adventures

Continuing General Ledger Case

(This is a continuation of the Great Adventures problem from earlier chapters.)

**RWP3–9** Tony and Suzie graduate from college in May 2024 and begin developing their new business. They begin by offering clinics for basic outdoor activities such as mountain biking or kayaking. Upon developing a customer base, they'll hold their first adventure races. These races will involve four-person teams that race from one checkpoint to the next using a combination of kayaking, mountain biking, orienteering, and trail running. In the long run, they plan to sell outdoor gear and develop a ropes course for outdoor enthusiasts.

On July 1, 2024, Tony and Suzie organize their new company as a corporation, Great Adventures Inc. The articles of incorporation state that the corporation will sell 20,000 shares of common stock for $1 each. Each share of stock represents a unit of ownership. Tony and Suzie will act as co-presidents of the company. The following business activities occur during July for Great Adventures.

| | |
|---|---|
| July 1 | Sell $10,000 of common stock to Suzie. |
| July 1 | Sell $10,000 of common stock to Tony. |
| July 1 | Purchase a one-year insurance policy for $4,800 ($400 per month) to cover injuries to participants during outdoor clinics. |
| July 2 | Pay legal fees of $1,500 associated with incorporation. |
| July 4 | Purchase office supplies of $1,800 on account. |
| July 7 | Pay $300 to a local newspaper for advertising to appear immediately for an upcoming mountain biking clinic to be held on July 15. Attendees will be charged $50 the day of the clinic. |
| July 8 | Purchase 10 mountain bikes, paying $12,000 cash. |

July 15    On the day of the clinic, Great Adventures receives cash of $2,000 from 40 bikers. Tony conducts the mountain biking clinic.

July 22    Because of the success of the first mountain biking clinic, Tony holds another mountain biking clinic and the company receives $2,300.

July 24    Pay $700 to a local radio station for advertising to appear immediately. A kayaking clinic will be held on August 10, and attendees can pay $100 in advance or $150 on the day of the clinic.

July 30    Great Adventures receives cash of $4,000 in advance from 40 kayakers for the upcoming kayak clinic.

**Required:**

1. Record each transaction in July for Great Adventures. [Note: These same transactions can be assigned as part of a more complete accounting cycle in Chapter 4's RWP4–9].
2. Post each transaction to T-accounts.
3. Prepare a trial balance.

## BRIEF EXERCISES

**Balance the accounting equation (LO3–1)**

**BE3–1** Suppose a local company has the following balance sheet accounts:

| Accounts | Balances |
| --- | --- |
| Land | $ 9,000 |
| Equipment | ? |
| Salaries Payable | 4,300 |
| Notes Payable | ? |
| Supplies | 2,100 |
| Cash | 7,200 |
| Stockholders' Equity | 13,500 |
| Accounts Payable | 1,700 |
| Prepaid Rent | 3,200 |

Calculate the missing amounts assuming the business has total assets of $37,500.

**Balance the accounting equation (LO3–1, 3–2)**

**BE3–2** Using the notion that the accounting equation (Assets = Liabilities + Stockholders' Equity) must remain in balance, indicate whether each of the following transactions is possible.

a. Cash increases; Accounts Payable decreases.

b. Service Revenue increases; Salaries Payable increases.

c. Advertising Expense increases; Cash decreases.

**Analyze the effects of transactions on the accounting equation (LO3–1, 3–2)**
*See JBE3–3 for journal entries.*

**BE3–3** The following transactions occur for the Panther Detective Agency during the month of July:

1. Purchase a truck and sign a note payable, $15,000.
2. Purchase office supplies for cash, $600.
3. Pay $800 in rent for the current month.

Analyze each transaction and show the effects of each on the accounting equation.

|   | Assets | = | Liabilities | + | Stockholders' Equity |
| --- | --- | --- | --- | --- | --- |
| 1. | ____ | | ____ | | ____ |
| 2. | ____ | | ____ | | ____ |
| 3. | ____ | | ____ | | ____ |

**Analyze the effects of transactions on the accounting equation (LO3–1, 3–2)**
*See JBE3–4 for journal entries.*

**BE3–4** The following transactions occur for T-Bird Music Academy during the month of October:

1. Provide music lessons to students for $17,000 cash.
2. Purchase prepaid insurance to protect musical equipment over the next year for $4,200 cash.
3. Purchase musical equipment for $20,000 cash.
4. Obtain a loan from a bank by signing a note for $30,000.

Analyze each transaction and show the effects of each on the accounting equation.

| | Assets | = | Liabilities | + | Stockholders' Equity |
|---|---|---|---|---|---|
| 1. | _____ | | _____ | | _____ |
| 2. | _____ | | _____ | | _____ |
| 3. | _____ | | _____ | | _____ |
| 4. | _____ | | _____ | | _____ |

**BE3–5** The following transactions occur for Badger Biking Company during the month of June:

1. Purchase bicycle inventory for $80,000 on account.
2. Sell inventory costing $40,000 for $65,000 in cash.
3. Provide repair services to customers on account for $50,000.
4. Receive cash of $42,000 from customers in (c) above.
5. Purchase bike repair equipment by signing a note with the bank for $35,000.
6. Pay utilities of $5,000 for the current month.

Analyze the effects of transactions on the accounting equation (LO3–1, 3–2) *See JBE3–5 for journal entries.*

Analyze each transaction and show the effects of each on the accounting equation.

| | Assets | = | Liabilities | + | Stockholders' Equity |
|---|---|---|---|---|---|
| 1. | _____ | | _____ | | _____ |
| 2. | _____ | | _____ | | _____ |
| 3. | _____ | | _____ | | _____ |
| 4. | _____ | | _____ | | _____ |
| 5. | _____ | | _____ | | _____ |
| 6. | _____ | | _____ | | _____ |

**BE3–6** The Cougar Creamery enters into the following transactions during the month of June:

1. Purchase inventory on account for $165,000;
2. Pay $40,000 in salaries to employees for work performed during the month;
3. Sell merchandise that cost $120,000 to customers on account for $200,000;
4. Collect $180,000 in cash from customers on account; and
5. Pay for inventory previously purchased on account for $145,000.

Analyze the effects of transactions on the accounting equation (LO3–1, 3–2) *See JBE3–6 for journal entries.*

Analyze each transaction and show the effects of each on the accounting equation.

| | Assets | = | Liabilities | + | Stockholders' Equity |
|---|---|---|---|---|---|
| 1. | _____ | | _____ | | _____ |
| 2. | _____ | | _____ | | _____ |
| 3. | _____ | | _____ | | _____ |
| 4. | _____ | | _____ | | _____ |
| 5. | _____ | | _____ | | _____ |

**BE3–7** Refer to the information in the BE3–6. Prepare a preliminary income statement based on those transactions.

Prepare a preliminary income statement (LO3–3)

**BE3–8** The following are account balances for M-E Corporation: sales revenue, $325,000; cost of goods sold, $168,000; salaries expense, $45,000; rent expense, $20,000; income tax expense, $30,000; and miscellaneous expense, $12,000. Prepare a preliminary income statement.

Prepare a preliminary income statement (LO3–3)

**BE3–9** The following are account balances for M-E Corporation: cash, $5,000; accounts receivable, $10,000; inventory, $16,000; equipment $60,000; accounts payable, $20,000; salaries payable, $12,000; retained earnings, $9,000; and common stock, $50,000. Prepare a preliminary balance sheet.

Prepare a preliminary balance sheet (LO3–3)

Analyze the effects of transactions on the accounting equation **(LO3–1, 3–2)**

**E3–1** Below are the external transactions for Shockers Incorporated.
1. Issue common stock in exchange for cash.
2. Purchase equipment by signing a note payable.
3. Provide services to customers on account.
4. Pay rent for the current month.
5. Pay insurance for the current month.
6. Collect cash from customers on account.

| | **Assets** | **=** | **Liabilities** | **+** | **Stockholders' Equity** |
|---|---|---|---|---|---|
| 1. | Increase | = | No effect | + | Increase |
| 2. | ___ | | ___ | | ___ |
| 3. | ___ | | ___ | | ___ |
| 4. | ___ | | ___ | | ___ |
| 5. | ___ | | ___ | | ___ |
| 6. | ___ | | ___ | | ___ |

**Required:**
Analyze each transaction. Under each category in the accounting equation, indicate whether the transaction increases, decreases, or has no effect. The first item is provided as an example.

Analyze the effects of transactions on the accounting equation **(LO3–1, 3–2)**

**E3–2** Green Wave Company plans to own and operate a storage rental facility. For the first month of operations, the company had the following transactions.
1. Issue 10,000 shares of common stock in exchange for $32,000 in cash.
2. Purchase land for $19,000. A note payable is signed for the full amount.
3. Purchase storage container equipment for $8,000 cash.
4. Hire three employees for $2,000 per month.
5. Receive cash of $12,000 in rental fees for the current month.
6. Purchase office supplies for $2,000 on account.
7. Pay employees $6,000 for the first month's salaries.

**Required:**
For each transaction, describe the dual effect on the accounting equation. For example, in the first transaction, (1) assets increase and (2) stockholders' equity increases.

Analyze the effects of transactions on the accounting equation **(LO3–1, 3–2)**

**E3–3** Boilermaker Paint Company incurs the following transactions for September.
1. Paint houses in the current month for $15,000 on account.
2. Purchase painting equipment for $16,000 cash.
3. Purchase inventory on account for $2,500.
4. Pay employee salaries of $3,200 for the current month.
5. Purchase advertising to appear in the current month, $1,200.
6. Pay office rent of $4,400 for the current month.
7. Receive $10,000 from customers in (1) above.
8. Receive cash of $5,000 in advance from a customer who plans to have his house painted in the following month.

**Required:**
For each transaction, describe the dual effect on the accounting equation. For example, for the first transaction, (1) assets increase and (2) stockholders' equity increases.

Understand the components of retained earnings **(LO3–2)**

**E3–4** At the beginning of April, Owl Corporation has a balance of $13,000 in the Retained Earnings account. During the month of April, Owl had the following external transactions.
1. Issue common stock for cash, $11,000.
2. Provide services to customers on account, $8,500.
3. Provide services to customers in exchange for cash, $3,200.
4. Purchase equipment and pay cash, $7,600.

5. Pay rent for April, $1,100.
6. Pay employee salaries for April, $3,500.
7. Pay dividends to stockholders, $2,000.

**Required:**

Using the external transactions above, compute the balance of Retained Earnings at April 30.

**E3–5** Terrapin Company engages in the following external transactions for November.
1. Purchase equipment in exchange for cash of $23,400.
2. Provide services to customers and receive cash of $6,800.
3. Pay the current month's rent of $1,300.
4. Purchase office supplies on account for $1,000.
5. Pay employee salaries of $2,100 for the current month.

Analyze the effects of transactions on the accounting equation (LO3–1, 3–2)
*See JE3–3 for journal entries.*

**Required:**

Analyze each transaction and show the effects of each on the accounting equation.

**E3–6** Sun Devil Hair Design has the following transactions during the month of February.

| | |
|---|---|
| February 2 | Pay $700 for radio advertising for February. |
| February 7 | Purchase beauty inventory of $1,300 on account. |
| February 14 | Provide beauty services of $2,900 to customers and receive cash. |
| February 15 | Pay employee salaries for the current month of $900. |
| February 18 | Sell beauty inventory costing $1,100 to customers for $2,000 in cash. |
| February 25 | Provide beauty services of $1,000 to customers on account. |
| February 28 | Pay utility bill for the current month of $300. |

Analyze the effects of transactions on the accounting equation (LO3–1, 3–2)
*See JE3–5 for journal entries.*

**Required:**

Analyze each transaction and show the effects of each on the accounting equation.

**E3–7** Bearcat Construction begins operations in March and has the following transactions.

| | |
|---|---|
| March 1 | Issue common stock for $21,000. |
| March 5 | Obtain $9,000 loan from the bank by signing a note. |
| March 10 | Purchase construction equipment for $25,000 cash. |
| March 15 | Purchase advertising for the current month for $1,100 cash. |
| March 22 | Provide construction services for $18,000 on account. |
| March 27 | Receive $13,000 cash on account from March 22 services. |
| March 28 | Pay salaries for the current month of $6,000. |

Analyze the effects of transactions on the accounting equation (LO3–1, 3–2)
*See JE3–6 for journal entries.*

**Required:**

Analyze each transaction and show the effects of each on the accounting equation.

**E3–8** Refer to the information in E3–4. Prepare a preliminary income statement for the month of April.

Prepare a preliminary income statement (LO3–3)

**E3–9** Below is the complete list of accounts of Sooner Company and the related balances. Cash, $1,900; Prepaid Rent, $7,400; Inventory, $6,000; Accounts Payable $4,300; Common Stock, $40,000; Service Revenue, $25,400; Sales Revenue, $14,000; Salaries Expense, $8,200; Accounts Receivable, $6,100; Land, $60,000; Cost of Goods Sold, $10,000; Deferred Revenue, $2,300; Retained Earnings, $34,800; Supplies Expense, $9,400.

Prepare preliminary financial statements (LO3–3)

**Required:**

Prepare a preliminary balance sheet and preliminary income statement for Sooner Company.

**E3–10** Below is the complete list of accounts of Cobras Incorporated and the related balances. Supplies, $1,000; Buildings, $55,000; Salaries Payable, $500; Common Stock, $35,000; Accounts Payable, $2,200; Utilities Expense, $3,700; Prepaid Insurance, $1,200; Service Revenue, $19,500; Accounts Receivable, $4,200; Cash, $3,500; Salaries Expense, $6,400; Retained Earnings, $27,200.

Prepare preliminary financial statements (LO3–3)

**Required:**

Prepare a preliminary balance sheet and preliminary income statement for Cobras Incorporated.

## PROBLEMS

**Analyze the effects of transactions on the accounting equation (LO3–1, 3–2)**

**P3–1** Below is a list of activities for Jayhawk Corporation.

| Transaction | Assets | = | Liabilities | + | Stockholders' Equity |
|---|---|---|---|---|---|
| 1. *Issue common stock in exchange for cash.* | *Increase* | *=* | *No effect* | *+* | *Increase* |
| 2. Purchase business supplies on account. | _____ | | _____ | | _____ |
| 3. Pay for legal services for the current month. | _____ | | _____ | | _____ |
| 4. Provide services to customers on account. | _____ | | _____ | | _____ |
| 5. Pay employee salaries for the current month. | _____ | | _____ | | _____ |
| 6. Provide services to customers for cash. | _____ | | _____ | | _____ |
| 7. Pay for advertising for the current month. | _____ | | _____ | | _____ |
| 8. Repay loan from the bank. | _____ | | _____ | | _____ |
| 9. Pay dividends to stockholders. | _____ | | _____ | | _____ |
| 10. Receive cash from customers in (4) above. | _____ | | _____ | | _____ |
| 11. Pay for supplies purchased in (2) above. | _____ | | _____ | | _____ |

**Required:**

For each activity, indicate whether the transaction increases, decreases, or has no effect on assets, liabilities, and stockholders' equity.

**Analyze the effects of transactions on the accounting equation (LO3–1, 3–2)**

**P3–2** Below is a list of activities for Purple Cow Incorporated.

| Transaction | Assets | = | Liabilities | + | Stockholders' Equity |
|---|---|---|---|---|---|
| 1. *Provide services to customers on account, $1,600.* | *+$1,600* | *=* | *$0* | *+* | *+$1,600* |
| 2. Pay $400 for current month's rent. | _____ | | _____ | | _____ |
| 3. Hire a new employee, who will be paid $500 at the end of each month. | _____ | | _____ | | _____ |
| 4. Pay $100 for advertising aired in the current period. | _____ | | _____ | | _____ |
| 5. Purchase office supplies for $400 cash. | _____ | | _____ | | _____ |
| 6. Receive cash of $1,000 from customers in (1) above. | _____ | | _____ | | _____ |
| 7. Obtain a loan from the bank for $7,000. | _____ | | _____ | | _____ |
| 8. Receive a bill of $200 for utility costs in the current period. | _____ | | _____ | | _____ |
| 9. Issue common stock for $10,000 cash. | _____ | | _____ | | _____ |
| 10. Pay $500 to employee in (3) above. | _____ | | _____ | | _____ |
| Totals | _____ | = | _____ | + | _____ |

*Required:*

For each activity, indicate the impact on the accounting equation. After doing so for all transactions, ensure that the accounting equation remains in balance.

**P3–3** Refer to the information in P3–2. Prepare a preliminary income statement for the month of April.

Prepare a preliminary income statement **(LO3–3)**

**P3–4** The following transactions occurred for the Wayne Corporation in March, its first month of operations. The company owns and operates a wholesale warehouse.

1. Issued 30,000 shares of common stock in exchange for $300,000 in cash.
2. Purchased equipment at a cost of $40,000. $10,000 cash was paid and a note payable to the seller was signed for the balance owed.
3. Purchased inventory on account at a cost of $90,000.
4. Credit sales for the month totaled $120,000. The cost of the goods sold was $70,000.
5. Paid $5,000 in rent on the warehouse building for the month of March.
6. Paid $6,000 to an insurance company for fire and liability insurance for a one-year period beginning in April.
7. Paid $70,000 on account for the merchandise purchased in 3.
8. Collected $55,000 from customers on account.
9. Paid utilities expense of $1,000 for the month.

Analyze the effects of transactions on the accounting equation and prepare preliminary financial statements **(LO3–1, 3–2, 3–3)**

*Required:*

1. Analyze each transaction and show the effect of each on the accounting equation for a corporation.
2. Prepare a preliminary balance sheet and preliminary income statement for Wayne Corporation for March.

## JOURNAL ENTRIES

Mc Graw Hill **connect**

## Journal Entries—Brief Exercises

**JBE3–1** For each of the following accounts, indicate whether a debit or credit is used to increase (+) or decrease (–) the balance of the account. The solution for the first one is provided as an example.

Understand the effect of debits and credits on accounts **(LO3–4)**

| Account | Debit | Credit |
| --- | --- | --- |
| Asset | + | – |
| Liability | _____ | _____ |
| Common Stock | _____ | _____ |
| Retained Earnings | _____ | _____ |
| Dividends | _____ | _____ |
| Revenue | _____ | _____ |
| Expense | _____ | _____ |

**JBE3–2** Fill in the blanks below with the word "debit" or "credit."

a. The balance of an asset account increases with a _____ and decreases with a _____.
b. The balance of a liability account increases with a _____ and decreases with a _____ .
c. The balance of a stockholders' equity account increases with a _____ and decreases with _____ .
d. The balance of a revenue account increases with a _____ and decreases with a _____ .
e. The balance of an expense account increases with a _____ and decreases with a _____ .

Understand the effect of debits and credits on accounts **(LO3–4)**

**JBE3–3** The following transactions occur for the Panther Detective Agency during the month of July:

1. Purchase a truck and sign a note payable, $15,000.
2. Purchase office supplies for cash, $600.
3. Pay $800 in rent for the current month.

Record transactions **(LO3–4)**
*See BE3–3 for analyzing effects.*

Record the transactions. The company uses the following accounts: Cash, Supplies, Equipment (for the truck), Notes Payable, and Rent Expense.

**Record transactions**
**(LO3–4)**
*See BE3–4 for analyzing effects.*

**JBE3–4** The following transactions occur for T-Bird Music Academy during the month of October:
1. Provide music lessons to students for $17,000 cash.
2. Purchase prepaid insurance to protect musical equipment over the next year for $4,200 cash.
3. Purchase musical equipment for $20,000 cash.
4. Obtain a loan from a bank by signing a note for $30,000.

Record the transactions. The company uses the following accounts: Cash, Prepaid Insurance, Equipment, Notes Payable, and Service Revenue.

**Record transactions**
**(LO3–4)**
*See BE3–5 for analyzing effects.*

**JBE3–5** The following transactions occur for Badger Biking Company during the month of June:
1. Purchase bicycle inventory for $80,000 on account.
2. Sell inventory costing $40,000 for $65,000 in cash.
3. Provide repair services to customers on account for $50,000.
4. Receive cash of $42,000 from customers in (c) above.
5. Purchase bike repair equipment by signing a note with the bank for $35,000.
6. Pay utilities of $5,000 for the current month.

Record the transactions.

**Record transactions**
**(LO3–4)**
*See BE3–6 for analyzing effects.*

**JBE3–6** The Cougar Creamery enters into the following transactions during the month of June:
1. Purchase inventory on account for $165,000.
2. Pay $40,000 in salaries to employees for work performed during the month.
3. Sell merchandise that cost $120,000 to customers on account for $200,000.
4. Collect $180,000 in cash from customers on account.
5. Pay for inventory previously purchased on account for $145,000.

Record the transactions.

**Analyze T-accounts**
**(LO3–5)**

**JBE3–7** Consider the following T-account for cash:

| Cash | |
|---|---|
| 13,000 | 8,200 |
| 4,400 | 1,900 |
| 3,500 | 5,500 |

1. Compute the balance of the Cash account.
2. Give some examples of transactions that would have resulted in the $4,400 posting to the account.
3. Give some examples of transactions that would have resulted in the $1,900 posting to the account.

**Record transactions and post to ledger**
**(LO3–4, 3–5)**

**JBE3–8** The following transactions occur for the Wolfpack Shoe Company during the month of June:
a. Provide services to customers for $30,000 and receive cash.
b. Purchase shoe inventory on account for $20,000.
c. Sell inventory costing $10,000 to customers for $18,000 in cash.
d. Pay $7,000 in salaries to employees for work performed during the month.

1. Record the transactions. The company uses the following accounts: Cash, Inventory, Accounts Payable, Cost of Goods Sold, Salaries Expense, Sales Revenue, and Service Revenue.
2. Post the transactions to T-accounts. Assume the opening balance in each of the accounts is zero.

**JBE3–9** Using the following information, prepare a trial balance. Assume all asset, dividend, and expense accounts have debit balances and all liability, stockholders' equity, and revenue accounts have credit balances. List the accounts in the following order: assets, liabilities, stockholders' equity, dividends, revenues, and expenses.

Prepare trial balance (LO3–6)

| | | | |
|---|---|---|---|
| Cash | $6,100 | Dividends | $ 500 |
| Salaries Payable | 700 | Rent Expense | 2,000 |
| Prepaid Rent | 900 | Accounts Receivable | 4,400 |
| Accounts Payable | 2,000 | Common Stock | 6,200 |
| Retained Earnings | 2,000 | Service Revenue | 7,100 |
| Salaries Expense | 3,000 | Advertising Expense | 1,100 |

**JBE3–10** Your study partner is having trouble getting total debits to equal total credits in the trial balance. Prepare a corrected trial balance by placing each account balance in the correct debit or credit column.

Correct a trial balance (LO3–6)

**Trial Balance**

| Accounts | Debit | Credit |
|---|---|---|
| Cash | $ 7,300 | |
| Accounts Receivable | | $ 2,100 |
| Inventory | 10,400 | |
| Accounts Payable | 3,900 | |
| Deferred Revenue | | 1,100 |
| Common Stock | 11,000 | |
| Retained Earnings | | 3,900 |
| Dividends | 600 | |
| Sales Revenue | | 4,500 |
| Cost of Goods Sold | 3,200 | |
| Utilities Expense | | 800 |
| Total | $36,400 | $12,400 |

## Journal Entries—Exercises

**JE3–1** Below is a list of common accounts.

Identify debits and credits (LO3–4)

| Accounts | Debit or Credit |
|---|---|
| Cash | 1. _____ |
| Sales Revenue | 2. _____ |
| Salaries Expense | 3. _____ |
| Accounts Payable | 4. _____ |
| Equipment | 5. _____ |
| Retained Earnings | 6. _____ |
| Cost of Goods Sold | 7. _____ |
| Accounts Receivable | 8. _____ |
| Dividends | 9. _____ |
| Common Stock | 10. _____ |

*Required:*

Indicate whether the normal balance of each account is a debit or a credit.

**Understand the effect of debits and credits on accounts (LO3–4)**

**JE3–2** Below are several external transactions for Hokies Company.

| | Account Debited | Account Credited |
|---|---|---|
| *Example: Purchase equipment in exchange for cash.* | *Equipment* | *Cash* |
| 1. Pay a cash dividend. | _____ | _____ |
| 2. Pay rent in advance for the next three months. | _____ | _____ |
| 3. Provide services to customers on account. | _____ | _____ |
| 4. Purchase office supplies on account. | _____ | _____ |
| 5. Pay salaries for the current month. | _____ | _____ |
| 6. Issue common stock in exchange for cash. | _____ | _____ |
| 7. Collect cash from customers for services provided in (3) above. | _____ | _____ |
| 8. Borrow cash from the bank and sign a note. | _____ | _____ |
| 9. Pay for the current month's utilities. | _____ | _____ |
| 10. Pay for office supplies purchased in (4) above. | _____ | _____ |

Hokies uses the following accounts:

| | | |
|---|---|---|
| Accounts Payable | Equipment | Accounts Receivable |
| Cash | Supplies | Utilities Expense |
| Prepaid Rent | Rent Expense | Service Revenue |
| Common Stock | Notes Payable | Retained Earnings |
| Salaries Payable | Salaries Expense | Dividends |

*Required:*
Indicate which accounts should be debited and which should be credited.

**Record transactions (LO3–4)**
*See E3–5 for analyzing effects.*

**JE3–3** Terrapin Company engages in the following external transactions for November.
1. Purchase equipment in exchange for cash of $23,400.
2. Provide services to customers and receive cash of $6,800.
3. Pay the current month's rent of $1,300.
4. Purchase office supplies on account for $1,000.
5. Pay employee salaries of $2,100 for the current month.

*Required:*
Record the transactions. Terrapin uses the following accounts: Cash, Supplies, Equipment, Accounts Payable, Service Revenue, Rent Expense, and Salaries Expense.

**Identify transactions (LO3–4)**

**JE3–4** Below are recorded transactions of Yellow Jacket Corporation for August.

| | Debit | Credit |
|---|---|---|
| 1. Equipment ............................................. | 8,800 | |
|     Cash............................................. | | 8,800 |
| 2. Accounts Receivable................................. | 3,200 | |
|     Service Revenue ............................. | | 3,200 |
| 3. Salaries Expense .................................... | 1,900 | |
|     Cash............................................. | | 1,900 |
| 4. Cash ................................................... | 1,500 | |
|     Deferred Revenue............................ | | 1,500 |
| 5. Dividends.............................................. | 900 | |
|     Cash............................................. | | 900 |
| 6. Inventory ............................................. | 2,400 | |
|     Cash............................................. | | 2,400 |

| | | |
|---|---|---|
| 7. Accounts Receivable................................... | 3,600 | |
|     Sales Revenue ........................................ | | 3,600 |
|     Cost of Goods Sold .................................... | 2,000 | |
|       Inventory.............................................. | | 2,000 |
| 8. Cash............................................................. | 3,600 | |
|     Accounts Receivable............................. | | 3,600 |

**Required:**

Provide an explanation for each transaction.

**JE3–5** Sun Devil Hair Design has the following transactions during the month of February.

Record transactions (LO3–4). See E3–6 for analyzing effects.

| | |
|---|---|
| February 2 | Pay $700 for radio advertising for February. |
| February 7 | Purchase beauty inventory of $1,300 on account. |
| February 14 | Provide beauty services of $2,900 to customers and receive cash. |
| February 15 | Pay employee salaries for the current month of $900. |
| February 18 | Sell beauty inventory costing $1,100 to customers for $2,000 in cash. |
| February 25 | Provide beauty services of $1,000 to customers on account. |
| February 28 | Pay utility bill for the current month of $300. |

**Required:**

Record each transaction. Sun Devil uses the following accounts: Cash, Accounts Receivable, Inventory, Accounts Payable, Service Revenue, Sales Revenue, Cost of Goods Sold, Advertising Expense, Salaries Expense, and Utilities Expense.

**JE3–6** Bearcat Construction begins operations in March and has the following transactions.

Record transactions (LO3–4). See E3–7 for analyzing effects.

| | |
|---|---|
| March 1 | Issue common stock for $21,000. |
| March 5 | Obtain $9,000 loan from the bank by signing a note. |
| March 10 | Purchase construction equipment for $25,000 cash. |
| March 15 | Purchase advertising for the current month for $1,100 cash. |
| March 22 | Provide construction services for $18,000 on account. |
| March 27 | Receive $13,000 cash on account from March 22 services. |
| March 28 | Pay salaries for the current month of $6,000. |

**Required:**

Record each transaction. Bearcat uses the following accounts: Cash, Accounts Receivable, Equipment, Notes Payable, Common Stock, Service Revenue, Advertising Expense, and Salaries Expense.

**JE3–7** Below are several transactions for Scarlet Knight Corporation. A junior accountant, recently employed by the company, proposes to record the following transactions.

Correct recorded transactions (LO3–4)

| External Transaction | Accounts | Debit | Credit |
|---|---|---|---|
| 1. Owners invest $15,000 in the company and receive common stock. | Common Stock<br>   Cash | 15,000 | 15,000 |
| 2. Receive cash of $4,000 for services provided in the current period. | Cash<br>    Service Revenue | 4,000 | 4,000 |
| 3. Purchase office supplies on account, $300. | Supplies<br>   Cash | 300 | 300 |
| 4. Pay $600 for next month's rent. | Rent Expense<br>   Cash | 600 | 600 |
| 5. Purchase office equipment with cash of $2,200. | Cash<br>    Equipment | 2,200 | 2,200 |

*Required:*

Assess whether the junior accountant correctly proposes how to record each transaction. If incorrect, provide the correction.

Correct recorded transactions (LO3–4)

**JE3–8** Below are several transactions for Crimson Tide Corporation. A junior accountant, recently employed by the company, proposes to record the following transactions.

| External Transaction | Accounts | Debit | Credit |
|---|---|---|---|
| 1. Pay cash dividends of $800 to stockholders. | Cash | 800 | |
| | Dividends | | 800 |
| 2. Provide services on account for customers, $3,400. | Cash | 3,400 | |
| | Service Revenue | | 3,400 |
| 3. Pay a $500 utilities bill for the current period. | Utilities Expense | 500 | |
| | Cash | | 500 |
| 4. Receive cash of $400 from previously billed customers. | Cash | 400 | |
| | Service Revenue | | 400 |
| 5. Pay for supplies previously purchased on account, $1,200. | Supplies Expense | 1,200 | |
| | Cash | | 1,200 |

*Required:*

Assess whether the junior accountant correctly proposes how to record each transaction. If incorrect, provide the correction.

Post transactions to Cash T-account (LO3–5)

**JE3–9** Consider the following transactions.
1. Receive cash from customers, $15,000.
2. Pay cash for employee salaries, $9,000.
3. Pay cash for rent, $3,000.
4. Receive cash from sale of equipment, $8,000.
5. Pay cash for utilities, $1,000.
6. Receive cash from a bank loan, $4,000.
7. Pay cash for advertising, $7,000.
8. Purchase supplies on account, $3,000.

*Required:*

Post transactions to the Cash T-account and calculate the ending balance. The beginning balance in the Cash T-account is $5,000.

Post transactions to T-accounts (LO3–5)

**JE3–10** Consider the recorded transactions below.

| | Debit | Credit |
|---|---|---|
| 1. Accounts Receivable............................... | 8,400 | |
|     Service Revenue ............................ | | 8,400 |
| 2. Supplies ............................................. | 2,300 | |
|     Accounts Payable .......................... | | 2,300 |
| 3. Cash.................................................. | 10,200 | |
|     Accounts Receivable........................ | | 10,200 |
| 4. Advertising Expense............................ | 1,000 | |
|     Cash........................................... | | 1,000 |
| 5. Accounts Payable................................ | 3,700 | |
|     Cash........................................... | | 3,700 |
| 6. Cash ................................................. | 1,100 | |
|     Deferred Revenue........................... | | 1,100 |

**Required:**
Post each transaction to T-accounts and compute the ending balance of each account. The beginning balance of each account before the transactions is Cash, $3,400; Accounts Receivable, $4,200; Supplies, $400; Accounts Payable, $3,500; Deferred Revenue, $300. Service Revenue and Advertising Expense each have a beginning balance of zero.

**JE3–11** Below are T-accounts. The first row in each is the beginning balance, and the numbers in parentheses are transaction numbers.

Identify transactions from T-accounts (LO3–5)

| | Cash | | | | Accounts Receivable | | | | | Supplies | |
|---|---|---|---|---|---|---|---|---|---|---|---|
| | 8,000 | | | | 2,000 | | | | | 1,000 | |
| (1) | 20,000 | 14,000 | (5) | (2) | 5,000 | 4,000 | (3) | (4) | | 6,000 | |
| (3) | 4,000 | 7,000 | (6) | | | | | | | | |
| | 11,000 | | | | 3,000 | | | | | 7,000 | |

| | Accounts Payable | | | | Service Revenue | | | | Salaries Expense | |
|---|---|---|---|---|---|---|---|---|---|---|
| | | 2,000 | | | | 0 | | | 0 | |
| (6) | 7,000 | 6,000 | (4) | | | 20,000 | (1) | (5) | 14,000 | |
| | | | | | | 5,000 | (2) | | | |
| | | 1,000 | | | | 25,000 | | | 14,000 | |

**Required:**
Provide an explanation for each transaction.

**JE3–12** Below is the complete list of accounts of Sooner Company and the related balance at the end of April. All accounts have their normal debit or credit balance. Cash, $1,900; Prepaid Rent, $7,400; Inventory, $6,000; Accounts Payable $4,300; Common Stock, $40,000; Service Revenue, $25,400; Sales Revenue, $14,000; Salaries Expense, $8,200; Accounts Receivable, $6,100; Land, $60,000; Cost of Goods Sold, $10,000; Deferred Revenue, $2,300; Retained Earnings, $23,000; Supplies Expense, $9,400.

Prepare a trial balance (LO3–6)

**Required:**
Prepare a trial balance with the list of accounts in the following order: assets, liabilities, stockholders' equity, revenues, and expenses.

**JE3–13** Below is the complete list of accounts of Cobras Incorporated and the related balance at the end of March. All accounts have their normal debit or credit balance. Supplies, $1,000; Buildings, $55,000; Salaries Payable, $500; Common Stock, $35,000; Accounts Payable, $2,200; Utilities Expense, $3,700; Prepaid Insurance, $1,200; Service Revenue, $19,500; Accounts Receivable, $4,200; Cash, $3,500; Salaries Expense, $6,400; Retained Earnings, $17,800.

Prepare a trial balance (LO3–6)

**Required:**
Prepare a trial balance with the list of accounts in the following order: assets, liabilities, stockholders' equity, revenues, and expenses.

**JE3–14** Green Wave Company plans to own and operate a storage rental facility. For the first month of operations, the company has the following transactions.
1. January 1 Issue 10,000 shares of common stock in exchange for $42,000 in cash.
2. January 5 Purchase land for $24,000. A note payable is signed for the full amount.
3. January 9 Purchase storage container equipment for $9,000 cash.
4. January 12 Hire three employees for $3,000 per month.
5. January 18 Receive cash of $13,000 in rental fees for the current month.
6. January 23 Purchase office supplies for $3,000 on account.
7. January 31 Pay employees $9,000 for the first month's salaries.

Record transactions, post to T-accounts and prepare a trial balance (LO3–4, 3–5, 3–6)

**Required:**

1. Record each transaction. Green Wave uses the following accounts: Cash, Supplies, Land, Equipment, Common Stock, Accounts Payable, Notes Payable, Service Revenue, and Salaries Expense.
2. Post each transaction to T-accounts and compute the ending balance of each account. Since this is the first month of operations, all T-accounts have a beginning balance of zero.
3. After calculating the ending balance of each account, prepare a trial balance.

**Record transactions, post to T-accounts and prepare a trial balance (LO3–4, 3–5, 3–6)**

**JE3–15** Boilermaker Paint Company incurs the following transactions for September.
1. September 3 Paint houses in the current month for $20,000 on account.
2. September 8 Purchase painting equipment for $21,000 cash.
3. September 12 Purchase office supplies on account for $3,500.
4. September 15 Pay employee salaries of $4,200 for the current month.
5. September 19 Purchase advertising to appear in the current month for $1,000 cash.
6. September 22 Pay office rent of $5,400 for the current month.
7. September 26 Receive $15,000 from customers in (1) above.
8. September 30 Receive cash of $6,000 in advance from a customer who plans to have his house painted in the following month.

**Required:**

1. Record each transaction. Boilermaker uses the following accounts: Cash, Accounts Receivable, Supplies, Equipment, Accounts Payable, Deferred Revenue, Common Stock, Retained Earnings, Service Revenue, Salaries Expense, Advertising Expense, and Rent Expense.
2. Post each transaction to T-accounts and compute the ending balance of each account. At the beginning of September, the company had the following account balances: Cash, $46,100; Accounts Receivable, $1,700; Supplies, $500; Equipment, $7,400; Accounts Payable, $1,200; Common Stock, $25,000; Retained Earnings, $29,500. All other accounts had a beginning balance of zero.
3. After calculating the ending balance of each account, prepare a trial balance.

## Journal Entries—Problems

**Understand the effect of debits and credits on accounts (LO3–4)**

**JP3–1** Below is a list of typical accounts.

| Accounts | Type of Account | Normal Balance (Debit or Credit) |
|---|---|---|
| 1. Salaries Payable | | |
| 2. Common Stock | | |
| 3. Prepaid Rent | | |
| 4. Buildings | | |
| 5. Utilities Expense | | |
| 6. Equipment | | |
| 7. Rent Expense | | |
| 8. Notes Payable | | |
| 9. Salaries Expense | | |
| 10. Cost of Goods Sold | | |
| 11. Cash | | |
| 12. Service Revenue | | |

**Required:**

For each account, indicate (1) the type of account and (2) whether the normal account balance is a debit or credit. For the type of account, choose from asset, liability, stockholders' equity, dividend, revenue, or expense.

**JP3–2** Jake owns a lawn maintenance company, and Luke owns a machine repair shop. For the month of July, the following transactions occurred:

**Record transactions (LO3–4)**

| | |
|---|---|
| July 3 | Jake provides lawn services to Luke's repair shop on account, $500. |
| July 6 | One of Jake's mowers malfunctions. Luke provides repair services to Jake on account, $450. |
| July 9 | Luke pays $500 to Jake for lawn services provided on July 3. |
| July 14 | Luke borrows $600 from Jake by signing a note. |
| July 18 | Jake purchases advertising in a local newspaper for the remainder of July and pays cash, $110. |
| July 20 | Jake pays $450 to Luke for services provided on July 6. |
| July 27 | Luke performs repair services for other customers for cash, $800. |
| July 30 | Luke pays employee salaries for the month, $300. |
| July 31 | Luke pays $600 to Jake for money borrowed on July 14. |

*Required:*
Record the transactions for Jake's Lawn Maintenance Company.

**JP3–3** Refer to the transactions described in JP3–2. Keep in mind that Jake may not need to record all transactions.

**Analyze the effects of transactions on the accounting equation and record transactions (LO3–2, 3–4)**

|  | Jake's Lawn Maintenance Company | | | | Luke's Repair Shop | | | |
|---|---|---|---|---|---|---|---|---|
|  | Assets | = | Liabilities | + | Stockholders' Equity | Assets | = | Liabilities | + | Stockholders' Equity |
| July 3 | +$500 | = | $0 | + | +$500 | $0 | = | +$500 | + | −$500 |
| 6 | ___ | ___ | ___ | | ___ | ___ | ___ | ___ | | ___ |
| 9 | ___ | ___ | ___ | | ___ | ___ | ___ | ___ | | ___ |
| 14 | ___ | ___ | ___ | | ___ | ___ | ___ | ___ | | ___ |
| 18 | ___ | ___ | ___ | | ___ | ___ | ___ | ___ | | ___ |
| 20 | ___ | ___ | ___ | | ___ | ___ | ___ | ___ | | ___ |
| 27 | ___ | ___ | ___ | | ___ | ___ | ___ | ___ | | ___ |
| 30 | ___ | ___ | ___ | | ___ | ___ | ___ | ___ | | ___ |
| 31 | ___ | ___ | ___ | | ___ | ___ | ___ | ___ | | ___ |

*Required:*
1. Record each transaction for Luke's Repair Shop. Keep in mind that Luke may not need to record all transactions.
2. Using the format shown above, indicate the effects of each transaction on the accounting equation for each company.

**JP3–4** Below are the account balances of Bruins Company at the end of November.

**Prepare a trial balance transactions (LO3–6)**

| Accounts | Balances | Accounts | Balances |
|---|---|---|---|
| Cash | $40,000 | Common Stock | $50,000 |
| Accounts Receivable | 50,000 | Retained Earnings | 35,000 |
| Supplies | 1,100 | Dividends | 1,100 |
| Prepaid Rent | 3,000 | Service Revenue | 65,000 |
| Equipment | ? | Salaries Expense | 30,000 |
| Accounts Payable | 17,000 | Rent Expense | 12,000 |
| Salaries Payable | 5,000 | Interest Expense | 3,000 |
| Interest Payable | 3,000 | Supplies Expense | 7,000 |
| Deferred Revenue | 9,000 | Utilities Expense | 6,000 |
| Notes Payable | 30,000 | | |

*Required:*

Prepare a trial balance by placing amounts in the appropriate debit or credit column and determining the balance of the Equipment account.

Record transactions, post to T-accounts and prepare a trial balance
(LO3–4, 3–5, 3–6)

**JP3–5** Below are the transactions for Ute Sewing Shop for March, the first month of operations.

March 1    Issue common stock in exchange for cash of $3,000.
March 3    Purchase sewing equipment by signing a note with the local bank, $2,700.
March 5    Pay rent of $600 for March.
March 7    Martha, a customer, places an order for alterations to several dresses. Ute estimates that the alterations will cost Martha $800. Martha is not required to pay for the alterations until the work is complete.
March 12   Purchase sewing supplies for $130 on account. This material will be used to provide services to customers.
March 15   Ute delivers altered dresses to Martha and receives $800.
March 19   Ute agrees to alter 10 business suits for Bob, who has lost a significant amount of weight recently. Ute receives $700 from Bob and promises the suits to be completed by March 25.
March 25   Ute delivers 10 altered business suits to Bob.
March 30   Pay utilities of $95 for the current period.
March 31   Pay dividends of $150 to stockholders.

*Required:*

1. Record each transaction.
2. Post each transaction to the appropriate T-accounts.
3. Calculate the balance of each account at March 31.
4. Prepare a trial balance as of March 31.

Ute uses the following accounts: Cash, Supplies, Equipment, Accounts Payable, Deferred Revenue, Notes Payable, Common Stock, Dividends, Service Revenue, Rent Expense, and Utilities Expense.

Record transactions, post to T-accounts and prepare a trial balance
(LO3–4, 3–5, 3–6)

**JP3–6** Pirates Incorporated had the following balances at the beginning of September.

| PIRATES INCORPORATED Trial Balance September 1 | | |
| --- | --- | --- |
| **Accounts** | **Debits** | **Credits** |
| Cash | $ 6,500 | |
| Accounts Receivable | 2,500 | |
| Supplies | 7,600 | |
| Land | 11,200 | |
| Accounts Payable | | $7,500 |
| Notes Payable | | 3,000 |
| Common Stock | | 9,000 |
| Retained Earnings | | 8,300 |
| Total | $27,800 | $27,800 |

The following transactions occur in September.

September 1    Provide services to customers for cash, $4,700.
September 2    Purchase land with a long-term note for $6,400 from Crimson Company.
September 4    Receive an invoice for $500 from the local newspaper for an advertisement that appeared on September 2.
September 8    Provide services to customers on account for $6,000.
September 10   Purchase supplies on account for $1,100.
September 13   Pay $4,000 to Crimson Company for a long-term note.

| September 18 | Receive $5,000 from customers on account. |
| September 20 | Pay $900 for September's rent. |
| September 30 | Pay September's utility bill of $2,000. |
| September 30 | Pay employees $4,000 for salaries for the month of September. |
| September 30 | Pay a cash dividend of $1,100 to shareholders. |

***Required:***

1. Record each transaction.
2. Post each transaction to the appropriate T-accounts.
3. Calculate the balance of each account at September 30. (*Hint:* Be sure to include the balance at the beginning of September in each T-account.)
4. Prepare a trial balance as of September 30.

**JP3–7** RiverHawk Expeditions provides guided tours in scenic mountainous areas. After the first 11 months of operations in 2024, RiverHawk has the following account balances.

Record transactions, post to T-accounts and prepare a trial balance
**(LO3–4, 3–5, 3–6)**

### RIVERHAWK EXPEDITIONS
### Trial Balance
### November 30, 2024

| Accounts | Debits | Credits |
|---|---|---|
| Cash | $   9,200 | |
| Accounts Receivable | 4,500 | |
| Prepaid Insurance | 400 | |
| Equipment | 24,100 | |
| Land | 170,000 | |
| Accounts Payable | | $   3,300 |
| Notes Payable | | 50,000 |
| Common Stock | | 120,000 |
| Retained Earnings | | 14,100 |
| Dividends | 5,000 | |
| Service Revenue | | 75,000 |
| Advertising Expense | 11,000 | |
| Salaries Expense | 28,300 | |
| Rent Expense | 9,900 | |
| Totals | $262,400 | $262,400 |

The following transactions occur during December 2021:

| December 1 | Pay rent for mountain lodges for the month of December, $900. |
| December 5 | Provide guided tour to customers in Grand Teton National Park for cash, $2,800. |
| December 8 | Borrow from a local bank by signing a note payable, $10,000. The note is due in one year with a 6% interest rate. |
| December 12 | Receive cash from customers as payment for a guided tour that occurred on November 28, $3,500. |
| December 13 | Issue additional shares of common stock for cash, $20,000. |
| December 15 | Pay employee salaries for the first half of the month, $1,200. |
| December 17 | Purchase advertising on several local radio stations to be aired during the following two weeks, $1,000. |
| December 22 | Provide guided tour to customers in Yellowstone National Park on account, $3,200. |
| December 23 | One of the customers from the December 22 tour claims to have seen the legendary creature Bigfoot. The company believes this exciting news will create additional revenue of $20,000 next year. |
| December 26 | Purchase several pieces of hiking equipment to give customers a more enjoyable adventure, such as night-vision goggles, GPS, long-range binoculars, and video cameras, for cash, $28,500. |

| December 28 | Pay cash on accounts payable, $1,500. |
| December 31 | Pay dividends to stockholders, $2,000. |

### Required:

1. Record each transaction.
2. Post each transaction to the appropriate T-accounts.
3. Calculate the balance of each account at December 31, 2024. (*Hint:* Be sure to include the balance at the beginning of December in each T-account.)
4. Prepare a trial balance as of December 31, 2024.

## DATA ANALYTICS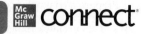

Visit Connect to view **Data Analytics** questions related to:

1. Applying Excel
2. Data Visualizations
3. Tableau Dashboard Activities
4. Applying Tableau

## ANSWERS TO THE SELF-STUDY QUESTIONS

1. c   2. d   3. c   4. c   5. d   6. a   7. c   8. c   9. a   10. d   11. b   12. c   13. a   14. c   15. d

# CHAPTER FOUR

# The Accounting Cycle: End of the Period

## Learning Objectives

## Self-Study Materials

## Feature Story

# Federal Express: Delivering Profits to Investors

Wouldn't it be great to put $1,000 into the stock market and watch your investment really grow? Which stock should you buy? Where should you buy it? There are thousands of stocks listed on stock exchanges in the United States and thousands of others listed throughout the world. With so many choices, how do you tell the winning stocks from the losing stocks? The single piece of information that best distinguishes them is *net income.*

To see an example of the power of net income in explaining movements in stock prices, consider the following information for **FedEx Corporation (FedEx)**. Over the 20-year period from 2001–2020, FedEx's net income increased in 14 of 20 years. For the other six years, net income decreased. What happened to FedEx's stock price in each of these years? In the years that net income increased, FedEx's stock price *rose* an average of 18.3%. In contrast, in

the years that net income decreased, FedEx's stock price *fell* an average of 8.6%. The goal is clear: Predict the direction of the change in net income, and you'll predict the change in stock prices.

Why does the change in net income provide a good indicator for the change in stock prices each year? Answer: Because it reliably measures the ability of a company to generate profits (or resources) for its investors, the stockholders.

An increase in net income typically signals the company has increased its ability to generate resources for its investors. As that ability increases, investors are willing to pay a higher price to own the stock. The opposite is true for activities that decrease the company's ability to generate resources. These activities will cause net income to decrease.

In this chapter, we'll discuss how a company reports its profits and available resources in financial statements. Important in this reporting process is making sure that amounts in these financial statements are updated at the end of the period to reflect the activities of a company.

## PART A

# THE MEASUREMENT PROCESS

In Chapter 3, we started the accounting cycle process by recording and posting transactions that occurred *during the period*. In this chapter, we'll complete the accounting cycle process at the *end of the period*. As summarized in Illustration 4–1, on the last day of the period we need to

1. Make **adjustments** to accounts (complete the measurement process).
2. Prepare **financial statements** (the reporting process).
3. **Close** temporary accounts (the closing process).

**■ ILLUSTRATION 4–1**

**The Accounting Cycle**

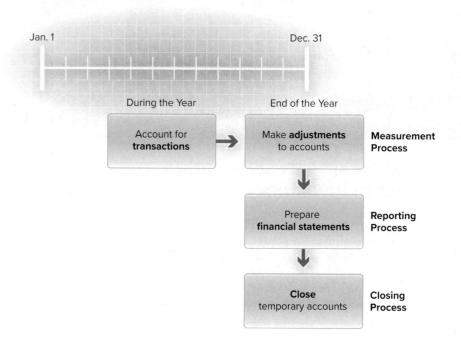

## Accrual-Basis Accounting

**■ LO4–1**

Understand when assets, liabilities, revenues, and expenses are reported.

Let's first look back at the measurement process we started in Chapter 3. In Chapter 3, we used accrual-basis accounting to record transactions. In simple terms, accrual-basis accounting means we report

**Assets**—at the time those resources are obtained.
**Liabilities**—at the time those obligations occur.
**Revenues**—at the time goods and services are provided to customers.
**Expenses**—at the time costs are used in running the company.

Under accrual-basis accounting, an attempt is made to report economic events as they occur. The intent is to provide accurate and timely information to financial statement users to make better decisions.

For example, when **FedEx** delivers a package, **American Eagle** sells a shirt, or **GEICO** provides insurance coverage, the company records revenue at that time. If a company sells goods or services to a customer in 2024, the company should report the revenue in its 2024 income statement. If the company sells goods or services to a customer in 2025, it should report the revenue in the 2025 income statement. This is the revenue recognition principle we discussed in Chapter 3.

Similarly, costs used in business operations to help generate revenues are reported as expenses in those periods. When FedEx delivers packages in 2024, the company will have costs of fuel for delivery trucks, salaries for delivery people, and supplies used in making deliveries. These costs will be reported as expenses in the 2024 income statement, along with the revenues they help to produce. Some costs (known as *period costs*) are more difficult to relate directly to a particular revenue activity, so we report those based on the period they occur (such as rent, advertising, or administrative salaries).

**KEY POINT**

Under accrual-basis accounting, economic events that affect assets, liabilities, revenues, and expenses are recorded as they occur.

## Accrual-Basis Compared with Cash-Basis Accounting

One way to better understand accrual-basis accounting is to compare it to an an alternative measurement method—cash-basis accounting. Under cash-basis accounting, we record transactions **only at the time** *cash* **is received or paid.** If cash is not received or paid, no transaction is recorded.

■ **LO4–2**
Distinguish between accrual-basis and cash-basis accounting.

### REVENUE-RELATED TRANSACTIONS

To demonstrate the timing difference between accrual-basis accounting versus cash-basis accounting, let's refer back to the transactions of Eagle Robotics. Illustration 4–2 lists two revenue-related transactions and summarizes revenue recognition under each method.

| | | Accrual Basis | | Cash Basis | |
|---|---|---|---|---|---|
| Transaction | Description | Good or Service Provided? | Revenue Recorded | Cash Received? | Revenue Recorded |
| (7) Dec. 17 | Sell 5 robots for: cash, $70,000, and on account, $280,000. | Yes ⟶ <br> Yes ⟶ | $70,000 <br> $280,000 | Yes ⟶ <br> **No** | $70,000 <br> $0 <br> Not recorded until cash received |
| (8) Dec. 23 | Receive cash in advance from customers for customization services to be performed in the future, $100,000. | **No** | $0 <br> Record as Deferred Revenue (liability) until services provided. | Yes ⟶ | $100,000 |

**ILLUSTRATION 4–2**

Accrual-Basis versus Cash-Basis for Revenue-Related Transactions

For accrual-basis accounting, we need to ask ourselves, "Was a good or service provided to customers at the time of the transaction?" The answer is "Yes" for transaction (7). Therefore, we recognize revenue on that date for the amount the company is entitled to receive, $350,000 (cash plus accounts receivable).

For transaction (8), no service has been provided to those customers, so no revenue is recognized at that time under accrual-basis accounting. Instead, we initially record Deferred Revenue (a liability account) for the cash received. Revenue is not recorded until those services are provided.

For cash-basis accounting, we simply ask ourselves, "Was *cash received* from customers?" The answer is "Yes" for part of transaction (7) and all of transaction (8). Under cash-basis accounting, we recognize revenue on those dates for the amount of cash received.

### EXPENSE-RELATED TRANSACTIONS

Illustration 4–3 lists several of the transactions of Eagle Robotics and summarizes accrual-basis accounting versus cash-basis accounting.

**ILLUSTRATION 4–3**

Accrual-Basis versus Cash-Basis for Expense-Related Transactions

| | | Accrual Basis | | Cash Basis | |
|---|---|---|---|---|---|
| Transaction | Description | Cost Used? | Expense Recorded | Cash Paid? | Expense Recorded |
| (4) Dec. 1 | Pay one year of rent in advance for retail and warehouse space, $180,000 ($15,000 per month). | No | $0<br>Record as Prepaid Rent (asset) until rent expires ($15,000/month) | Yes ⟶ $180,000 | |
| (5) Dec. 6 | Purchase supplies on account, $14,000. | No | $0<br>Record as Supplies (asset) until supplies used | No | $0<br>Not recorded until cash paid |
| (6) Dec. 12 | Purchase 15 robotics units as inventory, $750,000 ($50,000 per unit). | No | $0<br>Record as Inventory (asset) until inventory sold | Yes ⟶ $750,000 | |
| (7) Dec. 17 | Sell 5 robots with inventory cost of $250,000. | Yes ⟶ $250,000 | | No | $0<br>Expensed on Dec. 12 when cash paid |
| (9) Dec. 28 | Pay employee salaries of $28,000 for the month of December. | Yes ⟶ $28,000 | | Yes ⟶ $28,000 | |

For accrual-basis accounting, we need to ask ourselves, "Was a cost used at the time of the transaction?" The answer is "Yes" for transactions (7) and (9). On December 17, Eagle used 5 robot units from inventory to generate sales to customers. As a result, Eagle will record an expense equal to the cost of the 5 units sold. On December 28, employees are paid salaries for work they did in December. The cost of those salaries was used for activities of the company in December, so those costs should be expensed in December.

For transactions (4), (5), and (6), no costs were used at the time of the transaction, so no expense would be recorded under accrual-basis accounting. Instead, for transaction (4), we record Prepaid Rent (an asset). The cost of rent will be expensed as the rent expires. For transaction (5), we record Supplies (an asset). The cost of these supplies will be expensed once they are used. For transaction (6), we record Inventory (an asset). The cost of this inventory will be expensed once it is sold.

For cash-basis accounting, we simply ask ourselves, "Was *cash paid* for activities related to business operations?" The answer is "Yes" for transactions (4), (6), and (9). Under cash-basis accounting, we recognize expenses on those dates for the amount of cash paid. Nothing is recorded for transactions (5) and (7) because no cash was paid.

## TIMING DIFFERENCES

**Under both accrual-basis and cash-basis accounting, all revenues are eventually recorded for the same** *amount.* For example, the $100,000 received from customers in advance on December 23 eventually will be recognized as revenue under both accounting methods because the services will be provided at some point (accrual-basis), and cash has been received (cash-basis).

Similarly, for expenses, the $180,000 of rent purchased on December 1 will be expensed fully in one year under both accounting methods because the rental space will have been used (accrual-basis), and cash has been paid (cash-basis). The $14,000 of supplies purchased on December 6 will be expensed fully once those supplies are used (accrual-basis) and cash has been paid (cash-basis). **The difference between accrual-basis accounting and cash-basis accounting is in the** *timing* **of when we record those revenues and expenses.**

**COMMON MISTAKE**

It's easy at first to think that revenue should be recorded only when cash is received. However, under accrual-basis accounting, we record revenues when goods and services are provided to customers, regardless of when cash is received from those customers. Similarly, you might think that expenses can be recorded only when cash is paid, but we record expenses when costs are presumed to have been used, regardless of when cash is paid.

**No Timing Differences.**    Sometimes cash flows occur *at the same time* as the related revenue and expense activity; there are no timing differences. For example, in transaction (9), Eagle paid salaries of $28,000 for work done by employees in December. There is no timing difference between expense recognition under accrual-basis and cash-basis accounting. The outflow of cash occurs in the same period as the cost used for providing services.

**Generally Accepted Accounting Principles.**    Cash-basis accounting may seem appealing because it is essentially how we think about the inflow and outflow of cash from our bank accounts. However, **cash-basis accounting is not part of generally accepted accounting principles (GAAP).** All major companies use accrual-basis accounting to properly record revenues when goods and services are provided and to properly record expenses in the period those costs have been used in company operations. Accrual-basis accounting is focused on the *timing* of transactions and events in the accounting cycle.

Cash-basis accounting is not part of generally accepted accounting principles (GAAP).

**KEY POINT**

The difference between accrual-basis accounting and cash-basis accounting is *timing.* Under accrual-basis accounting, we record revenues when we provide goods and services to customers, and we record expenses when costs are used in company operations. Under cash-basis accounting, we record revenues when we receive cash, and we record expenses when we pay cash. Cash-basis accounting is not allowed for financial reporting purposes for most major companies.

Cavalier Company experienced the following set of events:

**Let's Review**

| | |
|---|---|
| May | *Receives cash* from customers for services to be provided in June. |
| June | *Provides services* to customers who prepaid in May. |
| May | *Pays cash* for supplies but does not use them. |
| June | *Uses supplies* purchased in May. |

*Required:*

1. Indicate in which month Cavalier records revenues under
   a. Accrual-basis accounting.
   b. Cash-basis accounting.
2. Indicate in which month Cavalier records expenses under
   a. Accrual-basis accounting.
   b. Cash-basis accounting.

*Solution:*

1a. June        1b. May        2a. June        2b. May

## Making Adjustments at the End of the Period

■ **LO4–3**
Adjust account balances at the end of the period.

As discussed earlier in this chapter, accrual-basis accounting creates timing differences between cash inflows and their related revenues and between cash outflows and their related expenses. **These timing differences are recorded as assets and liabilities under accrual-basis accounting.**

By the end of the year, we need to make sure all assets and liabilities are stated at their proper amounts. We'll use adjustments to update balances of assets and liabilities (and their related revenues and expenses). These adjustments are needed because transactions have occurred during the period but have not yet been recorded.

Let's first examine why adjustments to account balances are needed in the case of **cash flows occurring *before* the revenues and expenses are recognized.** This concept is demonstrated in Illustration 4–4A.

**ILLUSTRATION 4–4A**

Prepayments and Related Adjustments

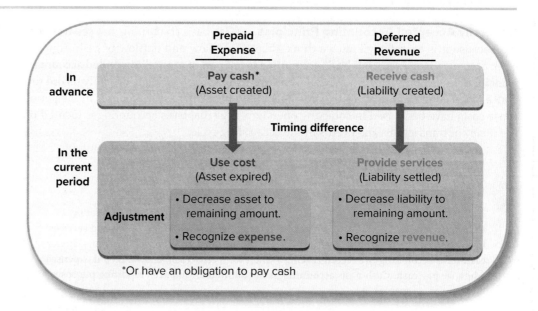

**Prepaid expenses** occur when a company pays cash to purchase an asset in advance of using that asset. For example, when cash is paid for rent in advance of the rental period, we record Prepaid Rent (an asset). That rent expires every day, but we don't need to decrease the balance of Prepaid Rent every day. Instead, we'll wait until the end of the reporting period to do a single adjustment to decrease the balance of Prepaid Rent to its remaining amount. We'll also recognize Rent Expense for the cost of rent expired during the period.

**Deferred revenues** occur when cash is received from customers in advance of the services to be provided. This creates an obligation for the company to provide services to the customer in the future. When those services are provided, we need an adjustment to decrease deferred revenue to its remaining amount and recognize service revenue.

Adjustments are also needed in the case of **cash flows occurring *after* the revenues and expenses are recognized.** This concept is demonstrated in Illustration 4–4B.

**Accrued expenses** occur when a company incurs costs, such as salaries, by the end of the current period but will not pay those salaries until the following period. An adjustment is needed in the current period to record salaries payable (a liability) and to recognize salaries expense for the amount to be paid.

**Accrued revenues** occur when a company provides goods and services and therefore generates the right to receive cash from a customer. An adjustment is needed in the current period to record the account receivable (an asset) and to recognize revenue, even though that cash won't be received until a future period.

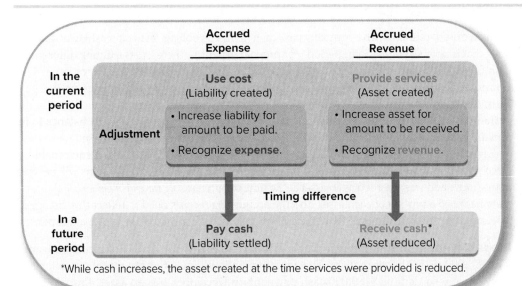

**ILLUSTRATION 4–4B**

Accruals and Related Adjustments

*While cash increases, the asset created at the time services were provided is reduced.

 **KEY POINT**

Making adjustments at the end of the period is a necessary part of accrual-basis accounting. They are used to record changes in assets and liabilities (and their related revenues and expenses) that have occurred during the period but have not yet been recorded by the end of the period.

In the sections to follow, we'll discuss each type of adjustment and work through several examples for Eagle Robotics. It will help if we first look back to the external transactions of Eagle Robotics from Chapter 3. For easy reference, we've restated these transactions in Illustration 4–5. These transactions have already been recorded in the month of December. In the next four sections, we'll prepare all adjustments on December 31 to account for other transactions that have occurred in the month of December but have not yet been recorded.

**ILLUSTRATION 4–5**

External Transactions of Eagle Robotics

| Transaction | Date | Description |
|---|---|---|
| (1) | Dec. 1 | Sell shares of common stock for $1,000,000 to obtain the funds necessary to start the business. |
| (2) | Dec. 1 | Borrow $500,000 from the local bank and sign a note promising to repay the full amount of the debt in three years. |
| (3) | Dec. 1 | Purchase equipment necessary for customizing robots, $240,000. |
| (4) | Dec. 1 | Pay one year of rent in advance for retail and warehouse space, $180,000 ($15,000 per month). |
| (5) | Dec. 6 | Purchase supplies on account, $14,000. |
| (6) | Dec. 12 | Purchase 15 robotics units as inventory, $750,000 ($50,000 per unit). |
| (7) | Dec. 17 | Sell 5 robots for cash, $70,000, and on account, $280,000. |
| (8) | Dec. 23 | Receive cash in advance from customers for customization services to be performed in the future, $100,000. |
| (9) | Dec. 28 | Pay employee salaries of $28,000 for the month of December. |
| (10) | Dec. 30 | Pay cash dividends of $14,000 to shareholders. |

## PREPAID EXPENSES

Prepaid expenses arise when a company pays cash (or has an obligation to pay cash) to acquire an asset that is not used until a later period. For prepaid expenses, there exists a timing difference—cash is paid now and, then later, the expense is recognized (refer back to Illustration 4–4A). Common examples include the purchase of buildings, equipment, or supplies or the payment of rent in advance. These payments are recorded as assets at the time of purchase. **In the period these assets are used, an adjustment is needed to (1) decrease the asset's balance to its remaining (unused) amount and (2) recognize an expense for the cost of asset used.**

Eagle Robotics had three prepaid expenses during December: It purchased equipment on December 1, rent on December 1, and supplies on December 6. Each of these items will be used in the future and was recorded as an asset at the time of purchase. *By the end of December,* the company has used a portion of each asset, and the accounting records need to reflect this change in assets and expenses. Let's now look at the adjustment needed for each of these prepaid expenses.

**Prepaid Rent.**   On December 1, Eagle Robotics purchased one year of rent in advance for $180,000 ($15,000 per month). The agreement allows Eagle to have rental space for one year, so we recorded the $180,000 cash payment on December 1 as an asset—Prepaid Rent. Eagle's ability to use the rented retail and warehouse space, however, will expire over time. By December 31, one month of rent has expired.

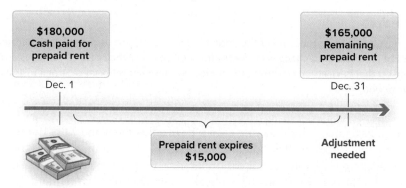

On December 31, we need to adjust the balance of Prepaid Rent by $15,000 for the rent expired during the month of December. After this adjustment, the Prepaid Rent account will now have a balance of $165,000 (= $180,000 − $15,000 adjustment), which equals the remaining amount of prepaid rent for the next 11 months. We also recognize Rent Expense for the cost of rent for the month.

|  | Prepaid Rent | Rent Expense |
|---|---|---|
| Balance—December 1 | $180,000 | $     0 |
| Adjustment for rent expired | (15,000) | 15,000 |
| Balance—December 31 | $165,000 | $15,000 |

---

**DEBITS & CREDITS**

An adjusting entry is needed to reduce the balance of Prepaid Rent to its remaining amount and to recognize an expense (Rent Expense) for the cost of rent for the month of December. The end-of-period adjusting entry for expiration of prepaid rent is below.

| | Debit | Credit |
|---|---|---|
| Rent Expense (+E, −SE) .................................................................... | 15,000 | |
| Prepaid Rent (−A) ............................................................. | | 15,000 |

Notice that this adjusting entry includes a $15,000 expense (+E), which reduces net income and stockholders' equity (−SE). The entry also reduces the balance in the asset account, Prepaid Rent (−A), by $15,000.

Rent Expense

| 0 | |
|---|---|
| Adj. 15,000 | |
| 15,000 | |

Prepaid Rent

| 180,000 | |
|---|---|
| | 15,000 Adj. |
| 165,000 | |

**Supplies.**   On December 6, Eagle purchased supplies for $14,000 on account. Those supplies were expected to be used at a later time and were recorded as an asset—Supplies. Assume that *at the end of December* a count of supplies reveals that only $4,000 of supplies remains. What happened to the other $10,000 of supplies? Apparently, this is the amount of supplies used throughout the month.

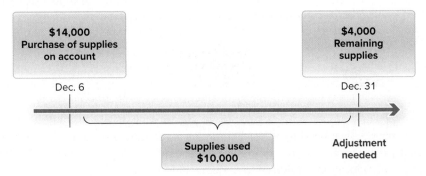

On December 31, we need to adjust the balance of Supplies by $10,000 to reflect the supplies used during the month of December. After this adjustment, the Supplies account will have a balance of $4,000 (= $14,000 − $10,000 adjustment), which equals the remaining amount of supplies. We also recognize Supplies Expense for the cost of supplies used for the month.

|  | Supplies | Supplies Expense |
|---|---|---|
| Balance—December 6 | $ 14,000 | $      0 |
| Adjustment for supplies used | (10,000) | 10,000 |
| Balance—December 31 | $   4,000 | $10,000 |

### DEBITS & CREDITS
An adjusting entry is needed to reduce the Supplies account to the remaining amount and to recognize the expense (Supplies Expense) for the cost of supplies used in December.

|  | Debit | Credit |
|---|---|---|
| Supplies Expense (+E, −SE) ............................................................... | 10,000 |  |
| Supplies (−A) .................................................................... |  | 10,000 |

   This adjusting entry includes a $10,000 expense, which reduces net income and stockholders' equity. The entry also reduces the balance in the asset account, Supplies, by $10,000.

Supplies Expense

| 0 |  |
|---|---|
| Adj. 10,000 |  |
| 10,000 |  |

Supplies

| 14,000 |  |
|---|---|
|  | 10,000 Adj. |
| 14,000 |  |

**Depreciable Assets.**   On December 1, Eagle purchased equipment for $240,000 cash. Let's assume that Eagle estimates the equipment will be used for the next five years (60 months), so the purchase was recorded as an asset—Equipment. As each month passes, the equipment will be used, and its benefits will expire. Therefore, by December 31, one month of the equipment's use has expired.

   Unlike prepayments for rent and supplies that typically expire within one year, equipment is an asset that typically expires in more than one year. We record the reduction in the cost of assets that have longer lives using a concept called *depreciation*. Depreciation is the process of allocating the cost of an asset, such as equipment, to expense over the asset's useful life. We discuss this in detail in Chapter 7; here we will cover just the basics.

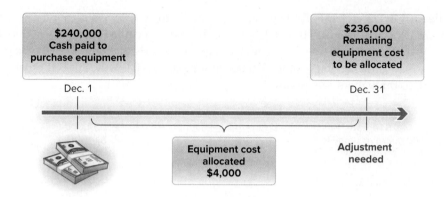

On December 31, we need to adjust Equipment to allocate a portion of its total cost to each period used. The cost of the equipment for one month's use is $4,000 (= $240,000 ÷ 60 months). This allocation is referred to as depreciation.

|  | Equipment, net | Depreciation Expense |
|---|---|---|
| Balance—December 1 | $240,000 | $    0 |
| Adjustment to allocate cost | (4,000) | 4,000 |
| Balance—December 31 | $236,000 | $4,000 |

### DEBITS & CREDITS

An adjusting entry is needed to reduce the equipment to the remaining amount to be used in the future and to recognize an expense for the cost of equipment allocated to expense in December.

|  | Debit | Credit |
|---|---|---|
| **Depreciation Expense (+E, −SE)** .................................................................... | **4,000** | |
| **Accumulated Depreciation (−A)** ......................................................... | | **4,000** |

This adjusting entry includes a $4,000 expense, which reduces net income and stockholders' equity. The entry also reduces assets by $4,000. Notice, however, that we didn't reduce Equipment directly by crediting the asset account itself. Instead, we reduce the asset indirectly by crediting an account called Accumulated Depreciation. The Accumulated Depreciation account is called a contra account. A **contra account** is an account with a balance opposite, or "contra," to that of its related accounts.

The normal balance in the Accumulated Depreciation contra asset account is a credit, which is opposite to the normal debit balance in an asset account. The reason we use a contra account is to keep the original balance of the asset intact while reducing its current balance indirectly. In the balance sheet, we report equipment at its current **book value,** which equals its original cost net of accumulated depreciation.

Depreciation Expense

| 0 | |
|---|---|
| Adj. 4,000 | |
| 4,000 | |

Equipment, net

| 240,000 | |
|---|---|
| | 4,000 Adj. |
| 236,000 | |

Illustration 4–6 shows how **FedEx** records its property and equipment at original cost and then subtracts accumulated depreciation. As you will see in Chapter 7, depreciation is an *estimate* based on expected useful life and is an attempt to *allocate the cost of the asset over its useful life.* Depreciation is a calculation internal to the company, and the cost of the asset less accumulated depreciation does not necessarily represent market value (what the asset could be sold for in the market).

| FedEx<br>Balance Sheet (partial)<br>($ in millions) | |
| --- | --- |
| *Property and Equipment, at Cost* | |
| Aircraft and related equipment | $24,518 |
| Package handling and ground support equipment | 11,382 |
| Information technology | 6,884 |
| Vehicles and trailers | 9,101 |
| Facilities and other | 13,139 |
| | 65,024 |
| Less accumulated depreciation | (31,416) |
| **Net property and equipment** | **$33,608** |

**ILLUSTRATION 4–6**

Reporting Depreciation of Property and Equipment for FedEx

## DEFERRED REVENUES

Deferred revenues arise when a company receives cash in advance from customers, but products and services won't be provided until a later period. This creates a timing difference between when the cash is received and when related revenue is recognized (refer back to Illustration 4–4A). Examples include receiving cash in advance from customers for subscriptions, memberships, and gift cards. When a company receives cash before providing services to customers, it *owes* the customer a service in return. This creates a liability. **In the period those services are provided, the liability is settled, and an adjustment is needed to (1) decrease the liability to its remaining amount owed and (2) recognize revenue.**

Eagle Robotics had deferred revenue tied to its transaction on December 23, in which Eagle received $100,000 from customers for future customization of robotics units to meet the customer's specific needs. At the time, these payments were received from customers, Eagle became obligated to provide that customization, so we recorded this transaction on December 23 as a liability—Deferred Revenue.

Assume that *by the end of December,* Eagle has provided $18,000 of customization services.

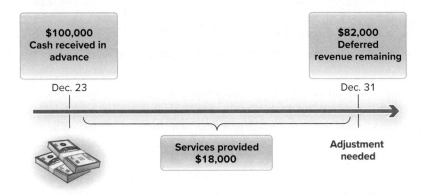

On December 31, we need to adjust the balance of Deferred Revenue by $18,000 for the services provided during December. After this adjustment, the Deferred Revenue account will now have a balance of $82,000 (= $100,000 − $18,000 adjustment), which equals the remaining amount of services owed to customers. We also recognize Service Revenue for these services provided during the month.

| | Deferred Revenue | Service Revenue |
|---|---|---|
| Balance—December 23 | $100,000 | $ 0 |
| Adjustment for services provided | (18,000) | 18,000 |
| Balance—December 31 | $ 82,000 | $18,000 |

**Deferred Revenue**

| Adj. 18,000 | 100,000 |
|---|---|
| | 82,000 |

**Service Revenue**

| | 0 |
|---|---|
| | 18,000 Adj. |
| | 18,000 |

### DEBITS & CREDITS

An adjusting entry is needed to account for the customization services provided during December to customers who paid in advance.

| | Debit | Credit |
|---|---|---|
| Deferred Revenue (−L) ........................................... | 18,000 | |
| Service Revenue (+R, +SE) ........................................... | | 18,000 |

This adjusting entry reduces the balance in the liability account, Deferred Revenue, by $18,000. The entry also includes an increase of $18,000 in Service Revenue, which increases net income and stockholders' equity.

Illustration 4–7 shows an example of deferred revenue for Lowe's.

**ILLUSTRATION 4–7**

Deferred Revenues and Other Current Liabilities for Lowe's

| LOWE'S Balance Sheet (partial) ($ in millions) | |
|---|---|
| **Current liabilities:** | |
| Short-term borrowings | $ 1,941 |
| Current maturities of long-term debt | 597 |
| Current operating lease liabilities | 501 |
| Accounts payable | 7,659 |
| Accrued compensation and employee benefits | 684 |
| **Deferred revenue** | **1,219** |
| Other current liabilities | 2,581 |
| **Total current liabilities** | **$15,182** |

In its annual report, Lowe's discusses that deferred revenues consist of "amounts received for which customers have not yet taken possession of merchandise or for which installation has not yet been completed." Deferred revenues also include "stored-value cards, which include gift cards and returned merchandise credits." The deferred liability will be settled as merchandise and services are provided to those customers.[1]

Now that we've discussed prepaid expenses and deferred revenues, let's look at the two other categories of adjustments—accrued expenses and accrued revenues. Accruals are the opposite of prepayments. **With accruals, the cash flow occurs *after* either the expense or**

---

[1]The Deferred Revenue account is sometimes referred to as the Unearned Revenue account. The use of the term "deferred revenue" is increasingly popular in practice and is more consistent with the FASB's 2014 update of the revenue recognition principle (ASU No. 2014-09), which eliminates the "earnings" process in defining revenue. The term "deferred revenue" is also helpful in emphasizing that revenue is initially deferred but will be recorded eventually when the service is provided.

**the revenue is recorded.** Walking through some examples using Eagle Robotics will demonstrate both types of accruals.

## ACCRUED EXPENSES

Accrued expenses occur when a company has used costs in the current period, but the company hasn't yet paid cash for those costs. This creates a timing differences between when an expense is recognized and when the related cash is paid (refer back to Illustration 4–4B). Common examples include the current cost of employee salaries, interest, and taxes that won't be paid until the following period. **Because the company has used these costs to operate the company in the current period and is obligated to pay them, an adjustment is needed to (1) recognize the cost as an expense and (2) record the liability to be paid.**

Eagle Robotics has three accrued expenses *by the end of December:* employee salaries, income taxes, and interest. How do we know these are accrued expenses? Each of these items represents costs of operating the company during the month of December, and the company is obligated to pay for these costs in the future. Let's now look at the adjustment needed for each of these accrued expenses.

**Accrued Salaries.**   Eagle's employees earn salaries of $1,000 per day. This means that for the first four weeks of December (28 days), Eagle's employees earned salaries of $28,000. On December 28, Eagle paid those salaries. These salaries were a cost used to operate the company during December, and therefore the company recorded the cash payment as an expense in December—Salaries Expense.

*By the end of December,* employees have earned $3,000 in additional salaries for the final three days of the month. But what if Eagle doesn't plan to pay the employees until the end of the week, January 4? Eagle still needs to record the obligation that exists as of December 31. Those salaries represent costs that have been used in December.

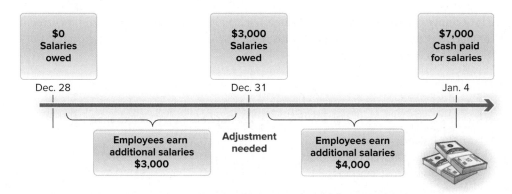

On December 31, we need to adjust Salaries Payable by $3,000 for the amount owed to employees. Later, in January, four more days of salaries expense ($4,000) will be recorded, and then workers will be paid for the entire week. We also recognize the cost of these additional salaries in December as Salaries Expense, adding to its current balance of $28,000.

|  | Salaries Payable | Salaries Expense |
|---|---|---|
| Balance—December 28 | $     0 | $28,000 |
| Adjustment for unpaid salaries | 3,000 | 3,000 |
| Balance—December 31 | $3,000 | $31,000 |

| Salaries Expense | |
|---|---|
| 28,000 | |
| Adj. 3,000 | |
| 31,000 | |

| Salaries Payable | |
|---|---|
| | 0 |
| | 3,000 Adj. |
| | 3,000 |

### DEBITS & CREDITS

An adjusting entry is needed to account for accrued salaries that remain unpaid by the end of December.

| | Debit | Credit |
|---|---|---|
| Salaries Expense (+E, −SE) ............................................................. | 3,000 | |
|     Salaries Payable (+L)............................................................ | | 3,000 |

This adjusting entry increases expenses, which decreases net income and stockholders' equity. The entry also increases liabilities for the amount incurred (but not paid for) in December.

**Accrued Taxes.**  Assume at the end of December, Eagle computes its corporate income tax bill to be $15,000. Eagle plans to pay the bill on April 15. Even though Eagle won't pay the cash until later, those taxes were incurred in December.

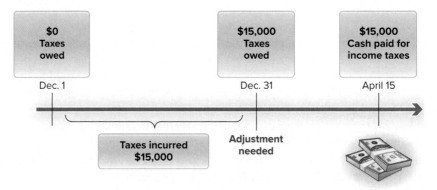

On December 31, we need to adjust Income Tax Payable by $15,000 for the taxes incurred in December. These taxes won't be paid until next year. We also recognize the cost of taxes in December as Income Tax Expense.

| | Income Tax Payable | Income Tax Expense |
|---|---|---|
| Balance—December 1 | $    0 | $    0 |
| Adjustment for unpaid taxes | 15,000 | 15,000 |
| Balance—December 31 | $15,000 | $15,000 |

| Income Tax Expense | |
|---|---|
| 0 | |
| Adj. 15,000 | |
| 15,000 | |

| Income Tax Payable | |
|---|---|
| | 0 |
| | 15,000 Adj. |
| | 15,000 |

### DEBITS & CREDITS

An adjusting entry is needed to account for accrued taxes that remain unpaid by the end of December.

| | Debit | Credit |
|---|---|---|
| Income Tax Expense (+E, −SE) ...................................................... | 15,000 | |
|     Income Tax Payable (+L)........................................................ | | 15,000 |

This adjusting entry increases expenses, which decreases net income and stockholders' equity. The entry also increases liabilities for the amount incurred (but not paid for) in December.

**Accrued Interest.**  In transaction (2) of Illustration 4–5, Eagle borrowed $500,000 from the bank to begin operations. Assume the bank charges Eagle annual interest of 12% (or 1% per month) on the borrowed amount. Interest is due in one year, but repayment of the

$500,000 borrowed is not due for three years. By the end of the first month, the loan has accrued interest of $5,000, calculated as follows:

| Amount of note payable | × | Annual interest rate | × | Fraction of the year | = | Interest |
|---|---|---|---|---|---|---|
| $500,000 | × | 12% | × | 1/12 | = | $5,000 |

Notice we multiplied by 1/12 to calculate the interest for one month. If we had calculated interest for a two-month period, we would have multiplied by 2/12; for three months, we would have multiplied by 3/12; and so on.

Although Eagle won't pay the interest until later, $5,000 is the cost of using the borrowed funds *by the end of December* and needs to be recorded.

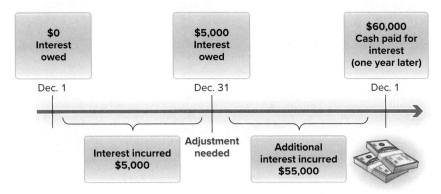

On December 31, we need to adjust Interest Payable by $5,000 for the interest incurred in December. Additional interest expense of $55,000 will be recorded over the next 11 months, and then the full year's interest will be paid. We also recognize the cost of interest in December as Interest Expense.

| | Interest Payable | Interest Expense |
|---|---|---|
| Balance—December 1 | $   0 | $   0 |
| Adjustment for unpaid interest | 5,000 | 5,000 |
| Balance—December 31 | $5,000 | $5,000 |

### DEBITS & CREDITS

An adjusting entry is needed to account for accrued interest that remains unpaid by the end of December.

| | Debit | Credit |
|---|---|---|
| **Interest Expense** (+E, −SE) ................................................................ | **5,000** | |
| **Interest Payable** (+L)................................................................ | | **5,000** |

This adjusting entry increases expenses, which decreases net income and stockholders' equity. The entry also increases liabilities for the amount incurred (but not paid for) in December.

Interest Expense

|  | 0 |  |
|---|---|---|
| Adj. | 5,000 | |
|  | 5,000 | |

Interest Payable

|  |  | 0 |  |
|---|---|---|---|
|  |  | 5,000 | Adj. |
|  |  | 5,000 | |

## ACCRUED REVENUES

Accrued revenues occur when a company provides products or services but hasn't yet received cash. This creates a timing difference between when revenue is recognized and when the related cash is received (refer back to Illustration 4–4B). Examples include selling products and services to customers on account or being owed interest on amounts lent to others. **Because the company has provided products and services in the current period and has the right to receive payment, an adjustment is needed to (1) record an asset for the amount expected to be received and (2) recognize revenue.**

**Accounts Receivable.** Eagle previously recorded Accounts Receivable of $280,000 for services provided to customers on account on December 17. Assume that *by the end of December,* Eagle has provided $7,000 of additional robotics customization to customers. The company has not yet collected cash or billed those customers. Eagle expects to receive cash from all customers in the future (January 10).

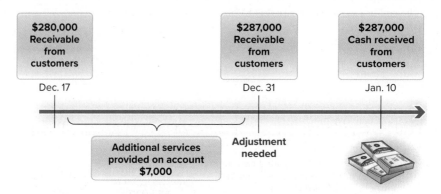

On December 31, we need to adjust Accounts Receivable by $7,000 for the additional amount to be received from customers. After this adjustment, the Accounts Receivable account will now have a balance of $287,000 (= $280,000 + $7,000 adjustment). We also recognize Services Revenue for these services provided in December.

|  | Accounts Receivable | Service Revenue |
| --- | --- | --- |
| Balance—December 17 | $280,000 | $18,000 |
| Adjustment for accrued revenue | 7,000 | 7,000 |
| Balance—December 31 | $287,000 | $25,000 |

Accounts Receivable

| 280,000 | |
| Adj. 7,000 | |
| 287,000 | |

Service Revenue

| | 18,000 |
| | 7,000  Adj. |
| | 25,000 |

**DEBITS & CREDITS**

An adjusting entry is needed to account for services provided but yet to be collected by the end of December.

| | Debit | Credit |
| --- | --- | --- |
| Accounts Receivable (+A) ................................................................... | **7,000** | |
| Service Revenue (+R, +SE) ................................................................... | | **7,000** |

This adjusting entry increases assets for an additional amount to be collected. The entry also increases revenues, which increases net income and stockholders' equity.

**KEY POINT**

End-of-period adjustments are needed when cash flows or obligations occur *before* the revenue- or expense-related activity (prepayment) or when cash flows occur *after* the revenue- or expense-related activity (accrual).

## NO ADJUSTMENT NECESSARY

Notice that we didn't make any adjustments associated with transaction (1) or (10) for Eagle Robotics in Illustration 4–5. Transaction (1) is the sale of common stock, and transaction (10) is the payment of dividends to common stockholders. **These are transactions with *owners* and therefore do not involve the recognition of revenues or expenses.**

Similarly, transaction (9) did not require adjustment because there is *no timing difference.* That is, when Eagle pays salaries to employees on December 28, the company records Salaries Expense at the same time it records cash paid, and no corresponding period-end adjustment is needed. The same would be true for revenue recorded at the same time when the cash is received.

**In summary, transactions in which we receive cash at the same time we record revenue or in which we pay cash at the same time we record an expense do not require adjustments.**

**KEY POINT**

Adjustments are *unnecessary* in two cases: (1) for transactions that do not involve the recognition of revenues or expenses and (2) for transactions that result in revenues or expenses being recorded at the same time as the cash flow.

---

**Let's Review**

Below are four scenarios for a local **Midas Muffler** shop for the month of December.

**Scenario 1:** On December 1, the balance of Supplies totals $400. On December 15, the shop purchases an additional $200 of maintenance supplies with cash. By the end of December, only $100 of maintenance supplies remain.

**Scenario 2:** On December 4, Midas receives $6,000 cash from a local moving company in an agreement to provide truck maintenance of $1,000 each month for the next six months, beginning in December.

**Scenario 3:** Mechanics have worked the final four days in December, earning $600, but have not yet been paid. Midas plans to pay its mechanics on January 2.

**Scenario 4:** Customers receiving $250 of maintenance services from Midas on December 29 have not been billed as of the end of the month. These customers will be billed on January 3 and are expected to pay the full amount owed on January 6.

*Required:*

For each of the scenarios, determine the accounts to be adjusted, the amount of the adjustment, and the ending balances. Assume no adjustments were previously made during the year.

*Solution:*

**Scenario 1:** Adjustment type: Prepaid Expense

| | Supplies | Supplies Expense |
|---|---|---|
| Balance—Before adjustment | $ 600 | $ 0 |
| Adjustment for supplies used | (500) | 500 |
| Balance—After adjustment | $ 100 | $500 |

**Scenario 2:** Adjustment type: Deferred Revenue

| | Deferred Revenue | Service Revenue |
|---|---|---|
| Balance—Before adjustment | $6,000 | $ 0 |
| Adjustment for services provided | (1,000) | 1,000 |
| Balance—After adjustment | $5,000 | $1,000 |

**Scenario 3:** Adjustment type: Accrued Expense

| | Salaries Payable | Salaries Expense |
|---|---|---|
| Balance—Before adjustment | $ 0 | $ 0 |
| Adjustment for unpaid salaries | 600 | 600 |
| Balance—After adjustment | $600 | $600 |

**Scenario 4:** Adjustment type: Accrued Revenue

| | Accounts Receivable | Service Revenue |
|---|---|---|
| Balance—Before adjustment | $ 0 | $1,000 |
| Adjustment for accrued revenue | 250 | 250 |
| Balance—After adjustment | $250 | $1,250 |

## Adjustments Summary

■ LO4–4
Calculate adjusted balances of all accounts.

As part of the adjustment process in the previous section, we have updated the balances of assets, liabilities, revenues, and expenses. We did so by making adjustments that update the balances of each account.

Let's verify the accounting equation remains in balance after calculating adjusted balances. Recall that Assets = Liabilities + Stockholders' Equity. We'll list assets in column (1) and liabilities and equities in column (2). Because Accumulated Depreciation is a contra (negative) asset, we can move that account to column (2) to show it as a positive amount. Similarly, both expenses and dividends are negative equity accounts, so we'll move those accounts to column (1) to show them as positive amounts. With these simple algebraic modifications to the expanded accounting equation, we see from looking at the total of both columns in Illustration 4–8 that the equation remains in balance.

---

### DEBITS & CREDITS

Illustration 4–8 is an example of an adjusted trial balance. An **adjusted trial balance** is a list of all accounts and their balances after we've updated account balances for adjusting entries. Column (1) includes all accounts with debit balances. Column (2) includes all accounts with credit balances. Note that total debits equal total credits.

**ILLUSTRATION 4–8**

Adjusted Account
Balances for Eagle
Robotics

| EAGLE ROBOTICS<br>Adjusted Account Balances<br>December 31, 2024 | | | |
|---|---|---|---|
| **Accounts** | **(1)** | **=** | **(2)** |
| Cash | $  458,000 | | |
| Accounts Receivable | 287,000 | | |
| Supplies | 4,000 | | |
| Prepaid Rent | 165,000 | | |
| Inventory | 500,000 | | |
| Equipment | 240,000 | | |
| Accumulated Depreciation | | | $      4,000 |
| Accounts Payable | | | 14,000 |
| Salaries Payable | | | 3,000 |
| Income Tax Payable | | | 15,000 |
| Interest Payable | | | 5,000 |
| Deferred Revenue | | | 82,000 |
| Notes Payable | | | 500,000 |
| Common Stock | | | 1,000,000 |
| Retained Earnings | | | – |
| Dividends | 14,000 | | |
| Sales Revenue | | | 350,000 |
| Service Revenue | | | 25,000 |
| Cost of Goods Sold | 250,000 | | |
| Salaries Expense | 31,000 | | |
| Rent Expense | 15,000 | | |
| Supplies Expense | 10,000 | | |
| Depreciation Expense | 4,000 | | |
| Income Tax Expense | 15,000 | | |
| Interest Expense | 5,000 | | |
| Totals | $1,998,000 | | $1,998,000 |

**KEY POINT**

After we have made adjustments to all accounts, the sum of assets, expenses and dividends
should equal the sum of liabilities, stockholders' equity, and revenue accounts.

# THE REPORTING PROCESS: PREPARE
# FINANCIAL STATEMENTS

**PART B**

Once the adjustments are complete, we prepare financial statements. Illustration 4–9
describes the relationship between the adjusted account balances and the financial statements. Notice the color coding of the accounts to indicate their relationships to the financial statements.

■ **LO4–5**
Prepare financial
statements using the
adjusted account balances.

Revenue and expense accounts are reported in the income statement. The difference
between total revenues and total expenses equals net income. All asset, liability, and stockholders' equity accounts are reported in the balance sheet. The balance sheet confirms the
equality of the basic accounting equation.

**ILLUSTRATION 4–9** Relationship between Adjusted Account Balances and Financial Statements

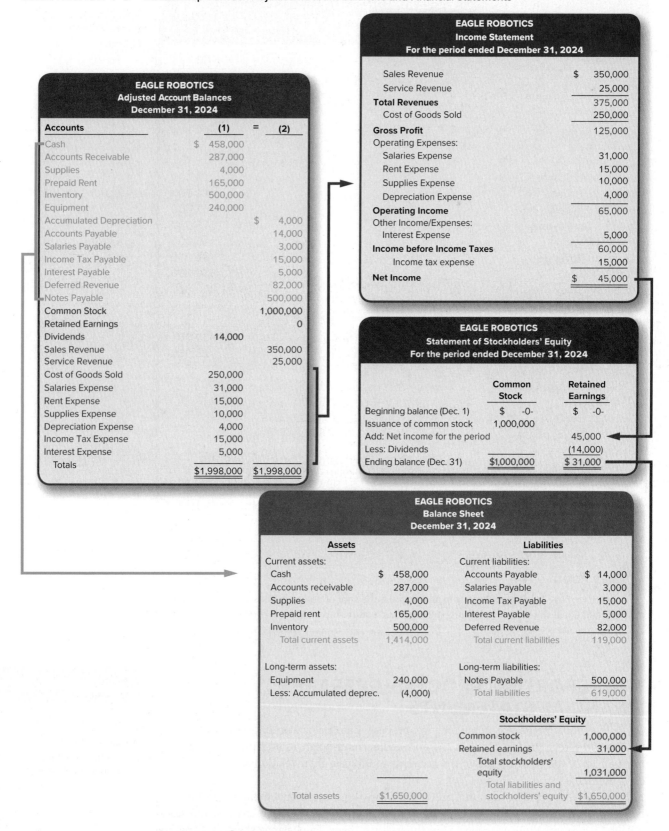

## Income Statement

Illustration 4–10 shows the income statement of Eagle Robotics for the period ended December 31, 2024. The income statement is presented in a multiple-step format, as discussed in Chapter 2.

ILLUSTRATION 4–10

Income Statement for Eagle Robotics

**EAGLE ROBOTICS**
**Income Statement**
**For the period ended December 31, 2024**

| | |
|---|---:|
| Sales revenue | $350,000 |
| Service revenue | 25,000 |
| **Total revenues** | 375,000 |
| Cost of goods sold | 250,000 |
| **Gross profit** | 125,000 |
| Operating expenses: | |
| Salaries expense | 31,000 |
| Rent expense | 15,000 |
| Supplies expense | 10,000 |
| Depreciation expense | 4,000 |
| **Operating income** | 65,000 |
| Other income/expenses: | |
| Interest expense | 5,000 |
| **Income before income taxes** | 60,000 |
| Income tax expense | 15,000 |
| **Net income** | $ 45,000 |

We'll highlight several items about Eagle's income statement:

1. The income statement reports revenues and expenses *over an interval of time.* In this example, Eagle started operations on December 1, 2024, so the revenues and expenses reported in the income statement are those occurring from December 1 through December 31, 2024.

2. **Total revenues** include revenues related to products and services provided to customers during the reporting period. Eagle reports total revenues of **$375,000** for the year, which is made up of revenue from the sale of robotics inventory ($350,000) as well as revenue from the customization of those robots ($25,000).

3. **Gross profit** represents the difference between total revenues and the cost of goods sold. Gross profit captures the profitability after subtracting inventory costs and is a key measure for a company's stakeholders. Eagle reports gross profit of **$125,000**.

4. **Operating income** represents the company's profits from normal operations. It's calculated as gross profit less operating expenses, such as expenses related to advertising, salaries, rent, utilities, supplies, and depreciation. These costs are normal operating expenses for most companies. Eagle reports operating income of **$65,000**.

5. **Income before income taxes** includes all revenues and expenses except income tax expense. Eagle reports income before income taxes of **$60,000**, which accounts for its operating income less $5,000 in interest expense related to its long-term notes payable.

6. **Net income** is computed simply as all revenues minus all expenses. Eagle pays a 25% tax rate, so its tax expense is $15,000. After taking the tax expense into account, Eagle reports net income of **$45,000**. This amount represents profit generated by the company for its owners and provides some indication of management's success in operating the company.

## Statement of Stockholders' Equity

The statement of stockholders' equity summarizes the changes in each stockholders' equity account over the reporting period. Illustration 4–11 shows the statement of stockholders' equity for Eagle Robotics.

**ILLUSTRATION 4–11**

Statement of Stockholders' Equity for Eagle Robotics

**EAGLE ROBOTICS**
**Statement of Stockholders' Equity**
**For the period ended December 31, 2024**

| | Common Stock | Retained Earnings | Total Stockholders' Equity |
|---|---|---|---|
| Beginning Balance (Dec. 1) | $          0 | $          0 | $          0 |
| Issuance of Common Stock | 1,000,000 | | 1,000,000 |
| Add: Net income for the period | | 45,000 | 45,000 |
| Less: Dividends | | (14,000) | (14,000) |
| Ending balance (Dec. 31) | **$1,000,000** | **$31,000** | **$1,031,000** |

From the income statement →

Total stockholders' equity increases from **$0** at the beginning of December to **$1,031,000** by the end of December. The increase occurs as a result of a **$1,000,000** investment by the owners (stockholders) when they bought common stock plus an increase of **$31,000** when the company generated a profit of **$45,000** for its stockholders and distributed $14,000 of dividends.

You've seen that retained earnings has three components: revenues, expenses, and dividends. For Eagle Robotics, the beginning balance of Retained Earnings equals $0 since this is the first month of operations. Ending Retained Earnings equals its beginning balance of $0 plus the effects of all revenue and expense transactions (net income of **$45,000**) less dividends of $14,000 paid to stockholders. Since dividends represent the payment of company resources (typically cash) to owners, they will have a negative effect on the stockholders' equity (retained earnings) of the company.

## Balance Sheet

The balance sheet you saw in Chapter 1 contained the key asset, liability, and stockholders' equity accounts, presented as a rather simple list. Here, we introduce a slightly more complex form, called the classified balance sheet. A classified balance sheet groups a company's asset and liability accounts into current and long-term categories. We'll use the numbers from the adjusted account balances to present the classified balance sheet for Eagle Robotics in Illustration 4–12.

There are five items to note about the classified balance sheet for Eagle Robotics.

1. **Total assets** are separated into current and long-term assets. Eagle reports $1,414,000 in current assets, including cash, accounts receivable, supplies, prepaid rent, and inventory. It reports $236,000 (= $240,000 − $4,000) in net long-term assets for its robotics customization equipment. The total of current and long-term assets is $1,650,000.

2. **Total liabilities** are separated into current and long-term liabilities. Eagle reports $119,000 in current liabilities, including accounts payable, salaries payable, income tax payable, interest payable, and deferred revenue. It reports $500,000 in long-term liabilities related to its notes payable of $500,000. The total of current and long-term liabilities is $619,000.

3. **Total stockholders' equity** includes common stock and retained earnings from the statement of stockholders' equity. Eagle reports $1,000,000 in common stock and $31,000 in retained earnings, for total stockholders' equity of **$1,031,000**.

4. Total assets must equal total liabilities plus stockholders' equity. This rule holds true for Eagle's balance sheet where both equal $1,650,000.

5. The balance sheet reports assets, liabilities, and stockholders' equity at a **point in time**.

**ILLUSTRATION 4–12**

Classified Balance
Sheet for Eagle Robotics

### EAGLE ROBOTICS
### Balance Sheet
### December 31, 2024

| Assets | | Liabilities | |
|---|---|---|---|
| Current assets: | | Current liabilities: | |
| Cash | $  458,000 | Accounts payable | $    14,000 |
| Accounts Receivable | 287,000 | Salaries payable | 3,000 |
| Supplies | 4,000 | Income Tax Payable | 15,000 |
| Prepaid Rent | 165,000 | Interest payable | 5,000 |
| Inventory | 500,000 | Deferred revenue | 82,000 |
| Total current assets | 1,414,000 | Total current liabilities | 119,000 |
| | | | |
| Long-term assets: | | Long-term liabilities: | |
| Equipment | 240,000 | Notes payable | 500,000 |
| Less: Accumulated deprec. | (4,000) | Total liabilities | 619,000 |
| | | | |
| | | Stockholders' Equity | |
| | | Common stock | 1,000,000 |
| | | Retained earnings | 31,000 |
| | | Total stockholders' equity | 1,031,000 |
| | | Total liabilities and stockholders' equity | $1,650,000 |
| Total assets | $1,650,000 | | |

← From the statement of stockholders' equity

**KEY POINT**

We prepare the income statement, statement of stockholders' equity, and balance sheet after adjusting all appropriate accounts. The income statement provides a measure of net income (profitability), calculated as revenues minus expenses. The balance sheet demonstrates that assets equal liabilities plus stockholders' equity (the basic accounting equation).

# Statement of Cash Flows

The final financial statement we need to prepare is the statement of cash flows. As discussed in previous chapters, the statement of cash flows reports all cash receipts and cash payments, separated into a company's operating, investing, and financing activities. Here's the statement of cash flows for Eagle Robotics in Illustration 4–13.

There are several items to note regarding Eagle's statement of cash flows.

1. Eagle shows *negative* net operating cash flows of $788,000. The fact that these cash flows are negative (in parentheses) implies that, on net, there were cash *out*flows. Some of the activities were cash inflows from sales to customers, but the majority were cash outflows for operating activities, such as purchasing inventory, paying salaries, paying interest, and paying taxes. Negative operating cash flows are common for a start-up like Eagle.

2. Eagle also shows *negative* net investing cash flows of $240,000. Investing cash flows relate to the acquisition and sale of long-lived assets and investments. In this case, Eagle's investing cash outflow relates to its purchase of equipment. Again, negative investing cash flows are common for a start-up like Eagle.

ILLUSTRATION 4–13
Statement of Cash
Flows for Eagle Robotics

**EAGLE ROBOTICS**
**Statement of Cash Flows**
**For the month ended December 31, 2024**

| | | |
|---|---:|---:|
| Net income | | $    45,000 |
| *Adjustments for noncash items:* | | |
| Depreciation expense | $    4,000 | |
| *Adjustments in operating assets and liabilities* | | |
| Increase in operating assets | (956,000) | |
| Increase in operating liabilities | 119,000 | |
| **Net cash flows from operating activities** | | **(788,000)** |
| Cash flows from investing activities | | |
| Purchase of equipment | (240,000) | |
| **Net cash flows from investing activities** | | **(240,000)** |
| Cash flows from financing activities | | |
| Issuance of common stock | 1,000,000 | |
| Issuance of long-term note | 500,000 | |
| Dividends paid to stockholders | (14,000) | |
| **Net cash flows from financing activities** | | **1,486,000** |
| Net increase in cash | | 458,000 |
| Cash balance, December 1 | | 0 |
| Cash balance, December 31 | | $    458,000 |

3. Eagle shows highly *positive* net cash flows from financing activities of $1,486,000. Financing cash flows generally represent cash flows from two major financing activities: issuing equity and borrowing.

4. Similar to the income statement, the statement of cash flows is a *change* statement, summarizing the transactions that affected the balance of cash during the period. It shows that the change in cash was $458,000.

5. Finally, the change in cash of $458,000 equals the sum of operating, investing and financing cash flows for the year.

We'll discuss the statement of cash flows in further detail in Chapter 11.

## PART C

### THE CLOSING PROCESS

■ LO4–6
Close temporary account balances.

All accounts that appear in the balance sheet, including Retained Earnings, are permanent accounts. This means we carry forward their balances from one period to the next. For example, if Cash (an asset) or Accounts Payable (a liability) has a balance of $1,000 at the end of the year, then that's also the balance at the beginning of next year. However, that's not the case with temporary accounts—revenues, expenses, and dividends. For these accounts, we transfer each balance at the end of the year to one account—Retained Earnings—and then all revenue, expense, and dividend accounts start with a $0 balance at the beginning of next year. We accomplish the transfer of balances from temporary accounts to Retained Earnings by closing all revenue, expense, and dividend accounts.

### Closing Accounts

**To close accounts, we transfer the balances of all temporary accounts (revenues, expenses, and dividends) to the balance of the Retained Earnings account.** Revenues increase the equity of a company, so transferring those balances will increase the balance of Retained

Earnings. In contrast, expenses and dividends decrease the equity of a company, so transferring those balances will decrease the balance of Retained Earnings. To demonstrate this closing process, refer back to the revenues and expenses of Eagle Robotics in Illustration 4–10 and to dividends in Illustration 4–11.

First, we transfer the balances of revenue accounts into Retained Earnings. Sales Revenue had a balance of $350,000, and Service Revenue had a balance of $25,000 (see Illustration 4–10). We'll reduce these balances to $0 and increase the balance of Retained Earnings by $375,000 (= $350,000 + $25,000).

| Closing Revenues | Sales Revenue | Service Revenue | Retained Earnings |
|---|---|---|---|
| Balance—Before closing | $350,000 | $ 25,000 | $ 0 |
| Amount closed to Retained Earnings | (350,000) | (25,000) → | 375,000 |
| Balance—After closing | $ 0 | $ 0 | $375,000 |

Second, we transfer the balances of expense accounts into Retained Earnings. Eagle reported several expenses (see Illustration 4–10). We'll reduce each of these balances to $0 and decrease the balance of Retained Earnings by $330,000, which equals the sum of all closed-out expenses.

| Closing Expenses | Cost of Goods Sold | Salaries Expense | Rent Expense | Supplies Expense | Depreciation Expense | Interest Expense | Income Tax Expense | Retained Earnings |
|---|---|---|---|---|---|---|---|---|
| Balance—Before closing | $250,000 | $31,000 | $15,000 | $10,000 | $4,000 | $5,000 | $15,000 | (from above) $375,000 |
| Amount closed to Retained Earnings | (250,000) | (31,000) | (15,000) | (10,000) | (4,000) | (5,000) | (15,000) → | (330,000) |
| Balance—After closing | $ 0 | $ 0 | $ 0 | $ 0 | $ 0 | $ 0 | $ 0 | $ 45,000 |

Finally, we transfer the balance of Dividends into Retained Earnings. Eagle had $14,000 in dividends (see Illustration 4–11). We'll reduce the Dividends account to $0 and decrease the balance of Retained Earnings by $14,000.

| Closing Dividends | Dividends | Retained Earnings |
|---|---|---|
| Balance—Before closing | $ 14,000 | (from above) $ 45,000 |
| Amount closed to Retained Earnings | (14,000) → | (14,000) |
| Balance—After closing | $ 0 | $ 31,000 |

The ending balance of Retained Earnings on December 31, 2024, will be its beginning balance in the following period beginning January 1, 2025. Then we'll close revenues, expenses, and dividends in that period to Retained Earnings, and this cycle will continue each period.

## DEBITS & CREDITS

We transfer the balances of all revenue and expense accounts, and the dividend account, to the balance of the Retained Earnings account with **closing entries**.

| December 31 | Debit | Credit |
|---|---|---|
| **(a) Sales Revenue** ............................................................................ | 350,000 | |
| **Service Revenue** ...................................................................... | 25,000 | |
| **Retained Earnings** ............................................................. | | 375,000 |
| *(Close revenues to retained earnings)* | | |
| **(b) Retained Earnings** ....................................................................... | 330,000 | |
| **Cost of Goods Sold** ................................................................. | | 250,000 |
| **Salaries Expense** ...................................................................... | | 31,000 |
| **Rent Expense** ............................................................................ | | 15,000 |
| **Supplies Expense** .................................................................... | | 10,000 |
| **Depreciation Expense** ............................................................. | | 4,000 |
| **Interest Expense** ...................................................................... | | 5,000 |
| **Income Tax Expense** ................................................................ | | 15,000 |
| *(Close expenses to retained earnings)* | | |
| **(c) Retained Earnings** ....................................................................... | 14,000 | |
| **Dividends** ................................................................................. | | 14,000 |
| *(Close dividends to retained earnings)* | | |

| Retained Earnings | |
|---|---|
| | 0 |
| | 375,000 |
| 330,000 | |
| 14,000 | |
| | 31,000 |

- **Revenues**—All revenue accounts have credit balances. To transfer these balances to the Retained Earnings account, we debit each of these revenue accounts for its balance and credit Retained Earnings for the total.
- **Expenses**—All expense accounts have debit balances. To transfer these balances to the Retained Earnings account, we credit each of these accounts for its balance and debit Retained Earnings for the total.
- **Dividends**—The Dividends account has a debit balance. To transfer this balance to the Retained Earnings account, we credit Dividends for its balance and debit Retained Earnings for the same amount.

**KEY POINT**

The closing process serves two purposes: (1) to transfer the balances of temporary accounts (revenues, expenses, and dividends) to the Retained Earnings account, and (2) to reduce the balances of these temporary accounts to zero to prepare them for measuring activity in the next period.

The closing process does *not affect the balances of permanent accounts* (assets, liabilities, and permanent stockholders' equity accounts) *other than retained earnings*. Permanent accounts carry a cumulative balance throughout the life of the company.

## Account Balances after Closing

■ **LO4–7**
Calculate closed balances of all accounts.

After the closing process has been completed, the **$31,000** balance of Retained Earnings now equals the amount shown in the balance sheet. In addition, the ending balances of all revenue, expense, and dividend accounts are now $0 and ready to begin the next period.

Illustration 4–14 shows that the accounting equation remains in balance after all accounts are closed. Column (1) lists the asset accounts, and column (2) lists the liabilities and stockholders' equity accounts. Because Accumulated Depreciation is a contra (negative) asset, we

**ILLUSTRATION 4–14**

Account Balances after Closing for Eagle Robotics

| EAGLE ROBOTICS<br>Account Balances after Closing<br>December 31, 2024 | | | |
|---|---|---|---|
| **Accounts** | **(1)** | **=** | **(2)** |
| Cash | $ 458,000 | | |
| Accounts Receivable | 287,000 | | |
| Supplies | 4,000 | | |
| Prepaid Rent | 165,000 | | |
| Inventory | 500,000 | | |
| Equipment | 240,000 | | |
| Accumulated Depreciation | | | $ 4,000 |
| Accounts Payable | | | 14,000 |
| Salaries Payable | | | 3,000 |
| Income Tax Payable | | | 15,000 |
| Interest Payable | | | 5,000 |
| Notes Payable | | | 500,000 |
| Deferred Revenue | | | 82,000 |
| Common Stock | | | 1,000,000 |
| Retained Earnings | | | 31,000 |
| Totals | $ 1,654,000 | | $1,654,000 |

can move that account to column (2) to show it as a positive amount. Notice that the illustration does not include any revenues, expenses, or dividends because these accounts all have $0 balances after the closing process.

### DEBITS & CREDITS

Illustration 4–14 is an example of a post-closing trial balance. A **post-closing trial balance** is a list of all accounts and their balances after we've updated account balances for closing entries. Column (1) includes all accounts with debit balances. Column (2) includes all accounts with credit balances. Note that total debits equal total credits.

 **KEY POINT**

After the closing process is completed, the balance of Retained Earnings equals the amount shown in the balance sheet. The balances of all revenue, expense, and dividend accounts are zero at that point.

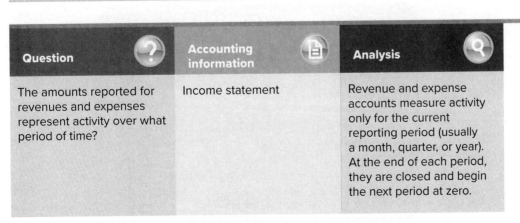

| Question | Accounting information | Analysis |
|---|---|---|
| The amounts reported for revenues and expenses represent activity over what period of time? | Income statement | Revenue and expense accounts measure activity only for the current reporting period (usually a month, quarter, or year). At the end of each period, they are closed and begin the next period at zero. |

**Manager Analysis**

**Let's Review**

Below are the adjusted account balances of Beckham Robotics for December 31, 2024.

**BECKHAM ROBOTICS**
**Adjusted Account Balances**
**December 31, 2024**

| Accounts | (1) | = | (2) |
|---|---|---|---|
| Cash | $ 2,600 | | |
| Supplies | 3,900 | | |
| Accounts Payable | | | $ 1,000 |
| Salaries Payable | | | 300 |
| Common Stock | | | 3,000 |
| Retained Earnings | | | 1,700 |
| Dividends | 200 | | |
| Service Revenue | | | 4,300 |
| Salaries Expense | 2,400 | | |
| Supplies Expense | 700 | | |
| Rent Expense | 500 | | |
| Totals | $10,300 | | $10,300 |

**Required:**

1. Transfer balances of temporary accounts to Retained Earnings and calculate its ending balance.
2. Calculate all account balances after closing.

**Solution:**

1. Transfer balances of temporary accounts to Retained Earnings.

| | Retained Earnings |
|---|---|
| Balance before closing | $1,700 |
| Service Revenue | 4,300 |
| Salaries Expense | (2,400) |
| Supplies Expense | (700) |
| Rent Expense | (500) |
| Dividends | (200) |
| Balance after closing | $2,200 |

2. Calculate all account balances after closing.

**BECKHAM ROBOTICS**
**Account Balances after Closing**
**December 31, 2024**

| Accounts | (1) | = | (2) |
|---|---|---|---|
| Cash | $2,600 | | |
| Supplies | 3,900 | | |
| Accounts Payable | | | $1,000 |
| Salaries Payable | | | 300 |
| Common Stock | | | 3,000 |
| Retained Earnings | | | 2,200 |
| Totals | $6,500 | | $6,500 |

## THE BOTTOM LINE

**LO4–1   Understand when assets, liabilities, revenues, and expenses are reported.**

Under accrual-basis accounting, economic events that affect assets, liabilities, revenues, and expenses are reported as they occur.

**LO4–2   Distinguish between accrual-basis and cash-basis accounting.**

The difference between accrual-basis accounting and cash-basis accounting is *timing*. Under accrual-basis accounting, we record revenues when we provide goods and services to customers, and we record expenses when costs are used in company operations. Under cash-basis accounting, we record revenues when we receive cash, and we record expenses when we pay cash. Cash-basis accounting is not allowed for financial reporting purposes for most major companies.

**LO4–3   Adjust account balances at the end of the period.**

Making adjustments at the end of the period is a necessary part of accrual-basis accounting. They are used to record changes in assets and liabilities (and their related revenues and expenses) that have occurred during the period but have not yet been recorded by the end of the period.

End-of-period adjustments are needed when cash flows or obligations occur *before* the revenue- or expense-related activity (prepayment) or when cash flows occur *after* the revenue- or expense-related activity (accrual).

Adjustments are *unnecessary* in two cases: (1) for transactions that do not involve the recognition of revenues or expenses and (2) for transactions that result in revenues or expenses being recorded at the same time as the cash flow.

**LO4–4   Calculate adjusted balances of all accounts.**

After we have made adjustments to all accounts, the sum of assets, expenses and dividends should equal the sum of liabilities, stockholders' equity, and revenue accounts.

**LO4–5   Prepare financial statements using the adjusted account balances.**

We prepare the income statement, statement of stockholders' equity, and balance sheet after adjusting all appropriate accounts. The income statement provides a measure of net income (profitability), calculated as revenues minus expenses. The balance sheet demonstrates that assets equal liabilities plus stockholders' equity (the basic accounting equation). The statement of cash flows measures activities involving cash receipts and cash payments, reflecting a company's operating, investing, and financing activities.

**LO4–6   Close temporary account balances.**

The closing process serves two purposes: (1) to transfer the balances of temporary accounts (revenues, expenses, and dividends) to the Retained Earnings account and (2) to reduce the balances of these temporary accounts to zero to prepare them for measuring activity in the next period.

**LO4–7   Calculate closed balances of all accounts.**

After the closing process is completed, the balance of Retained Earnings equals the amount shown in the balance sheet. The balances of all revenue, expense, and dividend accounts are zero at that point.

## GLOSSARY

**Accrual-basis accounting:** Record revenues when goods and services are provided to customers, and record expenses for the costs used to provide those goods and services to customers. **p. 156**

**Accrued expense:** Occur when a company has used costs in the current period, but the company hasn't yet paid cash for those costs. **p. 167**

**Accrued revenues:** Occur when a company provides products or services but hasn't yet received cash. **p. 169**

**Adjusted trial balance:** A list of all accounts and their balances after

we have updated account balances for adjusting entries. **p. 172**

**Adjustments:** Made at the end of the period used to update balances of revenues and expenses (and changes in their related assets and liabilities) that have occurred during the period but that we have not yet recorded. **p. 160**

**Adjusting entries:** the journal entries used to make adjustments. **p. 162**

**Book value:** An asset's original cost less accumulated depreciation. **p. 164**

**Cash-basis accounting:** Record revenues at the time cash is received and expenses at the time cash is paid. **p. 157**

**Classified balance sheet:** Groups a company's liability accounts into current and long-term categories. **p. 176**

**Closing entries:** Entries that transfer the balances of all temporary accounts (revenues, expenses, and dividends) to the balance of the Retained Earnings account. **p. 180**

**Contra account:** An account with a balance that is opposite, or "contra," to that of its related accounts. **p. 164**

**Deferred revenues:** Arise when a company receives cash in advance from customers, but goods and services won't be provided until a later period. **p. 165**

**Depreciation:** The process of allocating the cost of a long-term asset to expense over its useful life. **p. 163**

**Permanent accounts:** All accounts that appear in the balance sheet; account balances are carried forward from period to period. **p. 178**

**Post-closing trial balance:** A list of all accounts and their balances at a

particular date after we have updated account balances for closing entries. **p. 181**

**Prepaid expenses:** Arise when a company pays cash (or has an obligation to pay cash) to acquire an asset that is not used until a later period. **p. 162**

**Revenue recognition principle:** Record revenue in the period in which

we provide goods and services to customers. **p. 156**

**Temporary accounts:** All revenue, expense, and dividend accounts; account balances are maintained for a single period and then closed (or zeroed out) and transferred to the balance of the Retained Earnings account at the end of the period. **p. 178**

## SELF-STUDY QUESTIONS

1. On May 5, Johnson Plumbing receives a phone call from a customer needing a new water heater and schedules a service visit for May 7. On May 7, Johnson installs the new water heater. The customer pays for services on May 10. According to the revenue recognition principle, on which date should Johnson record service revenue? **(LO4–1)**
   a. May 5 (date of phone call).
   b. May 7 (date of service).
   c. May 10 (date of cash receipt).
   d. Evenly over the three dates.

2. On January 17, Papa's Pizza signs a contract with Bug Zappers for exterminating services related to a recent sighting of cockroaches in the restaurant. Papa's pays for the extermination service on January 29, and Bug Zappers sprays for bugs on February 7. On which date should Papa's Pizza record the extermination expense? **(LO4–1)**
   a. January 17 (date of the contract).
   b. January 29 (date of cash payment).
   c. February 7 (date of extermination service).
   d. Evenly over the three dates.

3. Refer to the information in Self-Study Question 1. Using cash-basis accounting, on which date should Johnson record service revenue? **(LO4–2)**
   a. May 5 (date of phone call).
   b. May 7 (date of service).
   c. May 10 (date of cash receipt).
   d. Evenly over the three dates.

4. Refer to the information in Self-Study Question 2. Using cash-basis accounting, on which date should Papa's Pizza record the extermination expense? **(LO4–2)**
   a. January 17 (date of the contract).
   b. January 29 (date of cash payment).
   c. February 7 (date of extermination service).
   d. Evenly over the three dates.

5. Which of the following is not a characteristic of making adjustments? **(LO4–3)**
   a. Reduce the balances of revenue, expense, and dividend accounts to zero.

   b. Allow for proper recognition of revenues and expenses.
   c. Are part of accrual-basis accounting.
   d. Are recorded at the end of the accounting period.

6. On November 1, 2024, a company receives cash of $6,000 from a customer for services to be provided evenly over the next six months. Deferred revenue is recorded at that time. Which of the following adjustments is needed on December 31, 2024? **(LO4–3)**
   a. Reduce Deferred Revenue for $2,000; Increase Cash for $2,000.
   b. Reduce Deferred Revenue for $2,000; Increase Service Revenue for $2,000.
   c. Reduce Deferred Revenue for $6,000; Increase Service Revenue for $6,000.
   d. Reduce Service Revenue for $2,000; Increase Deferred Revenue for $4,000.

7. A company owes employee salaries of $5,000 on December 31 for work completed in the current year, but the company doesn't plan to pay those salaries until the following year. What adjustment, if any, is needed on December 31? **(LO4–3)**
   a. Reduce Salaries Payable for $5,000; Reduce Salaries Expense for $5,000.
   b. Reduce Salaries Payable for $5,000; Reduce Cash for $5,000.
   c. Increase Salaries Expense for $5,000; Increase Salaries Payable for $5,000.
   d. No adjustment is needed.

8. Ambassador Hotels purchases one year of fire insurance coverage on December 1 for $24,000 ($2,000 per month), increasing Prepaid Insurance. On December 31, Ambassador would record the following year-end adjustment: **(LO4–3)**
   a. Increase Insurance Expense for $24,000; Reduce Prepaid Insurance for $24,000.
   b. Increase Insurance Expense for $2,000; Reduce Prepaid Insurance for $2,000.
   c. Increase Insurance Expense for $22,000; Reduce Prepaid Insurance for $22,000.
   d. No adjustment is needed.

9. After completing all adjustments for the fiscal period, **(LO4–4)**
   a. Revenues, expenses, and dividends are closed to zero.
   b. The financial statements are complete.
   c. The balances of prepayments and accruals are zero.
   d. We are ready to prepare financial statements.

10. Which of the following describes the information reported in the income statement? **(LO4–5)**
    a. Net income for the period is calculated as revenues minus expenses.
    b. Total assets equal total liabilities plus stockholders' equity.
    c. Change in stockholders' equity through changes in common stock and retained earnings.
    d. Net cash flows from operating, investing, and financing activities.

11. Which of the following describes the information reported in the statement of stockholders' equity? **(LO4–5)**
    a. Net income for the period is calculated as revenues minus expenses.
    b. Total assets equal total liabilities plus stockholders' equity.
    c. Change in stockholders' equity through changes in common stock and retained earnings.
    d. Net cash flows from operating, investing, and financing activities.

12. In a classified balance sheet, liabilities are separated into two categories based on **(LO4–5)**
    a. The amount of the obligation to be satisfied—large versus small.

b. To whom the obligation is owed—those inside versus those outside of the company.
c. The nature of the obligation—determinable amount versus estimated amount.
d. The length of time until the obligation is expected to be satisfied—within one year versus more than one year.

13. In a classified balance sheet, long-term assets used in the normal course of business are known as **(LO4–5)**
    a. Investments.
    b. Property, plant, and equipment.
    c. Other assets.
    d. Total assets.

14. Which of the following describes the purpose(s) of the closing process? **(LO4–6)**
    a. Adjust the balances of asset and liability accounts for unrecorded activity during the period.
    b. Transfer the balances of temporary accounts (revenues, expenses, and dividends) to Retained Earnings.
    c. Reduce the balances of the temporary accounts to zero to prepare them for measuring activity in the next period.
    d. Both b. and c.

15. Which of the following accounts is a temporary account closed to Retained Earnings? **(LO4–7)**
    a. Prepaid Rent.
    b. Accounts Payable.
    c. Salaries Expense.
    d. Retained Earnings.

*Note: For answers, see the last page of the chapter.*

## REAL WORLD PERSPECTIVES

### McDonald's Corporation (ticker: MCD)

EDGAR Case

**RWP4–1** Visit **www.sec.gov/edgar** and search for the **McDonald's** annual report (10-K) for the year ended December 31, 2019, using EDGAR (Electronic Data Gathering, Analysis, and Retrieval system). Search or scroll within the annual report to find the financial statements, typically found in Item 8 of the 10-K.

*Required:*

Determine the following from the company's financial statements:
1. Do the company's revenues exceed expenses? What is the amount of net income?
2. Did net income increase in the most recent year compared to the previous year?
3. Which assets are listed as current assets? Why are the other assets not listed as current assets?
4. Which liabilities are listed as current liabilities? Why are the other liabilities not listed as current liabilities?
5. By how much did retained earnings increase/decrease in the most recent year compared to the previous year?
6. What is the amount of dividends paid to common stockholders? This information can be found in the statement of shareholders' equity or the statement of cash flows.
7. Does the change in retained earnings (from requirement 4) equal net income (requirement 1) minus dividends (requirement 6)?

## BJ's Wholesale Club Holdings, Inc. (ticker: BJ)

**RWP4–2** Visit www.sec.gov/edgar and search for the **BJ's Wholesale** annual report (10-K) for the year ended February 1, 2020, using EDGAR (Electronic Data Gathering, Analysis, and Retrieval system). Search or scroll within the annual report to find the balance sheet, labeled "Consolidated Balance Sheets."

**_Required:_**

1. Find the amounts reported for accumulated depreciation for the period ended February 1, 2020, and February 2, 2019. Assuming no depreciable assets were sold during the year, determine the adjustment for BJ's depreciation for the year and compute the adjusted balances of the related accounts.
2. For simplicity, assume the entire amount reported for "Prepaid expenses and other current assets" represents the balance of the Supplies account. If the year-end balance of the Supplies account prior to any adjustment is $200,000 (in thousands), determine the adjustment that was made to Supplies (and Supplies Expense) at the end of the current year and compute the adjusted balances of the related accounts.
3. For simplicity, assume that 10% of the amount reported for "Accrued expenses and other current liabilities" represents the balance of the Salaries Payable account (rounded to the nearest dollar). Assuming all salaries from the previous year were paid in full and Salaries Expense was $600,000 prior to adjustment, determine the adjustment that was made to Salaries Payable (and Salaries Expense) at the end of the current year and compute the adjusted balances of the related accounts.

## Chipotle Mexican Grill, Inc (ticker: CMG)

**RWP3–3** Visit www.sec.gov/edgar and search for the **Chipotle** annual report (10-K) for the year ended December 31, 2019, using EDGAR (Electronic Data Gathering, Analysis, and Retrieval system). Locate its income statement sheet, labeled "Consolidated Statements of Income." Use this information to answer the questions below.

**_Required:_**

1. Close Revenue and Interest and Other Income to determine the increase (decrease) in Retained Earnings.
2. Close all expenses to determine the increase (decrease) in Retained Earnings. _Hint:_ There are _nine_ expense accounts that should be closed.

## Build-A-Bear Workshop, Inc (ticker: BBW)

**RWP4–4** Visit www.sec.gov/edgar and search for the **Build-A-Bear Workshop** annual report (10-K) for the year ended February 1, 2020, using EDGAR (Electronic Data Gathering, Analysis, and Retrieval system). Locate its balance sheet, labeled "Consolidated Balance Sheets." Use this information to answer the questions below.

**_Required:_**

1. Using the information from the financial statements, create a list of accounts and demonstrate that the accounting equation remains in balance after closing (sometimes referred to as a post-closing trial balance). In column (1), list all account balances on the left side of the accounting equation. In column (2), list all account balances on the right side of the accounting equation.
2. Here is a template to get you started:

<br>

**Build-A-Bear Workshop, Inc.**
**Account Balances after Closing**
**February 1, 2020**

| Accounts | (1) | (2) |
|---|---|---|
| Cash and cash equivalents | $26,726 | |
| Inventories, net | 53,381 | |

## American Eagle Outfitters, Inc.

Continuing Financial
Analysis Case

**RWP4–5** Financial information for **American Eagle** is presented in **Appendix A** at the end of the book.

*Required:*
1. For the most recent year, what amount does American Eagle report for current assets? What is the ratio of current assets to total assets?
2. For the most recent year, what amount does American Eagle report for current liabilities? What is the ratio of current liabilities to total liabilities?
3. What is the change in retained earnings reported in the balance sheet?
4. For the most recent year, what is the amount of net income reported in the income statement?

## The Buckle, Inc.

Continuing Financial
Analysis Case

**RWP4–6** Financial information for **Buckle** is presented in **Appendix B** at the end of the book.

*Required:*
1. For the most recent year, what amount does Buckle report for current assets? What is the ratio of current assets to total assets?
2. For the most recent year, what amount does Buckle report for current liabilities? What is the ratio of current liabilities to total liabilities?
3. For the most recent year, what is the change in retained earnings reported in the balance sheet?
4. For the most recent year, what is the amount of net income reported in the income statement?
5. Using your answers in 3 and 4 above, calculate the amount of dividends paid during the year. Verify your answer by looking at the retained earnings column in the statement of stockholders' equity.

## American Eagle Outfitters, Inc. vs. The Buckle, Inc.

Continuing Comparative
Analysis Case

**RWP4–7** Financial information for **American Eagle** is presented in **Appendix A** at the end of the book, and financial information for **Buckle** is presented in **Appendix B** at the end of the book.

*Required:*
1. Determine which company maintains a higher ratio of current assets to total assets. How might this be an advantage for the company?
2. Determine which company maintains a higher ratio of current liabilities to total liabilities. How might this be a disadvantage for the company?
3. The dividend payout ratio equals dividends paid during the year divided by net income. Determine which company has a higher dividend payout ratio. Why might this be the case?

## Ethics

Ethics Case

**RWP4–8** You have recently been hired as the assistant controller for Stanton Temperton Corporation, which rents building space in major metropolitan areas. Customers are required to pay six months of rent in advance. At the end of 2021, the company's president, Jim Temperton, notices net income has fallen compared to last year. In 2020, the company reported pretax profit of $330,000, but in 2021 the pretax profit is only $280,000. This concerns Jim for two reasons. First, his year-end bonus is tied directly to pretax profits. Second, shareholders may see a decline in profitability as a weakness in the company and begin to sell their stock. With the sell-off of stock, Jim's personal investment in the company's stock, as well as his company-operated retirement plan, will be in jeopardy of severe losses.

After close inspection of the financial statements, Jim notices the balance of the Deferred Revenue account is $120,000. This amount represents payments in advance from long-term customers ($80,000) and from relatively new customers ($40,000). Jim comes to you, the company's accountant, and suggests the company should recognize as revenue in 2021 the $80,000 received in advance from long-term customers. He offers the following explanation: "First, we have received these customers' cash by the end of 2021, so there is no question about their ability to pay. Second, we have a long-term history of fulfilling our obligation to these customers. We have always stood by our commitments to our customers and we always will. We earned that money when we got them to sign the six-month contract."

### *Required:*

1. Understand the reporting effect: What are the effects on pretax profits of reporting the $80,000 as service revenue?
2. Specify the options: Instead of reporting the $80,000 as revenue, how else might you report this amount?
3. Identify the impact: Are investors and creditors potentially affected by Jim's suggestion?
4. Make a decision: As a staff employee, should you follow Jim's suggestion?

**Continuing General Ledger Case**

## Great Adventures

**RWP4–9** (This is a continuation of the Great Adventures problem from earlier chapters.) You may refer to the opening story of Tony and Suzie and their decision to start Great Adventures in Chapter 1's RWP1–9. More of their story and the first set of transactions for the company in July are presented in RWP3–9 and repeated here.

| | |
|---|---|
| July 1 | Sell $10,000 of common stock to Suzie. |
| July 1 | Sell $10,000 of common stock to Tony. |
| July 1 | Purchase a one-year insurance policy for $4,800 ($400 per month) to cover injuries to participants during outdoor clinics. |
| July 2 | Pay legal fees of $1,500 associated with incorporation. |
| July 4 | Purchase office supplies of $1,800 on account. |
| July 7 | Pay $300 to a local newspaper for advertising of $300 to appear immediately for an upcoming mountain biking clinic to be held on July 15. Attendees will be charged $50 the day of the clinic. |
| July 8 | Purchase 10 mountain bikes, paying $12,000 cash. |
| July 15 | On the day of the clinic, Great Adventures receives cash of $2,000 from 40 bikers. Tony conducts the mountain biking clinic. |
| July 22 | Because of the success of the first mountain biking clinic, Tony holds another mountain biking clinic, and the company receives $2,300. |
| July 24 | Pay $700 to a local radio station for advertising to appear immediately. A kayaking clinic will be held on August 10, and attendees can pay $100 in advance or $150 on the day of the clinic. |
| July 30 | Great Adventures receives cash of $4,000 in advance from 40 kayakers for the upcoming kayak clinic. |

The following transactions occur over the remainder of 2024.

| | |
|---|---|
| Aug. 1 | Great Adventures obtains a $30,000 low-interest loan for the company from the city council, which has recently passed an initiative encouraging business development related to outdoor activities. The loan is due in three years, and 6% annual interest is due each year on July 31. |
| Aug. 4 | The company purchases 14 kayaks, paying $28,000 cash. |
| Aug. 10 | Twenty additional kayakers pay $3,000 ($150 each), in addition to the $4,000 that was paid in advance on July 30, on the day of the clinic. Tony conducts the first kayak clinic. |
| Aug. 17 | Tony conducts a second kayak clinic, and the company receives $10,500 in cash. |
| Aug. 24 | Office supplies of $1,800 purchased on July 4 are paid in full. |
| Sep. 1 | To provide better storage of mountain bikes and kayaks when not in use, the company rents a storage shed for one year, paying $2,400 ($200 per month) in advance. |
| Sep. 21 | Tony conducts a rock-climbing clinic. The company receives $13,200 cash. |
| Oct. 17 | Tony conducts an orienteering clinic. Participants practice how to understand a topographical map, read an altimeter, use a compass, and orient through heavily wooded areas. The company receives $17,900 cash. |

| Dec. 1 | Tony decides to hold the company's first adventure race on December 15. Four-person teams will race from checkpoint to checkpoint using a combination of mountain biking, kayaking, orienteering, trail running, and rock-climbing skills. The first team in each category to complete all checkpoints in order wins. The entry fee for each team is $500. |
|---|---|
| Dec. 5 | To help organize and promote the race, Tony hires his college roommate, Victor. Victor will be paid $50 in salary for each team that competes in the race. His salary will be paid after the race. |
| Dec. 8 | The company pays $1,200 to purchase a permit from a state park where the race will be held. The amount is recorded as a miscellaneous expense. |
| Dec. 12 | The company purchases racing supplies for $2,800 on account due in 30 days. Supplies include trophies for the top-finishing teams in each category, promotional shirts, snack foods and drinks for participants, and field markers to prepare the racecourse. |
| Dec. 15 | The company receives $20,000 cash from a total of forty teams, and the race is held. |
| Dec. 16 | The company pays Victor's salary of $2,000. |
| Dec. 31 | The company pays a dividend of $4,000 ($2,000 to Tony and $2,000 to Suzie). |
| Dec. 31 | Using his personal money, Tony purchases a diamond ring for $4,500. Tony surprises Suzie by proposing they get married. Suzie accepts and they get married! |

The following information relates to year-end adjusting entries as of December 31, 2024.

a. Depreciation of the mountain bikes purchased on July 8 and kayaks purchased on August 4 totals $8,000.
b. Six months of the one-year insurance policy purchased on July 1 has expired.
c. Four months of the one-year rental agreement purchased on September 1 has expired.
d. Of the $1,800 of office supplies purchased on July 4, $300 remains.
e. Interest expense on the $30,000 loan obtained from the city council on August 1 should be recorded.
f. Of the $2,800 of racing supplies purchased on December 12, $200 remains.
g. Suzie calculates that the company owes $14,000 in income taxes.

**Required:**
1. Record transactions from July 1 through December 31.
2. Record adjusting entries as of December 31, 2024.
3. Post transactions from July 1 through December 31 and adjusting entries on December 31 to T-accounts.
4. Prepare an adjusted trial balance as of December 31, 2024.
5. For the period July 1 to December 31, 2024, prepare an income statement and statement of stockholders' equity. Prepare a classified balance sheet as of December 31, 2024.
6. Record closing entries as of December 31, 2024
7. Post closing entries to T-accounts.
8. Prepare a post-closing trial balance as of December 31, 2024.

## BRIEF EXERCISES

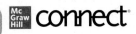

**BE4–1** Below are transactions for Lobos, Inc., during the month of December. Determine whether each transaction increases, decreases, or has no effect on assets, liabilities, and revenues in December.

a. Receive $1,200 cash from customers for services to be provided next month.
b. Perform $900 of services during the month and bill customers. Customers are expected to pay next month.
c. Perform $2,300 of services during the month and receive full cash payment from customers at the time of service.

Determine effects of revenue-related transactions (LO4–1)

Determine effects
of expense-related
transactions (LO4–1)

**BE4–2** Below are transactions for Bronco Corporation during the month of June. Determine whether each transaction increases, decreases, or has no effect on assets, liabilities, and expenses in June.

a. Pay $600 cash to employees for work performed during June.

b. Receive a $200 telephone bill for the month of June, but Bronco does not plan to pay the bill until early next month.

c. Pay $500 on account for supplies purchased last month. All supplies were used last month.

Calculate net
income (LO4–1)

**BE4–3** Hoya Corporation reports the following amounts: Assets = $18,000; Liabilities = $3,000; Stockholders' equity = $15,000; Dividends = $3,000; Revenues = $17,000; and Expenses = $12,000. What amount is reported for net income?

Distinguish between
accrual-basis and cash-
basis accounting (LO4–2)

**BE4–4** Consider the following set of transactions occurring during the month of May for Bison Consulting Company. For each transaction, indicate the impact on (1) the balance of cash, (2) cash-basis net income, and (3) accrual-basis net income for May. The first answer is provided as an example.

| Impact on: | Cash Balance | Cash-Basis Net Income | Accrual-Basis Net Income |
|---|---|---|---|
| (a) *Receive $1,500 from customers who were billed for services in April.* | *+$1,500* | *+$1,500* | *$0* |
| (b) Provide $3,200 of consulting services to a local business. Payment is not expected until June. | | | |
| (c) Purchase office supplies for $400 on account. All supplies are used by the end of May. | | | |
| (d) Pay $600 to workers. $400 is for work in May and $200 is for work in April. | | | |
| (e) Pay $200 to advertise in a local newspaper in May. | | | |
| Totals | | | |

Determine accrual-basis
and cash-basis net
income (LO4–2)

**BE4–5** Rebel Technology maintains its records using cash-basis accounting. Consider the following:

- During the year, the company received cash from customers, $50,000, and paid cash for salaries, $21,900.
- At the beginning of the year, customers owe Rebel $1,100. By the end of the year, customers owe $8,000.
- At the beginning of the year, Rebel owes salaries of $7,000. At the end of the year, Rebel owes salaries of $4,000.

Determine cash-basis net income and accrual-basis net income for the year.

Determine the adjustment
for supplies (LO4–3)
See JBE4–1 for journal
entries.

**BE4–6** At the beginning of the year, Golden Gopher Company reports a balance in Supplies of $500. During the year, Golden Gopher purchases an additional $3,300 of supplies for cash. By the end of the year, only $300 of supplies remains. Determine the accounts to be adjusted on December 31, the amount of the adjustment, and the ending balances. Assume no adjustments were previously made during the year.

Determine the adjustment
for prepaid rent (LO4–3)
See JBE4–2 for journal
entries.

**BE4–7** Suppose Hoosiers, a specialty clothing store, rents space at a local mall for one year, paying $25,200 ($2,100/month) in advance on October 1. The balance of Prepaid Rent at the beginning of the year is $0. Determine the accounts to be adjusted on December 31, the amount of the adjustment, and the ending balances. Assume no adjustments were previously made during the year.

Determine the
adjustment for prepaid
insurance (LO4–3)
See JBE4–3 for journal
entries.

**BE4–8** Mountaineer Excavation operates in a low-lying area subject to heavy rains and flooding. Because of this, Mountaineer purchases one year of flood insurance in advance on March 1, paying $36,000 ($3,000/month). The balance of Prepaid Insurance at the beginning of the year is

$0. Determine the accounts to be adjusted on December 31, the amount of the adjustment, and the ending balances. Assume no adjustments were previously made during the year.

**BE4–9** Beaver Construction purchases new equipment for $50,400 cash on April 1, 2024. At the time of purchase, the equipment is expected to be used in operations for seven years (84 months) and has no resale or scrap value at the end. Beaver depreciates equipment evenly over the 84 months ($600/month). The balance of Accumulated Depreciation at the beginning of 2024 is $0. Determine the accounts to be adjusted on December 31, the amount of the adjustment, and the ending balances. Assume no adjustments were previously made during the year.

*Determine the adjustment for depreciation (LO4–3)*
*See JBE4–4 for journal entries.*

**BE4–10** Suppose a customer rents a vehicle for three months from Commodores Rental on November 1, paying $6,000 ($2,000/month). Service Revenue is $19,000 prior to adjustment. The balance of Deferred Revenue at the beginning of the year is $0. Determine the accounts to be adjusted on December 31, the amount of the adjustment, and the ending balances. Assume no adjustments were previously made during the year.

*Determine the adjustment for deferred revenue (LO4–3)*
*See JBE4–5 for journal entries.*

**BE4–11** Fighting Irish Incorporated pays its employees $5,600 every two weeks ($400/day). The current two-week pay period ends on December 28, 2024, and employees are paid $5,600. The next two-week pay period ends on January 11, 2025, at which point employees will be paid $5,600. Prior to adjustment, Salaries Expense is $144,800. The balance of Salaries Payable before adjustment in 2024 is $0. Determine the accounts to be adjusted on December 31, the amount of the adjustment, and the ending balances. Assume no adjustments were previously made during the year.

*Determine the adjustment for salaries payable (LO4–3)*
*See JBE4–6 for journal entries.*

**BE4–12** Midshipmen Company borrows $15,000 from Falcon Company on July 1, 2024. Midshipmen repays the amount borrowed and will pay interest of 12% (1%/month) on June 30, 2025. The balance of Interest Payable at the beginning of the year is $0. Determine the accounts to be adjusted by Midshipmen on December 31, the amount of the adjustment, and the ending balances. Assume no adjustments were previously made during the year.

*Determine the adjustment for interest payable (LO4–3)*
*See JBE4–7 for journal entries.*

**BE4–13** Refer to the information in BE4–12. For Falcon Company, the balance of Interest Receivable at the beginning of the year is $0. Determine the accounts to be adjusted by Falcon on December 31, the amount of the adjustment, and the ending balances. Assume no adjustments were previously made during the year.

*Determine the adjustment for interest receivable (LO4–3)*
*See JBE4–8 for journal entries.*

**BE4–14** For each of the following accounts, indicate whether the account is shown in the income statement or the balance sheet:

*Assign accounts to financial statements (LO4–5)*

| Accounts | Financial Statement |
|---|---|
| 1. Accounts Receivable | _____ |
| 2. Deferred Revenue | _____ |
| 3. Supplies Expense | _____ |
| 4. Salaries Payable | _____ |
| 5. Depreciation Expense | _____ |
| 6. Service Revenue | _____ |

**BE4–15** Below are the four primary financial statements. Match each financial statement with its primary purpose to investors.

*Understand the purpose of financial statements (LO4–5)*

**Financial Statements**

1. _____ Income statement
2. _____ Statement of stockholders' equity
3. _____ Balance sheet
4. _____ Statement of cash flows

**Purposes**

a. Provides measures of resources and claims to those resources at the end of the year.

b. Provides an indication of the company's ability to make a profit during the current year.

c. Provides a measure of net increases and decreases in cash for the current year.

d. Shows changes in owners' claims to resources for the current year.

**Prepare an income statement (LO4–5)**

**BE4–16** Beavers Corporation has the following adjusted account balances on December 31, 2024: Sales Revenue, $275,000; Cost of Goods Sold, $95,000; Salaries Expense, $50,000; Supplies Expense, $20,000; Rent Expense, $26,000; Advertising Expense, $44,000; and Delivery Expense, $18,000. Prepare an income statement for the year ended December 31, 2024, including computations of both gross profit and net income.

**Prepare a statement of stockholders' equity (LO4–5)**

**BE4–17** Spiders Corporation has the following adjusted account balances on December 31, 2024: Common Stock, $30,000; Retained Earnings, $8,000; Dividends, $1,000; Service Revenue, $28,000; Salaries Expense, $16,000; and Rent Expense, $9,000. No common stock was issued during the year. Prepare the statement of stockholders' equity for the year ended December 31, 2024.

**Prepare a classified balance sheet (LO4–5)**

**BE4–18** Blue Devils Corporation has the following adjusted account balances on December 31, 2024: Cash, $5,000; Accounts Receivable, $9,000; Supplies, $19,000; Land, $75,000; Accounts Payable, $26,000; Salaries Payable, $16,000; Common Stock, $60,000; and Retained Earnings, _____. Prepare the December 31, 2024, classified balance sheet including the correct balance for retained earnings.

**Close temporary accounts to retained earnings (LO4–6)**
*See JBE4–9 for journal entries.*

**BE4–19** Aggies Corporation has the following year-end adjusted account balances (before closing): Retained Earnings, $230,000; Sales Revenue, $900,000; Cost of Goods Sold, $390,000; Rent Expense, $150,000; Interest Expense, $85,000; and Dividends, $60,000. Calculate the balance of Retained Earnings after the closing process has been completed.

**Calculate account balances after closing (4–7)**
*See JBE4–10 for journal entries.*

**BE4–20** Hilltoppers Corporation has the following year-end adjusted account balances (before closing): Cash, $5,000; Equipment, $17,000; Accounts Payable, $3,000; Common Stock, $11,000; Retained Earnings, $8,100; Dividends, $1,100; Service Revenue, $16,000; Salaries Expense, $11,000; and Utilities Expense, $4,000. Determine the account balances of all permanent accounts after the closing process has been completed.

## EXERCISES

**Determine the timing of revenue recognition (LO4–1)**

**E4–1** Consider the following situations:

1. **American Airlines** collects cash on June 12 from the sale of a ticket to a customer. The flight occurs on August 16.
2. A customer purchases sunglasses from **Eddie Bauer** on January 27 on account. Eddie Bauer receives payment from the customer on February 2.
3. On March 30, a customer preorders 10 supreme pizzas (without onions) from **Pizza Hut** for a birthday party. The pizzas are prepared and delivered on April 2. The company receives cash at the time of delivery.
4. A customer pays in advance for a three-month subscription to *Sports Illustrated* on July 1. Issues are scheduled for delivery each week from July 1 through September 30.

***Required:***

For each situation, determine the date for which the company recognizes the revenue under accrual-basis accounting.

**Determine the timing of expense recognition (LO4–2)**

**E4–2** Consider the following situations:

1. **American Airlines** operates a flight from Dallas to Los Angeles on August 16. The pilots' salaries associated with the flight are paid on September 2.
2. **Eddie Bauer** pays cash on January 6 to purchase sunglasses from a wholesale distributor. The sunglasses are sold to customers on January 27.
3. On January 1, **Pizza Hut** pays for a one-year property insurance policy with coverage starting immediately.
4. *Sports Illustrated* signs an agreement with CBS on January 12 to provide television advertisements during the Super Bowl. Payment is due within 3 weeks after February 4, the day of the Super Bowl. *Sports Illustrated* makes the payment on February 23.

*Required:*

For each situation, determine the date for which the company recognizes the expense under accrual-basis accounting.

**E4–3** Refer to the situations discussed in E4–1.

Differentiate cash-basis revenues from accrual-basis revenues (LO4–2)

*Required:*

For each situation, determine the date for which the company recognizes revenue using cash-basis accounting.

**E4–4** Refer to the situation discussed in E4–2.

Differentiate cash-basis expenses from accrual-basis expenses (LO4–2)

*Required:*

For each situation, determine the date for which the company recognizes the expense using cash-basis accounting.

**E4–5** During the course of your examination of the financial statements of Trojan Corporation for the year ended December 31, 2024, you come across several items needing further consideration. Currently, net income is $100,000.

Determine the amount of net income (LO4–1)

1. An insurance policy covering 12 months was purchased on October 1, 2024, for $24,000. The entire amount was recorded in Prepaid Insurance, and no adjustment was made for this item during 2024.
2. During 2024, the company received a $4,000 cash advance from a customer for services to be performed in 2025. The $4,000 was incorrectly recorded in Service Revenue.
3. Purchases of supplies during the year were incorrectly recorded to Supplies Expense. You discover that supplies costing $2,750 were on hand on December 31, 2024.
4. Trojan borrowed $70,000 from a local bank on September 1, 2024. Principal and interest at 9% will be paid on August 31, 2025. No accrual was made for interest in 2024.

*Required:*

Using the information in 1 through 4 above, determine the proper amount of net income as of December 31, 2024.

**E4–6** Golden Eagle Company has the following balances at the end of the year before any adjustments:

Determine year-end adjustments to accounts (LO4–3)
*See JE4–1 for journal entries.*

| | Balance |
| --- | --- |
| Supplies | $37,000 |
| Prepaid Insurance | 12,000 |
| Salaries Payable | 0 |
| Deferred Revenue | 18,000 |

The following additional information is known on December 31:

1. Supplies purchased during the year were recorded to the Supplies account. Supplies on hand at the end of December equal $4,000.
2. Insurance for 12 months was purchased on September 1 and recorded to Prepaid Insurance.
3. Salaries paid for the first 11 months of the year total $94,000. Salaries for December were $16,000 but have not been paid.
4. On December 1, Golden Eagle received $18,000 from a customer for rent for the period December through February and recorded Deferred Revenue at that time. By the end of December, one month of this rent has been provided. Revenue for rent provided to other customers during the year totaled $70,000.

*Required:*

For each item, determine the accounts to be adjusted on December 31, the amount of the adjustment, and the ending balance. Assume no adjustments were previously made during the year.

Determine year-end
adjustments **(LO4–3)**
*See JE4–2 for journal
entries.*

**E4–7** Consider the following items for Huskies Insurance Company:

1. Income taxes for the year total $42,000 but won't be paid until next April 15.
2. On June 30, the company lent its chief financial officer $50,000; principal and interest at 7% are due in one year.
3. On October 1, the company received $16,000 from a customer for a one-year property insurance policy. Deferred Revenue was recorded on October 1. Insurance services provided to other customers during the year totaled $100,000.

***Required:***

For each item, determine the accounts to be adjusted on December 31, the amount of the adjustment, and the ending balance. Assume no adjustments were previously made during the year.

Calculate the effects
on net income
of not recording
adjustments **(LO4–3)**

**E4–8** Refer to the information in E4–7.

***Required:***

For each of the adjustments in E4–7, indicate by how much net income in the income statement is higher or lower if the adjustment is not recorded.

Determine year-end
adjustments **(LO4–3)**
*See JE4–3 for journal
entries.*

**E4–9** Consider the following items for Shocker Enterprises:

1. On November 30, 2024, Shocker received a $4,500 payment from a customer for services to be rendered evenly over the next three months. Deferred Revenue was recorded on November 30. Revenue for other services during the year provided totaled $60,000.
2. On December 1, 2024, the company paid a local radio station $2,700 for 30 radio ads to be aired, 10 per month, throughout December, January, and February. Prepaid Advertising was recorded for the full amount on December 1. Shocker had no other advertising during the year.
3. Employee salaries for the month of December totaling $8,000 will be paid on January 7, 2025. Salaries paid for the first 11 months of the year total $108,000.
4. On August 31, 2024, Shocker borrowed $70,000 from a local bank. A note was signed with principal with 9% interest to be paid on August 31, 2025.

***Required:***

For each item, determine the accounts to be adjusted on December 31, the amount of the adjustment, and the ending balance. Assume no adjustments were previously made during the year.

Calculate the effects
on the accounting
equation of not recording
adjustments **(LO4–3, 4–4)**

**E4–10** Refer to the information in E4–9.

***Required:***

For each of the adjustments recorded in E4–9, indicate by how much the assets, liabilities, and stockholders' equity in the December 31, 2024, balance sheet is higher or lower if the adjustment is not recorded.

Determine year-end
adjustments **(LO4–3)**
*See JE4–4 for journal
entries.*

**E4–11** Consider the following items for Wolverine Properties during 2024.

1. On December 1, 2024, Wolverine received $4,000 cash from a company renting office space from Wolverine. The payment, representing rent for December and January, was recorded to Deferred Revenue on December 1. Revenue for other rentals totaled $125,000.
2. Wolverine purchases a one-year property insurance policy on July 1, 2024, for $13,200. The payment was recorded in Prepaid Insurance for the entire amount on July 1. Wolverine had $5,400 in insurance costs for the first six months of the year.
3. Employee salaries of $3,000 for the month of December will be paid in early January 2025. Salaries paid for the first 11 months of the year total $42,000.
4. On November 1, 2024, the company borrowed $15,000 from a bank. The loan requires principal and interest at 10% to be paid on October 30, 2025.
5. Office supplies at the beginning of 2024 totaled $1,000. On August 15, Wolverine purchased an additional $3,400 of office supplies, recorded to the Supplies account. By the end of the year, $500 of office supplies remains.

***Required:***

For each item, determine the accounts to be adjusted on December 31, 2024, the amount of the adjustment, and the ending balance. Assume no adjustments were previously made during the year.

**E4–12** Below are transactions for Hurricane Company during 2024.

1. On October 1, 2024, Hurricane lent $9,000 to another company. The other company signed a note indicating principal and 12% interest will be paid to Hurricane on September 30, 2025.
2. On November 1, 2024, Hurricane paid its landlord $4,500, representing rent for the months of November through January. The payment was recorded in Prepaid Rent for the entire amount on November 1. Costs related to rent for the first 11 months of the year total $15,000.
3. On August 1, 2024, Hurricane collected $13,200 in advance from another company to provide consulting services for one year. The entire amount was recorded in Deferred Revenue. Hurricane generates $160,000 in other Service Revenue during the year.
4. Utilities owed at the end of the year are $400. For the first 11 months of the year, Hurricane has paid $4,000 for utilities.
5. Salaries for the December earned by employees but not paid to them or recorded are $5,000. For the first 11 months of the year, Hurricane has paid $45,000 for salaries.
6. Hurricane began the year with $500 in supplies. During the year, the company purchased $2,500 in supplies. At year-end, supplies costing $600 remain on hand.

*Required:*

1. For each item, determine the accounts to be adjusted on December 31, 2024, the amount of the adjustment, and the ending balance. Assume no adjustments were previously made during the year.
2. Prepare an income statement for the year ended December 31, 2024 based on the items above.

Determine year-end adjustments and account balances and prepare an income statement **(LO4–3, 4–4, 4–5)**
*See JE4–5 for journal entries.*

**E4–13** The December 31, 2024, unadjusted account balances for Demon Deacons Corporation are presented below.

Determine year-end adjustments and account balances **(LO4–3, 4–4)**
*See JE4–6 for journal entries.*

| Accounts | Balance |
| --- | --- |
| Cash | $10,000 |
| Accounts Receivable | 15,000 |
| Prepaid Rent | 7,200 |
| Supplies | 4,000 |
| Deferred Revenue | 3,000 |
| Common Stock | 11,000 |
| Retained Earnings | 6,000 |
| Service Revenue | 51,200 |
| Salaries Expense | 35,000 |
| Rent Expense | 9,000 |

At year-end, the following additional items are available:

1. The balance of Prepaid Rent, $7,200, represents payment on October 31, 2024, for rent from November 1, 2024, to April 30, 2025.
2. The balance of Deferred Revenue, $3,000, represents payment in advance from a customer. By the end of the year, $750 of the services have been provided.
3. An additional $700 in salaries is owed to employees at the end of the year but will not be paid until January 4, 2025.
4. The balance of Supplies, $4,000, consists of $1,700 of office supplies on hand at the beginning of the year plus an additional $2,300 purchased throughout 2024. By the end of 2024, only $800 of supplies remains.

*Required:*

1. For each item, determine the accounts to be adjusted on December 31, 2024, the amount of the adjustment, and the ending balance. Assume no adjustments were previously made during the year.
2. Determine ending account balances of *all* accounts as of December 31, 2024.

**Calculate the balance of retained earnings (LO4–5)**

**E4–14** Below are the net income and retained earnings for Volunteers Inc. and Raiders Inc. for the period 2015–2024. Volunteers began operations in 2016, while Raiders began several years earlier.

|  | VOLUNTEERS INC.<br>($ in millions) | | RAIDERS INC.<br>($ in millions) | |
| --- | --- | --- | --- | --- |
| Year | Net Income<br>(Loss) | Retained<br>Earnings | Net Income<br>(Loss) | Retained<br>Earnings |
| 2015 | — | $0 | $ 35 | $11 |
| 2016 | $ 30 | _____ | (43) | _____ |
| 2017 | (7) | _____ | 63 | _____ |
| 2018 | 41 | _____ | 63 | _____ |
| 2019 | 135 | _____ | 102 | _____ |
| 2020 | 30 | _____ | 135 | _____ |
| 2021 | (131) | _____ | (42) | _____ |
| 2022 | 577 | _____ | 74 | _____ |
| 2023 | 359 | _____ | 110 | _____ |
| 2024 | 360 | _____ | 162 | _____ |

*Required:*

Calculate the balance of retained earnings each year for each company. Neither company paid dividends during this time.

**Prepare financial statements from account balances (LO4–5)**
*See JE4–7 for adjusted trial balance.*

**E4–15** The December 31, 2024, account balances for Fightin' Blue Hens Corporation are presented below. The balances have already been appropriately adjusted.

| Accounts | Balance |
| --- | --- |
| Cash | $ 12,000 |
| Accounts Receivable | 150,000 |
| Prepaid Rent | 6,000 |
| Supplies | 30,000 |
| Land | 265,000 |
| Accounts Payable | 12,000 |
| Salaries Payable | 11,000 |
| Interest Payable | 5,000 |
| Notes Payable (due in two years) | 40,000 |
| Common Stock | 300,000 |
| Retained Earnings | 60,000 |
| Service Revenue | 500,000 |
| Salaries Expense | 400,000 |
| Rent Expense | 20,000 |
| Utilities Expense | 40,000 |
| Interest Expense | 5,000 |

*Required:*

1. Prepare an income statement for the year ended December 31, 2024.
2. Prepare a statement of stockholders' equity for the year ended December 31, 2024, assuming no common stock was issued during 2024.
3. Prepare a classified balance sheet as of December 31, 2024.

**E4–16** Seminoles Corporation's fiscal year-end is December 31, 2024. The following is a partial listing of adjusted account balances as of December 31.

Prepare income statement
and close accounts
**(LO4–5, LO4–6, 4–7)**
*See JE4–8 for journal
entries.*

| Accounts | Balance |
|---|---|
| Retained Earnings | $30,000 |
| Dividends | 3,000 |
| Sales Revenue | 50,000 |
| Interest Revenue | 6,000 |
| Cost of Goods Sold | 15,000 |
| Rent Expense | 6,000 |
| Advertising Expense | 3,000 |
| Insurance Expense | 11,000 |
| Interest Expense | 5,000 |

*Required:*

1. Based on the information above, prepare the Income Statement for Seminoles Corporation for December 31, 2024.
2. Transfer balances of temporary accounts to Retained Earnings and calculate its ending balance.

**E4–17** The December 31, 2024, adjusted account balances for the Cowboys Corporation are presented below.

Prepare financial
statements and close
accounts **(LO4–5, LO4–6,
LO4–7)**
*See JE4–9 for journal
entries.*

| Accounts | Balance |
|---|---|
| Cash | $ 21,000 |
| Accounts Receivable | 300,000 |
| Prepaid Rent | 10,000 |
| Inventory | 50,000 |
| Office Equipment | 600,000 |
| Accumulated Depreciation | 250,000 |
| Accounts Payable | 60,000 |
| Notes Payable (due in six months) | 60,000 |
| Salaries Payable | 8,000 |
| Interest Payable | 2,000 |
| Common Stock | 400,000 |
| Retained Earnings | 100,000 |
| Sales Revenue | 800,000 |
| Cost of Goods Sold | 480,000 |
| Salaries Expense | 120,000 |
| Rent Expense | 30,000 |
| Depreciation Expense | 60,000 |
| Interest Expense | 4,000 |
| Advertising Expense | 5,000 |

*Required:*

1. Prepare an income statement for the year ended December 31, 2024, and a classified balance sheet as of December 31, 2024.
2. Transfer balances of temporary accounts to Retained Earnings and calculate its ending balance.

**Determine ending account balances after closing (LO4–6, 4–7)**
*See JE4–10 for journal entries.*

**E4–18** Laker Incorporated's fiscal year-end is December 31, 2024. The following is a listing of adjusted account balances as of December 31.

| Accounts | Balance |
|---|---|
| Cash | $12,000 |
| Supplies | 39,000 |
| Prepaid Rent | 30,000 |
| Accounts Payable | 3,000 |
| Notes Payable | 30,000 |
| Common Stock | 40,000 |
| Retained Earnings | 9,000 |
| Dividends | 4,000 |
| Service Revenue | 54,000 |
| Salaries Expense | 20,000 |
| Advertising Expense | 13,000 |
| Rent Expense | 10,000 |
| Utilities Expense | 8,000 |

**Required:**

1. Transfer balances of temporary accounts to Retained Earnings and calculate its ending balance.
2. Calculate all account balances after closing.

**Determine ending account balances after closing (LO4–5; LO4–6, 4–7)**
*See JE4–11 for journal entries.*

**E4–19** Refer to E4–15 for adjusted account balances for Fightin' Blue Hens Corporation as of December 31, 2024.

**Required:**

1. Transfer balances of temporary accounts to Retained Earnings and calculate its ending balance.
2. Calculate all account balances after closing.

## PROGRAMS

**PROBLEMS**

Mc Graw Hill **connect**

**Determine accrual-basis and cash-basis revenues and expenses (LO4–1, 4–2)**

**P4–1** Consider the following transactions.

| Transaction | Accrual Basis Revenue | Accrual Basis Expense | Cash Basis Revenue | Cash Basis Expense |
|---|---|---|---|---|
| 1. Receive cash from customers in advance of services to be provided, $600. | ___ | ___ | ___ | ___ |
| 2. Pay utilities bill for the previous period, $150. | ___ | ___ | ___ | ___ |
| 3. Pay for insurance in advance of the period to be covered, $2,000. | ___ | ___ | ___ | ___ |
| 4. Pay workers' salaries for the current period, $800. | ___ | ___ | ___ | ___ |
| 5. Incur costs for employee salaries in the current period but do not pay, $1,000. | ___ | ___ | ___ | ___ |
| 6. Receive cash from customers at the time of service, $1,700. | ___ | ___ | ___ | ___ |
| 7. Purchase office supplies on account, $330. | ___ | ___ | ___ | ___ |
| 8. Borrow cash from the bank, $4,000. | ___ | ___ | ___ | ___ |
| 9. Receive cash from customers for services performed in the previous period, $750. | ___ | ___ | ___ | ___ |
| 10. Pay for advertising to appear in the current period, $450. | ___ | ___ | ___ | ___ |
| 11. Purchase inventory for $600 in cash. | ___ | ___ | ___ | ___ |
| 12. Sell inventory on account, $800. The inventory had a cost of $600. | ___ | ___ | ___ | ___ |

**Required:**

For each transaction, determine the amount of revenue or expense, if any, that is recorded under accrual-basis accounting and under cash-basis accounting in the current period.

**P4–2** Minutemen Law Services maintains its books using cash-basis accounting. However, the company decides to borrow $100,000 from a local bank, and the bank requires Minutemen to provide annual financial statements prepared using accrual-basis accounting as part of the creditworthiness verification. During 2024, the company records the following cash flows:

*Convert cash-basis accounting to accrual-basis accounting (LO4–1, 4–2)*

| | | |
|---|---:|---:|
| Cash collected from customers | | $70,000 |
| Cash paid for: | | |
| Salaries | $36,000 | |
| Supplies | 4,000 | |
| Rent | 5,000 | |
| Insurance | 7,000 | |
| Utilities | 3,000 | 55,000 |
| Net cash flows | | $15,000 |

You are able to determine the following information:

| | January 1, 2021 | December 31, 2021 |
|---|---:|---:|
| Accounts Receivable | $21,000 | $24,000 |
| Prepaid Insurance | -0- | 3,700 |
| Supplies | 5,000 | 2,000 |
| Salaries Payable | 2,700 | 4,400 |

**Required:**

Prepare an accrual-basis income statement for the year ended December 31, 2024, by calculating accrual-basis revenues and expenses.

**P4–3** The following items are necessary for preparing the 2024 year-end adjustments for Gamecock Advertising Agency. Gamecock's fiscal year-end is December 31.

*Determine year-end adjustments and ending balances (LO4–3, 4–4)*
*See JP4–1 for journal entries.*

1. On July 1, 2024, Gamecock received $6,000 from a customer for advertising services to be given evenly over the next 10 months. Revenues related to other advertising provided during the year total $96,000

2. At the end of the year, income taxes owed are $7,000. These taxes won't be paid until next April 15.

3. On May 1, 2024, the company paid $4,800 for a two-year fire and liability insurance policy. The amount was recorded in Prepaid Insurance on May 1. Insurance costs prior to May total $1,100.

4. On September 1, 2024, the company borrowed $20,000 from a local bank and signed a note. Principal and interest at 12% will be paid on August 31, 2025.

5. At year-end, there is a $2,700 balance in the Supplies account. Only $1,000 of supplies remains on hand at the end of the year.

**Required:**

For each item, determine the accounts to be adjusted on December 31, 2024, the balances before adjustment, the amount of the adjustment, and the ending balances. Assume no adjustments were previously made during the year.

**P4–4** Buzzard Bicycle specializes in custom painting and design of bicycles. December 31 is the company's fiscal year-end. Information necessary to prepare the year-end adjustments appears below.

*Determine year-end adjustments, ending balances, and prepare an income statement (LO4–3, 4–4, 4–5)*
*See JP4–2 for journal entries.*

1. A three-year fire insurance policy was purchased on July 1, 2024, for $18,000. The company recorded the amount in Prepaid Insurance on July 1. The cost of insurance prior to July totals $2,500.

2. Employee salaries of $25,000 for the month of December will be paid in early January. Salaries paid in the first 11 months of the year totaled $190,000.

3. On November 1, 2024, the company received $6,000 in cash from a customer requesting a custom design for six identical bikes ($1,000 each). The entire amount is recorded in Deferred Revenue on November 1. By the end of the year, four of the bikes have been completed. Other revenues generated during the year total $280,000.

4. Supplies at the beginning of the year totaled $2,000. During 2024, additional supplies of $18,000 were purchased and recorded in Supplies at the time of purchase. Supplies remaining at the end of the year total $4,000.

5. Buzzard paid a local radio station $12,000 for four months of advertising on December 1, 2024. The advertising will appear evenly over the four-month period. The company recorded the entire amount in Prepaid Advertising on December 1. Advertising costs the first 11 months of the year total $15,000.

6. Buzzard borrowed $36,000 on March 1, 2024. The principal is due to be collected in five years. Interest is receivable each March 1 at an annual rate of 10%.

**Required:**

1. Determine the adjustments needed on December 31, 2024.
2. Prepare an income statement for Buzzard Bicycle for the year ended December 31, 2024.

**Prepare financial statements from adjusted account balances (LO4–5)**

**P4–5** Boilermaker Unlimited specializes in building new homes and remodeling existing homes. Remodeling projects include adding game rooms, changing kitchen cabinets and countertops, and updating bathrooms. Below are the year-end adjusted account balances of Boilermaker Unlimited.

| **BOILERMAKER UNLIMITED** Adjusted Account Balances December 31, 2024 | | |
|---|---|---|
| **Accounts** | **(1)** | **(2)** |
| Cash | $ 16,000 | |
| Accounts Receivable | 25,000 | |
| Supplies | 32,000 | |
| Prepaid Insurance | 7,000 | |
| Land | 425,000 | |
| Accounts Payable | | 31,000 |
| Salaries Payable | | 28,000 |
| Utilities Payable | | 5,000 |
| Notes Payable (due in 5 years) | | 150,000 |
| Common Stock | | 200,000 |
| Retained Earnings | | 31,000 |
| Dividends | 26,000 | |
| Service Revenue—new construction | | 450,000 |
| Service Revenue—remodeling | | 280,000 |
| Salaries Expense | 160,000 | |
| Supplies Expense | 285,000 | |
| Rent Expense | 50,000 | |
| Insurance Expense | 25,000 | |
| Utilities Expense | 42,000 | |
| Interest Expense | 9,000 | |
| Service Fee Expense | 73,000 | |
| Totals | $1,375,000 | $1,375,000 |

*Required:*

Prepare an income statement, statement of stockholders' equity, and classified balance sheet. In preparing the statement of stockholders' equity, note that during the year, the company issued additional common stock for $30,000. This amount is included in the amount for Common Stock's adjusted balance.

**P4–6** The year-end financial statements of Rattlers Tax Services are provided below.

Transfer balances of temporary accounts and determine ending account balances after closing **(LO4–6, 4–7)**
*See JP4–4 for journal entries.*

### RATTLERS TAX SERVICES
### Income Statement

| | | |
|---|---|---|
| Service revenue | | $77,500 |
| Expenses: | | |
| Salaries | $46,000 | |
| Utilities | 8,200 | |
| Insurance | 5,800 | |
| Supplies | 2,100 | 62,100 |
| Net income | | $15,400 |

### RATTLERS TAX SERVICES
### Statement of Stockholders' Equity

| | Common Stock | Retained Earnings | Total S. Equity |
|---|---|---|---|
| Beg. bal., Jan. 1 | $60,000 | $24,500 | $ 84,500 |
| Issue stock | 30,000 | | 30,000 |
| Net income | | 15,400 | 15,400 |
| Dividends | | (6,000) | (6,000) |
| Ending bal., Dec. 31 | $90,000 | $33,900 | $123,900 |

### RATTLERS TAX SERVICES
### Balance Sheet

| Assets | | | Liabilities | | |
|---|---|---|---|---|---|
| Cash | $ 4,700 | | Accounts payable | | $ 3,000 |
| Accounts receivable | 7,200 | | **Stockholders' Equity:** | | |
| Land | 115,000 | | Common stock | $90,000 | |
| | | | Retained earnings | 33,900 | 123,900 |
| Total assets | $126,900 | | Total liabs. and equities | | 126,900 |

*Required:*

1. Transfer balances of all temporary accounts to Retained Earnings and calculate its ending balance. (*Hint:* The balance of Retained Earnings after closing will be the amount shown in the balance sheet.)
2. Calculate all account balances after closing.

## JOURNAL ENTRIES

## Journal Entries—Brief Exercises

**JBE4–1** At the beginning of the year, Golden Gopher Company reports a balance in Supplies of $500. On May 15, Golden Gopher purchases an additional $3,300 of supplies for cash. By the end of the year, only $300 of supplies remains. (1) Record the purchase of supplies on May 15. (2) Record the adjusting entry on May 31.

Record adjusting entry for supplies **(LO4–3)**
*See BE4–6 for financial statement effects.*

**JBE4–2** Suppose Hoosiers, a specialty clothing store, rents space at a local mall for one year, paying $25,200 ($2,100/month) in advance on October 1. (1) Record the payment of rent in advance on October 1. (2) Record the adjusting entry on December 31.

Record adjusting entry for prepaid rent **(LO4–3)**
*See BE4–7 for financial statement effects.*

Record adjusting entry for
prepaid insurance (LO4–3)
See BE4–8 for financial
statement effects.

**JBE4–3** Mountaineer Excavation operates in a low-lying area subject to heavy rains and flooding. Because of this, Mountaineer purchases one year of flood insurance in advance on March 1, paying $36,000 ($3,000/month). (1) Record the purchase of insurance in advance on March 1. (2) Record the adjusting entry on December 31.

Record adjusting entry for
depreciation (LO4–3)
See BE4–9 for financial
statement effects.

**JBE4–4** Beaver Construction purchases new equipment for $50,400 cash on April 1, 2024. At the time of purchase, the equipment is expected to be used in operations for seven years (84 months) and has no resale or scrap value at the end. Beaver depreciates equipment evenly over the 84 months ($600/month). (1) Record the purchase of equipment on April 1. (2) Record the adjusting entry for depreciation on December 31, 2024.

Record adjusting entry for
deferred revenue (LO4–3)
See BE4–10 for financial
statement effects.

**JBE4–5** Suppose a customer rents a vehicle for three months from Commodores Rental on November 1, paying $6,000 ($2,000/month). (1) Record the rental for Commodores on November 1. (2) Record the adjusting entry on December 31.

Record adjusting entry for
salaries payable (LO4–3)
See BE4–11 for financial
statement effects.

**JBE4–6** Fighting Irish Incorporated pays its employees $5,600 every two weeks ($400/ day). The current two-week pay period ends on December 28, 2024, and employees are paid $5,600. The next two-week pay period ends on January 11, 2025, and employees are paid $5,600. Record the adjusting entry on December 31, 2024.

Record adjusting entry for
interest payable (LO4–3)
See BE4–12 for financial
statement effects.

**JBE4–7** Midshipmen Company borrows $15,000 from Falcon Company on July 1, 2024. Midshipmen repays the amount borrowed and will pay interest of 12% (1%/month) on June 30, 2025. (1) Record the borrowing for Midshipmen on July 1, 2024. (2) Record the adjusting entry for Midshipmen on December 31, 2024.

Record adjusting entry for
interest receivable (LO4–3)
See BE4–13 for financial
statement effects.

**JBE4–8** Refer to the information in JBE4–7. (1) Record the lending for Falcon on July 1, 2024. (2) Record the adjusting entry for Falcon on December 31, 2024.

Record closing
entries (LO4–6)
See BE4–19 for financial
statement effects.

**JBE4–9** Aggies Corporation has the following year-end adjusted account balances (before closing): Retained Earnings, $230,000; Sales Revenue, $900,000; Cost of Goods Sold, $390,000; Rent Expense, $150,000; Interest Expense, $85,000; and Dividends, $60,000. Record the necessary closing entries.

Record closing entries
(LO4–6, 4–7)
See BE4–20 for financial
statement effects.

**JBE4–10** Hilltoppers Corporation has the following year-end adjusted account balances (before closing): Cash, $5,000; Equipment, $17,000; Accounts Payable, $3,000; Common Stock, $11,000; Retained Earnings, $8,100; Dividends, $1,100; Service Revenue, $16,000; Salaries Expense, $11,000; and Utilities Expense, $4,000. (1) Record the necessary closing entries. (2) Complete the post-closing trial balance.

## Journal Entries—Exercises

Record adjusting
entries (LO4–3)
See E4–6 for financial
statement effects.

**JE4–1** Golden Eagle Company has the following balances at the end of the year before any adjustments:

|  | Balance |
| --- | --- |
| Supplies | $37,000 |
| Prepaid Insurance | 12,000 |
| Salaries Payable | 0 |
| Deferred Revenue | 18,000 |

The following additional information is known on December 31:

1. Supplies purchased during the year were recorded to the Supplies account. Supplies on hand at the end of December equal $4,000.
2. Insurance for 12 months was purchased on September 1 and recorded to Prepaid Insurance.
3. Salaries paid for the first 11 months of the year total $94,000. Salaries for December were $16,000 but have not been paid.

4. On December 1, Golden Eagle received $18,000 from a customer for rent for the period December through February and recorded Deferred Revenue at that time. By the end of December, one month of this rent has been provided. Rent provided to other customers during the year totaled $70,000.

**Required:**

Prepare the adjusting entries for supplies, prepaid insurance, salaries payable, and deferred revenue on December 31.

**JE4–2** Consider the following items for Huskies Insurance Company:

1. Income taxes for the year total $42,000 but won't be paid until next April 15.
2. On June 30, the company lent its chief financial officer $50,000; principal and interest at 7% are due in one year.
3. On October 1, the company received $16,000 from a customer for a one-year property insurance policy. Deferred Revenue was recorded on October 1.

**Required:**

For each item, record the necessary adjusting entry for Huskies Insurance at its year-end of December 31. Assume no adjustments were previously made during the year.

**JE4–3** Consider the following items for Shocker Enterprises:

1. On November 30, 2024, Shocker received a $4,500 payment from a customer for services to be rendered evenly over the next three months. Deferred Revenue was recorded on November 30.
2. On December 1, 2024, the company paid a local radio station $2,700 for 30 radio ads to be aired, 10 per month, throughout December, January, and February. Prepaid Advertising was recorded for the full amount on December 31. Shocker had no other advertising during the year.
3. Employee salaries for the month of December totaling $8,000 will be paid on January 7, 2025.
4. On August 31, 2024, Shocker borrowed $70,000 from a local bank. A note was signed with principal and 9% interest to be paid on August 31, 2025.

**Required:**

Record the necessary adjusting entries for Shocker on December 31, 2024. No prior adjusting entries were made during the year.

**JE4–4** Consider the following items for Wolverine Properties during 2024.

1. On December 1, 2024, Wolverine received $4,000 cash from a company renting office space from Wolverine. The payment, representing rent for December and January, was recorded to Deferred Revenue on December 1.
2. Wolverine purchases a one-year property insurance policy on July 1, 2024, for $13,200. The payment was recorded in Prepaid Insurance for the entire amount on July 1.
3. Employee salaries of $3,000 for the month of December will be paid in early January 2025.
4. On November 1, 2024, the company borrowed $15,000 from a bank. The loan requires principal and interest at 10% to be paid on October 30, 2025.
5. Office supplies at the beginning of 2024 totaled $1,000. On August 15, Wolverine purchased an additional $3,400 of office supplies, recorded to the Supplies account. By the end of the year, $500 of office supplies remains.

**Required:**

Record the necessary adjusting entries on December 31, 2024, for Wolverine Properties. You do not need to record transactions made during the year. Assume no financial statements were prepared during the year, and no adjustments were previously recorded.

**JE4–5** Below are transactions for Hurricane Company during 2024.

1. On October 1, 2024, Hurricane lent $9,000 to another company. The other company signed a note indicating principal and 12% interest will be paid to Hurricane on September 30, 2025.

---

*Side notes (right margin):*

Record adjusting entries **(LO4–3)**
*See E4–7 for financial statement effects.*

Record adjusting entries **(LO4–3)**
*See E4–9 for financial statement effects.*

Record adjusting entries **(LO4–3)**
*See E4–11 for financial statement effects.*

Record adjusting entries **(LO4–3)**
*See E4–12 for financial statement effects.*

2. On November 1, 2024, Hurricane paid its landlord $4,500, representing rent for the months of November through January. The payment was properly recorded in Prepaid Rent for the entire amount on November 1.

3. On August 1, 2024, Hurricane collected $13,200 in advance from another company to provide consulting services for one year. The entire amount properly was recorded in Deferred Revenue.

4. Utilities owed at the end of the year are $400.

5. Salaries for the December earned by employees but not paid to them or recorded are $5,000.

6. Hurricane began the year with $500 in supplies. During the year, the company purchased $2,500 in supplies. At year-end, supplies costing $600 remain on hand.

**Required:**

Record the necessary adjusting entries on December 31, 2024, for Hurricane Company for each of the situations. Assume no financial statements were prepared during the year, and no adjustments were previously made.

**JE4–6** The December 31, 2024, unadjusted account balances for Demon Deacons Corporation are presented below.

**Record adjusting entries and prepare an adjusted trial balance (LO4–3, 4–4)**
*See E4–13 for financial statement effects.*

| Accounts | Debit | Credit |
|---|---|---|
| Cash | $10,000 | |
| Accounts Receivable | 15,000 | |
| Prepaid Rent | 7,200 | |
| Supplies | 4,000 | |
| Deferred Revenue | | $3,000 |
| Common Stock | | 11,000 |
| Retained Earnings | | 6,000 |
| Service Revenue | | 51,200 |
| Salaries Expense | 35,000 | |
| Rent Expense | 9,000 | |

At year-end, the following additional items are available:

1. The balance of Prepaid Rent, $7,200, represents payment on October 31, 2024, for rent from November 1, 2024, to April 30, 2025.

2. The balance of Deferred Revenue, $3,000, represents payment in advance from a customer. By the end of the year, $750 of the services have been provided.

3. An additional $700 in salaries is owed to employees at the end of the year but will not be paid until January 4, 2025.

4. The balance of Supplies, $4,000, represents the amount of office supplies on hand at the beginning of the year of $1,700 plus an additional $2,300 purchased throughout 2024. By the end of 2024, only $800 of supplies remains.

**Required:**

1. Update account balances for the year-end information by recording any necessary adjusting entries. No prior adjustments have been made in 2024.

2. Prepare an adjusted trial balance as of December 31, 2024.

**Prepare financial statements from an adjusted trial balance (LO4–4, 4–5)**
*See E4–15 for financial statement effects.*

**JE4–7** The December 31, 2024, adjusted trial balance for Fightin' Blue Hens Corporation is presented below.

| Accounts | Debit | Credit |
|---|---|---|
| Cash | $ 12,000 | |
| Accounts Receivable | 150,000 | |
| Prepaid Rent | 6,000 | |
| Supplies | 30,000 | |
| Land | 265,000 | |
| Accounts Payable | | $ 12,000 |
| Salaries Payable | | 11,000 |
| Interest Payable | | 5,000 |
| Notes Payable (due in two years) | | 40,000 |
| Common Stock | | 300,000 |
| Retained Earnings | | 60,000 |
| Service Revenue | | 500,000 |
| Salaries Expense | 400,000 | |
| Rent Expense | 20,000 | |
| Utilities Expense | 40,000 | |
| Interest Expense | 5,000 | |
| Totals | $1,063,000 | $1,063,000 |

**Required:**

1. Prepare an income statement for the year ended December 31, 2024.
2. Prepare a statement of stockholders' equity for the year ended December 31, 2024, assuming no common stock was issued during 2024.
3. Prepare a classified balance sheet as of December 31, 2024.

**JE4–8** Seminoles Corporation's fiscal year-end is December 31, 2024. The following is a partial adjusted trial balance as of December 31.

Record closing entries and determine ending retained earnings **(LO4–6, 4–7)**
*See E4–16 for financial statement effects.*

| Accounts | Debit | Credit |
|---|---|---|
| Retained Earnings | | $30,000 |
| Dividends | $3,000 | |
| Service Revenue | | 50,000 |
| Interest Revenue | | 6,000 |
| Salaries Expense | 15,000 | |
| Rent Expense | 6,000 | |
| Advertising Expense | 3,000 | |
| Depreciation Expense | 11,000 | |
| Interest Expense | 5,000 | |

**Required:**

1. Prepare the necessary closing entries.
2. Calculate the ending balance of Retained Earnings.

Prepare financial
statements and closing
entries (LO4–5, LO4–6,
LO4–7)
See E4–17 for financial
statement effects.

**JE4–9** The December 31, 2024, adjusted trial balance for the Cowboys Corporation is presented below.

| Accounts | Debits | Credits |
|---|---|---|
| Cash | $ 21,000 | |
| Accounts Receivable | 300,000 | |
| Prepaid Rent | 10,000 | |
| Inventory | 50,000 | |
| Office Equipment | 600,000 | |
| Accumulated Depreciation | | $250,000 |
| Accounts Payable | | 60,000 |
| Notes Payable (due in six months) | | 60,000 |
| Salaries Payable | | 8,000 |
| Interest Payable | | 2,000 |
| Common Stock | | 400,000 |
| Retained Earnings | | 100,000 |
| Sales Revenue | | 800,000 |
| Cost of Goods Sold | 480,000 | |
| Salaries Expense | 120,000 | |
| Rent Expense | 30,000 | |
| Depreciation Expense | 60,000 | |
| Interest Expense | 4,000 | |
| Advertising Expense | 5,000 | |

*Required:*

1. Prepare an income statement for the year ended December 31, 2024, and a classified balance sheet as of December 31, 2024.
2. Prepare the necessary closing entries on December 31, 2024.

Record closing entries and
prepare a post-closing
trial balance (LO4–6, 4–7)
See E4–18 for financial
statement effects.

**JE4–10** Laker Incorporated's fiscal year-end is December 31, 2024. The following is an adjusted trial balance as of December 31.

| Accounts | Debit | Credit |
|---|---|---|
| Cash | $ 12,000 | |
| Supplies | 39,000 | |
| Prepaid Rent | 30,000 | |
| Accounts Payable | | $  3,000 |
| Notes Payable | | 30,000 |
| Common Stock | | 40,000 |
| Retained Earnings | | 9,000 |
| Dividends | 4,000 | |
| Service Revenue | | 54,000 |
| Salaries Expense | 20,000 | |
| Advertising Expense | 13,000 | |
| Rent Expense | 10,000 | |
| Utilities Expense | 8,000 | |
| Totals | $136,000 | $136,000 |

*Required:*

1. Prepare the necessary closing entries.
2. Calculate the ending balance of Retained Earnings.
3. Prepare a post-closing trial balance.

**JE4–11** Refer to JE4–7 for the adjusted trial balance for Fightin' Blue Hens Corporation as of December 31, 2024.

**Required:**

1. Prepare the necessary closing entries.
2. Calculate the ending balance of Retained Earnings.
3. Prepare a post-closing trial balance.

Record closing entries and prepare a post-closing trial balance **(LO4–6, 4–7)**
*See E4–19 for financial statement effects.*

**JE4–12** On January 1, 2024, Red Flash Photography had the following balances: Cash, $12,000; Supplies, $8,000; Land, $60,000; Deferred Revenue, $5,000; Common Stock $50,000; and Retained Earnings, $25,000. During 2024, the company had the following transactions:

| | |
|---|---|
| February 15 | Issue additional shares of common stock, $20,000. |
| May 20 | Provide services to customers for cash, $35,000, and on account, $30,000. |
| August 31 | Pay salaries to employees for work in 2024, $23,000. |
| October 1 | Purchase rental space for one year, $12,000. |
| November 17 | Purchase supplies on account, $22,000. |
| December 30 | Pay dividends, $2,000. |

Record transactions and prepare adjusting entries, adjusted trial balance, financial statements, and closing entries **(LO4–3, 4–4, 4–5, 4–6, 4–7)**

The following information is available on December 31, 2024:

1. Employees are owed an additional $4,000 in salaries.
2. Three months of the rental space has expired.
3. Supplies of $5,000 remain on hand.
4. All of the services associated with the beginning deferred revenue have been performed.

**Required:**

1. Record the transactions that occurred during the year.
2. Record the adjusting entries at the end of the year.
3. Prepare an adjusted trial balance.
4. Prepare an income statement, statement of stockholders' equity, and classified balance sheet.
5. Prepare closing entries.

**JE4–13** On January 1, 2024, the general ledger of Dynamite Fireworks includes the following account balances:

Complete the accounting cycle **(LO4–3, 4–4, 4–5, 4–6, 4–7)**

| Accounts | Debit | Credit |
|---|---|---|
| Cash | $23,800 | |
| Accounts Receivable | 5,200 | |
| Supplies | 3,100 | |
| Land | 50,000 | |
| Accounts Payable | | $ 3,200 |
| Common Stock | | 65,000 |
| Retained Earnings | | 13,900 |
| Totals | $82,100 | $82,100 |

During January 2024, the following transactions occur:

| | |
|---|---|
| January 2 | Purchase rental space for one year in advance, $6,000 ($500/month). |
| January 9 | Purchase additional supplies on account, $3,500 |
| January 13 | Provide services to customers on account, $25,500. |
| January 17 | Receive cash in advance from customers for services to be provided in the future, $3,700. |
| January 20 | Pay cash for salaries, $11,500. |
| January 22 | Receive cash on accounts receivable, $24,100. |
| January 29 | Pay cash on accounts payable, $4,000. |

*Required:*

1. Record each of the transactions listed above.
2. Record adjusting entries on January 31.
   a. Rent for the month of January has expired.
   b. Supplies remaining at the end of January total $2,800.
   c. By the end of January, $3,200 of services has been provided to customers who paid in advance on January 17.
   d. Unpaid salaries at the end of January are $5,800.
3. Prepare an adjusted trial balance as of January 31, 2024, after updating beginning balances (above) for transactions during January (Requirement 1) and adjusting entries at the end of January (Requirement 2).
4. Prepare an income statement for the period ended January 31, 2024.
5. Prepare a classified balance sheet as of January 31, 2024.
6. Record closing entries.
7. Analyze the following features of Dynamite Fireworks' financial condition:
   a. What is the amount of profit reported for the month of January?
   b. Calculate the ratio of current assets to current liabilities at the end of January.
   c. Based on Dynamite Fireworks' profit and ratio of current assets to current liabilities, indicate whether Dynamite Fireworks appears to be in good or bad financial condition.

## Journal Entries—Problems

**Record adjusting entries (LO4–3)**

*See P4–3 for financial statement effects.*

**JP4–1** The following items are necessary for preparing the 2024 year-end adjusting entries for Gamecock Advertising Agency. Gamecock's fiscal year-end is December 31.

1. On July 1, 2024, Gamecock received $6,000 from a customer for advertising services to be given evenly over the next 10 months.
2. At the end of the year, income taxes owed are $7,000. These taxes won't be paid until next April 15.
3. On May 1, 2024, the company paid $4,800 for a two-year fire and liability insurance policy. The amount was recorded in Prepaid Insurance on May 1.
4. On September 1, 2024, the company borrowed $20,000 from a local bank and signed a note. Principal and interest at 12% will be paid on August 31, 2025.
5. At year-end, there is a $2,700 balance in the Supplies account. Only $1,000 of supplies remains on hand at the end of the year.

*Required:*

Record the necessary adjusting entries on December 31, 2024, for the following accounts: Deferred Revenue, Income Tax Expense, Prepaid Insurance, Interest Expense, and Supplies. No prior adjustments have been made during 2024.

**Record adjusting entries (LO4–3)**

*See P4–4 for financial statement effects.*

**JP4–2** Buzzard Bicycle specializes in custom painting and design of bicycles. December 31 is the company's fiscal year-end. Information necessary to prepare the year-end adjustments appears below.

1. A three-year fire insurance policy was purchased on July 1, 2024, for $18,000. The company recorded the amount in Prepaid Insurance on July 1.
2. Employee salaries of $25,000 for the month of December will be paid in early January.
3. On November 1, 2024, the company received $6,000 in cash from a customer requesting a custom design for six identical bikes ($1,000 each). The entire amount is recorded in Deferred Revenue on November 1. By the end of the year, four of the bikes have been completed.
4. Supplies at the beginning of the year totaled $2,000. During 2024, additional supplies of $18,000 were purchased and recorded in Supplies at the time of purchase. Supplies remaining at the end of the year total $4,000.
5. Buzzard paid a local radio station $12,000 for four months of advertising on December 1, 2024. The advertising will appear evenly over the four-month period. The company recorded the entire amount in Prepaid Advertising on December 1.
6. Buzzard borrowed $36,000 on March 1, 2024. The principal is due to be collected in five years. Interest is receivable each March 1 at an annual rate of 10%.

***Required:***

Record the necessary adjusting entries on December 31, 2024.

**JP4–3** Tar Heels Unlimited began business on January 1, 2024. During January, the following transactions occurred:

Record adjusting entries and prepare an adjusted trial balance (LO4–3, 4–4)

| Jan. | 1 | Issue common stock in exchange for $100,000 cash. |
|---|---|---|
| | 2 | Purchase inventory on account for $35,000. |
| | 4 | Pay an insurance company $2,400 for a one-year insurance policy. |
| | 10 | Sell inventory on account for $12,000. The cost of the inventory was $7,000. |
| | 15 | Borrow $30,000 from a local bank and signed a note. Principal and interest at 10% is to be repaid in six months. |
| | 20 | Pay employees $6,000 salaries for the first half of the month. |
| | 22 | Sell inventory for $10,000 cash. The cost of the inventory was $6,000. |
| | 24 | Pay $15,000 to suppliers for the inventory purchased on January 2. |
| | 26 | Collect $6,000 on account from customers. |
| | 28 | Pay $1,000 to the local utility company for January gas and electricity. |
| | 30 | Pay $4,000 rent for the building. Of this amount, $2,000 is for January rent, and $2,000 is for February rent. Prepaid Rent and Rent Expense are debited for their appropriate amounts. |

***Required:***

1. Record each transaction.
2. Record adjusting entries for (a) one month of expired insurance related to January 4 purchase, (b) one-half month of interest owed related to January 15 borrowing, and (c) salaries payable at the end of January of $6,000.
3. Prepare an adjusted trial balance as of January 30, 2024. All accounts had a balance of $0 at the beginning of January.

**JP4–4** The year-end financial statements of Rattlers Tax Services are provided below.

Record closing entries and prepare a post-closing trial balance (LO4–6, 4–7)
*See P4–6 for financial statement effects.*

**RATTLERS TAX SERVICES**
**Income Statement**

| Service revenue | | $77,500 |
|---|---|---|
| Expenses: | | |
| Salaries | $46,000 | |
| Utilities | 8,200 | |
| Insurance | 5,800 | |
| Supplies | 2,100 | 62,100 |
| Net income | | $15,400 |

**RATTLERS TAX SERVICES**
**Statement of Stockholders' Equity**

| | Common Stock | Retained Earnings | Total S. Equity |
|---|---|---|---|
| Beg. bal., Jan. 1 | $ 60,000 | $ 24,500 | $ 84,500 |
| Issue stock | 30,000 | | 30,000 |
| Net income | | 15,400 | 15,400 |
| Dividends | | (6,000) | (6,000) |
| Ending bal., Dec. 31 | $ 90,000 | $ 33,900 | $123,900 |

**RATTLERS TAX SERVICES**
**Balance Sheet**

| Assets | | | Liabilities | | |
|---|---|---|---|---|---|
| Cash | $ | 4,700 | Accounts payable | $ | 3,000 |
| Accounts receivable | | 7,200 | **Stockholders' Equity:** | | |
| Land | | 115,000 | Common stock | $90,000 | |
| | | | Retained earnings | 33,900 | 123,900 |
| Total assets | | $126,900 | Total liabs. and equities | | $126,900 |

**Required:**

1. Record year-end closing entries.

2. Prepare a post-closing trial balance. (*Hint:* The balance of Retained Earnings will be the amount shown in the balance sheet.)

Record transactions and prepare adjusting entries, adjusted trial balance, financial statements, and closing entries (LO4–3, 4–4, 4–5, 4–6, 4–7)

**JP4–5** Crimson Tide Music Academy offers lessons in playing a wide range of musical instruments. The *unadjusted* trial balance as of December 31, 2024, appears below. December 31 is the company's fiscal year-end.

| Accounts | Debit | Credit |
|---|---|---|
| Cash | $ 10,300 | |
| Accounts Receivable | 9,500 | |
| Interest Receivable | -0- | |
| Supplies | 2,000 | |
| Prepaid Rent | 7,200 | |
| Land | 78,000 | |
| Notes Receivable | 20,000 | |
| Accounts Payable | | $   7,700 |
| Salaries Payable | | -0- |
| Deferred Revenue | | 5,300 |
| Utilities Payable | | -0- |
| Common Stock | | 79,000 |
| Retained Earnings | | 19,700 |
| Service Revenue | | 42,200 |
| Interest Revenue | | -0- |
| Salaries Expense | 24,500 | |
| Rent Expense | -0- | |
| Supplies Expense | -0- | |
| Utilities Expense | 2,400 | |
| Totals | $153,900 | $ 153,900 |

In addition, the company had the following year-end adjusting entries.

| | Debit | Credit |
|---|---|---|
| a. Salaries Expense | 2,100 | |
|    Salaries Payable | | 2,100 |
| b. Interest Receivable | 800 | |
|    Interest Revenue | | 800 |
| c. Supplies Expense | 1,300 | |
|    Supplies | | 1,300 |
| d. Deferred Revenue | 3,300 | |
|    Service Revenue | | 3,300 |
| e. Rent Expense | 5,400 | |
|    Prepaid Rent | | 5,400 |
| f. Utilities Expense | 200 | |
|    Utilities Payable | | 200 |

**Required:**

Complete the following steps:

1. Prepare an adjusted trial balance.

2. Prepare an income statement and a statement of shareholders' equity for the year ended December 31, 2024, and a classified balance sheet as of December 31, 2024. Assume no common stock is issued during the year.

3. Record closing entries.

4. Prepare a post-closing trial balance.

## DATA ANALYTICS

Visit Connect to view **Data Analytics** questions related to:

1. Applying Excel
2. Data Visualizations
3. Tableau Dashboard Activities
4. Applying Tableau

## ANSWERS TO THE SELF-STUDY QUESTIONS

1. b   2. c   3. c   4. b   5. a   6. b   7. c   8. b   9. d   10. a   11. c   12. d   13. b   14. d   15. c

# 5 Revenue and Receivables

## Learning Objectives

## Self-Study Materials

Shutterstock/Rocketclips, Inc.

## Feature Story

## Tenet Healthcare: Bad Debts Cause Pain to Investors

**Tenet Healthcare Corporation** is one of the largest hospital chains in the United States. The company operates 65 hospitals and 500 other health-care facilities, employs over 110,000 people, and sees millions of patients each year. Everything seems fine, right?

Wrong. Over the period 2017–2019, Tenet reported net losses of $825 million. One of the key reasons for Tenet's poor operating performance was "uncompensated care." Uncompensated care occurs when patients receive services but are either unable or unwilling to pay. Though hospitals try to minimize these costs, federal law requires that patients not be denied emergency treatment due to their inability to pay.

Companies, like Tenet, can report revenue only for the amount they are *entitled* to receive. In the case of Tenet, the company must reduce its reported amount of revenue for discounted services provided to uninsured and underinsured patients. Estimates of this uncompensated care over the 2017–2019 period may have been as much as $5 billion, easily enough to have turned the company's losses into large profits.

In addition, Tenet provides some services to customers without receiving immediate payments, but for which it is unconditionally entitled to receive payment. Tenet bills these customers, hoping to receive cash in the future. These amounts to be received are reported as accounts receivable. Most customers end up paying, but some customers don't ever pay. At the end of each year, Tenet is required to *estimate* the amount of receivables not expected to be collected (bad debts), further reducing the company's reported profitability and total assets.

As you can see from this discussion, health-care providers face enormous challenges in providing individuals with necessary health care while maintaining profitability. At the end of the chapter, we'll analyze how well management of **Tenet Healthcare Corporation** collects cash from customers and compare the results with **LifePoint Hospitals.** Generally, the better a company is at collecting cash from customers, the more efficiently managers can run the business and the more profitable the company will be.

## PART A

# REVENUE

What is revenue? Revenues are inflows of assets or settlements of liabilities (or a combination of both) from delivering goods or services as part of a business entity's core operations. In simpler terms, revenue is the inflow of cash or accounts receivable that a business receives when it provides goods or services to its customers.

For many companies, revenue is the single largest number reported in the financial statements. Its pivotal role in helping to understand the performance and value of a business makes measuring and reporting revenue one of the most critical aspects of financial reporting. It is important not only to determine *how much* revenue to recognize, but also *when* to recognize it. A one-year income statement should report a company's revenues during only that one-year period. Sometimes, though, it's difficult to determine how much revenue to recognize in a particular period. Also, you can imagine that a manager who is evaluated according to how much revenue the company generates each period might be tempted to recognize more revenue than is appropriate. Revenue recognition accounting standards help ensure that the appropriate amount of revenue appears in each period's income statement.

## Revenue Recognition

Let's start with the core revenue recognition principle and the key steps we use to apply that principle. These are shown in Illustration 5–1.

**ILLUSTRATION 5–1**

**Revenue Recognition Principle and the Five Steps Used to Apply the Principle**

**Core Revenue Recognition Principle**

Companies recognize revenue when goods or services are transferred to customers for the amount the company expects to be entitled to receive in exchange for those goods or services.*

**Five Steps Used to Apply the Principle**

Step 1 • Identify the contract with a customer.

Step 2 • Identify the performance obligation(s) in the contract.

Step 3 • Determine the transaction price.

Step 4 • Allocate the transaction price to each performance obligation.

Step 5 • Recognize revenue when (or as) each performance obligation is satisfied.

*FASB ASC 606-10-05-4: Revenue from Contracts with Customers—Overall—Overview and Background—General [previously "Revenue from Contracts with Customers (Topic 606)" Accounting Standards Update 2014–09 (Norwalk, CT: FASB, 2014)].

All revenue recognition starts with a contract between a seller and a customer. Contracts contain one or more performance obligations, which are promises made by the seller to transfer goods, services, or both to a customer. The seller recognizes revenue when it satisfies a performance obligation by transferring the promised good or service. We consider transfer to have occurred when the customer has *control* of the good or service. *Control* means that the customer has direct influence over the use of the good or service and obtains its benefits.

## Recognizing Revenues at a Single Point in Time

■ **LO5–1**

Explain when revenue should be recognized at a single point in time.

First, we consider a simple contract that includes only one performance obligation that is satisfied at a single point in time. For such contracts, working through the five-step process to apply the revenue recognition principle is straightforward, as we typically just have to decide when the seller has satisfied the performance obligation by delivering goods or providing a service.

To illustrate, assume **Nordstrom** sells a skirt to a customer for $75 that Nordstrom previously purchased from a wholesaler for $40. How would Nordstrom account for the sale?

1. **Identify the contract with a customer:** In this case, the contract may not be written, but it is clear—Nordstrom delivers the skirt to the customer, and the customer agrees to pay $75 to Nordstrom.
2. **Identify the performance obligation(s) in the contract:** Nordstrom has only one performance obligation—to deliver the skirt.
3. **Determine the transaction price:** Nordstrom is entitled to receive $75 from the customer.
4. **Allocate the transaction price to each performance obligation:** With only one performance obligation, Nordstrom allocates the full transaction price of $75 to delivery of the skirt.
5. **Recognize revenue when (or as) each performance obligation is satisfied:** Nordstrom satisfies its performance obligation when it delivers the skirt to the customer.

The financial statement effects of the transaction are as follows:

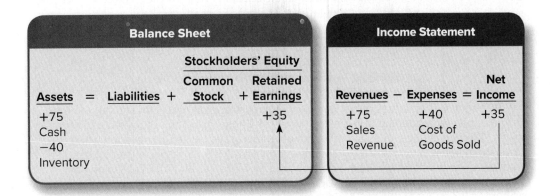

It's typically obvious when the performance obligation has been satisfied. In the Nordstrom example, the obligation is satisfied when the customer walks out of the store with the skirt. But what if the skirt was ordered by the customer online and shipped to their home address. When is the performance obligation satisfied? As presented in Illustration 5–2, Nordstrom discloses in its annual report that revenue associated with online orders is recognized when the goods are shipped to customers (at "shipping point").

**ILLUSTRATION 5–2**

Excerpt from Nordstrom's Annual Report

| **NORDSTROM** |
| **Notes to the Financial Statements (excerpt)** |
| Revenue from sales to customers shipped from our Supply Chain Network facilities, stores and directly from our vendors ("shipped revenues"), which includes shipping revenue when applicable, is recognized at shipping point, the point in time where control has transferred to the customer. |

Several indicators can be used to determine when a performance obligation is satisfied because a good has been delivered or a service provided. A performance obligation is likely satisfied if the customer has any of the following:

1. An obligation to pay the seller.
2. Received legal title to the good or received the service.
3. Physical possession of the asset.
4. Assumed the risk and reward of ownership to the good or receiving the service.
5. Accepted the goods or service.

## DEFERRED REVENUE (AT A SINGLE POINT IN TIME)

Contracts often involve receiving cash in advance of satisfying a performance obligation, which requires recognition of a liability called deferred revenue, which is also sometimes referred to as *unearned revenue*. For example, **American Airlines** generally receives payments from customers in advance (often months in advance) in order for the customer to reserve a seat of an upcoming flight (see Illustration 5–3).

**ILLUSTRATION 5–3**

Excerpt from American Airlines' Annual Report

**AMERICAN AIRLINES**
**Notes to the Financial Statements (excerpt)**

We recognize all revenues generated from transportation on American and our regional flights operated under the brand name American Eagle, including associated baggage fees, ticketing change fees, and other inflight services, as passenger revenue when transportation is provided. Ticket and other related sales for transportation that has not yet been provided are initially deferred and recorded as air traffic liability on our consolidated balance sheets. The air traffic liability principally represents tickets sold for future travel on American and partner airlines, as well as estimated future refunds and exchanges of tickets sold for past travel.

To illustrate the process of recording deferred revenue, suppose on March 15, American Airlines received $350 from a customer for a flight that was to take place on May 3. The financial statement effects of the transaction on March 15 when the cash is received are as follows:

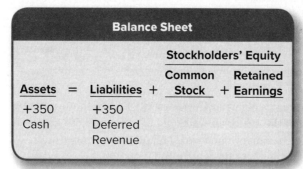

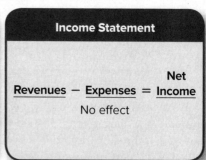

Then, on May 3 when the flight takes place, American Airlines has satisfied its performance obligation and can recognize revenue. The financial statement effects are as follows:

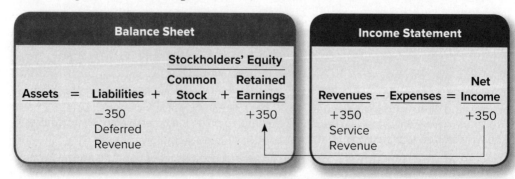

**DEBITS & CREDITS**

To record the receipt of cash on March 15, American Airlines would record the following journal entry:

|  | Debit | Credit |
|---|---|---|
| **Cash**........................................................................... | **350** | |
|    **Deferred Revenue**......................................................... | | **350** |

To recognize revenue at the conclusion of the flight on May 3, American Airlines would record the following journal entry:

|  | Debit | Credit |
|---|---|---|
| **Deferred Revenue**......................................................... | **350** | |
|    **Service Revenue**............................................................ | | **350** |

| Cash | |
|---|---|
| 350 | |

| Deferred Revenue | |
|---|---|
| | 350 |

| Deferred Revenue | |
|---|---|
| 350 | |

| Service Revenue | |
|---|---|
| | 350 |

**KEY POINT**

Revenue should be recognized at a single point in time when control of a good or service is transferred to the customer on a specific date. Indicators that transfer has occurred and that revenue should be recognized include the seller having the right to receive payment, the customer having legal title and physical possession of the asset, the customer formally accepting the asset, and the customer assuming the risks and rewards of ownership.

## Recognizing Revenues over a Period of Time

Services such as lending money, performing audits, and providing consulting advice are performed over a period of time. Some construction contracts require construction over months or even years. In these situations, should a company recognize revenue continuously over time as a product or service is being provided, or wait to recognize revenue at the single point in time when the company has finished providing the product or service? As we'll see next, in most situations like these, companies should recognize revenue over time as the service or product is being provided.

Revenue should be recognized over time if either:

1. The customer consumes the benefit of the seller's work as it is performed, or
2. The customer controls the asset as it is created, or
3. The seller is creating an asset that has no alternative use to the seller, and the seller has the legal right to be paid.

If a performance obligation meets at least one of these criteria, then we recognize revenue over time *in proportion to the amount of the performance obligation that has been satisfied*. If, say, one-third of a service has been performed, then one-third of the performance obligation has been satisfied and one-third of the revenue should be recognized. For example, **Vail Resorts** recognizes revenue from season pass sales throughout the entire ski season (see Illustration 5–4).

■ **LO5–2**
Explain when revenue should be recognized over a period of time.

**ILLUSTRATION 5–4**
**Excerpt from Vail Resorts' Annual Report**

**VAIL RESORTS**
**Notes to the Financial Statements (excerpt)**

The number of season pass holder visits is estimated based on historical data and the revenue is recognized throughout the ski season based on this estimate, or on a straight-line basis if usage patterns cannot be determined based on available historical data.

If a performance obligation doesn't meet any of the three criteria for recognizing revenue over time, then we recognize revenue at the point in time when the performance obligation has been completely satisfied, which usually occurs at the end of the contract. Many services are so short term in nature that companies don't bother with recognizing revenue over time, even if they qualify for doing so. For example, a two-week IT project may provide benefit to a customer as the work is being performed, so it meets the first criterion for revenue recognition over time. However, from a practical perspective, it likely is easier to simply recognize revenue for the service at the conclusion of work. This departure from generally accepted accounting principles (GAAP) is immaterial given the short duration of the service and the lack of additional useful information that would be provided by more precise timing of revenue recognition.

## DEFERRED REVENUE (OVER A PERIOD OF TIME)

In the deferred revenue example for American Airlines discussed previously, the company satisfies the performance obligation at a point in time (e.g., at the time of the flight). But how is deferred revenue impacted if the performance obligation is satisfied over time? In its annual report, **Dropbox** discloses that it generally takes payments from customers in advance in a subscription model that allows customers to access its platform over a specified period of time in the future (see Illustration 5–5). Because Dropbox satisfies its performance obligation over time, it should recognize revenue over time.

**ILLUSTRATION 5–5**

Excerpt from Dropbox's Annual Report

### DROPBOX
### Notes to the Financial Statements (excerpt)

The Company's subscription agreements generally have monthly or annual contractual terms and a small percentage have multi-year contractual terms. Revenue is recognized ratably over the related contractual term beginning on the date that the platform is made available to a customer. Access to the platform represents a series of distinct services as the Company continually provides access to, and fulfills its obligation to the end customer over the subscription term. The series of distinct services represents a single performance obligation that is satisfied over time. The Company recognizes revenue ratably because the customer receives and consumes the benefits of the platform throughout the contract period. The Company's contracts are generally non-cancelable.

To illustrate the process, suppose on October 1, Dropbox receives a payment of $120 for an annual plan that offers 1TB of storage space. The financial statement effects of the receipt of cash and the start of the subscription on October 1 are as follows:

| Balance Sheet | | | | | Income Statement | | |
|---|---|---|---|---|---|---|---|
| | | | **Stockholders' Equity** | | | | |
| | | | Common | Retained | | | **Net** |
| **Assets** | = | **Liabilities** + | **Stock** + | **Earnings** | **Revenues** − | **Expenses** = | **Income** |
| +120 | | +120 | | | | No effect | |
| Cash | | Deferred | | | | | |
| | | Revenue | | | | | |

Notice that Dropbox recognizes no revenue on October 1. Rather, Dropbox recognizes a deferred revenue liability of $120 associated with receiving cash prior to satisfying its performance obligation to provide customers with storage for one year. Dropbox subscribers receive benefits each day they have access to the platform, so Dropbox uses "proportion of time" as its measure of progress toward completion. At the end of each of the 12 months following the sale, Dropbox would recognize one-twelfth of the total amount, or $10 in revenue, and reduce the Deferred Revenue account by a corresponding $10. For example, on October 31, one month later, the financial statement effects of recognizing revenue for the month of October would be as follows:

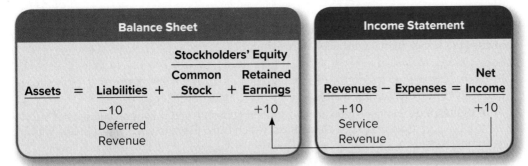

| Balance Sheet | | | | | | Income Statement | | | |
|---|---|---|---|---|---|---|---|---|---|
| | | | **Stockholders' Equity** | | | | | | |
| | | | **Common** | **Retained** | | | | | **Net** |
| **Assets** | = | **Liabilities** + | **Stock** + | **Earnings** | | **Revenues** − | **Expenses** = | **Income** | |
| −10 | | | | +10 | | +10 | | +10 | |
| Deferred | | | | | | Service | | | |
| Revenue | | | | | | Revenue | | | |

After 12 months, Dropbox will have recognized the entire $120 of subscription revenue and the Deferred Revenue account will be reduced to zero.

---

**DEBITS & CREDITS**

To record the receipt of cash on October 1, Dropbox would record the following journal entry:

|  | Debit | Credit |
|---|---|---|
| **Cash**............................................................................ | **120** | |
| **Deferred Revenue**............................................... | | **120** |

To recognize revenue at the conclusion of the first month of service, Dropbox box would record the following journal entry on October 31:

|  | Debit | Credit |
|---|---|---|
| **Deferred Revenue ($120 ÷ 12 months)**.................. | **10** | |
| **Service Revenue** ............................................... | | **10** |

| Cash | |
|---|---|
| 120 | |

| Deferred Revenue | |
|---|---|
| | 120 |

| Deferred Revenue | |
|---|---|
| 10 | |

| Service Revenue | |
|---|---|
| | 10 |

---

**KEY POINT**

Revenue should be recognized over time when a performance obligation is satisfied over time. That occurs if (1) the customer consumes the benefit of the seller's work as it is performed, (2) the customer controls the asset as the seller creates it, or (3) the asset has no alternative use to the seller, and the seller has a legal right to be paid.

---

## Recognizing Revenue for Contracts That Contain Multiple Performance Obligations

Revenue recognition becomes more complicated when a contract contains multiple performance obligations, particularly if the performance obligations are satisfied at different points in time. For example, **IBM** discloses in its annual report that it often provides a basket of goods and services under a single contract that includes consulting services, hardware, software, and related financing (see Illustration 5–6).

**■ LO5–3**
Allocate a contract's price to multiple performance obligations.

**ILLUSTRATION 5–6**
Excerpt from IBM's Annual Report

---

**IBM**
**Notes to the Financial Statements (excerpt)**

The company's global capabilities as a cognitive solutions and cloud platform company include services, software, hardware and related financing. The company enters into revenue arrangements that may consist of any combination of these products and services based on the needs of its clients. For example, a client may purchase a server that includes operating system software. In addition, the arrangement may include post-contract support for the software and a contract for post-warranty maintenance service for the hardware. These types of arrangements may also include financing provided by the company. These arrangements consist of multiple products and services, whereby the hardware and software may be delivered in one period and the software support and hardware maintenance services are delivered over time.

We will illustrate how to recognize revenue using the five-step process for contracts with multiple performance obligations using **Microsoft**'s Xbox All Access bundle. Illustration 5–7 provides the key elements on the All Access bundle.

**ILLUSTRATION 5–7**

All Access Bundle Elements

Microsoft's Xbox All Access bundle:

- For $480, customers receive an Xbox gaming console and a 24-month subscription to Xbox Live Gold and Xbox Game Pass, which allow users to play games online with other users.
- This bundle is priced such that purchasing an Xbox console and then subscribing to Xbox Live Gold and Xbox Game Pass separately would be significantly more expensive for the customer.
- Microsoft sells Xbox consoles separately for $360.
- Microsoft sells a 24-month subscription to Xbox Live Gold and Xbox Game Pass at a cost of $10 per month ($240 total).

## STEP 1: IDENTIFY THE CONTRACT

Microsoft agreed to provide the console and the 24-month subscription service, and the customer agrees to pay the bundle price. Generally this indicates the existence of a contract, so step 1 of the revenue recognition process is satisfied.

## STEP 2: IDENTIFY THE PERFORMANCE OBLIGATION(S) IN THE CONTRACT

Sellers account for a promise to provide a good or service as a performance obligation if the good or service is distinct from other goods or services in the contract. The idea is to separate contracts into parts that can be viewed on a stand-alone basis. That way, the financial statements can better reflect the timing of the transfer of separate goods and services and the profit generated on each one. Goods or services that are not distinct are combined and treated as a single performance obligation.

A good or service is distinct if it is *both:*

1. *Capable of being distinct.* The customer could use the good or service on its own or in combination with other goods or services it could obtain elsewhere, and
2. *Separately identifiable from other goods or services in the contract.* The promises to transfer goods and services are distinct in the context of the contract, because the seller is promising to provide goods and services individually as opposed to promising to provide a combined good or service for which the individual goods or services are inputs.

In the case of the Microsoft All Access bundle, do the Xbox console and the 24-month subscription service qualify as performance obligations?

**Which of the goods and services promised in the contract are distinct?** Both the gaming console and the 24-month subscription can be used on their own by a customer, so they are capable of being distinct. The console and subscription are not highly interrelated and do not modify or customize each other, and the nature of Microsoft's promise is not to integrate the console and subscription into a combined unit, so they are separately identifiable in the context of the contract.

**Conclusion:** The console and subscription are distinct, so the contract has two performance obligations: (1) delivery of an Xbox console and (2) fulfillment of a 24-month online gaming subscription.

## STEP 3: DETERMINE THE TRANSACTION PRICE

The transaction price is the amount the seller expects to be entitled to receive from the customer in exchange for providing goods or services. Determining the transaction price is simple if the customer pays a fixed amount immediately or soon after the sale. That's not the case with the Xbox All Access bundle. The transaction price is $480, but how much of this amount is for the console and how much is for the subscription?

## STEP 4: ALLOCATE THE TRANSACTION PRICE TO EACH PERFORMANCE OBLIGATION

If a contract includes more than one performance obligation, the seller (Microsoft) allocates the transaction price to each one in proportion to the stand-alone selling prices of the goods or services in the contract. The stand-alone selling price is the amount at which the good or service is sold separately under similar circumstances. If a stand-alone selling price can't be directly observed, the seller should estimate it. Illustration 5–8 shows how this allocation is performed.

**ILLUSTRATION 5–8**

Allocating the Transaction Price to Performance Obligations Based on Relative Selling Prices

Assume the same facts as provided in Illustration 5–7, namely:

- The transaction price is $480.
- The stand-alone price of the console is $360.
- The stand-alone price of the 24-month subscription service is $240 ($10 × 24 months).

Because the stand-alone price of the console ($360) represents 60% of the sum of the stand-alone selling prices [$360 ÷ ($360 + $240)], and the stand-alone price of a subscription comprises 40% of the total [$240 ÷ ($360 + $240)], we allocate 60% of the transaction price to the console and 40% of the transaction price to the subscription, as follows:

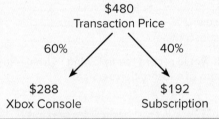

$480
Transaction Price

60%          40%

$288              $192
Xbox Console      Subscription

## STEP 5: RECOGNIZE REVENUE WHEN (OR AS) EACH PERFORMANCE OBLIGATION IS SATISFIED

Suppose Microsoft receives cash of $480 from a customer for an Xbox All Access contract on January 1 and delivered the Xbox console on that same day. Based on the allocation determined in Step 4, the $288 of revenue associated with the Xbox console is recognized immediately when the console is delivered to the customer on January 1. However, the $192 of revenue associated with the subscription service is initially deferred and will be recognized over the 24-month subscription period. The financial statement effects on January 1 are as follows:[1]

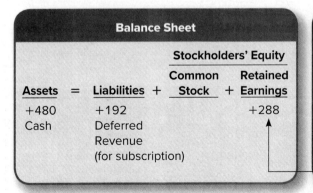

| Balance Sheet | | | | | Income Statement | | | |
|---|---|---|---|---|---|---|---|---|
| | | | **Stockholders' Equity** | | | | | |
| | | | **Common** | **Retained** | | | | **Net** |
| **Assets** | **=** | **Liabilities +** | **Stock +** | **Earnings** | **Revenues −** | **Expenses** | **=** | **Income** |
| +480 | | +192 | | +288 | +288 | | | +288 |
| Cash | | Deferred | | | Sales | | | |
| | | Revenue | | | Revenue | | | |
| | | (for subscription) | | | (for console) | | | |

---

[1]The financial statement effects also would include cost of goods sold (expense) and decrease to inventory (asset) to recognize the cost of inventory sold. For simplicity, we ignore those effects here to focus on revenue recognition.

At the end of each of the next 24 months, Microsoft then would recognize revenue of $8, which equals one-twenty-fourth of the total subscription amount of $192. For example, at the end of January (after the first month), the financial statement effects of recognizing revenue would be as follows:

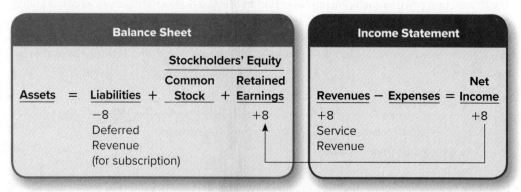

### DEBITS & CREDITS

On January 1, Microsoft would record the following journal entry when the contract is signed, and the gaming console is provided to the customer:

|  | Debit | Credit |
|---|---|---|
| Cash................................................................................... | 480 | |
|    Sales Revenue (for console)............................................. | | 288 |
|    Deferred Revenue (for subscription)................................ | | 192 |

On January 31, Microsoft would record the following journal entry to recognize revenue at the end of the first month of subscription service:

|  | Debit | Credit |
|---|---|---|
| Deferred Revenue (for subscription)................................ | 8 | |
|    Service Revenue ............................................................... | | 8 |

**Discounts in Contracts with Multiple Performance Obligations.**    Note that the Microsoft Xbox All Access example shows that the bundle is sold at a discount—Microsoft sells the bundle for a transaction price ($480) that's less than the sum of the stand-alone selling prices of the gaming console and subscription service ($600 = $360 console + $240 subscription). This type of bundled discount is very common. Because there is no evidence that the discount relates to only one of the performance obligations, it is spread between them in the allocation process. If Microsoft had clear evidence from sales of those goods and services that the discount related to only one of them, the entire discount would be allocated to that good or service.

 **KEY POINT**

A contract's transaction price is allocated to its performance obligations. The allocation is based on the stand-alone selling prices of the goods and services underlying those performance obligations. The stand-alone selling price must be estimated if a good or service is not sold separately.

## Manager Analysis

| Question | Accounting information | Analysis |
|---|---|---|
| Is a company more aggressively recognizing revenue over time? | Revenue and deferred revenue | A significant decrease in the ratio of deferred revenue to total revenue may indicate that the company is being more aggressive in applying revenue recognition rules. |

Macrovision sells a variety of satellite TV packages. The popular $600 Basic Package includes a hardware component (consisting of a dish and receiver) along with a 12-month subscription to 130 channels. Macrovision sells the hardware component without a subscription for $180 and sells a 12-month subscription to the same 130 channels without hardware for $540/year. Let's account for the sale of one Basic Package for $600 on January 1, 2024.

**Required:**

1. Identify the performance obligations in the Basic Package contract, and determine when revenue for each should be recognized.
2. For the single Basic Package sold on January 1, 2024, allocate the $600 transaction price to the performance obligations in the contract.
3. How much revenue associated with the Basic Package is recognized on January 1, 2024 and how much is deferred?
4. How much revenue associated with the Basic Package is recognized on January 31, 2024 and how much remains in the Deferred Revenue account?

**Solution:**

1. The hardware component and the 12-month subscription are capable of being sold separately and are separately identifiable (the hardware and services are not highly intertwined, so it makes sense to consider them separately). Therefore, the hardware component and the 12-month subscription are distinct from each other and should be treated as separate performance obligations.

   Revenue for the hardware component should be recognized on January 1, 2024, because transfer of control of the hardware occurs when the hardware is delivered to the customer. Revenue for the subscription should be recognized over the next 12 months as the customer receives the benefit of having access to TV channels.

2. Because the stand-alone price of the hardware component ($180) represents 25% of the total of all the stand-alone selling prices ($180 ÷ [$180 + $540]), and the stand-alone price of the 12-month subscription comprises 75% of the total ($540 ÷ [$180 +$540]), we allocate 25% of the transaction price to the hardware component and 75% of the transaction price to the 12-month subscription.

   Hardware component:        $600 × 25% = $150
   12-month subscription:      $600 × 75% = $450

3. On January 1, 2024, revenue of $150 associated with the hardware component is recognized, and $450 is deferred.

4. On January 31, 2024, one month worth of revenue associated with the monthly subscription, or $37.50 ($450.00 ÷ 12 = $37.50), is recognized. The deferred revenue balance is now $412.50 ($450.00 – $37.50 = $412.50).

**Let's Review**

## Net Revenues

Now that we've discussed the revenue recognition principle, let's examine how revenues are presented in the financial statements. You might be surprised to learn the amount of revenues reported in the income statement may not reflect the total amount (or "gross amount") of revenue recognized during the period. Rather, it represents a "net" amount after considering various "allowances." It's common for companies to offer their customers a variety of allowances associated with sales, including discounts and the right to return products. These allowances reduce the amount of cash the company is entitled to receive. Companies can report revenues only for the amount they are entitled to receive in cash after considering the effects of such allowances. The resulting number is called net revenue. To calculate net revenues, managers must estimate the amount of sales returns and discounts customers will take advantage of in the future.

■ LO5–4
Calculate net revenues using sales returns and sales discounts.

## SALES RETURNS

A **sales return** is when a customer returns a product. In the notes to the financial statements, **Macy's** discloses it has reserved (in a current liability account) $269 million for possible merchandise returns and that this estimate is based on historical data (see Illustration 5–9). This estimate reduces the amount of sales revenue reported in the income statement.

**ILLUSTRATION 5–9**

Excerpt from Macy's Annual Report

**MACY'S**
**Notes to the Financial Statements (excerpt)**

Sales of merchandise are recorded at the time of shipment to the customer and are reported net of estimated merchandise returns and certain customer incentives.

*Merchandise Returns*

The Company estimates merchandise returns using historical data and recognizes an allowance that reduces net sales and cost of sales. The liability for merchandise returns is included in accounts payable and accrued liabilities on the Company's Consolidated Balance Sheets and was $213 million as of February 1, 2020 and $269 million as of February 2, 2019.

## DISCOUNTS

Companies can offer two types of discounts to customers: trade discounts and sales discounts. **Trade discounts** represent a reduction in the listed price of a good or service. Companies typically use trade discounts to provide incentives to larger customers or consumer groups to purchase from the company. Trade discounts also can be used to encourage customers to make purchases in certain periods of time. For example, **Deere and Company** discloses that it uses trade discounts in an effort to reduce the effects of seasonality of sales on its production schedules (see Illustration 5–10). Trade discounts are reported *indirectly* by simply reporting revenue equal to the discounted price.

**ILLUSTRATION 5–10**

Excerpt from Deere & Company's Annual Report

**DEERE & COMPANY**
**Notes to the Financial Statements (excerpt)**

*Seasonality.*

Seasonal patterns in retail demand for agricultural equipment result in substantial variations in the volume and mix of products sold to retail customers during the year. Seasonal demand must be estimated in advance, and equipment must be manufactured in anticipation of such demand in order to achieve efficient utilization of manpower and facilities throughout the year. For certain equipment, John Deere offers early order discounts to retail customers. Production schedules are based, in part, on these early order programs.

A **sales discount** represents a reduction, not in the selling price of a good or service, but in the amount received from a credit customer if collection occurs within a specified period of time (we will discuss credit sales in more detail in Part B of this chapter). A sales discount is intended to provide incentive to the customer for quick payment. Discount terms, such as 2/10, n/30, are a shorthand way to communicate the amount of the discount and the time period within which it's available. The term "2/10," pronounced "two ten," for example, indicates the customer will receive a 2% discount if the amount owed is paid within 10 days. The term "n/30," pronounced "net thirty," means that if the customer does not take the discount, full payment net of any returns or allowances is due within 30 days. Suppose a company sells $100 of goods to a customer and offers a 2% sales discount if payment is received within 10 days. If the company expects the customer to pay within the discount period, the company is entitled to receive $98 and should report revenue for that amount.

**KEY POINT**

Sales returns, trade discounts, and sales discounts are subtracted from total revenues to calculate net revenues reported on the income statement.

**Manager Analysis**

| Question | Accounting information | Analysis |
|---|---|---|
| Does a company have a recurring problem with customer satisfaction? | Total sales, sales returns, and sales allowances | If sales returns and sales allowances are routinely high relative to total sales, this might indicate that customers are not satisfied with the company's goods or services. |

**SUSTAINABILITY**

Sustainability accounting seeks to provide information on factors that help a company create long-term value (SASB Conceptual Framework 2020), which can only be accomplished if the company can promote a sustainable revenue stream. This is especially important for companies that rely on natural resources to generate their revenues stream. **Neenah, Inc.**, is recognized as a world-class manufacturer of premium paper, used for writing, text, book covers, and specialty watermark papers. For this company, sourcing tree "fiber" from sustainable forests is a critical environmental and business consideration.

In its 2020 Sustainability Report, Neenah discloses that it takes the following actions to protect the forests that provide its fiber.

> . . .we only purchase fiber from sources that demonstrate sustainable practices and have third-party forest management certification programs, including Sustainable Forestry Initiative (SFI), Forest Stewardship Council (FSC), and the Programme for the Endorsement of Forest Certification schemes (PEFC.)
>
> Neenah will never knowingly procure any pulp or forest products from illegally harvested wood, and we require all vendors and sub-vendors to demonstrate compliance with legal requirements. Similarly, we won't knowingly procure any pulp or forest products from areas where traditional or civil rights are violated; or from uncertified forests having high conservation values threatened by forest management activities; or harvested from genetically modified trees.
>
> We are proud that 100% of Neenah's wood fiber purchases are coming from FSC certified materials and other controlled sources. Our premium fine paper business was the first in our industry to receive FSC certification.

**PART B**

# RECOGNIZING ACCOUNTS RECEIVABLE AND ESTIMATING UNCOLLECTIBLE ACCOUNTS

Companies often provide goods or services to customers, not for cash, but on account. Formally, accounts receivable represent the amount of cash owed to a company by its customers from the sale of goods or services on account.

## Credit Sales and Accounts Receivable

Credit sales transfer goods or services to a customer today while bearing the risk of collecting payment from that customer in the future. Credit sales transactions are also known

■ **LO5–5**
Recognize accounts
receivable at the time of
credit sales.

as *sales on account*. Similarly, credit service transactions are also called *services on account*. Credit sales are common for many businesses. Extending credit to customers makes it more convenient for them to purchase goods or services. It can also potentially increase customer loyalty and boost sales, especially if the company's competitors are not offering credit to their customers. However, extending credit comes with specific costs that all managers must carefully consider. Extending credit delays the collection of cash associated with the sale and thus negatively impacts operating cash flows. There's also the possibility that some customers will fail to pay the amount due.

Credit sales typically include an informal credit agreement supported by an invoice. An invoice is a source document that identifies the date of sale, the customer, the specific items sold, the dollar amount of the sale, and the payment terms. Payment terms typically require the customer to pay within 30 to 60 days after the sale. Even though no cash is received at the time of the credit sale, the seller may be able to recognize revenue immediately if the performance obligation is met and future collection of cash from the customer is probable.

The legal right to *receive* cash in the future is valuable and represents an asset of the company. This asset is referred to as *accounts receivable* (sometimes called trade receivables, receivables, or just "AR").

**Example.** To see how companies recognize credit sales, consider a hypothetical example. On March 1, a company provides services to a customer for $500. The customer doesn't pay cash at the time of service, but instead promises to pay the $500 by March 31. The company has provided the service and is entitled to received $500. The financial statement effects of the transaction are as follows:

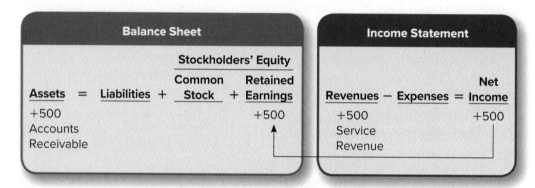

Notice that instead of reporting an increase in Cash, as in a cash sale, the company reports an increase in another asset—Accounts Receivable—for the credit sale. Later, when $500 cash is received from the customer, the company then accounts for the increase to Cash. Also, Accounts Receivable is reduced because the customer no longer owes money to the company. It's important to note that the subsequent receipt of cash does not affect the income statement in any way. The income statement was already affected at the time of sale.

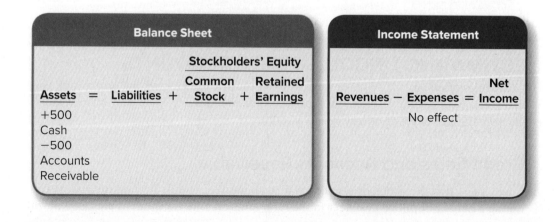

---

**DEBITS & CREDITS**

In the example above, the company would record the following journal entry at the time of the service on March 1:

|  | Debit | Credit |
|---|---|---|
| Accounts Receivable............................................................... | 500 | |
|    Service Revenue ............................................................. | | 500 |

The company would then record the following journal entry when the cash is collected on March 31:

|  | Debit | Credit |
|---|---|---|
| Cash........................................................................................ | 500 | |
|    Accounts Receivable ....................................................... | | 500 |

| Accounts Receivable | |
|---|---|
| 500 | |

| Service Revenue | |
|---|---|
| | 500 |

| Cash | |
|---|---|
| 500 | |

| Accounts Receivable | |
|---|---|
| | 500 |

---

Recall from Part A of this chapter that sellers recognize an amount of revenue equal to the amount they are entitled to receive in exchange for satisfying a performance obligation. Sellers allocate the transaction price to the various performance obligations in a contract and then recognize revenue (and the corresponding receivable for credit sales) when performance obligations are satisfied. Clearly, revenue recognition and accounts receivable recognition are closely related. This means that some of the complexities that affect revenue recognition also affect accounts receivable.

 **KEY POINT**

Companies report an asset (accounts receivable) and revenue when they sell goods or services to their customers on account, expecting collection in the future. Once the receivable is collected, the balance of accounts receivable is reduced.

## Estimating Uncollectible Accounts

The *upside* of extending credit to customers is that it boosts sales by allowing customers the ability to purchase on account and pay cash later. Many customers may not have cash readily available to make a purchase or, for other reasons, simply prefer to buy on credit.

**■ LO5–6**
Establish an allowance for uncollectible accounts.

Even though companies extending credit to their customers do not receive cash at the time of the sale, they have a right to receive cash in the future. This right is a valuable resource for the company. This is why the accounts receivable account is an asset, reported in the company's balance sheet. If the company expects to receive the cash within one year from the date of the balance sheet, then it classifies the receivable as a current asset; otherwise, it classifies the receivable as a long-term asset.

The *downside* of extending credit to customers is that not all customers will pay fully on their accounts. Even the most well-meaning customers may find themselves in difficult financial circumstances beyond their control, limiting their ability to repay debt. Customers' accounts we no longer expect to collect are referred to as uncollectible accounts, doubtful accounts, or *bad debts*.

## Allowance Method

Generally accepted accounting principles (GAAP) require that we account for uncollectible accounts using what's called the allowance method. **Under the allowance method, a company reports its accounts receivable for the net amount *expected* to be collected.** To do this, the company must estimate the amount of *current* accounts receivable that will prove uncollectible in the *future* and report this estimate as a contra asset to its accounts receivable.[2]

Accounts receivable we do not expect to collect have no benefit to the company. Thus, to avoid overstating the assets of the company, we need to reduce accounts receivable in

---

[2]In Appendix A, we'll look at a second method—the direct write-off method. The direct write-off method is used for tax purposes but is generally not permitted for financial reporting.

the balance sheet by an estimate of the amount expected not to be collected. The resulting amount is called "net accounts receivable."

It's important to understand the following key point. Using the allowance method, we account for events (customers' bad debts) that have *not yet* occurred, but that are likely to occur. This is different from other transactions you've learned about up to this point. Those earlier transactions involved reporting events that have already occurred, such as purchasing supplies, paying employees, and providing services to customers. **Under the allowance method, companies are required to estimate *future* uncollectible accounts and report those estimates in the *current* year.** This estimate requires judgment, and companies typically use a variety of information to establish such estimates. For example, **Whirlpool** provides the following disclosure in its annual report about the allowance for doubtful accounts (see Illustration 5–11).

**ILLUSTRATION 5–11**

Excerpt from Whirlpool Annual Report

> ### WHIRLPOOL
> #### Notes to the Financial Statements (excerpt)
>
> **Accounts Receivable and Allowance for Doubtful Accounts**
>
> We carry accounts receivable at sales value less an allowance for doubtful accounts. We periodically evaluate accounts receivable and establish an allowance for doubtful accounts based on a combination of specific customer circumstances, credit conditions and the history of write-offs and collections. We evaluate items on an individual basis when determining accounts receivable write-offs.

To understand how to apply the allowance method, we'll consider the following three stages in the process:

1. At the end of the initial year, establish an allowance by estimating future uncollectible accounts.
2. During the subsequent year, write off actual bad debts as uncollectible. Note that *actual* write-offs may differ from the previous year's *estimate* of future uncollectible accounts.
3. At the end of the subsequent year, once again estimate future uncollectible accounts.

## ESTABLISHING AN ALLOWANCE FOR UNCOLLECTIBLE ACCOUNTS

We will now illustrate the three-stage process by considering the following example. In 2024, its first year of operations, Kimzey Medical Clinic bills customers $50 million for emergency care services provided. By the end of the year, $20 million remains due from customers. Those receivables are assets of the company. However, because Kimzey cannot always verify patients' ability to pay before administering care, it does *not* expect to receive the full $20 million. **The receivables not expected to be collected should not be counted in assets of the company.**

Because this is Kimzey's first year of operations, it hasn't established a record of customer bad debts. Kimzey's credit manager relies on industry data and decides that 30% of the total year-end accounts receivable of $20 million is a reasonable estimate of amounts that won't be collected. The creation of an allowance for future uncollectible accounts affects the reported financial position of the company by reducing assets and increasing expenses by $6 million (=$20 million × 30%) as follows:

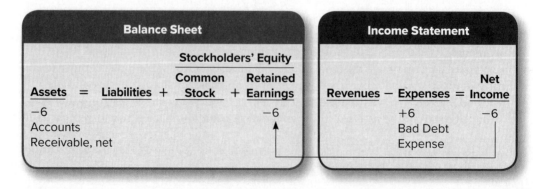

The decrease to "Accounts Receivable, net" represents an increase in Allowance for Uncollectible Accounts (a contra asset account) of $6 million. The balance of the Accounts Receivable account itself remains unchanged. Kimzey also recognizes Bad Debt Expense for the expected uncollectible receivables.

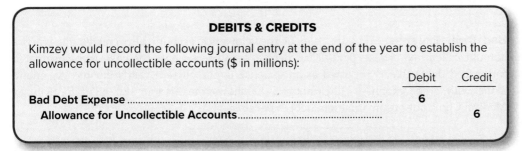

**DEBITS & CREDITS**

Kimzey would record the following journal entry at the end of the year to establish the allowance for uncollectible accounts ($ in millions):

|  | Debit | Credit |
|---|---|---|
| Bad Debt Expense .......................................... | 6 |  |
|    Allowance for Uncollectible Accounts.................. |  | 6 |

Because the nature of these accounts differs somewhat from those we covered in previous chapters, let's take a closer look at each of the accounts involved.

**Allowance for Uncollectible Accounts.** Companies report their estimate of future bad debts using an allowance for uncollectible accounts. Allowance for Uncollectible Accounts is a contra asset account that represents the amount of accounts receivable not expected to be collected. The allowance account provides a way to *reduce accounts receivable* indirectly, rather than decreasing the accounts receivable balance itself.

**We report the allowance for uncollectible accounts in the asset section of the balance sheet, but it represents a reduction in the balance of accounts receivable.** The difference between total (or "gross") accounts receivable and the allowance for uncollectible accounts equals net accounts receivable. Illustration 5–12 demonstrates the concept behind accounting for future uncollectible accounts and how the accounts receivable portion of Kimzey's year-end balance sheet appears.

*Common Terms*
The allowance for uncollectible accounts is sometimes referred to as the *allowance for doubtful accounts*.

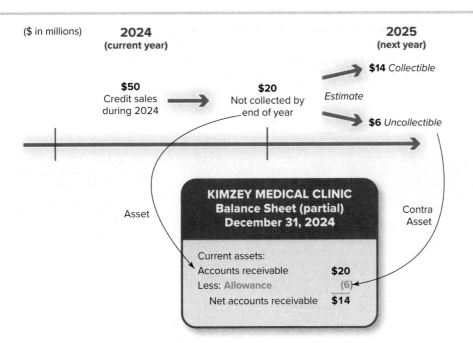

**ILLUSTRATION 5–12**

**Accounting for Uncollectible Accounts and the Accounts Receivable Portion of the Balance Sheet**

After we estimate uncollectible accounts to be $6 million, we reduce the $20 million balance of accounts receivable and report them at their estimated collectible amount of $14 million. But is this estimate correct? Only time will tell. Kimzey's prediction of $6 million for uncollectible accounts might be too high or too low. In either case, it's generally more informative than making no estimate at all. (Later in the chapter, we'll find out how close the estimate is.)

**COMMON MISTAKE**

Because Allowance for Uncollectible Accounts has a normal credit balance, students sometimes misclassify this account as a liability, which also has a normal credit balance. Instead, a contra asset represents a reduction in a related asset.

*Common Terms*
Bad debt expense sometimes is referred to as *uncollectible accounts expense* or *provision for doubtful accounts.*

**Bad Debt Expense.**   The creation of the allowance account also creates an expense account called bad debt expense. Bad debt expense represents the cost of the estimated future bad debts that is reported as an expense in the current year's income statement, along with other expenses. Illustration 5–13 shows the income statement for Kimzey Medical Clinic after estimating bad debt expense.

**ILLUSTRATION 5–13**

Income Statement Showing Bad Debt Expense

| KIMZEY MEDICAL CLINIC<br>Income Statement<br>For the year ended 2024 | | |
| --- | --- | --- |
| ($ in millions) | | |
| Revenue from credit sales | | $50 |
| Expenses: | | |
| Bad debt expense | $ 6 | |
| Other operating expenses | 34 | 40 |
| Net income | | $10 |

In the 2024 income statement, we reduce the $50 million of revenue from credit sales by total expenses of $40 million, of which $6 million is for estimated future bad debts.

**KEY POINT**

Customers' accounts receivable we no longer expect to collect are referred to as uncollectible accounts, or bad debts. Under the allowance method, accounts receivable are reported for the net amount expected to be collected. At the end of the current year, estimated future uncollectible accounts are reported in a contra asset account, reducing net accounts receivable. Establishing an allowance for uncollectible accounts correctly reports accounts receivable in the balance sheet at the amount expected to be collected. Bad debt expense is reported in the income statement.

**Manager Analysis**

| Question | Accounting information | Analysis |
| --- | --- | --- |
| Are the company's credit sales policies too lenient? | Accounts receivable and the allowance for uncollectible accounts | A high ratio of the allowance for uncollectible accounts to total accounts receivable could be an indication that the company extends too much credit to high-risk customers. |

### WRITING OFF ACCOUNTS RECEIVABLE

■ **LO5–7**
Write off accounts receivable as uncollectible.

To continue with our example of Kimzey Medical Clinic, let's suppose on February 23, 2025 (the following year), Kimzey receives notice that one of its former patients, Bruce Easley, has filed for bankruptcy protection against all creditors. Based on this information, Kimzey believes it is unlikely Bruce will pay his account of $4,000. Remember, Kimzey previously allowed for the likelihood that *some* of its customers would not pay, though it didn't know which ones.

Now that it *knows* a specific customer will not pay, it can adjust the allowance and reduce the accounts receivable balance itself. Upon receiving the news, Kimzey will reduce the contra asset allowance account, which will increase net accounts receivable and will also reduce accounts receivables by the same amount. The net effect is no change to net accounts receivable:

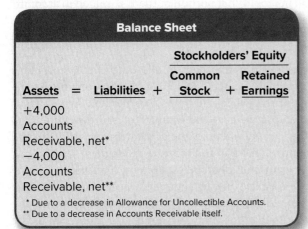

**Balance Sheet**

| Assets | = | Liabilities | + | Stockholders' Equity | |
|---|---|---|---|---|---|
| | | | | Common Stock | + Retained Earnings |
| +4,000 Accounts Receivable, net* | | | | | |
| −4,000 Accounts Receivable, net** | | | | | |

\* Due to a decrease in Allowance for Uncollectible Accounts.
\*\* Due to a decrease in Accounts Receivable itself.

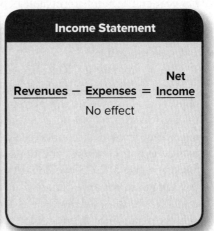

**Income Statement**

| Revenues | − | Expenses | = | Net Income |
|---|---|---|---|---|
| | | No effect | | |

**DEBITS & CREDITS**

Kimzey would record the following journal entry upon receiving news of the uncollectible account on February 23:

| | Debit | Credit |
|---|---|---|
| Allowance for Uncollectible Accounts .................................................. | 4,000 | |
|    Accounts Receivable .................................................. | | 4,000 |

Allowance for
Uncollectible Accounts

| | 4,000 |

Accounts Receivable

| 4,000 | |

**Overall, the write-off of the account receivable has no effect on total amounts reported in the balance sheet or in the income statement.** There is no decrease in total assets and no decrease in net income with the write-off. Here's why: **We have already reported the negative effects of the bad news.** Kimzey reported those effects when it *estimated* future bad debts at the end of 2024 in bad debt expense and the allowance account. So, when Bruce declares bankruptcy in the following year, 2025, we had already allowed for this bad debt. The write-off on February 23, 2025, reduces both an asset account (Accounts Receivable) and its contra asset account (Allowance for Uncollectible Accounts), leaving the *net* receivable unaffected. Thus, the actual write-off results in no change to total assets and no change to net income. What happens if a cash payment is made on a previously written-off account? If this happens, then the financial statement effects of the write-off are simply reversed, and the cash collection on account is recorded.

**COMMON MISTAKE**

Students often mistakenly believe bad debt expense is reported when an uncollectible account is written off. The bad debt expense was reported in a prior year at the time of estimating uncollectible accounts.

**KEY POINT**

Writing off a customer's account as uncollectible reduces the balance of accounts receivable but also reduces the contra asset—allowance for uncollectible accounts. The net effect is that there is no change in the *net* receivable (accounts receivable less the allowance) or in total assets.

## ADJUSTING THE ALLOWANCE IN SUBSEQUENT YEARS

■ LO5–8
Adjust the allowance for
uncollectible accounts in
subsequent years.

At the end of 2025 (the clinic's second year in operations), Kimzey Medical Clinic must once again prepare financial statements. This means once again making a year-end adjustment to estimate uncollectible accounts. Suppose Kimzey has credit sales of $80 million in 2025 and has year-end accounts receivable of $30 million. What portion of the $30 million in accounts receivable does Kimzey not expect to collect? Kimzey is required to report that estimate in allowance for uncollectible accounts in its year-end balance sheet as a contra asset to accounts receivable.

In our example for Kimzey, we previously established an allowance for uncollectible accounts in 2024 by applying a *single* estimated percentage (30%) to total accounts receivable. This is known as the percentage-of-receivables method. This method sometimes is referred to as a *balance sheet method* because we base the estimate of bad debts on a balance sheet account—accounts receivable.[3] For this method, the percentage may be estimated using current economic conditions, company history, and industry guidelines.

At the end of 2025, we could once again multiply total accounts receivable by a single percentage to get an estimate of future uncollectible accounts. However, a more accurate method is to consider the various *ages* of individual accounts receivable, using a higher percentage of uncollectible for "old" accounts than for "new" accounts. This is known as the aging method. For instance, accounts that are 120 days past due are older than accounts that are 60 days past due. **The older the account, the less likely it is to be collected.** The aging method is a more detailed application of the percentage-of-receivables method, so it also is a balance sheet method.

Illustration 5–14 lists eight of Kimzey's individual patients' accounts, including the amount owed by each patient and the number of days past due by the end of 2025. For simplicity, all remaining patients' accounts are summarized in the "Others" row. Shirley Akin owes $12,000, and this amount is not yet due; Cara Lott owes $4,000, and this amount is more than 120 days past due; and so on.

**ILLUSTRATION 5–14**

Kimzey's Accounts
Receivable Aging
Schedule

| Patients | Not Yet Due | Days Past Due 1–60 | Days Past Due 61–120 | Days Past Due More than 120 | Total |
|---|---|---|---|---|---|
| Shirley Akin | $   12,000 | | | | $   12,000 |
| Cara Lott | | | | $   4,000 | 4,000 |
| Ben Greene | | $   5,000 | | | 5,000 |
| Anita Hand | | | $   7,000 | | 7,000 |
| Ima Hertz | 9,000 | | | | 9,000 |
| Noah Luck | | 8,000 | | | 8,000 |
| Phil Sikley | 6,000 | | | | 6,000 |
| Justin Payne | | | | 10,000 | 10,000 |
| Others | 15,973,000 | 8,987,000 | 3,993,000 | 986,000 | 29,939,000 |
| Total Accounts Receivable | $16,000,000 | $ 9,000,000 | $ 4,000,000 | $1,000,000 | $30,000,000 |
| Estimated Percent Uncollectible | 10% | 30% | 50% | 70% | |
| Estimated Amount Uncollectible | $ 1,600,000 | $2,700,000 | $2,000,000 | $ 700,000 | $ 7,000,000 |

The estimated percent
uncollectible increases
with age.

---

[3]In Appendix A to this chapter, we'll consider an income statement method—percentage-of-credit-sales method. In practice, companies are required to use a balance sheet method for financial reporting purposes, so that will be our focus here.

Notice that each age group has its own estimate of the percent uncollectible, and this percentage increases with the age of the account. The "Not Yet Due" column has an estimated 10% percent uncollectible. The "1–60" days past due column has an estimated 30% uncollectible, since these accounts are older and less likely to be collected. The estimated percentage uncollectible continues to increase as the account becomes more past due. Summing the estimated amount uncollectible for each age group results in a total estimate of $7,000,000.

### KEY POINT

Using the aging method to estimate uncollectible accounts is more accurate than applying a single percentage to all accounts receivable. The aging method recognizes that the longer accounts are past due, the less likely they are to be collected.

So, if the estimated amount uncollectible is $7 million, then Allowance for Uncollectible Accounts needs to have an ending balance of $7 million. We need to (1) know the current balance of Allowance for Uncollectible Accounts and then (2) determine the adjustment needed so that the ending balance will be $7 million. Illustration 5–15 provides an illustration of how to determine these amounts.

**ILLUSTRATION 5–15**

Balance of Kimzey's Allowance for Uncollectible Accounts

| **Allowance for Uncollectible Accounts** ($ in millions) | |
| --- | --- |
| Beginning balance in 2025 | 6 |
| *Less:* Write-offs in 2025 | (4) |
| Current balance before adjustment | 2 |
| *Plus:* Year-end adjustment (bad debt expense) | ? |
| Estimated ending balance for 2025 | 7 |

At the end of 2024 (previous year) Kimzey estimated future bad debts to be $6 million. This is the beginning balance of Allowance for Uncollectible Accounts in 2025. Let's assume, however, that only $4 million of accounts were actually written off in 2025. This means the balance of the allowance account at the end of 2025, prior to any year-end adjustment, has a leftover amount of **$2 million.** If we want the ending balance to be $7 million, by how much does the $2 million current balance need to be adjusted?

Kimzey needs an adjustment of $5 million to increase the current balance of $2 million to the estimated ending balance of $7 million.

The financial statement effects of the year-end adjustment to the allowance for uncollectible accounts are as follows:

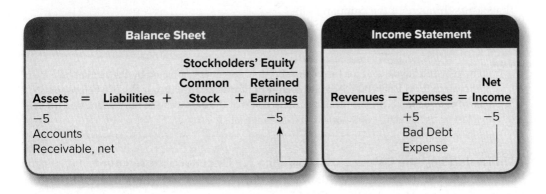

Bad Debt Expense

_____
5 |

Allowance for
Uncollectible Accounts
_____
| 5

**DEBITS & CREDITS**

Kimzey would record the following year-end adjusting entry:

|  | Debit | Credit |
|---|---|---|
| Bad Debt Expense ............................................................. | 5 | |
|     Allowance for Uncollectible Accounts................................. | | 5 |

After the adjusting entry, the allowance account will have a balance of $7 million, and Kimzey can report this amount in its balance sheet. This is shown in Illustration 5–16.

**ILLUSTRATION 5–16**

Accounts Receivable Portion of the Balance Sheet

**KIMZEY MEDICAL CLINIC**
**Balance Sheet (partial)**
**December 31, 2025**

| ($ in millions) | **Assets** | |
|---|---|---|
| Current assets: | | |
|   Accounts receivable | $30 | |
|   Less: Allowance for uncollectible accounts | (7) | |
|     Net accounts receivable | | $23 |

In its 2025 income statement, Kimzey will report bad debt expense of only $5 million (not $7 million). This is the amount of the adjustment to the allowance account in Illustration 5–15. The income statement is shown in Illustration 5–17, along with credit sales of $80 million and other operating expenses of $50 million.

**ILLUSTRATION 5–17**

Bad Debt Expense in the Income Statement

**KIMZEY MEDICAL CLINIC**
**Income Statement**
**For the year ended 2025**

| ($ in millions) | | |
|---|---|---|
| Revenue from credit sales | | $80 |
| Expenses: | | |
|   Bad debt expense | $ 5 | |
|   Other operating expenses | 50 | 55 |
| Net income | | $25 |

The process of estimating an allowance for uncollectible accounts, writing off bad debts in the following period, and then reestimating the allowance at the end of the period is one that occurs throughout the company's life.

 **KEY POINT**

The year-end adjustment for future uncollectible accounts is affected by the current balance of Allowance for Uncollectible Accounts before adjustment. The current balance before adjustment equals the balance of the allowance account at the beginning of the current year (or end of last year) less actual write-offs in the current year.

**Understanding the Balance of Allowance for Uncollectible Accounts.**    Notice in our example that the balance of Allowance for Uncollectible Accounts in 2025 before the year-end adjustment is $2 million. That $2 million is the result of estimating bad debts at the end of 2024 to be $6 million but actual bad debts in 2025 being only $4 million. Therefore, **a *positive* balance before adjustment indicates that the balance of the allowance account at the beginning of the year (or end of last year) may have been too high.** However, it's possible that some of the estimated uncollectible accounts have not proven bad yet.

**A *negative* balance before adjustment indicates that the balance of the allowance account at the beginning of the year was too low.** In the case of a negative balance, we've written off more bad debts in the current year than we had estimated. We'll discuss an example that involves a negative balance in the Let's Review problem at the end of this section. **The year-end adjustment is affected by the extent to which the previous year's ending balance of Allowance for Uncollectible Accounts differs from the current year's actual amount of uncollectible accounts.**

Users of financial statements must realize that some of the amounts reported in financial statements are estimates, and estimating the future almost always results in some inaccuracy. Illustration 5–18 provides an excerpt from the annual report of **Tenet Healthcare Corporation**.

**ILLUSTRATION 5–18**

Excerpt from Tenet Healthcare Corporation's Annual Report

### TENET HEALTHCARE CORPORATION
### Notes to the Financial Statements (excerpt)

The preparation of financial statements, in conformity with accounting principles generally accepted in the United States of America ("GAAP"), requires us to make estimates and assumptions that affect the amounts reported in our Consolidated Financial Statements and these accompanying notes. We regularly evaluate the accounting policies and estimates we use. In general, we base the estimates on historical experience and on assumptions that we believe to be reasonable given the particular circumstances in which we operate. Although we believe all adjustments considered necessary for a fair presentation have been included, actual results may vary from those estimates.

Illustration 5–19 presents Tenet Healthcare's policy of estimating uncollectible accounts using the aging method.

**ILLUSTRATION 5–19**

Excerpt from Tenet Healthcare Corporation's Annual Report

### TENET HEALTHCARE CORPORATION
### Notes to the Financial Statements (excerpt)

We provide for an allowance against accounts receivable that could become uncollectible by establishing an allowance to reduce the carrying value of such receivables to their estimated net realizable value. Generally, we estimate this allowance based on the aging of our accounts receivable by hospital, our historical collection experience by hospital and for each type of payer over a look-back period, and other relevant factors. There are various factors that can impact collection trends, such as changes in the economy, which in turn have an impact on unemployment rates and the number of uninsured and underinsured patients, the volume of patients through our emergency departments, the increased burden of co-pays and deductibles to be made by patients with insurance, and business practices related to collection efforts. These factors continuously change and can have an impact on collection trends and our estimation process.

The following tables present the approximate aging by payer of our net accounts receivable from the continuing operations:

| Age | Medicare | Medicaid | Managed Care | Indemnity, Self-Pay, and Other | Total |
|---|---|---|---|---|---|
| 0–60 days | $372 | $34 | $1,199 | $ 75 | $1,680 |
| 61–120 days | 20 | 7 | 295 | 43 | 365 |
| 121–180 days | 8 | 2 | 157 | 31 | 198 |
| Over 180 days | 4 | 3 | 314 | 161 | 482 |
| Total | $404 | $46 | $1,965 | $310 | $2,725 |

**Subsidiary Ledgers.** Using the aging method requires a company to maintain records for individual customer accounts to help track amounts expected to be received and the portion of those amounts estimated to be uncollectible. This idea was demonstrated in Illustration 5–14. A subsidiary ledger contains a group of individual sub-accounts associated with a particular general ledger account. For example, the subsidiary ledger for accounts receivable keeps track of all increases and decreases to individual customers' accounts. The balances of all individual accounts then sum to the balance of total accounts receivable in the general ledger and reported in the balance sheet. Subsidiary ledgers are also used for accounts payable, property and equipment, investments, and other accounts.

**Let's Review**

Community Medical is an outpatient health facility that provides minor surgical and other health-related services to the local community. Many of the patients do not have medical insurance. These customers are required to pay for services within 30 days of receiving treatment. At the beginning of 2024, Community Medical's allowance for uncollectible accounts was a positive balance of $100,000.

*Required:*

1. What impact will the write-off of $120,000 of actual accounts receivable that became uncollectible during 2024 have on the balance sheet at the end of 2024?

2. Estimate the allowance for future uncollectible accounts using the following age groups, amount of accounts receivable within each age group, and estimated percent uncollectible at the end of 2024:

| Age Group | Amount Receivable | Estimated Percent Uncollectible | Estimated Amount Uncollectible |
|---|---|---|---|
| Not yet due | $600,000 | 10% | |
| 1–45 days past due | 200,000 | 20% | |
| More than 45 days past due | 50,000 | 60% | |
| Total | $850,000 | | |

3. Determine bad debt expense for 2024.

4. Prepare a partial balance sheet showing accounts receivable and the allowance for uncollectible accounts.

*Solution:*

1. The write-off of $120,000 in accounts receivable will decrease both Accounts Receivables and the Allowance for Uncollectible Accounts. Thus, the balance in Net Accounts Receivable reported in the balance sheet will not change.

| The journal entry to record the write-off is as follows: | Debit | Credit |
|---|---|---|
| Allowance for Uncollectible Accounts | 120,000 | |
| Accounts Receivable | | 120,000 |

2. Estimate of the allowance for future uncollectible accounts:

| Age Group | Amount Receivable | Estimated Percent Uncollectible | Estimated Amount Uncollectible |
|---|---|---|---|
| Not yet due | $600,000 | 10% | $ 60,000 |
| 1–45 days past due | 200,000 | 20% | 40,000 |
| More than 45 days past due | 50,000 | 60% | 30,000 |
| Total | $850,000 | | $130,000 |

3. Bad Debt Expense is determined using the following T-account:

| Allowance for Uncollectible Accounts | |
|---|---:|
| Beginning balance in 2024 | 100,000 |
| *Less:* Write-offs in 2024 | (120,000) |
| Current balance before adjustment | (20,000) |
| *Plus:* Year-end adjustment (bad debt expense) | ? |
| Estimated ending balance for 2024 | 130,000 |

Bad Debt Expense for 2024 is $150,000.*

The journal entry to record Bad Debt Expense:

| December 31, 2024 | Debit | Credit |
|---|---|---|
| **Bad Debt Expense** .................................................................. | **150,000** | |
| **Allowance for Uncollectible Accounts**....................................... | | **150,000**\* |

*Notice from the calculation in requirement 3 that the balance of the allowance account before adjustment is a $20,000 *negative*. Based on the estimated allowance of a $130,000, we need an adjustment of $150,000. Of this adjustment, $20,000 is needed to get the allowance account to a zero balance, and the remaining $130,000 adjusts the account to the estimated ending balance.

4. Partial Balance Sheet:

**COMMUNITY MEDICAL**
**Balance Sheet (partial)**
**December 31, 2024**

**Assets**

| | | |
|---|---:|---:|
| Current assets: | | |
| Accounts receivable | $850,000 | |
| Less: Allowance for uncollectible accounts | (130,000) | |
| Net accounts receivable | | $720,000 |

**Direct Write-Off Method (Not GAAP).** We've just seen how the *allowance method* for uncollectible accounts works. This is the method required for financial reporting by generally accepted accounting principles (GAAP). However, for tax reporting, companies use an alternative method commonly referred to as the *direct write-off method.* Under the direct write-off method, we write off bad debts only at the time they actually become uncollectible, unlike the allowance method that requires estimating uncollectible accounts before they even occur.

**It is important to emphasize that the direct write-off method is generally not allowed for financial reporting under GAAP.** It is only used in financial reporting if uncollectible accounts are not anticipated or are expected to be very small. This is an application of the concept of materiality because financial statement users are unlikely to deem it significant in their decision-making process. **The direct write-off method is primarily used for tax reporting.** Companies do not report a tax deduction for bad debts until those bad debts are actually uncollectible.

Under the allowance method, future bad debts are *estimated* and reported as an expense and a reduction in assets in the same period as the revenue it helps to create. Under the direct write-off method, though, we make no attempt to estimate future bad debts. We report bad debt expense in the period the account proves uncollectible.

**The difference between the two methods is in the timing.** The direct write-off method is less timely in recognizing uncollectible accounts.

 **COMMON MISTAKE**

Some students erroneously think firms should reduce total assets and increase bad debt expense at the time the bad debt actually occurs. However, companies *anticipate* future bad debts and establish an allowance for those estimates.

# Decision Maker's Perspective

## Managing Bad Debt Estimates

While the allowance method is conceptually superior to the direct write-off method and more accurately reports assets, it does have one disadvantage. This disadvantage arises from the fact that reported amounts under the allowance method represent management estimates. If so inclined, management could use these estimates to manipulate reported earnings. For example, if management wants to boost earnings in the current year, it can intentionally *underestimate* future uncollectible accounts. Similarly, if a company is having an especially good year and management wants to "reserve" earnings for the future, it can intentionally *overestimate* future uncollectible accounts. Having a large expense in the current year means there is less of a charge to bad debt expense in a future year, increasing future earnings. Other expenses, such as rent expense, are much more difficult to manipulate because their reported amounts don't rely on management estimates. These expenses are evidenced by past transactions, and their amounts are verifiable to the penny using a receipt or an invoice.

HealthSouth Corporation appears to have used estimates of uncollectible accounts to manipulate earnings. In the early 1990s, HealthSouth reported large amounts of bad debt expense, building large reserves in the allowance account. Then in the mid-1990s, as additional earnings were needed to meet analysts' expectations, HealthSouth was able to report low amounts for bad debt expense because of the previously inflated allowance account. In 1999, when it became apparent that HealthSouth's earnings were falling dramatically, the company took a "big bath" by reporting a very large charge to bad debt expense. Some companies feel that if they are going to have a bad year, they might as well release all the bad news at once. This makes it possible to report better news in future years.

 **ETHICAL DILEMMA**

SDI Productions/Getty Images

Philip Stanton, the executive manager of Thomson Pharmaceutical, receives a bonus if the company's net income in the current year exceeds net income in the past year. By the end of 2024, it appears that net income for 2024 will easily exceed net income for 2023. Philip has asked Mary Beth Williams, the company's controller, to try to reduce this year's income and "bank" some of the profits for future years. Mary Beth suggests the company's bad debt expense as a percentage of accounts receivable for 2024 be increased from 10% to 15%. She believes 10% is the more accurate estimate but knows both the corporation's internal and external auditors allow some flexibility in estimates. What is the effect of increasing the estimate of bad debts from 10% to 15% of accounts receivable? How does this "bank" income for future years? Why does Mary Beth's proposal present an ethical dilemma?

# RECEIVABLES ANALYSIS
## Managing Receivables: Tenet vs. LifePoint

■ **LO5–9**
Calculate key ratios to assess the company's effectiveness at managing receivables and the quality of the receivables.

The amount of a company's accounts receivable is influenced by a variety of factors, including the level of sales, the nature of the product or service sold, and credit and collection policies. These factors are, of course, related. For example, a change in credit policies could affect sales. More liberal credit policies—allowing customers a longer time to pay or offering cash discounts for early payment—often are initiated with the specific objective of increasing sales volume.

Management's choice of credit and collection policies results in trade-offs. For example, when a company attempts to boost sales by allowing customers more time to pay, that policy also creates an increase in the required investment in receivables and may increase bad debts because older accounts are less likely to be collected. Offering discounts for early payment may increase sales volume, accelerate customer payment, and reduce bad debts, but at the same time it reduces the amount of cash collected from customers who take advantage of the discounts.

Investors, creditors, and financial analysts can gain important insights by monitoring a company's receivables. Two important ratios that help us understand the company's effectiveness in managing receivables are the *receivables turnover ratio* and the *average collection period*. We will discuss those measures and then compare them for **Tenet Healthcare Corporation** and **LifePoint Hospitals**.

### RECEIVABLES TURNOVER RATIO

Because collection of cash is vital to the company's operations, management closely monitors their ability to collect cash from customers. The more quickly a company is able to collect cash, the more quickly that cash can be used for company operations and the less likely the customer is to default on payment.

The receivables turnover ratio provides a measure of a company's ability to collect cash from customers. The ratio shows the *number of times* during a year that the average accounts receivable balance is collected (or "turns over"). We calculate it as follows:

$$\text{Receivables turnover ratio} = \frac{\text{Net credit sales}}{\text{Average accounts receivable}}$$

The "net" in net credit sales refers to total credit sales net of discounts, returns, and allowances (similar to net revenues calculated earlier in the chapter). The amount for net credit sales is obtained from the current period's income statement. Average accounts receivable equals the average of total (or "gross") accounts receivable reported in this period's and last period's balance sheets. Last period's ending accounts receivable are this period's beginning accounts receivable. As a practical matter, companies often do not separately report net credit sales versus net cash sales. They report only net sales as a total. Because of this, the receivables turnover ratio is most commonly calculated as net sales divided by average accounts receivable. This ratio can be interpreted as how well management collects cash from all sales to customers. **The more frequently a business is able to "turn over" its average accounts receivable, the more effective a company is at granting credit to and collecting cash from its customers.**

### AVERAGE COLLECTION PERIOD

The average collection period is another way to express the same efficiency measure. This ratio shows the approximate *number of days* the average accounts receivable balance is outstanding. It is calculated as 365 days divided by the receivables turnover ratio.

$$\text{Average collection period} = \frac{365 \text{ days}}{\text{Receivables turnover ratio}}$$

The receivables turnover ratio and average collection period are typically calculated over a year using *annual* financial statement information. These ratios, however, can also be calculated over shorter periods, most commonly, a fiscal quarter. In this case, to calculate the receivables turnover ratio net credit sales *for the quarter* would be the numerator of the ratio, and the denominator would be average accounts receivable calculated using the beginning and ending balances *for the quarter*. Then, to calculate the average collection period, 90 days is typically used in the numerator instead of 365.

Companies typically strive for a high receivables turnover ratio and a correspondingly low average collection period. As a company's sales increase, receivables also likely will increase. If the percentage increase in receivables is greater than the percentage increase in sales, the receivables turnover ratio will decline (and the average collection period will increase). A declining turnover ratio could indicate that customers are dissatisfied with the product, the company is selling to high-risk customers, or the company's payment terms for attracting new customers are too generous, all of which could increase sales returns and bad debts.

Of course, what's "high" and "low" for these ratios depends on the situation. Companies may wish to evaluate these ratios relative to the prior year's ratios, ratios of other firms in the same industry, or specific targets set by management.

Let's compare Tenet Healthcare Corporation to LifePoint Hospitals. Below are relevant amounts for each company, along with their bad debt expense.

| ($ in millions) | Net Sales | Beginning Accounts Receivable | Ending Accounts Receivable | Bad Debt Expense |
|---|---|---|---|---|
| Tenet Healthcare | $21,070 | $3,591 | $3,928 | $1,449 |
| LifePoint Hospitals | 7,274 | 1,541 | 1,804 | 910 |

To compute the receivables turnover ratio, we need the average accounts receivable, which is the beginning amount plus the ending amount, divided by 2.

**Tenet Healthcare**    Average accounts receivable
= ($3,591 + $3,928) ÷ 2 = **$3,759.5**

**LifePoint Hospitals**    Average accounts receivable
= ($1,541 + $1,804) ÷ 2 = **$1,672.5**

As shown in Illustration 5–20, we divide net sales by average accounts receivable to compute the receivables turnover ratio. Then, we divide 365 days by the receivables turnover ratio to compute the average collection period.

**ILLUSTRATION 5–20**

Comparison of Receivables Ratios between Tenet Healthcare Corporation and LifePoint Hospitals

| | Receivables Turnover Ratio | Average Collection Period |
|---|---|---|
| **Tenet Healthcare** | $21,070 ÷ **$3,759.5** = 5.6 times | 365 ÷ 5.6 = 65.2 days |
| **LifePoint Hospitals** | $7,274 ÷ **$1,672.5** = 4.3 times | 365 ÷ 4.3 = 84.9 days |

From Illustration 5–20, we see that Tenet has a higher receivables turnover and a shorter collection period, indicating that the company more efficiently collects cash from patients than does LifePoint. The difference can be seen in the ratio of bad debt expense to net sales. For Tenet, bad debt expense represents a 6.9% reduction in net sales (= $1,449 ÷ $21,070). This same ratio for LifePoint is 12.5% (= $910 ÷ $7,274). Thus, LifePoint's less efficient cash collection causes a larger reduction in profitability.

Having enough cash is important to running any business. The more quickly a company can collect its receivables, the more quickly it can use that cash to generate even more cash by reinvesting in the business and generating additional sales.

 **KEY POINT**

The receivables turnover ratio and average collection period provide an indication of management's ability to collect cash from customers in a timely manner.

| Question | | Accounting information | | Analysis | |
|---|---|---|---|---|---|
| Is the company effectively managing its receivables? | | Receivables turnover ratio and average collection period | | A high receivables turnover ratio (or low average collection period) generally indicates that the company's credit sales and collection policies are effective. | |

**Manager Analysis**

## Assessing Receivables Quality: Whirlpool

As discussed earlier in this chapter, the amount of receivables reported in the balance sheet is not the gross or total amount. Rather it's a net amount, called net accounts receivables, that the company expects to collect in cash after considering the possibility that some customers will not pay. To arrive at net accounts receivable, managers exercise their professional judgment, which raises the possibility for bias or manipulation. For example, a manager may be tempted to decrease the amount of the reserve for uncollectible accounts in order to inflate net accounts receivable and total assets. Such manipulation would also inflate net income.

Investors, creditors, and financial analysts can assess the quality of the reported net account receivable balance by examining the allowance ratio, which we calculate as follows:

$$\text{Allowance Ratio} = \frac{\text{Allowance for uncollectible accounts receivable}}{\text{Accounts receivable}}$$

It's important to note that "gross" accounts receivable is used in the denominator of the ratio and not "net" accounts receivable. Gross accounts receivable represent the total amount of outstanding receivables at a given point in time and, therefore, is not influenced by manager's potentially biased expectations of which customers will fail to pay. We can calculate gross accounts receivable by simply adding net accounts receivable and the allowance for uncollectible accounts together. Net accounts receivable is provided in the balance sheet and some companies choose to disclose the allowance amount on the same line. Illustrations 5–21 and 5–22 provide an example from **Whirlpool Corporation**:

**ILLUSTRATION 5–21**

Excerpt from Whirlpool Coporation's Annual Report

| WHIRLPOOL CORPORATION<br>Balance Sheet (excerpt) | | |
|---|---|---|
| | **Dec. 31, 2020** | **Dec. 31, 2019** |
| **Assets** | | |
| Accounts receivable, net of allowance of $132 and $132, respectively . . . . . . . . . . | $3,109 | $2,198 |

**ILLUSTRATION 5–22**

**Allowance Ratios for Whirlpool**

The calculations for Whirlpool's allowance ratio in 2020 and 2019 are as follows:

|  | **2020** | **2019** |
|---|---|---|
| Allowance Ratio | $\dfrac{\$132}{\$3,109 + \$132} = 4.1\%$ | $\dfrac{\$132}{\$2,198 + \$132} = 5.7\%$ |

As you can see from this example, even though Whirlpool's accounts receivable balance increased from 2019 to 2020, its allowance for doubtful accounts did not change. This resulted in a significant decline in the allowance ratio from 5.7% in 2019 to 4.1% in 2020. This decrease in the allowance is a little surprising given the financial impact of the COVID-19 pandemic on its customers in 2020, which would likely increase the likelihood of bad debt. If we expand to a seven-year window (see Illustration 5–23), we can see that Whirlpool's historic allowance ratio generally ranges between 5.3% and 6.4%. This provides another indication that the allowance ratio in 2020 may be low. This raises potential concerns that Whirlpool has under-estimated the amount of uncollectible accounts that it will experience in the future. By under-estimating the allowance, Whirlpool has potentially over-estimated net accounts receivable and under-estimated bad debt expense for 2020.

**ILLUSTRATION 5–23**

**Whirpool's Allowance Ratio over Time**

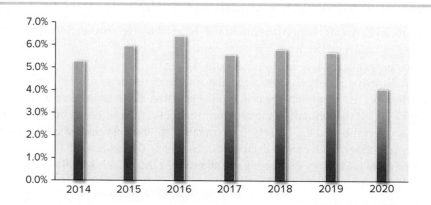

However, it's also useful to compare allowance ratios between other companies in the industry. It could be the case that industry or economic conditions are such that the probability of not receiving payment from a customer is lower in any particular period for the entire sector. Illustration 5–24 provides the allowance ratios for Whirlpool and four U.S. competitors in 2020. This comparison indicates that Whirlpool's allowance ratio is near the higher end of the range observed in its industry, which eases concerns that its allowance ratio is too low.

**ILLUSTRATION 5–24**

**Allowance Ratio for Whirlpool and Selected Competitors**

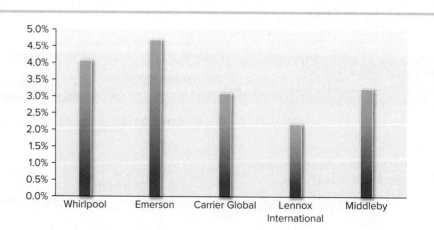

**KEY POINT**

The receivables turnover ratio and average collection period can provide an indication of management's ability to collect cash from customers in a timely manner. The allowance ratio captures the discretion used by managers to establish the allowance for uncollectible accounts. Comparing this ratio across time and related companies can provide an indication of the quality of the net accounts receivable balance reported in the balance sheet.

# PERCENTAGE-OF-CREDIT-SALES METHOD

**APPENDIX A**

■ **LO5–10**
Estimate uncollectible accounts using the percentage-of-credit-sales method.

In the chapter, we estimated uncollectible accounts based on a percentage of total accounts receivable (*percentage-of-receivables method*) or based on the age of individual accounts receivable (*aging method*). We refer to both of these as a *balance sheet method,* because we base the estimate of bad debts on a balance sheet account—accounts receivable.

As an alternative, we can estimate uncollectible accounts using an income statement account—credit sales. Estimating uncollectible accounts using a percentage of credit sales is aptly referred to as the *percentage-of-credit-sales method* or the *income statement method.* In this appendix, we consider the percentage-of-credit-sales method.

Assume Kimzey bills customers $80 million for services, with $30 million in accounts receivable remaining at the end of 2025. Also assume the balance of the allowance account, before adjustment, is a $2 million credit. Consider the following estimates of uncollectible accounts:

1.  Percentage-of-receivables approach = 20% of total accounts receivable.
2.  Percentage-of-credit-sales approach = 10% of credit sales.

Illustration 5–25 demonstrates the differences in the two methods when adjusting for estimates of uncollectible accounts. **Notice that the two methods for estimating uncollectible accounts result in different adjustments.**

| Percentage-of-Receivables Method | Percentage-of-Credit-Sales Method |
|---|---|
| Estimate of Uncollectible Accounts | Estimate of Uncollectible Accounts |
| • 20% of accounts receivable at the end of 2025 will not be collected. | • 10% of credit sales in 2025 will not be collected. |
| • 20% of $30 million = $6 million. | • 10% of $80 million = $8 million. |
| • Adjust Allowance account from $2 million existing balance to estimate of $6 million. | • Ignore $2 million existing balance of Allowance account and add $8 million. |
| Adjustment | Adjustment |
| $6 million − $2 million = $4 million | $8 million |

**ILLUSTRATION 5–25**
Adjusting for Estimates of Uncollectible Accounts

Because the amounts of the adjustments differ, the effects on the financial statements differ. Recall that the balance of the allowance account before adjustment is a $2 million credit. After adjustment, the balance of the allowance account will differ between the two methods, as will the amount of bad debt expense. Illustration 5–26 summarizes the differences in financial statement effects.

**ILLUSTRATION 5–26**

Financial Statement
Effects of Estimating
Uncollectible Accounts

| Percentage-of-Receivables Method ($ in millions) | | Percentage-of-Credit-Sales Method ($ in millions) | |
|---|---|---|---|
| Income Statement Effect | | Income Statement Effect | |
| Revenues | $80 | Revenues | $80 |
| Bad debt expense | (4) | Bad debt expense | (8) |
| Net income | $76 | Net income | $72 |
| Balance Sheet Effect | | Balance Sheet Effect | |
| Accounts receivable | $30 | Accounts receivable | $30 |
| Less: Allowance | (6)* | Less: Allowance | (10)* |
| Net accounts receivable | $24 | Net accounts receivable | $20 |
| *$6 = $2 + $4 (adjustment) | | *$10 = $2 + $8 (adjustment) | |

From an income statement perspective, some argue that the percentage-of-credit-sales method provides a better method for estimating bad debts because expenses (bad debts) are better matched with revenues (credit sales). A better matching of expenses and revenues results in a more accurate measure of net income for the period. From a balance sheet perspective, though, the percentage-of-receivables method is preferable because assets (net accounts receivable) are reported closer to the amount expected to be collected.

The current emphasis on better measurement of assets (balance sheet focus) outweighs the emphasis on better measurement of net income (income statement focus). **This is why the percentage-of-receivables method (balance sheet method) is the preferable method, while the percentage-of-credit-sales method (income statement method) is allowed only if amounts do not differ significantly from estimates using the percentage-of-receivables method.**

 **KEY POINT**

When applying the percentage-of-credit-sales method, we adjust the allowance for uncollectible accounts for the current year's credit sales we don't expect to collect (rather than adjusting at the end of the year for the percentage of accounts receivable we don't expect to collect).

# APPENDIX B   NOTES RECEIVABLE AND INTEREST

Notes receivable are similar to accounts receivable but are more formal credit arrangements evidenced by a written debt instrument, or *note*. Notes receivable typically arise from loans to other entities (including affiliated companies), loans to stockholders and employees, and occasionally the sale of merchandise, other assets, or services.

## Accounting for Notes Receivable

■ **LO5–11**
Account for notes receivable and interest revenue.

Like accounts receivable, notes receivable are assets. We classify notes receivable as either *current* or *noncurrent* (long term), depending on the expected collection date. If the time to maturity is longer than one year, the note receivable is a long-term asset.

**Example.**   On February 1, 2024, Kimzey Medical Clinic provides services of $10,000 to a patient, Justin Payne, who is not able to pay immediately. In place of payment, Justin offers Kimzey a six-month, 12% promissory note. Because of the large amount of the receivable, Kimzey agrees to accept the promissory note as a way to increase the likelihood of eventually receiving payment. In addition, because of the delay in payment, Kimzey would like to charge interest on the outstanding balance. A formal promissory note provides an explicit statement of the interest charges. Illustration 5–27 shows an example of a typical note receivable.

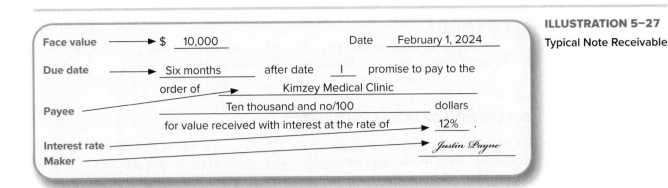

**ILLUSTRATION 5–27**
Typical Note Receivable

The financial statement effects of accepting the note receivable on February 1 are as follows:

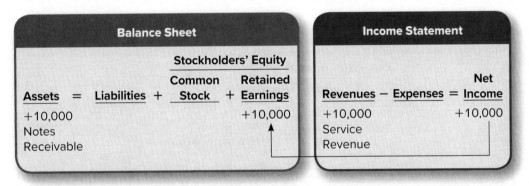

| | Debit | Credit |
|---|---|---|
| Notes Receivable | 10,000 | |
| Service Revenue | | 10,000 |

| Notes Receivable | |
|---|---|
| 10,000 | |

| Service Revenue | |
|---|---|
| | 10,000 |

**KEY POINT**

Notes receivable are similar to accounts receivable, except that notes receivable are formal credit arrangements made with a written debt instrument, or *note*.

## INTEREST CALCULATION

Many of the same issues we discussed concerning accounts receivable, such as allowing for uncollectible accounts, also apply to notes receivable. The one issue that usually applies to notes receivable, but not to accounts receivable, is interest. You're probably familiar with the concept of interest. You may be earning interest on money in a savings account, and you might be paying interest on student loans, a car loan, or a credit card.

In the previous example, Kimzey accepted a six-month, 12% promissory note. The "12%" indicates the *annual* interest rate charged by the payee. The terms of the six-month note mean that Kimzey will charge Justin Payne one-half year of interest, or 6%, on the face value. Interest on Kimzey's note receivable is calculated as follows.

| Interest | = | Face value | × | Annual interest rate | × | Fraction of the year | |
|---|---|---|---|---|---|---|---|
| $600 | = | $10,000 | × | 12% | × | 6/12 | |

Interest calculation

**KEY POINT**

We calculate interest as the face value of the note multiplied by the stated annual interest rate multiplied by the appropriate fraction of the year that the note is outstanding.

## COLLECTION OF NOTES RECEIVABLE

We account for the collection of notes receivable the same way as collection of accounts receivable, except we also have interest revenue to report in the income statement.

Continuing the previous example, suppose on August 1, 2024, the maturity date, Justin repays the note and interest in full as promised. The financial statement effects of the repayment of the note receivable on August 1 are as follows:

| Balance Sheet | | | | | | Income Statement | | |
|---|---|---|---|---|---|---|---|---|
| | | | | **Stockholders' Equity** | | | | |
| | | | | Common | Retained | | | Net |
| **Assets** | = | **Liabilities** | + | **Stock** | + **Earnings** | **Revenues** | − **Expenses** = | **Income** |
| +10,600 Cash | | | | | +600 | +600 Interest Revenue | | +600 |
| −10,000 Notes Receivable | | | | | | | | |

### DEBITS & CREDITS

Kimzey would record the following journal entry on August 1:

| | Debit | Credit |
|---|---|---|
| Cash........................................................................................ | **10,600** | |
|    Notes Receivable ............................................................ | | **10,000** |
|    Interest Revenue ............................................................. | | **600** |

| Cash | |
|---|---|
| 10,600 | |

| Notes Receivable | |
|---|---|
| | 10,000 |

| Interest Revenue | |
|---|---|
| | 600 |

Over the six-month period, Kimzey earns interest revenue of $600. The credit to Notes Receivable reduces the balance in that account to $0, which is the amount Justin owes after payment to Kimzey.

## ACCRUED INTEREST

It frequently happens that a note is issued in one year and the maturity date occurs in the following year. For example, what if Justin Payne issued the previous six-month note to Kimzey on November 1, 2024, instead of February 1, 2024? In that case, the $10,000 face value (principal) and $600 interest on the six-month note are not due until May 1, 2025. The length of the note (six months) and interest rate (12%) remain the same, and so the total interest of $600 charged to Justin remains the same. However, Kimzey will earn interest revenue in two separate accounting periods (assuming Kimzey uses a calendar year): for two months of the six-month note in 2024 (November and December), and for four months in the next year (January through April). Illustration 5–28 demonstrates the calculation of interest revenue over time. Interest receivable from Kimzey's six-month, $10,000, 12% note is $100 per month (= $10,000 × 12% × 1/12).

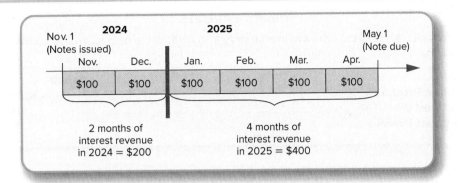

Because Kimzey earns two months of interest in 2024, it must accrue that interest of $200 on December 31, 2024 (even though no cash has been collected). The financial statement effects of accruing interest revenue are as follows:

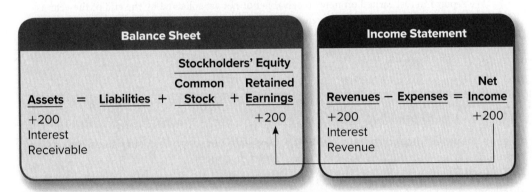

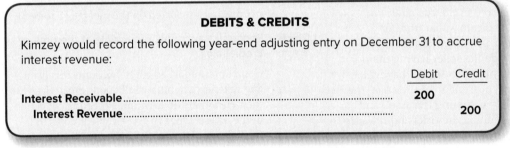

On May 1, 2025, the maturity date, Kimzey collects the note receivable of $10,000 plus interest of $600. Notice that the cash collected for interest includes $200 receivable from 2024, as well as $400 of additional interest revenue related to four months in 2025. The financial statement effect at the maturity date of the note receivable is as follows:

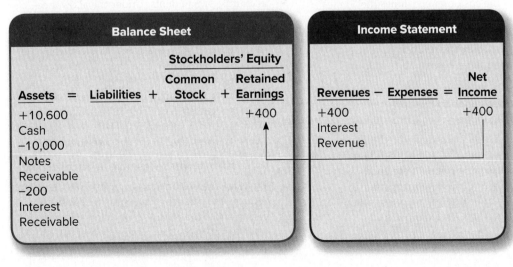

| Cash | |
|---|---|
| 10,600 | |

| Notes Receivable | |
|---|---|
| | 10,000 |

| Interest Receivable | |
|---|---|
| | 200 |

| Interest Revenue | |
|---|---|
| | 400 |

**DEBITS & CREDITS**

Kimzey would record the following journal entry at maturity of the note receivable on May 1:

| | Debit | Credit |
|---|---|---|
| Cash............................................................................................ | 10,600 | |
|    Notes Receivable ..................................................................... | | 10,000 |
|    Interest Receivable................................................................... | | 200 |
|    Interest Revenue...................................................................... | | 400 |

The entry on May 1, 2025, eliminates the balances of the note receivable and interest receivable reported in 2024.

 **KEY POINT**

We report interest earned on notes receivable but not yet collected by the end of the year as interest receivable and interest revenue.

 **THE BOTTOM LINE**

**LO5–1**    Explain when revenue should be recognized at a single point in time.

Revenue should be recognized at a single point in time when control of a good or service is transferred to the customer on a specific date. Indicators that transfer has occurred and that revenue should be recognized include the seller having the right to receive payment, the customer having legal title and physical possession of the asset, the customer formally accepting the asset, and the customer assuming the risks and rewards of ownership.

**LO5–2**    Explain when revenue should be recognized over a period of time.

Revenue should be recognized over time when a performance obligation is satisfied over time. That occurs if (1) the customer consumes the benefit of the seller's work as it is performed, (2) the customer controls the asset as the seller creates it, or (3) the asset has no alternative use to the seller and the seller has a legal right to be paid.

**LO5–3**    Allocate a contract's price to multiple performance obligations.

A contract's transaction price is allocated to its performance obligations. The allocation is based on the stand-alone selling prices of the goods and services underlying those performance obligations. The stand-alone selling price must be estimated if a good or service is not sold separately.

**LO5–4**    Calculate net revenues using sales returns and sales discounts.

Sales returns, trade discounts, and sales discounts are subtracted from total revenues to calculate net revenues reported on the income statement.

**LO5–5**    Recognize accounts receivable at the time of credit sales.

Companies report an asset (accounts receivable) and revenue when they sell goods or services to their customers on account, expecting collection in the future. Once the receivable is collected, the balance of accounts receivable is reduced.

**LO5–6**    Establish the allowance for uncollectible accounts.

Customers' accounts receivable we no longer expect to collect are referred to as uncollectible accounts, or bad debts. Under the allowance method, accounts receivable are reported for the net amount expected to be collected. At the end of the current year, estimated future uncollectible accounts are reported in a contra asset account, reducing net accounts receivable. Establishing an allowance for uncollectible accounts correctly reports accounts receivable in the balance sheet at the amount expected to be collected. Bad debt expense is reported in the income statement.

**LO5–7**    Write off accounts receivable as uncollectible.

Writing off a customer's account as uncollectible reduces the balance of accounts receivable but also reduces the contra asset—allowance for uncollectible accounts. The net effect is that there is no change in the net receivable (accounts receivable less the allowance) or in total assets.

**LO5–8  Adjust the allowance for uncollectible accounts in subsequent years.**

Using the aging method to estimate uncollectible accounts is more accurate than applying a single percentage to all accounts receivable. The aging method recognizes that the longer accounts are past due, the less likely they are to be collected.

The year-end adjustment for future uncollectible accounts is affected by the current balance of Allowance for Uncollectible Accounts before adjustment. The current balance before adjustment equals the balance of the allowance account at the beginning of the current year (or end of last year) less actual write-offs in the current year.

**LO5–9  Calculate key ratios to assess the company's effectiveness at managing receivables and the quality of the receivables.**

The receivables turnover ratio and average collection period can provide an indication of management's ability to collect cash from customers in a timely manner.

The allowance ratio captures the discretion used by managers to establish the allowance for uncollectible accounts. Comparing this ratio across time and related companies can provide an indication of the quality of the net accounts receivable balance reported in the balance sheet.

**LO5–10  Estimate uncollectible accounts using the percentage-of-credit-sales method.**

When applying the percentage-of-credit-sales method, we adjust the allowance for uncollectible accounts for the current year's credit sales that we don't expect to collect (rather than adjusting at the end of the year for the percentage of accounts receivable we don't expect to collect).

**LO5–11  Account for notes receivable and interest revenue.**

Notes receivable are similar to accounts receivable except that notes receivable are formal credit arrangements made with a written debt instrument, or note.

We calculate interest as the face value of the note multiplied by the stated annual interest rate multiplied by the appropriate fraction of the year that the note is outstanding.

We report interest earned on notes receivable but not yet collected by the end of the year as interest receivable and interest revenue.

## GLOSSARY

**Accounts receivable:** The amount of cash owed to the company by its customers from the sale of goods or services on account. **p. 225**

**Aging method:** Basing the estimate of future bad debts on the various ages of individual accounts receivable, using a higher percentage for "old" accounts than for "new" accounts. **p. 232**

**Allowance for uncollectible accounts:** Contra asset account representing the amount of accounts receivable not expected to be collected. **p. 229**

**Allowance method:** Method of reporting accounts receivable for the net amount expected to be collected. **p. 227**

**Average collection period:** Approximate number of days the average accounts receivable balance is outstanding. It equals 365 divided by the receivables turnover ratio. **p. 239**

**Bad debt expense:** The cost of estimated future bad debts that is reported as an expense in the current year's income statement. **p. 230**

**Credit sales:** Transfer of goods or services to a customer today while bearing the risk of collecting payment from that customer in the future. Also known as *sales on account* or *services on account*. **p. 225**

**Deferred Revenue:** Cash received in advance from a customer for goods or servies to be provided in the future. **p. 216**

**Direct write-off method:** Recording bad debt expense at the time we know the account is actually uncollectible. **p. 237**

**Invoice:** A source document that identifies the date of sale, the customer, the specific items sold, the dollar amount of the sale, and the payment terms. **p. 226**

**Net accounts receivable:** The difference between total accounts receivable and the allowance for uncollectible accounts. **p. 229**

**Net revenue:** A company's total revenues less any discounts, returns, and allowances. **p. 223**

**Notes receivable:** Formal credit arrangements evidenced by a written debt instrument, or *note*. **p. 244**

**Percentage-of-receivables method:** Method of estimating uncollectible accounts based on the percentage of accounts receivable expected not to be collected. **p. 232**

**Performance obligations:** Promises to deliver goods or services to a customer. **p. 214**

**Receivables turnover ratio:** Number of times during a year that the average accounts receivable balance is collected (or "turns over"). It equals net credit sales divided by average accounts receivable. **p. 239**

**Revenue:** Inflows of assets or settlements of liabilities (or a combination of both) from delivering goods or services as part of a business entity's primary operations. **p. 214**

**Sales discount:** Reduction in the amount to be received from a credit customer if collection on account occurs within a specified period of time. **p. 224**

**Sales return:** Customer returns a product. **p. 224**

**Stand-alone selling price:** The amount at which a good or service is sold separately under similar circumstances. **p. 221**

**Subsidiary ledger:** A group of individual accounts associated with a particular general ledger control account. **p. 236**

**Trade discount:** Reduction in the listed price of a good or service. **p. 224**

**Transaction Price:** The amount the seller expects to receive from a customer in exchange for goods or services. **p. 220**

**Uncollectible accounts:** Customers' accounts that no longer are considered collectible. **p. 227**

# SELF-STUDY QUESTIONS

1. Zoomies manufactures furniture for children and receives payment on a large retail order in December of 2024. The manufacturing is complete in 2024, and the order ships to the customer in January of 2025. When does Zoomies record the revenue on this sale? **(LO5–1)**
   a. In 2024.
   b. In 2025.
   c. In both 2024 and 2025.

2. Estate Construction is constructing a large warehouse for CyberB, an online retailing company. Under the construction agreement, Estate will complete construction within 16 months. When should Estate recognize revenue? **(LO5–2)**
   a. Before the building is constructed.
   b. As the building is constructed.
   c. After construction is completed.
   d. As cash is received.

3. eLean is an online fitness company. The company sells fitness clothing, exercise books, and one-year access to workout videos. Customers can buy these items individually or become a member for an annual fee of $300. With payment of annual membership, individuals gain immediate access to exercise videos for one year, receive one exercise book of their choice, and receive a coupon to be used at any time over the year to purchase fitness clothing. How many performance obligations exist in the annual membership contract? **(LO5–3)**
   a. One.
   b. Two.
   c. Three.
   d. Four.

4. On March 17, Fox Lumber sells materials to Whitney Construction for $12,000. Whitney pays for the materials on March 23. What amount would Fox recognize as gross revenue on March 17? **(LO5–4)**
   a. $12,400.
   b. $11,760.
   c. $12,000.
   d. $12,240.

5. Refer to the information in the previous question. What is the amount of net revenues (sales minus sales discounts) as of March 23? **(LO5–4)**
   a. $0.
   b. $11,760.
   c. $12,000.
   d. $12,240.

6. Accounts receivable are best described as **(LO5–5)**
   a. Liabilities of the company that represent the amount owed to suppliers.
   b. Amounts previously received from customers.
   c. Assets of the company representing the amount owed by customers.
   d. Amounts previously paid to suppliers.

7. The allowance method for uncollectible accounts **(LO5–6)**
   a. Is required by generally accepted accounting principles.
   b. Allows for the possibility that some accounts will not be collected.
   c. Reports net accounts receivable for the amount of cash expected to be collected.
   d. All of the above are correct.

8. At the end of its first year of operations, a company estimates future uncollectible accounts to be $4,500. This estimate would impact the current year's financial statements by **(LO5–6)**
   a. Decreasing accounts receivable, gross.
   b. Increasing the allowance for uncollectible accounts.
   c. Decreasing the allowance for uncollectible accounts.
   d. Decreasing bad debt expense.

9. Using the allowance method, the write-off of accounts receivable will have which effect at the time of the write-off? **(LO5–7)**
   a. Increase bad debt expense.
   b. Decrease the allowance for uncollectible accounts.
   c. Increase the allowance for uncollectible accounts.
   d. Decrease accounts receivable, net.

10. Using the allowance method, the effect on the current year's financial statements of writing off an account receivable generally is to **(LO5–7)**
    a. Decrease total assets.
    b. Decrease net income.
    c. Both a. and b.
    d. Neither a. nor b.

11. A company has the following account balances at the end of the year: **(LO5–8)**
    - Credit Sales = $400,000
    - Accounts Receivable = $80,000
    - Allowance for Uncollectible Accounts = $400 (*positive, credit balance*)

    The company estimates future uncollectible accounts to be 4% of accounts receivable. At what amount would Bad Debt Expense be reported in the current year's income statement?
    a. $400.                  c. $3,200.
    b. $2,800.                d. $3,600.

12. A company has the following account balances at the end of the year: **(LO5–8)**
    - Credit Sales = $400,000
    - Accounts Receivable = $80,000
    - Allowance for Uncollectible Accounts = $400 (*negative, debit balance*)

    The company estimates future uncollectible accounts to be 4% of accounts receivable. At what amount would Bad Debt Expense be reported in the current year's income statement?
    a. $400.
    b. $2,800.
    c. $3,200.
    d. $3,600.

13. At the beginning of the year, Clay Ventures has total accounts receivable of $100,000. By the end of the year, Clay reports net credit sales of $900,000 and total accounts receivable of $200,000.

*Note: For answers, see the last page of the chapter.*

What is the receivables turnover ratio for Clay Ventures? **(LO5–9)**
a. 2.0.                  c. 6.0.
b. 4.5.                  d. 9.0.

14. At the end of the year, the balance sheet of Burn Inc. reports accounts receivable (net) of $40,500 and an allowance for uncollectible accounts of $2,500. Burn Inc.'s allowance ratio at the end of the year is **(LO5–9)**
a. 6.5%                  c. 5.8%
b. 6.2%                  d. 5.5%

15. A company has the following account balances at the end of the year: **(LO5–10)**
    - Credit Sales = $400,000
    - Accounts Receivable = $80,000
    - Allowance for Uncollectible Accounts = $400 (*positive, credit balance*)

    The company estimates 1% of credit sales will be uncollectible. At what amount would Allowance for Uncollectible Accounts be reported in the current year's balance sheet?
    a. $4,000.                c. $3,600.
    b. $4,400.                d. $800.

16. On May 1, 2024, Nees Manufacturing lends $10,000 to Roberson Supply using a 9% note due in 12 months. Nees has a December 31 year-end. Calculate the amount of interest revenue Nees will report in its 2024 and 2025 income statements. **(LO5–11)**
    a. 2024 = $300; 2025 = $600.
    b. 2024 = $600; 2025 = $300.
    c. 2024 = $900; 2025 = $0.
    d. 2024 = $0; 2025 = $900.

17. On January 1, 2024, Nees Manufacturing lends $10,000 to Roberson Supply using a 9% note due in eight months. Calculate the amount of interest revenue Nees will report in its 2024 income statement. **(LO5–11)**
    a. $300.                  c. $900.
    b. $600.                  d. $1,000.

## REAL WORLD PERSPECTIVES

### Delta Airlines (ticker: DAL)

**EDGAR Case**

**RWP5–1** Visit **www.sec.gov/edgar** and search for the **Delta Air Lines** annual report (10-K) for the year ended December 31, 2018, using EDGAR (Electronic Data Gathering, Analysis, and Retrieval system). Locate the note titled "Revenue Recognition."

*Required:*

1. What percent of total revenue in 2018 came from ticket sales?
2. In which liability account does Delta record the sales of passenger tickets for flights that have not yet flown?
3. When does Delta recognize revenue of tickets that were purchased, but never used?

EDGAR Case

## Apple (ticker: AAPL)

**RWP5–2** Visit www.sec.gov/edgar and search for the **Apple** annual report (10-K) for the year ended September 28, 2019, using EDGAR (Electronic Data Gathering, Analysis, and Retrieval system). Locate the note titled "Revenue Recognition."

### Required:

What are the three performance obligations regularly identified in the sale of Apple's products (e.g., iPhones, Mac, etc.).

EDGAR Case

## Dropbox (ticker: DBX)

**RWP5–3** Visit www.sec.gov/edgar and search for the **Dropbox** annual report (10-K) for the year ended December 31, 2018, using EDGAR (Electronic Data Gathering, Analysis, and Retrieval system). Locate the note titled "Description of the Business and Summary of Significant Accounting Policies."

### Required:

Dropbox refers to its uncollectible accounts as doubtful accounts. What factors does Dropbox consider when it establishes an allowance for doubtful accounts (also commonly referred to as allowance for uncollectible accounts) for trade and other receivables?

EDGAR Case

## General Mills (ticker: GIS)

**RWP5–4** Visit www.sec.gov/edgar and search for the **General Mills** annual report (10-K) for the year ended May 26, 2019, using EDGAR (Electronic Data Gathering, Analysis, and Retrieval system). Locate the consolidated balance sheet and the note titled "Schedule II–Valuation of qualifying accounts."

### Required:

1. The balance sheet reports Accounts Receivable $1,679.7 million at May 26, 2019. This amount is reported net of the allowance for doubtful accounts (also commonly referred to as allowance for uncollectible accounts). Calculate the gross (or total) amount of accounts receivable using the information about the allowance for doubtful accounts in Schedule II.
2. How much bad debt expense did General Mill recognize in the income statement for the year ending May 26, 2019?
3. How much receivables did General Mill write off for the year ending May 26, 2019?

Continuing Financial Analysis Case

## American Eagle Outfitters, Inc.

**RWP5–5** Financial information for **American Eagle** is presented in **Appendix A** at the end of the book.

### Required:

1. Determine whether the trend in net sales has been increasing or decreasing for the past three years.
2. In which financial statement is the balance of accounts receivable reported? Explain why using net sales to calculate the receivables turnover ratio might not be a good indicator of a company's ability to efficiently manage receivables for a retail company like American Eagle, which typically sells clothing for cash.
3. Does American Eagle indicate in the balance sheet that the company likely has an allowance for uncollectible accounts?

Continuing Financial Analysis Case

## The Buckle, Inc.

**RWP5–6** Financial information for **Buckle** is presented in **Appendix B** at the end of the book.

### Required:

1. Determine whether the trend in net sales has been increasing or decreasing for the past three years.

2. In which financial statement is the balance of accounts receivable reported? Explain why using net sales to calculate the receivables turnover ratio might not be a good indicator of a company's ability to efficiently manage receivables for a retail company like Buckle, which typically sells clothing for cash.

3. Does Buckle indicate in the balance sheet that the company likely has an allowance for uncollectible accounts?

## American Eagle Outfitters, Inc. vs. The Buckle, Inc.

**Continuing Comparative Analysis Case**

**RWP5–7** Financial information for **American Eagle** is presented in **Appendix A** at the end of the book, and financial information for **Buckle** is presented in **Appendix B** at the end of the book.

### Required:

Try to estimate each company's ratio of total current receivables to total current assets. Do you see problems with either company's management of receivables?

## Ethics

**Ethics Case**

**RWP5–8** You have recently been hired as the assistant controller for Stanton Industries. Your immediate superior is the controller who, in turn, reports to the vice president of finance. The controller assigned you the task of preparing the year-end adjusting entries. For receivables, you prepared an aging of accounts receivable and have applied historical percentages to the balances of each of the age categories. The analysis indicates an appropriate balance for Allowance for Uncollectible Accounts is $180,000. The existing balance in the allowance account prior to any adjusting entry is a $20,000 credit balance.

After showing your analysis to the controller, he tells you to change the aging category of a large account from over 120 days to current status and to prepare a new invoice to the customer with a revised date that agrees with the new aging category. This will change the required allowance for uncollectible accounts from $180,000 to $135,000. Tactfully, you ask the controller for an explanation for the change and he tells you, "We need the extra income; the bottom line is too low."

### Required:

1. Understand the reporting effect: What is the effect on income before taxes of lowering the allowance estimate from $180,000 to $135,000, as requested by the controller?
2. Specify the options: If you do not make the change, how would the additional $45,000 of Allowance for Uncollectible Accounts affect total assets?
3. Identify the impact: Are investors and creditors potentially harmed by the controller's suggestion?
4. Make a decision: Should you follow the controller's suggestion?

## Sustainability

**Sustainability Case**

**RWP5–9** Go to the SASB website (**https://www.sasb.org/company-use/sasb-reporters/**) and search for the 2020 Environmental, Social, and Governance Report for **PotlatchDeltic** (search "Potlatch"), which is a large forest products company traded in the Nasdaq. PotlatchDeltic relies on 1.9 million acres of timberland to produce timber and plywood in 7 different U.S. manufacturing facilities.

In the report, read "A Message from our Chief Executive Officer" on page 6. The CEO states that environmental, social and governance issues are important to the shareholders of PotlatchDeltic because they are tied to what specific factors?

## Earnings Management

**Earnings Management Case**

**RWP5–10** Ernie Upshaw is the supervising manager of Sleep Tight Bedding. At the end of the year, the company's accounting manager provides Ernie with the following information, before any adjusting entry.

| Accounts receivable | $500,000 |
| Estimated percent uncollectible | 9% |
| Allowance for uncollectible accounts | $20,000 (*debit*) |
| Operating income | $320,000 |

In the previous year, Sleep Tight Bedding reported operating income (after adjusting entries) of $275,000. Ernie knows it's important to report an upward trend in earnings. This is important not only for Ernie's compensation and employment, but also for the company's stock price. If investors see a decline in earnings, the stock price could drop significantly, and Ernie owns a large amount of the company's stock. This has caused Ernie many sleepless nights.

### Required:

1. Record the adjusting entry for uncollectible accounts using the accounting manager's estimate of 9% of accounts receivable.
2. After the adjusting entry is recorded in requirement 1, what is the revised amount of operating income? Does operating income increase or decrease compared to the previous year?
3. Ernie instructs the accounting manager to record the adjusting entry for uncollectible accounts using 4% rather than 9% of accounts receivable. After this adjusting entry, does operating income increase or decrease compared to the previous year?
4. By how much would total assets and expenses be misstated using the 4% amount?

Continuing General Ledger Case

## Great Adventures

(This is a continuation of the Great Adventures problem from earlier chapters.)

**RWP5–11** Tony and Suzie are ready to expand Great Adventures even further in 2025. Tony believes that many groups in the community (for example, Boys and Girls Clubs, church groups, civic groups, and local businesses) would like to hold one-day outings for their members. Groups would engage in outdoor activities, such as rock climbing, fishing, capture the flag, paintball, treasure hunts, scavenger hunts, nature hikes, and so on. The purpose of these one-day events would be for each member of the group to learn the importance of TEAM (Together Everyone Achieves More).

Tony knows that most people are not familiar with these types of activities, so to encourage business he allows groups to participate in the event before paying. He offers a 5% quick-payment discount to those who pay within 10 days after the event. He also guarantees at least eight hours of outdoor activities will be provided or the customer will receive a 20% discount. For the first six months of the year, the following activities occur for TEAM operations.

| Jan. | 24 | Great Adventures purchases outdoor gear such as ropes, helmets, harnesses, compasses, and other miscellaneous equipment for $5,000 cash. |
| Feb. | 25 | Kendall's Boys and Girls Club participates in a one-day TEAM adventure. Normally, Tony would charge a group of this size $3,500, but he wants to encourage kids to exercise more and enjoy the outdoors, so he charges the group only $3,000. Great Adventures provides these services on account. |
| Feb. | 28 | Great Adventures receives payment from the Kendall Club Kendall for the full amount owed, less the 5% quick-payment discount. |
| Mar. | 19 | Reynold's Management has its employees participate in a one-day TEAM adventure. Great Adventures provides services on account for $4,000, and Reynold's agrees to pay within 30 days. |
| Mar. | 27 | Great Adventures receives payment from Reynolds for the full amount owed, less the 5% quick-payment discount. |
| Apr. | 7 | Several men from the Elks Lodge decide to participate in a TEAM adventure. Great Adventures receives $7,500 immediately, and the event is scheduled for the following week. |
| Apr. | 14 | The TEAM adventure is held for members of the Elks Lodge. |
| Apr. | 30 | Myers Manufacturing participates in a TEAM adventure. Great Adventures provides services on account for $6,000, and Myers agrees to pay within 30 days. |

| May | 31 | Myers Manufacturing fails to pay the amount owed within the specified period and agrees to sign a three-month, 8% note receivable to replace the existing account receivable. |
|---|---|---|
| Jun. | 15 | Several MBA groups participate in TEAM adventures. Great Adventures provides services on account for $24,000 to these groups, with payment due in July. |

**Required:**

1. Record TEAM adventure transactions occurring during the first six months of 2025.
2. Consider the following information as of June 30, 2025.
    a. Suzie estimates uncollectible accounts to be 10% of accounts receivable (which does not include the $6,000 note receivable from Myers Manufacturing). Record the adjusting entry for uncollectible accounts.
    b. Accrue one month of interest on the note receivable from Myers Manufacturing.
    c. Prepare a partial balance sheet showing the net accounts receivable section.

The Great Adventures continuing problem also can be assigned using the General Ledger software in Connect. Students will be given an existing trial balance and asked to prepare (1) the journal entries above, (2) financial statements, and (3) closing entries.

## BRIEF EXERCISES

**BE5–1** What are the five key steps a company follows to apply the core revenue recognition principle?

*Identify steps in the revenue recognition principle (LO5–1, 5–2, 5–3)*

**BE5–2** On July 1, 2024, Apache Company, sold and delivered to a customer a large piece of equipment for $3,000 (on account). The cost to manufacture the equipment was $1,200. How much revenue will Apache recognize on July 1, 2024?

*Recognize revenue at a point in time (LO5–1)*
*See JBE5–1 for journal entries.*

**BE5–3** On May 1, 2024, Varga Tech Services signed a $6,000 consulting contract with Shaffer Holdings. The contract requires Varga to provide computer technology support services whenever requested over the period from May 1, 2024, to April 30, 2025, with Shaffer paying the entire $6,000 on May 1, 2024.

How much revenue and deferred revenue should Varga recognize in its year-ended December 31, 2024, financial statements?

*Determine timing of revenue recognition (LO5–2)*
*See JBE5–2 for journal entries.*

**BE5–4** Sarjit Systems sold software to a customer for $80,000. As part of the contract, Sarjit promises to provide "free" technical support over the next six months. Sarjit sells the same software without technical support for $70,000 and a stand-alone six-month technical support contract for $30,000, so these products would sell for $100,000 if sold separately. Sarjit delivered the software and received cash of $80,000 on May 15. Allocate the transaction price to software and technical support, and determine the financial statements effects of the transaction on May 15.

*Allocate the transaction price (LO5–3)*
*See JBE5–3 for journal entries.*

**BE5–5** During 2024, its first year of operations, Hollis Industries recorded sales of $10,600,000 and experienced returns of $720,000. Cost of goods sold totaled $6,360,000 (60% of sales). The company estimates that 8% of all sales will be returned. How much net revenue will Hollis Industries report at the end of its first year of operations?

*Determine net revenue after sales returns (LO5–4)*
*See JBE5–4 for journal entries.*

**BE5–6** RUHC Corp ships a large order of chemicals to a customer near of the end of March 2025. The sale price on the order is $15,000. The customer has 60 days to pay for the order. Payment is received in early May of 2025. Determine the financial statement effects of the sale in March and the cash receipt in May.

*Account for credit sales (LO5–5)*
*See JBE5–5 for journal entries.*

**Establish an allowance for uncollectible accounts (LO5–6)**
See JBE5–6 for journal entries.

**BE5–7** At the end of the first year of operations, Mayberry Advertising had accounts receivable of $20,000. Management of the company estimates 10% of the accounts will not be collected. Determine the financial statement effects of establishing an allowance for uncollectible accounts.

**Write off uncollectible accounts (LO5–7)**
See JBE5–7 for journal entries.

**BE5–8** At the beginning of the year, Mitchum Enterprises allows for estimated uncollectible accounts of $15,000. By the end of the year, write-offs of bad debts total $17,000. Determine the financial statement effects of the write-offs of $17,000 and compute the ending balance of Allowance for Uncollectible Accounts?

**Calculate bad debt expense (LO5–8)**
See JBE5–8 for journal entries.

**BE5–9** At the end of the year, Mercy Cosmetics' balance of Allowance for Uncollectible Accounts before adjustment is $600 (*positive, credit balance*). The balance of Accounts Receivable is $25,000. The company estimates 12% of accounts will not be collected over the next year. Calculate bad debt expense for Mercy Cosmetics for the year.

**Calculate bad debt expense (LO5–8)**
See JBE5–9 for journal entries.

**BE5–10** Refer to the information in BE5–9, but now assume that the balance of Allowance for Uncollectible Accounts before adjustment is $600 (*negative, debit balance*). The company still estimates future uncollectible accounts to be 12% of Accounts Receivable. Calculate bad debt expense for Mercy Cosmetics for the year. Is the amount of bad debt expense greater or less than the amount in BE5–9? Why?

**Calculate uncollectible accounts using the aging method (LO5–8)**

**BE5–11** Williamson Distributors separates its accounts receivable into three age groups for purposes of estimating the percentage of uncollectible accounts.

1. Accounts not yet due = $40,000; estimated uncollectible = 5%.
2. Accounts 1-30 days past due = $11,000; estimated uncollectible = 20%.
3. Accounts more than 30 days past due = $5,000; estimated uncollectible = 30%.

Compute the total estimated uncollectible accounts.

**Calculate uncollectible accounts using the aging method (LO5–8)**
See JBE5–10 for journal entries.

**BE5–12** Spade Agency separates its accounts receivable into three age groups for purposes of estimating the percentage of uncollectible accounts.

1. Accounts not yet due = $25,000; estimated uncollectible = 4%.
2. Accounts 1-60 days past due = $10,000; estimated uncollectible = 25%.
3. Accounts more than 60 days past due = $5,000; estimated uncollectible = 50%.

In addition, the balance of Allowance for Uncollectible Accounts before adjustment is $1,000 (*positive, credit balance*). Compute the total estimated uncollectible accounts.

**Calculate receivables ratios (LO5–9)**

**BE5–13** Atlantic Sunwear reports accounts receivable of $20,000 and $36,000 at the end of 2023 and 2024, respectively. Credit sales during 2024 totaled $425,000. Calculate the receivables turnover ratio and average collection period for Atlantic Sunwear for 2024.

**Calculate the allowance ratio (LO5–9)**

**BE5–14** At the end of 2023, Indell Semiconductors balance sheet reports $3,500,000 in receivables, which are presented net of an allowance for uncollectible accounts of $202,000. Calculate the allowance ratio at the end of 2023.

**Use the percentage-of-credit-sales method to calculate bad debt expense (LO5–10)**
See JBE5–11 for journal entries.

**BE5–15** At the end of the year, Brinkley Incorporated's balance of Allowance for Uncollectible Accounts before adjustment is $4,000 (*positive, credit balance*). The company estimates future uncollectible accounts to be 3% of credit sales for the year. Credit sales for the year total $135,000. Calculate bad debt expense for the year using the percentage-of-credit-sales method.

**Use the percentage-of-credit-sales method to calculate bad debt expense (LO5–10)**
See JBE5–12 for journal entries.

**BE5–16** Refer to the information in BE5–15, but now assume that the balance of Allowance for Uncollectible Accounts before adjustment is $4,000 (*negative, debit balance*). The company still estimates future uncollectible accounts to be 3% of credit sales for the year. Calculate bad debt expense for the year using the percentage-of-credit-sales method.

**BE5–17** Calculate the missing amount for each of the following notes receivable.

Calculate amounts related to interest (LO5–11)

| Face Value | Annual Interest Rate | Fraction of the Year | Interest |
|---|---|---|---|
| $11,000 | 6% | 4 months | (a) |
| $30,000 | 5% | (b) | $1,500 |
| $35,000 | (c) | 6 months | $1,225 |
| (d) | 8% | 6 months | $ 700 |

**BE5–18** On October 1, 2024, Oberley Corporation loans one of its employees $40,000 and accepts a 12-month, 9% note receivable. Calculate the amount of interest revenue Oberley will recognize in 2024 and 2025.

Calculate interest revenue of notes receivable (LO5–11)

**BE5–19** Match each of the following terms with its definition.

Define terms related to receivables (LO5–4, 5–5, 5–6, 5–8)

| Terms | Definitions |
|---|---|
| _____ 1. Accounts receivable | a. Reductions in amount owed by customers because of deficiency in products or services. |
| _____ 2. Credit sales | b. Formal credit arrangements evidenced by a written debt instrument. |
| _____ 3. Sales allowances | |
| _____ 4. Allowance method | c. Amount of cash owed to the company by customers from the sale of products or services on account. |
| _____ 5. Notes receivable | |
| _____ 6. Net revenues | d. Sales on account to customers. |
| _____ 7. Sales discounts | e. Reductions in amount owed by customers if payment on account is made within a specified period of time. |
| _____ 8. Aging method | |

f. Total revenues less returns, allowances, and discounts.

g. At the end of each period, account for the estimate of future uncollectible accounts.

h. Estimated percentage of uncollectible accounts is greater for "old" accounts than for "new" accounts.

## EXERCISES

**E5–1** B-Rides, Inc., manufactures bicycles that can fold to a compact size. On March 15, the company receives a large order from a big box specialty retailer. Due to the size of the order, B-Rides required this customer to pay $1,000 immediately, reflecting a 10 percent down payment. The remaining balance of $9,000 was received from the customer in April (the following month) at delivery.

Recognize revenue at a point in time (LO5–1)

*Required:*
1. How much revenue should be recognized in March?
2. How much deferred revenue should be recognized in March?
3. How much revenue should be recognized in April?
4. How much deferred revenue should be recognized in April?

**E5–2** Ski West, Inc., operates a downhill ski area near Lake Tahoe, California. An all-day adult lift ticket can be purchased for $85. Adult customers also can purchase a season pass that entitles the pass holder to ski any day during the season, which typically runs from December 1 through April 30. Ski West expects its season pass holders to use their passes equally throughout the season. The company's fiscal year ends on December 31.

On November 6, 2024, Ski West sells a season pass to Jake Lawson for $450.

Recognize revenue over time (LO5–2)
*See JE5–1 for journal entries.*

*Required:*
1. When should Ski West recognize revenue from the sale of its season passes?

2. What are the financial statement effects from the sale of the season pass on November 6, 2024?
3. What will be included in Ski West's 2024 income statement and balance sheet related to the sale of the season pass to Jake Lawson?

**Allocate the transaction price (LO5–3)**

**E5–3** Video Planet (VP) sells a big screen TV package consisting of a 60-inch QLED TV, a universal remote, and onsite installation by VP staff. The installation includes programming the remote to have the TV interface with other parts of the customer's home entertainment system. VP concludes that the TV, remote, and installation service are separate performance obligations. VP sells the 60-inch TV separately for $1,700, sells the remote separately for $100, and offers the installation service separately for $200. The entire package sells for $1,900.

***Required:***

How much revenue would be allocated to the TV, the remote, and the installation service?

**Determine performance obligations and recognize revenue (LO5–1, LO5–3)**
*See JE5–2 for journal entries.*

**E5–4** On March 1, 2024, Gold Examiner receives $147,000 from a local bank and promises to deliver 100 units of certified 1-oz. gold bars on a future date. The contract states that ownership passes to the bank when Gold Examiner delivers the products to Brink's, a third-party carrier. In addition, Gold Examiner agreed to provide a replacement shipment at no additional cost if the product is lost in transit. The stand-alone price of a gold bar is $1,440 per unit, and Gold Examiner estimates the stand-alone price of the replacement insurance service to be $60 per unit. Brink's picked up the gold bars from Gold Examiner on March 30, and delivery to the bank occurred on April 1.

***Required:***
1. How many performance obligations are in this contract?
2. How does this sale impact the financial statements on March 1?
3. How does this sale impact the financial statements on March 30?
4. How does this sale impact the financial statements on April 1?

**Calculate sales returns and net revenues (LO5–4)**

**E5–5** WTC Shoes reports gross revenues of $6,200,000 for the year ended January 31, 2025. Past history suggests that 3% of sales will be returned.

***Required:***
1. How much will WTC Shoes reserve for sales returns in 2025?
2. How much net revenues will be reported in the income statement for the year ended January 31, 2025?

**Calculate net revenues (LO5–4)**

**E5–6** Medical Waste Services provides services on account to hospitals with terms 2/10, n/30. During the year, gross revenues were $45,000,000. Medical Waste Services estimates that customers will take advantage of $500,000 in discounts.

***Required:***

How much net revenues will be reported in Medical Waste Services' income statement for the year?

**Account for credit sale (LO5–5)**
*See JE5–3 for journal entries.*

**E5–7** On May 7, Juanita Construction provides services on account to Michael Wolfe for $4,000. Michael pays for those services on May 13.

***Required:***
1. For Juanita Construction, what are the financial statement effects when the service is rendered on May 7?
2. For Juanita Construction, what are the financial statement effects when the cash is collected on May 13?

**Identify the financial statement effects of transactions related to accounts receivable and allowance for uncollectible accounts (LO5–5, 5–6, 5–7, 5–8)**

**E5–8** Consider the following transactions associated with accounts receivable and the allowance for uncollectible accounts.

| Credit Sales Transaction Cycle | Assets | Liabilities | Stockholders' Equity | Revenues | Expenses |
|---|---|---|---|---|---|
| 1. Provide services on account | ____ | ____ | ____ | ____ | ____ |
| 2. Estimate uncollectible accounts | ____ | ____ | ____ | ____ | ____ |
| 3. Write off accounts as uncollectible | ____ | ____ | ____ | ____ | ____ |
| 4. Collect on account previously written off | ____ | ____ | ____ | ____ | ____ |

**Required:**

For each transaction, indicate whether it would increase (I), decrease (D), or have no effect (NE) on the account totals. (*Hint:* Make sure the accounting equation, Assets = Liabilities + Stockholders' Equity, remains in balance after each transaction.)

**E5–9** Physicians' Hospital has the following balances on December 31, 2024, before any adjustment: Accounts Receivable = $60,000; Allowance for Uncollectible Accounts = $1,100 (*positive, credit balance*). On December 31, 2024, Physicians' estimates uncollectible accounts to be 15% of accounts receivable.

*Account for uncollectible accounts and calculate net accounts receivable* **LO5–6, 5–8**

**Required**
1. Determine the amount at which Bad Debt Expense is reported in the income statement and the Allowance for Uncollectible Accounts is reported in the balance sheet.
2. Calculate net accounts receivable reported in the balance sheet.

**E5–10** Mercy Hospital has the following balances on December 31, 2024, before any adjustment: Accounts Receivable = $70,000; Allowance for Uncollectible Accounts = $1,400 (*positive, credit balance*). Mercy estimates uncollectible accounts based on an aging of accounts receivable as shown below.

*Account for uncollectible accounts using the aging method* **(LO5–6, 5–8)**

**Required**
1. Determine the amount at which Bad Debt Expense is reported in the income statement and the Allowance for Uncollectible Accounts is reported in the balance sheet.
2. Calculate net accounts receivable reported in the balance sheet.

| Age Group | Amount Receivable | Estimated Percent Uncollectible |
|---|---|---|
| Not yet due | $50,000 | 15% |
| 0–30 days past due | 11,000 | 20% |
| 31–90 days past due | 8,000 | 45% |
| More than 90 days past due | 1,000 | 85% |
| Total | $70,000 | |

**E5–11** During 2024, its first year of operations, Pave Construction provides services on account of $160,000. By the end of 2024, cash collections on these accounts total $110,000. Pave estimates that 25% of the uncollected accounts will be uncollectible. In 2025, the company writes off uncollectible accounts of $10,000.

*Establish an allowance for uncollectible accounts and write off accounts receivable* **(LO5–6, 5–7)**
*See JE5–4 for journal entries.*

**Required**
1. Determine bad debt expense for the year ended December 31, 2024.
2. Describe the financial statement effects of the write-offs in 2025.

Account for uncollectible accounts using the aging method (LO5–6, 5–8)
See JE5–5 for journal entries.

**E5–12** The Physical Therapy Center specializes in helping patients regain motor skills after serious accidents. The center has the following balances on December 31, 2024, before any adjustment: Accounts Receivable = $110,000; Allowance for Uncollectible Accounts = $4,000 (*negative, debit balance*). The center estimates uncollectible accounts based on an aging of accounts receivable as shown below.

| Age Group | Amount Receivable | Estimated Percent Uncollectible |
|---|---|---|
| Not yet due | $ 60,000 | 4% |
| 0–60 days past due | 26,000 | 20% |
| 61–120 days past due | 16,000 | 30% |
| More than 120 days past due | 8,000 | 85% |
| Total | $110,000 | |

**Required:**
1. Estimate bad debt expense for the year ended December 31, 2024.
2. Calculate net accounts receivable reported in the balance sheet at December 31, 2024.

Calculate receivables ratios (LO5–9)

**E5–13** Below are amounts (in millions) from three companies' annual reports.

| | Beginning Accounts Receivable | Ending Accounts Receivable | Net Sales |
|---|---|---|---|
| WalCo | $1,815 | $2,762 | $322,427 |
| TarMart | $6,166 | $6,694 | $ 67,878 |
| CostGet | $ 629 | $ 665 | $ 68,963 |

**Required:**
For each company, calculate the receivables turnover ratio and the average collection period (rounded to one decimal place). Which company appears most efficient in collecting cash from sales?

Analyze receivables ratios (LO5–9)

**E5–14** WalCo, Inc.'s receivable turnover ratio has been steadying increasing over time.

**Require:**
1. Is WalCo getting more or less efficient at managing its receivables?
2. Identify several possible explanations for such a change in the receivable turnover ratio.

Calculate the allowance ratio (LO5–9)

**E5–15** Below are the amounts (in millions) from three companies' annual reports at the end of the year.

| | Net Accounts Receivable | Allowance for Uncollectible Accounts |
|---|---|---|
| WalCo | $2,762 | 650 |
| TarMart | $6,694 | 875 |
| CostGet | $ 665 | 45 |

**Required:**
For each company, calculate the allowance ratio (rounded to one decimal place).

Analyze the allowance ratio (LO5–9)

**E5–16** The allowance ratio for Jacobs & Jacobs Pharmaceuticals has consistently been around the industry average of 4.5 percent. The most recent financial statements reveal that the allowance ratio declined to 2.5 percent, while the industry remained at its historical average.

**Required:**
1. Describe how this decrease in the allowance ratio impacts reported net income in the income statement.
2. Describe how this decrease in the allowance ratio impacts reported accounts receivable in the balance sheet.

**E5–17** Suzuki Supply reports the following amounts at the end of 2024 (before adjustment)

Compare the percentage-of-receivables method and the percentage-of-credit-sales method (LO5–6,5–8, 5–10)

| | |
|---|---|
| Credit Sales for 2024 | $260,000 |
| Accounts Receivable, December 31, 2024 | 55,000 |
| Allowance for Uncollectible Accounts, December 31, 2024 | 1,100 *(positive, credit balance)* |

*Required:*
1. Calculate bad debt expense using the percentage-of-receivables method. Suzuki estimates 12% of receivables will not be collected.
2. Calculate bad debt expense using the percentage-of-credit-sales method. Suzuki estimates 3% of credit sales will not be collected.
3. Which method results in higher pretax income?

**E5–18** Refer to the information in E5–17, but now assume the balance of the Allowance for Uncollectible Accounts on December 31, 2024, is $2,100 *(negative, debit balance)* (before adjustment).

Compare the percentage-of-receivables method and the percentage-of-credit-sales method (LO5–6,5–8, 5–10)

*Required:*
1. Calculate bad debt expense using the percentage-of-receivables method. Suzuki estimates 12% of receivables will not be collected.
2. Calculate bad debt expense using the percentage-of-credit-sales method. Suzuki estimates 3% of credit sales will not be collected.
3. Which method results in higher pretax income?

**E5–19** On March 1, Terrell & Associates provides legal services to Whole Grain Bakery regarding some recent food poisoning complaints. Legal services total $11,000. In payment for the services, Whole Grain Bakery signs a 9% note requiring the payment of the face amount and interest to Terrell & Associates on September 1.

Account for notes receivable and interest revenue (LO5–11) *See JE5–6 for journal entries.*

*Required:*
1. For Terrell & Associates, how are the financial statements affected by the acceptance of the note receivable on March 1?
2. For Terrell & Associates, how are the financial statement affected by the cash collection on September 1?

**E5–20** On April 1, 2024, Shoemaker Corporation realizes that one of its main suppliers is having difficulty meeting delivery schedules, which is hurting Shoemaker's business. The supplier explains that it has a temporary lack of funds that is slowing its production cycle. Shoemaker agrees to lend $600,000 to its supplier using a 12-month, 11% note.

Account for notes receivable and interest revenue (LO5–11) *See JE5–7 for journal entries.*

*Required:*
Describe the financial statement effects of the following transactions for Shoemaker Corporation.
1. The loan of $600,000 and acceptance of the note receivable on April 1, 2024.
2. Interest accrued on December 31, 2024.
3. Cash collection of the note and interest on April 1, 2025.

## PROBLEMS

**P5–1** Assume the following scenarios.

Calculate the amount of revenue to recognize (LO5–1)

Scenario 1:   During 2024, **IBM** provides consulting services on its mainframe computer for $11,000 on account. The customer does not pay for those services until 2025.

Scenario 2:   On January 1, 2024, **Gold's Gym** sells a one-year membership for $1,200 cash. Normally, this type of membership would cost $1,600, but the company is offering a 25% "New Year's Resolution" discount.

Scenario 3:   During 2024, **The Manitowoc Company** provides shipbuilding services to the U.S. Navy for $450,000. The U.S. Navy will pay $150,000 at the end of each year for the next three years, beginning in 2024.

**Scenario 4:**     During 2024, **Goodyear** sells tires to customers on account for $35,000. By the end of the year, collections total $30,000. At the end of 2025, it becomes apparent that the remaining $5,000 will never be collected from customers.

**Required:**

For each scenario, calculate the amount of revenue to be recognized in 2024.

Identify performance obligations and recognize revenue (LO5–3)

**P5–2** Accorsi & Sons specializes in selling and installing upscale home theater systems. On March 1, 2024, Accorsi sold a premium home theater package that includes a projector, set of surround speakers, and high-quality leather seats, along with complete installation service, for $32,500. If sold separately, each of these goods or services would have cost $15,000 (projector), $12,500 (speakers), $17,500 (seats), and $3,000 (installation), respectively.

**Required:**

How much of the transaction price would be allocated to the projector, the speakers, the leather seats, and the installation service, assuming that each of these four parts of the contract is a separate performance obligation?

Calculate revenues from credit sales (LO5–4)
*See JP5–1 for journal entries.*

**P5–3** Outdoor Expo provides guided fishing tours. The company charges $300 per person but offers a 20% discount to parties of four or more. Consider the following transactions during the month of May.

| | |
|---|---|
| May 2 | Charlene books a fishing tour with Outdoor Expo for herself and four friends at the group discount price ($1,200 = $240 × 5). The tour is scheduled for May 7. |
| May 7 | The fishing tour occurs. Outdoor Expo asks that payment be made within 30 days of the tour and offers a 6% discount for payment within 15 days. |
| May 9 | Charlene is upset that no one caught a single fish and asks management for a discount. Outdoor Expo has a strict policy of no discounts related to number of fish caught. |
| May 15 | Upon deeper investigation, management of Outdoor Expo discovers that Charlene's tour was led by a new guide who did not take the group to some of the better fishing spots. In concession, management offers a sales allowance of 30% of the amount due. |
| May 20 | Outdoor Expo receives the amount owed by Charlene. |

**Required:**

1. Determine the financial statement effects for each date.
2. Calculate net revenues for Outdoor Expo by May 20.

Calculate net accounts receivable
(LO5–5, 5–6, 5–7, 5–8)
*See JP5–2 for journal entries.*

**P5–4** The following events occur for The Underwood Corporation during 2024 and 2025, its first two years of operations.

| | |
|---|---|
| June 12, 2024 | Provide services to customers on account for $41,000. |
| September 17, 2024 | Receive $25,000 from customers on account. |
| December 31, 2024 | Estimate that 45% of accounts receivable at the end of the year will not be received. |
| March 4, 2025 | Provide services to customers on account for $56,000. |
| May 20, 2025 | Receive $10,000 from customers for services provided in 2024. |
| July 2, 2025 | Write off the remaining amounts owed from services provided in 2024. |
| October 19, 2025 | Receive $45,000 from customers for services provided in 2025. |
| December 31, 2025 | Estimate that 45% of accounts receivable at the end of the year will not be received. |

**Required:**

1. Determine the financial statement effects for each date.
2. Calculate net accounts receivable reported in the balance sheet at the end of 2024 and 2025.

Determine bad debt expense and the allowance for uncollectible accounts (LO5–6, 5–7)
*See JP5–3 for journal entries.*

**P5–5** Pearl E. White Orthodontist specializes in correcting misaligned teeth. During 2024, Pearl provides services on account of $590,000. Of this amount, $80,000 remains receivable at the end of the year. An aging schedule as of December 31, 2024, is provided below.

| Age Group | Amount Receivable | Estimated Percent Uncollectible |
|---|---|---|
| Not yet due | $40,000 | 4% |
| 0–90 days past due | 16,000 | 20% |
| 91–180 days past due | 11,000 | 25% |
| More than 180 days past due | 13,000 | 80% |
| Total | $80,000 | |

**Required:**

1. Calculate the allowance for uncollectible accounts.
2. Calculate bad debt expense for 2024, assuming the balance of Allowance for Uncollectible Accounts before adjustment is $5,000 (*positive, credit balance*).
3. On July 19, 2025, a customer's account balance of $8,000 is written off as uncollectible. Show the financial statement effects of this write-off.

**P5–6** Willie Cheetum is the CEO of Happy Foods, a distributor of produce to grocery store chains throughout the Midwest. At the end of the year, the company's accounting manager provides Willie with the following information, before any adjustment.

*Use estimates of uncollectible accounts to overstate income (LO5–6)*

| | |
|---|---|
| Accounts receivable | $1,100,000 |
| Estimated percentage uncollectible | 9% |
| Allowance for uncollectible accounts | $40,000 (*positive, credit balance*) |
| Operating income | $260,000 |

Willie's compensation contract states that if the company generates operating income of at least $210,000, he will get a salary bonus early next year.

**Required:**

1. Calculate bad debt expense for the year using the accountant's estimate that 9% of accounts receivable will be uncollectible.
2. After the calculation in requirement 1, what is the revised amount of operating income? Will Willie get his salary bonus?
3. Willie instructs the accountant to estimate uncollectible accounts using 6% rather than 9% of accounts receivable. Now will Willie get his salary bonus? Explain.
4. By how much would total assets and operating income be misstated using the 6% amount?

**P5–7** Humanity International sells medical and food supplies to those in need in underdeveloped countries. Customers in these countries are often very poor and must purchase items on account. At the end of 2024, total accounts receivable equal $1,300,000. The company understands it is dealing with high-credit-risk clients. These countries are often in the middle of a financial crisis, civil war, severe drought, or some other difficult circumstance. Because of this, Humanity International typically estimates the percentage of uncollectible accounts to be 35% (= $455,000). Actual write-offs in 2025 total only $300,000, which means that the company significantly overestimated uncollectible accounts in 2024. It appears that efforts by the International Monetary Fund (IMF) and the United Nations (UN), and a mild winter mixed with adequate spring rains, have provided for more stable economic conditions than were expected, helping customers to pay on their accounts.

*Overestimate future uncollectible accounts (LO5–6)*

**Required:**

1. Calculate bad debt expense for 2024 assuming there is no balance in Allowance for Uncollectible Accounts at the end of 2024 before any adjustment.
2. By the end of 2025, Humanity International has the benefit of hindsight to know that estimates of uncollectible accounts in 2024 were too high. How did this overestimation affect the reported amounts of total assets and expenses at the end of 2024? Ignore tax effects.
3. Should Humanity International prepare new financial statements for 2024 to show the correct amount of uncollectible accounts? Explain.

Calculate and analyze ratios (LO5–9)

**P5–8** Assume selected financial data for **Walmart** and **Target**, two close competitors in the retail industry, are as follows:

| ($ in millions) | Net Sales | Beginning Accounts Receivable | Ending Accounts Receivable |
|---|---|---|---|
| Walmart | $443,854 | $5,089 | $5,937 |
| Target | 68,466 | 6,153 | 5,927 |

*Required:*
1. Calculate the receivables turnover ratio and average collection period for Walmart and Target. Round your answers to one decimal place. Which company has more favorable ratios?

## JOURNAL ENTRIES

### Journal Entries—Brief Exercises

Recognize revenue at a point in time (LO5–1)
See BE5–2 for financial statement effects.

**JBE5–1** On July 1, 2024, Apache Company, sold and delivered to a customer a large piece of equipment for $3,000 (on account). The cost to manufacture the equipment was $1,200. The customer. Record the journal entry to recognize revenue for the sale of the equipment.

Recognize revenue over time (LO5–2)
See BE5–3 for financial statement effects.

**JBE5–2** On May 1, 2024, Varga Tech Services signed a $6,000 consulting contract with Shaffer Holdings. The contract requires Varga to provide computer technology support services whenever requested over the period from May 1, 2024, to April 30, 2025, with Shaffer paying the entire $6,000 on May 1, 2024. Record the journal entries for Varga on May 1 and December 31, 2024?

Allocate the transaction price (LO5–3)
See BE5–4 for financial statement effects.

**JBE5–3** Sarjit Systems sold software to a customer for $80,000. As part of the contract, Sarjit promises to provide "free" technical support over the next six months. Sarjit sells the same software without technical support for $70,000 and a stand-alone six-month technical support contract for $30,000, so these products would sell for $100,000 if sold separately. Record Sarjit's journal entry for the sale of the software.

Record sales returns (LO5–4)
See BE5–5 for financial statement effects.

**JBE5–4** During 2024, its first year of operations, Hollis Industries recorded sales of $10,600,000 and experienced returns of $720,000. Cost of goods sold totaled $6,360,000 (60% of sales). The company estimates that 8% of all sales will be returned. Record the year-end adjusting journal entries to account for anticipated sales returns under the assumption that all sales are made for cash (no accounts receivable are outstanding).

Record credit sales (LO5–5)
See BE5–6 for financial statement effects.

**JBE5–5** RUHC Corp ships a large order of chemicals to a customer near of the end of March 2025. The sale price on the order is $15,000. The customer has 60 days to pay for the order. Cash is collected from the customer in early May of 2002. Record the journal entries for the sale of the goods and the cash collection.

Establish an allowance for uncollectible accounts (LO5–6)
See BE5–7 for financial statement effects.

**JBE5–6** At the end of the first year of operations, Mayberry Advertising had accounts receivable of $20,000. Management of the company estimates that 10% of the accounts will not be collected. What adjusting entry would Mayberry Advertising record to establish Allowance for Uncollectible Accounts?

Record the write-off of uncollectible accounts (LO5–7)
See BE5–8 for financial statement effects.

**JBE5–7** At the beginning of the year, Mitchum Enterprises allows for estimated uncollectible accounts of $15,000. By the end of the year, write-offs of bad debts total $17,000. Record the journal entries needed to write off the uncollectible accounts.

Record the adjusting entry for uncollectible accounts (LO5–8)
See BE5–9 for financial statement effects.

**JBE5–8** At the end of the year, Mercy Cosmetics' balance of Allowance for Uncollectible Accounts before adjustment is $600 (*credit balance*). The balance of Accounts Receivable is $25,000. The company estimates that 12% of accounts will not be collected over the next year. What adjusting entry would Mercy Cosmetics record for uncollectible accounts at the end of the year?

**JBE5-9** Refer to the information in JBE5-8, but now assume that the balance of Allowance for Uncollectible Accounts before adjustment is $600 (*debit balance*). The company still estimates future uncollectible accounts to be 12% of Accounts Receivable. What adjusting entry would Mercy Cosmetics record for uncollectible accounts at the end of the year?

*Record the adjusting entry for uncollectible accounts (LO5–8)*
*See BE5–10 for financial statement effects.*

**JBE5-10** Spade Agency separates its accounts receivable into three age groups for purposes of estimating the percentage of uncollectible accounts.
1. Accounts not yet due = $25,000; estimated uncollectible = 4%.
2. Accounts 1-60 days past due = $10,000; estimated uncollectible = 25%.
3. Accounts more than 60 days past due = $5,000; estimated uncollectible = 50%.

In addition, the balance of Allowance for Uncollectible Accounts before making an adjusting entry is $1,000 (*credit balance*). Record the year-end adjusting entry.

*Calculate uncollectible accounts using the aging method (LO5–8)*
*See BE5–12 for financial statement effects.*

**JBE5-11** At the end of the year, Brinkley Incorporated's balance of Allowance for Uncollectible Accounts is $4,000 (*credit balance*) before making an adjusting entry. The company estimates future uncollectible accounts to be 3% of credit sales for the year. Credit sales for the year total $135,000.

What is the adjusting entry Brinkley would record for Allowance for Uncollectible Accounts using the percentage-of-credit-sales method?

*Use the percentage-of-credit-sales method to adjust for uncollectible accounts (LO5–10)*
*See BE5–15 for financial statement effects.*

**JBE5-12** Refer to the information in JBE5-11, but now assume that the balance of Allowance for Uncollectible Accounts before making an adjusting entry is $4,000 (*debit balance*). The company still estimates future uncollectible accounts to be 3% of credit sales for the year. What adjusting entry would Brinkley record for Allowance for Uncollectible Accounts using the percentage-of-credit-sales method?

*Use the percentage-of-credit-sales method to adjust for uncollectible accounts (LO5–10)*
*See BE5–16 for financial statement effects.*

## Journal Entries—Exercises

**JE5-1** Ski West, Inc., operates a downhill ski area near Lake Tahoe, California. An all-day adult lift ticket can be purchased for $85. Adult customers also can purchase a season pass that entitles the pass holder to ski any day during the season, which typically runs from December 1 through April 30. Ski West expects its season pass holders to use their passes equally throughout the season. The company's fiscal year ends on December 31.

On November 6, 2024, Ski West sells a season pass to Jake Lawson for $450.

*Timing of revenue recognition (LO5–2)*
*See E5–2 for financial statement effects.*

*Required:*
1. Record the appropriate journal entries for Ski West on November 6 and December 31.

**JE5-2** On March 1, 2024, Gold Examiner receives $147,000 from a local bank and promises to deliver 100 units of certified 1-oz. gold bars on a future date. The contract states that ownership passes to the bank when Gold Examiner delivers the products to Brink's, a third-party carrier. In addition, Gold Examiner agreed to provide a replacement shipment at no additional cost if the product is lost in transit. The stand-alone price of a gold bar is $1,440 per unit, and Gold Examiner estimates the stand-alone price of the replacement insurance service to be $60 per unit. Brink's picked up the gold bars from Gold Examiner on March 30, and delivery to the bank occurred on April 1.

*Determine performance obligations (LO5–1, LO5–3)*
*See E5–4 for financial statement effects.*

*Required:*
1. Record the journal entry for Gold Examiner on March 1.
2. Record the journal entry for Gold Examiner on March 30.
3. Record the journal entry for Gold Examiner on April 1.

**JE5-3** On May 7, Juanita Construction provides services on account to Michael Wolfe for $4,000. Michael pays for those services on May 13.

*Record credit sale (LO5–5)*
*See E5–7 for financial statement effects.*

*Required:*
For Juanita Construction, record the service on account on May 7 and the collection of cash on May 13.

Establish an allowance
for uncollectible accounts
and write off accounts
receivable (LO5–6, 5–7)
See E5–11 for financial
statement effects.

**JE5–4** During 2024, its first year of operations, Pave Construction provides services on account of $160,000. By the end of 2024, cash collections on these accounts total $110,000. Pave estimates that 25% of the uncollected accounts will be uncollectible. In 2025, the company writes off uncollectible accounts of $10,000.

**Required**

1. What is the journal entry to record bad debt expense for the year ended December 31, 2024?
2. What is the journal entry to write off accounts receivables in 2025?

Record the adjusting
entry for uncollectible
accounts using the aging
method (LO5–6, 5–7)
See E5–12 for financial
statement effects.

**JE5–5** The Physical Therapy Center specializes in helping patients regain motor skills after serious accidents. The center has the following balances on December 31, 2024, before making any adjusting entry: Accounts Receivable = $110,000; Allowance for Uncollectible Accounts = $4,000 (*debit balance*). The center estimates uncollectible accounts based on an aging of accounts receivable as shown below.

| Age Group | Amount Receivable | Estimated Percent Uncollectible |
|---|---|---|
| Not yet due | $ 60,000 | 4% |
| 0–60 days past due | 26,000 | 20% |
| 61–120 days past due | 16,000 | 30% |
| More than 120 days past due | 8,000 | 85% |
| Total | $110,000 | |

**Required:**

What is the adjusting entry for uncollectible accounts for the year ended December 31, 2024?

Record notes
receivable and interest
revenue (LO5–11)
See E5–19 for financial
statement effects.

**JE5–6** On March 1, Terrell & Associates provides legal services to Whole Grain Bakery regarding some recent food poisoning complaints. Legal services total $11,000. In payment for the services, Whole Grain Bakery signs a 9% note requiring the payment of the face amount and interest to Terrell & Associates on September 1.

**Required:**

Record the following transactions for Terrell & Associates:
1. Acceptance of the note receivable on March 1.
2. Collection of cash on September 1.

Record notes
receivable and interest
revenue (LO5–11)
See E5–20 for financial
statement effects.

**JE5–7** On April 1, 2024, Shoemaker Corporation realizes one of its main suppliers is having difficulty meeting delivery schedules, which is hurting Shoemaker's business. The supplier explains that it has a temporary lack of funds that is slowing its production cycle. Shoemaker agrees to lend $600,000 to its supplier using a 12-month, 11% note.

**Required:**

Record the following transactions for Shoemaker Corporation.
1. The loan of $600,000 and acceptance of the note receivable on April 1, 2024.
2. The adjusting entry for accrued interest on December 31, 2024.
3. Cash collection of the note and interest on April 1, 2025.

## Journal Entries–Problems

Record transactions
related to credit sales and
contra revenues (LO5–4)
See P5–3 for financial
statement effects.

**JP5–1** Outdoor Expo provides guided fishing tours. The company charges $300 per person but offers a 20% discount to parties of four or more. Consider the following transactions during the month of May.

| | |
|---|---|
| May 2 | Charlene books a fishing tour with Outdoor Expo for herself and four friends at the group discount price ($1,200 = $240 × 5). The tour is scheduled for May 7. |
| May 7 | The fishing tour occurs. Outdoor Expo asks that payment be made within 30 days of the tour and offers a 6% discount for payment within 15 days. |
| May 9 | Charlene is upset that no one caught a single fish and asks management for a discount. Outdoor Expo has a strict policy of no discounts related to number of fish caught. |

May 15   Upon deeper investigation, management of Outdoor Expo discovers that Charlene's tour was led by a new guide who did not take the group to some of the better fishing spots. In concession, management offers a sales allowance of 30% of the amount due.

May 20   Outdoor Expo receives the amount owed by Charlene.

**Required:**

Record the journal entries for each transaction.

**JP5–2** The following events occur for The Underwood Corporation during 2024 and 2025, its first two years of operations.

*Record transactions related to accounts receivable (LO5–5, 5–6, 5–7, 5–8)*
*See P5–4 for financial statement effects.*

| | |
|---|---|
| June 12, 2024 | Provide services to customers on account for $41,000. |
| September 17, 2024 | Receive $25,000 from customers on account. |
| December 31, 2024 | Estimate that 45% of accounts receivable at the end of the year will not be received. |
| March 4, 2025 | Provide services to customers on account for $56,000. |
| May 20, 2025 | Receive $10,000 from customers for services provided in 2024. |
| July 2, 2025 | Write off the remaining amounts owed from services provided in 2024. |
| October 19, 2025 | Receive $45,000 from customers for services provided in 2025. |
| December 31, 2025 | Estimate that 45% of accounts receivable at the end of the year will not be received. |

**Required:**

Record the journal entries for each transaction.

**JP5–3** Pearl E. White Orthodontist specializes in correcting misaligned teeth. During 2024, Pearl provides services on account of $590,000. Of this amount, $80,000 remains receivable at the end of the year. An aging schedule as of December 31, 2024, is provided below.

*Record transactions related to uncollectible accounts (LO5–6, 5–7)*
*See P5–5 for financial statement effects.*

| Age Group | Amount Receivable | Estimated Percent Uncollectible |
|---|---|---|
| Not yet due | $40,000 | 4% |
| 0–90 days past due | 16,000 | 20% |
| 91–180 days past due | 11,000 | 25% |
| More than 180 days past due | 13,000 | 80% |
| Total | $80,000 | |

**Required:**

1. Record the December 31, 2024, adjusting entry, assuming the balance of Allowance for Uncollectible Accounts before the adjusting entry is $5,000 (*credit balance*).
2. On July 19, 2025, a customer's account balance of $8,000 is written off as uncollectible. Record the write-off.

## DATA ANALYTICS

Visit Connect to view **Data Analytics** questions related to:

1. Applying Excel
2. Data Visualizations
3. Tableau Dashboard Activities
4. Applying Tableau

## ANSWERS TO THE SELF-STUDY QUESTIONS

1. b   2. b   3. c   4. c   5. b   6. c   7. d   8. b   9. b   10. d   11. b   12. d   13. c   14. c   15. b   16. b   17. b

# CHAPTER SIX

# Inventory and Cost of Goods Sold

## Learning Objectives

## Self-Study Materials

Sergey Yechikov/Shutterstock

## Feature Story

# Best Buy: Taking Inventory of Electronics Sold

**Best Buy** is the largest consumer electronics retailer in the United States. You are probably familiar with most of the products offered by Best Buy—computers, computer software, TVs, video games, music, mobile phones, digital and video cameras, home appliances (washing machines, dryers, and refrigerators), and other related merchandise.

Merchandise inventory for sale to customers is the single largest asset owned by Best Buy, as it is for many retail companies. At any given time, Best Buy holds about $5 billion in inventory, or about 35% of the company's total assets. Proper management of inventory and inventory risks is key to the company's success.

Management of Best Buy knows there is a fine line between having too little and too much inventory. Having too little inventory reduces the selection of products available to customers, ultimately reducing sales revenue. On the other hand, in a technology-based industry where changes occur rapidly, having too much inventory can leave the store holding outdated inventory. Besides obsolescence, other risks associated with holding large inventories are seasonalities, product life cycle fluctuations, and changes in consumer preferences. Holding less inventory also provides access to money that can be invested elsewhere within the company.

For now, Best Buy seems to be taking the right steps with its inventory. Look below at the company's revenues from sales of inventory compared to the cost of the inventory sold. These amounts are reported in the company's income statement ($ in millions). The difference between net sales (a revenue) and cost of goods sold (an expense) is called *gross profit,* and it has averaged more than $10 billion over the period 2019–2021.

|                    | 2019     | 2020     | 2021     |
|--------------------|----------|----------|----------|
| Net sales          | $42,879  | $43,638  | $47,262  |
| Cost of goods sold | 32,918   | 33,590   | 36,689   |
| Gross profit       | $ 9,961  | $10,048  | $10,573  |

In this chapter, we explore how to account for the purchase and sale of inventory items. We'll see how inventory (an asset in the balance sheet) turns into cost of goods sold (an expense in the income statement) once it is sold, and how these amounts can affect business decisions. At the end of the chapter, we'll analyze inventory transactions of **Best Buy** versus **Tiffany** and **Target**.

# REPORTING INVENTORY AND COST OF GOODS SOLD

In preceding chapters, we dealt with companies that provide a service. **Service companies** such as **FedEx**, **Zoom**, **AT&T**, and **Marriott** generate revenues by providing services to their customers. FedEx delivers packages, Zoom provides video conferencing, AT&T provides media and telecommunications services, and Marriott offers a place to stay the night. Many companies, though, generate revenues by selling inventory rather than a service.

Part A of this chapter introduces the concept of inventory and demonstrates the different methods used to calculate the cost of inventory for external reporting. Once you understand this, then you're ready to learn in Part B how companies actually maintain their own internal records of inventory transactions and the adjustments that are sometimes needed to prepare financial statements. In Part C, we'll examine how to measure a company's efficiency in managing its inventory.

## Types of Inventory

**■ LO6–1**

Understand that inventory flows from manufacturing companies to merchandising companies and is reported as an asset on the balance sheet.

*Inventory is a current asset.*

Inventory includes items a company intends to sell to customers in the ordinary course of business. You already are familiar with several types of inventory—clothes at **H&M**, shoes at **Zappos.com**, grocery items at **Sprouts Markets**, digital equipment at **Best Buy**, building supplies at **Home Depot**, and so on. Inventory also includes items that are not yet finished products. For instance, lumber at a cabinet manufacturer, steel at a construction firm, and rubber at a tire manufacturer are also part of inventory because the firm will use them to make a finished product for sale to customers. We typically report inventory as a current asset in the balance sheet—an *asset* because it represents a valuable resource to the company, and *current* because the company expects to convert it to cash in the near term.

### MANUFACTURING COMPANIES

**Manufacturing companies** produce the inventories they sell, rather than buying them as a finished product from suppliers. **Apple**, **Coca-Cola**, **Harley-Davidson**, **ExxonMobil**, **Ford**, **Sony**, and **Intel** are manufacturers. Manufacturing companies buy the inputs for the products they manufacture. Thus, we classify inventory for a manufacturer into three categories: (1) raw materials, (2) work in process, and (3) finished goods:

- *Raw materials* inventory includes the cost of components that will become part of the finished product but have not yet been used in production.
- *Work-in-process* inventory refers to the products that have been started in the production process but are not yet complete at the end of the period. The total costs include raw materials, direct labor, and indirect manufacturing costs called *overhead*.
- *Finished goods* inventory is the cost of fully assembled but unshipped inventory at the end of the reporting period.

Intel manufactures the components that are used to build computers. At any given time, Intel's inventory includes the cost of materials that will be used to build computer components (raw materials), partially manufactured components (work-in-process), and fully assembled but unsold components (finished goods). These separate inventory accounts are added together and reported by Intel as total inventories.

### MERCHANDISING COMPANIES

*Common Terms*
Inventory is sometimes referred to as *merchandise inventory.*

**Merchandising companies,** such as **Best Buy**, don't manufacture computers or their components. Instead, Best Buy purchases finished computers from manufacturers, and then these computers are sold to customers like you. Merchandising companies may assemble, sort, repackage, redistribute, store, refrigerate, deliver, or install the inventory, but they do not manufacture it. They simply serve as intermediaries in the process of moving inventory from the manufacturer to the end user. Illustration 6–1 shows the different inventory accounts for Intel (a manufacturing company) and Best Buy (a merchandising company), as reported in their balance sheets.

| INVENTORY (from balance sheets) | | |
|---|---|---|
| Inventory accounts ($ in millions) | Intel | Best Buy |
| Raw materials | $ 908 | |
| Work in process | 6,007 | |
| Finished goods | 1,512 | |
| Merchandise inventories | | $5,612 |
| Total inventories | $8,427 | $5,612 |

**ILLUSTRATION 6–1**

**Inventory Amounts for a Manufacturing Company (Intel) versus a Merchandising Company (Best Buy)**

**Wholesalers and Retailers.**  Merchandising companies can further be classified as wholesalers or retailers. *Wholesalers* resell inventory to retail companies or to professional users. For example, a wholesale food service company like **Sysco** supplies food to restaurants, schools, and sporting events but generally does not sell food directly to the public. Also, Sysco does not transform the food prior to sale; it just stores the food, repackages it as necessary, and delivers it.

*Retailers* purchase inventory from manufacturers or wholesalers and then sell this inventory to end users. You probably are more familiar with retail companies because these are the companies from which you buy products. **Amazon**, **Best Buy**, **Target**, **Lowe's**, **Macy's**, **Gap**, **Costco**, and **McDonald's** are retailers. Merchandising companies typically hold their inventories in a single category simply called *inventory.*

Illustration 6–2 shows the largest 10 U.S. companies ranked by total inventory. The list includes both manufacturers (**Boeing**, **General Electric**) and merchandising companies (**Walmart**, **Amazon**). For these companies, inventory represents a major portion of their assets.

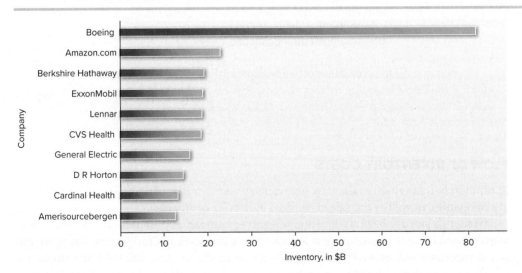

**ILLUSTRATION 6–2**

**Largest 10 Companies Ranked by Total Inventory**

*Source:* Standard & Poor's

**KEY POINT**

Service companies report revenues when providing services to customers. Merchandising and manufacturing companies report revenues when selling inventory to customers.

**SUSTAINABILITY**

The SASB aims to enable standardized, comparable reporting of sustainability metrics for many topics, including inventory sourcing. This goal of standardization and comparability implies that similar companies report similar sustainability measures in similar ways. Comparability will allow investors and other stakeholders to credibly assess and compare the quality of a company's sustainability numbers to other similar companies.

This issue can be seen in the SASB standards for the Apparel, Accessories & Footwear industry, which ask companies to disclose accounting metrics related to product inventory. The following table presents some of the important quantitative metrics requested by the SASB for apparel companies:

| Topic | Accounting Metric | Unit of Measure | SASB Code |
|---|---|---|---|
| Raw Material Sourcing & Innovation | Top five raw materials used in products | Metric tons | CN0501-03 |
| | Percentage of raw materials third-party certified to meet sustainability standards | Percentage (%) by weight | CN0501-04 |
| Labor Conditions in the Supply Chain | Percentage of suppliers that have committed to a labor code of conduct. | Percentage (%) | CN0501-05 |
| | Non-conformance rate for suppliers' labor code of conduct audits | Rate | CN0501-06 |
| Environmental Impacts in the Supply Chain | Percentage of supplier facilities with wastewater discharge meeting or exceeding legal requirements | Percentage (%) | CN0501-08 |
| | Percentage of suppliers who have completed an independent assessment on environmental data collection | Percentage (%) | CN0501-09 |

By encouraging the consistent measurement and disclosure of these important metrics, the SASB is aiming to improve practices on responsible inventory sourcing.

**Source:** https://www.sasb.org/wp-content/uploads/2015/09/CN0501_Apparel-Accessories-Footwear_Standard.pdf

## FLOW OF INVENTORY COSTS

Illustration 6–3 summarizes the flow of inventory costs for manufacturing and merchandising companies, as well as the sale of services by service companies.

Inventory's journey begins when manufacturing companies purchase raw materials, hire workers, and incur manufacturing overhead during production. Once the products are finished, manufacturers normally pass finished goods inventory to merchandising companies, whether wholesalers or retailers. Merchandising companies then sell finished goods to you, the end user. In some cases, manufacturers may sell directly to end users.

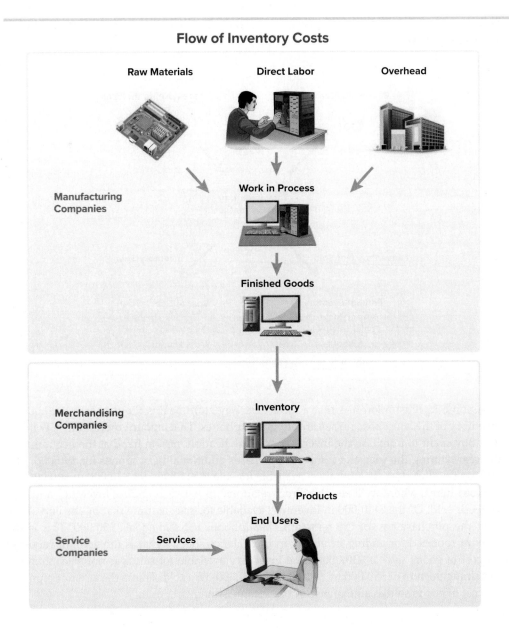

**Flow of Inventory Costs**

**ILLUSTRATION 6–3**

Types of Companies and Flow of Inventory Costs

Some companies sell goods and also provide services to customers. For example, **IBM** generates about half its revenues from selling its inventories of hardware and software and the other half from providing services like consulting, systems maintenance, and financing.

In this chapter, we focus on merchandising companies, both wholesalers and retailers. Still, most of the accounting principles and procedures discussed here also apply to manufacturing companies. We do not attempt to address all the unique problems of accumulating the direct costs of raw materials and labor and allocating manufacturing overhead. We leave those details for managerial and cost accounting courses. We also do not examine these costs for companies without traditional inventory, such as service companies (e.g., **Accenture**) or tech companies with digital inventory (e.g., **Netflix**). These companies report *cost of services*. In this course, we focus on the financial reporting implications of inventory cost flows.

## Cost of Goods Sold in the Income Statement

We've discussed that inventory is reported as an asset in the balance sheet. The amount reported is the cost of inventory *not yet sold* at the end of the year. Now let's discuss how we

■ **LO6–2**
Understand how cost of goods sold is reported in a multiple-step income statement.

report cost of goods sold, an expense in the income statement, for the cost of the inventory *sold* during the year.

**ILLUSTRATION 6–4**

Relationship between
Inventory and Cost of
Goods Sold

Assume in Illustration 6–4 that a local **Best Buy** store begins the year with $20,000 of inventory of the latest Bose noise-canceling headphones. That amount represents how much Best Buy spent to purchase the inventory of these headphones on hand at the beginning of the year. During the year, the company purchases additional headphones for $90,000. The total cost of inventory (headphones) available for sale is $110,000 (= $20,000 + $90,000).

Now, here's where we'll see the direct relationship between ending inventory and cost of goods sold. Of the $110,000 in inventory available for sale, assume that by the end of the year, the purchase cost of the remaining headphones *not sold* equals $30,000. This is the amount reported for ending inventory in the balance sheet. What is the amount reported for cost of goods *sold*? If $30,000 of the inventory available for sale was not sold, then the remaining portion of $80,000 (= $110,000 − $30,000) was sold. This is the amount reported for cost of goods sold as an expense in the income statement.

 **KEY POINT**

Inventory is a current asset reported in the balance sheet and represents the cost of inventory *not yet sold* at the end of the period. Cost of goods sold is an expense reported in the income statement and represents the cost of inventory *sold*.

To see how Best Buy actually reports its cost of goods sold as an expense, as well as its other income statement items, let's look at Illustration 6–5.

## LEVELS OF PROFITABILITY

Inventory transactions are typically the most important activities of a merchandising company. For this reason, companies report the revenues and expenses directly associated with these transactions in the top section of a multiple-step income statement, which reports multiple levels of profitability.

*Revenues* include the sale of products and services to customers. Inventory sales are commonly referred to as *sales revenue,* while providing services is referred to as *service revenue.* Best Buy reports its revenues after subtracting customer returns, allowances, and discounts,

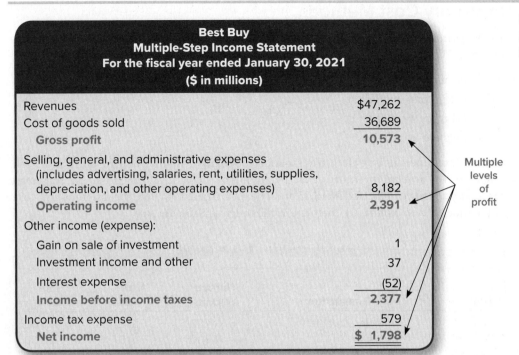

**ILLUSTRATION 6–5**

Multiple-Step Income Statement for Best Buy

as discussed in Chapter 5, although the company does not list these amounts separately in the income statement. The net amount of revenues is commonly referred to as **net sales.**

*Cost of goods sold* is the cost of inventory sold during the year. Best Buy's cost of goods sold includes not only the cost of the physical merchandise purchased from suppliers, but also costs related to getting inventory ready for sale, such as shipping and other costs for its distribution network.

Gross profit equals net revenues (or net sales) minus cost of goods sold. Gross profit is the first level of profit shown in the multiple-step income statement and is a key measure of profitability for the company's primary business activities. Best Buy's gross profit is over $10 billion for $47 billion in sales.

After gross profit, the next items reported are *selling, general, and administrative expenses,* often referred to as **operating expenses,** such as salaries, rent, and depreciation.

Operating income (sometimes referred to as income from operations) equals gross profit minus operating expenses. It measures profitability from *normal* operations, a key performance measure for predicting the future profit-generating ability of the company.

After operating income, a company reports *nonoperating* revenues and expenses, which typically includes interest expense, interest income and gains/losses on the sale of investments. Best Buy refers to these items as *Other income (expense).*

Income before income taxes is the combination of operating income and nonoperating income.

Net income equals income before income taxes minus income tax expense. Income tax expense is reported separately from other expenses because it represents a significant expense. Best Buy's net income is its "bottom line," which amounted to nearly $1.8 billion.

**Common Terms**
Cost of goods sold is sometimes referred to as *cost of sales, cost of merchandise sold,* or *cost of products sold.* For example, Target calls it *cost of sales* and Nvidia calls it *cost of revenues.* These different terms all point to the same concept: cost of goods sold.

**KEY POINT**

A multiple-step income statement reports multiple levels of profitability. **Gross profit** equals net revenues (or net sales) minus cost of goods sold. **Operating income** equals gross profit minus operating expenses. **Income before income taxes** equals operating income plus nonoperating revenues and minus nonoperating expenses. **Net income** equals all revenues minus all expenses.

■ LO6-3
Determine the cost of
goods sold and ending
inventory using different
inventory cost methods.

# Inventory Cost Methods

To this point, we've discussed the cost of inventory without considering how we determine that cost. We do that now by considering four methods for inventory costing.

1. Specific identification
2. First-in, first-out (FIFO)
3. Last-in, first-out (LIFO)
4. Weighted-average cost

We'll examine the inventory transactions for Mario's Game Shop in Illustration 6–6. There are 100 units of inventory at the beginning of the year, and then two purchases are made during the year—one on April 25 and one on October 19. (Note the different unit costs at the time of each purchase.) There are **1,000** units available for sale.

**ILLUSTRATION 6–6**

**Inventory Transactions for Mario's Game Shop**

| Date | Transaction | Number of Units | Unit Cost | Total Cost |
|---|---|---|---|---|
| Jan. 1 | Beginning inventory | 100 | $ 7 | $ 700 |
| Apr. 25 | Purchase | 300 | 9 | 2,700 |
| Oct. 19 | Purchase | 600 | 11 | 6,600 |
| | Total available for sale | 1,000 | | $10,000 |
| Jul. 17 | Sale (for $15 each) | 300 | | |
| Dec. 15 | Sale (for $15 each) | 500 | | |
| | Total units sold | 800 | | |
| Dec. 31 | Ending inventory | 200 | | |

During the year, the company sells **800** units of inventory for $15 each. While most companies sell their products continuously throughout the year, for simplicity we'll assume 300 units are sold on July 17, and 500 units are sold on December 15.

There are **200** units remaining in ending inventory at the end of the year (1,000 available − 800 sold). But which 200? Do they include some of the $7 units from beginning inventory? Are they 200 of the $9 units from the April 25 purchase? Or, do they include some $11 units from the October 19 purchase? **The answer depends on which of the four inventory methods is used.**

## SPECIFIC IDENTIFICATION

The specific identification
method reports *actual*
units sold.

The **specific identification method** is the method you might think of as the most logical. It matches—or *identifies*—each unit of inventory with its actual cost. For example, an automobile has a unique serial number that we can match to an invoice identifying the actual purchase price. Fine jewelry and pieces of art are other possibilities. Specific identification works well in such cases.

In our example for Mario's Game Shop, we might have been able to track each of the 800 units sold. Suppose the *actual* units sold include 100 units of beginning inventory, 200 units of the April 25 purchase, and 500 units of the October 19 purchase. The cost of those units would be reported as cost of goods sold. The cost of the 200 units remaining (consisting of 100 from the April 25 purchase and 100 from the October 19 purchase) would be reported as ending inventory.

However, keeping track of each unit of inventory is not practicable for most companies. Consider the inventory at **Home Depot** or **Macy's**: large stores and numerous items, many of which are relatively inexpensive. Specific identification would be very difficult for such merchandisers. Although bar codes and RFID tags now make it possible to instantly track purchases and sales of specific types of inventory, it may be too costly to know the specific unit cost for each individual sale. **For that reason, the specific identification method is used primarily by companies with unique or expensive products with low sales volume.**

FIFO, LIFO, and weighted-average *assume* which units are sold.

Most companies instead use one of the three inventory cost flow assumptions—FIFO, LIFO, or weighted-average cost. Note the use of the word *assumptions*. FIFO, LIFO, and weighted-average cost *assume* a particular pattern of inventory cost flows. However, the *actual* flow of physical units of inventory does not need to match the *assumed* cost flow in order for the company to use a particular method. This is a crucial point. **Companies are allowed to report inventory costs by *assuming* which units of inventory are sold and not sold, even if this does not match the *actual* flow.** This is another example of using estimates in financial accounting.

### FIRST-IN, FIRST-OUT

Using the first-in, first-out (FIFO) method, we assume that the first units purchased (the first in) are the first ones sold (the first out). We assume that beginning inventory sells first, followed by the inventory from the first purchase during the year, followed by the inventory from the second purchase during the year, and so on.

As shown previously in Illustration 6–6 for Mario's Game Shop, 800 units were sold during the year. Using the FIFO method, we assume they were the *first* 800 units purchased. The remaining 200 units represent ending inventory. The calculations for cost of goods sold and ending inventory are shown in Illustration 6–7.

**ILLUSTRATION 6–7**

Inventory Calculation Assuming the FIFO Method

**Inventory Transactions for Mario's Game Shop—FIFO METHOD**

| Beginning Inventory and Purchases | Number of Units | × | Unit Cost | = | Total Cost | | | |
|---|---|---|---|---|---|---|---|---|
| Jan. 1 | 100 | | $ 7 | | $ 700 | Sold first | $ 700 | |
| Apr. 25 | 300 | | 9 | | 2,700 | 800 | 2,700 | |
| Oct. 19 | 400 | | 11 | | 4,400 | units | 4,400 | |
| | 200 | | 11 | | 2,200 } | Not sold | | $2,200 |
| | 1,000 | | | | $10,000 | = | $7,800 + | $2,200 |
| | | | | | Cost of Goods Available for Sale | = | Cost of Goods Sold + | Ending Inventory |

**Cost of Goods Sold.**    The first 800 units assumed sold include 100 units of beginning inventory, 300 units from the April 25 purchase, and 400 units from the October 19 purchase. Multiplying these units by their respective unit costs, Mario's reports cost of goods sold in the income statement as $7,800.

**Ending Inventory.**    Of the 600 units purchased on October 19, 200 are assumed not to be sold. These units cost $11 each, so the amount of ending inventory Mario's reports in the balance sheet will be $2,200.

**COMMON MISTAKE**

When calculating cost of goods sold using FIFO, students sometimes forget to count beginning inventory as the first purchase. These units were purchased last period, which was before any purchases this period, so they are assumed to be the first units sold.

You may have noticed that we don't actually need to directly calculate both cost of goods sold and inventory. Once we calculate one, the other is apparent. Because the two amounts always add up to the cost of goods available for sale (**$10,000** in our example), knowing either amount allows us to subtract to find the other.

## LAST-IN, FIRST-OUT

Using the last-in, first-out (LIFO) method, we assume that the last units purchased (the last in) are the first ones sold (the first out). In other words, the very *last unit purchased* for the year is assumed to be the very *first unit sold*. While this pattern of inventory flow is unrealistic for nearly all companies, LIFO is an allowable reporting practice. **Companies that use LIFO for reporting purposes calculate cost of goods sold and ending inventory only once per period—*at the end.*** This means that companies don't keep a continual record of LIFO amounts throughout the year.

Recall Mario's Game Shop sold 800 units during the year. Using the LIFO method, we assume they were the *last* 800 units purchased. The remaining 200 units represent ending inventory. The calculations for cost of goods sold and ending inventory are shown in Illustration 6–8.

**ILLUSTRATION 6–8**

Inventory Calculation Assuming the LIFO Method

**Inventory Transactions for Mario's Game Shop—LIFO METHOD**

| Beginning Inventory and Purchases | Number of Units | × | Unit Cost | = | Total Cost | | | | |
|---|---|---|---|---|---|---|---|---|---|
| Jan. 1 | 100 | | $ 7 | | $ 700 | Not sold | | | $ 700 |
| Apr. 25 | 100 | | 9 | | 900 | | | | 900 |
| | 200 | | 9 | | 1,800 | Sold last 800 units | $1,800 | | |
| Oct. 19 | 600 | | 11 | | 6,600 | | 6,600 | | |
| | 1,000 | | | | $10,000 | | $8,400 | + | $1,600 |

Cost of Goods Available for Sale = Cost of Goods Sold + Ending Inventory

**Cost of Goods Sold.**    The last 800 units assumed sold include the 600 units purchased on October 19 and 200 from the units purchased on April 25. Multiplying these units by their respective unit costs, Mario's reports cost of goods sold in the income statement as $8,400.

**Ending Inventory.**    Of the units purchased on April 25, 100 are assumed not to be sold. These units, along with the 100 units of beginning inventory, will be multiplied by their respective unit costs to reporting ending inventory of $1,600.

 **COMMON MISTAKE**

Many students find it surprising that companies are allowed to report inventory costs using assumed amounts rather than actual amounts. Nearly all companies sell their actual inventory in a FIFO manner, but they are allowed to report it as if they sold it in a LIFO manner. Later, we'll see why that's advantageous.

## WEIGHTED-AVERAGE COST

Using the weighted-average cost method, we assume that both cost of goods sold and ending inventory consist of a random mixture of all the goods available for sale. We assume each unit of inventory has a cost equal to the weighted-average unit cost of all inventory items. We calculate that cost at the end of the year as

$$\text{Weighted-average unit cost} = \frac{\text{Cost of goods available for sale}}{\text{Number of units available for sale}}$$

Illustration 6–9 demonstrates the calculation of cost of goods sold and ending inventory using the weighted-average cost method. Notice that the weighted-average cost of each unit is $10, even though none of the units actually cost $10. However, on average, all the units cost $10, and this is the amount we use to calculate cost of goods sold and ending inventory under the weighted-average cost method.

**ILLUSTRATION 6–9**

Inventory Calculation Assuming the Weighted-Average Cost Method

### Inventory Transactions for Mario's Game Shop— WEIGHTED-AVERAGE COST METHOD

| | | Cost of Goods Available for Sale | | | |
| | | Number of Units | × Unit Cost | = | Total Cost |
| Date | Transaction | | | | |
| --- | --- | --- | --- | --- | --- |
| Jan. 1 | Beginning inventory | 100 | $ 7 | | $ 700 |
| Apr. 25 | Purchase | 300 | 9 | | 2,700 |
| Oct. 19 | Purchase | 600 | 11 | | 6,600 |
| | | 1,000 | | | $10,000 |

| | | | | | |
| --- | --- | --- | --- | --- | --- |
| Weighted-average unit cost | = | $10,000 / 1,000 units | = | $10 per unit | |
| Cost of goods sold | = | 800 sold | × $10 | = | $ 8,000 |
| Ending inventory | = | 200 not sold | × 10 | = | 2,000 |
| | | | | | $10,000 |

**COMMON MISTAKE**

In calculating the weighted-average unit cost, be sure to use a *weighted* average of the unit cost instead of the *simple* average. In the example above, there are three unit costs: $7, $9, and $11. A simple average of these amounts is $9 [= ($7 + $9 + $11) ÷ 3]. The simple average, though, fails to take into account that more units were purchased at $11 than at $7 or $9. So we need to *weight* the unit costs by the number of units purchased. We do that by taking the total cost of goods available for sale ($10,000) divided by the total number of units available for sale (1,000) for a weighted average of $10.

Illustration 6–10 depicts the concept behind the three inventory cost flow assumptions for Mario's Game Shop. If Mario sells 800 units of inventory, which 800 are they?

- Using FIFO, we assume inventory is sold in the order purchased: Beginning inventory is sold first, the first purchase during the year is sold second, and part of the second purchase during the year is sold third.

- Using LIFO, we assume inventory is sold in the opposite order that we purchased it: The last purchase is sold first, and part of the second-to-last purchase is sold second.
- Using average cost, we assume inventory is sold using an average of all inventory purchased, including the beginning inventory.

**ILLUSTRATION 6–10**

Comparison of Cost of Goods Sold and Ending Inventory under the Three Inventory Cost Flow Assumptions for Mario's Game Shop

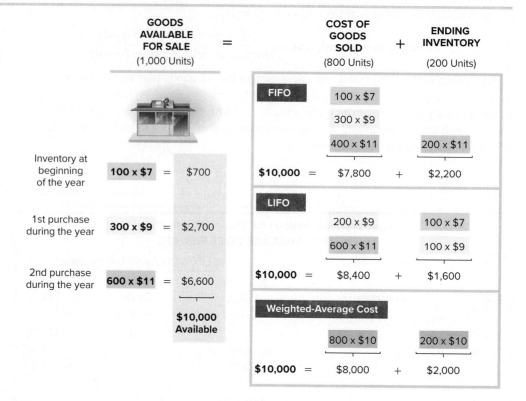

### COMMON MISTAKE

FIFO and LIFO describe more directly the calculation of *cost of goods sold,* rather than ending inventory. For example, FIFO (first-in, first-out) directly suggests which inventory units are assumed sold (the first ones in) and therefore used to calculate cost of goods sold. It is implicit under FIFO that the inventory units *not* sold are the last ones in and are used to calculate ending inventory.

### KEY POINT

Companies are allowed to report inventory costs by *assuming* which specific units of inventory are sold and not sold, even if this does not match the *actual* flow. The three major inventory cost flow assumptions are FIFO (first-in, first-out), LIFO (last-in, first-out), and weighted-average cost.

**Let's Review**

HOVER Unlimited sells low-cost mini-drones for kids and hobbyists. The company has the following beginning inventory and purchase for the year.

| Date | Transaction | Number of Units | Unit Cost | Total Cost |
|---|---|---|---|---|
| Jan. 1 | Beginning inventory | 120 | $20 | $2,400 |
| Aug. 15 | Purchase | 180 | 15 | 2,700 |
| | Total | 300 | | $5,100 |

Because of technological advances, HOVER Unlimited has seen a decrease in the unit cost of its inventory. Throughout the year, the company maintained a selling price of $30 for each mini-drone and sold a total of 280 units, which leaves 20 units in ending inventory.

**Required:**

1. Calculate cost of goods sold and ending inventory using the FIFO method.
2. Calculate cost of goods sold and ending inventory using the LIFO method.
3. Calculate cost of goods sold and ending inventory using the weighted-average cost method.

**Solution:**

1. Cost of goods sold and ending inventory using the **FIFO method:**

| Beginning Inventory and Purchases | Number of Units | × | Unit Cost | = | Total Cost | | | |
|---|---|---|---|---|---|---|---|---|
| Jan. 1 | 120 | | $20 | | $2,400 ⎤ | Sold first | $2,400 | |
| Aug. 15 { | 160 | | 15 | | 2,400 ⎦ | 280 units | 2,400 | |
| | 20 | | 15 | | 300 } | Not sold | | $300 |
| | 300 | | | | **$5,100** | = | **$4,800** + | **$300** |
| | | | | | Cost of Goods Available for Sale | = | Cost of Goods Sold | + Ending Inventory |

2. Cost of goods sold and ending inventory using the **LIFO method:**

| Beginning Inventory and Purchases | Number of Units | × | Unit Cost | = | Total Cost | | | |
|---|---|---|---|---|---|---|---|---|
| Jan. 1 { | 20 | | $20 | | $ 400 } | Not sold | | $400 |
| | 100 | | 20 | | 2,000 ⎤ | Sold last | $2,000 | |
| Aug. 15 | 180 | | 15 | | 2,700 ⎦ | 280 units | 2,700 | |
| | 300 | | | | **$5,100** | = | **$4,700** + | **$400** |
| | | | | | Cost of Goods Available for Sale | = | Cost of Goods Sold | + Ending Inventory |

3. Cost of goods sold and ending inventory using the **weighted-average cost method:**

$$\text{Weighted-average unit cost} = \frac{\$5,100}{300 \text{ units}} = \$17 \text{ per unit}$$

| Cost of goods sold | = 280 sold | × $17 = | $4,760 |
|---|---|---|---|
| Ending inventory | = 20 not sold | × 17 = | 340 |
| | 300 | | **$5,100** |

■ LO6–4
Explain the financial
statement effects and tax
effects of inventory cost
methods.

# Effects of Inventory Cost Methods

Companies not using the specific identification method are free to choose FIFO, LIFO, or weighted-average cost to report inventory and cost of goods sold. However, because inventory costs generally change over time, the reported amounts for ending inventory and cost of goods sold will not be the same across inventory reporting methods. These differences could mislead investors and creditors if they are not aware of differences in inventory assumptions.

Illustration 6–11 compares the FIFO, LIFO, and weighted-average cost methods for Mario's Game Shop. (Recall from earlier discussion in this chapter that *gross profit* is a key measure of profitability, calculated as the difference between revenues and cost of goods sold.)

**ILLUSTRATION 6–11**

Comparison of
Inventory Cost
Methods, when Costs
Are Rising

|  | FIFO | LIFO | Weighted-Average |
|---|---|---|---|
| Balance sheet: | | | |
| Ending inventory | $ 2,200 | $ 1,600 | $ 2,000 |
| Income statement: | | | |
| Sales revenue (800 × $15) | $12,000 | $12,000 | $12,000 |
| Cost of goods sold | 7,800 | 8,400 | 8,000 |
| Gross profit | $ 4,200 | $ 3,600 | $ 4,000 |

**When inventory costs are *rising* (as in our example), FIFO results in**

1. Higher reported amount for inventory in the balance sheet.
2. Higher reported gross profit in the income statement.

The reason is that FIFO assumes the lower costs of the earlier purchases become cost of goods sold first. This leaves the higher costs of the later purchases in ending inventory. **If inventory costs had been *falling*,** then it's LIFO that would have produced higher reported inventory and gross profit. The weighted-average cost method typically produces amounts that fall between the FIFO and LIFO amounts for both cost of goods sold and ending inventory.

FIFO has a balance-sheet focus.

Accountants often call FIFO the *balance-sheet approach:* The amount it reports for ending inventory (which appears in the *balance sheet*) better approximates the current cost of inventory. The ending inventory amount reported under LIFO, in contrast, generally includes "old" inventory costs that do not realistically represent the cost of today's inventory.

LIFO has an income-statement focus.

Accountants often call LIFO the *income-statement approach:* The amount it reports for cost of goods sold (which appears in the *income statement*) more realistically matches the current costs of inventory needed to produce current revenues. Recall that LIFO assumes the last purchases are sold first, reporting the most recent inventory cost in cost of goods sold. However, also note that the most recent cost is not the same as the actual cost. FIFO better approximates actual cost of goods sold for most companies, since most companies' actual physical flow follows FIFO.

# Decision Maker's Perspective

## FIFO or LIFO?

Management must weigh the benefits of FIFO and LIFO when deciding which inventory cost flow assumption will produce a better outcome for the company. Here we review the logic behind that decision.

### Why Choose FIFO?

**Most companies' actual physical flow follows FIFO.** Think about a supermarket, sporting goods store, clothing shop, electronics store, or just about any company with whom you're familiar. These companies generally sell their oldest inventory first (first-in, first-out). If a company wants to choose an inventory method that most closely approximates its *actual physical flow* of inventory, then for most companies, FIFO makes the most sense.

Another reason managers may want to use FIFO relates to its effect on the financial statements. **During periods of rising costs, which is the case for most companies (including our example for Mario's Game Shop), FIFO results in a (1)** *higher* **ending inventory, (2)** *lower* **cost of goods sold, and (3)** *higher* **reported profit than does LIFO.** Managers may want to report higher assets and profitability to increase their bonus compensation, decrease unemployment risk, satisfy shareholders, meet lending agreements, or increase stock price.

## Why Choose LIFO?

If FIFO results in higher total assets and higher net income and produces amounts that most closely follow the actual flow of inventory, why would any company choose LIFO? **The primary benefit of choosing LIFO is tax savings.** LIFO results in the lowest amount of reported profits (when inventory costs are rising). While that might not look so good in the income statement, it's a welcome outcome in the tax return. When taxable income is lower, the company owes less in taxes to the Internal Revenue Service (IRS).

Can a company have its cake and eat it too by using FIFO for financial reporting and LIFO for the tax return? No. The IRS established the LIFO conformity rule, which requires a company that uses LIFO for tax reporting to also use LIFO for financial reporting, although companies must provide justification for doing so. For example, Illustration 6–12 provides an excerpt of **Bassett Furniture**'s footnote explaining that they use LIFO because it "provides better matching of revenue and expenses."

**BASSETT FURNITURE**
**Notes to the Financial Statements (excerpt)**

Cost is determined for domestic manufactured furniture inventories using the last-in, first-out ("LIFO") method because we believe this methodology provides better matching of revenue and expenses.

## REPORTING THE LIFO DIFFERENCE

As Mario's Game Shop demonstrates, the choice between FIFO and LIFO results in different amounts for ending inventory in the balance sheet and cost of goods sold in the income statement. This complicates the way we compare financial statements: One company may be using FIFO, while a competing company may be using LIFO. **To better compare each company's inventory and profitability, investors must adjust for the fact that managers' choice of inventory method has an effect on reported amounts.**

Companies that report using LIFO must also report the difference between the LIFO amount and what that amount would have been if they had used FIFO. This difference is often referred to as the *LIFO reserve.*

For example, Illustration 6–13 shows the current asset section of **Kroger Company**'s balance sheet. Kroger is a retail company that serves millions of people each day in its supermarkets. Supermarkets don't actually sell the last units first, but they are allowed to report inventory under that assumption. Kroger maintains its internal inventory records throughout the year using FIFO. This results in ending inventory of $8,464 million. Kroger then uses a year-end adjusting entry to convert that FIFO amount to LIFO for financial reporting purposes. Its LIFO inventory is lower by $1,380 million.

**ILLUSTRATION 6–13**

Effect of the LIFO Difference on Reported Inventory of Kroger Company

### KROGER COMPANY
### Balance Sheet (partial)

| ($ in millions) | 2020 |
| --- | --- |
| Current assets | |
| Cash and temporary cash investments | $   399 |
| Store deposits in-transit | 1,179 |
| Receivables | 1,706 |
| **FIFO inventory** | **8,464** |
| **LIFO reserve** | **(1,380)** |
| Prepaid and other current assets | 522 |
| Total current assets | 10,890 |

## Manager Analysis

| Question | Accounting information | Analysis |
| --- | --- | --- |
| When comparing inventory amounts between two companies, does the choice of inventory method matter? | The LIFO difference reported in the balance sheet or notes to the financial statements | When inventory costs are rising, FIFO results in a *higher* reported inventory. The LIFO difference can be used to compare inventory of two companies if one uses FIFO and the other uses LIFO. |

## CONSISTENCY IN REPORTING

Companies can choose which inventory method they use, even if the method does not match the actual physical flow of goods. However, once the company chooses a method, it is not allowed to frequently change to another one.[1] For example, a retail store cannot use FIFO in the current year because inventory costs are rising and then switch to LIFO in the following year because inventory costs are now falling.

However, a company need not use the same method for all its inventory. **International Paper**, for instance, uses LIFO for its raw materials and finished pulp and paper products, and both FIFO and weighted-average cost for other inventories. Another example is **McKesson**, which uses LIFO for its domestic inventory and FIFO for its foreign inventory, consistent with locally prevailing accounting standards and tax laws. Because of the importance of inventories and the possible differential effects of different methods on the financial statements, a company informs its stockholders of the inventory method(s) being used in a note to the financial statements. Illustration 6–14 shows that the proportion of companies with a LIFO reserve is trending downward, suggesting that LIFO usage is declining over time.

 **KEY POINT**

Generally, FIFO more closely resembles the actual physical flow of inventory. When inventory costs are rising, FIFO results in higher reported inventory in the balance sheet and higher reported income in the income statement. Conversely, LIFO results in a lower reported inventory and net income, reducing the company's income tax obligation.

---

[1]When a company changes from LIFO for tax purposes, it cannot change back to LIFO until it has filed five tax returns using the non-LIFO method.

**ILLUSTRATION 6–14**

**Proportion of Retail and Manufacturing Companies with LIFO Reserve**

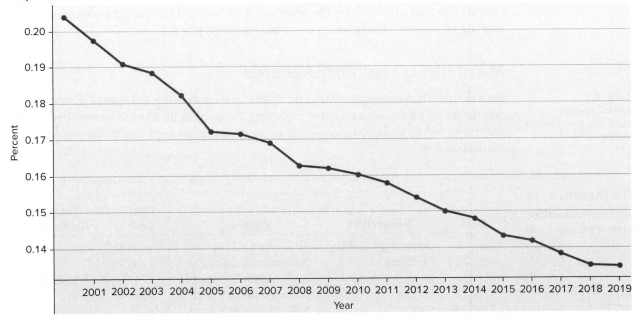

Source: Standard & Poor's

# MAINTAINING INVENTORY RECORDS

**PART B**

So far, we've talked about how companies report inventory amounts (ending inventory and cost of goods sold) using various cost flow assumptions (FIFO, LIFO, and weighted average). Now let's examine how companies track costs in the accounting system. It's the ability of the accounting system to accurately track inventory transactions that allows managers to make timely decisions related to purchases of inventory.

A perpetual inventory system is used by nearly all companies to record inventory transactions. This system involves recording inventory purchases and sales on a perpetual (continual) basis. Managers know that to make good decisions, they need to keep a pulse on which inventory is selling and which is not. This information will affect nearly every other facet of the business, including purchasing, pricing, product development, marketing, and employee management. Thus, because decisions for these related business activities need to be made on a real-time basis, maintaining inventory records on a continual basis is necessary.

The demand for real-time inventory information has led to significant technological advances in recent years, which allow managers to instantly track inventory purchases and sales. Large companies can employ enterprise resource planning (ERP) systems that manage inventory, such as SAP or NetSuite. In addition, there are even a number of popular apps that make a perpetual inventory system possible for even very small companies. Thus, maintaining a perpetual inventory system has never been simpler, more cost-effective or more accessible.

In contrast, a periodic inventory system does not continually record inventory amounts. Instead, it calculates the balance of inventory once per period, at the end, based on a physical count of inventory on hand. The Appendix to the chapter shows how to record transactions using the periodic inventory system.

As we'll see in the next example, for companies that report using FIFO, recording transactions on a continual basis under a perpetual inventory system will produce the same amounts for cost of goods sold and ending inventory as under a periodic system (computed previously in Illustration 6–7). However, this would not be true for LIFO. In practice, companies that report using LIFO typically maintain their own inventory records on a perpetual FIFO basis (as demonstrated in the example below) and then prepare a year-end adjusting entry to convert to LIFO periodic amounts (as computed previously in Illustration 6–8). We'll show this simple LIFO adjustment below. **The inventory recording and reporting procedures we demonstrate below most closely reflect those used in actual practice.**

## Maintaining Inventory Records

■ **LO6–5**

Maintain inventory records using a perpetual inventory system.

Let's examine how companies maintain inventory records using a perpetual inventory system. To do so, let's look again at the inventory transactions for Mario's Game Shop, which are shown below in Illustration 6–15 and are the same transactions shown previously in Illustration 6–6.

**ILLUSTRATION 6–15**

Inventory Transactions for Mario's Game Shop

| Date | Transaction | Details | Total Cost | Total Revenue |
|---|---|---|---|---|
| Jan. 1 | Beginning inventory | 100 units for $7 each | $ 700 | |
| Apr. 25 | Purchase | 300 units for $9 each | 2,700 | |
| Jul. 17 | Sale | 300 units for $15 each | | $ 4,500 |
| Oct. 19 | Purchase | 600 units for $11 each | 6,600 | |
| Dec. 15 | Sale | 500 units for $15 each | | 7,500 |
| | Totals | | $10,000 | $12,000 |

### INVENTORY PURCHASES AND SALES

**Purchase.**    When a company purchases inventory, it gains an asset, which is paid for with either cash or with credit via Accounts Payable. Thus, when Mario's purchases on account 300 units of inventory at $9 each for a total of $2,700, it increases the left-hand side of the balance sheet via an increase to Inventory (an asset account) and increases the right-hand side of the balance sheet via an increase to Accounts Payable (a liability account). Notice that the income statement is unaffected by inventory purchase transactions. The financial statement effects of the inventory purchase on April 25 are as follows:

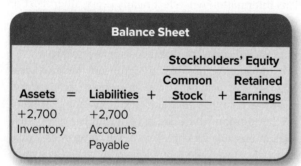

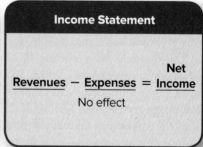

Inventory

2,700

Accounts Payable

2,700

**DEBITS & CREDITS**

Mario's would record the purchase of inventory on account on April 25 as follows:

| | Debit | Credit |
|---|---|---|
| Inventory................................................................................. | 2,700 | |
| Accounts Payable................................................................. | | 2,700 |

**Sale.**   Let's examine how the financial statements are affected when a company makes a sale of inventory—you'll see that this seemingly simple transaction actually affects a number of different accounts. We'll record these effects in two parts.

The first part of the transaction involves recording the sale to the customer. On July 17, Mario sold 300 units of inventory on account for $15 each. Thus, the company has generated $4,500 in sales revenue, which will directly increase the top line of the income statement. We'll also assume the inventory units were sold on account—this generates an Account Receivable (an asset) of $4,500 in the balance sheet.

The second part of the transaction tracks the cost of the inventory sold, which will depend on the inventory accounting assumption chosen by Mario's (FIFO, LIFO, or weighted average). Let's assume that Mario's, like most retail companies, maintains its inventory records using FIFO, because that method most closely matches its actual business practice of selling oldest inventory first (we'll show you how to adjust to LIFO in a bit). Using FIFO, the cost of the 300 units sold on July 17 is assumed to be $2,500, consisting of 100 units of beginning units ($700) plus 200 units from the April 25 purchase ($1,800). Also, because these units of inventory have been sold to the customer, they need to be removed from Mario's inventory records for an amount equal to their cost of $2,500.

In summary, the financial statement effects of this sale of inventory are as follows:

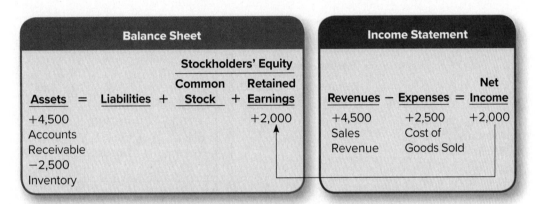

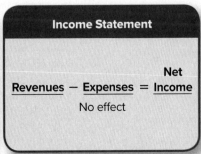

### DEBITS & CREDITS

Mario's would record the sale of inventory on account on July 17 as follows:

|  | Debit | Credit |
|---|---|---|
| Accounts Receivable............................................................................ | 4,500 | |
|    Sales Revenue.............................................................................. | | 4,500 |

Mario's also would record the cost of the inventory sold:

|  | Debit | Credit |
|---|---|---|
| Cost of Goods Sold............................................................................ | 2,500 | |
|    Inventory........................................................................................ | | 2,500 |

**Additional Purchase.**   On October 19, Mario purchased 600 additional units of inventory for $6,600 on account. That transaction affects only the balance sheet:

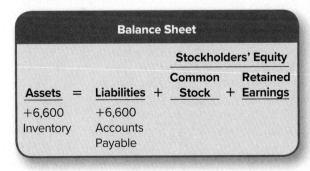

Inventory

| 6,600 | |

Accounts Payable

| | 6,600 |

---

**DEBITS & CREDITS**

Mario's would record the purchase of additional inventory on October 19 as follows:

| | Debit | Credit |
|---|---|---|
| **Inventory**........................................................................ | **6,600** | |
|     **Accounts Payable**........................................................ | | **6,600** |

---

**Additional Sale.**    On December 15, Mario sold another 500 units for $15 each on account. Again, this sales transaction will affect both the income statement (via Sales Revenue and Cost of Goods Sold) and the balance sheet (via Accounts Receivable and Inventory). Computing the value of the revenue is simple: price times quantity. Thus, Sales Revenue and Accounts Receivable both increase by $7,500 (500 units × $15).

What did the inventory sold on December 15 cost Mario? *The answer depends on the accounting assumption.* Using the FIFO assumption, the cost of the 500 units sold is $5,300. This includes $900 of remaining units from the April 25 purchase (100 units × $9) plus $4,400 from the October 19 purchase (400 units × $11). Thus, the financial statement effects of this sale on December 15 are:

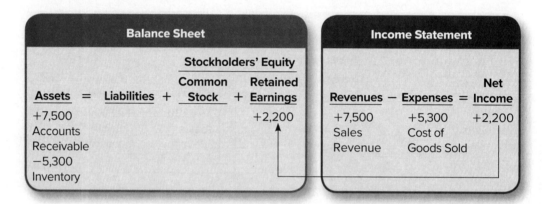

Accounts Receivable

| 7,500 | |

Sales Revenue

| | 7,500 |

Cost of Goods Sold

| 5,300 | |

Inventory

| | 5,300 |

---

**DEBITS & CREDITS**

Mario's would record the sale of inventory on account on December 15 as follows:

| | Debit | Credit |
|---|---|---|
| **Accounts Receivable**.................................................... | **7,500** | |
|     **Sales Revenue**.......................................................... | | **7,500** |

Mario's also would record the cost of the inventory sold:

| | Debit | Credit |
|---|---|---|
| **Cost of Goods Sold**...................................................... | **5,300** | |
|     **Inventory**.................................................................. | | **5,300** |

---

Thus, Mario's ending Inventory balance is $2,200, as shown in Illustration 6–16. Refer back to Illustration 6–7 to verify the ending balance of inventory using FIFO.

---

**ILLUSTRATION 6–16**

**Inventory Account for Mario's Game Shop**

| Jan. 1 | Beginning | $ 700 |
|---|---|---|
| Apr. 25 | Purchase | 2,700 |
| Jul. 17 | Sale | (2,500) |
| Oct. 19 | Purchase | 6,600 |
| Dec. 15 | Sale | (5,300) |
| Dec. 31 | Ending (FIFO) | $2,200 |

You can also verify the balance of cost of goods sold. In the two transactions above, the Cost of Goods Sold account was recorded for $2,500 and $5,300. That's an ending balance of $7,800, and that's the same amount calculated in Illustration 6–7 as the cost of the first 800 units sold.

### KEY POINT

The perpetual inventory system maintains a continual record of inventory purchased and sold. When companies *purchase* inventory using a perpetual inventory system, they increase Inventory in the balance sheet. When companies *sell* inventory, they (1) increase an asset account (Cash or Accounts Receivable) in the balance sheet, (2) increase Sales Revenue in the income statement, (3) increase Cost of Goods Sold in the income statement, and (4) decrease Inventory in the balance sheet.

**Simple Year-End Adjustment from FIFO to LIFO.**   In the example above, we recorded inventory transactions using the FIFO assumption. Thus, Mario assumed that the 800 units sold during the year came from the first 800 units purchased. **In practice, most companies maintain their own inventory records throughout the year using the FIFO assumption, because that's how they typically sell their actual inventory.** However, as discussed earlier in the chapter, for preparing financial statements, many companies choose to report their inventory using the LIFO assumption. So, at the end of the year, how does a company adjust its own FIFO inventory records to a LIFO basis for preparing financial statements? The company must make a year-end LIFO adjustment.

To see how easy the year-end LIFO adjustment can be, let's refer back to our example involving Mario's Game Shop. As summarized in Illustration 6–7, Mario's ending balance of Inventory using FIFO is $2,200. Under LIFO, it would be only $1,600 (see Illustration 6–8). As a result, if Mario's Game Shop wants to adjust its FIFO inventory records to LIFO for preparing financial statements, it needs to adjust the Inventory account downward by $600 (decreasing the balance from $2,200 to $1,600).

The LIFO adjustment increases Cost of Goods Sold in the Income Statement and decreases Inventory in the Balance Sheet, as follows:

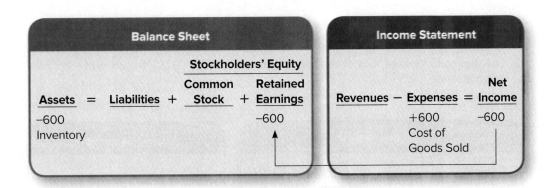

| Balance Sheet | | | | | Income Statement | | | |
|---|---|---|---|---|---|---|---|---|
| | | | **Stockholders' Equity** | | | | | |
| | | | **Common** | **Retained** | | | | **Net** |
| **Assets** | **=** | **Liabilities +** | **Stock** | **+ Earnings** | **Revenues** | **− Expenses** | **=** | **Income** |
| −600 | | | | −600 | | +600 | | −600 |
| Inventory | | | | | | Cost of | | |
| | | | | | | Goods Sold | | |

**DEBITS & CREDITS**

To make the LIFO adjustment, Mario's would record the following adjusting entry on December 31:

|  | Debit | Credit |
|---|---|---|
| Cost of Goods Sold.............................................................. | **600** | |
|    Inventory........................................................................ | | **600** |

Cost of Goods Sold

| 600 | |
|---|---|

Inventory

| | 600 |
|---|---|

In rare situations where the LIFO Inventory balance is *greater* than the FIFO Inventory balance (such as when inventory costs are declining), the LIFO adjustment would be reversed.

Illustration 6–17 shows the Inventory account for Mario's Game Shop after the year-end LIFO adjustment. Notice that the balance of Inventory has decreased to reflect the amount reported under the LIFO method.

**ILLUSTRATION 6–17**

Inventory Account for
Mario's Game Shop,
after LIFO Adjustment

| | | |
|---|---|---:|
| Jan. 1 | Beginning | $ 700 |
| Apr. 25 | Purchase | 2,700 |
| Jul. 17 | Sale | (2,500) |
| Oct. 19 | Purchase | 6,600 |
| Dec. 15 | Sale | (5,300) |
| Dec. 31 | Ending (FIFO) | 2,200 |
| Dec. 31 | **LIFO Adjustment** | (600) |
| Dec. 31 | Ending (LIFO) | $1,600 |

**KEY POINT**

Most companies maintain their own inventory records on a FIFO basis, and then some prepare financial statements on a LIFO basis. To adjust their FIFO inventory records to LIFO for financial reporting, companies use a LIFO adjustment at the end of the year.

**Let's Review**

Vintage Sound sells vintage 80s electronics, such as Sony Walkmans. It accounts for its inventory using FIFO with a perpetual system. At the beginning of March, the company has inventory of $24,000 (= $240 × 100 units).

*Required:*

Determine the financial statement effects for the following inventory transactions for Vintage Sound.
1. On March 7, Vintage Sound purchases on account 200 Walkmans for $250 each.
2. On March 16, Vintage Sound makes full payment for inventory purchased on March 7.
3. On March 20, Vintage Sound sells 260 Walkmans for $78,000 ($300 each). All sales are for cash.

*Solution:*

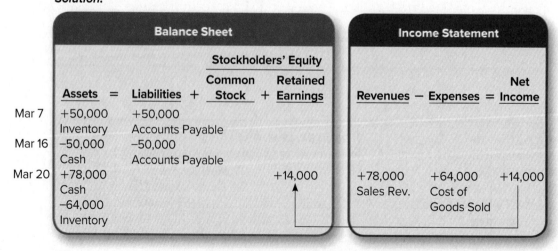

**DEBITS & CREDITS**

| March 7 | Debit | Credit |
|---|---|---|
| Inventory......................................................................................... | 50,000 | |
|    Accounts Payable.......................................................................... | | 50,000 |
|    *(Purchase units on account)* | | |
|    *($50,000 = $250 × 200 units)* | | |
| | | |
| **March 16** | | |
| Accounts Payable............................................................................. | 50,000 | |
|    Cash................................................................................................ | | 50,000 |
|    *(Make full payment for March 7 purchase)* | | |
| | | |
| **March 20** | | |
| Cash.................................................................................................... | 78,000 | |
|    Sales Revenue................................................................................ | | 78,000 |
|    *(Sell 260 units for cash)* | | |
|    *($78,000 = $300 × 260 units)* | | |
| Cost of Goods Sold............................................................................ | 64,000 | |
|    Inventory......................................................................................... | | 64,000 |
|    *(Record cost of units sold using FIFO)* | | |
|    *(Cost of 100 units in beginning inventory = $24,000)* | | |
|    *(Cost of 160 units purchased on March 7 = $250 × 160 = $40,000)* | | |

# INVENTORY ANALYSIS
## Best Buy vs. Tiffany

■ LO6–6
Analyze management of inventory using the inventory turnover ratio and gross profit ratio.

**PART C**

As discussed in the previous section, inventory can subject the company to significant risks, which a manager will want to prepare for using techniques to effectively manage inventory.

There are several key metrics that are used to evaluate the management of inventory. Outside analysts as well as managers often use the *inventory turnover ratio* to evaluate a company's effectiveness in managing its investment in inventory. In addition, investors often rely on the *gross profit ratio* to determine the core profitability of a merchandising company's operations. We discuss these ratios next, using **Best Buy** and **Tiffany** to illustrate the power of these ratios for understanding inventory management. Later, we will look at these ratios for Best Buy relative to those for a more natural competitor, **Target**.

### INVENTORY TURNOVER RATIO

The inventory turnover ratio shows the *number of times* the firm sells its average inventory balance during a reporting period. It is calculated as cost of goods sold divided by average inventory.

$$\text{Inventory turnover ratio} = \frac{\text{Cost of goods sold}}{\text{Average inventory}}$$

The amount for cost of goods sold is obtained from the current period's income statement; average inventory equals the average of inventory reported in this period's and last period's balance sheets. Last period's ending inventory is this period's beginning inventory. The more frequently a business is able to sell or "turn over" its average inventory balance, the less the company needs to invest in inventory for a given level of sales. Other things equal, a higher ratio indicates greater effectiveness of a company in managing its investment in inventory.

**COMMON MISTAKE**

Many students use ending inventory rather than average inventory in calculating the inventory turnover ratio. Generally, when you calculate a ratio that includes an income statement item (an amount generated over a period) with a balance sheet item (an amount at a particular date), the balance sheet item needs to be converted to an amount *over the same period*. This is done by averaging the beginning and ending balances of the balance sheet item.

## AVERAGE DAYS IN INVENTORY

Another way to measure the same activity is to calculate the average days in inventory. This ratio indicates the approximate *number of days* the average inventory is held. It is calculated as 365 days divided by the inventory turnover ratio.

$$\text{Average days in inventory} = \frac{365}{\text{Inventory turnover ratio}}$$

We can analyze the inventory of Best Buy and Tiffany by calculating these ratios for both companies. Best Buy sells a large volume of commonly purchased products. In contrast, Tiffany is a specialty retailer of luxury jewelry, watches, and other accessories. Below are relevant amounts for each company.

| ($ in millions) | Cost of Goods Sold | Beginning Inventory | Ending Inventory |
|---|---|---|---|
| Best Buy | $32,918 | $5,209 | $5,409 |
| Tiffany | 1,631 | 2,254 | 2,428 |

To compute the inventory turnover ratio we need the *average* inventory, which is the beginning amount of inventory plus the ending amount, divided by 2.

| Best Buy | Average inventory = ($5,209 + $5,409) ÷ 2 = **$5,309** |
|---|---|
| Tiffany | Average inventory = ($2,254 + $2,428) ÷ 2 = **$2,341** |

We put average inventory in the denominator to compute the inventory turnover ratio, as shown in Illustration 6–18. We divide 365 by the inventory turnover ratio to compute the average days in inventory.

**ILLUSTRATION 6–18**

Inventory Turnover and Average Days in Inventory for Best Buy and Tiffany

| | Inventory Turnover Ratio | Average Days in Inventory |
|---|---|---|
| Best Buy | $32,918 ÷ **$5,309** = 6.2 times | $\frac{365}{6.2}$ = 59 days |
| Tiffany | $1,631 ÷ **$2,341** = 0.7 times | $\frac{365}{0.7}$ = 521 days |

The turnover ratio is much higher for Best Buy. On average, each dollar of inventory is sold in 59 days. In contrast, each dollar of inventory at Tiffany is sold every 521 days. If the two companies had the same business strategies, this would indicate that Best Buy is better at managing inventory. In this case, though, the difference in inventory turnover relates to the different types of products the two companies sell. Best Buy sells mostly common household electronics and accessories, while Tiffany has very expensive jewelry (like engagement rings) that takes time to sell to the right customer. As we see in the next section, Tiffany offsets its low inventory turnover with a higher gross profit margin.

**Manager Analysis**

| Question | Accounting information | Analysis |
|---|---|---|
| Is the company effectively managing its inventory? | Inventory turnover ratio and average days in inventory | A high inventory turnover ratio (or low average days in inventory) generally indicates that the company's inventory policies are effective. |

### GROSS PROFIT RATIO

Another important indicator of the company's successful management of inventory is the gross profit ratio (also called *gross profit percentage*). It measures the amount by which the sale of inventory exceeds its cost per dollar of sales. We calculate the gross profit ratio as gross profit divided by net sales. (Net sales equal total sales revenue less sales discounts, returns, and allowances.)

$$\text{Gross profit ratio} = \frac{\text{Gross profit}}{\text{Net sales}}$$

The higher the gross profit ratio, the higher is the "markup" a company is able to achieve on its inventories. Best Buy and Tiffany report the following information.

| ($ in millions) | Net Sales | − | Cost of Goods Sold | = | Gross Profit |
|---|---|---|---|---|---|
| Best Buy | $42,879 | | $32,918 | | **$9,961** |
| Tiffany | 4,442 | | 1,631 | | **2,811** |

Illustration 6–19 shows calculation of the gross profit ratio for Best Buy and Tiffany.

| | Gross Profit/Net Sales | = | Gross Profit Ratio |
|---|---|---|---|
| Best Buy | **$9,961/$42,879** | = | 23% |
| Tiffany | **$2,811/$4,442** | = | 63% |

**ILLUSTRATION 6–19**

Gross Profit Ratios for Best Buy and Tiffany

For Best Buy, the gross profit ratio is 23%, which means that for every $1 of net sales, the company spends $0.77 on inventory, resulting in a gross profit of $0.23. In contrast, the gross profit ratio for Tiffany is 63%. We saw earlier that Tiffany inventory turnover is much lower than that of Best Buy. But, we see now that Tiffany makes up for that lower turnover with a much higher gross profit margin. Overall, these ratios help us see the tradeoffs that companies like Best Buy and Tiffany strategically make between sales volume and margins.

## Best Buy vs. Target

The previous comparison of **Best Buy** to **Tiffany** helps us see how different inventory strategies can lead to very different inventory turnover and gross margin ratios. However, in real-world analysis, we often evaluate companies relative to their direct competitors to see how they are doing in their own product space. So, who are Best Buy's competitors? The answer to this question can be found in its recent annual report (see Illustration 6–20), in which Best Buy discusses the competition it currently faces.

ILLUSTRATION 6-20

Excerpt from Best Buy's Recent Annual Report

> **Best Buy**
> **Notes to the Financial Statements (excerpt)**
>
> Our competitors are primarily multi-channel retailers, e-commerce businesses, technology service providers, traditional store-based retailers, vendors and mobile network carriers who offer their products and services directly to customers. We believe our ability to help customers online, in stores and in their homes and to connect technology product and solutions with customer needs offers us key competitive advantages.

Thus, there are a number of Best Buy's competitors in consumer electronics, including **Amazon**, **Walmart**, **GameStop**, **NewEgg.com**, and **Costco**. We will compare Best Buy to **Target**, which sells many of the same goods, has a similar geographic footprint, and operates both brick-and-mortar and online sales fronts.

## INVENTORY TURNOVER RATIO

As noted, the inventory turnover ratio shows the number of times the firm sells through its inventory during a given period. As shown in Illustration 6–21, Best Buy has an inventory turnover ratio of 6.2, compared to 5.9 for Target. This indicates that these companies sell through their inventory about 6 times per year. The average days in inventory for each company is around 60 days. Thus, the two companies are comparable in inventory turnover.

ILLUSTRATION 6-21

Inventory Turnover Ratios for Best Buy and Target

|  | **Inventory Turnover Ratio** | **Average Days in Inventory** |
|---|---|---|
| Best Buy | $\$32{,}918 \div \mathbf{\$5{,}309} = 6.2$ times | $\frac{365}{6.2} = 59$ days |
| Target | $\$53{,}299 \div \mathbf{\$9{,}047} = 5.9$ times | $\frac{365}{5.9} = 62$ days |

Illustration 6–22 shows average days in inventory over the past two decades for Best Buy and Target. It shows that Best Buy dominated Target with faster movement through its inventory, but in more recent years, the two companies' average days in inventory converged to around 60 days. We can conclude that Best Buy has lost a step in recent years with regard to its inventory management; a good analyst or manager will use this information to dig deeper into why this is happening for Best Buy.

We can also compare Best Buy and Target to the rest of the retail industry. In Illustration 6–22, retail stores average about seven turns through inventory per year. Thus, both Best Buy and Target show days in inventory metrics that are slightly below the median for the retail industry. Illustration 6–23 shows that there are certain industries that, because of the types of inventory they sell, tend to turn over their inventory much faster (or slower). For example, we see that the oil and petroleum industry has an average days in inventory of around 18 days, indicating that these inventories are sold through rather quickly (nearly 20 times a year). On the other hand, pharmaceuticals have an average days in inventory of almost 120 days, indicating that these inventories sell through much more slowly (only three times a year).

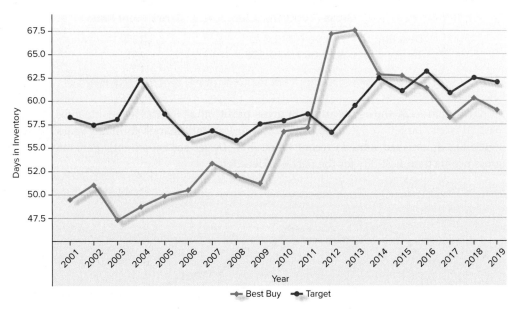

**ILLUSTRATION 6–22**

**Average Days in Inventory for Best Buy vs. Target**

*Source:* Standard & Poor's

**ILLUSTRATION 6–23**

**Average Days in Inventory by Industry**

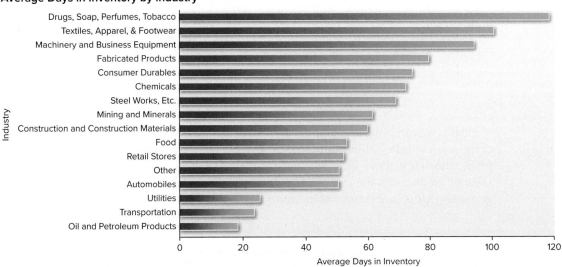

Source: Standard & Poor's

## GROSS PROFIT RATIO

Finally, we compare Best Buy to Target in terms of gross profit ratio, which tells us how much profit the company generates per dollar of inventory sold. Here, Target seems to dominate with a gross profit ratio of 29% compared to 23% for Best Buy. This suggests that Target generates nearly 6 cents more for every dollar of inventory sold than does Best Buy.

| ($ in millions) | Net Sales | − | Cost of Goods Sold | = | Gross Profit |
|---|---|---|---|---|---|
| Best Buy | $42,879 | | $32,918 | | **$9,961** |
| Target | 75,356 | | 53,299 | | **22,057** |

| | Gross Profit/Net Sales | = | Gross Profit Ratio |
|---|---|---|---|
| Best Buy | **$9,961**/$42,879 | = | 23% |
| Target | **$22,057**/$75,356 | = | 29% |

Illustration 6–24 shows the trend in gross profit ratios for the two companies over the past 20 years. Target averaged more than 30% gross profit margin for many years, but that figure has diminished some in recent years. Still, Target has consistently generated higher gross profits than Best Buy for the past two decades.

**ILLUSTRATION 6–24**

**Gross Profit Ratio for Best Buy vs. Target**

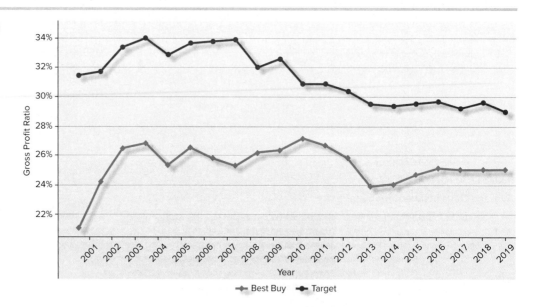

Finally, we can compare the gross profit ratio for Best Buy and Target to that for the rest of the retail industry in Illustration 6–25. On average, retail stores report an average gross profit ratio of just above 30%. This suggests that the profits Target generates from inventory sales are in line with the rest of the industry, while Best Buy has fallen slightly behind in generating gross profits from its inventory.

**ILLUSTRATION 6–25**

**Gross Profit Ratio by Industry**

*Source:* Standard & Poor's

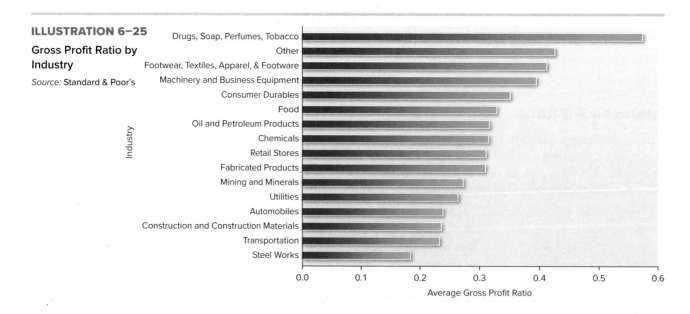

Overall, these analyses examine the efficiency with which Best Buy and Target manage their inventory. While both companies are generating profits, the previous analyses show Best Buy is losing its edge at selling through its inventory, and relatedly, is generating less profits on inventory sales than its competition.

 **KEY POINT**

The inventory turnover ratio indicates the number of times the firm sells, or turns over, its average inventory balance during a reporting period. The gross profit ratio measures the amount by which the sale of inventory exceeds its cost per dollar of sales.

**Manager Analysis**

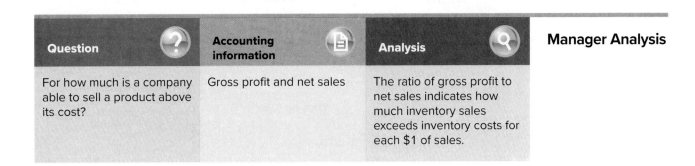

| Question | Accounting information | Analysis |
|---|---|---|
| For how much is a company able to sell a product above its cost? | Gross profit and net sales | The ratio of gross profit to net sales indicates how much inventory sales exceeds inventory costs for each $1 of sales. |

# OTHER INVENTORY ISSUES

**APPENDIX**

In this Appendix, we present several additional issues that arise with inventory management. These include:

- Additional inventory transactions, such as freight charges, purchase discounts, and purchase returns.
- Maintaining inventory records using the periodic inventory system.
- Lower of cost and net realizable value.
- Inventory errors.

## Additional Inventory Transactions

To this point, we've recorded inventory purchases and inventory sales transactions. Let's add three more inventory-related transactions to our Mario's Game Shop example, as follows:

■ **LO6–7**
Examine additional inventory transactions.

1. On April 25, pays freight charges of $300 for inventory purchased on April 25.
2. On April 30, pays for the units purchased on April 25, less a 2% purchase discount.
3. On October 22, returns 50 defective units from the October 19 purchase.

Next, we discuss how to record each of these three transactions.

### FREIGHT CHARGES

A significant cost associated with inventory for most merchandising companies includes freight (also called shipping or delivery) charges. This includes the cost of shipments of inventory from suppliers, as well as the cost of shipments to customers. When goods are shipped, they are shipped with terms *FOB shipping point* or *FOB destination.* FOB stands for "free on board" and indicates *when* title (ownership) passes from the seller to the buyer.

1. **FOB** *shipping point* means title passes when the seller *ships* the inventory.
2. **FOB** *destination* means title passes when the inventory reaches the buyer's *destination.*

For example, suppose that when Mario purchased 300 units for $2,700 ($9 per unit) on April 25, the terms of the purchase were FOB shipping point. The inventory was shipped from the supplier's warehouse on April 25 but did not arrive at Mario's location until April 29. Mario would record the purchase when title passes—April 25—even though Mario does not have actual physical possession of the inventory until April 29. If, instead, the terms of the purchase were FOB destination, Mario would have waited until the inventory was received on April 29 to record the purchase. This idea is demonstrated in Illustration 6–26.

**ILLUSTRATION 6–26**

**Shipping Terms**

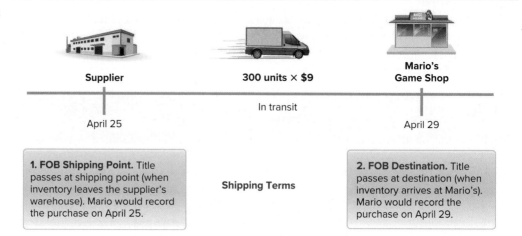

Freight charges on incoming shipments from suppliers are commonly referred to as **freight-in. We add the cost of freight-in to the balance of Inventory.** In this case, the cost of freight is considered a cost of the purchased inventory. When Mario pays $300 for freight charges associated with the purchase of inventory on April 25, those charges would be added to the balance of inventory, as follows:

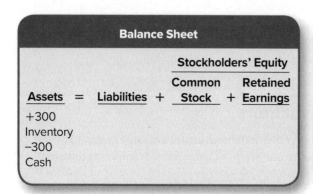

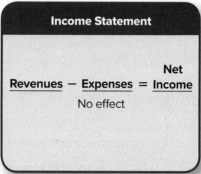

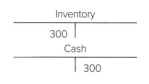

**DEBITS & CREDITS**

Mario's would record the freight-in charges on April 25 as follows:

|  | Debit | Credit |
|---|---|---|
| Inventory | 300 | |
| Cash | | 300 |

**Later, when that inventory is sold, those freight charges become part of the cost of goods sold.** In Mario's case, all of the units purchased on April 25 are sold by the end of the year, so the $300 freight charge would be reported as part of cost of goods sold in the income statement at the end of the year.

The cost of freight on shipments *to* customers is called **freight-out.** Shipping charges for outgoing inventory are reported in the income statement either as part of cost of goods sold or as an operating expense, usually among selling expenses. If a company adopts a policy of not including shipping charges in cost of goods sold, both the amounts incurred during the period as well as the income statement classification of the expense must be disclosed.[2]

To see an example of how **Amazon.com** accounts for freight charges, look at Illustration 6–27.

---

**AMAZON.COM**
**Notes to the Financial Statements (excerpt)**

Cost of sales primarily consists of the purchase price of consumer products, inbound and outbound shipping costs. . .

Shipping costs . . . were $27.7 billion and $37.9 billion in 2018 and 2019.

**ILLUSTRATION 6–27**

Accounting for Shipping Costs by Amazon.com

---

## PURCHASE DISCOUNTS

As discussed in Chapter 5, sellers often encourage prompt payment by offering *discounts* to buyers. From the seller's point of view, these are sales discounts; from the buyer's point of view, they are *purchase discounts*. **Purchase discounts allow buyers to trim a portion of the cost of the purchase in exchange for payment within a certain period of time.** Buyers are not required to take purchase discounts, but many find it advantageous to do so.

Let's assume that Mario's supplier, Luigi Software, Inc., offers terms 2/10, n/30 for the April 25 purchase on account. This means that Mario can receive a 2% discount if payment is made within 10 days, but the total invoice is due within 30 days.

Recall that on April 25, Mario purchased 300 units on account for $9 each (or $2,700 total). When Mario makes payment on April 30, the discount would be $54 (= $2,700 × 2%). Mario has to pay only $2,646 (= $2,700 − $54) to eliminate the $2,700 amount owed. To account for the purchase discount, we subtract the discount from the balance in the Inventory account.

| Balance Sheet | | | | | Income Statement | | |
|---|---|---|---|---|---|---|---|
| | | | **Stockholders' Equity** | | | | |
| | | | **Common** | **Retained** | | | **Net** |
| **Assets** | = | **Liabilities** | + **Stock** | + **Earnings** | **Revenues** | − **Expenses** | = **Income** |
| −2,646 | | −2,700 | | | | No effect | |
| Cash | | Accounts | | | | | |
| −54 | | Payable | | | | | |
| Inventory | | | | | | | |

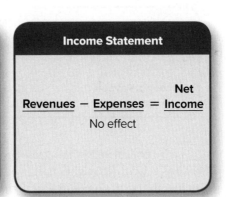

**DEBITS & CREDITS**

Mario's would record the purchase discount on April 30 as follows:

| | Debit | Credit |
|---|---|---|
| Accounts Payable ......................................................... | 2,700 | |
| Inventory ($2,700 × 2%)............................................. | | 54 |
| Cash .............................................................................. | | 2,646 |

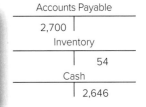

---

[2]FASB ASC 605–45–50–2: Revenue Recognition–Principal Agent Considerations–Disclosure–Shipping and Handling Fees and Costs [previously "Accounting for Shipping and Handling Fees and Costs," *EITF Issue No. 00–10* (Norwalk, CT: FASB, 2000), par. 6].

Just as freight charges *add* to the cost of inventory and therefore increase the cost of goods sold once those items are sold, purchase discounts *subtract* from the cost of inventory and therefore reduce cost of goods sold once those items are sold. When Mario sells the 300 units purchased on April 25, the cost of goods sold associated with those items will be the cost of the actual units ($2,700) plus freight charges ($300) less the purchase discount ($54), totaling $2,946.

## PURCHASE RETURNS

Occasionally, a company will find inventory items to be unacceptable for some reason—perhaps they are damaged or are different from what was ordered. In those cases, the company returns the items to the supplier and records the purchase return as a reduction in both Inventory and Accounts Payable. For example, when Mario decides on October 22 to return 50 defective units from the 600 units purchased on October 19 for $11 each, it would affect the financial statements as follows:

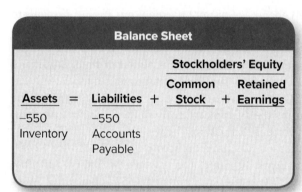

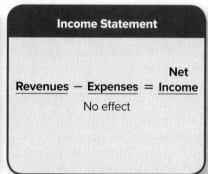

**DEBITS & CREDITS**

Mario's would record the return of inventory previously purchased on account on October 22 as follows:

|  | Debit | Credit |
|---|---|---|
| Accounts Payable .................................................................... | 550 | |
| Inventory.................................................................................. | | 550 |

Let's recalculate Mario's gross profit after accounting for the additional inventory transactions related to freight charges and the purchase discount. The calculations are demonstrated in Illustration 6–28. Recall that Mario sold 800 units during the year for $15 each (or $12,000 total). This is the amount reported as sales revenue. From sales revenue, we subtract the cost of the 800 units sold. To calculate this amount, we need to look back at transactions related to the purchase cost of those 800 units, including the cost of freight charges and the purchase discount associated with the purchase on April 25. Mario would report $8,046 as the cost of goods sold, resulting in a gross profit of $3,954.

**KEY POINT**

For most companies, freight charges are added to the cost of inventory, whereas purchase returns and purchase discounts are deducted from the cost of inventory. Some companies choose to report freight charges on outgoing shipments as part of selling expenses instead of cost of goods sold.

| | Units | Unit Price | Total |
|---|---|---|---|
| Sales revenue | 800 | $15 | $12,000 |
| | **Units** | **Unit Cost** | **Total** |
| Cost of goods sold: | | | |
| Beginning inventory | 100 | $ 7 | $    700 |
| Purchase on April 25 | 300 | 9 | 2,700 |
| Freight charges | | | 300 |
| Purchase discount | | | (54) |
| Purchase on October 19 | 400 | 11 | 4,400 |
| | 800 | | $ 8,046 |
| Gross profit | | | $ 3,954 |

**ILLUSTRATION 6–28**

Gross Profit for Mario's Game Shop after Additional Inventory Transactions

## Using a Periodic Inventory System

In this chapter, we discussed how to record inventory transactions using a *perpetual* inventory system. Here we discuss how to record inventory transactions using a *periodic* inventory system.

Recall that under a **perpetual inventory system** we maintain a continual—or *perpetual—*record of inventory purchased and sold. In contrast, using a periodic inventory system we do not continually modify inventory amounts. Instead, we *periodically* adjust for purchases and sales of inventory at the end of the reporting period, based on a physical count of inventory on hand.

To demonstrate the differences in these two systems, let's record inventory transactions under the periodic system using the same information (from Illustration 6–15) that we used to demonstrate the perpetual inventory system. We repeat those transactions in Illustration 6–29.

**■ LO6–8**
Maintain inventory records using a periodic inventory system.

**ILLUSTRATION 6–29**
Inventory Transactions for Mario's Game Shop

| Date | Transaction | Details | Total Cost | Total Revenue |
|---|---|---|---|---|
| Jan. 1 | Beginning inventory | 100 units for $7 each | $    700 | |
| Apr. 25 | Purchase | 300 units for $9 each | 2,700 | |
| Jul. 17 | Sale | 300 units for $15 each | | $ 4,500 |
| Oct. 19 | Purchase | 600 units for $11 each | 6,600 | |
| Dec. 15 | Sale | 500 units for $15 each | | 7,500 |
| | Totals | | $10,000 | $12,000 |

To make the distinction between the perpetual system and the periodic system easier, in the next section we look at side-by-side comparisons. The perpetual entries are repeated from those in the chapter and shown on the left side of each comparison.

### INVENTORY PURCHASES AND SALES

The first transaction on April 25 involves the purchase of $2,700 of inventory on account. Under the periodic system, instead of debiting the Inventory account, we debit a Purchases account. Remember, we're not continually adjusting the Inventory account under the periodic method. We use the Purchases account to temporarily track increases in inventory.

| **Perpetual System** | | **Periodic System** | |
|---|---|---|---|
| Inventory ................................. 2,700 | | Purchases............................ 2,700 | |
| Accounts Payable ............. | 2,700 | Accounts Payable ............ | 2,700 |

The transaction on July 17 involves the sale on account of 300 units of inventory for $4,500. We record that transaction as follows.

| Perpetual System | | | Periodic System | | |
|---|---|---|---|---|---|
| Accounts Receivable ............. | 4,500 | | Accounts Receivable............ | 4,500 | |
| Sales Revenue ................... | | 4,500 | Sales Revenue.................. | | 4,500 |
| Cost of Goods Sold................ | 2,500 | | | | |
| Inventory............................ | | 2,500 | No entry for cost of goods sold | | |

Notice that under the periodic system, we record the sales revenue, but we don't record the reduction in inventory or the increase in cost of goods sold at the time of the sale. Instead, we will record these at the end of the period.

The final two transactions are (1) the purchase of 600 additional units of inventory for $6,600 on account on October 19 and (2) the sale of 500 units for $7,500 on account on December 15. We record these transactions as follows.

| Perpetual System | | | Periodic System | | |
|---|---|---|---|---|---|
| Inventory ................................. | 6,600 | | Purchases................................ | 6,600 | |
| Accounts Payable .............. | | 6,600 | Accounts Payable .............. | | 6,600 |

| Perpetual System | | | Periodic System | | |
|---|---|---|---|---|---|
| Accounts Receivable ............. | 7,500 | | Accounts Receivable............ | 7,500 | |
| Sales Revenue ................... | | 7,500 | Sales Revenue................... | | 7,500 |
| Cost of Goods Sold................ | 5,300 | | | | |
| Inventory............................ | | 5,300 | No entry for cost of goods sold | | |

In addition to purchases and sales of inventory, we also looked at additional inventory transactions for Mario's Game Shop that related to freight charges, purchase discounts, and purchase returns:

1. On April 25, Mario pays freight charges of $300 for inventory purchased on April 25.
2. On April 30, Mario pays for the units purchased on April 25, less a 2% purchase discount.
3. On October 22, Mario returns 50 defective units from the October 19 purchase.

Next, let's also compare the perpetual system and periodic system for these transactions.

## FREIGHT CHARGES

Under the perpetual system discussed in the chapter, we saw that freight charges are included as an additional cost of inventory. Here we'll see that under the periodic system, we record these charges in a separate account called Freight-in. That account will later be closed in a period-end adjustment. For freight charges of $300 associated with the April 25 purchase, we record the following transaction.

| Perpetual System | | | Periodic System | | |
|---|---|---|---|---|---|
| Inventory ................................. | 300 | | Freight-in ................................. | 300 | |
| Cash ........................................ | | 300 | Cash........................................ | | 300 |

Pay freight-in charges

## PURCHASE DISCOUNTS AND RETURNS

Under the perpetual system, purchase discounts and purchase returns are recorded as a reduction in inventory cost. Under the periodic system, these transactions are recorded in separate accounts—Purchase Discounts and Purchase Returns. In the perpetual system, we credit purchase returns and purchase discounts to Inventory. The Purchase Returns and Purchase Discounts accounts used in the periodic system are referred to as *contra purchases accounts.*

For our examples in the chapter, Mario (1) makes payment on April 30 for inventory purchased on April 25 for $2,700, receiving a $54 discount and (2) returns 50 defective units on October 22 from the 600 units purchased on account on October 19 for $11 each. We record these transactions as follows.

| Perpetual System | | | Periodic System | | |
|---|---|---|---|---|---|
| Accounts Payable | 2,700 | | Accounts Payable | 2,700 | |
| Inventory | | 54 | Purchase Discounts | | 54 |
| Cash | | 2,646 | Cash | | 2,646 |

| Perpetual System | | | Periodic System | | |
|---|---|---|---|---|---|
| Accounts Payable | 550 | | Accounts Payable | 550 | |
| Inventory | | 550 | Purchase Returns | | 550 |

## PERIOD-END ADJUSTMENT

**A period-end adjustment is needed only under the periodic system.** The adjustment serves the following purposes:

1. Adjusts the balance of inventory to its proper ending balance.
2. Records the cost of goods sold for the period, to match inventory costs with the related sales revenue.
3. Closes (or zeros out) the temporary purchases accounts (Purchases, Freight-in, Purchase Discounts, and Purchase Returns).

Let's see what the period-end adjustment would look like for Mario's Game Shop using the transactions described in this appendix. In addition, recall that beginning inventory equals $700 (= 100 units × $7 unit cost) and ending inventory equals $1,650 (= 150 units × $11 unit cost).

| Perpetual System | Periodic System | | |
|---|---|---|---|
| No entry | Inventory (ending) | 1,650 | |
| | Cost of Goods Sold | 8,046 | |
| | Purchase Discounts | 54 | |
| | Purchase Returns | 550 | |
| | Purchases | | 9,300 |
| | Freight-in | | 300 |
| | Inventory (beginning) | | 700 |

Temporary accounts closed

Notice that (1) the balance of Inventory is updated for its ending amount of $1,650, while its beginning balance of $700 is eliminated; (2) Cost of Goods Sold is recorded for $8,046; and (3) temporary accounts related to purchases are closed to zero. Purchase Discounts and Purchase Returns are credit balance accounts so they need to be debited to close them. Likewise, Purchases and Freight-in are debit balance accounts so they need to be credited to close them.

If you look carefully, you may notice that the amount of Cost of Goods Sold above calculated under the periodic system is exactly the same as that calculated under the perpetual system. To see a detailed example of this, let's examine the first section of the multiple-step income statement, shown again in Illustration 6–30.

**ILLUSTRATION 6–30**

Calculation of Gross Profit in a Multiple-Step Income Statement

| MARIO'S GAME SHOP | | |
|---|---|---|
| **Multiple-Step Income Statement (partial)** | | |
| **For the year ended December 31, 2024** | | |
| Sales revenue | | $12,000 |
| **Cost of goods sold:** | | |
| Beginning inventory | $ 700 | |
| Add: Purchases | 9,300 | |
| Freight-in | 300 | |
| Less: Purchase discounts | (54) | |
| Purchase returns | (550) | |
| Cost of goods available for sale | 9,696 | |
| Less: Ending inventory | (1,650) | |
| Cost of goods sold | | 8,046 |
| **Gross profit** | | $ 3,954 |

The periodic system and perpetual system will always produce the same amounts for cost of goods sold (and therefore also ending inventory) when the FIFO inventory method is used.

However, when using LIFO or weighted-average, the amounts for cost of goods sold may differ between the periodic system and perpetual system. The reason for this difference is discussed further in more advanced accounting courses; it happens because determining which units of inventory are assumed sold occurs at the time of each sale throughout the period using a perpetual system but just once at the end of the period using a periodic system. For those interested, the book's online resources include additional discussion and problems related to FIFO, LIFO, and weighted-average using the perpetual inventory system.

As discussed in Part B of the chapter, some companies maintain their own records on a FIFO basis and then adjust for the LIFO difference in preparing financial statements. **The inventory recording and reporting procedures discussed in Part B of the chapter most closely reflect those used in actual practice.**

 **KEY POINT**

Using the periodic inventory system, we record purchases, freight-in, purchase returns, and purchase discounts to *temporary accounts* rather than directly to Inventory. These temporary accounts are closed in a period-end adjustment. In addition, at the time inventory is sold, we do not record a decrease in inventory sold; instead, we update the balance of Inventory in the period-end adjustment.

# Lower of Cost and Net Realizable Value

**■ LO6–9**

Apply the lower of cost and net realizable value rule for inventories.

Think about the store where you usually buy your clothes. You've probably noticed the store selling leftover inventory at deeply discounted prices after the end of each selling season to make room for the next season's clothing line. The value of the company's old clothing inventory has likely fallen below its original cost. Is it appropriate to still report the reduced-value inventory at its original cost?

When the value of inventory falls below its original cost, companies are required to report inventory at the lower net realizable value of that inventory. Net realizable value is the estimated selling price of the inventory in the ordinary course of business, less any costs of completion, disposal, and transportation. In other words, it's the *net* amount a company expects to *realize* in cash from the sale of the inventory.

Once a company has determined both the cost and the net realizable value of inventory, it reports ending inventory in the balance sheet at the *lower* of the two amounts. This method of recording inventory is lower of cost and net realizable value.[3]

Illustration 6–31 demonstrates the concept behind the lower of cost and net realizable value (NRV).

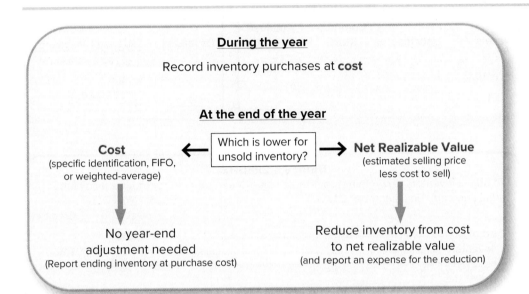

**ILLUSTRATION 6–31**

Lower of Cost and Net Realizable Value

To see how we apply the lower of cost and net realizable value to inventory amounts, assume Mario's Game Shop sells FunStation 2 and FunStation 3. Illustration 6–32 shows information related to ending inventory at the end of the year.

**ILLUSTRATION 6–32**

Calculating the Lower of Cost and Net Realizable Value

| Inventory Items | Quantity | Cost Per unit | Cost Total | NRV Per unit | NRV Total | Lower of Cost and NRV | Year-end Adjustment Needed* |
|---|---|---|---|---|---|---|---|
| FunStation 2 | 15 | $300 | $ 4,500 | $200 | $3,000 | = $ 3,000 | $1,500 |
| FunStation 3 | 20 | 400 | 8,000 | 450 | 9,000 | = 8,000 | 0 |
| | | | $12,500 | | | $11,000 | $1,500 |
| | | | Recorded Cost | | | Ending Inventory | |

\* The year-end adjustment is recorded when NRV is below cost. The adjustment equals the difference between cost and net realizable value.

Mario reports the FunStation 2 in ending inventory at net realizable value ($200 per unit) because that's lower than its original cost ($300 per unit). The 15 FunStation 2s were originally reported in inventory at their cost of $4,500 (= 15 × $300). To reduce the inventory from that original cost of $4,500 to its lower net realizable value of $3,000 (= 15 × $200),

[3]The method of reporting inventory using the lower of cost and net realizable value applies to companies that use FIFO and weighted-average, but not LIFO. For LIFO, companies report inventory using the lower of cost or market, where market is typically defined as replacement cost. Market value is never greater than net realizable value. The lower of cost or market method is covered in intermediate accounting books.

Mario needs to reduce inventory by $1,500, which has the following financial statement effects:

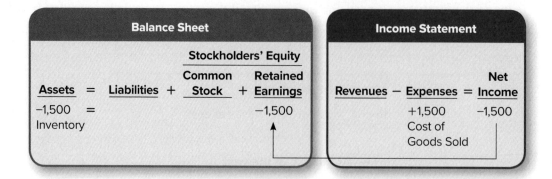

| Balance Sheet | | | | | | Income Statement | | |
|---|---|---|---|---|---|---|---|---|
| | | | **Stockholders' Equity** | | | | | |
| | | | Common | Retained | | | | Net |
| **Assets** | = | **Liabilities** + | **Stock** + | **Earnings** | | **Revenues** − | **Expenses** = | **Income** |
| −1,500 Inventory | = | | | −1,500 | | | +1,500 Cost of Goods Sold | −1,500 |

**DEBITS & CREDITS**

To adjust inventory down to net realizable value, Mario's would record the following adjusting entry on December 31:

| | Debit | Credit |
|---|---|---|
| Cost of Goods Sold ........................................................................ | 1,500 | |
|     Inventory ........................................................................ | | 1,500 |

Notice that the write-down of inventory has the effect not only of reducing total assets, but also of reducing net income and retained earnings.

The FunStation 3 inventory, on the other hand, remains on the books at its original cost of $8,000 (= $400 × 20), since cost is less than net realizable value. Mario does not need to make any adjustment for these inventory items.

After adjusting inventory to the lower of cost and net realizable value, the store calculates its ending balance of inventory as follows:

| | Inventory |
|---|---|
| Balance before adjustment | 12,500 |
| **Adjustment to NRV** | **(1,500)** |
| Ending balance | 11,000 |

 **KEY POINT**

We report inventory at the lower of cost and net realizable value; that is, at cost (specific identification, FIFO, or weighted-average cost) or net realizable value (selling price minus cost of completion, disposal, and transportation), whichever is lower. When net realizable value falls below cost, we adjust downward the balance of inventory from cost to net realizable value.

## Inventory Errors

■ **LO6–10**

Determine the financial statement effects of inventory errors.

Nobody's perfect, and even accountants make mistakes. When we discover accounting errors, we correct them. However, we don't always know when we've made an error. Errors can unknowingly occur in inventory amounts if there are mistakes in a physical count of inventory or in the pricing of inventory quantities.

### EFFECTS IN THE CURRENT YEAR

To understand the effects of an inventory error in the financial statements, let's think again about the formula for cost of goods sold, shown in Illustration 6–33.

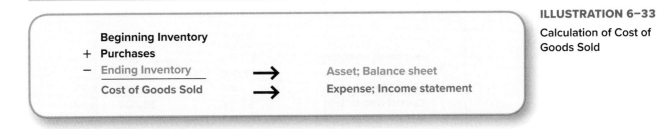

**ILLUSTRATION 6–33**

Calculation of Cost of Goods Sold

Notice that an error in calculating ending inventory (an asset in the balance sheet) causes an error in calculating cost of goods sold (an expense in the income statement). If cost of goods sold is misstated, gross profit will be misstated as well, but in the opposite direction. This is true because gross profit equals sales *minus* cost of goods sold. Furthermore, if gross profit is misstated, then net income and retained earnings will be misstated in the same direction; any mistake in net income is closed to retained earnings. The effect of the inventory error in the current year is summarized in Illustration 6–34.

| Inventory Error | Cost of Goods Sold | Gross Profit | Net Income | Retained Earning |
|---|---|---|---|---|
| Overstate ending inventory | Understate | Overstate | Overstate | Overstate |
| Understate ending inventory | Overstate | Understate | Understate | Understate |

**ILLUSTRATION 6–34**

Summary of Effects of Inventory Error in the Current Year

## EFFECTS IN THE FOLLOWING YEAR

To understand the effects of a current-year inventory error on financial statements in the following year, remember that the amount of ending inventory this year is the amount of beginning inventory next year. An error in ending inventory this year will create an error in beginning inventory next year. This is demonstrated in Illustration 6–35.

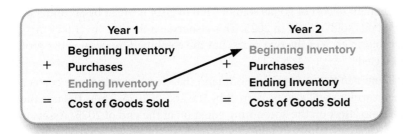

**ILLUSTRATION 6–35**

Relationship between Cost of Goods Sold in the Current Year and the Following Year

Notice that ending inventory is *subtracted* in calculating cost of goods sold in year 1 (the year of the inventory error). That same amount becomes beginning inventory in the following year and is *added* in calculating cost of goods sold. Because of this, **an error in calculating ending inventory in the current year will automatically affect cost of goods sold in the following year** *in the opposite direction.*

Consider a simple example to see how this works. Illustration 6–36 shows the correct inventory amounts for 2024 and 2025.

**ILLUSTRATION 6–36**

Correct Inventory
Amounts

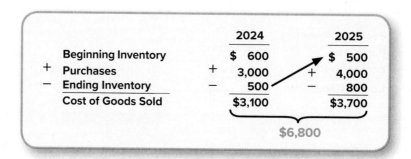

Now, assume the company mistakenly reports ending inventory in 2024 as **$400**, instead of $500. The effect of the mistake is shown in Illustration 6–37.

**ILLUSTRATION 6–37**

Incorrect Inventory
Amounts

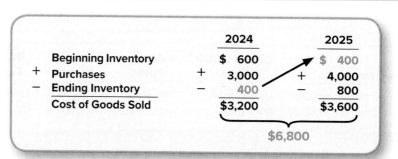

Notice three things:

1. The amount reported for inventory is correct by the end of the second year, $800. This is true *even if the company had never discovered its inventory mistake* in 2024.

2. The total amount reported for cost of goods sold over the two-year period from 2024 to 2025 is the same ($6,800) whether the error occurs or not. That's because the overstatement to cost of goods sold of $100 in 2024 is offset by an understatement to cost of goods sold of $100 in 2025. This also means that the inventory error affects gross profit in each of the two years, but the combined two-year gross profit amount is unaffected.

3. If the combined two-year gross profit (and therefore net income) is correct, then retained earnings will also be correct by the end of 2025. Thus, the inventory error in 2024 has no effect on the accounting equation at the end of 2025. Assets (inventory) and stockholders' equity (retained earnings) are correctly stated.

 **KEY POINT**

In the current year, inventory errors affect the amounts reported for inventory and retained earnings in the balance sheet and amounts reported for cost of goods sold and gross profit in the income statement. At the end of the following year, the error has no effect on ending inventory or retained earnings but reverses for cost of goods sold and gross profit.

**THE BOTTOM LINE**

**LO6–1** **Understand that inventory flows from manufacturing companies to merchandising companies and is reported as an asset on the balance sheet.**

Service companies report revenues when providing services to customers. Merchandising and manufacturing companies report revenues when selling inventory to customers.

**LO6–2** **Understand how cost of goods sold is reported in a multiple-step income statement.**

Inventory is a current asset reported in the balance sheet and represents the cost of inventory *not yet sold* at the end of the period. Cost of goods sold is an expense reported in the income statement and represents the cost of inventory *sold*.

A multiple-step income statement reports multiple levels of profitability. Gross profit equals net revenues (or net sales) minus cost of goods sold. Operating income equals gross profit minus operating expenses. Income before income taxes equals operating income plus nonoperating revenues and minus nonoperating expenses. Net income equals all revenues minus all expenses.

**LO6–3** **Determine the cost of goods sold and ending inventory using different inventory cost methods.**

Companies are allowed to report inventory costs by *assuming* which specific units of inventory are sold and not sold, even if this does not match the *actual* flow. The three major inventory cost flow assumptions are FIFO (first-in, first-out), LIFO (last-in, first-out), and weighted-average cost.

**LO6–4** **Explain the financial statement effects and tax effects of inventory cost methods.**

Generally, FIFO more closely resembles the actual physical flow of inventory. When inventory costs are rising, FIFO results in higher reported inventory in the balance sheet and higher reported income in the income statement. Conversely, LIFO results in a lower reported inventory and net income, reducing the company's income tax obligation.

**LO6–5** **Maintain inventory records using a perpetual inventory system.**

The perpetual inventory system maintains a continual record of inventory purchased and sold. When companies *purchase* inventory using a perpetual inventory system, they increase Inventory in the balance sheet. When companies *sell* inventory, they (1) increase an asset account (Cash or Accounts Receivable) in the balance sheet, (2) increase Sales Revenue in the income statement, (3) increase Cost of Goods Sold in the income statement, and (4) decrease Inventory in the balance sheet.

Most companies maintain their own inventory records on a FIFO basis, and then some prepare financial statements on a LIFO basis. To adjust their FIFO inventory records to LIFO for financial reporting, companies use a LIFO adjustment at the end of the year.

**LO6–6** **Analyze management of inventory using the inventory turnover ratio and gross profit ratio.**

The inventory turnover ratio indicates the number of times the firm sells, or turns over, its average inventory balance during a reporting period. The gross profit ratio measures the amount by which the sale of inventory exceeds its cost per dollar of sales.

**LO6–7** **Examine additional inventory transactions.**

For most companies, freight charges are added to the cost of inventory, whereas purchase returns and purchase discounts are deducted from the cost of inventory. Some companies choose to report freight charges on outgoing shipments as part of selling expenses instead of cost of goods sold.

**LO6–8** **Maintain inventory records using a periodic inventory system.**

Using the periodic inventory system, we record purchases, freight-in, purchase returns, and purchase discounts to temporary accounts rather than directly to Inventory. These temporary accounts are closed in a period-end adjustment. In addition, at the time inventory is sold, we do not record a decrease in inventory sold; instead, we update the balance of Inventory in the period-end adjustment.

**LO6–9** **Apply the lower of cost and net realizable value rule for inventories.**

We report inventory at the lower of cost and net realizable value; that is, at cost (specific identification, FIFO, or weighted-average cost) or net realizable value (selling price minus cost of completion, disposal, and transportation), whichever is lower. When net realizable value falls below cost, we adjust downward the balance of Inventory from cost to net realizable value.

**LO6–10** **Determine the financial statement effects of inventory errors.**

In the current year, inventory errors affect the amounts reported for inventory and retained earnings in the balance sheet and amounts reported for cost of goods sold and gross profit in the income statement. At the end of the following year, the error has no effect on ending inventory or retained earnings but reverses for cost of goods sold and gross profit.

## GLOSSARY

**Average days in inventory:** Approximate number of days the average inventory is held. It equals 365 days divided by the inventory turnover ratio. **p. 292**

**Cost of goods sold:** Cost of the inventory that was sold during the period. **p. 274**

**First-in, first-out method (FIFO):** Inventory costing method that assumes the first units purchased (the first in) are the first ones sold (the first out). **p. 277**

**Freight-in:** Cost to transport inventory to the company, which is included as part of inventory cost. **p. 298**

**Freight-out:** Cost of freight on shipments to customers, which is included in the income statement either as part of cost of goods sold or as a selling expense. **p. 298**

**Gross profit:** The difference between net sales and cost of goods sold. **p. 275**

**Gross profit ratio:** Measure of the amount by which the sale of inventory exceeds its cost per dollar of sales. It equals gross profit divided by net sales. **p. 293**

**Income before income taxes:** Operating income plus nonoperating revenues less nonoperating expenses. **p. 275**

**Inventory:** Items a company intends for sale to customers in the ordinary course of business. **p. 270**

**Inventory turnover ratio:** The number of times a firm sells its average inventory balance during a reporting period. It equals cost of goods sold divided by average inventory. **p. 291**

**Last-in, first-out method (LIFO):** Inventory costing method that assumes the last units purchased (the last in) are the first ones sold (the first out). **p. 278**

**LIFO adjustment:** An adjustment used to convert a company's own inventory records maintained throughout the year on a FIFO basis to LIFO basis for preparing financial statements at the end of the year. **p. 289**

**LIFO conformity rule:** IRS rule requiring a company that uses LIFO for tax reporting to also use LIFO for financial reporting. **p. 283**

**Lower of cost and net realizable value:** Method where companies report inventory in the balance sheet at the lower of cost and net realizable value, where net realizable value equals estimated selling price of the inventory in the ordinary course of business less any costs of completion, disposal, and transportation. **p. 305**

**Multiple-step income statement:** An income statement that reports *multiple* levels of income (or profitability). **p. 274**

**Net income:** Difference between all revenues and all expenses for the period. **p. 275**

**Net realizable value:** Estimated selling price of the inventory in the ordinary course of business less any costs of completion, disposal, and transportation. **p. 304**

**Operating income:** Profitability from normal operations that equals gross profit less operating expenses. **p. 275**

**Periodic inventory system:** Inventory system that periodically adjusts for purchases and sales of inventory at the end of the reporting period based on a physical count of inventory on hand. **p. 285**

**Perpetual inventory system:** Inventory system that maintains a continual record of inventory purchased and sold. **p. 285**

**Specific identification method:** Inventory costing method that matches or identifies each unit of inventory with its actual cost. **p. 276**

**Weighted-average cost method:** Inventory costing method that assumes both cost of goods sold and ending inventory consist of a random mixture of all the goods available for sale. **p. 279**

## SELF-STUDY QUESTIONS

1. Which of the following companies report revenues by selling inventory? **(LO6–1)**
   a. Service companies.
   b. Manufacturing companies.
   c. Merchandising companies.
   d. Both manufacturing and merchandising companies.

2. At the beginning of the year, Bennett Supply has inventory of $3,500. During the year, the company purchases an additional $12,000 of inventory. An inventory count at the end of the year reveals remaining inventory of $4,000. What amount will Bennett report for cost of goods sold? **(LO6–2)**
   a. $11,000.
   b. $11,500.
   c. $12,000.
   d. $12,500.

3. Which of the following levels of profitability in a multiple-step income statement represents revenues

from the sale of inventory less the cost of that inventory? **(LO6–2)**
   a. Gross profit.
   b. Operating income.
   c. Income before income taxes.
   d. Net income.

4. Madison Outlet has the following inventory transactions for the year: **(LO6–3)**

| Date | Transaction | Number of Units | Unit Cost | Total Cost |
|------|-------------|-----------------|-----------|------------|
| Jan. 1 | Beginning inventory | 10 | $200 | $2,000 |
| Mar. 14 | Purchase | 15 | 300 | 4,500 |
| | | | | $6,500 |
| Jan. 1–Dec. 31 | Total sales to customers | 12 | | |

What amount would Madison report for cost of goods sold using FIFO?

a. $2,600.

b. $2,900.

c. $3,600.

d. $3,900.

5. Using the information in Question 4, what amount would Madison report for ending inventory using FIFO? **(LO6–3)**

a. $2,600.

b. $2,900.

c. $3,600.

d. $3,900.

6. Using the information in Question 4, what amount would Madison report for cost of goods sold using LIFO? **(LO6–3)**

a. $2,600.

b. $2,900.

c. $3,600.

d. $3,900.

7. Using the information in Question 4, what amount would Madison report for ending inventory using weighted-average cost? **(LO6–3)**

a. $3,380.

b. $3,250.

c. $3,120.

d. $3,000.

8. Which inventory cost flow assumption generally results in the lowest reported amount for cost of goods sold when inventory costs are rising? **(LO6–4)**

a. Lower of cost and net realizable value.

b. First-in, first-out (FIFO).

c. Last-in, first-out (LIFO).

d. Weighted-average cost.

9. Using a perpetual inventory system, the purchase of inventory on account would **(LO6–5)**

a. Increase Cost of Goods Sold; decrease Inventory.

b. Increase Inventory; decrease Sales Revenue.

c. Increase Cost of Goods Sold; increase Accounts Payable.

d. Increase Inventory; increase Accounts Payable.

10. Using a perpetual inventory system, the sale of inventory on account would **(LO6–5)**

a. Increase Cost of Goods Sold; decrease Inventory.

b. Increase Inventory; decrease Sales Revenue.

c. Increase Accounts Receivable; increase Sales Revenue.

d. Both a. and c. are correct.

11. Emmie's Pet World reports net sales of $400,000 and cost of goods sold of $320,000 for the year. At the beginning of the year, it had $60,000 of inventory on hand, whereas, at the end of the year, it has $70,000 of inventory on hand. What is Emmie's inventory turnover for the year? **(LO6–6)**

a. 4.9 times.

b. 5.3 times.

c. 4.6 times.

d. 5.7 times.

12. Using the information in the previous question, determine Emmie's average days in inventory. **(LO6–6)**

a. 68 days.

b. 80 days.

c. 74 days.

d. 64 days.

13. For the year, Simmons Incorporated reports net sales of $100,000, cost of goods sold of $80,000, and an average inventory balance of $40,000. What is Simmons' gross profit ratio? **(LO6–6)**

a. 20%.

b. 25%.

c. 40%.

d. 50%.

14. Which of the following is added to (increases) the balance of inventory? **(LO6–7)**

a. Freight-out.

b. Freight-in.

c. Purchase discounts.

d. Purchase returns.

15. Using a *periodic* inventory system, the purchase of inventory on account would be recorded as **(LO6–8)**

a. Increase Cost of Goods Sold; decrease Inventory.

b. Increase Inventory; increase Sales Revenue.

c. Increase Purchases; increase Accounts Payable.

d. Increase Inventory; increase Accounts Payable.

16. When a company determines the net realizable value of its ending inventory is lower than its cost, what would be the effect(s) of the adjustment to write down inventory to net realizable value? **(LO6–9)**

a. Decrease total assets.

b. Decrease net income.

c. Decrease retained earnings.

d. All of these answer choices are correct.

17. Maxwell Corporation has the following inventory information at the end of the year: **(LO6–9)**

| Inventory | Quantity | Unit Cost | Unit NRV |
|-----------|----------|-----------|----------|
| Item A | 20 | $20 | $35 |
| Item B | 50 | 30 | 25 |
| Item C | 40 | 10 | 15 |

Using the lower of cost and net realizable method, for what amount would Maxwell report ending inventory?

a. $2,050.

b. $2,300.

c. $2,550.

d. $2,800.

18. Suppose Ajax Corporation overstates its ending inventory amount. What effect will this have on the reported amount of cost of goods sold in the year of the error? **(LO6–10)**

   a. Overstate cost of goods sold.
   b. Understate cost of goods sold.
   c. Have no effect on cost of goods sold.
   d. Not possible to determine with the information given.

*Note: For answers, see the last page of the chapter.*

## REAL WORLD PERSPECTIVES CASES

**EDGAR Case**

### Sprouts Farmers Market, Inc. (ticker: SFM)

**RWP6–1** Visit www.sec.gov/edgar and search for the **Sprouts** annual report (10-K) for the year ended December 29, 2019, using EDGAR (Electronic Data Gathering, Analysis, and Retrieval system). Locate the note titled "Inventories." Use the information in this note to answer the questions below.

*Required:*
1. Does Sprouts typically purchase its inventory ready for resale, or does it manufacture its inventory?
2. Does Sprouts use FIFO, LIFO, weighted average, or some other inventory costing method?
3. Sprouts reports its inventory at cost or net realizable value. What does this mean?

**EDGAR Case**

### Gamestop Corporation (ticker: GME)

**RWP6–2** Visit www.sec.gov/edgar and search for the **Gamestop** annual report (10-K) for the year ended February 1, 2020, using EDGAR (Electronic Data Gathering, Analysis, and Retrieval system). The ending balances for inventory for the fiscal years ended 2020, 2019, and 2018 are $860, $1,251, and $1,250 ($ in millions), respectively. Using other information from the income statement, complete the following requirements.

*Required:*
1. Compute the inventory turnover ratio for fiscal years ended in 2020 and 2019. Has the ratio increased or decreased?
2. Compute the average days in inventory for fiscal years ended in 2020 and 2019. Has the number of days increased or decreased?

**EDGAR Case**

### Broadcom (ticker: AVGO)

**RWP6–3** Visit www.sec.gov/edgar and search for the **Broadcom** annual report (10-K) for the year ended November 3, 2019, using EDGAR (Electronic Data Gathering, Analysis, and Retrieval system). Find the income statement, which is titled "Consolidated Statements of Operations."

*Required:*
1. Compute Broadcom's gross profit ratio focusing on revenues and costs from products.
2. Now Compute Broadcom's gross profit ratio focusing on revenues and costs from subscriptions and services. Ignore amortization and restructuring charges.
3. Based on gross profit percentage, is Broadcom more profitable selling products or providing subscriptions and services?

**EDGAR Case**

### Caterpillar, Inc (ticker: CAT)

**RWP6–4** Visit www.sec.gov/edgar and search for the **Caterpillar** annual report (10-K) for the year ended December 29, 2019, using EDGAR (Electronic Data Gathering, Analysis, and Retrieval system). Locate the note titled "Inventories."

*Required:*
1. What inventory method does the company principally use?
2. Does Caterpillar primarily purchase completed inventory or manufacture its own inventory?

3. Compute the proportion of the company's total inventory contained in raw materials, work-in-process, and finished goods. Include "supplies" in work-in-process inventory.

## American Eagle Outfitters, Inc.

**Continuing Financial Analysis Case**

**RWP6–5** Financial information for **American Eagle** is presented in **Appendix A** at the end of the book.

*Required:*
1. For the most recent year, what is the amount of inventory in the balance sheet? What does this amount represent?
2. American Eagle refers to its cost of goods sold using a different name. What is it?
3. For the most recent year, what is the amount of cost of goods sold in the income statement? What does this amount represent?
4. Calculate American Eagle's inventory turnover ratio and average days in inventory for the most recent year.
5. Calculate American Eagle's gross profit ratio for each of the three years. Do you notice any trends?
6. For the most recent year, calculate American Eagle's ratio of operating expenses (other than cost of goods sold) to net sales. (*Hint:* These operating expenses include those amounts subtracted from gross profit to calculate operating income.)

## The Buckle, Inc.

**Continuing Financial Analysis Case**

**RWP6–6** Financial information for **Buckle** is presented in **Appendix B** at the end of the book.

*Required:*
1. For the most recent year, what is the amount of inventory in the balance sheet? What does this amount represent?
2. Buckle refers to its cost of goods sold using a different name. What is it?
3. For the most recent year, what is the amount of cost of goods sold in the income statement? What does this amount represent?
4. Calculate Buckle's inventory turnover ratio and average days in inventory for the most recent year.
5. Calculate Buckle's gross profit ratio for each of the three years. Do you notice any trends?
6. For the most recent year, calculate Buckle's ratio of operating expenses (other than cost of goods sold) to net sales.

## American Eagle Outfitters, Inc. vs. The Buckle, Inc.

**Continuing Comparative Analysis Case**

**RWP6–7** Financial information for **American Eagle** is presented in **Appendix A** at the end of the book, and financial information for **Buckle** is presented in **Appendix B** at the end of the book.

*Required:*
1. Which company carries a greater inventory balance as a percentage of total assets?
2. Which company has a higher inventory turnover ratio and, therefore, lower average days in inventory?
3. Which company's operations are more profitable using the gross profit ratio?
4. Considering the companies' ratio of operating expenses (other than cost of goods sold) to net sales, does your answer to requirement 3 change? Explain.

## Ethics

**Ethics Case**

**RWP6–8** Horizon Corporation manufactures personal computers. The company began operations in 2012 and reported profits for the years 2012 through 2022. Due primarily to increased competition and price slashing in the industry, 2023's income statement reported a loss of $20 million. Just before the end of the 2024 fiscal year, a memo from the company's chief financial officer (CFO) to Jim Fielding, the company controller, included the following comments:

> If we don't do something about the large amount of unsold computers already manufactured, our auditors will require us to report a write-down. The resulting loss for 2024 will cause a violation of our debt covenants and force the company into bankruptcy. I suggest that you ship half of our inventory to J.B. Sales, Inc., in Oklahoma City. I know the company's president, and he will accept the inventory and acknowledge the shipment as a purchase. We can report the sale in 2024, which will boost our loss to a profit. Then J.B. Sales will simply return the inventory in 2025 after the financial statements have been issued.

### Required:

1. Understand the reporting effect: What is the effect on income before taxes of the sales transaction requested by the CFO?
2. Specify the options: If Jim does not report the sales transaction requested by the CFO, what is the effect on total assets and income before taxes of the inventory write-down?
3. Identify the impact: Are investors and creditors potentially harmed by the CFO's suggestion?
4. Make a decision: Should Jim follow the CFO's suggestion?

Sustainability Case

## Sustainability

**RWP6–9** Part of sustainability accounting is responsible sourcing of inventory. That is, sustainability accounting for inventory considers more than costs, but also how raw material is sourced, labor conditions in the supply chain, and the impact of inventory sourcing on the environment. To learn more about the idea of sustainable inventory sourcing and supply chain management, let's review the sustainability disclosures of **The Gap**.

Go to the SASB website (https://www.sasb.org/company-use/sasb-reporters/) and search for The Gap. Click on the Corporate Responsibility Report for 2019 and go to the section titled "Assessment + Remediation" starting on page 33.

### Required:

1. To formalize its dedication to sustainability in inventory sourcing, Gap monitors its inventory suppliers based on its own Code of Vendor Conduct (COVC), which uses a color-coded system to rate the quality of suppliers' sustainability. What percentage of The Gap's supplier facilities were rated as red in 2016? In 2019?
2. Gap attempts to identify and resolve COVC issues of its suppliers. Issues include factors such as workers' well-being, human rights violations, and negative environmental impact. If these issues cannot be resolve, Gap will create an exit plan to no longer use the supplier. How many open COVC issues did Gap have at the start of its fiscal year on February 1, 2019?
3. Which country had the most open COVC issues?
4. What percent of total COVC issues did GAP resolve within 12 months of discovery?

Earnings Management Case

## Earnings Management

**RWP6–10** Eddie's Galleria sells billiard tables. The company has the following purchases and sales for 2024.

| Date | | Transactions | Units | Unit Cost | Total Cost |
|------|---|-------------|-------|-----------|-----------|
| January | 1 | Beginning inventory | 150 | $540 | $ 81,000 |
| March | 8 | Purchase | 120 | 570 | 68,400 |
| August | 22 | Purchase | 100 | 600 | 60,000 |
| October | 29 | Purchase | 80 | 640 | 51,200 |
| | | | 450 | | $260,600 |
| Jan. 1–Dec. 31 | | Sales ($700 each) | 400 | | |

Eddie is worried about the company's financial performance. He has noticed an increase in the purchase cost of billiard tables, but at the same time, competition from other billiard table stores and other entertainment choices have prevented him from increasing the sales price. Eddie is worried if the company's profitability is too low, stockholders will demand he be replaced. Eddie does not want to lose his job. Since 60 of the 400 billiard tables sold have not yet been picked up by the customers as of December 31, 2024, Eddie decides incorrectly to include these tables in ending inventory. He appropriately includes the sale of these 60 tables as part of total revenues in 2024.

### Required:

1. What amount will Eddie calculate for ending inventory and cost of goods sold using FIFO, assuming he erroneously reports 110 tables remain in ending inventory?
2. What amount would Eddie calculate for cost of goods sold using FIFO if he correctly reports only 50 tables remain in ending inventory?
3. What effect will the inventory error have on reported amounts for (a) ending inventory, (b) retained earnings, (c) cost of goods sold, and (d) net income (ignoring tax effects) in 2024?
4. Assuming ending inventory is correctly counted at the end of 2025, what effect will the inventory error in 2024 have on reported amounts for (a) ending inventory, (b) retained earnings, (c) cost of goods sold, and (d) net income (ignoring tax effects) in 2025?

## Great Adventures

Continuing General Ledger Case

(This is a continuation of the Great Adventures problem from earlier chapters.)

**RWP6–11** Now that operations for outdoor clinics and TEAM events are running smoothly, Suzie thinks of another area for business expansion. She notices a few clinic participants wear multiuse (MU) watches. Beyond the normal timekeeping features of most watches, MU watches can report temperature, altitude, and barometric pressure. MU watches are waterproof, so moisture from kayaking, rain, fishing, or even diving up to 100 feet won't damage them. Suzie decides to have MU watches available for sale at the start of each clinic. The following transactions relate to purchases and sales of watches during the second half of 2025. All watches are sold for $500 each.

| | |
|---|---|
| Jul.  17 | Purchased 50 watches for $7,500 ($150 per watch) on account. |
| Jul.  31 | Sold 40 watches for $20,000 cash. |
| Aug. 12 | Purchased 40 watches for $6,400 ($160 per watch) cash. |
| Aug. 22 | Sold 30 watches for $15,000 on account. |
| Sep. 19 | Paid for watches purchased on July 17. |
| Sep. 27 | Receive cash of $9,000 for watches sold on account on August 22. |
| Oct. 27 | Purchased 80 watches for $13,600 ($170 per watch) cash. |
| Nov. 20 | Sold 90 watches for $45,000 cash. |
| Dec.  4 | Purchased 100 watches for $18,000 ($180 per watch) on account. |
| Dec.  8 | Sold 40 watches for $20,000 on account. |

### Required:

1. (a) Calculate sales revenue, cost of goods sold, and ending inventory as of December 31, 2025, assuming Suzie uses FIFO to account for inventory.
   (b) Prepare the gross profit section of a partial income statement for transactions related to MU watches.
2. Late in December, the next generation of multiuse (MU II) watches are released. In addition to all of the features of the MU watch, the MU II watches are equipped with a global positioning system (GPS) and have the ability to download and play songs and videos off the Internet. The demand for the original MU watches is greatly reduced. As of December 31, the estimated net realizable value of MU watches is only $100 per watch.
   (a) Record any necessary adjusting entry on December 31, 2025, related to this information.
   (b) For what amount would MU inventory be reported in the December 31, 2025, balance sheet?
   (c) Prepare an updated gross profit section of a partial income statement accounting for this additional information. Compare your answer to requirement 1(b).

The Great Adventures continuing problem also can be assigned using the General Ledger software in Connect. Students will be given an existing trial balance and asked to prepare (1) the journal entries above, (2) financial statements, and (3) closing entries.

Understand inventory
flows (LO6–1)

**BE6–1** Match each of the following types of companies with its definition.

| Types of Companies | Definitions |
|---|---|
| 1. _____ Service company | a. Purchases goods that are primarily in finished form for resale to customers. |
| 2. _____ Merchandising company | b. Records revenues when providing services to customers. |
| 3. _____ Manufacturing company | c. Produces the goods they sell to customers. |

Understand inventory
flows (LO6–1)

**BE6–2** Match each of the following inventory classifications with its definition.

| Inventory Classifications | Definitions |
|---|---|
| 1. _____ Raw materials | a. Cost of items not yet complete by the end of the period. |
| 2. _____ Work-in-process | b. Cost of fully assembled but unshipped inventory at the end of the reporting period. |
| 3. _____ Finished goods | c. Basic components used to build a product. |

Understand cost of goods
sold (LO6–2)

**BE6–3** At the beginning of the year, Bryers Incorporated reports inventory of $8,000. During the year, the company purchases additional inventory for $23,000. At the end of the year, the cost of inventory remaining is $10,000. Calculate cost of goods sold for the year.

Understand how cost of
goods sold is reported in
a multiple-step income
statement (LO6–2)

**BE6–4** For each company, calculate the missing income statement amount.

| Company | Sales Revenue | Cost of Goods Sold | Gross Profit | Operating Expenses | Net Income |
|---|---|---|---|---|---|
| Lennon | $18,000 | (a) | $8,000 | $3,500 | $4,500 |
| Harrison | 20,000 | $11,000 | (b) | 6,000 | 3,000 |
| McCartney | 13,000 | 9,000 | 4,000 | (c) | 1,500 |
| Starr | 16,000 | 6,000 | 10,000 | 6,500 | (d) |

Determine the cost
of goods sold and
ending inventory using
FIFO (LO6–3)

**BE6–5** During the year, Wright Company sells 470 remote-control airplanes for $110 each. The company has the following inventory purchase transactions for the year.

| Date | Transaction | Number of Units | Unit Cost | Total Cost |
|---|---|---|---|---|
| Jan. 1 | Beginning inventory | 60 | $82 | $ 4,920 |
| May 5 | Purchase | 250 | 85 | 21,250 |
| Nov. 3 | Purchase | 200 | 90 | 18,000 |
| | | 510 | | $44,170 |

Calculate ending inventory and cost of goods sold for the year, assuming the company uses FIFO.

Determine the cost of goods
sold and ending inventory
using LIFO (LO6–3)

**BE6–6** Refer to the information in BE6–5. Calculate ending inventory and cost of goods sold for the year, assuming the company uses LIFO.

Determine the cost of
goods sold and ending
inventory using weighted-
average cost (LO6–3)

**BE6–7** Refer to the information in BE6–5. Calculate ending inventory and cost of goods sold for the year, assuming the company uses weighted-average cost.

Determine the cost of
goods sold and ending
inventory using specific
identification (LO6–3)

**BE6–8** Refer to the information in BE6–5. Calculate ending inventory and cost of goods sold for the year, assuming the company uses specific identification. The company's actual sales include its entire beginning inventory, 230 units of inventory from the May 5 purchase, and 180 units from the November 3 purchase.

**BE6–9** For each item below, indicate whether FIFO or LIFO will generally result in a higher reported amount when inventory costs are rising versus falling. The first answer is provided as an example.

Inventory costing when prices are rising (LO6–4)

| Inventory Costs | Higher Total Assets | Higher Cost of Goods Sold | Higher Net Income |
|---|---|---|---|
| Rising | FIFO | | |
| Declining | | | |

**BE6–10** Shankar Company uses a perpetual system to account for inventory transactions. The company purchases inventory on account on February 2 for $40,000 and then sells this inventory on account on March 17 for $60,000. Determine the financial statement effects of the purchase of inventory on account and sale of inventory on account.

Using a perpetual inventory system (LO6–5)
See JBE6–1 for journal entries.

**BE6–11** Litton Industries uses a perpetual inventory system. The company began its fiscal year with inventory of $267,000. Purchases of merchandise on account during the year totaled $845,000. Merchandise costing $902,000 was sold on account for $1,420,000. Determine the financial statement effects of these transactions.

Using a perpetual inventory system (LO6–5)
See JBE6–2 for journal entries.

**BE6–12** Using the amounts below, calculate the inventory turnover ratio, average days in inventory, and gross profit ratio.

Analyze inventory efficiency (LO6–6)

| | |
|---|---|
| Net Sales | $250,000 |
| Cost of goods sold | 180,000 |
| Beginning inventory | 55,000 |
| Ending inventory | 45,000 |

**BE6–13** Cloud X and Cloud Y are two competitors in manufacturing and selling large-capacity digital storage. Cloud X reports gross profit ratio of 16%, while Cloud Y reports a gross profit ratio of 20%. Given that Cloud X and Cloud Y report cost of goods sold of $140,000 and $160,000, respectively, determine which company has higher net sales revenues for the year.

Analyze inventory efficiency (LO6–6)

**BE6–14** Kelly Corporation shipped goods to a customer f.o.b. destination on December 29, 2024. The goods arrived at the customer's location in January. In addition, one of Kelly's major suppliers shipped goods to Kelly f.o.b. shipping point on December 30. The merchandise arrived at Kelly's location in January. Which shipments should be included in Kelly's December 31 inventory?

Understand shipping point (LO6–7)

**BE6–15** Shankar Company uses a perpetual system to account for inventory transactions. The company purchases inventory on account on February 2 for $40,000. In addition to the cost of inventory, the company also pays $600 for freight charges associated with the purchase on the same day. Determine the financial statement effects of the purchase of inventory on account and the payment of freight charges on February 2.

Understand freight charges (LO6–7)
See JBE6–3 for journal entries.

**BE6–16** Shankar Company uses a perpetual system to account for inventory transactions. The company purchases 1,500 units of inventory on account on February 2 for $60,000 ($40 per unit) but then returns 100 defective units on February 5. Determine the financial statement effects of the inventory purchase on account on February 2 and the inventory return on February 5.

Understand purchase returns (LO6–7)
See JBE6–4 for journal entries.

**BE6–17** Shankar Company uses a perpetual system to account for inventory transactions. The company purchases inventory on account on February 2 for $40,000, with terms 3/10, n/30. On February 10, the company pays on account for the inventory. Determine the financial statement effects of the inventory purchase on account on February 2 and the payment on February 10.

Understand purchase discounts (LO6–7)
See JBE6–5 for journal entries.

Understand purchase discounts (LO6–7)
*See JBE6–6 for journal entries.*

**BE6–18** On December 28, 2024, Videotech Corporation (VTC) purchased 10 units of a new satellite uplink system from Tristar Communications for $25,000 each. The terms of each sale were 1/10, n/30. VTC paid the net-of-discount amount on January 6, 2025. Determine the financial statement effects of these transactions.

Maintain inventory records using a periodic inventory system (LO6–8)

**BE6–19** Samuelson and Messenger (SAM) began 2024 with 200 units of its one product. These units were purchased near the end of 2023 for $25 each. During the month of January, 100 units were purchased on January 8 for $28 each, and another 200 units were purchased on January 19 for $30 each. Sales of 125 units and 100 units were made on January 10 and January 25, respectively. There were 275 units on hand at the end of the month. SAM uses a periodic inventory system. Calculate ending inventory and cost of goods sold for January using FIFO.

Apply the lower of cost and net realizable value (LO6–9)

**BE6–20** Powder Ski Shop reports inventory using the lower of cost and net realizable value (NRV). Information related to its year-end inventory appears below. Calculate the total amount to be reported for ending inventory in the balance sheet.

| Inventory | Quantity | Unit Cost | Unit NRV |
|---|---|---|---|
| Ski jackets | 20 | $115 | $ 95 |
| Skis | 25 | 300 | 350 |

Apply the lower of cost and net realizable value (LO6–9)

**BE6–21** Creative Technology reports inventory using the lower of cost and net realizable value (NRV). Below is information related to its year-end inventory. Calculate the total amount to be reported for ending inventory in the balance sheet.

| Inventory | Quantity | Unit Cost | Unit NRV |
|---|---|---|---|
| Optima cameras | 20 | $115 | $ 95 |
| Inspire speakers | 25 | 300 | 350 |

Determine the financial statement effects of inventory errors (LO6–10)

**BE6–22** Ebbers Corporation overstated its ending inventory balance by $15,000 in the current year. What impact will this error have on cost of goods sold and gross profit in the current year and following year?

Determine the financial statement effects of inventory errors (LO6–10)

**BE6–23** Refer to the information in BE6–22. What impact will this error have on ending inventory and retained earnings in the current year and following year? Ignore any tax effects.

## EXERCISES

Understand inventory flows (LO6–1)

**E6–1** Quality Retail Group begins the year with inventory of $55,000 and ends the year with inventory of $45,000. During the year, the company has four purchases for the following amounts.

| | |
|---|---|
| Purchase on February 17 | $210,000 |
| Purchase on May 6 | 130,000 |
| Purchase on September 8 | 160,000 |
| Purchase on December 4 | 410,000 |

*Required:*
Calculate cost of goods available for sale and cost of goods sold for the year.

Prepare a multiple-step income statement (LO6–2)

**E6–2** Wayman Corporation reports the following amounts in its December 31, 2024, income statement.

| | | | |
|---|---|---|---|
| Sales revenue | $390,000 | Income tax expense | $ 50,000 |
| Interest expense | 20,000 | Cost of goods sold | 130,000 |
| Salaries expense | 40,000 | Advertising expense | 30,000 |
| Utilities expense | 50,000 | | |

*Required:*
Prepare a multiple-step income statement.

**E6–3** Tisdale Incorporated reports the following amount in its December 31, 2024, income statement.

Prepare a multiple-step income statement (LO6–2)

| | | | |
|---|---|---|---|
| Sales revenue | $300,000 | Income tax expense | $ 30,000 |
| Nonoperating revenue | 110,000 | Cost of goods sold | 190,000 |
| Selling expenses | 60,000 | Administrative expenses | 40,000 |
| General expenses | 50,000 | | |

*Required:*

1. Prepare a multiple-step income statement.
2. Explain how analyzing the multiple levels of profitability can help in understanding the future profit-generating potential of Tisdale Incorporated.

**E6–4** During the year, TRC Corporation has the following inventory transactions.

Determine the cost of goods sold and ending inventory using different inventory cost methods amid rising prices (LO6–3, 6–4)

| Date | Transaction | Number of Units | Unit Cost | Total Cost |
|---|---|---|---|---|
| Jan. 1 | Beginning inventory | 60 | $52 | $ 3,120 |
| Apr. 7 | Purchase | 140 | 54 | 7,560 |
| Jul. 16 | Purchase | 210 | 57 | 11,970 |
| Oct. 6 | Purchase | 120 | 58 | 6,960 |
| | | 530 | | $29,610 |

For the entire year, the company sells 450 units of inventory for $70 each.

*Required:*

1. Using FIFO, calculate (a) ending inventory, (b) cost of goods sold, (c) sales revenue, and (d) gross profit.
2. Using LIFO, calculate (a) ending inventory, (b) cost of goods sold, (c) sales revenue, and (d) gross profit.
3. Using weighted-average cost, calculate (a) ending inventory, (b) cost of goods sold, (c) sales revenue, and (d) gross profit.
4. Determine which method will result in higher profitability when inventory costs are rising.

**E6–5** During the year, Triumph Incorporated has the following inventory transactions.

Determine the cost of goods sold and ending inventory using different inventory cost methods amid rising prices (LO6–3, 6–4)

| Date | Transaction | Number of Units | Unit Cost | Total Cost |
|---|---|---|---|---|
| Jan. 1 | Beginning Inventory | 20 | $22 | $ 440 |
| Mar. 4 | Purchase | 25 | 21 | 525 |
| Jun. 9 | Purchase | 30 | 20 | 600 |
| Nov. 11 | Purchase | 30 | 18 | 540 |
| | | 105 | | $2,105 |

For the entire year, the company sells 81 units of inventory for $30 each.

*Required:*

1. Using FIFO, calculate (a) ending inventory, (b) cost of goods sold, (c) sales revenue, and (d) gross profit.
2. Using LIFO, calculate (a) ending inventory, (b) cost of goods sold, (c) sales revenue, and (d) gross profit.
3. Using weighted-average cost, calculate (a) ending inventory, (b) cost of goods sold, (c) sales revenue, and (d) gross profit.
4. Determine which method will result in higher profitability when inventory costs are declining.

**Maintain inventory records using a perpetual inventory system (LO6–5)**
*See JE6–1 for journal entries.*

**E6–6** Bingerton Industries began the year with inventory of $85,000. Purchases of inventory on account during the year totaled $310,000. Inventory costing $335,000 was sold on account for $520,000.

**Required:**
Determine the financial statement effects of the purchase of inventory on account and the sale of inventory on account using a perpetual system.

**Maintain inventory records using a perpetual inventory system with a purchase return (LO6–5, LO6–7)**
*See JE6–2 for journal entries.*

**E6–7** On June 5, Staley Electronics purchases 200 units of inventory on account for $20 each. After closer examination, Staley determines 40 units are defective and returns them to its supplier for full credit on June 9. All remaining inventory is sold on account on June 16 for $35 each.

**Required:**
Determine the financial statement effects of transactions for the purchase of inventory on account, return of defective inventory, and sale of inventory on account using a perpetual system.

**Maintain inventory records using a perpetual inventory system with a purchase discount (LO6–5, LO6–7)**
*See JE6–3 for journal entries.*

**E6–8** On June 5, Staley Electronics purchases 200 units of inventory on account for $19 each, with terms 2/10, n/30. Staley pays for the inventory on June 12.

**Required:**
1. Determine the financial statement effects of transactions for the purchase of inventory on account and payment on account using a perpetual system.
2. Now, assume payment is made on June 22. Determine the financial statement effects of the payment on account.

**Determine cost of goods sold and the inventory turnover ratio (LO6–2, LO6–6)**

**E6–9** Lewis Incorporated and Clark Enterprises report the following amounts for the year.

|  | Lewis | Clark |
|---|---|---|
| Inventory (beginning) | $ 24,000 | $ 50,000 |
| Inventory (ending) | 18,000 | 60,000 |
| Purchases | 261,000 | 235,000 |
| Purchase returns | 15,000 | 60,000 |

**Required:**
1. Calculate cost of goods sold for each company.
2. Calculate the inventory turnover ratio for each company.
3. Calculate the average days in inventory for each company.
4. Explain which company appears to be managing its inventory more efficiently.

**Prepare a multiple-step income statement and compute gross profit ratio (LO6–2, LO6–6)**

**E6–10** Below are amounts found in the income statements of three companies.

| Company | Sales Revenue | Cost of Goods Sold | Operating Expenses | Nonoperating Expenses | Income Tax Expense |
|---|---|---|---|---|---|
| Henry | $32,000 | $ 4,800 | $ 5,000 | $2,000 | $2,000 |
| Grace | 35,000 | 24,500 | 13,100 | 7,000 | 0 |
| James | 40,000 | 24,800 | 3,000 | 0 | 3,000 |

**Required:**
1. For each company, calculate (a) gross profit, (b) operating income, (c) income before income taxes, and (d) net income.
2. For each company, calculate the gross profit ratio and indicate which company has the most favorable ratio.

**E6–11** Littleton Books has the following transactions during May.

| | |
|---|---|
| May 2 | Purchases books on account from Readers Wholesale for $3,300, terms 1/10, n/30. |
| May 3 | Pays cash for freight costs of $200 on books purchased from Readers. |
| May 5 | Returns books with a cost of $400 to Readers because part of the order is incorrect. |
| May 10 | Pays the full amount due to Readers. |
| May 30 | Sells all books purchased on May 2 (less those returned on May 5) for $4,000 on account. |

Examine additional inventory transactions (LO6–7)
See JE6–4 for journal entries.

*Required:*

1. Determine the financial statement effects of the transactions of Littleton Books, assuming the company uses a perpetual inventory system.
2. Assume payment to Readers is made on May 24 instead of May 10. Determine the financial statement effects of this payment.

**E6–12** Sundance Systems has the following transactions during July.

| | |
|---|---|
| July 5 | Purchases 40 LCD televisions on account from Red River Supplies for $2,500 each, terms 3/10, n/30. |
| July 8 | Returns to Red River two televisions that had defective sound. |
| July 13 | Pays the full amount due to Red River. |
| July 28 | Sells remaining 38 televisions from July 5 for $3,000 each on account. |

Examine additional inventory transactions (LO6–7)
See JE6–5 for journal entries.

*Required:*

Determine the financial statement effects of the transactions of Sundance Systems, assuming the company uses a perpetual inventory system.

**E6–13** DS Unlimited has the following transactions during August.

| | |
|---|---|
| August 6 | Purchases 70 handheld game devices on account from GameGirl, Inc., for $200 each, terms 1/10, n/60. |
| August 7 | Pays $400 to Sure Shipping for freight charges associated with the August 6 purchase. |
| August 10 | Returns to GameGirl six game devices that were defective. |
| August 14 | Pays the full amount due to GameGirl. |
| August 23 | Sells 50 game devices purchased on August 6 for $220 each to customers on account. The total cost of the 50 game devices sold is $10,212.50. |

Examine additional inventory transactions (LO6–7)
See JE6–6 for journal entries.

*Required:*

Determine the financial statement effects of the transactions of DS Unlimited, assuming the company uses a perpetual inventory system.

**E6–14** The June 30, 2024, year-end balances for Askew Company include the following:

Maintain inventory records using a periodic inventory system (LO6–8)

| Account | Balance |
|---|---|
| Inventory, 7/1/2023 | $ 32,000 |
| Sales revenue | 380,000 |
| Sales returns | 12,000 |
| Purchases | 240,000 |
| Purchase discounts | 6,000 |
| Purchase returns | 10,000 |
| Freight-in | 17,000 |

In addition, you determine that the June 30, 2024, inventory balance is $40,000.

*Required:*

Calculate the cost of goods sold for the Askew Company for the year ending June 30, 2024.

**E6–15** Home Furnishings reports inventory using the lower of cost and net realizable value (NRV). Below is information related to its year-end inventory.

Apply lower of cost and net realizable value (LO6–9)
See JE6–10 for journal entries.

| Inventory | Quantity | Unit Cost | Unit NRV |
|---|---|---|---|
| Furniture | 200 | $ 85 | $100 |
| Electronics | 50 | 400 | 300 |

**Required:**

1. Calculate the total cost of ending inventory before any adjustments.
2. Calculate ending inventory using the lower of cost and net realizable value.
3. Determine the financial statement effects of any adjustment to inventory for the lower of cost and net realizable value.

**Apply lower of cost and net realizable value (LO6–9)**
*See JE6–11 for journal entries.*

**E6–16** A company like **Golf USA** that sells golf-related inventory typically will have inventory items such as golf clothing and golf equipment. As technology advances the design and performance of the next generation of drivers, the older models become less marketable and therefore decline in value. Suppose that in the current year, **Ping** (a manufacturer of golf clubs) introduces the MegaDriver II, the new and improved version of the MegaDriver. Below are year-end amounts related to Golf USA's inventory.

| Inventory | Quantity | Unit Cost | Unit NRV |
|---|---|---|---|
| Shirts | 35 | $ 60 | $ 70 |
| MegaDriver | 15 | 360 | 250 |
| MegaDriver II | 30 | 350 | 420 |

**Required:**

1. Calculate the total cost of ending inventory before any adjustments.
2. Calculate ending inventory using the lower of cost and net realizable value.
3. Determine the financial statement effects of any adjustment to inventory for the lower of cost and net realizable value.

**Examine additional inventory transactions and inventory errors (LO6–7, LO6–10)**

**E6–17** Mulligan Corporation purchases inventory on account with terms FOB shipping point. The goods are shipped on December 30, 2024, but do not reach Mulligan until January 5, 2025. Mulligan correctly accounts for accounts payable associated with the purchase but does not include this inventory in its 2024 ending inventory count.

**Required:**

1. If an error has been made, explain why.
2. If an error has been made, indicate whether there is an understatement (U), overstatement (O), or no effect (N) on the reported amount of each financial statement element in the current year and following year. Ignore any tax effects.

| | Balance Sheet | | | Income Statement | | |
|---|---|---|---|---|---|---|
| Year | Assets | Liabilities | Stockholders' Equity | Revenues | Cost of Goods Sold | Gross Profit |
| Current | ___ | ___ | ___ | ___ | ___ | ___ |
| Following | ___ | ___ | ___ | ___ | ___ | ___ |

## Mc Graw Hill connect | PROBLEMS

**Understand inventory cost flows, and determine the cost of goods sold and ending inventory using different inventory cost methods (LO6–1, 6–3)**

**P6–1** Sandra's Purse Boutique has the following transactions related to its top-selling **Gucci** purse for the month of October.

| Date | Transactions | Units | Unit Cost | Total Cost |
|---|---|---|---|---|
| October 1 | Beginning inventory | 6 | $900 | $ 5,400 |
| October 4 | Sale | 4 | | |
| October 10 | Purchase | 5 | 910 | 4,550 |
| October 13 | Sale | 3 | | |
| October 20 | Purchase | 4 | 920 | 3,680 |
| October 28 | Sale | 7 | | |
| October 30 | Purchase | 7 | 930 | 6,510 |
| | | | | $20,140 |

**Required:**

1. Calculate ending inventory and cost of goods sold at October 31, using the specific identification method. The October 4 sale consists of purses from beginning inventory, the October 13 sale consists of one purse from beginning inventory and two purses from the October 10 purchase, and the October 28 sale consists of three purses from the October 10 purchase and four purses from the October 20 purchase.
2. Using FIFO, calculate ending inventory and cost of goods sold at October 31.
3. Using LIFO, calculate ending inventory and cost of goods sold at October 31.
4. Using weighted-average cost, calculate ending inventory and cost of goods sold at October 31.

**P6–2** Greg's Bicycle Shop has the following transactions related to its top-selling Mongoose mountain bike for the month of March.

*Understand different inventory cost methods and different inventory cost methods (LO6–3, 6–4)*

| Date | Transactions | Units | Unit Cost | Total Cost |
|------|-------------|-------|-----------|-----------|
| March 1 | Beginning inventory | 20 | $250 | $ 5,000 |
| March 5 | Sale ($400 each) | 15 | | |
| March 9 | Purchase | 10 | 270 | 2,700 |
| March 17 | Sale ($450 each) | 8 | | |
| March 22 | Purchase | 10 | 280 | 2,800 |
| March 27 | Sale ($475 each) | 12 | | |
| March 30 | Purchase | 9 | 300 | 2,700 |
| | | | | $13,200 |

**Required:**

1. Calculate ending inventory and cost of goods sold at March 31, using the specific identification method. The March 5 sale consists of bikes from beginning inventory, the March 17 sale consists of bikes from the March 9 purchase, and the March 27 sale consists of four bikes from beginning inventory and eight bikes from the March 22 purchase.
2. Using FIFO, calculate ending inventory and cost of goods sold at March 31.
3. Using LIFO, calculate ending inventory and cost of goods sold at March 31.
4. Using weighted-average cost, calculate ending inventory and cost of goods sold at March 31.
5. Calculate sales revenue and gross profit under each of the four methods.
6. Comparing FIFO and LIFO, which one provides the more meaningful measure of ending inventory? Explain.

**P6–3** At the beginning of July, Fick_3D Corp. has a balance in inventory of $3,400 of 3D printing accessories. The following transactions occur during the month of July.

*Prepare a multiple-step income statement, maintain inventory records using a perpetual inventory system and compute gross profit ratio (LO6–2, 6–5, 6–6, 6–7)*
*See JP6–1 for journal entries.*

July 3  Purchase inventory on account from Wholesale 3D for $2,300, terms 1/10, n/30.
July 4  Pay cash for freight charges related to the July 3 purchase from Wholesale 3D, $110.
July 9  Return incorrectly ordered 3D printing accessories to Wholesale 3D and receive credit, $200.
July 11  Pay Wholesale 3D in full.
July 12  Sell 3D printing accessories to customers on account, $5,800, that had a cost of $3,000.
July 15  Receive full payment from customers related to the sale on July 12.
July 18  Purchase 3D printing accessories on account from 3D Supply for $3,100, terms 1/10, n/30.
July 22  Sell 3D printing accessories to customers for cash, $4,200, that had a cost of $2,500.
July 28  Return 3D printing accessories to 3D Supply and receive credit of $300.
July 30  Pay 3D Supply in full.

**Required:**

1. Assuming Fick_3D uses a perpetual inventory system, determine the financial statement effects for each of the transactions.

2. Prepare the top section of the multiple-step income statement through gross profit for the month of July.

3. Compute the gross profit ratio for the month of July.

Apply lower of cost and net realizable value **(LO6–9)**
*See JP6–3 for journal entries.*

**P6–4** A local **Chevrolet** dealership carries the following types of vehicles:

| Inventory Items | Quantity | Unit Cost | Unit NRV | Lower of Cost and NRV |
|---|---|---|---|---|
| Vans | 4 | $27,000 | $25,000 | _____ |
| Trucks | 7 | 18,000 | 17,000 | _____ |
| 2-door sedans | 3 | 13,000 | 15,000 | _____ |
| 4-door sedans | 5 | 17,000 | 20,000 | _____ |
| Sports cars | 1 | 37,000 | 40,000 | _____ |
| SUVs | 6 | 30,000 | 28,000 | _____ |

Because of recent increases in gasoline prices, the car dealership has noticed a reduced demand for its SUVs, vans, and trucks.

**Required:**

1. Compute the total cost of the entire inventory.

2. Determine whether each inventory item would be reported at cost or net realizable value (NRV). Multiply the quantity of each inventory item by the appropriate cost or NRV amount and place the total in the "Lower of Cost and NRV" column. Then determine the total for that column.

3. From the information in the previous requirements, determine the financial statement effects of using lower of cost and net realizable value to report inventory.

Determine the cost of goods sold and ending inventory using different inventory cost methods and apply lower of cost and net realizable value **(LO6–3, 6–9)**
*See JP6–4 for journal entries.*

**P6–5** For the current year, Parker Games has the following inventory transactions related to its traditional board games.

| Date | Transaction | Units | Unit Cost | Total Cost |
|---|---|---|---|---|
| Jan. 1 | Beginning inventory | 120 | $21 | $2,520 |
| Mar. 12 | Purchase | 90 | 16 | 1,440 |
| Sep. 17 | Purchase | 60 | 9 | 540 |
| | | 270 | | $4,500 |
| Jan. 1–Dec. 31 | Sales | 170 | | |

**Required:**

1. Using FIFO, calculate ending inventory and cost of goods sold.

2. Using LIFO, calculate ending inventory and cost of goods sold.

3. Because of the increasing popularity of electronic video games, Parker Games continues to see a decline in the demand for board games. Sales prices have decreased by over 50% during the year. At the end of the year, Parker estimates the net realizable value of the 100 units of unsold inventory to be $500. Determine the amount of ending inventory to report using lower of cost and net realizable value under FIFO. 4. Determine the financial statement effects of any necessary adjustment to the amount of ending inventory for the lower of cost and net realizable value.

Maintain inventory records, examine additional inventory transactions, apply lower of cost and net realizable value, and compute the gross profit ratio **(LO6–5, 6–6, 6–7, 6–9)**
*See JP6–5 for journal entries.*

**P6–6** At the beginning of October, Bowser Co.'s inventory consists of 50 units with a cost per unit of $50. The following transactions occur during the month of October.

| October | 4 | Purchase 130 units of inventory on account from Waluigi Co. for $50 per unit, terms 2/10, n/30. |
|---|---|---|
| October | 5 | Pay cash for freight charges related to the October 4 purchase, $600. |

| | |
|---|---|
| October  9 | Return 10 defective units from the October 4 purchase and receive credit. |
| October 12 | Pay Waluigi Co. in full. |
| October 15 | Sell 160 units of inventory to customers on account, $12,800. (Hint: The cost of units sold from the October 4 purchase includes $50 unit cost plus $5 per unit for freight less $1 per unit for the purchase discount, or $54 per unit.) |
| October 19 | Receive full payment from customers related to the sale on October 15. |
| October 20 | Purchase 100 units of inventory from Waluigi Co. for $70 per unit, terms 2/10, n/30. |
| October 22 | Sell 100 units of inventory to customers for cash, $8,000. |

**Required:**

1. Assuming Bowser Co. uses a FIFO perpetual inventory system to maintain its inventory records, determine the financial statement effects for each of the transactions.
2. Suppose by the end of October the remaining inventory is estimated to have a net realizable value per unit of $35. Determine the financial statement effects of any necessary adjustment for the lower of cost and net realizable value.
3. Compute the gross profit ratio for the month of October after the adjustment for lower of cost and net realizable value.

**P6–7 Baskin-Robbins** is one of the world's largest specialty ice cream shops. The company offers dozens of different flavors, from Very Berry Strawberry to low-fat Espresso 'n Cream. Assume a local Baskin-Robbins in Chapel Hill, North Carolina, has the following amounts for the month of July 2024.

*Prepare a multiple-step income statement and analyze inventory efficiency (LO6–2, 6–6)*

| | | | |
|---|---|---|---|
| Salaries expense | $13,700 | Sales revenue | $69,800 |
| Inventory (July 1, 2021) | 2,300 | Interest income | 3,300 |
| Sales returns | 1,100 | Cost of goods sold | 28,700 |
| Utilities expense | 3,600 | Rent expense | 6,700 |
| Income tax expense | 6,000 | Interest expense | 400 |
| | | Inventory (July 31, 2021) | 1,100 |

**Required:**

1. Prepare a multiple-step income statement for the month ended July 31, 2024.
2. Calculate the inventory turnover ratio for the month of July. Would you expect this ratio to be higher or lower in December 2024? Explain.
3. Calculate the gross profit ratio for the month of July.

**P6–8 Wawa Food Markets** is a convenience store chain located primarily in the Northeast. The company sells gas, candy bars, drinks, and other grocery-related items. **St. Jude Medical Incorporated** sells medical devices related to cardiovascular needs. Suppose a local Wawa Food Market and St. Jude sales office report the following amounts in the same year (company names are disguised):

*Analyze inventory efficiency (LO6–6)*

| | Company 1 | Company 2 |
|---|---|---|
| Net sales | $400,000 | $400,000 |
| Cost of goods sold | 180,000 | 330,000 |
| Gross profit | $220,000 | $ 70,000 |
| Average inventory | $ 40,000 | $ 30,000 |

**Required:**

1. For Company 1 and Company 2, calculate the inventory turnover ratio.
2. For Company 1 and Company 2, calculate the gross profit ratio.
3. After comparing the inventory turnover ratios and gross profit ratios, which company do you think is Wawa and which is St. Jude? Explain.

Analyze inventory
efficiency and inventory
errors (LO6–6, 6–10)

**P6–9** Over a four-year period, Jackie Corporation reported the following series of gross profits.

|  | 2021 | 2022 | 2023 | 2024 |
|---|---|---|---|---|
| Net sales | $60,000 | $66,000 | $74,000 | $90,000 |
| Cost of goods sold | 32,000 | 46,000 | 28,000 | 48,000 |
| Gross profit | $28,000 | $20,000 | $46,000 | $42,000 |

In 2024, the company performed a comprehensive review of its inventory accounting procedures. Based on this review, company records reveal that ending inventory was understated by $11,000 in 2022. Inventory in all other years is correct.

**Required:**
1. Calculate the gross profit ratio for each of the four years based on amounts originally reported.
2. Calculate the gross profit ratio for each of the four years based on corrected amounts. Describe the trend in the gross profit ratios based on the original amounts versus the corrected amounts.
3. Total gross profit over the four-year period based on the amounts originally reported equals $136,000 (= $28,000 + $20,000 + $46,000 + $42,000). Compare this amount to total gross profit over the four-year period based on the corrected amounts.

Analyze periodic inventory,
discounts, returns and
freight-in (LO6–7, 6–8)

**P6–10** La Playa Company has the following information in its records. Certain data have been intentionally omitted ($ in thousands).

|  | 2024 | 2025 | 2026 |
|---|---|---|---|
| Beginning inventory | ? | ? | 225 |
| Cost of goods sold | 627 | 621 | ? |
| Ending inventory | ? | 225 | 216 |
| Cost of goods available for sale | 876 | ? | 800 |
| Purchases (gross) | 630 | ? | 585 |
| Purchase discounts | 18 | 15 | ? |
| Purchase returns | 24 | 30 | 14 |
| Freight-in | 13 | 32 | 16 |

**Required:**
1. Determine the missing numbers. Show computations where appropriate.

## JOURNAL ENTRIES

### Journal Entries–Brief Exercises

Record inventory
transactions (LO6–5)
See BE6–10 for financial
statement effects.

**JBE6–1** Shankar Company uses a perpetual system to record inventory transactions. The company purchases inventory on account on February 2 for $40,000 and then sells this inventory on account on March 17 for $60,000. Record the transactions for the purchase and sale of inventory.

Record inventory
transactions (LO6–5)
See BE6–11 for financial
statement effects.

**JBE6–2** Litton Industries uses a perpetual inventory system. The company began its fiscal year with inventory of $267,000. Purchases of merchandise on account during the year totaled $845,000. Merchandise costing $902,000 was sold on account for $1,420,000. Record the journal entries for these transactions.

**JBE6–3** Shankar Company uses a perpetual system to record inventory transactions. The company purchases inventory on account on February 2 for $40,000. In addition to the cost of inventory, the company also pays $600 for freight charges associated with the purchase on the same day. Record the purchase of inventory on February 2, including the freight charges.

Record additional inventory transactions **(LO6–7)**
*See BE6–15 for financial statement effects.*

**JBE6–4** Shankar Company uses a perpetual system to record inventory transactions. The company purchases 1,500 units of inventory on account on February 2 for $60,000 ($40 per unit) but then returns 100 defective units on February 5. Record the inventory purchase on February 2 and the inventory return on February 5.

Record additional inventory transactions **(LO6–7)**
*See BE6–16 for financial statement effects.*

**JBE6–5** Shankar Company uses a perpetual system to record inventory transactions. The company purchases inventory on account on February 2 for $40,000, with terms 3/10, n/30. On February 10, the company pays on account for the inventory. Record the inventory purchase on February 2 and the payment on February 10.

Record additional inventory transactions **(LO6–7)**
*See BE6–17 for financial statement effects.*

**JBE6–6** On December 28, 2024, Videotech Corporation (VTC) purchased 10 units of a new satellite uplink system from Tristar Communications for $25,000 each. The terms of each sale were 1/10, n/30. VTC paid the net-of-discount amount on January 6, 2025. Record the journal entries for these transactions using the perpetual inventory system.

Record additional inventory transactions **(LO6–7)**
*See BE6–18 for financial statement effects.*

**JBE6–7** Refer to the information in JBE6–1, but now assume Shankar uses a *periodic* system to record inventory transactions. Record transactions for the purchase and sale of inventory.

Record inventory transactions using a periodic inventory system **(LO6–8)**

**JBE6–8** Refer to the information in JBE6–3, but now assume Shankar uses a *periodic* system to record inventory transactions. Record the purchase of inventory on February 2, including the freight charges.

Record inventory transactions using a periodic inventory system **(LO6–8)**

**JBE6–9** Refer to the information in JBE6–4, but now assume Shankar uses a *periodic* system to record inventory transactions. Record the inventory purchase on February 2 and the inventory return on February 5.

Record inventory transactions using a periodic inventory system **(LO6–8)**

**JBE6–10** Refer to the information in JBE6–5, but now assume Shankar uses a *periodic* system to record inventory transactions. Record the inventory purchase on February 2 and the payment on February 10.

Record inventory transactions using a periodic inventory system **(LO6–8)**

## Journal Entries—Exercises

**JE6–1** Bingerton Industries began the year with inventory of $85,000. Purchases of inventory on account during the year totaled $310,000. Inventory costing $335,000 was sold on account for $520,000.

**Required:**
Record transactions for the purchase and sale of inventory using a perpetual system.

Record inventory transactions **(LO6–5)**
*See E6–6 for financial statement effects.*

**JE6–2** On June 5, Staley Electronics purchases 200 units of inventory on account for $20 each. After closer examination, Staley determines 40 units are defective and returns them to its supplier for full credit on June 9. All remaining inventory is sold on account on June 16 for $35 each.

**Required:**
Record transactions for the purchase, return, and sale of inventory using a perpetual system.

Record inventory transactions with an inventory return **(LO6–5, LO6–7)**
*See E6–7 for financial statement effects.*

**JE6–3** On June 5, Staley Electronics purchases 200 units of inventory on account for $19 each, with terms 2/10, n/30. Staley pays for the inventory on June 12.

**Required:**
1. Record transactions for the purchase of inventory and payment on account using a perpetual system.
2. Now, assume payment is made on June 22. Record the payment on account.

Record inventory transactions with a purchase discount **(LO6–5, LO6–7)**
*See E6–8 for financial statement effects.*

Record additional inventory
transactions **(LO6–7)**
*See E6–11 for financial
statement effects.*

**JE6–4** Littleton Books has the following transactions during May.

| May | 2 | Purchases books on account from Readers Wholesale for $3,300, terms 1/10, n/30. |
|---|---|---|
| May | 3 | Pays cash for freight costs of $200 on books purchased from Readers. |
| May | 5 | Returns books with a cost of $400 to Readers because part of the order is incorrect. |
| May | 10 | Pays the full amount due to Readers. |
| May | 30 | Sells all books purchased on May 2 (less those returned on May 5) for $4,000 on account. |

**Required:**

1. Record the transactions of Littleton Books, assuming the company uses a perpetual inventory system.
2. Assume payment to Readers is made on May 24 instead of May 10. Record this payment.

Record additional inventory
transactions **(LO6–7)**
*See E6–12 for financial
statement effects.*

**JE6–5** Sundance Systems has the following transactions during July.

| July | 5 | Purchases 40 LCD televisions on account from Red River Supplies for $2,500 each, terms 3/10, n/30. |
|---|---|---|
| July | 8 | Returns to Red River two televisions that had defective sound. |
| July | 13 | Pays the full amount due to Red River. |
| July | 28 | Sells remaining 38 televisions from July 5 for $3,000 each on account. |

**Required:**

Record the transactions of Sundance Systems, assuming the company uses a perpetual inventory system.

Record additional inventory
transactions **(LO6–7)**
*See E6–13 for financial
statement effects.*

**JE6–6** DS Unlimited has the following transactions during August.

| August | 6 | Purchases 70 handheld game devices on account from GameGirl, Inc., for $200 each, terms 1/10, n/60. |
|---|---|---|
| August | 7 | Pays $400 to Sure Shipping for freight charges associated with the August 6 purchase. |
| August | 10 | Returns to GameGirl six game devices that were defective. |
| August | 14 | Pays the full amount due to GameGirl. |
| August | 23 | Sells 50 game devices purchased on August 6 for $220 each to customers on account. The total cost of the 50 game devices sold is $10,212.50. |

**Required:**

Record the transactions of DS Unlimited, assuming the company uses a perpetual inventory system.

Record inventory
transactions using
a periodic inventory
system **(LO6–8)**

**JE6–7** Refer to the transactions in JE6–4.

**Required:**

1. Record the transactions of Littleton Books, assuming the company uses a periodic inventory system.
2. Record the period-end adjusting entry to cost of goods sold on May 31, assuming the company has no beginning or ending inventory.

Record inventory
transactions using
a periodic inventory
system **(LO6–8)**

**JE6–8** Refer to the transactions in JE6–5.

**Required:**

1. Record the transactions of Sundance Systems, assuming the company uses a periodic inventory system.
2. Record the period-end adjusting entry to cost of goods sold on July 31, assuming the company has no beginning inventory.

Record inventory
transactions using
a periodic inventory
system **(LO6–8)**

**JE6–9** Refer to the transactions in JE6–6.

**Required:**

1. Record the transactions of DS Unlimited, assuming the company uses a periodic inventory system.

2. Record the period-end adjusting entry to cost of goods sold on August 31, assuming the company has no beginning inventory and ending inventory has a cost of $2,859.50.

**JE6–10** Home Furnishings reports inventory using the lower of cost and net realizable value (NRV). Below is information related to its year-end inventory.

*Apply lower of cost and net realizable value (LO6–9)*
*See E6–15 for financial statement effects.*

| Inventory | Quantity | Unit Cost | Unit NRV |
|---|---|---|---|
| Furniture | 200 | $ 85 | $100 |
| Electronics | 50 | 400 | 300 |

**Required:**
1. Calculate the total recorded cost of ending inventory before any adjusting entries.
2. Calculate ending inventory using the lower of cost and net realizable value.
3. Record any necessary adjusting entry for the lower of cost and net realizable value.

**JE6–11** A company like **Golf USA** that sells golf-related inventory typically will have inventory items such as golf clothing and golf equipment. As technology advances the design and performance of the next generation of drivers, the older models become less marketable and therefore decline in value. Suppose that in the current year, **Ping** (a manufacturer of golf clubs) introduces the MegaDriver II, the new and improved version of the MegaDriver. Below are year-end amounts related to Golf USA's inventory.

*Apply lower of cost and net realizable value (LO6–9)*
*See E6–16 for financial statement effects.*

| Inventory | Quantity | Unit Cost | Unit NRV |
|---|---|---|---|
| Shirts | 35 | $ 60 | $ 70 |
| MegaDriver | 15 | 360 | 250 |
| MegaDriver II | 30 | 350 | 420 |

**Required:**
1. Calculate the total recorded cost of ending inventory before any adjusting entries.
2. Calculate ending inventory using the lower of cost and net realizable value.
3. Record any necessary adjusting entry for the lower of cost and net realizable value.

**JE6–12** On January 1, 2024, the general ledger of Big Blast Fireworks includes the following account balances:

*Comprehensive example (LO 6–2, 6–3, 6–5, 6–6, 6–7, 6–9)*

| Accounts | Debit | Credit |
|---|---|---|
| Cash | $ 21,900 | |
| Accounts Receivable | 36,500 | |
| Allowance for Uncollectible Accounts | | $  3,100 |
| Inventory | 30,000 | |
| Land | 61,600 | |
| Accounts Payable | | 32,400 |
| Notes Payable (8%, due in 3 years) | | 30,000 |
| Common Stock | | 56,000 |
| Retained Earnings | | 28,500 |
| Totals | $150,000 | $150,000 |

The $30,000 beginning balance of inventory consists of 300 units, each costing $100. During January 2024, Big Blast Fireworks had the following inventory transactions:

| | |
|---|---|
| January  3 | Purchase 1,200 units for $126,000 on account ($105 each). |
| January  8 | Purchase 1,300 units for $143,000 on account ($110 each). |
| January 12 | Purchase 1,400 units for $161,000 on account ($115 each). |
| January 15 | Return 100 of the units purchased on January 12 because of defects. |

| January 19 | Sell 4,000 units on account for $600,000. The cost of the units sold is determined using a FIFO perpetual inventory system. |
| January 22 | Receive $580,000 from customers on accounts receivable. |
| January 24 | Pay $410,000 to inventory suppliers on accounts payable. |
| January 27 | Write off accounts receivable as uncollectible, $2,500. |
| January 31 | Pay cash for salaries during January, $128,000. |

***Required:***

1. Record each of the transactions listed above, assuming a FIFO perpetual inventory system.
2. Record adjusting entries on January 31.
   a. At the end of January, the company estimates that the remaining units of inventory are expected to sell in February for only $100 each.
   b. At the end of January, $4,000 of accounts receivable are past due, and the company estimates that 40% of these accounts will not be collected. Of the remaining accounts receivable, the company estimates that 4% will not be collected.
   c. Accrued interest expense on notes payable for January. Interest is expected to be paid each December 31.
   d. Accrued income taxes at the end of January are $12,300.
3. Prepare an adjusted trial balance as of January 31, 2024, after updating beginning balances (above) for transactions during January (requirement 1) and adjusting entries at the end of January (requirement 2).
4. Prepare a multiple-step income statement for the period ended January 31, 2024.
5. Prepare a classified balance sheet as of January 31, 2024.
6. Record closing entries.
7. Analyze how well Big Blast Fireworks' manages its inventory:
   a. Calculate the inventory turnover ratio for the month of January. If the industry average of the inventory turnover ratio for the month of January is 18.5 times, is the company managing its inventory more or less efficiently than other companies in the same industry?
   b. Calculate the gross profit ratio for the month of January. If the industry average gross profit ratio is 33%, is the company more or less profitable per dollar of sales than other companies in the same industry?
   c. Used together, what might the inventory turnover ratio and gross profit ratio suggest about Big Blast Fireworks' business strategy? Is the company's strategy to sell a higher volume of less expensive items, or does the company appear to be selling a lower volume of more expensive items?

## Journal Entries—Problems

**Prepare a multiple-step income statement, maintain inventory records using a perpetual inventory system and compute gross profit ratio (LO6–2, 6–5, 6–6, 6–7)**

*See P6–3 for financial statement effects.*

**JP6–1** At the beginning of July, Fick_3D Corp. has a balance in inventory of $3,400 of 3D printing accessories. The following transactions occur during the month of July.

| July 3 | Purchase inventory on account from Wholesale 3D for $2,300, terms 1/10, n/30. |
| July 4 | Pay cash for freight charges related to the July 3 purchase from Wholesale 3D, $110. |
| July 9 | Return incorrectly ordered 3D printing accessories to Wholesale 3D and receive credit, $200. |
| July 11 | Pay Wholesale 3D in full. |
| July 12 | Sell 3D printing accessories to customers on account, $5,800, that had a cost of $3,000. |
| July 15 | Receive full payment from customers related to the sale on July 12. |
| July 18 | Purchase 3D printing accessories on account from 3D Supply for $3,100, terms 1/10, n/30. |
| July 22 | Sell 3D printing accessories to customers for cash, $4,200, that had a cost of $2,500. |

July 28      Return 3D printing accessories to 3D Supply and receive credit of $300.
July 30      Pay 3D Supply in full.

**Required:**

1. Assuming Fick_3D uses a perpetual inventory system, record the transactions.
2. Prepare the top section of the multiple-step income statement through gross profit for the month of July.
3. Compute the gross profit ratio for the month of July.

**JP6–2** Refer to the transactions of Fick_3D Corp. in P6–3.

**Required:**

1. Assuming Fick_3D uses a periodic inventory system, record the transactions.
2. Record the month-end adjusting entry to inventory, assuming that a final count reveals ending inventory with a cost of $2,889.
3. Prepare the top section of the multiple-step income statement through gross profit for the month of July.
4. Compute the gross profit ratio for the month of July.

Prepare a multiple-step income statement, maintain inventory records using a periodic inventory system, and compute gross profit ratio **(LO6–2, 6–6, 6–8)**

**JP6–3** A local **Chevrolet** dealership carries the following types of vehicles:

Apply the lower of cost and net realizable value rule for inventories **(LO6–9)**
*See P6–4 for financial statement effects.*

| Inventory Items | Quantity | Unit Cost | Unit NRV | Lower of Cost and NRV |
|---|---|---|---|---|
| Vans | 4 | $27,000 | $25,000 | ——— |
| Trucks | 7 | 18,000 | 17,000 | ——— |
| 2-door sedans | 3 | 13,000 | 15,000 | ——— |
| 4-door sedans | 5 | 17,000 | 20,000 | ——— |
| Sports cars | 1 | 37,000 | 40,000 | ——— |
| SUVs | 6 | 30,000 | 28,000 | ——— |

Because of recent increases in gasoline prices, the car dealership has noticed a reduced demand for its SUVs, vans, and trucks.

**Required:**

1. Compute the total cost of the entire inventory.
2. Determine whether each inventory item would be reported at cost or net realizable value (NRV). Multiply the quantity of each inventory item by the appropriate cost or NRV amount and place the total in the "Lower of Cost and NRV" column. Then determine the total for that column.
3. Compare your answers in requirement 1 and requirement 2 and then record any necessary adjustment to inventory for the lower of cost and net realizable value.

**JP6–4** For the current year, Parker Games has the following inventory transactions related to its traditional board games.

Apply different inventory cost methods and apply lower of cost and net realizable value **(LO6–3, 6–9)**
*See P6–5 for financial statement effects.*

| Date | Transaction | Units | Unit Cost | Total Cost |
|---|---|---|---|---|
| Jan.  1 | Beginning inventory | 120 | $21 | $2,520 |
| Mar. 12 | Purchase | 90 | 16 | 1,440 |
| Sep. 17 | Purchase | 60 | 9 | 540 |
| | | 270 | | $4,500 |
| Jan. 1– Dec. 31 | Sales | 170 | | |

*Required:*

1. Using FIFO, calculate ending inventory and cost of goods sold.

2. Using LIFO, calculate ending inventory and cost of goods sold.

3. Because of the increasing popularity of electronic video games, Parker Games continues to see a decline in the demand for board games. Sales prices have decreased by over 50% during the year. At the end of the year, Parker estimates the net realizable value of the 100 units of unsold inventory to be $500. Determine the amount of ending inventory to report using lower of cost and net realizable value under FIFO. 4. Record any potential adjustment to inventory for the lower of cost and net realizable value.

**Comprehensive example (LO6–3, 6–5, 6–6, 6–7, 6–9)**

*See P6–6 for financial statement effects.*

**JP6–5** At the beginning of October, Bowser Co.'s inventory consists of 50 units with a cost per unit of $50. The following transactions occur during the month of October.

| | |
|---|---|
| October  4 | Purchase 130 units of inventory on account from Waluigi Co. for $50 per unit, terms 2/10, n/30. |
| October  5 | Pay cash for freight charges related to the October 4 purchase, $600. |
| October  9 | Return 10 defective units from the October 4 purchase and receive credit. |
| October 12 | Pay Waluigi Co. in full. |
| October 15 | Sell 160 units of inventory to customers on account, $12,800. (*Hint:* The cost of units sold from the October 4 purchase includes $50 unit cost plus $5 per unit for freight less $1 per unit for the purchase discount, or $54 per unit.) |
| October 19 | Receive full payment from customers related to the sale on October 15. |
| October 20 | Purchase 100 units of inventory from Waluigi Co. for $70 per unit, terms 2/10, n/30. |
| October 22 | Sell 100 units of inventory to customers for cash, $8,000. |

*Required:*

1. Assuming Bowser Co. uses a FIFO perpetual inventory system to maintain its inventory records, record the transactions.

2. Suppose by the end of October, the remaining inventory is estimated to have a net realizable value per unit of $35. Record any necessary adjustment to inventory for lower of cost and net realizable value.

3. Compute the gross profit ratio for the month of October after the adjustment to inventory for lower of cost and net realizable value.

## DATA ANALYTICS

Visit Connect to view **Data Analytics** questions related to:

1. Applying Excel
2. Data Visualizations
3. Tableau Dashboard Activities
4. Applying Tableau

## ANSWERS TO THE SELF-STUDY QUESTIONS

1. d    2. b    3. a    4. a    5. d    6. c    7. a    8. b    9. d    10. d    11. a    12. c    13. a    14. b    15. c    16. d    17. a    18. b

# Long-Term Assets

## Learning Objectives

## Self-Study Materials

## Feature Story

# Disney: Assets Abound

**The Walt Disney Company** (hereafter: Disney) is an iconic worldwide entertainment company. If you're like most people, in the last month, you've probably watched a Disney movie, watched sports on its networks, streamed entertainment via its online services, taken a cruise on one of its cruise lines, or if you're very lucky, you've even gone to Disney World! Disney specializes in entertainment, with an incredible array of entertaining and iconic resources. Just think of the many icons related to Disney, including characters (Mickey and Minnie Mouse, Ironman, Luke Skywalker), physical properties (Magic Kingdom, Disneyland Parks and Resorts), cable networks (ESPN and ABC), and production studios (Marvel and Lucasfilms).

Many of these assets show up in Disney's balance sheet as **long-term assets.** However, measuring the value of the assets that Disney reports in the balance sheet can be challenging. For example, Disney has acquired dozens of other companies throughout the years, including **Pixar, Marvel, Lucasfilms, Hulu,** and most recently, **21st Century Fox.** These acquisitions often lead to the creation of an intangible asset in the balance sheet called **goodwill,** an asset that is notoriously hard to value. Of its $100 billion in assets, Disney reports a whopping $31 billion in goodwill. Disney also has other **long-term assets,** such as amusement parks and resorts, which are also challenging to value. Disney reports that the historic cost of its parks is over $55 billion, but those parks have **accumulated depreciation** of nearly $31 billion over the years. Finally, Disney reports nearly $6 billion of other **intangible assets** (trademarks, licenses, etc.).

However, despite boasting $100 billion in assets in the balance sheet, Disney has many other assets that are *not* reported in the balance sheet, including the brand value of iconic figures like Mickey and Minnie Mouse. Other iconic characters such as the brand value of Captain America and Thor are reported in the balance sheet. Why?

In this chapter, we'll answer that question and more related to how we account for the acquisition of long-term assets; allocate the cost of long-term assets through depreciation or amortization; and report the sale, retirement, or exchange of long-term assets at the end of their service life.

At the end of the chapter, we compare the return on assets for **Disney** and **Netflix.** We separate return on assets into two parts: profit margin (how much a company makes for each dollar in sales) and asset turnover (how much sales a company generates for each dollar in assets). We then examine whether the ratios support our expectations regarding Disney and Netflix, two close competitors in the entertainment industry.

**Hershey** cannot make chocolate without its manufacturing facilities and the equipment in those facilities. In contrast, it's not physical assets but copyrights on its computer software that give **Alphabet** the ability to generate billions of dollars in revenue each year. Both of these types of revenue-producing assets are considered *long-term assets,* the topic of this chapter.

We classify long-term assets into two major categories:

1. **Tangible assets.** Assets in this category include land, land improvements, buildings, equipment, and natural resources. Hershey's land, buildings, and equipment fall into this category.

2. **Intangible assets.** Assets in this category include patents, trademarks, copyrights, franchises, and goodwill. We distinguish these assets from property, plant, and equipment by their lack of physical substance. The evidence of their existence often is based on a legal contract. Alphabet's copyrights are intangible assets.

Illustration 7–1 presents a breakdown of the total assets for **Workday**, a fin-tech company that provides cloud-based applications for finance and human resources. In terms of long-term assets, Workday reports three major categories: property and equipment, intangible assets, and goodwill.

**ILLUSTRATION 7–1**

Balance Sheet for Workday

| WORKDAY, INC. Balance Sheet (partial) ($ in millions) | |
|---|---:|
| Current Assets: | |
| Cash and cash equivalents | $  639 |
| Marketable securities | 1,140 |
| Trade receivables | 750 |
| Other current assets | 217 |
| Total current assets | 2,746 |
| Property and equipment, net | 797 |
| Intangible assets, net | 313 |
| Goodwill | 1,379 |
| Other long-term assets | 331 |
| **Total assets** | **$5,566** |

To properly report both tangible and intangible assets, we need to address a variety of issues, including (1) which amounts to include in their initial cost, (2) how to expense their costs while using them, and (3) how to account for their sale or disposal at the end of their service life. These three issues are the basis for the major parts of the chapter.

## PART A

## ASSET ACQUISITION

The first issue to consider in accounting for long-term assets is how to report their cost at the time of acquisition. To do this, we need to understand the major types of tangible and intangible assets. We begin with tangible assets, also referred to as property, plant, and equipment.

## Property, Plant, and Equipment

■ **LO7–1**

Identify the major types of property, plant, and equipment.

The property, plant, and equipment category consists of land, land improvements, buildings, equipment, and natural resources. The general rule for reporting all such long-term assets can be simply stated as: **We report a long-term asset at its cost *plus* all expenditures**

**necessary to get the asset ready for use.** Thus, the initial cost of a long-term asset might be more than just its purchase price; it also will include any additional amounts the company paid to bring the asset to its desired condition and location for use.

To capitalize an expenditure means to account for the expenditure as an asset. **The capitalized expenditure will be expensed** *over time* **as the asset is used in company operations.**

To **expense** an expenditure means to **account for the full expenditure as an expense** *immediately.* We'll discuss both types of expenditures in this chapter. Whether management capitalizes an expenditure or expenses it fully in the current year can have a significant effect on a company's financial statements.

M_D_A/iStock/Getty Images

## LAND

The Land account represents land a company is using in its operations. (In contrast, land purchased for investment purposes is reported in a separate investment account.) We capitalize to Land all expenditures necessary to get the land ready for its intended use.

Such capitalized costs include the purchase price of the land plus closing costs such as fees for the attorney, real estate agent commissions, title, title search, and recording fees. If the property is subject to back taxes or other obligations, we include these amounts as well. In fact, any additional expenditure such as clearing, filling, and leveling the land, or even removing existing buildings to prepare the land for its intended use, become part of the land's capitalized cost. If we receive any cash from selling salvaged building materials, we reduce the cost of land by that amount.

Assume, for instance, **Workday** purchases a two-acre tract of land and an existing building for $2,500,000. In addition to the purchase price, the company incurs several other costs, listed in Illustration 7–2. Using the guideline of **cost plus all expenditures necessary to get the asset ready for use,** what amount should Workday report as the total cost of the land?

**ILLUSTRATION 7–2**

Computation of the Capitalized Cost of Land

| Costs necessary to get the land ready for use | |
| --- | --- |
| Purchase price of land and existing building | $2,500,000 |
| Commissions to sales agent | 150,000 |
| Title insurance | 15,000 |
| Back property taxes (seller's unpaid taxes)* | 30,000 |
| Property taxes for the current year ($10,000)* | – |
| Removing existing building | 250,000 |
| Less: Salvaged materials from existing building | (25,000) |
| Leveling the land | 30,000 |
|   Total capitalized cost of land | $2,950,000 |

*Property taxes paid for the seller's unpaid taxes in previous years are necessary to get title clearance for the land. Any property taxes for the current period after the purchase are not included and instead expensed as incurred.

 **COMMON MISTAKE**

Many students incorrectly add or ignore the cash received from the sale of salvaged materials. Cash received from the sale of salvaged materials *reduces* the total cost of land.

## LAND IMPROVEMENTS

Beyond the cost of the land, **Workday** likely will spend additional amounts to improve the land by adding a parking lot, sidewalks, security fencing, landscaping, lighting systems, fences, sprinklers, and similar additions. These are land improvements. Because land improvements have limited useful lives (parking lots eventually wear out), and land has an unlimited useful life, we report land improvements separately from the land itself.

Chine Nouvelle/SIPA/
Shutterstock

## BUILDINGS

Buildings include administrative offices, retail stores, manufacturing facilities, and storage warehouses. **The cost of acquiring a building usually includes realtor commissions and legal fees in addition to the purchase price.** The new owner sometimes needs to remodel or otherwise modify the building to suit its needs. These additional costs are part of the building's acquisition cost.

Unique accounting issues arise when a firm constructs a building rather than purchasing it. Of course, the cost of construction includes architect fees, material costs, and construction labor. New building construction likely also includes costs such as manager supervision, overhead (costs indirectly related to the construction), and interest costs incurred during construction.

## EQUIPMENT

Equipment is a broad term that includes machinery used in manufacturing, computers and other office equipment, vehicles, furniture, and fixtures. **The cost of equipment is the actual purchase price plus all other costs necessary to prepare the asset for use.** These can be any of a variety of other costs including sales tax, shipping, delivery insurance, assembly, installation, testing, and even legal fees incurred to establish title.

What about recurring costs related to equipment, such as annual property insurance and annual property taxes on vehicles? Rather than including recurring costs as part of the cost of the equipment, we expense them as we incur them. The question to ask yourself when deciding whether to add a cost to the asset account or report it as an expense of the current period is, *"Is this a cost of acquiring the asset and getting it ready for use, or is it a recurring cost that benefits the company in the current period?"*

Assume **Workday** purchases new equipment for $82,000 plus $6,500 in sales tax. Additional costs incurred by Workday include: freight of $800 to transport the equipment and $200 for shipping insurance, installation of the equipment for $1,500, and liability insurance of $1,600 to cover the equipment's first year of operation. Illustration 7–3 shows the calculation of the amount at which Workday should report the cost of the equipment.

**ILLUSTRATION 7–3**

Computation of the Capitalized Cost of Equipment

| Costs necessary to get the equipment ready for use | |
| --- | ---: |
| Purchase price | $ 82,000 |
| Sales tax | 6,500 |
| Transportation | 800 |
| Shipping insurance | 200 |
| Installation | 1,500 |
| Annual insurance ($1,600)* | – |
| Total capitalized cost of equipment | $ 91,000 |

*The annual insurance of $1,600 initially will be recorded as Prepaid Insurance and allocated to Insurance Expense over the first year of coverage.

## BASKET PURCHASES

Sometimes companies purchase more than one asset at the same time for one purchase price. This is known as a basket purchase. For example, assume a company purchases land, building, and equipment together for $900,000. We need to report land, building, and equipment in separate accounts. How much should we report in the separate accounts for land, building, and equipment? The simple answer is that **we allocate the total purchase price of $900,000 based on the estimated *fair values* of each of the individual assets.** The fair value of an asset is its estimated stand-alone selling price.

The difficulty, though, is that the estimated fair values of the individual assets often exceed the total purchase price, in this case, $900,000. Let's say the estimated fair values of the land, building, and equipment are $200,000, $700,000, and $100,000, respectively, for a total estimated fair value of $1 million. In that case, the total purchase of $900,000 will be allocated to the separate accounts for Land, Building, and Equipment based on their relative fair values, shown in Illustration 7–4.

| | Estimated Fair Value | Allocation Percentage | | Amount of Basket Purchase | Reported Amount |
|---|---|---|---|---|---|
| Land | $ 200,000 | $200,000/$1,000,000 = 20% | × | $900,000 | $180,000 |
| Building | 700,000 | $700,000/$1,000,000 = 70% | × | $900,000 | 630,000 |
| Equipment | 100,000 | $100,000/$1,000,000 = 10% | × | $900,000 | 90,000 |
| Total | $1,000,000 | | 100% | | $900,000 |

**ILLUSTRATION 7–4**

Allocation of Cost in a Basket Purchase

## NATURAL RESOURCES

Many companies depend heavily on natural resources, such as oil, natural gas, timber, and salt. **ExxonMobil**, for example, maintains oil and natural gas deposits on six of the world's seven continents. **Weyerhaeuser** is one of the largest pulp and paper companies in the world, with major investments in timber forests. Even salt is a natural resource, with the largest supply in the United States mined under the Great Lakes of North America.

We can distinguish natural resources from other property, plant, and equipment by the fact that we can physically use up, or *deplete,* natural resources. ExxonMobil's oil reserves are a natural resource that deplete as the firm extracts oil. Similarly, timber land is used up to produce materials in the construction industry, and salt is extracted from salt mines for use in cooking and melting icy roads.

**KEY POINT**

Tangible assets such as land, land improvements, buildings, equipment, and natural resources are reported at cost plus all costs necessary to get the asset ready for its intended use.

**SUSTAINABILITY**

Sustainability accounting encourages companies to report the impact of their long-term assets on the environment, including factors related to emissions, air quality, energy use, and climate change (see the SASB Materiality Map). To understand this point, we can examine sustainability disclosures from **Delta Air Lines** related to its most visible assets—its airplanes.

In its Sustainability Report, Delta discloses the actions it is undertaking related to climate opportunities, with a specific discussion of reducing airplane fuel consumption and greenhouse gas emissions. Here are some of the climate actions disclosed by Delta:

*Our commitment to addressing climate change is a factor in the way we manage our fleet. We balance technological improvements available in new aircraft with a desire to build a fleet that is sustainable for the long-term and that maximizes the useful life of our planes.*

*. . . New, more efficient aircraft will produce the biggest impact on our efficiency and our ability to reduce absolute greenhouse gas emissions. Over the past few years, we have reduced the number of regional aircraft and depended on larger aircraft, such as the Boeing 717–200, to achieve the same capacity with fewer takeoffs and landings, thereby improving overall efficiency.*

The purchase and deployment of long-term assets that are sustainable will be crucial for the long-term success of asset-intensive companies, such as Delta Air Lines.

# Intangible Assets

■ **LO7–2**
Identify the major types of intangible assets.

The other major category of long-term assets, intangible assets, have no physical substance and generally represent exclusive rights that provide benefits to owners. Assets in this category include patents, trademarks, copyrights, franchises, and goodwill.

Despite their lack of physical substance, intangible assets can be very valuable. One of the most valuable intangible assets for many companies is their trademark or brand. *Interbrand* publishes an annual list of the 100 most valuable brands. Illustration 7–5 summarizes the top 10 most valuable brands. As you can see, the **Apple** brand has an estimated value of $234.2 billion. Despite this value, Apple reports no intangible assets on its balance sheet. Later, we'll see why many intangible assets are *not* reported in the balance sheet at their estimated values.

**ILLUSTRATION 7–5**

**World's Top 10 Brands**

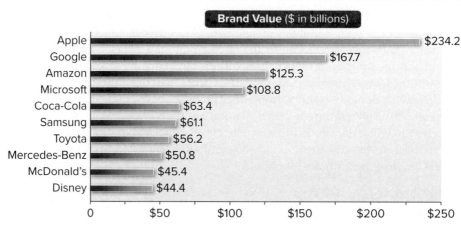

*Source:* "Best Gobal Brands 2019 Rankings," Interbrand.com, 2019, www.interbrand.com.

The issues involved in accounting for intangible assets are similar to those of property, plant, and equipment. One key difference, though, is that the future benefits that we attribute to intangible assets usually are much less certain than those attributed to tangible assets. For example, the productive capacity and service life of a delivery truck is fairly easy to determine in most situations. However, will expenditures for the exclusive right to sell a product (a patent) provide future benefits? If so, for how long? Will expenditures to acquire a franchise or customer list provide future benefits? If so, for how long? This uncertainty is a discriminating characteristic of intangible assets that perhaps better distinguishes them from tangible assets than their lack of physical substance.

Companies acquire intangible assets in two ways:

1. They *purchase* intangible assets like patents, copyrights, trademarks, or franchise rights from other companies. We account for purchased intangible assets at their original cost plus all other costs, such as legal fees, necessary to get the asset ready for use.

2. They *develop* intangible assets internally, for instance by developing a new product or process and obtaining a protective patent. Rather than reporting these in the balance sheet as intangible assets, we expense in the income statement most of the costs for internally developed intangible assets in the period we incur those costs.

Research and development costs are expensed as incurred.

**Research and Development (R&D).**    Costs incurred to conduct research and to develop a new product or process are not reported as an intangible asset in the balance sheet. Instead, they are expensed directly in the income statement. For example, Apple spends approximately $15–$20 billion in research and development every year. All of this cost is reported by Apple as an expense in the income statement rather than as an intangible asset in the balance sheet. The reason we expense all R&D costs is the difficulty in determining the portion of R&D that benefits future periods. Conceptually, we should report as an intangible asset the portion that benefits future periods. Due to the difficulties in arriving at this estimate, current U.S. accounting rules require firms to expense all R&D costs as incurred.[1]

Take a look at the list of the largest 10 companies ranked by their R&D expenses (see Illustration 7–6). These companies spend an incredible amount of money on R&D, but under U.S. GAAP, these costs are expensed in the income statement rather than capitalized as an intangible asset in the balance sheet. For example, **Amazon** tops the list below with nearly $30 billion in annual R&D expenditures in the income statement. In contrast, its balance sheet shows $19 billion in intangible assets were purchased. This amount includes about $15 billion related to acquisitions of other companies and another $4 billion for intangible assets acquired specifically related to marketing, contracts, technology, and entertainment content.

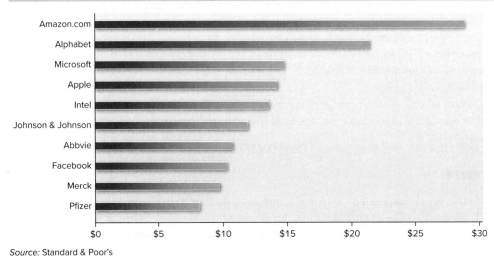

**ILLUSTRATION 7–6**

Companies with the Largest Amount of Research and Development ($ in billions)

*Source:* Standard & Poor's

This illustration is intended to highlight a debate in accounting, which is whether the current accounting standards lead to an understatement of a company's total assets by systematically failing to report certain assets in the balance sheet. Some academics and investors consider this to be a major flaw in the accounting system.[2] Regardless of where you stand in the debate, a good manager or analyst will not ignore value-creating expenditures just because they do not appear in the balance sheet as an asset.

Referring back to the case of Disney discussed at the start of this chapter, the difference in accounting for purchased intangibles versus the accounting for internally developed intangibles explains why Mickey Mouse is not on Disney's balance sheet. Because Mickey Mouse is an internally generated intangible asset, it is not directly placed on the balance sheet as an asset, but rather the costs to develop the Mickey character and brand were expensed as incurred. On the other hand, other purchased intangible assets, including some very noteworthy characters, such as Captain America and Thor, are included as assets (with the official label, "Character/Franchise Intangibles") on the balance sheet with annual amortization on the income statement.

**Advertising.**   A similar argument about the difficulty of estimating benefits in future periods can be made for advertising expenses. Advertising at Apple clearly has made its trademark more valuable. Because we cannot tell what portion of today's advertising benefits future periods and for how many periods it might benefit, advertising costs are not reported as an intangible asset in the balance sheet. Instead, advertising costs are recorded as expenses and are reported in the income statement in the period incurred.

---

[1]A major exception to this rule is for software development costs, which under certain circumstances can be capitalized as an intangible asset and subsequently amortized.

[2]For instance, see Lev & Gu (2016), The End of Accounting and the Path Forward for Investors and Managers, or Govindarajan, Rajgopal, Srivastava, & Enache (2019), It's Time to Stop Treating R&D as a Discretionary Expenditure.

**KEY POINT**

We report purchased intangibles as long-term assets at their purchase price plus all costs necessary to get the asset ready for use. We expense internally generated intangibles, such as R&D and advertising costs, as we incur them.

There are many types of intangible assets, and there is a large variety of ways companies list these assets for reporting purposes. Some of the more common types of intangible assets include:

- *Technology-based* intangible assets such as patents, computer software, and purchased research and development.
- *Customer-related* intangible assets such as customer lists, customer contracts, and customer relationships.
- *Marketing-related* intangible assets such as trademarks, trade names, and internet domain names.
- *Contract-based* intangible assets such as licenses, royalty agreements, and franchises.
- *Artistic-based* intangible assets such as copyrights to books, songs, advertising jingles, pictures, and movies.
- *Goodwill* when one company purchases another company for an amount greater than the fair value of the identifiable net assets of the acquired company.

Let's discuss a few of these intangible assets in more detail.

## PATENTS

A patent is an exclusive right to manufacture a product or to use a process. The U.S. Patent and Trademark Office grants this right for a period of 20 years. **When a firm *purchases* a patent, it records the patent as an intangible asset at its purchase price plus other costs such as legal and filing fees to secure the patent.** Filing fees include items such as the fee to register a patent with the U.S. Patent and Trademark Office.

In contrast, when a firm engages in its own research activities to develop a new product or process, it expenses those costs as it incurs them. For example, major pharmaceutical companies like **Amgen** and **Gilead Sciences** spend over a billion dollars each year developing new drugs. Most of these research and development costs are reported as operating expenses in the income statement.[3]

Let's look at an example of purchased versus internally developed patents in Illustration 7–7. Suppose a company obtains two patents during the year. Patent #1 was purchased from another company for $200,000, while Patent #2 was developed internally at a cost of $200,000 (cost of salaries, supplies, equipment, and facilities). Both patents had legal and filing fees of $40,000 and $5,000, respectively. While these two situations may seem similar, Patent #1 will result in an intangible asset being reported for $245,000, while only the legal and filing fees would be reported as an intangible asset for Patent #2. All internal costs for research and development would be expensed immediately.

**ILLUSTRATION 7–7**

Computation of the Capitalized Cost of Patent

|  | Patent #1 (*externally* purchased) | Patent #2 (*internally* developed) |
|---|---|---|
| Cash expenditures | $200,000 | $200,000 |
| Legal fees | 40,000 | 40,000 |
| Filing fees | 5,000 | 5,000 |
| Patent (intangible asset) | $245,000 | $ 45,000 |
| Research and development expense |  | $200,000 |

[3]An exception to this rule is legal fees. The firm will report in the Patent asset account the legal and filing fees to secure a patent, even if it developed the patented item or process internally.

## COPYRIGHTS

A copyright is an exclusive right of protection given by the U.S. Copyright Office to the creator of a published work such as a song, film, painting, photograph, book, or computer software. Copyrights are protected by law and give the creator (and heirs) the exclusive right to reproduce and sell the artistic or published work for the life of the creator plus 70 years. A copyright also allows the copyright holder to pursue legal action against anyone who attempts to infringe the copyright. Accounting for the costs of copyrights is virtually identical to that of patents.

## TRADEMARKS

A trademark, like the name **Apple**, is a word, slogan, or symbol that distinctively identifies a company, product, or service. The firm can register its trademark with the U.S. Patent and Trademark Office to protect it from use by others for a period of 10 years. The registration can be renewed for an indefinite number of 10-year periods, so a trademark is an example of an intangible asset whose useful life can be indefinite.

Grzegorz Czapski/Shutterstock

Firms often acquire trademarks through acquisition. As an example, in 2017, luxury retailer, **Michael Kors**, bought another luxury retailer, **Jimmy Choo**. As part of the deal, the trademarks related to the Jimmy Choo brand were included in the acquisition.[4]

## FRANCHISES

**Subway**, **McDonald's**, and **Starbucks** are three of the world's largest franchises. Many popular retail businesses such as restaurants, auto dealerships, and hotels are set up as franchises. These are local outlets that pay for the exclusive right to use the franchisor company's name and to sell its products within a specified geographical area. Many franchisors provide other benefits to the franchisee, such as participating in the construction of the retail outlet, training employees, and purchasing national advertising.

To report the cost of a franchise, the franchisee records the initial fee as an intangible asset. Additional periodic payments to the franchisor usually are for services the franchisor provides on a continuing basis, and the franchisee will expense them as incurred.

## GOODWILL

Goodwill often is the largest (and the most unique) intangible asset in the balance sheet. **It is reported *only* when one company acquires another company.** Goodwill is reported by the acquiring company for the amount that the purchase price exceeds the fair value of the acquired company's identifiable net assets.

Let's look at a real-world example of the computation of goodwill. We will use the example of Michael Kors' acquisition of Jimmy Choo. Kors paid $1.447 billion for Choo, which had identifiable assets and liabilities shown in Illustration 7–8 ($ in millions).

**ILLUSTRATION 7–8**

Identifiable Assets and Liabilities for Jimmy Choo ($ in millions)

| Fair value of assets | | | Fair value of liabilities | | |
|---|---|---|---|---|---|
| Cash | $ | 34 | Accounts Payable | $ | 129 |
| Accounts Receivable | | 31 | Other Liabilities | | 262 |
| Inventory | | 126 | | | |
| Property | | 51 | | | |
| Jimmy Choo Brand | | 578 | | | |
| Customer Relationships | | 213 | | | |
| Other Assets | | 120 | | | |
| Total fair value of assets | | $1,153 | Total fair value of liabilities | | $391 |

In this example, Jimmy Choo has *identifiable* net assets of $762 million (= $1,153 − $391). Some of Jimmy Choo's identifiable assets are tangible (inventory, property) and others are intangible (Jimmy Choo brand, customer relationships).

---

[4]As with patents, the legal fees to develop and defend trademarks can be capitalized as an asset.

As you can see, Michael Kors paid a large premium for Jimmy Choo, as the purchase price of $1.447 billion far exceeds the value of Jimmy Choo's identifiable net assets. To justify this premium, Michael Kors must believe that there are other *unidentified* assets that justify the purchase price in excess of the value of the *identifiable* assets. Indeed, Michael Kors states in its subsequent annual report that "this combination will further strengthen its future growth opportunities while also increasing both product and geographic diversification and will allow it to grow its international presence through the formation of a global fashion luxury group, bringing together industry-leading luxury fashion brands." The other unidentified assets (in this case: growth opportunities, diversification, international presence) are recorded in the accounting system under goodwill, which amounts to **$685** million. The computation of goodwill for this transaction is shown in Illustration 7–9 ($ in millions).

**ILLUSTRATION 7–9**

**Goodwill for Michael Kors' Acquisition of Jimmy Choo ($ in millions)**

| | | |
|---|---:|---:|
| Purchase price | | $1,447 |
| Less: | | |
| Total Assets (at fair value) | $1,153 | |
| Less: Total Liabilities (at fair value) | 391 | |
| Equals: Fair value of identifiable net assets | | 762 |
| **Goodwill** | | **$ 685** |

As a result of the acquisition, Michael Kors will effectively place all of Jimmy Choo's assets and liabilities in its own balance sheet. Here is a summary of the financial statement effects of this acquisition for Michael Kors (the acquirer):

**Balance Sheet**

| Assets | | = | Liabilities | + | Common Stock | + | Retained Earnings |
|---|---|---|---|---|---|---|---|
| +34 | Cash* | | +129 Accts. Pay. | | | | |
| +31 | Accts. Rec. | | +262 Other Liab. | | | | |
| +126 | Inventory | | | | | | |
| +51 | Property | | | | | | |
| +578 | Jimmy Choo | | | | | | |
| +213 | Cust. Rel. | | | | | | |
| +120 | Other Assets | | | | | | |
| +685 | Goodwill | | | | | | |
| −1,447 | Cash | | | | | | |

Stockholders' Equity

**Income Statement**

| Revenues | − | Expenses | = | Net Income |
|---|---|---|---|---|
| | | No effect | | |

*represents acquired cash

**DEBITS & CREDITS**

Michael Kors would record the acquisition of the net assets of Jimmy Choo as follows:

| | Debit | Credit |
|---|---:|---:|
| **Cash** (acquired) | 34 | |
| **Accounts Receivable** | 31 | |
| **Inventory** | 126 | |
| **Property** | 51 | |
| **Jimmy Choo Brand** | 578 | |
| **Customer Relationships** | 213 | |
| **Other Assets** | 120 | |
| **Goodwill** | 685 | |
| **Accounts Payable** | | 129 |
| **Other Liabilities** | | 262 |
| **Cash** (purchase price) | | 1,447 |

Most companies also create goodwill to some extent through advertising, employee train-ing, and other efforts. However, as it does for other internally generated intangibles, a com-pany must *expense* costs incurred in the internal generation of goodwill. Imagine how difficult it would be to estimate the amount and future benefits of internally generated goodwill. Due to this difficulty, we report goodwill only when it is part of the acquisition of another business.

In Illustration 7–10, the companies with the largest amounts of intangible assets are presented.

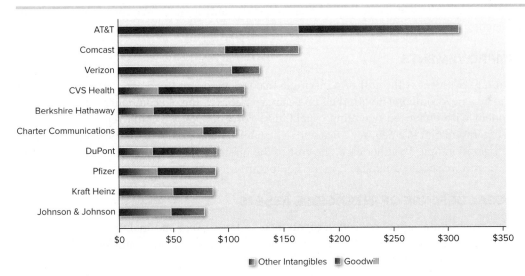

**ILLUSTRATION 7–10**

**Companies with the Largest Amount of Intangible Assets ($ in billions)**

These are large household name companies, such as **AT&T** and **DuPont**, and they have billions of dollars of total intangible assets, which include things like patents, copyrights, customer lists, and goodwill. What is apparent from this figure is that a large portion of their total intangible assets is made up of goodwill. This indicates that these companies have made numerous acquisitions over the years, which leads to a large amount of goodwill included on their balance sheet.

 **KEY POINT**

Intangible assets have no physical substance and generally represent exclusive rights that pro-vide benefits to owners. Common types include patents, copyrights, trademarks, franchises, and goodwill.

## Expenditures after Acquisition

Over the life of a long-term asset, the owners often incur additional expenditures associated with the asset. We can do one of two things with these additional expenditures:

**■ LO7–3**
Describe the accounting treatment of expenditures after acquisition.

1. We **capitalize** an expenditure as an asset if it increases **future** benefits.
2. We **expense** an expenditure if it benefits only the **current** period.

To see the choice more clearly, let's look at different types of expenditures: repairs and maintenance, additions, and improvements.

### REPAIRS AND MAINTENANCE

The cost of an engine tune-up, oil change, or repair of a minor engine part for a delivery truck allows the truck to continue its productive activity in the *current* period. We expense repairs and maintenance expenditures like these in the period incurred because they main-tain a given level of benefits. They also are likely to recur again in the following period. More extensive repairs that increase the *future* benefits of the delivery truck would be capitalized as assets. These include major repairs that are unlikely to recur each period, such as a new transmission or an engine overhaul.

### ADDITIONS

An addition occurs when we add a new major component to an existing asset. We should capitalize the cost of additions if they increase, rather than maintain, the future benefits from the expenditure. For example, adding a refrigeration unit to a delivery truck increases the capability of the truck beyond that originally anticipated, thus increasing its future benefits.

### IMPROVEMENTS

An improvement is the cost of replacing a major component of an asset. The replacement can be a new component with the same characteristics as the old component or a new component with enhanced operating capabilities. For example, we could replace an existing refrigeration unit in a delivery truck with a new but similar unit or with a new and improved refrigeration unit. In either case, the cost of the improvement usually increases future benefits, and we should capitalize it to the Equipment account.

### LEGAL DEFENSE OF INTANGIBLE ASSETS

The expenditures after acquisition mentioned so far—repairs and maintenance, additions, and improvements—generally relate to property, plant, and equipment. Intangible assets, though, also can require expenditures after their acquisition, the most frequent being the cost of legally defending the right that gives the asset its value. For example, **Apple** spends millions of dollars every year defending its patents related to the iPhone and other products. The costs of successfully defending a patent, including attorneys' fees, are added to the Patent account. However, if the defense of an intangible right is unsuccessful, then the firm should expense the litigation costs as incurred because they provide no future benefit.

Illustration 7–11 provides a summary of expenditures after acquisition.

**ILLUSTRATION 7–11**

Expenditures after Acquisition

| Type of Expenditure | Definition | Period Benefited | Usual Accounting Treatment |
|---|---|---|---|
| Repairs and maintenance | Maintaining a given level of benefits | Current | **Expense** |
| Repairs and maintenance | Making major repairs that increase future benefits | Future | **Capitalize** |
| Additions | Adding a new major component | Future | **Capitalize** |
| Improvements | Replacing a major component | Future | **Capitalize** |
| Legal defense of intangible assets | Incurring litigation costs to defend the legal right to the asset | Future | **Capitalize** (Expense if defense is unsuccessful) |

 **KEY POINT**

We capitalize (report as an asset) expenditures that benefit *future* periods. We expense items that benefit only the *current* period.

**Let's Review**

Lincoln Driving Academy purchased a pre-owned car for its driver's education program. Lincoln incurred the following expenses related to the car.

1. Replaced the car's transmission at a cost of $4,100. The repairs are considered extensive and increase future benefits.
2. Installed a passenger side brake to be used by the instructor, if necessary, at a cost of $1,100.
3. Paid the annual registration fees of $185.
4. Changed the oil and had an engine tune-up at a cost of $350.
5. Overhauled the engine at a cost of $2,200, increasing the service life of the car by an estimated four years.

**Required:**

Indicate whether Lincoln should capitalize or expense each of these expenditures. How could Lincoln fraudulently use expenditures like these to increase reported earnings?

**Solution:**

1. Capitalize. It benefits future periods.
2. Capitalize. It benefits future periods.
3. Expense. It benefits only the current period.
4. Expense. It benefits only the current period.
5. Capitalize. It benefits future periods.

Lincoln could increase reported earnings by improperly reporting expenses as assets. For example, Lincoln could report maintenance and repair expense (like item 4) as part of the equipment asset account. This would lower expenses and increase earnings reported in the current year.

# ASSET DEPRECIATION, AMORTIZATION, AND DISPOSAL

**PART B**

When people talk about a car depreciating, they usually are talking about how much the value of the car has decreased. Depreciation in accounting, though, is different. The primary dictionary definition of depreciation differs from the definition of depreciation used in accounting:

> **Dictionary definition** = Decrease in value (or selling price) of an asset.
> **Accounting definition** = Allocation of an asset's cost to an expense over time.

If depreciation were calculated based on the dictionary definition, we would need to estimate the value of every long-term asset each period. Due to the difficulty and subjectivity involved, long-term assets are not adjusted to fair value each period. Rather, long-term assets are recorded at their cost, and then this cost is allocated to expense over time. We use the term *depreciation* to describe that process when it applies to property, plant, and equipment. For intangible assets, the cost allocation process is called *amortization*.

## Depreciation of Property, Plant, and Equipment

Depreciation in accounting is allocating the cost of an asset to an expense over its service life. An asset provides benefits (revenues) to a company in future periods. We allocate a portion of the asset's cost to depreciation expense in each year the asset provides a benefit. If the asset will provide benefits to the company for four years, for example, then we allocate a portion of the asset's cost to depreciation expense in each year for four years. Illustration 7–12 portrays this concept of depreciating an asset's original purchase cost over the periods benefited.

■ **LO7–4**

Calculate depreciation of property, plant, and equipment.

**ILLUSTRATION 7–12**

Depreciation of Long-Term Assets

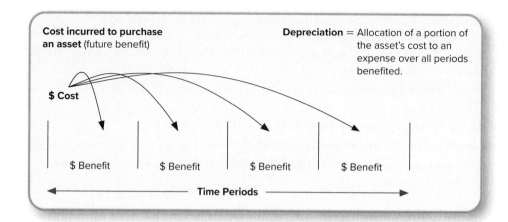

### COMMON MISTAKE

Students sometimes mistake accounting depreciation as recording the decrease in value of an asset. Depreciation in accounting is *not* a valuation process. Rather, depreciation in accounting is an allocation of an asset's cost to expense over time.

To illustrate, let's assume the local **Starbucks** pays $1,200 for equipment—say, an espresso machine. The machine is expected to have a service life of four years.

Annual depreciation on this asset will equal $300 (=$1,200 ÷ 4 years). How does this annual depreciation of $300 affect the financial statements? Total assets in the balance sheet are reduced (via Accumulated Depreciation) and net income in the income statement is reduced (via Depreciation Expense).

| Balance Sheet | | | | | Income Statement | | |
|---|---|---|---|---|---|---|---|
| | | | **Stockholders' Equity** | | | | |
| | | | Common | Retained | | | **Net** |
| **Assets** | = | **Liabilities** + | **Stock** | + **Earnings** | **Revenues** | − **Expenses** | = **Income** |
| −300 | | | | −300 | | +300 | −300 |
| Equipment, net | | | | | | Depreciation | |
| | | | | | | Expense | |

Depreciation
Expense

| 300 | |
|---|---|

Accumulated
Depreciation

| | 300 |
|---|---|

### DEBITS & CREDITS

We record the annual depreciation on the equipment as:

| | Debit | Credit |
|---|---|---|
| **Depreciation Expense**................................................................ | **300** | |
| **Accumulated Depreciation**......................................................... | | **300** |

Pay attention to several important insights. First, notice that depreciation does not affect the Cash account–it's a noncash expense. Second, notice that the balance of "Equipment, net" declines in the balance sheet. This reduction happens through an increase in **Accumulated Depreciation**, which is a contra asset account (meaning that its balance is netted with a related asset account). Rather than reduce the balance of the Equipment account directly, we instead increase its contra account and then report the net amount of Equipment minus Accumulated Depreciation in the balance sheet. The name Accumulated Depreciation comes from the fact that the depreciation we report each period *accumulates* in the account.

After one year, for instance, we have

| | |
|---|---|
| Equipment (cost) | $1,200 |
| Less: Accumulated depreciation ($300 × 1 year) | (300) |
| = Book value | $ 900 |

**Book value**, also referred to as carrying value, equals the original cost of the asset minus the current balance in Accumulated Depreciation. Note that by increasing accumulated depreciation each period, we are reducing the book value of equipment. The Accumulated Depreciation account allows us to reduce the book value of assets through depreciation, while maintaining the original cost of each asset in the accounting records.

After two years, we have

| | |
|---|---|
| Equipment (cost) | $1,200 |
| Less: Accumulated depreciation ($300 × 2 years) | (600) |
| = Book value | $ 600 |

Each year the Accumulated Depreciation account increases by $300, and the book value decreases by $300. By the end of the fourth year, Accumulated Depreciation will be $1,200 and the book value will be $0.

**KEY POINT**

Depreciation refers to the allocation of the asset's original cost to an expense during the periods benefited. Depreciation does *not* refer to the change in value or selling price.

Recording depreciation requires accountants to establish three factors at the time the asset is put into use:

1. **Service life** (or useful life)—The estimated use the company expects to receive from the asset before disposing of it.
2. **Residual value** (or salvage value)—The amount the company expects to receive from selling the asset at the end of its service life.
3. **Depreciation method**—The pattern in which the asset's depreciable cost (original cost minus residual value) is allocated over time.

**Service Life.** We can measure service life in units of time or in units of activity. For example, the estimated service life of a delivery truck might be either five years or 100,000 miles. Different asset types have very different estimated service lives. For instance, **Alaska Airlines** reports an estimated service life for certain airplanes of between 20 and 25 years, while it reports an estimated service life for computer hardware of up to 10 years. We use the terms service life and useful life interchangeably because both terms are used in practice.

**Residual Value.** At the end of an asset's useful life, a company may sell or trade the asset for a new one. The residual value is the selling price or the trade-in value of the asset. A company might estimate residual value from prior experience or by researching the resale values of similar types of assets. Due to the difficulty in estimating residual value, it's not uncommon to assume a residual value of zero.

**Depreciation Method.** In determining how much of an asset's cost to allocate to each year, a company should choose a depreciation method that corresponds to the pattern of benefits received from using the asset. The most common depreciation method used (by far) in practice is straight-line, followed by declining-balance and activity-based.[5]

---

[5]Some introductory financial accounting textbooks illustrate a fourth depreciation method called *sum-of-the-years'-digits*. However, use of this method has decreased dramatically over the years to the point that this method is now rarely seen in actual practice. A recent survey of depreciation methods used by large public companies is provided in Illustration 7–24.

1. **Straight-line.** This method allocates an equal amount of depreciation to each year. The implication is that the asset is used evenly over its service life. This method is by far the simplest and most common depreciation method used in financial accounting.

2. **Declining-balance.** This method is an accelerated method, meaning that more depreciation expense is taken in the earlier years than in the later years of an asset's life. The U.S. Internal Revenue Service (IRS) requires that all companies use a declining-balance depreciation method for tax purposes.

3. **Activity-based.** This method calculates depreciation based on the activity associated with the asset. For example, a vehicle can be depreciated based on the miles driven, or a machine can be depreciated based on the hours used. The method is commonly used to allocate the cost of natural resources.

The concepts of historical cost, service life and depreciation method are illustrated in a recent footnote provided by **Disney** (Illustration 7–13), as they discussed the depreciation of its theme parks and resorts:

**ILLUSTRATION 7–13**

Excerpt from Disney's Annual Report

> **DISNEY**
> **Notes to the Financial Statements (excerpt)**
>
> Parks, resorts and other property are carried at historical cost. Depreciation is computed on the straight-line method, generally over estimated useful lives as follows:
>
> | | |
> |---|---|
> | Attractions, buildings and improvements | 20 – 40 years |
> | Furniture, fixtures and equipment | 3 – 25 years |
> | Land improvements | 20 – 40 years |

Let's illustrate each of the three methods using the same business situation: Little King Sandwiches, a local submarine sandwich restaurant, purchased a new delivery truck. The specific details of that purchase are described in Illustration 7–14.

**ILLUSTRATION 7–14**

Data to Illustrate Depreciation Methods

| | |
|---|---|
| Cost of the new truck | $40,000 |
| Estimated residual value | $5,000 |
| Estimated service life | 5 years or 100,000 miles |

## STRAIGHT-LINE DEPRECIATION

By far the most easily understood and widely used depreciation method is straight-line. With the straight-line method, we allocate an *equal* amount of the depreciable cost to each year of the asset's service life. The *depreciable cost* is the asset's cost minus its estimated residual value. Depreciable cost represents the total depreciation to be taken over the asset's service life. To calculate depreciation expense for a given year, we simply divide the depreciable cost by the number of years in the asset's life, as shown in Illustration 7–15.

**ILLUSTRATION 7–15**

Formula for Straight-Line Depreciation

$$\text{Depreciation expense} = \frac{\text{Asset's cost} - \text{Residual value}}{\text{Service life}} = \frac{\text{Depreciable cost}}{\text{Service life}}$$

$$\text{Depreciation expense} = \frac{\$40,000 - \$5,000}{5 \text{ years}} = \$7,000 \text{ per year}$$

Note that dividing the depreciable cost each year by five is the same as multiplying the depreciable cost each year by 20% ($1/5 = 0.20$).

Illustration 7–16 provides a depreciation schedule for the delivery truck using the straight-line method. Notice that the asset is depreciated until its book value equals the residual value ($5,000). **The residual value is never depreciated.**

ILLUSTRATION 7–16

Straight-Line
Depreciation Schedule

| | **Calculation** | | | | **End-of-Year Amounts** | |
|---|---|---|---|---|---|---|
| **Year** | **Depreciable Cost** | × | **Depreciation Rate** | = | **Depreciation Expense** | **Accumulated Depreciation** | **Book Value*** |

**LITTLE KING SANDWICHES**
**Depreciation Schedule—Straight-Line**

| Year | Depreciable Cost | × | Depreciation Rate | = | Depreciation Expense | Accumulated Depreciation | Book Value* |
|---|---|---|---|---|---|---|---|
| | | | | | | | $40,000 |
| 1 | $35,000 | | 0.20 | | $ 7,000 | $ 7,000 | 33,000 |
| 2 | 35,000 | | 0.20 | | 7,000 | 14,000 | 26,000 |
| 3 | 35,000 | | 0.20 | | 7,000 | 21,000 | 19,000 |
| 4 | 35,000 | | 0.20 | | 7,000 | 28,000 | 12,000 |
| 5 | 35,000 | | 0.20 | | 7,000 | 35,000 | **5,000** |
| Total | | | | | **$35,000** | | |

*Book value is the original cost of the asset ($40,000) minus accumulated depreciation. Book value of $33,000 at the end of year 1, for example, is $40,000 minus $7,000 in accumulated depreciation.

**Partial-Year Depreciation.** In the example above, we assumed Little King Sandwiches bought the truck *at the beginning of Year 1.* What if the company bought the truck *partially through Year 1?* In this case, the truck should be depreciated only for the portion of Year 1 it was used. For example, if Little King bought the truck on November 1 and its year-end is December 31, depreciation in Year 1 is calculated for only two of the 12 months. This calculation is shown in Illustration 7–17. Notice that we depreciate the truck in Year 1 for only 2/12 of the full-year amount because we've used the truck for only 2/12 of the year.

ILLUSTRATION 7–17

Partial-Year Straight-Line Depreciation

| | **Calculation** | | | | **End-of-Year Amounts** | |
|---|---|---|---|---|---|---|
| **Year** | **Depreciable Cost** | × | **Depreciation Rate*** | = | **Depreciation Expense** | **Accumulated Depreciation** | **Book Value*** |
| | | | | | | | $40,000 |
| 1 | $35,000 | | 0.20 × 2/12 | | $ 1,167 | $ 1,167 | 38,833 |
| 2 | 35,000 | | 0.20 | | 7,000 | 8,167 | 31,833 |
| 3 | 35,000 | | 0.20 | | 7,000 | 15,167 | 24,833 |
| 4 | 35,000 | | 0.20 | | 7,000 | 22,167 | 17,833 |
| 5 | 35,000 | | 0.20 | | 7,000 | 29,167 | 10,833 |
| 6 | 35,000 | | 0.20 × 10/12 | | 5,833 | 35,000 | **5,000** |
| Total | | | | | **$35,000** | | |

*Depreciation in Year 1 assumes the asset is purchased on November 1. The asset is depreciated using the straight-line method, assuming a five-year service life and residual value of $5,000.

Depreciation for the second, third, fourth, and fifth years is for the full-year amount. The partial-year depreciation for the first year doesn't affect depreciation in those subsequent years because the truck is utilized for those entire years.

The truck's five-year service life will extend to Year 6. Since the company depreciated the truck for only two months in Year 1, the final 10 months of depreciation will occur in Year 6. The amount of depreciation expense in Year 6 is 10/12 of the full-year amount. By the end of Year 6, the truck has been fully depreciated (from its original cost of $40,000 down to its residual value of $5,000).

You can determine partial year depreciation for any month. If an asset is purchased at the beginning of April (nine months until the year end), its first year of annual depreciation will be multiplied by 9/12, and its final year of annual depreciation will be multiplied by 3/12.

**COMMON MISTAKE**

Many students think March 1 to the end of the year is nine months because December is the twelfth month and March is the third month. March 1 to the end of the year is actually ten months; it is every month except January and February.

**Land.**    We report depreciation for land improvements, buildings, and equipment, but we *don't* report depreciation for land. Unlike other long-term assets, land is not "used up" over time.

**COMMON MISTAKE**

Some students mistakenly depreciate land because it's part of property, plant, and equipment. Land is *property*, but it is *not* depreciated because its service life never ends.

**Change in Depreciation Estimate.**    Depreciation is an *estimate*. Remember the amount of depreciation allocated to each period is based on management's estimates of service life and of residual value—as well as the depreciation method chosen. Management needs to periodically review these estimates. If a change in estimate is required, the company changes depreciation in current and future years, but not in prior periods.

For example, assume that after three years, Little King Sandwiches estimates the remaining service life of the delivery truck to be four more years, for a total service life of seven years rather than the original five. At this time, Little King also changes the estimated residual value to $3,000 from the original estimate of $5,000. How much should Little King report each year for depreciation in years 4 to 7? Take the book value at the end of year 3 ($19,000), subtract the new estimated residual value ($3,000), and then divide by the new remaining service life (four more years). Little King Sandwiches will report depreciation in years 4 to 7 as $4,000 per year. Illustration 7–18 shows the calculations.

**ILLUSTRATION 7–18**

**Change in Depreciation Estimate**

| | |
|---|---:|
| Book value, end of year 3 | $19,000 |
| − New residual value | (3,000) |
| New depreciable cost | 16,000 |
| ÷ New remaining service life | 4 |
| Annual depreciation in years 4 to 7 | $  4,000 |

Notice that Little King Sandwiches makes all the changes in years 4 to 7. The company does not go back and change the calculations for depreciation already reported during the first three years.

**ETHICAL DILEMMA**

Caiaimage/Glow Images

James Wright is the chief financial officer (CFO) for The Butcher Block, a major steakhouse restaurant chain. As CFO, James has the final responsibility for all aspects of financial reporting. James tells investors that The Butcher Block should post earnings of at least $1 million.

In examining the preliminary year-end numbers, James notices that earnings are coming in at $950,000. He also is aware that The Butcher Block has been depreciating most of its restaurant equipment over a five-year service life. He proposes to change the estimated service life for a subset of the equipment to a service life of seven years rather than five. By depreciating over a longer service life, depreciation expense will be lower in the current year, increasing earnings to just over $1 million. It looks like The Butcher Block is going to exceed earnings of $1 million after all.

Do you think James Wright's change in the depreciable life of assets is ethical? What concerns might you have?

Straight-line depreciation assumes that the benefits we derive from the use of an asset are the same each year. In some situations, it might be more reasonable to assume that the asset will provide greater benefits in the earlier years of its life than in the later years. In these cases, we achieve a better matching of depreciation with revenues by using an accelerated depreciation method, with higher depreciation in the earlier years of the asset's life and lower depreciation in later years. We look at one such method next.

## DECLINING-BALANCE DEPRECIATION

The declining-balance method is an accelerated depreciation method. Declining-balance depreciation will be higher than straight-line depreciation in earlier years, but lower in later years. **However, both declining-balance and straight-line will result in the same total depreciation over the asset's service life.** No matter what allocation method we use, total depreciation over the asset's service life will be equal to the depreciable cost (asset cost minus residual value).

The depreciation rate we use under the declining-balance method is a multiple of the straight-line rate, such as 125%, 150%, or 200% of the straight-line rate. The most common declining-balance rate is 200%, which we refer to as the *double*-declining-balance method since the rate is double the straight-line rate. In our illustration for Little King Sandwiches, the double-declining-balance rate would be 40% (double the straight-line rate of 20%). Illustration 7–19 provides a depreciation schedule using the double-declining-balance method.

**ILLUSTRATION 7–19**

Double-Declining-Balance Depreciation Schedule

| | **LITTLE KING SANDWICHES** Depreciation Schedule—Double-Declining-Balance | | | | |
|---|---|---|---|---|---|
| | **Calculation** | | | **End-of-Year Amounts** | |
| **Year** | **Beginning Book Value** × | **Depreciation Rate** = | **Depreciation Expense** | **Accumulated Depreciation** | **Book Value*** |
| | | | | | $40,000 |
| 1 | $40,000 | 0.40 | **$16,000** | $16,000 | 24,000 |
| 2 | 24,000 | 0.40 | **9,600** | 25,600 | 14,400 |
| 3 | 14,400 | 0.40 | **5,760** | 31,360 | 8,640 |
| 4 | 8,640 | 0.40 | **3,456** | 34,816 | 5,184 |
| 5 | 5,184 | | **184**** | 35,000 | **5,000** |
| Total | | | **$35,000** | | |

*Book value is the original cost of the asset minus accumulated depreciation. Book value at the end of year 1 is $24,000, equal to the cost of $40,000 minus accumulated depreciation of $16,000. Book value at the end of **year 1** in the last column is equal to book value at the beginning of **year 2** in the second column of the schedule.
**Amount necessary to reduce book value to residual value.

A simple way to get the depreciation rate for double-declining-balance is to divide the number 2 by the estimated service life. In our example of a five-year asset, that would be 2 divided by 5 years, which equals 0.40. The depreciation rate for double-declining-balance depreciation is determined by the following general equation:

$$\text{Double-declining depreciation rate} = 2/\text{Estimated service life}$$

If the service life had been four years instead of five, what depreciation rates would we use under straight-line and under double-declining-balance? The straight-line rate is 1 divided by the four-year service life, or $1/4 = 0.25$. The double-declining-balance rate is 2 divided by the four-year service life, or $2/4 = 0.50$.

Notice two unusual features of declining-balance depreciation.

1. We multiply the depreciation rate by beginning *book value* (cost minus accumulated depreciation), rather than by the depreciable cost (cost minus residual value).

2. In year 5, we do not report depreciation expense for the entire $5,184 times 0.40, because doing so would cause the book value to fall below the expected residual value. Instead, depreciation expense in the final year is the amount that reduces book value to the estimated residual value (book value beginning of year, $5,184, minus estimated residual value, $5,000, = $184).

If the estimated residual value is high enough, the asset will reach its residual value in fewer years than its expected service life. For instance, if the estimated residual value had been $10,000 rather than $5,000, the delivery truck would be fully depreciated under the double-declining-balance method in only three years, even though we used a five-year life in determining the depreciation rate.

 **COMMON MISTAKE**

When using the declining-balance method, mistakes are commonly made in the first and last year of the calculation. In the first year, students sometimes calculate depreciation incorrectly as cost minus residual value times the depreciation rate. The correct way in the first year is to simply multiply cost times the depreciation rate. In the final year, some students incorrectly calculate depreciation expense in the same manner as in earlier years, multiplying book value by the depreciation rate. However, under the declining-balance method, depreciation expense in the final year is the amount necessary to reduce book value down to residual value.

## ACTIVITY-BASED DEPRECIATION

*Common Terms*
Activity-based depreciation is also called *units of production* or *units of output*.

Straight-line and declining-balance methods measure depreciation based on time. In an activity-based method, we instead allocate an asset's cost based on its *use*. For example, we could measure the service life of a machine in terms of its output (units, pounds, barrels). This method also works for vehicles such as our delivery truck, whose use we measure in miles.

We first compute the average *depreciation rate per unit* by dividing the depreciable cost (cost minus residual value) by the number of units expected to be produced. In our illustration, the depreciation rate is $0.35 per mile, calculated as shown in Illustration 7–20.

**ILLUSTRATION 7–20**

**Formula for Activity-Based Depreciation**

$$\text{Depreciation rate per unit} = \frac{\text{Depreciable cost}}{\text{Total units expected to be produced}}$$

$$\text{Depreciation rate} = \frac{\$40,000 - \$5,000}{100,000 \text{ expected miles}} = \$0.35 \text{ per mile}$$

To calculate the depreciation expense for the reporting period, we then multiply the per unit rate by the number of units of activity each period. Illustration 7–21 shows a depreciation schedule using the activity-based method. The actual miles driven in years 1 to 5 were 30,000, 22,000, 15,000, 20,000, and 13,000. Notice that the activity-based method is very similar to the straight-line method, except that rather than dividing the depreciable cost by the service life in years, we divide it by the service life in expected miles.

**ILLUSTRATION 7–21**

**Activity-Based Depreciation Schedule**

| | | | Calculation | | | End-of-Year Amounts | |
|---|---|---|---|---|---|---|---|
| Year | Miles Driven | × | Depreciation Rate | = | Depreciation Expense | Accumulated Depreciation | Book Value* |
| | | | | | | | $40,000 |
| 1 | 30,000 | | $0.35 | | **$10,500** | $10,500 | 29,500 |
| 2 | 22,000 | | 0.35 | | **7,700** | 18,200 | 21,800 |
| 3 | 15,000 | | 0.35 | | **5,250** | 23,450 | 16,550 |
| 4 | 20,000 | | 0.35 | | **7,000** | 30,450 | 9,550 |
| 5 | 13,000 | | 0.35 | | **4,550** | 35,000 | **5,000** |
| Total | | | | | **$35,000** | | |

LITTLE KING SANDWICHES
Depreciation Schedule—Activity-Based

*Book value is the original cost of the asset ($40,000) minus accumulated depreciation. Book value of $29,500 in year 1 is $40,000 minus $10,500 in accumulated depreciation.

In our illustration, the delivery truck is driven exactly 100,000 miles over the five years. What if we drive the delivery truck *less than* 100,000 miles by the end of the fifth year? Then we will continue to depreciate the truck past five years until we reach 100,000 miles. Similarly, if we drive the delivery truck *more than* 100,000 miles by the end of the fifth year, we will stop depreciating the truck at 100,000 miles before the five years are up. In either case, we need to depreciate the asset until the book value (cost minus accumulated depreciation) declines to the estimated residual value.

# Decision Maker's Perspective

## Selecting a Depreciation Method

Assume you are the chief financial officer (CFO) responsible for your company's accounting and reporting policies. Which depreciation method would you choose? Illustration 7–22 compares annual depreciation for the delivery truck under the three alternatives we discussed.

| Year | Straight-Line | Double-Declining-Balance | Activity-Based |
|------|---------------|--------------------------|----------------|
| 1 | $ 7,000 | $16,000 | $10,500 |
| 2 | 7,000 | 9,600 | 7,700 |
| 3 | 7,000 | 5,760 | 5,250 |
| 4 | 7,000 | 3,456 | 7,000 |
| 5 | 7,000 | 184 | 4,550 |
| Total | $35,000 | $35,000 | $35,000 |

**ILLUSTRATION 7–22**

**Comparison of Depreciation Methods**

Comparing methods, we see that all three alternatives result in total depreciation of $35,000 ($40,000 cost minus $5,000 residual value). Straight-line creates an equal amount of depreciation each year. Double-declining-balance creates more depreciation in earlier years and less depreciation in later years. Activity-based depreciation varies depending on the miles driven each year. Illustration 7–23 provides a graph that shows depreciation expense over time for each of these three methods.

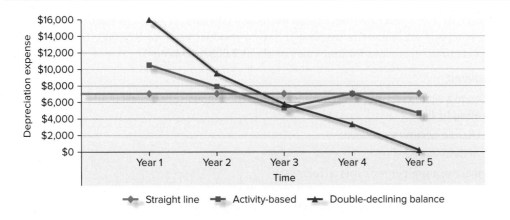

**ILLUSTRATION 7–23**

**Depreciation Expense over Time for Three Depreciation Methods**

Companies are free to choose the depreciation method they believe best reflects the pattern of an asset's use and the revenues it creates. Illustration 7–24 shows a recent survey of depreciation methods used by large public companies.

Why do so many companies use the straight-line method? Many probably believe they realize benefits from their plant assets approximately evenly over these assets' service lives. Certainly, another motivating factor is that straight-line is the easiest method to apply. One more important motivation is straight-line's positive effect on reported income. Straight-line

ILLUSTRATION 7–24

Use of Various
Depreciation Methods

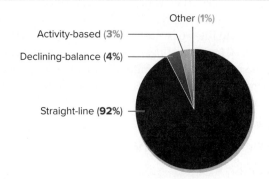

ILLUSTRATION 7–24

Use of Various
Depreciation Methods

produces a higher net income than accelerated methods in the earlier years of an asset's life. Higher net income can improve bonuses paid to management, increase stock prices, and reduce the likelihood of violating debt agreements with lenders.

## TAX DEPRECIATION

Conflicting with the desire to report higher net income is the desire to reduce taxes by *reducing* taxable income. An accelerated method serves this objective by reducing taxable income more in the earlier years of an asset's life than does straight-line. As a result, most companies use the straight-line method for financial reporting and the Internal Revenue Service's prescribed accelerated method (called MACRS[6]) for income tax purposes. Thus, companies report higher net income using straight-line depreciation and lower taxable income using MACRS depreciation. MACRS combines declining-balance methods in earlier years with straight-line in later years to allow for a more advantageous tax depreciation deduction. Congress, not accountants, approved MACRS rules to encourage greater investment in long-term assets by U.S. companies.

 **KEY POINT**

Straight-line, declining-balance, and activity-based depreciation all are acceptable depreciation methods for financial reporting. Most companies use straight-line depreciation for financial reporting and an accelerated method called MACRS for tax reporting.

---

**Let's Review**

University Hero purchases new bread ovens at a cost of $110,000. On the date of purchase, the company estimates the ovens will have a residual value of $20,000. University Hero expects to use the ovens for four years or about 9,000 total hours.

*Required:*

Prepare a depreciation schedule using each of the following methods:
1. Straight-line.
2. Double-declining-balance.
3. Activity-based.

Actual oven use per year was as follows:

| Year | Hours Used |
|------|-----------|
| 1 | 2,200 |
| 2 | 2,600 |
| 3 | 2,300 |
| 4 | 2,100 |
| Total | 9,200 |

---

[6]Modified accelerated cost recovery system.

*Solution:*

1. Straight-line:

**UNIVERSITY HERO**
**Depreciation Schedule—Straight-Line**

| | Calculation | | | | End-of-Year Amounts | |
|---|---|---|---|---|---|---|
| Year | Depreciable Cost | × Depreciation Rate* | = | Depreciation Expense | Accumulated Depreciation | Book Value** |
| 1 | $90,000 | 0.25 | | **$22,500** | $22,500 | $87,500 |
| 2 | 90,000 | 0.25 | | **22,500** | 45,000 | 65,000 |
| 3 | 90,000 | 0.25 | | **22,500** | 67,500 | 42,500 |
| 4 | 90,000 | 0.25 | | **22,500** | 90,000 | **20,000** |
| Total | | | | **$90,000** | | |

*1 ÷ 4 years = 0.25 per year
**$110,000 cost minus accumulated depreciation.

2. Double-declining-balance:

**UNIVERSITY HERO**
**Depreciation Schedule—Double-Declining-Balance**

| | Calculation | | | | End-of-Year Amounts | |
|---|---|---|---|---|---|---|
| Year | Beginning Book Value | × Depreciation Rate* | = | Depreciation Expense | Accumulated Depreciation | Book Value** |
| 1 | $110,000 | 0.50 | | **$55,000** | $55,000 | $55,000 |
| 2 | 55,000 | 0.50 | | **27,500** | 82,500 | 27,500 |
| 3 | 27,500 | 0.50 | | **7,500*** | 90,000 | **20,000** |
| 4 | | | | **0** | 90,000 | **20,000** |
| Total | | | | **$90,000** | | |

*2 ÷ 4 years = 0.50 per year
**$110,000 cost minus accumulated depreciation.
***Amount needed to reduce book value to residual value.

3. Activity-based:

**UNIVERSITY HERO**
**Depreciation Schedule—Activity-Based**

| | Calculation | | | | End-of-Year Amounts | |
|---|---|---|---|---|---|---|
| Year | Hours Used | × Depreciation Rate* | = | Depreciation Expense | Accumulated Depreciation | Book Value** |
| 1 | 2,200 | $10 | | **$22,000** | $22,000 | $88,000 |
| 2 | 2,600 | 10 | | **26,000** | 48,000 | 62,000 |
| 3 | 2,300 | 10 | | **23,000** | 71,000 | 39,000 |
| 4 | 2,100 | | | **19,000*** | 90,000 | **20,000** |
| Total | 9,200 | | | **$90,000** | | |

*$90,000 ÷ 9,000 hours = $10/hour
**$110,000 cost minus accumulated depreciation.
***Amount needed to reduce book value to residual value.

# Amortization of Intangible Assets

Allocating the cost of property, plant, and equipment to expense is called depreciation. Similarly, allocating the cost of *intangible* assets to expense is called amortization. The major challenge in understanding the amortization of intangibles is that some intangible assets are amortized and others are not.

## INTANGIBLE ASSETS SUBJECT TO AMORTIZATION

■ **LO7–5**
Calculate amortization of intangible assets.

Many intangible assets have a finite useful life that we can estimate. The service life of an intangible asset usually is limited by legal, regulatory, or contractual provisions. For example, the legal life of a patent is 20 years. However, the estimated useful life of a patent often is less than 20 years if the benefits are not expected to continue for the patent's entire legal life. The patent for the Apple Watch, for example, is amortized over fewer than 20 years, since new technology will cause the watch to become outdated in a shorter period.

The expected residual value of most intangible assets is zero. This might not be the case, though, if at the end of its useful life to the reporting entity, the asset will benefit another entity. For example, if **Apple** has a commitment from another company to purchase one of its patents at the end of the patent's useful life at a determinable price, we use that price as the patent's residual value.

Companies use *straight-line amortization* for intangibles. Also, many companies report amortization as a direct reduction to the intangible asset account itself rather than to a related contra asset account (Accumulated Amortization). That's the approach illustrated in the chapter and the approach to be used for homework in Connect. However, using a contra account such as Accumulated Amortization is also acceptable in practice.

**Example.**  In early January, Little King Sandwiches acquires from University Hero two intangible assets—a franchise and a patent. The details of the transaction include:

- Purchase price of the franchise is $800,000, and the agreement is for a period of 20 years.
- Purchase price of the patent is $72,000. The original legal life of the patent was 20 years, and there are 12 years remaining. However, due to expected technological obsolescence, the Little King estimates that the useful life of the patent is only 8 more years. Little King uses straight-line amortization for all intangible assets. The company's fiscal year-end is December 31.

Let's first compute the annual amortization expense related to the franchise, calculated as its purchase cost divided by the life of the franchise agreement:

$$\text{Franchise amortization expense} = \$800{,}000 \div 20 \text{ years} = \$40{,}000/\text{year.}$$

Next, let's compute the annual amortization expense related to the patent, calculated as its purchase cost divided by the estimated remaining useful life of the patent:

$$\text{Patent amortization expense} = \$72{,}000 \div 8 \text{ years} = \$9{,}000/\text{year.}$$

The franchise and patent will be amortized for these amounts each year over their useful lives.

How does the amortization of the franchise and patent affect the financial statements? In the income statement, the annual amortization reduces net income. In the balance sheet, Franchises and Patents are reduced by their annual amortization, and retained earnings is

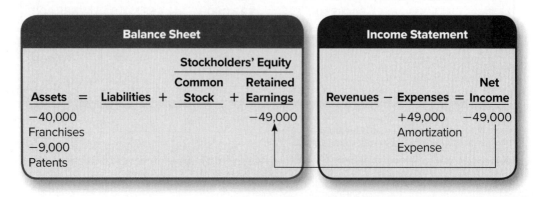

reduced via Amortization Expense in the income statement. The financial statement effects are summarized as follows:

**DEBITS & CREDITS**

Little King records the amortization expense for the franchise and the patent as follows:

| | Debit | Credit |
|---|---|---|
| Amortization Expense ............................................................ | 40,000 | |
|    Franchises.............................................................................. | | 40,000 |
| Amortization Expense ............................................................ | 9,000 | |
|    Patents.................................................................................... | | 9,000 |

Amortization Expense

| 40,000 | |
| 9,000 | |

Franchises

| | 40,000 |

Patents

| | 9,000 |

## INTANGIBLE ASSETS NOT SUBJECT TO AMORTIZATION

We don't depreciate land because it has an unlimited life. Similarly, we do *not* amortize intangible assets with indefinite (unknown or not determinable) useful lives. Illustration 7–25 provides some examples of intangible assets that are amortized and those that are not amortized. An asset's useful life is indefinite if there is no foreseeable limit on the period of time over which we expect it to contribute to the cash flows of the entity. For example, suppose Little King acquired a trademark for its name. Registered trademarks have a legal life of 10 years, but the trademark registration is renewable for an indefinite number of 10-year periods. We consider the life of Little King's trademark for its name to be indefinite, so we don't amortize it.

| Intangible Assets Subject to Amortization (those with finite useful life) | Intangible Assets Not Subject to Amortization (those with indefinite useful life) |
|---|---|
| • Patents | • Goodwill |
| • Computer software | • Trademarks (with indefinite life) |
| • Copyrights | • Domain names (with indefinite life) |
| • Trademarks (with finite life) | • Licenses (with indefinite life) |
| • Domain names (with finite life) | |
| • Franchises | |
| • Licenses (with finite life) | |
| • Royalty agreements | |
| • Customer lists | |

**ILLUSTRATION 7–25**

**Amortization Treatment of Intangible Assets**

Goodwill is the most common intangible asset with an indefinite useful life. Recall that we measure goodwill as the difference between the purchase price of a company and the fair value of all its identifiable net assets (tangible and intangible assets minus the liabilities assumed). Does this mean that goodwill and other intangible assets with indefinite useful lives will remain on a company's balance sheet at their original cost forever? Probably not. **Management must review long-term assets for a potential *impairment* or write-down when events or changes in circumstances indicate the asset's "recoverable amount" is *less than* its "reported amount" in the accounting records.** The recoverable amount is the cash expected to be received from using the asset over its remaining useful life. All long-term assets are subject to these impairment rules, which we discuss in more detail in the appendix to this chapter.

To conclude, let's examine the footnote for **PluralSight**, a cloud company that provides online educational content for corporations and individuals. Illustration 7–26 provides an excerpt of this footnote, in which the company lists its intangible assets, along with their useful lives, carrying amounts, accumulated amortization and book value.

ILLUSTRATION 7–26

Excerpt from
PluralSight's Annual
Report

### PluralSight
### Notes to the Financial Statements (excerpt)

Intangible assets are summarized as follows ($ in thousands):

|  | Remaining Useful Life | Gross Carrying Amount | Accumulated Amortization | Net Book Value |
|---|---|---|---|---|
| Technology | 2.4 | $ 4,500 | $ 2,080 | $2,420 |
| Trademarks | 4.8 | 1,162 | 773 | 389 |
| Noncompetition agreements | 0.8 | 390 | 390 | – |
| Customer relationships | 0.8 | 2,750 | 2,750 | – |
| Database | – | 40 | 40 | – |
| Domain names | Indefinite | 45 | – | 45 |
| Total |  | $ 8,887 | $ 6,033 | $2,854 |

PluralSight lists four intangible assets with a finite remaining useful life: technology, trademarks, noncompetition agreements, and customer relationships. It lists an intangible asset, database, which is fully amortized, resulting in a book value of $0. The final intangible asset it lists, domain names, has an indefinite useful life and is therefore not amortized. In summary, companies have a wide variety of intangible assets like these, and their amortization will depend on whether they have finite or indefinite useful lives—those with finite lives are amortized, those with indefinite lives are not.

### KEY POINT

Amortization is a process, similar to depreciation, in which we allocate the cost of intangible assets over their estimated service lives. Intangible assets with an indefinite useful life (goodwill and most trademarks) are *not* amortized.

## Asset Disposal: Sale, Retirement, or Exchange

■ LO7–6

Account for the disposal of
long-term assets.

In this section, we discuss what to do when we no longer use a long-term asset. Illustration 7–27 shows three different ways an asset can be disposed of. A *sale* is the most common method to dispose of an asset. When a long-term asset is no longer useful but cannot be sold, we have a *retirement*. For example, Little King Sandwiches might physically remove a baking oven that no longer works and also remove it from the accounting records. An *exchange* occurs when two companies trade assets. In an exchange, we often use cash to make up for any difference in fair value between the assets.

ILLUSTRATION 7–27

Three Methods of Asset
Disposal

Sale            Retirement            Exchange

### SALE OF LONG-TERM ASSETS

The sale of a long-term asset typically involves a transaction in which cash is received for the asset given up. The difference between the cash received and the book value of the asset given up is reported as a gain or loss in the income statement.

*Gains increase net income.*

A **gain** occurs when we sell an asset for *more than its book value*. In this case, the cash received is greater than the book value of the asset sold. The amount of the gain equals the net increase in assets. Gains, like revenues, are reported as an increase to net income.

A **loss** occurs when we sell an asset for *less than its book value.* In this case, the cash received is less than the book value of the asset sold. The amount of the loss equals the net decrease in assets. Losses, like expenses, are reported as a decrease to net income.

Remember, book value is the cost of the asset minus accumulated depreciation. In order to have the correct book value, it's important to compute depreciation as of the date of the sale.

 **COMMON MISTAKE** ——————————————

Some students forget to update depreciation prior to reporting the disposal of the asset. Depreciation must be computed up to the date of the sale, retirement, or exchange. Otherwise, the book value will be overstated, and the resulting gain or loss on disposal will be in error as well.

To illustrate the sale of an asset, let's return to our delivery truck example for Little King Sandwiches. Assume Little King uses straight-line depreciation and reports the delivery truck in the Equipment account. The specific details are summarized again in Illustration 7–28.

**ILLUSTRATION 7–28**

**Data to Illustrate Long-Term Asset Disposals**

| | |
|---|---|
| Original cost of the truck | $40,000 |
| Estimated residual value | $5,000 |
| Estimated service life | 5 years |
| Depreciation/year | $7,000 |

Let's play out a couple different scenarios for selling this delivery truck. First, let's assume Little King sells the delivery truck at the end of year 3 for $22,000. Did we have a gain or a loss on the truck's sale? To answer this question requires a bit of arithmetic, as we must first compute the book value of the truck as of the date of sale. Illustration 7–29 shows this calculation.

**ILLUSTRATION 7–29**

**Gain on Sale**

| | | |
|---|---|---|
| Sale amount | | $22,000 |
| Less: | | |
| Original cost of the truck | $40,000 | |
| Less: Accumulated depreciation (3 years × $7,000/year) | (21,000) | |
| Book value at the end of year 3 | | 19,000 |
| **Gain** | | **$ 3,000** |

The sale of the delivery truck will affect both the balance sheet and the income statement. Remember that the truck (equipment) will be removed from the balance sheet at its historical cost, along with all of the accumulated depreciation for that same truck. The cash received upon selling the truck increases assets in the balance sheet, and the gain on sale increases retained earnings through a gain in the income statement. The financial statement effects are summarized as follows:

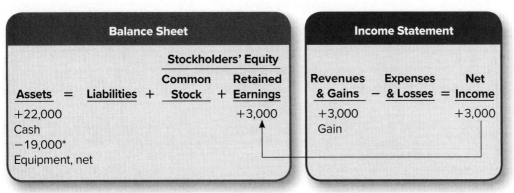

| Balance Sheet | | | | | | Income Statement | | |
|---|---|---|---|---|---|---|---|---|
| | | | **Stockholders' Equity** | | | | | |
| | | | **Common** | **Retained** | | **Revenues** | **Expenses** | **Net** |
| **Assets** | **=** | **Liabilities +** | **Stock** | **+ Earnings** | | **& Gains** | **— & Losses** | **= Income** |
| +22,000 | | | | +3,000 | | +3,000 | | +3,000 |
| Cash | | | | | | Gain | | |
| −19,000* | | | | | | | | |
| Equipment, net | | | | | | | | |

*= 40,000 − 21,000

Cash

| 22,000 | |

Accumulated
Depreciation

| 21,000 | |

Equipment

| | 40,000 |

Gain

| | 3,000 |

---

**DEBITS & CREDITS**

The sale of the delivery truck is recorded as:

| | Debit | Credit |
|---|---|---|
| Cash............................................................................ | 22,000 | |
| Accumulated Depreciation ............................................. | 21,000 | |
|    Equipment............................................................... | | 40,000 |
|    Gain........................................................................ | | 3,000 |

---

 **COMMON MISTAKE**

Students sometimes get confused by the amounts used for equipment ($40,000) and accumulated depreciation ($21,000). The key is to remember that the book value of the asset is equal to its historical cost less its accumulated depreciation. Thus, when we sell the equipment, both the *equipment at its historical cost* and the *accumulated depreciation to date* are removed from the balance sheet.

---

Now, let's change the assumptions a bit. Assume Little King sells the delivery truck at the end of year 3 for only $17,000 (instead of $22,000). Illustration 7–30 shows that this leads to a $2,000 loss on the sale.

**ILLUSTRATION 7–30**

**Loss on Sale**

| | | |
|---|---|---|
| Sale amount | | $17,000 |
| Less: | | |
| Original cost of the truck | $40,000 | |
| Less: Accumulated depreciation (3 years × $7,000/year) | (21,000) | |
|    Book value at the end of year 3 | | 19,000 |
| **Loss** | | **$ (2,000)** |

The financial statement effects of the sale of this equipment at a loss are as follows:

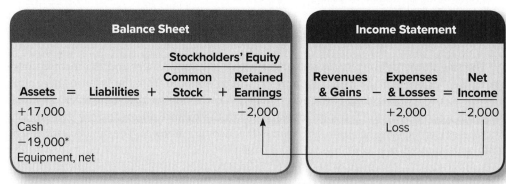

*= 40,000 − 21,000

Cash

| 17,000 | |

Loss

| 2,000 | |

Accumulated
Depreciation

| 21,000 | |

Equipment

| | 40,000 |

---

**DEBITS & CREDITS**

The sale of the delivery truck at a loss is recorded as:

| | Debit | Credit |
|---|---|---|
| Cash........................................................................... | 17,000 | |
| Loss............................................................................ | 2,000 | |
| Accumulated Depreciation ............................................ | 21,000 | |
|    Equipment.............................................................. | | 40,000 |

# Decision Maker's Perspective

## Understanding Gains and Losses

It's tempting to think of a "gain" and "loss" on the sale of a depreciable asset as "good" and "bad" news. For example, we commonly use the term "gain" in everyday language to mean we sold something for more than we bought it. Gain could also be misinterpreted to mean the asset was sold for more than its fair value (we got a "good deal"). However, neither of these represents the meaning of a gain on the sale of assets. Refer back to our example in Illustration 7–29. The sale of the truck resulted in a gain, but the truck was sold for *less than* its original cost, and there is no indication that Little King sold the machine for more than its fair value.

A gain on the sale of a depreciable asset simply means the asset was sold for more than its book value. In other words, the asset received (such as cash) is greater than the book value of the asset that was sold and removed from the accounting records. The net increase in the book value of total assets is an accounting gain (not an economic gain).

The same is true for losses. A loss signifies that the cash received is less than the book value of the asset that was sold; there is a net decrease in the book value of total assets.

## RETIREMENT OF LONG-TERM ASSETS

Now assume that Little King retires the delivery truck instead of selling it. If, for example, the truck is totaled in an accident at the end of year 3, we have a $19,000 loss on retirement as calculated in Illustration 7–31.

| | | |
|---|---:|---:|
| Sale amount | | $ 0 |
| Less: | | |
| Original cost of the truck | $40,000 | |
| Less: Accumulated depreciation (3 years × $7,000/year) | (21,000) | |
| Book value at the end of year 3 | | 19,000 |
| **Loss** | | **$(19,000)** |

**ILLUSTRATION 7–31**

**Loss on Retirement**

The financial statement effects of the retirement of the equipment at a complete loss are as follows:

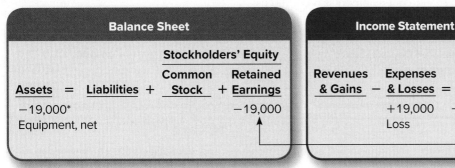

\*= 40,000 − 21,000

**DEBITS & CREDITS**

The loss on retirement is recorded as:

| | Debit | Credit |
|---|---:|---:|
| Loss............................................................................... | **19,000** | |
| **Accumulated Depreciation** ............................................. | **21,000** | |
| **Equipment**................................................................... | | **40,000** |

Loss
| 19,000 |

Accumulated Depreciation
| 21,000 |

Equipment
| 40,000

## EXCHANGE OF LONG-TERM ASSETS

Now assume that Little King exchanges (trades in) the delivery truck at the end of year 3 for a new truck valued at $45,000. The dealership gives Little King a trade-in allowance of $23,000 on the exchange, with the remaining $22,000 paid in cash. We have a $4,000 gain, as calculated in Illustration 7–32.

**ILLUSTRATION 7–32**

**Gain on Exchange**

| | | |
|---|---|---:|
| Trade-in allowance | | $23,000 |
| Less: | | |
| Original cost of the truck | $ 40,000 | |
| Less: Accumulated depreciation (3 years × $7,000/year) | (21,000) | |
| Book value at the end of year 3 | | 19,000 |
| **Gain** | | **$ 4,000** |

The financial statement effects of the trade-in of the equipment are as follows:

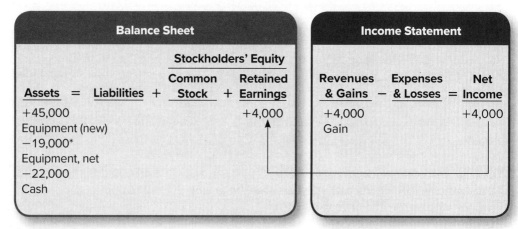

*= 40,000 − 21,000

Equipment

| 45,000 | 40,000 |

Accumulated
Depreciation

| | 21,000 |

Cash

| | 22,000 |

Gain

| | 4,000 |

**DEBITS & CREDITS**

The exchange of equipment is recorded as:

| | Debit | Credit |
|---|---:|---:|
| **Equipment** (new)............................................................. | **45,000** | |
| **Accumulated Depreciation** (old)..................................... | **21,000** | |
| Equipment (old)............................................................. | | 40,000 |
| Cash ................................................................................. | | 22,000 |
| Gain ................................................................................. | | 4,000 |

In summary, the equipment account increases and decreases with the exchange, representing purchase and sale of equipment, respectively. We add equipment (and other property) from the balance sheet at its historical cost. We also remove equipment from the balance sheet at its cost, remembering to also remove the related accumulated depreciation. Finally, the payment reduces the balance of cash, and the gain increases net income.

 **KEY POINT**

If we dispose of an asset for *more* than its book value, we report a gain. If we dispose of an asset for *less* than its book value, we report a loss.

# ASSET ANALYSIS
## Disney vs. Netflix

We have discussed the purchase, depreciation, and disposal of long-term assets. In this final section, we see how to use financial statement information to analyze the profitability of a company's assets. Illustration 7–33 provides selected financial data reported from **Disney** and **Netflix** for use in our analysis. These two companies are close competitors in the entertainment industry and both companies have significant investments in long-term assets.

■ **LO7–7**
Describe the links among return on assets, profit margin, and asset turnover.

**ILLUSTRATION 7–33**

Selected Financial Data for Disney and Netflix

| ($ in millions) | Disney | Netflix |
|---|---|---|
| Net sales | $59,434 | $15,794 |
| Net income | 12,598 | 1,211 |
| Total assets, beginning | 95,789 | 19,012 |
| Total assets, ending | 98,598 | 25,974 |

## RETURN ON ASSETS

Disney had net income of $12.6 billion, and Netflix had net income of $1.2 billion. Since Disney's net income is so much larger, does that imply that Disney is more profitable? In an absolute sense, yes; but in a comparative sense, not necessarily. We need to adjust profitability to make it comparable across different-sized companies. Disney is a much larger company, with about four times the total assets than Netflix has. A more comparable measure of profitability than net income is return on assets, or ROA for short, which equals net income divided by average total assets.

$$\text{Return on assets} = \frac{\text{Net income}}{\text{Average total assets}}$$

The average is calculated as the beginning amount plus the ending amount, divided by 2. Dividing net income by average total assets adjusts net income for differences in company size.

**COMMON MISTAKE**

Students sometimes divide by ending total assets rather than by average total assets. However, there is a good reason to use average total assets in the denominator: to align the *timing* of the numerator and denominator. That is, given that net income (the numerator) is measured over a fiscal period, we want total assets (the denominator) to reflect that same time period, so we use the *average* total assets over that time period. This is the standard approach in ratio analysis: Whenever we divide a number in the income statement by a number in the balance sheet, we use an average balance sheet number in the denominator so that both the numerator and denominator are aligned in time.

The return on assets ratio is calculated for Disney and Netflix in Illustration 7–34.

**ILLUSTRATION 7–34**

Return on Assets for Disney and Netflix

| ($ in millions) | Net Income | ÷ | Average Total Assets | = | Return on Assets |
|---|---|---|---|---|---|
| Disney | $12,598 | ÷ | ($95,789 + $98,598)/2 | = | 13.0% |
| Netflix | $ 1,211 | ÷ | ($19,012 + $25,974)/2 | = | 5.4% |

Return on assets indicates the amount of net income generated for each dollar invested in assets. Disney is generating an impressive ROA of 13.0%, indicating that it generates 13 cents of profit for every dollar of assets. Netflix's ROA of 5.4% indicates that it generates 5.4 cents of profit for every dollar of assets. After adjusting for company size (assets) using ROA, Disney is much more profitable than Netflix.

**Manager Analysis**

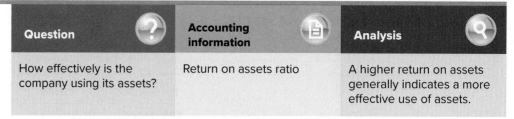

| Question | Accounting information | Analysis |
|---|---|---|
| How effectively is the company using its assets? | Return on assets ratio | A higher return on assets generally indicates a more effective use of assets. |

## PROFIT MARGIN AND ASSET TURNOVER

We can explore profitability further by separating return on assets into two components: profit margin and asset turnover, as shown in Illustration 7–35.

**ILLUSTRATION 7–35**

**Components of Return on Assets**

$$\text{Return on assets} = \text{Profit margin} \times \text{Asset turnover}$$
$$\frac{\text{Net income}}{\text{Average total assets}} = \frac{\text{Net income}}{\text{Net sales}} \times \frac{\text{Net sales}}{\text{Average total assets}}$$

As Illustration 7–35 indicates, profit margin is calculated as net income divided by net sales. This ratio indicates the earnings per dollar of sales. Asset turnover is calculated as net sales divided by average total assets. This ratio measures the sales per dollar of assets invested. In summary, we can break ROA into two components—profit margin and asset turnover—to better understand how a company is able to generate its return on assets.

Illustration 7–36 indicates that Disney's profit margin far exceeds that of Netflix. Disney's profit margin is nearly three times that of Netflix. However, Illustration 7–37 shows

**ILLUSTRATION 7–36**

**Profit Margin for Disney and Netflix**

| ($ in millions) | Net Income | ÷ | Net Sales | = | Profit Margin |
|---|---|---|---|---|---|
| Disney | $12,598 | ÷ | $59,434 | = | 21.2% |
| Netflix | $ 1,211 | ÷ | $15,794 | = | 7.7% |

**ILLUSTRATION 7–37**

**Asset Turnover for Disney and Netflix**

| ($ in millions) | Net Sales | ÷ | Average Total Assets | = | Asset Turnover |
|---|---|---|---|---|---|
| Disney | $59,434 | ÷ | ($95,789 + $98,598)/2 | = | 0.61 times |
| Netflix | $15,794 | ÷ | ($19,012 + $25,974)/2 | = | 0.70 times |

that both companies have similar asset turnover. Thus, Disney's higher return on assets, relative to that of Netflix, is driven by its superior profit margin and not by its ability to more efficiently generate sales from deploying assets.

**Manager Analysis**

| Question | Accounting information | Analysis |
|---|---|---|
| How much profit is being generated from sales? | Profit margin | A higher profit margin indicates a company generates a higher net income per dollar of sales. |
| Is the company effectively generating sales from its assets? | Asset turnover ratio | A higher asset turnover indicates a company generates a higher sales volume per dollar of assets invested. |

**Impact of Estimates on Financial Ratios.**   As noted previously, accounting estimates are necessary in the reporting of long-term assets. For instance, to calculate depreciation, managers must estimate the service life and residual value of an asset. By purposely *overestimating* the service life and/or residual value of an asset, a manager reduces the reported amount of depreciation expense and thereby inflates net income in the earlier years of an asset's life. This causes financial ratios—such as return on assets and profit margin—to create the appearance of better company performance.

**KEY POINT**

Return on assets indicates the amount of net income generated for each dollar invested in assets. Return on assets can be separated to examine two important business strategies: profit margin and asset turnover.

# IMPAIRMENT OF LONG-TERM ASSETS

**APPENDIX**

Depreciation and amortization represent a gradual consumption of the benefits inherent in property, plant, and equipment and intangible assets. Situations can arise, however, that cause a significant decline or impairment of the total benefits or service potential of specific long-term assets. For example, if a retail chain closed several stores and no longer used them in operations, the buildings and equipment may be subject to impairment. **Michael Kors**, designer of luxury accessories, recently reported impairment charges of $198 million related to the closing of selected stores.

■ **LO7–8**
Identify impairment situations and describe the two-step impairment process.

When operating conditions suggest a potential reduction in an asset's benefit or service potential, management must review the asset for impairment. Impairment occurs when the expected future cash flows (expected future benefits) generated for a long-term asset fall below its book value (original cost minus accumulated depreciation).

Reporting for impairment losses is a two-step process summarized in Illustration 7–38.

**ILLUSTRATION 7–38**

Two-Step Impairment
Process

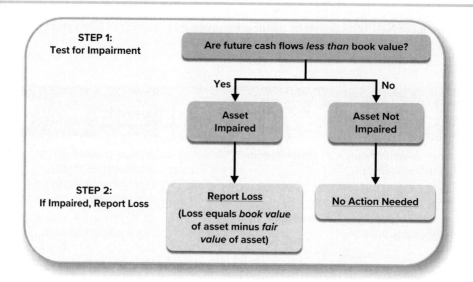

To illustrate asset impairment, suppose Little King pays $60,000 for the trademark rights to a line of specialty sandwiches. After several years, the book value is now $50,000, based on the initial cost of $60,000 less $10,000 in accumulated amortization. Unfortunately, sales for this line of specialty sandwiches are disappointing, and management estimates the total future cash flows from sales will be only $20,000. Due to the disappointing sales, the estimated fair value of the trademark is now only $12,000. Here's how Little King determines and reports the impairment loss.

## STEP 1: TEST FOR IMPAIRMENT

The long-term asset is impaired since future cash flows ($20,000) are less than book value ($50,000).

## STEP 2: IF IMPAIRED, REPORT THE LOSS

The loss is $38,000, calculated as the amount by which fair value ($12,000) is below book value ($50,000).

What is the overall financial statement effect of an impairment loss? The impairment loss reduces net income in the income statement by $38,000 and reduces total assets in the balance sheet by $38,000. The new balance in the Trademarks account is $12,000, which equals its current fair value. We can write down the trademark further through impairment in future years, but we cannot write it back up under current accounting rules.

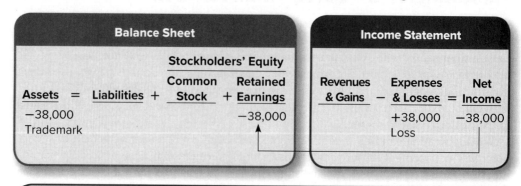

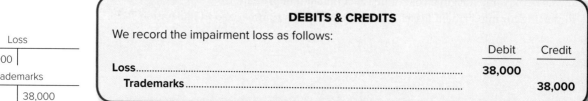

**COMMON MISTAKE**

Some students forget step 1 when considering impairment. An impairment loss (equal to book value minus fair value) is reported only when step 1 indicates that future cash flows are less than book value.

**Goodwill Impairment.**

We covered the basic impairment rules in this appendix. The two-step impairment process applies to property, plant, and equipment and to intangible assets with *finite* useful lives. For intangible assets with *indefinite* useful lives (such as goodwill and certain trademarks), we omit step 1. We omit step 1 for these types of intangible assets because they are presumed to provide cash flows indefinitely, so estimated future cash flows are not a good indicator of impairment in the current period.

Recall that goodwill is a unique intangible asset that is reported only when one company acquires control of another company. By its very nature, goodwill is inseparable from a particular *reporting unit.* A reporting unit is an operating segment of a company or a component of an operating segment for which discrete financial information is available, and segment management regularly reviews the operating results of that component.

So, for purposes of impairment testing, we compare the value of the reporting unit itself with its book value. A goodwill impairment loss is indicated when the fair value of the reporting unit is less than its book value. A goodwill impairment charge affects the financial statements by directly decreasing assets (goodwill) and decreasing retained earnings (via an impairment loss in the income statement).

Goodwill impairments are often quite large, with impairment charges commonly exceeding a billion dollars. For example, a few years ago, **Yahoo** announced an impairment charge of $400 million of goodwill related to its acquisition of the social media site **Tumblr**. Yahoo was subsequently acquired by **Verizon**. In an ironic turn of events, Verizon later announced a $4.6 billion goodwill impairment related to its acquisition of Yahoo. As this Yahoo example demonstrates, a goodwill impairment can be an indicator of a poor acquisition.

**KEY POINT**

Impairment is a two-step process: **Step 1: Test for impairment.** A long-term asset with a finite life is impaired if future cash flows are less than book value. **Step 2: If impaired, report impairment loss.** The impairment loss is the amount by which fair value is less than book value.

# Decision Maker's Perspective

## Taking a Big Bath

In practice, determining impairment losses can be subjective. Accounting research suggests that managers sometimes use the reporting of impairment losses to their advantage. Some companies time their impairment losses with other one-time losses, such as losses on sales of assets, inventory write-downs, and restructuring charges, to report a big loss in one year. We refer to this practice as taking a big bath—reporting all losses in one year to make a bad year even worse. Management thus cleans its slate and is able to report higher earnings in future years. Future earnings are higher because the write-down of assets in this year results in lower depreciation and amortization charges in the future. When analyzing financial statements, investors should be alert to this kind of manipulation.

**THE BOTTOM LINE**

**LO7–1** Identify the major types of property, plant, and equipment.

Tangible assets such as land, land improvements, buildings, equipment, and natural resources are reported at cost plus all costs necessary to get the asset ready for its intended use.

**LO7–2** Identify the major types of intangible assets.

We report purchased intangibles as long-term assets at their purchase price plus all costs necessary to get the asset ready for use. We expense internally generated intangibles, such as R&D and advertising costs, as we incur those costs.

Intangible assets have no physical substance and generally represent exclusive rights that provide benefits to owners. Common types include patents, copyrights, trademarks, franchises, and goodwill.

**LO7–3** Describe the accounting treatment of expenditures after acquisition.

We capitalize (report as an asset) expenditures that benefit *future* periods. We expense items that benefit only the *current* period.

**LO7–4** Calculate depreciation of property, plant, and equipment.

Depreciation refers to the allocation of an asset's original cost to an expense during the periods benefited. Depreciation does *not* refer to the change in value or selling price.

Straight-line, declining-balance, and activity-based depreciation all are acceptable depreciation methods for financial reporting. Most companies use straight-line depreciation for financial reporting and an accelerated method called MACRS for tax reporting.

**LO7–5** Calculate amortization of intangible assets.

Amortization is a process, similar to depreciation, in which we allocate the cost of intangible assets over their estimated service life. Intangible assets with an indefinite useful life (goodwill and most trademarks) are *not* amortized.

**LO7–6** Account for the disposal of long-term assets.

If we dispose of an asset for *more* than its book value, we report a gain. If we dispose of an asset for *less* than its book value, we report a loss.

**LO7–7** Describe the links among return on assets, profit margin, and asset turnover.

Return on assets indicates the amount of net income generated for each dollar invested in assets. Return on assets can be separated to examine two important business strategies: profit margin and asset turnover.

**LO7–8** Identify impairment situations and describe the two-step impairment process.

Impairment is a two-step process. **Step 1: Test for impairment.** A long-term asset with a finite life is impaired if future cash flows are less than book value. **Step 2: If impaired, report loss.** The impairment loss is the amount by which fair value is less than book value.

## GLOSSARY

**Accelerated depreciation method:** Allocates a higher depreciation in the earlier years of the asset's life and lower depreciation in later years. **p. 353**

**Accumulated Depreciation:** A contra asset account representing the total depreciation taken to date. **p. 348**

**Activity-based method:** Allocates an asset's cost based on its use. **p. 354**

**Addition:** Occurs when a new major component is added to an existing asset. **p. 346**

**Amortization:** Allocation of the cost of an intangible asset over its service life. **p. 358**

**Asset turnover:** Net sales divided by average total assets, which measures the sales per dollar of assets invested. **p. 366**

**Basket purchase:** Purchase of more than one asset at the same time for one purchase price. **p. 338**

**Big bath:** Reporting all losses in one year to make a bad year even worse. **p. 369**

**Book value:** An asset's original cost less accumulated depreciation. **p. 349**

**Capitalize:** Report an expenditure as an asset. **p. 337**

**Copyright:** An exclusive right of protection given to the creator of a published work such as a song, film, painting, photograph, book, or computer software. **p. 343**

**Declining-balance method:** An accelerated depreciation method that reports more depreciation in earlier years and less depreciation in later years. **p. 353**

**Depreciation:** Allocating the cost of a long-term asset to an expense over its service life. **p. 347**

**Depreciation method:** The pattern in which the asset's depreciable cost (original cost minus residual value) is allocated over time. **p. 349**

**Franchise:** Local outlets that pay for the exclusive right to use the franchisor company's name and to sell its products within a specified geographical area. **p. 343**

**Goodwill:** Equals the purchase price less the fair value of the net assets acquired. **p. 343**

**Impairment:** Occurs when the future cash flows (future benefits) generated for a long-term asset fall below its book value (cost minus accumulated depreciation). **p. 367**

**Improvement:** The cost of replacing a major component of an asset. **p. 346**

**Intangible assets:** Long-term assets that lack physical substance and whose existence is often based on a legal contract. **p. 340**

**Land improvements:** Improvements to land such as paving, lighting, and landscaping that, unlike land itself, are subject to depreciation. **p. 337**

**Natural resources:** Assets like oil, natural gas, and timber that we can physically use up or deplete. **p. 339**

**Patent:** An exclusive right to manufacture a product or to use a process. **p. 342**

**Profit margin:** Net income divided by net sales; indicates the earnings per dollar of sales. **p. 366**

**Repairs and maintenance:** Expenses that maintain a given level of benefits in the period incurred. **p. 345**

**Residual value:** The amount the company expects to receive from selling the asset at the end of its service life; also referred to as *salvage value.* **p. 349**

**Return on assets:** Net income divided by average total assets; measures the amount of net income generated for each dollar invested in assets. **p. 365**

**Service life:** How long the company expects to receive benefits from the asset before disposing of it; also referred to as *useful life.* **p. 349**

**Straight-line method:** Allocates an equal amount of depreciation to each year of the asset's service life. **p. 350**

**Trademark:** A word, slogan, or symbol that distinctively identifies a company, product, or service. **p. 343**

## SELF-STUDY QUESTIONS

1. We normally report a long-term asset at the **(LO7–1)**
   a. Cost of the asset only.
   b. Cost of the asset plus all costs necessary to get the asset ready for use.
   c. Appraised value.
   d. Cost of the asset, but subsequently adjust it up or down to appraised value.

2. Sandwich Express incurred the following costs related to its purchase of a bread machine. **(LO7–1)**

   | | |
   |---|---:|
   | Cost of the equipment | $20,000 |
   | Sales tax (8%) | 1,600 |
   | Shipping | 2,200 |
   | Installation | 1,400 |
   | Total costs | $25,200 |

   At what amount should Sandwich Express report the bread machine?
   a. $20,000.
   b. $21,600.
   c. $23,800.
   d. $25,200.

3. Research and development costs **(LO7–2)**
   a. Are reported as research and development assets.
   b. Are capitalized and then amortized.
   c. Should be included in the cost of the patent they relate to.
   d. Should be expensed.

4. Bryer Co. purchases all of the assets and liabilities of Stellar Co. for $1,500,000. The fair value of Stellar's assets is $2,000,000, and its liabilities have a fair value of $1,200,000. The book value of Stellar's assets and liabilities are not known. How much goodwill is associated with the purchase? **(LO7–2)**
   a. $800,000.
   b. $500,000.
   c. $700,000.
   d. $0.

5. Which of the following expenditures should be considered an expense? **(LO7–3)**
   a. Repairs and maintenance that maintain current benefits.
   b. Adding a major new component to an existing asset.
   c. Replacing a major component of an existing asset.
   d. Successful legal defense of an intangible asset.

6. Which of the following will maximize net income by minimizing depreciation expense in the first year of the asset's life? **(LO7–4)**
   a. Short service life, high residual value, and straight-line depreciation.
   b. Long service life, high residual value, and straight-line depreciation.
   c. Short service life, low residual value, and double-declining-balance depreciation.
   d. Long service life, high residual value, and double-declining-balance depreciation.

7. The balance in the Accumulated Depreciation account represents **(LO7–4)**
   a. The amount charged to expense in the current period.

b. A contra expense account.

c. A cash fund to be used to replace plant assets.

d. The amount charged to depreciation expense since the acquisition of the plant asset.

8. The book value of an asset is equal to the **(LO7–4)**

   a. Replacement cost.

   b. Asset's cost less accumulated depreciation.

   c. Asset's fair value less its historical cost.

   d. Historical cost plus accumulated depreciation.

9. Equipment was purchased for $50,000. At that time, the equipment was expected to be used eight years and have a residual value of $10,000. The company uses straight-line depreciation. At the beginning of the third year, the company changed its estimated service life to a total of six years (four years remaining) and the residual value to $8,000. What is depreciation expense in the third year? **(LO7–4)**

   a. $8,000.

   b. $5,000.

   c. $7,000.

   d. $5,500.

10. Equipment was purchased for $50,000. The equipment is expected to be used 15,000 hours over its service life and then have a residual value of $10,000. In the first two years of operation, the equipment was used 2,700 hours and 3,300 hours, respectively. What is the equipment's accumulated depreciation at the end of the second year using the activity-based method? **(LO7–4)**

    a. $16,000.

    b. $7,200.

    c. $8,800.

    d. $20,000.

11. Which of the following statements is true regarding the amortization of intangible assets? **(LO7–5)**

    a. Intangible assets with a limited useful life are not amortized.

    b. The useful life of an intangible asset is always equal to its legal life.

*Note: For answers, see the last page of the chapter.*

c. The expected residual value of most intangible assets is zero.

d. Accumulated Amortization is a contra-liability account.

12. Equipment originally costing $95,000 has accumulated depreciation of $30,000. If the equipment is sold for $55,000, the company has which of the following? **(LO7–6)**

    a. No gain or loss.

    b. A gain of $10,000.

    c. A loss of $10,000.

    d. A loss of $40,000.

13. The company's profitability on each dollar invested in assets is represented by which of the following ratios: **(LO7–7)**

    a. Profit margin.

    b. Asset turnover.

    c. Return on assets.

    d. Return on equity.

14. A company has a profit margin of 10% and reports net sales of $4,000,000 and average total assets of $5,000,000. Calculate the company's return on assets. **(LO7–7)**

    a. 12.5%.          c. 4.5%.

    b. 8.0%.           d. 5.0%.

15. A company has the following three assets with the information provided: **(LO7–8)**

| ($ in millions) | Equipment | Land | Building |
|---|---|---|---|
| Book value | $8 | $20 | $12 |
| Estimated total future cash flows | 6 | 35 | 14 |
| Fair value | 5 | 30 | 10 |

Determine the amount of the impairment loss, if any.

a. $0.

b. $5 million.

c. $10 million.

d. $3 million.

# REAL WORLD PERSPECTIVES

**EDGAR Case**

## Norfolk Southern (ticker: NSC)

**RWP7–1** Visit www.sec.gov/edgar and search for the Norfolk Southern annual report (10-K) for the year ended December 31, 2019, using EDGAR (Electronic Data Gathering, Analysis, and Retrieval system). Locate the note titled "7. Properties." Use the information in this note to answer the questions below.

*Required:*

1. Does the company have any assets that are *not* depreciated? If so, what are they?

2. What type of property has the highest depreciation rate?

3. Focus on Locomotives, which are one of Norfolk's major assets used in operations. Based on the stated depreciation rate, back into the implied service life of the company's locomotives.

## Texas Roadhouse, Inc. (ticker: TXRH)

**EDGAR Case**

**RWP7–2** Visit **www.sec.gov/edgar** and search for the **Texas Roadhouse** annual report (10-K) for the year ended December 31, 2019, using EDGAR (Electronic Data Gathering, Analysis, and Retrieval system). Use the note titled "Property and Equipment" to answer the questions below.

*Required:*

1. What does it mean that "property and equipment are stated at cost"?
2. What kinds of expenditures are capitalized, and what others are expensed as incurred?
3. What method does the company use to depreciate its property and equipment?

## Shoe Carnival, Inc. (ticker: SCVL)

**EDGAR Case**

**RWP7–3** Visit **www.sec.gov/edgar** and search for the **Shoe Carnival** annual report (10-K) for the year ended February 1, 2020, using EDGAR (Electronic Data Gathering, Analysis, and Retrieval system). Use the note titled "Note 5—Property and Equipment . . ." to answer the questions below.

*Required:*

1. List the four types of property and equipment.
2. Conceptually, what are "improvements"? Do they generally depreciate?
3. Compute the ratio of Accumulated Depreciation to Total Property and Equipment for the year ended February 1, 2020. What does this ratio tell you?

## Abercrombie & Fitch Co. (ticker: ANF)

**EDGAR Case**

**RWP7–4** Visit **www.sec.gov/edgar** and search for the **Abercrombie & Fitch** annual report (10-K) for the year ended February 1, 2020, using EDGAR (Electronic Data Gathering, Analysis, and Retrieval system). Use the Balance Sheet and Income Statement to answer the questions below, assuming Total Assets in 2018 were $2,325,692.

*Required:*

1. Calculate the company's return on assets and profit margin for the years ended February 1, 2020, and February 2, 2019. Be sure to use the line item entitled "Net Income" as opposed to other measures of income.
2. What can we infer about trends in the company's performance?
3. Calculate the company's asset turnover for the years ended February 1, 2020, and February 2, 2019.
4. What can we infer about trends in the company's asset efficiency?

## American Eagle Outfitters, Inc.

**Continuing Financial Analysis Case**

**RWP7–5** Financial information for **American Eagle** is presented in **Appendix A** at the end of the book.

*Required:*

1. The summary of significant accounting policies is located in note 2 to the financial statements. Locate the section on property and equipment. What depreciation method does American Eagle use? What are the estimated useful lives for buildings and for fixtures and equipment?
2. Find note 7 for Property and Equipment. What are the cost and the book value of property and equipment for the most recent year? What is the trend in depreciation expense for the past three years?
3. Find note 8 for Intangible Assets. What intangible asset is listed? What are listed as the cost and the book value of intangible assets for the most recent year? What is the trend in amortization expense for the past three years?

## The Buckle, Inc.

**Continuing Financial Analysis Case**

**RWP7–6** Financial information for **Buckle** is presented in **Appendix B** at the end of the book.

*Required:*

1. The summary of significant accounting policies is located in note A to the financial statements. Locate the section on property and equipment. What depreciation method does Buckle use? What are the estimated useful lives for property and equipment? What are the estimated useful lives for buildings?

2. Find note D entitled Property and Equipment. What is the cost of property and equipment for the most recent year? What is the trend in property and equipment for the past two years?
3. From the balance sheet, what two other types of long-term assets are listed?

## American Eagle Outfitters, Inc. vs. The Buckle, Inc.

**RWP7–7** Financial information for **American Eagle** is presented in **Appendix A** at the end of the book, and financial information for **Buckle** is presented in **Appendix B** at the end of the book.

### Required:
1. Calculate American Eagle's return on assets, profit margin, and asset turnover ratio for the most recent year.
2. Calculate Buckle's return on assets, profit margin, and asset turnover ratio for the most recent year.
3. Which company is doing better based on return on assets? Which company has the higher profit margin? Which company has the higher asset turnover?

## Ethics

**RWP7–8** Companies often are under pressure to meet or beat Wall Street earnings projections in order to increase stock prices and also to increase the value of stock options. Such pressure may cause some managers to alter their estimates for depreciation to artificially create desired results.

### Required:
1. Understand the reporting effect: Do estimates by management affect the amount of depreciation in its company's financial statements?
2. Specify the options: To increase earnings in the initial years following the purchase of a depreciable asset, would management (a) choose straight-line or double-declining balance, (b) estimate a longer or shorter service life, or (c) estimate a higher or lower residual value?
3. Identify the impact: Are decisions of investors and creditors affected by accounting estimates?
4. Make a decision: Should a company alter depreciation estimates for the sole purpose of meeting expectations of Wall Street analysts?

## Sustainability

**RWP7–9** Go to the SASB website (**https://www.sasb.org/company-use/sasb-reporters/**) and search for **Adobe Inc.** Click on the Corporate Responsibility Report for 2020. Adobe is a software-as-a-service (SAAS) company that provides products and services to help users create and manage digital media. The company has grown substantially in the last decade and is now generating over $11 billion in revenues. As it grows, it must acquire and deploy long-term assets.

In its Corporate Social Responsibility Report, it discloses metrics—called Key ESG Performance Indicators—that provide information on sustainability related to its long-term assets, namely its buildings (see page 12). Use those metrics to answer the questions below.

### Required:
1. In 2019, how much square footage did Adobe own or lease? Did this square footage increase or decrease from the prior year?
2. In 2019, what percentage of Adobe's total square footage was in "LEED/ Green-certified" space? Did this percentage increase or decrease from the prior year?
3. In 2019, what percentage of total energy consumption is renewable energy? Did this percentage increase or decrease from the prior year?
4. In 2019, by what year does the company have as a goal to be using 100% renewable energy?

## Earnings Management

**RWP7–10** Edward L. Vincent is CFO of Energy Resources, Inc. The company specializes in the exploration and development of natural gas. It's near year-end, and Edward is feeling terrific. Natural gas prices have risen throughout the year, and Energy Resources is set to report record-breaking performance that will greatly exceed analysts' expectations. However, during an executive meeting this morning, management agreed to "tone down" profits due to concerns that reporting excess profits could encourage additional government regulations in the industry, hindering future profitability.

At the beginning of the current year, the company purchased equipment for $4,200,000. The company's standard practice for equipment like this is to use straight-line depreciation over 12 years using an estimated residual value of $600,000. To address the issue discussed in the meeting, Edward is considering three options. Option 1: Adjust the estimated service life of the equipment from 12 years to 6 years. Option 2: Adjust estimated residual values on the equipment from $600,000 to $0. Option 3: Make both adjustments.

*Required:*
1. Calculate annual depreciation using the company's standard practice.
2. Calculate annual depreciation for each of the three options and state whether the option would increase or decrease net income.
3. Which option has the biggest effect on net income?

## Great Adventures

(This is a continuation of the Great Adventures problem from earlier chapters.)

**RWP7–11** Tony and Suzie see the need for a rugged all-terrain vehicle to transport participants and supplies. They decide to purchase a used Suburban on July 1, 2025, for $12,000. They expect to use the Suburban for five years and then sell the vehicle for $4,500. The following expenditures related to the vehicle were also made on July 1, 2025:

- The company pays $1,800 to **GEICO** for a one-year insurance policy.
- The company spends an extra $3,000 to repaint the vehicle, placing the Great Adventures logo on the front hood, back, and both sides.
- An additional $2,000 is spent on a deluxe roof rack and a trailer hitch.

The painting, roof rack, and hitch are all expected to increase the future benefits of the vehicle for Great Adventures. In addition, on October 22, 2025, the company pays $400 for basic vehicle maintenance related to changing the oil, replacing the windshield wipers, rotating the tires, and inserting a new air filter.

*Required:*
1. Record the expenditures related to the vehicle on July 1, 2025. Note: The capitalized cost of the vehicle is recorded in the Equipment account.
2. Record the expenditure related to vehicle maintenance on October 22, 2025.
3. Prepare a depreciation schedule using the straight-line method. Follow the example in Illustration 7–15, except the calendar years 2025 (first year) and 2030 (last year) will have a half-year of depreciation to reflect the five-year service life beginning on July 1, 2025.
4. Record the depreciation expense and any other adjusting entries related to the vehicle on December 31, 2025.
5. Record the sale of the vehicle two years later on July 1, 2027, for $10,000.

The Great Adventures continuing problem also can be assigned using the General Ledger software in Connect. Students will be given an existing trial balance and asked to prepare (1) the journal entries for the transactions above in 2025, (2) financial statements, and (3) closing entries.

**Determine cost of land (LO7–1)**

**BE7–1** Fresh Veggies, Inc. (FVI), purchases land and a warehouse for $490,000. In addition to the purchase price, FVI makes the following expenditures related to the acquisition: broker's commission, $29,000; title insurance, $1,900; and miscellaneous closing costs, $6,000. The warehouse is immediately demolished at a cost of $29,000 in anticipation of building a new warehouse. Determine the total the cost of the land.

**Determine cost of equipment (LO7–1)**
*See JBE7–1 for journal entries.*

**BE7–2** Whole Grain Bakery purchases an industrial bread machine for $30,000. In addition to the purchase price, the company makes the following expenditures: freight, $2,000; installation, $4,000; testing, $1,500; and property tax on the machine for the first year, $600. What is the initial cost of the bread machine?

**Allocate costs in basket purchase (LO7–1)**

**BE7–3** Finley Co. is looking for a new office location and sees a building with a fair value of $400,000. Finley also notices that much of the equipment in the existing building would be useful to its own operations. Finley estimates the fair value of the equipment to be $80,000. Finley offers to buy both the building and the equipment for $450,000, and the offer is accepted. Determine the amounts Finley should allocate to the separate accounts for building and equipment.

**Compute goodwill (LO7–2)**

**BE7–4** Kosher Pickle Company acquires all the outstanding stock of Midwest Produce for $19 million. The fair value of Midwest's assets is $14.3 million. The fair value of Midwest's liabilities is $2.5 million. Calculate the amount paid for goodwill.

**Compute R&D expense (LO7–2)**

**BE7–5** West Coast Growers incurs the following costs during the year related to the creation of a new disease-resistant tomato plant.

| | |
|---|---|
| Salaries for R&D | $540,000 |
| Depreciation on R&D facilities and equipment | 145,000 |
| Utilities incurred for the R&D facilities | 7,000 |
| Patent filing and related legal costs | 27,000 |
| Payment to another company for part of the development work | 13,000 |

What amount should West Coast Growers report as research and development (R&D) expense in its income statement?

**Determine expenditures after acquisition (LO7–3)**

**BE7–6** Hanoi Foods incurs the following expenditures during the current fiscal year: (1) annual maintenance on its machinery, $8,900; (2) remodeling of offices, $42,000; (3) improvement of the shipping and receiving area, resulting in an increase in productivity, $25,000; and (4) addition of a security system to the manufacturing facility, $35,000. How should Hanoi account for each of these expenditures?

**Legal defense of intangible assets (LO7–3)**

**BE7–7** Betty Foods has separate patents for its chocolate chip cookie dough and vanilla ice cream. In the current year, both patents were challenged in court. Betty Foods spent $240,000 in legal fees to successfully defend its cookie dough and $300,000 in legal fees in an unsuccessful defense of its vanilla ice cream. For what amount can Betty Foods capitalize these costs?

**Understand depreciation (LO7–4)**

**BE7–8** Early in the fiscal year, The Beanery purchases a delivery vehicle for $40,000. At the end of the year, the vehicle has a fair value of $33,000. The company controller reports depreciation expense of $7,000 for the year, the decline in the vehicle's value. Is the company controller's approach to reporting depreciation expense correct?

**Calculate partial-year depreciation (LO7–4)**

**BE7–9** El Tapitio purchased restaurant furniture on September 1, 2024, for $45,000. Residual value at the end of an estimated 10-year service life is expected to be $6,000. Calculate depreciation expense for 2024 and 2025, using the straight-line method and assuming a December 31 year-end.

**BE7–10** On January 1, Hawaiian Specialty Foods purchased equipment for $30,000. Residual value at the end of an estimated four-year service life is expected to be $3,000. Calculate depreciation expense for the first year using the straight-line method

*Calculate depreciation using straight-line method (LO7–4)*
*See JBE7–2 for journal entries.*

**BE7–11** Refer to the information in BE7–10. Calculate depreciation expense for the first year using the double-declining-balance method.

*Calculate depreciation using double-declining-balance method (LO7–4)*
*See JBE7–3 for journal entries.*

**BE7–12** Refer to the information in BE7–10. In addition, the machine operated for 3,100 hours in the first year, and the company expects the machine to operate for a total of 20,000 hours over its service life. Calculate depreciation expense for the first year using the activity-based method.

*Calculate depreciation using activity-based method (LO7–4)*
*See JBE7–4 for journal entries.*

**BE7–13** On January 1, Omaha Beef Co. purchased a delivery truck for $50,000. The residual value at the end of an estimated eight-year service life is expected to be $10,000. The company uses straight-line depreciation for the first six years. In the seventh year, the company now believes the truck will be useful for a total of 10 years (four more years), and the residual value will remain at $10,000. Calculate depreciation expense for the seventh year.

*Change in depreciation estimate (LO7–4)*

**BE7–14** In early January, Burger Mania acquired 100% of the common stock of the Crispy Taco restaurant chain. The purchase price allocation included the following items: $4 million, patent; $5 million, trademark considered to have an indefinite useful life; and $6 million, goodwill. Burger Mania's policy is to amortize intangible assets with finite useful lives using the straight-line method, no residual value, and a five-year service life. What is the total amount of amortization expense that would appear in Burger Mania's income statement for the first year ended December 31 related to these items?

*Calculate amortization of intangible assets (LO7–5)*

**BE7–15** Granite Stone Creamery sold ice cream equipment for $16,000. Granite Stone originally purchased the equipment for $90,000, and depreciation through the date of sale totaled $71,000. What was the gain or loss on the sale of the equipment?

*Account for the disposal of long-term assets (LO7–6)*

**BE7–16** Piper's Pizza sold baking equipment for $25,000. The equipment was originally purchased for $72,000, and depreciation through the date of sale totaled $51,000. What was the gain or loss on the sale of the equipment?

*Account for the disposal of long-term assets (LO7–6)*

**BE7–17** On January 1, Masterson Supply purchased a small storage building for $20,000 to be used over a five-year period. The building has no residual value. Early in the fourth year, the storage building burned down. Determine the financial statement effects of the removal of the storage building from the accounting records.

*Account for the disposal of long-term assets (LO7–6)*
*See JBE7–5 for journal entries.*

**BE7–18** China Inn and Midwest Chicken exchanged assets. China Inn received delivery equipment and gave restaurant equipment. The fair value and book value of the restaurant equipment were $22,000 and $12,000 (original cost of $45,000 less accumulated depreciation of $33,000), respectively. To equalize market values of the exchanged assets, China Inn paid $9,000 in cash to Midwest Chicken. Determine the financial statement effects of this asset exchange for China Inn.

*Account for the exchange of long-term assets (LO7–6)*
*See JBE7–6 for journal entries.*

**BE7–19** The balance sheet of Cedar Crest Resort reports total assets of $840,000 and $930,000 at the beginning and end of the year, respectively. The return on assets for the year is 20%. Calculate Cedar Crest's net income for the year.

*Compute return on assets (LO7–7)*

**BE7–20** Elder's Bread and Bakery reports net sales and net income for the year of $600,000 and $63,000, respectively. The company had assets of $350,000 and $390,000 at the beginning and end of the year, respectively. Calculate Elder's return on assets, profit margin, and asset turnover.

*Analyze assets (LO7–7)*

**BE7–21** Vegetarian Delights has been experiencing declining market conditions for its specialty foods division. Management decided to test the operational assets of the division for possible impairment. The test revealed the following: book value of the division's assets, $33.5 million;

*Determine the impairment loss (LO7–8)*

fair value of the division's assets, $30 million; sum of estimated future cash flows generated from the division's assets, $38 million. What amount of impairment loss, if any, should Vegetarian Delights report?

**Determine the impairment loss (LO7–8)**

**BE7–22** Refer to the situation described in BE7–21. Assume the sum of estimated future cash flows is $32 million instead of $38 million. What amount of impairment loss should Vegetarian Delights report?

## EXERCISES

**Determine cost of land (LO7–1)**

**E7–1** McCoy's Fish House purchases a tract of land and an existing building for $1,000,000. The company plans to remove the old building and construct a new restaurant on the site. In addition to the purchase price, McCoy pays closing costs, including title insurance of $3,000. The company also pays $14,000 in property taxes, which includes $9,000 of back taxes (unpaid taxes from previous years) paid by McCoy on behalf of the seller and $5,000 due for the current fiscal year after the purchase date. Shortly after closing, the company pays a contractor $50,000 to tear down the old building and remove it from the site. McCoy is able to sell salvaged materials from the old building for $5,000 and pays an additional $11,000 to level the land.

*Required:*
Determine the total cost of the land.

**Determine cost of equipment (LO7–1)**
*See JE7–1 for journal entries.*

**E7–2** Orion Flour Mills purchased new equipment and made the following expenditures:

| | |
|---|---:|
| Purchase price | $75,000 |
| Sales tax | 6,000 |
| Shipment of equipment | 1,000 |
| Insurance on the equipment for the first year | 700 |
| Installation of equipment | 2,000 |

*Required:*
Determine the financial statement effects of the above expenditures for the new equipment. All expenditures were paid in cash.

**Allocate costs in basket purchase (LO7–1)**

**E7–3** Red Rock Bakery purchases land, building, and equipment for a single purchase price of $600,000. However, the estimated fair values of the land, building, and equipment are $175,000, $455,000, and $70,000, respectively, for a total estimated fair value of $700,000.

*Required:*
Determine the amounts Red Rock should allocate to the separate accounts for the land, the building, and the equipment.

**Determine costs of intangible assets (LO7–2)**

**E7–4** Brick Oven Corporation made the following expenditures during the first month of operations:

| | |
|---|---:|
| Attorneys' fees to organize the corporation | $  9,000 |
| Purchase of a patent | 40,000 |
| Legal and other fees for transfer of the patent | 2,500 |
| Advertising | 80,000 |
| Total | $131,500 |

*Required:*
Determine the financial statement effects of the $131,500 in cash expenditures.

**Determine goodwill (LO7–2)**
*See JE7–2 for journal entries.*

**E7–5** Mainline Produce Corporation acquired all the outstanding common stock of Iceberg Lettuce Corporation for $30,000,000 in cash. The book values and fair values of Iceberg's assets and liabilities were as follows:

| | Book Value | Fair Value |
|---|---|---|
| Current assets | $11,400,000 | $14,400,000 |
| Property, plant, and equipment | 20,200,000 | 26,200,000 |
| Other assets | 3,400,000 | 4,400,000 |
| Current liabilities | 7,800,000 | 7,800,000 |
| Long-term liabilities | 13,200,000 | 12,200,000 |

**Required:**
1. Calculate the amount paid for goodwill.
2. Determine the financial statement effects of the acquisition.

**E7–6** Satellite Systems modified its model Z2 satellite to incorporate a new communication device. The company made the following expenditures:

Compute patent and R&D expense (LO7–2)

| | |
|---|---|
| Basic research to develop the technology | $3,900,000 |
| Engineering design work | 1,180,000 |
| Development of a prototype device | 590,000 |
| Testing and modification of the prototype | 390,000 |
| Legal fees for patent application | 79,000 |
| Legal fees for successful defense of the new patent | 39,000 |
| Total | $6,178,000 |

During your year-end review of the accounts related to intangibles, you discover that the company has capitalized all the above as costs of the patent. Management contends that the device represents an improvement of the existing communication system of the satellite and, therefore, should be capitalized.

**Required:**
1. Which of the above costs should Satellite Systems capitalize to the Patent account in the balance sheet?
2. Which of the above costs should Satellite Systems report as Research and Development Expense in the income statement?
3. What are the basic criteria for determining whether to capitalize or expense intangible related costs?

**E7–7** Listed below are several terms and phrases associated with operational assets. Pair each item from List A (by letter) with the item from List B that is most appropriately associated with it.

Match terms used in the chapter (LO7–2, 7–4)

List A

_____ 1. Depreciation
_____ 2. Goodwill
_____ 3. Amortization
_____ 4. Natural resources
_____ 5. Intangible assets
_____ 6. Copyright
_____ 7. Trademark

List B

a. Exclusive right to display a word, a symbol, or an emblem.
b. Exclusive right to benefit from a creative work.
c. Assets that represent contractual rights.
d. Oil and gas deposits, timber tracts, and mineral deposits.
e. Purchase price less fair value of net identifiable assets.
f. The allocation of cost for plant and equipment.
g. The allocation of cost for intangible assets.

**E7–8** Sub Sandwiches of America made the following expenditures related to its restaurant:
1. Replaced the heating equipment at a cost of $250,000.
2. Covered the patio area with a clear plastic dome and enclosed it with glass for use during the winter months. The total cost of the project was $750,000.
3. Performed annual building maintenance at a cost of $24,000.

Determine expenditures after acquisition (LO7–3)

See JE7–3 for journal entries.

4. Paid for annual insurance for the facility at $8,800.

5. Built a new sign above the restaurant, putting the company name in bright neon lights, for $9,900.

6. Paved a gravel parking lot at a cost of $65,000.

**Required:**

Sub Sandwiches of America pays cash for each of these expenditures. Determine the financial statement effects for each.

**Calculate depreciation using different methods (LO7–4)**

**E7–9** On January 1, Super Saver Groceries purchased store equipment for $29,500. Super Saver estimates that at the end of its 10-year service life, the equipment will be worth $3,500. During the 10-year period, the company expects to use the equipment for a total of 13,000 hours. Super Saver used the equipment for 1,700 hours the first year.

**Required:**

Calculate depreciation expense for the first year, using each of the following methods. Round all amounts to the nearest dollar.

1. Straight-line.
2. Double-declining-balance.
3. Activity-based.

**Calculate depreciation using different methods (LO7–4)**

**E7–10** On January 1, Speedy Delivery Company purchases a delivery van for $90,000. Speedy estimates that at the end of its six-year service life, the van will be worth $30,000. During the six-year period, the company expects to drive the van 200,000 miles.

**Required:**

Calculate annual depreciation for the first two years using each of the following methods. Round all amounts to the nearest dollar.

1. Straight-line.
2. Double-declining-balance.
3. Activity-based. Actual miles driven each year were 32,000 miles in year 1 and 35,000 miles in year 2.

**Calculate partial-year depreciation (LO7–4)**
*See JE7–4 for journal entries.*

**E7–11** Togo's Sandwiches acquired equipment on April 1, 2024, for $18,000. The company estimates a residual value of $2,000 and a five-year service life.

**Required:**

1. Calculate depreciation expense using the straight-line method for 2024 and 2025, assuming a December 31 year-end.
2. Determine the financial statement effects of the depreciation in 2024.

**Calculate partial-year depreciation (LO7–4)**
*See JE7–5 for journal entries.*

**E7–12** Tasty Subs acquired a food-service truck on October 1, 2024, for $120,000. The company estimates a residual value of $40,000 and a four-year service life.

**Required:**

1. Calculate depreciation expense using the straight-line method for 2024 and 2025, assuming a December 31 year-end.
2. Determine the financial statement effects of the depreciation in 2024.

**Calculate depreciation of property, plant, and equipment (LO7–4)**
*See JE7–6 for journal entries.*

**E7–13** The Donut Stop acquired equipment for $19,000. The company uses straight-line depreciation and estimates a residual value of $3,000 and a four-year service life. At the end of the second year, the company estimates that the equipment will be useful for four additional years, for a total service life of six years rather than the original four. At the same time, the company also changed the estimated residual value to $1,200 from the original estimate of $3,000.

**Required:**

1. Calculate annual depreciation in years 3 to 6.
2. Determine the financial statement effects of the annual depreciation in years 3 to 6.

**E7–14** Tasty Subs acquired a food-service truck on October 1, 2024, for $120,000. The company estimates a residual value of $40,000 and a four-year service life. It expects to drive the truck 100,000 miles. Actual mileage was 5,000 miles in 2024 and 28,000 miles in 2025.

*Compute activity-based depreciation (LO7–4)*
*See JE7–7 for journal entries.*

**Required:**

1. Calculate depreciation expense using the activity-based method for 2024 and 2025, assuming a December 31 year-end.
2. Determine the financial statement effects of the depreciation in 2024.

**E7–15** On January 1, 2024, Weaver Corporation purchased a patent for $237,000. The remaining legal life is 20 years, but the company estimates the patent will be useful for only six more years. In January 2026, the company incurred legal fees of $57,000 in successfully defending a patent infringement suit. The successful defense did not change the company's estimate of useful life. Weaver Corporation's year-end is December 31.

*Calculate amortization of intangible assets (LO7–5)*
*See JE7–8 for journal entries.*

**Required:**

Determine the financial statement effects of the following: the purchase in 2024; amortization in 2024; amortization in 2025; legal fees in 2026; and amortization in 2026.

**E7–16** Abbott Landscaping purchased a tractor at a cost of $42,000 and sold it three years later for $21,600. Abbott accounted for depreciation using the straight-line method, a five-year service life, and a $3,000 residual value. Tractors are included in the Equipment account.

*Account for the disposal of long-term assets (LO7–6)*
*See JE7–9 for journal entries.*

**Required:**

1. Determine the financial statement effects of the sale of the tractor.
2. Assume the tractor was sold for $13,600 instead of $21,600. Determine the financial statement effects of the sale.

**E7–17** Salad Express exchanged land it had been holding for future plant expansion for a more suitable parcel of land along distribution routes. Salad Express reported the old land on the previously issued balance sheet at its original cost of $70,000. According to an independent appraisal, the old land currently is worth $132,000. Salad Express paid $19,000 in cash to complete the transaction.

*Account for the exchange of long-term assets (LO7–6)*
*See JE7–10 for journal entries.*

**Required:**

1. What is the fair value of the new parcel of land received by Salad Express?
2. Determine the financial statement effects of the exchange.

**E7–18** Brad's BBQ reported sales of $735,000 and net income of $28,000. Brad's also reported ending total assets of $496,000 and beginning total assets of $389,000.

*Compute return on assets, profit margin, and asset turnover (LO7–7)*

**Required:**

Calculate the return on assets, the profit margin, and the asset turnover ratio for Brad's BBQ.

**E7–19** Midwest Services, Inc., operates several restaurant chains throughout the Midwest. One restaurant chain has experienced sharply declining profits. The company's management has decided to test the property and equipment of the restaurants for possible impairment. The relevant information for these assets is presented below.

*Determine the impairment loss of property and equipment (LO7–8)*
*See JE7–11 for journal entries.*

| | |
|---|---|
| Book value | $8.6 million |
| Estimated total future cash flows | 7.1 million |
| Fair value | 5.9 million |

**Required:**

1. Determine the amount of the impairment loss, if any.
2. Determine the financial statement effects of the impairment loss, if any.

**E7–20** In 2018, Northeast Technologies purchased a patent for $450,000 to provide cloud computing services to customers. By the end of 2024, the patent had a book value of $300,000. Due to increased competition and new delivery methods in cloud computing services, management believes it should test the patent for impairment. Management estimates the

*Determine the impairment loss of patent (LO7–8)*
*See JE7–12 for journal entries.*

patent will generate future cash flows of $375,000 over its remaining legal life and currently has a fair value of $330,000 at the end of 2024.

**Required:**

1. Determine the amount of the impairment loss, if any, and its financial statement effects.
2. Now assume management estimates future cash flows of $220,000 and fair value of $180,000. Determine the amount of the impairment loss, if any, and its financial statement effects.

## PROBLEMS

**Determine cost of land (LO7–1)**

**P7–1** The Italian Bread Company purchased land as a factory site for $70,000. An old building on the property was demolished, and construction began on a new building. Costs incurred during the first year are listed as follows:

| | |
|---|---:|
| Demolition of old building | $ 9,000 |
| Sale of salvaged materials | (1,100) |
| Architect fees (for new building) | 20,000 |
| Legal fees (for title investigation of land) | 3,000 |
| Property taxes on the land (for the first year) | 4,000 |
| Building construction costs | 600,000 |
| Interest costs related to the construction | 23,000 |

**Required:**

Determine the separate amounts that will be reported in the Land and Building accounts.

**Determine cost of equipment (LO7–1)**

**P7–2** Great Harvest Bakery purchased bread ovens from New Morning Bakery. New Morning Bakery was closing its bakery business and sold its two-year-old ovens at a discount for $700,000. Great Harvest incurred and paid freight costs of $35,000, and its employees ran special electrical connections to the ovens at a cost of $5,000. Labor costs were $37,800. Unfortunately, one of the ovens was damaged during installation, and repairs cost $4,000. Great Harvest then consumed $900 of bread dough in testing the ovens. It installed safety guards on the ovens at a cost of $1,500 and placed the machines in operation.

**Required:**

1. Compute the amounts that will be included in the Equipment account.
2. Indicate how any amounts not included in the Equipment account should be reported.

**Compute goodwill (LO7–2)**

*See JP7–1 for journal entries.*

**P7–3** Fresh Cut Corporation purchased all the outstanding common stock of Premium Meats for $12,000,000 in cash. The book values and fair values of Premium Meats' assets and liabilities were

| | Book Value | Fair Value |
|---|---:|---:|
| Accounts Receivable | $1,800,000 | $ 1,600,000 |
| Equipment | 8,500,000 | 9,900,000 |
| Patents | 300,000 | 1,700,000 |
| Notes Payable | (2,700,000) | (2,700,000) |
| Net assets | $7,900,000 | $10,500,000 |

**Required:**

1. Calculate the amount Fresh Cut should report for goodwill.
2. Determine the financial statement effects for Fresh Cut as a result of its acquisition of Premium Meats.

**Account for expenditures after acquisition (LO7–3)**

**P7–4** Several years ago, Health Services acquired a helicopter for use in emergency situations. Health Services incurred the following expenditures related to the helicopter delivery operations in the current year:

1. Overhauled the engine at a cost of $7,500. Health Services estimated the work would increase the service life for an additional five years.

2. Cleaned, repacked, and sealed the bearings on the helicopter at a cost of $800. This repair is performed annually.
3. Added new emergency health equipment to the helicopter for $25,000.
4. Modified the helicopter to reduce cabin noise by installing new sound barrier technology at a cost of $15,000.
5. Paid insurance on the helicopter for the current year, which increased 15% over the prior year to $9,000.
6. Performed annual maintenance and repairs at a cost of $39,000.

*Required:*
For each expenditure, indicate whether Health Services should capitalize or expense each item.

**P7–5** University Car Wash built a deluxe car wash across the street from campus. The new machines cost $270,000, including installation. The company estimates that the equipment will have a residual value of $24,000. University Car Wash also estimates it will use the machine for six years or about 12,000 total hours.

*Calculate depreciation using multiple methods (LO7–4)*

*Required:*
Prepare a depreciation schedule for six years using the following methods:
1. Straight-line.
2. Double-declining-balance.
3. Activity-based.
Actual use per year was as follows:

| Year | Hours Used |
|------|-----------|
| 1 | 3,100 |
| 2 | 1,100 |
| 3 | 1,200 |
| 4 | 2,800 |
| 5 | 2,600 |
| 6 | 1,200 |

**P7–6** The following information relates to the intangible assets of University Testing Services (UTS):
a. On January 1, 2024, UTS completed the purchase of Heinrich Corporation for $3,510,000 in cash. The fair value of the net identifiable assets of Heinrich was $3,200,000.
b. Included in the assets purchased from Heinrich was a patent valued at $82,250. The original legal life of the patent was 20 years; there are 12 years remaining, but UTS believes the patent will be useful for only 7 more years.
c. UTS acquired a franchise on July 1, 2024, by paying an initial franchise fee of $333,000. The contractual life of the franchise is nine years.

*Compute goodwill and amortization of intangible assets (LO7–2, 7–5)*
*See JP7–2 for journal entries.*

*Required:*
1. Compute goodwill arising from the purchase of Heinrich Corporation.
2. Determine amortization expense for the intangible assets at December 31, 2024.
3. Prepare the intangible asset section of the December 31, 2024, balance sheet.

**P7–7** Solich Sandwich Shop had the following long-term asset balances as of January 1, 2024:

*Calculate depreciation of property and equipment and amortization of intangible assets (LO7–4, 7–5)*
*See JP7–3 for journal entries.*

| | Cost | Accumulated Depreciation | Book Value |
|------|------|--------------------------|-----------|
| Land | $ 95,000 | – | $ 95,000 |
| Building | 460,000 | $(165,600) | 294,400 |
| Equipment | 235,000 | (50,000) | 185,000 |
| Patent | 250,000 | (100,000) | 150,000 |

Additional information:
• Solich purchased all the assets at the beginning of 2022.

- The building is depreciated over a 10-year service life using the double-declining-balance method and estimating no residual value.
- The equipment is depreciated over a nine-year service life using the straight-line method with an estimated residual value of $10,000.
- The patent is estimated to have a five-year service life with no residual value and is amortized using the straight-line method.
- Depreciation and amortization have been recorded for 2022 and 2023 (first two years).

**Required:**

1. For the year ended December 31, 2024 (third year), determine the financial statement effects of the depreciation of buildings and equipment. Land is not depreciated.
2. For the year ended December 31, 2024, determine the financial statement effects of the amortization of the patent.
3. Calculate the book value for each of the four long-term assets at December 31, 2024.

**Account for the disposal of long-term assets (LO7–6)**
*See JP7–4 for journal entries.*

**P7–8** New Morning Bakery is in the process of closing its operations. It sold its two-year-old bakery ovens to Great Harvest Bakery for $700,000. The ovens originally cost $910,000, had an estimated service life of 10 years, had an estimated residual value of $60,000, and were depreciated using straight-line depreciation. Complete the requirements below for New Morning Bakery.

**Required:**

1. Calculate the balance in the Accumulated Depreciation account at the end of the second year.
2. Calculate the book value of the ovens at the end of the second year.
3. What is the gain or loss on the sale of the ovens at the end of the second year?
4. Determine the financial statement effects of the sale of the ovens at the end of the second year.

**Compute return on assets, profit margin, and asset turnover (LO7–7)**

**P7–9** Sub Station and Planet Sub reported the following selected financial data ($ in thousands). Sub Station's business strategy is to sell the best-tasting sandwich with the highest-quality ingredients. Planet Sub's business strategy is to sell the lowest-cost sub on the planet.

|  | Sub Station | Planet Sub |
|---|---|---|
| Net sales | $108,249 | $62,071 |
| Net income | 25,922 | 3,492 |
| Total assets, beginning | 75,183 | 38,599 |
| Total assets, ending | 116,371 | 44,533 |

**Required:**

1. Calculate Sub Station's return on assets, profit margin, and asset turnover ratio.
2. Calculate Planet Sub's return on assets, profit margin, and asset turnover ratio.
3. Which company has the more favorable profit margin, and which company has the more favorable asset turnover? Is this consistent with the primary business strategies of these two companies?

**Compute return on assets, profit margin, and asset turnover (LO7–7)**

**P7–10** University Hero is considering expanding operations beyond its healthy sandwiches. Jim Axelrod, vice president of marketing, would like to add a line of smoothies with a similar health emphasis. Each smoothie would include two free health supplements such as vitamins, antioxidants, and protein. Jim believes smoothie sales should help fill the slow mid-afternoon period. Adding the line of smoothies would require purchasing additional freezer space, machinery, and equipment. Jim provides the following projections of net sales, net income, and average total assets in support of his proposal.

|  | Sandwiches Only | Sandwiches and Smoothies |
|---|---|---|
| Net sales | $900,000 | $1,500,000 |
| Net income | 170,000 | 260,000 |
| Average total assets | 500,000 | 900,000 |

*Required:*

1. Calculate University Hero's return on assets, profit margin, and asset turnover for sandwiches only.
2. Calculate University Hero's return on assets, profit margin, and asset turnover for sandwiches and smoothies.
3. Based on these ratios, what recommendation would you make?

**P7–11** Optic Corporation operates a manufacturing plant in Arizona. Due to a significant decline in demand for the product manufactured at the Arizona site, an impairment test is deemed appropriate. Management has acquired the following information for the assets at the plant:

| | |
|---|---|
| Cost | $32,500,000 |
| Accumulated Depreciation | 14,200,000 |
| Estimated total cash flows to be generated by the Arizona plant | 15,000,000 |

Determine the impairment loss (LO7–8)
*See JP7–5 for journal entries.*

The fair value of the Arizona plant is estimated to be $11,000,000.

*Required:*

1. Determine the amount of impairment loss, if any.
2. If a loss is indicated, determine the financial statement effects of the loss.
3. Repeat requirement 1, assuming that the estimated future cash flows are $12,000,000 instead of $15,000,000.
4. Repeat requirement 1, assuming that the estimated future cash flows are $19,000,000 instead of $15,000,000.

## JOURNAL ENTRIES

## Journal Entries—Brief Exercises

**JBE7–1** Whole Grain Bakery purchases an industrial bread machine for $30,000. In addition to the purchase price, the company makes the following expenditures: freight, $2,000; installation, $4,000; testing, $1,500; and property tax on the machine for the first year, $600. Record the purchase of the bread machine.

Record purchase of equipment (LO7–1)
*See BE7–2 for financial statement effects.*

**JBE7–2 On January 1,** Hawaiian Specialty Foods purchased equipment for $30,000. Residual value at the end of an estimated four-year service life is expected to be $3,000. Calculate and record depreciation expense for the first year using the straight-line method.

Record depreciation using straight-line (LO7–4)
*See BE7–10 for financial statement effects.*

**JBE7–3** Refer to the information in JBE7–2. Calculate and record depreciation expense for the first year using the double-declining-balance method.

Record depreciation using double-declining-balance (LO7–4)
*See BE7–11 for financial statement effects.*

**JBE7–4** Refer to the information in JBE7–2. In addition, the machine operated for 3,100 hours in the first year, and the company expects the machine to operate for a total of 20,000 hours over its service life. Calculate and record depreciation expense for the first year using the activity-based method.

Record depreciation using activity-based (LO7–4)
*See BE7–12 for financial statement effects.*

**JBE7–5** Masterson Supply purchased a small storage building for $20,000 to be used over a five-year period. The building has no residual value. Early in the fourth year, the storage building burned down. Record the retirement of the remaining book value of the storage building.

Record the disposal of long-term assets (LO7–6)
*See BE7–17 for financial statement effects.*

**JBE7–6** China Inn and Midwest Chicken exchanged assets. China Inn received delivery equipment and gave restaurant equipment. The fair value and book value of the restaurant equipment were $22,000 and $12,000 (original cost of $45,000 less accumulated depreciation

Record the exchange of long-term assets (LO7–6)
*See BE7–18 for financial statement effects.*

of $33,000), respectively. To equalize market values of the exchanged assets, China Inn paid $9,000 in cash to Midwest Chicken. Record the exchange of the delivery equipment and restaurant equipment for China Inn?

## Journal Entries—Exercises

Record purchase of equipment (LO7–1)
See E7–2 for financial statement effects.

**JE7–1** Orion Flour Mills purchased new equipment and made the following expenditures:

| | |
|---|---|
| Purchase price | $75,000 |
| Sales tax | 6,000 |
| Shipment of equipment | 1,000 |
| Insurance on the equipment for the first year | 700 |
| Installation of equipment | 2,000 |

**Required:**

Record the above expenditures for the new equipment. All expenditures were paid in cash.

Record goodwill (LO7–2)
See E7–5 for financial statement effects.

**JE7–2** Mainline Produce Corporation acquired all the outstanding common stock of Iceberg Lettuce Corporation for $30,000,000 in cash. The book values and fair values of Iceberg's assets and liabilities were as follows:

| | Book Value | Fair Value |
|---|---|---|
| Current assets | $11,400,000 | $14,400,000 |
| Property, plant, and equipment | 20,200,000 | 26,200,000 |
| Other assets | 3,400,000 | 4,400,000 |
| Current liabilities | 7,800,000 | 7,800,000 |
| Long-term liabilities | 13,200,000 | 12,200,000 |

**Required:**

1. Calculate the amount paid for goodwill.
2. Record the acquisition.

Record expenditures after acquisition (LO7–3)
See E7–8 for financial statement effects.

**JE7–3** Sub Sandwiches of America made the following expenditures related to its restaurant:
1. Replaced the heating equipment at a cost of $250,000.
2. Covered the patio area with a clear plastic dome and enclosed it with glass for use during the winter months. The total cost of the project was $750,000.
3. Performed annual building maintenance at a cost of $24,000.
4. Paid for annual insurance for the facility at $8,800.
5. Built a new sign above the restaurant, putting the company name in bright neon lights, for $9,900.
6. Paved a gravel parking lot at a cost of $65,000.

**Required:**

Sub Sandwiches of America credits Cash for each of these expenditures. Indicate the account it debits for each.

Record partial-year depreciation (LO7–4)
See E7–11 for financial statement effects.

**JE7–4** Togo's Sandwiches acquired equipment on April 1, 2024, for $18,000. The company estimates a residual value of $2,000 and a five-year service life.

**Required:**

Calculate and record the year-end adjusting entry for straight-line depreciation expense for 2024 and 2025, assuming a December 31 year-end.

Record partial-year depreciation (LO7–4)
See E7–12 for financial statement effects.

**JE7–5** Tasty Subs acquired a food-service truck on October 1, 2024, for $120,000. The company estimates a residual value of $40,000 and a four-year service life.

**Required:**

Calculate and record straight-line depreciation expense for 2024 and 2025, assuming a December 31 year-end.

**JE7–6** The Donut Stop acquired equipment for $19,000. The company uses straight-line depreciation and estimates a residual value of $3,000 and a four-year service life. At the end of the second year, the company estimates that the equipment will be useful for four additional years, for a total service life of six years rather than the original four. At the same time, the company also changed the estimated residual value to $1,200 from the original estimate of $3,000.

*Record depreciation of property, plant, and equipment (LO7–4)*
*See E7–13 for financial statement effects.*

*Required:*

Calculate and record the depreciation expense for years 3 through 6.

**JE7–7** Tasty Subs acquired a food-service truck on October 1, 2024, for $120,000. The company estimates a residual value of $40,000 and a four-year service life. It expects to drive the truck 100,000 miles. Actual mileage was 5,000 miles in 2024 and 28,000 miles in 2025.

*Record activity-based depreciation (LO7–4)*
*See E7–14 for financial statement effects.*

*Required:*

Calculate and record the depreciation expense using the activity-based method for 2024 and 2025, assuming a December 31 year-end.

**JE7–8** On January 1, 2024, Weaver Corporation purchased a patent for $237,000. The remaining legal life is 20 years, but the company estimates the patent will be useful for only six more years. In January 2026, the company incurred legal fees of $57,000 in successfully defending a patent infringement suit. The successful defense did not change the company's estimate of useful life. Weaver Corporation's year-end is December 31.

*Record amortization of intangible assets (LO7–5)*
*See E7–15 for financial statement effects.*

*Required:*

1. Record the purchase in 2024; amortization in 2024; amortization in 2025; legal fees in 2026; and amortization in 2026.
2. What is the balance in the Patent account at the end of 2026?

**JE7–9** Abbott Landscaping purchased a tractor at a cost of $42,000 and sold it three years later for $21,600. Abbott accounted for depreciation using the straight-line method, a five-year service life, and a $3,000 residual value. Tractors are included in the Equipment account.

*Record the disposal of long-term assets (LO7–6)*
*See E7–16 for financial statement effects.*

*Required:*

1. Record the sale.
2. Assume the tractor was sold for $13,600 instead of $21,600. Record the sale.

**JE7–10** Salad Express exchanged land it had been holding for future plant expansion for a more suitable parcel of land along distribution routes. Salad Express reported the old land on the previously issued balance sheet at its original cost of $70,000. According to an independent appraisal, the old land currently is worth $132,000. Salad Express paid $19,000 in cash to complete the transaction.

*Record the exchange of long-term assets (LO7–6)*
*See E7–17 for financial statement effects.*

*Required:*

1. What is the fair value of the new parcel of land received by Salad Express?
2. Record the exchange.

**JE7–11** Midwest Services, Inc., operates several restaurant chains throughout the Midwest. One restaurant chain has experienced sharply declining profits. The company's management has decided to test the property and equipment of the restaurants for possible impairment. The relevant information for these assets is presented below.

*Record impairment loss on property and equipment (LO7–8)*
*See E7–19 for financial statement effects.*

| | |
|---|---|
| Book value | $8.6 million |
| Estimated total future cash flows | 7.1 million |
| Fair value | 5.9 million |

*Required:*

1. Determine the amount of the impairment loss, if any.
2. Record the impairment loss, if any.

Record impairment loss on patent (LO7–8)
See E7–20 for financial statement effects.

**JE7–12** In 2018, Northeast Technologies purchased a patent for $450,000 to provide cloud computing services to customers. By the end of 2024, the patent had a book value of $300,000. Due to increased competition and new delivery methods in cloud computing services, management believes it should test the patent for impairment. Management estimates the patent will generate future cash flows of $375,000 over its remaining legal life and currently has a fair value of $330,000 at the end of 2024.

***Required:***

1. Determine and record the amount of the impairment loss, if any.
2. Now assume management estimates future cash flows of $220,000 and fair value of $180,000. Determine and record the amount of the impairment loss, if any.

## Journal Entries—Problems

Record goodwill (LO7–2)
See P7–3 for financial statement effects.

**JP7–1** Fresh Cut Corporation purchased all the outstanding common stock of Premium Meats for $12,000,000 in cash. The book values and fair values of Premium Meats' assets and liabilities were

|  | Book Value | Fair Value |
|---|---|---|
| Accounts Receivable | $ 1,800,000 | $ 1,600,000 |
| Equipment | 8,500,000 | 9,900,000 |
| Patents | 300,000 | 1,700,000 |
| Notes Payable | (2,700,000) | (2,700,000) |
| Net assets | $ 7,900,000 | $10,500,000 |

***Required:***

1. Calculate the amount Fresh Cut should report for goodwill.
2. Record Fresh Cut's acquisition of Premium Meats.

Compute goodwill and record amortization of intangible assets (LO7–2, 7–5)
See P7–6 for financial statement effects.

**JP7–2** The following information relates to the intangible assets of University Testing Services (UTS):

a. On January 1, 2024, UTS completed the purchase of Heinrich Corporation for $3,510,000 in cash. The fair value of the net identifiable assets of Heinrich was $3,200,000.

b. Included in the assets purchased from Heinrich was a patent valued at $82,250. The original legal life of the patent was 20 years; there are 12 years remaining, but UTS believes the patent will be useful for only 7 more years.

c. UTS acquired a franchise on July 1, 2024, by paying an initial franchise fee of $333,000. The contractual life of the franchise is nine years.

***Required:***

1. Record the year-end adjusting entry for amortization expense, if any, for the intangible assets at December 31, 2024.
2. Prepare the intangible asset section of the December 31, 2024, balance sheet.

Record depreciation of property and equipment and amortization of intangible assets (LO7–4, 7–5)
See P7–7 for financial statement effects.

**JP7–3** Solich Sandwich Shop had the following long-term asset balances as of January 1, 2024:

|  | Cost | Accumulated Depreciation | Book Value |
|---|---|---|---|
| Land | $ 95,000 | – | $ 95,000 |
| Building | 460,000 | $(165,600) | 294,400 |
| Equipment | 235,000 | (50,000) | 185,000 |
| Patent | 250,000 | (100,000) | 150,000 |

Additional information:

- Solich purchased all the assets at the beginning of 2022.
- The building is depreciated over a 10-year service life using the double-declining-balance method and estimating no residual value.

- The equipment is depreciated over a nine-year service life using the straight-line method with an estimated residual value of $10,000.
- The patent is estimated to have a five-year service life with no residual value and is amortized using the straight-line method.
- Depreciation and amortization have been recorded for 2022 and 2023 (first two years).

***Required:***

1. For the year ended December 31, 2024 (third year), record the adjusting entry for depreciation expense for buildings and equipment. Land is not depreciated.
2. For the year ended December 31, 2024, record the adjusting entry for amortization expense for the patent.
3. Calculate the book value for each of the four long-term assets at December 31, 2024.

**JP7–4** New Morning Bakery is in the process of closing its operations. It sold its two-year-old bakery ovens to Great Harvest Bakery for $700,000. The ovens originally cost $910,000, had an estimated service life of 10 years, had an estimated residual value of $60,000, and were depreciated using straight-line depreciation. Complete the requirements below for New Morning Bakery.

**Record the disposal of long-term assets (LO7–6)**
*See P7–8 for financial statement effects.*

***Required:***

1. Calculate the balance in the Accumulated Depreciation account at the end of the second year.
2. Calculate the book value of the ovens at the end of the second year.
3. What is the gain or loss on the sale of the ovens at the end of the second year?
4. Record the sale of the ovens at the end of the second year.

**JP7–5** Optic Corporation operates a manufacturing plant in Arizona. Due to a significant decline in demand for the product manufactured at the Arizona site, an impairment test is deemed appropriate. Management has acquired the following information for the assets at the plant:

**Record the impairment loss (LO7–8)**
*See P7–11 for financial statement effects.*

| | |
|---|---|
| Cost | $32,500,000 |
| Accumulated Depreciation | 14,200,000 |
| Estimated total cash flows to be generated by the Arizona plant | 15,000,000 |

The fair value of the Arizona plant is estimated to be $11,000,000.

***Required:***

1. Determine the amount of impairment loss, if any.
2. If a loss is indicated, record the loss.
3. Repeat requirement 1, assuming that the estimated future cash flows are $12,000,000 instead of $15,000,000.
4. Repeat requirement 1, assuming that the estimated future cash flows are $19,000,000 instead of $15,000,000.

**JP7–6** On January 1, 2024, the general ledger of TNT Fireworks includes the following account balances:

**Comprehensive problem**

| Accounts | Debit | Credit |
|---|---|---|
| Cash | $ 58,700 | |
| Accounts Receivable | 25,000 | |
| Allowance for Uncollectible Accounts | | $ 2,200 |
| Inventory | 36,300 | |
| Notes Receivable (5%, due in 2 years) | 12,000 | |
| Land | 155,000 | |
| Accounts Payable | | 14,800 |
| Common Stock | | 220,000 |
| Retained Earnings | | 50,000 |
| Totals | $287,000 | $287,000 |

During January 2024, the following transactions occur:

January 1    Purchase equipment for $19,500. The company estimates a residual value of $1,500 and a five-year service life.
January 4    Pay cash on accounts payable, $9,500.
January 8    Purchase additional inventory on account, $82,900.
January 15   Receive cash on accounts receivable, $22,000
January 19   Pay cash for salaries, $29,800.
January 28   Pay cash for January utilities, $16,500.
January 30   Firework sales for January total $220,000. All of these sales are on account. The cost of the units sold is $115,000.

*Required:*

1. Record each of the transactions listed above.
2. Record adjusting entries on January 31.
   a. Depreciation on the equipment for the month of January is calculated using the straight-line method.
   b. At the end of January, $3,000 of accounts receivable are past due, and the company estimates that 50% of these accounts will not be collected. Of the remaining accounts receivable, the company estimates that 3% will not be collected. The note receivable of $12,000 is considered fully collectible and therefore is not included in the estimate of uncollectible accounts.
   c. Accrued interest revenue on notes receivable for January.
   d. Unpaid salaries at the end of January are $32,600.
   e. Accrued income taxes at the end of January are $9,000.
3. Prepare an adjusted trial balance as of January 31, 2024, after updating beginning balances (above) for transactions during January (requirement 1) and adjusting entries at the end of January (requirement 2).
4. Prepare a multiple-step income statement for the period ended January 31, 2024.
5. Prepare a classified balance sheet as of January 31, 2024.
6. Record closing entries.
7. Analyze how well TNT Fireworks manages its assets:
   a. Calculate the return on assets ratio for the month of January. If the average return on assets for the industry in January is 2%, is the company more or less profitable than other companies in the same industry?
   b. Calculate the profit margin for the month of January. If the industry average profit margin is 4%, is the company more or less efficient at converting sales to profit than other companies in the same industry?
   c. Calculate the asset turnover ratio for the month of January. If the industry average asset turnover is 0.5 times per month, is the company more or less efficient at producing revenues with its assets than other companies in the same industry?

## DATA ANALYTICS

    Visit Connect to view **Data Analytics** questions related to:

1. Applying Excel
2. Data Visualizations
3. Tableau Dashboard Activities
4. Applying Tableau

## ANSWERS TO THE SELF-STUDY QUESTIONS

1. b   2. d   3. d   4. c   5. a   6. b   7. d   8. b   9. a   10. a   11. c   12. c   13. c   14. b   15. d

# Cash and Investments

## Learning Objectives

## Self-Study Materials

## Feature Story

### Is Microsoft a Bank?

**Microsoft** is one of the most successful tech companies in the world with operations around the globe. Microsoft is also one of the largest tech companies, reporting total assets of approximately $259 billion in its balance sheet. Would it surprise you to learn that $136 billion of these assets are in cash and investments? This level of cash and investment holdings is greater than most mid-sized banks in the United States, which typically have cash and investment holdings between $8 billion and $50 billion. Would it also surprise you that Microsoft doesn't earn a very high return on these investments, generally less than 5 percent annually? If Microsoft is a bank, then it's not a very good one.

So why would Microsoft hold so much cash and low-return investments rather than pumping those resources back into more productive assets? Microsoft is not alone in this investing endeavor. In fact, most technology companies have cash and investment balances that make up more than half of all assets reported in the balance sheet. **Apple**, **Google**, **Cisco**, and **Oracle** all maintain large balances in their cash and investment accounts. Having liquid resources on hand allows tech companies to quickly respond to the rapidly changing landscape of their industry. In order to remain competitive, when the next big idea comes along, tech companies need to be able to quickly deploy resources towards that new idea.

In this chapter, you'll learn why companies like Microsoft make investments in equity and debt securities and how these investments impact the financial statements. You'll see that investment accounting includes a number of different methods of accounting, which depend on factors such as the nature of the investments, the percentage of ownership represented by the investments (in the case of equity investments), and the intended holding period of the investment.

■ **LO8–1**
Define cash and cash equivalents

# CASH AND CASH EQUIVALENTS

The amount of **cash** held by a company is reported in its balance sheet. This balance includes currency, coins, and balances in savings and checking accounts, as well as items acceptable for deposit in these accounts, such as checks received from customers. The amount also includes the cash to be collected from sales to customers who use credit cards or debit cards, because cash from those transactions typically will be deposited electronically into the company's bank account within a few days.

The balance of cash also includes **cash equivalents**, which are short-term investments that have a maturity date no longer than three months from the date of purchase. Common examples of such investments are money market funds, Treasury bills, and certificates of deposit. These investments are reported in the balance sheet at their **fair value**, which is the amount an investment could be bought or sold for in a current transaction between willing parties.

Cash equivalents provide a good alternative to holding idle cash. Idle cash earns no returns for the company or its shareholders until that cash is spent on productive assets. For that reason, companies often make short-term investments in cash equivalents until that cash is put to use.

Companies typically disclose the different components of the cash balance in the notes to the financial statements. For example, **Adobe**'s balance sheet reports cash and cash equivalents of $1,642,755. In the notes to the financial statements, Adobe then discloses the following additional information provided in Illustration 8-1.

**ILLUSTRATION 8–1**

Excerpt from Adobe's Annual Report

> ### ADOBE
> #### Notes to the Financial Statements (excerpt)
>
> Cash equivalents consist of instruments with remaining maturities of three months or less at the date of purchase. In general, these investments are free of trading restrictions. We carry these investments at fair value, based on quoted market prices or other readily available market information.
>
> |  | Estimated Fair Value |
> |---|---|
> | Cash | $    368,564 |
> | Cash equivalents: |  |
> | Money market mutual funds | 1,234,188 |
> | Time deposits | 40,023 |
> | Total cash and cash equivalents | $1,642,775 |

Several factors affect the amount of cash held by a company. One factor is the volatility or seasonality of operations. Companies that are more susceptible to short-term dips in the business cycle often tend to hold more cash to reduce the risk of default on their debt. In addition, companies prefer to have sufficient cash available to make timely purchases of long-term operating assets or invest strategically in other companies. Having sufficient cash allows the company to respond quickly to these opportunities. The use of internal cash also represents a lower-cost alternative to external financing. We'll discuss external financing through debt in Chapter 9 and through equity in Chapter 10. Next, we discuss why companies sometimes use their cash holdings to invest in other companies.

 **KEY POINT**

Cash includes coins and currency, checks received, and balances in savings and checking accounts. The cash balance also includes credit card and debit card sales, as well as cash equivalents, defined as investments that mature within three months from the date of purchase (such as money market funds, Treasury bills, and certificates of deposit).

# Why Companies Invest in Other Companies

■ **LO8–2**
Explain why companies invest in other companies.

Beyond investments in cash equivalents, companies also invest in other companies. We'll discuss the two basic types of investments in this chapter—equity investments (Part B) and debt investments (Part C). There are a variety of reasons for making these investments:

1. To receive dividends, earn interest, or gain from the increase in the value of their investment.
2. To temporarily invest excess cash created by operating in seasonal industries.
3. To build strategic alliances, increase market share, enter new industries, or enter markets in new countries.

Companies purchase *equity securities* for dividend income and for appreciation in the value of the stock. Many companies pay a stable dividend stream to their investors. Historically, **General Electric** has been one of the most reliable, highest-dividend-paying stocks on the New York Stock Exchange. In contrast, some companies pay little or no dividends. Companies with large expansion plans, called *growth companies,* prefer to reinvest earnings in the growth of the company rather than distribute earnings to investors in the form of cash dividends. For example, **Starbucks**, founded in 1987, did not pay a cash dividend until March 2010. Even without receiving dividends, investors still benefit when companies reinvest earnings, leading to even more profits in the future and eventually higher stock prices.

Companies purchase *debt securities* primarily for the interest revenue they provide, although investment returns also are affected when the values of debt securities change over time. The value of a debt security with fixed interest payments changes in the opposite direction of interest rates. For example, when general market interest rates decrease, the market value of a bond with fixed interest payments goes up because the fixed interest payments are now more attractive to investors.

The seasonal nature of some companies' operations also influences their investment balances. *Seasonal* refers to the revenue activities of a company varying based on the time (or season) of the year. For instance, agricultural and construction companies enjoy more revenues in the summer, and ski resorts earn most of their revenues in the winter. Most retail companies see their sales revenues increase dramatically during the holiday season. As a result of having seasonal operations, companies save excess cash generated during the busy part of the year to maintain operations during the slower time of the year. With this excess cash, companies tend to purchase low-risk investments such as money market funds (savings accounts), government bonds, or highly-rated corporate bonds. These low-risk investments enable companies to earn interest while ensuring the funds will be available when needed during the slow season. Investing excess cash in stocks is more risky because the value of stocks varies more than the value of bonds. Stocks typically have greater upside potential, providing a higher average return to their investors than do bonds over the long run. However, stocks can lose value in the short run, making them a better choice for investments that are more long-term in nature.

Companies also can make sizable long-term stock investments in other companies for strategic purposes. For instance, **AT&T** acquired **Cingular Wireless** to gain a stronger presence in the market for cell phones. **Coca-Cola** acquired **Minute Maid** and **PepsiCo** purchased **Tropicana** in order to diversify beyond soft drinks. Sometimes, a company will remove competition and increase market share by purchasing a controlling interest (more than 50% of its voting stock) in a competing company. Companies also might purchase a controlling interest in an established company in a *different* industry to expand into that industry and avoid many of the start-up costs associated with beginning a new business from scratch.

 **KEY POINT**

Companies invest in other companies primarily to receive dividends, earn interest, and gain from the increase in the value of their investment. Companies in seasonal industries often invest excess funds generated during the busy season and draw on these funds in the slow season. Many companies also make investments for strategic purposes to develop closer business ties, increase market share, or expand into new industries.

## PART B

# EQUITY INVESTMENTS

**Equity investments** are the "flip side" of issuing stock. One company issues stock, and another company invests by purchasing that stock. We've discussed the issuance of stock briefly in prior chapters and will discuss it in more depth in Chapter 10. Here, we discuss how companies that purchase stock account for their investment.

The way we account for equity investments is determined by the *degree of influence* an investor has over the company in which it invests. **A guideline for determining the degree of influence is the percentage of stock held by the investor.** Illustration 8–2 summarizes the reporting methods for equity investments.

**ILLUSTRATION 8–2**

Accounting for Equity Investments

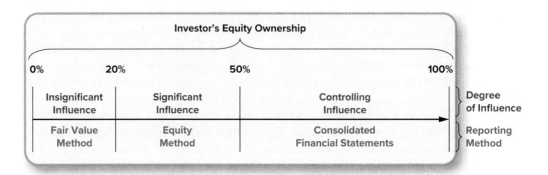

The **fair value method** is used when a company (investor) purchases less than 20% of the voting shares of another company's stock (investee). In this case, the investor typically is presumed to have *insignificant* influence over the investee. Under the fair value method:

1. Equity securities are reported in the balance sheet at their fair value.
2. Changes in fair value from one period to the next are reported as gains and losses in the income statement.

As discussed previously, fair value is the amount an investment could be bought or sold for in a current transaction between willing parties. For example, when you purchased your car, you and the car dealership (or whomever you bought the car from) came to an agreement on the purchase price, or fair value, of the car. What could you sell that car for today? That's the car's current fair value.

The **equity method** is used when an investor purchases between 20% and 50% of the voting stock of a company. In this case, the investor typically is presumed to have *significant influence* over the investee. By voting all those shares with a single intent, the investor can influence decisions in the direction it desires.

**Consolidated financial statements** are prepared when an investor purchases more than 50% of the voting stock of a company. In this case, the investor typically is presumed to have *controlling influence;* by voting those shares, the investor (referred to as the parent) actually can control the operations of the investee (referred to as the subsidiary). Both companies continue to operate as separate legal entities, but because they are viewed as a single economic entity, the parent company prepares one set of financial statements as if the two companies were operating as a combined company.

## Equity Investments with Insignificant Influence

■ **LO8–3**

Account for investments in equity securities when the investor has *insignificant* influence.

The critical events over the life of an equity investment in another company include the following:

1. Purchasing the equity security.
2. Receiving dividends (for some equity securities).

3. Holding the investment during periods in which the investment's fair value changes (*unrealized* holding gains and losses).

4. Selling the investment (*realized* gains and losses).

Let's go through each of these events.

## PURCHASE EQUITY INVESTMENTS

To see how a company accounts for the purchase of an equity investment, let's assume Nathan's Sportswear purchases 1,000 shares of Canadian Falcon common stock for $30 per share on December 6, 2024. Canadian Falcon's total number of shares outstanding is 20,000, so Nathan's Sportswear owns 5% of the shares (= 1,000/20,000 shares), requiring it to account for the investment using the fair value method.

The financial statement effects of the investment in Canadian Falcon are as follows:

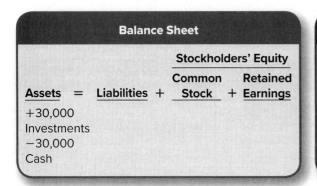
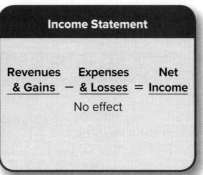

## RECEIVE CASH DIVIDENDS

The receipt of dividends is reported in the income statement as dividend revenue. If Canadian Falcon pays cash dividends of $0.50 per share on December 15, 2024, then Nathan's Sportswear will receive $500 in cash on its 1,000 shares of the stock.

The financial statement effects of receiving this dividend are as follows:

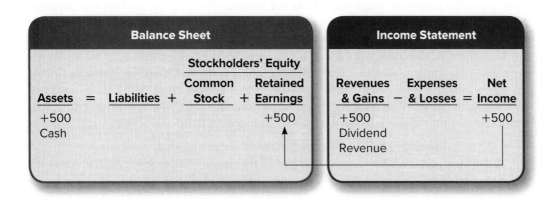

Cash
---
| 500 | |

Dividend Revenue
---
| | 500 |

**DEBITS & CREDITS**

To report dividends received from the investment:

| | Debit | Credit |
|---|---|---|
| Cash.................................................................................. | 500 | |
|    Dividend Revenue ................................................... | | 500 |

## ADJUST TO FAIR VALUE

At the end of each period, we report these investment assets at their *fair value*. We do this by changing the value of the investment to the current fair value on the balance sheet. If Canadian Falcon's stock at the end of 2024 has a current price of $28 per share, then Nathan's Sportswear needs to decrease the reported amount of the investment ($30 per share) to its current fair value ($28 per share). This requires a downward adjustment to the Investments account of $2 for each of the 1,000 shares or $2,000 in total. Nathan's Sportswear would also report a $2,000 unrealized loss in the income statement to reflect the decline in value of the Canadian Falcon investment.

The financial statement effects of reporting the investment in Canadian Falcon at its fair value are as follows:

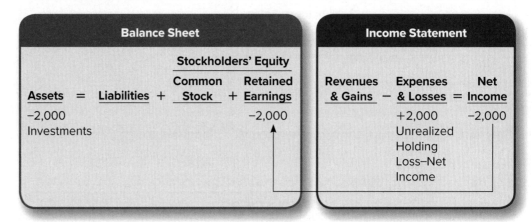

Unrealized Holding
Loss—Net Income
---
| 2,000 | |

Investments
---
| | 2,000 |

**DEBITS & CREDITS**

To report the investment at its fair value:

| | Debit | Credit |
|---|---|---|
| Unrealized Holding Loss—Net Income ....................................... | 2,000 | |
|    Investments .......................................................................... | | 2,000 |

The process of reporting investments at their fair value in the balance sheet involves an account we've not yet discussed called *Unrealized Holding Loss—Net Income*. The term *unrealized* means the loss has not been realized (has not been obtained) in the form of less cash received (or the right to receive less cash). The loss is *realized* when the investment has been sold, and the loss is "locked in." **The unrealized holding loss is reported in the current year's income statement when calculating net income.** Even though the loss is unrealized, reporting it as part of current net income helps to reflect that most equity investments could be sold immediately, and any fair value changes would be realized in cash.

Unrealized holding gains and losses are reported as part of nonoperating revenues and expenses. Illustration 8–3 shows an example of the income statement for Nathan's Sportswear. To complete the income statement, we assume sales revenue totals $100,000 and operating expenses are $60,000 for the year ended December 31, 2024. From the transactions above, the income statement also reports as nonoperating items:

- **$500** in dividend revenue from December 15.
- **$2,000** unrealized holding loss resulting from the downward fair value adjustment at the end of the year.

**ILLUSTRATION 8–3**

Income Statement for
Nathan's Sportswear

| NATHAN'S SPORTSWEAR<br>Income Statement<br>For the year ended December 31, 2024 | |
| --- | --- |
| Sales revenue | $100,000 |
| Operating expenses | 60,000 |
| Operating income | 40,000 |
| Dividend revenue | 500 |
| Unrealized holding loss | (2,000) |
| Net income | $ 38,500 |

If the fair value of Canadian Falcon's stock had *increased* by $2 per share by the end of the year, Nathan's Sportswear would have reported a $2,000 *Unrealized Holding Gain–Net Income*.

## SELL EQUITY INVESTMENTS

We report the sale of equity investments similar to the sale of many other assets, such as land (discussed in Chapter 7).

- If the investment sells for *more* than its recorded amount, we realize a *gain* on the sale of investments.
- If the investment sells for *less* than its recorded amount, we realize a *loss* on the sale of investments.

Realized gains and losses on the sale of investments are reported as nonoperating revenues and expenses in the income statement.

Suppose Nathan's Sportswear sells 100 shares of Canadian Falcon for $24 per share on January 18, 2025. How much is the gain or loss on the sale? Let's first remember that at the end of 2024 (prior year), Nathan's Sportswear adjusted the Investments account by decreasing it $2,000. Since the investment was originally recorded for $30,000, the investment is now in the accounting records at $28,000, or $28 per share for 1,000 shares. By selling shares at $24 per share, there is a $4 loss per share on each of the 100 shares sold.

The financial statement effects of selling the 100 shares are as follows:

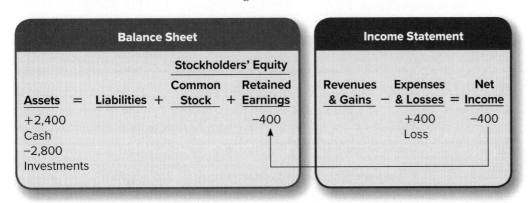

| Balance Sheet | | | | |
| --- | --- | --- | --- | --- |
| | | | Stockholders' Equity | |
| | | | Common | Retained |
| Assets | = | Liabilities + | Stock + | Earnings |
| +2,400<br>Cash<br>−2,800<br>Investments | | | | −400 |

| Income Statement | | |
| --- | --- | --- |
| Revenues<br>& Gains − | Expenses<br>& Losses = | Net<br>Income |
| | +400<br>Loss | −400 |

| DEBITS & CREDITS | | |
| --- | --- | --- |
| To record the sale of 100 shares at $24 per share: | | |
| | Debit | Credit |
| **Cash** (100 shares × $24) ............................................ | **2,400** | |
| **Loss**............................................................................. | **400** | |
| Investments (100 shares × $28)................................. | | **2,800** |

Cash
2,400 |
Loss
400 |
Investments
| 2,800

Now suppose the price of the stock has risen to $32 per share by February 26, 2025, and Nathan's Sportswear decides to sell another 100 shares. Since these shares are carried at $28 per share, there is a $4 gain per share on each of the 100 shares sold.

The financial statement effects of this sale are as follows:

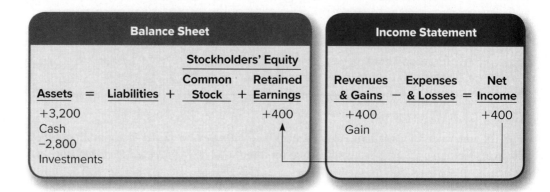

| Balance Sheet | | | | | | Income Statement | | |
|---|---|---|---|---|---|---|---|---|
| | | | **Stockholders' Equity** | | | | | |
| | | | Common | Retained | | Revenues | Expenses | Net |
| Assets | = | Liabilities + | Stock | + Earnings | | & Gains | − & Losses | = Income |
| +3,200 Cash | | | | +400 | | +400 Gain | | +400 |
| −2,800 Investments | | | | | | | | |

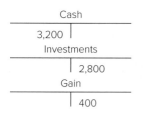

| Cash | |
|---|---|
| 3,200 | |

| Investments | |
|---|---|
| | 2,800 |

| Gain | |
|---|---|
| | 400 |

**DEBITS & CREDITS**

To record the sale of 100 shares at $24 per share:

| | Debit | Credit |
|---|---|---|
| **Cash** (100 shares × $32) | **3,200** | |
| **Investments** (100 shares × $28) | | **2,800** |
| **Gain** | | **400** |

### KEY POINT

We report investments at fair value when a company has an insignificant influence over another company in which it invests, often indicated by an ownership interest of less than 20%. Dividends received are reported as dividend revenue in net income. Unrealized holding gains and losses and realized gains and losses from the sale of the investments are included in net income.

## Let's Review

Sheer Designs, a custom clothing designer, has heard great things about Slacks 5th Avenue and decided to make a small investment (insignificant influence) in the corporation's common stock. Sheer Designs has the following transactions relating to its investment in Slacks 5th Avenue.

| January | 15 | Purchase 500 shares of common stock for $20 per share. |
|---|---|---|
| June | 30 | Receive a cash dividend of $2 per share. |
| October | 1 | Sell 100 shares of common stock for $25 per share. |
| December | 31 | The fair value of Slacks 5th Avenue's stock equals $23 per share. |

**Required:**

1. Determine the financial statement effects of these transactions, including the fair value adjustment on December 31.

2. Calculate the balance in the Investments account on December 31.

**Solution:**

1. The financial statement effects are as follows:

| | | Balance Sheet | | | | | Income Statement | | |
|---|---|---|---|---|---|---|---|---|---|
| | | | | | **Stockholders' Equity** | | | | |
| | | | | | **Common** | **Retained** | **Revenues** | **Expenses** | **Net** |
| | **Assets** | = | **Liabilities** | + | **Stock** | + **Earnings** | **& Gains** | − **& Losses** | = **Income** |
| January 15: (Purchase) | +10,000 Investments −10,000 Cash | | | | | | | | |
| June 30: (Dividend) | +1,000 Cash | | | | | +1,000 | +1,000 Dividend Revenue | | +1,000 |
| October 1: (Sale) | +2,500 Cash −2,000 Investments | | | | | +500 | +500 Gain | | +500 |
| December 31: (Fair value) | +1,200 Investments | | | | | +1,200 | +1,200 Unrealized Holding Gain–Net Income | | +1,200 |

The journal entries associated with these transactions are as follows:

| | Debit | Credit |
|---|---|---|
| **January 15** | | |
| **Investments** ............................................................................... | **10,000** | |
|     **Cash** .................................................................................. | | **10,000** |
|     *(Purchase common stock)* | | |
|     ($10,000 = 500 *shares* × $20) | | |
| **June 30** | | |
| **Cash** ....................................................................................... | **1,000** | |
|     **Dividend Revenue** ............................................................. | | **1,000** |
|     *(Receive cash dividends)* | | |
|     ($1,000 = 500 *shares* × $2) | | |
| **October 1** | | |
| **Cash** (100 *shares* × $25) ............................................................. | **2,500** | |
|     **Investments** (100 *shares* × $20) ....................................... | | **2,000** |
|     **Gain** (difference) ............................................................... | | **500** |
|     *(Sell investments above recorded amount)* | | |
| **December 31** | | |
| **Investments** ............................................................................... | **1,200** | |
|     **Unrealized Holding Gain—Net Income** .................................. | | **1,200** |
|     *(Adjust investments to fair value)* | | |
|     ($1,200 = 400 *shares* × $3) | | |

2. The balance in the Investments account on December 31 is $9,200, which equals the 400 remaining shares times $23 per share fair value.

| **Investments** | |
|---|---|
| Initial investment | $10,000 |
| *Less*: Sale of shares | (2,000) |
| *Plus*: Increase in fair value | 1,200 |
| Ending balance (400 shares × $23) | $ 9,200 |

# Equity Investments with Significant Influence

■ **LO8–4**
Account for investments in equity securities when the investor has *significant* influence.

When a company owns between 20% and 50% of the common stock in another company, it is presumed that the investing company exercises *significant influence* over the investee. Share ownership provides voting rights, and by voting these shares, the investing company can sway decisions in the direction it desires, such as the selection of members of the board of directors or the payment of dividends. This significant influence changes the accounting for the investment. When a company has significant influence over an investee, the company is required to use the equity method. Under the equity method, the investment is initially recorded at cost. After that, the investment balance is

1. Increased by the investor's percentage share of the investee's net income (or decreased by its share of a loss).
2. Decreased by the investor's percentage share of the investee's dividends paid.
3. Not adjusted for changes in fair value while held.

The rationale for this approach is the presumption that the fortunes of the investor and investee are so intertwined that, as the investee prospers, the investor prospers proportionately. Stated differently, as the investee earns additional net assets (income), the investor's share of those net assets increases. When the investee pays out assets (dividends), the investor's share of the remaining net assets decreases. **It's also important to recognize that the equity method ignores fair value changes in the investment.**[1] Let's now walk through the financial statement effects of the equity method.

## PURCHASE EQUITY INVESTMENTS

On January 2, 2025, Nathan's Sportswear purchases 5,000 shares of International Outfitter's common stock for $30 per share. International Outfitter's total number of shares outstanding is 20,000, so Nathan's owns 25% of the common stock (= 5,000/20,000 shares). By holding 25% of the stock, Nathan's Sportswear can exert significant influence over the operations of International Outfitter and is required to account for its investment using the equity method.

The financial statement effects of the initial investment are as follows:

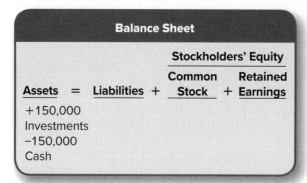

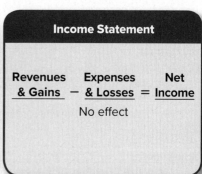

**DEBITS & CREDITS**
To record the initial investment in International Outfitters:

| | Debit | Credit |
|---|---|---|
| Investments | 150,000 | |
| Cash | | 150,000 |

## RECOGNIZE EQUITY INCOME

Under the equity method, the investor (Nathan's Sportswear) includes in net income its portion of the investee's (International Outfitter's) net income. Assume on December 31, 2025, International Outfitter reports net income of $30,000 for the year. Nathan's Sportswear

---

[1]Adjustment to fair value is an allowable alternative under the equity method but is not common in practice.

reports $7,500 of equity income, which represents its 25% share of International Outfitter's net income of $30,000.

The financial statement effects of accounting for the proportionate share of net income are:

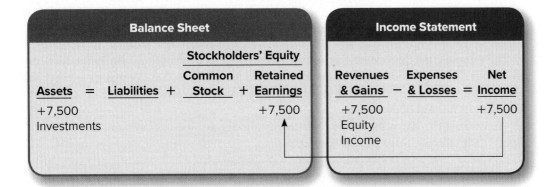

| Balance Sheet | | | | | |
|---|---|---|---|---|---|
| | | | **Stockholders' Equity** | |
| | | | **Common** | **Retained** |
| **Assets** | **=** | **Liabilities** | **+** | **Stock** | **+** | **Earnings** |
| +7,500 | | | | | +7,500 |
| Investments | | | | | |

| Income Statement | | | |
|---|---|---|---|
| **Revenues & Gains** | **−** | **Expenses & Losses** | **=** | **Net Income** |
| +7,500 | | | +7,500 |
| Equity | | | |
| Income | | | |

| DEBITS & CREDITS | | |
|---|---|---|
| To report equity method income from the investment in International Outfitters: | | |
| | **Debit** | **Credit** |
| Investments ($30,000 × 25% ownership)..................................................... | **7,500** | |
|    Equity Income ......................................................................................... | | **7,500** |

| Investments | |
|---|---|
| 7,500 | |

| Equity Income | |
|---|---|
| | 7,500 |

The investee's net income increases the investor's Investments account and Equity Income account. Equity Income is a revenue account included as a nonoperating revenue in the income statement. The reason Nathan's Sportswear can report a portion of International Outfitter's net income as its own is that significant ownership essentially eliminates the independent operations of the two companies. Nathan's Sportswear can significantly influence the operations of International Outfitter. **Therefore, the success (or failure) of International Outfitter's operations should be partially assigned to Nathan's Sportswear and recognized as income (or loss) in its income statement, based on its portion of ownership.**

## RECEIVE CASH DIVIDENDS

Because we record equity income when the investee reports net income, it would be inappropriate to record equity income again when the investee distributes that same net income as dividends to the investor. To do so would be to double-count equity income. Instead, the investor records dividend payments received from the investee as a *reduction* in the Investments account. One way to think about this dividend is as a return of capital to the stockholders. Assuming International Outfitter pays total dividends of $10,000 to all shareholders on December 31, 2025, Nathan's Sportswear receives its share of $2,500 (= $10,000 × 25% ownership).

The financial statement effects of the receipt of the dividend are as follows:

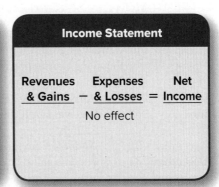

| Balance Sheet | | | | | |
|---|---|---|---|---|---|
| | | | **Stockholders' Equity** | |
| | | | **Common** | **Retained** |
| **Assets** | **=** | **Liabilities** | **+** | **Stock** | **+** | **Earnings** |
| +2,500 | | | | | |
| Cash | | | | | |
| −2,500 | | | | | |
| Investments | | | | | |

| Income Statement | | | |
|---|---|---|---|
| **Revenues & Gains** | **−** | **Expenses & Losses** | **=** | **Net Income** |
| | No effect | | |

Cash

| 2,500 | |

Investments

| 2,500 | |

**DEBITS & CREDITS**

To record the receipt of dividends from International Outfitters:

|  | Debit | Credit |
|---|---|---|
| **Cash** ($10,000 × 25% ownership)............................................................... | **2,500** | |
| **Investments** ................................................................................. | | **2,500** |

The rationale for this accounting is that the investee is distributing cash in the form of dividends. This distribution of assets by the investee reduces that company's equity. To account for the investee's decrease in equity, the investor decreases its Investments account based on its portion of ownership.

We can see the balances in the Investments and Equity Income accounts for Nathan's Sportswear after the three transactions above.

| Investments | |
|---|---|
| Initial investment | $150,000 |
| *Plus*: 25% of investee net income | 7,500 |
| *Less*: 25% of investee dividends | (2,500) |
| Ending balance | $155,000 |
| **Equity Income** | |
| 25% of investee net income | $  7,500 |

The Investments account increases by the initial investment and the investor's share of the investee's net income, and it decreases by the investor's share of the investee's dividends. The Equity Income account reflects the investor's share of net income rather than its share of dividends.

The equity method can differ significantly from reporting investments under the fair value method. Under the fair value method, the investment by Nathan's Sportswear would be reported at the purchase price of $150,000 and then be adjusted to fair value at the end of each period. Under the equity method, no adjustment is made to fair value. In addition, Nathan's Sportswear would report only $2,500 of dividend revenue under the fair value method, rather than the $7,500 of equity income reported using the equity method.

 **KEY POINT**

We initially record equity method investments at cost. Under the equity method, the balance of the Investments account increases for the investor's share of the investee's net income and decreases for the investor's share of the investee's cash dividends. Equity Income reflects the investor's share of the investee's net income.

**Let's Review**    To help ensure control over availability and delivery of its inventory, Designer Dresses purchases a 40% investment (significant influence) in Anderson Textile's common stock. Designer Dresses has the following transactions relating to its investment in Anderson Textile.

| January | 1 | Purchase 500 shares of common stock for $20 per share. |
|---|---|---|
| June | 30 | Receive a cash dividend of $500 (or 40% of Anderson's total dividend of $1,250). |
| December | 31 | Anderson Textile reports total net income of $5,000 for the year. |
| December | 31 | The fair value of Anderson Textile's stock equals $23 per share. |

**Required:**

1. Determine the financial statement effects of each of these transactions.

2. Calculate the balance of the Investments account on December 31.

**Solution:**

1. The financial statement effects are as follows:

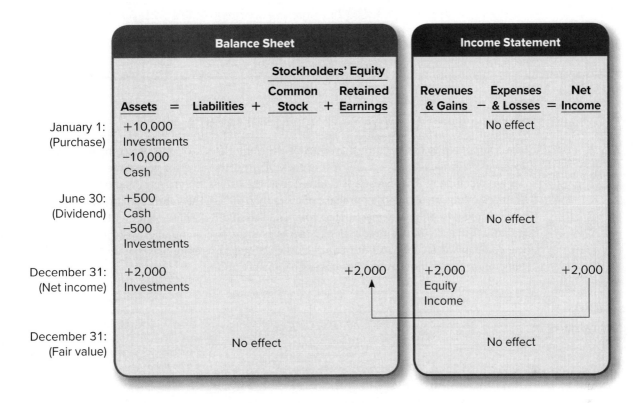

| | Balance Sheet | | | | | Income Statement | | |
|---|---|---|---|---|---|---|---|---|
| | | | | **Stockholders' Equity** | | | | |
| | | | | **Common** | **Retained** | **Revenues** | **Expenses** | **Net** |
| | **Assets** | **= Liabilities** | **+** | **Stock** | **+ Earnings** | **& Gains** | **− & Losses** | **= Income** |
| January 1: | +10,000 | | | | | | No effect | |
| (Purchase) | Investments | | | | | | | |
| | −10,000 | | | | | | | |
| | Cash | | | | | | | |
| June 30: | +500 | | | | | | | |
| (Dividend) | Cash | | | | | | No effect | |
| | −500 | | | | | | | |
| | Investments | | | | | | | |
| December 31: | +2,000 | | | | +2,000 | +2,000 | | +2,000 |
| (Net income) | Investments | | | | | Equity | | |
| | | | | | | Income | | |
| December 31: | | No effect | | | | | No effect | |
| (Fair value) | | | | | | | | |

Note that the financial statements are not adjusted on December 31 to fair value because we are using the equity method of accounting.

The journal entries associated with these transactions are as follows:

| | Debit | Credit |
|---|---|---|
| January 1 | | |
| **Investments** .......................................................... | **10,000** | |
| Cash ................................................................... | | **10,000** |
| (Purchase common stock) | | |
| June 30 | | |
| **Cash** .......................................................................... | **500** | |
| Investments ...................................................... | | **500** |
| (Receive cash dividends) | | |
| ($500 = $1,250 × 40% ownership) | | |
| December 31 | | |
| **Investments** .......................................................... | **2,000** | |
| Equity Income ................................................... | | **2,000** |
| (Earn equity income) | | |
| ($2,000 = $5,000 × 40% ownership) | | |
| December 31 | | |
| No adjustments are recorded for fair value changes when using the equity method. | | |

2. The balance of the Investments account on December 31 is $11,500.

| Investments | |
| --- | --- |
| Initial investment | $10,000 |
| *Less*: 40% of Anderson's dividends | (500) |
| *Plus*: 40% of Anderson's net income | 2,000 |
| Ending balance | $11,500 |

# Equity Investments with Controlling Influence

**■ LO8–5**

Account for investments in equity securities when the investor has *controlling* influence.

If a company purchases more than 50% of the voting stock of another company, it's said to have a *controlling influence.* By voting these shares, the investor actually can control the acquired company. The investor is referred to as the *parent;* the investee is the *subsidiary.*

Investments involving the purchase of more than 50% of the voting stock require the parent company to prepare consolidated financial statements. These statements combine the parent's and subsidiary's financial statements as if the two companies were a *single* reporting company, even though both companies continue to operate as separate legal entities. Illustration 8–4 demonstrates the concept of consolidation.

**ILLUSTRATION 8–4**

**Consolidation Method**

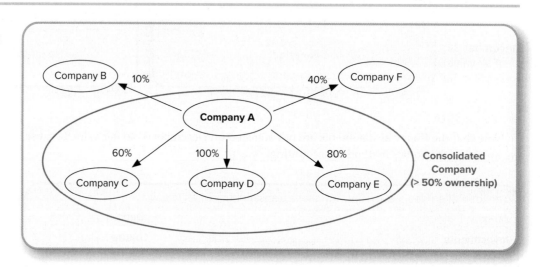

Suppose Company A owns common stock in five other companies. When preparing financial statements, Company A combines its financial statement results with all companies in which it has greater than 50% ownership (in this instance, Companies C, D, and E). For example, if Company A has $10 million cash, and Companies C, D, and E have $2 million, $4 million, and $6 million, respectively, the consolidated balance sheet would report cash of $22 million.[2] The cash balances for Companies B and F are not included in the consolidated financial statements of Company A. The 10% ownership (insignificant

---

[2]Any transactions between Companies A, C, D, and E are eliminated from consolidated reporting because these transactions are not with external parties. This avoids "double-counting" those amounts in the consolidated statements. For example, we report amounts owed by Company C to Company D as accounts payable in Company C's balance sheet and as accounts receivable in Company D's balance sheet. However, these amounts are not included in the consolidated balance sheet because a company can't owe money to itself, and the consolidated company is treated as a single company for financial reporting purposes.

influence) in Company B is accounted for using the fair value method, while the 40% ownership (significant influence) in Company F is accounted for using the equity method. The process of consolidating financial statements is beyond the scope of this introductory textbook and is covered in intermediate and advanced accounting textbooks.

 **KEY POINT**

Investments involving one company (parent) purchasing more than 50% of the voting stock of another company (subsidiary) require the parent company to prepare consolidated financial statements. These statements combine the parent's and subsidiary's financial statements as if the two companies were a single reporting company.

# DEBT INVESTMENTS

**PART C**

■ **LO8–6**
Account for investments in debt securities and understand the three classifications of debt investments.

Debt investments are the "flip side" of long-term debt: One party *borrows* by issuing a debt instrument, while another party *lends* by investing in the debt instrument. In Chapter 9, we will discuss how to report the issuance of bonds (a specific type of debt instrument recorded as bonds payable). While bonds payable incur interest expense, investment in bonds earns interest revenue. Here, we discuss how to report an *investment* in bonds and the interest revenue.

The critical events over the life of a debt investment in another company include the following:

1. Purchasing the debt security.
2. Receiving interest (for some debt securities).
3. Holding the investment during periods in which the investment's fair value changes (*unrealized* holding gains and losses).
4. Either selling the investment before maturity (*realized* gains and losses) or receiving principal payment at maturity.

Let's go through each of these events.

## PURCHASE DEBT INVESTMENTS

Assume on January 1, 2024, Nathan's Sportswear purchases $100,000 of 7%, 10-year bonds issued by California Coasters, with interest receivable semiannually on June 30 and December 31 each year. The bonds are issued "at par," which means that they are issued at their face amount.[3]

For Nathan's Sportswear, the financial statement effects of the investment in the bonds are as follows:

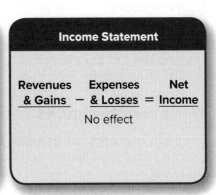

| Balance Sheet | | | | |
|---|---|---|---|---|
| | | | **Stockholders' Equity** | |
| | | | **Common** | **Retained** |
| **Assets** | **=** | **Liabilities +** | **Stock +** | **Earnings** |
| +100,000 Investments −100,000 Cash | | | | |

| Income Statement | | |
|---|---|---|
| **Revenues & Gains** | **Expenses − & Losses** | **Net = Income** |
| | No effect | |

---

[3]Bonds are sometimes issued at an amount different from their face amount (either a discount or premium). We'll discuss bonds issued at discounts or premiums in more detail in Chapter 9.

Investments

| 100,000 | |

Cash

| | 100,000 |

**DEBITS & CREDITS**

To record Nathan's investment in the bonds of California Coasters:

| | Debit | Credit |
|---|---|---|
| Investments ........................................................................................ | 100,000 | |
|   Cash ............................................................................................. | | 100,000 |

## EARN INTEREST REVENUE

On June 30, 2024, six months after the initial bond investment, Nathan's Sportswear will receive cash from California Coasters equal to the investment's face amount ($100,000) times the stated rate (7% annually, or 3.5% semiannually). Interest revenue will also be reported as follows:

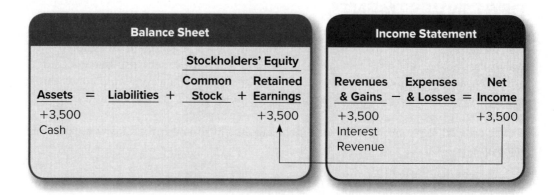

Cash

| 3,500 | |

Interest Revenue

| | 3,500 |

**DEBITS & CREDITS**

To report the semiannual interest received from the bond investment:

| | Debit | Credit |
|---|---|---|
| Cash............................................................................................... | 3,500 | |
|   Interest Revenue .......................................................................... | | 3,500 |

Nathan's Sportswear will receive this same semiannual interest payment of $3,500, and recognize $3,500 in interest revenue, every six months until the bond matures 10 years later on December 31, 2033.

 **KEY POINT**

Bond investments are the "flip side" of bonds payable. Bond investments are long-term assets that earn interest revenue, while bonds payable are long-term liabilities that incur interest expense.

## THREE CLASSIFICATIONS OF DEBT INVESTMENTS

The bonds issued by California Coasters had a 7% rate of interest and a fair value (or issue price) of $100,000 on January 1, 2024. This fair value reflected the price investors were willing to pay at the time of the issuance for the future cash flows of the bonds—principal at maturity and periodic interest payments. However, market conditions may change over time, causing investors to apply a different discount rate to the future cash flows of the bonds.

If market conditions cause investors' discount rate to increase, the fair value of the bonds will decrease. In that case, the investors holding the bonds suffer an *unrealized* holding loss.

The loss hasn't been realized because the investment hasn't been sold. Alternatively, market conditions could lower investors' discount rate applied to future cash flows of the bonds. In this case, the fair value of the bonds will increase, and investors will enjoy an unrealized holding gain.

**Accounting for these changes in fair value depends on the classification of the debt investment.** There are three types:

- Held-to-maturity securities are debt securities a company expects to hold until they *mature*, which means until the issuer is required to repay the full amount of the bonds to the investors. Companies are not required to adjust held-to-maturity securities to fair value because there is not an expectation of selling these securities in the bond market before they mature. Instead, these securities are carried at historical cost (or at amortized cost if the bonds were issued at a discount or premium).[4]

- Trading securities are debt investments the investor expects to sell (trade) in the near future. These securities are reported the same way we report equity investments with insignificant influence; we report trading securities as current assets at their fair value, and any unrealized gains or losses are recognized in the income statement as part of net income.

- Available-for-sale securities are debt investments held for reasons other than attempting to profit from trading in the near future and can be classified as either current or long-term assets. Like trading securities, these securities are reported at their fair value. However, unlike trading securities, unrealized gains and losses are reported as *other comprehensive income*, which we discuss next.

## ADJUST TO FAIR VALUE: AVAILABLE-FOR-SALE SECURITIES

As discussed in the section above, we don't adjust held-to-maturity securities for changes in fair value, because we don't plan to sell them. We do adjust trading securities to fair value, and the accounting is the same as we saw in Part B of this chapter for equity investments with insignificant influence. Here, we discuss how to adjust available-for-sale securities for changes in fair value.

Continuing our previous example, assume Nathan's Sportswear accounts for its $100,000 investment in California Coaster's bond as an available-for-sale security. Suppose interest rates fall during the year, and the bond's fair value increases to $101,035. This means the Investments account needs a fair value adjustment of $1,035 (= $101,035 − $100,000).

Because this investment is classified as available-for-sale, the unrealized holding gain associated with the increase in the fair value of the bond investment will be reported as *other comprehensive income*.

Comprehensive income consists of two components. You've already been introduced to the first component—net income. Net income consists of *all* revenues and expenses and *most* gains and losses. These items are reported in the income statement. However, there are a *few* gains and losses from nonowner transactions that we don't report in the income statement; instead, we report these gains and losses separately as the second component of comprehensive income known as other comprehensive income. Together, net income and other comprehensive income from comprehensive income.

$$\text{Net income} + \text{Other comprehensive income} = \text{Comprehensive income}$$

Other comprehensive income (OCI) items are reported as a component of stockholders' equity, in an account called Accumulated Other Comprehensive Income (or AOCI), that is separate from other components such as common stock, retained earnings, and treasury stock. This means any balance at the end of the year carries forward into the next year.

---

[4]However, U.S. GAAP does allow companies to elect a fair value option. Under this option, companies may report held-to-maturity securities at fair value, with unrealized gains and losses recognized in income in the period in which they occur—the same approach we use to account for trading securities.

In order to present the financial statement effects of the fair value adjustment to the bonds, we need to add Accumulated Other Comprehensive Income (AOCI) to the Stockholders' Equity section of the balance sheet as follows:

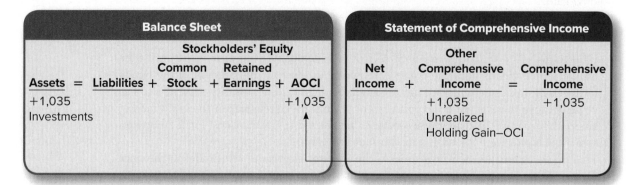

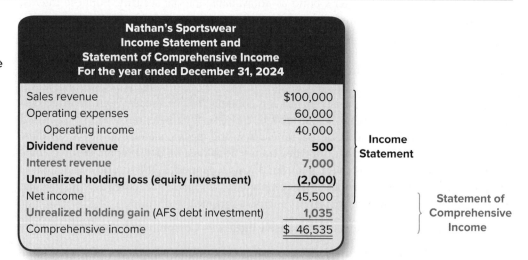

Illustration 8–5 shows an example of the income statement and the statement of comprehensive income for Nathan's Sportswear. Recall the income statement for Nathan's Sportswear in Illustration 8–3 included **$500** dividend revenue from the equity investment in Canadian Falcon, as well as the unrealized holding loss of **$2,000** for the change in that investment's fair value. For the investment in California Coaster's available-for-sale debt security, we also need to report:

- **$7,000** as interest revenue during 2024 ($3,500 on June 30 plus $3,500 on December 31)
- **$1,035** unrealized holding gain for the increase in fair value as of December 31, 2024.

**ILLUSTRATION 8–5**

Income Statement
and Statement of
Comprehensive Income

| Nathan's Sportswear<br>Income Statement and<br>Statement of Comprehensive Income<br>For the year ended December 31, 2024 | | |
|---|---:|---|
| Sales revenue | $100,000 | |
| Operating expenses | 60,000 | |
| Operating income | 40,000 | Income |
| **Dividend revenue** | **500** | Statement |
| Interest revenue | 7,000 | |
| **Unrealized holding loss (equity investment)** | **(2,000)** | |
| Net income | 45,500 | Statement of |
| Unrealized holding gain (AFS debt investment) | 1,035 | Comprehensive |
| Comprehensive income | $ 46,535 | Income |

Nathan's Sportswear would report the available-for-sale security as an asset in the balance sheet for its fair value of $101,035.

## SELL DEBT INVESTMENTS

Let's assume in the following year on July 1, 2025, Nathan's Sportswear sells the bonds for $102,000.

When an actual sale of a debt security occurs, the first thing we do is to remove the effects of any unrealized holding gains or losses that have previously been recorded. In this case, we would remove the $1,035 unrealized holding gain, which would bring the investment balance back to its original value of $100,000. We then record any realized gain or loss on the sale in net income equal to the difference between the carrying value of the investment ($100,000) and the amount of cash received on the sale ($102,000). In this case, a gain of $2,000 is realized.

The financial statement effects of the sale of the bond are as follows:

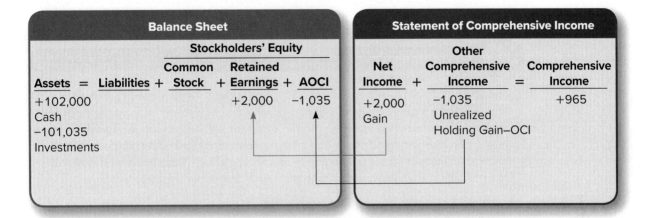

| | | | Balance Sheet | | | | | Statement of Comprehensive Income | | |
|---|---|---|---|---|---|---|---|---|---|---|
| | | | | Stockholders' Equity | | | | Other | | |
| | | | Common | Retained | | | Net | Comprehensive | Comprehensive | |
| Assets | = | Liabilities + | Stock | + Earnings | + | AOCI | Income + | Income | = | Income |
| +102,000 Cash | | | | +2,000 | | −1,035 | +2,000 Gain | −1,035 Unrealized Holding Gain–OCI | | +965 |
| −101,035 Investments | | | | | | | | | | |

**DEBITS & CREDITS**

To report the sale of the bond before maturity:

| | Debit | Credit |
|---|---|---|
| Cash | 102,000 | |
| Unrealized Holding Gain—OCI | 1,035 | |
| Investments | | 101,035 |
| Gain | | 2,000 |

Cash
| 102,000 | |

Unrealized Holding Gain—OCI
| 1,035 | |

Investments
| | 101,035 |

Gain
| | 2,000 |

**Held to Maturity.** If Nathan's Sportswear decides to hold the bonds for 10 years until maturity, then it will receive the principal payment equal to the face value of the bond of $100,000. The financial statement effects are as follows:

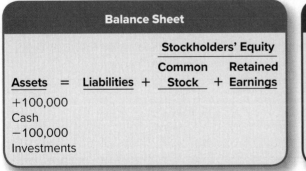

| | | | Balance Sheet | | | Income Statement | | |
|---|---|---|---|---|---|---|---|---|
| | | | | Stockholders' Equity | | | | |
| | | | Common | Retained | Revenues | Expenses | Net | |
| Assets | = | Liabilities + | Stock | + Earnings | & Gains | − & Losses | = Income | |
| +100,000 Cash | | | | | | No effect | | |
| −100,000 Investments | | | | | | | | |

**DEBITS & CREDITS**

To record the cash received from the principal of the bond at maturity:

| | Debit | Credit |
|---|---|---|
| Cash | 100,000 | |
| Investments | | 100,000 |

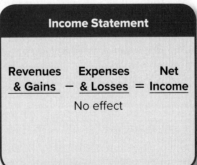

Cash
| 100,000 | |

Investments
| | 100,000 |

**KEY POINT**

For debt investments, trading securities and available-for-sale securities are reported at fair value, while held-to-maturity securities are carried at historical cost if they are issued at par. Unrealized holding gains and losses from fair value changes are reported as part of net income for trading securities and as part of other comprehensive income for available-for-sale securities.

**SUSTAINABILITY**

The SASB maintains sustainability accounting standards that are specific to the financial industry. In particular, companies are asked to disclose information regarding how their investments take account of social capital, human capital, and business ethics. **BlackRock** is one of the world's largest asset managers with trillions in assets under management. In its sustainability report, BlackRock describes how and why it incorporates sustainability considerations into its investment strategy as follows:

*BlackRock defines ESG integration as the practice of incorporating material environmental, social, and governance information into investment decisions in order to **enhance risk-adjusted returns**. ESG integration centers on material sustainability-related information as part of the total mix of economic and financial indicators associated with an investment—whether used in the research and due diligence phase, or in actively monitoring portfolios. ESG integration is not only about increasing the quantity of information available to portfolio managers, **but also identifying information that is additive to the investment process, whether those insights are intended to mitigate risks or contribute to long-term outperformance.***

BlackRock clearly believes that sustainability issues are business issues that can help them decrease investment risk and increase investment return. The sustainability report goes on to identify the people responsible for ensuring that sustainability issues are considered.

*At BlackRock, the people responsible for investment decisions are also responsible for integrating ESG information into the investment analyses that support those decisions. Our investment teams develop views on the materiality of specific sustainability-related topics by considering external and proprietary ESG research from a variety of sources. **Currently, every active investment team at BlackRock considers ESG factors in its investment process.** By the end of 2020, all active portfolios and advisory strategies will be fully ESG integrated—meaning that, at the portfolio level, our portfolio managers will be accountable for appropriately managing exposure to ESG risks and documenting how those considerations have affected investment decisions.*

**Let's Review**    Assume on January 1, 2024, Wally World issues $200,000 of 9% bonds, due in 10 years, with interest payable semiannually on June 30 and December 31 each year. American Life Insurance Company (ALICO) purchases all of the bonds.

***Required:***

1. Describe the financial statement effects of the investment in bonds by ALICO on January 1, 2024, and receipt of the first semiannual interest payment on June 30, 2024, assuming the bonds were issued at par.

*Solution:*

1. The financial statement effects are as follows:

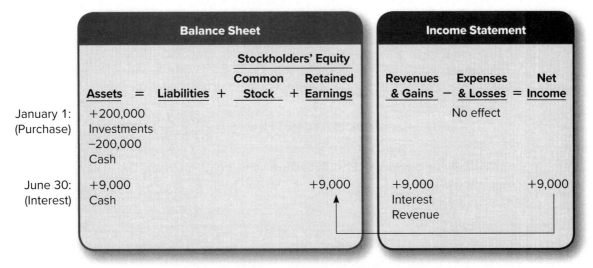

The journal entries associated with these transactions are as follows:

| January 1, 2024 | Debit | Credit |
| --- | --- | --- |
| **Investments** ................................................................ | **200,000** | |
| **Cash** ................................................................ | | **200,000** |
| *(Purchase bonds)* | | |

| June 30, 2024 | | |
| --- | --- | --- |
| **Cash** ................................................................ | **9,000** | |
| **Interest Revenue** ................................................................ | | **9,000** |
| *(Receive semiannual interest revenue)* | | |
| *($9,000 = $200,000 × 9% × ½)* | | |

# CASH AND INVESTMENT ANALYSIS
## Assessing Cash Holdings

**PART D**

■ **LO8–7**
Assess cash holdings.

Companies hold cash for a variety of reasons and several factors could explain why one company holds more cash than another. Some of these factors include:

- **Growth**. Growth companies tend to have less cash available because of their higher capital spending on new opportunities.
- **Changing technology**. Companies that operate in industries with rapidly changing technology tend to have more cash in order to quickly respond to technological advances.
- **Volatility of operations**. Companies with more volatile operations tend to hold more cash. Short-term negative shocks in the business cycle can cause a company to default on its debt and enter bankruptcy. These companies tend to keep more cash in reserve.
- **Foreign operations**. Historically, companies in the United States had to pay additional income taxes on foreign profits once those profits were returned as cash to the United States. To avoid these additional taxes, companies with major international operations (such as **Apple**, **Microsoft**, and **Google**) often kept the cash from foreign profits in those foreign countries, causing them to have higher overall cash balances.
- **Dividend policy**. Companies that pay greater dividends tend to have less cash available. Some companies choose to return a higher portion of their earnings to stockholders in the form of cash dividends.

The amount of cash a company is holding can be compared across time and across companies using the cash holdings ratio, which is calculated as follows:

$$\text{Cash holdings ratio} = \frac{\text{Cash} + \text{Cash equivalents}}{\text{Total assets}}$$

Microsoft reports $8,759 million in cash and cash equivalents and $258,848 million of total assets. Thus, Microsoft's cash holdings ratio is calculated as follows:

$$\text{Cash holdings ratio for Microsoft} = \frac{\$8,759}{\$258,848} = 3.4\%$$

Illustration 8–6 presents the cash holdings ratio for Microsoft and two of its competitors: Apple and Google.

**ILLUSTRATION 8–6**

**Cash Holdings Ratio for Microsoft and Peers**

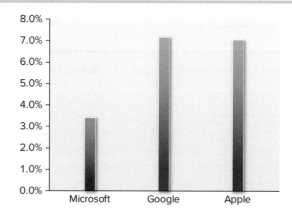

We see that Microsoft's cash holdings are about half as large as the cash holdings of Google and Apple. What factors could help explain why Microsoft is holding less cash? Microsoft is much more involved in providing goods and services (e.g., servers, software, cloud services) to commercial enterprises than are these two competitors. This could mean its business operations are less volatile and less subject to seasonality. It also may be that differences in dividend policies explain some of the difference. Microsoft paid cash dividends of $12,699 million, which represents 77% of its net income of $16,571. In contrast, Google does not pay cash dividends, and Apple paid cash dividends of $13,712 million, which represents 23% of its net income of $59,531. It may also be the case that Microsoft chooses to invest more of its cash into short-term and long-term securities, which we will examine next.

**KEY POINT**

The cash holdings ratio measures the amount of cash and cash equivalents a company is holding in relation to its total assets. Holding cash provides companies with flexibility to grow and deal with seasonality. However, holding too much cash comes at the cost of foregone returns.

## INVESTMENT ANALYSIS

■ **LO8–8**
Assess the level of investment and return on investments.

The balance sheet reports the total amount of short-term and long-term investments a company has made. The notes to the financial statements often will provide a more detailed breakdown of these investments and any associated unrealized holding gains or losses. This disclosure allows financial statement users to assess the amount of risk associated with the investments and the potential rewards. For example, Microsoft reports approximately $124 billion in short-term and long-term investments in its balance sheet and, as shown in Illustration 8–7, provides the breakdown in a disclosure note.

ILLUSTRATION 8–7

Excerpt from Microsoft's Annual Report

**MICROSOFT**
**Notes to the Financial Statements (excerpt)**

| ($ in millions) | Cost Basis | Unrealized Gains | Unrealized Losses | Recorded Basis (Fair Value) |
|---|---|---|---|---|
| Commercial paper | $    298 | $    0 | $    0 | $    298 |
| Certificates of deposit | 193 | 0 | 0 | 193 |
| U.S. government and agency securities | 106,184 | 62 | (1,167) | 105,079 |
| Foreign government bonds | 5,182 | 1 | (10) | 5,173 |
| Mortgage- and asset-backed securities | 3,868 | 4 | (13) | 3,859 |
| Corporate notes and bonds | 6,947 | 21 | (56) | 6,912 |
| Municipal securities | 271 | 37 | (1) | 307 |
| Common and preferred stock | 1,220 | 95 | (10) | 1,305 |
| Other investments | 558 | 0 | 0 | 558 |
| **Total** | **$124,721** | **$220** | **$(1,257)** | **$123,684** |

This breakdown of investment types is sorted by risk, starting with very low-risk investments such as commercial paper and certificates of deposit and ending with higher-risk investments such as common stock. For Microsoft, this note reveals that the vast majority of its investments are in lower-risk securities, including very short-term investments and government-backed securities.

The disclosure also provides information on the performance of the investments. The "Cost Basis" provided in the note is the historical cost of the investment, and the "Recorded Basis" is the fair value of the investments reported in the balance sheet date. In aggregate, we see that the fair value of the investments is lower than the cost basis by $1,037 million (= $123,684 − $124,721). This aggregate unrealized loss on all of its investments reflects the performance of the investments from their original purchase price (which could have been several years ago).

The level of investments can be compared across companies. This type of analysis allows financial statement users to assess whether a company is potentially over- or under-invested in securities compared to its peers. The investment-to-assets ratio measures the level of investment a company has made (relative to its asset base) and is calculated as follows:

$$\text{Investment-to-assets ratio} = \frac{\text{Short-term investments} + \text{Long-term investments}}{\text{Total assets}}$$

The investment-to-assets ratio at Microsoft is calculated as follows:

$$\text{Investment-to-assets ratio for Microsoft} = \frac{\$123,684}{\$258,848} = 47.8\%$$

Illustration 8–8 presents investment-to-assets ratios for Microsoft and its competitors. Here we see that Microsoft's level of investment is roughly on par with that of Google. The level of investment by Microsoft and Google, however, is markedly lower than that observed in Apple. This suggests Apple could potentially be over-investing in marketable securities. In fact, Apple has had a large investment balance for years and has even been sued over it. In 2013, hedge fund billionaire David Einhorn filed a lawsuit against Apple for holding too much cash and investments, demanding the company pay out more shareholder dividends.

**ILLUSTRATION 8-8**

Investment-to-Assets
Ratio for Microsoft and
Peers

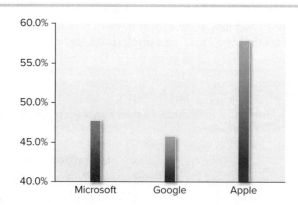

While the lawsuit was subsequently dropped, it did draw the attention of management who committed in a shareholder meeting to revisit their investment strategy.

It is also important to examine the impact of these investments on the income statement. Many companies (unless they are a bank) do not report investment income as a separate line item on the income statement, but instead include this amount in an *"other* income and expense" account. The breakdown of this account will usually be provided in the financial statement notes. For example, Microsoft's income statement reports $1,416 million in a line item called "Other income (expense), net." A separate financial statement note then provides a break down of this account as shown in Illustration 8–9.

**ILLUSTRATION 8-9**

Excerpt from
Microsoft's Annual
Report

| MICROSOFT<br>Notes to the Financial Statements (excerpt) | |
| --- | --- |
| **($ in millions)** | |
| **Dividends and interest income** | **$2,214** |
| Interest expense | (2,733) |
| **Net recognized gains on investments** | **2,399** |
| **Net losses on derivatives** | **(187)** |
| Net losses on foreign currency remeasurements | (218) |
| Other, net | (59) |
| **Total** | **$1,416** |

This note reveals that Microsoft's income statement includes $2,214 million from dividend and interest income, $2,399 in recognized gains on investments, and a $187 loss on derivatives. Together, this means that the income statement includes a total of $4,426 million in investment-related income (pretax). We divide this by the average investments balance from the balance sheet to estimate the return on investments as reported in the income statement. The average short-term and long-term investments balances are calculated by summing the beginning (prior year's ending balance) and ending balances reported in the balance sheet and then dividing by 2. The return on investments ratio is calculated as follows:

$$\text{Return on investments ratio} = \frac{\text{Investment-related income (loss)}}{\text{Average short-term investments} + \text{Average long-term investments}}$$

The return on investments ratio at Microsoft is calculated as follows:

$$\text{Return on investments ratio for Microsoft} = \frac{\$4,426}{\$127,513} = 3.5\%$$

Illustration 8–10 presents the return on investments ratio for Microsoft and its competitors.

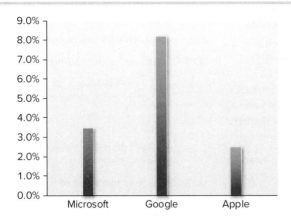

**ILLUSTRATION 8–10**
Return on Investments
for Microsoft and Peers

We learn that Microsoft's investment return is on par with that of Apple, but quite a bit lower than that of Google. Microsoft's relatively low investment return is driven by the fact that the vast majority of its investments are in low-risk cash equivalents and U.S. government-backed securities. By investing in such low-risk investments, Microsoft is potentially sacrificing returns.

**KEY POINT**

The investments-to-assets ratio measures the level of investment that a company has made. Holding lots of investments can be good or bad depending on the strategic purposes of the investments.

The return on investments ratio can be used to determine the income statement impact of the investments held by a company. This return is a function of the riskiness of the investments held.

**THE BOTTOM LINE**

**LO8–1** Define cash and cash equivalents.

Cash includes coins and currency, checks received, and balances in savings and checking accounts. The cash balance also includes credit card and debit card sales, as well as cash equivalents, defined as investments that mature within three months from the date of purchase (such as money market funds, Treasury bills, and certificates of deposit).

**LO8–2** Explain why companies invest in other companies.

Companies invest in other companies primarily to receive dividends, earn interest, and gain from the increase in the value of their investment. Companies in seasonal industries often invest excess funds generated during the busy season and draw on these funds in the slow season. Many companies also make investments for strategic purposes to develop closer business ties, increase market share, or expand into new industries.

**LO8–3** Account for investments in equity securities when the investor has *insignificant* influence.

We report investments at fair value when a company has an insignificant influence over another company in which it invests, often indicated by an ownership interest of less than 20%. Dividends received are reported as dividend revenue in net income. Unrealized holding gains and losses and realized gains and losses from the sale of the investments are included in net income.

**LO8–4** Account for investments in equity securities when the investor has *significant* influence.

We initially record equity investments at cost. Under the equity method, the balance of the Investments account increases for the investor's share of the investee's net income and decreases for the investor's share of the investee's cash dividends. Equity Income reflects the investor's share of the investee's net income.

**LO8–5** **Account for investments in equity securities when the investor has *controlling* influence.**

Investments involving one company (parent) purchasing more than 50% of the voting stock of another company (subsidiary) require the parent company to prepare consolidated financial statements. These statements combine the parent's and subsidiary's financial statements as if the two companies were a single reporting company.

**LO8–6** **Account for investments in debt securities and understand the three classifications of debt investments.**

Bond investments are the "flip side" of bonds payable. Bond investments are long-term assets that earn interest revenue, while bonds payable are long-term liabilities that incur interest expense.

For debt investments, trading securities and available-for-sale securities are reported at fair value, while held-to-maturity securities are carried at historical cost if they are issued at par. Unrealized holding gains and losses from fair value changes are reported as part of net income for trading securities and as part of other comprehensive income for available-for-sale securities.

**LO8–7** **Assess cash holdings.**

The cash holdings ratio measures the amount of cash and cash equivalents that a company is holding in relation to its total assets. Holding cash provides companies with flexibility to grow and deal with seasonality. However, holding too much cash comes at the cost of forgone returns.

**LO8–8** **Assess the level of investments and return on investments.**

The investment-to-assets ratio measures the level of investment a company has made. Holding lots of investments can be good or bad depending on strategic purposes of the investments.

The return on investments ratio can be used to determine the income statement impact of the investments held by a company. This return is a function of the riskiness of the investments held.

## GLOSSARY

**Available-for-sale securities:** Debt securities held for reasons other than attempting to profit from trading in the near future. **p. 409**

**Cash:** currency and coins, balances in checking accounts, and items acceptable for deposit in these accounts, such as checks and money orders received from customers. **p. 394**

**Cash equivalents** short-term investments that have a maturity date no longer than three months from the date of purchase. **p. 394**

**Cash holdings ratio:** Cash and cash equivalents divided by total assets. **p. 414**

**Comprehensive income:** A broader definition of income that includes *all* revenues, expenses, gains, and losses; it's all changes in stockholders' equity other than investments by stockholders and distributions to stockholders. **p. 409**

**Consolidated financial statements:** Combination of the separate financial statements of the parent (purchasing company) and the subsidiary (acquired company) into a single set of financial statements. **pp. 396, 406**

**Debt investments:** Investments made in the debt issued by another party. **p. 407**

**Equity investments:** Investments made in the equity (or stock) issued by another party. **p. 396**

**Equity method:** Method of recording equity investments when an investor has significant influence over, yet does not control, the operations of the investee, often indicated by ownership of between 20% and 50% of the voting shares. Under this method, the investor company records the investment as if the investee is a part of the company. **pp. 396, 402**

**Fair value:** The amount for which the investment could be bought or sold in a current transaction between willing parties. **p. 396**

**Fair value method:** Method of recording equity investments when an investor has insignificant influence, often indicated by ownership of less than 20% of the voting shares. Under this method, equity securities are reported in the balance sheet at their fair value, with changes in fair value from one period to the next being reported as gains and losses in the income statement. **p. 396**

**Held-to-maturity securities:** Debt securities that are expected to be held until they *mature,* which means until the issuer is required to repay the full amount of the bonds to the investors. **p. 409**

**Investment-to-assets ratio:** Short-term investments and long-term investments dividend by total assets; measures the level of investments that a company has made. **p. 415**

**Net income:** Profitability reported in the income statement, consisting of all revenues and expenses and most gains and losses **p. 409**

**Other comprehensive income:** Gains and losses from non-owner transactions that are not reported in the income statement. **p. 409**

**Return on investments ratio:** Investment-related income divided by average total investments (sum of short-term investments and long-term investments); measures the return of the investments that a company holds. **p. 416**

**Trading securities:** Debt securities that the investor expects to sell in the near future. **p. 409**

## SELF-STUDY QUESTIONS

1. Which of the following is considered cash for financial reporting purposes? **(LO8–1)**
   a. Accounts receivable from customers who are expected to pay.
   b. Investments with maturity dates less than three months from the date of purchase.
   c. Credit cards used by the company to purchase office supplies.
   d. Accounts payable to local vendors used on a regular basis.

2. One of the primary reasons for investing in equity securities includes **(LO8–2)**
   a. Receiving dividend payments.
   b. Acquiring debt of competing companies.
   c. Earning interest revenue.
   d. Deducting dividend payments for tax purposes.

3. One of the primary reasons for investing in debt securities includes **(LO8–2)**
   a. Deducting interest payments for tax purposes.
   b. Receiving dividend payments.
   c. Earning interest revenue.
   d. Acquiring ownership control in other companies.

4. On November 17, Tasty Foods purchased 1,000 shares (10%) of Eco-Safe Packaging's voting stock for $12 per share. By the end of the year, Eco-Safe Packaging's stock price dropped to $10 per share. How would the drop in stock price affect Tasty Foods' net income for the year? **(LO8–3)**
   a. Decrease net income by $12,000.
   b. Decrease net income by $10,000.
   c. Decrease net income by $2,000.
   d. No effect.

5. On November 17, Tasty Foods purchased 1,000 shares (10%) of Eco-Safe Packaging's voting stock for $12 per share. By the end of the year, Eco-Safe Packaging's stock price increased to $14 per share. How would the increase in stock price affect Tasty Foods' net income for the year? **(LO8–3)**
   a. Increase net income by $12,000.
   b. Increase net income by $10,000.
   c. Increase net income by $2,000.
   d. No effect.

6. On January 1, Tasty Foods purchased 3,000 shares (30%) of Eco-Safe Packaging's voting stock for $12 per share. On December 31, Eco-Safe Packaging reports net income $10,000 and a total dividend payment of $2,000, and the stock price dropped to $10 per share. For how much would Tasty Foods report its investment in Eco-Safe Packaging at the end of the year? **(LO8–4)**
   a. $30,000.
   b. $38,400.
   c. $36,000.
   d. $39,000.

7. On January 1, Tasty Foods purchased 10,000 shares (100%) of Eco-Safe Packaging's voting stock for $12 per share. Throughout the year, both companies continue to operate as separate legal entities. By December 31, Eco-Safe Packaging's cash balance is $2,000, and Tasty Foods' cash balance is $5,000. In preparing its year-end financial statements, how much would Tasty Foods report as its cash balance? **(LO8–5)**
   a. $7,000.
   b. $5,000.
   c. $3,000.
   d. $2,000.

8. On January 1, Eco-Safe Packaging issues $100,000 of 8%, 5-year bonds with interest payable semiannually on June 30 and December 31. Tasty Foods purchases all of the bonds for $100,000 and plans to hold them to maturity. How much would Tasty Foods report its investment in Eco-Safe Packaging's bonds at the end of the year? **(LO8–6)**
   a. $100,000.
   b. $108,000.
   c. $92,000
   d. $96,000

9. Refer to Question 8. How much interest revenue would Tasty Foods record at the time it receives the first semiannual payment on June 30? **(LO8–6)**
   a. $800.
   b. $8,000.
   c. $1,600.
   d. $4,000.

10. Which of the following is a potential reason one company would hold more cash than another company does? **(LO8–7)**
    a. The company has a policy of reinvesting all of its earnings rather than paying dividends.
    b. The company is in a more stable industry.
    c. The company does not rely on technical innovations.
    d. The company does not have foreign operations.

11. The investment-to-assets ratio is **(LO8–8)**
    a. Cash, short-term investments and long-term investments all divided by total assets.
    b. Long-term investments divided by total assets.
    c. Short-term investments and long-term investments divided by total assets.
    d. Short-term investments divided by total assets.

12. The return on investments ratio can provide an indication of the **(LO8–8)**
    a. Operating performance of the company.
    b. Financial leverage of the company.
    c. Operating efficiency of the company.
    d. Riskiness of the company's investment strategy.

*Note: For answers, see the last page of the chapter.*

**EDGAR Case**

## Gilead Sciences (ticker: GILD)

**RWP8–1** Visit www.sec.gov/edgar and search for the **Gildead Sciences** annual report (10-K) for the year ended December 31, 2019, using EDGAR (Electronic Data Gathering, Analysis, and Retrieval system). Locate the Consolidated Balance Sheet.

***Required:***
1. Calculate the cash holdings ratio for the most recent year and the previous year. Did the ratio go up or down?
2. Calculate the investment-to-assets ratio for the most recent year and the previous year. Did the ratio go up or down?

**EDGAR Case**

## Zoom Video Communications (ticker: ZM)

**RWP8–2** Visit www.sec.gov/edgar and search for the **Zoom** annual report (10-K) for the year ended January 31, 2020, using EDGAR (Electronic Data Gathering, Analysis, and Retrieval system).

***Required:***
1. Locate the note titled "Summary of Business and Significant Accounting Policies," and then find the subsection titled "Cash, Cash Equivalents, and Restricted Cash." Which items does Zoom include in cash equivalents?
2. Now locate the note titled "Marketable securities." What percentage of the fair value of the marketable securities is invested in "Corporate and other debt securities"?

**EDGAR Case**

## Cisco Systems (ticker: CSCO)

**RWP8–3** Visit www.sec.gov/edgar and search for the **Cisco** annual report (10-K) for the year ended July 27, 2019, using EDGAR (Electronic Data Gathering, Analysis, and Retrieval system). Locate the note titled "Available-for-Sale Debt Investments and Equity Investments."

***Required:***
1. What type of securities makes up the majority of Cisco's Available-for-Sale debt investments in the most recent year?
2. Does Cisco have a net unrealized gain or net unrealized loss on its Corporate debt securities in the most recent year?

**EDGAR Case**

## Biogen Inc. (ticker: BIIB)

**RWP8–4** Visit www.sec.gov/edgar and search for the **Biogen** annual report (10-K) for the year ended December 31, 2019, using EDGAR (Electronic Data Gathering, Analysis, and Retrieval system).

***Required:***
1. Locate the noted titled "Other Consolidated Financial Statement Details" and then find the subsection labeled "Other Income (Expense), Net." How much investment-related income does Biogen report in the most recent year?
2. Calculate the return on investments ratio for Biogen for the most recent year.

**Continuing Financial Analysis Case**

## American Eagle Outfitters, Inc.

**RWP8–5** Financial information for **American Eagle** is presented in **Appendix A** at the end of the book.

***Required:***
1. Calculate the cash holdings ratio for the most recent year and the prior year. Determine whether the cash holdings ratio in the most recent year increased, decreased, or remained the same from the prior year.
2. Calculate the investment-to-asset ratio for the most recent year and the prior year. Determine whether the investment-to-asset ratio in the most recent year increased, decreased, or remained the same from the prior year.

## The Buckle, Inc.

**Continuing Financial Analysis Case**

**RWP8–6** Financial information for **Buckle** is presented in **Appendix B** at the end of the book.

**Required:**
1. Calculate the cash holdings ratio for the most recent year and the prior year. Determine whether the cash holdings ratio in the most recent year increased, decreased, or remained the same from the prior year?
2. Calculate the investment-to-asset ratio for the most recent year. Determine whether the investment-to-asset ratio in the most recent year increased, decreased, or remained the same from the prior year.

## American Eagle Outfitters, Inc. vs. The Buckle, Inc.

**Continuing Comparative Analysis Case**

**RWP8–7** Financial information for **American Eagle** is presented in **Appendix A** at the end of the book, and financial information for **Buckle** is presented in **Appendix B** at the end of the book.

**Required:**
1. Calculate the cash holdings ratio for both companies for the most recent year. Which company has the higher ratio?
2. Calculate the investment-to-asset ratio for both companies for the most recent year. Which company has the higher ratio?

## Ethics

**Ethics Case**

**RWP8–8** Rock Canyon Enterprises has a five-year loan with a large bank. This loan includes a covenant requiring Rock Canyon Enterprises to have "*tangible* net assets of at least $50 million." The loan agreement calculates tangible net assets as follows:

$$Tangible\ net\ assets = (Total\ assets - Intangible\ assets) - Total\ liabilities$$

If the company's tangible net assets drop below $50 million, then the entire loan amount becomes due. At the end of the year, Rock Canyon Enterprises has total assets of $250 million, which includes $57 million in intangible assets (i.e., goodwill, patents, copyrights) and total liabilities of $145 million.

One of Rock Canyon Enterprises investments includes a 10% stake in a private company. The fair value of this investment currently is stated on the balance sheet at $7 million. However, Eric Yost, the chief accountant, would like to alter a few of the assumptions used to value this investment to achieve a fair value of $10 million. He explains that valuing private company investments "is very squishy business" and that the bank is unlikely to push back on their valuation.

**Required:**
1. Understand the reporting effect: Calculate Rock Canyon Enterprises tangible net assets before Eric Yost's proposed change. Is the debt covenant violated?
2. Specify the options: Calculate Rock Canyon Enterprises tangible net assets after Eric Yost's proposed change. Is the debt covenant violated?
3. Identify the impact: Does the change in assumption potentially affect the bank?
4. Make a decision: Should Rock Canyon Enterprises revalue the private company investment?

## Sustainability

**Sustainability Case**

**RWP8–9** Go to the SASB website (**https://www.sasb.org/company-use/sasb-reporters/**) and search for **BlackRock's** sustainability report for 2019 (publication year 2021). Go to the section titled "Incorporation of ESG Factors in Investment Management & Advisory."

1. What is the amount of assets under management (AUM) that have integrated ESG issues at the end of 2019, and by how much did this change over the prior year?
2. What is the amount of AUM that include "screened investments" that exclude specific companies or sectors that are associated with one or more objectionable activities, and by how much did this amount change over the prior year?

## Earnings Management

**RWP8–10** Boost Semiconductors is a new tech company that recently went public. Growth expectations among investors are high. Near the end of the year, it became clear the company's earnings would fall short of analyst expectations of $2.15 per share. For growth companies like Boost, missing analyst expectations would have a significantly detrimental effect on its stock price.

The company's CFO, Jonathon Glazier, forecasts that Boost's net income will be $65.0 million. Mr. Glazier then had an idea, however, on how to use some of the company's investment securities to increase net income. Boost's balance sheet currently includes $40.0 million in corporate debt investments that are classified as held-to-maturity. Many of these investments have appreciated in value, such that the fair value of the entire held-to-maturity portfolio is $40.9 million. Mr. Glazier proposes reclassifying these securities from held-to-maturity to trading securities. He explained that under U.S. GAAP, when securities are reclassified from held-to-maturity to trading securities, the securities are revalued at their fair value and that the associated unrealized gain or loss is included in net income as if all of it occurred in the current year. Of course, the reclassification would have to be disclosed in the notes, but Mr Glazier argued that investors rarely pick-up on this type of "accounting magic."

Boost Semiconductor has 30.5 million outstanding shares of common stock.

### Required:

1. Calculate Boost Semiconductor's forecasted earnings per share by dividing Mr. Glazier's forecast by the number of shares outstanding? Is forecasted earnings per share expected to be above or below analyst expectations of $2.15?
2. Calculate forecasted earnings per share assuming all held-to-maturity investments are reclassified to trading securities (ignore any potential tax implications of the reclassification). Is the revised forecasted earnings per share expected to be above or below analyst expectations of $2.15?

## Great Adventures

(This is a continuation of the Great Adventures problem from earlier chapters.)

**RWP8–11** Recall that Great Adventures originally was financed with $10,000 in equity financing from Tony (common stock), $10,000 in equity financing from Suzie (common stock), and $30,000 in debt financing (bank loan). This financing structure means that Tony and Suzie each own 50% of the company and is commonly referred to as a "50-50 joint venture." The equity method of accounting is used to account for 50-50 joint ventures.

In Chapter 3, we accounted for the equity contributions from Tony and Suzie from the perspective of Great Adventures (see RWP3–9). We'll now consider this investment from the perspective of Suzie, one of the Great Adventures investors.

The following transactions occurred during 2024 and relate to Suzie's investment in Great Adventures:

| | |
|---|---|
| July 1 | Suzie buys $10,000 in Great Adventures common stock. |
| Dec 31 | Suzie receives a $2,000 dividend from Great Adventures |
| Dec 31 | Great Adventures reports net income of $37,150. |
| Dec 31 | Suzie estimates that the fair value of her investment in Great Adventures is $18,000. |

### Required:

1. Assume Suzie accounts for her investment in Great Adventures using the equity method.
   (a) Record Suzie's investment in Great Adventures on July 1.
   (b) Record the receipt of dividends from Great Adventures on December 31 using the equity method.
   (c) Record Suzie's share of Great Adventures 2024 net income using the equity method.
   (d) Record the adjusting entry for the fair value on December 31.
   (e) Determine the ending balance in Suzie's Investment account related to Great Adventures.
2. Now assume Suzie could not exercise significant influence over Great Adventures and would thus use the fair value method to account for her investment.

(a) Record Suzie's investment in Great Adventures on July 1.
(b) Record the receipt of dividends from Great Adventures on December 31 using the fair value method.
(c) Record Suzie's share of Great Adventures 2024 net income using the fair value method.
(d) Record the adjusting entry for the fair value on December 31 (assume Suzie classifies the investment as available-for-sale securities).
(e) Determine the ending balance in Suzie's Investment account related to Great Adventures.

## BRIEF EXERCISES

**BE8–1** Determine whether the firm reports each of the following items as part of cash and cash equivalents in the balance sheet.

Identify cash and cash equivalents (LO 8–1)

| Item | Cash or Cash Equivalent? (yes/no) |
|---|---|
| 1. Currency | _____ |
| 2. Inventory for sale to customers | _____ |
| 3. Balance in savings account | _____ |
| 4. Checks | _____ |
| 5. Accounts receivable | _____ |
| 6. Investments purchased with maturities of less than three months | _____ |

**BE8–2** Indicate with an "X" any of the following that represent a common reason companies invest in other companies.

Identify reasons companies invest (LO 8–2)

_____ 1.     To invest excess cash created by operating in seasonal industries.
_____ 2.     To increase employees' morale.
_____ 3.     To build strategic alliances.
_____ 4.     To reduce government regulation.
_____ 5.     To receive interest and dividends.

**BE8–3** On September 1, Leather Suppliers, Inc., purchases 150 shares of Western Wear Clothing for $13 per share. On November 1, Leather Suppliers sells the investment for $17 per share. How will the purchase and sale of the investment in Western Wear Clothing affect the financial statements of Leather Suppliers?

Account for equity investments using the fair value method (LO 8–3)
See JBE8–1 for journal entries.

**BE8–4** On December 28, Summit purchased **Microsoft** common shares for $485,000. On December 31, the shares had a fair value of $483,000. How will the initial investment by Summit and the decrease in fair value affect the financial statements?

Account for equity investments using the fair value method (LO 8–3)
See JBE8–2 for journal entries.

**BE8–5** On December 28, Summit purchased **Microsoft** common shares for $485,000. On December 31, the shares had a fair value of $487,000. How will the initial investment by Summit and the increase in fair value affect the financial statements?

Account for equity investments using the fair value method (LO 8–3)
See JBE8–3 for journal entries.

**BE8–6** On December 29, 2024, Adams Apples purchased 1,000 shares of **General Electric** common stock for $19 per share. On December 31, the market value of the stock increased to $20 per share. On January 24, 2025, all of the shares are sold for $22 per share. Describe the financial statement effects of the initial investment, any fair value adjustment needed at the end of 2024, and the sale in 2025.

Account for equity investments using the fair value method (LO 8–3)
See JBE8–4 for journal entries.

**BE8–7** On December 29, 2024, Adams Apples purchased 1,000 shares of **General Electric** common stock for $19 per share. On December 31, the market value of the stock increased to $20 per share. On January 24, 2025, all of the shares are sold for $16 per share. Describe the financial statement effects of the initial investment, any fair value adjustment needed at the end of 2024, and the sale in 2025.

Account for equity investments using the fair value method (LO 8–3)
See JBE8–5 for journal entries.

Account for dividend revenue using the fair value method (LO 8–3)
See JBE8–6 for journal entries.

**BE8–8** Wendy Day Kite Company owns 10% of the outstanding stock of Strong String Company. During the current year, Strong String paid total dividends of $10 million to all stockholders. What effect does receiving dividends from Strong String have on Wendy Day's financial statements?

Understand the effect of net income by the investee in an equity method investment (LO 8–4)
See JBE8–7 for journal entries.

**BE8–9** Wendy Day Kite Company owns 40% of the outstanding stock of Strong String Company. During the current year, Strong String reported net income of $15 million. What effect does Strong String's reported net income have on Wendy Day's financial statements?

Understand the effect of dividends by the investee in an equity method investment (LO 8–4)
See JBE8–8 for journal entries.

**BE8–10** Wendy Day Kite Company owns 40% of the outstanding stock of Strong String Company. During the current year, Strong String paid a $10 million cash dividend on all of its common shares. What effect does Strong String's dividend have on Wendy Day's financial statements?

Calculate consolidated amounts (LO 8–5)

**BE8–11** Wendy Day Kite Company owns 100% of the outstanding stock of Strong String Company. At the end of the year, Wendy Day has total inventory of $14,000, and Strong String has total inventory of $8,000. Determine the amount of inventory that would be reported in Wendy Day's consolidated financial statements (assuming no transactions involving inventory occurred between the two companies).

Account for investment in bonds at face value (LO 8–6)
See JBE8–9 for journal entries.

**BE8–12** Salt Foods purchases forty $1,000, 7%, 10-year bonds issued by Pretzelmania, Inc., for $40,000 on January 1. Salt Foods receives interest semiannually on June 30 and December 31. How will the investment in bonds and the receipt of the first interest payment affect the financial statements?

Account for investment in debt securities (LO 8–6)

**BE8–13** Indicate which of the following debt securities are reported at their fair value on the balance sheet at the end of the year.

    ___ Held-to-maturity securities

    ___ Trading securities

    ___ Available-for-sale securities

Adjust trading securities to their fair value (LO 8–6)
See JBE8–10 for journal entries.

**BE8–14** Q&M Apparel purchased debt securities on January 1 for $150,000 and classified the investments as trading securities. On December 31, the debt securities are valued at $148,000. What effects will the year-end adjustment of these securities to their fair value have on the financial statements?

Adjust available-for-sale securities to their fair value (LO 8–6)
See JBE8–11 for journal entries.

**BE8–15** Use the same facts as in BE8–14, but now assume the debt securities are classified as available-for-sale securities. What effects will the year-end adjustment of these securities to their fair value have on the financial statements?

Calculate the cash holdings ratio (LO 8–7)

**BE8–16** J-Mark Superstores provides the following selected financial data. Calculate the cash holdings ratio for 2024.

| | 2024 | 2023 |
|---|---|---|
| Cash and cash equivalents | $ 852,540 | $ 750,235 |
| Short-term investments | 45,050 | 39,194 |
| Accounts receivable | 1,120,545 | 1,030,901 |
| Inventory | 2,812,020 | 2,615,179 |
| Property, plant and equipment | 4,212,686 | 3,749,291 |
| Long-term investments | 96,555 | 82,072 |
| Total asset | 9,139,396 | 8,266,871 |
| Total liabilities | 4,204,122 | 3,968,098 |
| Total stockholders' equity | 4,935,274 | 4,298,773 |
| | | |
| Net sales | $15,579,865 | $13,710,281 |
| Operating income | 5,452,953 | 4,661,496 |
| Interest expense | 157,655 | 148,804 |
| Investment income | 5,947 | 4,851 |

**BE8–17** Refer to the financial information for J-Mark Superstores presented in BE8–16. Calculate the investment-to-assets ratio for 2024.

Calculate the investment-to-asset ratio (LO 8–8)

**BE8–18** Refer to the financial information for J-Mark Superstores presented in BE8–16. Calculate the return on investments ratio for 2024.

Calculate the return on investments ratio (LO 8–8)

## EXERCISES

**E8–1** Below are several amounts reported at the end of the year.

Determine the amount of cash to report (LO 8–1)

| | |
|---|---:|
| Currency located at the company | $1,050 |
| Supplies | 3,200 |
| Short-term investments that mature within three months | 1,950 |
| Accounts receivable | 3,500 |
| Balance in savings account | 8,500 |
| Checks received from customers but not yet deposited | 650 |
| Prepaid rent | 1,450 |
| Coins located at the company | 110 |
| Equipment | 9,400 |
| Balance in checking account | 6,200 |

*Required:*
Calculate the amount of cash to report in the balance sheet.

**E8–2** Consider the following statements.

Identify reasons why companies invest (LO 8–2)

_____ 1. A reason companies invest in other companies is to build strategic alliances.

_____ 2. All companies are required to pay dividends to their investors.

_____ 3. When market interest rates increase, the market value of a bond increases as well.

_____ 4. One way for a company to expand operations into a new industry is to acquire the majority of common stock in another company that already operates in that industry.

_____ 5. Stocks typically have greater upside potential, providing a higher average return to their investors over the long run than do bonds.

_____ 6. Companies purchase debt securities primarily for the dividend revenue they provide.

*Required:*
Indicate whether each statement is true (T) or false (F).

**E8–3** First National Bank buys and sells securities. The company's fiscal year ends on December 31. The following selected transactions relating to First National's trading account occurred during the year.

Account for equity investments using the fair value method (LO 8–3)
See JE8–1 for journal entries.

| | |
|---|---|
| December 20 | Purchases 300,000 shares in Classic Computers common stock for $1,500,000 ($5 per share). |
| December 28 | Receives cash dividends of $6,000 from the Classic Computers shares. |
| December 31 | The fair value of Classic Computers' stock is $4.80 per share. |

*Required:*
1. How will each of these transactions, including an adjustment on December 31 for the investment's fair value, affect the financial statements?
2. Calculate the balance of the Investments account on December 31.

Account for equity investments using the fair value method **(LO 8–3)**
See JE8–2 for journal entries.

**E8–4** Mr. T's Fashions, once a direct competitor to Italian Stallion's clothing line, has formed a friendship in recent years leading to a small investment (less than 5%) by Mr. T in the common stock of Italian Stallion. Mr. T's engages in the following transactions relating to its investment.

| | | |
|---|---|---|
| February | 1 | Purchases 150 shares of Italian Stallion common stock for $16 per share. |
| June | 15 | Sells 50 shares of Italian Stallion stock for $14 per share. |
| October | 31 | Receives a cash dividend of $0.50 per share. |
| December | 31 | The fair value of Italian Stallion's stock is $12 per share. |

**Required:**

1. How will each of these transactions, including an adjustment on December 31 for the investment's fair value, affect the financial statements?
2. Calculate the balance of the Investments account on December 31.

Account for equity investments using the fair value method **(LO 8–3)**
See JE8–3 for journal entries.

**E8–5** Gator Shoes, Inc., manufactures a line of stylish waterproof footwear. The following transactions relate to investments in common stock during 2024.

| | | |
|---|---|---|
| March | 1 | Purchases 3,000 shares (10%) of Power Drive Corporation's common stock for $62 per share. |
| July | 1 | Receives a cash dividend of $1.25 per share. |
| December | 31 | The fair value of Power Drive Corporation's common stock is $75 per share. |

On February 1, 2025 (the following year), Gator Shoes sells 1,000 shares of Power Drive Corporation's common stock for $70 per share.

**Required:**

1. How will each of these transactions in 2024, including an adjustment on December 31 for the investment's fair value, affect the financial statements?
2. How will the sale on February 1, 2025, affect the financial statements?

Account for equity investments using the fair value method **(LO 8–3)**
See JE8–4 for journal entries.

**E8–6** Refer to the transactions in E8–5, but now assume the 1,000 shares are sold on February 1, 2025, for $80 per share.

**Required:**

1. How will each of these transactions in 2024, including an adjustment on December 31 for the investment's fair value, affect the financial statements?
2. How with the sale on February 1, 2025, affect the financial statements.

Account for equity investments using the fair value method **(LO 8–3)**

**E8–7** The investments of Harlon Enterprises included the following cost and fair value amounts ($ in millions):

| | | Fair Value, Dec. 31 | |
|---|---|---|---|
| **Equity Investments** | **Cost** | **2024** | **2025** |
| A Corporation shares | $ 20 | $14 | N/A |
| B Corporation shares | 35 | 38 | $ 37 |
| C Corporation shares | 15 | N/A | 14 |
| D Industries shares | 45 | 46 | 50 |
| Totals | $115 | $95 | $101 |

Additional information:

- Harlon accounts for its equity investment portfolio using the fair value method.
- Harlon sold its holdings of A Corporation shares on June 1, 2025, for $17 million.
- On September 12, 2025, Harlon purchased the C Corporation shares for $15 million.

**Required:**

1. What is the effect of the sale of the A Corporation shares and the purchase and holding of the C Corporation shares on Harlon's 2025 net income (ignore tax effects)?
2. What is the effect of holding the B Corporation shares and D Corporation shares on Harlon's 2025 net income (ignore tax effects)?

3. At what amount should Harlon report its equity investment portfolio in its 2025 balance sheet?

**E8–8** On January 1, Lifestyle Pools purchased 25% of Marshall Fence's common stock for $700,000 cash. By the end of the year, Marshall Fence reported net income of $160,000 and paid dividends of $60,000 to all shareholders.

Account for investments using the equity method (LO 8–4)
See JE8–5 for journal entries.

**Required:**

1. For Lifestyle Pools, what are the financial statement effects of the initial investment in Marshall Fence?
2. For Lifestyle Pools, how will its share of Marshall Fence's net income and dividends for the year affect its financial statements?

**E8–9** On January 1, Marcum's Landscape purchased 10,000 shares (35%) of the common stock of Atlantic Irrigation for $600,000. Below are amounts reported by both companies for the year.

Account for investments using the equity method (LO 8–4)
See JE8–6 for journal entries.

|  | Marcum's Landscape | Atlantic Irrigation |
|---|---|---|
| Stock price on January 1 | $85 | $60 |
| Net income for the year | $500,000 | $130,000 |
| Dividends paid for the year | $60,000 | $40,000 |
| Stock price on December 31 | $94 | $68 |

**Required:**

For Marcum's Landscape, how will the initial purchase, its share of Atlantic's net income and dividends, and the adjustment for Atlantic's fair value at the end of the year affect its financial statements?

**E8–10** As a long-term investment, Fair Company purchased 20% of Midlin Company's 300,000 shares for $360,000 at the beginning of the reporting year of both companies. During the year, Midlin earned net income of $135,000 and distributed cash dividends of $0.25 per share. At year-end, the fair value of the shares is $375,000.

Compare the fair value method to the equity method (LO 8–3, LO 8–4)
See JE8–7 for journal entries.

**Required:**

1. Assume no significant influence was acquired. How will the investment in Midlin Company be reflected in the balance sheet and income statement of Fair Company at year-end?
2. Assume significant influence was acquired. How will the investment in Midlin Company be reflected in the balance sheet and income statement of Fair Company at year-end?

**E8–11** Alpha has made the following investments.

Determine which companies to consolidate (LO 8–5)

_____ 1. 10% of the common stock of Beta.
_____ 2. 40% of the bonds of Gamma.
_____ 3. 75% of the common stock of Delta.
_____ 4. 15% of the bonds of Epsilon.
_____ 5. 25% of the common stock of Zeta.
_____ 6. 60% of the bonds of Eta.
_____ 7. 100% of the common stock of Theta.

**Required:**

Indicate with an "X" which of the companies above would be accounted for using the consolidation method.

**E8–12** On January 1, Dora purchases 175 of the $1,000, 7%, 15-year bonds issued by Splash City, with interest receivable semiannually on June 30 and December 31 each year. The bonds were issued at face amount.

Account for investment in bonds issued at face amount (LO 8–6)
See JE8–8 for journal entries.

**Required:**

1. How will the purchase of the bonds by Dora on January 1 affect the financial statements?
2. How will the receipt of the first semiannual interest payment on June 30 affect the financial statements?

Account for debt
investments classified as
trading securities **(LO 8–6)**

**E8–13** Q&M Apparel buys and sells securities, which it classifies as trading securities. On December 27, 2024, Q&M purchases bonds at face amount for $875,000, and sells the bonds on January 3, 2025, for $880,000. At December 31, 2024, the bonds had a fair value of $873,000.

***Required:***
1. How would the investment in bonds affect the 2024 income statement?
2. How would the investment in bonds affect the 2025 income statement?

Account for debt
investments classified
as available-for-sale
securities **(LO 8–6)**

**E8–14** Use the same facts as in E8–13, but now assume Q&M Apparel classifies the debt securities as available-for-sale securities.

***Required:***
1. How would the investment in bonds affect the 2024 income statement?
2. How would the investment in bonds affect the 2025 income statement?

Account for debt
investments classified
as held-to-maturity
securities **(LO 8–6)**
*See JE8–9 for journal
entries.*

**E8–15** Tanner-UNF Corporation acquired as a long-term investment $200 million of 6% bonds, dated July 1, on July 1, 2024. Company management has the positive intent and ability to hold the bonds until maturity. Tanner-UNF paid $200 million for the bonds. The company will receive interest semiannually on June 30 and December 31. As a result of changing market conditions, the fair value of the bonds at December 31, 2024, was $210 million.

***Required:***
1. How will Tanner-UNF's investment in the bonds on July 1, 2024, affect the financial statements?
2. How will Tanner-UNF's receipt of interest on December 31, 2024, affect the financial statements?
3. At what amount will Tanner-UNF report its investment in the December 31, 2024, balance sheet?
4. Suppose Moody's bond rating agency downgraded the risk rating of the bonds motivating Tanner-UNF to sell the investment on January 2, 2025, for $190 million. How will the sale of the bond investment affect Tanner-UNF's financial statements?

Account for debt
investments classified as
trading securities **(LO 8–6)**
*See JE8–10 for journal
entries.*

**E8–16** Assume the same facts as in E8–15, but now assume Tanner-UNF management is holding the bonds in a trading portfolio.

***Required:***
1. How will Tanner-UNF's investment in the bonds on July 1, 2024, affect the financial statements?
2. How will Tanner-UNF's receipt of interest on December 31, 2024, affect the financial statements?
3. How will the fair value adjustment at December 31 affect the financial statements? At what amount will Tanner-UNF report its investment in the December 31, 2024, balance sheet?
4. Suppose Moody's bond rating agency downgraded the risk rating of the bonds motivating Tanner-UNF to sell the investment on January 2, 2025, for $190 million. How will the sale of the bond investment affect Tanner-UNF's financial statements?

Account for debt
investments classified as
available-for-sale **(LO 8–6)**
*See JE8–11 for journal
entries.*

**E8–17** Assume the same facts as in E8–15, but now assume Tanner-UNF management classifies the investment as available-for-sale securities.

***Required:***
1. How will Tanner-UNF's investment in the bonds on July 1, 2024, affect the financial statements?
2. How will Tanner-UNF's receipt of interest on December 31, 2024, affect the financial statements?
3. How will the fair value adjustment at December 31 affect the financial statements? At what amount will Tanner-UNF report its investment in the December 31, 2024, balance sheet?
4. Suppose Moody's bond rating agency downgraded the risk rating of the bonds motivating Tanner-UNF to sell the investment on January 2, 2025, for $190 million. How will the sale of the bond investment affect Tanner-UNF's financial statements?

**E8–18** DEFT Records and Q Records provide the following selected financial data.

Calculate and analyze the cash holdings ratio (LO 8–7)

| | DEFT Records | | Q Records | |
|---|---|---|---|---|
| | **2024** | **2023** | **2024** | **2023** |
| Cash and cash equivalents | $ 150,250 | $ 132,220 | $ 486,810 | $ 428,393 |
| Short-term investments | 85,540 | 74,420 | 132,587 | 115,351 |
| Accounts receivable | 750,890 | 690,819 | 1,178,897 | 1,084,586 |
| Inventory | 650,425 | 604,895 | 1,040,680 | 967,832 |
| Property, plant and equipment | 2,156,850 | 1,919,597 | 3,558,803 | 3,167,334 |
| Long-term investments | 110,540 | 93,959 | 182,391 | 155,032 |
| Total asset | 3,904,495 | 3,515,909 | 6,580,168 | 5,918,528 |
| Total liabilities | 1,249,438 | 1,160,250 | 2,500,464 | 2,249,041 |
| Total stockholders' equity | 2,655,057 | 2,355,659 | 4,079,704 | 3,669,487 |
| Net sales | $6,549,875 | $5,763,890 | $9,824,813 | $8,645,835 |
| Operating income | 2,095,960 | 1,815,625 | 3,536,933 | 3,026,042 |
| Interest expense | 56,225 | 53,952 | 97,518 | 97,833 |
| Investment income | 5,686 | 5,388 | 13,229 | 10,815 |

*Required:*

1. Calculate the cash holdings ratio for DEFT Records in 2024.
2. Calculate the cash holdings ratio for Q Records in 2024.
3. Companies in this industry typically have cash holding ratios between 7% and 9%. Which company's cash holdings ratio are you concerned about?

**E8–19** Refer to the financial information for DEFT Records and Q Records presented in E8–18.

Calculate and analyze the investment-to-asset ratio (LO 8–8)

*Required:*

1. Calculate the investment-to-assets ratio for DEFT Records in 2024.
2. Calculate the investment-to-assets for Q Records in 2024.
3. Companies in this industry typically have investment-to-assest ratios between 4% and 6%. Which company's investment-to-assets ratio are you concerned about?

**E8–20** Refer to the financial information for DEFT Records and Q Records presented in E8–18.

Calculate and analyze the return on investments ratio (LO 8–8)

*Required:*

1. Calculate the return on investments ratio for DEFT Records in 2024.
2. Calculate the return on investments ratio for Q Records in 2024.
3. Which company's investments delivered a more favorable return in 2024?

## PROBLEMS

Mc Graw Hill **connect**

**P8–1** Barry, Hank, and Babe form a company named Long Ball Investments, hoping to find that elusive home run stock. A new clothing company by the name of Major League Apparel caught their eye. Major League Apparel has two classes of stock authorized: Class A stock and Class B stock. Class A stock has voting rights but pays no dividends, while Class B stock offers guaranteed dividends of $1.50 per share but has no voting rights. Long Ball Investments has the following transactions during the year. None of the investments are large enough to exert a significant influence.

Account for investments using the fair value method (LO 8–3) See JP8–1 for journal entries.

| | | |
|---|---|---|
| January | 2 | Purchase 1,500 shares of Major League Class A stock for $70 per share. |
| February | 14 | Purchase 600 shares of Major League Class B stock for $12 per share. |
| May | 15 | Sell 300 shares of Class A stock for $62 per share. |
| December | 30 | Receive a cash dividend on Class B stock of $1.50 per share. |
| December | 31 | The fair values of Class A and Class B shares are $73 and $14, respectively. |

*Required*

1. Determine the financial statement effects of each of these investment transactions.
2. Calculate the balance in the Investments account as of December 31.

Account for investments using the equity method **(LO 8–4)**
See JP8–2 for journal entries.

**P8–2** As a long-term investment at the beginning of the year, Willie Winn Track Shoes purchased 25% of Betty Will Company's 34 million shares outstanding for $178 million. During the first year of the investment, Betty Will earned net income of $130 million and distributed cash dividends of $1.10 per share. During the second year of the investment, Betty Will earned net income of $142 million and again distributed cash dividends of $1.10 per share.

**Required:**

1. Determine the financial statement effects of Willie Winn Track Shoes' initial investment in the Betty Will Company in the first year.
2. How will Willie Winn Track Shoes' share of Betty Will's net income and dividends affect its financial statements in the first year?
3. How will Willie Winn Track Shoes' share of Betty Will's net income and dividends affect its financial statements in the second year?
4. Determine the balance in the Betty Will Investments account at the end of the second year.

Account for investments in debt securities **(LO 8–6)**
See JP8–3 for journal entries.

**P8–3** On January 1, Twister Enterprises issues $600,000 of 6% bonds, due in 20 years, with interest payable semiannually on June 30 and December 30 each year. The bonds were issued at their face amount. National Hydraulics, a supplier of mechanical parts to Twister Enterprises, purchases 25% of the bond issue ($150,000 face amount). National Hydraulics sells the bonds on December 31 for $145,000.

**Required:**

1. Determine the financial statement effects of the investment in bonds by National Hydraulics.
2. Determine the financial statement effects of the first two semiannual interest payments on June 30 and December 30.
3. Determine the financial statement effects of the sale of the bonds by National Hydraulics on December 31.
4. What happened to market interest rates between the beginning and end of the year?

Analyze investment ratios **(LO 8–7, 8–8)**

**P8–4** New Corp, an up-and-coming biotech company, provides the following selected financial statement information. Financial information for Benchmark Corp, a well-established biotech company whose financial ratios represent the gold-standard in the industry, is also provided.

| | New Corp | | Benchmark Corp | |
| --- | --- | --- | --- | --- |
| | **2024** | **2023** | **2024** | **2023** |
| Cash and cash equivalents | $ 350,656 | $ 238,446 | $ 4,207,872 | $ 3,997,478 |
| Short-term investments | 490,545 | 353,192 | 9,320,355 | 8,947,541 |
| Accounts receivable | 32,588 | 23,137 | 782,112 | 766,470 |
| Property, plant and equip. | 852,459 | 588,197 | 18,754,098 | 17,816,393 |
| Intangible assets | 2,565,875 | 1,796,113 | 41,054,000 | 39,822,380 |
| Long-term investments | 1,545,856 | 1,082,099 | 46,375,680 | 45,448,166 |
| Total asset | 5,837,979 | 4,081,184 | 120,494,117 | 116,798,428 |
| Total liabilities | 875,697 | 571,366 | 45,787,764 | 43,215,419 |
| Total stockholders' equity | 4,962,282 | 3,509,819 | 74,706,353 | 73,583,010 |
| | | | | |
| Net sales | $7,865,315 | $5,112,455 | $245,253,656 | $240,348,583 |
| Operating income | 1,179,797 | 1,610,423 | 88,291,316 | 84,122,004 |
| Interest expense | 39,406 | 26,569 | 1,373,633 | 1,361,286 |
| Investment income | 81,456 | 45,929 | 1,670,881 | 1,523,080 |

**Required:**

1. Calculate the cash holdings ratio for both companies. What conclusions do you draw about the cash holdings of New Corp?
2. Calculate the investment-to-assets ratio for both companies. What conclusions do you draw about the New Corp's level of investment?
3. Calculate the return on investments ratio for both companies. What conclusions do you draw about the riskiness of New Corp's investments?

## JOURNAL ENTRIES

## Journal Entries—Brief Exercises

**JBE8–1** On September 1, Leather Suppliers, Inc., purchases 150 shares of Western Wear Clothing for $13 per share. On November 1, Leather Suppliers sells the investment for $17 per share. Record the transactions made by Leather Suppliers for the purchase and sale of the investment in Western Wear Clothing.

Record equity investments using the fair value method **(LO 8–3)**
*See BE8–3 for financial statement effects.*

**JBE8–2** On December 28, Summit purchased **Microsoft** common shares for $485,000. On December 31, the shares had a fair value of $483,000. Record the initial investment by Summit and, if appropriate, an adjusting entry to record the investment at fair value.

Record equity investments using the fair value method **(LO 8–3)**
*See BE8–4 for financial statement effects.*

**JBE8–3** On December 28, Summit purchased **Microsoft** common shares for $485,000. On December 31, the shares had a fair value of $487,000. Record the initial investment by Summit and, if appropriate, an adjusting entry to record the investment at fair value.

Record equity investments using the fair value method **(LO 8–3)**
*See BE8–5 for financial statement effects.*

**JBE8–4** On December 29, 2024, Adams Apples purchased 1,000 shares of **General Electric** common stock for $19 per share. On December 31, the market value of the stock increased to $20 per share. On January 24, 2025, all of the shares are sold for $22 per share. Record the initial investment, any fair value adjustment at the end of 2024, and the sale in 2025.

Record equity investments using the fair value method **(LO 8–3)**
*See BE8–6 for financial statement effects.*

**JBE8–5** On December 29, 2024, Adams Apples purchased 1,000 shares of **General Electric** common stock for $19 per share. On December 31, the market value of the stock increased to $20 per share. On January 24, 2025, all of the shares are sold for $16 per share. Record the initial investment, any fair value adjustment at the end of 2024, and the sale in 2025.

Record equity investments using the fair value method **(LO 8–3)**
*See BE8–7 for financial statement effects.*

**JBE8–6** Wendy Day Kite Company owns 10% of the outstanding stock of Strong String Company. During the current year, Strong String paid total dividends of $10 million to all stockholders. Record the receipt of cash dividends from Strong String.

Record dividend revenue using the fair value method **(LO 8–3)**
*See BE8–8 for financial statement effects.*

**JBE8–7** Wendy Day Kite Company owns 40% of the outstanding stock of Strong String Company. During the current year, Strong String reported net income of $15 million. Record Wendy Day Kit Company's share of Strong String's net income.

Understand the effect of net income by the investee in an equity method investment **(LO 8–4)**
*See BE8–9 for financial statement effects.*

**JBE8–8** Wendy Day Kite Company owns 40% of the outstanding stock of Strong String Company. During the current year, Strong String paid a $10 million cash dividend on all of its common shares. Record the receipt of cash dividends from Strong String.

Understand the effect of dividends received by the investee in an equity method investment **(LO 8–4)**
*See BE8–10 for financial statement effects.*

**JBE8–9** Salt Foods purchases forty $1,000, 7%, 10-year bonds issued by Pretzelmania, Inc., for $40,000 on January 1. Salt Foods receives interest semiannually on June 30 and December 31. Record the investment in bonds and the receipt of the first interest payment on June 30.

Record investment in bonds at face value **(LO 8–6)**
*See BE8–12 for financial statement effects.*

**JBE8–10** Q&M Apparel purchased debt securities on January 1 for $150,000 and classified the investments as trading securities. On December 31, the debt securities are valued at $148,000. Record the year-end entry to adjust these securities to their fair value.

Adjust trading securities to their fair value **(LO 8–6)**
*See BE8–14 for financial statement effects.*

**JBE8–11** Use the same facts as in JBE8–10, but now assume the debt securities are classified as available-for-sale securities. Record the year-end entry to adjust these securities to their fair value.

Adjust available-for-sale securities to their fair value **(LO 8–6)**
*See BE8–15 for financial statement effects.*

## Journal Entries—Exercises

Record equity investments using the fair value method (LO 8–3)
*See E8–3 for financial statement effects.*

**JE8–1** First National Bank buys and sells securities. The company's fiscal year ends on December 31. The following selected transactions relating to First National's trading account occurred during the year.

| December 20 | Purchases 300,000 shares in Classic Computers common stock for $1,500,000 ($5 per share). |
| December 28 | Receives cash dividends of $6,000 from the Classic Computers shares. |
| December 31 | The fair value of Classic Computers' stock is $4.80 per share. |

**Required:**

1. Record each of these transactions, including an adjusting entry on December 31 for the investment's fair value, if appropriate
2. Calculate the balance of the Investments account on December 31.

Record equity investments using the fair value method (LO 8–3)
*See E8–4 for financial statement effects.*

**JE8–2** Mr. T's Fashions, once a direct competitor to Italian Stallion's clothing line, formed a friendship in recent years leading to a small investment (less than 5%) by Mr. T in the common stock of Italian Stallion. Mr. T's engages in the following transactions relating to its investment.

| February | 1 | Purchases 150 shares of Italian Stallion common stock for $16 per share. |
| June | 15 | Sells 50 shares of Italian Stallion stock for $14 per share. |
| October | 31 | Receives a cash dividend of $0.50 per share. |
| December | 31 | The fair value of Italian Stallion's stock is $12 per share. |

**Required:**

1. Record each of these transactions, including an adjusting entry on December 31 for the investment's fair value, if appropriate.
2. Calculate the balance of the Investments account on December 31.

Record equity investments using the fair value method (LO 8–3)
*See E8–5 for financial statement effects.*

**JE8–3** Gator Shoes, Inc., manufactures a line of stylish waterproof footwear. The following transactions relate to investments in common stock during 2024.

| March | 1 | Purchases 3,000 shares (10%) of Power Drive Corporation's common stock for $62 per share. |
| July | 1 | Receives a cash dividend of $1.25 per share. |
| December | 31 | The fair value of Power Drive Corporation's common stock is $75 per share. |

On February 1, 2025, Gator Shoes sells 1,000 shares of Power Drive Corporation's common stock for $70 per share.

**Required:**

1. Record each of these transactions in 2024, including an adjusting entry on December 31 for the investment's fair value, if appropriate.
2. Record the sale on February 1, 2025.

Record equity investments using the fair value method (LO 8–3)
*See E8–6 for financial statement effects.*

**JE8–4** Refer to the transactions in JE8–3, but now assume the 1,000 shares are sold on February 1, 2025, for $80 per share.

**Required:**

1. Record each of these transactions in 2024, including an adjusting entry on December 31 for the investment's fair value, if appropriate.
2. Record the sale on February 1, 2025.

Record investments using the equity method (LO 8–4)
*See E8–8 for financial statement effects.*

**JE8–5** On January 1, Lifestyle Pools purchased 25% of Marshall Fence's common stock for $700,000 cash. By the end of the year, Marshall Fence reported net income of $160,000 and paid dividends of $60,000 to all shareholders.

**Required:**

For Lifestyle Pools, record the initial purchase and its share of Marshall Fence's net income and dividends for the year.

**JE8–6** On January 1, Marcum's Landscape purchased 10,000 shares (35%) of the common stock of Atlantic Irrigation for $600,000. Below are amounts reported by both companies for the year.

Record investments using the equity method **(LO 8–4)**
*See E8–9 for financial statement effects.*

| | Marcum's Landscape | Atalantic Irrigation |
|---|---|---|
| Stock price on January 1 | $85 | $60 |
| Net income for the year | $500,000 | $130,000 |
| Dividends paid for the year | $60,000 | $40,000 |
| Stock price on December 31 | $94 | $68 |

**Required:**

For Marcum's Landscape, record the initial purchase, its share of Atlantic's net income and dividends, and the adjusting entry for Atlantic's fair value at the end of the year, if appropriate.

**JE8–7** As a long-term investment, Fair Company purchased 20% of Midlin Company's 300,000 shares for $360,000 at the beginning of the reporting year of both companies. During the year, Midlin earned net income of $135,000 and distributed cash dividends of $0.25 per share. At year-end, the fair value of the shares is $375,000.

Compare the fair value method to the equity method **(LO 8–3, LO 8–4)**
*See E8–10 for financial statement effects.*

**Required:**

1. Assume no significant influence was acquired. Record the transactions from the purchase through the end of the year, including any adjusting entry for the investment's fair value, if appropriate.
2. Assume significant influence was acquired. Record the transactions from the purchase through the end of the year, including any adjusting entry for the investment's fair value, if appropriate.

**JE8–8** On January 1, Dora purchases 175 of the $1,000, 7%, 15-year bonds issued by Splash City, with interest receivable semiannually on June 30 and December 31 each year. The bonds were issued at face amount.

Compare the fair value method to the equity method **(LO 8–6)**
*See E8–12 for financial statement effects.*

**Required:**

Record the initial purchase of the bonds and the receipt of the first semiannual interest payment on June 30.

**JE8–9** Tanner-UNF Corporation acquired as a long-term investment $200 million of 6% bonds, dated July 1, 2024. Company management has the positive intent and ability to hold the bonds until maturity. Tanner-UNF paid $200 million for the bonds. The company will receive interest semiannually on June 30 and December 31. As a result of changing market conditions, the fair value of the bonds at December 31, 2024, was $210 million.

Account for debt investments classified as held-to-maturity securities **(LO 8–6)**
*See E8–15 for financial statement effects.*

**Required:**

1. Prepare the journal entry to record Tanner-UNF's investment in the bonds on July 1, 2024.
2. Prepare the journal entry by Tanner-UNF to record interest on December 31, 2024, at the effective (market) rate.
3. Prepare the journal entry, if needed, to record the fair value adjustment at December 31. At what amount will Tanner-UNF report its investment in the December 31, 2024, balance sheet?
4. Suppose Moody's bond rating agency downgraded the risk rating of the bonds motiving Tanner-UNF to sell the investment on January 2, 2025, for $190 million. Prepare the journal entry to record the sale.

**JE8–10** Assume the same facts as in JE8–9, but now assume Tanner-UNF management is holding the bonds in a trading portfolio.

Account for debt investments classified as trading securities **(LO 8–6)**
*See E8–16 for financial statement effects.*

**Required:**

1. Prepare the journal entry to record Tanner-UNF's investment in the bonds on July 1, 2024.
2. Prepare the journal entry by Tanner-UNF to record interest on December 31, 2024, at the effective (market) rate.
3. Prepare the journal entry, if needed, to record the fair value adjustment at December 31.

4. Suppose Moody's bond rating agency downgraded the risk rating of the bonds motiving Tanner-UNF to sell the investment on January 2, 2025, for $190 million. Prepare the journal entry to record the sale.

Account for debt investments classified as available-for-sale securities **(LO 8–6)** *See E8–17 for financial statement effects.*

**JE8–11** Assume the same facts as in JE8–9, but now assume Tanner-UNF management is holding the bonds as available-for-sale securities.

*Required:*

1. Prepare the journal entry to record Tanner-UNF's investment in the bonds on July 1, 2024.
2. Prepare the journal entry by Tanner-UNF to record interest on December 31, 2024, at the effective (market) rate.
3. Prepare the journal entry, if needed, to record the fair value adjustment at December 31.
4. Suppose Moody's bond rating agency downgraded the risk rating of the bonds motiving Tanner-UNF to sell the investment on January 2, 2025, for $190 million. Prepare the journal entry to record the sale.

## Journal Entries—Problems

Record investment transactions using the fair value method **(LO 8–3)** *See P8–1 for financial statement effects.*

**JP8–1** Barry, Hank, and Babe form a company named Long Ball Investments, hoping to find that elusive home run stock. A new clothing company by the name of Major League Apparel caught their eye. Major League Apparel has two classes of stock authorized: Class A stock and Class B stock. Class A stock has voting rights but pays no dividends, while Class B stock offers guaranteed dividends of $1.50 per share but has no voting rights. Long Ball Investments has the following transactions during the year. None of the investments are large enough to exert a significant influence.

| | | |
|---|---|---|
| January | 2 | Purchase 1,500 shares of Major League Class A stock for $70 per share. |
| February | 14 | Purchase 600 shares of Major League Class B stock for $12 per share. |
| May | 15 | Sell 300 shares of Major League's Class A stock for $62 per share. |
| December 30 | | Receive a cash dividend on Major League's Class B stock of $1.50 per share. |
| December 31 | | The fair values of the Class A and Class B shares are $73 and $14, respectively. |

*Required*

1. Record each of these investment transactions.
2. Calculate the balance in the Investments account as of December 31.

Record investment transactions using the equity method **(LO 8–4)** *See P8–2 for financial statement effects.*

**JP8–2** As a long-term investment at the beginning of the year, Willie Winn Track Shoes purchased 25% of Betty Will Company's 34 million shares outstanding for $178 million. During the first year of the investment, Betty Will earned net income of $130 million and distributed cash dividends of $1.10 per share. During the second year of the investment, Betty Will earned net income of $142 million and again distributed cash dividends of $1.10 per share.

*Required:*

1. Record Willie Winn Track Shoes' investment in the Betty Will Company in the first year.
2. Record Willie Win Track Shoes' share of Betty Will's net income and dividends in the first year?
3. Record Willie Win Track Shoes' share of Betty Will's net income and dividends in the second year?

Record investments in debt securities **(LO 8–6)** *See JP8–3 for financial statement effects.*

**JP8–3** On January 1, Twister Enterprises issues $600,000 of 6% bonds, due in 20 years, with interest payable semiannually on June 30 and December 30 each year. The bonds were issued at their face amount. National Hydraulics, a supplier of mechanical parts to Twister Enterprises, purchases 25% of the bond issue ($150,000 face amount). National Hydraulics sells the bonds on December 31 for $145,000.

*Required:*

1. Record the investment in bonds by National Hydraulics.
2. Record the first two semiannual interest payments on June 30 and December 30.
3. Record the sale of the bonds by National Hydraulics on December 31.

## DATA ANALYTICS

Visit Connect to view **Data Analytics** questions related to:

1. Applying Excel
2. Data Visualizations
3. Tableau Dashboard Activities
4. Applying Tableau

## ANSWERS TO THE SELF-STUDY QUESTIONS

1. b    2. a    3. c    4. c    5. c    6. b    7. a    8. a    9. d    10. a    11. c    12. d

# Liabilities

## 9

## Feature Story

# United Airlines: A Future up in the Air

You might think airlines like **American**, **Delta**, or **United** are highly profitable, low-risk companies. Commercial airlines typically fly more than 40,000 flights each day. However, American, Delta, and United Airlines have all filed for bankruptcy over the years, and external factors such as the COVID-19 pandemic represent significant operating risks to their ability to pay debts.

Companies must file for bankruptcy protection when they no longer are able to pay their liabilities as they become due. By carefully examining information in financial statements, investors and creditors can assess a company's *profitability*, its *liquidity* (its ability to pay current debts), and its *solvency* (its ability to pay long-term debts). Profitability, liquidity, and solvency help indicate a company's risk of filing for bankruptcy.

What are some of the current liabilities reported by companies in the airline industry? The airline industry is very labor-intensive, resulting in extensive payroll liabilities. Another substantial current liability for airlines is advance ticket sales. This liability, representing tickets sold for future flights, is in the billions of dollars for several major U.S. airlines. Airlines are also well known for their frequent-flyer programs. These programs have created liabilities for frequent-flyer incentives exceeding $100 million. Finally, a somewhat different type of liability airlines face is contingent liabilities. A *contingent liability* is a possible liability for which payment is contingent upon another event. An example is pending litigation. All of the major airlines report contingent liabilities related to unsettled litigation. Airlines also typically have high levels of long-term debt such as installment notes, leases, and bonds. Airlines need long-term debt to finance their extensive investments in physical assets such as planes and equipment. These assets serve as collateral for the debt, which lowers the cost of debt to the airline because it reduces the risk to the lender. Ultimately, the goal of long-term borrowing is to earn a rate of return on the financed assets that is greater than the interest rate on the borrowing. However, high levels of debt increase the risk of bankruptcy.

In this chapter, we'll cover various types of current and long-term liabilities. At the end of the chapter, we'll discuss liquidity ratios of **United Airlines** versus **American Airlines** and the solvency ratios of **Coca-Cola** versus **Pepsi** to understand how to assess a company's ability to pay its liabilities as they come due.

## PART A

# CURRENT LIABILITIES

In the four preceding chapters, we worked our way down the asset side of the balance sheet, examining cash, accounts receivable, inventory, investments, and long-term assets. We now turn to the other half of the balance sheet—liabilities (Chapter 9) and stockholders' equity (Chapter 10).

**■ LO9–1**

Explain financing alternatives and characteristics of liabilities.

## Financing Alternatives

Let's begin by reviewing the basic accounting equation reported in the balance sheet:

| Assets | = | Liabilities | + | Stockholders' Equity |
|---|---|---|---|---|
| (resources) | | (creditors' claims) | | (owners' claims) |

Assets are the resources of the company. To help maintain those assets and continue to grow operations, companies need funds. Some of the funds needed to pay for assets can come from the profits generated by the company's own operations. Profits generated by the company are a source of *internal financing*. Managers generally turn to internal financing first as a source of funds because it's "free" in the sense that it's not associated with a cost such as interest.

Frequently, though, companies must rely on funds from those outside the company to pay for operations and expansion. Funds coming from those outside of the company are sources of *external financing*. The right side of the accounting equation reveals the two sources of external financing—debt financing and equity financing. Debt financing refers to borrowing money from creditors (liabilities). Equity financing refers to obtaining investment from stockholders (stockholders' equity).

Capital-intensive companies (i.e., those with lots of property, plant and equipment) typically use debt financing to a greater extent for their financing because their capital investments can be used as collateral. Companies that rely more heavily on research and development ("ideas") use equity financing to a greater extent to finance their asset growth. The mixture of liabilities and equity a business uses is called its capital structure. Illustration 9–1 shows how capital structure varies across a variety of companies.

**ILLUSTRATION 9–1**

**Debt versus Equity for Five Companies in Different Industries**

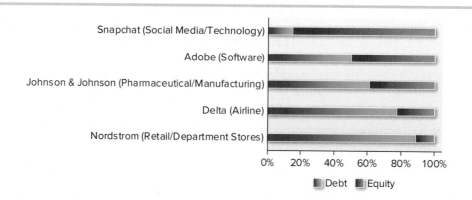

Another reason a company would choose to borrow money rather than issue additional stock relates to taxes. **Interest expense incurred when borrowing money is tax-deductible, whereas dividends paid to stockholders are not tax-deductible.** Interest expense incurred on debt reduces taxable income; paying dividends to stockholders does not reduce taxable income because dividends are not an expense. Therefore, debt can be a less costly source of external financing. In this chapter, we'll discuss the various liabilities used by companies as a source of debt financing.

 **KEY POINT**

Companies obtain external funds through debt financing (liabilities) and equity financing (stockholders' equity). One advantage of debt financing is that interest on borrowed funds is tax-deductible.

## CHARACTERISTICS OF LIABILITIES

A liability is an obligation of a company to transfer some economic benefit in the future. Most liabilities require the payment of cash in the future. For instance, accounts payable, notes payable, and salaries payable usually are paid in cash. Other liabilities, such as deferred revenue, arise when a company receives cash in advance from customers. These liabilities represent an obligation of the company to transfer inventory or perform services to those customers in the future.

## CURRENT VS. LONG-TERM CLASSIFICATION

In the balance sheet, we categorize liabilities as either current or long-term. **In most cases, current liabilities are payable within one year from the balance sheet date, and long-term liabilities are payable in more than one year.**

*Common Terms*
Current liabilities are also sometimes called *short-term liabilities.*

Current liabilities are *usually*, but not always, due within one year. If a company has an operating cycle longer than one year (a winery, for example), its current liabilities are defined by the operating cycle rather than by the length of a year. An *operating cycle* is the length of time from incurring costs to provide goods and services to a customer until collection of cash from that customer. For now, remember that in most cases (but not all), current liabilities are due within one year.

Distinguishing between current and long-term liabilities is important in helping investors and creditors assess risk. Given a choice, most companies would prefer to report a liability as long-term rather than current because doing so may cause the company to appear less risky. In turn, less-risky companies may enjoy lower interest rates on borrowing and command higher stock prices for new stock listings.

The Feature Story at the beginning of this chapter pointed out that the U.S. airline industry has experienced financial difficulties over the years, resulting in greater risk to investors. Several major airlines were forced into bankruptcy because they were unable to pay current liabilities as they became due. In Illustration 9–2, an excerpt from the annual report of **United Airlines** discusses some of the risk factors faced by the airline industry.

**ILLUSTRATION 9–2**
Risk Factors of United Airlines

**UNITED AIRLINES**
**Management Discussion and Analysis (excerpt)**

The global pandemic resulting from a novel strain of coronavirus has had an adverse impact that has been material to the Company's business, operating results, financial condition, and liquidity, and the duration and spread of the pandemic could result in additional adverse impacts. The outbreak of another disease or similar public health threat in the future could also have an adverse effect on the Company's business, operating results, financial condition, and liquidity.

The Company has a significant amount of financial leverage from fixed obligations and intends to seek material amounts of additional financial liquidity in the short-term, and insufficient liquidity may have a material adverse effect on the Company's financial condition and business.

What obligations do companies most frequently report as current liabilities? Loan amounts due within the next year, accounts payable, and payroll liabilities are three main categories. In addition, companies report a variety of other current liabilities, including deferred revenue, sales tax payable, and the current portion of long-term debt. There is no prescribed order for presenting accounts within the current liabilities section of the balance sheet.

Illustration 9–3 presents the current liabilities section for **Southwest Airlines**. For a company like Southwest Airlines, accounts payable and accrued liabilities consist of amounts owed for items such as employee compensation, taxes, airplane maintenance, and fuel. Air traffic liability is a liability recognized when tickets are first sold (deferred revenue). Southwest Airlines owes the customer a service until that flight is provided. Long-term debt is sometimes referred to as a note. When a note (or a portion of a long-term note) becomes due in the next year, the amount due is classified as a current liability.

**ILLUSTRATION 9–3**

Current Liabilities Section for Southwest Airlines

| SOUTHWEST AIRLINES Balance Sheet (partial) ($ in millions) | |
| --- | --- |
| Current liabilities: | |
| Accounts payable | $1,574 |
| Accrued liabilities | 1,749 |
| Current operating lease liabilities | 353 |
| Air traffic liability | 4,457 |
| Current maturities of long-term debt | 819 |
| Total current liabilities | $8,952 |

**KEY POINT**

In most cases, current liabilities are payable within one year from the balance sheet date, and long-term liabilities are payable in more than one year.

## Notes Payable

■ **LO9–2**

Account for notes payable and interest expense.

When a company borrows cash from a bank, the bank requires the company to sign a note promising to repay the amount borrowed plus interest. The borrower reports its liability as *notes payable*. About two-thirds of bank loans are short-term. Companies often use short-term debt because it usually offers lower interest rates than does long-term debt because the risk of default is lower with loans of shorter durations.

**Example.**  Assume **Southwest Airlines** borrows $100,000 from **Bank of America** on September 1, 2024, signing a 6%, six-month note for the amount borrowed plus accrued interest due six months later on March 1, 2025. On September 1, 2024, Southwest will receive $100,000 in cash.

The financial statement effects of the transaction are as follows:

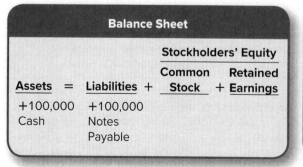

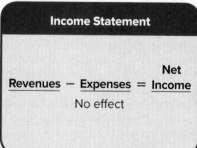

---

**DEBITS & CREDITS**
To record the issuance of the note payable:

|  | Debit | Credit |
|---|---|---|
| Cash ......................................................................... | 100,000 | |
| Notes Payable ...................................................... | | 100,000 |

Cash
100,000

Notes Payable
| 100,000

When a company borrows money, it pays the lender interest in return for using the lender's money during the term of the loan. Interest is stated in terms of an annual percentage rate to be applied to the face amount of the loan. Because the stated interest rate is an *annual* rate, when calculating interest for a current note payable, we must adjust for the fraction of the year the loan spans. We calculate interest on notes as

$$\text{Interest} = \frac{\text{Face}}{\text{amount}} \times \frac{\text{Annual}}{\text{interest rate}} \times \frac{\text{Fraction}}{\text{of the year}}$$

In the example above, how much interest cost does Southwest incur for the six-month period of the note from September 1, 2024, to March 1, 2025?

$$\$3,000 = \$100,000 \times 6\% \times 6/12$$

However, if Southwest's reporting period ends on December 31, 2024, then the company should not wait until March 1, 2025, to recognize the interest cost. Instead, the company reports the four months' interest incurred during 2024 ($2,000 for September, October, November, and December) as interest expense in its 2024 income statement. The remaining $1,000 of interest expense (for January and February) will be reported in its 2025 income statement. In addition, because the company will not pay the 2024 interest until the note becomes due (March 1, 2025), the 2024 balance sheet needs to report four months of **interest payable** as of December 31, 2024. The financial statement effects are as follows in 2024:

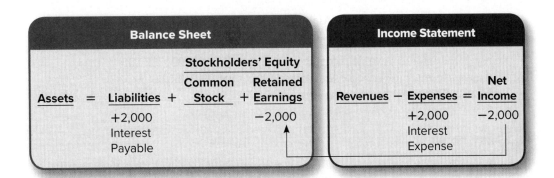

---

**DEBITS & CREDITS**
To accrue interest expense for the first four months of the note ending December 31, 2024:

|  | Debit | Credit |
|---|---|---|
| Interest Expense ($100,000 × 6% × 4/12) ....................................... | 2,000 | |
| Interest Payable ................................................................................ | | 2,000 |

Interest Expense
2,000 |

Interest Payable
| 2,000

 **COMMON MISTAKE** ⎯⎯⎯⎯⎯⎯⎯⎯⎯⎯⎯⎯⎯⎯⎯⎯⎯⎯⎯⎯⎯

When calculating the number of months of interest, students sometimes mistakenly subtract December (month 12) from September (month 9) and get three months. However, the time from September 1 to December 31 includes both September and December, so there are four months.

When the note comes due on March 1, 2025, Southwest Airlines will pay the face amount of the loan ($100,000) plus the entire $3,000 interest incurred ($100,000 × 6% × 6/12). The $3,000 represents six months of interest—the four months of interest ($2,000) in 2024 previously reported as interest payable and two months of interest ($1,000) in 2025. Repayment of the note and interest would have the following financial statement effects in 2025:

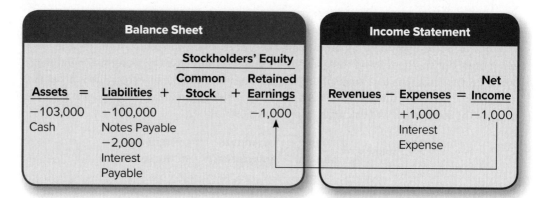

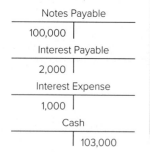

**DEBITS & CREDITS**

To record the repayment of the loan and the payment of six months of interest (first four months accrued in 2024 and the final two months in 2025):

| | Debit | Credit |
|---|---|---|
| Notes Payable | 100,000 | |
| Interest Payable | 2,000 | |
| Interest Expense ($100,000 × 6% × 2/12) | 1,000 | |
| Cash | | 103,000 |

Notice that with the payment on March 1, 2025, the company:

- Removes the note payable recognized on September 1, 2024 ($100,000).
- Removes the interest payable recognized on December 31, 2024 ($2,000).
- Recognizes interest expense for January and February 2025 ($1,000).
- Reduces cash for the total amount paid ($103,000).

 **KEY POINT**

We report interest expense in the period in which we *incur* it, rather than in the period in which we pay it.

## Let's Review

Assume **Delta Air Lines** borrows $500,000 from **Chase Bank** on November 1, 2024, signing a 9%, six-month note payable.

*Required:*

1. What effect will the issuance of the note have on Delta's balance sheet and income statement on November 1, 2024?
2. Delta will accrue interest on December 31, 2024 (the end of the fiscal year). How will this accrual affect the balance sheet and income statement?
3. How will the balance sheet and income statement be affected when Delta repays the loan to Chase in 2025?

***Solution:***

1. In the balance sheet, the issuance of the note will increase Cash (an asset) by $500,000 and increase Notes Payable (a liability) by $500,000. There is no income statement effect at issuance.

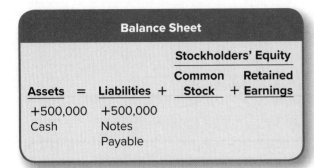
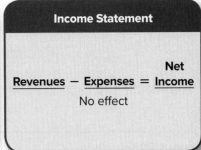

| November 1, 2024 | | Debit | Credit |
|---|---|---|---|
| **Cash** ...................................................................................................... | | **500,000** | |
|     **Notes Payable** ........................................................................... | | | **500,000** |
|     (*Issue note payable*) | | | |

2. At December 31, 2024, Delta will accrue for two months of interest totaling $7,500 (=$500,000 × 9% × 2/12). The income statement will reflect interest expense of $7,500 and the balance sheet will include $7,500 in Interest Payable.

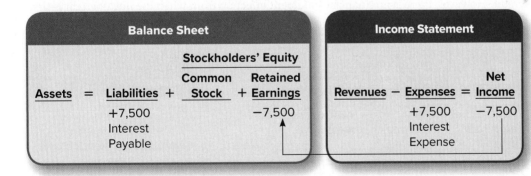

| December 31, 2024 | | Debit | Credit |
|---|---|---|---|
| **Interest Expense** ($500,000 × 9% × 2/12) ...................................... | | **7,500** | |
|     **Interest Payable** ...................................................................... | | | **7,500** |
|     (*Record interest incurred, but not paid*) | | | |

3. At maturity (May 1, 2025), Delta will repay the $500,000 note and will also pay $22,500 for all six months of interest that has accrued. In addition, Delta will need to recognize interest expense for the four months in 2025 that have passed (January through April). Thus, the income statement will reflect interest expense of $15,000 (= $500,000 × 9% × 4/12). In the balance sheet, Notes Payable will decrease by $500,000, Interest Payable accrued from the prior year will decrease by $7,500, and Cash will decrease by $522,500.

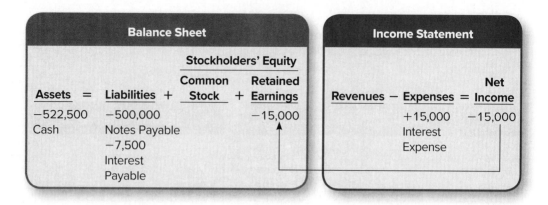

| May 1, 2025 | Debit | Credit |
|---|---|---|
| Notes Payable ..................................................................... | 500,000 | |
| Interest Payable (from 2024) ........................................... | 7,500 | |
| Interest Expense ($500,000 × 9% × 4/12) ........................ | 15,000 | |
| Cash ............................................................................... | | 522,500 |
| (*Pay note and interest*) | | |

Many companies prearrange the terms of a note payable by establishing a line of credit with a bank. A **line of credit** is an informal agreement that permits a company to borrow up to a prearranged limit without having to follow formal loan procedures and prepare paperwork. Notes payable is recorded each time the company borrows money under the line of credit. However, there is no financial statement effect up front when the line of credit is first negotiated because no money has yet been borrowed.

**Manager Analysis**

| Question ❓ | Accounting information 📄 | Analysis 🔍 |
|---|---|---|
| How can you tell the amount and interest rate of a company's line of credit? | Notes to the financial statements | Companies are required to disclose the terms of available lines of credit such as the amounts, maturity dates, and interest rates. |

If a company borrows from another company rather than from a bank, the note is referred to as **commercial paper**. The reporting for commercial paper is exactly the same as the reporting for notes payable described earlier. Commercial paper is sold with maturities normally ranging from 30 to 270 days. Since a company is borrowing directly from another company, the interest rate on commercial paper is usually lower than on a bank loan. Because of this, commercial paper has thus become an increasingly popular way for large companies to raise funds.

 **KEY POINT**

Many short-term loans are arranged under an existing line of credit with a bank, or for larger corporations in the form of commercial paper, a loan from one company to another.

# Other Common Current Liabilities

Beyond notes payable discussed in the previous section, there are many other common current liabilities that companies report in their balance sheet. These current liabilities reflect obligations that are expected to be settled within one year of the balance sheet date.

## ACCOUNTS PAYABLE

Accounts payable, sometimes called *trade accounts payable,* are amounts the company owes to suppliers of merchandise or services that it has bought on credit. We previously discussed accounts payable when we studied inventory purchases in Chapter 6. Briefly, recall that when a company purchases inventory on account (if it does not pay immediately with cash), it increases Inventory and Accounts Payable. Later, when the company pays the amount owed, it decreases both Cash and Accounts Payable. Most accounts are payable within one year and are therefore classified as current liabilities. Any accounts payable in more than one year would be classified as long-term liabilities.

■ **LO9–3**
Explain the accounting for common current liabilities.

Accounts payable are an attractive form of financing for companies because suppliers generally do not charge interest on the amount owed. Large retailers, such as **Target** and **Walmart**, rely heavily on this type of free supplier financing. In its recent annual report, Walmart reports an accounts payable balance of approximately $49 billion, representing 30% of its total liabilities.

## PAYROLL LIABILITIES

Many companies, including those in the airline industry, are very labor-intensive. Payroll liabilities make up a significant portion of current liabilities for these companies.

Salaries Payable is a current liability in the balance sheet that reflects that amount owed, but not yet paid, to employees for their past work. Payroll costs also include federal and state unemployment taxes, the employer's matched portion of Social Security and Medicare (FICA taxes), the employer's contributions for health, disability, and life insurance, and the employer's contributions to retirement or other savings plans. Liabilities associated with these amounts are also reflected in the balance sheet any time the amounts are accrued in one reporting period, but paid out in the subsequent reporting period.

**Robert Half** is a global human resource consulting firm that relies heavily on human labor with approximately 19,000 full-time employees and over 200,000 temporary employees. In its recent balance sheet, Robert Half reports accrued payroll and benefits costs of $398 million and employee deferred compensation plan obligations of $435 million in the current liabilities section. The annual report also discloses a breakdown of the accrued payroll and benefits costs as provided in Illustration 9–4.

**ILLUSTRATION 9–4**

Excerpt from Robert Half's Annual Report

| ROBERT HALF<br>Notes to the Financial Statements (excerpt) | |
| --- | --- |
| Accrued payroll and benefit costs and employee deferred compensation plan (in thousands): | |
| Payroll and benefits | $ 311,169 |
| Worker's compensation | 18,996 |
| Payroll taxes | 67,712 |
| **Accrued payroll and benefit costs** | **$397,877** |
| **Employee deferred compensation plan obligations** | **$435,121** |

Given Robert Half's business model, it may not surprise you to learn that payroll-related liabilities make up a significant portion of the company's total liabilities. A little more than 80% of its total liabilities relate to payroll.

## DEFERRED REVENUES

As we discussed in Chapter 5, some companies collect cash payments in advance of providing services or delivering goods. In such cases, a current liability account in the balance sheet called deferred revenue is increased when the cash is received. Later, when those services are rendered or goods are delivered, deferred revenue is decreased and revenue is recognized.

For example, suppose you purchase a $400 ticket from **United Airlines** on March 15 but the flight is not scheduled until August 4. United would recognize deferred revenue of $400 on March 15, at the time it receives your cash for the ticket purchase. Then, once the flight occurs on August 4 and United has satisfied its obligation to you, the company would decrease its deferred revenue and would recognize revenue of $400.

## SALES TAX PAYABLE

Most states impose a state sales tax, and many areas include a local sales tax as well. Yet, some states do not have a sales tax, including Alaska, Delaware, Montana, New Hampshire, and Oregon. However, many cities in Alaska have *local* sales taxes. The other four states impose sales-type taxes on specific transactions such as lodging, tobacco, or gasoline sales.

Each company selling products subject to sales tax is responsible for collecting the sales tax directly from customers and periodically sending the sales taxes collected to the state and local governments. The selling company reports sales revenue in one account and sales tax payable in another. **When the company collects the sales taxes, it increases Cash and increases Sales Tax Payable.**

**COMMON MISTAKE**

Some students want to report sales taxes paid by the company as Sales Tax Expense. While sales tax is an expense for the consumer, it is not an expense for the company selling the goods or service. For the company, sales taxes are simply additional cash the company collects from customers for taxes that the customer owes to local or state government.

## CURRENT PORTION OF LONG-TERM DEBT

The current portion of long-term debt is the amount that will be paid within one year from the balance sheet date. Management needs to know this amount in order to budget the cash flow necessary to pay the current portion as it comes due. Investors and lenders also pay attention to current debt because it provides information about a company's bankruptcy risk.

Long-term obligations (notes, mortgages, bonds) usually are reclassified and reported as current liabilities when they become payable within the upcoming year (or operating cycle, if longer than a year). For example, when a company obtains a 10-year note payable, it will classify the portion due within one year from the balance sheet date as a current liability and the portion due in more than one year as a long-term liability. With each passing year, the portion that becomes due in the following year will be reclassified from long-term liabilities to current liabilities.

**Southwest Airlines** had total borrowings of $3,387 million. Of that amount, $566 million is due in the next year, and the remaining $2,821 million is due in more than a year. In its balance sheet, the company reports these amounts separately, as shown in Illustration 9–5.

**ILLUSTRATION 9–5**

Current Portion of Long-Term Debt

| SOUTHWEST AIRLINES Balance Sheet (partial) ($ in millions) | |
| --- | --- |
| Current liabilities: | |
| Current maturities of long-term debt | $   566 |
| Long-term liabilities: | |
| Long-term debt less current maturities | 2,821 |
| Total borrowings | $3,387 |

**KEY POINT**

Common current liabilities include (1) accounts payable to vendors and suppliers; (2) payroll liabilities for unpaid salaries, unemployment taxes, employer portion of FICA taxes, and employer portion of insurance and retirement contributions; (3) deferred revenue for cash received in advance from customers; (4) sales taxes collected from customers by the seller to be paid to the government; and (5) the current portion of a long-term debt that will be paid within one year from the balance sheet date.

## Decision Maker's Perspective

### Current or Long Term?

Given a choice, do you suppose management would prefer to report an obligation as a current liability or a long-term liability? Other things being equal, most managers would choose the long-term classification. The reason is that outsiders such as banks, bondholders, and shareholders usually consider debt that is due currently to be riskier than debt that is not due for some time. Riskier debt means paying higher interest rates for borrowing. So, be aware that management has incentives to report current obligations as long-term.

## Contingencies

A contingent liability is an existing uncertain situation that *might* result in a loss depending on the outcome of a future event. Examples include lawsuits, product warranties, environmental problems, and premium offers. **Philip Morris**'s tobacco litigation, **Motorola**'s cell phone warranties, **BP**'s environmental obligations, and **United**'s frequent-flyer program are all contingent liabilities. Should companies wait until these uncertainties are settled before reporting to shareholders, or do they go ahead and report the details of the expected future costs? In this section, we discuss how to report these uncertain situations, which are broadly called contingencies. We'll look at two common types of contingent liabilities—litigation and product warranties—and then briefly discuss contingent gains.

■ **LO9–4**
Apply the appropriate accounting treatment for contingencies.

### LITIGATION

**Deloitte** was the auditor for a client we'll call Jeeps, Inc. The client sold accessories for jeeps, such as tops, lights, cargo carriers, and hitches. One of the major issues that appeared in Deloitte's audit of Jeeps, Inc., was outstanding litigation. Several lawsuits against the company alleged that the jeep top (made of vinyl) did not hold in a major collision. The jeep manufacturer, **Chrysler**, also was named in the lawsuits. The damages claimed were quite large, about $100 million. Although the company had litigation insurance, there was some question whether the insurance company could pay because the insurance carrier was undergoing financial difficulty. The auditor discussed the situation with the outside legal counsel representing Jeeps, Inc.

What, if anything, should the auditor require Jeeps, Inc., to report because of the litigation? The outcome of the litigation was not settled by the end of the year, so no amount is yet legally owed. There are three options to consider for Jeeps, Inc.:

1. Report a liability in the balance sheet for the full $100 million (or perhaps some lesser amount that is more likely to be owed).

2. Do not report a liability in the balance sheet, but provide full disclosure of the litigation in a note to the financial statements.

3. Do not report a liability in the balance sheet and provide no disclosure in a note.

The option we choose depends on (1) the likelihood of payment and (2) the ability to estimate the amount of payment. Illustration 9–6 provides details for each of these criteria.

**ILLUSTRATION 9–6**

Criteria for Reporting a
Contingent Liability

1. **The likelihood of payment is**
   a. *Probable*—likely to occur.
   b. *Reasonably possible*—more than remote but less than probable.
   c. *Remote*—the chance is slight.

2. **The amount of payment is**
   a. *Reasonably estimable.*
   b. *Not reasonably estimable.*

A contingent liability is reported only if a loss is probable *and* the amount is reasonably estimable. In the case of Jeeps, Inc., above, if the auditor believes it is probable that Jeeps, Inc., will lose the $100 million lawsuit at some point in the future, then Jeeps, Inc., would report a contingent liability for $100 million at the end of the year in the balance sheet.

The contingent liability is reported as either a current or a long-term liability depending on when management expects the probable loss to be paid. A loss of $100 million is reported in the income statement as either an operating or a nonoperating expense.

If the likelihood of payment is probable and if one amount within a range appears more likely, we report that amount. When no amount within the range appears more likely than others, we report the *minimum* amount and disclose the range of potential loss.

If the likelihood of payment is only *reasonably possible* rather than probable, we do not report an amount in the financial statements but make full disclosure in a note to the financial statements to describe the contingency. Finally, if the likelihood of payment is *remote,* disclosure usually is not required. Illustration 9–7 provides a summary of the accounting for contingent liabilities.

**ILLUSTRATION 9–7**

Accounting Treatment
of Contingent Liabilities

| | Amount of payment is: | |
| Likelihood of payment is: | Reasonably Estimable | Not Reasonably Estimable |
| --- | --- | --- |
| **Probable** | Liability reported | Disclosure required |
| **Reasonably possible** | Disclosure required | Disclosure required |
| **Remote** | Disclosure not required | Disclosure not required |

 **KEY POINT**

A contingent liability is reported only if a loss is **probable** *and* the amount is **reasonably estimable.**

Back to the example of Jeeps, Inc.: How do you think Deloitte, as the auditor of Jeeps, Inc., treated the litigation described earlier? Based on the response of legal counsel, the likelihood of the payment occurring was considered to be remote, so disclosure was not required. Although this additional disclosure may not be required, it still may prove useful to investors and creditors evaluating the financial stability of a company involved in litigation. Since the amount was so large, and because there were concerns about the company's primary insurance carrier undergoing financial difficulty, Deloitte insisted on full disclosure of the litigation in the notes to the financial statements.

**Manager Analysis**

| Question | Accounting information | Analysis |
|---|---|---|
| Is the company involved in any litigation? | Notes to the financial statements | Companies are required to disclose all contingencies, including litigation, with at least a reasonable possibility of payment. This information can then be used to help estimate their potential financial effect. |

Illustration 9–8 provides an excerpt from the disclosure of contingencies made by ExxonMobil.

**ILLUSTRATION 9–8**

Disclosure of Contingencies by ExxonMobil

---

**EXXONMOBIL**
**Notes to the Financial Statements (excerpt)**

**Litigation.** A variety of claims have been made against ExxonMobil and certain of its consolidated subsidiaries in a number of pending lawsuits. The Corporation accrues an undiscounted liability for those contingencies where the incurrence of a loss is probable and the amount can be reasonably estimated. The Corporation does not record liabilities when the likelihood that the liability has been incurred is probable but the amount cannot be reasonably estimated or when the liability is believed to be only reasonably possible or remote. For contingencies where an unfavorable outcome is reasonably possible and which are significant, the Corporation discloses the nature of the contingency and, where feasible, an estimate of the possible loss. ExxonMobil will continue to defend itself vigorously in these matters.

---

 **SUSTAINABILITY**

Sustainability accounting encourages companies to report important information related to the impact its operations are having on the environment. **DuPont's** annual report (Form 10-K) discloses that the company had "accrued obligations of $80 million for probable environmental remediation and restoration costs." These obligations are likely contingent liabilities. The company further stated that "it is reasonably possible that the ultimate cost with respect to these particular matters could range up to $170 million above the amount accrued." This provides a clear example of how environmental issues are also business issues for DuPont.

In its recent Sustainability report, DuPont discloses that one of the company's Core Values is to *Protect the Planet.* This value states its commitment to ". . . find science-enabled sustainable solutions for our customers, always managing our businesses to protect the environment and preserve the Earth's natural resources—for today and for future generations." The company's *Zero Waste* initiative is one example of its efforts to protect the environment. As part of this initiative, the company discloses that it has created its own internal waste standards and has a group tasked specifically with ensuring the standards are met. The company also discloses that it has signed on with various international waste programs such as Operation Clean Sweep, which is designed to help keep plastic materials out of marine environments. These efforts reduce the impact DuPont is having on the environment and could potentially save the company millions in remediation and restoration costs in the future, reducing environment-related contingent liabilities.

## WARRANTIES

Warranties are perhaps the most common example of contingent liabilities. When you buy a new **Dell** laptop, it comes with a warranty covering the hardware from defect for either a 90-day, one-year, or two-year period depending on the product. Dell offers such warranties to increase sales.

The warranty for the computer represents a liability at the time of the sale because it meets the criteria for reporting a contingent liability.

1. **Probable.** Warranties almost always entail an eventual expenditure.
2. **Reasonably estimable.** Even though a company doesn't know precisely what the warranty costs will be next year, it can formulate a reasonable prediction from past experiences, industry statistics, and other current business conditions.

**Example.**    Suppose Dell introduces a new laptop computer in December 2024 that carries a one-year warranty against manufacturer's defects. Suppose new laptop sales for the entire month of December are $1.5 million. How much does Dell "owe" these customers? Even though no laptops are currently needing warranty work, Dell expects future warranty costs to be 3% of sales. This means the probable warranty cost in the next year is estimated to be $45,000 (=$1.5 million × 3%). This contingent liability affects the financial statements in 2024 as follows:

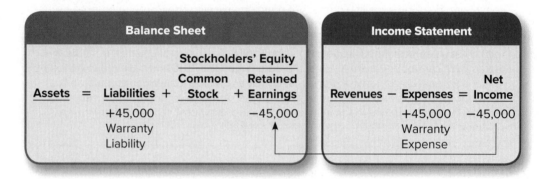

When customers make warranty claims and Dell incurs costs to satisfy those claims, the liability is reduced. Let's say that customers make warranty claims costing Dell $12,000 in January of 2025 (the following year). These claims would have the following effect in the balance sheet only in 2025:

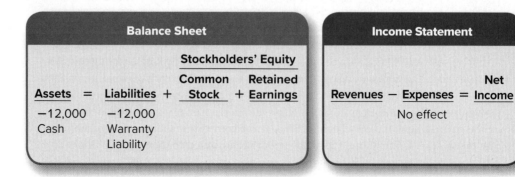

**DEBITS & CREDITS**

To record actual warranty costs:

| | Debit | Credit |
|---|---|---|
| Warranty Liability ........................................................................ | 12,000 | |
|    Cash ................................................................................... | | 12,000 |

Warranty Liability

| | |
|---|---|
| 12,000 | |

Cash

| | |
|---|---|
| | 12,000 |

The transaction above assumes Dell pays for all warranty costs with cash. Companies may also use employee labor hours, inventory parts, or supplies in satisfying warranty claims.

The balance in the Warranty Liability account at the end of January is $33,000.

**Warranty Liability**

| | |
|---|---|
| Beginning balance | $45,000 |
| *Minus:* Actual payment | (12,000) |
| Current balance | $33,000 |

Because Dell provides a one-year warranty, any balance remaining in Warranty Liability will expire at the end of one year and can be written off. However, it's likely that Dell will have additional laptop sales in the following year, and those laptops also have a one-year warranty. Any remaining balance in Warranty Liability at the end of the year is adjusted for whatever amount is needed to equal Dell's new estimate of future warranty costs.

**COMMON MISTAKE**

Some students think the balance in the Warranty Liability account is always equal to Warranty Expense. Remember, the Warranty Liability account is increased when the warranty cost is estimated, but then is reduced over time by actual warranty expenditures.

**Contingent Gain.**    Sometimes an existing uncertain situation might result in a *gain* to the company, referred to as a contingent gain. For example, **Polaroid** sued **Kodak** for patent infringement. Polaroid had a contingent gain, while Kodak faced a contingent loss. Companies **usually are not allowed to report contingent gains until the gain is known with** *certainty.* This is different from contingent liabilities that are reported when the loss is *probable*, and the amount is reasonably estimable. The nonparallel treatment of contingent gains and contingent losses reflects a general tendency toward conservatism in financial reporting through more timely recognition of losses.

**KEY POINT**

Unlike contingent liabilities, contingent gains are not recognized until the gain is certain and no longer a contingency.

# LONG-TERM LIABILITIES

**PART B**

Companies have three primary sources of long-term debt financing: notes, leases, and bonds. We discuss each of these sources of long-term debt financing next.

## Installment Notes

You may have purchased a car or a house. If so, unless you paid cash, you signed a note promising to pay the purchase price over, say, 4 years for the car or 30 years for the house. Car loans and home loans usually call for payment in monthly installments rather than by a single amount at maturity. Companies, too, often borrow cash using installment notes. **Each installment payment includes both an amount that represents interest and an amount that represents a reduction of the outstanding loan balance.** The periodic reduction of the balance is enough that at maturity, the note is completely paid.

To illustrate, assume that a start-up in the custom art business, Master Peace, Inc., obtains a $25,000, 6%, four-year loan for the purchase of a new delivery truck on November 1, 2024. Payments of $587.13 (rounded) are required at the end of each month for 48 months.[1] An amortization schedule provides a table format detailing the cash payment each period, the portions of each cash payment that represent interest and the change in carrying value, and the balance of the carrying value. For an installment note payable, the interest portion is recognized as interest expense and the carrying value is the loan's remaining balance. Illustration 9–9 provides a partial amortization schedule. The full amortization schedule would have a row for each of the 48 payments. We use asterisks to denote periods omitted.

**ILLUSTRATION 9–9**

Amortization Schedule for an Installment Note

| (1)<br>Date | (2)<br>Cash Paid | (3)<br>Interest<br>Expense<br>Carrying Value ×<br>Interest Rate | (4)<br>Decrease in<br>Carrying Value<br>(2) − (3) | (5)<br>Carrying Value<br>Prior Carrying<br>Value − (4) |
|---|---|---|---|---|
| 11/1/2024 | | | | $25,000.00 |
| 11/30/2024 | $587.13 | $125.00 | $462.13 | 24,537.87 |
| 12/31/2024 | 587.13 | 122.69 | 464.44 | 24,073.43 |
| * | * | * | * | * |
| 12/31/2025 | 587.13 | 94.04 | 493.09 | 18,315.65 |
| * | * | * | * | * |
| 9/30/2028 | 587.13 | 5.83 | 581.30 | 584.21 |
| 10/31/2028 | 587.13 | 2.92 | 584.21 | 0 |
| Total | $28,182.24 = | $3,182.24 + | $25,000.00 | |

Notice the following features of the amortization schedule:

1. **Date.** Payments are made at the end of each month.
2. **Cash Paid.** Monthly payments remain the same over the loan period. Notice the 48 payments of $587.13 add up to $28,182.24. This amount represents total interest on borrowing ($3,182.24) plus repayment of the loan amount ($25,000).
3. **Interest Expense.** Interest expense equals the prior month's carrying value times the interest rate (in this example, the monthly interest rate is 0.5% = 6% annual rate × 1/12).
4. **Decrease in Carrying Value.** The cash paid in excess of interest expense reduces the carrying value (remaining loan balance).
5. **Carrying Value.** The carrying value begins at $25,000, the original amount of the loan. With each monthly cash payment, the portion assigned to interest expense becomes less, and the portion that reduces the carrying value becomes more. By the end of the four-year loan, the $25,000 loan has been paid off, and the carrying value equals $0.

---

[1]The monthly payment of $587.13 is based on the following financial calculator inputs: future value, $0; present value, $25,000; interest rate, 0.5% (6% ÷ 12 periods each year); periods to maturity, 48 (4 years × 12 periods each year)—and solving for the monthly payment (PMT).

The issuance of the $25,000 installment note, and the first two monthly payments would have the following financial statement effects:

| | Balance Sheet | | | | | Income Statement | | |
|---|---|---|---|---|---|---|---|---|
| | | | | **Stockholders' Equity** | | | | |
| | | | | **Common Stock** | **Retained Earnings** | | | **Net** |
| | **Assets** | = | **Liabilities** + | + | | **Revenues** − | **Expenses** = | **Income** |
| Issuance | +25,000 Cash | | +25,000 Notes Payable | | | | No effect | |
| First monthly payment | −587.13 Cash | | −462.13 Notes Payable | | −125.00 | | +125.00 Interest Expense | −125.00 |
| Second monthly payment | −587.13 Cash | | −464.44 Notes Payable | | −122.69 | | +122.69 Interest Expense | −122.69 |

**DEBITS & CREDITS**

| | Debit | Credit |
|---|---|---|
| To record the issuance of the $25,000 installment note: | | |
| **Cash** | **25,000** | |
| Notes Payable | | 25,000 |
| | | |
| To record the first monthly payment: | | |
| **Notes Payable** | 462.13 | |
| **Interest Expense** | 125.00 | |
| Cash | | 587.13 |
| | | |
| To record the second monthly payment: | | |
| **Notes Payable** | 464.44 | |
| **Interest Expense** | 122.69 | |
| Cash | | 587.13 |

Cash
| 25,000 | |

Notes Payable
| | 25,000 |

Notes Payable
| 462.13 | |

Interest Expense
| 125.00 | |

Cash
| | 587.13 |

Notes Payable
| 464.44 | |

Interest Expense
| 122.69 | |

Cash
| | 587.13 |

Master Peace, Inc., will make its first monthly payment on November 30, another monthly payment on December 31, and so on. The amounts used in recording the monthly payments come directly from the amortization schedule. Notice that the amount of cash paid is the same for each payment but (a) the amount of interest expense is decreasing and (b) the amount paid on the note's principal balance is increasing. After the second payment, the note will have a balance of $24,073.43.

In the example above, we increased Cash because that's the asset that was received at the time the note was issued. If we instead used the note to purchase a noncash asset, such as equipment, buildings, or land, we would increase that asset account instead.

**Classification of Debt.**   By the end of 2024, the remaining balance of the note is $24,073.43. **For financial reporting, this amount needs to be split into its current and long-term portions.** The *current portion* is the amount of the loan that will be settled *within one year* of the balance sheet date. We can determine this amount by looking back at Illustration 9–9. After 12 additional monthly payments in 2025, the loan's remaining balance on December 31, 2025, will be reduced to 18,315.65. That means $5,757.78 of the loan's balance (= $24,073.43 − $18,315.65) will be settled in 2025. In its 2024 balance sheet, Master Peace reports separately the note's current portion as a current liability ($5,757.78) and its long-term portion as a long-term liability ($18,315.65).

 **KEY POINT**

Most notes payable require periodic installment payments. Each installment payment includes an amount that represents interest expense and an amount that represents a reduction of the carrying value (remaining loan balance).

# Leases

■ **LO9–6**
Understand how leases are reported.

Leasing is a very common form of external financing. A lease is a contractual arrangement by which the *lessor* (owner) provides the *lessee* (user) the right to use an asset for a specified period of time. Most U.S. companies will engage in some type of lease, whether it be to lease office space, equipment, or other operating assets. Companies choose to lease an asset, rather than to buy it, for a number of reasons including the following:

1. **Leasing may reduce the upfront cash needed to use an asset.** Instead of paying cash upfront for the full purchase of an asset, only the first month's lease payment is needed to begin using the asset. This is especially important for companies that have high credit risk and may not be able to borrow enough cash to purchase an asset.

2. **Lease payments often are lower than installment payments.** Lease payments often are tied only to the portion of value related to the period of use, while the installment payments are tied to the entire value of the asset regardless of the borrower's intended period of use. This means the monthly payments associated with leasing often are lower.

3. **Leasing may offer flexibility and lower costs when disposing of an asset.** Returning a leased asset at the end of the lease term requires little effort or cost. Selling an asset, however, may require more time to find a buyer, especially for unique assets. Selling an asset also can require significant costs, such as selling commissions and legal fees.

4. **Leasing may offer protection against the risk of declining asset values.** In certain lease agreements, lessees don't have to worry about declining fair values (selling prices) while using the asset. Of course, the lessee also misses out on any increase in fair value.

You may have heard that another benefit of leasing is that it is a form off-balance sheet financing that keeps the obligation to make future lease payments off the books (that is, off the balance sheet). This was historically true for certain types of leases called "operating" leases. The accounting standards surrounding leases recently changed. Under the new rules, the liability associated with all leases is reported in the balance-sheet. Thus, leasing is no longer considered to be a form of off-balance sheet financing.

## REPORTING A LEASE

A long-term lease creates an asset and a liability for the lessee (user).

The lease arrangement gives the lessee (user) the right to use an asset for a period of time. This right is reported as a right-of-use *asset* in the balance sheet as its own line item or together with property, plant, and equipment. The user also has an obligation to make payments over the lease period. This obligation is reported as a *liability*.

Let's look at an example recognizing a lease by modifying our earlier example of Master Peace. Instead of purchasing a new delivery truck, Master Peace agrees to make lease payments of $352.28 at the end of each month for 48 months. Master Peace doesn't own the leased truck, but the company has the right to use the truck by agreeing to terms of the lease. At the beginning of the lease period, Master Peace recognizes a lease asset and lease payable for the *present value of the lease payments.* In this example, the present value of the 48 lease payments using a 6% borrowing rate is $15,000 (calculation discussed below). The financial statement effects to report the long-term lease are as follows:

Report a long-term lease for the present value of payments.

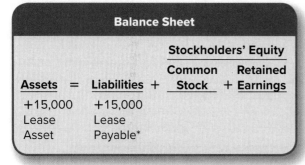

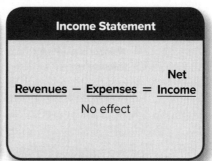

*present value of ordinary annuity; $n = 48$, $i = 6\% \div 12$.

**DEBITS & CREDITS**

To record the issuance of the long-term lease:

| | Debit | Credit |
|---|---|---|
| **Lease Asset** | 15,000 | |
| **Lease Payable** | | 15,000 |
| ($15,000 = present value of lease payments) | | |

| Lease Asset | |
|---|---|
| 15,000 | |

| Lease Payable | |
|---|---|
| | 15,000 |

Even though lease payments total $16,909.44 over the four-year period ($352.28 × 48 payments), we report the lease payable for only $15,000, the present value of those future payments. The additional payment of $1,909.44 essentially represents the cost of borrowing for four years. As lease payments are made over time, the carrying values of the asset and the liability will be reduced to zero. These adjustments are beyond the scope of this introductory book and are covered in intermediate accounting books.

**Calculating the Present Value of Lease Payments (Annuity).** Table 4 at the back of this book provides present values of annuities of $1 for many variations in number of periods ($n$) and interest rates ($i$). These values are multiplied by the monthly lease payment to get the present value of the total lease payments. For combinations of $n$ and $i$ not shown, you can calculate the present value of the lease payments using a financial calculator or Excel.

In our example, the lease period is 48 months, and the interest rate per month is 0.5% (= 6% annual rate ÷ 12). Illustration 9–10 shows the calculator inputs used to obtain the present value of $15,000.

**ILLUSTRATION 9–10**<br>Present Value of Lease Payments Using a Financial Calculator

**CALCULATOR INPUT**

| Lease Characteristics | Key | Amount |
|---|---|---|
| 1. Future value | FV | $0 |
| 2. Lease payment | PMT | $352.28 |
| 3. Number of payments | N | 48 = 4 years × 12 periods each year |
| 4. Interest rate | I | 0.5 = 6% ÷ 12 periods each year |

**CALCULATOR OUTPUT**

| | | |
|---|---|---|
| Present value of payments | PV | $15,000 |

An alternative to using a financial calculator is to use Excel. Illustration 9–11 demonstrates the inputs and the formula used to calculate the present value of lease payments.

**ILLUSTRATION 9–11**

Present Value of Lease Payments Using Excel

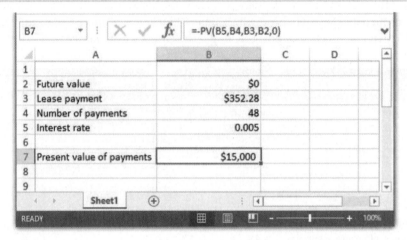

Microsoft Corporation

Companies are required to disclose their future lease payments for the next five years and for all years thereafter in the notes to the financial statements. Illustration 9–12 presents the total future lease payments for **Delta Air Lines** and **American Airlines** as shown in their 2018 annual reports. Delta discloses that it has leased 376 aircraft with remaining terms ranging from one month to 13 years. American discloses that it has leased 660 aircraft with remaining terms ranging from one to 12 years.

**ILLUSTRATION 9–12**

Future Lease Payments for Delta and American

|  | Delta | American |
|---|---|---|
| 2019 | $ 1,299 | $ 2,036 |
| 2020 | 1,089 | 1,958 |
| 2021 | 894 | 1,754 |
| 2022 | 725 | 1,560 |
| 2023 | 681 | 1,360 |
| Thereafter | 4,311 | 3,902 |
| Total lease payments | 8,999 | 12,570 |
| Less: amount representing interest | (1,840) | (2,320) |
| Present value of lease payments | $ 7,159 | $10,250 |

**Initial Down Payment.**    In addition to having the obligation of future lease payments, companies often are required to pay an initial amount at the beginning of the lease. In this case, the initial amount of the Lease Asset would be the cash down payment plus the Lease Payable.

**KEY POINT**

While not transferring ownership as in a purchase, a lease gives the lessee (user) the right to use the asset over the lease period. This right is reported as an asset, and the obligation to make lease payments is reported as a liability.

## Bonds

■ **LO9–7**

Identify bond characteristics and account for bonds issued at face amount.

A **bond** is a formal debt contract issued by a company to borrow money. The issuing company (borrower) receives cash by selling a bond to an investor (lender). In return, the issuing company promises to pay back to the investor: (1) a stated amount, referred to as the *principal* or *face amount,* at a specified maturity date, and (2) periodic interest payments over the life of the bond. Bonds are very similar to notes. Bonds, though, usually are for greater amounts and are issued to many lenders, while notes most often are issued to a single lender such as a bank. Traditionally, interest on bonds is paid twice a year (semiannually) on designated interest dates, beginning six months after the original bond issue date.

TungCheung/Shutterstock

For most large corporations, bonds are sold, or *underwritten,* by investment banks. The three largest bond underwriters are **JPMorgan Chase**, **Citigroup**, and **Bank of America**.

A company issuing a bond pays a fee for these underwriting services. Other costs include legal, accounting, registration, and printing fees. To keep costs down, the issuing company may choose to sell the bonds directly to a single investor, such as a large investment fund or an insurance company. This is referred to as a private placement.

Why do some companies issue bonds rather than borrow money directly from a bank? A company that borrows by issuing bonds is effectively bypassing the bank and borrowing directly from the investing public—which may lead to a lower interest rate than it would in a bank loan. Bonds typically have fewer restrictions (called debt covenants) than bank loans, which provides more flexibility to the borrower. However, issuing bonds entails significant bond issue costs that can exceed 5% of the amount borrowed. For smaller loans, the additional bond issuance costs exceed the savings from a lower interest rate, making it more economical to borrow from a bank. For loans of $20 million or more, the interest rate savings often exceed the additional bond issuance costs, making a bond issue more attractive.

## BOND CHARACTERISTICS

Bonds can have any number of different features. Secured bonds are backed by a specific asset that is pledged as collateral. On default, the borrowers are entitled to the collateral. Unsecured bonds are not backed by collateral and are called *debentures.* Due to the increased risk, unsecured bonds typically have a higher rate of interest than secured bonds. Term bonds require a single payment in full at the bond maturity date, while serial bonds require periodic payments throughout the life of the bond. Callable bonds allow the borrower to repay the bond early (before the scheduled maturity date). This option allows borrowers to hedge against future decreases in interest rates. Finally, convertible bonds allow the investor to convert the bond into a specific number of shares of common stock. The convertible feature is considered a "sweetener" that can make a bond more attractive to investors.

Illustration 9–13 provides a summary of these common bond characteristics.

**ILLUSTRATION 9–13**

Summary of Bond Characteristics

| Bond Characteristic | Definition |
|---|---|
| Secured | Bonds are backed by collateral. |
| Unsecured | Bonds are not backed by collateral. |
| Term | Bonds mature on a single date. |
| Serial | Bonds mature in installments. |
| Callable | Issuing company can pay off bonds early. |
| Convertible | Investor can convert bonds to common stock. |

## ACCOUNT FOR BONDS ISSUED AT FACE AMOUNT

We will now learn how to account for bonds. Corporations normally issue bonds in the millions of dollars. However, to simplify the illustrations in this chapter, we drop three digits and illustrate the issuance of bonds in thousands rather than in millions. We will use the following example to illustrate bond accounting.

**Example.** Assume that on January 1, 2024, California Coasters decides to raise money for development of its new roller coaster by issuing $100,000 of bonds paying interest of 7% each year. The bonds are due in 10 years, with interest payable semiannually on June 30 and December 31 each year. **In practice, most corporate bonds pay interest semiannually (every six months) rather than paying interest monthly, quarterly, or annually.**

In this example, California Coasters will receive cash of $100,000 on the issue date. In return, California Coasters promises the following cash payments back to investors:

1. **Face amount** of $100,000 at the end of 10 years, plus
2. **Interest payments** of $3,500 (= $100,000 × 7% × 1/2 year) every six months for 10 years. That's a total of 20 interest payments of $3,500 each ($70,000).

Illustration 9–14 provides a timeline of the cash flows related to the bond issue.

**ILLUSTRATION 9–14**

Timeline of a Bond Issue

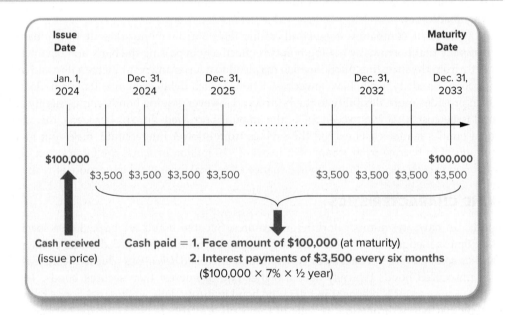

Over the 10-year period, investors will receive a total of $170,000, which is the face amount of $100,000 due at maturity plus 20 semiannual interest payments of $3,500, totaling $70,000. In return for the right to receive these payments, investors pay cash to the company on the issue date. The amount investors pay to the company is known as the *issue price* of the bond. In this example, the bonds had an issue price equal to their face amount of $100,000. The majority of bonds are issued at their face amount (or "par").[2] In the appendix, we'll see how companies account for the issuance of bonds for amounts greater (premium) and less (discount) than face amount.

Let's now see how the issuance of the bonds and their related interest payments are reported. The financial statement effects of the bond issuance on January 1, 2024, are as follows:

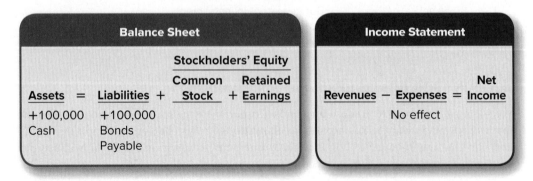

---

[2]Amiram et al. (2018) report that the median bond is issued at par. Amiram, D., Kalay, Al., Kalay, Av., & Ozel, N. B. (2017). Information Asymmetry and the Bond Coupon Choice. *The Accounting Review* 93(2): 37–59.

---

## DEBITS & CREDITS

To record the issuance of the bonds:

|  | Debit | Credit |
|---|---|---|
| **Cash** ............................................................................. | **100,000** |  |
| **Bonds Payable** ......................................................... |  | **100,000** |

Cash
| 100,000 |

Bonds Payable
|  | 100,000 |

---

California Coasters reports bonds payable in the long-term liabilities section of the balance sheet. Nine years from now, when the bonds are within one year of maturity, the firm will reclassify the bonds as current liabilities.

On June 30, 2024, California Coasters recognizes the first semiannual interest payment based on the bond's stated interest rate. The stated interest rate is the rate specified in the bond contract used to calculate the cash payments for interest.

The financial statement effects of each semiannual interest payment are as follows:

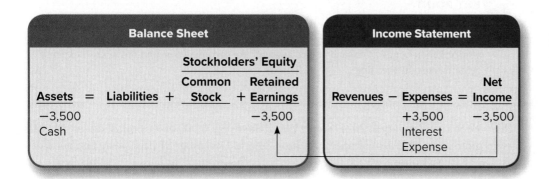

---

## DEBITS & CREDITS

To record each semiannual interest payment:

|  | Debit | Credit |
|---|---|---|
| **Interest Expense** ($100,000 × 7% × 1/2) ............................... | **3,500** |  |
| **Cash** ........................................................................ |  | **3,500** |

Interest Expense
| 3,500 |

Cash
|  | 3,500 |

---

The firm will recognize another semiannual interest payment on December 31, 2024. In fact, it will recognize this same semiannual interest payment at the end of every six-month period for the next 10 years.

## BOND RETIREMENT

A company retires a bond by paying back the borrowed amount at maturity. For California Coasters, the financial statement effects of the bond retirement at maturity are as follows:

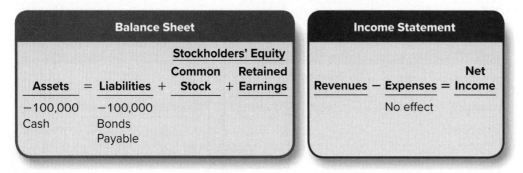

Bonds Payable

| | |
|---|---|
| | 100,000 |

Cash

| | |
|---|---|
| | 100,000 |

**DEBITS & CREDITS**

To record the retirement of bonds at maturity:

| | Debit | Credit |
|---|---|---|
| Bonds Payable ......................................................................................... | 100,000 | |
|     Cash .......................................................................................................... | | 100,000 |

**Retirement Before Maturity.** Bonds that are retired before maturity can be retired at a cost that differs from their current carrying value, depending on current market conditions. If the cost to retire the bonds is less than their carrying value, then a *gain on early extinguishment of debt* is reported in the income statement. If the cost to retire the bonds is greater than their carrying value, then a *loss on early extinguishment of debt* is reported in the income statement. The amount of the gain or loss is equal to the difference between the current carrying value of the bonds and the retirement cost. The way we account for any gains or losses on the retirement of debt is a topic covered in intermediate accounting books.

**KEY POINT**

Bonds are distinguished whether they are backed by collateral, become due at a single specified date or over a period of time, can be redeemed prior to maturity, or can be converted to equity. When bonds are issued at face amount, the carrying value and the interest expense remain constant over time.

## Let's Review

Assume that on January 1, 2024, Water World issues $200,000 of 9% bonds, due in 10 years, with interest payable semiannually on June 30 and December 31 each year. The bonds are issued at face amount for $200,000.

**Required:**

1. Describe the financial statement effects of the bond issuance on January 1, 2024.

2. Describe the financial statement effects of the first semiannual interest payments on June 30, 2024.

3. Describe the financial statement effects of the bond retirement on December 31, 2033.

**Solution:**

1. The financial statement effects of the bond issuance are as follows:

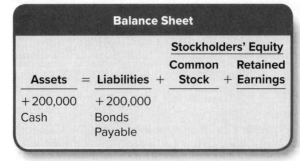

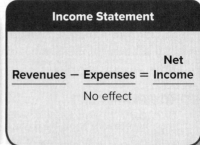

| | | Balance Sheet | | | | | Income Statement | | |
|---|---|---|---|---|---|---|---|---|---|
| | | | | **Stockholders' Equity** | | | | | |
| | | | | Common | Retained | | | | **Net** |
| Assets | = | Liabilities | + | Stock | + Earnings | | Revenues | − Expenses = | Income |
| +200,000 | | +200,000 | | | | | | No effect | |
| Cash | | Bonds Payable | | | | | | | |

2. The financial statement effects of the first semiannual interest payment are as follows:

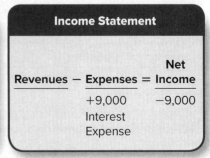

| | | Balance Sheet | | | | | Income Statement | | |
|---|---|---|---|---|---|---|---|---|---|
| | | | | **Stockholders' Equity** | | | | | |
| | | | | Common | Retained | | | | **Net** |
| Assets | = | Liabilities | + | Stock | + Earnings | | Revenues | − Expenses = | Income |
| −9,000 | | | | | − 9,000 | | | +9,000 | −9,000 |
| Cash | | | | | | | | Interest Expense | |

3. The financial statement effects of the bond retirement are as follows:

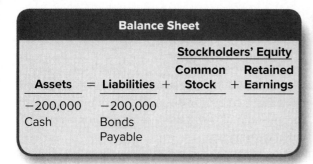
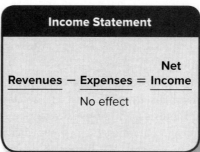

The journal entries for the transactions above are as follows:

| | Debit | Credit |
|---|---|---|
| **January 1, 2024** | | |
| **Cash** ......................................................................................... | 200,000 | |
|     **Bonds Payable** ...................................................................... | | 200,000 |
|     *(Issue bonds at face amount)* | | |
| **June 30, 2024** | | |
| **Interest Expense** ..................................................................... | 9,000 | |
|     **Cash** (= $200,000 × 9% × 1/2) ........................................ | | 9,000 |
|     *(Pay semiannual interest)* | | |
| **December 31, 2033** | | |
| **Bonds Payable** ........................................................................ | 200,000 | |
|     **Cash** ....................................................................................... | | 200,000 |
|     *(Retire bonds at maturity date)* | | |

# LIQUIDITY AND SOLVENCY ANALYSIS
## Liquidity: United Airlines vs. American Airlines

**PART C**

Liquidity refers to having sufficient cash (or other current assets convertible to cash in a relatively short time) to pay currently maturing liabilities. Because a lack of liquidity can result in financial difficulties or even bankruptcy, it is critical that managers as well as outside investors and lenders maintain a close watch on this aspect of a company's well-being. Here we look at three liquidity measures: working capital, the current ratio, and the acid-test ratio. All three measures are calculated using current assets and current liabilities.

**■ LO9–8**
Assess liquidity and solvency using ratios.

### WORKING CAPITAL

The concept of working capital is straightforward. It is simply the difference between current assets and current liabilities.

Working capital = Current assets − Current liabilities

Working capital answers the question, "After paying our current obligations, how much in current assets will we have to work with?" A large positive working capital is an indicator of liquidity—whether a company will be able to pay its current obligations on time.

However, working capital is not the best measure of liquidity when comparing one company with another, because it does not account for the relative size of each company. In comparing companies, the current ratio and the acid-test ratio are better measures of a company's ability to pay its obligations on time.

## CURRENT RATIO

We calculate the current ratio by dividing current assets by current liabilities.

$$\text{Current ratio} = \frac{\text{Current assets}}{\text{Current liabilities}}$$

A current ratio greater than 1 indicates that there are more current assets than current liabilities. Recall that current assets include cash, current investments, accounts receivable, inventories, and prepaid expenses. A current ratio of, say, 1.5 indicates that for every $1 of current liabilities, the company has $1.50 of current assets.

In general, the higher the current ratio, the greater the company's liquidity. But we should evaluate the current ratio, like other ratios, in the context of the industry in which the company operates. An acceptable level of liquidity as captured by the current ratio in one industry may not be an acceptable level in another industry. Illustration 9–15 presents average current ratios for various industries.

**ILLUSTRATION 9–15    Current Ratios by Industry**

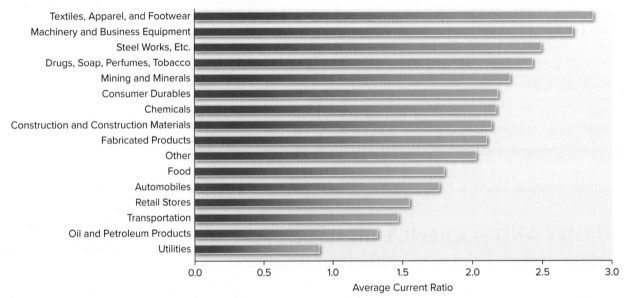

Source: Standard and Poor's

## ACID-TEST RATIO

*Common Terms*
The acid-test ratio is also called the *quick ratio.*

It is important to recognize that not all current assets are equally liquid. Some current assets can be converted into cash more quickly than others. Our next ratio takes this into account. The acid-test ratio, or *quick ratio,* is similar to the current ratio but is based on a more limited measure of current assets available to pay current liabilities. We calculate it by dividing "quick assets" by current liabilities. Quick assets include only cash, current investments, and accounts receivable.

Because the numerator contains only a portion of the current assets used in the current ratio, the acid-test ratio will be smaller than the current ratio. By eliminating other current assets, such as inventory and prepaid expenses, that are less readily convertible into cash, the acid-test ratio may provide a better indication of a company's liquidity than does the current ratio.

$$\text{Acid-test ratio} = \frac{\text{Cash} + \text{Current investments} + \text{Accounts receivable}}{\text{Current liabilities}}$$

We interpret the acid-test ratio much like the current ratio, with one difference: We know that current assets in the numerator are only those that can be quickly converted to cash. Thus, an acid-test ratio of, say, 1.5 would indicate that for every $1 of current liabilities, the company has $1.50 of current assets that are easily convertible to cash that might be used to help pay the current liabilities as they come due. As is true for other ratios, the acid-test ratio should be evaluated in the context of the industry in which the company operates.

Illustration 9–16 presents average acid-test ratios for various industries. Many companies in the airline industry struggle to maintain adequate liquidity. **United Airlines** declared bankruptcy in 2002 and emerged from bankruptcy in 2006. Similarly, **American Airlines** declared bankruptcy in 2011 and came out of bankruptcy two years later in late 2013. The recovery by American Airlines has been remarkable. Its share price increased from around $25 per share when it first came out of bankruptcy in December 2013 to over $50 per share, just one year later.

**ILLUSTRATION 9–16**   Acid-test Ratios by Industry

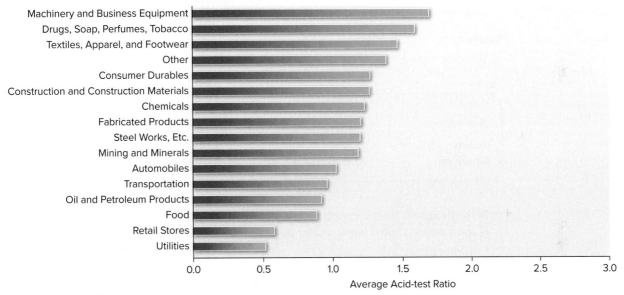

Source: Standard and Poor's

Let's compare **United Airlines'** liquidity ratios to those of **American Airlines** and see if the recovery from bankruptcy of American Airlines is reflected in stronger liquidity ratios. Selected financial data regarding current assets and current liabilities for United and American Airlines[3] are as follows.

**Let's Review**

| ($ in millions) | United | American |
|---|---|---|
| Current assets: | | |
|    Cash and cash equivalents | $2,756 | $   280 |
|    Current investments | 2,182 | 3,704 |
|    Net receivables | 1,364 | 1,750 |
|    Inventory | 1,072 | 1,851 |
|    Other current assets | 814 | 621 |
|      Total current assets | $8,188 | $8,206 |

---

[3]American Airlines Group (Ticker AAL) includes American Airlines, US Airways, and Envoy Aviation.

| ($ in millions) | United | American |
|---|---|---|
| Current liabilities: | | |
| Current debt | $ 2,139 | $ 2,861 |
| Accounts payable | 2,703 | 2,062 |
| Salaries payable | 2,271 | 1,541 |
| Deferred revenue | 7,259 | 8,001 |
| Other current liabilities | 571 | 3,846 |
| Total current liabilities | $14,943 | $18,311 |

**Required:**

1. Calculate and compare working capital for United Airlines and American Airlines.
2. Calculate the current ratio for United Airlines and American Airlines. Which company has a higher current ratio?
3. Calculate the acid-test (quick) ratio for United Airlines and American Airlines. Which company has a higher acid-test ratio?

**Solution:**

1. Working capital:

| ($ in millions) | Current Assets | − | Current Liabilities | = | Working Capital |
|---|---|---|---|---|---|
| United | $8,188 | − | $14,943 | = | $ (6,755) |
| American | $8,206 | − | $18,311 | = | $(10,105) |

Both companies have a negative working capital, in which current liabilities exceed current assets. United has a smaller negative working capital of $6,755 million.

2. Current ratio:

| ($ in millions) | Current Assets | ÷ | Current Liabilities | = | Current Ratio |
|---|---|---|---|---|---|
| United | $8,188 | ÷ | $14,943 | = | 0.55 |
| American | $8,206 | ÷ | $18,311 | = | 0.45 |

United has a higher current ratio, which would indicate better liquidity than American.

3. Acid-test (quick) ratio:

| ($ in millions) | Quick Assets | ÷ | Current Liabilities | = | Acid-Test Ratio |
|---|---|---|---|---|---|
| United | $6,302 | ÷ | $14,943 | = | 0.42 |
| American | $5,734 | ÷ | $18,311 | = | 0.31 |

Remember that *quick assets* equal cash + current investments + net receivables.

By eliminating less-liquid current assets such as inventory and other current assets, the acid-test ratio often provides a better indicator of liquidity. Again, United has a higher acid-test ratio.

We should be careful to evaluate liquidity measures in the context of an industry. The airlines have faced tough times, and many airlines have struggled to maintain adequate liquidity. So, while United current ratio and acid-test ratio exceed those for American, the liquidity for both companies likely does not compare well with companies in most other industries.

## Decision Maker's Perspective

### Indicators of Liquidity

If the company's current ratio or acid-test ratio is lower than that of the industry as a whole, does that mean liquidity is a problem? Perhaps, but perhaps not. It does, though, raise a red flag that suggests caution when assessing other aspects of the company.

It's important to remember that each ratio is but one piece of the puzzle. For example, profitability is probably the best long-run indicator of liquidity. It is difficult to maintain liquidity over a string of consecutive loss years. Another consideration is that management may be very efficient in managing current assets so that some current assets—receivables or inventory—remain at minimum amounts. This is good for the company overall, but it may result in less-impressive current and acid-test ratios. The turnover ratios we discussed in Chapters 5 and 6, such as receivables turnover and inventory turnover, help measure the efficiency of asset management in this regard.

 **COMMON MISTAKE**

As a general rule, a higher current ratio is better. However, a high current ratio is not always a positive signal. Companies having difficulty collecting receivables or holding excessive inventory will also have a higher current ratio. Managers must balance the incentive for strong liquidity (yielding a higher current ratio) with the need to minimize levels of receivables and inventory (yielding a lower current ratio).

### EFFECT OF TRANSACTIONS ON LIQUIDITY RATIOS

How are the ratios affected by changes in current assets? It depends on which current asset changes. Both ratios include cash, current investments, and accounts receivable. An increase in any of those will increase *both* ratios. However, only the current ratio includes inventory and other current assets. An increase in inventory or other current assets will increase the current ratio, but not the acid-test ratio.

What about changes in current liabilities? Total current liabilities is in the denominator for both ratios. Therefore, an increase in current liabilities will decrease both ratios, since we are dividing by a larger amount. Likewise, a decrease in current liabilities will increase both ratios. Illustration 9–17 summarizes the effect of changes in current assets and current liabilities on the liquidity ratios.

### LIQUIDITY MANAGEMENT

Can management influence the ratios that measure liquidity? Yes, at least to some extent. A company can influence the timing of inventory and accounts payable recognition by asking suppliers to change their delivery schedules. For instance, a large airplane manufacturer

**ILLUSTRATION 9–17**

Effect of Various
Changes on the
Liquidity Ratios

|  | Changes That Increase the Ratio | Changes That Decrease the Ratio |
|---|---|---|
| **Current Ratio** | • Increase in current assets<br>• Decrease in current liabilities | • Decrease in current assets<br>• Increase in current liabilities |
| **Acid-Test Ratio** | • Increase in quick assets<br>• Decrease in current liabilities | • Decrease in quick assets<br>• Increase in current liabilities |

like **Boeing** might delay the shipment and billing of certain inventory parts to receive them in early January rather than late December, reducing inventory and accounts payable at year-end. It can also choose to make additional purchases in late December, increasing inventory and accounts payable at year-end. Let's see how changes in the delivery of inventory affect the current ratio.

Assume a company with a current ratio of 1.25 (current assets of $5 million and current liabilities of $4 million) has a *debt covenant* with its bank that requires a minimum current ratio exceeding 1.25. A debt covenant is an agreement between a borrower and a lender that requires certain minimum financial measures be met or the lender can recall the debt. By delaying the receipt of $1 million in goods until early January, inventory and accounts payable would both be lower by $1 million than they would be without the delay. This, in turn, increases the current ratio to 1.33 (current assets of $4 million and current liabilities of $3 million), and the requirement of the debt covenant is met.

Now, let's look at what happens when the current ratio is less than 1.00. Assume the company has a current ratio of 0.75 (current assets of $3 million and current liabilities of $4 million) and has a *debt covenant* with its bank that requires a minimum current ratio exceeding 0.75. In this situation, delaying the delivery of $1 million decreases the current ratio even further to 0.67 (current assets of $2 million and current liabilities of $3 million).

Rather than delay delivery, the company could choose instead to purchase $1 million in additional inventory on credit. Then, inventory and accounts payable both increase by $1 million, raising the current ratio from 0.75 to 0.80 (current assets of $4 million and current liabilities of $5 million). Investors and creditors should be aware of managerial activities that increase liquidity ratios, such as large fluctuations in inventory purchases near year-end or unusual variations in accounts payable balances.

 **KEY POINT**

Working capital is the difference between current assets and current liabilities. The current ratio is equal to current assets divided by current liabilities. The acid-test ratio is equal to quick assets (cash, current investments, and accounts receivable) divided by current liabilities. Each measures a company's liquidity; its ability to pay currently maturing debts.

**Manager Analysis**

| Question 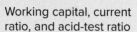 | Accounting information | Analysis  |
|---|---|---|
| Does the company have enough cash to pay current liabilities as they come due? | Working capital, current ratio, and acid-test ratio | A high working capital, current ratio, or acid-test ratio generally indicates the ability to pay current liabilities on a timely basis. |

# Solvency: Coca-Cola vs. PepsiCo

Solvency refers to a company's ability to make interest payments and pay back its debts as they become due. Thus, long-term debt is one of the first places decision makers look when trying to get a handle of the solvency and financial risk of the company. The year before **Toys R Us** declared bankruptcy, the company described in its annual report the risks of its growing long-term liabilities. Excerpts are provided in Illustration 9–18.

**ILLUSTRATION 9–18**

Toys R Us Notes to the Financial Statements (excerpt)

---

**TOYS R US**
**Notes to the Financial Statements (excerpt)**

Our substantial indebtedness could have significant consequences, including, among others,

- increasing our vulnerability to general economic and industry conditions;
- reducing our ability to fund our operations and capital expenditures, capitalize on future business opportunities, expand our business and execute our strategy;
- increasing the difficulty for us to make scheduled payments on our outstanding debt;
- exposing us to the risk of increased interest expense;
- causing us to make non-strategic divestitures;
- limiting our ability to obtain additional financing;
- limiting our ability to adjust to changing market conditions and reacting to competitive pressure, placing us at a competitive disadvantage compared to our competitors who are less leveraged.

---

Next, we look at two ratios frequently used to measure solvency: (1) debt to equity and (2) times interest earned.

## DEBT TO EQUITY RATIO

To measure a company's solvency risk, we often calculate the debt to equity ratio:

$$\text{Debt to equity ratio} = \frac{\text{Total interest-bearing debt}}{\text{Stockholders' equity}}$$

It's first important to recognize that the debt to equity ratio often uses total interest-bearing debt in the numerator instead of total liabilities. Interest-bearing liabilities include bank loans, bonds, and leases. There are several types of liabilities that are generally not considered to be "debt," including accounts payable, wages payable, and deferred revenue. Companies are required to disclose the amount of debt in a financial statement footnote. Illustration 9–19 shows the debt disclosure of **Coca-Cola**.

The debt disclosure reveals Coca-Cola's total amount of debt, $43.6 billion (= $13.2 + $30.4), as well as the interest rates associated with the different types of debt. Coca-Cola's balance sheet reports total liabilities of approximately $64.2 billion. Thus, 67.9% (=$43.6/$64.2) of its total liabilities are interest-bearing. We focus on interest-bearing debt because it generally requires payment on specific dates.

Failure to repay debt or the interest associated with the debt on a timely basis may result in default and perhaps even bankruptcy for a company. Other things being equal, the higher the debt to equity ratio, the higher the risk of bankruptcy. When a company assumes more debt, risk increases.

Debt also can be an advantage. It can enhance the return to stockholders. If a company earns a return in excess of the cost of borrowing the funds, stockholders are provided with a total return greater than what could have been earned with equity funds alone. Unfortunately, borrowing is not always favorable. Sometimes the cost of borrowing the funds exceeds the returns they generate. This illustrates the risk–reward trade-off faced by stockholders.

**ILLUSTRATION 9–19**

Excerpt from Coca-Cola's Annual Report

**COCA-COLA**
**Notes to the Financial Statements (excerpt)**

| Short-term borrowings | Amount | Average Rate |
|---|---|---|
| Commercial paper | $13,063 | 2.6% |
| Lines of credit | 131 | Not disclosed |
| Total | $13,194 | |
| **Long-term debt** | Amount | Average Rate |
| U.S. dollar notes due 2019–2093 | $13,619 | 2.6% |
| U.S. dollar debentures due 2020–2098 | 1,390 | 5.2 |
| U.S. dollar zero coupon notes due 2020 | 163 | 8.4 |
| Australian dollar notes due 2020–2024 | 723 | 2.2 |
| Euro notes due 2019–2036 | 12,994 | 0.6 |
| Swiss franc notes due 2022–2028 | 1,128 | 3.6 |
| Other, due through 2098 | 282 | 3.4 |
| Adjustments | 62 | N/A |
| Total | $30,361 | 1.9 |

Let's examine the debt to equity ratio for two competitors: Coca-Cola and **PepsiCo**. Illustration 9–20 provides selected financial data for these companies.

**ILLUSTRATION 9–20**

Financial Information for Coca-Cola and PepsiCo

**SELECTED BALANCE SHEET DATA**
**($ in millions)**

| | Coca-Cola | PepsiCo |
|---|---|---|
| Total assets | $83,216 | $77,648 |
| Accounts payable and accrued expenses | $ 8,932 | $18,112 |
| Loan and notes payable | 13,194 | 73 |
| Current maturities of long-term debt | 4,997 | 3,953 |
| Other current liabilities | 2,100 | 0 |
| Current liabilities | 29,223 | 22,138 |
| Long-term debt | 25,364 | 28,295 |
| Other liabilities | 9,571 | 12,613 |
| Total liabilities | $64,158 | $63,046 |
| Total equity | $19,058 | $14,602 |

**SELECTED INCOME STATEMENT DATA**
**($ in millions)**

| | Coca-Cola | PepsiCo |
|---|---|---|
| Sales | $31,856 | $64,661 |
| Operating expenses | 23,156 | 54,551 |
| Operating income | 8,700 | 10,110 |
| Other income | 318 | 604 |
| Interest expense | 919 | 1,525 |
| Tax expense (benefit) | 1,623 | (3,370) |
| Net income | $ 6,476 | $12,559 |

Illustration 9–21 compares the debt to equity ratio for Coca-Cola and PepsiCo.

| | Total Debt | Equity | Debt to Equity Ratio |
|---|---|---|---|
| Coca-Cola | $13,194 + $4,997 + $25,364 = $43,555 | $19,058 | 2.29 |
| PepsiCo | $73 + $3,953 + $28,295 = $32,321 | $14,602 | 2.21 |

**ILLUSTRATION 9–21**

Debt to Equity Ratio for Coca-Cola and PepsiCo

The debt to equity ratio for Coca-Cola and PepsiCo are similar, with Coca-Cola being slightly more leveraged. This is not uncommon. Companies in similar industries often gravitate towards similar capital structures due to the opportunities, risks, and economics of the industry.

**Manager Analysis**

| Question | Accounting information | Analysis |
|---|---|---|
| Which company has higher leverage? | Debt to equity ratio | Debt to equity is a measure of financial leverage. Companies with more debt will have a higher debt to equity ratio and higher leverage. |

## TIMES INTEREST EARNED RATIO

Lenders require interest payments in return for the use of their money. Failure to pay interest when it is due may invoke penalties, possibly leading to bankruptcy. A ratio often used to measure this risk is the times interest earned ratio. This ratio provides an indication to creditors of how many "times" greater earnings are than interest expense. A company's earnings (or profitability) provide an indication of its ability to generate cash from operations in the current year and in future years, and its cash that will be used to pay interest payments. So, **the higher a company's earnings relative to its interest expense, the more likely it will be able to make current and future interest payments.**

At first glance, you might think we can calculate the times interest earned ratio as net income divided by interest expense. But remember, interest is one of the expenses subtracted in determining net income. So, to measure how many times greater earnings are than interest expense, we need to add interest expense back to net income. Similarly, because interest is deductible for income tax purposes, we also need to add back income tax expense to get a measure of earnings *before* the effects of interest and taxes. This measure is often called EBIT or earnings before interest and taxes. We compute the times interest earned ratio as

$$\text{Times interest earned ratio} = \frac{\text{Net income} + \text{Interest expense} + \text{Tax expense}}{\text{Interest expense}}$$

To further understand why we need to add back interest expense and income tax expense to net income, assume a company has the following income statement:

| | |
|---|---|
| Income before interest and taxes | $ 90,000 |
| **Interest expense** | **(10,000)** |
| Income before taxes | 80,000 |
| Income tax expense (25%) | (20,000) |
| Net income | $ 60,000 |

How many times greater is the company's earnings than interest expense? Is it 6.0 times greater (= $60,000 ÷ $10,000)? No, it's 9.0 times greater (= $90,000 ÷ $10,000). If current earnings provide an indication of the ability of a company to generate cash from operations in the current year and in future years, then a ratio of 9.0 suggests that the company will have plenty of cash available to pay current and future interest payments.

Illustration 9–22 computes the times interest earned ratios for Coca-Cola and PepsiCo to compare the companies' ability to make interest payments.

**ILLUSTRATION 9–22**

Times Interest Earned Ratio for Coca-Cola and PepsiCo

| ($ in millions) | Net Income + Interest Expense + Tax Expense | ÷ | Interest Expense | = | Times Interest Earned Ratio |
|---|---|---|---|---|---|
| Coca-Cola | $ 9,018 | ÷ | $ 919 | = | 9.8 |
| PepsiCo | $10,714 | ÷ | $1,525 | = | 7.0 |

Coca-Cola has a higher times interest earned ratio than PepsiCo, indicating Coca-Cola is better able to meet its long-term interest obligations. However, both companies exhibit strong earnings in relation to their interest expense, and both companies appear well able to meet interest payments.

 **KEY POINT**

The debt to equity ratio is a measure of financial leverage. Taking on more debt (higher leverage) can be good or bad depending on whether the company earns a return in excess of the cost of borrowed funds. The times interest earned ratio measures a company's ability to meet interest payments as they become due.

**Manager Analysis**

| Question | Accounting information | Analysis |
|---|---|---|
| Can a company meet its interest obligations? | Times interest earned ratio | A high times interest earned ratio indicates the ability of a company to meet its interest obligations. |

## APPENDIX

## ADDITIONAL BOND TOPICS

■ **LO9–9**
Account for bonds issued at a discount or premium.

In Part B of this chapter, we discussed how to account for bonds issue for their face amount. However, that's not always the case. Bonds will sometimes issue for an amount different from their face amount when the bond's *stated rate* differs from their *market rate*. In this appendix, we'll cover two topics: (1) how to account for the issuance of bonds for a price other than the face amount (referred to as a *discount* or *premium*) and (2) how to calculate that issue price.

### BOND DISCOUNTS AND PREMIUMS

*Common Terms*
The market interest rate is also known as the *effective-interest rate* or *yield rate*.

The *stated interest rate* is specified in the bond contract as the interest rate to be paid by the company to investors in the bond. The market interest rate is not specified in the bond contract. The market rate is an implied rate based on the price investors pay to purchase a bond in return for the right to receive the face amount at maturity and periodic interest payments over the remaining life of the bond.

All else equal, investors demand a higher market rate for bonds that have a higher default risk. Default risk refers to the possibility that a company will be unable to pay the bond's face amount or interest payments as they become due. **As the default risk of the bond increases, investors can *increase* their rate of return over the life of the bond by paying a *lower* price at the issue date.**

If the bonds' stated interest rate is *less than* the market interest rate, then the bonds will issue below face amount (discount). If the bonds' stated interest rate is *more than* the market interest rate, the bonds will issue above face amount (premium).

## BONDS ISSUED AT A DISCOUNT

Let's return to our example of California Coasters issuing a bond from earlier in the chapter. Now let's assume that California Coasters issues the same $100,000 of 7% bonds, but due to the company's higher default risk, investors require a market rate of return of 8%. California Coasters' bonds are less attractive to investors because they will receive a stated interest rate of 7% per year, which is less than their required rate of 8%. Because of the unfavorable interest rate, investors will pay less than $100,000 to purchase the bonds. These bonds will issue at a discount of $93,205.[4]

California Coasters recognizes the cash received of $93,205 by increasing Cash. The company also increases Bonds Payable for the full face amount of $100,000 that must be paid to investors in 10 years. The difference between these two amounts is reported as an increase to an account called Discount on Bonds Payable.

The financial statement effect of the bond issued at a discount is as follows:

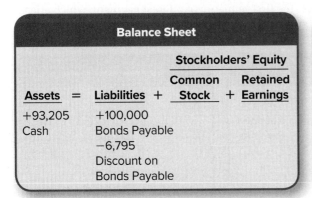

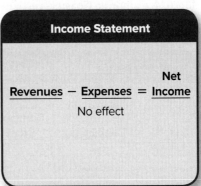

The Discount account is a contra liability, which is deducted from Bonds Payable in the balance sheet as shown below:

| Long-term liabilities: | |
| --- | --- |
| Bonds payable | $100,000 |
| *Minus*: Discount on bonds payable | (6,795) |
| Carrying value | $ 93,205 |

---

[4]In this example, the issue price of $93,205 is given. To see the details of how the issue price is calculated, see Illustration 9–29, 9–30, or 9–31 in this appendix to the chapter.

These bonds initially will be reported in the balance sheet at their carrying value of $93,205, which equals bonds payable less the bond discount. The discount ($6,795 in this example) effectively represents the additional cost of borrowing when issuing bonds for $93,205 but being required to pay back principal of $100,000. We'll report this amount as additional interest expense over the 10-year life of the bonds as we recognize each period's interest payment, as shown next.

**Interest Paid versus Interest Expense.**    The bond agreement specifies that cash paid for interest will be the same every six months—the face amount times the stated rate:

$$\begin{array}{ccccc} \text{Cash paid for} \\ \text{interest} \end{array} = \begin{array}{c} \text{Face amount} \\ \text{of bond} \end{array} \times \begin{array}{c} \text{Stated interest rate} \\ \text{per period} \end{array}$$

$$\$3{,}500 = \$100{,}000 \times 7\% \times 1/2$$

However, interest expense is not based on the *stated* rate. The amount to recognize for interest expense equals the current carrying value times the *market* rate (4% semiannually or 8% annually, in our example). This method of calculating interest is referred to as the *effective-interest method.*[5] For the first interest payment, interest expense is calculated as

$$\begin{array}{c} \text{Interest} \\ \text{expense} \end{array} = \begin{array}{c} \text{Carrying value} \\ \text{of bond} \end{array} \times \begin{array}{c} \text{Market interest rate} \\ \text{per period} \end{array}$$

$$\$3{,}728 = \$93{,}205 \times 8\% \times 1/2$$

When a bond sells at a discount, interest expense ($3,728) will be more than the cash paid for interest ($3,500). The difference represents the reduction in the discount. On June 30, 2024, California Coasters recognizes the first semiannual interest payment, which effects the financial statements as follows:

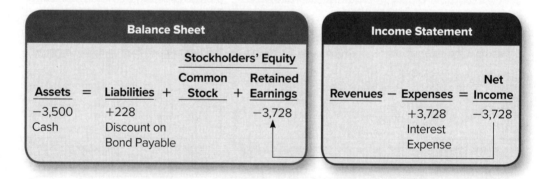

Interest Expense

| 3,728 | |

Discount on Bonds Payable

| | 228 |

Cash

| | 3,500 |

**DEBITS & CREDITS**

To record the first semiannual interest payment of a bond issued at a discount:

|  | Debit | Credit |
|---|---|---|
| Interest Expense ($93,205 × 8% × 1/2) | 3,728 | |
| Discount on Bonds Payable | | 228 |
| Cash ($100,000 × 7% × 1/2) | | 3,500 |

 **COMMON MISTAKE**

Students sometimes incorrectly record interest expense using the stated rate rather than the market rate. Remember that interest expense is the carrying value times the market rate, while the cash paid for interest is the face amount times the stated rate.

---

[5]We cover the effective-interest method, as this is the generally accepted method under both U.S. GAAP and IFRS. The straight-line amortization method, which is allowed only if it does not materially differ from the effective-interest method, is discussed as an alternative approach in intermediate accounting.

After the first interest payment, the balance of the discount has decreased by $228, which increases the bond's carrying value to $93,433 (= $93,205 + $228). We use the revised carrying value to calculate interest expense for the second semiannual interest period, which affects the financial statements as follows:

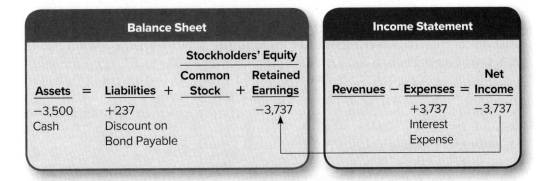

| Balance Sheet | | | | | Income Statement | | | |
|---|---|---|---|---|---|---|---|---|
| | | | **Stockholders' Equity** | | | | | |
| | | | **Common** | **Retained** | | | | **Net** |
| **Assets** | = | **Liabilities** + | **Stock** + | **Earnings** | **Revenues** − | **Expenses** | = | **Income** |
| −3,500 | | +237 | | −3,737 | | +3,737 | | −3,737 |
| Cash | | Discount on | | | | Interest | | |
| | | Bond Payable | | | | Expense | | |

**DEBITS & CREDITS**

To record the second semiannual interest payment of a bond issued at a discount:

| | Debit | Credit |
|---|---|---|
| Interest Expense ($93,433 × 8% × 1/2) ........................................... | 3,737 | |
| Discount on Bonds Payable ............................................................ | | 237 |
| Cash ($100,000 × 7% × 1/2) ........................................................... | | 3,500 |

Interest Expense
3,737 |
Discount on Bonds Payable
| 237
Cash
| 3,500

A bond amortization schedule summarizes the cash paid for interest, interest expense, and changes in the bond's carrying value for each semiannual interest period. Illustration 9–23 provides an amortization schedule for the bonds issued at a discount. Note that the amounts for the June 30, 2024, and the December 31, 2024, semiannual interest payments shown above can be taken directly from the amortization schedule.

**ILLUSTRATION 9–23**

Amortization Schedule for Bonds Issued at a Discount

| (1) | (2) | (3) | (4) | (5) |
|---|---|---|---|---|
| | | **Interest** | **Increase in** | **Carrying** |
| **Date** | **Cash Paid** | **Expense** | **Carrying Value** | **Value** |
| | Face Amount × Stated Rate | Carrying Value × Market Rate | (3) − (2) | Prior Carrying Value + (4) |
| 1/1/2024 | | | | $ 93,205 |
| 6/30/2024 | $3,500 | $3,728 | $228 | 93,433 |
| 12/31/2024 | 3,500 | 3,737 | 237 | 93,670 |
| * | * | * | * | * |
| * | * | * | * | 99,057 |
| 6/30/2033 | 3,500 | 3,962 | 462 | 99,519 |
| 12/31/2033 | 3,500 | 3,981 | 481 | 100,000 |

The amortization schedule shows interest calculations every six months because interest is paid semiannually. The entire amortization schedule would include 20 more rows (10 years × 2 periods per year) after the initial balance on January 1, 2024. To save space, we show only the amortization for the first and last years. The eight years in the middle are represented by asterisks. Cash paid is $3,500 (= $100,000 × 7% × 1/2) every six months. Interest expense is the carrying value times the market rate. Interest expense for the six months ended June 30, 2024, is $3,728 (= $93,205 × 8% × 1/2). The difference between interest expense and the cash paid increases the carrying value of the bonds. At the maturity date, the carrying value will equal the face amount of $100,000.

## BONDS ISSUED AT A PREMIUM

Now let's assume that California Coasters issues the same $100,000 of 7% bonds, but, for this example, investors require a rate of return of only 6%. Investors will pay *more* than $100,000 for these bonds since the bonds' 7% stated rate is relatively attractive to investors requiring only 6%. The bonds will issue at a premium of $107,439.

California Coasters recognizes the cash received of $107,439 by increasing Cash. The company increases Bonds Payable for the full face amount of $100,000 that must be paid to investors in 10 years. The difference is reported as an increase to an account called Premium on Bonds Payable.

The financial statement effect of the bond issued at a premium is as follows:

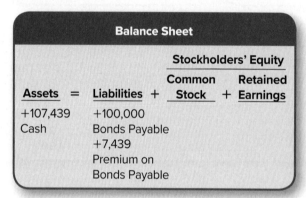

| | Balance Sheet | | | | | Income Statement | | |
|---|---|---|---|---|---|---|---|---|
| | | | **Stockholders' Equity** | | | | | |
| **Assets** | = | **Liabilities** | + | **Common Stock** | + | **Retained Earnings** | | |
| +107,439 Cash | | +100,000 Bonds Payable +7,439 Premium on Bonds Payable | | | | | | |

Income Statement: Revenues − Expenses = Net Income — No effect

**Cash**
107,439 |

**Bonds Payable**
| 100,000

**Premium on Bonds Payable**
| 7,439

### DEBITS & CREDITS
To record the issuance of the bonds issued at a premium:

| | Debit | Credit |
|---|---|---|
| **Cash** | **107,439** | |
| **Bonds Payable** | | **100,000** |
| **Premium on Bonds Payable** | | **7,439** |

The balance of Premium on Bonds Payable is added to Bonds Payable in the balance sheet as shown below:

| **Long-term liabilities:** | |
|---|---|
| Bonds payable | $100,000 |
| *Plus:* Premium on bonds payable | 7,439 |
| Carrying value | $107,439 |

Initially, the bonds will be reported in the balance sheet at their carrying value of $107,439. The premium ($7,439 in this example) effectively represents the reduction in cost of borrowing when issuing bonds for $107,439 but being required to pay back principal of only $100,000. We'll report this cost saving as reduced interest expense over the 10-year life of the bonds as we recognize each period's interest payment.

On June 30, 2024, California Coasters recognizes the first semiannual interest payment. Because the bonds sold at a premium, interest expense ($3,223) will be less than the cash paid for interest ($3,500). The difference is the reduction in the premium. The financial statement effects are as follows:

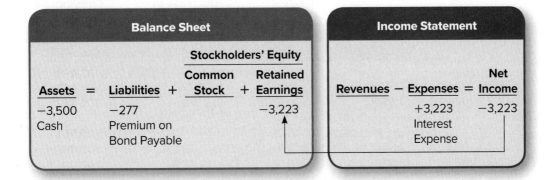

**DEBITS & CREDITS**

To record the first semiannual interest payment of a bond issued at a premium:

| | Debit | Credit |
|---|---|---|
| Interest Expense ($107,439 × 6% × 1/2) | 3,223 | |
| Premium on Bonds Payable | 277 | |
| Cash ($100,000 × 7% × 1/2) | | 3,500 |

Interest Expense
3,223

Premium on Bonds Payable
277

Cash
3,500

After the first interest payment, the balance of the premium has decreased by $277, which decreases the bond's carrying value to $107,162 (= $107,439 − $277). We use the revised carrying value to calculate interest expense for the second semiannual interest period on December 31, 2024, which affects the financial statements as follows:

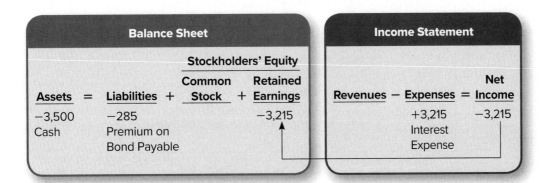

**DEBITS & CREDITS**

To record the second semiannual interest payment of a bond issued at a premium:

| | Debit | Credit |
|---|---|---|
| Interest Expense ($107,162 × 6% × 1/2) | 3,215 | |
| Premium on Bonds Payable | 285 | |
| Cash ($100,000 × 7% × 1/2) | | 3,500 |

Interest Expense
3,215

Premium on Bonds Payable
285

Cash
3,500

The amortization schedule in Illustration 9–24 summarizes the reporting of interest expense for the bonds issued at a premium.

**ILLUSTRATION 9–24**

Amortization Schedule for Bonds Issued at a Premium

| (1) Date | (2) Cash Paid Face Amount × Stated Rate | (3) Interest Expense Carrying Value × Market Rate | (4) Decrease in Carrying Value (2) − (3) | (5) Carrying Value Prior Carrying Value − (4) |
|---|---|---|---|---|
| 1/1/2024 | | | | $107,439 |
| 6/30/2024 | $3,500 | $3,223 | $277 | 107,162 |
| 12/31/2024 | 3,500 | 3,215 | 285 | 106,877 |
| * | * | * | * | * |
| * | * | * | * | 100,956 |
| 6/30/2033 | 3,500 | 3,029 | 471 | 100,485 |
| 12/31/2033 | 3,500 | 3,015 | 485 | 100,000 |

Just as in the discount example, the amounts for the June 30, 2024, and the December 31, 2024, semiannual interest payments can be obtained directly from the amortization schedule. Now, however, with a bond premium, the difference between cash paid and interest expense *decreases* the carrying value each period from $107,439 at bond issue down to $100,000 (the face amount) at bond maturity.

Illustration 9–25 shows how carrying value changes as a bond approaches its maturity date.

**ILLUSTRATION 9–25**

Changes in Carrying Value over Time

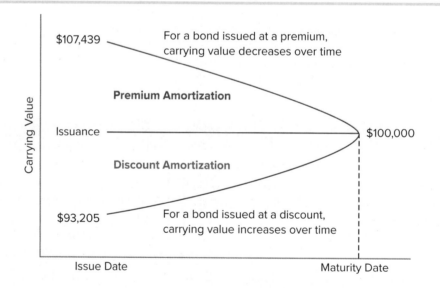

 **KEY POINT**

When bonds issue at face amount, the carrying value and the corresponding interest expense *remain constant* over time. When bonds issue at a discount (below face amount), the carrying value and the corresponding interest expense *increase* over time. When bonds issue at a premium (above face amount), the carrying value and the corresponding interest expense *decrease* over time.

## Pricing a Bond

■ **LO9–10**

Calculate bond prices.

So far, in the examples used in the chapter and in this appendix, the issue price of the bond was given. In this section, we demonstrate how that issue price is calculated. **The issue price of a bond equals the *present value* of the bond's face amount plus the *present value* of its periodic interest payments.** To calculate these present values, we need to know

1. The face amount of the bond.
2. The interest payment each period based on the stated interest rate of the bond.
3. The number of periods until the bond matures.
4. The market interest rate per period.

The first three items are stated in the bond contract. In our example for California Coasters, the *face amount* equals $100,000. The *interest payment* every six months is $3,500 (= $100,000 × 7% × 1/2 year) based on the bond's stated interest rate of 7%. The *number of periods* to maturity is 20 because the bonds pay interest semiannually (twice per year) for 10 years.

As discussed previously, the *market interest rate* is not stated in the bond contract. This rate is implied based on the issue price of the bond. **It's the market rate that we'll use to determine the present value of the face amount and the present value of the interest payments.** When the market rate equals the bond's stated rate, the issue price equals the face amount. When the market rate is greater than (less than) the stated rate, the bonds will issue at a discount (premium).

## BONDS ISSUED AT FACE AMOUNT

Let's first assume the market interest rate is 7%, the same as the issuing company's stated interest rate. One way to determine the issue price of bonds is to use your financial calculator. Illustration 9–26 shows the calculator inputs used to obtain an issue price at the face amount of $100,000.

**ILLUSTRATION 9–26**

Pricing Bonds Issued at Face Amount Using a Financial Calculator

**CALCULATOR INPUT**

| Bond Characteristics | Key | Amount |
|---|---|---|
| 1. Face amount | FV | $100,000 |
| 2. Interest payment | PMT | $3,500 = 100,000 × 7% × 1/2 year |
| 3. Number of periods | N | 20 = 10 years × 2 periods each year |
| 4. Market interest rate | I | 3.5 = 7% ÷ 2 periods each year |

**CALCULATOR OUTPUT**

| | | |
|---|---|---|
| Issue price | PV | $100,000 |

An alternative to using a financial calculator is to calculate the price of bonds in Excel. Illustration 9–27 demonstrates the inputs and the formula used to calculate the issue price.

**ILLUSTRATION 9–27**

Pricing Bonds Issued at Face Amount Using Excel

| B7 | fx | =-PV(B5,B4,B3,B2,0) |
|---|---|---|

| | A | B |
|---|---|---|
| 2 | Face amount | $100,000 |
| 3 | Interest payment | $3,500 |
| 4 | Number of periods | 20 |
| 5 | Market interest rate | 0.035 |
| 7 | Issue price | $100,000 |

Microsoft Corporation

A third alternative is to calculate the price of the bonds using present value tables. In Illustration 9–28, we calculate the price of the bonds using the present value tables provided at the back of this book.

**ILLUSTRATION 9–28**

**Pricing Bonds Issued at Face Amount Using Present Value Tables**

| | | |
|---|---|---|
| Present value of face amount | = $100,000 × 0.50257* | = $ 50,257 |
| Present value of interest payments | = $3,500† × 14.21240** | = 49,743 |
| Issue price of the bonds | | $100,000 |

†$100,000 × 7% × 1/2 year = $3,500
*Table 2, $i$ = 3.5%, $n$ = 20
**Table 4, $i$ = 3.5%, $n$ = 20

We use Table 2 at the back of the book, the present value of $1, to calculate the present value of the face amount since it's just one amount ($100,000) due at maturity. We use Table 4 at the back of the book, the present value of an ordinary annuity of $1, to calculate the present value of the interest payments since they are a series of equal amounts ($3,500 each) paid every semiannual interest period. A series of equal amounts over equal time periods is called an *annuity*.

Using any of these three alternatives, the issue price of the bonds is equal to $100,000. All three methods have their advantages. A financial calculator and Excel are simple to use and provide greater flexibility regarding the choice of different interest rates and time periods. On the other hand, present value tables provide a more detailed understanding of how bond prices are determined.

## BONDS ISSUED AT A DISCOUNT

Now let's assume that California Coasters issues the same $100,000 of 7%, bonds, but investors require a market rate of return of 8%. These bonds will issue for less than $100,000 (at a *discount*). Illustration 9–29 shows the calculation of this issue price using a market rate of 8% (4% every semiannual period).

**ILLUSTRATION 9–29**

**Pricing Bonds Issued at a Discount Using a Financial Calculator**

**CALCULATOR INPUT**

| Bond Characteristics | Key | Amount |
|---|---|---|
| 1. Face amount | FV | $100,000 |
| 2. Interest payment | PMT | $3,500 = $100,000 × 7% × 1/2 year |
| 3. Number of periods | N | 20 = 10 years × 2 periods each year |
| 4. Market interest rate | I | 4 = 8% ÷ 2 periods each year |

**CALCULATOR OUTPUT**

| | | |
|---|---|---|
| Issue price | PV | $93,205 |

Illustration 9–30 demonstrates how to use Excel to determine the issue price.

**ILLUSTRATION 9–30**

**Pricing Bonds Issued at a Discount Using Excel**

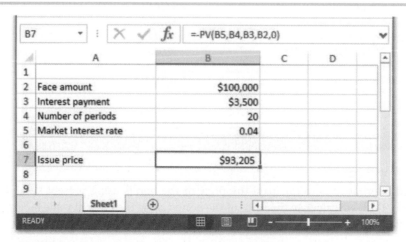

Microsoft Corporation

In Illustration 9–31, we calculate the price of the bonds using the present value tables provided at the back of this textbook, assuming the market rate of interest is 8% per year, or 4% every semiannual period.

**ILLUSTRATION 9–31**

Pricing Bonds Issued at a Discount Using Present Value Tables

| | | | |
|---|---|---|---|
| Present value of principal | = $100,000 × 0.45639* | = | $45,639 |
| Present value of interest payments | = $3,500[1] × 13.59033** | = | 47,566 |
| Issue price of the bonds | | | $93,205 |

[1]$100,000 × 7% × 1/2 year = $3,500
*Table 2, $i = 4\%$, $n = 20$
**Table 4, $i = 4\%$, $n = 20$

By investing only $93,205 to receive the face amount of $100,000 and semiannual interest payments of $3,500, investors *effectively* earn the market rate of 8% on their investment. **In other words, an investor paying $93,205 for the 7% bonds will earn the same rate of return (8%) as an investor paying $100,000 for bonds with a stated rate of 8%.**

**COMMON MISTAKE**

The interest rate we use to calculate the bond issue price is always the *market* rate, never the stated rate. Some students get confused and incorrectly use the stated rate to calculate present value. Use the stated rate to calculate the interest payment each period, but use the market rate to calculate the present value of the cash flows.

## BONDS ISSUED AT A PREMIUM

Now let's assume that California Coasters issues $100,000 of 7% bonds when investors require a rate of only 6%. These bonds will issue for more than $100,000 (a *premium*). Illustration 9–32 shows the calculation of this issue price using a market rate of 6% (3% every semiannual period).

**ILLUSTRATION 9–32**

Pricing Bonds Issued at a Premium Using a Financial Calculator

**CALCULATOR INPUT**

| Bond Characteristics | Key | Amount |
|---|---|---|
| 1. Face amount | FV | $100,000 |
| 2. Interest payment | PMT | $3,500 = $100,000 × 7% × 1/2 year |
| 3. Number of periods | N | 20 = 10 years × 2 periods each year |
| 4. Market interest rate | I | 3 = 6% ÷ 2 periods each year |

**CALCULATOR OUTPUT**

| | | |
|---|---|---|
| Issue price | PV | $107,439 |

Illustration 9–33 demonstrates how to use Excel to determine the issue price.

**ILLUSTRATION 9–33**

Pricing Bonds Issued at a Premium Using Excel

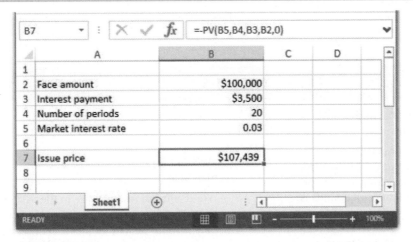

Microsoft Corporation

Illustration 9–34 calculates the price of the bonds using the present value tables provided at the back of this book, again assuming the market rate of interest is 6% (3% semiannually).

**ILLUSTRATION 9–34**

**Pricing Bonds Issued at a Premium Using Present Value Tables**

| | | | |
|---|---|---|---|
| Present value of principal | = $100,000 × 0.55368* | = | $ 55,368 |
| Present value of interest payments | = $3,500[1] × 14.87747** | = | 52,071 |
| Issue price of the bonds | | | $107,439 |

[1]$100,000 × 7% × 1/2 year = $3,500
*Table 2, $i = 3\%$, $n = 20$
**Table 4, $i = 3\%$, $n = 20$

By investing $107,439 to receive the face amount of $100,000 and semiannual interest payments of $3,500, investors *effectively* earn the market rate of 6% on their investment. **In other words, an investor paying $107,439 for the 7% bonds will earn the same rate of return (6%) as an investor paying $100,000 for bonds with a stated rate of 6%.**

Illustration 9–35 shows the relation between the stated interest rate, the market interest rate, and the bond issue price.

**ILLUSTRATION 9–35**

**Stated Rate, Market Rate, and the Bond Issue Price**

| Bonds Issued at a Discount | Bonds Issued at a Face Amount | Bonds Issued at a Premium |
|---|---|---|
| Stated rate (7%) less than **Market rate (8%)** | Stated rate (7%) equal to **Market rate (7%)** | Stated rate (7%) greater than **Market rate (6%)** |

If the bonds' stated interest rate is less than the market interest rate, then the bonds will issue below face amount (discount). If the bonds' stated interest rate equals the market interest rate, then the bonds will issue at face amount. Finally, if the bonds' stated interest rate is more than the market interest rate, the bonds will issue above face amount (premium).

Which is most common in practice—bonds issued at face amount, a discount, or a premium? Most bonds initially are issued at a slight discount. Because there is a delay between when the company determines the characteristics of the bonds and when the bonds actually are issued, the company must estimate the market rate of interest. Bond issuers usually adopt a stated interest rate close to, but just under, the expected market interest rate. However, in future periods, the bonds may trade at either a discount or a premium, depending on changes in market interest rates.

 **KEY POINT**

The issue price of a bond is equal to the present value of the face amount (principal) payable at maturity, plus the present value of the periodic interest payments. Bonds can be issued at face amount, below face amount (at a discount), or above face amount (at a premium).

 **THE BOTTOM LINE**

**LO9–1   Explain financing alternatives and characteristics of liabilities.**

Companies obtain external funds through debt financing (liabilities) and equity financing (stockholders' equity). One advantage of debt financing is that interest on borrowed funds is tax-deductible.

In most cases, current liabilities are payable within one year from the balance sheet date,

and long-term liabilities are payable in more than one year.

**LO9–2   Account for notes payable and interest expense.**

We report interest expense in the period we incur it, rather than in the period in which we pay it. Many short-term loans are arranged under an existing line of credit with a bank, or for larger corporations in the form of commercial paper, a loan from one company to another.

**LO9–3 Explain the accounting for common current liabilities.**

Common current liabilities include (1) accounts payable to vendors and suppliers; (2) payroll liabilities for unpaid salaries, unemployment taxes, employer portion of FICA taxes, and employer portion of insurance and retirement contributions; (3) deferred revenue for cash received in advance from customers; (4) sales taxes collected from customers by the seller to be paid to the government; and (5) the current portion of a long-term debt that will be paid within one year from the balance sheet date.

**LO9–4 Apply the appropriate accounting treatment for contingencies.**

A contingent liability is reported only if a loss is probable and the amount is reasonably estimable. Unlike contingent liabilities, contingent gains are not recognized until the gain is certain and no longer a contingency.

**LO9–5 Account for installment notes payable.**

Most notes payable require periodic installment payments. Each installment payment includes an amount that represents interest expense and an amount that represents a reduction of the carrying value (remaining loan balance).

**LO9–6 Understand how leases are reported.**

While not transferring ownership as in a purchase, a lease gives the lessee (user) the right to use the asset over the lease period. This right is reported as an asset, and the obligation to make lease payments is reported as a liability.

**LO9–7 Identify bond characteristics and account for bonds issued a face amount.**

The distinguishing characteristics of bonds include whether they are backed by collateral (secured or unsecured), become due at a single specified date or over a series of years (term or serial), can be redeemed prior to maturity (callable), or can be converted into common stock (convertible). When bonds are issued at face amount, the carrying value and the corresponding interest expense remain constant over time.

**LO9–8 Assess liquidity and solvency using ratios.**

Working capital is the difference between current assets and current liabilities. The current ratio is equal to current assets divided by current liabilities. The acid-test ratio is equal to quick assets (cash, short-term investments, and accounts receivable) divided by current liabilities. Each measures a company's liquidity, its ability to pay currently maturing debts.

The debt to equity ratio is a measure of financial leverage. Assuming more debt (higher leverage) can be good or bad depending on whether the company earns a return in excess of the cost of borrowed funds. The times interest earned ratio measures a company's ability to meet interest payments as they become due.

**LO9–9 Account for bonds issued at a discount or premium.**

When bonds issue at a discount (below face amount), the carrying value and the corresponding interest expense increase over time. When bonds issue at a premium (above face amount), the carrying value and the corresponding interest expense decrease over time.

**LO9–10 Calculate bond prices.**

The issue price of a bond is equal to the present value of the face amount (principal) payable at maturity, plus the present value of the periodic interest payments. Bonds can be issued at face amount, below face amount (at a discount), or above face amount (at a premium).

## GLOSSARY

**Accounts payable:** Obligations to suppliers for purchases of inventory or supplies on account. **p. 445**

**Acid-test ratio:** Cash, current investments, and accounts receivable divided by current liabilities; measures the availability of liquid current assets to pay current liabilities. **p. 462**

**Amortization schedule:** Provides a table format detailing the cash payment each period, the portions of each cash payment that represents interest and the change in carrying value, and balance of the carrying value. **p. 452**

**Annuity:** Cash payments of equal amounts over equal time periods. **p. 478**

**Bond:** A formal debt instrument issued by a company to borrow money. The issuing company (borrower) is obligated to pay back to the investor (lender): (1) a stated amount, referred to as the *principal* or *face amount,* at a specified maturity date, and (2) periodic interest payments over the life of the bond. **p. 456**

**Callable bond:** A bond feature that allows the borrower to repay the bonds before their scheduled maturity date at a specified call price. **p. 457**

**Capital structure:** The mixture of liabilities and stockholders' equity in a business. **p. 438**

**Commercial paper:** Borrowing from another company rather than from a bank. **p. 444**

**Contingencies:** Uncertain situations that can result in a gain or a loss for a company. **p. 447**

**Contingent gain:** An existing uncertain situation that might result in a gain. **p. 451**

**Contingent liability:** An existing uncertain situation that might result in a loss. **p. 447**

**Convertible bond:** A bond feature that allows the lender (or investor) to convert each bond into a specified number of shares of common stock. **p. 457**

**Current liabilities:** Debts that, in most cases, are due within one year from the balance sheet date. However, when a company has an operating cycle of longer than a year, its current liabilities are defined by the length of the operating cycle, rather than by the length of one year. **p. 439**

**Current portion of long-term debt:** Debt that will be paid within one year from the balance sheet date. **p. 446**

**Current ratio:** Current assets divided by current liabilities; measures the availability of current assets to pay current liabilities. **p. 462**

**Debt covenant:** An agreement between a borrower and a lender requiring certain minimum financial measures be met, or the lender can recall the debt. **p. 466**

**Deferred revenue:** Cash received in advance from a customer for products or services to be provided in the future. **p. 446**

**Debt financing:** Borrowing money from creditors (liabilities). **p. 438**

**Debt to equity ratio:** Total interest-bearing debt divided by total stockholders' equity; measures a company's risk. **p. 467**

**Default risk:** The risk that a company will be unable to pay the bond's face amount or interest payments as they become due. **p. 471**

**Discount:** A bond's issue price is below the face amount. **p. 471**

**Equity financing:** Obtaining investment from stockholders (stockholders' equity). **p. 438**

**Installment payment:** Includes both an amount that represents interest and an amount that represents a reduction of the outstanding balance. **p. 452**

**Interest:** "rent" paid for the use of money for some period of time. **p. 441**

**Lease:** A contractual arrangement by which the lessor (owner) provides the lessee (user) the right to use an asset for a specified period of time. **p. 454**

**Liability:** A present responsibility to sacrifice assets in the future due to a transaction or other event that happened in the past. **p. 439**

**Line of credit:** An informal agreement that permits a company to borrow up to a prearranged limit without having to follow formal loan procedures and prepare paperwork. **p. 444**

**Liquidity:** Having sufficient cash (or other assets convertible to cash in a relatively short time) to pay currently maturing debts. **p. 461**

**Market interest rate:** An implied rate based on the price investors are willing to pay to purchase a bond in return for the right to receive the face amount at maturity and periodic interest payments over the remaining life of the bond. **p. 470**

**Notes payable:** Written promises to repay amounts borrowed plus interest. **p. 440**

**Premium:** A bond's issue price is above the face amount. **p. 471**

**Private placement:** Sale of debt securities directly to a single investor. **p. 457**

**Quick assets:** Includes only cash, current investments, and accounts receivable. **p. 462**

**Sales tax payable:** Sales tax collected from customers by the seller, representing current liabilities payable to the government. **p. 446**

**Secured bonds:** Bonds that are supported by specific assets pledged as collateral. **p. 457**

**Serial bonds:** Bonds that require payment of the principal amount of the bond over a series of maturity dates. **p. 457**

**Stated interest rate:** The rate specified in the bond contract used to calculate the cash payments for interest. **p. 459**

**Term bonds:** Bonds that require payment of the full principal amount at a single maturity date. **p. 457**

**Times interest earned ratio:** Ratio that compares interest expense with income available to pay those charges. **p. 469**

**Unsecured bonds:** Bonds that are *not* supported by specific assets pledged as collateral. **p. 457**

**Working capital:** The difference between current assets and current liabilities. **p. 461**

# SELF-STUDY QUESTIONS

1. Which of the following is not a primary source of corporate debt financing? **(LO9–1)**
   a. Bonds.
   b. Notes.
   c. Leases.
   d. Receivables.

2. Which of the following statements regarding liabilities is not true? **(LO9–1)**
   a. Liabilities can be for services rather than cash.
   b. Liabilities are reported in the balance sheet for almost every business.
   c. Liabilities result from future transactions.
   d. Liabilities represent probable future sacrifices of benefits.

3. Current liabilities **(LO9–1)**
   a. May include contingent liabilities.
   b. Include obligations payable within one year or one operating cycle, whichever is shorter.
   c. Can be satisfied only with the payment of cash.
   d. Are preferred by most companies over long-term liabilities.

4. Express Jet borrows $100 million on October 1, 2024, for one year at 6% interest. For what amount does Express Jet report interest payable for the year ended December 31, 2024? **(LO9–2)**
   a. $0.
   b. $4.5 million.
   c. $1.5 million.
   d. $6 million.

5. We report interest expense on a note payable in the period in which **(LO9–2)**
   a. We pay cash for interest.
   b. We incur interest.
   c. We pay cash and incur interest.
   d. We pay cash or incur interest.

6. The seller collects sales taxes from the customer at the time of sale and reports the sales taxes as **(LO9–3)**
   a. Sales tax expense.
   b. Sales tax revenue.
   c. Sales tax receivable.
   d. Sales tax payable.

7. Management can estimate the amount of loss that will occur due to litigation against the company. If the likelihood of loss is reasonably possible, a contingent liability should be **(LO9–4)**
   a. Disclosed but not reported as a liability.
   b. Disclosed and reported as a liability.
   c. Neither disclosed nor reported as a liability.
   d. Reported as a liability but not disclosed.

8. A company purchased new equipment for $31,000 with a two-year installment note requiring 5% interest. The required monthly payment is $1,360. For the first month's payment, what amount represents interest expense? **(LO9–5)**
   a. $120.
   b. $129.
   c. $68.
   d. $155.

9. A company purchased new equipment for $31,000 with a two-year installment note requiring 5% interest. The required monthly payment is $1,360. After the first month's payment, what is the balance of the note? **(LO9–5)**
   a. $30,723.
   b. $29,640.
   c. $29,769.
   d. $30,871.

10. Which of the following typically represents an advantage of leasing over purchasing an asset with an installment note? **(LO9–6)**
    a. Lease payments often are lower than installment payments.
    b. Leasing generally requires less cash up front.
    c. Leasing typically offers greater flexibility and lower costs in disposing of an asset.
    d. All of the above are advantages of leasing.

11. A company needs construction equipment to complete a project over the next 20 months. The equipment costs $10,000. Instead of purchasing the equipment with a 12% note, the company leases the equipment with payments of $300 due at the end of each month. For what amount would the company report the lease liability at the beginning of the lease? **(LO9–6)**
    a. $5,414.
    b. $6,000.
    c. $4,586.
    d. $10,000.

12. Serial bonds are **(LO9–7)**
    a. Bonds backed by collateral.
    b. Bonds that mature in installments.
    c. Bonds the issuer can repurchase at a fixed price.
    d. Bonds issued below the face amount.

13. A company issues $50,000 of 4% bonds, due in five years, with interest payable semiannually. The bonds were issued at par. Calculate interest expense as of the first semiannual interest payment. **(LO9–7)**
    a. $1,570.
    b. $1,000.
    c. $785.
    d. $375.

14. The acid-test ratio is **(LO9–8)**
    a. Current assets divided by current liabilities.
    b. Cash and current investments divided by current liabilities.
    c. Cash, current investments, and accounts receivable divided by current liabilities.
    d. Cash, current investments, accounts receivable, and inventory divided by current liabilities.

15. Assuming a current ratio of 1.00 and an acid-test ratio of 0.75, how will the purchase of inventory with cash affect each ratio? **(LO9–8)**
    a. Increase the current ratio and increase the acid-test ratio.
    b. No change to the current ratio and decrease the acid-test ratio.
    c. Decrease the current ratio and decrease the acid-test ratio.
    d. Increase the current ratio and decrease the acid-test ratio.

16. Which of the following ratios measures financial leverage? **(LO9–8)**
    a. The return on assets ratio.
    b. The inventory turnover ratio.
    c. The times interest earned ratio.
    d. The debt to equity ratio.

*Note: For answers, see the last page of the chapter.*

17. Which of the following is true for bonds issued at a discount? **(LO9–9)**
    a. The stated interest rate is greater than the market interest rate.
    b. The market interest rate is greater than the stated interest rate.
    c. The stated interest rate and the market interest rate are equal.
    d. The stated interest rate and the market interest rate are unrelated.

18. A company issues $50,000 of 4% bonds, due in five years, with interest payable semiannually. Assuming a market rate of 3%, the bonds issue for $52,306. Calculate the carrying value of the bonds after the first semiannual interest payment. **(LO9–9)**
    a. $51,306.
    b. $52,091.
    c. $49,000.
    d. $51,521.

19. A company issues $50,000 of 4% bonds, due in five years, with interest payable semiannually. Calculate the issue price of the bonds, assuming a market interest rate of 5%. **(LO9–10)**
    a. $47,835.
    b. $52,246.
    c. $58,983.
    d. $47,812.

## REAL WORLD PERSPECTIVES

**EDGAR Case**

### Tesla (ticker: TSLA)

**RWP9–1** Visit **www.sec.gov/edgar** and search for the **Tesla** annual report (10-K) for the year ended December 31, 2019, using EDGAR (Electronic Data Gathering, Analysis, and Retrieval system). Locate the note titled "Note 2 - Summary of Significant Accounting Policies." Then, find the sub-section in Note 2 titled "*Warranties.*"

*Required:*
1. How much did Tesla reserve for warranties at the beginning of 2019?
2. How much did Tesla reserve for warranties at the end of 2019?
3. How many warranty-related costs were incurred in the 2019 income statement?

**EDGAR Case**

### Chevron (ticker: CVX)

**RWP9–2** Visit **www.sec.gov/edgar** and search for the **Chevron** annual report (10-K) for the year ended December 31, 2019, using EDGAR (Electronic Data Gathering, Analysis, and Retrieval system). Locate note 22 titled "Other Contingencies and Commitments." Then, find the sub-section in Note 2 titled "*Environmental.*"

*Required:*
1. How much is in Chevron's environmental reserve at December 31, 2019?
2. These environmental liabilities are primarily associated with what types of activities?

**EDGAR Case**

### PepsiCo (ticker: PEP)

**RWP9–3** Visit **www.sec.gov/edgar** and search for the **PepsiCo** annual report (10-K) for the year ended December 28, 2019, using EDGAR (Electronic Data Gathering, Analysis, and Retrieval system). Locate the Consolidated Balance Sheet and the note titled "Debt Obligations."

*Required:*

1. What percentage of PepsiCo's total liabilities of $63,679 million at December 28, 2019, constitutes interest-bearing debt?
2. How much debt does PepsiCo expect to pay down in fiscal 2020?
3. What is the range of interest rates PepsiCo incurs on its long-term debt obligations (identify the lowest and highest rate)?

## Nike (ticker: NKE)

EDGAR Case

**RWP9–4** Visit **www.sec.gov/edgar** and search for the **Nike** annual report (10-K) for the year ended May 31, 2019, using EDGAR (Electronic Data Gathering, Analysis, and Retrieval system). Locate the note titled "Note 8 - Long-term Debt."

*Required:*

1. How many different bonds does Nike have at May 31, 2019?
2. How often do these bonds pay interest?
3. Were the bonds issued at face amount, a discount, or a premium? How do you know?
4. How much will Nike have to pay the bondholders of the 2.38% bond on November 1, 2029?

## American Eagle Outfitters, Inc.

Continuing Financial Analysis Case

**RWP9–5** Financial information for **American Eagle** is presented in **Appendix A** at the end of the book.

*Required:*

1. Calculate the current ratio for the past two years. Did the current ratio improve or weaken in the more recent year?
2. Calculate the acid-test (quick) ratio for the past two years. Did the acid-test ratio improve or weaken in the more recent year?
3. If American Eagle used $100 million in cash to pay $100 million in accounts payable, how would its current ratio and acid-test ratio change? Show your calculations.
4. Review the balance sheet and note 9 to the financial statements. Based on this information, how would you rate the bankruptcy risk of American Eagle?

## The Buckle, Inc.

Continuing Financial Analysis Case

**RWP9–6** Financial information for **Buckle** is presented in **Appendix B** at the end of the book.

*Required:*

1. Calculate the current ratio for the past two years. Did the current ratio improve or weaken in the more recent year?
2. Calculate the acid-test (quick) ratio for the past two years. Did the acid-test ratio improve or weaken in the more recent year?
3. If Buckle purchased $50 million of inventory by debiting Inventory and crediting Accounts Payable, how would its current ratio and acid-test ratio change? Show your calculations.
4. Review the balance sheet and note E to the financial statements. Based on this information, how would you rate the bankruptcy risk of Buckle?

## American Eagle Outfitters, Inc. vs. The Buckle, Inc.

Continuing Comparative Analysis Case

**RWP9–7** Financial information for **American Eagle** is presented in **Appendix A** at the end of the book, and financial information for **Buckle** is presented in **Appendix B** at the end of the book.

*Required:*

1. Calculate the current ratio for both companies for the year ended February 3, 2018. Which company has the better ratio? Compare your calculations with those for **United Airlines** and **American Airlines** reported in the chapter text. Which industry maintains a higher current ratio?
2. Calculate the acid-test (quick) ratio for both companies for the year ended February 3, 2018. Which company has the better ratio? Compare your calculations with those for United Airlines and American Airlines reported in the chapter text. Which industry maintains a higher acid-test ratio?
3. How would the purchase of additional inventory with accounts payable affect the current ratio for these two companies?

Ethics Case

## Ethics

**RWP9–8** The Tony Hawk Skate Park was built in early 2024. The construction was financed by a $3,000,000, 7% note due in six years, with payments of $51,147 required each month. The first year has not been as profitable as hoped. The discussion at the executive board meeting at the end of 2024 focused on the potential need to obtain additional financing. However, board members are concerned the company's debt level at the end of 2024 will make the company appear too risky to additional lenders. The balance of the note at the end of 2024 is $2,583,026. By the end of 2025, the 12 monthly payments will reduce the balance by an additional $447,116. Separate from the note, the company has the following amounts at the end of 2024: current assets of $3,100,000; current liabilities of $2,700,000; total equity of $4,000,000.

Jim Trost, the VP of finance, tells board members that he plans to classify the full balance of the note at the end of 2024 as long-term because the full length of the note is six years. He explains that lenders will be more willing to let the company borrow and will offer a lower interest rate if the company reports fewer current liabilities. Plus, he plans to tell lenders that there is no problem with long-term solvency because the company's long-term profits will be used to pay its long-term debt.

### Required:
1. Understand the reporting effect: How does Jim's decision affect the reported amount of current liabilities versus long-term liabilities as of December 31, 2024?
2. Specify the options: Calculate the current ratio and the debt to equity ratio at the end of 2024 (a) with and (b) without Jim's assumption. Assume all liabilities are interest-bearing.
3. Identify the impact: Can Jim's decision affect lenders?
4. Make a decision: Should Jim report the full balance of the note as a long-term liability in its balance sheet as of December 31, 2024?

Sustainability Case

## Sustainability

**RWP9–9** Go to the SASB website (https://www.sasb.org/company-use/sasb-reporters/) and search for the 2020 Sustainability Report for **DuPont de Nemours Inc.** Then read the subsection titled "Acting on climate" on page 30.
1. By how much would the company like to reduce greenhouse gas emissions from their facilities by 2030?
2. In 2019, what percent of the company's electricity came from renewable sources?
3. What percent of its electricity use would the company like to come from renewable energy sources by 2030?

Earnings Management Case

## Earnings Management

**RWP9–10** Quattro Technologies, a hydraulic manufacturer in the aeronautics industry, has reported steadily increasing net income over the past few years. The company reported net income of $120 million in 2022 and $140 million in 2023. The stock is receiving increasing analyst attention because many investors expect the steady growth in net income to continue well into the future.

One of the factors increasing sales is the superior warranty Quattro offers. Based on experience, warranty expense in 2024 should be around $40 million. However, in a recent executive meeting, it was suggested the CFO report a larger, more conservative, estimate of warranty expense of $50 million this year.

### Required:
1. Can Quattro use warranty expense to manage its reported amount of net income?
2. Assume net income before warranty expense is $210 million in 2024 and $210 million in 2025, and total warranty expense over the two years is $80 million. Calculate net income after warranty expense based on the suggestion in the executive meeting to report $50 million in warranty expense in 2024. Calculate net income after warranty expense in 2025.
3. Does reporting warranty expense of $50 million in 2024 and $30 million in 2025 produce a steadier growth in net income than does reporting $40 million each year?

## Great Adventures –Part 1

Continuing General
Ledger Case

(This is a continuation of the Great Adventures problem from earlier chapters.)

**RWP9–11** At the end of 2025, the following information is available for Great Adventures.

- Additional interest for five months needs to be accrued on the $30,000, 6% loan obtained on August 1, 2024. Recall that annual interest is paid each July 31.
- Assume $10,000 of the $30,000 loan discussed above is due next year.
- By the end of the year, $20,000 in gift cards have been redeemed. The company had sold gift cards of $25,000 during the year and recorded those as Deferred Revenue.
- Great Adventures is a defendant in litigation involving a biking accident during one of its adventure races. The company believes the likelihood of payment occurring is probable, and the estimated amount to be paid is $12,000.
- For sales of MU watches, Great Adventures offers a warranty against defects for one year. At the end of the year, the company estimates future warranty costs to be $4,000.

*Required:*
1. Record each of the transactions above on December 31, 2025.
2. If the likelihood of payment for the litigation is determined to be reasonably possible, what should Great Adventures record for this possible payment?

The Great Adventures continuing problem also can be assigned using the General Ledger software in Connect. Students will be given an existing trial balance and asked to prepare (1) the journal entries for the transactions above in 2025, (2) financial statements, and (3) closing entries.

## Great Adventures–Part 2

Continuing General
Ledger Case

(This is a continuation of the Great Adventures problem from earlier chapters.)

**RWP9–12** Tony's favorite memories of his childhood were the times he spent with his dad at camp. Tony was daydreaming of those days a bit as he and Suzie jogged along a nature trail and came across a wonderful piece of property for sale. He turned to Suzie and said, "I've always wanted to start a camp where families could get away and spend some quality time together. If we just had the money, I know this would be the perfect place." On November 1, 2025, Great Adventures purchased the land by issuing a $500,000, 6%, 10-year installment note to the seller. Payments of $5,551 are required at the end of each month over the life of the 10-year loan. Each monthly payment of $5,551 includes both interest expense and principal payments (i.e., reduction of the loan amount).

Late that night, Tony exclaimed, "We now have land for our new camp; this has to be the best news ever!" Suzie said, "There's something else I need to tell you. I'm expecting!" They decided right then, if it was a boy, they would name him Venture.

*Required:*
1. Complete the first three rows of an amortization schedule.
2. Record the purchase of land with the issuance of a long-term note payable on November 1, 2025.
3. Record the first two payments on November 30, 2025, and December 31, 2025, and calculate the remaining balance of the note payable as of December 31, 2025.
4. The 12 monthly payments in 2026 (following year) will reduce the note's balance by an additional $38,014. How would the remaining balance of the note payable be reported in the balance sheet as of December 31, 2025?

The Great Adventures continuing problem also can be assigned using the General Ledger software in Connect. Students will be given an existing trial balance and asked to prepare (1) the journal entries for the transactions above in 2025, (2) financial statements, and (3) closing entries.

## BRIEF EXERCISES

**BE9–1** On September 1, 2024, **Southwest Airlines** borrows $41 million, of which $10 million is due next year. Show how Southwest Airlines would report the $41 million debt in its December 31, 2024, balance sheet.

Report current portion of long-term debt **(LO9–1)**

Account for notes
payable and interest
expense (LO9–2)
See JBE9–1 for journal
entries.

**BE9–2**  On November 1, Bahama Cruise Lines borrows $4 million and issues a six-month, 6% note payable. Interest is payable at maturity. How would the issuance of the note on November 1 and the recognition of interest on December 31 affect the financial statements?

Determine interest
expense (LO9–2)

**BE9–3**  On July 1, Alaskan Adventures issues a $160,000, eight-month, 6% note. Interest is payable at maturity. What is the amount of interest expense the company would report on December 31 of the current year?

Record deferred
revenue (LO9–3)

**BE9–4**  On December 18, **Intel** receives $260,000 from a customer toward a cash sale of $2.6 million for computer chips to be completed on January 23. The computer chips had a total production cost of $1.6 million. How will this receipt of cash be reflected in financial statements on December 31?

Determine the current
portion of long-term
debt (LO9–3)

**BE9–5**  **United Airlines** borrowed $500 million from a bank on March 15. The principal amount of this loan is be paid back in equal amounts over the next five years. How will this loan be reflected in the December 31 financial statements?

Calculate warranty
liability (LO9–4)

**BE9–6**  **Sony** introduces a new compact music player to compete with **Apple**'s iPod that carries a two-year warranty against manufacturer's defects. Based on industry experience with similar product introductions, warranty costs are expected to be approximately 3% of sales. By the end of the first year of selling the product, total sales are $31 million, and actual warranty expenditures are $300,000. What amount (if any) should Sony report as a liability at the end of the year?

Determine the
financial statement
effect of a contingent
liability (LO9–4)

**BE9–7**  Consultants notify management of Discount Pharmaceuticals that a stroke medication poses a potential health hazard. Counsel indicates a product recall is probable and is estimated to cost the company $8 million. How will this affect the company's income statement and balance sheet this period?

Account for installment
notes (LO9–5)
See JBE9–2 for journal
entries.

**BE9–8**  On January 1, 2024, Corvallis Carnivals borrows $30,000 to purchase a delivery truck by agreeing to a 5%, five-year loan with the bank. Payments of $566.14 are due at the end of each month, with the first installment due on January 31, 2024. How will the issuance of the note payable and the first monthly payment affect the financial statements?

Account for installment
notes (LO9–5)
See JBE9–3 for journal
entries.

**BE9–9**  On January 1, 2024, Beaver Tours financed the purchase of a new building by borrowing $600,000 from the bank using a 30-year, 6% note payable. Payments of $3,597.30 are due at the end of each month, with the first installment due on January 31, 2024. How will the issuance of the note payable and the first monthly payment affect the financial statements?

Account for leases
(LO9–6)
See JBE9–4 for journal
entries.

**BE9–10** On April 1, 2024, Primer Corp. signs a five-year lease to use office space. The present value of the monthly lease payments is $100,000. How will the financial statements be affected when the lease is signed on April 1, 2024?

Understand balance sheet
effect of leases (LO9–6)

**BE9–11** Suppose a company signs a three-year lease agreement. The lease payments have a present value of $40,000. Prior to signing the lease, the company had total assets of $600,000, total liabilities of $400,000, and total stockholders' equity of $200,000. Calculate the balance of total assets, total liabilities, and total stockholders' equity immediately after signing the lease.

Match bond terms with
their definitions (LO9–7)

**BE9–12** Listed below are terms and definitions associated with bonds. Match (by letter) the bond terms with their definitions. Each letter is used only once.

**Terms**

| | |
|---|---|
| _____ 1. Secured bond. | _____ 4. Serial bond. |
| _____ 2. Unsecured bond. | _____ 5. Callable bond. |
| _____ 3. Term bond. | _____ 6. Convertible bond. |

**Definitions**

a.  Allows the issuer to pay off the bonds early at a fixed price.

b.  Matures in installments.

c.  Secured only by the "full faith and credit" of the issuing corporation.

d.  Allows the investor to transfer each bond into shares of common stock.

e.  Matures on a single date.

f.  Supported by specific assets pledged as collateral by the issuer.

**BE9–13** Pretzelmania, Inc., issues 7%, 10-year bonds at face amount of $70,000 on January 1, 2024. Interest is paid semiannually on June 30 and December 31. How will the issuance of the bonds on January 1 and the first interest payment on June 30, 2024, affect the financial statements?

*Account for bonds issued at face amount and related semiannual interest (LO9–7)*
*See JBE9–5 for journal entries.*

**BE9–14** Airline Accessories has the following current assets: cash, $112 million; receivables, $104 million; inventory, $192 million; and other current assets, $28 million. Airline Accessories has the following liabilities: accounts payable, $118 million; current portion of long-term debt, $45 million; and long-term debt, $33 million. Based on these amounts, calculate the current ratio and the acid-test ratio for Airline Accessories.

*Calculate current ratio and acid-test ratio (LO9–8)*

**BE9–15** For each of the transactions below, determine the effect on (a) the current ratio and (b) the acid-test ratio.
1. Provide services to customers on account.
2. Borrow cash from the bank by signing a long-term note payable.
3. Purchase office supplies with cash.
4. Pay rent for the current period.

*Determine effect of transactions on liquidity ratios (LO9–8)*

**BE9–16** Surf's Up, a manufacturer of surfing supplies and training equipment, has the following selected data ($ in millions):

*Calculate ratios (LO9–8)*

**SURF'S UP**
**Selected Balance Sheet Data:**

|  | 2024 | 2023 |
|---|---|---|
| Total assets | $727 | $718 |
| Interest-bearing debt | 505 | 425 |
| Other liabilities | 123 | 105 |
| Total liabilities | 628 | 530 |
| Total equity | 99 | 188 |

**Selected Income Statement Data:**

|  | 2024 |
|---|---|
| Sales revenue | $795 |
| Interest expense | 15 |
| Tax expense | 44 |
| Net income | 66 |

Based on these amounts, calculate the following ratios for 2024:
1. Debt to equity ratio.
2. Times interest earned ratio.

**BE9–17** Pretzelmania, Inc., issues 7%, 15-year bonds with a face amount of $70,000 for $63,948 on January 1, 2024. The market interest rate for bonds of similar risk and maturity is 8%. Interest is paid semiannually on June 30 and December 31. How will the issuance of the bonds on January 1 and the first interest payment on June 30, 2024, affect the financial statements?

*Account for bonds issued at a discount and related semiannual interest (LO9–9)*
*See JBE9–6 for journal entries.*

**BE9–18** Pretzelmania, Inc., issues 7%, 15-year bonds with a face amount of $70,000 for $76,860 on January 1, 2024. The market interest rate for bonds of similar risk and maturity is 6%. Interest is paid semiannually on June 30 and December 31. How will the issuance of the bonds on January 1 and the first interest payment on June 30, 2024, affect the financial statements?

*Account for bonds issued at a premium and related semiannual interest (LO9–9)*
*See JBE9–7 for journal entries.*

**BE9–19** On January 1, 2024, Lizzy's Lemonade issues 5%, 20-year bonds with a face amount of $100,000 for $88,443, priced to yield 6%. Interest is paid semiannually. What is the amount of interest expense on June 30, 2024, the first interest payment date?

*Calculate interest expense (LO9–9)*

**BE9–20** On January 1, 2024, Lyle's Limeade issues 4%, 10-year bonds with a face amount of $90,000 for $82,985, priced to yield 5%. Interest is paid semiannually. What is the amount of interest expense in the December 31, 2024, annual income statement?

*Calculate interest expense (LO9–9)*

Interpret a bond
amortization schedule
(LO9–9)
See JBE9–8 for journal
entries.

**BE9–21** Presented below is a partial amortization schedule for Discount Pizza. How will the issuance of the bonds and the first interest payment six months later affect the financial statements assuming the face amount of bonds payable is $70,000?

| (1) Period | (2) Cash Paid for Interest | (3) Interest Expense | (4) Increase in Carrying Value | (5) Carrying Value |
|---|---|---|---|---|
| Issue date | | | | $63,948 |
| 1 | $2,450 | $2,558 | $108 | 64,056 |
| 2 | 2,450 | 2,562 | 112 | 64,168 |

Calculate the issue price of bonds (LO9–10)

**BE9–22** Ultimate Butter Popcorn issues 7%, *15-year* bonds with a face amount of $60,000. The market interest rate for bonds of similar risk and maturity is 8%. Interest is paid semiannually. At what price will the bonds issue?

Calculate the issue price of bonds (LO9–10)

**BE9–23** Ultimate Butter Popcorn issues 7%, *20-year* bonds with a face amount of $60,000. The market interest rate for bonds of similar risk and maturity is 6%. Interest is paid semiannually. At what price will the bonds issue?

## EXERCISES

Compare financing alternatives (LO9–1)

**E9–1** Penny Arcades, Inc., is trying to decide between the following two alternatives to finance its new $35 million gaming center:
a. Issue $35 million, 7% note.
b. Issue 1 million shares of common stock for $35 per share.

| | Issue Bonds | Issue Stock |
|---|---|---|
| Operating income | $11,000,000 | $11,000,000 |
| Interest expense (note only) | | |
| Income before tax | | |
| Income tax expense (35%) | | |
| Net income | $ | $ |
| Number of shares | 4,000,000 | 5,000,000 |
| Earnings per share (Net income/# of shares) | $ | $ |

*Required:*
1. Assuming the note or shares of stock are issued at the beginning of the year, complete the income statement for each alternative.
2. Which alternative results in the higher earnings per share?

Determine proper classification of liabilities (LO9–1, 9–2, 9–3, 9–4)

**E9–2** Match (by letter) the correct reporting method for each of the items listed below.

**Reporting Method**

C = Current liability
L = Long-term liability
D = Disclosure note only
N = Not reported

**Item**

| | | | |
|---|---|---|---|
| _____ | 1. Accounts payable. | _____ | 4. Notes payable due next year. |
| _____ | 2. Current portion of long-term debt. | _____ | 5. Notes payable due in two years. |
| _____ | 3. Sales tax collected from customers. | _____ | 6. Advance payments from customers. |

_____ 7. Commercial paper.
_____ 8. Unused line of credit.
_____ 9. A contingent liability with a *probable* likelihood of occurring within the next year and can be estimated.

_____ 10. A contingent liability with a *reasonably possible* likelihood of occurring within the next year and can be estimated.

**E9–3** On November 1, 2024, Aviation Training Corp. borrows $60,000 cash from Community Savings and Loan. Aviation Training signs a three-month, 7% note payable. Interest is payable at maturity. Aviation's year-end is December 31.

*Account for notes payable (LO9–2)*
*See JE9–1 for journal entries.*

**Required:**
1. How will the issuance of the note on November 1, 2024, affect the financial statements?
2. How will accrued interest on December 31, 2024, affect the financial statements?
3. How will the payment of the note and interest at maturity affect the financial statements?

**E9–4** OS Environmental provides cost-effective solutions for managing regulatory requirements and environmental needs specific to the airline industry. Assume on July 1, the company issues a one-year note for the amount of $6 million. Interest is payable at maturity.

*Determine interest expense (LO9–2)*

**Required:**
Determine the amount of interest expense that should be reported in the fiscal year-end income statement under each of the following independent assumptions:

| Interest Rate | Fiscal Year-End |
|---|---|
| 1. 11% | December 31 |
| 2. 9% | September 30 |
| 3. 10% | October 31 |
| 4. 7% | January 31 |

**E9–5** During December, Luxury Cruise Lines incurs employee salaries of $3 million. Withholdings in December are $229,500 for the employee portion of FICA, $450,000 for federal income tax, and $187,500 for state income tax. The company incurs an additional $186,000 for federal and state unemployment tax. These costs and expenses will be paid in January.

*Determine payroll liabilities (LO9–3)*

**Required:**
Determine the amount of accrued payroll and benefit costs Luxury Cruise Lines will report in its December balance sheet.

**E9–6** Pacific Cruise Lines is a defendant in litigation involving a swimming accident on one of its three cruise ships.

*Determine proper treatment of a contingent liability (LO9–4)*

**Required:**
For each of the following scenarios, determine the appropriate way to report the situation. Determine any financial statement effects that may occur.
1. The likelihood of a payment occurring is probable, and the estimated amount is $1.3 million.
2. The likelihood of a payment occurring is probable, and the amount is estimated to be in the range of $1.1 to $1.6 million.
3. The likelihood of a payment occurring is reasonably possible, and the estimated amount is $1.3 million.
4. The likelihood of a payment occurring is remote, while the estimated potential amount is $1.3 million.

**E9–7** Computer Wholesalers restores and resells notebook computers. It originally acquires the notebook computers from corporations upgrading their computer systems, and it backs each notebook it sells with a 90-day warranty against defects. Based on previous experience, Computer Wholesalers expects warranty costs to be approximately 6% of sales. Sales for the

*Analyze and account for contingent liability— warranties (LO9–4)*
*See JE9–2 for journal entries.*

month of December are $600,000. Actual warranty expenditures in January of the following year were $13,000.

**Required:**

1. Does this situation represent a contingent liability? Why or why not?
2. How will the warranties affect the financial statements at the end of December?
3. How will the payment of the actual warranty expenditures of $13,000 in January of the following year affect the financial statements?
4. What is the balance in the Warranty Liability account after the transactions in requirements 2 and 3?

**Analyze disclosure of contingent liabilities (LO9–4)**

**E9–8 Dow Chemical Company** provides chemical, plastic, and agricultural products and services to various consumer markets. The following excerpt is taken from the disclosure notes of Dow's annual report.

> **DOW CHEMICAL**
> **Notes to the Financial Statements (excerpt)**
>
> Dow Chemical had accrued obligations of $381 million for environmental remediation and restoration costs, including $40 million for the remediation of Superfund sites. This is management's best estimate of the costs for remediation and restoration with respect to environmental matters for which the Company has accrued liabilities, although the ultimate cost with respect to these particular matters could range up to twice that amount. Inherent uncertainties exist in these estimates primarily due to unknown conditions, changing governmental regulations and legal standards regarding liability, and evolving technologies for handling site remediation and restoration.

**Required:**

1. Does the excerpt describe a contingent liability?
2. Under what conditions would Dow report such a contingency?
3. How did the $381 million affect Dow's financial statements?

**Account for installment notes (LO9–5)**
*See JE9–3 for journal entries.*

**E9–9** On January 1, 2024, Tropical Paradise borrows $50,000 by agreeing to a 6%, six-year note with the bank. The funds will be used to purchase a new BMW convertible for use in promoting resort properties to potential customers. Loan payments of $828.64 are due at the end of each month, with the first installment due on January 31, 2024.

**Required:**

1. How will the issuance of the installment notes payable affect the financial statements?
2. How will the first two monthly payments affect the financial statements?

**Account for installment notes (LO9–5)**
*See JE9–4 for journal entries.*

**E9–10** On January 1, 2024, Jalen Company purchased land costing $800,000. Instead of paying cash at the time of purchase, Jalen plans to make four installment payments of $215,221.64 on June 30 and December 31 in 2024 and 2025. The payments include interest at a rate of 6%.

**Required:**

1. How will the purchase of land with a note affect the financial statements?
2. How will the first installment payment on June 30, 2024, and the second installment payment on December 31, 2024, affect the financial statements?
3. Calculate the balance of Notes Payable and Interest Expense on December 31, 2024.

**Understand the effect of leases on financial ratios (LO9–6)**

**E9–11** Coney Island enters into a lease agreement for a new ride. The lease payments have a present value of $2 million. Prior to this agreement, the company's total assets are $25 million, and its total liabilities are $15 million.

*Required:*

1. Calculate total stockholders' equity prior to the lease agreement.
2. Prior to the lease being signed, calculate the debt to equity ratio.
3. Immediately after the lease being signed, calculate the debt to equity ratio.
4. Does the direction of the change in the debt to equity ratio typically indicate that the company has higher leverage risk?

**E9–12** On June 1, 2024, Florida National leased a building. The lease agreement calls for Florida National to make lease payments of $3,618.18 each month for the next two years, with the first lease payment beginning June 30. The company's normal borrowing rate is 8%.

Account for leases
(**LO9–6**)
*See JE9–5 for journal entries.*

*Required:*

1. Calculate the present value of the lease payments. Round to the nearest whole dollar. (*Hint:* Use a financial calculator or Excel)
2. How will the signing of the lease agreement on June 1, 2024, affect the financial statements?

**E9–13** On January 1, 2024, Splash City issues $500,000 of 9% bonds, due in 20 years, with interest payable semiannually on June 30 and December 31 each year. The bonds issue at $500,000.

Account for bonds issued at face amount and related *semiannual* interest
(**LO9–7**)
*See JE9–6 for journal entries.*

*Required:*

1. How will the bond issuance on January 1, 2024, affect the financial statements?
2. How will the first two semiannual interest payments on June 30, 2024, and December 31, 2024, affect the financial statements?

**E9–14** On January 1, 2024, White Water issues $600,000 of 7% bonds, due in 10 years, with interest payable semiannually on June 30 and December 31 each year. The bonds issue at $600,000.

Account for bonds issued at face amount and related *semiannual* interest (**LO9–7**)
*See JE9–7 for journal entries.*

*Required:*

1. How will the bond issuance on January 1, 2024, affect the financial statements?
2. How will the first two semiannual interest payments on June 30, 2024, and December 31, 2024, affect the financial statements?

**E9–15** Selected financial data regarding current assets and current liabilities for Queen's Line, a competitor in the cruise line industry, is provided:

Calculate and analyze liquidity ratios (**LO9–8**)

| ($ in millions) | |
| --- | ---: |
| Current assets: | |
| Cash and cash equivalents | $ 331 |
| Current investments | 63 |
| Net receivables | 230 |
| Inventory | 116 |
| Other current assets | 135 |
| Total current assets | $ 875 |
| Current liabilities: | |
| Accounts payable | $1,025 |
| Short-term debt | 694 |
| Other current liabilities | 919 |
| Total current liabilities | $2,638 |

*Required:*

1. Calculate the current ratio and the acid-test ratio for Queen's Line.
2. Compare your calculations with those for United Airlines and American Airlines reported in the chapter text. Which company appears more likely to have difficulty paying its currently maturing debts?

Calculate and analyze
ratios (LO9–8)

**E9–16** Two online travel companies, E-Travel and Pricecheck, provide the following selected financial data:

| | E-Travel | Pricecheck |
|---|---|---|
| Total asset | $7,437,156 | $2,094,224 |
| Interest-bearing debt | 3,900,500 | 405,285 |
| Other liabilities | 353,975 | 81,325 |
| Total stockholders' equity | 3,182,681 | 1,607,614 |
| Sales revenue | $3,455,426 | $2,838,212 |
| Interest expense | 94,233 | 34,084 |
| Tax expense | 174,400 | 57,168 |
| Net income | 319,526 | 509,472 |

*Required:*

1. Calculate the debt to equity ratio for E-Travel and Pricecheck. Which company has the higher solvency ratio?
2. Calculate the times interest earned ratio for E-Travel and Pricecheck. Which company is better able to meet interest payments as they become due?

Account for bonds
issued at a discount
and related *semiannual*
interest (LO9–9)
See JE9–8 for journal
entries.

**E9–17** On January 1, 2024, Splash City issues $500,000 of 9% bonds, due in 20 years, with interest payable semiannually on June 30 and December 31 each year.

*Required:*

Assuming the market interest rate on the issue date is 10%, the bonds will issue at $457,102.

1. Complete the first three rows of an amortization schedule.
2. How will the bond issuance on January 1, 2024, affect the financial statements?
3. How will the first two semiannual interest payments on June 30, 2024, and December 31, 2024, affect the financial statements?

Account for bonds
issued at a premium
and related *semiannual*
interest (LO9–9)
See JE9–9 for journal
entries.

**E9–18** On January 1, 2024, Splash City issues $500,000 of 9% bonds, due in 20 years, with interest payable semiannually on June 30 and December 31 each year.

*Required:*

Assuming the market interest rate on the issue date is 8%, the bonds will issue at $549,482.

1. Complete the first three rows of an amortization schedule.
2. How will the bond issuance on January 1, 2024, affect the financial statements?
3. How will the first two semiannual interest payments on June 30, 2024, and December 31, 2024, affect the financial statements?

Calculate the issue price of
bonds (LO9–10)

**E9–19** On January 1, 2024, Frontier World issues $41 million of 9% bonds, due in 20 years, with interest payable semiannually on June 30 and December 31 each year. The proceeds will be used to build a new ride that combines a roller coaster, a water ride, a dark tunnel, and the great smell of outdoor barbeque, all in one ride.

*Required:*

1. If the market rate is 8%, will the bonds issue at face amount, a discount, or a premium? Calculate the issue price.
2. If the market rate is 9%, will the bonds issue at face amount, a discount, or a premium? Calculate the issue price.
3. If the market rate is 10%, will the bonds issue at face amount, a discount, or a premium? Calculate the issue price.

Calculate the issue price of
bonds (LO9–10)

**E9–20** On January 1, 2024, Water World issues $26 million of 7% bonds, due in 10 years, with interest payable semiannually on June 30 and December 31 each year. Water World intends to use the funds to build the world's largest water avalanche and the "tornado"—a giant outdoor vortex in which riders spin in progressively smaller and faster circles until they drop through a small tunnel at the bottom.

*Required:*

1. If the market rate is 6%, will the bonds issue at face amount, a discount, or a premium? Calculate the issue price.
2. If the market rate is 7%, will the bonds issue at face amount, a discount, or a premium? Calculate the issue price.
3. If the market rate is 8%, will the bonds issue at face amount, a discount, or a premium? Calculate the issue price.

## PROBLEMS

**P9–1** Listed below are several terms and phrases associated with current liabilities. Pair each item from List A (by letter) with the item from List B that is most appropriately associated with it.

Review current liability terms and concepts **(LO9–1)**

| List A | List B |
|---|---|
| _____ 1. An IOU promising to repay the amount borrowed plus interest. | a. Recording of a contingent liability. |
| _____ 2. Payment amount is reasonably possible and is reasonably estimable. | b. Deferred revenue. |
| | c. The riskiness of a business's obligations. |
| _____ 3. Mixture of liabilities and equity a business uses. | d. Disclosure of a contingent liability. |
| | e. Interest on debt. |
| _____ 4. Payment amount is probable and is reasonably estimable. | f. Payroll taxes. |
| | g. Line of credit. |
| _____ 5. A liability that requires the sacrifice of something other than cash. | h. Capital structure. |
| | i. Note payable. |
| _____ 6. Long-term debt maturing within one year. | j. Current portion of long-term debt. |
| _____ 7. FICA and FUTA. | |
| _____ 8. Informal agreement that permits a company to borrow up to a prearranged limit. | |
| _____ 9. Classifying liabilities as either current or long-term helps investors and creditors assess this. | |
| _____ 10. Amount of note payable × annual interest rate × fraction of the year. | |

**P9–2** Precision Castparts, a manufacturer of processed engine parts in the automotive and airline industries, borrows $41 million cash on October 1, 2024, to provide working capital for anticipated expansion. Precision signs a one-year, 9% promissory note to Midwest Bank under a prearranged short-term line of credit. Interest on the note is payable at maturity. Precision Castparts has a December 31 year-end.

Account for notes payable **(LO9–2)**
*See JP9–1A for journal entries.*

*Required:*

1. How will the issuance of the note payable affect the financial statements of Precision Castparts on October 1, 2024?
2. How will the accrued interest on the note payable affect the financial statements of Precision Castparts at the end of the fiscal year (December 31, 2024)?
3. How will the repayment of the note and interest on September 30, 2025, affect the financial statements of Precision Castparts?

**P9–3** The University of Michigan football stadium, built in 1927, is the largest college stadium in America, with a seating capacity of 114,000 fans. Assume the stadium sells out all six home games before the season begins, and the athletic department collects $102.6 million in ticket sales.

Account for deferred revenue **(LO9–3)**

*Required:*

1. What is the average price per season ticket and average price per individual game ticket sold?

2. How will the advance collection of $102.6 million in ticket sales affect the financial statements?

3. How much revenue will the University recognize after the first home game is completed?

Account for contingencies
(LO9–4)

**P9–4** Dinoco Petroleum faces three potential contingency situations, described below. Dinoco's fiscal year ends December 31, 2024, and it issues its 2024 financial statements on March 15, 2025.

**Required:**

Determine the contingent amount Dinoco would report in each situation for the year ended December 31, 2024.

1. In the initial trial in October, Dinoco lost a $130 million lawsuit resulting from a dispute with a supplier. Although Dinoco feels it is probable it will have to pay the full amount, the case is under appeal at the end of the year. Dinoco does not expect the case to have a material adverse effect on the company.

2. In November 2023, the state of Texas filed suit against Dinoco, seeking civil penalties and injunctive relief for violations of environmental laws regulating hazardous waste. On January 12, 2025, Dinoco reached a settlement with state authorities. Based upon discussions with legal counsel, it is probable Dinoco will require $150 million to cover the cost of violations.

3. Dinoco is the plaintiff in a $300 million lawsuit filed against a customer for damages due to lost profits from rejected contracts and for unpaid receivables. The case is in final appeal, and legal counsel advises that it is probable Dinoco will prevail and be awarded $150 million.

Account for and analyze installment notes
(LO9–5)
See JP9–2 for journal entries.

**P9–5** On January 1, 2024, Gundy Enterprises purchases an office building for $360,000, paying $60,000 down and borrowing the remaining $300,000, signing a 7%, 10-year mortgage. Installment payments of $3,483.25 are due at the end of each month, with the first payment due on January 31, 2024.

**Required:**

1. How will the purchase of the building on January 1, 2024, affect the financial statements?

2. Complete the first three rows of an amortization schedule similar to Illustration 9–9.

3. How will the first monthly mortgage payment on January 31, 2024, affect the financial statements? How much of the first payment goes to interest expense, and how much goes to reducing the carrying value of the loan?

4. Total payments over the 10 years are $417,990 ($3,483.25 × 120 monthly payments). How much of this is interest expense, and how much is actual payment of the loan?

Prepare amortization schedule and account for installment notes
(LO9–5)
See JP9–3 for journal entries.

**P9–6A** On January 1, 2024, Strato Corporation borrowed $2 million from a local bank to construct a new building over the next three years. The loan will be paid back in three equal installments of $776,067 on December 31 of each year. The payments include interest at a rate of 8%.

**Required:**

1. How will the loan affect the financial statements on January 1, 2024?

2. Prepare an amortization schedule over the three-year life of the installment note. Round answers to the nearest dollar.

3. How will each of the three equal installment payments affect the financial statements?

Explore the impact of leases on the debt to equity ratio (LO9–6, 9–8)

**P9–7** Thrillville has $41 million in bonds payable. One of the contractual agreements in the bond is that the debt to equity ratio cannot exceed 2.0. Thrillville's total stockholders' equity is $29 million, and its debt other than the bonds payable are $11 million. The company is considering some additional financing through leasing.

**Required:**

1. Calculate the debt to equity ratio before entering any lease agreement.

2. The company enters a lease agreement requiring lease payments with a present value of $16 million. How does the lease agreement affect the financial statements?

3. Recalculate the debt to equity ratio after the lease agreement. Will entering into the lease cause the debt to equity ratio to be in violation of the contractual agreement in the bond?

Account for bonds issued and related interest
(LO9–7, 9–9)
See JP9–4 for journal entries.

**P9–8** On January 1, 2024, Twister Enterprises, a manufacturer of a variety of transportable spin rides, issues $600,000 of 8% bonds, due in 20 years, with interest payable semiannually on June 30 and December 31 each year.

**Required:**

1. If the market interest rate is 8%, the bonds will issue at $600,000. How will the bond issue affect the financial statements on January 1, 2024? How will the first two semiannual interest payments on June 30, 2024, and December 31, 2024, affect the financial statements?
2. If the market interest rate is 9%, the bonds will issue at $544,795. How will the bond issue affect the financial statements on January 1, 2024? How will the first two semiannual interest payments on June 30, 2024, and December 31, 2024, affect the financial statements?
3. If the market interest rate is 7%, the bonds will issue at $664,065. How will the bond issue affect the financial statements on January 1, 2024? How will the first two semiannual interest payments on June 30, 2024, and December 31, 2024, affect the financial statements?

**P9–9** On January 1, 2024, Vacation Destinations issues $40 million of bonds that pay interest semiannually on June 30 and December 31. Portions of the bond amortization schedule appear below:

*Understand a bond amortization schedule (LO9–7, 9–9)*

| (1) Date | (2) Cash Paid for Interest | (3) Interest Expense | (4) Increase in Carrying Value | (5) Carrying Value |
|---|---|---|---|---|
| 1/1/2024 | | | | $37,281,935 |
| 6/30/2024 | $1,400,000 | $1,491,277 | $91,277 | 37,373,212 |
| 12/31/2024 | 1,400,000 | 1,494,928 | 94,928 | 37,468,140 |

**Required:**

1. Were the bonds issued at face amount, a discount, or a premium?
2. What is the original issue price of the bonds?
3. What is the face amount of the bonds?
4. What is the stated annual interest rate?
5. What is the market annual interest rate?
6. What is the total cash paid for interest assuming the bonds mature in 10 years?

**P9–10** Selected financial data regarding current assets and current liabilities for ACME Corporation and Wayne Enterprises are as follows:

*Calculate and analyze ratios (LO9–8)*

| ($ in millions) | ACME Corporation | Wayne Enterprises |
|---|---|---|
| Current assets: | | |
| Cash and cash equivalents | $ 2,494 | $ 541 |
| Current investments | | 125 |
| Net receivables | 1,395 | 217 |
| Inventory | 10,710 | 8,600 |
| Other current assets | 773 | 301 |
| Total current assets | $15,372 | $9,784 |
| Current liabilities | | |
| Current debt | $ 1,321 | $ 47 |
| Accounts payable | 8,871 | 5,327 |
| Other current liabilities | 1,270 | 2,334 |
| Total current liabilities | $11,462 | $7,708 |

**Required:**

1. Calculate the current ratio for ACME Corporation and Wayne Enterprises. Which company has the higher ratio?
2. Calculate the acid-test (quick) ratio for ACME Corporation and Wayne Enterprises. Which company has the higher ratio?
3. How would the purchase of additional inventory on credit affect the current ratio? How would it affect the acid-test ratio?

**Calculate and analyze ratios (LO9–8)**

**P9–11** Selected financial data for Bahama Bay and Caribbean Key are as follows:

| | Bahama Bay | | Caribbean Key | |
| --- | --- | --- | --- | --- |
| | 2024 | 2023 | 2024 | 2023 |
| Total asset | $8,861 | $9,560 | $ 7,640 | $7,507 |
| Interest-bearing debt | 3,895 | 4,105 | 1,215 | 980 |
| Other liabilities | 1,826 | 2,501 | 1,604 | 1,709 |
| Total stockholders' equity | 3,137 | 2,954 | 4,821 | 4,818 |
| Sales revenue | $6,321 | | $ 3,949 | |
| Interest expense | 170 | | 70 | |
| Tax expense | 148 | | 8 | |
| Net income | 562 | | 88 | |

**Required:**

1. Calculate the debt to equity ratio for Bahama Bay and Caribbean Key for the most recent year. Which company has the higher ratio?
2. Calculate the times interest earned ratio for Bahama Bay and Caribbean Key. Which company is better able to meet interest payments as they become due?

**Calculate the issue price of a bond and prepare amortization schedules (LO9–10)**

**P9–12** On January 1, 2024, Coney Island Entertainment issues $1,300,000 of 7% bonds, due in 15 years, with interest payable semiannually on June 30 and December 31 each year.

**Required:**

Calculate the issue price of a bond and complete the first three rows of an amortization schedule when

1. The market interest rate is 7% and the bonds issue at face amount.
2. The market interest rate is 8% and the bonds issue at a discount.
3. The market interest rate is 6% and the bonds issue at a premium.

## JOURNAL ENTRIES

## Journal Entries—Brief Exercises

**Record notes payable (LO9–2)**
*See BE9–2 for financial statement effects.*

**JBE9–1** On November 1, Bahama Cruise Lines borrows $4 million and issues a six-month, 6% note payable. Interest is payable at maturity. Record the issuance of the note and the appropriate adjusting entry for accrued interest at December 31, the end of the reporting period.

**Record installment notes (LO9–5)**
*See BE9–8 for financial statement effects.*

**JBE9–2** On January 1, 2024, Corvallis Carnivals borrows $30,000 to purchase a delivery truck by agreeing to a 5%, five-year loan with the bank. Payments of $566.14 are due at the end of each month, with the first installment due on January 31, 2024. Record the issuance of the note payable and the first monthly payment.

**Record installment notes (LO9–5)**
*See BE9–9 for financial statement effects.*

**JBE9–3** On January 1, 2024, Beaver Tours financed the purchase of a new building by borrowing $600,000 from the bank using a 30-year, 6% note payable. Payments of $3,597.30 are due at the end of each month, with the first installment due on January 31, 2024. Record the issuance of the note payable and the first monthly payment.

**Record leases (LO9–6)**
*See BE9–10 for financial statement effects.*

**JBE9–4** On April 1, 2024, Primer Corp. signs a five-year lease to use office space. The present value of the monthly lease payments is $100,000. Record the lease.

**JBE9–5** Pretzelmania, Inc., issues 7%, 10-year bonds at face amount of $70,000 on January 1, 2024. Interest is paid semiannually on June 30 and December 31. Record the bond issue at January 1, 2024, and the first interest payment on June 30, 2024.

*Record bond issue at face amount and related semiannual interest* **(LO9–7)**
*See BE9–13 for financial statement effects.*

**JBE9–6** Pretzelmania, Inc., issues 7%, 15-year bonds with a face amount of $70,000 for $63,948 on January 1, 2024. The market interest rate for bonds of similar risk and maturity is 8%. Interest is paid semiannually on June 30 and December 31. Record the bond issue at January 1, 2024, and the first interest payment on June 30, 2024.

*Record bond issue at a discount and related semiannual interest* **(LO9–9)**
*See BE9–17 for financial statement effects.*

**JBE9–7** Pretzelmania, Inc., issues 7%, 15-year bonds with a face amount of $70,000 for $76,860 on January 1, 2024. The market interest rate for bonds of similar risk and maturity is 6%. Interest is paid semiannually on June 30 and December 31. Record the issuance of the bond on January 1, 2024, and the first interest payment on June 30, 2024.

*Record bond issue at a premium and related semiannual interest* **(LO9–9)**
*See BE9–18 for financial statement effects.*

**JBE9–8** Presented below is a partial amortization schedule for Discount Pizza. Record the bond issue and the first interest payment assuming the face amount of the bonds is $70,000.

*Interpret a bond amortization schedule* **(LO9–9)**
*See BE9–21 for financial statement effects.*

| (1)<br>Period | (2)<br>Cash Paid<br>for Interest | (3)<br>Interest<br>Expense | (4)<br>Increase in<br>Carrying Value | (5)<br>Carrying<br>Value |
|---|---|---|---|---|
| Issue date | | | | $63,948 |
| 1 | $2,450 | $2,558 | $108 | 64,056 |
| 2 | 2,450 | 2,562 | 112 | 64,168 |

## Journal Entries—Exercises

**JE9–1** On November 1, 2024, Aviation Training Corp. borrows $60,000 cash from Community Savings and Loan. Aviation Training signs a three-month, 7% note payable. Interest is payable at maturity. Aviation's year-end is December 31.

*Record notes payable* **(LO9–2)**
*See E9–3 for financial statement effects.*

*Required:*

1. Record the issuance of the note payable by Aviation Training.
2. Record the appropriate adjusting entry for accrued interest on the note by Aviation Training on December 31, 2024.
3. Record the payment of the note and interest at maturity.

**JE9–2** Computer Wholesalers restores and resells notebook computers. It originally acquires the notebook computers from corporations upgrading their computer systems, and it backs each notebook it sells with a 90-day warranty against defects. Based on previous experience, Computer Wholesalers expects warranty costs to be approximately 6% of sales. Sales for the month of December are $600,000. Actual warranty expenditures in January of the following year were $13,000.

*Analyze and record a contingent liability— warranties* **(LO9–4)**
*See E9–7 for financial statement effects.*

*Required:*

1. Record warranty expense and warranty liability for the month of December based on 6% of sales.
2. Record the payment of the actual warranty expenditures of $13,000 in January of the following year.

**JE9–3** On January 1, 2024, Tropical Paradise borrows $50,000 by agreeing to a 6%, six-year note with the bank. The funds will be used to purchase a new BMW convertible for use in promoting resort properties to potential customers. Loan payments of $828.64 are due at the end of each month, with the first installment due on January 31, 2024.

*Record installment notes* **(LO9–5)**
*See E9–9 for financial statement effects.*

*Required:*

Record the issuance of the installment note payable and the first two monthly payments.

Record installment notes
(LO9–5)
See E9–10 for financial
statement effects.

**JE9–4** On January 1, 2024, Jalen Company purchased land costing $800,000. Instead of paying cash at the time of purchase, Jalen plans to make four installment payments of $215,221.64 on June 30 and December 31 in 2024 and 2025. The payments include interest at a rate of 6%.

*Required:*

1. Record the purchase of land when the note is issued.
2. Record the first installment payment on June 30, 2024, and the second installment payment on December 31, 2024.
3. Calculate the balance of Notes Payable and Interest Expense on December 31, 2024.

Record leases  (LO9–6)
See E9–12 for financial
statement effects.

**JE9–5** On June 1, 2024, Florida National leased a building. The lease agreement calls for Florida National to make lease payments of $3,618.18 each month for the next two years, with the first lease payment beginning June 30. The company's normal borrowing rate is 8%.

*Required:*

1. Calculate the present value of the lease payments. Round to the nearest whole dollar. (*Hint:* Use a financial calculator or Excel)
2. Record the lease on June 1, 2024.

Record bonds issued at
face amount and related
*semiannual* interest
(LO9–7)
See E9–13 for financial
statement effects.

**JE9–6** On January 1, 2024, Splash City issues $500,000 of 9% bonds, due in 20 years, with interest payable semiannually on June 30 and December 31 each year.

*Required:*

Assuming the market interest rate on the issue date is 9%, the bonds will issue at $500,000. Record the bond issue on January 1, 2024, and the first two semiannual interest payments on June 30, 2024, and December 31, 2024.

Record bonds issued at
face amount and related
*semiannual* interest
(LO9–7)
See E9–14 for financial
statement effects.

**JE9–7** On January 1, 2024, White Water issues $600,000 of 7% bonds, due in 10 years, with interest payable semiannually on June 30 and December 31 each year.

*Required:*

Assuming the market interest rate on the issue date is 7%, the bonds will issue at $600,000. Record the bond issue on January 1, 2024, and the first two semiannual interest payments on June 30, 2024, and December 31, 2024.

Record bonds issued at
a discount and related
*semiannual* interest
(LO9–9)
See E9–17 for financial
statement effects.

**JE9–8** On January 1, 2024, Splash City issues $500,000 of 9% bonds, due in 20 years, with interest payable semiannually on June 30 and December 31 each year.

*Required:*

Assuming the market interest rate on the issue date is 10%, the bonds will issue at $457,102.
1. Complete the first three rows of an amortization schedule.
2. Record the bond issue on January 1, 2024, and the first two semiannual interest payments on June 30, 2024, and December 31, 2024.

Record bonds issued at
a premium and related
*semiannual* interest
(LO9–9)
See E9–18 for financial
statement effects.

**JE9–9** On January 1, 2024, Splash City issues $500,000 of 9% bonds, due in 20 years, with interest payable semiannually on June 30 and December 31 each year.

*Required:*

Assuming the market interest rate on the issue date is 8%, the bonds will issue at $549,482.
1. Complete the first three rows of an amortization schedule.
2. Record the bond issue on January 1, 2024, and the first two semiannual interest payments on June 30, 2024, and December 31, 2024.

## Journal Entries—Problems

Record notes payable
(LO9–2)
See P9–2 for financial
statement effects.

**JP9–1** Precision Castparts, a manufacturer of processed engine parts in the automotive and airline industries, borrows $41 million cash on October 1, 2024, to provide working capital for anticipated expansion. Precision signs a one-year, 9% promissory note to Midwest Bank under a prearranged short-term line of credit. Interest on the note is payable at maturity. Precision Castparts has a December 31 year-end.

*Required:*

1. Prepare the journal entry on October 1, 2024, to record the issuance of the note payable for Precision Castparts.
2. Record the adjusting entry for accrued interest on December 31, 2024, for Precision Castparts.
3. Prepare the journal entry on September 30, 2025, to record payment of the note and interest for Precision Castparts.

**JP9–2** On January 1, 2024, Gundy Enterprises purchases an office building for $360,000, paying $60,000 down and borrowing the remaining $300,000, signing a 7%, 10-year mortgage. Installment payments of $3,483.25 are due at the end of each month, with the first payment due on January 31, 2024.

*Required:*

1. Record the purchase of the building on January 1, 2024.
2. Complete the first three rows of an amortization schedule similar to Illustration 9–9.
3. Record the first monthly mortgage payment on January 31, 2024. How much of the first payment goes to interest expense, and how much goes to reducing the carrying value of the loan?
4. Total payments over the 10 years are $417,990 ($3,483.25 × 120 monthly payments). How much of this is interest expense, and how much is actual payment of the loan?

> Record and analyze installment notes
> **(LO9–5)**
> *See P9–5 for financial statement effects.*

**JP9–3** On January 1, 2024, Strato Corporation borrowed $2 million from a local bank to construct a new building over the next three years. The loan will be paid back in three equal installments of $776,067 on December 31 of each year. The payments include interest at a rate of 8%.

*Required:*

1. Record the cash received when the note is issued.
2. Prepare an amortization schedule over the three-year life of the installment note. Round answers to the nearest dollar.
3. Use amounts from the amortization schedule to record each installment payment.

> Prepare amortization schedule and record installment notes
> **(LO9–5)**
> *See P9–6 for financial statement effects.*

**JP9–4** On January 1, 2024, Twister Enterprises, a manufacturer of a variety of transportable spin rides, issues $600,000 of 8% bonds, due in 20 years, with interest payable semiannually on June 30 and December 31 each year.

*Required:*

1. If the market interest rate is 8%, the bonds will issue at $600,000. Record the bond issue on January 1, 2024, and the first two semiannual interest payments on June 30, 2024, and December 31, 2024.
2. If the market interest rate is 9%, the bonds will issue at $544,795. Record the bond issue on January 1, 2024, and the first two semiannual interest payments on June 30, 2024, and December 31, 2024.
3. If the market interest rate is 7%, the bonds will issue at $664,065. Record the bond issue on January 1, 2024, and the first two semiannual interest payments on June 30, 2024, and December 31, 2024.

> Record bond issue and related interest
> **(LO9–7, 9–9)**
> *See P9–8 for financial statement effects.*

## DATA ANALYTICS

Visit Connect to view **Data Analytics** questions related to:

1. Applying Excel
2. Data Visualizations
3. Tableau Dashboard Activities
4. Applying Tableau

## ANSWERS TO THE SELF-STUDY QUESTIONS

1. d   2. c   3. a   4. c   5. b   6. d   7. a   8. b   9. c   10. d   11. a   12. b   13. b   14. c   15. b   16. d   17. b   18. b   19. d

# 10

# Stockholders' Equity

## Feature Story

# The Evolving Equity Market

When a company first issues stock to the public, it is called an initial public offering (IPO). The public equity market was once the primary place for a company to raise significant amounts of equity capital via an IPO. In the 1980s and 1990s, the market averaged over 300 IPOs a year. However, in more recent decades, the average number of annual IPOs has declined to half that. In the past, the end-game for a successful private start-up company (sometimes referred to as a unicorn company) was an IPO, which would greatly enrich the founders and early investors. However, the trend suggests the glamor of an IPO is diminishing.

Pinning down a single root cause for the decline in IPO activity is challenging. Rather, there are likely several factors at play. First, issuing public stock subjects the company to substantial disclosure requirements—private companies (i.e., those without publicly issued stock) don't have to provide financial statements to the investing public. Second, there is substantial and increasing access to private capital, such as financing from hedge funds, private equity funds, and endowments. Third, many companies have access to debt financing that is cheaper than ever before. Finally, company founders seem to have changing preferences for issuing stock, which by its nature, dilutes the ownership and control of the company across thousands of investors.

Having public equity leads the company to significantly more market pressures, and founders seem less willing to deal with those pressures.

Regardless of the trend in IPOs, a number of companies continue to have IPOs, including the unicorns, **Uber** and **Lyft**. Uber's IPO brought in over $8 billion in cash and valued the company at $82 billion dollars. Other major recent IPOs include **Zoom Video**, **Pinterest**, **DoorDash**, **Zscalar**, **Snap**, **Slack**, and **Airbnb**. Some companies with clear opportunities to go public, such as **Cargill**, choose to remain private and forgo the opportunity to raise cash through stock issuance.

Other equity-related activities are changing too. Companies are increasingly engaging in share repurchases as a way to return cash to investors, while at the same time, companies are paying less in cash dividends than in the past. Finally, companies are paying their employees more frequently with stock-based compensation. Clearly, the market for equity is evolving.

This chapter discusses the accounting for these major issues related to shareholders' equity. In particular, the chapter discusses the reporting of stock issuances, stock repurchases, stock splits, cash dividends, and stock-based compensation. The chapter concludes with an analysis of the equity for a company that was once a unicorn, **Facebook**, as well as for one of the most stable tech companies in the market, **IBM**.

**Common Terms**
Stockholders' equity
sometimes is referred to
as shareholders' equity.

A major decision for a manager is how to raise capital for the company. The manager must consider whether to finance the company via debt, equity, or most commonly, both. The previous chapter discusses financing with debt, such as notes, leases, and bonds. In this chapter, we'll examine financing with equity, which entails exchanging ownership of the company for capital. We focus on the financial statement impact of major equity transactions, including issuing stock, stock repurchases, paying dividends, and stock splits.

Recall the accounting equation, which captures the intuition that a company's assets arise from one of two forms of financing: debt financing or equity financing. Illustration 10–1 shows the primary components of stockholders' equity.

**ILLUSTRATION 10–1**

Accounting Equation and Components of Stockholders' Equity

| Assets (resources) | = | Liabilities (creditors' claims) | + | Stockholders' Equity (owners' claims) |
|---|---|---|---|---|

**Primary Components of Stockholders' Equity**

1. **Contributed capital** is the amount stockholders have invested in the company.
2. **Retained earnings** is the amount of earnings the company has kept or retained—that is, the earnings not distributed in dividends to stockholders over the life of the company.
3. **Treasury stock** is a company's own issued stock that it has repurchased.
4. **Accumulated other comprehensive income (AOCI)** is the accumulation of components of other comprehensive income, including unrealized gains and losses from available-for-sale debt investments and other items related to foreign currency translation, derivatives, and pensions.*

*See Chapter 2 for a discussion of AOCI and comprehensive income.

In Part A of the chapter, we discuss transactions involving invested or paid-in capital. A better description might be "contributed capital" since it's the amount stockholders *contribute* when they purchase a company's stock. This discussion includes treasury stock for company repurchases of its own shares. In Part B, we examine transactions involving retained earnings. A better description might be "earned capital," since it's the amount the company *earned* for the stockholders and retained in the business. In Part C, we look at the reporting of total stockholders' equity.

**PART A**

# CONTRIBUTED CAPITAL

**Contributed capital** is the amount of money paid into a company by its owners. That is why contributed capital is sometimes called "invested capital," because it represents owner investments of capital to the business. While sole proprietorships and partnerships are the most common form of business ownership, corporations are typically far larger in terms of total sales, assets, earnings, and employees. A **corporation** is an entity that is legally separate from its owners and even pays its own income taxes. Most corporations are owned by many stockholders, although some corporations are owned entirely by one individual.

## Corporations: Advantages and Disadvantages

**■ LO10–1**

Identify the advantages and disadvantages of the corporate form of ownership.

Corporations are formed in accordance with the laws of individual states. The state incorporation laws guide corporations as they write their **articles of incorporation** (sometimes called the corporate charter). The articles of incorporation describe (a) the nature of the firm's business activities, (b) the shares of stock to be issued, and (c) the initial board of directors. The board of directors establishes corporate policies and appoints officers who manage the corporation. Illustration 10–2 presents an **organization chart** tracing the line of authority for a typical corporation.

**ILLUSTRATION 10-2**

Organization Chart

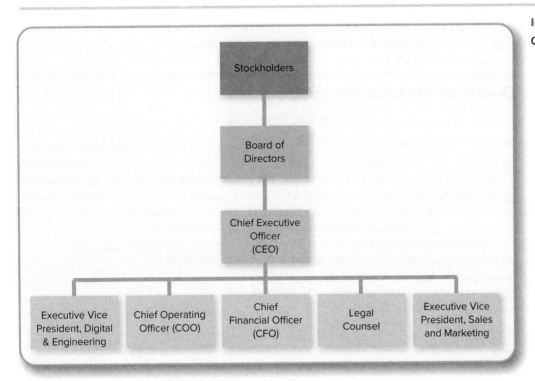

Ultimately, stockholders control the company. They are the owners of the corporation. By voting their shares, stockholders determine the makeup of the board of directors, which in turn appoints the management to run the company.

Corporations may be either public or private. The stock of a publicly held corporation trades on a public market (or exchange), such as the New York Stock Exchange (NYSE) or Nasdaq. Most of the companies we've highlighted in this book, such as **Amazon, Netflix,** and **Pinterest,** are publicly held corporations.

A privately held corporation does not allow investment by the general public and normally has fewer stockholders than a public corporation. Three of the largest private corporations in the United States are **Cargill** (agricultural commodities), **Koch Industries** (oil and gas), and **Mars** (food and candy). Generally, corporations whose stock is privately held do not need to file financial statements with the SEC.

Corporations offer their owners certain **rights** and allow for certain **advantages** over sole proprietorships and partnerships.

1. The right to vote (including electing the board of directors).
2. The right to receive dividends.
3. The right to share in the distribution of assets if the company is dissolved.
4. Limited liability.
5. Greater ability to raise capital and transfer ownership.

Limited liability guarantees that stockholders in a corporation can lose no more than the amount they invested in the company, even in the event of bankruptcy. In contrast, owners in a sole proprietorship or a partnership can be held personally liable for debts the company has incurred, above and beyond the investment they have made.

However, corporations also have **disadvantages,** such as:

1. Additional taxes (often referred to as double taxation).
2. More paperwork imposed by federal and state governments and by securities regulators.

Double taxation refers to the current legal requirement where owners of a corporation are taxed twice—once at the corporate level on the company's earnings and then again at the individual level when those earnings are distributed to stockholders in dividends. In contrast, owners of sole proprietorships and partnerships are taxed once when they include their share of earnings in their personal income tax returns.

# Decision Maker's Perspective

### Limited Liability *and* Beneficial Tax Treatment

Wouldn't it be nice to get the best of both worlds—enjoy the limited liability of a corporation and the tax benefits of a sole proprietorship or partnership? An S corporation allows a company to enjoy limited liability as a corporation but tax treatment as a partnership. Because of these benefits, many companies that qualify choose to incorporate as S corporations. One of the major restrictions is that the corporation cannot have more than 100 stockholders, so S corporations appeal more to smaller, less widely held businesses.

Two additional business forms have evolved in response to liability issues and tax treatment—*limited liability companies* (LLCs) and *limited liability partnerships* (LLPs). Most accounting firms in the United States adopt one of these two business forms because they offer limited liability and avoid double taxation, but with no limits on the number of owners as in an S corporation.

 **KEY POINT**

The primary advantages of the corporate form of business are limited liability and the ability to raise capital. The primary disadvantages are additional taxes and more paperwork.

# Common Stock

■ **LO10–2**
Understand the issuance of common stock.

We can think of the common stockholders as the true "owners" of the business. In most cases, each share of common stock represents one unit of ownership.

## AUTHORIZED, ISSUED, OUTSTANDING, AND TREASURY STOCK

For our discussion in this chapter, we need to make clear the different types of shares.

• Authorized stock is the total number of shares available to sell, as stated in the company's articles of incorporation.
• Issued stock is the number of shares that have been sold to investors. A company usually does not issue all its authorized stock.

The total number of issued shares can then be divided into two categories.

• Outstanding stock is the number of issued shares held *by investors*. Only these shares receive dividends.
• Treasury stock is the number of issued shares repurchased *by the company*.

Illustration 10–3 summarizes the differences among authorized, issued, outstanding, and treasury stock.

**ILLUSTRATION 10–3**

Authorized, Issued, Outstanding, and Treasury Stock

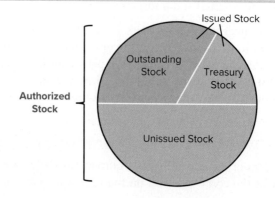

| Types of Stock | Definition |
|---|---|
| Authorized | Shares available to sell (= Issued + Unissued) |
| Issued | Shares actually sold (= Outstanding + Treasury) |
| Outstanding | Shares issued and held *by investors* |
| Treasury | Shares issued and repurchased *by the company* |

## Manager Analysis

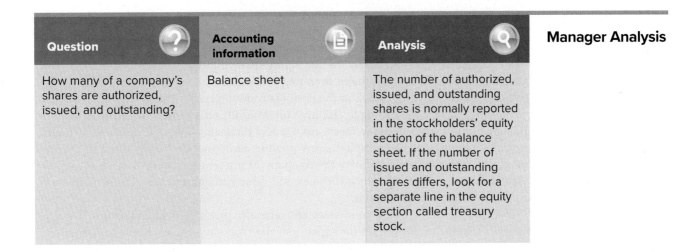

| Question | Accounting information | Analysis |
|---|---|---|
| How many of a company's shares are authorized, issued, and outstanding? | Balance sheet | The number of authorized, issued, and outstanding shares is normally reported in the stockholders' equity section of the balance sheet. If the number of issued and outstanding shares differs, look for a separate line in the equity section called treasury stock. |

To illustrate the concepts of authorized, issued, outstanding and treasury shares, let's take a look at the annual report of **Applied Materials**, a large manufacturer of semiconductors. Illustration 10–4 provides its disclosure of number of shares. As you can see, shares issued equals the sum of shares outstanding and treasury stock.

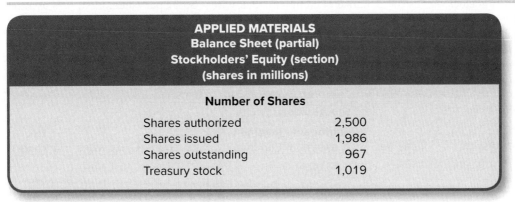

**APPLIED MATERIALS**
**Balance Sheet (partial)**
**Stockholders' Equity (section)**
**(shares in millions)**

| Number of Shares | |
|---|---|
| Shares authorized | 2,500 |
| Shares issued | 1,986 |
| Shares outstanding | 967 |
| Treasury stock | 1,019 |

**ILLUSTRATION 10–4**

Number of Shares for Applied Materials

## PAR VALUE

Par value is the legal capital per share of stock assigned when the corporation is first established. Par value originally indicated the real value of a company's shares of stock. Today, **par value has no relationship to the market value of the common stock.** For instance, **Facebook**'s common stock has traded above $100 per share since 2015, but it has a par value of $0.000006 per share.

Laws in many states permit corporations to issue no-par stock. No-par value stock is common stock that has not been assigned a par value. Many new corporations, and even some established corporations such as **Nike** or **Procter & Gamble**, issue no-par value common stock.

**COMMON MISTAKE**

Some students confuse par value with market value. Par value is the legal capital per share that is set when the corporation is first established and actually is unrelated to "value." The market value per share is equal to the current share price. In most cases, the market value per share will far exceed the par value.

## COMMON STOCK ISSUANCE

Equity financing typically follows a progression of financing stages, in which the company seeks out capital from more and more investors until it ultimately leads to a public offering. In the beginning, most corporations raise money by selling stock to the founders of the business and their friends and family. As the equity financing needs of the corporation grow, companies seek outside investment from angel investors and venture capital firms. Angel investors are wealthy individuals in the business community, like those featured in the television show *Shark Tank*, willing to risk investment funds on a promising business venture. Individual angel investors may invest from a few thousand dollars to millions of dollars in the corporation. Venture capital firms provide additional financing, often in the millions, for a percentage ownership in the company. Many venture capital firms look to invest in promising companies to which they can add value through business contacts, financial expertise, or marketing channels.

Through this stage, these companies are generally privately held companies. Then, as success broadens opportunities for expansion, the corporation may choose to "go public." The first time a corporation issues stock to the public is called an initial public offering (IPO).

When a company issues stock to an equity investor—angel investors, venture capitalists, or common shareholders via an IPO—it typically does so in exchange for cash. Thus, the issuance of stock will affect two general accounts on the balance sheet: Cash and Common Stock. Let's look at how the issuance of common stock affects the balance sheet of a hypothetical healthcare information company, Sakul Analytics.

We'll consider two different scenarios for Sakul Analytics: the issuance of no-par common stock versus the issuance of common stock with a $0.01 par value. First, let's assume Sakul issues 1,000 shares of no-par value common stock at $30 per share. What are the effects on the financial statements?

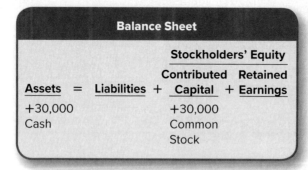

As it turns out, the issuance of no-par stock has no effect on the income statement. Instead, issuing no-par stock increases assets via Cash and increases equity via Common Stock.

If the company issues par value stock rather than no-par value stock, the Cash account is still involved, but now there are two equity accounts involved: Common Stock and Additional Paid-in Capital. The balance of Common Stock increases by the proceeds of the stock issuance up to the par value, while the balance of Additional Paid-in Capital increases by the portion of the cash proceeds above par value.

For example, assume that Sakul Analytics issues 1,000 shares of $0.01 par value common stock at $30 per share. The transaction would increase Cash in the balance sheet (as with the no-par example). The issuance would also increase Common Stock by the par value of the shares, $10 (= 1,000 shares × $0.01) and increase Additional Paid-in Capital for the portion of the cash proceeds above par value, $29,990.

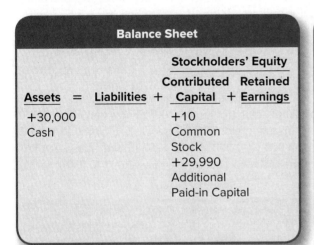

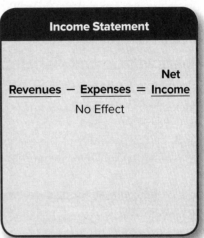

| DEBITS & CREDITS | | |
|---|---|---|
| Sakul Analytics would record the common stock issuance (par) as | Debit | Credit |
| Cash (= 1,000 shares × $30).............................................................. | 30,000 | |
| Common Stock (= 1,000 shares × $0.01)............................................. | | 10 |
| Additional Paid-in Capital (difference)............................................. | | 29,990 |

Cash
30,000

Common Stock
10

Additional
Paid-in Capital
29,990

 **KEY POINT**

If no-par value stock is issued, the corporation increases Cash and Common Stock. If par value or stated value stock is issued, the corporation increases Cash and two equity accounts—Common Stock at the par value per share and Additional Paid-in Capital for the portion above par value.

## Preferred Stock

In order to attract wider investment, some corporations issue preferred stock in addition to common stock. For example, **Wells Fargo** has issued over $23 billion in preferred stock. Preferred stock is "preferred" over common stock in two ways:

**■ LO10–3**
Understand the issuance of preferred stock.

1. Preferred stockholders usually have first rights to a specified amount of dividends (a stated dollar amount per share or a percentage of par value per share). If the board of directors declares dividends, preferred shareholders will receive the designated dividend before common shareholders receive any.

2. Preferred stockholders receive preference over common stockholders in the distribution of assets in the event the corporation is dissolved.

About 20% of the largest U.S. companies have issued preferred stock. However, unlike common stock, most preferred stock does not have voting rights. Control of the company remains with common stockholders.

It is important to note that the categories of stock (common vs. preferred) can change over time with changing circumstances at the company. Many privately-held startup companies issue preferred stock to the founders and early investors. These shares represent a way for these investors to maintain ownership rights that are different than the common stock issued to other investors. Some of these preferred shares have voting rights, and others don't. Once the company goes public via an IPO, the founders' preferred stock typically converts to common stock. For example, **Snap Inc.** (parent company of Snapchat) raised over $1 billion in cash *prior* to its IPO by issuing preferred stock to the founder and other early investors. Once the company went public via an IPO, it raised an additional $2.7 billion in cash by issuing common stock; at the same time, the preferred stock held by early investors converted into common stock—the same kind of common stock that any of us could buy on any given day.

### PREFERRED STOCK ISSUANCE

Issuing preferred stock has a similar effect on the balance sheet as does issuing common stock at par. For example, assume that Sakul Analytics issues 1,000 shares of $30 par value preferred stock at $40 per share. The transaction would increase Cash, increase Preferred Stock by the par value of the shares, $30,000 (= 1,000 shares × $30), and increase Additional Paid-in Capital for the portion of the cash proceeds above par value, $10,000.

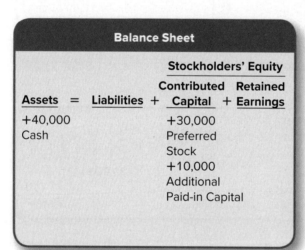

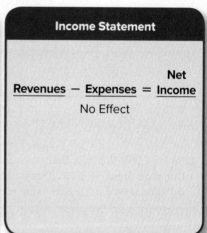

Cash

| 40,000 | |

Preferred Stock

| | 30,000 |

Additional
Paid-in Capital

| | 10,000 |

**DEBITS & CREDITS**

Sakul Analytics would record the preferred stock issuance (par) as

| | Debit | Credit |
|---|---|---|
| **Cash** (= 1,000 shares × $40)............................................................... | **40,000** | |
| **Preferred Stock** (= 1,000 shares × $30)............................................... | | **30,000** |
| **Additional Paid-in Capital** (difference)............................................... | | **10,000** |

Illustration 10–5 displays the stockholders' equity section of the balance sheet for Sakul Analytics following the issuance of both common and preferred stock. The balance of retained earnings is discussed later in this chapter.

### DIVIDENDS FOR PREFERRED STOCK

One of the key features of preferred stock is the payment of dividends—companies that issue preferred stock generally commit to pay dividends to the preferred shareholders. These dividends typically have a fixed, preset dividend rate and typically are paid quarterly. The computation of the preferred dividend is directly tied to its par value:

**Preferred dividend per share = Par value × Dividend rate**

| SAKUL ANALYTICS  Balance Sheet (partial) | |
|---|---|
| Stockholders' equity: | |
| Preferred stock, $30 par value; 100,000 shares authorized; | |
| 1,000 shares issued and outstanding | $ 30,000 |
| Common stock, $0.01 par value; 1 million shares authorized; | |
| 1,000 shares issued and outstanding | 10 |
| Additional paid-in capital | 39,990 |
| Total contributed capital | 70,000 |
| Retained earnings | 30,000 |
| Total stockholders' equity | $100,000 |

The par value and dividend rate are both publicly available to investors, who will consider the preferred dividend as they make the decision of whether to invest in preferred stock. Although preferred dividends are preset at issuance, they are not guaranteed—a company can generally fail to pay a preferred dividend without direct consequences, although shareholders will likely be disappointed.

**Debt or Equity.**   Is preferred stock considered debt or equity? The answer to this question is not as straightforward as you might think because the attributes of preferred stock have some similarities to those of common stock (equity) and some to those of long-term debt (liabilities). Preferred stock does provide equity ownership in the company but without voting rights that accrue to common shareholders. Preferred stock generally pays out a consistent dividend that is akin to an interest payment made for long-term debt, such as a bond. Illustration 10–6 provides a comparison of common stock, preferred stock, and bonds along several dimensions. In short, preferred stock has attributes of both equity and debt.

| Factor | Common Stock | Preferred Stock | Bonds |
|---|---|---|---|
| Voting rights | Yes | Usually no | No |
| Risk to the investor | Highest | Middle | Lowest |
| Expected return to the investor | Highest | Middle | Lowest |
| Preference for dividends/interest | Lowest | Middle | Highest |
| Preference in distribution of assets | Lowest | Middle | Highest |
| Tax deductibility of payments | No | Usually no | Yes |

**KEY POINT**

Preferred stock has preference over common stock in receiving dividends and in the distribution of assets in the event the corporation is dissolved. Issuing preferred stock increases Cash, Preferred Stock, and Additional Paid-in Capital in the balance sheet. The preferred dividend per share is equal to the par value times the dividend rate.

## Share Repurchases

■ **LO10–4**
Account for share
repurchases.

The previous section discusses the issuance of common and preferred stock. In this section, we look at what happens when companies buy back or "repurchase" shares they have previously issued.[1] **Treasury stock** is the name given to a company's own issued stock that it has repurchased.

Over two-thirds of all publicly traded companies report treasury stock in their balance sheets. Illustration 10–7 provides a summary of cash dividends and stock repurchases for the 1,000 largest companies in the U.S.

*Common Terms*
Purchases of treasury stock are commonly referred to as *buybacks* or *repurchases of treasury stock.*

For the 1,000 largest U.S. companies, stock repurchases are larger than cash dividends paid in recent years. In addition, cash dividends are relatively steady over time, while stock repurchases are more volatile. Both cash dividends and stock repurchases return cash to investors, but companies have different reasons for choosing which method to return that cash.

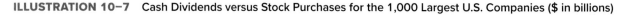

**ILLUSTRATION 10–7**   Cash Dividends versus Stock Purchases for the 1,000 Largest U.S. Companies ($ in billions)

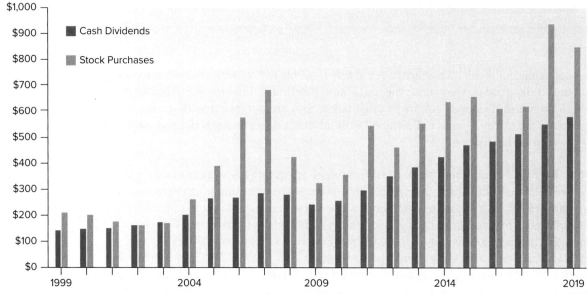

Source: Standard & Poor's

## Decision Maker's Perspective

### Why Corporations Repurchase Their Stock

What would motivate a company to buy back its own stock? Companies acquire their own stock for various reasons:

1. **To boost underpriced stock.** When company management believes the market price of its stock is too low, it may attempt to support the price by decreasing the supply of stock in the marketplace. An announcement by **Johnson & Johnson** that it planned to buy up to $5 billion of its outstanding shares triggered a public buying spree that pushed the stock price up by more than 3%.

2. **To distribute surplus cash without paying dividends.** While dividends usually are a good thing, investors do pay personal income tax on them. Another way for a

---

[1]The common term for a company buying back its stock is a "share repurchase." However, the word repurchase is somewhat of a misnomer because it implies a *repeat purchase* of stock, when in reality, the company is simply buying back stock. However, throughout the book, we maintain the convention used by market participants by using the term "share repurchase" to denote a stock buyback.

company to distribute surplus cash to shareholders without giving them taxable *dividend* income is to use the excess cash to repurchase its own stock. Under a stock repurchase, only shareholders selling back their stock to the company at a profit incur taxable income.

3.  **To boost earnings per share.** Earnings per share is calculated as earnings divided by the number of shares outstanding. Stock repurchases reduce the number of shares outstanding, thereby increasing earnings per share. However, with less cash in the company, it may become more difficult for companies to maintain the same level of earnings following a share repurchase.

4.  **To satisfy employee stock ownership plans.** Another motivation for stock repurchases is to acquire shares used in employee stock award and stock option compensation programs. Microsoft, for example, reported that its board of directors had approved a program to repurchase shares of its common stock to offset the increase in shares from stock option and stock repurchase plans.

## ACCOUNTING FOR TREASURY STOCK

Treasury stock is the purchase of a company's own issued stock. **Just as issuing shares increases stockholders' equity, buying back those shares decreases stockholders' equity.** Unlike other equity accounts, however, treasury stock is a *contra-equity account*. What does that mean? It means the more of its own stock a company purchases, the less stock is available for the other shareholders. Therefore, increases in treasury stock reduce the amount of equity in the balance sheet. In fact, because treasury stock is a contra-equity account, it shows up in the balance sheet as "negative" equity. For example, take a look at a recent balance sheet for Boeing in Illustration 10–8.

**ILLUSTRATION 10–8**

Shareholders' Equity for Boeing in the Balance Sheet

| THE BOEING COMPANY Balance Sheet (partial) ($ in millions) | |
| --- | --- |
| Common stock (at par value, $5.00) | $ 5,061 |
| Additional paid-in capital | 6,768 |
| Treasury stock, at cost | (52,348) |
| Retained earnings | 55,941 |
| Accumulated other comprehensive loss | (15,083) |
| Total shareholders' equity | $ 339 |

Boeing has had a major stock repurchase program over the past few decades. On the balance sheet, the cumulative effect of the many years' worth of Boeing's stock repurchases shows up as negative equity (treasury stock) to the tune of *negative* $52 billion dollars.

Boeing also uses the phrase "at cost" to describe the balance of treasury stock. This phrase captures the notion that treasury stock affects the balance sheet based on the *historical cost* to repurchase the shares in the market. That is, even though the subsequent market price of the shares will change over time, the balance sheet will not be updated based on these price changes—the amount of treasury stock on the balance sheet will always be its cost on the purchase date.

**COMMON MISTAKE**

Sometimes students confuse the purchase of treasury stock with investments in another company. An equity investment is the purchase of stock *in another corporation,* and we report it as an increase in assets. Treasury stock is the purchase of a *corporation's own stock,* and we report it as a reduction in stockholders' equity.

Let's continue our example for Sakul Analytics. Assume it repurchases 100 shares of its own $0.01 par value common stock at $30 per share. The balance sheet effects of this stock repurchase are as follows:

An increase in treasury stock, denoted by the up arrow because it increases a contra-equity account, leads to a decrease in contributed capital, and vice versa.

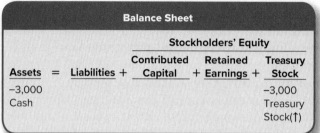

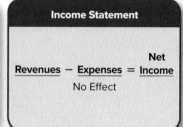

Treasury Stock

| 3,000 | |

Cash

| | 3,000 |

**DEBITS & CREDITS**

We record the stock repurchase as follows:

| | Debit | Credit |
|---|---|---|
| Treasury stock (at cost, 100 shares × $30)................................................. | **3,000** | |
|    Cash................................................................................................. | | **3,000** |

It's important to highlight several things. First, and most importantly, the overall equity of the company is reduced by the $3,000 increase in Treasury Stock—an increase to a contra-equity account (treasury stock) decreases stockholders' equity. Second, the income statement is unaffected by the purchase of treasury stock. Third, the stock's par value has no bearing on the balance sheet effect of stock repurchases.

Illustration 10–9 displays the stockholders' equity section of the balance sheet before and after the purchase of treasury stock. Treasury stock is reported as a contra equity, or negative amount, because treasury stock reduces total stockholders' equity.[2]

**ILLUSTRATION 10–9**

Stockholders' Equity before and after Purchase of Treasury Stock

| SAKUL ANALYTICS Balance Sheet (partial) | | |
|---|---|---|
| **Stockholders' equity:** | **Before** | **After** |
| Preferred stock, $30 par value; 100,000 shares authorized; | | |
|    1,000 shares issued and outstanding | $ 30,000 | $30,000 |
| Common stock, $0.01 par value; 1 million shares authorized; | | |
|    1,000 shares issued and 900 shares outstanding | 10 | 10 |
| Additional paid-in capital | 39,990 | 39,990 |
|    Total contributed capital | 70,000 | 70,000 |
| Retained earnings | 30,000 | 30,000 |
| Treasury stock (at cost, 100 shares) | 0 | (3,000) |
|    Total stockholders' equity | $100,000 | $97,000 |

Now let's assume that Sakul Analytics resells the 100 shares of treasury stock for $35. Recall that these shares originally were purchased for $30 per share, so the $35 resale price

[2]Some companies present treasury stock in their balance sheet without putting parentheses around the number. In this case, the amount still reduces total stockholders' equity. In other words, treasury stock always reduces total equity regardless of whether the amount is in parentheses or not.

represents a $5 per share increase in additional paid-in capital. It's *not* considered a $5 per share gain in the income statement, as it would be for the sale of an investment in another company, since the company is reselling its own stock.

Instead, reselling the treasury stock at an increased price of $35 affects only the balance sheet:

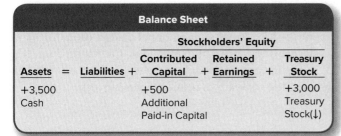
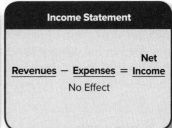

**DEBITS & CREDITS**

The resale of treasury stock is recorded as follows:

|  | Debit | Credit |
|---|---|---|
| Cash (= 100 shares × $35)...................................................................... | **3,500** | |
| Treasury Stock (= 100 shares × $30)...................................................... | | **3,000** |
| Additional Paid-in Capital[3] (= 100 shares × $5).................................. | | **500** |

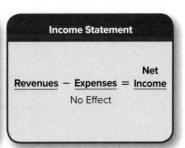

Cash increases by $3,500 (=100 shares × $35) as a result of the inflow of cash from reselling treasury stock. Equity increases by $3,500, representing 1) the decrease in treasury stock by its original cost of $3,000 and 2) the increase in additional paid-in capital by the difference of $500.

The effect of the resale of the treasury stock on stockholders' equity is to remove the treasury stock from the balance sheet and increase additional paid-in capital.

Now, let's consider a different scenario: What if the stock price goes down, and we resell the treasury stock for less than the $30 per share we paid to buy back the shares? Let's assume Sakul Analytics resells the 100 shares of treasury stock for only $25.

The balance sheet effects of reselling the treasury stock at a decreased price of $25 are:

| Balance Sheet | | | | | | Income Statement | | |
|---|---|---|---|---|---|---|---|---|
| | | | **Stockholders' Equity** | | | | | |
| | | | **Contributed** | **Retained** | **Treasury** | | | **Net** |
| **Assets** | **= Liabilities +** | | **Capital** | **+ Earnings +** | **Stock** | **Revenues − Expenses = Income** | | |
| +2,500 | | | −500 | | +3,000 | No Effect | | |
| Cash | | | Additional | | Treasury | | | |
| | | | Paid-in Capital | | Stock(↓) | | | |

---

[3]Some companies credit "Additional Paid-in Capital from Treasury Stock Transactions" as a separate account from "Additional Paid-in Capital from Common Stock Transactions." We combine all additional paid-in capital entries into one "Additional Paid-in Capital" account, similar to how most companies report additional paid-in capital on the balance sheet.

Cash

| | |
|---|---|
| | 2,500 |

Additional Paid-in Capital

| | |
|---|---|
| | 500 |

Treasury stock

| | |
|---|---|
| 3,000 | |

**DEBITS & CREDITS**

The resale of treasury stock is recorded as follows:

| | Debit | Credit |
|---|---|---|
| Cash (= 100 × $25) | **2,500** | |
| Additional Paid-in Capital[4] (= 100 × $5) | **500** | |
| Treasury Stock (= 100 × $30) | | **3,000** |

By purchasing 100 shares of its own stock for $30 per share and reselling them for only $25 per share, Sakul Analytics experienced a decrease in additional paid-in capital. This is reflected in the balance sheet as a decrease to the Additional Paid-in Capital account. It's not reported as a $5 per share loss in the income statement, as we would for the sale of an investment in another company, because the company is reselling its own stock.

 **KEY POINT**

When a company repurchases its own stock, it increases an account called Treasury Stock. Treasury Stock is a contra-equity account—increases in Treasury Stock decrease stockholders' equity. When a company resells treasury stock, the amount of the sale price above (below) the stock's original purchase cost is reported as an increase (decrease) in additional paid-in capital.

**PART B**

# EARNED CAPITAL

In Part A of the chapter, we discussed transactions involving "contributed capital" because when investors buy a corporation's stock, they are contributing to the company. Here, in Part B, we examine transactions involving "earned capital." This component of equity represents the net assets of the company that have been *earned* for the stockholders rather than *contributed* by the stockholders. We'll also see that some of this earned capital is distributed back to stockholders in the form of dividends. Thus, we end up with a component of equity that represents earned capital that has been retained in the company, commonly referred to as *Retained Earnings*.

## Retained Earnings

**■ LO10–5**
Describe retained earnings and account for cash dividends.

As noted at the beginning of the chapter, retained earnings represent the earnings retained in the company—earnings not distributed as dividends to stockholders over the life of the company. In other words, the balance in retained earnings equals all net income, less all dividends, since the company began operations.

$$\text{Retained earnings} = \text{All net income since the company began} - \text{All dividends since the company began}$$

Let's look at an example. Illustration 10–10 shows how net income and dividends impact the balance in retained earnings over a four year period.

**ILLUSTRATION 10–10**

Retained Earnings over a Four-Year Period

| | Net Income (Net Loss) | Dividends | Balance in Retained Earnings |
|---|---|---|---|
| Year 1 | $ (1,000) | $ 0 | $ (1,000) |
| Year 2 | 3,000 | 0 | 2,000 |
| Year 3 | 4,000 | 1,000 | 5,000 |
| Year 4 | 10,000 | 3,000 | 12,000 |

---

[4]Companies debit Retained Earnings rather than Additional Paid-in Capital if there is not a sufficient prior credit balance in Additional Paid-in Capital from treasury stock transactions. The details are covered in intermediate financial accounting courses.

It is important to note the following:

- Year 1 (first year of operations): The company reports a net loss of $1,000. The net loss results in a balance of −$1,000 in retained earnings.
- Year 2: The company reports net income of $3,000. This means that by the end of year 2, all net income (−$1,000 in year 1 and $3,000 in year 2) minus all dividends ($0 in years 1 and 2) results in a cumulative balance in retained earnings of $2,000.
- Year 3: The difference between net income and dividends is $3,000 (= $4,000 − $1,000), and this amount adds to the cumulative balance of retained earnings from Year 2.
- Year 4: The difference between net income and dividends is $7,000 and adds to the cumulative balance of retained earnings in Year 3.

**This process of adding net income and subtracting dividends each year to calculate the cumulative balance of retained earnings continues over the life of the company.**

 **COMMON MISTAKE**

Some students think, incorrectly, that retained earnings represents a *cash* balance set aside by the company. In fact, the size of retained earnings can differ greatly from the balance in the Cash account. Facebook reported approximately $60 billion in retained earnings, but only about $20 billion in cash.

**Negative Retained Earnings (or Accumulated Deficit).**   In a company's early years, the balance in retained earnings tends to be small, and total contributed capital—money invested into the corporation—tends to be large. As the years go by, the earnings retained in the business continue to grow and, for many profitable companies, can exceed the total amount originally invested in the corporation. Unfortunately, for some companies, expenses sometimes are more than revenues, so a net loss is recorded. Just as net income increases retained earnings, a net loss *decreases* retained earnings.

Retained earnings generally has a positive balance. However, if losses exceed income since the company began, or if dividends paid exceed profits, the balance of Retained Earnings will be negative. A negative balance is called an accumulated deficit. In Illustration 10–10, we saw an example of an accumulated deficit in year 1. We subtract an accumulated deficit from total contributed capital in the balance sheet to arrive at total stockholders' equity. Many companies in the start-up phase or when experiencing financial difficulties report an accumulated deficit.

 **KEY POINT**

Retained earnings are the cumulative profits of a company less the cumulative dividends paid since the company began.

## Cash Dividends

Dividends are distributions by a corporation to its stockholders. Investors pay careful attention to cash dividends. A change in the quarterly or annual cash dividend paid by a company can provide useful information about its future prospects. For instance, an increase in dividends often is perceived as good news. Companies tend to increase dividends when the company is doing well and future prospects look bright.

## Decision Maker's Perspective

### Why Don't Some Companies Pay Dividends?

Many companies that are unprofitable choose not to pay dividends. Management of these companies may instead need to use that cash for strategic purposes to keep the company from bankruptcy. However, many profitable companies also choose not to pay cash dividends. Companies with large expansion plans, called *growth companies,* prefer to reinvest earnings in the growth of the company rather than distribute earnings back to investors in the form of cash dividends. **Facebook, Alphabet** (Google), and **Berkshire Hathaway** are highly profitable companies that have yet to pay any dividends, although these companies may buy back their own stock from time to time.

As companies mature and their growth opportunities diminish, they tend to pay out more dividends. **Microsoft** and **Apple** did not pay dividends in their early growth years, but have been paying them in more recent years.

Why do investors buy stock in companies like Facebook if they do not receive dividends? Investors hope a company's share price increases, and then they can sell the stock for a profit. Illustration 10–11 presents the disclosure of Facebook's dividend policy.

**ILLUSTRATION 10–11**

Facebook's Dividend Policy

---

**FACEBOOK, INC.**
**Notes to the Financial Statements (excerpt)**

We have never declared or paid cash dividends on our capital stock. We currently intend to retain any future earnings to finance the operation and expansion of our business, and we do not expect to declare or pay any cash dividends in the foreseeable future. As a result, you may only receive a return on your investment in our Class A common stock and, if issued, our Class C capital stock if the trading price of your shares increases.

Source: Facebook, Inc.

---

For companies that do pay dividends, the date the board of directors announces the next dividend to be paid is known as the declaration date. The declaration of a dividend creates a binding legal obligation for the company declaring the dividend. On that date, we (a) increase Dividends, a temporary account that is closed into Retained Earnings at the end of each period, and (b) increase a liability account, Dividends Payable.

The board of directors also indicates a specific date on which the company looks at its records to determine who the stockholders of the company are. This date is called the record date. An investor must be a stockholder on the record date to have the right to receive the dividend.[5] The date of the actual distribution is the payment date. Dividends are paid only on shares outstanding. **Dividends are not paid on treasury shares.**

To illustrate the payment of a cash dividend, assume that on March 15 Sakul Analytics declares a $0.25 per share dividend on its 2,000 outstanding shares.

The balance sheet effects of declaring a cash dividend are:

An increase in dividends (denoted by the up arrow) leads to a decrease in retained earnings.

| Balance Sheet | | | | Income Statement | | |
|---|---|---|---|---|---|---|
| | | **Stockholders' Equity** | | | | |
| | | Contributed | Retained | | | **Net** |
| **Assets** = | **Liabilities** + | **Capital** + | **Earnings** | **Revenues** − | **Expenses** = | **Income** |
| | +500 | | −500 | | No Effect | |
| | Dividends | | Dividends(↑) | | | |
| | Payable | | | | | |

---

[5]The stock exchange on which the company's stock is traded sets an ex-dividend date, which typically is one business day before the record date. Investors must own the stock at least one day prior to the ex-dividend date to receive the dividend. The reason the ex-dividend date is one day before the record date is that in the United States, the Securities and Exchange Commission (SEC) requires stock trades to settle two days after purchase. So, to own the stock by the record date and have the right to receive the dividend, an investor would need to purchase the stock at least two business days before the date of record, which is one day before the ex-dividend date.

| DEBITS & CREDITS | | |
|---|---|---|
| The declaration of cash dividends is recorded on March 15 as follows: | | |
| | Debit | Credit |
| Dividends (= 2,000 shares × $0.25)............................................................ | 500 | |
|    Dividends Payable ............................................................................... | | 500 |

Dividends
500 |

Dividends Payable
| 500

The Dividends account is a *temporary* stockholders' equity account that is closed into Retained Earnings at the end of each period. When dividends are declared, we increase the Dividends account, which ultimately reduces the equity of the company. In addition, once declared by the board of directors, dividends are legally payable, so Dividends Payable increases.

**COMMON MISTAKE**

Some students incorrectly calculate dividends based on the number of issued shares. Dividends are based on the number of outstanding shares since dividends are not paid on treasury stock.

Let's continue our example and assume the dividend declared by Sakul Analytics is paid on April 15 to stockholders of record at March 31. On the record date (March 31), the dividends have no effect on the balance sheet. The balance is affected by the payment of dividends on April 15 as follows:

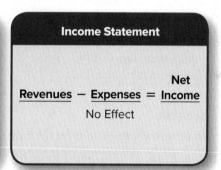

| DEBITS & CREDITS | | |
|---|---|---|
| The payment of cash dividends is recorded on April 15 as follows: | | |
| | Debit | Credit |
| Dividends Payable (= 2,000 shares × $0.25)............................................ | 500 | |
|    Cash................................................................................................. | | 500 |

Dividends Payable
500 |

Cash
| 500

Because cash is the asset most easily distributed to stockholders, most corporate dividends are cash dividends. In concept, though, any asset can be distributed to stockholders as a dividend. When a noncash asset is distributed to stockholders, it is referred to as a property dividend. Securities held as investments are the assets most often distributed in a property dividend. The actual recording of property dividends is covered in intermediate accounting.

**KEY POINT**

The declaration of cash dividends decreases Retained Earnings and increases Dividends Payable. The payment of cash dividends decreases Dividends Payable and decreases Cash. The net effect, then, is a reduction in both Retained Earnings and Cash.

**Manager Analysis**

| Question | Accounting information | Analysis |
|---|---|---|
| How much profit has the company made for its stockholders that has not been distributed back to them in dividends? | Balance in Retained Earnings | The balance in Retained Earnings shows all net income less dividends since the company began operations. |

**Let's Review**

MMPay, a microcredit company that facilitates digital payments by cell phone, has two classes of stock authorized: $100 par preferred and $1 par common. As of the beginning of the year, 1,000 shares of common stock and no preferred shares have been issued. The following transactions affect stockholders' equity during the year:

| | | |
|---|---|---|
| January | 15 | Issue 2,000 additional shares of common stock for $20 per share. |
| February | 1 | Issue 100 shares of preferred stock for $110 per share. |
| June | 1 | Declare a cash dividend of $5 per share on preferred stock and $1 per share on common stock to all stockholders of record on June 15. |
| June | 30 | Pay the cash dividend declared on June 1. |
| October | 1 | Purchase 200 shares of treasury stock for $25 per share. |
| November | 1 | Resell 100 shares of the treasury stock purchased on October 1 for $28 per share. |

**Required:**

1. Indicate the effect of each transaction on the balance sheet by indicating increases (+), decreases (−), or has no effect (NE), on total assets, total liabilities, and total stockholders' equity.

2. Record the journal entry for each transaction.

**Solution:**

1. Effects of transactions on the balance sheet:

| Transaction | Total Assets | Total Liabilities | Total Stockholders' Equity |
|---|---|---|---|
| Issue common stock | + | NE | + |
| Issue preferred stock | + | NE | + |
| Declare cash dividends | NE | + | − |
| Pay cash dividends | − | − | NE |
| Purchase treasury stock | − | NE | − |
| Resell treasury stock | + | NE | + |

2. Entries to record each transaction:

| January 15 | Debit | Credit |
|---|---|---|
| **Cash** (= 2,000 × $20)............................................................ | 40,000 | |
| **Common Stock** (= 2,000 × $1)......................................... | | 2,000 |
| **Additional Paid-in Capital** (difference)................................ | | 38,000 |
| (Issue common stock above par) | | |
| February 1 | | |
| **Cash** (= 100 × $110).......................................................... | 11,000 | |
| **Preferred Stock** (= 100 × $100)...................................... | | 10,000 |
| **Additional Paid-in Capital** (difference)................................ | | 1,000 |
| (Issue preferred stock above par) | | |

| June 1 | Debit | Credit |
|---|---|---|
| **Dividends*** ............................................................................................ | 3,500 | |
|    **Dividends Payable** ....................................................................... | | 3,500 |
|    *(Declare cash dividends)* | | |
|    *=(100 preferred shares × $5) + (3,000 common shares × $1)* | | |
| June 30 | | |
| **Dividends Payable** ............................................................................ | 3,500 | |
|    **Cash** ................................................................................................ | | 3,500 |
|    *(Pay cash dividends)* | | |
| October 1 | | |
| **Treasury Stock** (= 200 shares × $25) ............................................. | 5,000 | |
|    **Cash** ................................................................................................ | | 5,000 |
|    *(Purchase treasury stock)* | | |
| November 1 | | |
| **Cash** (= 100 shares × $28)............................................................... | 2,800 | |
|    **Treasury Stock** (= 100 shares × $25)............................................ | | 2,500 |
|    **Additional Paid-in Capital** (= 100 × $3) ....................................... | | 300 |
|    *(Resell treasury stock above cost)* | | |

## Stock Splits and Stock Dividends

Rather than distribute cash dividends to shareholders, sometimes corporations distribute additional shares of their own stock. These are known as stock dividends or stock splits, depending on the size of the stock distribution. Suppose you own 100 shares of stock. Assuming the company issues a 10% stock dividend, you'll get 10 additional shares. If the company declares a 2-for-1 stock split, you'll covert each of your shares into two shares and now have 200 shares. This type of stock split would be equivalent to a 100% stock dividend.

Stock splits are declared primarily due to the effect they have on stock prices. Let's say that before the stock split, the shares are trading at $40 a share, so your 100 shares are worth $4,000. After the 100% stock dividend, you will have twice as many shares, 200. That sounds good, but let's look closer. Because the company as a whole still has the same value, each share of stock is now worth half as much—$20 rather than $40 per share. Your 200 shares still have a value of $4,000, the same as your 100 shares before the stock dividend. However, now each share is worth half as much—$20 rather than $40 per share.

Stock splits occur much more frequently than stock dividends, which are relatively rare. Because stock splits are quite newsworthy, you can find "split calendars" from credible data providers, such as **Nasdaq** and **Zacks**, which provide detail listings of companies who are planning to split their stocks. However, despite the publicity that stock splits create, the question remains: do stock splits truly enrich shareholders? The answer to that question is not clear.

Think of the company as a pizza. A 100% stock dividend is like changing an 8-slice pizza into 16 slices by cutting each slice in half. You are no better off with 16 half-slices than with the original 8 slices. Whether it's cut in 8 large slices or 16 smaller slices, it's still the same-sized pizza. Whether a company is represented by 1 million shares worth $40 each or 2 million shares worth $20 each, it's the same $40 million company. So, from this pizza perspective, shareholders are not better off because of a stock split.

However, in general, the market seems to view stock splits as a good signal because they represent past price appreciation and future growth opportunities. Research shows that in the years following a stock split, companies tend to perform well.[6] The opposite is true for a "reverse stock split," in which more shares are exchanged for less. For example, **TOP Ships** underwent a 1-for-20 reverse stock split of its common shares. The effect of the reverse split

■ **LO10–6**
Explain the effect of stock dividends, stock splits, and stock-based compensation.

---

[6]See, for example, Smith (2019): https://joi.pm-research.com/content/28/4/21.abstract

was to reduce shares outstanding from about 31.7 million to about 1.6 million shares. If you owned 40 shares of TOP Ships' stock before the reverse split, you'd own 2 shares after.[7] How did the market react to this reverse split? Shares of TOP Ships dropped by nearly 7% at the announcement of the reverse split.

What are the effects of stock splits and stock dividends on the financial statements? For the sake of simplicity, we will avoid some of the detail-oriented accounting related to small stock dividends, large stock dividends, and stock splits—we leave these for more advanced accounting courses. For now, keep this one punchline top of mind: **stock dividends and stock splits have no effect on the balance sheet! Total assets, total liabilities, and total stockholders' equity do not change as a result of a stock split or stock dividend.**

 **KEY POINT**

Declaring stock dividends and stock splits is like cutting a pizza into more slices. Everyone has more shares, but each share is worth proportionately less than before. Neither stock splits nor stock dividends have any effect on total assets, total liabilities, and total stockholders' equity.

## Stock-Based Compensation

Employee compensation plans frequently include stock-based awards, in which employees are paid in some form of equity. For example, **Autodesk** reports that it has given its employees over 800,000 stock options and 4.3 million shares of stock as part of their overall employment compensation. The goal of stock-based compensation is to align the incentives of the employees with those of the shareholders. When the company does well (as measured by stock price appreciation), both shareholders and employees win.

There are two accounting questions in regards to share-based compensation plans:

(1) *How much* compensation expense should be reported by the employer?
(2) *When* should the compensation expense be reported by the employer?

We'll answer these two questions for restricted stock units, leaving the accounting for other types of stock-based compensation for more advanced accounting courses.

### RESTRICTED STOCK UNITS

An increasingly popular form of stock-based compensation is restricted stock units (RSUs). A restricted stock unit is a right to receive a specified number of shares of company stock. The employee doesn't receive the stock right away because the shares are, in fact, restricted. Instead, the shares are distributed as the recipient of RSUs satisfies the "vesting" requirement, which is typically an obligation to work for the company for a preset number of years. For example, assume a tech company grants 100,000 RSUs to key executives on January 1, when the market price is $8. The shares will vest after four years of employment.

As noted, we need to answer two questions regarding RSUs.

*How much share-based compensation expense should be reported?* The answer depends on the total fair value of the RSUs on the date they are granted to employees. For public companies, the fair value of the RSUs is the market value on the grant date. In our example above, total compensation expense is $800,000 (= $8 price on grant date × 100,000 RSUs).

*When should the share-based compensation expense be reported?* Not on January 1 (the grant date). On the date the RSUs are granted to employees, there is no effect on the financial statements. Why? At that point, the company hasn't incurred any expense because the employees haven't "earned" their RSUs yet. The RSUs are restricted in the sense that the employees must remain with the company for four years to take ownership of the RSUs

---

[7]With some splits and reverse splits, there is the potential for fractions of shares. In practice, these shares are simply cashed out. For instance, in the TOP Ships 1-for-20 reverse split example, a shareholder with 52 shares would end up with 2 shares and would be cashed out for the remaining 12 shares.

(i.e., a four-year vesting period). Instead, we allocate the total value in even amounts over the vesting period—this is done using the straight-line method you've learned in prior chapters. Continuing our example, we take the total fair value of the RSUs on the grant date ($800,000) divided by the vesting period of four years to get an annual compensation expense of $200,000 in each of the four vesting years.[8]

This expense is unique in that it represents a non-cash expense (i.e., an expense that reduces net income without also reducing cash flows) because the employee is paid in equity rather than in cash. However, while the compensation expense each year decreases net income (and therefore stockholders' equity via retained earnings), there is an offsetting increase to stockholders' equity via paid-in capital from the issuance of RSUs. **This means that total assets, total liabilities, and total stockholders' equity in the balance sheet remain unaffected by the issuance of RSUs.**

The accounting for restricted stock—including the answers to the above two questions—is summarized in the following disclosure from Autodesk:

---

### AUTODESK
### Notes to the Financial Statements

We measure stock-based compensation cost at the grant date fair value of the award, and recognize expense ratably over . . . the vesting period. The value of the portion of the award that is ultimately expected to vest is recognized as [an] expense in our [Income Statement].

---

**ILLUSTRATION 10–12**

Excerpt from Autodesk's annual report

**KEY POINT**

Companies often reward employees with restricted stock, which is treated as an expense and allocated evenly over the period when the employee is restricted from selling the stock.

---

### SUSTAINABILITY

We've covered contributed capital and earned capital at this point in the chapter. However, an often-overlooked component of a company's equity is its human capital. Sustainability accounting accounts for human capital with disclosures related to labor practices, employee health, and diversity and inclusion initiatives. To illustrate the importance of human capital, we can examine the sustainability disclosures for **Goldman Sachs**. These disclosures emphasize the importance of "inclusive growth":

> *It is imperative that the global economy generate growth that is more inclusive—that enables people to contribute to society, expands the middle class, and helps businesses and communities grow. Our firm is focused on driving a range of inclusive growth opportunities, spanning innovative financial products and services that reach more people, expanded access to education and healthcare, as well as greater investment in housing and infrastructure development in underserved communities.*
>
> *At its core, our approach to inclusive growth draws upon innovative ideas that mitigate unequal access, increase affordability and improve quality. Leaning on the principles of inclusivity and disruptive thinking, paired with our core capabilities as an advisor, financier and provider of capital, we support concrete solutions that make inclusive growth possible.*

These initiatives to drive more inclusive growth will not only enhance the human capital at Goldman Sachs, but also for many of its clients and customers.

---

[8]If the employee leaves prior to the vesting period, she forfeits the RSUs altogether. As a result, stock-based compensation expense is reduced by the amount of forfeitures.

PART C

# REPORTING STOCKHOLDERS' EQUITY

■ **LO10–7**
Prepare and analyze the stockholders' equity section of a balance sheet and the statement of stockholders' equity.

We now can apply what we've learned so far in the chapter to analyze the stockholders' equity of an actual company—**Nvidia Corporation**. In this section, we show the financial statement presentation of stockholders' equity in the balance sheet and differentiate it from the statement of stockholders' equity.

## Stockholders' Equity in the Balance Sheet

Illustration 10–13 presents the stockholders' equity section of the balance sheet for Nvidia Corporation, which designs graphics processing units (GPUs) for the gaming, cryptocurrency, and professional markets.

**ILLUSTRATION 10–13**

Stockholders' Equity Section for Nvidia

**NVIDIA CORPORATION**
**Balance Sheet (partial)**
($ and shares in millions)

| | |
|---|---:|
| Preferred stock, $0.001 par value, no shares issued | $ – |
| Common stock, $0.001 par value, 955 shares issued | 1 |
| Additional paid-in capital | 7,045 |
| Total contributed capital | 7,046 |
| Treasury stock, 342 shares | (9,814) |
| Accumulated other comprehensive income | 1 |
| Retained earnings | 14,971 |
| **Total stockholders' equity** | **$12,204** |

Preferred stock is usually is listed before common stock in the balance sheet, given its preference over common stock. The dollar amounts shown for common stock and preferred stock are based on the number of shares issued times their par value. Because Nvidia hasn't issued any preferred shares, this amount is $0. The company has issued 955 million shares of common stock. With a par value of $0.001, that rounds to a common stock balance of $1 million.

Additional paid-in capital represents amounts above par value that have been received from investors. For Nvidia, this balance is much larger than the Common Stock account balance. This is to be expected. Remember, Nvidia has a par value of only $0.001 per share, so most of the money invested in the company was added to Additional Paid-in Capital rather than Common Stock.

Now look at retained earnings. When a company is started, most of the equity is in the contributed capital section because that's the amount invested by stockholders. However, if a company is profitable over time, like Nvidia, and pays little in dividends, the retained earnings section of equity grows and often exceeds the amount invested by stockholders. For Nvidia, the balance in retained earnings is so large that it actually exceeds total stockholders' equity. How can this happen? Nvidia has used a portion of cash generated from earnings to buy back treasury stock, which decreases stockholders' equity. Nvidia has applied this strategy to such an extent that the balance in treasury stock (representing the cost of shares repurchased by the company) now exceeds total paid-in capital (representing the total price of shares originally issued).

## Decision Maker's Perspective

### Why Doesn't Stockholders' Equity Equal the Market Value of Equity?

The *market* value of equity is the price investors are willing to pay for a company's stock. The market value of equity equals the stock price times the number of shares outstanding. On the other hand, the *book* value of equity equals total stockholders' equity reported in the balance sheet. Market value and book value generally are not the same and often are vastly different. For example, Nvidia reported total stockholders' equity of about $12 billion, yet its market value at this same time was over $144 billion. Why?

Keep in mind that stockholders' equity is equal to assets minus liabilities. An asset's book value usually equals its market value *on the date it's purchased.* However, the two aren't necessarily the same after that. For instance, an asset such as a building often increases in value over time, but it continues to be reported in the balance sheet at historical cost minus accumulated depreciation. Consider another example. Nvidia spends well over $3 billion each year on research and development (R&D). These activities increase the long-term profit generating ability of the company, but under accounting rules, Nvidia expenses all its R&D costs as it incurs them. This causes the true market value of assets and stockholders' equity to be greater than the amount recorded for assets and stockholders' equity in the accounting records. Even when investors see the increase in a company's value and its stock price moves higher, common stock in the company's balance sheet continues to be reported at its original issue price rather than its higher market value.

## Statement of Stockholders' Equity

The stockholders' equity section of the balance sheet, like the one we just examined for Nvidia, shows the balance in each equity account *at a point in time.* In contrast, the statement of stockholders' equity summarizes the *changes* in the balance in each stockholders' equity account *over time.*

To contrast the *stockholders' equity section* of the balance sheet and the *statement of stockholders' equity,* let's compare both for Sakul Analytics. Illustration 10–14 shows the stockholders' equity section reported in Sakul Analytic's balance sheet.

| SAKUL ANALYTICS Balance Sheet (partial) December 31, 2024 | |
|---|---:|
| **Stockholders' equity:** | |
| Preferred stock, $30 par value; 100,000 shares authorized; | |
| 1,000 shares issued and outstanding | $ 30,000 |
| Common stock, $0.01 par value; 1 million shares authorized; | |
| 1,000 shares issued and outstanding | 10 |
| Additional paid-in capital | 40,490 |
| Total contributed capital | 70,500 |
| Retained earnings | 29,500 |
| Treasury stock | –0– |
| Total stockholders' equity | $100,000 |

**ILLUSTRATION 10–14**

Stockholders' Equity Section—Sakul Analytics

Compare that snapshot of stockholders' equity at the end of 2024 with Illustration 10–15, showing the statement of stockholders' equity for Sakul Analytics.

The statement of stockholders' equity reports how each equity account changed during the year. The beginning balances in Illustration 10–15 are zero because this is the first year of operations. It is important to note the following:

- Common Stock increased because Sakul Analytics issued common stock during the year.
- Additional Paid-in Capital increased from the issuance of common stock, the issuance of preferred stock, and the sale of treasury stock for more than its original cost.

ILLUSTRATION 10–15

Statement of
Stockholders' Equity—
Sakul Analytics

**SAKUL ANALYTICS**
**Statement of Stockholders' Equity**
**For the year ended December 31, 2024**

| | Preferred Stock | Common Stock | Additional Paid-in Capital | Retained Earnings | Treasury Stock | Total Stockholders' Equity |
|---|---|---|---|---|---|---|
| **Balance, January 1** | $ –0– | $–0– | $ –0– | $ –0– | $ –0– | $ –0– |
| Issue common stock | | 10 | 29,990 | | | 30,000 |
| Issue preferred stock | 30,000 | | 10,000 | | | 40,000 |
| Purchase treasury stock | | | | | (3,000) | (3,000) |
| Resell treasury stock | | | 500 | | 3,000 | 3,500 |
| Cash dividends | | | | (500) | | (500) |
| Net income | | | | 30,000 | | 30,000 |
| **Balance, December 31** | **$30,000** | **$ 10** | **$40,490** | **$29,500** | **$ –0–** | **$100,000** |

- Retained Earnings increased due to net income and decreased due to cash dividends. The retained earnings column is sometimes shown separately and referred to as a statement of retained earnings.
- Treasury stock was initially purchased, reducing total stockholders' equity. The treasury stock was then resold by the end of the year, eliminating its negative effect.

The ending balances of each stockholders' equity account are shown in the stockholders' equity section of the balance sheet. These ending balances will be the beginning balances next year in the statement of stockholders' equity.

**KEY POINT**

The stockholders' equity section of the balance sheet presents the balance of each equity account *at a point in time.* The statement of stockholders' equity shows the change in each equity account balance *over time.*

**Let's Review**

This is a continuation of the Let's Review exercise presented earlier in the chapter. Recall that MMPay has two classes of stock authorized: $100 par preferred and $1 par value common. As of the beginning of 2024, 1,000 shares of common stock have been issued and no shares of preferred stock have been issued. The following transactions affect stockholders' equity during 2024:

| | | |
|---|---|---|
| January | 15 | Issue 2,000 additional shares of common stock for $20 per share. |
| February | 1 | Issue 100 shares of preferred stock for $110 per share. |
| June | 1 | Declare a cash dividend of $5 per share on preferred stock and $1 per share on common stock to all stockholders of record on June 15. |
| June | 30 | Pay the cash dividend declared on June 1. |
| October | 1 | Purchase 200 shares of common treasury stock for $25 per share. |
| November | 1 | Resell 100 shares of treasury stock purchased on October 1 for $28 per share. |

MMPay has the following beginning balances in its stockholders' equity accounts on January 1, 2024: Preferred Stock, $0; Common Stock, $1,000; Additional Paid-in Capital, $14,000; and Retained Earnings, $5,000. Net income for the year ended December 31, 2024, is $4,000.

*Required:*

Taking into consideration the beginning balances and all of the transactions during 2024, prepare the following:

1. The stockholders' equity section of the balance sheet as of December 31, 2024.
2. The statement of stockholders' equity for the year ended December 31, 2024.

*Solution:*

1. Stockholders' equity section of the balance sheet:

| MMPAY<br>Balance Sheet (partial)<br>December 31, 2024 | |
| --- | ---: |
| Stockholders' equity: | |
| Preferred stock, $100 par value | $10,000 |
| Common stock, $1 par value | 3,000 |
| Additional paid-in capital | 53,300 |
| Total contributed capital | 66,300 |
| Retained earnings | 5,500 |
| Treasury stock | (2,500) |
| Total stockholders' equity | $69,300 |

2. Statement of stockholders' equity:

| MMPAY<br>Statement of Stockholders' Equity<br>For the year ended December 31, 2024 | | | | | | |
| --- | ---: | ---: | ---: | ---: | ---: | ---: |
| | Preferred Stock | Common Stock | Additional Paid-in Capital | Retained Earnings | Treasury Stock | Total Stockholders' Equity |
| Balance, January 1 | $ –0– | $1,000 | $14,000 | $5,000 | $ –0– | $20,000 |
| Issue common stock | | 2,000 | 38,000 | | | 40,000 |
| Issue preferred stock | 10,000 | | 1,000 | | | 11,000 |
| Dividends | | | | (3,500) | | (3,500) |
| Purchase treasury stock | | | | | (5,000) | (5,000) |
| Resell treasury stock | | | 300 | | 2,500 | 2,800 |
| Net income | | | | 4,000 | | 4,000 |
| Balance, December 31 | $10,000 | $3,000 | $53,300 | $5,500 | $(2,500) | $69,300 |

# EQUITY ANALYSIS
## Facebook vs. IBM

**PART D:
ANALYSIS**

Earnings are the key to a company's long-run survival. However, we need to evaluate earnings in comparison to the size of the investment. For instance, earnings of $500,000 may be quite large for a small business but would be a rather disappointing outcome for a major corporation like **International Business Machines (IBM)**. A useful summary measure of earnings that considers the relative size of the business is the return on equity.

■ **LO10–8**
Evaluate company performance using information on stockholders' equity.

## RETURN ON EQUITY

The return on equity (ROE) measures the ability of company management to generate earnings from the resources that owners provide. We compute the ratio by dividing net income by average total stockholders' equity.

$$\text{Return on equity} = \frac{\text{Net income}}{\text{Average stockholders' equity}}$$

Let's compare the return on equity of **Facebook** and **IBM**. Illustration 10–16 provides selected financial data for each company.

**ILLUSTRATION 10–16**

Selected Financial Data for Facebook and IBM

| ($ in millions except per share data) | Facebook | IBM |
|---|---|---|
| Net sales | $55,838 | $ 79,591 |
| Net income | $22,111 | $ 11,872 |
| Total liabilities | $13,207 | $106,452 |
| Stockholders' equity, beginning | $74,347 | $ 17,725 |
| Stockholders' equity, ending | $84,127 | $ 16,929 |
| Stock price, ending | $131.08 | $ 113.67 |
| Dividends per share | $  — | $   6.21 |
| Average shares outstanding | 2,895 million | 907 million |

The return on equity for both companies is calculated in Illustration 10–17.

**ILLUSTRATION 10–17**

Return on Equity for Facebook and IBM

| ($ in millions) | Net Income | ÷ | Average Stockholders' Equity | = | Return on Equity |
|---|---|---|---|---|---|
| Facebook | $22,111 | ÷ | ($74,347 + $84,127)/2 | = | 27.9% |
| IBM | $11,872 | ÷ | ($17,725 + $16,929)/2 | = | 68.5% |

Facebook has a return on equity of 27.9%, compared to 68.5% for IBM. At first, you might think this means that Facebook's performance is much poorer than is IBM's performance, and in terms of return on equity, that is true. However, a key reason for the difference in return on equity is that Facebook relies to a greater extent on equity financing, while IBM relies on debt financing. The ratio of total liabilities to equity for Facebook is only 15.7% (= $13,207 / $84,127) compared to that of IBM of 628.8% (= $106,452 / $16,929). While shareholders of IBM earn more per dollar of equity, a higher portion of those earnings are devoted to repaying debt. Facebook actually has a much higher return on total assets.

## DIVIDEND YIELD

Investors are also interested in knowing how much a company pays out in dividends relative to its share price. The dividend yield is computed as dividends per share divided by the stock price.

$$\text{Dividend yield} = \frac{\text{Dividends per share}}{\text{Stock price}}$$

Dividend yield for Facebook and IBM is shown in Illustration 10–18.

**ILLUSTRATION 10–18**

Dividend Yield for Facebook and IBM

| ($ in millions) | Dividends per Share | ÷ | Stock Price | = | Dividend Yield |
|---|---|---|---|---|---|
| Facebook | $0 | ÷ | $131.08 | = | 0.0% |
| IBM | $6 | ÷ | $113.67 | = | 5.5% |

Small growth companies tend not to pay dividends, while larger, more mature companies do. Facebook does not pay dividends, so its dividend yield is 0%. IBM pays a relatively high dividend yield of 5.5%. Shareholders of Facebook earn a total stock return equal to the change in stock price for the year. Shareholders of IBM earn a total stock return equal to the change in stock price for the year plus the dividend yield.

## EARNINGS PER SHARE

Earnings per share (EPS) measures the net income per share of common stock. We calculate earnings per share as net income minus preferred stock dividends divided by the average shares outstanding during the period:

$$\text{Earnings per share} = \frac{\text{Net income} - \text{Dividends on preferred stock}}{\text{Average shares of common stock outstanding}}$$

The numerator measures the income available to common stockholders. We subtract any dividends on preferred stock from net income to arrive at the income available to the true owners of the company—the common stockholders. If a company does not issue preferred stock, the numerator is simply net income. We then divide income available to common stockholders by the average shares outstanding during the period to calculate earnings per share.

**Earnings per share is useful in comparing earnings performance for the same company over time.** It is *not* useful for comparing earnings performance of one company with another because of wide differences in the number of shares outstanding among companies. For instance, assume two companies, Alpha and Beta, both report net income of $1 million and are valued by the market at $20 million. Quite comparable, right? Not if we are talking about their earnings per share. If Alpha has one million shares outstanding and Beta has two million shares outstanding, their earnings per share amounts will not be comparable. Alpha will have a share price of $20 (= $20 million ÷ 1 million shares) and an EPS of $1.00 (= $1 million in earnings ÷ 1 million shares). Beta, on the other hand, will have a share price of $10 ($20 million ÷ 2 million shares) and an EPS of $0.50 ($1 million in earnings ÷ 2 million shares). Is the earnings performance for Alpha better than that for Beta? Of course not. They both earned $1 million. Alpha's earnings per share is higher simply because it has half as many shares outstanding. (Same pizza, fewer slices.)

If Alpha declared a 2-for-1 stock split, its earnings per share would match Beta's exactly. The key point is that earnings per share is useful in comparing either Alpha's earnings over time or Beta's earnings over time, but it is not useful in comparing the companies with each other.

Investors use earnings per share extensively in evaluating the earnings performance of a company over time. Investors are looking for companies with the potential to increase earnings per share. Analysts also forecast earnings on a per share basis. If reported earnings per share fall short of analysts' forecasts, this is considered negative news, usually resulting in a decline in a company's stock price.

## PRICE-EARNINGS RATIO

Another measure widely used by analysts is the price-earnings ratio (PE ratio). It indicates how the stock is trading relative to current earnings. We calculate the PE ratio as the stock price divided by earnings per share, so that both stock price and earnings are expressed on a per share basis:

$$\text{Price-earnings ratio} = \frac{\text{Stock price}}{\text{Earnings per share}}$$

Intuitively, the price-earnings ratio measures what you pay (price) for what you expect to receive (earnings). Price-earnings ratios commonly are in the range of 15 to 25. A high PE ratio indicates that the market has high hopes for a company's stock and has bid up the price. Growth stocks are stocks whose future earnings investors expect to be higher. Their stock prices are high in relation to current earnings because investors expect future earnings to be higher. For example, **Peleton** recently had a price-earnings ratio of over 2,000, indicating extremely high expectations for future growth. On the other hand, value stocks are stocks that are priced low in relation to current earnings. The low price in relation to earnings may be justified due to poor future prospects, or it might suggest an underpriced stock that could boom in the future. For example, several airlines had price-earnings ratios below 5 during Covid-19, indicating expectations of poor future performance. Illustration 10–19 calculates the price-earnings ratios for Facebook and IBM.

**ILLUSTRATION 10–19**

Price-Earnings Ratios for Facebook and IBM

| | Stock Price | ÷ | Earnings per Share | = | Price-Earnings Ratio |
|---|---|---|---|---|---|
| Facebook | $131.08 | ÷ | $22,111/2,895 | = | 17.16 |
| IBM | $113.67 | ÷ | $11,872/907 | = | 8.68 |

The price-earnings ratios for Facebook is much higher, indicating investors expect greater growth in future earnings. Based on these ratios, we'd probably consider Facebook to be a growth stock, and IBM to be a value stock. Only time will tell whether those growth expectations are correct.

**KEY POINT**

Return on equity measures the ability to generate earnings from the owners' investment. It is calculated as net income divided by average stockholders' equity. Dividend yield measures how much a company pays out in dividends in relation to its stock price. Earnings per share measures the net income per share of common stock. The price-earnings ratio indicates how the stock is trading relative to current earnings.

**Manager Analysis**

| Question | Accounting information | Analysis |
|---|---|---|
| Do investors expect future earnings to grow? | Price-earnings ratio (PE ratio) | A high PE ratio indicates investors expect future earnings to be higher. A low PE ratio indicates investors' lack of confidence in future earnings growth. |

**THE BOTTOM LINE**

**LO10–1 Identify the advantages and disadvantages of the corporate form of ownership.**

The primary advantages of the corporate form of business are limited liability and the ability to raise capital. The primary disadvantages are additional taxes and more paperwork.

**LO10–2 Understand the issuance of common stock.**

If no-par value stock is issued, the corporation increases both Cash and Common Stock. If par value stock is issued, the corporation increases Cash and increases two equity accounts—Common

Stock at the par value per share and Additional Paid-in Capital for the portion above par.

**LO10–3 Understand the issuance of preferred stock.**

Preferred stock has preference over common stock in receiving dividends, and in the distribution of assets in the event the corporation is dissolved. Issuing preferred stock increases Cash, Preferred Stock, and Additional Paid-in Capital in the balance sheet. The preferred dividend per share is equal to the par value times the dividend rate.

**LO10–4 Account for share repurchases.**

When a company repurchases its stock, it increases an account called Treasury Stock. Treasury Stock is a contra-equity account—increases in Treasury Stock decrease stockholders' equity. When a company resells treasury stock, the amount of the sale price above (below) the stock's original purchase cost is reported as an increase (decrease) in Additional Paid-in Capital.

**LO10–5 Describe retained earnings and account for cash dividends.**

Retained earnings are the cumulative profits of a company less the cumulative dividends paid since the company began. The declaration of cash dividends creates a liability on the balance sheet (Dividends Payable) and reduces shareholders' equity via the Dividends account, which in turn reduces Retained Earnings. The payment of cash dividends decreases Dividends Payable and decreases Cash. The net effect, then, is a reduction in both Retained Earnings and Cash.

**LO10–6 Explain the effect of stock dividends, stock splits, and stock-based compensation.**

Declaring stock splits and stock dividends is like cutting a pizza into more slices. Everyone has more shares, but each share is worth proportionately less than before. Neither stock splits nor stock dividends have any effect on total assets, total liabilities, and total stockholders' equity. Companies often reward employees with restricted stock, which is treated as an expense and allocated evenly over the period when the employee is restricted from selling the stock.

**LO10–7 Prepare and analyze the stockholders' equity section of a balance sheet and the statement of stockholders' equity.**

The stockholders' equity section of the balance sheet presents the balance of each equity account *at a point in time*. The statement of stockholders' equity shows the change in each equity account balance *over time*.

**LO10–8 Evaluate company performance using information on stockholders' equity.**

Return on equity measures the ability to generate earnings from the owners' investment. It is calculated as net income divided by average stockholders' equity. Dividend yield measures how much a company pays out in dividends in relation to its stock price. Earnings per share measures the net income per outstanding share of common stock. The price-earnings ratio indicates how the stock is trading relative to current earnings.

## GLOSSARY

**Accumulated other comprehensive income:** A component of stockholders' equity that reports the accumulated amount of other comprehensive income items in the current and prior periods. **p. 504**

**Accumulated deficit:** A negative balance in Retained Earnings. **p. 517**

**Additional paid-in capital:** The portion of the cash proceeds from issuing stock above par value. **p. 509**

**Angel investors:** Wealthy individuals in the business community willing to risk investment funds on a promising business venture. **p. 508**

**Articles of incorporation:** Describes the nature of the firm's business activities, the shares to be issued, and the composition of the initial board of directors. **p. 504**

**Authorized stock:** Shares available to sell, as stated in the company's articles of incorporation. **p. 506**

**Contributed capital:** The amount of money paid into a company by its owners. **p. 504**

**Corporation:** An entity that is legally separate from its owners and even pays its own income taxes. **p. 504**

**Declaration date:** The date the board of directors announces the next dividend to be paid. **p. 518**

**Dividends:** Distributions to stockholders, typically in the form of cash. **p. 517**

**Dividend yield:** Dividends per share divided by the stock price. **p. 528**

**Double taxation:** Corporate income is taxed once on earnings at the corporate level and again on dividends at the individual level. **p. 505**

**Earnings per share (EPS):** Net income available to common shareholders divided by average shares of common stock outstanding. **p. 529**

**Growth stocks:** Stocks that tend to have higher price-earnings ratios and are expected to have higher future earnings. **p. 530**

**Initial public offering (IPO):** The first time a corporation issues stock to the public. **p. 508**

**Issued stock:** Shares sold to investors; includes treasury shares. **p. 506**

**Limited liability:** Stockholders in a corporation can lose no more than the amount they invested in the company. **p. 505**

**No-par value stock:** Common stock that has not been assigned a par value. **p. 507**

**Organization chart:** Traces the line of authority within the corporation. **p. 504**

**Outstanding stock:** Issued shares that currently are held by investors; does not include treasury shares. **p. 506**

**Par value:** The legal capital assigned per share of stock. **p. 507**

**Payment date:** The date of the actual distribution of dividends. **p. 518**

**Preferred stock:** Stock with preference over common stock in the payment of dividends and the distribution of assets. **p. 509**

**Price-earnings ratio:** The stock price divided by earnings per share so that both stock price and earnings are expressed on a per share basis. **p. 529**

**Privately held corporation:** Does not allow investment by the general public and normally has fewer stockholders. **p. 505**

**Property dividend:** The distribution of a noncash asset to stockholders. **p. 519**

**Publicly held corporation:** Allows investment by the general public and is regulated by the Securities and Exchange Commission. **p. 505**

**Record date:** The date on which a company looks at its records to determine who the stockholders of the company are. **p. 518**

**Restricted stock unit (RSU):** Shares of a company's stock given to employees as a form of compensation. **p. 522**

**Retained earnings:** Earnings not distributed as dividends to stockholders over the life of the company. **pp. 504, 516**

**Return on equity (ROE):** Net income divided by average stockholders' equity; measures the income generated per dollar of equity. **p. 528**

**S corporation:** Allows a company to enjoy limited liability as a corporation, but tax treatment as a partnership. **p. 506**

**Statement of stockholders' equity:** A financial statement that summarizes the changes in stockholders' equity over the fiscal period. **p. 525**

**Stock dividends:** Additional shares of a company's own stock given to stockholders. **p. 521**

**Stock split:** A large stock dividend that includes a reduction in the par or stated value per share. **p. 521**

**Treasury stock:** A company's own issued stock that it has repurchased. **pp. 504, 512**

**Value stocks:** Stocks that tend to have lower price-earnings ratios and are priced low in relation to current earnings. **p. 530**

**Venture capital firms:** Provide additional financing, often in the millions, for a percentage ownership in the company. **p. 508**

## SELF-STUDY QUESTIONS

1. Which of the following is a publicly traded company? **(LO10–1)**
   a. Facebook.
   b. Cargill.
   c. Ernst & Young.
   d. Koch Industries.

2. The advantages of owning a corporation include **(LO10–1)**
   a. Difficulty in transferring ownership.
   b. Limited liability.
   c. Lower taxes.
   d. Less paperwork.

3. The correct order from the smallest number of shares to the largest number of shares is: **(LO10–2)**
   a. Authorized, issued, and outstanding.
   b. Outstanding, issued, and authorized.
   c. Issued, outstanding, and authorized.
   d. Issued, authorized, and outstanding.

4. A company issues 10,000 shares of $0.05 par value common stock for $25 per share. What are the financial statement effects of the issuance? **(LO10–2)**
   a. Increase Common Stock by $250,000.
   b. Increase Additional Paid-In Capital by $250,000.
   c. Increase Common Stock for $500.
   d. Increase Additional Paid-In Capital for $500.

5. Preferred stock: **(LO10–3)**
   a. Is always reported as a liability.
   b. Is always reported as part of stockholders' equity.

   c. Can have features of both liabilities and stockholders' equity.
   d. Is not included in either liabilities or stockholders' equity.

6. Treasury stock **(LO10–4)**
   a. Can have features of both liabilities and stockholders' equity.
   b. Decreases stockholders' equity.
   c. Is reported as an investment.
   d. Increases stockholders' equity.

7. Suppose a company repurchases 2,000 shares of its own $1 par value common stock for $16 per share. How does this transaction affect the financial statements at the time of the repurchase? **(LO10–4)**
   a. Increases total assets.
   b. Increases stockholders' equity.
   c. Decreases total liabilities.
   d. Decreases stockholders' equity.

8. Suppose a company repurchases 2,000 shares of its own $1 par value common stock for $16 per share. The company then resells 400 of these shares for $20 per share. How does the resale of treasury stock affect the financial statements? **(LO10–4)**
   a. Increases total assets.
   b. Decreases total assets.
   c. Decreases total liabilities.
   d. Decreases total stockholders' equity.

9. Retained earnings: **(LO10–5)**
   a. Is part of the income statement.
   b. Decreases stockholders' equity.

c. Is equal to the balance in cash.

d. Increases stockholders' equity.

10. In its first three years of operations, a company has net income of $2,000; $5,000; and $8,000. It also pays dividends of $1,000 in the second year, and $3,000 in the third year. What is the balance of Retained Earnings at the end of the third year? **(LO10–5)**

a. $5,000.

b. $11,000.

c. $15,000.

d. $4,000.

11. The liability related to cash dividends increases on the: **(LO10–5)**

a. Payment date.

b. Record date.

c. Declaration date.

d. Never.

12. Suppose a company declares a dividend of $0.50 per share. At the time of declaration, the company has 100,000 shares issued and 90,000 shares outstanding. On the declaration date, dividends would be **(LO10–5)**

a. $0.

b. $50,000.

c. $45,000.

d. $95,000.

13. Both cash dividends and stock dividends: **(LO10–6)**

a. Reduce total assets.

b. Reduce total liabilities.

c. Reduce total stockholders' equity.

d. Reduce retained earnings.

14. How does the stockholders' equity section in the balance sheet differ from the statement of stockholders' equity? **(LO10–7)**

a. The stockholders' equity section shows balances at a point in time, whereas the statement of stockholders' equity shows activity over the fiscal period.

b. The stockholders' equity section shows activity over the fiscal period, whereas the statement of stockholders' equity is at a point in time.

c. There are no differences between them.

d. The stockholders' equity section is more detailed than the statement of stockholders' equity.

15. The PE ratio **(LO10–8)**

a. Measures a company's profitability per share.

b. Tends to be higher for value stocks.

c. Tends to be higher for growth stocks.

d. Typically is less than 1.

*Note: For answers, see the last page of the chapter.*

## REAL WORLD PERSPECTIVES

### Lyft, Inc. (ticker: LYFT)

EDGAR Case

**RWP10–1** Visit **www.sec.gov/edgar** and search for the **Lyft** annual report (10-K) for the year ended December 31, 2019, using EDGAR (Electronic Data Gathering, Analysis, and Retrieval system). Locate the note titled "Item 5." Use the information in this note to answer the questions below.

**Required:**

1. Lyft has two classes of common stock, Class A and Class B. Which of these is publicly traded?
2. On what stock exchange does the common stock trade?
3. Who owns the Class B common stock?
4. Does Lyft pay cash dividends?

### AbbVie Inc. (ticker: ABBV)

EDGAR Case

**RWP10–2** Visit **www.sec.gov/edgar** and search for the **AbbVie** annual report (10-K) for the year ended December 31, 2019, using EDGAR (Electronic Data Gathering, Analysis, and Retrieval system). Locate the "Consolidated Statements of Equity," and use it to answer the following questions.

**Required:**

1. What caused Retained Earnings to increase between the fiscal years ended in 2019 and 2018?
2. Did AbbVie undertake stock repurchases in 2019? If so, what was the effect on total stockholders' equity?
3. Did AbbVie compensate some its employees in stock during 2019? If so, what was the effect on paid-in capital?

EDGAR Case

## Marriott International, Inc. (ticker: MAR)

**RWP10–3** Visit www.sec.gov/edgar and search for the Marriott annual report (10-K) for the year ended December 31, 2019, using EDGAR (Electronic Data Gathering, Analysis, and Retrieval system). Focus on its "Consolidated Statements of Shareholders' Equity" to answer the following questions.

***Required:***

1. What is the par value on Marriott's common stock?
2. Does Marriott have preferred stock authorized? Outstanding?
3. In 2019, Marriott repurchased millions of its own shares. What was the average cost per share of the treasury stock acquired?
4. By December 31, 2019, Marriott's shares were trading for $151/share. If the shares purchased in #3 had been sold on December 31, how much higher would net income have been for 2019?

EDGAR Case

## The Clorox Company (ticker: CLX)

**RWP10–4** Visit www.sec.gov/edgar and search for the Clorox annual report (10-K) for the year ended December 31, 2019, using EDGAR (Electronic Data Gathering, Analysis, and Retrieval system). Locate the balance sheet, income statement, and statement of shareholders' equity. In addition, on June 30, 2019, the stock price was $153. Use these to answer the following questions.

***Required:***

1. Compute return on equity for the year ended June 30, 2019.
2. Compute dividend yield for the year ended June 30, 2019.
3. Compute earnings per share for the year ended June 30, 2019. Hint: use weighted average shares outstanding (basic) from the income statement.
4. Compute the price-earnings ratio for the year ended June 30, 2019.

Continuing Financial Analysis Case

## American Eagle Outfitters, Inc.

**RWP10–5** Financial information for American Eagle is presented in **Appendix A** at the end of the book. Using the financial information presented in **Appendix A,** answer the following.

***Required:***

1. What is the par value per share for the common stock?
2. How many common shares were issued at the end of the most recent year?
3. Did the company have any treasury stock? How many shares?
4. How much did the company pay in cash dividends in the most recent year? (Hint: Look in the statement of stockholders' equity in the retained earnings column.)

Continuing Financial Analysis Case

## The Buckle, Inc.

**RWP10–6** Financial information for Buckle is presented in **Appendix B** at the end of the book.

***Required:***

1. What is the par value per share for the common stock?
2. How many common shares were issued at the end of the most recent year?
3. Did the company have any treasury stock? How many shares?
4. How much did the company pay in cash dividends in the most recent year? (Hint: Look in the statement of stockholders' equity in the retained earnings column.)

Continuing Comparative Analysis Case

## American Eagle Outfitters, Inc. vs. The Buckle, Inc.

**RWP10–7** Financial information for American Eagle is presented in **Appendix A** at the end of the book, and financial information for Buckle is presented in **Appendix B** at the end of the book.

**Required:**

1. Calculate the return on equity for American Eagle and Buckle for the most recent year. Which company is more profitable?
2. Determine the amount reported for basic earnings per share (or net income per share) for the most recent year for each company. Basic earnings per share are provided for each company near the bottom of the income statement.
3. Determine the amount of dividends per share for the most recent year for each company. (*Hint:* Find dividends per share in the statement of stockholders' equity). Using your answers for requirement 2, which company has a higher ratio of cash dividends to earnings? Which company has more treasury stock purchases?

## Ethics

Ethics Case

**RWP10-8** Brooke Remming is the Chief Executive Officer of Dundem Corp. The board of directors agreed to pay Brooke a salary of $400,000 plus a 15% bonus if the company's pretax income increases by at least 10% from the prior year. In the prior year, Dundem reported pretax income of $3,000,000.

In the final week of the current year, Brooke projects pretax income will be $3,250,000. While this is a nice increase over the prior year, she realizes the increase is below the 10% required for her bonus. Brooke has devoted many years to the company and feels the company has had another successful year thanks to her efforts and good decisions.

As one example of a good decision, Brooke noticed earlier in the year that the company's stock price had fallen to $42 per share. She felt the price was too low, so she used some of the company's available cash to purchase 10,000 shares. The current price has risen to $50 per share, and she is considering whether to sell the stock. She calculates the company will make a profit of $80,000 (= 10,000 shares × $8 increase per share) on the sale, and she would include the gain in pretax income. She feels this profit is possible only because of her good intuition, so it should be used in calculating whether she gets a bonus.

**Required:**

1. Understand the reporting effect: If Brooke sells the stock and includes the $80,000 gain in pretax income, will she get her bonus? Assume any bonus paid to Brooke is not included in calculating pretax income.
2. Specify the options: Instead of reporting the gain as part of pretax income, how else might Brooke report the gain on the sale?
3. Identify the impact: Does Brooke's decision affect the company?
4. Make a decision: Should Brooke record the gain on the sale of stock as part of pretax income?

## Sustainability

Sustainability Case

**RWP10-9** Go to the SASB website (https://www.sasb.org/company-use/sasb-reporters/) and search for **Columbia Sportswear Co.** Click on the Corporate Responsibility Report for 2019. Columbia Sportswear is an outdoor apparel company with such prominent brands as Columbia, SOREL, Mountain Hardwear, and prAna.

In its Corporate Social Responsibility Report, it discusses its endeavors to improve human capital, an important (but often unrecognized) element of equity. In particular, it discusses initiatives related to "Empowering People" (starting on page 13), including:

- Igniting human potential for growth
- Empowering people in our supply chain
- Investing in healthy communities

In this case, we will dig deeper to better understand what these initiatives entail.

**Required:**

1. In 2019, under "IGNITING HUMAN POTENTIAL FOR GROWTH" on page 13, what percentage of employees identified as underrepresented groups? What percentage of manager-level employees were women?

2. In 2019, under "EMPOWERING PEOPLE IN OUR SUPPLY CHAIN" on page 19, what two areas does Columbia focus on to achieve its aim to empower people along the supply chain?
3. In 2019, under "INVESTING IN HEALTHY COMMUNITIES" on page 21, how much did the company raise for Open Outdoors for Kids? Approximately how many college students were provided access to quality outdoor products?

**Earnings Management Case**

## Earnings Management

**RWP10–10** Renegade Clothing is struggling to meet analysts' forecasts. It's early December 2024, and the year-end projections are in. Listed below are the projections for the year ended 2024 and the comparable actual amounts for 2023.

|  | Projected 2024 | Actual 2023 |
|---|---|---|
| Sales | $14,000,000 | $16,023,000 |
| Net Income | 878,000 | 1,113,000 |
| Total assets | $ 6,500,000 | $ 6,821,000 |
| Total liabilities | $ 2,500,000 | $ 2,396,000 |
| Stockholders' equity | 4,000,000 | 4,425,000 |
| Total liabilities and stockholders' equity | $ 6,500,000 | $ 6,821,000 |
| Shares outstanding at year-end | 950,000 | 950,000 |

Analysts forecast earnings per share for 2024 to be $0.95 per share. It looks like earnings per share will fall short of expectations in 2024.

Ronald Outlaw, the director of marketing, has a creative idea to improve earnings per share and the return on equity. He proposes the company borrow additional funds and use the proceeds to purchase some of its own stock—treasury shares. Is this a good idea?

***Required:***

1. Calculate the projected earnings per share and return on equity for 2024 before any purchase of stock.

Now assume Renegade Clothing borrows $1 million and uses the money to purchase 100,000 shares of its own stock at $10 per share. The projections for 2024 will change as follows:

|  | 2024 | 2023 |
|---|---|---|
| Sales | $14,000,000 | $16,023,000 |
| Net Income | 878,000 | 1,113,000 |
| Total assets | $ 6,500,000 | $ 6,821,000 |
| Total liabilities | $ 3,500,000 | $ 2,396,000 |
| Stockholders' equity | 3,000,000 | 4,425,000 |
| Total liabilities and stockholders' equity | $ 6,500,000 | $ 6,821,000 |
| Shares outstanding at year-end | 850,000 | 950,000 |

2. Calculate the new projected earnings per share and return on equity for 2024, assuming the company goes through with the treasury stock purchase. (*Hint:* In computing earnings per share, average shares outstanding is now 900,000 = (850,000 + 950,000)/2.)
3. Does the purchase of treasury stock near year-end improve earnings per share and the return on equity ratio? Explain.

**Continuing General Ledger Case**

## Great Adventures

(This is a continuation of the Great Adventures problem from earlier chapters.)

**RWP10–11** Tony and Suzie have purchased land for a new camp. Now they need money to build the cabins, dining facility, a ropes course, and an outdoor swimming pool. Tony and

Suzie first checked with Summit Bank to see if they could borrow an additional $1 million, but unfortunately the bank turned them down as too risky. Undeterred, they promoted their idea to close friends they had made through the outdoor clinics and TEAM events. They decided to go ahead and sell shares of stock in the company to raise the additional funds for the camp.

Great Adventures has authorized $1 par value common stock. When the company began on July 1, 2024, Tony and Suzie each purchased 10,000 shares (20,000 shares total) of $1 par value common stock at $1 per share. The following transactions affect stockholders' equity during the remainder of 2025:

| | |
|---|---|
| November 5 | Issue an additional 100,000 shares of common stock for $10 per share. |
| November 16 | Purchase 10,000 shares of its own common stock (i.e., treasury stock) for $15 per share. |
| November 24 | Resell 4,000 shares of treasury stock at $16 per share. |
| Devember 1 | Declare a cash dividend on its common stock of $11,400 ($0.10 per share) to all stockholders of record on December 15. |
| December 20 | Pay the cash dividend declared on December 1. |
| December 30 | Pay $800,000 for construction of new cabins and other facilities. The entire expenditure is recorded in the Buildings account. |

### Required:

1. Record each of these transactions.
2. Great Adventures has net income of $35,835 in 2025. Retained earnings at the beginning of 2025 was $33,450. Prepare the stockholders' equity section of the balance sheet for Great Adventures as of December 31, 2025.

The Great Adventures continuing problem also can be assigned using the General Ledger software in Connect. Students will be given an existing trial balance and asked to prepare: (1) the journal entries for the transactions above in 2025, (2) financial statements, and (3) closing entries.

## BRIEF EXERCISES

**BE10–1** Waldo is planning to start a clothing store helping big and tall men blend in with the crowd. Explain to Waldo the advantages and disadvantages of a corporation in comparison to a sole proprietorship or partnership.

*Identify the advantages of various corporate forms of ownership (LO10–1)*

**BE10–2** Renaldo heard that an S corporation combines the benefits of a corporation with the benefits of a partnership. Explain to Renaldo the specific benefits of an S corporation and any drawbacks to organizing as an S corporation.

*Identify the advantages and disadvantages of S corporations (LO10–1)*

**BE10–3** Western Wear Clothing issues 3,000 shares of its $0.01 par value common stock to provide funds for further expansion. Assuming the issue price is $11 per share, determine the financial statement effects of the issuance of common stock.

*Understand the issuance of common stock (LO10–2)*
*See JBE10–1 for journal entries.*

**BE10–4** Gothic Architecture is a new chain of clothing stores. Gothic issues 1,000 shares of its $1 par value common stock at $30 per share. Determine the financial statement effects of the issuance of the stock. How would the financial statement effects differ if Gothic issued no-par value stock?

*Understand par value versus no-par value stock (LO10–2)*
*See JBE10–2 for journal entries.*

**BE10–5** Equinox Outdoor Wear issues 1,000 shares of its $0.01 par value preferred stock for cash at $32 per share. Determine the financial statement effects of the issuance of the preferred shares.

*Understand preferred stock (LO10–3)*
*See JBE10–3 for journal entries.*

**BE10–6** Josie's Flip Flops issued 400,000 shares of 5.5% preferred stock with par value of $2. Determine the total preferred dividend for the year.

*Understand dividends on preferred stock (LO10–3)*

Account for purchase of treasury stock (LO10–4)
See JBE10–4 for journal entries.

**BE10–7** California Surf Clothing Company issues 1,000 shares of $1 par value common stock at $35 per share. Later in the year, the company decides to repurchase 100 shares at a cost of $38 per share. Determine the financial statement effects of the repurchase of treasury stock.

Account for sale of treasury stock (LO10–4)
See JBE10–5 for journal entries.

**BE10–8** Refer to the situation described in BE10–7. Determine the financial statement effects of the transaction if California Surf resells the 100 shares of treasury stock at $40 per share.

Account for sale of treasury stock (LO10–4)
See JBE10–6 for journal entries.

**BE10–9** Refer to the situation described in BE10–7. Determine the financial statement effects of the transaction if California Surf resells the 100 shares of treasury stock at $35 per share.

Calculate retained earnings (LO10–5)

**BE10–10** Diamond Dresses began the year with a balance of $425,000 in Retained Earnings. During the year, the company had net income of $100,000 and declared no dividends. (a) Calculate the ending balance of Retained Earnings. (b) Now assume the company declared dividends of $25,000. Calculate the ending balance of Retained Earnings.

Understand dividend dates (LO10–5)
See JBE10–7 for journal entries.

**BE10–11** Divine Apparel has 4,000 shares of common stock outstanding. On October 1, the company declares a $0.75 per share dividend to stockholders of record on October 15. The dividend is paid on October 31. Determine the financial statement effects for all transactions on the appropriate dates for cash dividends.

Identify effects of stock splits (LO10–6)

**BE10–12** On June 30, the board of directors of Sandals, Inc., declares a 2-for-1 stock split on its 30,000, $1 par, common shares. The market price of Sandals common stock is $35/share on June 30. What are the number of shares, par value per share, and market price per share immediately after the 2-for-1 stock split?

Identify effects of stock-based compensation (LO10–6)
See JBE10–8 for journal entries.

**BE10–13** Kerrie Mi Enterprises grants stock to its executive team on June 30, subject to the restriction that they remain employed with the company for at least three years. The market value of the stock on June 30 is $900,000. Determine the financial statement effects of the grant of restricted stock on June 30.

Identify effects of stock-based compensation (LO10–6)
See JBE10–9 for journal entries.

**BE10–14** Refer to the situation described in BE10–13. Determine the financial statement effects of stock-based compensation expense for the fiscal year ended December 31 (six months later), assuming all employees remain with the company.

Analyze effects on stockholders' equity (LO10–7)

**BE10–15** Indicate whether each of the following transactions increases (+), decreases (−), or has no effect (NE) on total assets, total liabilities, and total stockholders' equity. The first transaction is completed as an example.

| Transaction | Total Assets | Total Liabilities | Total Stockholders' Equity |
|---|---|---|---|
| *Issue common stock* | *+* | *NE* | *+* |
| Issue preferred stock | | | |
| Purchase treasury stock | | | |
| Resell treasury stock | | | |

Prepare the stockholders' equity section of a balance sheet (LO10–7)

**BE10–16** Summit Apparel has the following accounts at December 31: Common Stock, $1 par value, 2,000,000 shares issued; Additional Paid-in Capital, $18 million; Retained Earnings, $11 million; and Treasury Stock, 60,000 shares, $1.32 million. Prepare the stockholders' equity section of the balance sheet.

Compute return on equity (LO10–8)

**BE10–17** The financial statements of Colorado Outfitters include the following selected data ($ in millions): sales, $9,543; net income, $320; beginning stockholders' equity, $3,219; and ending stockholders' equity, $2,374. Calculate the return on equity.

Compute earnings per share (LO10–8)

**BE10–18** Refer to the situation described in BE10–17. Assuming Colorado Outfitters has 630 shares outstanding and 650 shares issued (shares in millions), calculate the earnings per share.

**BE10–19** KC Gardens pays an annual dividend of $0.65 per share on earnings per share of $2.20. Its stock price at the end of the year is $36. Calculate the dividend yield.

Compute dividend yield (LO10–8)

**BE10–20** Refer to the situation described in BE10–19. Calculate the price-earnings ratio.

Compute the price-earnings ratio (LO10–8)

## EXERCISES

Mc Graw Hill **connect**

**E10–1** Match (by letter) the following terms with their definitions. Each letter is used only once.

Understand the advantages and disadvantages of the corporate form of ownership (LO10–1)

Terms:

_____ 1. Publicly held corporation.
_____ 2. Organization chart.
_____ 3. Articles of incorporation.
_____ 4. Limited liability.
_____ 5. Initial public offering.
_____ 6. Double taxation.
_____ 7. S corporation.
_____ 8. Limited liability company.

Definitions

a. Shareholders can lose no more than the amount they invest in the company.
b. Corporate earnings are taxed twice—at the corporate level and individual shareholder level.
c. Like an S corporation, but there are no limitations on the number of owners as in an S corporation.
d. Traces the line of authority within the corporation.
e. Allows for legal treatment as a corporation, but tax treatment as a partnership.
f. Has stock traded on a stock exchange such as the New York Stock Exchange (NYSE).
g. The first time a corporation issues stock to the public.
h. Describes (a) the nature of the firm's business activities, (b) the shares to be issued, and (c) the composition of the initial board of directors.

**E10–2** Match (by letter) the following terms with their definitions. Each letter is used only once.

Understand common terms (LO10–2, 10–3, 10–4)

Terms:

_____ 1. Authorized stock
_____ 2. Issued stock
_____ 3. Outstanding stock
_____ 4. Preferred stock
_____ 5. Treasury stock

Definitions:

a. Shares held by investors (shares issued that have not been repurchased by the corporation).
b. Shares that have been sold to investors.
c. Shares of a company's own stock it has repurchased.
d. Shares available to sell, stated in the company's articles of incorporation.
e. Shares that have preference over common stockholders to receive dividends.

**E10–3** DEFT Adventures began operations on January 1 and engages in the following transactions during the year related to stockholders' equity.

Understand the issuance of common stock (LO10–2) See JE10–1 for journal entries.

January 1     Issues 700 shares of common stock for $50 per share.
April   1     Issues 110 additional shares of common stock for $54 per share.

*Required:*

1. Determine the financial statement effects of the transactions, assuming DEFT Adventures has no-par common stock.
2. Determine the financial statement effects of the transactions, assuming DEFT Adventures has $1 par value common stock.

**Understand the issuance of common stock (LO10–2)**
*See JE10–2 for journal entries.*

**E10–4** Major Sports plans to raise $5,000,000 in an initial public offering of its common stock. The company is considering three options:

a. Issue 100,000 shares of $1 par value common stock for $50 per share.
b. Issue 500,000 shares of $1 par value common stock for $10 per share.
c. Issue 1,000,000 shares of $1 par value common stock for $5 per share.

*Required:*
Determine the financial statement effects for each option.

**Understand the issuance of common stock (LO10–2)**
*See JE10–3 for journal entries.*

**E10–5** Datadog (Ticker: DDOG) underwent an initial public offering (IPO) in 2019 by issuing 24 million shares of common stock at $27.00/share. The par value is $0.00001 per share.

*Required:*

1. Determine the financial statement effects of the IPO.
2. The stock price for DDOG increased to $37 at the end of 2019. Assuming no other changes, determine the financial statement effects of the stock price increase, if any.

**Understand dividends on preferred stock (LO10–3, 10–5)**
*See JE10–4 for journal entries.*

**E10–6** Prints Charles Custom T-shirts issued 2,000 shares of 5%, $100 par value preferred stock on January 1 for $500,000. The company declares and pays the full preferred dividend on December 31.

*Required:*

1. Determine the financial statement effects of the preferred stock issuance on January 1.
2. Determine the amount and financial statement effects of the preferred dividend declared and paid on December 31.

**Understand effects of share repurchases (LO10–4)**
*See JE10–5 for journal entries.*

**E10–7** Chubb Limited (ticker: CG) reports the following share repurchase activity for the last quarter of 2019:

| Month | Total Number of Shares Purchased | Average Price Paid per Share |
|---|---|---|
| October | 703,200 | $153.65 |
| November | 677,600 | $151.41 |
| December | 654,400 | $153.84 |

*Required:*

1. Determine the financial statement effects of all share repurchases for the full quarter.
2. Assume Chubb resells 100,000 shares of treasury stock on December 31 for $150/share. These shares relate to the shares repurchased in October. Determine the financial statement effects of this transaction.

**Determine financial statement effects of share issuance and dividends (LO10–2, 10–3, 10–5)**
*See JE10–6 for journal entries.*

**E10–8** Italian Stallion has the following transactions during the year related to stockholders' equity.

| February 1 | Issues 6,000 shares of no-par common stock for $16 per share. |
|---|---|
| May 15 | Issues 700 shares of $10 par value, 12.5% preferred stock for $13 per share. |
| October 1 | Declares a cash dividend of $1.25 per share to all stockholders of record (both common and preferred) on October 15. |
| October 15 | Date of record. |
| October 31 | Pays the cash dividend declared on October 1. |

**Determine the effects of common stock issuance, preferred stock issuance and share repurchases (LO10–2, 10–3, 10–4)**
*See JE10–7 for journal entries.*

*Required:*
Determine the financial statement effects of each of these transactions.

**E10–9** Finishing Touches has two classes of stock authorized: 8%, $10 par preferred, and $1 par value common. The following transactions affect stockholders' equity during 2024, its first year of operations:

| January | 2 | Issues 100,000 shares of common stock for $35 per share. |
|---|---|---|
| February | 6 | Issues 3,000 shares of 8% preferred stock for $11 per share. |
| September | 10 | Repurchases 11,000 shares of its own common stock for $40 per share. |
| December | 15 | Resells 5,500 shares of treasury stock at $45 per share. |

*Required:*

Determine the financial statement effects of each of these transactions.

**E10–10** Consider each of the following independent situations:

Find missing amounts for retained earnings (LO10–5)

|  | Beginning Retained Earnings | Net Income for the Year | Dividends for the Year | Ending Retained Earnings |
|---|---|---|---|---|
| a. | $320,000 | $120,000 | $20,000 | _____ |
| b. | $540,000 | $230,000 | _____ | $700,000 |
| c. | $290,000 | _____ | $50,000 | $360,000 |
| d. | _____ | $170,000 | $30,000 | $490,000 |

*Required:*

For each situation, calculate the missing amount.

**E10–11** In its first five years of operations, Monster Hats reports the following net income and dividends (the first year is a net loss).

Calculate retained earnings each year (LO10–5)

| Year | Net Income (Loss) for the Year | Dividends for the Year | Ending Retained Earnings |
|---|---|---|---|
| 1 | $ (35,000) | $ 0 | _____ |
| 2 | 52,000 | 0 | _____ |
| 3 | 87,000 | 20,000 | _____ |
| 4 | 128,000 | 20,000 | _____ |
| 5 | 153,000 | 25,000 | _____ |

*Required:*

Calculate the balance of Retained Earnings at the end of each year.

**E10–12** On March 15, **American Eagle** declares a quarterly cash dividend of $0.125 per share payable on April 13 to all stockholders of record on March 30.

Account for cash dividends (LO10–5) See JE10–8 for journal entries.

*Required:*

Determine the financial statement effects of American Eagle's declaration and payment of cash dividends for its 210 million shares.

**E10–13** On September 15, 2024, MD Soccer Academy declares a quarterly cash dividend of $0.10 per share payable on October 10, 2024 to all stockholders of record on October 7, 2024. On December 15, 2024, MD Soccer declares a quarterly cash dividend of $0.10 per share payable on January 10, 2025 to all stockholders of record on January 7, 2025. The company has 400,000 shares outstanding.

Account for cash dividends and retained earnings (LO10–5)

*Required:*

1. Compute the total dividends declared for the year ended December 31, 2024.
2. Compute the total dividends paid for the year ended December 31, 2024.
3. Assuming net income of $63,000 and a beginning balance in retained earnings of $1,060,000, determine the balance of retained earnings as of the year ended December 31, 2024.

**E10–14** Power Drive Corporation designs and produces a line of golf equipment and golf apparel. Power Drive has 100,000 shares of common stock outstanding as of the beginning of 2024. Power Drive has the following transactions affecting stockholders' equity in 2024.

Understand stock issuance, treasury stock, cash dividends, and retained earnings (LO10–2, 10–4, 10–5) See JE10–9 for journal entries.

| March | 1 | Issues 65,000 additional shares of $1 par value common stock for $62 per share. |
|---|---|---|
| May | 10 | Purchases 6,000 shares of treasury stock for $65 per share. |
| June | 1 | Declares a cash dividend of $2.00 per share to all stockholders of record on June 15. (*Hint:* Dividends are not paid on treasury stock.) |
| July | 1 | Pays the cash dividend declared on June 1. |
| October | 21 | Resells 3,000 shares of treasury stock purchased on May 10 for $70 per share. |

**Required:**

Determine the financial statement effects of each of these transactions.

**Prepare the stockholders' equity section of a balance sheet (LO10–7)**

**E10–15** Refer to the information in E10–14. Power Drive Corporation has the following beginning balances in its stockholders' equity accounts on January 1, 2024: Common Stock, $100,000; Additional Paid-in Capital, $5,500,000; and Retained Earnings, $3,000,000. Net income for the year ended December 31, 2024, is $700,000.

**Required:**

Taking into consideration all of the transactions in E10–14, prepare the stockholders' equity section of the balance sheet for Power Drive Corporation as of December 31, 2024.

**Prepare the statement of stockholders' equity (LO10–7)**

**E10–16** Refer to the information in E10–14. Power Drive Corporation has the following beginning balances in its stockholders' equity accounts on January 1, 2024: Common Stock, $100,000; Additional Paid-in Capital, $5,500,000; and Retained Earnings, $3,000,000. Net income for the year ended December 31, 2024, is $700,000.

**Required:**

Taking into consideration all the transactions in E10–14, prepare the statement of stockholders' equity for Power Drive Corporation for the year ended December 31, 2024, using the format provided.

**POWER DRIVE CORPORATION**
**Statement of Stockholders' Equity**
**For the year ended December 31, 2024**

| | Common Stock | Additional Paid-In Capital | Retained Earnings | Treasury Stock | Total Stockholders' Equity |
|---|---|---|---|---|---|
| Balance, January 1 | $100,000 | $5,500,000 | $3,000,000 | $ -0- | $8,600,000 |
| Issue common stock | | | | | |
| Purchase treasury stock | | | | | |
| Declare dividends | | | | | |
| Resell treasury stock | | | | | |
| Net income | ___ | ___ | ___ | ___ | ___ |
| Balance, December 31 | ═══ | ═══ | ═══ | ═══ | ═══ |

**Indicate effects on total stockholders' equity (LO10–7)**

**E10–17** Indicate whether each of the following transactions increases (+), decreases (−), or has no effect (NE) on total assets, total liabilities, and total stockholders' equity. The first transaction is completed as an example.

| Transaction | Total Assets | Total Liabilities | Total Stockholders' Equity |
|---|---|---|---|
| *Issue common stock* | + | NE | + |
| Issue preferred stock | | | |
| Repurchase shares | | | |
| Resell treasury stock | | | |
| Declare cash dividend | | | |
| Pay cash dividend | | | |
| 2-for-1 stock split | | | |

**Prepare the stockholders' equity section of a balance sheet (LO10–7)**

**E10–18** United Apparel has the following balances in its stockholders' equity accounts on December 31, 2024: Treasury Stock, $850,000; Common Stock, $600,000; Preferred Stock, $3,600,000; Retained Earnings, $2,200,000; and Additional Paid-in Capital, $8,800,000.

**Required:**

Prepare the stockholders' equity section of the balance sheet for United Apparel as of December 31, 2024.

**E10–19** The financial statements of Friendly Fashions include the following selected data (in millions):

Evaluate company performance using information on stockholders' equity (LO10–8)

| ($ in millions except per share amounts) | 2024 | 2023 |
|---|---|---|
| Sales | $10,043 | $11,134 |
| Net income | $ 312 | $ 818 |
| Stockholders' equity | $ 1,850 | $ 2,310 |
| Average shares outstanding (in millions) | 675 | – |
| Dividends per share | $ 0.31 | – |
| Stock price per share | $ 6.20 | – |

**Required:**

1. Calculate the return on equity in 2024.
2. Calculate the dividend yield in 2024.
3. Calculate earnings per share in 2024.
4. Calculate the price-earnings ratio in 2024.

**E10–20** Financial information for Forever 18 includes the following selected data:

Evaluate company performance using information on stockholders' equity (LO10–8)

| ($ in millions except per share amounts) | 2024 | 2023 |
|---|---|---|
| Net income | $ 129 | $ 308 |
| Dividends on preferred stock | $ 20 | $ 15 |
| Average shares outstanding | 150 | 400 |
| Stock price per share | $12.02 | $10.97 |

**Required:**

1. Calculate earnings per share in 2024 and 2023. Did earnings per share increase in 2024?
2. Calculate the price-earnings ratio in 2024 and 2023. In which year is the stock priced lower in relation to reported earnings?

## PROBLEMS

**P10–1** Donnie Hilfiger has two classes of stock authorized: $1 par preferred and $0.01 par value common. As of the beginning of 2024, 300 shares of preferred stock and 4,000 shares of common stock have been issued. The following transactions affect stockholders' equity during 2024:

Understand stock issuance, share repurchases, and cash dividends (LO10–2, 10–3, 10–4, 10–5)
See JP10–1 for journal entries.

| March | 1 | Issue 1,100 shares of common stock for $42 per share. |
|---|---|---|
| May | 15 | Repurchase 400 shares of stock for $35 per share. |
| July | 10 | Resell 200 shares of treasury stock purchased on May 15 for $40 per share. |
| October | 15 | Issue 200 shares of preferred stock for $45 per share. |
| December | 1 | Declare a cash dividend on both common and preferred stock. |
| December | 31 | Pay the cash dividends declared on December 1. |

**Required:**

Indicate whether each of these transactions would increase (+), decrease (−), or have no effect (NE) on total assets, total liabilities, and total stockholders' equity by completing the following chart.

| Transaction | Total Assets | Total Liabilities | Total Stockholders' Equity |
|---|---|---|---|
| Issue common stock | | | |
| Purchase treasury stock | | | |
| Resell treasury stock | | | |
| Issue preferred stock | | | |
| Declare cash dividends | | | |
| Pay cash dividends | | | |

**Understand common stock issuance, preferred stock issuance, treasury stock and cash dividends. (LO10–2, 10–3, 10–4, 10–5)**
*See JP10–2 for journal entries.*

**P10–2** Major League Apparel has two classes of stock authorized: 6%, $10 par preferred, and $1 par value common. The following transactions affect stockholders' equity during 2024, its first year of operations:

| | | |
|---|---|---|
| January | 2 | Issue 110,00 shares of common stock for $70 per share. |
| February | 14 | Issue 60,000 shares of preferred stock for $12 per share. |
| May | 8 | Purchase 11,000 shares of its own common stock for $60 per share. |
| May | 31 | Resell 5,500 shares of treasury stock for $65 per share. |
| December | 1 | Declare a cash dividend on its common stock of $0.25 per share and a $36,000 (6% of par value) cash dividend on its preferred stock payable to all stockholders of record on December 15. The dividend is payable on December 30. (*Hint:* Dividends are not paid on treasury stock.) |
| December | 30 | Pay the cash dividends declared on December 1. |

*Required:*
Determine the financial statement effects of each of these transactions 2024.

**Identify dividend dates, account for cash dividends, and compute dividend yield (LO10–5, 10–8)**
*See JP10–3 for journal entries.*

**P10–3** On Nov. 21, 2019, **Chubb Limited** issued the following press release: *The Board of Directors of Chubb Limited (NYSE: CB) today declared a quarterly dividend equal to $0.75 per share, payable on January 10, 2020 to shareholders of record at the close of business on December 20, 2019.*

*Required:*
1. From the information above, identify the dividend declaration date, record date, and payment date.
2. Determine the financial statement effects of Chubb's declaration and payment of cash dividends for its 452 million shares.
3. Based on a stock price of $156, compute the dividend yield. (*Hint:* Annualize the dividend per share by multiplying the quarterly dividend per share by 4.)

**Explain the effect of stock dividends and stock splits (LO10–6)**

**P10–4** Sammy's Sportshops has been very profitable in recent years and has seen its stock price steadily increase to over $100 per share. The CFO thinks the company should consider a 2-for-1 stock split.

*Required:*
1. Complete the following chart showing the effects of a 2-for-1 stock split on the stockholders' equity accounts, shares outstanding, par value, and share price.

| | Before | After 2-for-1 Stock Split |
|---|---|---|
| Common stock, $1 par value | $ 1,100 | |
| Additional paid-in capital | 59,000 | _____ |
| Total paid-in capital | 60,100 | |
| Retained earnings | 23,850 | _____ |
| Total stockholders' equity | $83,950 | _____ |
| Shares outstanding | 1,100 | _____ |
| Par value per share | $    1 | _____ |
| Share price | $  130 | _____ |

2. What is the primary reason companies declare a stock split?

**P10–5** The stockholders' equity section of the balance sheet for Velcro World is presented here.    Analyze stockholders' equity (LO10–7)

### VELCRO WORLD
### Balance Sheet (partial)

| ($ and shares in thousands)<br>Stockholders' equity: | |
| --- | --- |
| Preferred stock, $1 par value | $        6,000 |
| Common stock, $1 par value | 30,000 |
| Additional paid-in capital | 1,164,000 |
| Total paid-in capital | 1,200,000 |
| Retained earnings | 288,000 |
| Treasury stock, 11,000 common shares | (352,000) |
| Total stockholders' equity | $1,136,0000 |

**Required:**

Based on the stockholders' equity section of the balance sheet for Velcro World, answer the following questions. Remember that all amounts are presented in thousands.

1. How many shares of preferred stock have been issued?
2. How many shares of common stock have been issued?
3. If the common shares were issued at $30 per share, at what average price per share were the preferred shares issued?
4. If retained earnings at the beginning of the period was $250 million and $30 million was paid in dividends during the year, what was the net income for the year?
5. What was the average cost per share of the treasury stock acquired?

**P10–6** Khaki Republic sells clothing and accessories through premium outlet locations and online. Selected financial data for Khaki Republic is provided as follows:     Evaluate company performance using information on stockholders' equity (LO10–8)

| ($ in millions) | |
| --- | --- |
| Sales | $4,158 |
| Net income | $    144 |
| Stockholders' equity, beginning | $1,890 |
| Stockholders' equity, ending | $1,931 |
| Average shares outstanding | 85.6 |
| Dividends per share | $  0.75 |
| Stock price, ending | $47.23 |

**Required:**

1. Calculate the return on equity for Khaki Republic. How does it compare with the return on equity for Facebook and IBM reported in the chapter?
2. Calculate the dividend yield for Khaki Republic. How does it compare with the dividend yield for Facebook and IBM reported in the chapter?
3. Calculate the price-earnings ratio for Khaki Republic. How does it compare with the price-earnings ratio for Facebook and IBM reported in the chapter?

## JOURNAL ENTRIES

## Journal Entries—Brief Exercises

**JBE10–1** Western Wear Clothing issues 3,000 shares of its $0.01 par value common stock to provide funds for further expansion. Assuming the issue price is $11 per share, record the issuance of common stock.

Record the issuance of common stock (LO10–2)
*See BE10–3 for financial statement effects.*

Record the issuance of par
value versus no-par value
stock (LO10–2)
See BE10–4 for financial
statement effects.

**JBE10–2** Gothic Architecture is a new chain of clothing stores. Gothic issues 1,000 shares of its $1 par value common stock at $30 per share. Record the issuance of the stock. How would the entry differ if Gothic issued no-par value stock?

Record the issuance of
preferred stock (LO10–3)
See BE10–5 for financial
statement effects.

**JBE10–3** Equinox Outdoor Wear issues 1,000 shares of its $0.01 par value preferred stock for cash at $32 per share. Record the issuance of the preferred shares.

Record the repurchase of
treasury stock (LO10–4)
See BE10–7 for financial
statement effects.

**JBE10–4** California Surf Clothing Company issues 1,000 shares of $1 par value common stock at $35 per share. Later in the year, the company decides to repurchase 100 shares at a cost of $38 per share. Record the share repurchase.

Record the sale of treasury
stock (LO10–4)
See BE10–8 for financial
statement effects.

**JBE10–5** Refer to the situation described in JBE–4. Record the transaction if California Surf resells the 100 shares of treasury stock at $40 per share.

Record the sale of treasury
stock (LO10–4)
See BE10–9 for financial
statement effects.

**JBE10–6** Refer to the situation described in JBE–4. Record the transaction if California Surf resells the 100 shares of treasury stock at $35 per share

Record cash
dividends (LO10–5)
See BE10–11 for financial
statement effects.

**JBE10–7** Divine Apparel has 4,000 shares of common stock outstanding. On October 1, the company declares a $0.75 per share dividend to stockholders of record on October 15. The dividend is paid on October 31. Record all transactions on the appropriate dates for cash dividends.

Record stock-based
compensation
(LO10–6)
See BE10–13 for financial
statement effects.

**JBE10–8** Kerrie Mi Enterprises grants common stock to its executive team on June 30, subject to the restriction they remain employed with the company for at least 3 years. The market value of the stock on June 30 is $900,000. If needed, record the grant of restricted stock on June 30.

Record stock-based
compensation
(LO10–6)
See BE10–14 for financial
statement effects.

**JBE10–9** Refer to the situation described in JBE10–8. Determine the amount of stock-based compensation expense for the fiscal year ended December 31, assuming all employees remain with the company. Record the stock-based compensation expense for the year ended December 31.

## Journal Entries—Exercises

Record the issuance of
common stock (LO10–2)
See E10–3 for financial
statement effects.

**JE10–1** DEFT Adventures began operations on January 1 and engages in the following transactions during the year related to stockholders' equity.

January 1       Issues 700 shares of common stock for $50 per share.
April   1       Issues 110 additional shares of common stock for $54 per share.

*Required:*
1. Record the transactions, assuming DEFT Adventures has no-par common stock.
2. Record the transactions, assuming DEFT Adventures has $1 par value common stock.

Record the issuance of
common stock (LO10–2)
See E10–4 for financial
statement effects.

**JE10–2** Major Sports plans to raise $5,000,000 in an initial public offering of its common stock. The company is considering three options:
a. Issue 100,000 shares of $1 par value common stock for $50 per share.
b. Issue 500,000 shares of $1 par value common stock for $10 per share.
c. Issue 1,000,000 shares of $1 par value common stock for $5 per share.

*Required:*
Record the issuance of common stock for each option.

**JE10–3** Datadog (Ticker: DDOG) underwent an initial public offering (IPO) in 2019 by issuing 24 million shares of common stock at $27.00/share. The par value is $0.00001 per share.

*Record the issuance of common stock (LO10–2)*

*See E10–5 for financial statement effects.*

**Required:**

1. Record the issuance of common stock via the IPO.
2. The stock price for DDOG increased to $37 at the end of 2019. Assuming no other changes, record the stock price increase, if needed.

**JE10–4** Prints Charles Custom T-shirts issued 2,000 shares of 5%, $100 par value preferred stock on January 1 for $500,000. The company declares and pays the full preferred dividend on December 31.

*Record the issuance of preferred stock and preferred dividends (LO10–3)*

*See E10–6 for financial statement effects.*

**Required:**

1. Record the preferred stock issuance on January 1.
2. Compute and record the preferred dividend declared and paid on December 31.

**JE10–5** Chubb Limited (Ticker: CG) reports the following share repurchase activity for the last quarter of 2019:

*Record share repurchases (LO10–4)*

*See E10–7 for financial statement effects.*

| Month | Total Number of Shares Purchased | Average Price Paid per Share |
|---|---|---|
| October | 703,200 | $153.65 |
| November | 677,600 | $151.41 |
| December | 654,400 | $153.84 |

**Required:**

1. Record the share repurchases for each month.
2. Assume Chubb resells 100,000 shares of treasury stock on December 31 for $150/share. These shares relate to the shares repurchased in October. Record this transaction.

**JE10–6** Italian Stallion has the following transactions during the year related to stockholders' equity.

*Record share issuance and dividends (LO10–2, 10–3, 10–5)*

*See E10–8 for financial statement effects.*

| | | |
|---|---|---|
| February | 1 | Issues 6,000 shares of no-par common stock for $16 per share. |
| May | 15 | Issues 700 shares of $10 par value preferred stock for $13 per share. |
| October | 1 | Declares a cash dividend of $1.25 per share to all stockholders of record (both common and preferred) on October 15. |
| October | 15 | Date of record. |
| October | 31 | Pays the cash dividend declared on October 1. |

**Required:**

Record each of these transactions.

**JE10–7** Finishing Touches has two classes of stock authorized: 8%, $10 par preferred, and $1 par value common. The following transactions affect stockholders' equity during 2024, its first year of operations:

*Record common stock issuance, preferred stock issuance and share repurchases (LO10–2, 10–3, 10–4)*

*See E10–9 for financial statement effects.*

**Required:**

Record each of these transactions.

| | | |
|---|---|---|
| January | 2 | Issues 100,000 shares of common stock for $35 per share. |
| February | 6 | Issues 3,000 shares of 8% preferred stock for $11 per share. |
| September | 10 | Repurchases 11,000 shares of its own common stock for $40 per share. |
| December | 15 | Resells 5,500 shares of treasury stock at $45 per share. |

**JE10–8** On March 15, American Eagle declares a quarterly cash dividend of $0.125 per share payable on April 13 to all stockholders of record on March 30.

*Record cash dividends (LO10–5)*

*See E10–12 for financial statement effects.*

**Required:**

Record American Eagle's declaration and payment of cash dividends for its 210 million shares.

Record stock issuance, treasury stock, and cash dividends (LO10–2, 10–4, 10–5)
See E10–14 for financial statement effects.

**JE10–9** Power Drive Corporation designs and produces a line of golf equipment and golf apparel. Power Drive has 100,000 shares of common stock outstanding as of the beginning of 2024. Power Drive has the following transactions affecting stockholders' equity in 2024.

| | | |
|---|---|---|
| March | 1 | Issues 65,000 additional shares of $1 par value common stock for $62 per share. |
| May | 10 | Purchases 6,000 shares of treasury stock for $65 per share. |
| June | 1 | Declares a cash dividend of $2.00 per share to all stockholders of record on June 15. (*Hint:* Dividends are not paid on treasury stock.) |
| July | 1 | Pays the cash dividend declared on June 1. |
| October | 21 | Resells 3,000 shares of treasury stock purchased on May 10 for $70 per share. |

**Required:**
Record each of these transactions.

## Journal Entries—Problems

Record stock issuance, share repurchases, and cash dividends (LO10–2, 10–3, 10–4, 10–5)
See P10–1 for financial statement effects.

**JP10–1** Donnie Hilfiger has two classes of stock authorized: $1 par preferred and $0.01 par value common. As of the beginning of 2024, 300 shares of preferred stock and 4,000 shares of common stock have been issued. The following transactions affect stockholders' equity during 2024:

| | | |
|---|---|---|
| March | 1 | Issue 1,100 shares of common stock for $42 per share. |
| May | 15 | Repurchase 400 shares of stock for $35 per share. |
| July | 10 | Resell 200 shares of treasury stock purchased on May 15 for $40 per share. |
| October | 15 | Issue 200 shares of preferred stock for $45 per share. |
| December | 1 | Declare a cash dividend on both common and preferred stock of $0.50 per share to all stockholders of record on December 15. (*Hint:* Dividends are not paid on treasury stock.) |
| December | 31 | Pay the cash dividends declared on December 1. |

**Required:**
Record each of these transactions.

Record stock issuance, share repurchases, and cash dividends   (LO10–2, 10–3, 10–4, 10–5)
See P10–2 for financial statement effects.

**JP10–2** Major League Apparel has two classes of stock authorized: 6%, $10 par preferred, and $1 par value common. The following transactions affect stockholders' equity during 2024, its first year of operations:

| | | |
|---|---|---|
| January | 2 | Issue 110,000 shares of common stock for $70 per share. |
| February | 14 | Issue 60,000 shares of preferred stock for $12 per share. |
| May | 8 | Purchase 11,000 shares of its own common stock for $60 per share. |
| May | 31 | Resell 5,500 shares of treasury stock for $65 per share. |
| December | 1 | Declare a cash dividend on its common stock of $0.25 per share and a $36,000 (6% of par value) cash dividend on its preferred stock payable to all stockholders of record on December 15. The dividend is payable on December 30. (*Hint:* Dividends are not paid on treasury stock.) |
| December | 30 | Pay the cash dividends declared on December 1. |

**Required:**
1. Record each of these transactions.
2. Prepare the stockholders' equity section of the balance sheet as of December 31, 2024. Net income for the year was $490,000.

Record cash dividends and compute dividend yield (LO10–5, 10–8)
See P10–3 for financial statement effects.

**JP10–3** On Nov. 21, 2019, **Chubb Limited** (Ticker: CB) issued the following press release:

*The Board of Directors of Chubb Limited (NYSE: CB) today declared a quarterly dividend equal to $0.75 per share, payable on January 10, 2020 to shareholders of record at the close of business on December 20, 2019.*

***Required:***

1. From the information above, identify the dividend declaration date, record date, and payment date.
2. Record Chubb's declaration and payment of cash dividends for its 452 million shares.
3. Based on a stock price of $156, compute the dividend yield. (*Hint:* Annualize the dividend per share by multiplying the quarterly dividend per share by 4.)

**JP10–4** On January 1, 2024, the general ledger of Grand Finale Fireworks includes the following account balances:

Comprehensive problem **(LO10–2, 10–3, 10–4, 10–5)**

| Accounts | Debit | Credit |
|---|---|---|
| Cash | $ 42,700 | |
| Accounts Receivable | 44,500 | |
| Supplies | 7,500 | |
| Equipment | 64,000 | |
| Accumulated Depreciation | | $ 9,000 |
| Accounts Payable | | 14,600 |
| Common Stock, $1 par value | | 10,000 |
| Additional Paid-in Capital | | 80,000 |
| Retained Earnings | | 45,100 |
| Totals | $158,700 | $158,700 |

During January 2024, the following transactions occur:

| | |
|---|---|
| January 2 | Issue an additional 2,000 shares of $1 par value common stock for $40,000. |
| January 9 | Provide services to customers on account, $14,300. |
| January 10 | Purchase additional supplies on account, $4,900. |
| January 12 | Purchase 1,000 shares of treasury stock for $18 per share. |
| January 15 | Pay cash on accounts payable, $16,500. |
| January 21 | Provide services to customers for cash, $49,100. |
| January 22 | Receive cash on accounts receivable, $16,600. |
| January 29 | Declare a cash dividend of $0.30 per share to all shares outstanding on January 29. |
| | The dividend is payable on February 15. (*Hint:* Grand Finale Fireworks had 10,000 shares outstanding on January 1, 2024, and dividends are not paid on treasury stock.) |
| January 30 | Resell 600 shares of treasury stock for $20 per share. |
| January 31 | Pay cash for salaries during January, $42,000. |

***Required:***

1. Record each of the transactions listed above.
2. Record adjusting entries on January 31.
   a. Unpaid utilities for the month of January are $6,200.
   b. Supplies at the end of January total $5,100.
   c. Depreciation on the equipment for the month of January is calculated using the straight-line method. At the time the equipment was purchased, the company estimated a service life of three years and a residual value of $10,000.
   d. Accrued income taxes at the end of January are $2,000.
3. Prepare an adjusted trial balance as of January 31, 2024, after updating beginning balances (above) for transactions during January (requirement 1) and adjusting entries at the end of January (requirement 2).
4. Prepare an income statement for the period ended January 31, 2024.
5. Prepare a classified balance sheet as of January 31, 2024.
6. Record closing entries.

7. Analyze the following for Grand Finale Fireworks:
   a. Calculate the return on equity for the month of January. If the average return on equity for the industry for January is 2.5%, is the company more or less profitable than other companies in the same industry?
   b. How many shares of common stock are outstanding as of January 31, 2024?
   c. Calculate earnings per share for the month of January. (*Hint:* To calculate average shares of common stock outstanding take the beginning shares outstanding plus the ending shares outstanding and divide the total by 2.) If earnings per share was $3.60 last year (i.e., an average of $0.30 per month), is earnings per share for January 2024 better or worse than last year's average?

 **DATA ANALYTICS**

  Visit Connect to view **Data Analytics** questions related to:

1. Applying Excel
2. Data Visualizations
3. Tableau Dashboard Activities
4. Applying Tableau

**ANSWERS TO THE SELF-STUDY QUESTIONS**

1. a   2. b   3. b   4. c   5. c   6. b   7. d   8. a   9. d   10. b   11. c   12. c   13. d   14. a   15. c

# Statement of Cash Flows

## Feature Story

## Apple Inc.: Cash Flows at the Core

Net income represents all revenues less expenses of a company during a reporting period. Operating cash flows represent the cash inflows less cash outflows related to the very same revenue and expense activities. Although you might expect these two amounts to be fairly similar, large differences can occur. Below are the net income and operating cash flows for three well-known companies in the technology industry ($ in millions):

| Company Name | Net Income | Operating Cash Flows |
|---|---|---|
| Apple | $59,531 | $77,434 |
| Alphabet | $19,478 | $36,036 |
| Amazon | $21,856 | $30,723 |

All three companies report much higher operating cash flows than net income. One reason that operating cash flows are often higher than net income is that certain items, like depreciation expense, decrease net income but have no effect on operating cash flows.

So, which is more important for understanding the performance of a company—net income or cash flows? The previous chapters of this book focused on accrual-basis net income. Under accrual accounting, net income measures performance for the period as the net economic resources generated from operations, regardless of when the cash associated with those economic events changes hands. Therefore, net income provides a timely measure of performance, and that's why academic research finds a correlation between a company's net income and its stock returns.[1]

However, the inflows and outflows of cash during the period are also critical in understanding a company's success. Ultimately, the company must generate cash to sustain operations, pay off its debt, and provide a return to shareholders. Further, accrual accounting requires managers to use judgments and estimates to measure performance, which sometimes can be wrong or even purposely manipulated. In contrast, judgments and estimates are not needed to determine the amount of cash flow that a company produces during a period; therefore, it is less susceptible to managerial manipulation. It's also the case that net income provides only limited information about a company's investing and financing activities during the year, and these activities can have important implications on future cash flows. Because of the additional benefits in understanding a company's cash flows, standard setters have mandated the reporting of the statement of cash flows in addition to the income statement.

An investor or creditor who analyzes both net income and operating cash flow will do better than one who focuses solely on one or the other. In this chapter, we will learn how to prepare and analyze the operating, investing, and financing sections of the statement of cash flows. At the end of the chapter, we'll perform a cash flow analysis for **Apple** vs. **Alphabet**.

[1]P. Dechow. 1994. "Accounting Earnings and Cash Flow as Measures of Firm Performance: The Role of Accounting Accruals." *Journal of Accounting and Economics* (July): 3–42.

553

# CLASSIFICATION OF CASH FLOW ACTIVITIES

A statement of cash flows provides a summary of cash inflows and cash outflows during the reporting period. A cash *inflow* simply means cash received by the company during the period. Similarly, a cash *outflow* is cash paid by the company during the period. The difference between cash inflows and cash outflows is called *net cash flows*. The statement of cash flows reports separately the net cash flows from operating, investing, and financing activities. The sum of the net cash flows from those three activities equals the change in total cash for the period that should reconcile to the difference in the cash balances reported in the balance sheet. Illustration 11–1 presents the statement of cash flows for E-Games, Inc.

We will use this statement as an example throughout the chapter. Don't be concerned about the details yet. That's what the rest of the chapter is all about.

**ILLUSTRATION 11–1**

Statement of Cash Flows (Indirect Method)

| E-GAMES, INC.<br>Statement of Cash Flows<br>For the year ended December 31, 2024 | | |
|---|---:|---:|
| **Cash Flows from Operating Activities** | | |
| Net income | $42,000 | |
| *Adjustments to reconcile net income to net cash flows from operating activities:* | | |
| Depreciation expense | 9,000 | |
| Loss on sale of land | 4,000 | |
| Increase in accounts receivable | (7,000) | |
| Decrease in inventory | 10,000 | |
| Increase in prepaid rent | (2,000) | |
| Decrease in accounts payable | (5,000) | |
| Increase in interest payable | 1,000 | |
| Decrease in income tax payable | (2,000) | |
| Net cash flows from operating activities | | $50,000 |
| **Cash Flows from Investing Activities** | | |
| Purchase of investments | (35,000) | |
| Sale of land | 6,000 | |
| Net cash flows from investing activities | | (29,000) |
| **Cash Flows from Financing Activities** | | |
| Issuance of common stock | 5,000 | |
| Payment of cash dividends | (12,000) | |
| Net cash flows from financing activities | | (7,000) |
| Net increase (decrease) in cash | | 14,000 |
| Cash at the beginning of the period | | 48,000 |
| Cash at the end of the period | | $62,000 |
| **Note: Noncash Activities** | | |
| Purchased equipment by issuing a note payable | | $20,000 |

## Classification of Transactions

■ **LO11–1**

Classify cash transactions as operating, investing, or financing activities.

The three primary categories of cash flows are (1) cash flows from operating activities, (2) cash flows from investing activities, and (3) cash flows from financing activities. Classifying each cash flow by source (operating, investing, or financing activities) is more informative than simply listing the various cash flows.

### CASH FLOW ACTIVITIES

Operating activities include cash receipts and cash payments for transactions involving revenue and expense activities during the period. In other words, operating activities include the cash effects of the same activities that are reported in the income statement to calculate net income. Common examples of operating activities include the collection of cash from customers or the payment of cash for inventory, salaries, and rent.

Investing activities include transactions involving the purchase and sale of long-term assets and investments. Companies periodically invest cash to replace or expand productive facilities such as buildings, land, and equipment. These are included in investing activities because they represent investments in capital assets or capital investments. In fact, cash outflows for capital assets have a specific name you might be familiar with: **capital expenditures** or CAPEX. Companies might also invest cash in other assets, such as stocks or bonds of other companies, with the expectation of a return on those investments—think of these as portfolio investments. In addition, when companies acquire other companies with cash or sell off parts of their own company for cash, these cash flows are classified as investing activities. The purchase and sale of long-term assets and investments are common examples of investing activities.

Financing activities include transactions with lenders, such as borrowing money and repaying debt, and with stockholders, such as issuing stock, paying dividends, and purchasing treasury stock. It's the lenders and stockholders who provide external financing to the company.

The total net cash flows from operating, investing, and financing activities equal the increase or decrease in total cash for the year. That is, the balance of cash at the beginning of the year, plus or minus net cash flows as reported in the statement of cash flows, equals the ending balance of cash reported in the balance sheet.

Illustration 11–2 lists common cash receipts and cash payments for operating, investing, and financing activities. **Review this illustration carefully** (you may even want to bookmark it); it will come in handy in solving many of the homework problems at the end of the chapter.

**ILLUSTRATION 11–2**

Operating, Investing, and Financing Activities

### Cash Flows from Operating Activities

| **Cash Inflows** | **Cash Outflows** |
|---|---|
| Sale of goods or services | Purchase of inventory |
| Collection of interest and dividends | Payment for operating expenses |
| | Payment of interest |
| | Payment of income taxes |

### Cash Flows from Investing Activities

| **Cash Inflows** | **Cash Outflows** |
|---|---|
| Sale of investments | Purchase of investments |
| Sale of long-term assets | Purchase of long-term assets (CAPEX) |
| Collection of notes receivable | Lending with notes receivable |
| Sale of subsidiary | Cash acquisition of another company |

### Cash Flows from Financing Activities

| **Cash Inflows** | **Cash Outflows** |
|---|---|
| Issuance of bonds or notes payable | Repayment of bonds or notes payable |
| Issuance of stock | Payments to repurchase stock (treasury stock) |
| | Payment of dividends |

Let's look at a few of the cash flows. For example, we report interest and dividends received from investments with operating activities rather than investing activities. Similarly, we report interest paid on bonds or notes payable with operating activities rather than financing activities. Why are these classified as operating activities? They are included in operating activities because each is a cash flow from an activity reported in the income statement—interest revenue, dividend revenue, and interest expense. As we discussed earlier, operating activities are those we report in the income statement.

On the other hand, we record dividends paid as a financing activity. Recall that dividends are not an expense and, therefore, paying dividends has no effect on net income. The payment of dividends simply reduces assets (cash) and stockholders' equity (retained earnings).

**COMMON MISTAKE**

Students sometimes misclassify dividends in preparing the statement of cash flows. Dividends *received* are included in operating activities. Dividends *paid* are included in financing activities.

We need information sources to determine the amounts necessary to prepare the statement of cash flows. Illustration 11–3 outlines the three primary sources.

**ILLUSTRATION 11–3**

**Information Sources for Preparing the Statement of Cash Flows**

| Information Sources | Explanation |
|---|---|
| 1. Income statement | Revenues and expenses provide information in determining cash flows from operating activities. |
| 2. Balance sheet | Changes in assets, liabilities, and stockholders' equity from the end of the last period to the end of this period help to identify cash flows from operating, investing, and financing activities. |
| 3. Detailed accounting records | Sometimes additional information from the accounting records is needed to determine specific cash inflows or cash outflows for the period. |

Illustration 11–4 summarizes the relationship of the income statement and balance sheet to the operating, investing, and financing sections in the statement of cash flows.

**ILLUSTRATION 11–4**

**Relationship of the Income Statement and Balance Sheet to the Statement of Cash Flows**

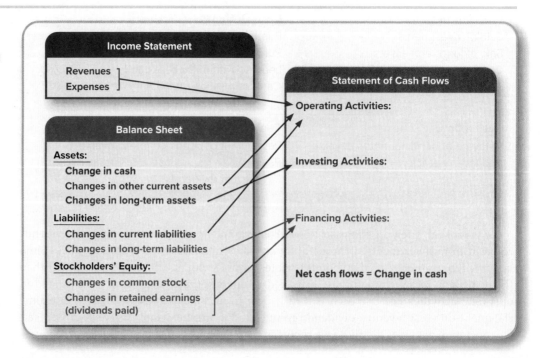

**KEY POINT**

Operating activities generally relate to income statement items and changes in current assets and current liabilities. Investing activities primarily involve changes in long-term assets. Financing activities primarily involve changes in long-term liabilities and stockholders' equity.

## NONCASH ACTIVITIES

Suppose a company borrows $200,000 in cash from a bank, issuing a long-term note payable for that amount. The company reports this transaction in a statement of cash flows as a *financing activity*. Suppose the company then uses that cash to purchase new equipment. The company reports this second transaction as an *investing activity*. But what if, instead of two separate transactions, the company had a *single transaction* that involved acquiring $200,000 of new equipment by issuing a $200,000 long-term note payable to the seller? **Since this single transaction does not affect cash, there are no investing or financing activities to report in the statement of cash flows.**

However, transactions that do not increase or decrease cash, but result in significant investing and financing activities, are reported as noncash activities either directly after the cash flow statement or in a note to the financial statements.

---

Indicate whether each of the following items is classified as an operating activity, investing activity, financing activity, or a significant noncash activity.

**Let's Review**

1. Dividends received from an investment.
2. Dividends paid to shareholders.
3. Property, plant, and equipment purchased for cash.
4. Property, plant, and equipment purchased by issuing stock.
5. Notes receivable accepted for lending cash.
6. Notes payable issued for borrowing cash.

*Solution:*

1. Operating.
2. Financing.
3. Investing.
4. Noncash.
5. Investing.
6. Financing.

---

# PREPARING THE STATEMENT OF CASH FLOWS

**PART B**

In this section, we first look at the steps involved in preparing the statement of cash flows, and its basic format. Then we work through these steps in preparing the operating, investing, and financing sections of the statement of cash flows.

## Steps in Preparing the Statement of Cash Flows

Illustration 11–5 summarizes the four basic steps in preparing the statement of cash flows.

■ **LO11–2**
Understand the steps and basic format in preparing the statement of cash flows.

**ILLUSTRATION 11–5**

**Steps in Preparing the Statement of Cash Flows**

**Step 1.** Calculate net cash flows from *operating activities,* using information from the income statement and changes in current assets (other than cash) and changes in current liabilities from the balance sheet.

**Step 2.** Determine the net cash flows from *investing activities,* by analyzing changes in long-term asset accounts from the balance sheet.

**Step 3.** Determine the net cash flows from *financing activities,* by analyzing changes in long-term liabilities and stockholders' equity accounts from the balance sheet.

**Step 4.** Combine the operating, investing, and financing activities, and make sure the total from these three activities equals the amount of cash reported in the balance sheet this year versus last year (the change in cash).

Illustration 11–6 provides the income statement, balance sheets, and additional information for E-Games, Inc. We will use this information to prepare the statement of cash flows following the four basic steps.

**ILLUSTRATION 11–6**

**Income Statement, Balance Sheets, and Additional Information for E-Games, Inc.**

### E-GAMES, INC.
### Income Statement
### For the year ended December 31, 2024

| | | |
|---|---:|---:|
| Net sales | | $1,012,000 |
| Expenses: | | |
| Cost of goods sold | $650,000 | |
| Operating expenses (salaries, rent, utilities) | 286,000 | |
| Depreciation expense | 9,000 | |
| Loss on sale of land | 4,000 | |
| Interest expense | 5,000 | |
| Income tax expense | 16,000 | |
| Total expenses | | 970,000 |
| Net income | | $    42,000 |

### E-GAMES, INC.
### Balance Sheets
### December 31, 2024 and 2023

| | 2024 | 2023 | Increase (I) or Decrease (D) |
|---|---:|---:|---:|
| **Assets** | | | |
| Current assets: | | | |
| Cash | $ 62,000 | $ 48,000 | $14,000 (I) |
| Accounts receivable | 27,000 | 20,000 | 7,000 (I) |
| Inventory | 35,000 | 45,000 | 10,000 (D) |
| Prepaid rent | 4,000 | 2,000 | 2,000 (I) |
| Long-term assets: | | | |
| Investments | 35,000 | 0 | 35,000 (I) |
| Land | 70,000 | 80,000 | 10,000 (D) |
| Equipment | 90,000 | 70,000 | 20,000 (I) |
| Accumulated depreciation | (23,000) | (14,000) | 9,000 (I) |
| Total assets | $300,000 | $251,000 | |

ILLUSTRATION 11–6

(*concluded*)

### E-GAMES, INC.
### Balance Sheets
### December 31, 2024 and 2023

|  | 2024 | 2023 | Increase (I) or Decrease (D) |
|---|---|---|---|
| **Liabilities and Stockholders' Equity** | | | |
| Current liabilities: | | | |
| Accounts payable | $ 22,000 | $ 27,000 | $ 5,000 (D) |
| Interest payable | 2,000 | 1,000 | 1,000 (I) |
| Income tax payable | 5,000 | 7,000 | 2,000 (D) |
| Long-term liabilities: | | | |
| Notes payable | 95,000 | 75,000 | 20,000 (I) |
| Stockholders' equity: | | | |
| Common stock | 105,000 | 100,000 | 5,000 (I) |
| Retained earnings | 71,000 | 41,000 | 30,000 (I) |
| Total liabilities and stockholders' equity | $300,000 | $251,000 | |

**Additional Information for 2024:**

1. Purchased stock in Intendo Corporation for $35,000.

2. Sold land for $6,000. The land originally was purchased for $10,000, resulting in a $4,000 loss being recorded at the time of the sale.

3. Purchased $20,000 in equipment by issuing a $20,000 note payable due in three years to the seller. No cash was exchanged in the transaction.

4. Issued common stock for $5,000 cash.

5. Declared and paid a cash dividend of $12,000.

Notice the first line of the balance sheets in 2023 and 2024. Cash increased from $48,000 in 2023 to $62,000 in 2024, an increase of **$14,000**. **The purpose of the statement of cash flows is to report the activities that caused the change in cash balances reported in the balance sheets from period to period.** Those activities are listed by type—operating, investing, or financing.

 **KEY POINT**

The steps in preparing the statement of cash flows involve calculating (1) net cash flows from operating activities, (2) net cash flows from investing activities, (3) net cash flows from financing activities, and (4) the sum of these three activities to verify it equals the amount of cash reported in the balance sheet this year versus last year (the change in cash).

## Basic Format

In preparing the statement of cash flows, it's helpful to first understand the basic format. As Illustration 11–7 shows, the statement of cash flows will always contain three sections, each of which has a total dollar amount for the section items listed. Thus, there will be a total for net cash flows from operating activities, from investing activities, and from financing activities. The total of these three net cash flow amounts will equal the net increase or net decrease in cash for the period. For our E-Games example, the **$14,000** change in the cash balance will be our "check figure," which means the cash inflows and cash outflows we identify must net to this amount.

After determining the net increase or decrease in cash for the period, we add cash at the beginning of the period to calculate cash at the end of the period. The amount of ending cash shown in the statement of cash flows will match the balance of cash shown in the balance sheet.

## OPERATING ACTIVITIES FORMAT—INDIRECT AND DIRECT METHODS

We have two ways to determine and report cash flows from operating activities in a statement of cash flows—the indirect method and the direct method.

Using the indirect method, we begin with net income and then list adjustments to net income to arrive at operating cash flows. An example of the indirect method was presented in Illustration 11–1 and the basic format is shown in Illustration 11–7. The indirect method is more popular because it is generally easier and less costly to prepare. In fact, nearly all major companies in the United States (about 99%) prepare the statement of cash flows using the indirect method.[2] For this reason, we emphasize the indirect method.

Using the direct method, we adjust the items in the income statement to directly show the cash inflows and outflows from operations such as cash received from customers and cash paid for inventory, salaries, rent, interest, and taxes. If a company decides to use the direct method to report operating activities, it must also report the indirect method either along with the statement of cash flows or in a separate note to the financial statements.

**The total net cash flows from operating activities are identical under both methods.** The methods differ only in the presentation format for operating activities. We discuss the indirect method in the next section. We present the direct method using the same example in an appendix to this chapter. Investing, financing, and noncash activities are reported identically under both methods.

**ILLUSTRATION 11–7**

Basic Format for the Statement of Cash Flows—Indirect Method

| E-GAMES, INC. Statement of Cash Flows For the year ended December 31, 2024 | | |
|---|---|---|
| **Cash Flows from Operating Activities** | | |
| Net income | $42,000 | |
| *Adjustments to reconcile net income to net cash flows from operating activities:* | | |
| (List individual reconciling items) | ———— | |
| Net cash flows from operating activities | | $50,000 |
| **Cash Flows from Investing Activities** | | |
| (List individual inflows and outflows) | ———— | |
| Net cash flows from investing activities | | (29,000) |
| **Cash Flows from Financing Activities** | | |
| (List individual inflows and outflows) | ———— | |
| Net cash flows from financing activities | | (7,000) |
| **Net increase (decrease) in cash** | | **14,000** |
| Cash at the beginning of the period | | 48,000 |
| Cash at the end of the period | | $62,000 |

[2]*Accounting Trends and Techniques–2011* (New York: American Institute of Certified Public Accountants).

**KEY POINT**

Companies choose between the indirect method and the direct method in reporting operating activities in the statement of cash flows. The indirect method begins with net income and then lists adjustments to net income in order to arrive at operating cash flows. The direct method specifically lists the various cash inflows and outflows from operations. The investing and financing sections of the statement of cash flows are identical under both methods.

## Operating Activities—Indirect Method

As summarized in Illustration 11–5, the first step in preparing the statement of cash flows is to calculate net cash flows from operating activities. With the indirect method, we start with net income. Net income includes all revenue and expense activities reported on an *accrual basis*. We need to remove the accruals from accrual-basis net income so that only the *cash portion* remains. Adjustments to net income include the following:

■ **LO11–3**
Prepare the operating activities section of the statement of cash flows using the indirect method.

1. **Income statement items.** (a) Remove noncash revenues and noncash expenses, such as depreciation expense, amortization expense, and stock-based compensation expense, and (b) remove nonoperating gains and nonoperating losses, such as gains and losses on the sale of land, buildings, equipment, and investments.

2. **Balance sheet items.** Adjust for changes in current assets and current liabilities. These changes represent differences between accrual-basis revenues/expenses and their corresponding operating cash flows. For example, an *increase* in accounts receivable represents sales to customers (accrual-basis revenue) that have not yet been collected (no operating cash inflow). We need to remove this amount of revenue from net income so that only the cash portion of sales revenue remains.

In the pages that follow, we'll cover many examples of both types of adjustments to net income. For now, understand the big picture—under the indirect method, the operating cash flows section provides a reconciliation from net income (accrual basis) to operating cash flows (cash basis). The adjustments are summarized in Illustration 11–8. This illustration is a helpful reference when completing the homework at the end of the chapter.

**ILLUSTRATION 11–8**

Summary of Adjustments to Net Income

| Cash Flows from Operating Activities | |
|---|---|
| | **Net income** (accrual basis) |
| | *Adjustments:* |
| Income Statement Adjustments | + Depreciation expense |
| | + Amortization expense |
| | + Stock-based compensation expense |
| | + Loss on sale of assets |
| | − Gain on sale of assets |
| Balance Sheet Adjustments | − Increase in a current asset |
| | + Decrease in a current asset |
| | + Increase in a current liability |
| | − Decrease in a current liability |
| | = **Net cash flows from operating activities** (cash basis) |

## INCOME STATEMENT ADJUSTMENTS—NONCASH ITEMS

To calculate operating cash flows using the indirect method, we first adjust net income for income statement items. The first set of these items are noncash items, which most often include expenses such as depreciation expense, amortization expense and stock-based compensation expense.

**Depreciation Expense.**    Depreciation expense reduces net income without any related cash outflows. Because we *deducted* this noncash expense in the determination of net income, we need to *add back* that amount in calculating operating cash flows. We add back depreciation expense and any other noncash expenses to net income in arriving at cash flows from operating activities.

E-Games, Inc., reports net income of $42,000 in its income statement. Included in this amount is depreciation expense of $9,000. Because depreciation expense reduces net income by $9,000 but has no effect on cash, E-Games will add back the $9,000 to net income in arriving at net cash flows from operations. Illustration 11–9 shows how E-Games reports depreciation expense in the statement of cash flows under the indirect method.

**ILLUSTRATION 11–9**

Adjustment for
Depreciation Expense

| E-GAMES, INC. Statement of Cash Flows (partial) | |
|---|---|
| **Cash Flows from Operating Activities** | |
| Net income | $42,000 |
| *Adjustments to reconcile net income to net cash flows from operating activities:* | |
| Depreciation expense | 9,000 |

**Stock-Based Compensation Expense.**    Many companies, especially tech companies, choose to compensate employees with stock-based awards, as noted in Chapter 10. **Amazon** recently offered over $5 billion of stock-based awards to its employees. Stock-based awards may include shares of stock given directly to the employee, restricted stock, or stock options. However, unlike salaries expense, stock-based compensation expense is a noncash expense; it reduces net income for the period, but there is no corresponding cash outflow. Therefore, because it's a noncash expense, we add back the amount of the stock-based compensation expense to net income in computing operating cash flows.

## INCOME STATEMENT ADJUSTMENTS—NONOPERATING ITEMS

The second set of income statement adjustments are gains and losses that do not affect operating cash flows. These gains and losses are typically related to investing activities, such as the sale of land, equipment, or investment securities, even though they are included in net income.

**Loss on Sale of Land.**    Losses on the sale of long-term assets decrease net income, while gains on the sale of those assets increase net income. Included in E-Games' net income is a $4,000 loss on the sale of land. The loss is not an *operating* cash inflow or cash outflow. (The actual cash received from the sale of land is an *investing* cash flow discussed later in the chapter.) This means we need to remove the loss in the calculation of operating cash flows. We remove the loss by adding back that amount to net income. Illustration 11–10 shows how E-Games adds back the loss on sale of land to net income in arriving at net cash flows from operating activities.

What if E-Games, Inc., had a gain of $4,000, rather than a loss, on the sale of land? Because we would have added the $4,000 gain in the determination of net income, we would need to subtract that amount from net income to calculate operating cash flows.

ILLUSTRATION 11–10

Adjustment for Loss on
Sale of Land

**E-GAMES, INC.**
**Statement of Cash Flows (partial)**

| Cash Flows from Operating Activities | |
| --- | --- |
| Net income | $42,000 |
| *Adjustments to reconcile net income to net cash* | |
| *flows from operating activities:* | |
| Depreciation expense | 9,000 |
| **Loss on sale of land** | **4,000** |

### COMMON MISTAKE

Students sometimes are unsure whether to add or subtract a loss on the sale of assets. Just remember that a loss is like an expense—both reduce net income. Treat a loss on the sale of assets like depreciation expense and add back that amount to net income. A gain on the sale of long-term assets is the opposite of an expense, so we subtract that amount from net income to arrive at net cash flows from operating activities.

## BALANCE SHEET ADJUSTMENTS

Finally, we adjust net income for balance sheet items. In particular, we adjust net income for changes in balance sheet accounts to convert the effects of those items to a cash basis. The accounts predominantly include current assets other than investments and notes receivable (often referred to as "working capital assets"), and current liabilities other than various forms of borrowing (often referred to as "working capital liabilities"). Adjusting for these changes in current assets and current liabilities helps to adjust accrual-basis revenues and expenses (within net income) to their related cash flow amounts. Let's look at the changes in current assets and current liabilities for E-Games to see how this works.

**Increase in Accounts Receivable.**    E-Games reports sales revenue of $1,012,000 in its income statement. This does not mean, however, that E-Games collected $1,012,000 cash from its customers during the reporting period. We know this because E-Games' accounts receivable increased $7,000 during the year (from $20,000 in 2023 to $27,000 in 2024). This tells us that the company must have collected less cash than its $1,012,000 in sales revenue. Why? Because customers owe the company $7,000 more than before. Here's a summary.

| | |
| --- | --- |
| Sales Revenue | $1,012,000 |
| − Increase in Accounts Receivable | − 7,000 |
| = Cash inflow from customers | $1,005,000 |

The $7,000 increase in accounts receivable represents $7,000 of sales revenue that E-Games reported as part of net income, but that did not result in operating cash inflows. Therefore, to adjust the sales revenue portion of net income (accrual basis = $1,012,000) to operating cash inflows from customers (cash basis = $1,005,000), we need to subtract the $7,000 increase in accounts receivable from net income, as shown in Illustration 11–11.

ILLUSTRATION 11–11

Adjustment for Change
in Accounts Receivable

**E-GAMES, INC.**
**Statement of Cash Flows (partial)**

| Cash Flows from Operating Activities | |
| --- | --- |
| Net income | $42,000 |
| *Adjustments to reconcile net income to net* | |
| *cash flows from operating activities:* | |
| Depreciation expense | 9,000 |
| Loss on sale of land | 4,000 |
| **Increase in accounts receivable** | **(7,000)** |

*Net income*
*− Incr. in A/R*
*+ Decr. in A/R*
*Oper. cash flows*

A decrease in accounts receivable would have the opposite effect. We would *add* a decrease in accounts receivable to net income to arrive at net cash flows from operating activities. A decrease in accounts receivable indicates that we collected more cash from customers than we reported as sales revenue.

**Decrease in Inventory.** E-Games' inventory balance decreased by $10,000 during the year. This tells us that the company sold $10,000 of inventory that was not replaced. This $10,000 is reported as cost of goods sold (an expense) in the income statement, reducing net income, but that amount had no effect on cash. To adjust for cash being greater by $10,000, we add the decrease in inventory to net income. Stated another way, we remove the $10,000 noncash portion of cost of goods sold by adding back that amount to net income. Illustration 11–12 shows the adjustment.

**ILLUSTRATION 11–12**

**Adjustment for Change in Inventory**

*Net income*
*− Incr. in Inventory*
*+ Decr. in Inventory*
‾‾‾‾‾‾‾‾‾‾‾‾‾‾‾‾
*Oper. cash flows*

**E-GAMES, INC.**
**Statement of Cash Flows (partial)**

| Cash Flows from Operating Activities | |
| --- | --- |
| Net income | $42,000 |
| Adjustments to reconcile net income to net cash flows from operating activities: | |
| Depreciation expense | 9,000 |
| Loss on sale of land | 4,000 |
| Increase in accounts receivable | (7,000) |
| **Decrease in inventory** | **10,000** |

If inventory had instead increased from year to year, the change in the balance would have been subtracted from net income to convert cost of goods sold from an accrual basis to a cash basis.

**Increase in Prepaid Rent.** E-Games' prepaid rent increased $2,000 during the year. This means the company paid $2,000 cash for an asset (prepaid rent) for which there is no corresponding expense (rent expense). In other words, the cash outflow to increase prepaid rent caused cash to decrease by $2,000, but net income remained unaffected. To adjust for cash being lower by $2,000, we subtract the increase in prepaid rent from net income. Illustration 11–13 shows this adjustment.

**ILLUSTRATION 11–13**

**Adjustment for Change in Prepaid Rent**

*Net income*
*− Incr. in Ppd. Rent*
*+ Decr. in Ppd. Rent*
‾‾‾‾‾‾‾‾‾‾‾‾‾‾‾‾
*Oper. cash flows*

**E-GAMES, INC.**
**Statement of Cash Flows (partial)**

| Cash Flows from Operating Activities | |
| --- | --- |
| Net income | $42,000 |
| Adjustments to reconcile net income to net cash flows from operating activities: | |
| Depreciation expense | 9,000 |
| Loss on sale of land | 4,000 |
| Increase in accounts receivable | (7,000) |
| Decrease in inventory | 10,000 |
| **Increase in prepaid rent** | **(2,000)** |

If prepaid rent had instead decreased from year to year, the change in the balance would have been added to net income to convert rent expense from an accrual basis to a cash basis.

**Decrease in Accounts Payable.** E-Games' accounts payable decreased $5,000 during the year. The decrease in accounts payable indicates that the company paid $5,000 cash to reduce its liability (accounts payable) for which there was no corresponding expense (cost of goods sold) during the period. In other words, the cash outflow to reduce accounts payable caused cash to decrease by $5,000, but net income remained unaffected. To adjust for cash being lower by $5,000, we subtract the decrease in accounts payable from net income, as shown in Illustration 11–14.

**ILLUSTRATION 11–14**

**Adjustment for Change in Accounts Payable**

**E-GAMES, INC.**
**Statement of Cash Flows (partial)**

| Cash Flows from Operating Activities | |
|---|---|
| Net income | $42,000 |
| Adjustments to reconcile net income to net cash flows from operating activities: | |
| Depreciation expense | 9,000 |
| Loss on sale of land | 4,000 |
| Increase in accounts receivable | (7,000) |
| Decrease in inventory | 10,000 |
| Increase in prepaid rent | (2,000) |
| **Decrease in accounts payable** | **(5,000)** |

*Net income*
*+ Incr. in A/P*
*− Decr. in A/P*
*Oper. cash flows*

If accounts payable had instead increased from year to year, the change in the balance would have been added to net income to convert associated expenses from an accrual basis to a cash basis. The expense most often associated with accounts payable is cost of goods sold.

**Increase in Interest Payable.** E-Games' interest payable increased $1,000 during the year. An increase in interest payable indicates that the company reported interest expense of $1,000 for which it did not pay cash. In other words, the $1,000 increase in interest payable reduces net income (because of interest expense) but has no effect on cash. To adjust for cash being greater by $1,000, we add the increase in interest payable to net income. This is shown in Illustration 11–15.

**ILLUSTRATION 11–15**

**Adjustment for Change in Interest Payable**

**E-GAMES, INC.**
**Statement of Cash Flows (partial)**

| Cash Flows from Operating Activities | |
|---|---|
| Net income | $42,000 |
| Adjustments to reconcile net income to net cash flows from operating activities: | |
| Depreciation expense | 9,000 |
| Loss on sale of land | 4,000 |
| Increase in accounts receivable | (7,000) |
| Decrease in inventory | 10,000 |
| Increase in prepaid rent | (2,000) |
| Decrease in accounts payable | (5,000) |
| **Increase in interest payable** | **1,000** |

*Net income*
*+ Incr. in Interest payable*
*− Decr. in Interest payable*
*Oper. cash flows*

If interest payable had instead decreased from year to year, the change in the balance would have been subtracted from net income to convert interest expense from an accrual basis to a cash basis.

**Decrease in Income Tax Payable.**    E-Games' income tax payable decreased $2,000 during the year. The decrease in income tax payable indicates that the company paid $2,000 cash to reduce its liability (income tax payable) but reported no corresponding expense (income tax expense) during the period. In other words, the cash outflow to reduce income tax payable caused cash to decrease by $2,000, but net income remained unaffected. To adjust for cash being lower by $2,000, we subtract the decrease in income tax payable from net income. Illustration 11–16 shows this adjustment and calculates total net cash flows from operating activities of $50,000.

**ILLUSTRATION 11–16**

**Adjustment for Change in Income Tax Payable**

| E-GAMES, INC. Statement of Cash Flows (partial) | |
|---|---|
| **Cash Flows from Operating Activities** | |
| Net income | $42,000 |
| *Adjustments to reconcile net income to net cash flows from operating activities:* | |
| Depreciation expense | 9,000 |
| Loss on sale of land | 4,000 |
| Increase in accounts receivable | (7,000) |
| Decrease in inventory | 10,000 |
| Increase in prepaid rent | (2,000) |
| Decrease in accounts payable | (5,000) |
| Increase in interest payable | 1,000 |
| **Decrease in income tax payable** | **(2,000)** |
| Net cash flows from operating activities | $50,000 |

*Net income*
*+ Incr. in Tax Pay.*
*− Decr. in Tax Pay.*
*Oper. cash flows*

If income tax payable had instead increased from year to year, the change in the balance would have been added to net income to convert operating activities from an accrual basis to a cash basis.

**KEY POINT**

Using the indirect method, we start with net income and adjust this number for income statement items (removing noncash revenues and noncash expenses and removing nonoperating gains and nonoperating losses) and  for balance sheet items (changes in current assets and changes in current liabilities).

Now let's look at the statement of cash flows for **Lowe's Companies** (Illustration 11–17) in order to further illustrate this three-step process for computing operating cash flows using the indirect method.

We can see from Illustration 11–17 that Lowe's uses the indirect method, which starts with net earnings of $2,314 million for the year. It then makes the three adjustments we've described in this section. First, it adds back the effects of any noncash expenses, including depreciation and amortization and share-based compensation. Second, it adds back nonoperating losses related to goodwill, property, and investments. Third, it adjusts for changes in each of the current asset and current liability accounts from the balance sheet.[3]

---

[3]We've made minor adjustments to other operating assets for simplicity.

**ILLUSTRATION 11–17**

**Operating Cash Flows (Indirect Method) for Lowe's Companies**

**Lowe's Companies Inc.**
**Statement of Cash Flows (partial)**
**($ in millions)**

| | |
|---|---:|
| Net earnings | $2,314 |
| *Adjustments to reconcile net earnings to net cash provided by operating activities* | |
| Depreciation and amortization | 1,607 |
| Share-based payment expense | 74 |
| Impairment of goodwill | 952 |
| Loss on property and other assets—net | 630 |
| Loss on investments | 9 |
| Changes in operating assets and liabilities: | |
| Merchandise inventory—net | (1,289) |
| Other operating assets | (261) |
| Accounts payable | 1,720 |
| Other operating liabilities | 437 |
| **Net cash provided by operating activities** | **$6,193** |

Adjustments to Compute Operating Cash Flows:

Add back noncash expenses

Add back nonoperating losses

Adjust for changes in current assets and current liabilities

**ILLUSTRATION 11–17**

**Operating Cash Flows (Indirect Method) for Lowe's Companies**

**Manager Analysis**

| Question | Accounting information | Analysis |
|---|---|---|
| Is a company's net income supported by strong operating cash flows? | Operating activities section of the statement of cash flows using the indirect method | The operating activities section using the indirect method reconciles net income to operating cash flows. Net income is considered to be of higher quality when backed by strong operating cash flows. |

**Let's Review**

Provided below are the income statement and partial balance sheet information for E-Phones, Inc.

**E-PHONES, INC.**
**Income Statement**
**For the year ended December 31, 2024**

| | | |
|---|---:|---:|
| Net sales | | $2,200,000 |
| Gain on sale of investment | | 5,000 |
| Expenses: | | |
| Cost of goods sold | $1,100,000 | |
| Operating expenses | 450,000 | |
| Depreciation expense | 25,000 | |
| Income tax expense | 217,000 | |
| Total expenses | | 1,792,000 |
| Net income | | $ 413,000 |

| Balance Sheet Information: | 2024 | 2023 | Increase (I) or Decrease (D) |
|---|---|---|---|
| Accounts receivable | $ 32,000 | $40,000 | $ 8,000 (D) |
| Inventory | 100,000 | 70,000 | 30,000 (I) |
| Accounts payable | 52,000 | 62,000 | 10,000 (D) |
| Income tax payable | 55,000 | 12,000 | 43,000 (I) |

**Required:**

Prepare the operating activities section of the statement of cash flows for E-Phones using the *indirect method*.

**Solution:**

**E-PHONES, INC.**
**Statement of Cash Flows—Indirect Method**
**For the year ended December 31, 2024**

| | | |
|---|---|---|
| **Cash Flows from Operating Activities** | | |
| Net income | $413,000 | |
| *Adjustments to reconcile net income to net cash flows from operating activities:* | | |
| Depreciation expense | 25,000 | |
| Gain on sale of investment | (5,000) | |
| Decrease in accounts receivable | 8,000 | |
| Increase in inventory | (30,000) | |
| Decrease in accounts payable | (10,000) | |
| Increase in income tax payable | 43,000 | |
| Net cash flows from operating activities | | $444,000 |

## Investing Activities

■ **LO11–4**
Prepare the investing activities section of the statement of cash flows.

The second step in preparing the statement of cash flows is to determine the net cash flows from *investing* activities. Companies periodically invest cash to replace or expand productive facilities such as property, plant, and equipment. Information concerning these investing activities can provide valuable insight to decision makers regarding the nature and amount of assets being acquired for future use, as well as provide clues concerning the company's ambitions for the future. In the investing activities section of the statement of cash flows, companies list separately cash inflows and cash outflows from transactions such as buying and selling property, plant, and equipment, making and collecting loans, and buying and selling investments in other companies. Let's now take a detailed look at how investing activities are determined, continuing our example of E-Games, Inc.

**We can find a firm's investing activities by analyzing changes in long-term asset accounts from the balance sheet.**[4] Looking at that section of E-Games' balance sheet, we determine the following cash flows from investing activities.

---

[4]Although not used as an example in this chapter, it's also possible to have investing activities related to changes in current investments or current notes receivable.

**Increase in Investments.** Investments increased $35,000 during the year (from $0 in 2023 to $35,000 in 2024). Additional-information item (1) in Illustration 11–6 reveals that this increase is due to the purchase of investments during the year. As Illustration 11–18 shows, we report the purchase of investments as a cash outflow of $35,000 from investing activities.

**Decrease in Land.** The Land account decreased $10,000 during the year, indicating that E-Games sold land costing $10,000. Additional-information item (2) in Illustration 11–6 indicates that we originally reported the land at a cost of $10,000 but sold it for only $6,000 (resulting in a loss on the sale of land of $4,000, as reported in the operating activities section). We report the actual cash proceeds of $6,000 from the sale as a cash inflow from investing activities. (See Illustration 11–18 below.)

**COMMON MISTAKE**

Some students mistakenly record a cash inflow from investing activities, like the sale of land for $6,000, at an amount that equals the change in the asset account, $10,000 in this case. Remember that the investing activities section reports the *actual* cash received or paid for an asset, which is usually not the same as the change in the asset account reported in the balance sheet.

**Increase in Equipment.** E-Games' Equipment account increased by $20,000 during the year. If E-Games purchased the equipment with cash, we would report a cash outflow from investing activities of $20,000. However, additional-information item (3) in Illustration 11–6 indicates that the firm paid for the equipment by issuing a $20,000 note payable to the seller. No cash was exchanged in the transaction. Therefore, the increase in equipment represents a noncash activity, which is disclosed either directly after the cash flow statement or in a note to the financial statements. Illustration 11–18 provides a summary of the cash flows from investing activities and disclosure of the noncash activity.

**ILLUSTRATION 11–18**

Cash Flows from Investing Activities

**E-GAMES, INC.**
**Statement of Cash Flows (partial)**

**Cash Flows from Investing Activities**

| | |
|---|---|
| Purchase of investments | $(35,000) |
| Sale of land | 6,000 |
| Net cash flows from investing activities | $ (29,000) |
| **Note: Noncash Activities** | |
| Purchased equipment by issuing a note payable | $ 20,000 |

**Other Investing Activities.** When a company acquires another business with cash, we classify this cash outflow as an investing activity. The intuition is that the acquisition represents an investment of one company to another company. For instance, **Activision Blizzard** spent $4.6 billion to acquire **King Digital Entertainment**, another digital entertainment company. Activision Blizzard then reported the $4.6 billion as a cash outflow in the investing section of its statement of cash flows. The same goes for cash-based divestitures, that is, when a company divests or spins off a subsidiary. When **eBay** sold its subsidiary, **Flipkart**, for $1.03 billion, it classified the cash inflow as an investing activity.

Again, we use **Lowe's** statement of cash flows to illustrate the construction of the investing activities section, presented in Illustration 11–19.

**ILLUSTRATION 11–19**

Cash Flows from Investing Activities for Lowe's Companies

| LOWE'S COMPANIES<br>Statement of Cash Flows (partial)<br>($ in millions) | |
|---|---|
| **Cash flows from investing activities:** | |
| Purchases of investments | $ (1,373) |
| Proceeds from sale/maturity of investments | 1,393 |
| Capital expenditures | (1,174) |
| Proceeds from sale of property and other long-term assets | 76 |
| Other—net | (2) |
| **Net cash used in investing activities** | **$(1,080)** |

Lowe's investing activities relate primarily to inflows and outflows from two sources: investments and capital expenditures. Investments include business acquisitions and sale or maturity of certain financial assets. Capital expenditures refer to expenditures on long-term assets (such as property) related to existing stores, expansion plans, and its existing distribution network.

**KEY POINT**

Cash transactions (inflows and outflows) involving long-term assets and current investments are reported in the investing activities section of the statement of cash flows. Typical investing activities include buying and selling property, plant, and equipment, as well as making and collecting loans.

# Financing Activities

**■ LO11–5**

Prepare the financing activities section of the statement of cash flows.

The third step in preparing the statement of cash flows is to determine the net cash flows from *financing* activities. To fund its operating and investing activities, a company must often rely on external financing from two sources—creditors and shareholders. In the financing activities section of the statement of cash flows, companies list separately cash inflows, such as borrowing money and issuing stock, and cash outflows, such as repaying amounts borrowed and paying dividends to shareholders. And like investing activities, the presentation of financing activities is the same whether we use the indirect or the direct method for operating cash flows.

**We can determine a company's financing activities by examining changes in long-term liabilities and stockholders' equity accounts from the balance sheet.**[5] Referring back to E-Games' balance sheet, we find the following cash flows from financing activities.

**Increase in Notes Payable.**  E-Games has only one long-term liability. The company reports an increase in notes payable of $20,000. As we saw earlier, this was in payment for equipment and represents a noncash activity disclosed in a note to the financial statements.

**Increase in Common Stock.**  Common stock increased by $5,000 during the year. Item (4) of the additional information in Illustration 11–6 confirms that this was the result of issuing $5,000 of common stock. As Illustration 11–20 shows, the $5,000 inflow of cash is reported as a financing activity.

---

[5]Although not used as an example in this chapter, it is also possible for financing activities to be indicated by changes in current liability accounts, such as current notes payable.

**Increase in Retained Earnings.** E-Games' Retained Earnings balance increased by $30,000 during the year (from $41,000 to $71,000). Recall from earlier chapters that the balance of retained earnings increases with net income and decreases with dividends declared.

Because net income is $42,000 and retained earnings increased by only $30,000, the company must have declared dividends of $12,000 during the year. Further, we know that the full $12,000 was paid out in cash because the balance sheet does not report any dividends payable at the end of the year.

| | |
|---|---|
| Retained earnings, beginning balance | $41,000 |
| + Net income | 42,000 |
| − **Payment of cash dividends** | **(12,000)** |
| Retained earnings, ending balance | $71,000 |

As shown in Illustration 11–20, we report the payment of cash dividends as a cash outflow from financing activities.

**E-GAMES, INC.**
**Statement of Cash Flows (partial)**

| Cash Flows from Financing Activities | | |
|---|---|---|
| Issuance of common stock | $ 5,000 | |
| Payment of cash dividends | (12,000) | |
| Net cash flows from financing activities | | (7,000) |

**ILLUSTRATION 11–20**

Cash Flows from Financing Activities

Only the dividends actually paid in cash during the year are reported in the statement of cash flows. If the company declares dividends in 2024 but does not pay them until 2025, it will report the dividends paid as a cash outflow in 2025, not in 2024.

The financing activities section of **Lowe's** statement of cash flows (Illustration 11–21) shows the cash received and paid for financing activities.

**LOWE'S COMPANIES**
**Statement of Cash Flows (partial)**
**($ in millions)**

| Cash flows from financing activities: | |
|---|---|
| Net change in short-term borrowings | $  (415) |
| Repayment of long-term debt | (326) |
| Proceeds from issuance of common stock under share-based payment plans | 114 |
| Cash dividend payments | (1,455) |
| Repurchase of common stock | (3,037) |
| Other—net | (5) |
| **Net cash used in financing activities** | **$(5,124)** |

**ILLUSTRATION 11–21**

Cash Flows from Financing Activities for Lowe's Companies

Aside from a minor cash inflow from stock-based compensation, Lowe's financing cash flows were largely negative, indicating cash outflows. Lowe's spent over $300 million to pay down long-term debt, nearly $1.5 billion to pay cash dividends, and over $3 billion to repurchase its common stock. The repurchase of stock is often a major financing cash outflow for large companies.

**KEY POINT**

Cash transactions (inflows and outflows) with creditors and shareholders are reported in the financing activities section of the statement of cash flows. Typical financing activities include borrowing money and repaying amounts borrowed from creditors, as well as issuing stock, repurchasing stock, and paying dividends to shareholders.

The fourth and final step in preparing the statement of cash flows is to combine the operating, investing, and financing activities and make sure the total of these three activities equals the net increase (decrease) in cash in the balance sheet. Illustration 11–22 shows the complete statement of cash flows for E-Games, with all three sections—operating, investing, and financing—included along with the note for noncash activities.

**ILLUSTRATION 11–22**

Complete Statement of Cash Flows for E-Games, Inc.

| E-GAMES, INC.<br>Statement of Cash Flows<br>For the year ended December 31, 2024 | | |
|---|---:|---:|
| **Cash Flows from Operating Activities** | | |
| Net income | $42,000 | |
| *Adjustments to reconcile net income to net cash flows*<br>*from operating activities:* | | |
| Depreciation expense | 9,000 | |
| Loss on sale of land | 4,000 | |
| Increase in accounts receivable | (7,000) | |
| Decrease in inventory | 10,000 | |
| Increase in prepaid rent | (2,000) | |
| Decrease in accounts payable | (5,000) | |
| Increase in interest payable | 1,000 | |
| Decrease in income tax payable | (2,000) | |
| Net cash flows from operating activities | | $50,000 |
| **Cash Flows from Investing Activities** | | |
| Purchase of investments | (35,000) | |
| Sale of land | 6,000 | |
| Net cash flows from investing activities | | (29,000) |
| **Cash Flows from Financing Activities** | | |
| Issuance of common stock | 5,000 | |
| Payment of cash dividends | (12,000) | |
| Net cash flows from financing activities | | (7,000) |
| **Net increase (decrease) in cash** | | **14,000** |
| Cash at the beginning of the period | | 48,000 |
| Cash at the end of the period | | $62,000 |
| | | |
| **Note: Noncash Activities** | | |
| Purchased equipment by issuing a note payable | | $20,000 |

This is the moment of truth. The sum of the net cash flows from operating, investing, and financing activities should equal the net increase (decrease) in cash for the period. In Illustration 11–22, we see that the total of the cash flows from operating (+$50,000), investing (−$29,000), and financing (−$7,000) activities equals the net increase in cash of **$14,000,** reconciling cash from the two consecutive balance sheets originally reported in Illustration 11–6.

Now let's look at it from the perspective of **Lowe's** cash flows as summarized in Illustration 11–23. The sum of its net cash flows from operating, investing, and financing activities is: $6,193 + $(1,080) + $(5,124) = $(11). With a minor adjustment for exchange rates of $(66), we see that the net decrease in cash and cash equivalents is $(77), which exactly equals the year-over-year change in cash shown in its balance sheet.

| LOWE'S COMPANIES Statement of Cash Flows (partial) ($ in millions) | |
| --- | --- |
| Net cash provided by operating activities | $6,193 |
| Net cash used in investing activities | (1,080) |
| Net cash used in investing activities | (5,124) |
| Other adjustments (exchange rate conversion, reclassification) | (66) |
| Net decrease in cash and cash equivalents | $ (77) |

**ILLUSTRATION 11–23**

**Summary of Statement of Cash Flows for Lowe's Companies**

We can see that Lowe's is spending nearly every dollar it generates in operations for investing activities and financing activities. In the next section, we delve deeper into the analysis of cash flows.

This is a continuation of the Let's Review exercise presented earlier in the chapter. Provided below are the income statement, balance sheets, and additional information for E-Phones, Inc.

**Let's Review**

| E-PHONES, INC. Income Statement For the year ended December 31, 2024 | | |
| --- | --- | --- |
| Net sales | | $2,200,000 |
| Gain on sale of investment | | 5,000 |
| Expenses: | | |
| Cost of goods sold | $1,100,000 | |
| Operating expenses | 450,000 | |
| Depreciation expense | 25,000 | |
| Income tax expense | 217,000 | |
| Total expenses | | 1,792,000 |
| Net income | | $ 413,000 |

### E-PHONES, INC.
### Balance Sheets
### December 31, 2024 and 2023

|  | 2024 | 2023 | Increase (I) or Decrease (D) |
|---|---|---|---|
| **Assets** | | | |
| Current assets: | | | |
| Cash | $ 32,000 | $ 48,000 | **$ 16,000 (D)** |
| Accounts receivable | 32,000 | 40,000 | 8,000 (D) |
| Inventory | 100,000 | 70,000 | 30,000 (I) |
| Long-term assets: | | | |
| Investments | 0 | 50,000 | 50,000 (D) |
| Land | 280,000 | 180,000 | 100,000 (I) |
| Equipment | 200,000 | 140,000 | 60,000 (I) |
| Accumulated depreciation | (53,000) | (28,000) | 25,000 (I) |
| Total assets | $591,000 | $500,000 | |
| **Liabilities and Stockholders' Equity** | | | |
| Current liabilities: | | | |
| Accounts payable | $ 52,000 | $ 62,000 | $ 10,000 (D) |
| Income tax payable | 55,000 | 12,000 | 43,000 (I) |
| Long-term liabilities: | | | |
| Bonds payable | 0 | 200,000 | 200,000 (D) |
| Stockholders' equity: | | | |
| Common stock | 200,000 | 100,000 | 100,000 (I) |
| Retained earnings | 284,000 | 126,000 | 158,000 (I) |
| Total liabilities and stockholders' equity | $591,000 | $500,000 | |

**Additional Information for 2024:**

1. Sold an investment in stock costing $50,000 for $55,000, resulting in a $5,000 gain on sale of investment.
2. Purchased $100,000 in land, issuing $100,000 of common stock as payment. No cash was exchanged in the transaction.
3. Purchased equipment for $60,000 cash.
4. Retired the $200,000 balance in bonds payable at the beginning of the year.
5. Declared and paid a cash dividend of $255,000.

*Required:*

Prepare the statement of cash flows using the *indirect method.* Disclose any noncash transactions in an accompanying note.

*Solution:*

### E-PHONES, INC.
### Statement of Cash Flows—Indirect Method
### For the year ended December 31, 2024

| Cash Flows from Operating Activities | |
|---|---|
| Net income | $413,000 |
| *Adjustments to reconcile net income to net cash flows from operating activities:* | |
| Depreciation expense | 25,000 |

(continued)

*(concluded)*

**E-PHONES, INC.**
**Statement of Cash Flows—Indirect Method**
**For the year ended December 31, 2024**

| | | |
|---|---:|---:|
| Gain on sale of investment | (5,000) | |
| Decrease in accounts receivable | 8,000 | |
| Increase in inventory | (30,000) | |
| Decrease in accounts payable | (10,000) | |
| Increase in income tax payable | 43,000 | |
| Net cash flows from operating activities | | $444,000 |
| **Cash Flows from Investing Activities** | | |
| Sale of investment | 55,000 | |
| Purchase of equipment | (60,000) | |
| Net cash flows from investing activities | | (5,000) |
| **Cash Flows from Financing Activities** | | |
| Retirement of bonds payable | (200,000) | |
| Payment of cash dividends | (255,000) | |
| Net cash flows from financing activities | | (455,000) |
| Net increase (decrease) in cash | | **(16,000)** |
| Cash at the beginning of the period | | 48,000 |
| Cash at the end of the period | | $ 32,000 |
| **Note: Noncash Activities** | | |
| Purchased land by issuing common stock | | $100,000 |

# CASH FLOW ANALYSIS
## Cash Flow Patterns and Company Life Cycle

**PART C**

Patterns in the statement of cash flows often provide an indication of the life cycle stage of the company. For example, cash flow patterns of start-up companies tend to look different from those companies that are in a steady state or decline. Illustration 11–24 provides a summary of the common cash flow patterns for four types of companies: Start-up, Growth, Steady State, and Decline.[6] A positive sign indicates that the cash flow activities typically result in a net cash inflow, and a negative sign indicates that those activities typically result in a net cash outflow.

| | Start-up | Growth | Steady State | Decline |
|---|:---:|:---:|:---:|:---:|
| Operating cash flows | − | + | + | − |
| Investing cash flows | − | − | − | + |
| Financing cash flows | + | + | − | +/ − |

**ILLUSTRATION 11–24**

Patterns in the Statement of Cash Flows

**Start-up** companies incur higher initial costs in starting the business but have not yet established a strong customer base to generate sales. This combination causes operating cash flows to be negative. Investing cash flows also tend to be negative because the company must invest in long-term assets needed in the new business (e.g., property and equipment). Finally, financing cash flows tend to be positive. These companies obtain the resources necessary to start the business by raising financing capital through new long-term debt or equity investments from owners. This pattern of negative-negative-positive cash flows from operating, investing, and financing activities, respectively, is quite common for start-ups.

[6]V. Dickinson, 2011. Cash Flow Patterns as a Proxy for Firm Life Cycle. *The Accounting Review, 86* (6): 1969–1994.

**Growth** companies typically exhibit a cash flow pattern of positive-negative-positive cash flows from operating, investing, and financing activities, respectively. This pattern suggests the company is generating positive cash flows from operations by growing sales from its day-to-day activities. The company attains this growth by purchasing additional investments and fixed assets, and finances these purchases by raising additional cash through financing via debt or equity.

**Steady-state** companies will typically exhibit a pattern of positive-negative-negative cash flows from operating, investing, and financing activities, respectively. This pattern indicates the company is generating substantial revenues and cash flows from providing products and services. These operating cash flows are sufficient to support the company's investing activities, such as buying more fixed assets or securities. At this stage, operating cash flows are sufficient to return capital to debt and equity providers by paying back loans, buying back stock, or paying dividends, each of which will show up as negative financing cash flows.

**Decline** companies will often exhibit a pattern of negative-positive-positive cash flows from operating, investing, and financing, respectively. These companies struggle to generate sufficient operating cash flows to cover expenses, which results in negative operating cash flows. Companies in decline also struggle to raise capital because the cost of doing such is high. This means that struggling companies often turn to selling off long-term assets to fund operations and remain afloat, resulting in positive cash flows from investing activities. This scenario is often called a "fire sale" and is typically a very bad sign. For companies in decline, financing cash flows can be positive or negative depending on whether the company is able to raise capital at a manageable cost or is forced to pay its debts without any additional financing.

Illustration 11–25 provides a summary of these patterns for several companies at each of the life cycle stages.

**ILLUSTRATION 11–25**

Patterns in Cash Flows for Lyft, Twilio, Anthem, and SunPower

| ($ in millions) | Lyft | Twilio | Anthem | SunPower |
|---|---|---|---|---|
| Operating cash flows | $ (105,702) | $ 32,654 | $10,688,000 | $(543,389) |
| Investing cash flows | (1,610,843) | (845,855) | (7,324,000) | 274,900 |
| Financing cash flows | 1,574,196 | 1,493,311 | (2,567,000) | 85,847 |

**Lyft** is a ridesharing transportation company that is in the start-up stage of its life cycle. As a result, its operating cash flows are negative, indicating that start-up costs exceed the cash inflows from sales. Its investing cash flows are negative as it purchased property and equipment, which were financed from financing cash flows related to its recent initial public offering (IPO).

**Twilio** is a cloud software company that is in the growth stage. It generates modest operating cash flows and reports substantial cash paid for investing activities. These investing activities were likely paid for with cash raised from an issuance of equity (financing activities).

**Anthem** is a successful, steady-state health-care company with over $100 billion in annual revenues. Its continued success leads to healthy cash inflows from normal operations. Meanwhile, it pays substantial cash for new investments (investing activities) and still has cash remaining to pay down debt and repurchase its stock (financing activities).

**SunPower** is a solar energy company that has experienced some troubles recently. It is generating negative cash flows from operations as a result of increased competition and declining margins in the solar power industry. To survive, it generates cash by selling equity method investments (investing activities) and using additional borrowing (financing activities).

As these examples demonstrate, a simple examination of the patterns in the statement of cash flows can provide useful indicators of a company's life cycle stage.

# Apple vs. Alphabet

Throughout this text, we have emphasized the analysis of financial statements from a decision maker's perspective. Often that analysis includes the development and comparison of financial ratios. The ratios discussed in Chapters 5 through 10 are all based on income statement and balance sheet amounts.

Now we reexamine the financial ratios introduced in Chapter 7—return on assets, profit margin, and asset turnover—substituting net cash flows from operating activities, also called **operating cash flows,** in place of net income. Illustration 11–26 provides selected financial data for **Apple** and **Alphabet** (formerly named **Google** until 2015).

**■ LO11–6**

Perform financial analysis using the statement of cash flows.

**ILLUSTRATION 11–26**

Selected Financial Data for Apple and Alphabet

| ($ in millions) | **Apple** | **Alphabet** |
|---|---|---|
| Net sales | $265,595 | $136,819 |
| Net income | 59,531 | 30,736 |
| Operating cash flows | 77,434 | 47,971 |
| Total assets, beginning | 375,319 | 197,295 |
| Total assets, ending | 365,725 | 232,792 |
| Capital expenditures | 13,313 | 25,139 |

## RETURN ON ASSETS

Return on assets, introduced in Chapter 7, is calculated as net income divided by average total assets. Illustration 11–27 presents return on assets for Apple and Alphabet.

**ILLUSTRATION 11–27**

Return on Assets for Apple and Alphabet

| ($ in millions) | **Net Income** | ÷ | **Average Total Assets** | = | **Return on Assets** |
|---|---|---|---|---|---|
| **Apple** | $59,531 | ÷ | ($375,319 + $365,725)/2 | = | 16.1% |
| **Alphabet** | $30,736 | ÷ | ($197,295 + $232,792)/2 | = | 14.3% |

Apple generated slightly more income for each dollar invested in assets.

## CASH RETURN ON ASSETS

We can gain additional insights by examining a similar measure called the cash return on assets by substituting operating cash flows for net income. We calculate it as

$$\text{Cash return on assets} = \text{Operating cash flows} \div \text{Average total assets}$$

Illustration 11–28 presents the cash return on assets for Apple and Alphabet.

**ILLUSTRATION 11–28**

Cash Return on Assets for Apple and Alphabet

| ($ in millions) | **Operating Cash Flows** | ÷ | **Average Total Assets** | = | **Cash Return on Assets** |
|---|---|---|---|---|---|
| **Apple** | $77,434 | ÷ | ($375,319 + $365,725)/2 | = | 20.9% |
| **Alphabet** | $47,971 | ÷ | ($197,295 + $232,792)/2 | = | 22.3% |

Now we see that it's Alphabet that shows a higher return on assets, in terms of operating cash flows. Do you think Alphabet's higher cash return on assets is due to higher pricing strategies or greater sales volume? We examine this question next.

## COMPONENTS OF CASH RETURN ON ASSETS

Let's explore the cash return on assets further by separating the ratio into two separate parts, as shown in Illustration 11–29.

**ILLUSTRATION 11–29**

Components of Cash
Return on Assets

| Cash return on assets | = | Cash flow to sales | × | Asset turnover |
|---|---|---|---|---|
| $\dfrac{\text{Operating cash flows}}{\text{Average total assets}}$ | = | $\dfrac{\text{Operating cash flows}}{\text{Net sales}}$ | × | $\dfrac{\text{Net sales}}{\text{Average total assets}}$ |

Cash return on assets can be separated into cash flow to sales and asset turnover. Cash flow to sales measures the operating cash flows generated for each dollar of sales. (It is the cash flow equivalent to profit margin, introduced in Chapter 7.) Asset turnover, also covered in Chapter 7, measures the sales revenue generated per dollar of assets. Cash flow to sales and asset turnover represent two primary strategies that companies have for increasing their cash return on assets. One strategy, pursued by both Apple and Alphabet, is to sell highly innovative products that yield very high cash inflows from customers in relationship to the cash outflows to produce their products. Another strategy is to pursue high asset turnover by selling at lower prices than the competition. In Illustrations 11–30 and 11–31, we calculate cash flow to sales and asset turnover for both companies.

**ILLUSTRATION 11–30**

Cash Flow to Sales for
Apple and Alphabet

| ($ in millions) | Operating Cash Flows | ÷ | Net Sales | = | Cash Flow to Sales |
|---|---|---|---|---|---|
| **Apple** | $77,434 | ÷ | $265,595 | = | 29.2% |
| **Alphabet** | $47,971 | ÷ | $136,819 | = | 35.1% |

**ILLUSTRATION 11–31**

Asset Turnover for
Apple and Alphabet

| ($ in millions) | Net Sales | ÷ | Average Total Assets | = | Asset Turnover |
|---|---|---|---|---|---|
| **Apple** | $265,595 | ÷ | ($375,319 + $365,725)/2 | = | 0.72 times |
| **Alphabet** | $136,819 | ÷ | ($197,295 + $232,792)/2 | = | 0.64 times |

Both companies have high cash flow to sales ratios, but Apple's is lower. This difference explains why Apple generates lower cash return on assets. However, this lower return is partially offset by Apple's higher asset turnover ratio. Apple uses its assets more efficiently to generate sales. To maximize cash flow from operations, a company strives to increase *both* cash flow per dollar of sales (cash flow to sales) and sales per dollar of assets invested (asset turnover).

Finally, we'll consider free cash flows. Conceptually, free cash flows represent the amount of internally-generated cash flows that are freely available for managers to spend, once major capital expenses are taken care of. Managers commonly spend free cash flows on financing activities, such as paying down debt early, paying dividends to shareholders, or repurchasing stock.

In practice, there are several acceptable ways to compute free cash flows. For simplicity, we'll compute it based on two numbers that come straight from the statement of cash flows, as follows:

$$\text{Free cash flows} = \text{Operating cash flows} - \text{Capital expenditures}$$

Let's compute free cash flows for Apple and Alphabet (Illustration 11–32). We'll also divide it by sales revenue to facilitate comparison between the two companies.

| ($ in millions) | Operating Cash Flows | − | Capital Expenditures | = | Free Cash Flows |
|---|---|---|---|---|---|
| **Apple** | $77,434 | − | $13,313 | = | $64,121 |
| **Alphabet** | $47,971 | − | $25,139 | = | $22,832 |

| ($ in millions) | Free Cash Flows | ÷ | Net Sales | = | Free Cash Flows to Sales |
|---|---|---|---|---|---|
| **Apple** | $64,121 | ÷ | $265,595 | = | 24.1% |
| **Alphabet** | $22,832 | ÷ | $136,819 | = | 16.7% |

Both companies generate billions of dollars of free cash flows, but Apple definitely generates more, both in terms of dollar amounts and as a percentage of sales. On the one hand, this could indicate that Apple is better than Alphabet at generating free cash flows, but it also may suggest that Apple is under-investing in capital assets that will potentially generate more free cash flows in the future. This is the power of examining free cash flows as a performance metric—it provides a joint assessment of the major source of cash flows (operations) together with a major use of cash flows (investment in capital assets).

Illustration 11–34 presents the Cash Cows in 2018, which are the 10 companies that generated the greatest free cash flows in terms of dollar amounts. Both Apple and Alphabet make the list—they are both cash cows!

**ILLUSTRATION 11–34**

Cash Cows: Largest 10 Companies by Free Cash Flows

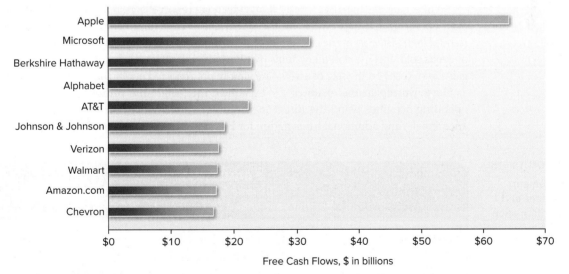

Free Cash Flows, $ in billions

Source: Standard & Poor's

**KEY POINT**

Cash return on assets indicates the amount of operating cash flow generated for each dollar invested in assets. We can separate cash return on assets into two components—cash flow to sales and asset turnover—to examine two important business strategies. Free cash flows measure the available cash flows for discretionary spending, often calculated as operating cash flows minus capital expenditures.

**ETHICAL DILEMMA**

Freedomz/Shutterstock

Ebenezer is CEO of a successful small business. One day he stops by to see Tim Cratchit, the new branch manager at First National Bank. Ebenezer and his partner Marley would like to double the size of their loan with the bank from $500,000 to $1 million. Ebenezer explains, "Business is booming, sales and earnings are up each of the past three years, and we could certainly use the funds for further business expansion." Tim Cratchit has a big heart, and Ebenezer has been a close friend of the family. He thinks to himself this loan decision will be easy, but he asks Ebenezer to e-mail the past three years' financial statements as required by bank policy.

In looking over the financial statements sent by Ebenezer, Tim becomes concerned. Sales and earnings have increased, just as Ebenezer said. However, receivables, inventory, and accounts payable have grown at a much faster rate than sales. Further, he notices a steady decrease in operating cash flows over the past three years, with negative operating cash flows in each of the past two years.

Who are the stakeholders, and what is the ethical dilemma? Do you think Tim should go ahead and approve the loan?

---

# APPENDIX

# OPERATING ACTIVITIES—DIRECT METHOD

**■ LO11–7**
Prepare the operating activities section of the statement of cash flows using the direct method.

There are two acceptable alternatives in reporting operating activities—the indirect method and the direct method. The presentation of operating activities in the main body of the chapter is referred to as the indirect method. By this method, we begin with reported net income and work backward to convert to a cash basis.

An alternative is the direct method, by which we report the cash inflows and cash outflows from operating activities directly in the statement of cash flows. For instance, we report *cash received from customers* as the cash effect of sales, and *cash paid to suppliers* as the cash effect of cost of goods sold. Income statement items that have *no* cash effect—such as depreciation expense or gains and losses on the sale of assets—are simply not reported under the direct method.

Here, we repeat the example for E-Games, Inc., this time presenting cash flows from operating activities using the direct method. For convenience, the income statement, balance sheets, and additional information for E-Games, Inc., are repeated in Illustration 11–35.

**ILLUSTRATION 11–35**

Income Statement, Balance Sheets, and Additional Information for E-Games, Inc.

| E-GAMES, INC. Income Statement For the year ended December 31, 2024 | | |
|---|---|---|
| Net sales | | $1,012,000 |
| Expenses: | | |
| Cost of goods sold | $650,000 | |
| Operating expenses (salaries, rent, utilities) | 286,000 | |
| Depreciation expense | 9,000 | |
| Loss on sale of land | 4,000 | |
| Interest expense | 5,000 | |
| Income tax expense | 16,000 | |
| Total expenses | | 970,000 |
| Net income | | $    42,000 |

(*continued*)

ILLUSTRATION 11–35

(concluded)

**E-GAMES, INC.**
**Balance Sheets**
**December 31, 2024 and 2023**

| | 2024 | 2023 | Increase (I) or Decrease (D) |
|---|---|---|---|
| **Assets** | | | |
| Current assets: | | | |
| Cash | $ 62,000 | $ 48,000 | $14,000 (I) |
| Accounts receivable | 27,000 | 20,000 | 7,000 (I) |
| Inventory | 35,000 | 45,000 | 10,000 (D) |
| Prepaid rent | 4,000 | 2,000 | 2,000 (I) |
| Long-term assets: | | | |
| Investments | 35,000 | 0 | 35,000 (I) |
| Land | 70,000 | 80,000 | 10,000 (D) |
| Equipment | 90,000 | 70,000 | 20,000 (I) |
| Accumulated depreciation | (23,000) | (14,000) | 9,000 (I) |
| Total assets | $300,000 | $251,000 | |
| **Liabilities and Stockholders' Equity** | | | |
| Current liabilities: | | | |
| Accounts payable | $ 22,000 | $ 27,000 | $ 5,000 (D) |
| Interest payable | 2,000 | 1,000 | 1,000 (I) |
| Income tax payable | 5,000 | 7,000 | 2,000 (D) |
| Long-term liabilities: | | | |
| Notes payable | 95,000 | 75,000 | 20,000 (I) |
| Stockholders' equity: | | | |
| Common stock | 105,000 | 100,000 | 5,000 (I) |
| Retained earnings | 71,000 | 41,000 | 30,000 (I) |
| Total liabilities and stockholders' equity | $300,000 | $251,000 | |

**Additional Information for 2024:**

1. Purchased stock in Intendo Corporation for $35,000.
2. Sold land for $6,000. The land originally was purchased for $10,000, resulting in a $4,000 loss being recorded at the time of the sale.
3. Purchased $20,000 in equipment by issuing a $20,000 note payable due in three years. No cash was exchanged in the transaction.
4. Issued common stock for $5,000 cash.
5. Declared and paid a cash dividend of $12,000.

Remember from Illustration 11–5 that the first step in preparing the statement of cash flows is to calculate net cash flows from *operating* activities using information from the income statement and changes in current assets and current liabilities from the balance sheet.

The income statement reports revenues recognized during the year, *regardless of when cash is received,* and the expenses incurred in generating those revenues, *regardless of when cash is paid.* This is the *accrual concept* of accounting that we've discussed throughout the book. Cash flows from operating activities, on the other hand, are both inflows and outflows of cash that result from activities reported in the income statement. In other words, it's the elements of net income, but **reported on a cash basis.** Using the direct method, we examine each account in the income statement and convert it from an accrual amount to a cash amount. We directly report the cash inflows and cash outflows. The relationships between items in the income statement and operating cash flows are shown in Illustration 11–36.

| Income Statement | Cash Flows from Operating Activities |
|---|---|
| **Revenues:** | **Cash inflows:** |
| Sales and service revenue | ➡ Cash received from customers |
| Investment revenue | ➡ Cash received from interest and dividends |
| Noncash revenues and gains (gains on sale of assets) | ➡ (Not reported) |
| **Less: Expenses** | **Less: Cash outflows** |
| Cost of goods sold | ➡ Cash paid to suppliers for inventory |
| Operating expense | ➡ Cash paid for salaries, rent, utilities, etc. |
| Noncash expenses and losses (loss on sale of assets, depreciation) | ➡ (Not reported) |
| Interest expense | ➡ Cash paid to creditors for interest |
| Income tax expense | ➡ Cash paid to the government for taxes |
| **= Net income** | **= Net cash flows from operating activities** |

The best way to apply the direct method is to convert each revenue and expense item to its cash-basis amount. We'll do this next using our E-Games example. Use the general guidelines in Illustration 11–36A for converting each income statement item to its operating cash flows.

**ILLUSTRATION 11–36A**

Convert Income Statement Items to Operating Cash Flows

| Revenue | Expense |
|---|---|
| − Increase in related current asset | + Increase in related current asset |
| + Decrease in related current asset | − Decrease in related current asset |
| + Increase in related current liability | − Increase in related current liability |
| − Decrease in related current liability | + Decrease in related current liability |
| **= Cash received** | **= Cash paid** |

**Cash Received from Customers.**   E-Games reports net sales of $1,012,000 as the first item in its income statement. Did E-Games receive $1,012,000 in cash from those sales? We can answer this by looking at the change in accounts receivable. If accounts receivable increases, this indicates that net sales exceed cash receipts from customers. That's why customers owe more than they did before. If accounts receivable decreases, the opposite will be true. Recall that accounts receivable increased $7,000. Therefore, we deduct the $7,000 increase in accounts receivable from net sales to obtain cash received from customers of $1,005,000, as shown in Illustration 11–37.

**ILLUSTRATION 11–37**

Cash Received from Customers

| | |
|---|---|
| Net sales | $ 1,012,000 |
| − Increase in accounts receivable | (7,000) |
| **= Cash received from customers** | **$1,005,000** |

Let's consider this again from a couple of different perspectives. Accounts receivable increases when we have credit sales to customers and decreases when we receive cash from customers. We can compare sales and the change in accounts receivable during the year to determine the amount of cash we received from customers. In T-account format the relationship looks like this:

| | **Accounts Receivable** | | |
|---|---|---|---|
| Beginning balance | 20,000 | | |
| Credit sales | 1,012,000 | ? | Cash received |
| (*increase A/R*) | | | (*decreases A/R*) |
| Ending balance | 27,000 | | |

We see from this analysis that *cash received from customers* must have been $1,005,000.

---

### DEBITS & CREDITS

Another way to view the situation is to think about how E-Games recorded these selling and collection activities during the year:

| | Debit | Credit |
|---|---|---|
| **Cash** (to balance) ......................................................................... | 1,005,000 | |
| **Accounts Receivable** (= $27,000 − $20,000)................................... | 7,000 | |
| **Sales Revenue** (from income statement) ......................................... | | 1,012,000 |

We record an increase in Sales Revenue with a credit and an increase in Accounts Receivable with a debit. Cash received from customers must be $1,005,000 for debits to equal credits. The journal entry above summarizes the many sales transactions that occurred during the period.

---

**Cash Paid to Suppliers.**   Moving down the income statement, we see that E-Games reports cost of goods sold of $650,000. Did E-Games pay cash of $650,000 to suppliers of those goods during the year? We'll approach this using both the equation and T-accounts. Solving for cash paid to suppliers takes two steps: solving for purchases (using changes inventory) and solving for cash paid to suppliers (using changes in accounts payable). Illustration 11–38 demonstrates these steps:

---

| | |
|---|---|
| Cost of goods sold | $650,000 |
| − Decrease in inventory | (10,000) |
| = Purchases | 640,000 |
| + Decrease in accounts payable | 5,000 |
| **= Cash paid to suppliers** | **$645,000** |

**ILLUSTRATION 11–38**

**Cash Paid to Suppliers**

---

Inventory decreased $10,000 for the year, so E-Games needed to purchase only $640,000 of goods in order to sell $650,000 of goods; $10,000 came from existing inventory. Because accounts payable decreased by $5,000, cash paid to suppliers must have been $5,000 more than purchases, so we add the decrease in accounts payable to purchases of $640,000 to arrive at cash paid to suppliers of $645,000.

The second way to do this is by looking at the T-accounts for the two current balance sheet accounts affected by merchandise purchases—Inventory and Accounts Payable. First, compare cost of goods sold with the change in inventory to determine the cost of goods purchased (not necessarily cash paid) during the year. Inventory decreased by $10,000. We can visualize the relationship in T-account format.

| | **Inventory** | | |
|---|---|---|---|
| Beginning balance | 45,000 | | |
| Cost of goods purchased | ? | 650,000 | Cost of goods sold |
| (*increases inventory*) | | | (*decreases inventory*) |
| Ending balance | 35,000 | | |

The number needed to explain the change is $640,000. That's the cost of goods purchased during the year. It's not necessarily true, though, that E-Games paid $640,000 cash to suppliers of these goods. We need to look at the change in accounts payable to determine the cash paid to suppliers.

**Accounts Payable**

| | | |
|---|---|---|
| | 27,000 | Beginning balance |
| Cash paid to suppliers | ?    640,000 | Cost of goods purchased |
| (*decreases A/P*) | | (*increases A/P*) |
| | 22,000 | Ending balance |

We now see that cash paid to suppliers must be $645,000.

---

**DEBITS & CREDITS**

We can confirm this by looking at how E-Games recorded inventory purchases and sales during the year:

| | Debit | Credit |
|---|---|---|
| **Cost of Goods Sold** (from income statement)........................................ | 650,000 | |
| **Accounts Payable** (= $27,000 − $22,000).......................................... | 5,000 | |
| **Inventory** (= $45,000 − $35,000)..................................................... | | 10,000 |
| **Cash** (to balance)......................................................................... | | 645,000 |

We record an increase in Cost of Goods Sold with a debit, a decrease in Inventory with a credit, and a decrease in Accounts Payable with a debit. Cash paid to suppliers is the "plug" figure we need for debits to equal credits in the journal entry. The journal entry above summarizes the many inventory transactions that occurred during the period.

---

With the exception of prepaid rent, we see no current assets or current liabilities associated with other operating expenses such as salaries expense or utilities expense, so we make no adjustments to these operating expenses. Therefore, the amounts we report for these operating expenses in the income statement must equal the amount of cash we paid for these items. Illustration 11–39 shows this computation.

---

**ILLUSTRATION 11–39**

Cash Paid for Operating Expenses

| | |
|---|---|
| Operating expenses | $286,000 |
| + Increase in prepaid rent | 2,000 |
| = **Cash paid for operating expenses** | **$288,000** |

---

**DEBITS & CREDITS**

Let's check our calculation by recording the payment for operating expenses during the year:

| | Debit | Credit |
|---|---|---|
| **Operating Expenses** (from income statement).................... | 286,000 | |
| **Prepaid Rent** (= $4,000 − $2,000)....................................... | 2,000 | |
| **Cash** (to balance)................................................................. | | 288,000 |

We record an increase in Operating Expenses with a debit and an increase in Prepaid Rent with a debit. Cash paid for operating expenses is the "plug" figure we need for debits to equal credits in the journal entry. The journal entry above summarizes the many operating transactions that occurred during the period.

---

**Depreciation Expense and Loss on Sale of Land.** The next expense listed in the income statement is depreciation expense of $9,000. Depreciation expense has no effect on cash flows. It is merely an allocation in the current period of a prior cash expenditure (to acquire the depreciable asset). Therefore, unlike the other expenses to this point, depreciation is *not* reported on the statement of cash flows under the direct method.

Similar to depreciation expense, the loss on sale of land is *not* reported because it, too, has no effect on *operating* cash flows. Additional-information item (2) in Illustration 11–35 indicates that land we originally purchased at a cost of $10,000 was sold for $6,000, resulting in a loss on the sale of land of $4,000.

**DEBITS & CREDITS**

E-Games records the sale as:

|  | Debit | Credit |
|---|---|---|
| **Cash** (selling price) | 6,000 | |
| **Loss** (difference) | 4,000 | |
| **Land** (cost) | | 10,000 |

As we discussed previously, we report the $6,000 cash inflow as an investing activity, because both investing in land and later selling the land are considered investing activities. The original cost of the land, and thus the loss, has no effect on operating cash flows.

**Cash Paid for Interest.**    E-Games next reports interest expense of $5,000 in the income statement. The related current asset or current liability in the balance sheet is interest payable. If interest payable increases, interest expense exceeds cash paid for interest. Interest payable increases $1,000. As shown in Illustration 11–40, we deduct the increase in interest payable from interest expense to arrive at cash paid for interest.

|  |  |
|---|---|
| Interest expense | $ 5,000 |
| − Increase in interest payable | (1,000) |
| = **Cash paid for interest** | **$ 4,000** |

**ILLUSTRATION 11–40**

**Cash Paid for Interest**

**DEBITS & CREDITS**

We can check our calculation by recording the payment for interest during the year:

|  | Debit | Credit |
|---|---|---|
| **Interest Expense** (from income statement) | 5,000 | |
| **Interest Payable** (= $2,000 − $1,000) | | 1,000 |
| **Cash** (to balance) | | 4,000 |

We record an increase in Interest Expense with a debit and an increase in Interest Payable with a credit. Cash paid for interest is the "plug" figure we need for debits to equal credits in the journal entry.

**Cash Paid for Income Taxes.**    The final item reported in the income statement is income tax expense of $16,000. The related current asset or current liability in the balance sheet is income tax payable. Income tax payable decreased $2,000. This means that E-Games paid $2,000 more than the income tax expense recorded. As shown in Illustration 11–41, we add the decrease in income tax payable to income tax expense to calculate cash paid for income taxes.

|  |  |
|---|---|
| Income Tax Expense | $16,000 |
| + Decrease in income tax payable | 2,000 |
| = **Cash paid for income taxes** | **$18,000** |

**ILLUSTRATION 11–41**

**Cash Paid for Income Taxes**

**DEBITS & CREDITS**

Recording the payment of taxes during the year confirms this:

|  | Debit | Credit |
|---|---|---|
| **Income Tax Expense** (from income statement) | 16,000 | |
| **Income Tax Payable** (= $7,000 − $5,000) | 2,000 | |
| **Cash** (to balance) | | 18,000 |

We record an increase in Income Tax Expense with a debit and a decrease in Income Tax Payable with a debit. Cash paid for income tax is the "plug" figure we need for debits to equal credits in the journal entry.

Illustration 11–42 shows the completed operating activities section using the direct method.

**ILLUSTRATION 11–42**

Operating Activities Using the Direct Method

### E-GAMES, INC.
### Statement of Cash Flows (partial)–Direct Method

**Cash Flows from Operating Activities**

| | |
|---|---:|
| Cash received from customers | $1,005,000 |
| Cash paid to suppliers | (645,000) |
| Cash paid for operating expenses | (288,000) |
| Cash paid for interest | (4,000) |
| Cash paid for income taxes | (18,000) |
| Net cash flows from operating activities | $50,000 |

Note that the net cash flows from operating activities is $50,000—**the same amount we calculated earlier in Illustration 11–16 using the indirect method.** This will always be the case. The indirect method begins with net income, whereas the direct method considers each of the individual accounts that make up net income. Both methods take into consideration the *same changes* in current asset and current liability accounts.

**KEY POINT**

The indirect method and direct method differ only in the presentation of operating activities. In the indirect method, we start with net income and make adjustments to arrive at net cash flows from operating activities. In the direct method, we convert each individual line item in the income statement to its cash basis and directly list the cash inflows and cash outflows from operating activities. The net cash flows from operating activities are *the same under both methods.*

**Let's Review**

The income statement, balance sheets, and additional information from the accounting records of E-Phones, Inc., are provided below.

### E-PHONES, INC.
### Income Statement
### For the year ended December 31, 2024

| | | |
|---|---:|---:|
| Net sales | | $2,200,000 |
| Gain on sale of investment | | 5,000 |
| Expenses: | | |
| Cost of goods sold | $1,100,000 | |
| Operating expenses | 450,000 | |
| Depreciation expense | 25,000 | |
| Income tax expense | 217,000 | |
| Total expenses | | 1,792,000 |
| Net income | | $  413,000 |

**E-PHONES, INC.**
**Balance Sheets**
**December 31, 2024 and 2023**

| Assets | 2024 | 2023 | Increase (I) or Decrease (D) |
|---|---|---|---|
| **Assets** | | | |
| Current assets: | | | |
| Cash | $ 32,000 | $ 48,000 | $ 16,000 (D) |
| Accounts receivable | 32,000 | 40,000 | 8,000 (D) |
| Inventory | 100,000 | 70,000 | 30,000 (I) |
| Long-term assets: | | | |
| Investments | 0 | 50,000 | 50,000 (D) |
| Land | 280,000 | 180,000 | 100,000 (I) |
| Equipment | 200,000 | 140,000 | 60,000 (I) |
| Accumulated depreciation | (53,000) | (28,000) | 25,000 (I) |
| Total assets | $591,000 | $500,000 | |
| **Liabilities and Stockholders' Equity** | | | |
| Current liabilities: | | | |
| Accounts payable | $ 52,000 | $ 62,000 | $ 10,000 (D) |
| Income tax payable | 55,000 | 12,000 | 43,000 (I) |
| Long-term liabilities: | | | |
| Bonds payable | 0 | 200,000 | 200,000 (D) |
| Stockholders' equity: | | | |
| Common stock | 200,000 | 100,000 | 100,000 (I) |
| Retained earnings | 284,000 | 126,000 | 158,000 (I) |
| Total liabilities and stockholders' equity | $591,000 | $500,000 | |

**Additional Information for 2024:**

1. Sold an investment in stock costing $50,000 for $55,000, resulting in a $5,000 gain on sale of investment.
2. Purchased $100,000 in land, issuing $100,000 of common stock as payment. No cash was exchanged in the transaction.
3. Purchased equipment for $60,000 cash.
4. Retired the $200,000 balance in bonds payable at the beginning of the year.
5. Declared and paid a cash dividend of $255,000.

*Required:*

Prepare the statement of cash flows using the *direct method* for reporting operating activities. Disclose any noncash transactions in a note to the statement of cash flows.

*Solution:*

**E-PHONES, INC.**
**Statement of Cash Flows—Direct Method**
**For the year ended December 31, 2024**

| | |
|---|---|
| **Cash Flows from Operating Activities** | |
| Cash received from customers | $2,208,000 |
| Cash paid to suppliers | (1,140,000) |

*(continued)*

(*concluded*)

**E-PHONES, INC.**
**Statement of Cash Flows—Direct Method**
**For the year ended December 31, 2024**

| | | |
|---|---:|---:|
| Cash paid for operating expenses | (450,000) | |
| Cash paid for income taxes | (174,000) | |
| Net cash flows from operating activities | | $444,000 |
| **Cash Flows from Investing Activities** | | |
| Sale of investment | 55,000 | |
| Purchase of equipment | (60,000) | |
| Net cash flows from investing activities | | (5,000) |
| **Cash Flows from Financing Activities** | | |
| Retirement of bonds payable | (200,000) | |
| Payment of cash dividends | (255,000) | |
| Net cash flows from financing activities | | (455,000) |
| Net increase (decrease) in cash | | **(16,000)** |
| Cash at the beginning of the period | | 48,000 |
| Cash at the end of the period | | $ 32,000 |
| **Note: Noncash Activities** | | |
| Purchased land by issuing common stock | | $100,000 |

Here are the supporting calculations for cash flows from operating activities under the direct method:

| | |
|---|---:|
| Net sales | $ 2,200,000 |
| + Decrease in accounts receivable | 8,000 |
| **= Cash received from customers** | **$2,208,000** |
| | |
| Cost of goods sold | $ 1,100,000 |
| + Increase in inventory | 30,000 |
| = Purchases | 1,130,000 |
| + Decrease in accounts payable | 10,000 |
| **= Cash paid to suppliers** | **$1,140,000** |
| | |
| **Cash paid for operating expenses** | **$   450,000** |
| | |
| Income tax expense | $   217,000 |
| − Increase in income tax payable | (43,000) |
| **= Cash paid for income taxes** | **$   174,000** |

---

 **THE BOTTOM LINE**

**LO11–1** **Classify cash transactions as operating, investing, or financing activities.**

Operating activities generally relate to income statement items and changes in current assets and current liabilities. Investing activities primarily involve changes in long-term assets.

Financing activities primarily involve changes in long-term liabilities and stockholders' equity.

**LO11–2** **Understand the steps and basic format in preparing the statement of cash flows.**

The steps in preparing the statement of cash flows involve calculating: (1) net cash flows from operating activities, (2) net cash flows from investing activities, (3) net cash flows from financing activities, and (4) the sum of these three activities to verify it equals the amount of cash reported in the balance sheet this year versus last year (the change in cash).

Companies choose between the indirect method and the direct method in reporting operating activities in the statement of cash flows. The indirect method begins with net income and then lists adjustments to net income, in order to arrive at operating cash flows. The direct method specifically lists the various cash inflows and outflows from operations. The investing and financing sections of the statement of cash flows are identical under both methods.

**LO11–3** Prepare the operating activities section of the statement of cash flows using the indirect method.

Using the indirect method, we start with net income and adjust this number for income statement items (removing noncash revenues and noncash expenses and removing nonoperating gains and nonoperating losses), and for balance sheet items (changes in current assets and changes in current liabilities).

**LO11–4** Prepare the investing activities section of the statement of cash flows.

Cash transactions (inflows and outflows) involving long-term assets and investments are reported in the investing activities section of the statement of cash flows. Typical investing activities include buying and selling property, plant, and equipment, as well as making and collecting loans.

**LO11–5** Prepare the financing activities section of the statement of cash flows.

Cash transactions (inflows and outflows) with creditors and shareholders are reported in the financing activities section of the statement of cash flows. Typical financing activities include borrowing money and repaying amounts borrowed from creditors, as well as issuing stock, repurchasing stock, and paying dividends to shareholders.

**LO11–6** Perform financial analysis using the statement of cash flows.

Cash return on assets indicates the amount of operating cash flow generated for each dollar invested in assets. We can separate cash return on assets into two components—cash flow to sales and asset turnover—to examine two important business strategies. Free cash flows measure the available cash flows for discretionary spending. It is often calculated as operating cash flows minus capital expenditures.

**LO11–7** Prepare the operating activities section of the statement of cash flows using the direct method.

The indirect method and direct method differ only in the presentation of operating activities. In the indirect method, we start with net income and make adjustments to arrive at net cash flows from operating activities. In the direct method, we convert each individual line item in the income statement to its cash basis and directly list the cash inflows and cash outflows from operating activities. The net cash flows from operating activities are *the same under both methods*.

## GLOSSARY

**Asset turnover:** Net sales divided by average total assets, which measures the sales per dollar of assets invested. **p. 578**

**Cash flow to sales:** Net cash flows from operating activities divided by sales revenue; measures the operating cash flow generated per dollar of sales. **p. 578**

**Cash return on assets:** Net cash flows from operating activities divided by average total assets; measures the operating cash flow generated per dollar of assets. **p. 577**

**Direct method:** Adjusts the items in the income statement to directly show the cash inflows and outflows from operations, such as cash received from customers and cash paid for inventory, salaries, rent, interest, and taxes. **pp. 560, 580**

**Financing activities:** Transactions with lenders, such as borrowing money and repaying debt, and with stockholders, such as issuing stock, paying dividends, and purchasing treasury stock. **p. 555**

**Free cash flows:** the difference between operating cash flows and capital expenditures; measures the cash flows available to spend at the manager's discretion. **p. 578**

**Indirect method:** Begins with net income and then lists adjustments to net income in order to arrive at operating cash flows. **p. 560**

**Investing activities:** Transactions involving the purchase and sale of long-term assets and current investments. **p. 555**

**Noncash activities:** Significant investing and financing activities that do not affect cash. **p. 557**

**Operating activities:** Transactions involving revenue and expense activities. **p. 554**

**Statement of cash flows:** A financial statement that measures activities involving cash receipts and cash payments over a period of time. **p. 554**

## SELF-STUDY QUESTIONS

1. The purchase of a long-term asset is classified in the statement of cash flows as a(n) **(LO11–1)**
   a. Operating activity.
   b. Investing activity.
   c. Financing activity.
   d. Noncash activity.

2. The issuance of common stock is classified in the statement of cash flows as a(n) **(LO11–1)**
   a. Operating activity.
   b. Investing activity.
   c. Financing activity.
   d. Noncash activity.

3. The issuance of notes payable is classified in the statement of cash flows as a(n) **(LO11–1)**
   a. Operating activity.
   b. Investing activity.
   c. Financing activity.
   d. Noncash activity.

4. Which of the following is an example of a noncash activity? **(LO11–1)**
   a. Cash received from the sale of land for more than its cost.
   b. Purchase of land by issuing common stock to the seller.
   c. Cash received from the sale of land for less than its cost.
   d. Purchase of land using cash proceeds from issuance of common stock.

5. The indirect and direct methods **(LO11–2)**
   a. Are used by companies about equally in actual practice.
   b. Affect the presentations of operating, investing, and financing activities.
   c. Arrive at different amounts for net cash flows from operating activities.
   d. Are two allowable methods to present operating activities in the statement of cash flows.

6. Which of the following best describes the indirect method of preparing the operating activities section of the statement of cash flows? **(LO11–3)**
   a. Net income reconciled from accrual basis to cash basis.
   b. A list of cash inflows and cash outflows from transactions involving the purchase and sale of long-term assets and current investments.
   c. A list of cash inflows and cash outflows from transactions related to revenue and expense activities.
   d. A list of cash inflows and cash outflows from transactions with lenders and stockholders.

7. Using the information below, calculate net cash flows from operating activities: **(LO11–3)**

| | |
|---|---|
| Net income | $120,000 |
| Receive cash from issuing stock | 80,000 |
| Pay cash for equipment | 90,000 |
| Increase in accounts receivable | 10,000 |
| Depreciation expense | 30,000 |
| Increase in accounts payable | 5,000 |
| Receive cash from sale of land | 75,000 |
| Pay cash dividends | 20,000 |

   a. $115,000.
   b. $155,000.
   c. $145,000.
   d. $190,000.

8. Which of the following is an example of a cash inflow from an investing activity? **(LO11–4)**
   a. Receipt of cash from the issuance of common stock.
   b. Receipt of cash from the sale of equipment.
   c. Receipt of cash from the issuance of a note payable.
   d. Receipt of cash from the sale of inventory.

9. Using the information in Question 7, calculate net cash flows from investing activities. **(LO11–4)**
   a. $(165,000).
   b. $15,000.
   c. $60,000.
   d. $(15,000).

10. Which of the following is an example of a cash outflow from a financing activity? **(LO11–5)**
    a. Payment of interest.
    b. Purchase of an intangible asset.
    c. Payment of cash dividends.
    d. Purchase of land.

11. Using the information in Question 7, calculate net cash flows from financing activities. **(LO11–5)**
    a. $60,000.
    b. $(15,000).
    c. $100,000.
    d. $80,000.

12. The balance of cash at the beginning of the year was $120,000, and at the end of the year was $140,000. Assuming operating cash flows equal $90,000 and investing cash flows equal $(40,000), calculate financing cash flows for the year. **(LO11–5)**
    a. $50,000.
    b. $(30,000).
    c. $10,000.
    d. $(70,000).

13. We can separate cash return on assets into **(LO11–6)**
    a. Cash flow to sales and return on assets.
    b. Profit margin and asset turnover.
    c. Cash flow to sales and profit margin.
    d. Cash flow to sales and asset turnover.

14. Which of the following items do we report in the statement of cash flows using the direct method? **(LO11–7)**
    a. Depreciation expense.
    b. Gain on sale of an asset.
    c. Cash paid to suppliers.
    d. Loss on sale of an asset.

15. Salaries expense for the year equals $240,000. Salaries payable at the beginning of the year were $25,000, and at the end of the year were $15,000. Calculate cash paid for salaries during the year. **(LO11–7)**
    a. $225,000.
    b. $250,000.
    c. $230,000.
    d. $265,000.

*Note: For answers, see the last page of the chapter.*

## REAL WORLD PERSPECTIVES

### Jabil Inc. (ticker: JBL)

**EDGAR Case**

**RWP11–1** Visit www.sec.gov/edgar and search for the **Jabil** annual report (10-K) for the year ended August 31, 2019, using EDGAR (Electronic Data Gathering, Analysis, and Retrieval system). Locate the "Consolidated Statements of Cash Flows," and use it to answer the following questions.

The following is a list of items pulled from Jabil's statement of cash flows:

- Changes in prepaid expenses and other current assets.
- Cash paid for business and intangible asset acquisitions.
- Depreciation and amortization.
- Acquisition of property, plant and equipment.
- Payments to acquire treasury stock.
- Changes in inventories.
- Proceeds and advances from sale of property, plant and equipment.
- Borrowings under debt agreements.
- Dividends paid to shareholders.
- Changes in accounts payable, accrued expenses and other liabilities.

*Required:*
1. Using the information in the 10-K, identify whether each of the above items is reported in the operating, investing or financing activities section of the statement of cash flows.

### Micron Technologies (ticker: MU)

**EDGAR Case**

**RWP11–2** Visit www.sec.gov/edgar and search for the **Micron** annual report (10-K) for the year ended August 29, 2019, using EDGAR (Electronic Data Gathering, Analysis, and Retrieval system). Locate the "Consolidated Statements of Cash Flows," which you'll use to answer the questions below.

*Required:*
1. What method (direct or indirect) does Micron use in the operating section of the statement of cash flows?
2. Identify the noncash items used in calculating operating cash flows and determine whether the item is added or subtracted from net income.
3. Identify the nonoperating items used in calculating operating cash flows and determine whether the item is added or subtracted from net income.
4. Identify the changes in current assets and current liabilities used in calculating operating cash flows and determine whether the item is added or subtracted from net income.

EDGAR Case

## Lam Research Corporation (ticker: LRCX)

**RWP11–3** Visit www.sec.gov/edgar and search for the **Lam Research** annual report (10-K) for the year ended June 30, 2019, using EDGAR (Electronic Data Gathering, Analysis, and Retrieval system). Focus on its "Consolidated Statements of Cash Flows" to answer the following questions.

### Required:
1. Did Lam Research purchase any available-for-sale securities in the most recent year? If so, how much?
2. Compute the year-over-year growth in CAPEX for the two most recent years.
3. What was the largest inflow of cash from financing activities?
4. What was the largest outflow of cash from financing activities?

EDGAR Case

## Oracle Corporation (ticker: ORCL)

**RWP11–4** Visit www.sec.gov/edgar and search for the **Oracle** annual report (10-K) for the year ended May 31, 2019, using EDGAR (Electronic Data Gathering, Analysis, and Retrieval system). Locate the balance sheet, income statement, and statement of cash flows. Use these to answer the following questions.

### Required:
1. Compute return on assets for the most recent year.
2. Compute cash return on assets for the most recent year.
3. Compute the cash flow to sales ratio and the asset turnover ratio for the most recent year.
4. Compute free cash flows and the free cash flow to sales ratio.

Continuing Financial Analysis Case

## American Eagle Outfitters, Inc.

**RWP11–5** Financial information for **American Eagle** is presented in **Appendix A** at the end of the book.

### Required:
1. What was the amount of increase or decrease in cash and cash equivalents for the most recent year?
2. What was net cash from operating activities for the most recent year? Is net cash from operating activities increasing in the most recent year? What is the largest reconciling item between net income and net operating cash flows during the most recent year?
3. What was net cash from investing activities for the most recent year? What is the largest investing activity during the most recent year?
4. What was net cash from financing activities for the most recent year? What is the largest financing activity during the most recent year?

Continuing Financial Analysis Case

## The Buckle, Inc.

**RWP11–6** Financial information for **Buckle** is presented in **Appendix B** at the end of the book.

### Required:
1. What was the amount of increase or decrease in cash and cash equivalents for the most recent year?
2. What was net cash from operating activities for the most recent year? Is net cash from operating activities increasing in the most recent year? What is the largest reconciling item between net income and net operating cash flows during the most recent year?
3. What was net cash from investing activities for the most recent year? What is the largest investing activity during the most recent year?
4. What was net cash from financing activities for the most recent year? What is the largest financing activity during the most recent year?

## American Eagle Outfitters, Inc. vs. The Buckle, Inc.

Continuing Comparative Analysis Case

**RWP11–7** Financial information for **American Eagle** is presented in **Appendix A** at the end of the book, and financial information for **Buckle** is presented in **Appendix B** at the end of the book.

*Required:*

1. Calculate American Eagle's cash return on assets, cash flow to sales, asset turnover ratio, free cash flows, and free cash flow to sales in the most recent year.
2. Calculate Buckle's cash return on assets, cash flow to sales, asset turnover ratio, free cash flows, and free cash flow to sales in the most recent year.
3. Which company is doing better based on cash return on assets? Which company has the higher cash flow to sales? Which company has the higher asset turnover? Which is doing better based on free cash flow to sales?

## Ethics

Ethics Case

**RWP11–8** Aggressive Corporation approaches Matt Taylor, a loan officer for Oklahoma State Bank, seeking to increase the company's borrowings with the bank from $100,000 to $200,000. Matt has an uneasy feeling as he examines the loan application from Aggressive Corporation, which just completed its first year of operations. The application included the following financial statements.

**AGGRESSIVE CORPORATION**
**Income Statement**
**For the year ended December 31, 2024**

| | | |
|---|---|---|
| Net sales | | $275,000 |
| Expenses: | | |
| Cost of goods sold | $150,000 | |
| Operating expenses | 50,000 | |
| Depreciation expense | 10,000 | |
| Total expenses | | 210,000 |
| Net income | | $ 65,000 |

**AGGRESSIVE CORPORATION**
**Balance Sheets**
**December 31, 2024**

| | 2024 | 2023 |
|---|---|---|
| **Assets** | | |
| Current assets: | | |
| Cash | $150,000 | $0 |
| Accounts receivable | 0 | 0 |
| Inventory | 0 | 0 |
| Long-term assets: | | |
| Equipment | 160,000 | 0 |
| Accumulated depreciation | (10,000) | 0 |
| Total assets | $300,000 | $0 |
| **Liabilities and Stockholders' Equity** | | |
| Current liabilities: | | |
| Accounts payable | $ 25,000 | $0 |
| Interest payable | 10,000 | 0 |
| Long-term liabilities: | | |
| Note payable | 100,000 | 0 |
| Stockholders' equity: | | |
| Common stock | 100,000 | 0 |
| Retained earnings | 65,000 | 0 |
| Total liabilities and stockholders' equity | $300,000 | $0 |

Matt notices the company has no ending accounts receivable and no ending inventory, which seems suspicious. Matt is also wondering why a company with $150,000 in cash is seeking an additional $100,000 in borrowing.

Seeing Matt's hesitation, Larry Bling, the CEO of Aggressive Corporation, closes the conference room door. He shares with Matt the following additional information:

- The ending accounts receivable balance is actually $60,000, but because those accounts are expected to be collected very soon, I assumed a balance of $0 and counted those receivables as cash collected.
- The ending inventory balance is actually $40,000, but I believe that inventory can easily be sold for $75,000 in the near future. So, I included sales revenue of $75,000 (and cost of goods of $40,000) in the income statement and cash collected of $75,000 (and no inventory) in the balance sheet.

Plus, Larry tells Matt that he'll be looking for a new CFO in another year to run Aggressive Corporation, along with his other businesses, and Matt is just the kind of guy he is looking for. Larry mentions that as CFO, Matt would receive a significant salary. Matt is flattered and says he will look over the loan application and get back to Larry concerning the additional $100,000 loan by the end of the week.

### Required:

1. Understand the reporting effect: Calculate operating cash flows using the financial statements provided by Larry.
2. Specify the options: Calculate operating cash flows without the two assumptions made by Larry.
3. Identify the impact: Could Larry's assumptions affect Matt's decision for the bank to lend an additional $100,000 to Larry?
4. Make a decision: Should Matt use Larry's assumption in analyzing the loan for Aggressive Corporation?

**Earnings Management Case**

## Earnings Management

**RWP11–9** Bryan Eubank began his accounting career as an auditor for a Big 4 CPA firm. He focused on clients in the high-technology sector, becoming an expert on topics such as inventory write-downs, stock options, and business acquisitions. Impressed with his technical skills and experience, General Electronics, a large consumer electronics chain, hired Bryan as the company controller responsible for all of the accounting functions within the corporation. Bryan was excited about his new position. To better understand the company's financial position, he began by making the following comparison over time ($ in millions):

|  | 2024 | 2023 | 2022 | 2021 |
|---|---|---|---|---|
| Operating income | $1,400 | $1,320 | $1,275 | $1,270 |
| Net income | 385 | 350 | 345 | 295 |
| Cash flows from operations | 16 | 110 | 120 | 155 |

Bryan also noticed a couple of other items:

a. The company's credit policy has been loosened, credit terms relaxed, and payment periods lengthened. This has resulted in a large increase in accounts receivable.
b. Several of the company's salary arrangements, including that of the CEO and CFO, are based on reported net income.

### Required:

1. What effect does relaxing credit terms and lengthening payment periods likely have on the balance of accounts receivable? Does the change in accounts receivable affect net income differently than operating cash flows?
2. Do salary arrangements for officers, such as the CEO and CFO, increase the risk of earnings management?
3. What trend in the information could be a source of concern for Bryan?

## Great Adventures

Continuing General
Ledger Case

(This is a continuation of the Great Adventures problem from earlier chapters.)

**RWP11–10** The income statement, balance sheets, and additional information for Great Adventures, Inc., are provided below.

### GREAT ADVENTURES, INC.
### Income Statement
### For the year ended December 31, 2025

| | | |
|---|---|---|
| Net revenues: | | $164,270 |
| Expenses: | | |
| Cost of goods sold | $38,500 | |
| Operating expenses | 51,400 | |
| Depreciation expense | 17,250 | |
| Interest expense | 6,785 | |
| Income tax expense | 14,500 | |
| Total expenses | | 128,435 |
| Net income | | $ 35,835 |

### GREAT ADVENTURES, INC.
### Balance Sheets
### December 31, 2025 and 2024

| | 2025 | 2024 | Increase (I) or Decrease (D) |
|---|---|---|---|
| **Assets** | | | |
| Current assets: | | | |
| Cash | $ 180,568 | $ 64,500 | $ 116,068 (I) |
| Accounts receivable | 47,600 | 0 | 47,600 (I) |
| Inventory | 7,000 | 0 | 7,000 (I) |
| Other current assets | 900 | 4,500 | 3,600 (D) |
| Long-term assets: | | | |
| Land | 500,000 | 0 | 500,000 (I) |
| Buildings | 800,000 | 0 | 800,000 (I) |
| Equipment | 62,000 | 40,000 | 22,000 (I) |
| Accumulated depreciation | (25,250) | (8,000) | 17,250 (I) |
| Total assets | $1,572,818 | $101,000 | |
| **Liabilities and Stockholders' Equity** | | | |
| Current liabilities: | | | |
| Accounts payable | $ 20,800 | $ 2,800 | $ 18,000 (I) |
| Interest payable | 750 | 750 | |
| Income tax payable | 14,500 | 14,000 | 500 (I) |
| Other current liabilities | 21,000 | 0 | 21,000 (I) |
| Notes payable (current and long-term) | 523,883 | 30,000 | 493,883 (I) |
| Stockholders' equity: | | | |
| Common stock | 120,000 | 20,000 | 100,000 (I) |
| Paid-in capital | 904,000 | 0 | 904,000 (I) |
| Retained earnings | 57,885 | 33,450 | 24,435 (I) |
| Treasury stock | (90,000) | 0 | (90,000) (I) |
| Total liabilities and stockholders' equity | $1,572,818 | $101,000 | |

**Additional Information for 2025:**
1. Land of $500,000 was obtained by issuing a note payable to the seller.
2. Buildings of $800,000 and equipment of $22,000 were purchased using cash.
3. Monthly payments during the year reduced notes payable by $6,117.
4. Issued common stock for $1,000,000.
5. Purchased 10,000 shares of treasury stock for $15 per share.
6. Sold 4,000 shares of treasury stock at $16 per share.
7. Declared and paid a cash dividend of $11,400.

*Required:*

Prepare the statement of cash flows for the year ended December 31, 2025, using the indirect method.

## BRIEF EXERCISES

Determine proper classification (LO11–1)

**BE11–1** Classify each of the following items as an operating, investing, or financing activity.
1. Dividends paid.
2. Repayment of notes payable.
3. Payment for inventory.
4. Purchase of equipment.
5. Interest paid.

Determine proper classification (LO11–1)

**BE11–2** The following selected transactions occur during the first year of operations. Determine how each should be reported in the statement of cash flows.
1. Issued one million shares of common stock at $20 per share.
2. Paid $75,000 to suppliers for inventory.
3. Paid a dividend of $1 per share to common stockholders.
4. Loaned $50,000 to an employee and accepted a note receivable.
5. Paid $45,000 in cash for computing equipment (CAPEX).

Understand the basic format for the statement of cash flows (LO11–2)

**BE11–3** Place the following items in the correct order as they would appear in the statement of cash flows.
Financing activities.
Net increase (decrease) in cash.
Operating activities.
Beginning cash balance.
Ending cash balance.
Investing activities.

Calculate operating activities—indirect method (LO11–3)

**BE11–4** 3-D Printing Supply reports net income of $650,000. Depreciation expense is $50,000, accounts receivable increases $11,000, and accounts payable decreases $30,000. Calculate net cash flows from operating activities using the indirect method.

Calculate operating activities—indirect method (LO11–3)

**BE11–5** Macrosoft Company reports net income of $75,000. The accounting records reveal stock-based compensation expense of $90,000 as well as increases in prepaid rent, accounts payable, and income tax payable of $70,000, $10,000, and $23,000, respectively. Prepare the operating activities section of Macrosoft's statement of cash flows using the indirect method.

Calculate operating activities—indirect method (LO11–3)

**BE11–6** Hi-Tech, Inc., reports net income of $70 million. Included in that number are depreciation expense of $6 million and a loss on the sale of equipment of $2 million. Records reveal increases in accounts receivable, accounts payable, and inventory of $3 million, $4 million, and $5 million, respectively. What are Hi-Tech's net cash flows from operating activities?

Calculate operating activities—indirect method (LO11–3)

**BE11–7** Engineering Wonders reports net income of $70 million. Included in that number is building depreciation expense of $6 million and a gain on the sale of land of $2 million. Records reveal decreases in accounts receivable, accounts payable, and inventory of $3 million,

$4 million, and $5 million, respectively. What are Engineering Wonders' net cash flows from operating activities?

**BE11–8** Creative Sound Systems sold investments, land, and its own common stock for $40 million, $16 million, and $42 million, respectively. Creative Sound Systems also purchased treasury stock, equipment, and a patent for $22 million, $26 million, and $13 million, respectively. What amount should the company report as net cash flows from investing activities?

Calculate net cash flows from investing activities (LO11–4)

**BE11–9** On April 1, 2023, Teleworks Company lent $100,000 to IT Industries. IT Industries pays back in full the note plus 10% interest on April 1, 2024. Determine the investing cash flows to be reported by Teleworks Company in 2024.

Determine investing cash flows from lending (LO11–4)

**BE11–10** Technologies Worldwide purchased land for $850,000 in 2023 with the intent to expand operations. In 2024, the company decides the land is no longer needed, and the land is sold for $900,000. Determine the investing cash flows to be reported in 2024. Determine the investing cash flows to be reported in 2024 if the land was purchased in 2023 for $950,000?

Determine investing cash flows from sale of land (LO11–4)

**BE11–11** Refer to the situation described in BE11–8. What amount should Creative Sound Systems report as net cash flows from financing activities?

Calculate net cash flows from financing activities (LO11–5)

**BE11–12** Refer to the situation described in BE11–9. Determine the financing cash flows to be reported by IT Industries in 2024.

Determine financing cash flows from borrowing (LO11–5)

**BE11–13** The balance sheet of Cranium Gaming reports total assets of $500,000 and $800,000 at the beginning and end of the year, respectively. Sales revenues are $2.10 million, net income is $75,000, and operating cash flows are $60,000. Calculate the cash return on assets, cash flow to sales, and asset turnover for Cranium Gaming.

Calculate the cash return on assets (LO11–6)

**BE11–14** The balance sheet of Innovative Products reports total assets of $620,000 and $820,000 at the beginning and end of the year, respectively. The cash return on assets for the year is 25%. Calculate Innovative Products' net cash flows from operating activities (operating cash flows) for the year.

Calculate the net cash flows from operating activities (LO11–6)

**BE11–15** The statement of cash flows of PKZ Gaming reports net sales of $1,800,000, net income of $240,000, operating cash flows of $340,000, and capital expenditures of $150,000. Calculate PKZ Gaming's free cash flows and free cash flow to sales ratio.

Calculate free cash flows (LO11–6)

**BE11–16** ELT company reports operating cash flows of $600,000, investing cash flows of ($850,000), and financing cash flows of $500,000. This pattern in cash flows indicates ELT is at what stage in its life cycle?

Analyze cash flow patterns (LO11–6)

**BE11–17** Video Shack's accounts receivable decreases during the year by $9 million. What is the amount of cash received from customers during the reporting period if its net sales are $73 million?

Determine cash received from customers (LO11–7)

**BE11–18** Electronic Superstore's inventory increases during the year by $5 million, and its accounts payable to suppliers increases by $7 million during the same period. What is the amount of cash paid to suppliers of merchandise during the reporting period if its cost of goods sold is $45 million?

Determine cash paid to suppliers (LO11–7)

**BE11–19** Wireless Solutions reports operating expenses of $985,000. Operating expenses include both rent expense and salaries expense. Prepaid rent increases during the year by $30,000 and salaries payable increases by $20,000. What is the cash paid for operating expenses during the year?

Determine cash paid for operating expenses (LO11–7)

**BE11–20** Computer World reports income tax expense of $340,000. Income taxes payable at the beginning and end of the year are $60,000 and $75,000, respectively. What is the cash paid for income taxes during the year?

Determine cash paid for income taxes (LO11–7)

**BE11–21** Wifi Around reports net income for the year of $220,000. Retained earnings at the beginning and end of the year are $810,000 and $930,000, respectively. What is the cash paid for dividends during the year (assume any dividends declared were paid)?

Determine cash paid for dividends (LO11–5, LO11–7)

Match terms with their definitions **(LO11–1, 11–2, 11–3, 11–4, 11–5, 11–6, 11–7)**

**E11–1** Match (by letter) the following items with the description or example that best fits. Each letter is used only once.

### Terms

_____ 1. Operating activities.
_____ 2. Investing activities.
_____ 3. Financing activities.
_____ 4. Noncash activities.
_____ 5. Indirect method.
_____ 6. Direct method.
_____ 7. Depreciation expense.
_____ 8. Cash return on assets.

### Descriptions

a. Begins with net income and then lists adjustments to net income in order to arrive at operating cash flows.
b. Item included in net income, but excluded from net operating cash flows.
c. Net cash flows from operating activities divided by average total assets.
d. Cash transactions involving lenders and investors.
e. Cash transactions involving net income.
f. Cash transactions for the purchase and sale of long-term assets.
g. Purchase of long-term assets by issuing stock to seller.
h. Shows the cash inflows and outflows from operations such as cash received from customers and cash paid for inventory, salaries, rent, interest, and taxes.

Determine proper classification **(LO11–1)**

**E11–2** Analysis of an income statement, balance sheet, and additional information from the accounting records of Gadgets, Inc., reveals the following items.
1. Purchase of a patent.
2. Depreciation expense.
3. Decrease in accounts receivable.
4. Issuance of a note payable.
5. Increase in inventory.
6. Collection of notes receivable.
7. Purchase of equipment.
8. Exchange of long-term assets.
9. Decrease in accounts payable.
10. Payment of dividends.

### Required:

Indicate in which section of the statement of cash flows each of these items would be reported: operating activities (indirect method), investing activities, financing activities, or a separate noncash activities note.

Determine proper classification **(LO11–1)**

**E11–3** Wi-Fi, Inc., has the following selected transactions during the year.
1. Issues $20 million in bonds.
2. Purchases equipment for $80,000.
3. Pays a $20,000 account payable.
4. Collects a $15,000 account receivable.
5. Exchanges land for a new patent. Both are valued at $300,000.
6. Declares and pays a cash dividend of $100,000.

7. Loans $50,000 to a customer, accepting a note receivable.
8. Pays $75,000 to suppliers for inventory.

**Required:**

Indicate in which section of the statement of cash flows each of these items would be reported: operating activities (indirect method), investing activities, financing activities, or a separate noncash activities note.

**E11–4** Ernie's Electronics had the following transactions with Bert's Bargain House:

1. Ernie sold Bert land, originally purchased for $180,000, at a sales price of $195,000, resulting in a gain on sale of land of $15,000.
2. Ernie borrowed $100,000 from Bert, signing a three-year note payable.
3. Ernie purchased $1 million in common stock in Bert's Bargain House through a private placement.
4. Ernie received a dividend of $40,000 from the common stock investment in Bert's Bargain House.

*Determine proper classification (LO11–1) Flip Side of E11–5*

**Required:**

Analyze each of the four transactions from the perspective of Ernie's Electronics. Indicate in which section of the statement of cash flows each of these items would be reported for Ernie's Electronics: operating activities (indirect method), investing activities, financing activities, or a separate noncash activities note.

**E11–5** Refer to the transactions between Ernie's Electronics and Bert's Bargain House recorded in E11–4.

*Determine proper classification (LO11–1) Flip Side of E11–4*

**Required:**

Analyze each of the four transactions from the perspective of Bert's Bargain House. Indicate in which section of the statement of cash flows each of these items would be reported for Bert's Bargain House: operating activities (indirect method), investing activities, financing activities, or a separate noncash activities note.

**E11–6** Hardware Suppliers reports net income of $165,000. Included in net income is a gain on the sale of land of $20,000. A comparison of this year's and last year's balance sheets reveals an increase in accounts receivable of $35,000, an increase in inventory of $20,000, and a decrease in accounts payable of $55,000.

*Calculate operating activities—indirect method (LO11–3)*

**Required:**

Prepare the operating activities section of the statement of cash flows using the indirect method. Do you see a pattern in Hardware Suppliers' adjustments to net income to arrive at operating cash flows? What might this imply?

**E11–7** Software Distributors reports net income of $65,000. Included in that number is depreciation expense of $15,000 and a loss on the sale of land of $6,000. A comparison of this year's and last year's balance sheets reveals a decrease in accounts receivable of $28,000, a decrease in inventory of $37,000, and an increase in accounts payable of $45,000.

*Calculate operating activities—indirect method (LO11–3)*

**Required:**

Prepare the operating activities section of the statement of cash flows using the indirect method. Do you see a pattern in Software Distributors' adjustments to net income to arrive at operating cash flows? What might this imply?

**E11–8** The balance sheets for Ultra HD Corporation, along with additional information, are provided below:

*Prepare a statement of cash flows—indirect method (LO11–3, 11–4, 11–5)*

**ULTRA HD CORPORATION**
**Balance Sheets**
**December 31, 2024 and 2023**

| | 2024 | 2023 |
|---|---|---|
| **Assets** | | |
| Current assets: | | |
| Cash | $ 108,900 | $ 126,800 |
| Accounts receivable | 82,000 | 97,000 |
| Inventory | 105,000 | 89,000 |
| Prepaid rent | 6,000 | 3,000 |
| Long-term assets: | | |
| Land | 530,000 | 530,000 |
| Equipment | 830,000 | 720,000 |
| Accumulated depreciation | (438,000) | (288,000) |
| Total assets | $1,223,900 | $1,277,800 |
| **Liabilities and Stockholders' Equity** | | |
| Current liabilities: | | |
| Accounts payable | $ 109,000 | $ 94,000 |
| Interest payable | 6,900 | 13,800 |
| Income tax payable | 10,000 | 6,000 |
| Long-term liabilities: | | |
| Notes payable | 115,000 | 230,000 |
| Stockholders' equity: | | |
| Common stock | 750,000 | 750,000 |
| Retained earnings | 233,000 | 184,000 |
| Total liabilities and stockholders' equity | $1,223,900 | $1,277,800 |

**Additional Information for 2024:**

1. Net income is $79,000.

2. The company purchases $110,000 in equipment.

3. Depreciation expense is $150,000.

4. The company repays $115,000 in notes payable.

5. The company declares and pays a cash dividend of $30,000.

*Required:*

Prepare the statement of cash flows using the indirect method.

Calculate operating activities—indirect method (LO11–3)

**E11–9** Portions of the financial statements for Peach Computer are provided below.

**PEACH COMPUTER**
**Income Statement**
**For the year ended December 31, 2024**

| | | |
|---|---|---|
| Net sales | | $2,050,000 |
| Expenses: | | |
| Cost of goods sold | $1,150,000 | |
| Operating expenses | 660,000 | |
| Stock-based compensation expense | 60,000 | |
| Income tax expense | 50,000 | |
| Total expenses | | 1,920,000 |
| Net income | | $ 130,000 |

**PEACH COMPUTER**
**Selected Balance Sheet Data**
**December 31, 2023 and 2024**

| | 2024 | 2023 | Increase (I) or Decrease (D) |
|---|---|---|---|
| Cash | $112,000 | $90,000 | $22,000 (I) |
| Accounts receivable | 46,000 | 54,000 | 8,000 (D) |
| Inventory | 85,000 | 60,000 | 25,000 (I) |
| Prepaid rent | 4,000 | 7,000 | 3,000 (D) |
| Accounts payable | 55,000 | 42,000 | 13,000 (I) |
| Income tax payable | 6,000 | 15,000 | 9,000 (D) |

**Required:**

Prepare the operating activities section of the statement of cash flows for Peach Computer using the *indirect* method.

**E11–10** The following summary transactions occurred during 2024 for Dinos Design:

Calculate investing cash flows (LO11–4)

| Cash received from: | |
|---|---|
| Collections from customers | $380,000 |
| Interest on notes receivable | 6,000 |
| Collection of notes receivable | 50,000 |
| Sale of investments | 30,000 |
| Issuance of notes payable | 100,000 |
| | |
| Cash received from: | |
| Purchase of inventory | 160,000 |
| Interest on notes payable | 5,000 |
| Purchase of equipment | 85,000 |
| Salaries to employees | 90,000 |
| Payment of notes payable | 25,000 |
| Dividends to shareholders | 20,000 |

**Required:**

Calculate net cash flows from investing activities.

**E11–11** Refer to the information in E11–10.

Calculate financing cash flows (LO11–5)

**Required:**

Calculate net cash flows from financing activities.

**E11–12** Dristell Inc. had the following activities during the year (all transactions are for cash unless stated otherwise):

Calculate investing cash flows (LO11–4)

a. A building with a book value of $400,000 was sold for $500,000.
b. Additional common stock was issued for $160,000.
c. Dristell purchased its own common stock as treasury stock at a cost of $75,000.
d. Land was acquired by issuing a 6%, 10-year, $750,000 note payable to the seller.
e. A dividend of $40,000 was paid to shareholders.
f. An investment in Fleet Corp.'s common stock was made for $120,000.
g. New equipment was purchased for $65,000.
h. A $90,000 note payable issued three years ago was paid in full.
i. A loan for $100,000 was made to one of Dristell's suppliers. The supplier plans to repay Dristell this amount plus 10% interest within 18 months.
j. Paid $280,000 to acquire another company, Elegido, Inc.

**Required:**

Calculate net cash flows from investing activities.

Calculate financing cash flows (LO11–5)

**E11–13** Refer to the information in E11–12.

*Required:*
Calculate net cash flows from financing activities.

Calculate cash flow ratios (LO11–6)

**E11–14** Zoogle has the following selected data ($ in millions):

| | |
|---|---:|
| Net sales | $24,651 |
| Net income | 6,620 |
| Operating cash flows | 9,326 |
| Total assets, beginning | 41,768 |
| Total assets, ending | 50,497 |
| Capital expenditures | 4,919 |

*Required:*
1. Calculate the return on assets.
2. Calculate the cash return on assets.
3. Calculate the cash flow to sales ratio and the asset turnover ratio.
4. Calculate free cash flows and the free cash flow to sales ratio.

Examine patterns in cash flows (LO11–6)

**E11–15** Aim Limited has the following selected data ($ in millions):

| | |
|---|---:|
| Cash balance, January 1 | $  180 |
| Financing cash flows | 1,090 |
| Capital expenditures | (400) |
| Investing cash flows | (500) |
| Operating cash flows | (440) |

*Required:*
1. Calculate the balance of cash at the end of the fiscal year, December 31.
2. Calculate free cash flows.
3. Based on the pattern in cash flows, determine Aim's life cycle stage.

Calculate operating activities—direct method (LO11–7)

**E11–16** Refer to the information provided for Peach Computer in E11–9.

*Required:*
Prepare the operating activities section of the statement of cash flows for Peach Computer using the *direct* method.

Calculate operating activities—direct method (LO11–7)

**E11–17** Mega Screens, Inc., reports net sales of $3,200,000, cost of goods sold of $2,000,000, and income tax expense of $150,000 for the year ended December 31, 2024. Selected balance sheet accounts are as follows:

| MEGA SCREENS, INC. Selected Balance Sheet Data December 31 | | |
|---|---|---|
| | **2024** | **2023** | **Increase (I) or Decrease (D)** |
| Cash | $150,000 | $195,000 | $45,000 (D) |
| Accounts receivable | 285,000 | 230,000 | 55,000 (I) |
| Inventory | 125,000 | 165,000 | 40,000 (D) |
| Accounts payable | 120,000 | 137,000 | 17,000 (D) |
| Income tax payable | 25,000 | 16,000 | 9,000 (I) |

*Required:*
Calculate cash received from customers, cash paid to suppliers, and cash paid for income taxes.

**E11–18** The income statement for Electronic Wonders reports net sales of $91,758 million and cost of goods sold of $69,278 million. An examination of balance sheet amounts indicates accounts receivable increased $1,733 million, inventory increased $883 million, and accounts payable to suppliers decreased $1,967 million.

Calculate operating activities—direct method (LO11–7)

*Required:*

Using the direct method, calculate (1) cash received from customers and (2) cash paid to suppliers.

**E11–19** Consider the three independent situations below (amounts are $ in millions):

Determine cash received from customers (LO11–7)

| Situation | Sales Revenue | Accounts Receivable Increase (Decrease) | Cash Received from Customers |
|---|---|---|---|
| 1. | $200 | $-0- | ? |
| 2. | 200 | 30 | ? |
| 3. | 200 | (30) | ? |

*Required:*
1. Calculate cash received from customers.
2. Prepare the summary journal entry for each situation.

**E11–20** Consider the four independent situations below.

Determine cash paid to suppliers (LO11–7)

| Situation | Cost of Goods Sold | Inventory Increase (Decrease) | Accounts Payable Increase (Decrease) | Cash Paid to Suppliers |
|---|---|---|---|---|
| 1. | $150 | $ 25 | $ 20 | ? |
| 2. | 150 | (25) | 20 | ? |
| 3. | 150 | 25 | (20) | ? |
| 4. | 150 | (25) | (20) | ? |

*Required:*
1. Calculate cash paid to suppliers.
2. Prepare the summary journal entry for each situation.

**E11–21** Consider the four independent situations below.

Determine cash paid for operating expenses (LO11–7)

| Situation | Operating Expenses | Prepaid Insurance Increase (Decrease) | Salaries Payable Increase (Decrease) | Cash Paid for Operating Expenses |
|---|---|---|---|---|
| 1. | $100 | $ 15 | $ 10 | ? |
| 2. | 100 | (15) | 10 | ? |
| 3. | 100 | 15 | (10) | ? |
| 4. | 100 | (15) | (10) | ? |

*Required:*
1. Calculate cash paid for operating expenses.
2. Prepare the summary journal entry for each situation.

## PROBLEMS

**Determine proper classification (LO11–1)**

**P11–1** Listed below are several transactions. For each transaction, indicate by letter whether the cash effect of each transaction is reported in a statement of cash flows as an operating (O), investing (I), financing (F), or noncash (NC) activity. Also, indicate whether the transaction is a cash inflow (CI) or cash outflow (CO), or has no effect on cash (NE). The first answer is provided as an example.

| Transaction | Type of Activity | Cash Inflow or Outflow |
|---|---|---|
| 1. *Payment of employee salaries.* | *O* | *CO* |
| 2. Sale of land for cash. | | |
| 3. Purchase of rent in advance. | | |
| 4. Collection of an account receivable. | | |
| 5. Issuance of common stock. | | |
| 6. Purchase of inventory. | | |
| 7. Collection of notes receivable. | | |
| 8. Payment of income taxes. | | |
| 9. Sale of equipment for a note receivable. | | |
| 10. Issuance of bonds. | | |
| 11. Loan to another company. | | |
| 12. Payment of a long-term note payable. | | |
| 13. Purchase of treasury stock. | | |
| 14. Payment of an account payable. | | |
| 15. Sale of equipment for cash. | | |

**Classify items and prepare the statement of cash flows (LO11–1, 11–3, 11–4, 11–5)**

**P11–2** Seth Erkenbeck, a recent college graduate, has just completed the basic format to be used in preparing the statement of cash flows (indirect method) for ATM Software Developers. All amounts are in thousands (000s).

**ATM SOFTWARE DEVELOPERS**
**Statement of Cash Flows**
**For the year ended December 31, 2024**

| | |
|---|---|
| **Cash Flows from Operating Activities** | |
| Net income | $ |
| *Adjustments to reconcile net income to net cash flows from operating activities:* | |
| Net cash flows from operating activities | _____ |
| **Cash Flows from Investing Activities** | |
| Net cash flows from investing activities | _____ |
| **Cash Flows from Financing Activities** | |
| Net cash flows from financing activities | |
| Net increase (decrease) in cash | $ 3,765 |
| Cash at the beginning of the period | 7,510 |
| Cash at the end of the period | $11,275 |

Listed below in random order are line items to be included in the statement of cash flows.

| | |
|---|---:|
| Cash received from the sale of land (no gain or loss) | $ 8,650 |
| Issuance of common stock | 13,075 |
| Depreciation expense | 5,465 |
| Increase in accounts receivable | 4,090 |
| Decrease in accounts payable | 1,760 |
| Issuance of long-term notes payable | 16,495 |
| Purchase of equipment | 39,865 |
| Decrease in inventory | 1,475 |
| Decrease in prepaid rent | 905 |
| Payment of dividends | 6,370 |
| Net income | 12,400 |
| Purchase of treasury stock | 2,615 |

**Required:**

Prepare the statement of cash flows for ATM Software Developers using the *indirect* method.

**P11–3** Portions of the financial statements for Alliance Technologies are provided below.

*Calculate operating activities—indirect method (LO11–3)*

**ALLIANCE TECHNOLOGIES**
**Income Statement**
**For the year ended December 31, 2024**

| | | |
|---|---:|---:|
| Net sales | | $405,000 |
| Expenses: | | |
| Cost of goods sold | $235,000 | |
| Operating expenses | 70,000 | |
| Depreciation expense | 17,000 | |
| Income tax expense | 27,000 | |
| Total expenses | | 349,000 |
| Net income | | $ 56,000 |

**ALLIANCE TECHNOLOGIES**
**Selected Balance Sheet Data**
**December 31, 2024, compared to December 31, 2023**

| | |
|---|---:|
| Decrease in accounts receivable | $ 7,000 |
| Increase in inventory | 14,000 |
| Decrease in prepaid rent | 10,000 |
| Increase in salaries payable | 6,000 |
| Decrease in accounts payable | 9,000 |
| Increase in income tax payable | 24,000 |

**Required:**

Prepare the operating activities section of the statement of cash flows for Alliance Technologies using the *indirect* method.

Prepare a statement
of cash flows—indirect
method (LO11–2, 11–3,
11–4, 11–5)

**P11–4** The income statement, balance sheets, and additional information for Cloud Mangu are provided.

### CLOUD MANGU
### Income Statement
### For the year ended December 31, 2024

| | | |
|---|---:|---:|
| Net sales | | $3,636,000 |
| Expenses: | | |
| Cost of goods sold | $2,450,000 | |
| Operating expenses | 958,000 | |
| Depreciation expense | 37,000 | |
| Loss on sale of land | 9,000 | |
| Interest expense | 20,000 | |
| Income tax expense | 58,000 | |
| Total expenses | | 3,532,000 |
| Net income | | $   104,000 |

### CLOUD MANGU
### Balance Sheets
### December 31

| | 2024 | 2023 |
|---|---:|---:|
| **Assets** | | |
| Current assets: | | |
| Cash | $   254,600 | $227,800 |
| Accounts receivable | 92,000 | 70,000 |
| Inventory | 105,000 | 145,000 |
| Prepaid rent | 14,400 | 7,200 |
| Long-term assets: | | |
| Investments | 115,000 | 0 |
| Land | 220,000 | 260,000 |
| Equipment | 290,000 | 220,000 |
| Accumulated depreciation | (81,000) | (44,000) |
| Total assets | $1,010,000 | $886,000 |
| **Liabilities and Stockholders' Equity** | | |
| Current liabilities: | | |
| Accounts payable | $     75,000 | $  91,000 |
| Interest payable | 7,000 | 12,000 |
| Income tax payable | 16,000 | 15,000 |
| Long-term liabilities: | | |
| Notes payable | 305,000 | 235,000 |
| Stockholders' equity: | | |
| Common stock | 400,000 | 400,000 |
| Retained earnings | 207,000 | 133,000 |
| Total liabilities and stockholders' equity | $1,010,000 | $886,000 |

**Additional Information for 2024:**

1. Purchased investment in bonds for $115,000.
2. Sold land for $31,000. The land originally was purchased for $40,000, resulting in a $9,000 loss being recorded at the time of the sale.
3. Purchased $70,000 in equipment by issuing a $70,000 long-term note payable to the seller. No cash was exchanged in the transaction.
4. Declared and paid a cash dividend of $30,000.

*Required:*

Prepare the statement of cash flows using the *indirect* method. Disclose any noncash transactions in an accompanying note.

**P11–5** Cyberdyne Systems and Virtucon are competitors focusing on the latest technologies. Selected financial data is provided below.

Calculate and analyze ratios (LO11–6)

| ($ in millions) | Cyberdyne | Virtucon |
|---|---|---|
| Net sales | $37,905 | $ 4,984 |
| Net income | 9,737 | 1,049 |
| Operating cash flows | 14,565 | 1,324 |
| Total assets, beginning | 57,851 | 14,928 |
| Total assets, ending | 72,574 | 14,783 |

*Required:*

1. Calculate the return on assets for both companies.
2. Calculate the cash return on assets for both companies.
3. Calculate the cash flow to sales ratio and the asset turnover ratio for both companies.
4. Which company has the more favorable ratios?

**P11–6** Refer to the information provided in P11–3 for Alliance Technologies.

Calculate operating activities—direct method (LO11–7)

*Required:*

Prepare the operating activities section of the statement of cash flows for Alliance Technologies using the *direct* method.

**P11–7** Data for Cloud Mangu are provided in P11–4.

Calculate operating activities—direct method (LO11–7)

*Required:*

Prepare the statement of cash flows for Cloud Mangu using the *direct* method. Disclose any noncash transactions in an accompanying note.

**P11–8** Cash flows from operating activities for both the indirect and direct methods are presented for Reverse Logic. All amounts are in thousands (000s).

Prepare an income statement using operating cash flow information—indirect and direct methods (LO11–3, 11–7)

| **Cash Flows from Operating Activities (Indirect method)** | | |
|---|---|---|
| Net income | | $174 |
| *Adjustments to reconcile net income to net cash flows from operating activities:* | | |
| Depreciation expense | 62 | |
| Increase in accounts receivable | (38) | |
| Decrease in inventory | 50 | |
| Increase in prepaid rent | (5) | |
| Decrease in accounts payable | (11) | |
| Decrease in income tax payable | (9) | |
| Net cash flows from operating activities | | $223 |
| **Cash Flows from Operating Activities (Direct method)** | | |
| Cash received from customers | $ 4,070 | |
| Cash paid to suppliers | (2,585) | |
| Cash paid for operating expenses | (1,163) | |
| Cash paid for income taxes | (99) | |
| Net cash flows from operating activities | | $223 |

*Required:*

Complete the following income statement for Reverse Logic. Assume all accounts payable are to suppliers.

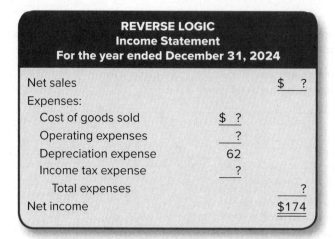

**REVERSE LOGIC**
**Income Statement**
**For the year ended December 31, 2024**

| | | |
|---|---:|---:|
| Net sales | | $ ? |
| Expenses: | | |
| Cost of goods sold | $ ? | |
| Operating expenses | ? | |
| Depreciation expense | 62 | |
| Income tax expense | ? | |
| Total expenses | | ? |
| Net income | | $174 |

[*Hint:* Use the following calculations and work backwards from bottom (in red) to top for each item.]

| | |
|---|---|
| Net sales | |
| ± Change in accounts receivable | _____ |
| = **Cash received from customers** | ========== |
| Cost of goods sold | |
| ± Change in inventory | _____ |
| = Purchases | |
| ± Change in accounts payable | _____ |
| = **Cash paid to suppliers** | ========== |
| Operating expenses | |
| ± Change in prepaid rent | _____ |
| = **Cash paid for operating expenses** | ========== |
| Income tax expense | |
| ± Change in income tax payable | _____ |
| = **Cash paid for income taxes** | ========== |

---

**DATA ANALYTICS**

Visit Connect to view **Data Analytics** questions related to:

1. Applying Excel
2. Data Visualizations
3. Tableau Dashboard Activities
4. Applying Tableau

---

**ANSWERS TO SELF-STUDY QUESTIONS**

1. b   2. c   3. c   4. b   5. d   6. a   7. c   8. b   9. d   10. c   11. a   12. b   13. d   14. c   15. b

# Financial Statement Analysis

## Feature Story

# VF Corporation: Making the Competition Sweat

**VF Corporation**'s (simply VF hereafter) desire is to outfit the world. The company was founded in 1899 as the Reading Glove and Mitten Manufacturing Company. It was rebranded to Vanity Fair in 1910 and has since grown into a massive conglomerate of some of the world's most recognizable brands, including **Vans**, The **North Face**, **JanSport**, **Dickies**, and **Timberland**.

VF's first major acquisition occurred in the 1960s when it acquired Lee Brands in an effort to diversify its product line. This acquisition prompted another name change to VF Corporation. Additional acquisitions were made over the next 50 years. The company's most recent acquisition was Altra, which designs and manufactures high-performance running shoes. In total, VF boasts 19 distinct brands in its portfolio.

VF's growth strategy over the years has largely relied on acquisitions. This is a common feature in the shoe and apparel industry. One of VF's primary competitors, **Nike**, also has acquired a few brands over the years (such as **Converse** and **Hurley**), but not nearly to the same extent as VF. Nike is almost three times the size of VF, and, for the most part, Nike has relied on organic growth to grow its business. Which strategy leads to stronger financial performance? The answer to this question is not as straight-forward as it seems. Given the differences in size of these two companies, how do we compare their financial performance?

In this chapter, we'll use financial analysis tools to analyze financial statements—the same statements you've learned to prepare in the preceding chapters. The techniques we introduce here—such as vertical analysis, horizontal analysis, and ratio analysis—help in evaluating the growth and performance of companies such as VF and comparing them to competitors like Nike.

At the end of the chapter, we provide examples of conservative and aggressive accounting practices. Accounting is not black and white. Many accounting decisions fall into a gray area subject to potential earnings manipulation and biases of managers.

## PART A

# COMPARISON OF FINANCIAL ACCOUNTING INFORMATION

Ratios are a common metric used to assess performance. Consider major sports. Batting averages provide feedback in baseball about how well a player is hitting. Basketball and football use points per game to compare teams' offensive and defensive performance. In each case, the ratio is more meaningful than a single number by itself. For example, whether 100 hits in baseball is a good number depends on the number of at-bats.

Likewise, managers, shareholders, and lenders use ratios to help evaluate a company's performance and financial position. Is net income of $10 million a cause for shareholders to celebrate? Probably not, if stockholders' equity is $1 billion, because $10 million is then only a 1% return on equity. But if stockholders' equity is $20 million, net income of $10 million is a 50% return on equity and definitely something to celebrate. Ratios are most useful when compared to some standard or benchmark. That standard of comparison may be the performance of a major competitor, last year's performance by the same company, or the average performance of companies in the same industry. Illustration 12–1 provides a summary of these three different types of comparisons.

**ILLUSTRATION 12–1    Three Types of Comparisons**

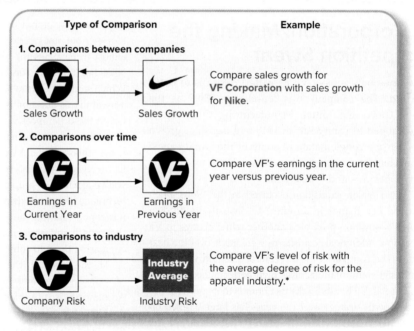

Rose Carson/Shutterstock; VF Corporation

*Industry averages can be obtained from websites such as Yahoo! Finance or from financial ratings agencies such as Dun & Bradstreet, Moody's, and Standard & Poor's.

When doing financial statement analysis, it's always important to learn about the company and its history and to let ratios guide further questioning about items. This will typically lead to further research before making final decisions about a company. In this chapter, we'll calculate ratios commonly used as bases for exploring financial statements and understanding company strategies.

## Vertical Analysis

■ **LO12–1**
Perform vertical analysis.

*Common Terms*
Vertical analysis is also known as common-size analysis.

In performing vertical analysis (also known as "common-sizing"), we express each item in a financial statement as a ratio that takes the form of a percentage of the same base amount measured in the same period. For instance, we can express each line item in an income statement as a percentage of sales. In a balance sheet, we can express each item as a percentage of total assets. Let's look at an example to see what a manager can learn from vertical analysis.

ILLUSTRATION 12–2

Common-Size Income
Statements

| VF AND NIKE<br>Common-Size Income Statements<br>For the years ended March 31, 2020, and May 31, 2020<br>($ in millions) | | | | |
| --- | --- | --- | --- | --- |
| | **VF** | | **NIKE** | |
| | **Amount** | **%** | **Amount** | **%** |
| Net sales | $10,489 | 100.0 | $37,403 | 100.0 |
| Cost of goods sold | 4,691 | 44.7 | 21,162 | 56.6 |
| Gross profit | 5,798 | 55.3 | 16,241 | 43.4 |
| Operating expenses | 4,870 | 46.4 | 13,126 | 35.1 |
| Operating income | 928 | 8.8 | 3,115 | 8.3 |
| Other income (expenses) | (201) | (1.9) | (228) | (0.6) |
| Income before tax | 727 | 6.9 | 2,887 | 7.7 |
| Income tax expense | 98 | 0.9 | 348 | 0.9 |
| Net income | $    629 | 6.0 | $ 2,539 | 6.8 |

The red arrow indicates
the direction in which
to read this statement.

## VERTICAL ANALYSIS OF THE INCOME STATEMENT

Illustration 12–2 provides common-size income statements for **VF** and **Nike**. Notice that the two companies end their fiscal years on different dates. VF's year-end is March 31 while Nike's is May 31. Even though the year-ends do not exactly match, they are relatively close and will still allow us to make meaningful comparisons between the two companies.

What do we learn from this comparison? Nike reports net income of $2,539 million while VF reports $629 million. Does this mean Nike's operations are much more profitable than VF's? Not necessarily. Nike is a larger company (almost four times as big), reporting sales of $37,403 million compared to $10,489 million for VF. Because of its greater size, we expect Nike to report a greater *amount* of net income. To better compare the performance of the two companies, we use vertical analysis to express each income statement item as a *percentage of sales.*

VF's gross profit equals 55.3% of sales ($5,798 ÷ $10,489) compared to Nike's 43.4%. This means that VF earns a higher gross profit for each dollar of sales, consistent with its business strategy of focusing on high-quality performance apparel. However, VF's higher gross profit is offset by its proportionately higher operating expenses, 46.4% of sales compared to 35.1% for Nike. The net result is that operating income, as a percentage of sales, is about the same for the two companies. Finally, Nike's net income, as a percentage of sales, slightly exceeds VF's.

| Question ? | Accounting information 🗎 | Analysis 🔍 |
| --- | --- | --- |
| How do we compare income between companies of different size? | Common-size income statements | A vertical analysis using common-size income statements allows for the comparison of income statement items between companies of different size. |

**Manager Analysis**

## VERTICAL ANALYSIS OF THE BALANCE SHEET

Vertical analysis of the balance sheet is useful, too. For this, we divide each balance sheet item by total assets to get an idea of its relative significance. Illustration 12–3 provides common-size balance sheets for VF and Nike.

What can we learn by analyzing the common-size balance sheets? Focusing on the asset portion of the balance sheet tells us about the *asset mix* of the company. Here we learn

**ILLUSTRATION 12–3**
Common-Size Balance Sheets

The red arrow indicates the direction in which to read this statement.

| | VF | | NIKE | |
|---|---|---|---|---|
| | Amount | % | Amount | % |
| **Assets** | | | | |
| Current assets | $ 5,027 | 45.2 | $20,556 | 65.6 |
| Property and equipment | 954 | 8.6 | 4,866 | 15.5 |
| Intangible assets | 3,011 | 27.0 | 497 | 1.6 |
| Other assets | 2,141 | 19.2 | 5,423 | 17.3 |
| Total assets | $11,133 | 100.0 | $31,342 | 100.0 |
| | | | | |
| **Liabilities and Stockholders' Equity** | | | | |
| Current liabilities | $ 3,024 | 27.2 | $ 8,284 | 26.4 |
| Long-term liabilities | 4,752 | 42.7 | 15,003 | 47.9 |
| Stockholders' equity | 3,357 | 30.2 | 8,055 | 25.7 |
| Total liabilities and equities | $11,133 | 100.0 | $31,342 | 100.0 |

**VF AND NIKE**
**Common-Size Balance Sheets**
**March 31, 2020, and May 31, 2020**
**($ in millions)**

that VF has a lower percentage of current assets and property, plant, and equipment, and a higher percentage of intangible assets than does Nike. These differences are consistent with the differences in the companies' growth strategies. VF primarily grows through acquisitions of other companies; Nike primarily grows through product innovation and branding. As we discussed in Chapter 7, acquisitions often result in the recording of goodwill, an intangible asset.

Looking at liabilities and stockholders' equity, we see little difference between the two companies. Later in Part B, we'll examine the current ratio and acid-test ratio to better understand the companies' ability to pay current liabilities with current assets. Both companies maintain similar proportions of liabilities and are financed approximately equally by equity and debt, suggesting they have a similar capital structure.

 **KEY POINT**

For vertical analysis, we express each item as a percentage of the same base amount, such as a percentage of sales in the income statement or as a percentage of total assets in the balance sheet.

■ **LO12–2**
Perform horizontal analysis.

*Common Terms*
Horizontal analysis is also known as trend analysis or time-series analysis.

# Horizontal Analysis

We use horizontal analysis to analyze trends in financial statement data for a single company over time. With horizontal analysis, we calculate the amount and percentage change in an account from last year to this year. We can then use this data to compare rates of change across accounts. Are sales growing faster than cost of goods sold? Are operating expenses growing faster than sales? Are any specific expenses increasing at a greater rate than others? Questions such as these can help identify areas of concern or, perhaps, indications of better things to come.

## HORIZONTAL ANALYSIS OF THE INCOME STATEMENT

Illustration 12–4 provides income statements over two years for VF. The final two columns show the dollar amount and percentage changes.

| VF<br>Income Statements<br>For the years ended March 31<br>($ in millions) | | | | |
|---|---|---|---|---|
| | Year | | Increase (Decrease) | |
| | 2020 | 2019 | Amount | % |
| Net sales | $10,489 | $10,267 | $ 222 | 2.2 |
| Cost of goods sold | 4,691 | 4,656 | 35 | 0.8 |
| Gross profit | 5,798 | 5,611 | 187 | 3.3 |
| Operating expenses | 4,870 | 4,421 | 449 | 10.2 |
| Operating income | 928 | 1,190 | (262) | (22.0) |
| Other income (expenses) | (201) | (152) | 49 | 32.2 |
| Income before tax | 727 | 1,038 | (311) | (30.0) |
| Income tax expense | 98 | 168 | (70) | (41.7) |
| Net income | $ 629 | $ 870 | $ (241) | (27.7) |

**ILLUSTRATION 12–4**

**Horizontal Analysis of VF's Income Statements**

The red arrow indicates the direction in which to read this statement.

We calculate the *amount* of the increases or decreases by simply subtracting the 2019 balance from the 2020 balance. A positive difference indicates the amount increased in 2020. A negative amount represents a decrease. We calculate the *percentage* increase or decrease based on the following formula:

$$\text{\% Increase (Decrease)} = \frac{\text{Current-year amount} - \text{Prior-year amount}}{\text{Prior-year amount}}$$

In our example, the calculation would be

$$\text{\% Increase (Decrease)} = \frac{\text{2020 amount} - \text{2019 amount}}{\text{2019 amount}}$$

For example, the amount of sales increased $222 million—equal to sales of $10,489 million in 2020 minus sales of $10,267 million in 2019. We calculate the percentage increase of 2.2% by dividing the $222 million increase in sales by 2019 sales of $10,267 million. If the base-year amount (2019 in our example) is ever zero, we can't calculate a percentage for that item.

The horizontal analysis for VF shows that while sales increased slightly, there was a decrease in profitability overall. You can see that the decrease is the result of an increase in operating expenses. Most of this decrease comes from a goodwill impairment charge related to VF's Timberland operation disclosed in the financial statement notes.

## HORIZONTAL ANALYSIS OF THE BALANCE SHEET

Illustration 12–5 provides a horizontal analysis of balance sheet information for VF for 2020 and 2019, with amount and percentage changes in the final two columns.

The horizontal analysis of VF's balance sheet further reflects its growth in operations during the year. Total assets grew by 7.5%. Much of that growth was funded through additional liabilities. The decline in total stockholders' equity is attributable to a decrease in retained earnings. The statement of stockholders' equity (not presented) reveals that the decline in retained earnings occurred because the amount of dividends and repurchased stock far exceeded the amount of net income.

**ILLUSTRATION 12–5**

Horizontal Analysis of VF's Balance Sheets

| VF<br>Balance Sheets<br>March 31<br>($ in millions) | | | | |
|---|---|---|---|---|
| | Year | | Increase (Decrease) | |
| | **2020** | **2019** | **Amount** | **%** |
| **Assets** | | | | |
| Current assets | $ 5,027 | $ 4,673 | $   354 | 7.6 |
| Property and equipment | 954 | 876 | 78 | 8.9 |
| Intangible assets | 3,011 | 3,399 | (388) | (11.4) |
| Other assets | 2,141 | 1,409 | 732 | 52.0 |
| Total assets | $11,133 | $10,357 | $   776 | 7.5 |
| | | | | |
| **Liabilities and Stockholders' Equity** | | | | |
| Current liabilities | $ 3,024 | $ 2,662 | $   362 | 13.6 |
| Long-term liabilities | 4,752 | 3,396 | 1,356 | 39.9 |
| Stockholders' equity | 3,357 | 4,299 | (942) | (21.9) |
| Total liabilities and equities | $11,133 | $10,357 | $   776 | 7.5 |

The red arrow indicates the direction in which to read this statement.

**KEY POINT**

We use horizontal analysis to analyze trends in financial statement data, such as the amount of change and the percentage change, for one company over time.

**Let's Review**

The income statements for Nike for the years ending May 31, 2020 and 2019, are as follows:

| NIKE<br>Income Statements<br>For the years ended May 31<br>($ in millions) | | | | |
|---|---|---|---|---|
| | | | Increase (Decrease) | |
| | **2020** | **2019** | **Amount** | **%** |
| Net sales | $37,403 | $39,117 | | |
| Cost of goods sold | 21,162 | 21,643 | | |
| Gross profit | 16,241 | 17,474 | | |
| Operating expenses | 13,126 | 12,702 | | |
| Operating income | 3,115 | 4,772 | | |
| Other income | (228) | 29 | | |
| Income before tax | 2,887 | 4,801 | | |
| Income tax expense | 348 | 772 | | |
| Net income | $ 2,539 | $ 4,029 | | |

**Required:**

Complete the "Amount" and "%" columns in a horizontal analysis of Nike's income statements. Discuss the meaning of the major fluctuations during the year.

**Solution:**

**NIKE**
**Income Statements**
**For the years ended May 31**
**($ in millions)**

| | 2020 | 2019 | Increase (Decrease) Amount | % |
|---|---|---|---|---|
| Net sales | $37,403 | $39,117 | $(1,714) | (4.4) |
| Cost of goods sold | 21,162 | 21,643 | (481) | (2.2) |
| Gross profit | 16,241 | 17,474 | (1,233) | (7.1) |
| Operating expenses | 13,126 | 12,702 | 424 | 3.3 |
| Operating income | 3,115 | 4,772 | (1,657) | (34.7) |
| Other income (expenses) | (228) | 29 | (257) | (886.2) |
| Income before tax | 2,887 | 4,801 | (1,914) | (39.9) |
| Income tax expense | 348 | 772 | (424) | (54.9) |
| Net income | $ 2,539 | $ 4,029 | $(1,490) | (37.0) |

All amounts for Nike declined in 2020 except for operating expenses. Nike's year end was May 31, 2020, approximately three months after the outbreak of COVID-19 in the United States. These three months were severely impacted, as individuals sheltered in place and businesses shut down. Thus, the decrease in operations and profitability was normal for many companies at this time.

# RATIO ANALYSIS

**PART B**

Beginning in Chapter 5 of the book, we discussed various ratios to help managers and capital providers (investors and lenders) assess a company's financial position and performance. We'll now bring many of those ratios together into a comprehensive framework that categorizes ratios into four groups. Each group of ratios captures a different financial attribute of the company. These groups are described as follows:

- **Return to Shareholders:** These ratios measure a company's ability to generate returns to its owners.
- **Profitability:** These ratios measure a company's ability to generate profits from its sales. They also measure operating effectiveness.
- **Asset Management:** These ratios measure a company's ability to use assets to generate sales. They also measure operating efficiency.
- **Credit Risk Management:** These ratios measure a company's ability to meet short-term obligations (liquidity) and long-term obligations (solvency).

One of the primary objectives of ratio analysis is to help managers and capital providers to understand more about the value of the company and its future prospects. Accordingly, the ratio analysis framework includes an assessment of company value at its center. Illustration 12–6 presents the ratio analysis framework, and Illustration 12–7 provides additional information about the ratios, including the chapters in which we discussed them.

**ILLUSTRATION 12–6**

Ratio Analysis
Framework

**ILLUSTRATION 12–7**    Ratio Analysis Framework

| Ratios | Chapter | Calculations |
|---|---|---|
| **Return to Shareholders** | | |
| Return on equity | 10 | $\dfrac{\text{Net income}}{\text{Average stockholders' equity}}$ |
| Return on assets | 7 | $\dfrac{\text{Net income}}{\text{Average total assets}}$ |
| **Profitability** | | |
| Gross profit ratio | 6 | $\dfrac{\text{Net sales} - \text{Cost of goods sold}}{\text{Net sales}}$ |
| Profit margin | 7 | $\dfrac{\text{Net income}}{\text{Net sales}}$ |
| **Asset Management** | | |
| Asset turnover | 7 | $\dfrac{\text{Net sales}}{\text{Average total assets}}$ |
| Receivables turnover ratio | 5 | $\dfrac{\text{Net credit sales}}{\text{Average accounts receivable}}$ |
| Average collection period | 5 | $\dfrac{365 \text{ days}}{\text{Receivables turnover ratio}}$ |
| Inventory turnover ratio | 6 | $\dfrac{\text{Cost of goods sold}}{\text{Average inventory}}$ |
| Average days in inventory | 6 | $\dfrac{365 \text{ days}}{\text{Inventory turnover ratio}}$ |
| **Credit Risk Management** | | |
| Current ratio | 9 | $\dfrac{\text{Current assets}}{\text{Current liabilities}}$ |
| Acid-test ratio | 9 | $\dfrac{\text{Cash} + \text{Current investments} + \text{Accounts receivable}}{\text{Current liabilities}}$ |
| Times interest earned ratio | 9 | $\dfrac{\text{Net income} + \text{Interest expense} + \text{Income tax expense}}{\text{Interest expense}}$ |
| Debt to equity ratio | 9 | $\dfrac{\text{Interest-bearing debt}}{\text{Stockholders' equity}}$ |
| **Valuation** | | |
| Price-earnings ratio | 10 | $\dfrac{\text{Stock price}}{\text{Earnings per share}}$ |

Let's now apply the ratio analysis framework to conduct a more detailed examination of **VF** and **Nike**. The income statement and the balance sheet for VF are presented in Illustration 12–8.

**ILLUSTRATION 12–8**

VF's Financial
Statements

**VF**
**Income Statement**
**For the year ended March 31, 2020**
**($ in millions)**

|  | 2020 |
|---|---|
| Net sales | $10,489 |
| Cost of goods sold | 4,691 |
| Gross profit | 5,798 |
| Operating expenses | 4,870 |
| Operating income | 928 |
| Other expense* | 201 |
| Income before tax | 727 |
| Income tax expense | 98 |
| Net income | $   629 |

*Other expense includes interest expense of $92 million

**VF CORPORATION**
**Balance Sheet**
**March 31**
**($ in millions)**

|  | 2020 | 2019 |
|---|---|---|
| **Assets** | | |
| Current assets: | | |
| Cash | $  1,369 | $    402 |
| Net receivables | 1,308 | 1,373 |
| Inventory | 1,294 | 1,173 |
| Other current assets | 1,056 | 1,725 |
| Total current assets | 5,027 | 4,673 |
| Property and equipment, net | 954 | 876 |
| Intangible assets, net | 3,011 | 3,399 |
| Other assets | 2,141 | 1,409 |
| Total assets | $11,133 | $10,357 |
| **Liabilities and Stockholders' Equity** | | |
| Accounts payable and accrued liabilities | $  1,667 | $  1,615 |
| Short-term debt and current portion of long-term debt | 1,230 | 664 |
| Other current liabilities | 127 | 382 |
| Current liabilities | 3,024 | 2,661 |
| Long-term debt | 3,629 | 2,116 |
| Other long-term liabilities | 1,123 | 1,281 |
| Stockholders' equity | 3,357 | 4,299 |
| Total liabilities and equity | $11,133 | $10,357 |

We'll now calculate and review the 14 ratios included in the ratio analysis framework for VF and Nike. When calculating ratios, remember how income statement accounts differ from balance sheet accounts: We measure income statement accounts over a period of time; we measure balance sheet accounts at a point in time. Therefore, ratios that compare an income statement account with a balance sheet account should express the balance sheet account as an average of the beginning and ending balances.

**COMMON MISTAKE**

In comparing an income statement account with a balance sheet account, some students incorrectly use the balance sheet account's ending balance rather than the *average* of its beginning and ending balances. Since income statement accounts are measured over a period of time, comparisons to related balance sheet accounts also need to be over time by taking the average of the beginning and ending balances.

■ **LO12–3**
Use ratios to analyze a company's return to shareholders.

*Common Terms*
Return on equity is referred to as ROE.

# Return to Shareholders

## RETURN ON EQUITY

Return on equity measures the income earned for each dollar in stockholders' equity. Return on equity relates net income to the investment made by owners of the business. The ratio is calculated as net income divided by average stockholders' equity. Average stockholders' equity is calculated as beginning stockholders' equity plus ending stockholders' equity, divided by 2. Illustration 12–9 shows the calculation of return on equity. VF has a return on equity of 16.4%. Its net income is 16.4 cents for every dollar invested in equity. Nike has a much higher return on equity of 29.7%.

**ILLUSTRATION 12–9**

**Return on Equity**

| Return on Equity | VF | Nike |
|---|---|---|
| $\dfrac{\text{Net Income}}{\text{Average stockholders' equity}}$ | $\dfrac{\$629}{(\$3,357 + \$4,299)/2} = 16.4\%$ | 29.7% |

## RETURN ON ASSETS

*Common Terms*
Return on assets is referred to as ROA.

Return on assets measures the income the company earns on each dollar invested in assets. We calculate this ratio as net income divided by average total assets. Average total assets are calculated as beginning total assets plus ending total assets, divided by 2. Illustration 12–10 provides the calculation of return on assets for VF and a comparison to Nike. VF earned a return on assets of 5.9% Nike has a much higher return on assets of 9.2%.

**ILLUSTRATION 12–10**

**Return on Assets**

| Return on Assets | VF | Nike |
|---|---|---|
| $\dfrac{\text{Net Income}}{\text{Average total assets}}$ | $\dfrac{\$629}{(\$11,133 + \$10,357)/2} = 5.9\%$ | 9.2% |

Our analysis of the return to shareholders ratios of VF and Nike reveal that Nike is delivering a higher return to its capital providers than is VF. What the return on equity and return on asset ratios do not reveal, however, is *how* Nike is delivering the higher returns. It could be that Nike is operating more profitably, managing its assets more efficiently, or some combination of the two. Let's now examine these financial attributes of the two companies to learn more.

**KEY POINT**

Return to shareholder ratios measure a company's ability to generate returns to its capital providers. These ratios capture the overall performance of a company over a period of time.

# Profitability

## GROSS PROFIT RATIO

■ **LO12–4**
Use ratios to analyze a company's profitability.

The gross profit ratio indicates the portion of each dollar of sales above its cost of goods sold. We calculate this ratio as gross profit (net sales minus cost of goods sold) divided by net sales. Gross profit ratios vary considerably by industry. For example, consider the average gross profit ratio, provided in parentheses, for the following major industries: retail grocery stores (25%), apparel stores (47%), major drug manufacturers (68%), and software (77%). Illustration 12–11 presents the calculation of the gross profit ratio for VF and Nike. With a gross profit ratio of 55.3%, VF sells its merchandise for about twice its cost. In comparison, Nike has a lower gross profit ratio of 43.4%. Nike's gross profit is still quite high, but not as high as VF's. Regardless of the difference between the two companies, they both are in the range of the apparel industry gross profit ratio (47%). Gross profit ratios normally decline as competition increases. For example, a patented drug can sell for many times its production cost. However, when the patent expires, competition from generic drug companies drives down selling prices, resulting in lower gross profit ratios for the drug manufacturer.

*Common Terms*
Gross profit is also called *gross margin* or *gross profit margin*.

| Gross Profit Ratio | VF | Nike |
|---|---|---|
| $\dfrac{\text{Net sales} - \text{Cost of goods sold}}{\text{Net sales}}$ | $\dfrac{\$5,798}{\$10,489} = 55.3\%$ | 43.4% |

**ILLUSTRATION 12–11**
Gross Profit Ratio

## PROFIT MARGIN

Profit margin measures the net income earned on each dollar of sales. We calculate this ratio as net income divided by net sales. Illustration 12–12 provides the calculation of profit margin for VF and Nike. VF has a profit margin of 6.0%, meaning that for every dollar of sales, 6 cents remains in net income after considering all expenses. Nike has a higher profit margin of 6.8%.

| Profit Margin | VF | Nike |
|---|---|---|
| $\dfrac{\text{Net income}}{\text{Net sales}}$ | $\dfrac{\$629}{\$10,489} = 6.0\%$ | 6.8% |

**ILLUSTRATION 12–12**
Profit Margin

Our analysis of profitability ratios suggests that Nike's slightly higher overall profitability is one reason why its return to shareholders ratios are higher than VF's. Several factors could potentially explain Nike's higher profitability. Nike is almost four times the size of VF, and larger companies are often able to generate cost savings, such as bulk inventory purchasing, streamlined supply chains, and superior contract negotiation, that smaller companies are unable to obtain. Economists call cost savings associated with size "economies of scale." In other words, Nike may be using its assets more effectively to reduce costs and therefore improve profits. We'll examine asset management next.

 **KEY POINT**

Profitability ratios measure a company's ability to generate profits from its sales. These ratios are used as a measure of the operating effectiveness of a company over a period of time, such as a year.

# Asset Management

## ASSET TURNOVER

■ **LO12–5**
Use ratios to analyze a company's asset management.

Asset turnover measures revenues in relation to the investment in assets—in other words, this ratio helps assess how well a company generates revenues with its assets in place. We calculate asset turnover as sales divided by average total assets. Illustration 12–13 presents the calculation of asset turnover. VF's asset turnover is 1.0. This means that VF generates revenues that are about one times its asset base. Another way to interpret this is that VF generates $1.00 in annual sales for every $1.00 it invests in assets. Nike's asset turnover is higher at 1.4.

**ILLUSTRATION 12–13**

Asset Turnover

| Asset Turnover | VF | Nike |
|---|---|---|
| $\dfrac{\text{Net sales}}{\text{Average total assets}}$ | $\dfrac{\$10,489}{(\$11,133 + \$10,357)/2} = 1.0 \text{ times}$ | 1.4 times |

Our assessment of the asset turnover ratio reveals that Nike is more efficient in managing its assets than is VF. In other words, the ratio shows that Nike is better at using its assets to generate revenues than is VF. Efficient asset management is another reason why Nike is able to deliver higher returns to its capital providers. What might explain Nike's superior asset efficiency? Conglomerates like VF are likely to have a more diverse set of assets to manage across the various brands in the portfolio, which could reduce its asset efficiency. In addition, different management teams at VF that govern these assets may even exhibit different management styles (you can imagine that managers at **Vans** and **Wrangler** might have different management philosophies than Nike). In contrast, Nike's approach to asset management is more likely to be focused and consistently applied across products within the company. This focus and consistency could lead to efficiencies within the organization. We'll now assess the management of two specific current assets that are important in this industry: accounts receivables and inventory.

## RECEIVABLES TURNOVER RATIO

The receivables turnover ratio measures how many times, on average, a company collects its entire receivables balance during the year. A low receivables turnover ratio may indicate that the company is having trouble collecting its accounts receivable. This often occurs when a company loosens its credit terms to generate additional sales. A high receivables turnover ratio is a positive sign that a company can quickly turn its receivables into cash. Illustration 12–14 shows the calculation of the receivables turnover ratio for VF and includes the ratio for Nike for comparison.

**ILLUSTRATION 12–14**

Receivables Turnover

| Receivables Turnover | VF | Nike |
|---|---|---|
| $\dfrac{\text{Net credit sales}}{\text{Average net accounts receivable}}$ | $\dfrac{\$10,489}{(\$1,308 + \$1,373)/2} = 7.8 \text{ times}$ | 10.7 times |

Recall receivables arise from sales *on account*—cash sales are not included. Therefore, in calculating the receivables turnover ratio, we have assumed that VF's sales are all credit sales. This is a reasonable assumption, as VF does not usually sell directly to customers, but to retailers, such as **Dick's Sporting Goods**. Most companies don't separately report their credit sales. The denominator of the ratio is the average accounts receivable during the year, calculated as beginning receivables plus ending receivables, divided by 2.

VF's receivables turnover ratio is 7.8, indicating that receivables turn over (are collected) 7.8 times per year. This is lower than Nike's receivables turnover ratio of 10.7.

## AVERAGE COLLECTION PERIOD

To help with interpretation, we often convert the receivables turnover ratio into a number of days and call it the average collection period. The shorter the average collection period, the better. Illustration 12–15 displays the average collection period for VF and Nike. VF's average collection period of 46.8 days is 365 days divided by the receivables turnover ratio of 7.8. It takes VF an average of over one month (46.8 days) to collect its accounts receivable. Nike's average collection period, at 34.1 days, indicates that it receives cash more quickly from customers.

| Average Collection Period | VF | Nike |
|---|---|---|
| $\dfrac{\text{365 days}}{\text{Receivables turnover}}$ | $\dfrac{365}{7.8} = 46.8$ days | 34.1 days |

**ILLUSTRATION 12–15**

Average Collection Period

## INVENTORY TURNOVER RATIO

The inventory turnover ratio measures how many times, on average, a company sells its entire inventory during the year. A high inventory turnover ratio usually is a positive sign. It indicates that inventory is selling quickly, less cash is tied up in inventory, and the risk of outdated inventory is lower. However, an extremely high inventory turnover ratio might be a signal that the company is losing sales due to inventory shortages. Illustration 12–16 provides the inventory turnover ratios for VF and Nike. Inventory at VF turns over, on average, 3.8 times per year compared to 3.3 times per year at Nike. The quicker inventory turnover at VF is a positive sign, indicating a lower risk of slow-moving inventory items.

| Inventory Turnover | VF | Nike |
|---|---|---|
| $\dfrac{\text{Cost of goods sold}}{\text{Average inventory}}$ | $\dfrac{\$4,691}{(\$1,294 + \$1,173)/2} = 3.8$ times | 3.3 times |

**ILLUSTRATION 12–16**

Inventory Turnover

## AVERAGE DAYS IN INVENTORY

We can convert the inventory turnover ratio into days and call it the average days in inventory. As you can imagine, companies try to minimize the number of days they hold inventory. We calculate the average days in inventory in Illustration 12–17. VF's average days in inventory is 96.1 days, calculated as 365 days divided by the inventory turnover ratio of 3.8. In comparison, Nike's average days in inventory is more than two weeks higher at 110.6 days.

| Average Days in Inventory | VF | Nike |
|---|---|---|
| $\dfrac{\text{365 days}}{\text{Inventory turnover}}$ | $\dfrac{365}{3.8} = 96.1$ days | 110.6 days |

**ILLUSTRATION 12–17**

Average Days in Inventory

As discussed in Chapter 6, inventory turnover ratios and the resulting average days in inventory vary significantly by industry. For example, compared with the sporting goods apparel industry, the dairy industry with its perishable products has a much higher inventory turnover, and car dealerships have a lower inventory turnover. Inventory turnover might even vary by product within the same industry. For instance, within the dairy industry, the inventory turnover for milk is much higher than for aged cheddar cheese. Similarly, within the auto industry, the inventory turnover for lower-priced cars like the Toyota Corolla is much higher than for the higher-priced Toyota Land Cruiser.

 **KEY POINT**

Asset management ratios measure a company's ability to use its assets to generate sales. These ratios are used as a measure of the operating efficiency of a company over a period of time, such as a year.

# CREDIT RISK MANAGEMENT

■ **LO12–6**

Use ratios to analyze a company's credit risk management.

As discussed in Chapter 9, we can break credit risk into two parts: liquidity risk and solvency risk. To review, liquidity refers to a company's ability to pay *current* liabilities, including debt obligations, as they come due. Solvency refers to a company's ability to pay its *long-term* debts as well. We will discuss ratios that capture each of these concepts.

## CURRENT RATIO

The current ratio compares current assets to current liabilities. It's probably the most widely used of all liquidity ratios. A high current ratio indicates that a company has sufficient current assets to pay current liabilities as they come due. Illustration 12–18 presents the current ratios for VF and Nike.

VF's current ratio of 1.7 means the company has $1.70 in current assets for each $1 in current liabilities. Nike has a higher current ratio of 2.5.

**ILLUSTRATION 12–18**

Current Ratio

| Current Ratio | VF | Nike |
|---|---|---|
| $\dfrac{\text{Current assets}}{\text{Current liabilities}}$ | $\dfrac{\$5{,}027}{\$3{,}024} = 1.7 \text{ to } 1$ | 2.5 to 1 |

A higher current ratio usually indicates less liquidity risk. In the cases of VF and Nike, both companies have sufficient current assets to cover their current obligations. However, a high current ratio is not always a good signal. A high current ratio might occur when a company has difficulty collecting receivables or carries too much inventory. Analysts become concerned if a company reports an increasing current ratio combined with either a lower receivables turnover ratio or a lower inventory turnover ratio.

## ACID-TEST RATIO

The acid-test ratio is similar to the current ratio but uses a more conservative measure of current assets available to pay current liabilities. Specifically, the numerator of the fraction includes only cash, current investments, and accounts receivable and eliminates current assets that are less readily convertible into cash, such as inventories and prepaid expenses. As a result, the acid-test ratio may provide a better indication of a company's liquidity than does the current ratio. We calculate the acid-test ratio in Illustration 12–19.

VF did not report any current investments, so $0 is recorded for current investments in the numerator of the ratio. VF's acid-test ratio is 0.9 and is lower than Nike's ratio of 1.4. VF's ratio is also lower than 1.0, suggesting that they do not have enough liquid assets available to pay current liabilities as they become due. This is a negative signal about VF's liquidity position.

ILLUSTRATION 12–19

Acid Test Ratio

| Acid Test Ratio | VF | Nike |
|---|---|---|
| Cash + Current investments<br>+ Accounts receivable<br>Current liabilities | $\dfrac{\$1{,}369 + \$0 + \$1{,}308}{\$3{,}024} = 0.9 \text{ to } 1$ | 1.4 to 1 |

## TIMES INTEREST EARNED RATIO

We use the times interest earned ratio to compare interest payments with a company's income available to make those payments. Some categorize this ratio as a liquidity ratio because it measures a company's ability to remain liquid by paying interest expense, a current period obligation. Others categorize it as a solvency ratio because interest payments are more often associated with long-term liabilities than with current liabilities. The exact classification is not really important as the ratio can be used as both a liquidity and solvency measure.

We calculate the times interest earned ratio by dividing net income before interest expense and income tax expense by interest expense. To get the numerator, we just add interest expense and income tax expense to net income. We use net income before interest expense and income tax expense as a reliable indicator of the income available to pay the interest. Illustration 12–20 shows how the ratio is calculated.

ILLUSTRATION 12–20

Times Interest Earned Ratio

| Times Interest Earned Ratio | VF | Nike |
|---|---|---|
| Net income + Interest<br>expense + Income tax expense<br>Interest expense | $\dfrac{\$629 + \$92 + \$98}{\$92} = 8.9 \text{ times}$ | 20.1 times |

The times interest earned ratio for VF is 8.9. That means VF's net income before interest and taxes was 8.9 times the amount it needed for interest expense alone. In comparison, Nike has an even better ratio of 20.1. Both VF and Nike generate more than enough income to cover their interest payments.

## DEBT TO EQUITY RATIO

The debt to equity ratio relates to solvency, or a company's ability to pay its current and long-term debt as it comes due. Other things being equal, the higher the debt to equity ratio, the greater the financial leverage in the company and the higher the risk of bankruptcy. The reason is that, unlike stockholders, debt holders have the ability to force a company into bankruptcy for failing to repay the debt in a timely manner. Illustration 12–21 shows the calculation of the debt to equity ratio for VF and Nike.

ILLUSTRATION 12–21

Debt to Equity Ratio

| Debt to Equity Ratio | VF | Nike |
|---|---|---|
| Total interest-bearing debt<br>Stockholders' equity | $\dfrac{\$1{,}230 + \$3{,}629}{\$3{,}357} = 144.7\%$ | 161.6% |

VF has a debt to equity ratio of 144.7%, or about $1.45 in interest-bearing debt for each $1 in stockholders' equity. Nike's debt to equity ratio is higher, at 161.6%.

Additional debt can be good for investors as long as a company earns a return on borrowed funds in excess of interest costs. However, taking on additional debt can also be bad for investors if interest costs exceed a company's return on borrowed funds. This highlights the trade-off between risk and return for debt. More debt increases the risk of bankruptcy, but it also increases the potential returns investors can enjoy.

Overall, the assessment of the credit risk management ratios for VF and Nike reveal that Nike is in a healthier credit position from a liquidity perspective. Nike has a greater ability to manage short-term obligations as they come due. However, Nike has more interest-bearing debt than does VF, which indicates it is in a poorer credit risk position from a longer-term solvency perspective.

 **KEY POINT**

Credit risk ratios measure a company's credit-worthiness. We categorize credit risk into liquidity ratios and solvency ratios. Liquidity ratios focus on a company's ability to pay current liabilities. Solvency ratios focus on a company's ability to pay long-term liabilities as well.

# Valuation

**■ LO12–7**
Use ratios to analyze a company's valuation.

Our ratio analysis of the return to shareholders, profitability, asset management, and credit risk management ratios suggests that, on balance, Nike is in a stronger financial position than is VF. In summary, Nike delivers a greater accounting return to shareholders, is operating more profitably, is managing total assets more efficiently, and has lower liquidity risk than VF does. These financial characteristic should be reflected in differences in the market valuations of the two companies.

Entire books are devoted to the study of how financial statement information informs valuation. A comprehensive discussion of the subject is beyond the scope of this introductory book. However, it's important to understand that market values reflect capital providers' (1) expectations of future growth and performance and (2) perceived underlying risks of a company.

Financial performance tends to be persistent over time—good performance in the current year generally suggests good performance in the future. Thus, companies with strong current period performance are generally awarded with high market valuations. At the same time, expectations of future performance contain a degree of uncertainty. To the extent economic and business conditions create uncertainty of future performance, investors' perceived risk increases and market valuations decline. We'll now discuss what is likely to be the most frequently used valuation ratio by investors: the price-earnings ratio.

## PRICE-EARNINGS RATIO

The price-earnings (PE) ratio compares a company's stock price per share with its earnings per share. Share price reflects the value of owning one share of the company's stock. This value ties closely to investors' expectations of a company's *future* profitability. In comparison, earnings per share (EPS) measures a company's *current* profitability per share. Therefore, one way to think about the PE ratio is that the ratio represents investors' expectations of earnings growth—the higher the expectations of growth, the higher the PE ratio. Illustration 12–22 presents the PE ratios for VF and Nike. At the end of 2020, VF's closing stock price was $54.08, and the company reported earnings per share for 2020 of $1.59. Putting these together leads to a PE ratio of 34.0. This indicates that the stock price is trading at about 34 times earnings. In contrast, the PE ratio for Nike is 60.5, which means that, at this point in time, investors are more optimistic about Nike's earnings growth potential than VF's, as shown by the higher price (per unit of earnings) they are willing to pay for Nike's stock.

**ILLUSTRATION 12–22**
Price-Earnings Ratio

| Price-Earnings Ratio | VF | Nike |
|---|---|---|
| $\dfrac{\text{Stock price}}{\text{Earnings per share}}$ | $\dfrac{\$54.08}{\$1.59} = 34.0$ | 60.5 |

It's also the case that a company's PE ratio is affected by the riskiness of its operations. As risk increases, investors are more averse to owning a company's stock and thus will pay less for a given level of earnings. While the lower PE ratio of VF likely occurs because of its lower growth expectations, the risk ratios we calculated previously also point to VF having higher risk. This higher risk further contributes to VF's lower PE ratio.

**Other Valuation Ratios.**   While the PE ratio is perhaps the most common valuation ratio, other ratios are often used in conjunction to further understand a company's valuation. It's common to compare companies on their ratios of price-to-book, price-to-sales, price-to-operating cash flows, and price-to-next year's forecasted earnings. Each of these ratios indicates the value investors place on a company relative to a particular accounting measure. These ratios enhance valuation comparisons across companies and help to understand investors' expectations of company growth.

 **KEY POINT**

Valuation ratios are constructed by dividing a company's measure of value (stock price per share) by a measure of the current profitability (earnings per share). The PE ratio captures the extent to which future earnings growth and the company's risk profile are reflected in stock price.

The income statement and balance sheets for **Nike** follow. In addition, Nike reported earnings per share for the year ended May 31, 2020, of $1.63, and the closing stock price on May 31, 2020, was $98.58.

**Let's Review**

*Required:*

Calculate the following ratios for Nike.

1. Return on equity
2. Return on assets
3. Gross profit ratio
4. Profit margin
5. Asset turnover
6. Price-earnings ratio

| NIKE Income Statement For the year ended May 31, 2020 ($ in millions) | |
|---|---:|
| Net sales | $37,403 |
| Cost of goods sold | 21,162 |
| Gross profit | 16,241 |
| Operating expenses | 13,126 |
| Operating income | 3,115 |
| Other income (expense) | (228)* |
| Income before tax | 2,887 |
| Income tax expense | 348 |
| Net income | $ 2,539 |

*Includes interest expense of $151 million.

| NIKE Balance Sheets May 31 ($ in millions) | | |
|---|---|---|
| | **2020** | **2019** |
| **Assets** | | |
| Current assets: | | |
| Cash | $ 8,348 | $ 4,466 |
| Current investments | 439 | 197 |
| Net receivables | 2,749 | 4,272 |
| Inventory | 7,367 | 5,622 |
| Other current assets | 1,653 | 1,968 |
| Total current assets | 20,556 | 16,525 |
| Property and equipment | 4,866 | 4,744 |
| Intangible assets | 497 | 437 |
| Other assets | 5,423 | 2,011 |
| Total assets | $31,342 | $23,717 |
| **Liabilities and Stockholders' Equity** | | |
| Current liabilities | $ 8,284 | $ 7,866 |
| Long-term liabilities | 15,003 | 6,811 |
| Stockholders' equity | 8,055 | 9,040 |
| Total liabilities and stockholders' equity | $31,342 | $23,717 |

*Solution:*

| Ratios | Calculations |
|---|---|
| Return on equity | $\dfrac{\$2,539}{(\$8,055 + \$9,040)/2} = 29.7\%$ |
| Return on assets | $\dfrac{\$2,539}{(\$31,342 + \$23,717)/2} = 9.2\%$ |
| Gross profit ratio | $\dfrac{\$16,241}{\$37,403} = 43.4\%$ |
| Profit margin | $\dfrac{\$2,539}{\$37,403} = 6.8\%$ |
| Asset turnover | $\dfrac{\$37,403}{(\$31,342 + \$23,717)/2} = 1.4 \text{ times}$ |
| Price-earnings ratio | $\dfrac{\$98.58}{\$1.63} = 60.5$ |

## PART C

# EARNINGS PERSISTENCE AND EARNINGS QUALITY

As we just saw when analyzing the PE ratio, investors expect VF's earnings will grow at a slower rate than Nike's. That's why VF's stock price is lower relative to its current earnings. If, for some reason, investors see VF's growth in earnings begin to speed up, then the stock price will rise. Because investors use current earnings to predict future earnings, they are interested in assessing both the persistence of earnings and the quality of earnings. We look at those topics in this section.

# Earnings Persistence and One-Time Income Items

To make predictions of future earnings, investors look for current earnings that will continue or *persist* into future years. Some items that are part of net income in the current year are not expected to persist. We refer to these as *one-time income items* or *transitory items.* Because one-time items are not expected to occur again in the future, they are not relevant to company value. It's important that investors identify and remove these items from their analyses so that they do not confound their assessments of company value. Discontinued operations, discussed below, is a prime example.

■ **LO12–8**
Distinguish persistent earnings from one-time items.

## DISCONTINUED OPERATIONS

A discontinued operation is a business, or a component of a business, that the organization has already discontinued or plans to discontinue. **Income from discontinued operations in the current year is reported separately from income on continuing operations.** This allows investors the opportunity to exclude discontinued operations in their estimate of income that will persist into future years.

Only disposals of businesses representing strategic shifts that have a major effect on an organization's operations and financial results are reported in discontinued operations. Examples include a disposal of a major geographical area, a major line of business, or a major investment in which the company has significant influence.

As an example, let's consider Q Sports Apparel, which has two business activities: a very profitable line of running apparel and a less profitable line of high-performance running shoes. Let's say that during 2024, the company decides to sell the high-performance running shoe business to a competitor. The running shoe business has income for the year, including a gain on disposal of its assets, of $1.5 million. We report the income from the discontinued segment "net of tax." This means the $1.5 million income (before tax), less $500,000 in related taxes, is reported in the income statement as $1 million of income from discontinued operations. Illustration 12–23 shows the income statement presentation of discontinued operations for Q Sports Apparel.

**ILLUSTRATION 12–23**

Presentation of a Discontinued Operation

| Q SPORTS APPAREL<br>Income Statement<br>For the year ended December 31, 2024<br>($ in thousands) | |
| --- | --- |
| Net sales | $15,500 |
| Cost of goods sold | 7,000 |
| Gross profit | 8,500 |
| Operating expenses | 1,200 |
| Depreciation expense | 1,000 |
| Other expenses | 300 |
| Income before tax | 6,000 |
| Income tax expense | 2,000 |
| Income from continuing operations | 4,000 |
| **Discontinued operation:** | |
| **Income from tennis shoe segment, net of tax** | 1,000 |
| Net income | $ 5,000 |

With discontinued operations reported separately in the income statement, investors can clearly see the reported net income *excluding* the effects of the discontinued running shoe segment, $4.0 million in this situation. Investors then can use the income from continuing operations, $4.0 million, to estimate income that persists into future periods.

**Manager Analysis**

| Question | Accounting information | Analysis |
|---|---|---|
| Are any parts of the company's earnings not expected to persist into the future? | Discontinued operations reported near the bottom of the income statement | Investors should normally exclude discontinued operations in estimating future earnings performance. |

## OTHER ONE-TIME ITEMS

As we just discussed, the income related to the sale or disposal of a significant component of a company's operations is reported separately as discontinued operations. What if instead, a company sells assets that are not classified as discontinued operations? For example, suppose Q Sports Apparel decides to sell the land, building, and equipment of a single store (rather than sell the entire tennis shoe division). The income from that store and any gain or loss on the sale of those assets would be reported as part of continuing operations, even though they are not expected to recur.

There are many other activities that impact net income that are not expected to recur. However, no matter how unusual or infrequent these activities are, they are not allowed to be reported as part of discontinued operations. They must be reported as part of continuing operations. Illustration 12–24 lists several common examples.

**ILLUSTRATION 12–24**

**Other Revenues and Expenses**

**Other One-Time Items**

**Examples**
1. Losses from write-down of receivables, inventory, or long-term assets (impairments).
2. Gains or losses on the sale of long-term assets.
3. Losses due to an employee strike.
4. Losses due to business restructuring.
5. Uninsured losses from a natural disaster such as a flood, earthquake, or hurricane.

# Decision Maker's Perspective

## Does Location in the Income Statement Matter?

As manager of a company, would you prefer to show an expense as part of continuing operations or as a part of discontinued operations? Your first response might be that it really doesn't matter since the choice affects only the location in the income statement and has no effect on the final net income number. True, but investors often use the location of items reported in the income statement as a signal of future profitability. Expenses and losses that are listed as part of discontinued operations are, by their classification, not expected to recur in the following year(s). For this reason, managers might prefer to report certain expenses and losses as part of discontinued operations to provide the appearance of more profitable, continuing operations.

However, managers do not have the choice of where to report expenses and losses in the income statement. Expenses and losses, no matter how unusual or infrequent, must be reported as part of income from continuing operations. Only those expenses and losses associated with the sale or disposal of a significant component of the business can be reported as part of discontinued operations.

**KEY POINT**

When using a company's current earnings to estimate future earnings performance, investors normally should exclude discontinued operations and other one-time items.

## Quality of Earnings

As we've learned throughout this book, accounting requires judgments and estimates. Managers must exercise their discretion in order to account for transactions. For example, in order to record bad debt expense, they must estimate the percentage of receivables that will not be collected. In order to record depreciation expense, they must estimate the useful life of the asset and the residual value of the asset.

For the most part, the judgment exercised by management is a good thing and improves the information provided to capital providers. However, given the discretion provided by the accounting rules, there are opportunities for managers to make judgments that mislead outside parties about their companies' earnings performance. Earnings management is the term used to describe how managers use assumptions, estimates, and discretion underlying many accounting rules to "manage" reported earnings. Managers face various incentives to engage in earnings management. We'll discuss a few examples.

*Delivering expected earnings to the stock market:* Each quarter, public companies are required to disclose their quarterly earnings to the market. When reported earnings meet or exceed expectations of analysts and investors (for example, analysts expect EPS of $2.00 and the company reports EPS of $2.01), the company is generally rewarded with a stock price increase. However, the opposite is also true. When reported earnings fail to meet expectations, the company is generally penalized with a stock price decrease. Because managers often have significant stock holdings in their company, they face incentives to manage earnings upward to meet or beat the earnings expectations. Meeting earnings expectations also helps to reduce managers' risk of being terminated by the board of directors if the company appears to be performing poorly.

*Avoiding debt covenant violations with a bank:* Most public and private companies will have a bank loan. These bank loans typically have debt covenants that require the company to maintain a certain level of financial performance or else face negative consequences (for example, when earnings performance falls below a certain threshold, the interest rate on the loan will automatically increase, or the loan will become due immediately). Because these covenants are frequently tied to a company's reported earnings, managers face incentives to manage reported earnings upward to avoid violating such covenants.

*Meeting a performance target tied to management bonus:* Many companies offer bonuses to high-level managers if a specified level of profitability is achieved. Because these managers have incentives to increase their own compensation, they face incentives to manage earnings upward to achieve the bonus. To some extent, the same could also be true for lower-level employees whose compensation is directly tied to the earnings performance of divisional profits.

When earnings are managed, it creates a difference between the earnings that is reported in the financial statements and the actual or true economic earnings of the company. When this difference is small, we say that the *quality of earnings* is high. When this difference is big, we say that the quality of earnings is poor. We'll now discuss how to assess the quality of earnings.

Quality of earnings refers to the ability of reported earnings to reflect the company's true earnings, as well as the usefulness of reported earnings to predict future earnings. To illustrate the concept, we continue our example of Q Sports Apparel.

Let's move one year forward to 2025 for our example company, Q Sports Apparel. Abbie Lynn, as chief financial officer (CFO), is responsible for all the accounting, finance, and MIS operations of the business. She has developed a reputation for her conservative yet powerful management style. Illustration 12–25 presents the preliminary financial statements for 2025, prepared under the supervision of CFO Lynn.

■ **LO12–9**
Distinguish between conservative and aggressive accounting practices.

**ILLUSTRATION 12–25**

Financial Statements Prepared by Abbie Lynn

**Q SPORTS APPAREL**
**Income Statement**
**For the year ended December 31, 2025**
**($ in thousands)**

| | |
|---|---:|
| Net sales | $18,800 |
| Cost of goods sold | 13,400 |
| Gross profit | 5,400 |
| Operating expenses | 1,600 |
| Depreciation expense | 1,000 |
| Loss (litigation) | 1,500 |
| Income before tax | 1,300 |
| Income tax expense | 450 |
| Net income | $ 850 |

**Q SPORTS APPAREL**
**Balance Sheets**
**December 31**
**($ in thousands)**

| | 2025 | 2024 |
|---|---:|---:|
| Cash | $ 2,300 | $ 800 |
| Accounts receivable | 1,500 | 1,200 |
| Inventory | 2,800 | 1,700 |
| Buildings | 11,000 | 11,000 |
| Less: Accumulated depreciation | (2,000) | (1,000) |
| Total assets | $15,600 | $13,700 |
| Accounts payable | $ 1,450 | $ 1,700 |
| Contingent liability | 1,500 | 0 |
| Common stock | 8,000 | 8,000 |
| Retained earnings | 4,650 | 4,000 |
| Total liabilities and stockholders' equity | $15,600 | $13,700 |

**Q SPORTS APPAREL**
**Statement of Cash Flows**
**For the year ended December 31, 2025**
**($ in thousands)**

| | | |
|---|---:|---:|
| **Cash Flows from Operating Activities** | | |
| Net income | $ 850 | |
| *Adjustments to reconcile net income to net cash flows from operating activities:* | | |
| Depreciation expense | 1,000 | |
| Increase in accounts receivable | (300) | |
| Increase in inventory | (1,100) | |
| Decrease in accounts payable | (250) | |
| Increase in contingent liability | 1,500 | |
| Net cash flows from operating activities | | $1,700 |
| **Cash Flows from Investing Activities** | | |
| Net cash flows from investing activities | | 0 |
| **Cash Flows from Financing Activities** | | |
| Payment of cash dividends | (200) | |
| Net cash flows from financing activities | | (200) |
| Net increase (decrease) in cash | | 1,500 |
| Cash at the beginning of the period | | 800 |
| Cash at the end of the period | | $2,300 |

## ABBIE LYNN RETIRES, AND MATTHEW DRAPER IS HIRED

After completing the preliminary financial statements for 2025, CFO Lynn retires, and the company hires a new CFO, Matthew Draper. In contrast to CFO Lynn, CFO Draper has a more aggressive management style. He has made it clear that he is now in charge, and changes will be made. Illustration 12–26 outlines four accounting changes CFO Draper proposes. They are based on accounting topics we discussed in Chapters 5, 6, 7, and 9.

**ILLUSTRATION 12–26**

Mr. Draper's Proposed Changes

### CFO Draper's Proposed Changes

1. **Estimate of bad debts**. At the end of 2025, CFO Lynn estimated that future bad debts would be 6% to 10% of current accounts receivable. She decided to play it safe and recorded an allowance equal to 10% of accounts receivable, or $150,000.

   CFO Draper proposes changing the estimate to be 6% of accounts receivable, or $90,000. This change would increase net accounts receivable and decrease bad debt expense by $60,000.

2. **Write-down of inventory**. CFO Lynn reported a $200,000 write-down of inventory that decreased inventory by $200,000 and increased Cost of Goods Sold by $200,000.

   CFO Draper insists the write-down was not necessary because the decline in inventory value was only temporary. Therefore, he proposes eliminating this write-down, which would increase inventory and decrease cost of goods sold by $200,000.

3. **Change in depreciation estimate**. For the building purchased for $11 million at the beginning of 2024, CFO Lynn recorded depreciation expense of $1 million in 2024 and 2025, using the straight-line method over 10 years with an estimated residual value of $1 million.

   Beginning in 2025, CFO Draper proposes calculating depreciation over a total of 20 years instead of 10 years and using an estimated residual value of $500,000. That change decreases accumulated depreciation and depreciation expense in 2025 by $500,000.

4. **Loss contingency**. At the end of 2025, the company's lawyer advised CFO Lynn that there was a 70% chance of losing a litigation suit of $1,500,000 filed against the company. CFO Lynn reported the possible loss as a contingent liability in the balance sheet for $1,500,000 and taking a $1,500,000 loss in the income statement.

   CFO Draper argues that the likelihood of losing the litigation is reasonably possible, but not probable. Therefore, he proposes removing the litigation liability and loss from the accounting records. The change would remove the loss and decrease liabilities by $1,500,000.

How will the proposed accounting changes affect net income? Illustration 12–27 presents the preliminary income statement prepared by CFO Lynn, the effect of the accounting changes, and the updated income statement prepared by CFO Draper.

**ILLUSTRATION 12–27**

Income Statement
Revised by CFO Draper

**Q SPORTS APPAREL**
**Income Statement**
**For the year ended December 31, 2025**
**($ in thousands)**

|  | CFO Lynn | Changes | CFO Draper |
|---|---|---|---|
| Net sales | $18,800 |  | $18,800 |
| Cost of goods sold | 13,400 | $ (200) | 13,200 |
| Gross profit | 5,400 |  | 5,600 |
| Operating expenses | 1,600 | (60) | 1,540 |
| Depreciation expense | 1,000 | (500) | 500 |
| Loss (litigation) | 1,500 | (1,500) | 0 |
| Income before tax | 1,300 | 2,260 | 3,560 |
| Income tax expense | 450 |  | 450 |
| Net income | $ 850 | $ 2,260 | $ 3,110 |

The four proposed accounting changes cause net income to more than triple, from $850 thousand to $3,110 thousand. Notice that all four changes proposed by CFO Draper increase net income: The reduction in bad debt expense for uncollectible accounts increases net income $60 thousand; the elimination of the inventory write-down in cost of goods sold increases net income $200 thousand; the reduction in depreciation expense estimate increases net income $500 thousand; and the elimination of the contingent litigation loss increases net income $1,500 thousand. **Note that income tax expense did not change because all of these changes affect financial income but not taxable income.**

How do positive changes to net income affect the balance sheet? Illustration 12–28 presents the balance sheet originally prepared by CFO Lynn, the effect of the four accounting changes, and the updated balance sheet prepared by CFO Draper.

**ILLUSTRATION 12–28**

Balance Sheet Revised
by CFO Draper

**Q SPORTS APPAREL**
**Balance Sheet**
**December 31, 2025**
**($ in thousands)**

|  | CFO Lynn | Changes | CFO Draper |
|---|---|---|---|
| **Assets** |  |  |  |
| Cash | $ 2,300 |  | $ 2,300 |
| Accounts receivable | 1,500 | $ 60 | 1,560 |
| Inventory | 2,800 | 200 | 3,000 |
| Buildings | 11,000 |  | 11,000 |
| Less: Accumulated depreciation | (2,000) | 500 | (1,500) |
| Total assets | $15,600 | $ 760 | $16,360 |
| **Liabilities and Stockholders' Equity** |  |  |  |
| Accounts payable | $ 1,450 |  | $ 1,450 |
| Contingent liability | 1,500 | $(1,500) | 0 |
| Common stock | 8,000 |  | 8,000 |
| Retained earnings | 4,650 | 2,260 | 6,910 |
| Total liabilities and equity | $15,600 | $ 760 | $16,360 |

The balance sheet also improves from the proposed adjustments. Total assets increase due to increases in receivables and inventory plus a decrease in accumulated depreciation. Total liabilities decrease due to the elimination of the $1.5 million litigation liability.

Stockholders' equity also goes up due to the increase in retained earnings caused by the increase in reported net income for the year.

What about the effects of the proposed adjustments on the statement of cash flows? Illustration 12–29 provides the statement of cash flows as revised by CFO Draper.

**ILLUSTRATION 12–29**

Statement of Cash Flows Revised by CFO Draper

| Q SPORTS APPAREL<br>Statement of Cash Flows<br>For the year ended December 31, 2025<br>($ in thousands) | CFO Lynn | Changes | CFO Draper |
|---|---|---|---|
| **Operating Activities** | | | |
| Net income | $ 850 | $ 2,260 | $ 3,110 |
| *Adjustments to reconcile net income to net cash flows from operating activities:* | | | |
| Depreciation expense | 1,000 | (500) | 500 |
| Increase in accounts receivable | (300) | (60) | (360) |
| Increase in inventory | (1,100) | (200) | (1,300) |
| Decrease in accounts payable | (250) | | (250) |
| Increase in contingent liability | 1,500 | (1,500) | 0 |
| Net cash flows from operating activities | 1,700 | 0 | 1,700 |
| **Investing Activities** | 0 | | 0 |
| **Financing Activities** | | | |
| Payment of cash dividends | (200) | | (200) |
| Net cash flows from financing activities | (200) | | (200) |
| **Net increase (decrease) in cash** | **1,500** | | **1,500** |
| Cash at the beginning of the period | 800 | | 800 |
| Cash at the end of the period | $2,300 | | $ 2,300 |

Interestingly, the proposed changes have **no effect at all on total operating cash flows or on the overall change in cash.** Net cash flows from operating activities remain at $1,700 thousand after the four proposed transactions. The net increase in cash remains at $1,500 thousand. None of the proposed changes affects the underlying cash flows of the company. **Rather, each proposed change improves the *appearance* of amounts reported in the income statement and the balance sheet.**

## Decision Maker's Perspective

Look Out for Earnings Management at Year-End

Let's assume you're an auditor and all four of the final changes to the accounting records near year-end increase income. Wouldn't you be just a little concerned? It may be that all four adjustments are perfectly legitimate, but it also may be an indication management is inflating earnings. Year-end adjustments, especially those with an increasing or decreasing pattern, should be investigated with greater skepticism.

### CONSERVATIVE VERSUS AGGRESSIVE ACCOUNTING

In our example above, CFO Lynn represents conservative accounting. Conservative accounting practices are those that result in reporting lower income, lower assets, and higher liabilities. The larger estimation of the allowance for uncollectible accounts, the write-down of overvalued inventory, the use of a shorter useful life for depreciation, and the recording of a contingent litigation loss are all examples of conservative accounting.

In contrast, CFO Draper represents aggressive accounting. Aggressive accounting practices result in reporting higher income, higher assets, and lower liabilities. CFO Draper's lower estimation of the allowance for uncollectible accounts, waiting to report an inventory write-down, choosing a longer useful life for depreciation, and waiting to record a litigation loss are examples of more aggressive accounting. Being able to distinguish between conservative and aggressive accounting practices is important. Everyone involved in business, not just accountants, needs to recognize that accounting is not just black and white. There are actually many gray areas in accounting, requiring management judgment in the application of accounting principles.

 **KEY POINT**

Changes in accounting estimates and practices alter the appearance of amounts reported in the income statement and the balance sheet. However, changes in accounting estimates and practices usually have no effect on a company's underlying cash flows.

**Let's Review**

Classify each of the following accounting practices as conservative or aggressive.
1. Increase the allowance for uncollectible accounts.
2. When costs are going up, change from LIFO to FIFO.
3. Increase the useful life for calculating depreciation.
4. Record a larger expense for warranties.
5. Wait to record revenue until the cash is collected.

*Solution:*

1. Conservative.
2. Aggressive.
3. Aggressive.
4. Conservative.
5. Conservative.

**APPENDIX**

■ **LO12–10**
Use the DuPont framework to analyze company performance.

# DUPONT FRAMEWORK

The return on equity (ROE) ratio is of particular interest to investors because it measures how well management uses the equity of a company to generate a profit. In the early part of the twentieth century, an electrical engineer working at **DuPont** developed a way to decompose ROE into three key components to better understand the underlying drivers of the ratio.

This DuPont framework includes the following components:

■ **Profitability,** measured by the profit margin (Net income ÷ Net sales). A higher profit margin indicates that a company generates more profit from each dollar of sales.

■ **Asset Efficiency,** measured by asset turnover (Net sales ÷ Average total assets). A higher asset turnover indicates that a company uses its assets more efficiently to generate sales.

■ **Financial Leverage,** measured by the equity multiplier (Average total assets ÷ Average total equity). A higher equity multiplier indicates that relatively more of the company's assets have been financed with debt; that is, the company is more leveraged.

In equation form, the DuPont framework looks like this:

$$\text{Return on equity} = \text{Profit margin} \times \text{Asset turnover} \times \text{Equity multiplier}$$

$$\frac{\text{Net income}}{\text{Avg. total equity}} = \frac{\text{Net income}}{\text{Net sales}} \times \frac{\text{Net sales}}{\text{Avg. total assets}} \times \frac{\text{Avg. total assets}}{\text{Avg. total equity}}$$

Notice that net sales and average total assets appear in the numerator of one ratio and the denominator of another, so they cancel to yield net income ÷ average total equity, or ROE. It is also important to recognize that another important ratio, return on assets (ROA), is determined by profit margin and asset turnover. So another way to compute ROE is by multiplying ROA by the equity multiplier:

$$\text{Return on equity} = \text{Return on assets} \times \text{Equity multiplier}$$

$$\frac{\text{Net income}}{\text{Avg. total equity}} = \frac{\text{Net income}}{\text{Avg. total assets}} \times \frac{\text{Avg. total assets}}{\text{Avg. total equity}}$$

We can see from this equation that an equity multiplier of greater than one will produce a return on equity that is higher than the return on assets. However, as with all ratio analyses, there are trade-offs to consider. If leverage is too high, creditors become concerned about the potential for default on the company's debt and require higher interest rates. Because interest is recognized as an expense, net income is reduced, so at some point, the benefits of a higher equity multiplier are offset by a lower profit margin. Part of the challenge of managing a company is to identify the combination of profitability, asset efficiency, and leverage that produces the highest return for equity holders. We can also see how leverage can multiply the effects of losses. When a company is operating at a loss, its ROA ratio will be negative, and the equity multiplier will magnify the effect of these losses. This is one of the risks of financial leverage.

Illustration 12–30 shows the application of the DuPont framework using **VF** and **Nike**.

**ILLUSTRATION 12–30**

DuPont Framework

| | VF | | Nike |
|---|---|---|---|
| **Profit Margin** | | | |
| $\times \quad \dfrac{\text{Net income}}{\text{Net sales}}$ | $\dfrac{\$629}{\$10,489}$ | = 6.00% | 6.79% |
| **Asset Turnover** | | | |
| $\times \quad \dfrac{\text{Net sales}}{\text{Average total assets}}$ | $\dfrac{\$10,489}{(\$11,133 + \$10,357)/2}$ | = 0.98 | 1.36 |
| **Equity Multiplier** | | | |
| $= \quad \dfrac{\text{Average total assets}}{\text{Average stockholders' equity}}$ | $\dfrac{(\$11,133 + \$10,357)/2}{(\$3,357 + \$4,299)/2}$ | = 2.80 | 3.22 |
| **Return on Equity** | | | |
| $\dfrac{\text{Net Income}}{\text{Average stockholders' equity}}$ | $\dfrac{\$629}{(\$3,357 + \$4,299)/2}$ | = 16.43% | 29.70% |

Note: any differences are due to rounding.

The first item to notice is that Nike's profit margin is higher than that of VF (6.79% for Nike compared to 6.00% for VF). This means that Nike generates 0.79 cents more profit for each $1 of sales. The asset turnover ratio further reveals that Nike is also better able to use its assets to generate sales. Nike's asset turnover ratio of 1.36 is noticeably higher than VF's ratio of only 0.98. Then, we see from the equity multiplier of each company that Nike also uses more debt (or conversely, less equity) to finance the purchase of its assets than does VF. This strategy has paid off for its shareholders. By using financial leverage to purchase more productive assets, Nike is able to generate a higher return on equity (ROE) for its shareholders (29.70% for Nike versus only 16.43% for VF). The DuPont analysis helps us understand how this occurs.

An important point of our discussion here and this entire chapter is that raw accounting numbers alone mean little to decision makers. The numbers gain value when viewed in relation to other numbers. Similarly, the financial ratios formed by those relationships provide an even greater perspective when compared with similar ratios of other companies or with averages for several companies in the same industry. Accounting information is useful in making decisions. Financial analysis that includes comparisons of financial ratios enhances the value of that information.

 **KEY POINT**

The DuPont framework is used to analyze the performance of a company as measured by the ROE ratio. ROE can be decomposed into three components: profitability, asset efficiency, and financial leverage.

 **THE BOTTOM LINE**

**LO12–1**   **Perform vertical analysis.**

For vertical analysis, we express each item as a percentage of the same base amount, such as a percentage of sales in the income statement or as a percentage of total assets in the balance sheet.

**LO12–2**   **Perform horizontal analysis.**

We use horizontal analysis to analyze trends in financial statement data, such as the amount of change and the percentage change, for one company over time.

**LO12–3**   **Use ratios to analyze a company's return to shareholders.**

Return on investment ratios measure a company's ability to generate returns to its capital providers. These ratios capture the overall performance of a company over a period of time.

**LO12–4**   **Use ratios to analyze a company's profitability.**

Profitability ratios measure a company's ability to generate profits from its sales. These ratios are used as a measure of the operating effectiveness of a company over a period of time, such as a year.

**LO12–5**   **Use ratios to analyze a company's asset management.**

Asset management ratios measure a company's ability to use its assets to generate sales. These ratios are used as a measure of the operating efficiency of a company over a period of time, such as a year.

**LO12–6**   **Use ratios to analyze a company's credit risk management.**

Credit risk ratios measure a company's creditworthiness. We categorize credit risk into

liquidity ratios and solvency ratios. Liquidity ratios focus on a company's ability to pay current liabilities. Solvency ratios focus on a company's ability to pay long-term liabilities as well.

**LO12–7**   **Use ratios to analyze a company's valuation.**

Valuation ratios are constructed by dividing a company's measure of value (stock price per share) by a measure of the current profitability (earnings per share). This ratio captures the extent to which future earnings growth and the company's risk profile are reflected in stock price.

**LO12–8**   **Distinguish persistent earnings from one-time items.**

When using a company's current earnings to estimate future earnings performance, investors normally should exclude discontinued operations and other one-time items.

**LO12–9**   **Distinguish between conservative and aggressive accounting practices.**

Changes in accounting estimates and practices alter the appearance of amounts reported in the income statement and the balance sheet. However, changes in accounting estimates and practices usually have no effect on a company's underlying cash flows.

**LO12–10**   **Use the DuPont framework to analyze company performance.**

The DuPont framework is used to analyze the performance of a company as measured by the ROE ratio. ROE can be decomposed into three components: profitability, asset efficiency, and financial leverage.

## GLOSSARY

**Acid-test ratio:** Cash, current investments, and accounts receivable divided by current liabilities; measures the availability of liquid current assets to pay current liabilities. **p. 624**

**Aggressive accounting:** Practices that result in reporting higher income, higher assets, and lower liabilities. **p. 636**

**Asset turnover:** Net sales divided by average total assets, which measures the sales per dollar of assets invested. **p. 622**

**Average collection period:** Approximate number of days the average accounts receivable balance is outstanding. It equals 365 days divided by the receivables turnover ratio. **p. 623**

**Average days in inventory:** Approximate number of days the average inventory is held. It equals 365 days divided by the inventory turnover ratio. **p. 623**

**Capital structure:** The mixture of liabilities and stockholders' equity in a business. **p. 614**

**Conservative accounting:** Practices that result in reporting lower income, lower assets, and higher liabilities. **p. 635**

**Current ratio:** Current assets divided by current liabilities; measures the availability of current assets to pay current liabilities. **p. 624**

**Debt to equity ratio:** Total interest-bearing debt divided by stockholders' equity; measures a company's risk. **p. 625**

**Discontinued operation:** The sale or disposal of a significant component of a company's operations. **p. 629**

**DuPont framework:** Depicts return on equity as determined by profit margin (representing profitability), asset turnover (representing efficiency), and the equity multiplier (representing leverage). **p. 636**

**Earnings management:** Managers use of assumptions, estimates, and discretion afforded by accounting rules to impact reported earnings in a way that influences some stakeholders views of the profitability of the company. **p. 631**

**Earnings per share (EPS):** Net income available to common shareholders divided by average shares of common stock outstanding. **p. 626**

**Gross profit ratio:** Measure of the amount by which the sale of inventory exceeds its cost per dollar of sales. It equals gross profit divided by net sales. **p. 621**

**Horizontal analysis:** Analyzes trends in financial statement data for a single company over time. **p. 614**

**Inventory turnover ratio:** The number of times a company sells its average inventory balance during a reporting period. It equals cost of goods sold divided by average inventory. **p. 623**

**Liquidity:** Having sufficient cash (or other assets convertible to cash in a relatively short time) to pay currently maturing debts. **p. 624**

**Price-earnings (PE) ratio:** Compares a company's share price with its earnings per share. **p. 626**

**Profit margin:** Net income divided by net sales; indicates the earnings per dollar of sales. **p. 621**

**Quality of earnings:** Refers to the ability of reported earnings to reflect the company's true earnings, as well as the usefulness of reported earnings to predict future earnings. **p. 631**

**Receivables turnover ratio:** Number of times during a year that the average accounts receivable balance is collected (or "turns over"). It equals net credit sales divided by average accounts receivable. **p. 622**

**Return on assets:** Net income divided by average total assets; measures the amount of net income generated for each dollar invested in assets. **p. 620**

**Return on equity:** Net income divided by average stockholders' equity; measures the income generated per dollar of stockholders' equity. **p. 620**

**Solvency:** Refers to a company's ability to pay its current and long-term debt. **p. 624**

**Times interest earned ratio:** Ratio that compares interest expense with income available to pay those charges. **p. 625**

**Vertical analysis:** Expresses each item in a financial statement as a percentage of the same base amount. **p. 612**

## SELF-STUDY QUESTIONS

1. When using vertical analysis, we express income statement accounts as a percentage of **(LO12–1)**
   a. Net income.
   b. Sales.
   c. Gross profit.
   d. Total assets.

2. When using vertical analysis, we express balance sheet accounts as a percentage of **(LO12–1)**
   a. Total assets.
   b. Total liabilities.
   c. Total stockholders' equity.
   d. Sales.

3. Horizontal analysis examines trends in a company **(LO12–2)**
   a. Between income statement accounts in the same year.
   b. Between balance sheet accounts in the same year.
   c. Between income statement and balance sheet accounts in the same year.
   d. Over time.

4. Which of the following is an example of horizontal analysis? **(LO12–2)**
   a. Comparing operating expenses with sales.
   b. Comparing the growth in sales with the growth in cost of goods sold.

c. Comparing property, plant, and equipment with total assets.

d. Comparing gross profit across companies.

5. A company's income statement reports sales of $30 million, operating income of $11 million, and net income of $2.5 million. From the balance sheets of the current year and previous year, the company reports average assets of $20 million, average stockholders' equity of $15 million, and average liabilities of $5 million. The company's return on equity is **(LO12–3)**

   a. 16.7%.
   b. 73.3%.
   c. 12.5%.
   d. 55.0%.

6. The Sports Shack reports net income of $120,000, sales of $1,200,000, and average assets of $960,000. The profit margin is **(LO12–4)**

   a. 10%.
   b. 12.5%.
   c. 80%.
   d. 125%.

7. The Sports Shack reports net income of $120,000, sales of $1,200,000, and average assets of $960,000. The asset turnover is **(LO12–5)**

   a. 0.10 times.
   b. 0.80 times.
   c. 8 times.
   d. 1.25 times.

8. Which of the following is a positive sign that a company can quickly turn its receivables into cash? **(LO12–5)**

   a. A low receivables turnover ratio.
   b. A high receivables turnover ratio.
   c. A low average collection period.
   d. Both a high receivables turnover ratio and a low average collection period.

9. The current ratio measures **(LO12–6)**

   a. The ability of a company to quickly collect cash from customers.
   b. The ability of a company to quickly sell its inventory to customers.
   c. The ability of a company to report profits in the current year.
   d. The ability of a company to pay its current obligations.

10. Which of the following ratios is most useful in evaluating solvency? **(LO12–6)**

    a. Receivables turnover ratio.
    b. Inventory turnover ratio.
    c. Debt to equity ratio.
    d. Current ratio.

11. Companies A and B are both in the retail industry. Company A has a price-earnings ratio of 25.5, and Company B has a price-earnings ratio of 18.5. Which of the following statements is most likely to be true? **(LO12–7)**

    a. Company A is more leveraged than Company B.
    b. Company A is much more profitable than Company B.
    c. Company A is larger than Company B.
    d. Company A has higher growth expectations by investors than Company B.

12. Which of the following items would we report in the income statement just before net income? **(LO12–8)**

    a. Losses due to the write-down of inventory.
    b. Gain on the sale of long-term assets.
    c. Discontinued operations.
    d. Losses due to restructuring.

13. A company suffers an inventory loss from water damage due to a broken pipe. The company has never incurred a loss of this type and does not expect this type of damage to occur again. The loss would be reported as **(LO12–8)**

    a. A reduction of sales revenue.
    b. Part of income from continuing operations.
    c. Part of income from discontinued operations.
    d. Not reported.

14. Which of the following is an example of a conservative accounting practice? **(LO12–9)**

    a. Estimate the allowance for uncollectible accounts to be a larger amount.
    b. Do not write down inventory for declines in net realizable value (estimated selling price).
    c. Record a lower amount of depreciation expense in the earlier years of an asset's life.
    d. Record sales revenue before it is actually earned.

15. Which of the following would be an example of conservative accounting? **(LO12–9)**

    a. Recording an increase in fair value of certain assets as a gain in net income but not recording a decrease in fair value as a loss.
    b. Estimating the percentage of bad debts as 6% of accounts receivable instead of 10% of accounts receivable.
    c. Estimating warranty costs to be 4% of sales instead of 9% of sales.
    d. Assessing the probability of a contingent liability as probable instead of reasonably likely.

16. The DuPont framework decomposes ROE into the following components except: **(LO12–10)**

    a. Asset efficiency.
    b. Leverage.
    c. Profitability.
    d. Liquidity.

*Note: For answers, see the last page of the chapter.*

## REAL WORLD PERSPECTIVES

### Raytheon (ticker: RTX) and Northrop Grumman (ticker: NOC)

**EDGAR Case**

**RWP12–1** Visit www.sec.gov/edgar and search for the annual reports (10-K) of **Raytheon/United Technolgies** and **Northrop Grumman** for the year ended December 31, 2019, using EDGAR (Electronic Data Gathering, Analysis, and Retrieval system). Locate the balance sheet and income statement of each company.

*Required:*
1. Calculate the return on equity (ROE) for both companies. Which company delivers a higher return to shareholders based on ROE?
2. Calculate the return on assets (ROA) for both companies. Which company delivers a higher return to shareholders based on ROA?
3. Explain how a company can have a slightly higher ROA than its competitor, but a much higher ROE.

### Kellogg (ticker: K) and General Mills (ticker: GIS)

**EDGAR Case**

**RWP12–2** Visit www.sec.gov/edgar and search for the annual reports (10-K) of **Kellogg** and **General Mills** for the year ended December 29, 2018, and May 26, 2019, respectively, using EDGAR (Electronic Data Gathering, Analysis, and Retrieval system). Locate the income statement of each company.

*Required:*
1. Calculate the profit margin for both companies. Which company is more profitable?
2. Using vertical analysis, which company has higher cost of goods sold?
3. Using vertical analysis, which company reports higher selling, general, and administrative expenses?

### Home Depot (ticker: HD) and Lowe's (ticker: LOW)

**EDGAR Case**

**RWP12–3** Visit www.sec.gov/edgar and search for the annual reports (10-K) of **Home Depot** and **Lowe's** for the year ended February 3, 2019, and February 1, 2019, respectively, using EDGAR (Electronic Data Gathering, Analysis, and Retrieval system). Locate the balance sheet and income statement of each company.

*Required:*
1. Calculate the inventory turnover ratio and average days in inventory for both companies. Which company more efficiently manages its inventory?
2. Calculate the average days in inventory for both companies in the prior year (note: this will require you to find the annual reports for the prior years). What additional insights do you learn by looking at the time trends in the average days in inventory of the two companies?

### Delta (ticker: DAL) and Southwest (ticker: LUV)

**EDGAR Case**

**RWP12–4** Visit www.sec.gov/edgar and search for the annual reports (10-K) of **Delta** and **Southwest** for the year ended December 31, 2018, using EDGAR (Electronic Data Gathering, Analysis, and Retrieval system). Locate the balance sheet and income statement of each company.

*Required:*
1. Calculate the current ratio and acid-test ratio for both companies. Which company has a greater liquidity risk?
2. Using a vertical analysis of the current assets, determine which company's total of cash, short-term investments, and accounts receivable is greater.
3. Calculate the times interest earned ratio and the debt to equity ratio for both companies. Which company has greater solvency risk?

## American Eagle Outfitters, Inc.

**RWP12–5** Financial information for **American Eagle** is presented in **Appendix A** at the end of the book.

### Required:
1. Calculate the following return to shareholders and profitability ratios for the most recent year:
   a. Return on equity.
   b. Return on assets.
   c. Gross profit ratio.
   d. Profit margin.

2. Calculate the following asset management and credit risk ratios for the most recent year:
   a. Asset turnover.
   b. Receivables turnover ratio.
   c. Average collection period.
   d. Inventory turnover ratio.
   e. Average days in inventory.
   f. Current ratio.
   g. Acid-test ratio.
   h. Debt to equity ratio (assume that other non-current liabilities are not interest-bearing).

## The Buckle, Inc.

**RWP12–6** Financial information for **Buckle** is presented in **Appendix B** at the end of the book.

### Required:
1. Calculate the following return to shareholders and profitability ratios for the most recent year:
   a. Return on equity.
   b. Return on assets.
   c. Gross profit ratio.
   d. Profit margin.

2. Calculate the following asset management and credit risk ratios for the most recent year:
   a. Asset turnover.
   b. Receivables turnover ratio.
   c. Average collection period.
   d. Inventory turnover ratio.
   e. Average days in inventory.
   f. Current ratio.
   g. Acid-test ratio.
   h. Debt to equity ratio.

## American Eagle Outfitters, Inc., vs. The Buckle, Inc.

**RWP12–7** Financial information for **American Eagle** is presented in **Appendix A** at the end of the book, and financial information for **Buckle** is presented in **Appendix B** at the end of the book.

### Required:
1. Calculate the following return to shareholders and profitability ratios for both companies for the most recent year. Based on these calculations, which company appears to deliver a higher return? Which company appears to be more profitable?
   a. Return on equity.
   b. Return on assets.
   c. Gross profit ratio.
   d. Profit margin.

2. Calculate the following asset management and credit risk ratios for both companies for the most recent year. Based on these calculations, which company appears to be more efficient? Which appears to have greater credit risk?
   a. Asset turnover.
   b. Receivables turnover ratio.

    c. Average collection period.

    d. Inventory turnover ratio.

    e. Average days in inventory.

    f. Current ratio.

    g. Acid-test ratio.

    h. Debt to equity ratio (assume that other non-current liabilities are not interest-bearing).

## Ethics

Ethics Case

**RWP12–8** After years of steady growth in net income, Performance Drug Company reported a preliminary net loss in 2024. The CEO, Joe Mammoth, notices the following estimates are included in reported performance:

1. Warranty expense and liability for estimated future warranty costs associated with sales in the current year.
2. Loss due to ending inventory's net realizable value (estimated selling price) falling below its cost. This type of inventory write down occurs most years.
3. Depreciation of major equipment purchased this year, which is estimated to have a 10-year service life.

    Joe is worried that the company's poor performance will have a negative impact on the company's risk and profitability ratios. This will cause the stock price to decline and hurt the company's ability to obtain needed loans in the following year. Before releasing the financial statements to the public, Joe asks his CFO to reconsider these estimates. He argues that (1) warranty work won't happen until next year, so that estimate can be eliminated, (2) there's always a chance we'll find the right customer and sell inventory above cost, so the estimated loss on inventory write-down can be eliminated, and (3) we may use the equipment for 20 years (even though equipment of this type has little chance of being used for more than 10 years). Joe explains that all of his suggestions make good business sense and reflect his optimism about the company's future. Joe further notes that executive bonuses (including his and the CFO's) are tied to net income, and if we don't show a profit this year, there will be no bonuses.

### Required:
1. Understand the reporting effect: How would excluding the warranty adjustment affect the debt to equity ratio? How would excluding the inventory adjustment affect the gross profit ratio? How would extending the depreciable life to 20 years affect the profit margin?
2. Specify the options: If the adjustments are kept, what will they indicate about the company's overall risk and profitability?
3. Identify the impact: Could these adjustments affect stockholders, lenders, and management?
4. Make a decision: Should the CFO follow Joe's suggestions of not including these adjustments?

## Earnings Management

Earnings Management Case

**RWP12–9** Major League Products provides merchandise carrying the logos of each fan's favorite major league team. In recent years, the company has struggled to compete against new Internet-based companies selling products at much lower prices. Andrew Ransom, in his second year out of college, was assigned to audit the financial statements of Major League Products. One of the steps in the auditing process is to examine the nature of year-end adjustments. Andrew's investigation reveals that the company has made several year-end adjustments, including (a) a decrease in the allowance for uncollectible accounts, (b) a reversal in the previous write-down of inventory, (c) an increase in the estimated useful life used to calculate depreciation expense, and (d) a decrease in the liability reported for litigation.

### Required:
1. Classify each adjustment as conservative or aggressive.
2. What effect do these adjustments have on expenses in the current year?

3. What effect do these adjustments have on the company's cash balance in the current year?

4. Do these year-end adjustments, taken together, raise concerns about earnings management?

**Continuing Problem**

## Great Adventures

(This is the conclusion of the Great Adventures problem from earlier chapters.)

**RWP12–10** Income statement and balance sheet data for Great Adventures, Inc., are provided below.

### GREAT ADVENTURES, INC.
### Income Statement
### For the year ended December 31, 2025

| | | |
|---|---:|---:|
| Net sales revenues | | $164,150 |
| Interest revenue | | 120 |
| Expenses: | | |
| Cost of goods sold | $38,500 | |
| Operating expenses | 51,400 | |
| Depreciation expense | 17,250 | |
| Interest expense | 6,785 | |
| Income tax expense | 14,500 | |
| Total expenses | | 128,435 |
| Net income | | $ 35,835 |

### GREAT ADVENTURES, INC.
### Balance Sheets
### December 31, 2025 and 2024

| | 2025 | 2024 |
|---|---:|---:|
| **Assets** | | |
| Current assets: | | |
| Cash | $ 180,568 | $ 64,500 |
| Accounts receivable | 47,600 | 0 |
| Inventory | 7,000 | 0 |
| Other current assets | 900 | 4,500 |
| Long-term assets: | | |
| Land | 500,000 | 0 |
| Buildings | 800,000 | 0 |
| Equipment | 62,000 | 40,000 |
| Accumulated depreciation | (25,250) | (8,000) |
| Total assets | $1,572,818 | $101,000 |
| **Liabilities and Stockholders' Equity** | | |
| Current liabilities: | | |
| Accounts payable | $ 20,800 | $ 2,800 |
| Interest payable | 750 | 750 |
| Income tax payable | 14,500 | 14,000 |
| Other current liabilities | 21,000 | 0 |
| Notes payable (current) | 48,014 | 0 |
| Notes payable (long-term) | 475,869 | 30,000 |
| Stockholders' equity: | | |
| Common stock | 120,000 | 20,000 |
| Paid-in capital | 904,000 | 0 |
| Retained earnings | 57,885 | 33,450 |
| Treasury stock | (90,000) | 0 |
| Total liabilities and equity | $1,572,818 | $101,000 |

As you can tell from the financial statements, 2025 was an especially busy year. Tony and Suzie were able to use the money received from borrowing and the issuance of stock to buy land and begin construction of cabins, dining facilities, ropes course, and the outdoor swimming pool. They even put in a baby pool to celebrate the birth of their first child.

**Required:**
1. Calculate the following return to shareholders and profitability ratios for 2025.
   a. Return on equity.
   b. Return on assets.
   c. Gross profit ratio. (*Hint:* Use net sales revenues.)
   d. Profit margin. (*Hint:* Use net sales revenues.)
2. Calculate the following asset management and credit risk ratios for 2025.
   a. Asset turnover.
   b. Receivables turnover ratio. (*Hint:* Use net sales revenues for net credit sales.)
   c. Average collection period.
   d. Inventory turnover ratio.
   e. Average days in inventory.
   f. Current ratio.
   g. Acid-test ratio. (*Hint:* There are no current investments.)
   h. Debt to equity ratio.
   i. Times interest earned ratio.

## BRIEF EXERCISES

**BE12–1** Perform a vertical analysis on the following information.

Prepare vertical analysis **(LO12–1)**

|                    | 2024         | 2023         |
| ------------------ | ------------ | ------------ |
| Cash               | $ 420,000    | $ 1,050,000  |
| Accounts receivable | 660,000     | 300,000      |
| Inventory          | 1,020,000    | 925,000      |
| Long-term assets   | 3,900,000    | 2,725,000    |
| Total assets       | $6,000,000   | $5,000,000   |

**BE12–2** Using the information presented in BE12–1, perform a horizontal analysis providing both the amount and percentage change.

Prepare horizontal analysis **(LO12–2)**

**BE12–3** Athletic World reports the following vertical analysis percentages.

Understand vertical analysis **(LO12–1)**

|                    | 2024 | 2023 |
| ------------------ | ---- | ---- |
| Sales              | 100% | 100% |
| Cost of goods sold | 48%  | 56%  |
| Operating expenses | 35%  | 30%  |

Did Athletic World's income before tax as a percentage of sales increase, decrease, or stay the same? If net income as a percentage of sales increases, does that mean net income also increases? Explain.

**BE12–4** Sales are $2.6 million in 2023, $2.7 million in 2024, and $2.5 million in 2025. What is the percentage change from 2023 to 2024? What is the percentage change from 2024 to 2025? Be sure to indicate whether the percentage change is an increase or a decrease.

Understand horizontal analysis **(LO12–2)**

**BE12–5** If sales are $1,150,000 in 2025 and this represents a 15% increase over sales in 2024, what were sales in 2024?

Understand percentage change **(LO12–2)**

**Calculate return on equity (LO12–3)**

**BE12–6** Wonder Wall Enterprises reports net income of $500,000 for the year ended 2025. The balance sheet for 2024 reports total assets of $4,500,000 and total stockholders' equity of $3,800,000. The balance sheet for 2025 reports total assets of $4,800,000 and total stockholders' equity of $3,900,000. Calculate the return on equity for 2025.

**Calculate return on assets (LO12–3)**

**BE12–7** Using the facts presented in BE12–6, calculate the return on assets for 2025.

**Calculate return to shareholders ratios (LO12–3)**

**BE12–8** LaDanion's Limos reports net income of $130,000, average total assets of $700,000, and average total liabilities of $340,000. Calculate LaDanion's return on assets and return on equity ratios.

**Calculate ratios (LO12–3, LO12–4, LO12–5)**

**BE12–9** Peyton's Palace has net income of $15 million on sales revenue of $130 million. Total assets were $96 million at the beginning of the year and $104 million at the end of the year. Calculate Peyton's return on assets, profit margin, and asset turnover ratios.

**Calculate receivables turnover (LO12–5)**

**BE12–10** Universal Sports Supply began the year with an accounts receivable balance of $200,000 and a year-end balance of $220,000. Credit sales of $750,000 generate a gross profit of $250,000. Calculate the receivables turnover ratio for the year.

**Calculate inventory turnover (LO12–5)**

**BE12–11** Universal Sports Supply began the year with an inventory balance of $65,000 and a year-end balance of $75,000. Sales of $750,000 generate a gross profit of $250,000. Calculate the inventory turnover ratio for the year.

**Understand inventory turnover (LO12–5)**

**BE12–12** The Intramural Sports Club reports sales revenue of $1,140,000. Inventory at both the beginning and end of the year totals $200,000. The inventory turnover ratio for the year is 4.9. What amount of gross profit does the company report in its income statement?

**Understand the current ratio (LO12–6)**

**BE12–13** Dungy Training Company has a current ratio of 0.70 to 1, based on current assets of $3.43 million and current liabilities of $4.90 million. How, if at all, will a $900,000 cash purchase of inventory affect the current ratio? How, if at all, will a $900,000 purchase of inventory on account affect the current ratio?

**Calculate the times interest earned ratio (LO12–6)**

**BE12–14** Calculate the times interest earned ratio using the following partial income statement.

| | |
|---|---:|
| Gross profit | $800,000 |
| Operating expenses | 650,000 |
| Operating income | 150,000 |
| Interest expense | 10,000 |
| Income before taxes | 140,000 |
| Income tax expense | 35,000 |
| Net income | $105,000 |

**Calculate the debt to equity ratio (LO12–6)**

**BE12–15** Right Help Inc. reports total debt of $16 million, total liabilities of $20 million, and total assets of $28 million. Calculate the debt to equity ratio.

**Calculate the price-earnings ratio (LO12–7)**

**BE12–16** The 23 million outstanding shares of Right Help Inc. stock is trading at $12.00 at the end of the year. The company's income statement reports sales of $900 million and net income of $250 million. Calculate the price-earnings ratio for Right Help Inc.

**Report discontinued operations (LO12–8)**

**BE12–17** Kobe's Clinics provides health services and career counseling. Net income from the health services business this year is $32 million after tax. During the year, Kobe's Clinics sold the career counseling side of the business at a loss after tax of $7.5 million. Show how Kobe's Clinics would report this loss in the income statement, beginning with income from continuing operations of $32 million.

**Classify income statement items (LO12–8)**

**BE12–18** Game Time Sports owns a recreational facility with basketball courts, pitching machines, and athletic fields. Determine whether the firm should report each of the following items as discontinued operations, other revenues, or other expenses.

1. Due to insurance concerns, Game Time sells a trampoline basketball game for a loss of $1,500.
2. Game Time experiences water damage due to a flood from a recent heavy storm. The company replaces the basketball floors at a cost of $75,000. Unfortunately, Game Time does not carry flood insurance.

3. Game Time has revenues from three sources: basketball, baseball, and football. It sells the baseball operations for a loss of $55,000 to focus on the more profitable basketball and football operations.
4. Game Time sells one of the buildings used for basketball operations at a gain of $250,000. The company has two other buildings for basketball and plans to build a new facility for basketball in another year or two.

**BE12–19** Classify each of the following accounting practices as conservative or aggressive.

1. Increase the allowance for uncollectible accounts.
2. When costs are rising, change from LIFO to FIFO.
3. Change from declining-balance to straight-line depreciation in the second year of an asset depreciated over 20 years.

*Distinguish between conservative and aggressive accounting practices (LO12–9)*

**BE12–20** Classify each of the following accepted accounting practices as conservative or aggressive.

1. Decrease warranty reserves below industry norms.
2. Expense all research and development costs rather than recording some research and development costs as an asset.
3. Record loss contingencies when they are probable and can be reasonably estimated, but do not record gain contingencies until they are certain.

*Distinguish between conservative and aggressive accounting practices (LO12–9)*

**BE12–21** The 2024 income statement for Anderson TV and Appliance reported net sales of $420,000 and net income of $65,000. Average total assets for 2024 was $800,000. Stockholders' equity at the beginning of the year was $500,000, and $20,000 was paid to shareholders as dividends. There were no other stockholders' equity transactions that occurred during the year. Show the DuPont framework's calculation of the three components of the 2024 return on equity for Anderson TV and Appliance.

*Calculate the DuPont framework ratios (LO12–10)*

## EXERCISES

**E12–1** Match (by letter) the following items with the description or example that best fits. Each letter is used only once.

*Match terms with their definitions (LO12–1, 12–2, 12–6, 12–8, 12–9)*

**Terms**

_____ 1. Vertical analysis.
_____ 2. Horizontal analysis.
_____ 3. Liquidity.
_____ 4. Solvency.
_____ 5. Discontinued operations.
_____ 6. Quality of earnings.
_____ 7. Conservative accounting practices.
_____ 8. Aggressive accounting practices.

**Descriptions**

a. A company's ability to pay its current liabilities.
b. Accounting choices that result in reporting lower income, lower assets, and higher liabilities.
c. Accounting choices that result in reporting higher income, higher assets, and lower liabilities.
d. The ability of reported earnings to reflect the company's true earnings as well as the usefulness of reported earnings to help investors predict future earnings.
e. A tool to analyze trends in financial statement data for a single company over time.
f. The sale or disposal of a significant component of a company's operations.
g. A means to express each item in a financial statement as a percentage of a base amount.
h. A company's ability to pay its current and long-term liabilities.

Prepare vertical
analysis **(LO12–1)**

**E12–2** The income statements for Federer Sports Apparel for 2025 and 2024 are presented below.

| FEDERER SPORTS APPAREL<br>Income Statements<br>For the years ended December 31<br>($ in thousands) | | |
|---|---|---|
| | **2025** | **2024** |
| Net sales | $18,800 | $15,500 |
| Cost of goods sold | 13,200 | 7,000 |
| Gross profit | 5,600 | 8,500 |
| Operating expenses | 1,600 | 1,200 |
| Depreciation expense | 1,000 | 1,000 |
| Inventory write-down | 200 | |
| Loss (litigation) | 1,500 | 300 |
| Income before tax | 1,300 | 6,000 |
| Income tax expense | 450 | 2,000 |
| Net income | $ 850 | $ 4,000 |

*Required:*

Prepare a vertical analysis of the data for 2025 and 2024.

Prepare horizontal
analysis **(LO12–2)**

**E12–3** Refer to the information provided in E12–2.

*Required:*

Prepare a horizontal analysis for 2025 using 2024 as the base year.

Prepare vertical
and horizontal
analyses **(LO12–1, 12–2)**

**E12–4** The balance sheets for Federer Sports Apparel for 2025 and 2024 are presented below.

| FEDERER SPORTS APPAREL<br>Balance Sheets<br>DECEMBER 31<br>($ in thousands) | | |
|---|---|---|
| | **2025** | **2024** |
| **Assets** | | |
| Cash | $ 2,300 | $ 800 |
| Accounts receivable | 1,500 | 2,200 |
| Inventory | 2,800 | 1,700 |
| Buildings | 11,000 | 11,000 |
| Less: Accumulated depreciation | (2,000) | (1,000) |
| Total assets | $15,600 | $14,700 |
| **Liabilities and Stockholders' Equity** | | |
| Accounts payable | $ 1,450 | $ 1,700 |
| Contingent liability | 1,500 | 1,000 |
| Common stock | 8,000 | 8,000 |
| Retained earnings | 4,650 | 4,000 |
| Total liabilities and stockholders' equity | $15,600 | $14,700 |

*Required:*

1. Prepare a vertical analysis of the balance sheet data for 2025 and 2024. Express each amount as a percentage of total assets.
2. Prepare a horizontal analysis for 2025 using 2024 as the base year.

**E12–5** The 2024 income statement of Adrian Express reports sales of $19,310,000, cost of goods sold of $12,250,000, and net income of $1,700,000. Balance sheet information is provided in the following table.

*Evaluate asset management and risk ratios (LO12–5, 12–6)*

**ADRIAN EXPRESS**
**Balance Sheets**
**December 31, 2024 and 2023**

| | 2024 | 2023 |
|---|---|---|
| **Assets** | | |
| Current assets: | | |
| Cash | $ 700,000 | $ 860,000 |
| Accounts receivable | 1,600,000 | 1,100,000 |
| Inventory | 2,000,000 | 1,500,000 |
| Long-term assets | 4,900,000 | 4,340,000 |
| Total assets | $9,200,000 | $7,800,000 |
| **Liabilities and Stockholders' Equity** | | |
| Current liabilities | $1,920,000 | $1,760,000 |
| Long-term debt | 2,400,000 | 2,500,000 |
| Common stock | 1,900,000 | 1,900,000 |
| Retained earnings | 2,980,000 | 1,640,000 |
| Total liabilities and stockholders' equity | $9,200,000 | $7,800,000 |

Industry averages for the following four ratios are as follows:

| | |
|---|---|
| Average collection period | 25 days |
| Average days in inventory | 60 days |
| Current ratio | 2 to 1 |
| Debt to equity ratio | 35% |

**Required:**

1. Calculate the four ratios listed above for Adrian Express in 2024 assuming all sales are on credit and current liabilities consist of accounts payable and salaries payable.
2. Do you think the company is more or less efficient at managing its current assets than the industry average? Explain your answer.
3. Do you think the company is more risky or less risky than the industry average? Explain your answer.

**E12–6** Refer to the information for Adrian Express in E12–5. Industry averages for the following ratios are as follows:

*Evaluate return to shareholders and profitability ratios (LO12–3, 12–4)*

| | |
|---|---|
| Gross profit ratio | 45% |
| Return on assets | 25% |
| Profit margin | 15% |
| Asset turnover | 2.5 times |
| Return on equity | 35% |

**Required:**

1. Calculate the five ratios listed above for Adrian Express.
2. Do you think the company is more profitable or less profitable than the industry average? Explain your answer.

Calculate asset
management and risk
ratios (LO12–5, 12–6)

**E12–7** The balance sheets for Plasma Screens Corporation and additional information are provided below.

**PLASMA SCREENS CORPORATION**
**Balance Sheets**
**December 31, 2024 and 2023**

| | 2024 | 2023 |
|---|---|---|
| **Assets** | | |
| Current assets: | | |
| Cash | $ 242,000 | $ 130,000 |
| Accounts receivable | 98,000 | 102,000 |
| Inventory | 105,000 | 90,000 |
| Investments | 5,000 | 3,000 |
| Long-term assets: | | |
| Land | 580,000 | 580,000 |
| Equipment | 890,000 | 770,000 |
| Less: Accumulated depreciation | (528,000) | (368,000) |
| Total assets | $1,392,000 | $1,307,000 |
| **Liabilities and Stockholders' Equity** | | |
| Current liabilities: | | |
| Accounts payable | $ 109,000 | $ 95,000 |
| Interest payable | 7,000 | 13,000 |
| Income tax payable | 9,000 | 6,000 |
| Long-term liabilities: | | |
| Notes payable | 110,000 | 220,000 |
| Stockholders' equity: | | |
| Common stock | 800,000 | 800,000 |
| Retained earnings | 357,000 | 173,000 |
| Total liabilities and equity | $1,392,000 | $1,307,000 |

**Additional Information for 2024:**

1. Net income is $184,000.
2. Sales on account are $1,890,000.
3. Cost of goods sold is $1,394,250.

*Required:*

1. Calculate the following ratios for 2024:
   a. Receivables turnover ratio.
   b. Inventory turnover ratio.
   c. Current ratio.
   d. Acid-test ratio.
   e. Debt to equity ratio.
2. When we compare two companies, can one have a higher current ratio while the other has a higher acid-test ratio? Explain your answer.

Calculate return to
shareholders and
profitability ratios
(LO12–3, 12–4)

**E12–8** Refer to the information provided for Plasma Screens Corporation in E12–7.

*Required:*

1. Calculate the following ratios for 2024:
   a. Gross profit ratio.
   b. Return on assets.
   c. Profit margin.

  d. Asset turnover.
  e. Return on equity.
2. When we compare two companies, can one have a higher return on assets while the other has a higher return on equity? Explain your answer.

**E12–9** The following condensed information is reported by Sporting Collectibles.

Calculate return to shareholders, profitability, asset management, and valuation ratios (LO12–3, 12–4, 12–5, 12–7)

|  | 2024 | 2023 |
|---|---|---|
| **Income Statement Information** |  |  |
| Sales revenue | $14,820,000 | $9,400,000 |
| Cost of goods sold | 9,544,080 | 6,900,000 |
| Net income | 418,000 | 348,000 |
| **Balance Sheet Information** |  |  |
| Current assets | $ 1,700,000 | $1,600,000 |
| Long-term assets | 2,300,000 | 2,000,000 |
| Total assets | $ 4,000,000 | $3,600,000 |
| Current liabilities | $ 1,300,000 | $1,000,000 |
| Long-term liabilities | 1,400,000 | 1,400,000 |
| Common stock | 900,000 | 900,000 |
| Retained earnings | 400,000 | 300,000 |
| Total liabilities and stockholders' equity | $ 4,000,000 | $3,600,000 |
| **Market Information** |  |  |
| Stock price | $    12.00 | $    10.90 |
| Shares Outstanding | 278,666 | $  278,666 |

*Required:*
1. Calculate the following ratios for 2024:
   a. Gross profit ratio.
   b. Return on assets.
   c. Profit margin.
   d. Asset turnover.
   e. Return on equity.
   f. Price-earnings ratio.
2. Determine the amount of dividends paid to shareholders in 2024.

**E12–10** The income statement for Stretch-Tape Corporation reports net sales of $540,000 and net income of $65,700. Average total assets for the year are $900,000. Stockholders' equity at the beginning of the year was $600,000, and $30,000 was paid to stockholders as dividends during the year. The stock price of the 262,800 shares outstanding at the end of the year was $2.50. There were no other stockholders' equity transactions that occurred during the year.

Calculate return to shareholders, profitability, asset management, and valuation ratios (LO12–3, 12–4, 12–5, 12–7)

*Required:*
Calculate the return on assets, profit margin, asset turnover, return on equity, and price-earnings ratios.

**E12–11** As an auditor for Bernard and Thomas, you are responsible for determining the proper classification of income statement items in the audit of California Sports Grill.

Classify income statement items (LO12–8)

  a. One of the company's restaurants was destroyed in a forest fire that raged through Southern California. Uninsured losses from the fire are estimated to be $450,000.
  b. California Sports Grill has three operating divisions: restaurants, catering, and frozen retail foods. The company sells the frozen retail foods division of the business for a profit of $2.4 million in order to focus more on the restaurant and catering business.

c. An employee strike to increase wages and benefits shut down operations for several days at an estimated cost of $200,000.

d. A restaurant waiter slipped on a wet floor and sued the company. The employee won a settlement for $100,000, but California Sports Grill has not yet paid the settlement.

e. The company owns and operates over 40 restaurants but sold one restaurant this year at a gain of $650,000.

**Required:**
Indicate whether each item should be classified as discontinued operations, other revenues, or other expenses.

**Report discontinued operations (LO12–8)**

**E12–12** Brighton Bookstores has two divisions: books and electronics. The electronics division had another great year in 2024 with net sales of $11 million, cost of goods sold of $6.5 million, operating expenses of $3 million, and income tax expense of $375,000. The book division did not do as well and was sold during the year. The loss from operations and sale of the book division was $900,000 before taxes and $675,000 after taxes.

**Required:**
Prepare the multiple-step income statement for Brighton Bookstores, including the proper reporting for the discontinued book division.

**Report discontinued operations and other expenses (LO12–8)**

**E12–13** Shack Corporation has operating income of $1.7 million, a loss on sale of investments of $200,000, and income tax expense of $425,000 for the year ended December 31, 2024, before considering the following item: a $275,000 gain, after tax, from the disposal of an operating segment.

**Required:**
Prepare the 2024 multiple step income statement for Shack Corporation beginning with operating income.

**Distinguish between conservative and aggressive accounting practices (LO12–9)**

**E12–14** Dwight's Trophy Shop is considering the following accounting changes:

a. Increase the allowance for uncollectible accounts.

b. When costs are going up, change from LIFO to FIFO.

c. Change from the straight-line method of depreciation to declining-balance in the second year of equipment with a 10-year life.

d. Record a smaller expense for warranties.

**Required:**
Classify each accounting change as either conservative or aggressive.

**Distinguish between conservative and aggressive accounting practices (LO12–9)**

**E12–15** Attached is a schedule of five proposed changes at the end of the year.

| ($ in millions) | Before the Change | Proposed Change | After the Change |
|---|---|---|---|
| Net sales | $18,800 | (a) $200 | $19,000 |
| Cost of goods sold | 13,200 | (b) 400 | 13,600 |
| Operating expenses | 1,600 | (c) (100) | 1,500 |
| Other revenue | 500 | (d) 50 | 550 |
| Other expense | 450 | (e) (50) | 400 |
| Net income | $ 4,050 | | $ 4,050 |

**Required:**
1. Indicate whether each of the proposed changes is conservative, aggressive, or neutral.
2. Indicate whether the total effect of all the changes is conservative, aggressive, or neutral.

**E12–16** The following condensed information was reported by Peabody Toys, Inc., for 2024 and 2023:

Calculate the DuPont framework ratios **(LO12–10)**

| ($ in thousands) | 2024 | 2023 |
|---|---|---|
| **Income Statement Information** | | |
| Net sales | $5,200 | $4,200 |
| Net income | 180 | 124 |
| **Balance sheet Information** | | |
| Current assets | $ 800 | $ 750 |
| Property, plant, and equipment (net) | 1,100 | 950 |
| Total assets | $1,900 | $1,700 |
| Current liabilities | $ 600 | $ 450 |
| Long-term liabilities | 750 | 750 |
| Common stock | 400 | 400 |
| Retained earnings | 150 | 100 |
| Liabilities and stockholders' equity | $1,900 | $1,700 |

**Required:**

1. Determine the following components of the DuPont framework for 2024:
   a. Profit margin.
   b. Asset turnover.
   c. Equity multiplier (leverage).
   d. Return on equity.
2. Write an equation that relates these components in calculating ROE. Use the Peabody Toys data to show the equation is correct.

## PROBLEMS

Mc Graw Hill **connect**

**P12–1** Sports Emporium has two operating segments: sporting goods and sports apparel. The income statement for each operating segment is presented below.

Perform vertical analysis **(LO12–1)**

**SPORTS EMPORIUM**
**Income Statement**
**For the year ended December 31, 2024**

| | Sporting Goods | | Sports Apparel | |
|---|---|---|---|---|
| | Amount | % | Amount | % |
| Net sales | $1,800,000 | | $970,000 | |
| Cost of goods sold | 1,040,000 | | 440,000 | |
| Gross profit | 760,000 | | 530,000 | |
| Operating expenses | 450,000 | | 340,000 | |
| Operating income | 310,000 | | 190,000 | |
| Other income (expense) | 20,000 | | (15,000) | |
| Income before tax | 330,000 | | 175,000 | |
| Income tax expense | 80,000 | | 70,000 | |
| Net income | $ 250,000 | | $105,000 | |

**Required:**

1. Complete the "%" columns to be used in a vertical analysis of Sports Emporium's two operating segments. Express each amount as a percentage of sales.
2. Use vertical analysis to compare the profitability of the two operating segments. Which segment is more profitable?

Perform horizontal
analysis (LO12–2)

**P12–2** The income statements for Anything Tennis for the years ending December 31, 2024 and 2023, are provided below.

### ANYTHING TENNIS
### Income Statements
### For the years ended December 31

| | 2024 | 2023 | Increase (Decrease) Amount | % |
|---|---|---|---|---|
| Net sales | $3,500,000 | $2,620,000 | | |
| Cost of goods sold | 2,150,000 | 1,380,000 | | |
| Gross profit | 1,350,000 | 1,240,000 | | |
| Operating expenses | 810,000 | 630,000 | | |
| Operating income | 540,000 | 610,000 | | |
| Other income (expense) | 10,000 | 6,000 | | |
| Income before tax | 550,000 | 616,000 | | |
| Income tax expense | 100,000 | 140,000 | | |
| Net income | $ 450,000 | $ 476,000 | | |

**Required:**

1. Complete the "Amount" and "%" columns to be used in a horizontal analysis of the income statements for Anything Tennis.
2. Discuss the major fluctuations in income statement items during the year.

Perform vertical and
horizontal analysis
(LO12–1, 12–2)

**P12–3** The balance sheets for Sports Unlimited for 2024 and 2023 are provided below.

### SPORTS UNLIMITED
### Balance Sheets
### For the years ended December 31

| | 2024 | 2023 |
|---|---|---|
| **Assets** | | |
| Current assets: | | |
| Cash | $103,500 | $ 70,400 |
| Accounts receivable | 46,800 | 32,000 |
| Inventory | 44,550 | 71,200 |
| Prepaid rent | 7,200 | 3,600 |
| Long-term assets: | | |
| Investment in bonds | 54,900 | |
| Land | 117,450 | 141,600 |
| Equipment | 106,200 | 102,000 |
| Less: Accumulated depreciation | (30,600) | (20,800) |
| Total assets | $450,000 | $400,000 |
| **Liabilities and Stockholders' Equity** | | |
| Current liabilities: | | |
| Accounts payable | $ 30,150 | $ 46,800 |
| Interest payable | 7,200 | 3,600 |
| Income tax payable | 12,150 | 10,000 |
| Long-term liabilities: | | |
| Notes payable | 138,150 | 127,600 |
| Stockholders' equity: | | |
| Common stock | 144,000 | 144,000 |
| Retained earnings | 118,350 | 68,000 |
| Total liabilities and equity | $450,000 | $400,000 |

**Required:**

1. Prepare a vertical analysis of Sports Unlimited's 2024 and 2023 balance sheets. Express each amount as a percentage of total assets for that year.
2. Prepare a horizontal analysis of Sports Unlimited's 2024 balance sheet using 2023 as the base year.

**P12–4** The following income statement and balance sheets for Virtual Gaming Systems are provided.

Calculate asset management and risk ratios (LO12–5, 12–6)

**VIRTUAL GAMING SYSTEMS**
**Income Statement**
**For the year ended December 31, 2024**

| | | |
|---|---|---|
| Net sales | | $3,086,000 |
| Cost of goods sold | | 1,960,000 |
| Gross profit | | 1,126,000 |
| Expenses: | | |
| Operating expenses | $868,000 | |
| Depreciation expense | 32,000 | |
| Loss on sale of land | 9,000 | |
| Interest expense | 20,000 | |
| Income tax expense | 58,000 | |
| Total expenses | | 987,000 |
| Net income | | $  139,000 |

**VIRTUAL GAMING SYSTEMS**
**Balance Sheets**
**December 31**

| | 2024 | 2023 |
|---|---|---|
| **Assets** | | |
| Current assets: | | |
| Cash | $196,000 | $154,000 |
| Accounts receivable | 91,000 | 70,000 |
| Inventory | 115,000 | 145,000 |
| Prepaid rent | 13,000 | 7,200 |
| Long-term assets: | | |
| Investment in bonds | 115,000 | 0 |
| Land | 220,000 | 250,000 |
| Equipment | 280,000 | 220,000 |
| Less: Accumulated depreciation | (84,000) | (52,000) |
| Total assets | $946,000 | $794,200 |
| **Liabilities and Stockholders' Equity** | | |
| Current liabilities: | | |
| Accounts payable | $  76,000 | $  91,000 |
| Interest payable | 8,000 | 4,000 |
| Income tax payable | 20,000 | 15,000 |
| Long-term liabilities: | | |
| Notes payable | 295,000 | 235,000 |
| Stockholders' equity: | | |
| Common stock | 310,000 | 310,000 |
| Retained earnings | 237,000 | 139,200 |
| Total liabilities and equity | $946,000 | $794,200 |

*Required:*

Assuming that all sales were on account, calculate the following ratios for 2024.

1. Receivables turnover ratio.
2. Average collection period.
3. Inventory turnover ratio.
4. Average days in inventory.
5. Current ratio.
6. Acid-test ratio.
7. Debt to equity ratio.
8. Times interest earned ratio.

Calculate return to
shareholders, profitability,
asset management, and
valuation ratios (LO12–3,
12–4, 12–5, 12–7)

**P12–5** Data for Virtual Gaming Systems are provided in P12–4. Earnings per share for the year ended December 31, 2024, are $1.40. The closing stock price on December 31, 2024, is $28.30.

*Required:*

Calculate the following ratios for 2024.

1. Gross profit ratio.
2. Return on assets.
3. Profit margin.
4. Asset turnover.
5. Return on equity.
6. Price-earnings ratio.

Use ratios to
analyze financial
statements (LO12–3,
12–4, 12–5, 12–6)

**P12–6** Income statement and balance sheet data for Virtual Gaming Systems are provided below.

### VIRTUAL GAMING SYSTEMS
### Income Statements
### For the years ended December 31

|  | 2025 | 2024 |
|---|---|---|
| Net sales | $3,560,000 | $3,086,000 |
| Cost of goods sold | 2,490,000 | 1,960,000 |
| Gross profit | 1,070,000 | 1,126,000 |
| Expenses: |  |  |
| Operating expenses | 965,000 | 868,000 |
| Depreciation expense | 40,000 | 32,000 |
| Loss on sale of land | 0 | 9,000 |
| Interest expense | 23,000 | 20,000 |
| Income tax expense | 9,000 | 58,000 |
| Total expenses | 1,037,000 | 987,000 |
| Net income | $   33,000 | $  139,000 |

### VIRTUAL GAMING SYSTEMS
### Balance Sheets
### December 31

|  | 2025 | 2024 | 2023 |
|---|---|---|---|
| **Assets** |  |  |  |
| Current assets: |  |  |  |
| Cash | $ 216,000 | $196,000 | $154,000 |
| Accounts receivable | 90,000 | 91,000 | 70,000 |
| Inventory | 140,000 | 115,000 | 145,000 |
| Prepaid rent | 15,000 | 13,000 | 7,200 |
| Long-term assets: |  |  |  |
| Investment in bonds | 115,000 | 115,000 | 0 |
| Land | 310,000 | 220,000 | 250,000 |
| Equipment | 310,000 | 280,000 | 220,000 |
| Less: Accumulated depreciation | (124,000) | (84,000) | (52,000) |
| Total assets | $1,072,000 | $946,000 | $794,200 |
| **Liabilities and Stockholders' Equity** |  |  |  |
| Current liabilities: |  |  |  |
| Accounts payable | $ 161,000 | $ 76,000 | $ 91,000 |
| Interest payable | 12,000 | 8,000 | 4,000 |
| Income tax payable | 13,000 | 20,000 | 15,000 |
| Long-term liabilities: |  |  |  |
| Notes payable | 450,000 | 295,000 | 235,000 |
| Stockholders' equity: |  |  |  |
| Common stock | 310,000 | 310,000 | 310,000 |
| Retained earnings | 126,000 | 237,000 | 139,200 |
| Total liabilities and stockholders' equity | $1,072,000 | $946,000 | $794,200 |

*Required:*

1. Calculate the following asset management and risk ratios for 2024 and 2025:
   a. Receivables turnover ratio.
   b. Inventory turnover ratio.
   c. Current ratio.
   d. Debt to equity ratio.
2. Calculate the following return to shareholders and profitability ratios for 2024 and 2025:
   a. Gross profit ratio.
   b. Return on assets.
   c. Profit margin.
   d. Asset turnover.
3. Based on the ratios calculated, determine whether overall financial position improved from 2024 to 2025.

## DATA ANALYTICS

Visit Connect to view **Data Analytics** questions related to:

1. Applying Excel
2. Data Visualizations
3. Tableau Dashboard Activities
4. Applying Tableau

## ANSWERS TO THE SELF-STUDY QUESTIONS

1. b   2. a   3. d   4. b   5. a   6. a   7. d   8. d   9. d   10. c   11. d   12. c   13. b   14. a   15. d   16. d

**UNITED STATES**
**SECURITIES AND EXCHANGE COMMISSION**
**WASHINGTON, D.C. 20549**

## FORM 10-K

☒ ANNUAL REPORT PURSUANT TO SECTION 13 OR 15(d) OF THE SECURITIES EXCHANGE ACT OF 1934

**For the fiscal year ended February 1, 2020**

OR

☐ TRANSITION REPORT PURSUANT TO SECTION 13 OR 15(d) OF THE SECURITIES EXCHANGE ACT OF 1934

Commission file number: **1-33338**

# AMERICAN EAGLE OUTFITTERS, INC.

(Exact name of registrant as specified in its charter)

| **Delaware** | **13-2721761** |
|---|---|
| (State or other jurisdiction of incorporation or organization) | (I.R.S. Employer Identification No.) |
| **77 Hot Metal Street, Pittsburgh, PA** | **15203-2329** |
| (Address of principal executive offices) | (Zip Code) |

Registrant's telephone number, including area code: **(412) 432-3300**

Securities registered pursuant to Section 12(b) of the Act:

| Title of each class | Trading Symbol(s) | Name of each exchange on which registered |
|---|---|---|
| **Common Stock, $0.01 par value** | **AEO** | **New York Stock Exchange** |

Securities registered pursuant to Section 12(g) of the Act: **None**

Indicate by check mark if the registrant is a well-known seasoned issuer, as defined in Rule 405 of the Securities Act.   YES ☒   NO ☐

Indicate by check mark if the registrant is not required to file reports pursuant to Section 13 or Sections 15(d) of the Act.   YES ☐   NO ☒

Indicate by check mark whether the registrant (1) has filed all reports required to be filed by Section 13 or 15(d) of the Securities Exchange Act of 1934 during the preceding 12 months (or for such shorter period that the registrant was required to file such reports), and (2) has been subject to the filing requirements for at the past 90 days.   YES ☒   NO ☐

Indicate by check mark whether the registrant has submitted electronically every Interactive Data File required to be submitted pursuant to Rule 405 of Regulation S-T (§232.405 of this chapter) during the preceding 12 months (or for such shorter period that the registrant was required to submit such files).   YES ☒   NO ☐

Indicate by check mark whether the registrant is a large accelerated filer, an accelerated filer, a non-accelerated filer, a smaller reporting company, or an emerging growth company. See the definitions of "large accelerated filer," "accelerated filer," "smaller reporting company," and "emerging growth company" in Rule 12b-2 of the Exchange Act.

| | | | |
|---|---|---|---|
| Large accelerated filer | ☒ | Accelerated filer | ☐ |
| Non-accelerated filer | ☐ | Smaller reporting company | ☐ |
| | | Emerging growth company | ☐ |

If an emerging growth company, indicate by check mark if the registrant has elected not to use the extended transition period for complying with any new or revised financial accounting standards provided pursuant to Section 13(a) of the Exchange Act. ☐

Indicate by check mark whether the registrant is a shell company (as defined in Rule 12b-2 of the Act).   YES ☐   NO ☒

The aggregate market value of voting and non-voting common equity held by non-affiliates of the registrant as of August 3, 2019 was $2,507,621,307.

Indicate the number of shares outstanding of each of the registrant's classes of common stock, as of the latest practicable date: 167,203,263 Common Shares were outstanding at March 9, 2020.

**DOCUMENTS INCORPORATED BY REFERENCE**

Portions of the Company's Proxy Statement for the 2020 Annual Meeting of Stockholders are incorporated into Part III herein.

**For the complete annual report, go online to http://investors.ae.com/financials-and-filings/annual-reports-and-proxy/default.aspx.**

**Report of Independent Registered Public Accounting Firm (in part)**

To the Stockholders and the Board of Directors of American Eagle Outfitters, Inc.

## Opinion on the Financial Statements

We have audited the accompanying consolidated balance sheets of American Eagle Outfitters, Inc. (the Company) as of February 1, 2020 and February 2, 2019, the related consolidated statements of operations, comprehensive income, stockholders' equity and cash flows for each of the three years in the period ended February 1, 2020, and the related notes (collectively referred to as the "consolidated financial statements"). In our opinion, the consolidated financial statements present fairly, in all material respects, the financial position of the Company at February 1, 2020 and February 2, 2019, and the results of its operations and its cash flows for each of the three years in the period ended February 1, 2020, in conformity with U.S. generally accepted accounting principles.

We also have audited, in accordance with the standards of the Public Company Accounting Oversight Board (United States) (PCAOB), the Company's internal control over financial reporting as of February 1, 2020, based on criteria established in Internal Control-Integrated Framework issued by the Committee of Sponsoring Organizations of the Treadway Commission (2013 Framework), and our report dated March 12, 2020 expressed an unqualified opinion thereon.

## Adoption of ASU No. 2016-02

As discussed in the paragraph under the caption "Recent Accounting Pronouncements" described in Note 2 to the consolidated financial statements, effective February 3, 2019, the Company changed its method of accounting for leases due to the adoption of Accounting Standards Update No. 2016-02, *Leases* (Topic 842).

## Basis for Opinion

These financial statements are the responsibility of the Company's management. Our responsibility is to express an opinion on the Company's financial statements based on our audits. We are a public accounting firm registered with the PCAOB and are required to be independent with respect to the Company in accordance with the U.S. federal securities laws and the applicable rules and regulations of the Securities and Exchange Commission and the PCAOB.

We conducted our audits in accordance with the standards of the PCAOB. Those standards require that we plan and perform the audit to obtain reasonable assurance about whether the financial statements are free of material misstatement, whether due to error or fraud. Our audits included performing procedures to assess the risks of material misstatement of the financial statements, whether due to error or fraud, and performing procedures that respond to those risks. Such procedures included examining, on a test basis, evidence regarding the amounts and disclosures in the financial statements. Our audits also included evaluating the accounting principles used and significant estimates made by management, as well as evaluating the overall presentation of the financial statements. We believe that our audits provide a reasonable basis for our opinion.

/s/ Ernst & Young LLP

We have served as the Company's auditor since 1993.
Pittsburgh, Pennsylvania
March 12, 2020

## AMERICAN EAGLE OUTFITTERS, INC.
### Consolidated Balance Sheets

| (In thousands, except per share amounts) | | February 1, 2020 | | February 2, 2019 |
|---|---|---|---|---|
| **Assets** | | | | |
| Current assets: | | | | |
| Cash and cash equivalents | $ | 361,930 | $ | 333,330 |
| Short-term investments (available for sale) | | 55,000 | | 92,135 |
| Merchandise inventory | | 446,278 | | 424,404 |
| Accounts receivable, net | | 119,064 | | 93,477 |
| Prepaid expenses and other | | 65,658 | | 102,907 |
| Total current assets | | 1,047,930 | | 1,046,253 |
| Property and equipment, at cost, net of accumulated depreciation | | 735,120 | | 742,149 |
| Operating lease right-of-use assets | | 1,418,916 | | - |
| Intangible assets, net, including goodwill | | 53,004 | | 58,167 |
| Non-current deferred income taxes | | 22,724 | | 14,062 |
| Other assets | | 50,985 | | 42,747 |
| Total assets | $ | 3,328,679 | $ | 1,903,378 |
| | | | | |
| **Liabilities and Stockholders' Equity** | | | | |
| Current liabilities: | | | | |
| Accounts payable | $ | 285,746 | $ | 240,671 |
| Current portion of operating lease liabilities | | 299,161 | | - |
| Accrued income and other taxes | | 9,514 | | 20,064 |
| Accrued compensation and payroll taxes | | 43,537 | | 82,173 |
| Unredeemed gift cards and gift certificates | | 56,974 | | 53,997 |
| Other current liabilities and accrued expenses | | 56,824 | | 145,740 |
| Total current liabilities | | 751,756 | | 542,645 |
| Non-current liabilities: | | | | |
| Non-current operating lease liabilities | | 1,301,735 | | - |
| Other non-current liabilities | | 27,335 | | 73,178 |
| Total non-current liabilities | | 1,329,070 | | 73,178 |
| Commitments and contingencies | | — | | — |
| Stockholders' equity: | | | | |
| Preferred stock, $0.01 par value; 5,000 shares authorized; none issued and outstanding | | — | | — |
| Common stock, $0.01 par value; 600,000 shares authorized; 249,566 shares issued; 166,993 and 172,436 shares outstanding, respectively | | 2,496 | | 2,496 |
| Contributed capital | | 577,856 | | 574,929 |
| Accumulated other comprehensive loss, net of tax | | (33,168) | | (34,832) |
| Retained earnings | | 2,108,292 | | 2,054,654 |
| Treasury stock, 82,573 and 77,130 shares, respectively, at cost | | (1,407,623) | | (1,309,692) |
| Total stockholders' equity | | 1,247,853 | | 1,287,555 |
| Total liabilities and stockholders' equity | $ | 3,328,679 | $ | 1,903,378 |

## AMERICAN EAGLE OUTFITTERS, INC.
### Consolidated Statements of Operations

| | | | | For the Years Ended | | |
|---|---|---|---|---|---|---|
| (In thousands, except per share amounts) | | February 1, 2020 | | February 2, 2019 | | February 3, 2018 |
| Total net revenue | $ | 4,308,212 | $ | 4,035,720 | $ | 3,795,549 |
| Cost of sales, including certain buying, occupancy and warehousing expenses | | 2,785,911 | | 2,548,082 | | 2,425,044 |
| Gross profit | | 1,522,301 | | 1,487,638 | | 1,370,505 |
| Selling, general and administrative expenses | | 1,029,412 | | 980,610 | | 879,685 |
| Impairment and restructuring charges | | 80,494 | | 1,568 | | 20,611 |
| Depreciation and amortization expense | | 179,050 | | 168,331 | | 167,421 |
| Operating income | | 233,345 | | 337,129 | | 302,788 |
| Other income (expense), net | | 11,933 | | 7,971 | | (15,615) |
| Income before income taxes | | 245,278 | | 345,100 | | 287,173 |
| Provision for income taxes | | 54,021 | | 83,198 | | 83,010 |
| Net income | $ | 191,257 | $ | 261,902 | $ | 204,163 |
| | | | | | | |
| Basic net income per common share | $ | 1.13 | $ | 1.48 | $ | 1.15 |
| | | | | | | |
| Diluted net income per common share | $ | 1.12 | $ | 1.47 | $ | 1.13 |
| | | | | | | |
| Weighted average common shares outstanding - basic | | 169,711 | | 176,476 | | 177,938 |
| Weighted average common shares outstanding - diluted | | 170,867 | | 178,035 | | 180,156 |

Refer to Notes to Consolidated Financial Statements

## AMERICAN EAGLE OUTFITTERS, INC.
### Consolidated Statements of Comprehensive Income

| (In thousands) | For the Years Ended | | |
| --- | --- | --- | --- |
| | February 1, 2020 | February 2, 2019 | February 3, 2018 |
| Net income | $ 191,257 | $ 261,902 | $ 204,163 |
| Other comprehensive gain (loss): | | | |
| Foreign currency translation gain (loss) | 1,664 | (4,037) | 5,667 |
| Other comprehensive gain (loss) | 1,664 | (4,037) | 5,667 |
| Comprehensive income | $ 192,921 | $ 257,865 | $ 209,830 |

## AMERICAN EAGLE OUTFITTERS, INC.
### Consolidated Statements of Stockholders' Equity

| (In thousands, except per share amounts) | Shares Outstanding (1) | Common Stock | Contributed Capital | Retained Earnings | Treasury Stock (2) | Accumulated Other Comprehensive Income (Loss) | Stockholders' Equity |
| --- | --- | --- | --- | --- | --- | --- | --- |
| Balance at January 28, 2017 | 181,886 | $ 2,496 | $ 603,890 | $ 1,775,775 | $ (1,141,130) | $ (36,462) | $ 1,204,569 |
| Stock awards | — | — | 17,202 | — | — | — | 17,202 |
| Repurchase of common stock as part of publicly announced programs | (6,000) | — | — | — | (87,672) | — | (87,672) |
| Repurchase of common stock from employees | (871) | — | — | — | (12,513) | — | (12,513) |
| Reissuance of treasury stock | 2,301 | — | (29,632) | (5,488) | 39,043 | — | 3,923 |
| Net income | — | — | — | 204,163 | — | — | 204,163 |
| Other comprehensive loss | — | — | — | — | — | 5,667 | 5,667 |
| Cash dividends and dividend equivalents ($0.50 per share) | — | — | 2,310 | (90,858) | — | — | (88,548) |
| Balance at February 3, 2018 | 177,316 | $ 2,496 | $ 593,770 | $ 1,883,592 | $ (1,202,272) | $ (30,795) | $ 1,246,791 |
| Stock awards | — | — | 27,057 | — | — | — | 27,057 |
| Repurchase of common stock as part of publicly announced programs | (7,300) | — | — | — | (144,405) | — | (144,405) |
| Repurchase of common stock from employees | (943) | — | — | — | (19,668) | — | (19,668) |
| Reissuance of treasury stock | 3,363 | — | (48,022) | 8,407 | 56,653 | — | 17,038 |
| Net income | — | — | — | 261,902 | — | — | 261,902 |
| Other comprehensive loss | — | — | — | — | — | (4,037) | (4,037) |
| Cash dividends and dividend equivalents ($0.55 per share) | — | — | 2,124 | (99,247) | — | — | (97,123) |
| Balance at February 2, 2019 | 172,436 | $ 2,496 | $ 574,929 | $ 2,054,654 | $ (1,309,692) | $ (34,832) | $ 1,287,555 |
| Stock awards | — | — | 22,742 | — | — | — | 22,742 |
| Repurchase of common stock as part of publicly announced programs | (6,336) | — | — | — | (112,381) | — | (112,381) |
| Repurchase of common stock from employees | (431) | — | — | — | (8,087) | — | (8,087) |
| Adoption of ASC 842, net of tax | — | — | — | (44,435) | — | — | (44,435) |
| Reissuance of treasury stock | 1,324 | — | (22,175) | 1,959 | 22,537 | — | 2,321 |
| Net income | — | — | — | 191,257 | — | — | 191,257 |
| Other comprehensive loss | — | — | — | — | — | 1,664 | 1,664 |
| Cash dividends and dividend equivalents ($0.55 per share) | — | — | 2,360 | (95,143) | — | — | (92,783) |
| Balance at February 1, 2020 | 166,993 | $ 2,496 | $ 577,856 | $ 2,108,292 | $ (1,407,623) | $ (33,168) | $ 1,247,853 |

(1)   600,000 authorized, 249,566 issued and 166,993 outstanding, $0.01 par value common stock at February 1, 2020; 600,000 authorized, 249,566 issued and 172,436 outstanding, $0.01 par value common stock at February 2, 2019; 600,000 authorized, 249,566 issued and 177,316 outstanding, $0.01 par value common stock at February 3, 2018; 600,000 authorized, 249,566 issued and 181,886 outstanding, $0.01 par value common stock at January 28, 2017. The Company has 5,000 authorized, with none issued or outstanding, $0.01 par value preferred stock for all periods presented.

(2)   82,573 shares, 77,130 shares and 72,250 shares at February 1, 2020, February 2, 2019 and February 3, 2018 respectively. During Fiscal 2019, Fiscal 2018, and Fiscal 2017, 1,324 shares, 3,363 shares, and 2,301 shares, respectively, were reissued from treasury stock for the issuance of share-based payments.

Refer to Notes to Consolidated Financial Statements

# AMERICAN EAGLE OUTFITTERS, INC.
## Consolidated Statements of Cash Flows

|  | For the Years Ended | | |
|---|---|---|---|
| (In thousands) | February 1, 2020 | February 2, 2019 | February 3, 2018 |
| Operating activities: | | | |
| Net income | $ 191,257 | $ 261,902 | $ 204,163 |
| Adjustments to reconcile net income to net cash provided by operating activities | | | |
| Depreciation and amortization | 181,379 | 170,504 | 169,473 |
| Share-based compensation | 23,038 | 27,506 | 16,890 |
| Deferred income taxes | 6,541 | (4,391) | 44,312 |
| Loss on impairment of assets | 66,252 | 546 | — |
| Changes in assets and liabilities: | | | |
| Merchandise inventory | (21,615) | (28,496) | (35,912) |
| Operating lease assets | 261,303 | — | — |
| Operating lease liabilities | (271,519) | — | — |
| Other assets | (32,845) | (22,206) | 13,755 |
| Accounts payable | 44,949 | 4,329 | (16,663) |
| Accrued compensation and payroll taxes | (38,603) | 28,043 | 1,289 |
| Accrued and other liabilities | 5,279 | 18,908 | (2,881) |
| Net cash provided by operating activities | 415,416 | 456,645 | 394,426 |
| Investing activities: | | | |
| Capital expenditures for property and equipment | (210,360) | (189,021) | (169,469) |
| Purchase of available-for-sale investments | (85,000) | (202,912) | — |
| Sale of available-for-sale investments | 122,135 | 109,776 | — |
| Other investing activities | (1,669) | (672) | (2,681) |
| Net cash used for investing activities | (174,894) | (282,829) | (172,150) |
| Financing activities: | | | |
| Repurchase of common stock as part of publicly announced programs | (112,381) | (144,405) | (87,682) |
| Repurchase of common stock from employees | (8,087) | (19,668) | (12,513) |
| Net proceeds from stock options exercised | 2,119 | 15,495 | 3,355 |
| Cash dividends paid | (92,783) | (97,123) | (88,548) |
| Other financing activities | (94) | (6,802) | (3,384) |
| Net cash used for financing activities | (211,226) | (252,503) | (188,772) |
| Effect of exchange rates on cash | (696) | (1,596) | 1,496 |
| Net change in cash and cash equivalents | 28,600 | (80,283) | 35,000 |
| Cash and cash equivalents - beginning of period | $ 333,330 | $ 413,613 | $ 378,613 |
| Cash and cash equivalents - end of period | 361,930 | 333,330 | 413,613 |

Refer to Notes to Consolidated Financial Statements

**AMERICAN EAGLE OUTFITTERS, INC.**

**Notes to Consolidated Financial Statements**
**For the Year Ended February 1, 2020**

## 1. Business Operations

American Eagle Outfitters, Inc. (the "Company," "we" and "our"), a Delaware corporation, operates under the American Eagle® ("AE") and Aerie® brands. We also operate Tailgate, a vintage, sports-inspired apparel brand with a college town store concept, and Todd Snyder New York, a premium menswear brand.

Founded in 1977, the Company is a leading multi-brand specialty retailer that operates more than 1,000 retail stores in the U.S. and internationally, online at www.ae.com and www.aerie.com, www.toddsnyder.com and more than 200 international store locations managed by third-party operators. Through its portfolio of brands, the Company offers high quality, on-trend clothing, accessories, and personal care products at affordable prices. The Company's online business, AEO Direct, ships to 81 countries worldwide.

### Merchandise Mix

The following table sets forth the approximate consolidated percentage of total net revenue from operations attributable to each merchandise group for each of the periods indicated:

|  | For the Years Ended | | |
|---|---|---|---|
|  | February 1, 2020 | February 2, 2019 | February 3, 2018 |
| Men's apparel and accessories | 29% | 32% | 34% |
| Women's apparel and accessories (excluding Aerie) | 52% | 52% | 53% |
| Aerie | 19% | 16% | 13% |
| Total | 100% | 100% | 100% |

## 2. Summary of Significant Accounting Policies

### Principles of Consolidation

The Consolidated Financial Statements include the accounts of the Company and its wholly owned subsidiaries. All intercompany transactions and balances have been eliminated in consolidation. At February 1, 2020, the Company operated in one reportable segment.

### Fiscal Year

Our fiscal year is a 52- or 53-week year that ends on the Saturday nearest to January 31. As used herein, "Fiscal 2020" refers to the 52-week period that will end on January 30, 2021. "Fiscal 2019" refers to the 52-week period ended February 1, 2020. "Fiscal 2018" refers to the 52-week period ended February 2, 2019. "Fiscal 2017" refers to the 53-week period ended February 3, 2018.

### Estimates

The preparation of financial statements in conformity with accounting principles generally accepted in the United States of America ("GAAP") requires the Company's management to make estimates and assumptions that affect the reported amounts of assets and liabilities and disclosure of contingent assets and liabilities at the date of the financial statements and the reported amounts of revenues and expenses during the reporting period. Actual results could differ from those estimates. On an ongoing basis, our management reviews its estimates based on currently available information. Changes in facts and circumstances may result in revised estimates.

### Cash, Cash Equivalents, and Short-term Investments

The Company considers all highly liquid investments purchased with a remaining maturity of three months or less to be cash equivalents.

Short-term investments classified as available-for-sale included certificates of deposit as of February 1, 2020, and they included certificates of deposit and commercial paper with a maturity of greater than three months, but less than one year as of February 2, 2019.

Refer to Note 3 to the Consolidated Financial Statements for information regarding cash, cash equivalents, and short-term investments.

### Merchandise Inventory

Merchandise inventory is valued at the lower of average cost or net realizable value, utilizing the retail method. Average cost includes merchandise design and sourcing costs and related expenses. The Company records merchandise receipts when control of the merchandise has transferred to the Company.

The Company reviews its inventory levels to identify slow-moving merchandise and generally uses markdowns to clear merchandise. Additionally, the Company estimates a markdown reserve for future planned permanent markdowns related to current inventory. Markdowns may occur when inventory exceeds customer demand for reasons of style, seasonal adaptation, changes in customer preference, lack of consumer acceptance of fashion items, competition, or if it is determined that the inventory in stock will not sell at its currently ticketed price. Such markdowns may have a material adverse impact on earnings, depending on the extent and amount of inventory affected.

The Company also estimates a shrinkage reserve for the period between the last physical count and the balance sheet date. The estimate for the shrinkage reserve, based on historical results, can be affected by changes in merchandise mix and changes in actual shrinkage trends.

### Property and Equipment

Property and equipment is recorded on the basis of cost with depreciation computed utilizing the straight-line method over the assets' estimated useful lives. The useful lives of our major classes of assets are as follows:

| | |
|---|---|
| Buildings | 25 years |
| Leasehold improvements | Lesser of 10 years or the term of the lease |
| Fixtures and equipment | Five years |
| Information technology | Three - five years |

As of February 1, 2020, the weighted average remaining useful life of our assets was approximately 7.5 years.

In accordance with ASC 360, *Property, Plant, and Equipment* ("ASC 360"), the Company's management evaluates the value of leasehold improvements, store fixtures, and operating lease ROU assets associated with retail stores, which have been open for a period sufficient to reach maturity. The Company evaluates long-lived assets for impairment at the individual store level, which is the lowest level at which individual cash flows can be identified. Impairment losses are recorded on long-lived assets used in operations when events and circumstances indicate that the assets might be impaired and the projected undiscounted cash flows estimated to be generated by those assets are less than the carrying amounts. When events such as these occur, the impaired assets are adjusted to their estimated fair value and an impairment loss is recorded separately as a component of operating income under impairment and restructuring charges.

During Fiscal 2019, the Company recorded asset impairment charges of $64.5 million on the assets of 20 retail stores. Of the total, $39.5 million related to the impairment of leasehold improvements and store fixtures, and $25.0 million related to the impairment of operating lease ROU assets. The impairments were recorded as a result of store performance up to and including the holiday selling season and a significant portfolio review in the fourth quarter of Fiscal 2019 that considered current and future performance projections and strategic real estate initiatives. The Company determined that these stores would not be able to generate sufficient cash flows over the expected remaining lease term to recover the carrying value of the respective stores' assets.

During Fiscal 2018, the Company recorded no significant asset impairment charges.

When the Company closes, remodels, or relocates a store prior to the end of its lease term, the remaining net book value of the assets related to the store is recorded as a write-off of assets within depreciation and amortization expense.

Refer to Note 7 to the Consolidated Financial Statements for additional information regarding property and equipment, and refer to Note 15 for additional information regarding impairment charges.

## Intangible Assets, including Goodwill

The Company's goodwill is primarily related to the acquisition of its importing operations, Canada business, and Tailgate and Todd Snyder brands. In accordance with ASC 350, *Intangibles – Goodwill and Other* ("ASC 350"), the Company evaluates goodwill for possible impairment on at least an annual basis and last performed an annual impairment test as of February 1, 2020. As a result, the Company concluded that certain goodwill was impaired resulting in a $1.7 million charge included within impairment and restructuring charges in the Consolidated Statements of Operations. There were no goodwill impairment charges recorded during Fiscal 2018.

Definite-lived intangible assets are recorded on the basis of cost with amortization computed utilizing the straight-line method over the assets' estimated useful lives. The Company's definite-lived intangible assets, which consist primarily of trademark assets, are generally amortized over 15 to 25 years.

The Company evaluates definite-lived intangible assets for impairment in accordance with ASC 360 when events or circumstances indicate that the carrying value of the asset may not be recoverable. Such an evaluation includes the estimation of undiscounted future cash flows to be generated by those assets. If the sum of the estimated future undiscounted cash flows is less than the carrying amounts of the assets, then the assets are impaired and are adjusted to their estimated fair value. No definite-lived intangible asset impairment charges were recorded for all periods presented.

Refer to Note 8 to the Consolidated Financial Statements for additional information regarding intangible assets, including goodwill.

## Gift Cards

Revenue is not recorded on the issuance of gift cards. The value of a gift card is recorded as a current liability upon issuance and revenue is recognized when the gift card is redeemed for merchandise. The Company estimates gift card breakage and recognizes revenue in proportion to actual gift card redemptions as a component of total net revenue.

The Company determines an estimated gift card breakage rate by continuously evaluating historical redemption data and the time when there is a remote likelihood that a gift card will be redeemed. The Company recorded $9.5 million, $8.9 million, and $10.1 million during Fiscal 2019, Fiscal 2018, and Fiscal 2017, respectively, of revenue related to gift card breakage.

## Customer Loyalty Program

In 2017, the Company launched a highly digitized loyalty program called AEO Connected™ (the "Program"). This Program integrates the credit card rewards program and the AEREWARDS® loyalty program into one combined customer offering. Under the Program, customers accumulate points based on purchase activity and earn rewards by reaching certain point thresholds. Customers earn rewards in the form of discount savings certificates. Rewards earned are valid through the stated expiration date, which is 45 days from the issuance date of the reward. Rewards not redeemed during the 45-day redemption period are forfeited. Additional rewards are also given for key items such as jeans and bras.

Points earned under the Program on purchases at American Eagle and Aerie are accounted for in accordance with ASC 606. The portion of the sales revenue attributed to the award points is deferred and recognized when the award is redeemed or when the points expire, using the relative stand-alone selling price method. Additionally, reward points earned using the co-branded credit card on non-AE or Aerie purchases are accounted for in accordance with ASC 606. As the points are earned, a current liability is recorded for the estimated cost of the award, and the impact of the adjustments are recorded in revenue.

## Sales Return Reserve

Revenue is recorded net of estimated and actual sales returns and deductions for coupon redemptions and other promotions. The Company records the impact of adjustments to its sales return reserve quarterly within total net revenue and cost of sales. The sales return reserve reflects an estimate of sales returns based on projected merchandise returns determined using historical average return percentages.

| | For the Years Ended | | |
| --- | --- | --- | --- |
| (In thousands) | February 1, 2020 | February 2, 2019 | February 3, 2018 |
| Beginning balance | $   4,620 | $   4,717 | $   3,639 |
| Returns | (121,513) | (113,805) | (103,393) |
| Provisions | 122,718 | 113,708 | 104,471 |
| Ending balance | $   5,825 | $   4,620 | $   4,717 |

The presentation on a gross basis consists of a separate right of return asset and liability. These amounts are recorded within (i) prepaid expenses and other and (ii) other current liabilities and accrued expenses, respectively, on the Consolidated Balance Sheets.

## Income Taxes

The Company calculates income taxes in accordance with ASC 740, *Income Taxes* ("ASC 740"), which requires the use of the asset and liability method. Under this method, deferred tax assets and liabilities are recognized based on the difference between the Consolidated Financial Statement carrying amounts of existing assets and liabilities and their respective tax bases as computed pursuant to ASC 740. Deferred tax assets and liabilities are measured using the tax rates, based on certain judgments regarding enacted tax laws and published guidance, in effect in the years when those temporary differences are expected to reverse. A valuation allowance is established against the deferred tax assets when it is more likely than not that some portion or all of the deferred taxes may not be realized. Changes in the Company's level and composition of earnings, tax laws or the deferred tax valuation allowance, as well as the results of tax audits, may materially affect the Company's effective income tax rate.

The Company evaluates its income tax positions in accordance with ASC 740, which prescribes a comprehensive model for recognizing, measuring, presenting, and disclosing in the financial statements tax positions taken or expected to be taken on a tax return, including a decision whether to file or not to file in a particular jurisdiction. Under ASC 740, a tax benefit from an uncertain position may be recognized only if it is more likely than not that the position is sustainable based on its technical merits.

The calculation of the deferred tax assets and liabilities, as well as the decision to recognize a tax benefit from an uncertain position and to establish a valuation allowance require management to make estimates and assumptions. The Company believes that its assumptions and estimates are reasonable, although actual results may have a positive or negative material impact on the balances of deferred tax assets and liabilities, valuation allowances or net income.

Refer to Note 14 to the Consolidated Financial Statements for additional information.

## Revenue Recognition

In May 2014, the FASB issued ASC 606, a comprehensive revenue recognition model that expands disclosure requirements and requires a company to recognize revenue to depict the transfer of goods or services to a customer at an amount that reflects the consideration it expects to receive in exchange for those goods or services. The Company adopted ASC 606 on February 4, 2018. Results for reporting periods beginning on or after February 4, 2018 are presented under ASC 606, while prior period amounts are not adjusted and continue to be reported in accordance with our historic accounting. The Company recorded a net increase to opening retained earnings of $0.2 million as of February 4, 2018 due to the cumulative impact of adoption. The impact was the result of accounting for customer loyalty programs using a relative stand-alone selling price method vs. incremental cost method. The Company defers a portion of the sales revenue attributed to the loyalty points and recognizes revenue when the points are redeemed or expire, consistent with the requirements of ASC 606. Refer to the Customer Loyalty Program caption above for additional information.

Revenue is recorded for store sales upon the purchase of merchandise by customers. The Company's e-commerce operation records revenue upon the estimated customer receipt date of the merchandise. Shipping and handling revenues are included in total net revenue on the Company's Consolidated Statements of Operations. Sales tax collected from customers is excluded from revenue and is included as part of accrued income and other taxes on the Company's Consolidated Balance Sheets.

Revenue is recorded net of estimated and actual sales returns and promotional price reductions. The Company records the impact of adjustments to its sales return reserve quarterly within total net revenue and cost of sales. The sales return reserve reflects an estimate of sales returns based on projected merchandise returns determined using historical average return percentages.

Revenue is not recorded on the issuance of gift cards. A current liability is recorded upon issuance, and revenue is recognized when the gift card is redeemed for merchandise. Additionally, the Company recognizes revenue on unredeemed gift cards based on an estimate of the amounts that will not be redeemed ("gift card breakage"), determined through historical redemption trends. Gift card breakage revenue is recognized in proportion to actual gift card redemptions as a component of total net revenue. For further information on the Company's gift card program, refer to the Gift Cards caption above.

The Company recognizes royalty revenue generated from its license or franchise agreements based upon a percentage of merchandise sales by the licensee/franchisee. This revenue is recorded as a component of total net revenue when earned and collection is probable.

## Cost of Sales, Including Certain Buying, Occupancy, and Warehousing Expenses

Cost of sales consists of merchandise costs, including design, sourcing, importing, and inbound freight costs, as well as markdowns, shrinkage and certain promotional costs (collectively "merchandise costs") and buying, occupancy and warehousing costs.

Design costs are related to the Company's Design Center operations and include compensation, travel and entertainment, supplies and samples for our design teams, as well as rent and depreciation for our Design Center. These costs are included in cost of sales as the respective inventory is sold.

Buying, occupancy and warehousing costs consist of: compensation, employee benefit expenses and travel and entertainment for our buyers and certain senior merchandising executives; rent and utilities related to our stores, corporate headquarters, distribution centers and other office space; freight from our distribution centers to the stores; compensation and supplies for our distribution centers, including purchasing, receiving and inspection costs; and shipping and handling costs related to our e-commerce operation. Gross profit is the difference between total net revenue and cost of sales.

## Selling, General, and Administrative Expenses

Selling, general, and administrative expenses consist of compensation and employee benefit expenses, including salaries, incentives, and related benefits associated with our stores and corporate headquarters. Selling, general, and administrative expenses also include advertising costs, supplies for our stores and home office, communication costs, travel, and entertainment, leasing costs and services purchased. Selling, general, and administrative expenses do not include compensation, employee benefit expenses and travel for our design, sourcing and importing teams, our buyers and our distribution centers as these amounts are recorded in cost of sales. Additionally, selling, general, and administrative expenses do not include rent and utilities related to our stores, operating costs of our distribution centers, and shipping and handling costs related to our e-commerce operations.

## Advertising Costs

Certain advertising costs, including direct mail, in-store photographs, and other promotional costs are expensed when the marketing campaign commences. As of February 1, 2020 and February 2, 2019, the Company had prepaid advertising expense of $14.5 million and $12.6 million, respectively. All other advertising costs are expensed as incurred. The Company recognized $151.5 million, $143.2 million, and $129.8 million in advertising expense during Fiscal 2019, Fiscal 2018, and Fiscal 2017, respectively.

## Store Pre-Opening Costs

Store pre-opening costs consist primarily of rent, advertising, supplies, and payroll expenses. These costs are expensed as incurred.

## Other Income (Expense), Net

Other income (expense), net consists primarily of foreign currency transaction gains (losses), interest income (expense), and realized investment gains (losses).

## Legal Proceedings and Claims

The Company is subject to certain legal proceedings and claims arising out of the conduct of its business. In accordance with ASC 450, *Contingencies* ("ASC 450"), the Company records a reserve for estimated losses when the loss is probable and the amount can be reasonably estimated. If a range of possible loss exists and no anticipated loss within the range is more likely than any other anticipated loss, the Company records the accrual at the low end of the range, in accordance with ASC 450. As the Company believes that it has provided adequate reserves, it anticipates that the ultimate outcome of any matter currently pending against the Company will not materially affect the consolidated financial position, results of operations or cash flows of the Company. However, our assessment of any litigation or other legal claims could potentially change in light of the discovery of facts not presently known or determinations by judges, juries, or other finders of fact that are not in accord with management's evaluation of the possible liability or outcome of such litigation or claims.

## Supplemental Disclosures of Cash Flow Information

The table below shows supplemental cash flow information for cash amounts paid during the respective periods:

|  | For the Years Ended | | |
|---|---|---|---|
| *(In thousands)* | February 1, 2020 | February 2, 2019 | February 3, 2018 |
| Cash paid during the periods for: | | | |
| Income taxes | $    69,689 | $    81,248 | $    47,094 |
| Interest | $       828 | $     1,207 | $     1,098 |

## 3. Cash, Cash Equivalents, and Short-term Investments

The following table summarizes the fair market value of our cash and short-term investments, which are recorded on the Consolidated Balance Sheets:

| *(In thousands)* | February 1, 2020 | February 2, 2019 |
|---|---|---|
| Cash and cash equivalents: | | |
| Cash | $    126,087 | $    108,216 |
| Interest bearing deposits | 235,843 | 165,274 |
| Commercial paper | — | 59,840 |
| Total cash and cash equivalents | $    361,930 | $    333,330 |
| Short-term investments: | | |
| Certificates of deposits | 55,000 | 70,000 |
| Commercial paper | — | 22,135 |
| Total short-term investments | 55,000 | 92,135 |
| Total cash and short-term investments | $    416,930 | $    425,465 |

## 4. Fair Value Measurements

ASC 820, *Fair Value Measurement Disclosures* ("ASC 820"), defines fair value, establishes a framework for measuring fair value in accordance with GAAP, and expands disclosures about fair value measurements. Fair value is defined under ASC 820 as the exit price associated with the sale of an asset or transfer of a liability in an orderly transaction between market participants at the measurement date.

## Financial Instruments

Valuation techniques used to measure fair value under ASC 820 must maximize the use of observable inputs and minimize the use of unobservable inputs. In addition, ASC 820 establishes a three-tier fair value hierarchy, which prioritizes the inputs used in measuring fair value. These tiers include:

- *Level 1* — Quoted prices in active markets.

- *Level 2* — Inputs other than Level 1 that are observable, either directly or indirectly.

- *Level 3* — Unobservable inputs that are supported by little or no market activity and that are significant to the fair value of the assets or liabilities.

The Company's cash equivalents and short-term investments are Level 1 financial assets and are measured at fair value on a recurring basis, for all periods presented. Refer to Note 3 to the Consolidated Financial Statements for additional information regarding cash equivalents and short-term investments.

The Company had no other financial instruments that required fair value measurement for any of the periods presented.

## Non-Financial Assets

The Company's non-financial assets, which include intangible assets and property and equipment, are not required to be measured at fair value on a recurring basis. However, if certain triggering events occur and the Company is required to evaluate the non-financial asset for impairment, a resulting impairment would require that the non-financial asset be recorded at the estimated fair value. During Fiscal 2019, the Company concluded that certain goodwill was impaired resulting in a $1.7 million charge included within impairment and restructuring charges in the Consolidated Statements of Operations. The measurement of the goodwill impairment included Level 3 measurements.

Certain long-lived assets were measured at fair value on a nonrecurring basis using Level 3 inputs as defined in ASC 820. During Fiscal 2019, the Company recorded asset impairment charges of $64.5 million on the assets of 20 retail stores. Of the total, $39.5 million related to the impairment of leasehold improvements and store fixtures and $25.0 million related to the impairment of operating lease ROU assets. The assets were adjusted to their fair value and the loss on impairment was recorded within impairment and restructuring charges in the Consolidated Statements of Operations. The fair value of the impaired assets on these stores, after the recorded loss, is approximately $145.2 million including $3.9 million of leasehold improvements and store fixtures and $141.3 million of operating lease ROU assets.

The fair value of the Company's stores was determined by estimating the amount and timing of net future cash flows and discounting them using a risk-adjusted rate of interest. The Company estimates future cash flows based on its experience and knowledge of the market in which the store is located.

## 5. Earnings per Share

The following is a reconciliation between basic and diluted weighted average shares outstanding:

|  | For the Years Ended | | |
|---|---|---|---|
| (In thousands, except per share amounts) | February 1, 2020 | February 2, 2019 | February 3, 2018 |
| Weighted average common shares outstanding: | | | |
| Basic number of common shares outstanding | 169,711 | 176,476 | 177,938 |
| Dilutive effect of stock options and non-vested restricted stock | 1,156 | 1,559 | 2,218 |
| Diluted number of common shares outstanding | 170,867 | 178,035 | 180,156 |
| | | | |
| Potentially issuable common shares excluded due to anti-dilutive effect | 700 | 393 | 3,082 |

Dilutive and anti-dilutive shares relate to share-based compensation.

Refer to Note 12 to the Consolidated Financial Statements for additional information regarding share-based compensation.

## 6. Accounts Receivable, net

Accounts receivable, net is comprised of the following:

| (In thousands) | February 1, 2020 | February 2, 2019 |
|---|---|---|
| Franchise and license receivable | $ 36,060 | $ 31,474 |
| Merchandise sell-offs and vendor receivables | 24,474 | 12,943 |
| Credit card program receivable | 30,578 | 21,129 |
| Tax refunds | 4,868 | 7,483 |
| Landlord construction allowances | 12,038 | 9,001 |
| Gift card receivable | 1,794 | 3,514 |
| Other items | 9,252 | 7,933 |
| Total | $ 119,064 | $ 93,477 |

## 7. Property and Equipment, net

Property and equipment, net consists of the following:

| (In thousands) | February 1, 2020 | February 2, 2019 |
|---|---|---|
| Land | $ 17,910 | $ 17,910 |
| Buildings | 211,814 | 209,487 |
| Leasehold improvements | 721,514 | 698,029 |
| Fixtures and equipment | 1,316,198 | 1,221,203 |
| Construction in progress | 46,992 | 34,221 |
| Property and equipment, at cost | $ 2,314,428 | $ 2,180,850 |
| Less:  Accumulated depreciation | (1,579,308) | (1,438,701) |
| Property and equipment, net | $ 735,120 | $ 742,149 |

Depreciation expense is as follows:

|  | For the Years Ended | | |
|---|---|---|---|
| (In thousands) | February 1, 2020 | February 2, 2019 | February 3, 2018 |
| Depreciation expense | $ 178,038 | $ 164,265 | $ 158,969 |

Additionally, during Fiscal 2019, Fiscal 2018, and Fiscal 2017, the Company recorded $4.3 million, $2.0 million and $6.0 million, respectively, related to asset write-offs within depreciation and amortization expense.

## 8. Intangible Assets, net, including Goodwill

Intangible assets, net, including goodwill, consists of the following:

| (In thousands) | February 1, 2020 | February 2, 2019 |
|---|---|---|
| Goodwill, gross | $ 17,353 | $ 17,383 |
| Accumulated impairment (1) | (4,196) | (2,484) |
| Goodwill, net | $ 13,157 | $ 14,899 |
| | | |
| Trademarks, at cost | 71,685 | 70,994 |
| Accumulated amortization | (31,838) | (27,726) |
| Trademarks, net | $ 39,847 | $ 43,268 |
| | | |
| Intangibles, net, including goodwill | $ 53,004 | $ 58,167 |

(1)   Accumulated impairment includes $2.5 million recorded in Fiscal 2016 and $1.7 million recorded in Fiscal 2019

Amortization expense is as follows:

|  | For the Years Ended | | |
|---|---|---|---|
| (In thousands) | February 1, 2020 | February 2, 2019 | February 3, 2018 |
| Amortization expense | $ 4,184 | $ 4,225 | $ 4,551 |

The table below summarizes the estimated future amortization expense for intangible assets existing as of February 1, 2020 for the next five Fiscal Years:

| (In thousands) | Future Amortization |
|---|---|
| 2020 | $ 3,493 |
| 2021 | $ 3,166 |
| 2022 | $ 3,164 |
| 2023 | $ 3,110 |
| 2024 | $ 2,902 |

## 9. Other Credit Arrangements

In January 2019, the Company entered into an amended and restated Credit Agreement ("Credit Agreement") for five-year, syndicated, asset-based revolving credit facilities (the "Credit Facilities"). The Credit Agreement provides senior secured revolving credit for loans and letters of credit up to $400 million, subject to customary borrowing base limitations. The Credit Facilities provide increased financial flexibility and take advantage of a favorable credit environment.

All obligations under the Credit Facilities are unconditionally guaranteed by certain subsidiaries. The obligations under the Credit Agreement are secured by a first-priority security interest in certain working capital assets of the borrowers and guarantors, consisting primarily of cash, receivables, inventory and certain other assets, and will be further secured by first-priority mortgages on certain real property.

As of February 1, 2020, the Company was in compliance with the terms of the Credit Agreement and had $7.9 million outstanding in stand-by letters of credit. No loans were outstanding under the Credit Agreement as of February 1, 2020 or at any time throughout Fiscal 2019.

## 10. Leases

The Company leases all store premises, some of its office space and certain information technology and office equipment. These leases are generally classified as operating leases.

Store leases generally provide for a combination of base rentals and contingent rent based on store sales. Additionally, most leases include lessor incentives such as construction allowances and rent holidays. The Company is typically responsible for tenant occupancy costs including maintenance costs, common area charges, real estate taxes, and certain other expenses.

Most leases include one or more options to renew. The exercise of lease renewal options is at the Company's discretion and is not reasonably certain at lease commencement. When measuring operating lease ROU assets and operating lease liabilities after the date of adoption of ASC 842 (February 3, 2019), the Company only includes cash flows related to options to extend or terminate leases once those options are executed.

Some leases have variable payments. However, because they are not based on an index or rate, they are not included in the measurement of operating lease ROU assets and operating lease liabilities.

When determining the present value of future payments for an operating lease that does not have a readily determinable implicit rate, the Company uses its incremental borrowing rate as of the date of initial possession of the leased asset.

For leases that qualify for the short-term lease exemption, the Company does not record an operating lease liability or operating lease ROU asset. Short-term lease payments are recognized on a straight-line basis over the lease term of 12 months or less.

The following table summarizes expense categories and cash payments for operating leases during the period. It also includes the total non-cash transaction activity for new operating lease ROU assets and related operating lease liabilities entered into during the period.

| (In thousands) | For the Year Ended February 1, 2020 |
|---|---|
| **Lease costs** | |
| Operating lease costs | $ 349,429 |
| Variable lease costs | 102,797 |
| Short-term leases and other lease costs | 37,293 |
| **Total lease costs** | $ 489,519 |
| | |
| **Other information** | |
| Cash paid for operating lease liability | $ (328,925) |
| New operating lease ROU asset entered into during the period | $ 277,562 |

The following table contains the average remaining lease term and discount rate, weighted by outstanding operating lease liability as of the end of the period:

| Lease term and discount rate | February 1, 2020 |
|---|---|
| Weighted-average remaining lease term - operating leases | 6.2 years |
| Weighted-average discount rate - operating leases | 5.1% |

The table below is a maturity analysis of the operating leases in effect as of the end of the period. Undiscounted cash flows for finance leases and short-term leases are not material for the periods reported and are excluded from the table below:

| (In thousands) | Undiscounted cash flows February 1, 2020 |
|---|---|
| Fiscal years: | |
| 2020 | $ 374,819 |
| 2021 | 331,578 |
| 2022 | 277,954 |
| 2023 | 255,695 |
| 2024 | 184,591 |
| Thereafter | 471,160 |
| Total undiscounted cash flows | $ 1,895,797 |
| Less: discount on lease liability | (294,901) |
| Total lease liability | $ 1,600,896 |

The Company adopted ASC 842 as of February 3, 2019 through the modified retrospective method. Prior period amounts have not been adjusted and continue to be reported in accordance with our historical accounting treatment. In accordance with the transition guidance within ASC 842, the following table provides the disclosures related to Fiscal Years 2018 and 2017 as required under ASC 840, *Leases*. Refer to Note 2 for further information about the Company's adoption of ASC 842.

| | For the Years Ended | | | |
| | February 2, 2019 | | February 3, 2018 | |
| *(In thousands)* | | | | |
| Store rent: | | | | |
| Fixed minimum | $ | 303,123 | $ | 298,458 |
| Contingent | | 13,883 | | 9,566 |
| Total store rent, excluding common area maintenance charges, real estate taxes and certain other expenses | $ | 317,006 | $ | 308,025 |
| Offices, distribution facilities, equipment and other | | 18,636 | | 26,960 |
| Total rent expense | $ | 335,642 | $ | 334,985 |

## 14. Income Taxes

On December 22, 2017, the U.S. government enacted comprehensive tax legislation in the form of the Tax Act. The Tax Act made broad and complex changes to the U.S. tax code including reducing the U.S. federal corporate tax rate from 35% to 21% effective January 1, 2018, and implementing a one-time transition tax on undistributed earnings of foreign subsidiaries. During the fourth quarter of Fiscal 2018, the Company completed its accounting for the tax effects of the Tax Act with no material net changes to the provisional amounts recorded for the one-time transition tax and the re-measurement of deferred tax assets and liabilities.

Additionally, the Tax Act included a provision designed to currently tax global intangible low-taxed income ("GILTI") earned by non-U.S. corporate subsidiaries of large U.S. shareholders starting in 2018. The Company has elected, as permitted in FASB Staff Q&A - Topic 740 - No. 5, to treat any future GILTI tax liabilities as period costs and will expense those liabilities in the period incurred. The Company therefore will not record deferred taxes associated with the GILTI provision of the Tax Act. The Company has no changes to this election for Fiscal 2019.

The components of income before income taxes from continuing operations were:

| | For the Years Ended | | | | | |
| | February 1, 2020 | | February 2, 2019 | | February 3, 2018 | |
| *(In thousands)* | | | | | | |
| U.S. | $ | 229,906 | $ | 308,424 | $ | 255,621 |
| Foreign | | 15,372 | | 36,676 | | 31,552 |
| Total | $ | 245,278 | $ | 345,100 | $ | 287,173 |

## 15. Impairment and Restructuring Charges

The following table represents impairment and restructuring charges. All amounts were recorded within impairment and restructuring charges on the Consolidated Statements of Operations, unless otherwise noted.

| | For the years ended | | | | | |
| | February 1, 2020 | | February 2, 2019 | | February 3, 2018 | |
| *(In thousands)* | | | | | | |
| Asset impairment charges [1] | $ | 66,252 | $ | — | $ | — |
| Severance and related employee costs | | 6,691 | | 1,568 | | 10,660 |
| Joint business venture exit charges [2] | | 4,194 | | — | | 7,964 |
| Japan market transition costs | | 1,814 | | — | | — |
| China restructuring [3] | | 1,543 | | — | | — |
| Lease termination and store closure costs | | — | | — | | 9,951 |
| Inventory charges [4] | | — | | — | | 1,669 |
| Total impairment and restructuring charges | $ | 80,494 | $ | 1,568 | $ | 30,244 |

[1]  Fiscal 2019 asset impairment charges of $64.5 million on the assets of 20 retail stores. Of the total, $39.5 million related to the impairment of leasehold improvements and store fixtures, and $25.0 million related to the impairment of operating lease ROU assets. The Company also concluded that certain goodwill was impaired resulting in a $1.7 million charge in Fiscal 2019.

[2]  Fiscal 2017 joint business venture exit charges were recorded within other (expense) income, net on the Consolidated Statements of Operations

[3]  Pre-tax corporate restructuring charges of $1.5 million, primarily consisting of severance and closure costs for our company-owned and operated stores in China recorded in the first quarter of Fiscal 2019

[4]  Fiscal 2017 inventory charges were recorded within cost of sales, including certain buying, occupancy, and warehousing expenses on the Consolidated Statements of Operations

A rollforward of the restructuring liabilities recognized in the Consolidated Balance Sheet is as follows:

| *(In thousands)* | February 1, 2020 | |
| Accrued liability as of February 2, 2019 | $ | 6,629 |
| Add: Costs incurred, excluding non-cash charges | | 10,686 |
| Less: Cash payments and adjustments | | (13,128) |
| Accrued liability as of February 1, 2020 | $ | 4,187 |

The accrued liability as of February 2, 2019 relates to previous restructuring activities disclosed in the Company's Fiscal 2018 Form 10-K, which remained unpaid at the beginning of Fiscal 2019.

## Item 9. Changes in and Disagreements with Accountants on Accounting and Financial Disclosure.

None.

## Item 9A. Controls and Procedures.

### Disclosure Controls and Procedures

We maintain disclosure controls and procedures that are designed to provide reasonable assurance that information required to be disclosed in our reports under the Securities Exchange Act of 1934, as amended (the "Exchange Act"), is recorded, processed, summarized and reported within the time periods specified in the SEC's rules and forms, and that such information is accumulated and communicated to the management of American Eagle Outfitters, Inc. (the "Management"), including our principal executive officer and our principal financial officer, as appropriate, to allow timely decisions regarding required disclosure. In designing and evaluating the disclosure controls and procedures, Management recognized that any controls and procedures, no matter how well designed and operated, can provide only reasonable assurance of achieving the desired control objectives.

As of the end of the period covered by this Annual Report on Form 10-K, the Company performed an evaluation under the supervision and with the participation of Management, including our principal executive officer and principal financial officer, of the design and effectiveness of our disclosure controls and procedures (as defined in Rules 13a-15(e) or 15d-15(e) under the Exchange Act). Based upon that evaluation, our principal executive officer and principal financial officer concluded that, as of the end of the period covered by this Annual Report, our disclosure controls and procedures were effective in the timely and accurate recording, processing, summarizing, and reporting of material financial and non-financial information within the periods specified within the SEC's rules and forms. Our principal executive officer and principal financial officer also concluded that our disclosure controls and procedures were effective to ensure that information required to be disclosed in the reports that we file or submit under the Exchange Act is accumulated and communicated to our Management, including our principal executive officer and principal financial officer, to allow timely decisions regarding required disclosure.

### Management's Annual Report on Internal Control over Financial Reporting

Our Management is responsible for establishing and maintaining adequate internal control over financial reporting (as defined in Rule 13a-15(f) or Rule 15(d)-15(f) under the Exchange Act). Our internal control over financial reporting is designed to provide a reasonable assurance to our Management and our Board that the reported financial information is presented fairly, that disclosures are adequate, and that the judgments inherent in the preparation of financial statements are reasonable.

All internal control systems, no matter how well designed, have inherent limitations, including the possibility of human error and the overriding of controls. Therefore, even those systems determined to be effective can provide only reasonable, not absolute, assurance with respect to financial statement preparation and presentation.

Our Management assessed the effectiveness of our internal control over financial reporting as of February 1, 2020. In making this assessment, our Management used the framework and criteria set forth in *Internal Control – Integrated Framework (2013)*, issued by the Committee of Sponsoring Organizations of the Treadway Commission (COSO). Based on this assessment, our Management concluded that the Company's internal control over financial reporting was effective as of February 1, 2020.

Our independent registered public accounting firm, Ernst & Young LLP, was retained to audit the Company's consolidated financial statements included in this Annual Report on Form 10-K and the effectiveness of the Company's internal control over financial reporting. Ernst & Young LLP has issued an attestation report on our internal control over financial reporting as of February 1, 2020, which is included herein.

### Changes in Internal Control over Financial Reporting

There were no changes in our internal control over financial reporting (as defined in Rules 13a-15(f) or 15d-15(f) of the Exchange Act) during our most recently-completed fiscal quarter that have materially affected, or are reasonably likely to materially affect, our internal control over financial reporting.

**Report of Independent Registered Public Accounting Firm**

To the Stockholders and the Board of Directors of American Eagle Outfitters, Inc.

**Opinion on Internal Control over Financial Reporting**

We have audited American Eagle Outfitters, Inc.'s internal control over financial reporting as of February 1, 2020, based on criteria established in Internal Control—Integrated Framework issued by the Committee of Sponsoring Organizations of the Treadway Commission (2013 framework) (the COSO criteria). In our opinion, American Eagle Outfitters, Inc. (the Company) maintained, in all material respects, effective internal control over financial reporting as of February 1, 2020, based on the COSO criteria.

We also have audited, in accordance with the standards of the Public Company Accounting Oversight Board (United States) (PCAOB), the consolidated balance sheets of the Company as of February 1, 2020 and February 2, 2019, the related consolidated statements of operations, comprehensive income, stockholders' equity and cash flows for each of the three years in the period ended February 1, 2020, and the related notes and our report dated March 12, 2020 expressed an unqualified opinion thereon.

**Basis for Opinion**

The Company's management is responsible for maintaining effective internal control over financial reporting and for its assessment of the effectiveness of internal control over financial reporting included in the accompanying Management's Annual Report on Internal Control over Financial Reporting. Our responsibility is to express an opinion on the Company's internal control over financial reporting based on our audit. We are a public accounting firm registered with the PCAOB and are required to be independent with respect to the Company in accordance with the U.S. federal securities laws and the applicable rules and regulations of the Securities and Exchange Commission and the PCAOB.

We conducted our audit in accordance with the standards of the PCAOB. Those standards require that we plan and perform the audit to obtain reasonable assurance about whether effective internal control over financial reporting was maintained in all material respects.

Our audit included obtaining an understanding of internal control over financial reporting, assessing the risk that a material weakness exists, testing and evaluating the design and operating effectiveness of internal control based on the assessed risk, and performing such other procedures as we considered necessary in the circumstances. We believe that our audit provides a reasonable basis for our opinion.

**Definition and Limitations of Internal Control Over Financial Reporting**

A company's internal control over financial reporting is a process designed to provide reasonable assurance regarding the reliability of financial reporting and the preparation of financial statements for external purposes in accordance with generally accepted accounting principles. A company's internal control over financial reporting includes those policies and procedures that (1) pertain to the maintenance of records that, in reasonable detail, accurately and fairly reflect the transactions and dispositions of the assets of the company; (2) provide reasonable assurance that transactions are recorded as necessary to permit preparation of financial statements in accordance with generally accepted accounting principles, and that receipts and expenditures of the company are being made only in accordance with authorizations of management and directors of the company; and (3) provide reasonable assurance regarding prevention or timely detection of unauthorized acquisition, use, or disposition of the company's assets that could have a material effect on the financial statements.

Because of its inherent limitations, internal control over financial reporting may not prevent or detect misstatements. Also, projections of any evaluation of effectiveness to future periods are subject to the risk that controls may become inadequate because of changes in conditions, or that the degree of compliance with the policies or procedures may deteriorate.

/s/ Ernst & Young LLP

Pittsburgh, Pennsylvania

March 12, 2020

**UNITED STATES**
**SECURITIES AND EXCHANGE COMMISSION**
**WASHINGTON, D.C. 20549**

**FORM 10-K**

☒ **ANNUAL REPORT PURSUANT TO SECTION 13 OR 15(d) OF THE SECURITIES EXCHANGE ACT OF 1934**

For the Fiscal Year Ended **February 1, 2020**

☐ **TRANSITION REPORT PURSUANT TO SECTION 13 OR 15(d) OF THE SECURITIES EXCHANGE ACT OF 1934**

For the Transition Period from _____ to _____

Commission File Number: 001-12951

**THE BUCKLE, INC.**
(Exact name of Registrant as specified in its charter)

| **Nebraska** | **47-0366193** |
|---|---|
| (State or other jurisdiction of incorporation or organization) | (I.R.S. Employer Identification No.) |

**2407 West 24th Street, Kearney, Nebraska  68845-4915**
(Address of principal executive offices)    (Zip Code)

Registrant's telephone number, including area code: **(308) 236-8491**

**Securities registered pursuant to Section 12(b) of the Act:**

| Title of each class | Trading Symbol(s) | Name of Each Exchange on Which Registered |
|---|---|---|
| Common Stock, $.01 par value | BKE | New York Stock Exchange |

**Securities registered pursuant to Section 12(g) of the Act: None**

Indicate by check mark if the registrant is a well-known seasoned issuer, as defined in Rule 405 of the Securities Act. Yes ☑  No ☐

Indicate by check mark if the registrant is not required to file reports pursuant to Section 13 or 15(d) of the Act. Yes ☐  No ☑

Indicate by check mark whether the registrant (1) has filed all reports required to be filed by Section 13 or 15(d) of the Securities Exchange Act of 1934 during the preceding 12 months (or for such shorter period that the Registrant was required to file such reports) and (2) has been subject to such filing requirements for the past 90 days. Yes ☑ No ☐

Indicate by check mark whether the registrant has submitted electronically every Interactive Data File required to be submitted pursuant to Rule 405 of Regulation S-T during the preceding 12 months (or for a shorter period that the registrant was required to submit such files). Yes ☑ No ☐

Indicate by check mark whether the registrant is a large accelerated filer, an accelerated filer, a non-accelerated filer, a smaller reporting company, or an emerging growth company. (See definition of "large accelerated filer," "accelerated filer," "smaller reporting company, " and "emerging growth company" in Rule 12b-2 of the Exchange Act). Check one.
☐  Large accelerated filer; ☑ Accelerated filer; ☐ Non-accelerated filer; ☐ Smaller Reporting Company; ☐ Emerging Growth Company

If an emerging growth company, indicate by check mark if the registrant has elected not to use the extended transition period for complying with any new or revised financial accounting standards provided pursuant to Section 13(a) of the Exchange Act. ☐

Indicate by check mark whether the registrant is a shell company (as defined in Rule 12b-2 of the Act). Yes ☐  No ☑

The aggregate market value (based on the closing price of the New York Stock Exchange) of the common stock of the registrant held by non-affiliates of the registrant was $554,715,851 on August 3, 2019. For purposes of this response, executive officers and directors are deemed to be the affiliates of the Registrant and the holdings by non-affiliates was computed as 28,229,814 shares.

The number of shares outstanding of the Registrant's Common Stock, as of March 27, 2020, was 49,408,181.

DOCUMENTS INCORPORATED BY REFERENCE

Portions of the definitive Proxy Statement for the registrant's 2020 Annual Meeting of Shareholders are incorporated by reference in Part III.

For the complete annual report, go online to corporate.buckle.com/investors/annual-reports.

## ITEM 8 - FINANCIAL STATEMENTS AND SUPPLEMENTARY DATA

## REPORT OF INDEPENDENT REGISTERED PUBLIC ACCOUNTING FIRM

To the stockholders and the Board of Directors of The Buckle, Inc.

### Opinion on the Financial Statements

We have audited the accompanying consolidated balance sheets of The Buckle, Inc. and subsidiary (the "Company") as of February 1, 2020 and February 2, 2019, the related consolidated statements of income, comprehensive income, stockholders' equity, and cash flows, for each of the three fiscal years in the period ended February 1, 2020, and the related notes and the schedule listed in the Index at Item 15 (collectively referred to as the "financial statements"). In our opinion, the financial statements present fairly, in all material respects, the financial position of the Company as of February 1, 2020 and February 2, 2019, and the results of its operations and its cash flows for each of the three fiscal years in the period ended February 1, 2020, in conformity with accounting principles generally accepted in the United States of America.

We have also audited, in accordance with the standards of the Public Company Accounting Oversight Board (United States) (PCAOB), the Company's internal control over financial reporting as of February 1, 2020 based on criteria established in *Internal Control - Integrated Framework (2013)* issued by the Committee of Sponsoring Organizations of the Treadway Commission and our report dated April 1, 2020, expressed an unqualified opinion on the Company's internal control over financial reporting.

### Change in Accounting Principle

As discussed in Note A to the financial statements, effective February 3, 2019, the Company adopted Financial Accounting Standards Board Accounting Standards Update No. 2016-02, *Leases (Topic 842)*.

### Basis for Opinion

These financial statements are the responsibility of the Company's management. Our responsibility is to express an opinion on the Company's financial statements based on our audits. We are a public accounting firm registered with the PCAOB and are required to be independent with respect to the Company in accordance with the U.S. federal securities laws and the applicable rules and regulations of the Securities and Exchange Commission and the PCAOB.

We conducted our audits in accordance with the standards of the PCAOB. Those standards require that we plan and perform the audit to obtain reasonable assurance about whether the financial statements are free of material misstatement, whether due to error or fraud. Our audits included performing procedures to assess the risks of material misstatement of the financial statements, whether due to error or fraud, and performing procedures that respond to those risks. Such procedures included examining, on a test basis, evidence regarding the amounts and disclosures in the financial statements. Our audits also included evaluating the accounting principles used and significant estimates made by management, as well as evaluating the overall presentation of the financial statements. We believe that our audits provide a reasonable basis for our opinion.

/s/ Deloitte & Touche LLP

Omaha, Nebraska
April 1, 2020

We have served as the Company's auditor since 1990.

**THE BUCKLE, INC.**

**CONSOLIDATED BALANCE SHEETS**
**(Amounts in Thousands Except Share and Per Share Amounts)**

| ASSETS | February 1, 2020 | February 2, 2019 |
|---|---:|---:|
| **CURRENT ASSETS:** | | |
| Cash and cash equivalents | $ 220,969 | $ 168,471 |
| Short-term investments (Notes B and C) | 12,532 | 51,546 |
| Receivables | 3,136 | 7,089 |
| Inventory | 121,258 | 125,190 |
| Prepaid expenses and other assets | 20,935 | 18,136 |
| Total current assets | 378,830 | 370,432 |
| | | |
| PROPERTY AND EQUIPMENT (Note E) | 452,205 | 452,187 |
| Less accumulated depreciation and amortization | (338,357) | (321,505) |
| | 113,848 | 130,682 |
| | | |
| OPERATING LEASE RIGHT-OF-USE ASSETS (Note D) | 350,088 | — |
| LONG-TERM INVESTMENTS (Notes B and C) | 15,863 | 18,745 |
| OTHER ASSETS (Notes G and H) | 9,261 | 7,443 |
| | | |
| Total assets | $ 867,890 | $ 527,302 |

**LIABILITIES AND STOCKHOLDERS' EQUITY**

| | | |
|---|---:|---:|
| **CURRENT LIABILITIES:** | | |
| Accounts payable | $ 26,491 | $ 29,008 |
| Accrued employee compensation | 22,929 | 21,452 |
| Accrued store operating expenses | 17,837 | 17,982 |
| Gift certificates redeemable | 15,319 | 16,634 |
| Current portion of operating lease liabilities (Note D) | 87,314 | — |
| Income taxes payable (Note G) | 2,751 | 5,142 |
| Total current liabilities | 172,641 | 90,218 |
| | | |
| DEFERRED COMPENSATION (Note J) | 15,863 | 13,978 |
| NON-CURRENT OPERATING LEASE LIABILITIES (Note D) | 290,238 | — |
| DEFERRED RENT LIABILITY | — | 29,229 |
| Total liabilities | 478,742 | 133,425 |
| | | |
| COMMITMENTS (Notes F and I) | | |
| | | |
| **STOCKHOLDERS' EQUITY (Note K):** | | |
| Common stock, authorized 100,000,000 shares of $.01 par value; 49,205,681 and 49,017,395 shares issued and outstanding at February 1, 2020 and February 2, 2019, respectively | 492 | 490 |
| Additional paid-in capital | 152,258 | 148,564 |
| Retained earnings | 236,398 | 244,823 |
| Total stockholders' equity | 389,148 | 393,877 |
| | | |
| Total liabilities and stockholders' equity | $ 867,890 | $ 527,302 |

See notes to consolidated financial statements.

**THE BUCKLE, INC.**

**CONSOLIDATED STATEMENTS OF INCOME**
(Amounts in Thousands Except Per Share Amounts)

| | Fiscal Years Ended | | |
| --- | --- | --- | --- |
| | February 1, 2020 | February 2, 2019 | February 3, 2018 |
| SALES, Net of returns and allowances | $ 900,254 | $ 885,496 | $ 913,380 |
| COST OF SALES (Including buying, distribution, and occupancy costs) | 522,780 | 519,423 | 533,357 |
| Gross profit | 377,474 | 366,073 | 380,023 |
| OPERATING EXPENSES: | | | |
| Selling | 204,480 | 202,032 | 206,068 |
| General and administrative | 41,497 | 43,113 | 39,877 |
| | 245,977 | 245,145 | 245,945 |
| INCOME FROM OPERATIONS | 131,497 | 120,928 | 134,078 |
| OTHER INCOME, Net | 6,210 | 5,716 | 5,407 |
| INCOME BEFORE INCOME TAXES | 137,707 | 126,644 | 139,485 |
| PROVISION FOR INCOME TAXES (Note G) | 33,278 | 31,036 | 49,778 |
| NET INCOME | $ 104,429 | $ 95,608 | $ 89,707 |
| EARNINGS PER SHARE (Note L): | | | |
| Basic | $ 2.15 | $ 1.97 | $ 1.86 |
| Diluted | $ 2.14 | $ 1.97 | $ 1.85 |

See notes to consolidated financial statements.

**THE BUCKLE, INC.**

**CONSOLIDATED STATEMENTS OF COMPREHENSIVE INCOME**
**(Amounts in Thousands)**

| | Fiscal Years Ended | | |
|---|---|---|---|
| | February 1, 2020 | February 2, 2019 | February 3, 2018 |
| NET INCOME | $        104,429 | $          95,608 | $          89,707 |
| | | | |
| OTHER COMPREHENSIVE INCOME, NET OF TAX: | | | |
| Change in unrealized loss on investments, net of tax of $0, $31, and $17, respectively | — | 89 | (7) |
| Other comprehensive income | — | 89 | (7) |
| | | | |
| COMPREHENSIVE INCOME | $        104,429 | $          95,697 | $          89,700 |

See notes to consolidated financial statements.

**THE BUCKLE, INC.**

**CONSOLIDATED STATEMENTS OF STOCKHOLDERS' EQUITY**
(Amounts in Thousands Except Share and Per Share Amounts)

| | Number of Shares | Common Stock | Additional Paid-in Capital | Retained Earnings | Accumulated Other Comprehensive Loss | Total |
|---|---|---|---|---|---|---|
| BALANCE, January 28, 2017 | 48,622,780 | $ 486 | $ 139,398 | $ 290,737 | $ (82) | $ 430,539 |
| Net income | — | — | — | 89,707 | — | 89,707 |
| Dividends paid on common stock, ($2.75 per share) | — | — | — | (133,874) | — | (133,874) |
| Issuance of non-vested stock, net of forfeitures | 193,390 | 2 | (2) | — | — | — |
| Amortization of non-vested stock grants, net of forfeitures | — | — | 4,883 | — | — | 4,883 |
| Change in unrealized loss on investments, net of tax | — | — | — | — | (7) | (7) |
| BALANCE, February 3, 2018 | 48,816,170 | $ 488 | $ 144,279 | $ 246,570 | $ (89) | $ 391,248 |
| Net income | — | — | — | 95,608 | — | 95,608 |
| Dividends paid on common stock, ($2.00 per share) | — | — | — | (97,744) | — | (97,744) |
| Issuance of non-vested stock, net of forfeitures | 201,225 | 2 | (2) | — | — | — |
| Amortization of non-vested stock grants, net of forfeitures | — | — | 4,287 | — | — | 4,287 |
| Change in unrealized loss on investments, net of tax | — | — | — | — | 89 | 89 |
| Cumulative effect of change in accounting upon adoption of ASC Topic 606 | — | — | — | 389 | — | 389 |
| BALANCE, February 2, 2019 | 49,017,395 | $ 490 | $ 148,564 | $ 244,823 | $ — | $ 393,877 |
| Net income | — | — | — | 104,429 | — | 104,429 |
| Dividends paid on common stock, ($2.30 per share) | — | — | — | (112,854) | — | (112,854) |
| Issuance of non-vested stock, net of forfeitures | 192,838 | 2 | (2) | — | — | — |
| Amortization of non-vested stock grants, net of forfeitures | — | — | 3,764 | — | — | 3,764 |
| Common stock purchased and retired | (4,552) | — | (68) | — | — | (68) |
| BALANCE, February 1, 2020 | 49,205,681 | $ 492 | $ 152,258 | $ 236,398 | $ — | $ 389,148 |

See notes to consolidated financial statements.

**THE BUCKLE, INC.**

**CONSOLIDATED STATEMENTS OF CASH FLOWS**
(Amounts in Thousands)

| | | Fiscal Years Ended | |
| --- | --- | --- | --- |
| | February 1, 2020 | February 2, 2019 | February 3, 2018 |
| CASH FLOWS FROM OPERATING ACTIVITIES: | | | |
| Net income | $ 104,429 | $ 95,608 | $ 89,707 |
| Adjustments to reconcile net income to net cash flows from operating activities: | | | |
| Depreciation and amortization | 23,789 | 26,848 | 30,745 |
| Amortization of non-vested stock grants, net of forfeitures | 3,764 | 4,287 | 4,883 |
| Deferred income taxes | (1,986) | (1,099) | (340) |
| Other | 504 | 1,925 | 1,628 |
| Changes in operating assets and liabilities: | | | |
| Receivables | 815 | (550) | (413) |
| Inventory | 3,932 | (7,487) | 7,687 |
| Prepaid expenses and other assets | (2,799) | (66) | (12,047) |
| Accounts payable | (2,667) | 276 | 4,584 |
| Accrued employee compensation | 1,477 | (855) | (4,599) |
| Accrued store operating expenses | (1,108) | 2,336 | 951 |
| Gift certificates redeemable | (1,315) | (1,568) | (2,997) |
| Income taxes payable | 747 | (5,173) | 1,662 |
| Other assets and liabilities | 1,083 | (5,755) | (1,730) |
| Net cash flows from operating activities | 130,665 | 108,727 | 119,721 |
| CASH FLOWS FROM INVESTING ACTIVITIES: | | | |
| Purchases of property and equipment | (7,322) | (10,021) | (13,462) |
| Proceeds from sale of property and equipment | 13 | 150 | 263 |
| Change in other assets | 168 | 158 | 92 |
| Purchases of investments | (25,629) | (74,215) | (56,631) |
| Proceeds from sales/maturities of investments | 67,525 | 76,330 | 52,441 |
| Net cash flows from investing activities | 34,755 | (7,598) | (17,297) |
| CASH FLOWS FROM FINANCING ACTIVITIES: | | | |
| Purchases of common stock | (68) | — | — |
| Payment of dividends | (112,854) | (97,744) | (133,874) |
| Net cash flows from financing activities | (112,922) | (97,744) | (133,874) |
| NET INCREASE (DECREASE) IN CASH AND CASH EQUIVALENTS | 52,498 | 3,385 | (31,450) |
| CASH AND CASH EQUIVALENTS, Beginning of year | 168,471 | 165,086 | 196,536 |
| CASH AND CASH EQUIVALENTS, End of year | $ 220,969 | $ 168,471 | $ 165,086 |

See notes to consolidated financial statements.

**THE BUCKLE, INC.**
**NOTES TO CONSOLIDATED FINANCIAL STATEMENTS**
**(Dollar Amounts in Thousands Except Share and Per Share Amounts)**

## A.  SUMMARY OF SIGNIFICANT ACCOUNTING POLICIES

*Fiscal Year* - The Buckle, Inc. (the "Company") has its fiscal year end on the Saturday nearest January 31. All references in these consolidated financial statements to fiscal years are to the calendar year in which the fiscal year begins. Fiscal 2019 represents the 52-week period ended February 1, 2020, fiscal 2018 represents the 52-week period ended February 2, 2019, and fiscal 2017 represents the 53-week period ended February 3, 2018.

*Nature of Operations* - The Company is a retailer of medium to better-priced casual apparel, footwear, and accessories for fashion-conscious young men and women. The Company operates its business as one reportable segment and sells its merchandise through its retail stores and e-Commerce platform. The Company operated 448 stores located in 42 states throughout the United States as of February 1, 2020.

During fiscal 2019, the Company opened 2 new stores, substantially remodeled 5 stores, and closed 4 stores. During fiscal 2018, the Company did not open any new stores, substantially remodeled 6 stores, and closed 7 stores. During fiscal 2017, the Company opened 2 new stores, substantially remodeled 8 stores, and closed 12 stores.

*Principles of Consolidation* - The consolidated financial statements include the accounts of The Buckle, Inc. and its wholly-owned subsidiary. All intercompany accounts and transactions have been eliminated in consolidation.

*Revenue Recognition* - Retail store sales are recorded, net of expected returns, upon the purchase of merchandise by customers. Online sales are recorded, net of expected returns, when the merchandise is tendered for delivery to the common carrier. Shipping fees charged to customers are included in revenue and shipping costs are included in selling expenses. The Company recognizes revenue from sales made under its layaway program upon delivery of the merchandise to the customer. Revenue is not recorded when gift cards and gift certificates are sold, but rather when a card or certificate is redeemed for merchandise. A current liability for unredeemed gift cards and certificates is recorded at the time the card or certificate is purchased. The liability recorded for unredeemed gift certificates and gift cards was $15,319 and $16,634 as of February 1, 2020 and February 2, 2019, respectively. Gift card and gift certificate breakage is recognized as revenue in proportion to the redemption pattern of customers by applying an estimated breakage rate. The estimated breakage rate is based on historical issuance and redemption patterns and is re-assessed by the Company on a regular basis. Sales tax collected from customers is excluded from revenue and is included as part of "accrued store operating expenses" on the Company's consolidated balance sheets.

The Company establishes a liability for estimated merchandise returns, based upon the historical average sales return percentage, that is recognized at the transaction value. The Company also recognizes a return asset and a corresponding adjustment to cost of sales for the Company's right to recover returned merchandise, which is measured at the estimated carrying value, less any expected recovery costs. The accrued liability for reserve for sales returns was $2,257 as of February 1, 2020 and $2,182 as of February 2, 2019.

The Company's Guest Loyalty program allows participating guests to earn points for every qualifying purchase, which (after achievement of certain point thresholds) are redeemable as a discount off a future purchase. Reported revenue is net of both current period reward redemptions and accruals for estimated future rewards earned under the Guest Loyalty program. A liability has been recorded for future rewards based on the Company's estimate of how many earned points will turn into rewards and ultimately be redeemed prior to expiration. As of February 1, 2020 and February 2, 2019, $9,615 and $10,910 was included in "accrued store operating expenses" as a liability for estimated future rewards.

Through partnership with Comenity Bank, the Company offers a private label credit card ("PLCC"). Customers with a PLCC are enrolled in our B-Rewards incentive program and earn points for every qualifying purchase on their card. At the end of each rewards period, customers who have exceeded a minimum point threshold receive a reward to be redeemed on a future purchase. The B-Rewards program also provides other discount and promotional opportunities to cardholders on a routine basis. Reported revenue is net of both current period reward redemptions, current period discounts and promotions, and accruals for estimated future rewards earned under the B-Rewards program. A liability has been recorded for future rewards based on the Company's estimate of how many earned points will turn into rewards and ultimately be redeemed prior to expiration, which is included in "gift certificates redeemable" on the Company's consolidated balance sheets.

*Cash and Cash Equivalents* - The Company considers all debt instruments with an original maturity of three months or less when purchased to be cash equivalents.

*Investments* - Investments classified as short-term investments include securities with a maturity of greater than three months and less than one year. Available-for-sale securities are reported at fair value, with unrealized gains and losses excluded from earnings and reported as a separate component of stockholders' equity (net of the effect of income taxes), using the specific identification method, until they are sold. Held-to-maturity securities are carried at amortized cost. Trading securities are reported at fair value, with unrealized gains and losses included in earnings, using the specific identification method.

*Inventory* - Inventory is valued at the lower of cost or net realizable value. Cost is determined using an average cost method that approximates the first-in, first-out (FIFO) method. Management makes adjustments to inventory and cost of goods sold, based upon estimates, to account for merchandise obsolescence and markdowns that could affect net realizable value, based on assumptions using calculations applied to current inventory levels within each different markdown level. Management also reviews the levels of inventory in each markdown group and the overall aging of the inventory versus the estimated future demand for such product and the current market conditions. The adjustment to inventory for markdowns and/or obsolescence reduced the Company's inventory valuation by $12,178 and $10,586 as of February 1, 2020 and February 2, 2019, respectively.

*Property and Equipment* - Property and equipment are stated on the basis of historical cost. Depreciation is provided using a combination of accelerated and straight-line methods based upon the estimated useful lives of the assets. The majority of property and equipment have useful lives of five to ten years with the exception of buildings, which have estimated useful lives of 31.5 to 39 years. Leasehold improvements are stated on the basis of historical cost and are amortized over the shorter of the life of the lease or the estimated economic life of the assets. When circumstances indicate the carrying values of long-lived assets may be impaired, an evaluation is performed on current net book value amounts. Judgments made by the Company related to the expected useful lives of property and equipment and the ability to realize cash flows in excess of carrying amounts of such assets are affected by factors such as changes in economic conditions and changes in operating performance. As the Company assesses the expected cash flows and carrying amounts of long-lived assets, adjustments are made to such carrying values.

*Pre-Opening Expenses* - Costs related to opening new stores are expensed as incurred.

*Advertising Costs* - Advertising costs are expensed as incurred and were $11,406, $10,661, and $18,075 for fiscal years 2019, 2018, and 2017, respectively.

**Health Care Costs** - The Company is self-funded for health and dental claims up to $200 per individual per plan year. The Company's plan covers eligible employees, and management makes estimates at period end to record a reserve for unpaid claims based upon historical claims information. The accrued liability as a reserve for unpaid health care claims was $685 and $890 as of February 1, 2020 and February 2, 2019, respectively.

**Leases** - The Company adopted Financial Accounting Standards Board ("FASB") Accounting Standards Update ("ASU") 2016-02, Leases (Topic 842) effective February 3, 2019. For fiscal years ending prior to this date, the Company followed the guidance for leases under FASB Accounting Standards Codification ("ASC") Topic 840, Leases. See Recently Issued Accounting Pronouncements below and Footnote D, Leases, for further details.

**Other Income** - The Company's other income is derived primarily from interest and dividends received on cash and investments.

**Use of Estimates** - The preparation of consolidated financial statements in conformity with accounting principles generally accepted in the United States of America requires management to make estimates and assumptions that affect the reported amounts of certain assets and liabilities, the disclosure of contingent assets and liabilities at the date of the financial statements, and the reported amounts of revenues and expenses during the reporting period. Actual results could differ from these estimates.

## D.  LEASES

The Company's lease portfolio is primarily comprised of leases for retail store locations. The Company also leases certain equipment and corporate office space. Store leases for new stores typically have an initial term of 10 years, with options to renew for an additional 1 to 5 years. The exercise of lease renewal options is at the Company's sole discretion and is included in the lease term for calculations of its right-of-use assets and liabilities when it is reasonably certain that the Company plans to renew these leases. Certain store lease agreements include rental payments based on a percentage of retail sales over contractual levels and others include rental payments adjusted periodically for inflation. Lease agreements do not contain any residual value guarantees, material restrictive covenants, or options to purchase the leased property.

The table below reconciles undiscounted future lease payments (e.g. fixed payments for rent, insurance, real estate taxes, and common area maintenance) for each of the next five fiscal years and the total of the remaining years to the operating lease liabilities recorded on the consolidated balance sheet as of February 1, 2020:

| Fiscal Year | Operating Leases [a] |
|---|---:|
| 2020 | $       100,016 |
| 2021 | 85,436 |
| 2022 | 72,503 |
| 2023 | 59,436 |
| 2024 | 44,677 |
| Thereafter | 55,391 |
| Total lease payments | 417,459 |
| Less: Imputed interest | 39,907 |
| Total operating lease liability | $       377,552 |

[a]   Operating lease payments exclude $1,355 of legally binding minimum lease payments for leases signed, but not yet commenced.

## E.  PROPERTY AND EQUIPMENT

|  | February 1, 2020 | February 2, 2019 |
|---|---:|---:|
| Land | $        2,491 | $        2,491 |
| Building and improvements | 43,267 | 43,243 |
| Office equipment | 12,494 | 12,388 |
| Transportation equipment | 21,010 | 20,993 |
| Leasehold improvements | 166,539 | 167,023 |
| Furniture and fixtures | 176,150 | 176,389 |
| Shipping/receiving equipment | 29,325 | 29,266 |
| Construction-in-progress | 929 | 394 |
| Total | $      452,205 | $      452,187 |

## F.  FINANCING ARRANGEMENTS

The Company has available an unsecured line of credit of $25,000 with Wells Fargo Bank, N.A. for operating needs and letters of credit. The line of credit agreement has an expiration date of July 31, 2021 and provides that $10,000 of the $25,000 line is available for letters of credit. Borrowings under the line of credit provide for interest to be paid at a rate based on LIBOR. The Company has, from time to time, borrowed against these lines of credit. There were no bank borrowings as of February 1, 2020 and February 2, 2019. There were no bank borrowings during fiscal 2019, 2018, and 2017. The Company had outstanding letters of credit totaling $1,523 and $1,986 as of February 1, 2020 and February 2, 2019, respectively.

## G.  INCOME TAXES

On December 22, 2017, the U.S. government enacted comprehensive tax legislation commonly referred to as the Tax Cuts and Jobs Act (the "Tax Act"). The Tax Act included many changes to the U.S. tax code including reducing the U.S. federal corporate tax rate from 35.0% to 21.0% effective January 1, 2018. This change reduced the Company's effective tax rate for the fiscal year ended February 3, 2018, based on the 21.0% rate being in effect for one month of the fiscal year, and then further reduced the Company's effective tax rate for the full fiscal years ended February 2, 2019 and February 1, 2020.

The provision for income taxes consists of:

|  | | Fiscal Years Ended | |
|---|---|---|---|
|  | February 1, 2020 | February 2, 2019 | February 3, 2018 |
| Current income tax expense: | | | |
| Federal | $ 29,660 | $ 27,278 | $ 46,158 |
| State | 5,604 | 4,857 | 3,960 |
| Deferred income tax expense (benefit) | (1,986) | (1,099) | (340) |
| Total | $ 33,278 | $ 31,036 | $ 49,778 |

## I.  COMMITMENTS AND CONTINGENCIES

*Litigation* - From time to time, the Company is involved in litigation relating to claims arising out of its operations in the normal course of business. As of the date of these consolidated financial statements, the Company was not engaged in any legal proceedings that are expected, individually or in the aggregate, to have a material effect on the Company's consolidated results of operations and financial position.

## L.  EARNINGS PER SHARE

The following table provides a reconciliation between basic and diluted earnings per share:

|  | | Fiscal Years Ended | | | | | | | |
|---|---|---|---|---|---|---|---|---|---|
|  | February 1, 2020 | | | February 2, 2019 | | | February 3, 2018 | | |
|  | Income | Weighted Average Shares (a) | Per Share Amount | Income | Weighted Average Shares (a) | Per Share Amount | Income | Weighted Average Shares (a) | Per Share Amount |
| Basic EPS | $ 104,429 | 48,587 | $ 2.15 | $ 95,608 | 48,413 | $ 1.97 | $ 89,707 | 48,250 | $ 1.86 |
| Effect of Dilutive Securities: | | | | | | | | | |
| Non-vested shares | — | 226 | (0.01) | — | 201 | — | — | 123 | (0.01) |
| Diluted EPS | $ 104,429 | 48,813 | $ 2.14 | $ 95,608 | 48,614 | $ 1.97 | $ 89,707 | 48,373 | $ 1.85 |

(a) Shares in thousands.

## M.  REVENUES

The Company is a retailer of medium to better priced casual apparel, footwear, and accessories for fashion conscious young men and women. The Company operates its business as one reportable segment. The Company sells its merchandise through its retail stores and e-Commerce platform. The Company operated 448 stores located in 42 states throughout the United States as of February 1, 2020.

During fiscal years 2019, 2018, and 2017, online revenues accounted for 12.3%, 11.7%, and 10.7%, respectively, of the Company's net sales. No sales to an individual customer or country, other than the United States, accounted for more than 10.0% of net sales.

The following is information regarding the Company's major product lines, stated as a percentage of the Company's net sales:

|  | | Fiscal Years Ended | |
|---|---|---|---|
| Merchandise Group | February 1, 2020 | February 2, 2019 | February 3, 2018 |
| Denims | 40.7% | 41.0% | 41.5% |
| Tops (including sweaters) | 32.2 | 32.8 | 32.3 |
| Accessories | 8.9 | 8.8 | 9.1 |
| Footwear | 8.0 | 6.7 | 6.1 |
| Sportswear/Fashions | 5.5 | 6.0 | 6.2 |
| Outerwear | 2.0 | 2.1 | 2.0 |
| Casual bottoms | 1.1 | 1.2 | 1.3 |
| Other | 1.6 | 1.4 | 1.5 |
| Total | 100.0% | 100.0% | 100.0% |

**ITEM 9 - CHANGES IN AND DISAGREEMENTS WITH ACCOUNTANTS ON ACCOUNTING AND FINANCIAL DISCLOSURE**

None.

**ITEM 9A – CONTROLS AND PROCEDURES**

The Company maintains a system of disclosure controls and procedures that are designed to provide reasonable assurance that material information, which is required to be timely disclosed, is accumulated and communicated to management in a timely manner. An evaluation of the effectiveness of the design and operation of the Company's disclosure controls and procedures (as defined in Rules 13a-15(e) of the Securities Exchange Act of 1934 (the "Exchange Act")) was performed as of the end of the period covered by this report. This evaluation was performed under the supervision and with the participation of the Company's Chief Executive Officer and Chief Financial Officer. Based upon that evaluation, the Chief Executive Officer and Chief Financial Officer concluded that the Company's disclosure controls and procedures as of the end of the period covered by this report were effective to provide reasonable assurance that information required to be disclosed by the Company in the Company's reports that it files or submits under the Exchange Act is accumulated and communicated to management, including its Chief Executive Officer and Chief Financial Officer, as appropriate, to allow timely decisions regarding required disclosure and are effective to provide reasonable assurance that such information is recorded, processed, summarized, and reported within the time periods specified by the SEC's rules and forms.

*Change in Internal Control Over Financial Reporting* - There were no changes in the Company's internal control over financial reporting that occurred during the Company's last fiscal quarter that have materially affected, or are reasonably likely to materially affect, the Company's internal control over financial reporting.

*Management's Report on Internal Control Over Financial Reporting* - Management of the Company is responsible for establishing and maintaining adequate internal control over financial reporting as defined in Rules 13a-15(f) and 15d-15(f) under the Securities Exchange Act of 1934. The Company's internal control over financial reporting is designed to provide reasonable assurance regarding the reliability of financial reporting and the preparation of financial statements for external purposes in accordance with accounting principles generally accepted in the United State of America ("GAAP").

All internal control systems, no matter how well designed, have inherent limitations. Therefore, even those systems determined to be effective can provide only reasonable assurance with respect to financial statement preparation and presentation. Because of its inherent limitations, internal control over financial reporting may not prevent or detect misstatements.

Management has assessed the effectiveness of the Company's internal control over financial reporting as of February 1, 2020, based on the criteria set forth by the Committee of Sponsoring Organizations ("COSO") of the Treadway Commission in their *Internal Control-Integrated Framework (2013)*. In making its assessment of internal control over financial reporting, management has concluded that the Company's internal control over financial reporting was effective as of February 1, 2020.

The Company's independent registered public accounting firm, Deloitte & Touche LLP, has audited the effectiveness of the Company's internal control over financial reporting. Their report appears herein.

**REPORT OF INDEPENDENT REGISTERED PUBLIC ACCOUNTING FIRM**

To the stockholders and the Board of Directors of The Buckle, Inc.

**Opinion on Internal Control over Financial Reporting**

We have audited the internal control over financial reporting of The Buckle, Inc. and subsidiary (the "Company") as of February 1, 2020, based on criteria established in *Internal Control - Integrated Framework (2013)* issued by the Committee of Sponsoring Organizations of the Treadway Commission (COSO). In our opinion, the Company maintained, in all material respects, effective internal control over financial reporting as of February 1, 2020, based on criteria established in *Internal Control - Integrated Framework (2013)* issued by COSO.

We have also audited, in accordance with the standards of the Public Company Accounting Oversight Board (United States) (PCAOB), the consolidated financial statements as of and for the fiscal year ended February 1, 2020, of the Company and our report dated April 1, 2020, expressed an unqualified opinion on those financial statements and included an explanatory paragraph regarding the Company's adoption of Financial Accounting Standards Board Accounting Standards Update No. 2016-02, *Leases (Topic 842).*

**Basis for Opinion**

The Company's management is responsible for maintaining effective internal control over financial reporting and for its assessment of the effectiveness of internal control over financial reporting, included in the accompanying *Management's Report on Internal Control Over Financial Reporting.* Our responsibility is to express an opinion on the Company's internal control over financial reporting based on our audit. We are a public accounting firm registered with the PCAOB and are required to be independent with respect to the Company in accordance with the U.S. federal securities laws and the applicable rules and regulations of the Securities and Exchange Commission and the PCAOB.

We conducted our audit in accordance with the standards of the PCAOB. Those standards require that we plan and perform the audit to obtain reasonable assurance about whether effective internal control over financial reporting was maintained in all material respects. Our audit included obtaining an understanding of internal control over financial reporting, assessing the risk that a material weakness exists, testing and evaluating the design and operating effectiveness of internal control based on the assessed risk, and performing such other procedures as we considered necessary in the circumstances. We believe that our audit provides a reasonable basis for our opinion.

**Definition and Limitations of Internal Control over Financial Reporting**

A company's internal control over financial reporting is a process designed to provide reasonable assurance regarding the reliability of financial reporting and the preparation of financial statements for external purposes in accordance with generally accepted accounting principles. A company's internal control over financial reporting includes those policies and procedures that (1) pertain to the maintenance of records that, in reasonable detail, accurately and fairly reflect the transactions and dispositions of the assets of the company; (2) provide reasonable assurance that transactions are recorded as necessary to permit preparation of financial statements in accordance with generally accepted accounting principles, and that receipts and expenditures of the company are being made only in accordance with authorizations of management and directors of the company; and (3) provide reasonable assurance regarding prevention or timely detection of unauthorized acquisition, use, or disposition of the company's assets that could have a material effect on the financial statements.

Because of its inherent limitations, internal control over financial reporting may not prevent or detect misstatements. Also, projections of any evaluation of effectiveness to future periods are subject to the risk that controls may become inadequate because of changes in conditions, or that the degree of compliance with the policies or procedures may deteriorate.

/s/ Deloitte & Touche LLP

Omaha, Nebraska
April 1, 2020

# Time Value of Money

## Learning Objectives

- **LO C–1**  Contrast simple and compound interest.
- **LO C–2**  Calculate the future value of a single amount.
- **LO C–3**  Calculate the present value of a single amount.
- **LO C–4**  Calculate the future value of an annuity.
- **LO C–5**  Calculate the present value of an annuity.

### SELF-STUDY MATERIALS

- Let's Review—Future value and present value of a single amount (p. C-8).
- Let's Review—Future value and present value of an annuity (p. C-12).
- The Bottom Line (Key Points by Learning Objective) (p. C-13).
- Glossary of Key Terms (p. C-13).
- Self-Study Questions with answers available (p. C-13).

Congratulations! Your new employment offer comes with a $1,000 signing bonus. The terms of the bonus give you the option of receiving (a) $1,000 today or (b) $1,000 one year from now. Which do you choose?

Probably, all of us would choose $1,000 today. Choosing to take the money today instead of one year from now just makes common sense. It also makes good economic sense. You could take your $1,000 bonus today, put it in a savings account, earn interest on it for one year, and have an amount greater than $1,000 a year from now. So, $1,000 today is not equal to $1,000 a year from now. This simple example demonstrates the time value of money, which means that interest causes the value of money received today to be greater than the value of that same amount of money received in the future.

Time value of money concepts are useful—in fact, essential—in solving many business decisions. These decisions include valuing assets and liabilities, making investment decisions, paying off debts, and establishing a retirement plan, to name just a few. We'll discuss some of these next.

## Simple versus Compound Interest

Interest is the cost of borrowing money. If you borrow $1,000 today and agree to pay 10% interest, you will pay back $1,100 a year from now. It is this interest that gives money its time value.

**LO C–1**
Contrast simple and compound interest.

Simple interest is interest you earn on the initial investment only. Calculate it as the initial investment times the applicable interest rate times the period of the investment or loan.

$$\text{Simple interest} = \text{Initial investment} \times \text{Interest rate} \times \text{Time}$$

For example, suppose you put $1,000 into a savings account that pays simple interest of 10% and then withdraw the money at the end of three years. Illustration C–1 demonstrates that the amount of simple interest you earned on your $1,000 in each of the three years is $100 (= $1,000 × 10%).

**ILLUSTRATION C–1**

Calculation of Simple Interest

| Time | Simple Interest (= Initial investment × Interest rate) | Outstanding Balance |
|---|---|---|
| Initial investment | | $1,000 |
| End of year 1 | $1,000 × 10% = $100 | $1,100 |
| End of year 2 | $1,000 × 10% = $100 | $1,200 |
| End of year 3 | $1,000 × 10% = $100 | **$1,300** |

With simple interest at 10% annually, the $1,000 initial investment generates $100 of interest each year and grows to **$1,300** by the end of the third year.

Compound interest works differently. Compound interest is interest you earn on the initial investment *and on previous interest.* Because you are earning "interest on interest" each period, compound interest yields increasingly larger amounts of interest earnings for each period of the investment (unlike simple interest, which yielded the same $100 in each year of our example above). Illustration C–2 shows calculations of compound interest for a $1,000, three-year investment that earns 10%.

**ILLUSTRATION C–2**

Calculation of Compound Interest

| Time | Compound Interest (= Outstanding balance × Interest rate) | Outstanding Balance |
|---|---|---|
| Initial investment | | $1,000 |
| End of year 1 | $1,000 × 10% = $100 | $1,100 |
| End of year 2 | $1,100 × 10% = $110 | $1,210 |
| End of year 3 | $1,210 × 10% = $121 | **$1,331** |

With compound interest at 10% annually, the $1,000 initial investment grows to **$1,331** at the end of three years. This compares to only **$1,300** for simple interest. The extra $31 represents *compounding,* or interest earned on interest. Nearly all business applications use compound interest, and compound interest is what we use in calculating the time value of money.

 **KEY POINT**

Simple interest is interest we earn on the initial investment only. Compound interest is the interest we earn on the initial investment plus previous interest. We use compound interest in calculating the time value of money.

## Time Value of a Single Amount

To better understand how compound interest affects the time value of money, we'll examine this topic from two perspectives. First, we'll calculate how much an amount today will grow to be at some point in the future (*future value*), and then we'll take the opposite perspective and examine how much an amount in the future is worth today (*present value*).

### FUTURE VALUE

■ **LO C–2**

Calculate the future value of a single amount.

In the example above, in which we invested $1,000 for three years at 10% compounded annually, we call $1,331 the future value. Future value is how much an amount today will grow to be in the future. The timeline in Illustration C–3 provides a useful way to visualize future values. Time $n = 0$ indicates today, the date of the initial investment.

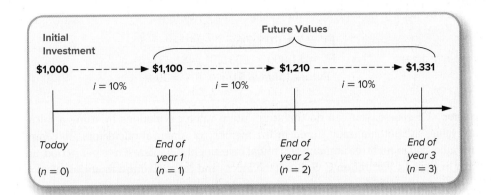

ILLUSTRATION C-3

Future Value of a Single Amount

Notice that at the end of each year, the investment grows by 10%. The future value at the end of the first year is **$1,100** (= $1,000 × 1.10). After three years, the investment has a future value of **$1,331** (= $1,000 × 1.10 × 1.10 × 1.10), representing 10% growth of a growing base amount each year.

To calculate future value, a variety of methods are available, such as a mathematical formula, time value of money tables, a financial calculator, or an Excel spreadsheet. We show all four methods below. You can use any of these approaches for completing the assignments at the end of the chapter.

*Formula.* We can determine the future value of any amount with a formula, as follows:

$$FV = I\,(1 + i)^n$$

where:          FV = future value of the invested amount
                I = initial investment
                i = interest rate
                n = number of compounding periods

*Table 1.* Instead of using a formula, we can also determine future value by using time value of money tables. Table 1, Future Value of $1, located at the end of this book, contains the future value of $1 invested for various periods of time, *n,* and various interest rates, *i.* With this table, it's easy to determine the future value of any invested amount. To do so, simply multiply the invested amount by the table value you find at the intersection of the *column* for the desired interest rate and the *row* for the number of periods. Illustration C-4 contains an excerpt from Table 1.

ILLUSTRATION C-4

Future Value of $1
(excerpt from Table 1)

|              | Interest Rates (*i*) | | | | | |
| --- | --- | --- | --- | --- | --- | --- |
| **Periods (*n*)** | **7%** | **8%** | **9%** | **10%** | **11%** | **12%** |
| 1 | 1.07000 | 1.08000 | 1.09000 | 1.10000 | 1.11000 | 1.12000 |
| 2 | 1.14490 | 1.16640 | 1.18810 | 1.21000 | 1.23210 | 1.25440 |
| 3 | 1.22504 | 1.25971 | 1.29503 | 1.33100 | 1.36763 | 1.40493 |
| 4 | 1.31080 | 1.36049 | 1.41158 | 1.46410 | 1.51807 | 1.57352 |
| 5 | 1.40255 | 1.46933 | 1.53862 | 1.61051 | 1.68506 | 1.76234 |
| 6 | 1.50073 | 1.58687 | 1.67710 | 1.77156 | 1.87041 | 1.97382 |
| 7 | 1.60578 | 1.71382 | 1.82804 | 1.94872 | 2.07616 | 2.21068 |
| 8 | 1.71819 | 1.85093 | 1.99256 | 2.14359 | 2.30454 | 2.47596 |

The table shows various values of $(1 + i)^n$ for different combinations of *i* and *n.* From the table you can find the future value factor for three periods (*n* = 3) at 10% interest to be 1.33100. This means that $1 invested at 10% compounded annually will grow to $1.331 (= $1 × 1.331) in three years. The table uses $1 as the initial investment, whereas our example used $1,000. Therefore, we need to multiply the future value factor by $1,000.

$$\textbf{FV} = \textbf{I} \times \textbf{FV factor}$$
$$\text{FV} = \$1,000 \times 1.33100^* = \$1,331$$
$$^*\text{Future value of } \$1; n = 3, i = 10\%$$

**Calculator.**  Of course, you can do the same future value calculations by using a calculator. Future values are automatically stored in the memory of financial calculators. To compute a future value, you input three amounts: (1) initial investment, (2) interest rate per period, and (3) number of periods. Illustration C–5 shows the inputs and output using a financial calculator.

**ILLUSTRATION C–5**

**Calculate the Future Value of a Single Amount Using a Financial Calculator**

The key symbols used to input the interest rate and number of periods differ across calculators, so be sure to check which key is appropriate for your calculator.

| CALCULATOR INPUTS | | |
|---|---|---|
| Inputs | Key | Amount |
| 1. Present value (initial investment) | PV | $1,000 |
| 2. Interest rate per period | *i* | 10% |
| 3. Number of periods | *n* | 3 |
| CALCULATOR OUTPUT | | |
| Future value | FV | $1,331 |

**Excel.**  Another option is to use an Excel spreadsheet, which has automatically stored the time value factors. To see how this is performed, see Illustration C–6.

**ILLUSTRATION C–6**

**Calculate the Future Value of a Single Amount Using Excel**

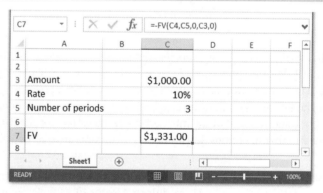

Microsoft Corporation

**Interest Compounding More Than Annually.**  In our example, interest was compounded annually (once per year). Remember the $n$ in the future value formula refers to the number of compounding *periods*—which is not necessarily the number of years. For example, suppose the three-year, $1,000 investment earns 10% compounded *semiannually*, or twice per year. The number of periods over three years is now 6 (= 3 years × 2 semiannual periods per year). The interest rate per period is 5% (= 10% annual rate ÷ 2).[1] The future value of the three-year, $1,000 investment that earns 10% compounded semiannually is calculated below.

$$\textbf{FV} = \textbf{I} \times \textbf{FV factor}$$
$$\text{FV} = \$1,000 \times 1.34010^* = \$1,340$$
$$^*\text{Future value of } \$1; n = 6, i = 5\%$$

---

[1]The rate of compounding can be broken into any number of periods. For example, if we instead assume *quarterly* compounding (four times per year), the number of periods over three years would be 12 (= 3 years × 4 quarters) and the interest rate per period would be 2.5% (= 10% ÷ 4 quarters).

Notice that the future amount is slightly higher for semiannual compounding ($1,340) compared to annual compounding ($1,331). **The more frequent the rate of compounding, the more interest we earn on previous interest, resulting in a higher future value.**

To confirm your understanding, let's look at a couple of examples of how to calculate the future value of a single amount.

**Example 1.** Suppose a company's top executive, Shirley McDaniel, currently owns stock in the company worth $800,000. Shirley is ready to retire but will not do so until her stock is worth at least $1,000,000. Over the next three years, the company's stock is expected to grow 8% annually. Will Shirley be ready to retire in three years?

The future value of $800,000 in three years with an annual interest rate of 8% equals $1,007,768 (= $800,000 × 1.25971, time value factor from Table 1, Future Value of $1, with $n = 3$ and $i = 8$%). With 8% growth, Shirley *will* be ready to retire in three years.

**Example 2.** Now suppose you are 20 years old and would like to retire by age 60. A goal of yours has always been to retire as a millionaire. You don't have any money to invest, but you do have a pretty nice car. If you sold your car for $28,000, bought a six-year-old car for $5,000, and invested the difference of $23,000 earning a 10% annual return, how much would you have at retirement?

The future value of $23,000 in 40 years (your proposed retirement age minus your present age) with an annual interest rate of 10% equals $1,040,963 (= $23,000 × 45.25926, time value factor from Table 1, Future Value of $1, with $n = 40$ and $i = 10$%). With a 10% annual return, just $23,000 today will grow to over one million dollars in 40 years. If you swap your expensive wheels, you'll have that million-dollar nest egg.

 **KEY POINT**

The future value of a single amount is how much that amount today will grow to be in the future.

## PRESENT VALUE

Present value is precisely the opposite of future value. Instead of telling us how much some amount today will grow to be in the future, present value tells us the value today of receiving some larger amount in the future. What is it worth today to receive $1,331 in three years? To answer this, we need to determine the discount rate. The discount rate is the rate at which we would be willing to give up current dollars for future dollars. If you would be willing to give up $100 today to receive $108 in one year, then your discount rate, or time value of money, equals 8%.

Continuing with our example, let's assume that your discount rate is 10%. In this case, the present value of receiving $1,331 in three years is $1,000. We could have figured this from Illustration C–3 by working backwards from the future value. The timeline in Illustration C–7 depicts this relationship between present value and future value.

■ LO C–3
Calculate the present value of a single amount.

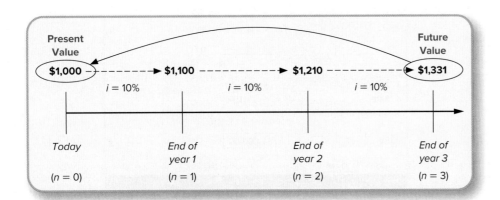

ILLUSTRATION C–7

Present Value of a Single Amount

To calculate present value, we can use a formula, time value of money tables, a calculator, or a computer spreadsheet. We show all four methods below.

**Formula.**   We can calculate present values with the following formula:

$$PV = \frac{FV}{(1 + i)^n}$$

**Table 2.**   Alternatively, we can use Table 2, Present Value of $1, located at the end of this book. Illustration C–8 shows an excerpt of Table 2.

**ILLUSTRATION C–8**

Present Value of $1
(excerpt from Table 2)

| Periods (*n*) | Interest Rates (*i*) | | | | | |
|---|---|---|---|---|---|---|
|  | **7%** | **8%** | **9%** | **10%** | **11%** | **12%** |
| 1 | 0.93458 | 0.92593 | 0.91743 | 0.90909 | 0.90090 | 0.89286 |
| 2 | 0.87344 | 0.85734 | 0.84168 | 0.82645 | 0.81162 | 0.79719 |
| 3 | 0.81630 | 0.79383 | 0.77218 | 0.75131 | 0.73119 | 0.71178 |
| 4 | 0.76290 | 0.73503 | 0.70843 | 0.68301 | 0.65873 | 0.63552 |
| 5 | 0.71299 | 0.68058 | 0.64993 | 0.62092 | 0.59345 | 0.56743 |
| 6 | 0.66634 | 0.63017 | 0.59627 | 0.56447 | 0.53464 | 0.50663 |
| 7 | 0.62275 | 0.58349 | 0.54703 | 0.51316 | 0.48166 | 0.45235 |
| 8 | 0.58201 | 0.54027 | 0.50187 | 0.46651 | 0.43393 | 0.40388 |

From the table you can find the present value factor for three periods ($n = 3$) at 10% is 0.75131. This means that $1 received in three years where there is interest of 10% compounded annually is worth about $0.75 today. So, the present value of $1,331 is approximately $1,000.

$$PV = FV \times PV \text{ factor}$$
$$PV = \$1,331 \times 0.75131 = \$1,000\,^*$$
$$^*\text{Rounded to the nearest whole dollar}$$

**Calculator.**   Illustration C–9 shows the same example worked out with a financial calculator.

**ILLUSTRATION C–9**

Calculate the Present
Value of a Single
Amount Using a
Financial Calculator

| CALCULATOR INPUTS | | |
|---|---|---|
| **Inputs** | **Key** | **Amount** |
| 1. Future value | FV | $1,331 |
| 2. Interest rate per period | *i* | 10% |
| 3. Number of periods | *n* | 3 |
| CALCULATOR OUTPUT | | |
| Present value | PV | $1,000 |

**Excel.**   In Illustration C–10, we see the same example worked out using an Excel spreadsheet.

**ILLUSTRATION C–10**

Calculate the Present
Value of a Single
Amount Using Excel

Microsoft Corporation

To confirm your understanding, let's look at a couple of examples of how to calculate the present value of a single amount.

**Example 1.**   Suppose Fisher Realtors lists for sale a 2,500-square-foot business building for $500,000. Someone offers to purchase the building, taking occupancy today, and then pay $575,000 in two years. If Fisher's discount rate is 7% compounded annually, should it accept the customer's offer?

The present value of receiving $575,000 in two years with an annual interest rate of 7% equals $502,228 (= $575,000 × 0.87344, time value factor from Table 2, Present Value of $1, with $n = 2$ and $i = 7\%$). Because the present value ($502,228) of the future payment is greater than the $500,000 listed selling price, Fisher should accept the offer.

**Example 2.**   Let's assume you would like to retire in 40 years with $1,000,000 in your retirement account. Investing aggressively in higher-risk securities, you are pretty confident you can earn an average return of 12% a year. How much do you need to invest today to have $1,000,000 in 40 years?

The present value of $1,000,000 in 40 years with an annual interest rate of 12% equals $10,750 (= $1,000,000 × 0.01075, time value factor from Table 2, Present Value of $1, with $n = 40$ and $i = 12\%$). An investment of only $10,750 today would grow to $1,000,000 in 40 years, assuming a 12% annual interest rate.

If you could earn only 6% annually rather than 12%, you would have to invest quite a bit more. The present value of $1,000,000 in 40 years with an interest rate of 6% equals $97,220 (= $1,000,000 × 0.09722, time value factor from Table 2, Present Value of $1, with $n = 40$ and $i = 6\%$). Over longer periods, the investment return you can achieve really makes a difference in the wealth you can accumulate.

**Discount Rates.**   As shown in Illustration C–11, as the interest rate increases, the more the present value of $1,000 grows in the future. For each of the four interest rates, the present value is the same ($1,000), but the future values are very different. Another way to look at this is by noticing that future values are discounted by a greater amount as the interest rate increases. For example, the present value of both (1) $1,728 discounted at 20% and (2) $1,061 discounted at 2% is $1,000. This illustration demonstrates the importance of understanding interest rates and the time value of money when making decisions over time.

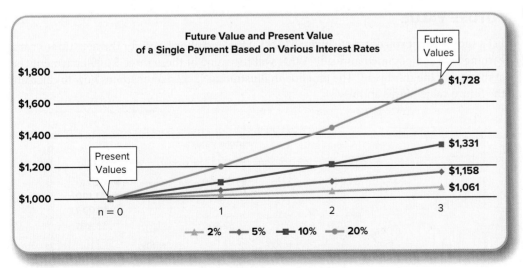

**ILLUSTRATION C–11**

Impact of Interest Rates on Present Value/Future Value Relationship

**KEY POINT**

The *present value* of a single amount is the value today of receiving that amount in the future.

**Let's Review**

Below are four scenarios related to the future value and present value of a single amount.

1. Manuel is saving for a new car. He puts $10,000 into an investment account today. He expects the account to earn 12% annually. How much will Manuel have in five years?

2. Ingrid would like to take her family to Disney World in three years. She expects the trip to cost $4,500 at that time. If she can earn 9% annually, how much should she set aside today so that she can pay for the trip in three years?

3. John puts $6,000 in a savings account today that earns 8% interest compounded semiannually. How much will John have in six years?

4. Anna purchases a ring with a selling price of $4,000 today but doesn't have to pay cash until one year from the purchase date. Assuming a discount rate of 16% compounded quarterly, what is Anna's actual cost of the ring today?

*Required:*

Calculate the time value of money for each scenario.

*Solution:*

(Rounded to the nearest whole dollar)
1. $10,000 × 1.76234 (FV of $1, $n = 5$, $i = 12\%$) = $17,623
2. $4,500 × 0.77218 (PV of $1, $n = 3$, $i = 9\%$) = $3,475
3. $6,000 × 1.60103 (FV of $1, $n = 12$, $i = 4\%$) = $9,606
4. $4,000 × 0.85480 (PV of $1, $n = 4$, $i = 4\%$) = $3,419

## Time Value of an Annuity

Up to now, we've focused on calculating the future value and present value of a *single* amount. However, many business transactions are structured as a series of receipts and payments of cash rather than a single amount. If we are to receive or pay the same amount each period, we refer to the cash flows as an annuity. Familiar examples of annuities are monthly payments for a car loan, house loan, or apartment rent. Of course, payments need not be monthly. They could be quarterly, semiannually, annually, or any interval. **An annuity includes cash payments of equal amounts over time periods of equal length.**

As with single amounts, we can calculate both the future value and the present value of an annuity.

### FUTURE VALUE

■ **LO C–4**
Calculate the future value of an annuity.

Let's suppose that you decide to invest $1,000 at the end of *each year* for the next three years, earning 10% compounded annually. What will the value of these three $1,000 payments be at the end of the third year? The timeline in Illustration C–12 demonstrates how to calculate the future value of this annuity.

**ILLUSTRATION C–12**

Future Value of an Annuity

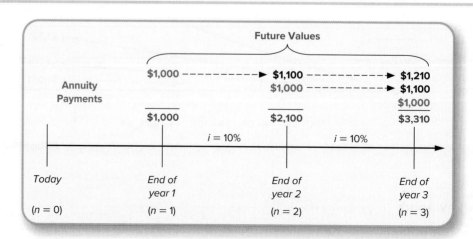

By the end of year 1, the investment's future value equals the $1,000 annuity payment. No interest has been earned because you invest the $1,000 at the *end* of the year. By the end of year 2, though, the first annuity payment has grown by 10% ($1,100 = $1,000 × 1.10), and you make the second $1,000 annuity payment. Adding these together, your total investment has grown to **$2,100**. By the end of the third year, the first annuity payment has grown by another 10% ($1,210 = $1,100 × 1.10), the second annuity payment has grown by 10% ($1,100 = $1,000 × 1.10), and you make the final $1,000 annuity payment. Add these together to find that the total investment has grown to **$3,310**. This is the future value of a $1,000 annuity for three years at 10% interest compounded annually.

**Table 3.**   Since annuities consist of multiple payments, calculating the future value of an annuity can be time-consuming, especially as the length of the annuity increases. To make this task more efficient, we can calculate the future value of an annuity using the time value of money tables located at the end of this book, a financial calculator, or a computer spreadsheet.[2]

Illustration C–13 shows an excerpt of Table 3, Future Value of an Annuity of $1.

**ILLUSTRATION C–13**

Future Value of an Annuity of $1 (excerpt from Table 3)

| Periods (*n*) | \multicolumn{6}{c}{Interest Rates (*i*)} |
|---|---|---|---|---|---|---|

| Periods (*n*) | 7% | 8% | 9% | 10% | 11% | 12% |
|---|---|---|---|---|---|---|
| 1 | 1.0000 | 1.0000 | 1.0000 | 1.0000 | 1.0000 | 1.0000 |
| 2 | 2.0700 | 2.0800 | 2.0900 | 2.1000 | 2.1100 | 2.1200 |
| 3 | 3.2149 | 3.2464 | 3.2781 | 3.3100 | 3.3421 | 3.3744 |
| 4 | 4.4399 | 4.5061 | 4.5731 | 4.6410 | 4.7097 | 4.7793 |
| 5 | 5.7507 | 5.8666 | 5.9847 | 6.1051 | 6.2278 | 6.3528 |
| 6 | 7.1533 | 7.3359 | 7.5233 | 7.7156 | 7.9129 | 8.1152 |
| 7 | 8.6540 | 8.9228 | 9.2004 | 9.4872 | 9.7833 | 10.0890 |
| 8 | 10.2598 | 10.6366 | 11.0285 | 11.4359 | 11.8594 | 12.2997 |

We calculate the future value of an annuity (FVA) by multiplying the annuity payment by the factor corresponding to three periods and 10% interest:

$$\text{FVA} = \$1,000 \times 3.3100 = \$3,310$$

**Calculator.**   You can also calculate the future value of an annuity using a financial calculator. To compute the future value of an annuity, you simply input three amounts: (1) payment amount, (2) interest rate per period, and (3) number of periods. Make sure the present value (PV) is set equal to zero. Illustration C–14 presents the inputs and output using a financial calculator.

**ILLUSTRATION C–14**

Calculate the Future Value of an Annuity Using a Financial Calculator

| CALCULATOR INPUTS | | |
|---|---|---|
| Inputs | Key | Amount |
| 1. Payment amount | PMT | $1,000 |
| 2. Interest rate per period | *i* | 10% |
| 3. Number of periods | *n* | 3 |
| CALCULATOR OUTPUT | | |
| Future value | FV | $3,310 |

---

[2]The mathematical formula for calculating the future value of an annuity is a bit more complicated than are these other methods, so we'll focus on those.

*Excel.* Illustration C–15 shows the Excel method for calculating the future value of an annuity.

ILLUSTRATION C–15

Calculate the Future
Value of an Annuity
Using Excel

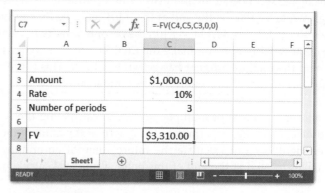

Microsoft Corporation

Again, let's look at two examples.

**Example 1.**   Suppose **Warner Bros.** borrows $300 million to produce another *Batman* movie and is required to pay back this amount in five years. If, at the end of each of the next five years, Warner Bros. puts $50 million in an account that is expected to earn 12% interest compounded annually, will the company have enough cash set aside to pay its debt?

The future value of a $50 million annuity over five years that earns 12% annually equals $317,640,000 (= $50,000,000 × 6.3528, time value factor from Table 3, Future Value of an Annuity of $1, with $n = 5$ and $i = 12\%$). Warner Bros. will have enough cash to pay its $300 million debt.

**Example 2.**   You still have aspirations of retiring in 40 years with $1,000,000 in your retirement account, but you do not have much money to invest right now. If you set aside just $2,500 at the end of each year with an average annual return of 10%, how much will you have at the end of 40 years?

The future value of a $2,500 annuity over 40 years that earns 10% annually equals $1,106,482 (= $2,500 × 442.5926, time value factor from Table 3, Future Value of an Annuity of $1, with $n = 40$ and $i = 10\%$). You will have quite a bit less assuming an average annual return of 8% ($647,641) and quite a bit more if you can achieve an average annual return of 12% ($1,917,729). Interest rates matter!

**KEY POINT**

Cash payments of equal amounts over time periods of equal length are called an annuity. The future value of an annuity is the sum of the future values of a series of cash payments.

## PRESENT VALUE

■ LO C–5
Calculate the present
value of an annuity.

One application of the present value of an annuity relates back to Chapter 9. There, you learned that we report certain liabilities in financial statements at their present values (leases and bonds). Most of these liabilities specify that the borrower must pay the lender periodic payments (or an annuity) over the life of the loan. As a result, we use the present value of an annuity to determine what portion of these future payments the borrower must report as a liability today.

To understand the idea behind the present value of an annuity, you need to realize that each annuity payment represents a single future amount. We calculate the present value of *each* of these future amounts and then add them together to determine the present value of an annuity. This idea is depicted in the timeline in Illustration C–16.

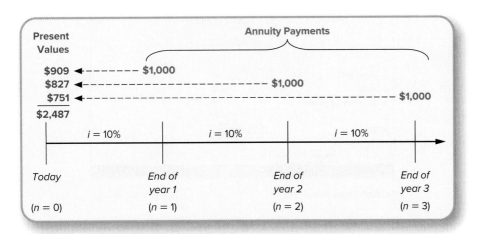

ILLUSTRATION C–16

Present Value of an Annuity

The present value of three $1,000 annual payments discounted at 10% equals the present value of the first payment ($909), plus the present value of the second payment ($827), plus the present value of the third payment ($751). You can verify these amounts by looking at the present value factors in Table 2, Present Value of $1, with $n = 1$, 2, and 3 and $i = 10\%$. The total present value of the annuity is $2,487.

**Table 4.**  Instead of calculating the present value of each annuity payment, a more efficient method is to use time value of money tables. An excerpt of Table 4, Present Value of an Annuity of $1, located at the end of this book, is shown in Illustration C–17.

**ILLUSTRATION C–17**

Present Value of an Annuity of $1 (excerpt from Table 4)

|  | Interest Rates (*i*) | | | | | |
|---|---|---|---|---|---|---|
| Periods (*n*) | 7% | 8% | 9% | 10% | 11% | 12% |
| 1 | 0.93458 | 0.92593 | 0.91743 | 0.90909 | 0.90090 | 0.89286 |
| 2 | 1.80802 | 1.78326 | 1.75911 | 1.73554 | 1.71252 | 1.69005 |
| 3 | 2.62432 | 2.57710 | 2.53129 | 2.48685 | 2.44371 | 2.40183 |
| 4 | 3.38721 | 3.31213 | 3.23972 | 3.16987 | 3.10245 | 3.03735 |
| 5 | 4.10020 | 3.99271 | 3.88965 | 3.79079 | 3.69590 | 3.60478 |
| 6 | 4.76654 | 4.62288 | 4.48592 | 4.35526 | 4.23054 | 4.11141 |
| 7 | 5.38929 | 5.20637 | 5.03295 | 4.86842 | 4.71220 | 4.56376 |
| 8 | 5.97130 | 5.74664 | 5.53482 | 5.33493 | 5.14612 | 4.96764 |

We calculate the present value of an annuity (PVA) by multiplying the annuity payment by the factor corresponding to three periods and 10% interest:

$$PVA = \$1,000 \times 2.48685 = \$2,487$$

**Calculator.**  Illustration C–18 shows the calculator solution.

**ILLUSTRATION C–18**

Calculate the Present Value of an Annuity Using a Financial Calculator

| CALCULATOR INPUTS | | |
|---|---|---|
| Inputs | Key | Amount |
| 1. Payment amount | PMT | $1,000 |
| 2. Interest rate per period | *i* | 10% |
| 3. Number of periods | *n* | 3 |
| CALCULATOR OUTPUT | | |
| Present value | PV | $2,487 |

**Excel.**  Illustration C–19 shows the Excel solution.

**ILLUSTRATION C–19**

Calculate the Present
Value of an Annuity
Using Excel

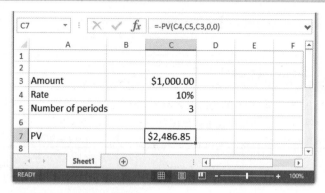

Microsoft Corporation

Again, let's look at some examples.

**Example 1.** A movie theatre considers upgrading its concessions area at a cost of $10,000. The upgrades are expected to produce additional cash flows from concession sales of $2,000 per year over the next six years. Should the movie theatre upgrade its concessions area if its discount rate is 8% annually?

The present value of a $2,000 annuity over six years at 8% interest is $9,245.76 (= $2,000 × 4.62288, time value factor from Table 4, Present Value of an Annuity of $1, with $n = 6$ and $i = 8\%$). The $10,000 cost of the upgrade is greater than the present value of the future cash flows of $9,245.76 generated. The theatre will be better off *not* making the investment.

**Example 2.** Each year you play the Monopoly game at **McDonald's**. This is your year: As you peel back the sticker, you realize you have both Park Place and Boardwalk. You have just won a million dollars payable in $50,000 installments over the next 20 years. Assuming a discount rate of 10%, how much did you really win?

The present value of a $50,000 annuity over 20 periods at 10% is $425,678 (= $50,000 × 8.51356, time value factor from Table 4, Present Value of an Annuity of $1, with $n = 20$ and $i = 10\%$). The value today of $50,000 per year for the next 20 years is actually less than half a million dollars, though you'd probably not be too disappointed with these winnings.

 **KEY POINT**

The *present* value of an annuity is the sum of the present values of a series of cash payments.

**Let's Review**

Below are four scenarios related to the future value and present value of an annuity.

1. Manuel is saving for a new car. He puts $2,000 into an investment account at the end of each year for the next five years. He expects the account to earn 12% annually. How much will Manuel have in five years?

2. Ingrid would like to take her family to Disney World in three years. She decides to purchase a vacation package that requires her to make three annual payments of $1,500 at the end of each year for the next three years. If she can earn 9% annually, how much should she set aside today so that the three annual payments can be made?

3. John puts $500 in a savings account at the end of each six months for the next six years that earns 8% interest compounded semiannually. How much will John have in six years?

4. Anna purchases a ring with a selling price of $4,000 and will make four payments of $1,000 at the end of each quarter for the next four quarters. Assuming a discount rate of 16% compounded quarterly, what is Anna's actual cost of the ring today?

*Required:*

Calculate the time value of money for each scenario.

*Solution:*

(Rounded to the nearest whole dollar)

1. $2,000 × 6.3528 (FV of annuity of $1, $n = 5$, $i = 12\%$) = $12,706
2. $1,500 × 2.53129 (PV of annuity of $1, $n = 3$, $i = 9\%$) = $3,797
3. $500 × 15.0258 (FV of annuity of $1, $n = 12$, $i = 4\%$) = $7,513
4. $1,000 × 3.62990 (PV of annuity of $1, $n = 4$, $i = 4\%$) = $3,630

---

## KEY POINTS BY LEARNING OBJECTIVE

**LO C–1   Contrast simple and compound interest.**

Simple interest is interest we earn on the initial investment only. Compound interest is the interest we earn on the initial investment plus previous interest. We use compound interest in calculating the time value of money.

**LO C–2   Calculate the future value of a single amount.**

The future value of a single amount is how much that amount today will grow to be in the future.

**LO C–3   Calculate the present value of a single amount.**

The present value of a single amount is the value today of receiving that amount in the future.

**LO C–4   Calculate the future value of an annuity.**

Cash payments of equal amounts over time periods of equal length are called an annuity. The future value of an annuity is the sum of the future values of a series of cash payments.

**LO C–5   Calculate the present value of an annuity.**

The present value of an annuity is the sum of the present values of a series of cash payments.

## GLOSSARY

**Annuity:** Cash payments of equal amounts over time periods of equal length. **p. C-8**

**Compound interest:** Interest earned on the initial investment and on previous interest. **p. C-2**

**Discount rate:** The rate at which someone would be willing to give up current dollars for future dollars. **p. C-5**

**Future value:** How much an amount today will grow to be in the future. **p. C-2**

**Present value:** The value today of receiving some amount in the future. **p. C-5**

**Simple interest:** Interest earned on the initial investment only. **p. C-1**

**Time value of money:** The value of money today is greater than the value of that same amount of money in the future. **p. C-1**

## SELF-STUDY QUESTIONS

1. How does simple interest differ from compound interest? **(LO C–1)**
   a. Simple interest includes interest earned on the initial investment plus interest earned on previous interest.
   b. Simple interest includes interest earned on the initial investment only.
   c. Simple interest is for a shorter time interval.
   d. Simple interest is for a longer time interval.

2. What is the future value of $100 invested in an account for eight years that earns 10% annual interest, compounded semiannually (rounded to the nearest whole dollar)? **(LO C–2)**
   a. $214.
   b. $216.
   c. $218.
   d. $220.

3. Present value represents **(LO C-3)**
   a. The value today of receiving money in the future.
   b. The amount that an investment today will grow to be in the future.
   c. The difference between the initial investment and the growth of that investment over time.
   d. A series of equal payments.

4. Cooper wants to save for college. Assuming he puts $5,000 into an account at the end of each year for five years and earns 12% compounded annually, how much will he have saved by the end of the fifth year (rounded to the nearest whole dollar)? **(LO C-4)**
   a. $25,000.
   b. $31,764.

    c. $18,024.
    d. $14,096.

5. A company agrees to pay $100,000 each year for five years for an exclusive franchise agreement. Assuming a discount rate of 8%, what is the cost today of the agreement (rounded to the nearest whole dollar)? **(LO C-5)**
   a. $500,000.
   b. $586,660.
   c. $399,271.
   d. $146,933.

*Note: For answers, see the last page of the appendix.*

---

## BRIEF EXERCISES

**Understand simple versus compound interest (LO C-1)**

**BEC-1** Oprah is deciding between investment options. Both investments earn an interest rate of 7%, but interest on the first investment is compounded annually, while interest on the second investment is compounded semiannually. Which investment would you advise Oprah to choose? Why?

**Understand simple versus compound interest for future value (LO C-1, C-2)**

**BEC-2** An investments account offers a 12% annual return. If $50,000 is placed in the account for two years, by how much will the investment grow if interest is compounded (a) annually, (b) semiannually, (c) quarterly, or (d) monthly?

**Calculate the future value of a single amount (LO C-2)**

**BEC-3** Dusty would like to buy a new car in six years. He currently has $15,000 saved. He's considering buying a car for around $19,000 but would like to add a Turbo engine to increase the car's performance. This would increase the price of the car to $23,000. If Dusty can earn 9% interest, compounded annually, will he be able to get a car with a Turbo engine in six years?

**Calculate the future value of a single amount (LO C-2)**

**BEC-4** Arnold and Helene would like to visit Austria in two years to celebrate their 25th wedding anniversary. Currently, the couple has saved $27,000, but they expect the trip to cost $31,000. If they put $27,000 in an account that earns 7% interest, compounded annually, will they be able to pay for the trip in two years?

**Calculate the future value of a single amount (LO C-2)**

**BEC-5** Calculate the future value of the following single amounts.

|  | Initial Investment | Annual Rate | Interest Compounded | Period Invested |
|---|---|---|---|---|
| 1. | $8,000 | 10% | Annually | 7 years |
| 2. | 6,000 | 12 | Semiannually | 4 years |
| 3. | 9,000 | 8 | Quarterly | 3 years |

**Calculate the present value of a single amount (LO C-3)**

**BEC-6** Maddy works at Burgers R Us. Her boss tells her that if she stays with the company for five years, she will receive a bonus of $6,000. With an annual discount rate of 8%, calculate the value today of receiving $6,000 in five years.

**Calculate the present value of a single amount (LO C-3)**

**BEC-7** Ronald has an investment opportunity that promises to pay him $55,000 in three years. He could earn a 6% annual return investing his money elsewhere. What is the most he would be willing to invest today in this opportunity?

**BEC–8** Calculate the present value of the following single amounts.

Calculate the present value of a single amount (LO C–3)

|  | Future Value | Annual Rate | Interest Compounded | Period Invested |
|---|---|---|---|---|
| 1. | $10,000 | 6% | Annually | 5 years |
| 2. | 7,000 | 8 | Semiannually | 8 years |
| 3. | 6,000 | 12 | Quarterly | 4 years |

**BEC–9** Tom and Suri decide to take a worldwide cruise. To do so, they need to save $30,000. They plan to invest $4,000 at the end of each year for the next seven years to earn 8% compounded annually. Determine whether Tom and Suri will reach their goal of $30,000 in seven years.

Calculate the future value of an annuity (LO C–4)

**BEC–10** Matt plans to start his own business once he graduates from college. He plans to save $3,000 every six months for the next five years. If his savings earn 10% annually (or 5% every six months), determine how much he will save by the end of the fifth year.

Calculate the future value of an annuity (LO C–4)

**BEC–11** Calculate the future value of the following annuities, assuming each annuity payment is made at the end of each compounding period.

Calculate the future value of an annuity (LO C–4)

|  | Annuity Payment | Annual Rate | Interest Compounded | Period Invested |
|---|---|---|---|---|
| 1. | $3,000 | 7% | Annually | 6 years |
| 2. | 6,000 | 8 | Semiannually | 9 years |
| 3. | 5,000 | 12 | Quarterly | 5 years |

**BEC–12** Tatsuo has just been awarded a four-year scholarship to attend the university of his choice. The scholarship will pay $8,000 each year for the next four years to reimburse normal school-related expenditures. Each $8,000 payment will be made at the end of the year, contingent on Tatsuo maintaining good grades in his classes for that year. Assuming an annual interest rate of 6%, determine the value today of receiving this scholarship if Tatsuo maintains good grades.

Calculate the present value of an annuity (LO C–5)

**BEC–13** Monroe Corporation is considering the purchase of new equipment. The equipment will cost $35,000 today. However, due to its greater operating capacity, Monroe expects the new equipment to earn additional revenues of $5,000 by the end of each year for the next 10 years. Assuming a discount rate of 10% compounded annually, determine whether Monroe should make the purchase.

Calculate the present value of an annuity (LO C–5)

**BEC–14** Calculate the present value of the following annuities, assuming each annuity payment is made at the end of each compounding period.

Calculate the present value of an annuity (LO C–5)

|  | Annuity Payment | Annual Rate | Interest Compounded | Period Invested |
|---|---|---|---|---|
| 1. | $4,000 | 7% | Annually | 5 years |
| 2. | 9,000 | 8 | Semiannually | 3 years |
| 3. | 3,000 | 8 | Quarterly | 2 years |

**EXERCISES**

Calculate the future value of a single amount (LO C–2)

**EC–1** The four people below have the following investments.

|  | Invested Amount | Interest Rate | Compounding |
|---|---|---|---|
| Jerry | $13,000 | 12% | Quarterly |
| Elaine | 16,000 | 6 | Semiannually |
| George | 23,000 | 8 | Annually |
| Kramer | 19,000 | 10 | Annually |

**Required:**

Determine which of the four people will have the greatest investment accumulation in six years.

Calculate the future value of a single amount (LO C–2)

**EC–2** You want to save for retirement. Assuming you are now 25 years old and you want to retire at age 55, you have 30 years to watch your investment grow. You decide to invest in the stock market, which has earned about 13% per year over the past 80 years and is expected to continue at this rate. You decide to invest $2,000 today.

**Required:**

How much do you expect to have in 30 years?

Calculate the future value of a single amount (LO C–2)

**EC–3** You are saving for a new car. You place $10,000 into an investment account today. How much will you have after four years if the account earns (a) 4%, (b) 6%, or (c) 8% compounded annually?

Calculate the future value of a single amount (LO C–2)

**EC–4** You are saving for a new boat. You place $25,000 in an investment account today that earns 6% compounded annually. How much will be in the account after (a) three years, (b) four years, or (c) five years?

Calculate the present value of a single amount (LO C–3)

**EC–5** The four actors below have just signed a contract to star in a dramatic movie about relationships among hospital doctors. Each person signs independent contracts with the following terms:

| | Contract Terms | |
|---|---|---|
| | **Contract Amount** | **Payment Date** |
| Derek | $600,000 | 2 years |
| Isabel | 640,000 | 3 years |
| Meredith | 500,000 | Today |
| George | 500,000 | 1 year |

**Required:**

Assuming an annual discount rate of 9%, which of the four actors is actually being paid the most?

Calculate the present value of a single amount (LO C–3)

**EC–6** Ray and Rachel are considering the purchase of two deluxe kitchen ovens. The first store offers the two ovens for $3,500 with payment due today. The second store offers the two ovens for $3,700 due in one year.

**Required:**

Assuming an annual discount rate of 9%, from which store should Ray and Rachel buy their ovens?

Calculate the present value of a single amount (LO C–3)

**EC–7** You have entered into an agreement for the purchase of land. The agreement specifies that you will take ownership of the land immediately. You have agreed to pay $50,000 today and another $50,000 in three years. Calculate the total cost of the land today, assuming a discount rate of (a) 5%, (b) 7%, or (c) 9%.

**EC–8** You believe you have discovered a new medical device. You anticipate it will take additional time to get the device fully operational, run clinical trials, obtain FDA approval, and sell to a buyer for $250,000. Assume a discount rate of 7% compounded annually. What is the value today of discovering the medical device, assuming you sell it for $250,000 in (a) two years, (b) three years, or (c) four years?

*Calculate the present value of a single amount (LO C–3)*

**EC–9** Lights, Camera, and More sells filmmaking equipment. The company offers three purchase options: (1) pay full cash today, (2) pay one-half down and the remaining one-half plus 10% in one year, or (3) pay nothing down and the full amount plus 15% in one year. George is considering buying equipment from Lights, Camera, and More for $150,000 and therefore has the following payment options:

*Calculate the present value of a single amount (LO C–3)*

|          | Payment Today | Payment in One Year | Total Payment |
|----------|---------------|---------------------|---------------|
| Option 1 | $150,000      | $        0          | $150,000      |
| Option 2 | 75,000        | 82,500              | 157,500       |
| Option 3 | 0             | 172,500             | 172,500       |

**Required:**
Assuming an annual discount rate of 11%, calculate which option's cost has the lowest present value.

**EC–10** GMG Studios plans to invest $60,000 at the end of each year for the next three years. There are three investment options available.

*Calculate the future value of an annuity (LO C–4)*

|          | Annual Rate | Interest Compounded | Period Invested |
|----------|-------------|---------------------|-----------------|
| Option 1 | 7%          | Annually            | 3 years         |
| Option 2 | 9           | Annually            | 3 years         |
| Option 3 | 11          | Annually            | 3 years         |

**Required:**
Determine the accumulated investment amount by the end of the third year for each of the options.

**EC–11** You would like to start saving for retirement. Assuming you are now 25 years old and you want to retire at age 55, you have 30 years to watch your investment grow. You decide to invest in the stock market, which has earned about 13% per year over the past 80 years and is expected to continue at this rate. You decide to invest $2,000 at the end of each year for the next 30 years.

*Calculate the future value of an annuity (LO C–4)*

**Required:**
Calculate how much your accumulated investment is expected to be in 30 years.

**EC–12** You are saving for a new house. You place $40,000 into an investment account each year for five years. How much will you have after five years if the account earns (a) 3%, (b) 6%, or (c) 9% compounded annually?

*Calculate the future value of an annuity (LO C–4)*

**EC–13** You want to buy a nice road bike. You place $3,000 each year in an investment account that earns 8% compounded annually. How much will be in the account after (a) two years, (b) three years, or (c) four years?

*Calculate the future value of an annuity (LO C–4)*

**EC–14** Denzel needs a new car. At the dealership, he finds the car he likes. The dealership gives him two payment options:
1. Pay $35,000 for the car today.
2. Pay $4,000 at the end of each quarter for three years.

*Calculate the present value of an annuity (LO C–5)*

**Required:**
Assuming Denzel uses a discount rate of 12% (or 3% quarterly), determine which option gives him the lower cost.

**Calculate the present value of an annuity (LO C–5)**

**EC–15** You have entered into an agreement to purchase a local accounting firm. The agreement specifies you will pay the seller $150,000 each year for six years. What is the cost today of the purchase, assuming a discount rate of (a) 8%, (b) 10%, or (c) 12%.

**Calculate the present value of an annuity (LO C–5)**

**EC–16** You have been issued a patent giving you exclusive rights to sell a new type of software. You believe the patent will produce sales of $200,000 each year as long as the software remains in demand. Assume a discount rate of 7% compounded annually. What is the value today of having the patent, assuming sales last for (a) three years, (b) four years, or (c) five years?

## PROBLEMS

**Calculate the future value of a single amount (LO C–2)**

**PC–1** Alec, Daniel, William, and Stephen decide today to save for retirement. Each person wants to retire by age 65 and puts $11,000 into an account earning 10% compounded annually.

| Person | Age | Initial Investment | Accumulated Investment by Retirement (age 65) |
|---|---|---|---|
| Alec | 55 | $11,000 | $_____ |
| Daniel | 45 | 11,000 | $_____ |
| William | 35 | 11,000 | $_____ |
| Stephen | 25 | 11,000 | $_____ |

*Required:*

Calculate how much each person will have accumulated by the age of 65.

**Consider present value (LO C–3, LO C–5)**

**PC–2** Bruce is considering the purchase of a restaurant named Hard Rock Hollywood. The restaurant is listed for sale at $1,000,000. With the help of his accountant, Bruce projects the net cash flows (cash inflows less cash outflows) from the restaurant to be the following amounts over the next 10 years:

| Years | Amount |
|---|---|
| 1–6 | $100,000 (each year) |
| 7 | 110,000 |
| 8 | 120,000 |
| 9 | 130,000 |
| 10 | 140,000 |

Bruce expects to sell the restaurant after 10 years for an estimated $1,300,000.

*Required:*

If Bruce wants to make at least 11% annually on his investment, should he purchase the restaurant? (Assume all cash flows occur at the end of each year.)

**Determine present value alternatives (LO C–3, C–5)**

**PC–3** Hollywood Tabloid needs a new state-of-the-art camera to produce its monthly magazine. The company is looking at two cameras that are both capable of doing the job and has determined the following:

Camera 1 costs $6,000. It should last for eight years and have annual maintenance costs of $300 per year. After eight years, the magazine can sell the camera for $300. Camera 2 costs $5,500. It will also last for eight years and have maintenance costs of $900 in year three, $900 in year five, and $1,000 in year seven. After eight years, the camera will have no resale value.

*Required:*

Determine which camera Hollywood Tabloid should purchase. Assume that an interest rate of 9% properly reflects the discount rate in this situation and that maintenance costs are paid at the end of each year.

## ANSWERS TO SELF-STUDY QUESTIONS

1. b   2. c   3. a   4. b   5. c

# Subject Index

Note: Page numbers followed by *n* indicate footnotes.

# Company Index

# Summary of Ratios Used in This Book

| | Chapter | Calculations |
|---|---|---|
| ***Return to Shareholders*** | | |
| Return on assets | 7 | $\dfrac{\text{Net income}}{\text{Average total assets}}$ |
| Return on equity | 10 | $\dfrac{\text{Net income}}{\text{Average stockholders' equity}}$ |
| Cash return on assets | 11 | $\dfrac{\text{Operating cash flow}}{\text{Average total assets}}$ |
| ***Profitability*** | | |
| Gross profit ratio | 6 | $\dfrac{\text{Net sales} - \text{Cost of goods sold}}{\text{Net sales}}$ |
| Profit margin | 7 | $\dfrac{\text{Net income}}{\text{Net sales}}$ |
| Earnings per share | 10 | $\dfrac{\text{Net income} - \text{Dividends on preferred stock}}{\text{Average shares of common stock outstanding}}$ |
| ***Asset Management*** | | |
| Receivables turnover ratio | 5 | $\dfrac{\text{Net credit sales}}{\text{Average accounts receivable}}$ |
| Average collection period | 5 | $\dfrac{\text{365 days}}{\text{Receivables turnover ratio}}$ |
| Inventory turnover ratio | 6 | $\dfrac{\text{Cost of goods sold}}{\text{Average inventory}}$ |
| Average days in inventory | 6 | $\dfrac{\text{365 days}}{\text{Inventory turnover ratio}}$ |
| Asset turnover | 7 | $\dfrac{\text{Net sales}}{\text{Average total assets}}$ |
| ***Credit Risk Management*** | | |
| Current ratio | 9 | $\dfrac{\text{Current assets}}{\text{Current liabilities}}$ |
| Acid-test ratio | 9 | $\dfrac{\text{Cash} + \text{Current investments} + \text{Accounts receivable}}{\text{Current liabilities}}$ |
| Debt to equity ratio | 9 | $\dfrac{\text{Total interest-bearing debt}}{\text{Stockholders' equity}}$ |
| Times interest earned ratio | 9 | $\dfrac{\text{Net income} + \text{Interest expense} + \text{Income tax expense}}{\text{Interest expense}}$ |
| ***Valuation*** | | |
| Price-earnings ratio | 10 | $\dfrac{\text{Stock price}}{\text{Earnings per share}}$ |
| ***Miscellaneous*** | | |
| Allowance ratio | 5 | $\dfrac{\text{Allowance for uncollectible accounts receivable}}{\text{Accounts receivable}}$ |
| Investment to asset ratio | 8 | $\dfrac{\text{Short-term investments} + \text{Long-term investments}}{\text{Total assets}}$ |
| Return on investments ratio | 8 | $\dfrac{\text{Investment-related income (loss)}}{\text{Average short-term investments} + \text{Average long-term investments}}$ |
| Cash holdings ratio | 8 | $\dfrac{\text{Cash} + \text{Cash equivalents}}{\text{Average total assets}}$ |
| Dividend yield | 10 | $\dfrac{\text{Dividends per share}}{\text{Stock price}}$ |
| Free cash flow | 11 | Operating cash flows − Capital expenditures |

# Framework for Financial Accounting

Two primary functions of financial accounting are to *measure* activities of a company and *communicate* those measurements to investors and other people for making decisions. The measurement process involves recording transactions into accounts. The balances of these accounts are used to communicate information in the four primary financial statements, which are linked. For more detailed illustrations of financial statements, see the corresponding illustrations in Chapter 2. A comprehensive list of accounts used to measure activities in this textbook is provided on the next page.

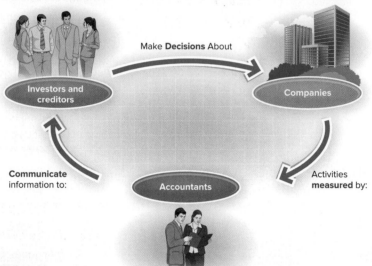

Make **Decisions** About

Investors and creditors

Companies

**Communicate** information to:

Accountants

Activities **measured** by:

## Financial Statements (in order)

### Income Statement

Revenues
− Expenses
= Net income

### Statement of Stockholders' Equity

| Common Stock | + | Retained Earnings | = | Stockholders' Equity |
|---|---|---|---|---|
| Beginning balance | | Beginning balance | | Beginning total |
| + New issuances | | | | + New issuances |
| | | + Net income | | + Net income |
| | | − Dividends | | − Dividends |
| Ending balance | + | Ending balance | = | Ending total |

### Balance Sheet

Assets = Liabilities + Stockholders' Equity
(including Cash)

### Statement of Cash Flows

Cash flows from operating activities
+ Cash flows from investing activities
+ Cash flows from financing activities
= Change in Cash

### Accounts Used to Measure Activities

1. **Assets**—Resources of a company
2. **Liabilities**—Amounts owed by the company
3. **Stockholders' Equity**—Owners' claims
4. **Dividends**—Distributions to owners
5. **Revenues**—Sales of products or services
6. **Expenses**—Costs of providing sales

### Effect of Debit and Credit on Account Balances

| Assets<br>Dividends<br>Expenses | Liabilities<br>Stockholders' Equity<br>Revenues |
|---|---|
| Debit = ↑ | Credit = ↑ |
| Credit = ↓ | Debit = ↓ |

### Recording Business Transactions

| Date | | Debit | Credit |
|---|---|---|---|
| Account Title | | Amount | |
|    Account Title | | | Amount |

# Representative Chart of Accounts*

## BALANCE SHEET

### ASSETS

Cash

Accounts Receivable

   Less: Allow. for Uncollectible Accts.

Notes Receivable

Interest Receivable

Supplies

Inventory

Prepaid Advertising

Prepaid Insurance

Prepaid Rent

Investments

Land

Land Improvements

Buildings

Equipment

   Less: Accumulated Depreciation

Lease Asset

Natural Resources

Patents

Copyrights

Trademarks

Franchises

Goodwill

### LIABILITIES

Accounts Payable

Notes Payable

Deferred Revenue

Salaries Payable

Interest Payable

Utilities Payable

Dividends Payable

Income Tax Payable

Contingent Liability

Warranty Liability

Lease Payable

Bonds Payable

### STOCKHOLDERS' EQUITY

Common Stock

Preferred Stock

Additional Paid-in Capital

Retained Earnings

   Less: Treasury Stock

Unrealized Holding Gain—Other Comprehensive Income

Unrealized Holding Loss—Other Comprehensive Income

## INCOME STATEMENT

### REVENUES

Service Revenue

Sales Revenue

   Less: Sales Discounts

   Less: Sales Returns

   Less: Sales Allowances

Interest Revenue

Dividend Revenue

Equity Income

Gain

Unrealized Holding Gain—Net Income

### EXPENSES

Advertising Expense

Amortization Expense

Bad Debt Expense

Cost of Goods Sold

Delivery Expense

Depreciation Expense

Income Tax Expense

Insurance Expense

Interest Expense

Legal Fees Expense

Postage Expense

Property Tax Expense

Rent Expense

Repairs and Maintenance Expense

Research and Development Expense

Salaries Expense

Stock-based Compensation Expense

Service Fee Expense

Supplies Expense

Utilities Expense

Warranty Expense

Loss

Unrealized Holding Loss—Net Income

## DIVIDENDS**

Dividends (Cash)

Stock Dividends

**Reported in the statement of stockholders' equity.

*You will see these account titles used in this book and in your homework. In practice, companies often use variations of these account titles, many of which are specific to particular industries or businesses.*

# Future Value and Present Value Tables

This table shows the future value of $1 at various interest rates ($i$) and time periods ($n$). It is used to calculate the future value of any single amount.

**TABLE 1** Future Value of $1

$$FV = \$1\,(1 + i)^n$$

| $n/i$ | 1.0% | 1.5% | 2.0% | 2.5% | 3.0% | 3.5% | 4.0% | 4.5% | 5.0% | 5.5% | 6.0% | 7.0% | 8.0% | 9.0% | 10.0% | 11.0% | 12.0% | 13.0% |
|---|---|---|---|---|---|---|---|---|---|---|---|---|---|---|---|---|---|---|
| 1 | 1.01000 | 1.01500 | 1.02000 | 1.02500 | 1.03000 | 1.03500 | 1.04000 | 1.04500 | 1.05000 | 1.05500 | 1.06000 | 1.07000 | 1.08000 | 1.09000 | 1.10000 | 1.11000 | 1.12000 | 1.13000 |
| 2 | 1.02010 | 1.03022 | 1.04040 | 1.05063 | 1.06090 | 1.07123 | 1.08160 | 1.09203 | 1.10250 | 1.11303 | 1.12360 | 1.14490 | 1.16640 | 1.18810 | 1.21000 | 1.23210 | 1.25440 | 1.27690 |
| 3 | 1.03030 | 1.04568 | 1.06121 | 1.07689 | 1.09273 | 1.10872 | 1.12486 | 1.14117 | 1.15763 | 1.17424 | 1.19102 | 1.22504 | 1.25971 | 1.29503 | 1.33100 | 1.36763 | 1.40493 | 1.44290 |
| 4 | 1.04060 | 1.06136 | 1.08243 | 1.10381 | 1.12551 | 1.14752 | 1.16986 | 1.19252 | 1.21551 | 1.23882 | 1.26248 | 1.31080 | 1.36049 | 1.41158 | 1.46410 | 1.51807 | 1.57352 | 1.63047 |
| 5 | 1.05101 | 1.07728 | 1.10408 | 1.13141 | 1.15927 | 1.18769 | 1.21665 | 1.24618 | 1.27628 | 1.30696 | 1.33823 | 1.40255 | 1.46933 | 1.53862 | 1.61051 | 1.68506 | 1.76234 | 1.84244 |
| 6 | 1.06152 | 1.09344 | 1.12616 | 1.15969 | 1.19405 | 1.22926 | 1.26532 | 1.30226 | 1.34010 | 1.37884 | 1.41852 | 1.50073 | 1.58687 | 1.67710 | 1.77156 | 1.87041 | 1.97382 | 2.08195 |
| 7 | 1.07214 | 1.10984 | 1.14869 | 1.18869 | 1.22987 | 1.27228 | 1.31593 | 1.36086 | 1.40710 | 1.45468 | 1.50363 | 1.60578 | 1.71382 | 1.82804 | 1.94872 | 2.07616 | 2.21068 | 2.35261 |
| 8 | 1.08286 | 1.12649 | 1.17166 | 1.21840 | 1.26677 | 1.31681 | 1.36857 | 1.42210 | 1.47746 | 1.53469 | 1.59385 | 1.71819 | 1.85093 | 1.99256 | 2.14359 | 2.30454 | 2.47596 | 2.65844 |
| 9 | 1.09369 | 1.14339 | 1.19509 | 1.24886 | 1.30477 | 1.36290 | 1.42331 | 1.48610 | 1.55133 | 1.61909 | 1.68948 | 1.83846 | 1.99900 | 2.17189 | 2.35795 | 2.55804 | 2.77308 | 3.00404 |
| 10 | 1.10462 | 1.16054 | 1.21899 | 1.28008 | 1.34392 | 1.41060 | 1.48024 | 1.55297 | 1.62889 | 1.70814 | 1.79085 | 1.96715 | 2.15892 | 2.36736 | 2.59374 | 2.83942 | 3.10585 | 3.39457 |
| 11 | 1.11567 | 1.17795 | 1.24337 | 1.31209 | 1.38423 | 1.45997 | 1.53945 | 1.62285 | 1.71034 | 1.80209 | 1.89830 | 2.10485 | 2.33164 | 2.58043 | 2.85312 | 3.15176 | 3.47855 | 3.83586 |
| 12 | 1.12683 | 1.19562 | 1.26824 | 1.34489 | 1.42576 | 1.51107 | 1.60103 | 1.69588 | 1.79586 | 1.90121 | 2.01220 | 2.25219 | 2.51817 | 2.81266 | 3.13843 | 3.49845 | 3.89598 | 4.33452 |
| 13 | 1.13809 | 1.21355 | 1.29361 | 1.37851 | 1.46853 | 1.56396 | 1.66507 | 1.77220 | 1.88565 | 2.00577 | 2.13293 | 2.40985 | 2.71962 | 3.06580 | 3.45227 | 3.88328 | 4.36349 | 4.89801 |
| 14 | 1.14947 | 1.23176 | 1.31948 | 1.41297 | 1.51259 | 1.61869 | 1.73168 | 1.85194 | 1.97993 | 2.11609 | 2.26090 | 2.57853 | 2.93719 | 3.34173 | 3.79750 | 4.31044 | 4.88711 | 5.53475 |
| 15 | 1.16097 | 1.25023 | 1.34587 | 1.44830 | 1.55797 | 1.67535 | 1.80094 | 1.93528 | 2.07893 | 2.23248 | 2.39656 | 2.75903 | 3.17217 | 3.64248 | 4.17725 | 4.78459 | 5.47357 | 6.25427 |
| 16 | 1.17258 | 1.26899 | 1.37279 | 1.48451 | 1.60471 | 1.73399 | 1.87298 | 2.02237 | 2.18287 | 2.35526 | 2.54035 | 2.95216 | 3.42594 | 3.97031 | 4.59497 | 5.31089 | 6.13039 | 7.06733 |
| 17 | 1.18430 | 1.28802 | 1.40024 | 1.52162 | 1.65285 | 1.79468 | 1.94790 | 2.11338 | 2.29202 | 2.48480 | 2.69277 | 3.15882 | 3.70002 | 4.32763 | 5.05447 | 5.89509 | 6.86604 | 7.98608 |
| 18 | 1.19615 | 1.30734 | 1.42825 | 1.55966 | 1.70243 | 1.85749 | 2.02582 | 2.20848 | 2.40662 | 2.62147 | 2.85434 | 3.37993 | 3.99602 | 4.71712 | 5.55992 | 6.54355 | 7.68997 | 9.02427 |
| 19 | 1.20811 | 1.32695 | 1.45681 | 1.59865 | 1.75351 | 1.92250 | 2.10685 | 2.30786 | 2.52695 | 2.76565 | 3.02560 | 3.61653 | 4.31570 | 5.14166 | 6.11591 | 7.26334 | 8.61276 | 10.19742 |
| 20 | 1.22019 | 1.34686 | 1.48595 | 1.63862 | 1.80611 | 1.98979 | 2.19112 | 2.41171 | 2.65330 | 2.91776 | 3.20714 | 3.86968 | 4.66096 | 5.60441 | 6.72750 | 8.06231 | 9.64629 | 11.52309 |
| 21 | 1.23239 | 1.36706 | 1.51567 | 1.67958 | 1.86029 | 2.05943 | 2.27877 | 2.52024 | 2.78596 | 3.07823 | 3.39956 | 4.14056 | 5.03383 | 6.10881 | 7.40025 | 8.94917 | 10.80385 | 13.02109 |
| 22 | 1.24472 | 1.38756 | 1.54598 | 1.72157 | 1.91610 | 2.13151 | 2.36992 | 2.63365 | 2.92526 | 3.24754 | 3.60354 | 4.43040 | 5.43654 | 6.65860 | 8.14027 | 9.93357 | 12.10031 | 14.71383 |
| 23 | 1.25716 | 1.40838 | 1.57690 | 1.76461 | 1.97359 | 2.20611 | 2.46472 | 2.75217 | 3.07152 | 3.42615 | 3.81975 | 4.74053 | 5.87146 | 7.25787 | 8.95430 | 11.02627 | 13.55235 | 16.62663 |
| 24 | 1.26973 | 1.42950 | 1.60844 | 1.80873 | 2.03279 | 2.28333 | 2.56330 | 2.87601 | 3.22510 | 3.61459 | 4.04893 | 5.07237 | 6.34118 | 7.91108 | 9.84973 | 12.23916 | 15.17863 | 18.78809 |
| 25 | 1.28243 | 1.45095 | 1.64061 | 1.85394 | 2.09378 | 2.36324 | 2.66584 | 3.00543 | 3.38635 | 3.81339 | 4.29187 | 5.42743 | 6.84848 | 8.62308 | 10.83471 | 13.58546 | 17.00006 | 21.23054 |
| 30 | 1.34785 | 1.56308 | 1.81136 | 2.09757 | 2.42726 | 2.80679 | 3.24340 | 3.74532 | 4.32194 | 4.98395 | 5.74349 | 7.61226 | 10.06266 | 13.26768 | 17.44940 | 22.89230 | 29.95992 | 39.11590 |
| 35 | 1.41660 | 1.68388 | 1.99989 | 2.37321 | 2.81386 | 3.33359 | 3.94609 | 4.66735 | 5.51602 | 6.51383 | 7.68609 | 10.67658 | 14.78534 | 20.41397 | 28.10244 | 38.57485 | 52.79962 | 72.06851 |
| 40 | 1.48886 | 1.81402 | 2.20804 | 2.68506 | 3.26204 | 3.95926 | 4.80102 | 5.81636 | 7.03999 | 8.51331 | 10.28572 | 14.97446 | 21.72452 | 31.40942 | 45.25926 | 65.00087 | 93.05097 | 132.78155 |
| 45 | 1.56481 | 1.95421 | 2.43785 | 3.03790 | 3.78160 | 4.70236 | 5.84118 | 7.24825 | 8.98501 | 11.12655 | 13.76461 | 21.00245 | 31.92045 | 48.32729 | 72.89048 | 109.53024 | 163.98760 | 244.64140 |
| 50 | 1.64463 | 2.10524 | 2.69159 | 3.43711 | 4.38391 | 5.58493 | 7.10668 | 9.03264 | 11.46740 | 14.54196 | 18.42015 | 29.45703 | 46.90161 | 74.35752 | 117.39085 | 184.56483 | 289.00219 | 450.73593 |

This table shows the present value of $1 at various interest rates (*i*) and time periods (*n*). It is used to calculate the present value of any single amount.

**TABLE 2** Present Value of $1

$$PV = \frac{\$1}{(1+i)^n}$$

| n/i | 1.0% | 1.5% | 2.0% | 2.5% | 3.0% | 3.5% | 4.0% | 4.5% | 5.0% | 5.5% | 6.0% | 7.0% | 8.0% | 9.0% | 10.0% | 11.0% | 12.0% | 13.0% |
|---|---|---|---|---|---|---|---|---|---|---|---|---|---|---|---|---|---|---|
| 1 | 0.99010 | 0.98522 | 0.98039 | 0.97561 | 0.97087 | 0.96618 | 0.96154 | 0.95694 | 0.95238 | 0.94787 | 0.94340 | 0.93458 | 0.92593 | 0.91743 | 0.90909 | 0.90090 | 0.89286 | 0.88496 |
| 2 | 0.98030 | 0.97066 | 0.96117 | 0.95181 | 0.94260 | 0.93351 | 0.92456 | 0.91573 | 0.90703 | 0.89845 | 0.89000 | 0.87344 | 0.85734 | 0.84168 | 0.82645 | 0.81162 | 0.79719 | 0.78315 |
| 3 | 0.97059 | 0.95632 | 0.94232 | 0.92860 | 0.91514 | 0.90194 | 0.88900 | 0.87630 | 0.86384 | 0.85161 | 0.83962 | 0.81630 | 0.79383 | 0.77218 | 0.75131 | 0.73119 | 0.71178 | 0.69305 |
| 4 | 0.96098 | 0.94218 | 0.92385 | 0.90595 | 0.88849 | 0.87144 | 0.85480 | 0.83856 | 0.82270 | 0.80722 | 0.79209 | 0.76290 | 0.73503 | 0.70843 | 0.68301 | 0.65873 | 0.63552 | 0.61332 |
| 5 | 0.95147 | 0.92826 | 0.90573 | 0.88385 | 0.86261 | 0.84197 | 0.82193 | 0.80245 | 0.78353 | 0.76513 | 0.74726 | 0.71299 | 0.68058 | 0.64993 | 0.62092 | 0.59345 | 0.56743 | 0.54276 |
| 6 | 0.94205 | 0.91454 | 0.88797 | 0.86230 | 0.83748 | 0.81350 | 0.79031 | 0.76790 | 0.74622 | 0.72525 | 0.70496 | 0.66634 | 0.63017 | 0.59627 | 0.56447 | 0.53464 | 0.50663 | 0.48032 |
| 7 | 0.93272 | 0.90103 | 0.87056 | 0.84127 | 0.81309 | 0.78599 | 0.75992 | 0.73483 | 0.71068 | 0.68744 | 0.66506 | 0.62275 | 0.58349 | 0.54703 | 0.51316 | 0.48166 | 0.45235 | 0.42506 |
| 8 | 0.92348 | 0.88771 | 0.85349 | 0.82075 | 0.78941 | 0.75941 | 0.73069 | 0.70319 | 0.67684 | 0.65160 | 0.62741 | 0.58201 | 0.54027 | 0.50187 | 0.46651 | 0.43393 | 0.40388 | 0.37616 |
| 9 | 0.91434 | 0.87459 | 0.83676 | 0.80073 | 0.76642 | 0.73373 | 0.70259 | 0.67290 | 0.64461 | 0.61763 | 0.59190 | 0.54393 | 0.50025 | 0.46043 | 0.42410 | 0.39092 | 0.36061 | 0.33288 |
| 10 | 0.90529 | 0.86167 | 0.82035 | 0.78120 | 0.74409 | 0.70892 | 0.67556 | 0.64393 | 0.61391 | 0.58543 | 0.55839 | 0.50835 | 0.46319 | 0.42241 | 0.38554 | 0.35218 | 0.32197 | 0.29459 |
| 11 | 0.89632 | 0.84893 | 0.80426 | 0.76214 | 0.72242 | 0.68495 | 0.64958 | 0.61620 | 0.58468 | 0.55491 | 0.52679 | 0.47509 | 0.42888 | 0.38753 | 0.35049 | 0.31728 | 0.28748 | 0.26070 |
| 12 | 0.88745 | 0.83639 | 0.78849 | 0.74356 | 0.70138 | 0.66178 | 0.62460 | 0.58966 | 0.55684 | 0.52598 | 0.49697 | 0.44401 | 0.39711 | 0.35553 | 0.31863 | 0.28584 | 0.25668 | 0.23071 |
| 13 | 0.87866 | 0.82403 | 0.77303 | 0.72542 | 0.68095 | 0.63940 | 0.60057 | 0.56427 | 0.53032 | 0.49856 | 0.46884 | 0.41496 | 0.36770 | 0.32618 | 0.28966 | 0.25751 | 0.22917 | 0.20416 |
| 14 | 0.86996 | 0.81185 | 0.75788 | 0.70773 | 0.66112 | 0.61778 | 0.57748 | 0.53997 | 0.50507 | 0.47257 | 0.44230 | 0.38782 | 0.34046 | 0.29925 | 0.26333 | 0.23199 | 0.20462 | 0.18068 |
| 15 | 0.86135 | 0.79985 | 0.74301 | 0.69047 | 0.64186 | 0.59689 | 0.55526 | 0.51672 | 0.48102 | 0.44793 | 0.41727 | 0.36245 | 0.31524 | 0.27454 | 0.23939 | 0.20900 | 0.18270 | 0.15989 |
| 16 | 0.85282 | 0.78803 | 0.72845 | 0.67362 | 0.62317 | 0.57671 | 0.53391 | 0.49447 | 0.45811 | 0.42458 | 0.39365 | 0.33873 | 0.29189 | 0.25187 | 0.21763 | 0.18829 | 0.16312 | 0.14150 |
| 17 | 0.84438 | 0.77639 | 0.71416 | 0.65720 | 0.60502 | 0.55720 | 0.51337 | 0.47318 | 0.43630 | 0.40245 | 0.37136 | 0.31657 | 0.27027 | 0.23107 | 0.19784 | 0.16963 | 0.14564 | 0.12522 |
| 18 | 0.83602 | 0.76491 | 0.70016 | 0.64117 | 0.58739 | 0.53836 | 0.49363 | 0.45280 | 0.41552 | 0.38147 | 0.35034 | 0.29586 | 0.25025 | 0.21199 | 0.17986 | 0.15282 | 0.13004 | 0.11081 |
| 19 | 0.82774 | 0.75361 | 0.68643 | 0.62553 | 0.57029 | 0.52016 | 0.47464 | 0.43330 | 0.39573 | 0.36158 | 0.33051 | 0.27651 | 0.23171 | 0.19449 | 0.16351 | 0.13768 | 0.11611 | 0.09806 |
| 20 | 0.81954 | 0.74247 | 0.67297 | 0.61027 | 0.55368 | 0.50257 | 0.45639 | 0.41464 | 0.37689 | 0.34273 | 0.31180 | 0.25842 | 0.21455 | 0.17843 | 0.14864 | 0.12403 | 0.10367 | 0.08678 |
| 21 | 0.81143 | 0.73150 | 0.65978 | 0.59539 | 0.53755 | 0.48557 | 0.43883 | 0.39679 | 0.35894 | 0.32486 | 0.29416 | 0.24151 | 0.19866 | 0.16370 | 0.13513 | 0.11174 | 0.09256 | 0.07680 |
| 22 | 0.80340 | 0.72069 | 0.64684 | 0.58086 | 0.52189 | 0.46915 | 0.42196 | 0.37970 | 0.34185 | 0.30793 | 0.27751 | 0.22571 | 0.18394 | 0.15018 | 0.12285 | 0.10067 | 0.08264 | 0.06796 |
| 23 | 0.79544 | 0.71004 | 0.63416 | 0.56670 | 0.50669 | 0.45329 | 0.40573 | 0.36335 | 0.32557 | 0.29187 | 0.26180 | 0.21095 | 0.17032 | 0.13778 | 0.11168 | 0.09069 | 0.07379 | 0.06014 |
| 24 | 0.78757 | 0.69954 | 0.62172 | 0.55288 | 0.49193 | 0.43796 | 0.39012 | 0.34770 | 0.31007 | 0.27666 | 0.24698 | 0.19715 | 0.15770 | 0.12640 | 0.10153 | 0.08170 | 0.06588 | 0.05323 |
| 25 | 0.77977 | 0.68921 | 0.60953 | 0.53939 | 0.47761 | 0.42315 | 0.37512 | 0.33273 | 0.29530 | 0.26223 | 0.23300 | 0.18425 | 0.14602 | 0.11597 | 0.09230 | 0.07361 | 0.05882 | 0.04710 |
| 30 | 0.74192 | 0.63976 | 0.55207 | 0.47674 | 0.41199 | 0.35628 | 0.30832 | 0.26700 | 0.23138 | 0.20064 | 0.17411 | 0.13137 | 0.09938 | 0.07537 | 0.05731 | 0.04368 | 0.03338 | 0.02557 |
| 35 | 0.70591 | 0.59387 | 0.50003 | 0.42137 | 0.35538 | 0.29998 | 0.25342 | 0.21425 | 0.18129 | 0.15352 | 0.13011 | 0.09366 | 0.06763 | 0.04899 | 0.03558 | 0.02592 | 0.01894 | 0.01388 |
| 40 | 0.67165 | 0.55126 | 0.45289 | 0.37243 | 0.30656 | 0.25257 | 0.20829 | 0.17193 | 0.14205 | 0.11746 | 0.09722 | 0.06678 | 0.04603 | 0.03184 | 0.02209 | 0.01538 | 0.01075 | 0.00753 |
| 45 | 0.63905 | 0.51171 | 0.41020 | 0.32917 | 0.26444 | 0.21266 | 0.17120 | 0.13796 | 0.11130 | 0.08988 | 0.07265 | 0.04761 | 0.03133 | 0.02069 | 0.01372 | 0.00913 | 0.00610 | 0.00409 |
| 50 | 0.60804 | 0.47500 | 0.37153 | 0.29094 | 0.22811 | 0.17905 | 0.14071 | 0.11071 | 0.08720 | 0.06877 | 0.05429 | 0.03395 | 0.02132 | 0.01345 | 0.00852 | 0.00542 | 0.00346 | 0.00222 |

This table shows the future value of an ordinary annuity of $1 at various interest rates (*i*) and time periods (*n*). It is used to calculate the future value of any series of equal payments made at the end of each compounding period.

**TABLE 3  Future Value of an Ordinary Annuity of $1**

$$FVA = \frac{(1+i)^n - 1}{i}$$

| n/i | 1.0% | 1.5% | 2.0% | 2.5% | 3.0% | 3.5% | 4.0% | 4.5% | 5.0% | 5.5% | 6.0% | 7.0% | 8.0% | 9.0% | 10.0% | 11.0% | 12.0% | 13.0% |
|---|---|---|---|---|---|---|---|---|---|---|---|---|---|---|---|---|---|---|
| 1 | 1.0000 | 1.0000 | 1.0000 | 1.0000 | 1.0000 | 1.0000 | 1.0000 | 1.0000 | 1.0000 | 1.0000 | 1.0000 | 1.0000 | 1.0000 | 1.0000 | 1.0000 | 1.0000 | 1.0000 | 1.0000 |
| 2 | 2.0100 | 2.0150 | 2.0200 | 2.0250 | 2.0300 | 2.0350 | 2.0400 | 2.0450 | 2.0500 | 2.0550 | 2.0600 | 2.0700 | 2.0800 | 2.0900 | 2.1000 | 2.1100 | 2.1200 | 2.1300 |
| 3 | 3.0301 | 3.0452 | 3.0604 | 3.0756 | 3.0909 | 3.1062 | 3.1216 | 3.1370 | 3.1525 | 3.1680 | 3.1836 | 3.2149 | 3.2464 | 3.2781 | 3.3100 | 3.3421 | 3.3744 | 3.4069 |
| 4 | 4.0604 | 4.0909 | 4.1216 | 4.1525 | 4.1836 | 4.2149 | 4.2465 | 4.2782 | 4.3101 | 4.3423 | 4.3746 | 4.4399 | 4.5061 | 4.5731 | 4.6410 | 4.7097 | 4.7793 | 4.8498 |
| 5 | 5.1010 | 5.1523 | 5.2040 | 5.2563 | 5.3091 | 5.3625 | 5.4163 | 5.4707 | 5.5256 | 5.5811 | 5.6371 | 5.7507 | 5.8666 | 5.9847 | 6.1051 | 6.2278 | 6.3528 | 6.4803 |
| 6 | 6.1520 | 6.2296 | 6.3081 | 6.3877 | 6.4684 | 6.5502 | 6.6330 | 6.7169 | 6.8019 | 6.8881 | 6.9753 | 7.1533 | 7.3359 | 7.5233 | 7.7156 | 7.9129 | 8.1152 | 8.3227 |
| 7 | 7.2135 | 7.3230 | 7.4343 | 7.5474 | 7.6625 | 7.7794 | 7.8983 | 8.0192 | 8.1420 | 8.2669 | 8.3938 | 8.6540 | 8.9228 | 9.2004 | 9.4872 | 9.7833 | 10.0890 | 10.4047 |
| 8 | 8.2857 | 8.4328 | 8.5830 | 8.7361 | 8.8923 | 9.0517 | 9.2142 | 9.3800 | 9.5491 | 9.7216 | 9.8975 | 10.2598 | 10.6366 | 11.0285 | 11.4359 | 11.8594 | 12.2997 | 12.7573 |
| 9 | 9.3685 | 9.5593 | 9.7546 | 9.9545 | 10.1591 | 10.3685 | 10.5828 | 10.8021 | 11.0266 | 11.2563 | 11.4913 | 11.9780 | 12.4876 | 13.0210 | 13.5795 | 14.1640 | 14.7757 | 15.4157 |
| 10 | 10.4622 | 10.7027 | 10.9497 | 11.2034 | 11.4639 | 11.7314 | 12.0061 | 12.2882 | 12.5779 | 12.8754 | 13.1808 | 13.8164 | 14.4866 | 15.1929 | 15.9374 | 16.7220 | 17.5487 | 18.4197 |
| 11 | 11.5668 | 11.8633 | 12.1687 | 12.4835 | 12.8078 | 13.1420 | 13.4864 | 13.8412 | 14.2068 | 14.5835 | 14.9716 | 15.7836 | 16.6455 | 17.5603 | 18.5312 | 19.5614 | 20.6546 | 21.8143 |
| 12 | 12.6825 | 13.0412 | 13.4121 | 13.7956 | 14.1920 | 14.6020 | 15.0258 | 15.4640 | 15.9171 | 16.3856 | 16.8699 | 17.8885 | 18.9771 | 20.1407 | 21.3843 | 22.7132 | 24.1331 | 25.6502 |
| 13 | 13.8093 | 14.2368 | 14.6803 | 15.1404 | 15.6178 | 16.1130 | 16.6268 | 17.1599 | 17.7130 | 18.2868 | 18.8821 | 20.1406 | 21.4953 | 22.9534 | 24.5227 | 26.2116 | 28.0291 | 29.9847 |
| 14 | 14.9474 | 15.4504 | 15.9739 | 16.5190 | 17.0863 | 17.6770 | 18.2919 | 18.9321 | 19.5986 | 20.2926 | 21.0151 | 22.5505 | 24.2149 | 26.0192 | 27.9750 | 30.0949 | 32.3926 | 34.8827 |
| 15 | 16.0969 | 16.6821 | 17.2934 | 17.9319 | 18.5989 | 19.2957 | 20.0236 | 20.7841 | 21.5786 | 22.4087 | 23.2760 | 25.1290 | 27.1521 | 29.3609 | 31.7725 | 34.4054 | 37.2797 | 40.4175 |
| 16 | 17.2579 | 17.9324 | 18.6393 | 19.3802 | 20.1569 | 20.9710 | 21.8245 | 22.7193 | 23.6575 | 24.6411 | 25.6725 | 27.8881 | 30.3243 | 33.0034 | 35.9497 | 39.1899 | 42.7533 | 46.6717 |
| 17 | 18.4304 | 19.2014 | 20.0121 | 20.8647 | 21.7616 | 22.7050 | 23.6975 | 24.7417 | 25.8404 | 26.9964 | 28.2129 | 30.8402 | 33.7502 | 36.9737 | 40.5447 | 44.5008 | 48.8837 | 53.7391 |
| 18 | 19.6147 | 20.4894 | 21.4123 | 22.3863 | 23.4144 | 24.4997 | 25.6454 | 26.8551 | 28.1324 | 29.4812 | 30.9057 | 33.9990 | 37.4502 | 41.3013 | 45.5992 | 50.3959 | 55.7497 | 61.7251 |
| 19 | 20.8109 | 21.7967 | 22.8406 | 23.9460 | 25.1169 | 26.3572 | 27.6712 | 29.0636 | 30.5390 | 32.1027 | 33.7600 | 37.3790 | 41.4463 | 46.0185 | 51.1591 | 56.9395 | 63.4397 | 70.7494 |
| 20 | 22.0190 | 23.1237 | 24.2974 | 25.5447 | 26.8704 | 28.2797 | 29.7781 | 31.3714 | 33.0660 | 34.8683 | 36.7856 | 40.9955 | 45.7620 | 51.1601 | 57.2750 | 64.2028 | 72.0524 | 80.9468 |
| 21 | 23.2392 | 24.4705 | 25.7833 | 27.1833 | 28.6765 | 30.2695 | 31.9692 | 33.7831 | 35.7193 | 37.7861 | 39.9927 | 44.8652 | 50.4229 | 56.7645 | 64.0025 | 72.2651 | 81.6987 | 92.4699 |
| 22 | 24.4716 | 25.8376 | 27.2990 | 28.8629 | 30.5368 | 32.3289 | 34.2480 | 36.3034 | 38.5052 | 40.8643 | 43.3923 | 49.0057 | 55.4568 | 62.8733 | 71.4027 | 81.2143 | 92.5026 | 105.4910 |
| 23 | 25.7163 | 27.2251 | 28.8450 | 30.5844 | 32.4529 | 34.4604 | 36.6179 | 38.9370 | 41.4305 | 44.1118 | 46.9958 | 53.4361 | 60.8933 | 69.5319 | 79.5430 | 91.1479 | 104.6029 | 120.2048 |
| 24 | 26.9735 | 28.6335 | 30.4219 | 32.3490 | 34.4265 | 36.6665 | 39.0826 | 41.6892 | 44.5020 | 47.5380 | 50.8156 | 58.1767 | 66.7648 | 76.7898 | 88.4973 | 102.1742 | 118.1552 | 136.8315 |
| 25 | 28.2432 | 30.0630 | 32.0303 | 34.1578 | 36.4593 | 38.9499 | 41.6459 | 44.5652 | 47.7271 | 51.1526 | 54.8645 | 63.2490 | 73.1059 | 84.7009 | 98.3471 | 114.4133 | 133.3339 | 155.6196 |
| 30 | 34.7849 | 37.5387 | 40.5681 | 43.9027 | 47.5754 | 51.6227 | 56.0849 | 61.0071 | 66.4388 | 72.4355 | 79.0582 | 94.4608 | 113.2832 | 136.3075 | 164.4940 | 199.0209 | 241.3327 | 293.1992 |
| 35 | 41.6603 | 45.5921 | 49.9945 | 54.9282 | 60.4621 | 66.6740 | 73.6522 | 81.4966 | 90.3203 | 100.2514 | 111.4348 | 138.2369 | 172.3168 | 215.7108 | 271.0244 | 341.5896 | 431.6635 | 546.6808 |
| 40 | 48.8864 | 54.2679 | 60.4020 | 67.4026 | 75.4013 | 84.5503 | 95.0255 | 107.0303 | 120.7998 | 136.6056 | 154.7620 | 199.6351 | 259.0565 | 337.8824 | 442.5926 | 581.8261 | 767.0914 | 1013.7042 |
| 45 | 56.4811 | 63.6142 | 71.8927 | 81.5161 | 92.7199 | 105.7817 | 121.0294 | 138.8500 | 159.7002 | 184.1192 | 212.7435 | 285.7493 | 386.5056 | 525.8587 | 718.9048 | 986.6386 | 1358.2300 | 1874.1646 |
| 50 | 64.4632 | 73.6828 | 84.5794 | 97.4843 | 112.7969 | 130.9979 | 152.6671 | 178.5030 | 209.3480 | 246.2175 | 290.3359 | 406.5289 | 573.7702 | 815.0836 | 1163.9085 | 1668.7712 | 2400.0182 | 3459.5071 |

This table shows the present value of an ordinary annuity of $1 at various interest rates (*i*) and time periods (*n*). It is used to calculate the present value of any series of equal payments made at the end of each compounding period.

**TABLE 4** Present Value of an Ordinary Annuity of $1

$$PVA = \frac{1 - \frac{1}{(1+i)^n}}{i}$$

| n/i | 1.0% | 1.5% | 2.0% | 2.5% | 3.0% | 3.5% | 4.0% | 4.5% | 5.0% | 5.5% | 6.0% | 7.0% | 8.0% | 9.0% | 10.0% | 11.0% | 12.0% | 13.0% |
|---|---|---|---|---|---|---|---|---|---|---|---|---|---|---|---|---|---|---|
| 1 | 0.99010 | 0.98522 | 0.98039 | 0.97561 | 0.97087 | 0.96618 | 0.96154 | 0.95694 | 0.95238 | 0.94787 | 0.94340 | 0.93458 | 0.92593 | 0.91743 | 0.90909 | 0.90090 | 0.89286 | 0.88496 |
| 2 | 1.97040 | 1.95588 | 1.94156 | 1.92742 | 1.91347 | 1.89969 | 1.88609 | 1.87267 | 1.85941 | 1.84632 | 1.83339 | 1.80802 | 1.78326 | 1.75911 | 1.73554 | 1.71252 | 1.69005 | 1.66810 |
| 3 | 2.94099 | 2.91220 | 2.88388 | 2.85602 | 2.82861 | 2.80164 | 2.77509 | 2.74896 | 2.72325 | 2.69793 | 2.67301 | 2.62432 | 2.57710 | 2.53129 | 2.48685 | 2.44371 | 2.40183 | 2.36115 |
| 4 | 3.90197 | 3.85438 | 3.80773 | 3.76197 | 3.71710 | 3.67308 | 3.62990 | 3.58753 | 3.54595 | 3.50515 | 3.46511 | 3.38721 | 3.31213 | 3.23972 | 3.16987 | 3.10245 | 3.03735 | 2.97447 |
| 5 | 4.85343 | 4.78264 | 4.71346 | 4.64583 | 4.57971 | 4.51505 | 4.45182 | 4.38998 | 4.32948 | 4.27028 | 4.21236 | 4.10020 | 3.99271 | 3.88965 | 3.79079 | 3.69590 | 3.60478 | 3.51723 |
| 6 | 5.79548 | 5.69719 | 5.60143 | 5.50813 | 5.41719 | 5.32855 | 5.24214 | 5.15787 | 5.07569 | 4.99553 | 4.91732 | 4.76654 | 4.62288 | 4.48592 | 4.35526 | 4.23054 | 4.11141 | 3.99755 |
| 7 | 6.72819 | 6.59821 | 6.47199 | 6.34939 | 6.23028 | 6.11454 | 6.00205 | 5.89270 | 5.78637 | 5.68297 | 5.58238 | 5.38929 | 5.20637 | 5.03295 | 4.86842 | 4.71220 | 4.56376 | 4.42261 |
| 8 | 7.65168 | 7.48593 | 7.32548 | 7.17014 | 7.01969 | 6.87396 | 6.73274 | 6.59589 | 6.46321 | 6.33457 | 6.20979 | 5.97130 | 5.74664 | 5.53482 | 5.33493 | 5.14612 | 4.96764 | 4.79877 |
| 9 | 8.56602 | 8.36052 | 8.16224 | 7.97087 | 7.78611 | 7.60769 | 7.43533 | 7.26879 | 7.10782 | 6.95220 | 6.80169 | 6.51523 | 6.24689 | 5.99525 | 5.75902 | 5.53705 | 5.32825 | 5.13166 |
| 10 | 9.47130 | 9.22218 | 8.98259 | 8.75206 | 8.53020 | 8.31661 | 8.11090 | 7.91272 | 7.72173 | 7.53763 | 7.36009 | 7.02358 | 6.71008 | 6.41766 | 6.14457 | 5.88923 | 5.65022 | 5.42624 |
| 11 | 10.36763 | 10.07112 | 9.78685 | 9.51421 | 9.25262 | 9.00155 | 8.76048 | 8.52892 | 8.30641 | 8.09254 | 7.88687 | 7.49867 | 7.13896 | 6.80519 | 6.49506 | 6.20652 | 5.93770 | 5.68694 |
| 12 | 11.25508 | 10.90751 | 10.57534 | 10.25776 | 9.95400 | 9.66333 | 9.38507 | 9.11858 | 8.86325 | 8.61852 | 8.38384 | 7.94269 | 7.53608 | 7.16073 | 6.81369 | 6.49236 | 6.19437 | 5.91765 |
| 13 | 12.13374 | 11.73153 | 11.34837 | 10.98319 | 10.63496 | 10.30274 | 9.98565 | 9.68285 | 9.39357 | 9.11708 | 8.85268 | 8.35765 | 7.90378 | 7.48690 | 7.10336 | 6.74987 | 6.42355 | 6.12181 |
| 14 | 13.00370 | 12.54338 | 12.10625 | 11.69091 | 11.29607 | 10.92052 | 10.56312 | 10.22283 | 9.89864 | 9.58965 | 9.29498 | 8.74547 | 8.24424 | 7.78615 | 7.36669 | 6.98187 | 6.62817 | 6.30249 |
| 15 | 13.86505 | 13.34323 | 12.84926 | 12.38138 | 11.93794 | 11.51741 | 11.11839 | 10.73955 | 10.37966 | 10.03758 | 9.71225 | 9.10791 | 8.55948 | 8.06069 | 7.60608 | 7.19087 | 6.81086 | 6.46238 |
| 16 | 14.71787 | 14.13126 | 13.57771 | 13.05500 | 12.56110 | 12.09412 | 11.65230 | 11.23402 | 10.83777 | 10.46216 | 10.10590 | 9.44665 | 8.85137 | 8.31256 | 7.82371 | 7.37916 | 6.97399 | 6.60388 |
| 17 | 15.56225 | 14.90765 | 14.29187 | 13.71220 | 13.16612 | 12.65132 | 12.16567 | 11.70719 | 11.27407 | 10.86461 | 10.47726 | 9.76322 | 9.12164 | 8.54363 | 8.02155 | 7.54879 | 7.11963 | 6.72909 |
| 18 | 16.39827 | 15.67256 | 14.99203 | 14.35336 | 13.75351 | 13.18968 | 12.65930 | 12.15999 | 11.68959 | 11.24607 | 10.82760 | 10.05909 | 9.37189 | 8.75563 | 8.20141 | 7.70162 | 7.24967 | 6.83991 |
| 19 | 17.22601 | 16.42617 | 15.67846 | 14.97889 | 14.32380 | 13.70984 | 13.13394 | 12.59329 | 12.08532 | 11.60765 | 11.15812 | 10.33560 | 9.60360 | 8.95011 | 8.36492 | 7.83929 | 7.36578 | 6.93797 |
| 20 | 18.04555 | 17.16864 | 16.35143 | 15.58916 | 14.87747 | 14.21240 | 13.59033 | 13.00794 | 12.46221 | 11.95038 | 11.46992 | 10.59401 | 9.81815 | 9.12855 | 8.51356 | 7.96333 | 7.46944 | 7.02475 |
| 21 | 18.85698 | 17.90014 | 17.01121 | 16.18455 | 15.41502 | 14.69797 | 14.02916 | 13.40472 | 12.82115 | 12.27524 | 11.76408 | 10.83553 | 10.01680 | 9.29224 | 8.64869 | 8.07507 | 7.56200 | 7.10155 |
| 22 | 19.66038 | 18.62082 | 17.65805 | 16.76541 | 15.93692 | 15.16712 | 14.45112 | 13.78442 | 13.16300 | 12.58317 | 12.04158 | 11.06124 | 10.20074 | 9.44243 | 8.77154 | 8.17574 | 7.64465 | 7.16951 |
| 23 | 20.45582 | 19.33086 | 18.29220 | 17.33211 | 16.44361 | 15.62041 | 14.85684 | 14.14777 | 13.48857 | 12.87504 | 12.30338 | 11.27219 | 10.37106 | 9.58021 | 8.88322 | 8.26643 | 7.71843 | 7.22966 |
| 24 | 21.24339 | 20.03041 | 18.91393 | 17.88499 | 16.93554 | 16.05837 | 15.24696 | 14.49548 | 13.79864 | 13.15170 | 12.55036 | 11.46933 | 10.52876 | 9.70661 | 8.98474 | 8.34814 | 7.78432 | 7.28288 |
| 25 | 22.02316 | 20.71961 | 19.52346 | 18.42438 | 17.41315 | 16.48151 | 15.62208 | 14.82821 | 14.09394 | 13.41393 | 12.78336 | 11.65358 | 10.67478 | 9.82258 | 9.07704 | 8.42174 | 7.84314 | 7.32998 |
| 30 | 25.80771 | 24.01584 | 22.39646 | 20.93029 | 19.60044 | 18.39205 | 17.29203 | 16.28889 | 15.37245 | 14.53375 | 13.76483 | 12.40904 | 11.25778 | 10.27365 | 9.42691 | 8.69379 | 8.05518 | 7.49565 |
| 35 | 29.40858 | 27.07559 | 24.99862 | 23.14516 | 21.48722 | 20.00066 | 18.66461 | 17.46101 | 16.37419 | 15.39055 | 14.49825 | 12.94767 | 11.65457 | 10.56682 | 9.64416 | 8.85524 | 8.17550 | 7.58557 |
| 40 | 32.83469 | 29.91585 | 27.35548 | 25.10278 | 23.11477 | 21.35507 | 19.79277 | 18.40158 | 17.15909 | 16.04612 | 15.04630 | 13.33171 | 11.92461 | 10.75736 | 9.77905 | 8.95105 | 8.24378 | 7.63438 |
| 45 | 36.09451 | 32.55234 | 29.49016 | 26.83302 | 24.51871 | 22.49545 | 20.72004 | 19.15635 | 17.77407 | 16.54773 | 15.45583 | 13.60552 | 12.10840 | 10.88120 | 9.86281 | 9.00791 | 8.28252 | 7.66086 |
| 50 | 39.19612 | 34.99969 | 31.42361 | 28.36231 | 25.72976 | 23.45562 | 21.48218 | 19.76201 | 18.25593 | 16.93152 | 15.76186 | 13.80075 | 12.23348 | 10.96168 | 9.91481 | 9.04165 | 8.30450 | 7.67524 |